PSYCHOLOGY

Frontiers and Applications

Michael W. Passer

University of Washington

Ronald E. Smith

University of Washington

McGraw Hill

Boston   Burr Ridge, IL   Dubuque, IA   Madison, WI   New York   San Francisco   St. Louis
Bangkok   Bogotá   Caracas   Kuala Lumpur   Lisbon   London   Madrid   Mexico City
Milan   Montreal   New Delhi   Santiago   Seoul   Singapore   Sydney   Taipei   Toronto

McGraw-Hill Higher Education

*A Division of The **McGraw-Hill** Companies*

PSYCHOLOGY: FRONTIERS AND APPLICATIONS

Published by McGraw-Hill, an imprint of The McGraw-Hill Companies, Inc., 1221 Avenue of the Americas, New York, NY 10020. Copyright © 2001 by The McGraw-Hill Companies, Inc. All rights reserved. No part of this publication may be reproduced or distributed in any form or by any means, or stored in a database or retrieval system, without the prior written consent of The McGraw-Hill Companies, Inc., including, but not limited to, in any network or other electronic storage or transmission, or broadcast for distance learning.

Some ancillaries, including electronic and print components, may not be available to customers outside the United States.

This book is printed on acid-free paper.

3 4 5 6 7 8 9 0 VNH/VNH 0 9 8 7 6 5 4 3 2 1

ISBN 0–07–365795–6

Vice president and editor-in-chief: *Thalia Dorwick*
Editorial director: *Jane E. Vaicunas*
Executive editor: *Joseph Terry*
Developmental editor: *Mindy De Palma*
Marketing manager: *Chris Hall*
Project manager: *Mary Lee Harms*
Media technology senior producer: *Sean Crowley*
Senior production supervisor: *Sandra Hahn*
Design manager: *Stuart D. Paterson*
Cover/interior designer: *Jamie O'Neal*
Cover images: (center photo) *Magnun Photos Inc. Photo by Steve McCurry*
MRI Courtesy, Information Services, University of Washington Health Sciences Center
(hands, plaza, and chimp) *PhotoDisc*
Senior photo research coordinator: *Lori Hancock*
Photo research: *Toni Michaels*
Supplement producer: *Brenda A. Ernzen*
Compositor: *Carlisle Communications, Ltd.*
Typeface: *10/12 Palatino*
Printer: *Von Hoffmann Press, Inc.*

The credits section for this book begins on page 718 and is considered an extension of the copyright page.

Library of Congress Cataloging-in-Publication Data

Passer, Michael W.
    Psychology : frontiers and applications / Michael W. Passer, Ronald E. Smith. — 1st ed.
        p.   cm.
    Includes bibliographical references and index.
    ISBN 0–07–365795–6
    1. Psychology. I. Smith, Ronald Edward, 1940–   . II. Title.

BF121 .P347   2001
150—dc21   00–048038
                                                                                          CIP

www.mhhe.com

ABOUT THE AUTHORS

Michael W. Passer, Ph.D.

Michael W. Passer coordinates the introductory psychology program at the University of Washington, which enrolls more than 3,000 students per year. He received his bachelor's degree from the University of Rochester, his Ph.D. in Social Psychology from the University of California, Los Angeles, and has been a faculty member at the University of Washington since 1977. A former Danforth Foundation Fellow and University of Washington Distinguished Teaching Award finalist, Dr. Passer has had a career-long love of teaching. He teaches introductory psychology twice yearly and has also taught courses in research methods, social psychology, industrial-organizational psychology, and attribution theory. Dr. Passer developed and annually offers a graduate course on Teaching of Psychology, which prepares students for careers in the college classroom. He has published over twenty scientific articles and chapters, primarily in the areas of attribution, stress, and anxiety.

Ronald E. Smith, Ph.D.

Ronald E. Smith is Professor of Psychology at the University of Washington, where he has served as Director of Clinical Psychology Training and as Head of the Social Psychology and Personality area. He received his bachelor's degree from Marquette University and his Ph.D. from Southern Illinois University, where he had dual specializations in physiological and clinical psychology. His major research interests are in personality, anxiety, stress and coping, and in performance enhancement research and intervention.

Dr. Smith is a Fellow of the American Psychological Association. He received a Distinguished Alumnus Award from the UCLA Neuropsychiatric Institute, where he did advanced clinical training, for his contributions to the field of psychology. He has published more than one hundred scientific articles and book chapters in his areas of interest and has authored or coauthored nineteen books on introductory psychology, stress and stress management, and human performance enhancement. An award-winning teacher, he has more than fifteen years of experience in teaching the introductory psychology course.

In memory of my parents, Jerome and Nathalie,
in gratitude to my mentors, Harold Kelley and
Harold Sigall, and to my wife, Bev, for everything.

mwp

To Kay, in gratitude for her loving
encouragement and support.

res

CONTENTS IN BRIEF

CONTENTS

As the scientific study of behavior and its causes, psychology is both a basic and an applied science. Historical roots in the physical and biological sciences, medicine, and philosophy provide us with six major perspectives for viewing behavior and studying its causes. Using depression as an example, we show how these perspectives allow psychologists to explore causal factors at biological, psychological, and environmental levels of analysis.

Science is about exploration and discovery. Like the wide-eyed child who sees the world and constantly asks "Why?", psychologists have an insatiable curiosity about behavior. And like the master detective, psychological researchers are incurable skeptics who collect and evaluate evidence before jumping to conclusions. We examine diverse methods that psychologists use to study behavior, discuss why all evidence is not created equal, and illustrate how analytic thinking can help you avoid reaching faulty conclusions in everyday life.

CHAPTER 3
BIOLOGICAL FOUNDATIONS OF BEHAVIOR 78

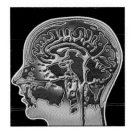

The biological perspective is creating some of the most exciting frontiers in psychology. Everything psychological reflects interactions between complex biological systems and the environment. You will learn about the workings of the nervous, endocrine, and immune systems, and how these systems work together and with environmental factors to affect our mental life, behavior, and well-being. We also examine recent work on evolutionary and genetic influences on behavior.

CHAPTER 4
SENSATION AND PERCEPTION 130

The miracle of perception results from our nervous system's translation of environmental stimuli into the language of nerve impulses. The brain uses this input to create our moment-to-moment experiences. We explore our windows to the external and internal worlds, as well as the role of social, cultural, personality, and experiential factors in forming our perceptions. We find that there are critical periods for the development of certain perceptual abilities.

CHAPTER 5
STATES OF CONSCIOUSNESS   180

The mysteries of consciousness have perplexed humankind for ages. After exploring some aspects of "normal" waking consciousness and differing views on the nature of the mind, you will learn how biological rhythms affect our mental states. Next, you will explore the fascinating world of sleep, sleep disorders, and dreams, and then examine how drugs influence consciousness. After seeing how drug effects depend on chemical, psychological, and environmental factors, you will learn about hypnosis and discover why it is controversial.

CHAPTER **6**

LEARNING AND ADAPTATION: THE ROLE OF EXPERIENCE   226

Learning enables us to adapt to diverse and ever-changing environments. Beyond the wide array of learned skills that we perform every day—from tying our shoes to telling time and using computers—you will see that learning also affects our emotional reactions, our attitudes, and even our physical health. The chapter explores the major psychological processes by which learning occurs, examines their applications, and provides you with practical guidelines for modifying behaviors that you wish to change.

CHAPTER **7**

MEMORY   272

Memory enriches our lives and enables us to learn from experience. After describing the case of a famous patient with amnesia (memory loss), we discuss how information is entered into memory, stored, and later retrieved. We explore the frailties of memory—reasons for forgetting and factors that distort what we remember—and examine societal controversies concerning eyewitness testimony, children's memory, and repressed memories of sexual abuse. You will discover ways to improve your memory, and learn about people with exceptional memory.

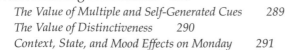

CHAPTER **8**

INTELLIGENT THOUGHT AND BEHAVIOR 314

Humans dominate their world because of their superior language, problem-solving, and intellectual abilities. The study of these cognitive skills has a long tradition in psychology and many exciting discoveries continue to emerge. Knowledge of the factors that affect intelligent thought and behavior can have important practical applications, as shown in guidelines you will be given for creative problem solving. We also analyze the influence of race and sex in cognitive functions.

CHAPTER 9
MOTIVATION   364

Whether in the context of striving for success, seeking thrills, finding a mate, or simply obtaining food to eat, motivation is a process that moves people toward their goals. We explore several perspectives about the nature of motivation, and then take a closer look at specific aspects of motivated behavior, such as hunger, sex, close relationships and love, achievement, and behavior in the workplace. You will see that motivation involves the interplay of biological, psychological, and environmental factors.

CHAPTER 10
EMOTION, STRESS, AND HEALTH   410

Emotions are complex events having physiological, mental, and behavioral components. We explore these interacting components and how they color our emotional experiences. We discuss the causes of happiness as well as the nature of stress, the ways people cope with it, and its impact on our physical and psychological well-being. On the practical side, we describe specific stress management coping skills that you can use in your life.

CHAPTER 11

DEVELOPMENT OVER THE LIFE SPAN   452

At the moment of conception you were a single-cell organism barely larger than a pinhead. Now, after following a wondrous path of development that will continue for the rest of your life, you have become an amazingly complex and sophisticated being. In this chapter you will explore important biological, psychological, and social changes that occur throughout the lifespan. While learning about human development, you will discover some common misconceptions in how people think about infancy, childhood, adolescence, and adulthood.

CHAPTER 12

BEHAVIOR IN A SOCIAL CONTEXT   498

Our social environment—the environment consisting of other people—profoundly affects how we think, feel, and behave. You will see how the "power of the situation" influences task performance, conformity, obedience, and antisocial behavior. After examining the nature of attitudes and the persuasion process, you will learn how to identify and resist specific persuasion techniques. You will learn about how people form impressions of one another, and then explore the nature prejudice, helping behavior and altruism, and aggression.

CHAPTER *13*
PERSONALITY 540

Every person is what all people are, what some people are, and what no other person is or ever will be. The fascinating spectrum of personality differences continues to stimulate theory development and research. You will learn about the major perspectives on personality, how personality differences are measured, and the many insights about individuality that personality psychologists have achieved through their research.

CHAPTER *14*
PSYCHOLOGICAL DISORDERS 584

Psychological disorders occur with distressing frequency in every culture. You will learn that judgments of normality are culturally influenced and that they have had major personal, social, and legal consequences. Using a framework that considers the interaction of personal vulnerability factors and life stressors, we describe the major disorders, present illustrative case studies, and discuss the biological, psychological, and environmental causes that have been identified in clinical research. We also provide guidelines for understanding and preventing suicide.

CHAPTER 15
TREATMENT OF PSYCHOLOGICAL DISORDERS   626

 Treating and preventing psychological disorders is an important psychological frontier. We describe the major psychological and biological approaches to treatment, illustrating them with case examples and reviewing evidence for their efficacy. You will learn that evaluating the effects of therapy is a major scientific challenge, as is the development of prevention approaches designed to increase personal resources, change harmful environmental factors, or both. Finally, we discuss the need for greater resources for community-based treatments.

CHAPTER *16*

PSYCHOLOGY AND SOCIETY: FROM BASIC RESEARCH TO SOCIAL APPLICATION   668

In this capstone chapter, we show how the results of psychological research can be used to create successful intervention programs that address major social problems. You will learn how psychologists have used principles you have already encountered to promote physical health, create growth-inducing environments for disadvantaged children, reduce substance abuse and violence, and promote multicultural understanding and harmony. Using the powerful tools of science, psychology is playing a key role in promoting human betterment.

PREFACE

This textbook reflects our experiences as undergraduate students and later as faculty who have taught the introductory psychology course many times (25 years and approximately 50 course offerings between us). As undergraduates, neither of us planned to become a psychologist. Mike planned to major in physics or chemistry, and Ron was a journalism major with a minor in philosophy. But the introductory psychology courses prompted both of us to change our majors to psychology. Because of instructors who brought psychology to life, we left our introductory courses with four goals that have remained with us ever since:

- To teach students that the world of behavior is downright fascinating;
- To help students think critically and analytically about behavior, and to dispel commonly held myths;
- To show how behavior can be studied with intellectually exciting scientific rigor.
- To bring the basic and applied aspects of psychology to life by applying scientific principles to real-world problems;

Years later, these themes remain our guideposts when we teach introductory psychology. As instructors, we want to pass on the torch of excitement about studying behavior that we received as undergraduates, and that we have experienced as scientists. To achieve this goal, we present the field from a perspective that emphasizes the interplay between basic science and applied science. Our goal is to bring both aspects of psychological science to life for our students. We strive to foster analytical thinking that teaches students how to view the world of behavior in a more sophisticated fashion, as most psychologists do. This approach has been well received by our students over the years.

Before describing how our book captures these themes, let's address one other key issue. In exit polls of graduating psychology majors at our university, most students report that the introductory psychology course was the most important stimulus for their deciding to major in psychology. Indeed, it is always gratifying to run into psychology majors who tell us that we helped shape their academic careers. But also important are the greater number of students who will not major in psychology or even take another psychology course. The introductory course is our one opportunity to inform and excite these students about psychological science and its contributions to their lives and to society.

〉 THEMES AND FEATURES OF THE TEXT

To provide a more cohesive approach to psychology, we have created a simple thematic framework that is integrated throughout the book. This framework is enhanced by our book's emphasis on the science of psychology and coverage that explicitly links basic and applied psychology.

Promoting Analytic Thinking: A Simple Framework That You Will Remember

"[One strength is] the use of themes that are carried throughout the book that emphasize basic concepts about psychology and behavior. These help to provide a more unified perspective on psychology. The chapters do not seem as disconnected as they often do in other books."

—Robert Kaleta, University of Wisconsin–Milwaukee

When teaching introductory psychology, we seek to enhance students' ability to think analytically about behavior, as psychologists do. To help students become more sophisticated in their everyday understanding of behavior, we present a simple framework that emphasizes the multicausal nature of psychology: *The causes of behavior can be studied at biological, psychological, and environmental levels of analysis.*

Our text establishes this theme in Chapter 1, where we describe the history of psychology in relation to the biological, cognitive, behavioral, psychodynamic, humanistic, and sociocultural perspectives that guide contemporary thinking in our field. We show how these perspectives contribute to the multilevel analysis of causal factors, and carry this unifying theme throughout the book in textual discussion and in special graphic features. These figures, entitled *Understanding the Causes of Behavior,* summarize the biological, psychological, and environmental causes discussed for specific topics. This levels-of-analysis framework is selectively applied within each chapter to achieve a unifying consistency without being overly repetitive.

Treating Cultural and Gender Issues

Cultural and gender issues are at the forefront of contemporary psychology, and it is crucial for any introductory textbook in psychology to nourish analytical thinking about these issues. Rather than isolating this material within one chapter, we have emphasized and integrated it throughout the text. Our multicausal levels of analysis approach represents culture at two levels: as an environmental factor and as a psychological factor that reflects the internalization of cultural influences. Cultural and gender issues are highlighted in several of the in-depth special features found throughout the book, spanning such diverse topics as pain, visual perception, psychopathology, self-concept, sexuality, cognitive skills, love and marriage, and coping strategies.

The textbook fosters analytic thinking in other ways. Without being overly repetitious, we return periodically to important themes, such as the inability to draw causal conclusions from correlational results. A special research feature within each chapter not only describes the methods and results of a specific study, but also critically evaluates it. Critical thinking questions at various places in the text also promote active learning. Finally, at the end of each chapter, a feature called *Applying Your Knowledge* consists of a set of ten multiple-choice questions that require students to analyze scenarios in light of what they have learned in the chapter.

Fostering an Understanding of Scientific Principles and Methods

"I find the style completely engaging—fresh, exciting illustrations of principles without oversimplification or "talking down" to the students. . . . The non-psych majors . . . will find it interesting and readable. . . . The psychology majors, who find some of the less challenging textbooks too simple, are also likely to be excited by the fascinating applications of concepts in the context of good scientific explanations of terms and processes."

—Kathleen Malley-Morrison
Boston University

Throughout the book, we emphasize the science of psychology. Psychological science is fascinating not only because of the rich insights it provides about human and animal behavior, but also because of its dynamic, evolving nature. To highlight this evolving feature of our science, each chapter includes an in-depth feature called **Psychological Frontiers** that presents cutting-edge scientific discoveries such as *Virtual Reality as a Therapeutic Technique* (Chapter 15).

Students need to know not only the findings derived from research, but also how the research is done. We live in an era in which students are bombarded with scientific information and misinformation. Therefore we have devoted special attention to Chapter 2, "Studying Behavior

Scientifically." There are two keys to a successful and engaging methods chapter: clear explanations and lively examples of scientific concepts and methods drawn from actual research. The chapter includes an exercise designed to help students experience the pitfalls of hindsight bias, a feature on paranormal phenomena that highlights the importance of not accepting conclusions at face value, and critical thinking exercises in which students are challenged to detect flaws in scientific reports or the popular press.

In addition to our research chapter, every chapter includes a special feature called *Research Close-Up* that presents a classic or recent study in journal format (background, method, results, and critical analysis). Together, these features provide a window to the researcher's world, an understanding of empirical methods, and an opportunity to think critically about research findings.

We also strive to emphasize the constantly evolving nature of psychological research. New findings appear monthly in hundreds of scientific journals around the world. Keeping up with the stream (or more accurately the torrent) of new studies is a special challenge for textbook authors. To provide an accurate portrait of our discipline, we have made every attempt to be as current as possible. As a result of our commitment to authoritative up-to-date coverage, nearly a quarter of the book's citations are post-1998, with more than 200 references from the year 2000. Yet our effort has not occurred at the expense of classic studies. Whenever possible, we try to include both a classic and a later study in our citations.

Emphasizing Relations Between Basic and Applied Science

"The authors . . . do a masterful job of demonstrating that psychology involves basic science but that it can be applied to real-life problems. The "capstone" chapter will be particularly valuable in terms of pulling these pieces together one more time."

—J. T. Ptacek
Bucknell University

Relations between basic and applied science are emphasized throughout the text. Students who read our book will understand that many questions studied from a basic science perspective are inspired by real-world questions and issues. They also will see that basic research findings often have implications for solving social and individual problems. When such applications occur, their effects should be evaluated empirically.

We emphasize scientific applications in three ways. First, numerous examples are woven throughout the main text. Second, a special feature called *Applications of Psychological Science*, presented in each chapter, demonstrates in greater depth how basic research principles can be applied directly to a social problem or to the student's own life. Finally, this basic/applied theme is reinforced once again in a capstone chapter, *Psychology and*

Society: From Basic Research to Social Application (Chapter 16). In this chapter, we link psychological principles and research findings discussed in previous chapters to successful social interventions in critical areas such as health promotion, violence reduction, early childhood intervention, and reduction of multicultural conflict. We want students to leave their introductory course with a solid appreciation for what psychology has to offer society and with an understanding of how challenging it is to design, implement, and evaluate social interventions. We were gratified when one reviewer of this chapter wrote, "It just may remind students of why they took the course in the first place."

❯ OUR PEDAGOGICAL FRAMEWORK

A textbook is, first and foremost, a learning tool. Consistent with our emphasis on the use of scientific data for applied purposes, within the book we have incorporated pedagogical tools that have an empirical basis. One important example is what we call *directed questions,* which occur in the margin of the book adjacent to important concepts and facts. These are designed to function as study guides and retrieval cues. Their inclusion was inspired by educational research on the value of "adjunct questions" in learning and retaining factual and conceptual material. In one major review, Richard Hamilton (1985) reviewed thirty-five experimental studies comparing the use of adjunct questions with control conditions in which participants simply read textual material. He found that questions like ours enhanced retention of facts and concepts by about 20 percent. This approach has proven so successful with our own students that we chose to make it an integral learning tool in this text.

An in-depth *Applications of Psychological Science* feature in Chapter 1 informs students about the scientific basis for the directed questions feature and instructs them in how to apply this tool in their studies. Instructors can also use the questions as a focus for homework assignments, as a study guide, and as a basis for test questions. Our directed questions should not be confused with the broader questions used in the SQ3R approach; ours are more numerous and specific. If students can answer all of them, they will have achieved a high level of content mastery and should perform very well on tests. Instructors may choose to supplement these questions with their own, or encourage their students to do so.

Four other *Applications* features throughout the book impart skills that can enhance student learning and course performance: behavioral self-regulation (Chapter 6); memory enhancement (Chapter 7); systematic goal setting (Chapter 13); and stress management (Chapter 10).

There are a number of pedagogical features throughout each chapter that contribute to student mastery of the content:

- Chapter Outline—this feature appears on the opening spread of every chapter to outline the major topics covered in each chapter
- Vignette—this feature opens each chapter with an interesting story provided to immediately draw students into each phychological topic
- Understanding the Causes of Behavior schema—three levels of analysis are presented in these figures to aid students understanding of the various causes of behavior in psychology
- Psychological Frontiers—this boxed feature presents students with cutting-edge scientific discoveries that will help students understand why psychology is so fascinating
- Applications of Psychological Science—this boxed feature explains how basic research principles can be applied directly to social problems and to student's own lives
- Research Close-Up—this boxed feature includes a classical or recent psychological study that is presented in a student-friendly, journal format to help students better understand the research process
- Chapter Summaries—presented in an easy-to-read bulleted format, this feature appears at the end of each chapter, facilitating student review of the content
- Key terms and concepts—this end-of-the-chapter feature presents students with a list of key words with page references that were highlighted throughout the chapter
- Applying Your Knowledge—this 10 question multiple choice quiz allows students to immediately test their comprehension of the material
- Directed Questions—these questions appear in the margins throughout each chapter are designed to act as retrieval cues to enhance student learning of psychology

❯ ACKNOWLEDGEMENTS/ REVIEWERS

A project having the scope of an introductory psychology text is truly a team enterprise, and we have been the lucky recipients of a great team effort. We wish to thank and acknowledge the contributions of the many people who made this book possible. Jane Vaicunas, Editorial Director, convinced us (quite correctly) that McGraw-Hill was a perfect match for us as a publisher. We thank her for her faith in this project. Shortly afterward, Joe Terry became our sponsoring editor and guided the project for the next two years. We express our gratitude to Joe for his wisdom and support. Mindy DePalma and Nancy Crochiere, our developmental editors, were wonderful to work with, and they helped keep the project on course through several rounds of reviews. On the production end, special thanks go to our Project Manager, Mary Lee Harms, for her cheerful and skillful coordination of the numerous production details. Her flexibility and wisdom was a constant source of support. Stuart Paterson guided the design and is largely responsible for the attractive appearance of the book. Bea Sussman did a wonderful job as copy editor, and photo editor Toni Morris worked tirelessly and with great tenacity. You will find many excellent and unique photos in this book, thanks to Toni's efforts. On our end of the production pipeline, we express a special debt of gratitude to Geraldine Williams, who helped us with the seemingly endless faxes and mailings during the course of the project.

In today's market, quality ancillaries are a critical element in the success of any text. Barbara Santoro, Editoral Coordinator, did a wonderful job coordinating the development of our supplementary materials, and she compiled an exceptional team. We thank Don Christensen (University of Washington), Kathleen Malley-Morrison (Boston University), and David Jones (Westminster College) for developing supplements that are second to none in quality.

A distinguished corps of colleagues reviewed the manuscript and gave us many helpful comments and suggestions. We want to first express our gratitude to several University of Washington colleagues who provided us with counsel and, at times, materials. These include David Corina, John Gottman, Hunter Hoffman, Earl Hunt, the late Neil Jacobson, Eileen Knight, G. Alan Marlatt, Lois McDermott, Lee Osterhout, and Yuichi Shoda.

We also express our gratitude for the input and suggestions received from Sarah Dunn a great many colleagues who reviewed several drafts of the manuscript. They include the following:

Ute J. Bayen
University of North Carolina, Chapel Hill

David Burrows
Beloit College

James Calhoun
University of Georgia

Marc Carter
Hofstra University

Betty Davenport
Campbell University

Rochelle Diogenes
Montclair, NJ

Dean E. Frost
Portland State University

Shepard B. Gorman
Nassau College Community

Robert A. Johnston
College of William & Mary

Robert Kaleta
University of Wisconsin–Milwaukee

Rick Kasschau
University of Houston

Karen Kopera-Frye
Buchtel College of Arts and Sciences

Alan J. Lipman
Georgetown University

Laura Madson
New Mexico State University

Kathleen Malley-Morrison
Boston University

David McDonald
University of Missouri

Mary Lee Meiners
San Diego Miramar College

Kevin Moore
De Pauw University

Donald J. Polzella
University of Dayton

Gary Poole
Simon Fraser University

J. T. Ptacek
Bucknell University

Jacqueline T. Ralston
Columbia College

Stephen Saunders
Marquette University

Alice H. Skeens
University of Toledo

Steven M. Smith
Texas A&M University

Sheldon Solomon
Skidmore College

Mary Hellen Spear
Prince Georges Community College

David Thomas
Oklahoma State University

David Uttal
Northwestern University

Lori Van Wallandael
University of North Carolina at Charlotte

Dennis Wanamaker
Bellevue College

Paul J. Watson
University of Tennessee

Clemens Weikert
Lund University

❯ SUPPLEMENTS FOR THE INSTRUCTOR

Print

Instructor's Manual.   A rich collection of lecture leads, learning objectives, in-class demonstrations, case studies, critical thinking questions, and current controversies will make course preparation a snap. This manual also provides many activity suggestions as well as handout and overhead transparency masters that will be sure to engage students' interest in class material.

Test Bank and Computerized Test Bank.   Keyed to the chapter learning objectives and marginal directed questions, the Test Bank contains approximately 250 questions per chapter to give maximum flexibility. Each chapter contains roughly 175 multiple-choice, 20 fill-in-the-blank, 20 matching, 20 true/false, and 5 essay questions. The printed TB is also available electronically in MAC and Windows to allow instructors to create their own tests.

Multimedia

On-Line Learning Center for Instructors.   This online resource contains PowerPoint lectures, the entire Instructor's Manual, an Image Bank, Web links, and a host of additional current resources to www.mhhe.com/passer to help prepare course materials.

Instructor's Resource CD-ROM.   This CD-ROM contains PowerPoint presentations, an Image Bank, Test Bank, and Instructor's Manual in addition to an easy-to-use interface for the design and delivery of multimedia classroom presentations.

Videos.   McGraw-Hill is committed to providing the video resources needed to supplement the introductory psychology course. Ask your sales representative for a brochure of current offerings and availability.

Transparency Acetates.   Over 50 key images drawn from the textbook are available for the instructor. In addition, the *Introductory Psychology Transparency Set* provides over 100 additional transparencies illustrating key concepts in general psychology.

Image Gallery.   This feature, located on the book's On-line Learning Center, consists of outstanding graphics that can be used for presentations in the classroom. The images can be downloaded into your favorite presentation program—for instance, PowerPoint.

PowerPoint Lecture.   Available on the Internet, these presentations cover the key points of the chapter and include images where relevant. They can be used as is or modified to meet your personal needs. Visit www.mhhe.com/passer

PageOut.   With PageOut even the most inexperienced computer user can quickly and easily create a professional-looking course website. Simply fill in our tempates with your information and with excellent content provided by McGraw-Hill, choose a design, and you've got a bang-up website specifically designed for your course! Best of all, it's FREE! Visit us at *www.pageout.net* to find out more.

❯ SUPPLEMENTS FOR THE STUDENT

Print

Student Study Guide.   Keyed to the directed questions in the text margin, the Study Guide contains helpful diagrams, a chapter overview and outline, key words and key people matching exercises, a chance to apply concepts, and practice chapter tests. In addition, the Study Guide includes a practice midterm and final! This is the perfect supplement for students *who are motivated to succeed.*

Multimedia

On-Line Learning Center for Students.   This rich collection of electronic resources features an interactive quizzing center, learning objectives, crossword puzzles, interactive exercises and drag-and-drop graphics. In attion, the OLC offers a statistics primer, Psychology Careers Appendix, and a study skills primer at www.mhhe.com/passer.

Making the Grade Student CD-ROM.   Packaged free with each copy of the text, this CD-ROM is designed to help students perform at their best. It contains practice quizzes for each text chapter, a learning styles assessment, study skills primer, guide to electronic research, and a link to the text website.

PRISM CD-ROM.   This student CD-ROM contains over 60 interactive exercises and activities, chapter outlined guided reviews, web links, a Psychology Careers Appendix, practice quizzes, Psychology Around the Globe interactive articles, and an Internet Primer. A great way to make studying a more effective exercise.

Psych On-Line.   This is designed to help students get the most out of the Internet for psychology research and provides general resource locations. Psychology sites are grouped by topic with a brief explanation of each site. Included are a number of genreal resouce sites for students seeking help.

Directed Questions

Each chapter has an average of forty to fifty directed questions that enhance student concept mastery, serve as retrieval clues during review, and act as a performance feedback measure for students.

Understanding the Causes of Behavior

This graphic feature occurs once in every chapter and accomplishes two important goals. First, it reinforces the central theme that behavior can be studied at biological, psychological, and environmental levels of analysis. Second, it summarizes the text's discussion of causal factors pertaining to a specific phenomenon, such as immune system functioning, learning, stress, aggression, and drug responses.

> 38. Which causal factors in depression are seen at the environmental level of analysis?

> 39. What is meant by the interaction of causal factors?

been subjected to severe loss and neglect may develop pessimistic personalities that predispose them to slide into depression in the face of later life stresses.

Finally, the environmental level of analysis reveals several factors that play a major role in depression. According to the behavioral view, depression is a reaction to a nonrewarding environment. A vicious cycle begins when the environment provides fewer rewards for the person. As depression intensifies, such people feel so badly that they to stop doing the things that ordinarily give them pleasure, a pattern that decreases environmental rewards still further. To make things worse, depressed people complain a good deal, seek excessive reassurance and support from others, and generally become less likeable. These behaviors eventually begin to alienate others and cause them to shy away from the depressed person. The net result is a worsening environment with fewer rewards, a reduction in support from others, and the unhappiness and hopeless pessimism that characterize chronic depression (Lewinsohn et al., 1985; Nezlek et al., 2000).

The sociocultural environment also affects depression. Although depression is found in virtually all cultures, both its symptom pattern and its causes may reflect cultural differences. For example, feelings of guilt and personal inadequacy seem to predominate in North American and western European countries, whereas bodily symptoms of fatigue, loss of appetite, and sleep difficulties are more often reported in Latin, Chinese, and African cultures (Brislin, 1993; Lopez & Guarnaccia, 2000). Cross-cultural studies have also shown that in developed countries like the United States, Canada, and other Western nations, women are about twice as likely as men to report feeling depressed, whereas no such sex difference is found in developing countries (Culbertson, 1997; Nolen-Hoeksema, 1990). Why should this be? At present, we do not have the answer, but we must wonder what it is about more technologically advanced cultures that would produce a sex difference that does not show up in developing countries.

Figure 1.23 summarizes causal factors in depression that are supported by theory and research. Although these causal factors are organized into three classes (biological, psychological, and environmental), we should keep two important points in mind. First, the specific causes of depression can not only differ from case to case, but they can also combine or *interact* with one another in ways that vary according to the person and the situation. **Interaction** means that the presence or strength of one factor can influence the effects of other factors. For example, a person who has a strong biological predisposition for depression may become de-

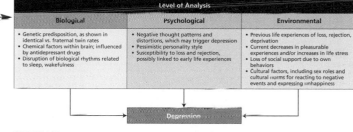

Level of Analysis		
Biological	**Psychological**	**Environmental**
• Genetic predisposition, as shown in identical vs. fraternal twin rates • Chemical factors within brain; influenced by antidepressant drugs • Disruption of biological rhythms related to sleep, wakefulness	• Negative thought patterns and distortions, which may trigger depression • Pessimistic personality style • Susceptibility to loss and rejection, possibly linked to early life experiences	• Previous life experiences of loss, rejection, deprivation • Current decreases in pleasurable experiences and/or increases in life stress • Loss of social support due to own behaviors • Cultural factors, including sex roles and cultural norms for reacting to negative events and expressing unhappiness

Depression

FIGURE 1.23 Understanding the Causes of Behavior: Biological, psychological, and environmental factors in depression.

PSYCHOLOGICAL FRONTIERS

Cultural and Psychological Influences on Pain

Our interpretation of pain impulses sent to the brain depends in part on our experiences and beliefs, and both of these factors are influenced by the culture in which we develop (Rollman, 1998). Consider childbirth, for example. This event is a painful ordeal for many mothers in Western cultures, and many women express considerable anxiety about going through it (Blechman & Brownell, 1998). Yet in certain cultures women show virtually no distress during childbirth. Indeed, in one culture studied by anthropologists, it was customarily for the woman's husband to get into bed and groan as if he were in great pain, while the woman calmly gave birth to the child. The husband stayed in bed with the baby to recover from his terrible ordeal while the mother returned to work in the fields almost immediately (Kroeber, 1948).

In certain parts of India, people practice an unusual hook-hanging ritual. A holy person is chosen to bless the children and crops in a number of neighboring villages. Large steel hooks attached by ropes to the top of a special ceremonial cart are then shoved under the skin and muscles on each side of his back, and he travels on the cart from village to village. At the climax of a ceremony in each village, the celebrant leaps from the cart and swings free, hanging only by the hooks embedded in his back (Figure 4.49). Incredibly, though impaled on the hooks with his entire body weight, the celebrant shows no evidence of pain during the ritual; on the contrary, he appears to be in a state of ecstasy. When the hooks are removed, the wounds heal rapidly and are scarcely visible within two weeks (Kosambi, 1967).

Although ethnic groups do not appear to differ in their ability to discriminate among pain stimuli, members of different cultural groups may differ greatly in their interpretation of pain and the amount of suffering they experience (Rollman, 1998; Zatzick & Dimsdale, 1990). In the Indian hook-hanging ceremony, for example, the religious meanings attached to the act seem to transform the interpretations and meaning of the sensory input from the hooks as well. The role of cultural factors in pain is found even within modern Western subcultures. In a study done in the Worcester, Massachusetts, area, researchers studied pain perception in 372 medical patients who represented six different ethnic groups: Old Americans (at least third-generation U.S.-born Caucasians who identified with no ethnic group except Americans), Hispanics, Italians, Irish, French Canadians, and Polish. All of the patients suffered from chronic pain conditions that had persisted for at least three months and were beyond the point of healing. The patients completed self-report measures about their pain experiences.

The ethnic groups did not differ overall in type of physical affliction, how long they had had it, or the kinds

FIGURE 4.49 A hook-swinging ceremony practiced in remote villages in India illustrates the importance of the meaning attributed to pain stimuli. After blessing all the children and farm fields in a village, the celebrant leaps from the cart and hangs suspended by the hooks in a state of ecstasy, showing no sign of pain.
Adapted from Kosambi, 1967.

of treatments and medications they were receiving. They did differ, however, in the pain levels they reported, and these differences were associated with different attitudes and beliefs about their pain. The Hispanic and Italian patients believed most strongly that they had no control over their pain, reported feeling worried and angry about it, and believed that they would be unhappy as long as they experienced it. They also believed that it is appropriate to express one's pain openly. These two ethnic groups reported the highest levels of pain and suffering. In contrast, the Old American and Polish patients felt it best to suppress the outward expression of pain, reported feeling less upset about their pain sensations, and believed that they had greater personal control over their lives. These attitudinal differences were associated with much lower levels of reported suffering (Bates et al., 1993).

Differences exist not only between cultural groups but also within them, as the physician Henry Beecher (1959) observed while working at Anzio Beachhead in World War II and later at Massachusetts General Hospital. Beecher found that only about 25 percent of the severely wounded

–Continued

Psychological Frontiers

This in-depth feature highlights cutting-edge research and issues in psychology. It emphasizes basic research and its relevance to societal applications. This feature illustrates the dynamic nature of psychological science and ways in which it can promote human betterment.

RESEARCH CLOSE-UP

Stalking a Deadly Illusion

▶ Background

When the Boeing Company introduced the 727 jet airliner in the mid-1960s, it was the latest word in aviation technology. The plane performed well in test flights, but four fatal crashes soon after it was placed in service raised fears that there might be some fatal flaw in its design.

The first accident occurred as a 727 made its approach to Chicago over Lake Michigan on a clear night. The plane plunged into the lake 19 miles offshore. About a month later, another 727 glided in over the Ohio River to land in Cincinnati. Unaccountably, it struck the ground about 12 feet below the runway elevation and burst into flames. The third accident occurred as an aircraft approached Salt Lake City over dark land. The lights of the city twinkled in the distance, but the plane made too rapid a descent and crashed short of the runway. Months later, a Japanese airliner approached Tokyo at night. The flight ended tragically as the plane, its landing gear not yet lowered, struck the waters of Tokyo Bay 6 miles from the runway.

Analysis of these four accidents, as well as others, suggested a common pattern. All occurred at night under clear weather conditions, so that the pilots were operating under visual flight rules rather than performing instrument landings. In each instance, the plane was approaching city lights over dark areas of water or land. In all cases, the lights in the background sloped upward to varying degrees. Finally, all of the planes crashed short of the runway. These observations led a Boeing psychologist, Conrad L. Kraft, to suspect that the cause of the crashes might be pilot error based on some sort of visual illusion.

▶ Method

To test this possibility, Boeing engineers constructed an apparatus to simulate night landings (Figure 4.46). It consisted of a cockpit and a miniature lighted "city" named Nightertown. The city moved toward the cockpit on computer-controlled rollers, and it could be tilted to simulate various terrain slopes. The pilot could control simulated air speed and rate of climb and descent, and the Nightertown scene was controlled by the pilot's responses just as a true visual scene would be.

The participants were 12 experienced Boeing flight instructors who made virtual reality "landings" at Nightertown under systematically varied conditions created by the computerized simulator. All of their landings were visual landings so as to be able to test whether a visual illusion was occurring. Every aspect of their approach and the manner in which they controlled the aircraft was measured precisely.

FIGURE 4.46 Conrad Kraft, a Boeing psychologist, created an apparatus to study how visual cues can affect the simulated landings of airline pilots. Pilots approached Nightertown in a simulated cockpit. The computer-controlled city could be tilted to reproduce the illusion thought to be responsible for fatal air crashes.

▶ Results

The landings made by the flight instructors were nearly flawless until Kraft duplicated the conditions of the fatal crashes by having the pilots approach an upward-sloping distant city over a dark area. When this occurred, the pilots were unable to detect the upward slope, assumed that the background city was flat, and consistently overestimated their altitude. On a normal landing, the preferred altitude at 4.5 miles from the runway is about 1,240 feet. As Figure 4.47 shows, the pilots approached at about this altitude when the simulated city was in a flat position. But when it was sloped upward, 11 of the 12 experienced pilot instructors crashed about 4.5 miles short of the runway.

▶ Critical Analysis

This study shows the value of being able to study behavior under highly controlled conditions and with precise measurements. By simulating the conditions under which the fatal crashes had occurred, Kraft identified the visual illusion that was the source of pilot error. He showed that the perceptual hypotheses of the flight instructors, like those of the pilots involved in the real crashes, were tragically incorrect. It would have been ironic if one of the finest jet liners ever built had been removed from service because of presumed mechanical defects while other aircraft remained at risk.

—Continued

Research Close-Ups

Each Research Close-Up describes and critically evaluates a high-interest study. Presented in a simplified journal format (background, method, results, critical analysis), these high-interest studies represent a diversity of research methods.

Applications of Psychological Science

This feature compellingly shows the student how principles derived from basic research have direct individual and social applications. Some features provide direct guidelines for the student's personal benefit, whereas others focus on more global societal issues.

APPLICATIONS OF PSYCHOLOGICAL SCIENCE

Making Close Relationships Work: Lessons From Psychological Research

Close relationships go through good times and bad, persisting or dissolving over time. Consider marriage. Though highly intimate, this union often is fragile. In the United States, about half of first marriages end in divorce, and the failure rate for second marriages is higher. How can people make their close relationships more satisfying and stable? Recent research on marriage suggests several answers that also can be applied to dating relationships and friendships.

For decades, most marital research simply asked people about their marriages. But as Figure 9.23 shows, researchers are now bringing couples into laboratories to videotape their interactions and to chart their facial and physiological responses as they discuss emotionally charged issues (Gottman et al., 1999; Kiecolt-Glaser et al., 1998). Rather than focusing only on unhappy couples to find out what is going wrong in their relationships, researchers are also studying happy couples to discover the secrets of their success.

Using these methods and new marital interview techniques, psychologists have predicted whether marriages will last or dissolve with impressive accuracy (Carrière et al., 2000). In one laboratory study, John Gottman and his coworkers (1998) collected behavioral and physiological data from 130 newlywed couples as they discussed areas of marital conflict (e.g., in-laws, finances, sex) during the first six months of their marriage. Six years later, participants reported being happily married, unhappily married, or divorced. Using data collected while the couples were newlyweds, the researchers predicted which marriages would end in divorce with 83 percent accuracy, and the degree of marital satisfaction in still-married couples with 80 percent accuracy.

Surprisingly, the amount of anger expressed by husbands and wives in their laboratory interactions predicted neither stability nor happiness six years later. Instead, the crucial factor was the manner in which couples dealt with their anger. Particularly important were four behaviors that Gottman (1994) calls "The Four Horsemen of the Apocalypse": *criticism, contempt, defensiveness,* and *stonewalling* (listener withdrawal and nonresponsiveness).

Couples headed for unhappiness or divorce often exhibit these behaviors while discussing conflict, thereby escalating their conflict and negative emotions. When the wife criticizes the husband, he often stonewalls and withdraws from her attempts to reach some resolution. Her resulting frustration leads to stronger emotional displays and criticism, and the interaction degenerates into exchanges of contempt in which the partners tear down

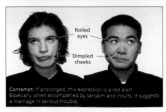

Rolled eyes

Dimpled cheeks

Contempt: if prolonged, this expression is a red alert. Especially when accompanied by sarcasm and insults, it suggests a marriage in serious trouble.

FIGURE 9.23 In John Gottman's "love lab," married couples (husband visible in rear) are filmed while interacting. Facial expressions, actions, heart rate, breathing rate, perspiration, fidgeting, and other responses are measured.

each other. Once this negative cycle develops, even positive overtures by one spouse are likely to evoke a negative response from the other (Margolin & Wampold, 1981).

Happily married couples experience conflict and anger too, but do not allow the spiral of negativity to get out of control. Instead, they make frequent "repair attempts" to resolve their differences in a spirit of mutual respect and support. Gottman and his coworkers (1998) found that in happy marriages, the wife often introduced the conflict topic in a softened or low-intensity manner, rather than

—Continued

Chapter Summary

The end-of-chapter summaries provide a bulleted list that highlights the major topics covered under each section within the chapter.

▼▼

CHAPTER SUMMARY

Perspectives on Motivation

- Motivation is a process that influences the direction, vigor, and persistence of behavior. Evolutionary psychologists propose that in our ancestral past, motivational tendencies that had adaptive significance were more likely to be passed from one generation to the next, eventually evolving into genetically based predispositions to act in certain ways.

- Homeostatic models view motivation as an attempt to maintain equilibrium in bodily systems. Drive theories propose that tissue deficits create drives, such as hunger, that motivate or "push" an organism from within to reduce that deficit and restore homeostasis.

- Incentive theories emphasize the role of environmental factors that "pull" people toward a goal. The cognitive expectancy × value theory explains why the same incentive may motivate some people, but not others.

- Psychodynamic theories emphasize that unconscious motives and mental processes guide much of our behavior. Humanist Abraham Maslow proposed that needs exist in a hierarchy, from basic biological needs to the ultimate need for self-actualization.

Hunger and Weight Regulation

- The body monitors several chemicals involved in energy utilization. Changing patterns of glucose usage provide one signal that helps initiate hunger. Upon eating, hormones such as CCK are released into the bloodstream and help signal the brain to stop eating. Fat cells release leptin, which acts as a long-term signal that helps to regulate appetite. The hypothalamus and other brain regions play a role in hunger regulation.

- The expected good taste of food motivates eating and the thought of food can trigger hunger. Our memory, attitudes, habits, and psychological needs affect our food intake.

- The availability, taste, and variety of food powerfully regulate eating. Through classical conditioning, neutral stimuli can acquire the capacity to trigger hunger. Cultural norms affect our food preferences and eating habits.

- Heredity and the environment affect our susceptibility to becoming obese. Homeostatic mechanisms make it difficult to lose substantial weight.

- Anorexia and bulimia are eating disorders that have serious physical consequences, occur more often in cultures that value thinness, and are associated with different psychological profiles and childhood patterns of family interaction.

Sensation-Seeking

- Humans and other animals tend to seek out novelty and stimulation. High sensation seekers are more likely to engage in risky activities than are low sensation seekers.

- Sensation seeking may have a biological basis. High sensation seekers may be less reactive to external stimulation than are low sensation seekers.

Sexual Motivation

- The last half century has witnessed changing patterns of sexual activity, such as an increase in premarital sex.

- During sexual intercourse people often experience a four-stage physiological response pattern consisting of excitement, plateau, orgasm, and resolution.

- Sex hormones have organizational effects that guide the prenatal development of internal and external organs along either a male or female pattern. Sex hormones also have activational effects that influence sexual desire.

- Sexual fantasy can trigger arousal, whereas stress and psychological difficulties can interfere with sexual arousal. Cultural norms determine the sexual practices and beliefs that are considered moral, proper, and desirable.

- Environmental stimuli affect sexual desire. Viewing sexual violence reinforces men's belief in rape myths and increases men's aggression toward women, at least temporarily.

- Sexual orientation involves dimensions of self-identity, sexual attraction, and actual sexual behavior. No single biological, social, or psychological factor—and no specific combination of causes—has been clearly identified as the cause of sexual orientation.

The Desire for Affiliation and Intimacy

- Affiliation has adaptive advantages and allows people to engage in social comparison.

- Proximity, mere exposure, similarity of attitudes, and physical attractiveness typically enhance our liking for someone else.

- Evolutionary theorists propose that cross-cultural gender differences in mate preferences reflect inherited biological tendencies, whereas social structure theory argues that they result from sex-role socialization and societal gender inequities in economic opportunities.

- Relationships deepen as partners self-disclose and exchanges between them become more intimate and broader. According to social exchange theory, people will be satisfied when their relationship outcomes exceed their comparison level, and they will remain in the relationship if the outcomes exceed their comparison level for alternatives.

- Different combinations of intimacy, commitment, and passion lead to different types of love. Due to transfer of excitation, arousal caused by some other factor may be misattributed as increased feelings of passion toward someone we find attractive.

- Partners are more likely to remain happily married when they understand each other and deal with conflicts by de-escalating their emotions and providing mutual support.

Achievement Motivation

- People who have a high motivation for success are attracted to the thrill of victory and value mastery and social comparison. People who have a high fear of failure experience anxiety in achievement settings. They are motivated by social comparison and a fear of performing poorly.

Key Terms and Concepts

This feature lists the key terms and concepts found throughout the chapter. Page references are provided with each key term to help students locate it within the chapter.

KEY TERMS AND CONCEPTS*

achievement test (341)
algorithm (332)
aptitude test (341)
availability heuristic (334)
belief bias (329)
cognitive process theories (348)
concept (323)
confirmation bias (335)
construct validity (343)
content validity (343)
crystallized intelligence (346)
deductive reasoning (327)
deep structure (318)
displacement (317)
divergent thinking (336)
emotional intelligence (347)
factor analysis (345)
fluid intelligence (346)
functional fixedness (336)
heuristics (332)
imaginal thought (323)
incubation (336)

inductive reasoning (328)
intelligence (337)
intelligence quotient (IQ) (338)
interjudge reliability (343)
internal consistency (343)
knowledge-acquisition components (349)
language (317)
linguistic relativity hypothesis (322)
means-ends analysis (332)
mental representations (316)
mental age (338)
mental set (331)
metacomponents (348)
morpheme (318)
motoric thought (323)
normal distribution (344)
norms (344)
performance components (349)
phoneme (318)
predictive validity (343)
primary mental abilities (345)

problem-solving schemas (331)
proposition (323)
propositional thought (323)
prototype (323)
psychological test (342)
psychometrics (344)
reaction range (351)
reliability (342)
representativeness heuristic (333)
savant (347)
semantics (318)
standardization (344)
stereotype threat (355)
subgoal analysis (332)
surface structure (317)
syntax (317)
telegraphic speech (320)
test-retest reliability (342)
triarchic theory of intelligence (348)
validity (343)

* Each term has been boldfaced in the text on the page indicated in parentheses.

Applying Your Knowledge

Applying Your Knowledge is an end-of-chapter set of ten multiple-choice questions that require students to apply the chapter's content to concrete situations.

APPLYING YOUR KNOWLEDGE

1. "Tom eats hamburgers. Pizza eats Tom." Which statement about these two sentences is correct?
   a) Both sentences are semantically correct.
   b) Only one sentence has correct syntax.
   c) Neither sentence is semantically correct.
   d) Both sentences have correct syntax.

2. A mother instructs her son to tell her neighbor, "I'll be home at four, but I'll be out until then." He tells the neighbor, "Mother will be gone most of the day, but she'll be back by four." The son clearly remembered the
   a) surface structure, but not the deep structure
   b) syntax of the message, but not the semantics
   c) deep structure, but not the surface structure
   d) phonemes, but not the morphemes

3. Shelley is trying to develop a theoretical principle. She considers the facts she knows to be true of the phenomenon she is studying. She then tries to reason from these facts to a conclusion about causal factors. Shelley is engaging in
   a) inductive reasoning
   b) propositional reasoning
   c) syllogistic inference
   d) deductive reasoning

4. You ask twenty of your acquaintances to rate the likelihood of the following statements: (a) There will be a flood in southern California; (b) There will be an earthquake in California that causes a flood. Sixteen of your participants

PSYCHOLOGY: THE SCIENCE OF BEHAVIOR

Perhaps the most fascinating and mysterious
universe of all is the one within us.
— *Carl Sagan*

1

CHAPTER OUTLINE

▼▼▼▼▼▼▼▼▼▼▼▼▼▼▼▼▼▼▼▼▼▼▼▼▼▼▼▼▼▼▼▼▼▼▼▼▼▼

Down through the ages . . . we have had political, economic and nationalistic revolutions. All of them, as our descendants will discover, are but ripples in an ocean of conservatism—trivial by comparison with the psychological revolution toward which we are so rapidly moving.

More than a half century has passed since the English literary master and visionary Aldous Huxley (1950) foresaw an age in which scientific knowledge about mind and behavior would provide us with greater understanding of ourselves and with powerful tools to improve our lives. We are now in the midst of the psychological revolution that Huxley predicted. On many fronts, important advances are being made in unraveling the mysteries of human behavior. Like the world in which we live, the face of modern-day psychology constantly changes as new discoveries deepen our knowledge and create new opportunities for the application of psychological science. In this book, we intend to share with you the sense of excitement that exists on these frontiers of our attempt to know, to understand, and to change ourselves and the world of the 21st century.

〉 THE NATURE OF PSYCHOLOGY

➤ 1. Define psychology and indicate what kinds of behaviors it studies.

Psychology is the scientific study of behavior and the factors that influence it. Psychologists use the term *behavior* very broadly to refer both to actions that we can directly observe and to inner processes such as thoughts, feelings, images, and physiological reactions. In their search for the causes of these diverse forms of behavior, psychologists take into account biological, psychological, and environmental factors.

The science of psychology relates to virtually every aspect of our lives. It explores the nature and causes of our behavior and feelings, our motives and thoughts. Psychology has also assumed an increasingly important role in solving human problems and promoting the welfare of the inhabitants of this complex and rapidly changing world. As you will discover, psychologists are concerned with an enormous range of questions about behavior. The following is just a sample of the issues we will be viewing through the window of psychology:

- How do we remember, think, and reason?
- How do drugs alter brain functioning and thereby affect consciousness and behavior?
- What makes us fall in love?
- How does one's culture influence behavior?
- What are the causes of aggression, and how can aggression be controlled?
- How do our genes affect our abilities, personality, and behavior?
- Which child-rearing methods produce psychologically healthy adults?
- Why do we sleep, and what functions do our dreams serve? What brain processes regulate sleep and dreaming?
- What are the causes of mental disorders and addictions, and how can they be treated or prevented?
- To what extent are our actions controlled by unconscious factors?
- Can stress kill? What are effective ways of coping with stress?

This book is your map. Follow us as we explore these and many other questions. Because behavior is so complex and so personal, its scientific study poses special challenges. As you become familiar with the kinds of evidence necessary to validate scientific conclusions, you can become a better informed

TABLE 1.1   WIDELY HELD BELIEFS ABOUT BEHAVIOR: FACTS OR FICTION?

1. Personality development is primarily influenced by the experiences that are shared by members of a family.
2. Intellectual abilities decline dramatically in old age.
3. The primary reason babies develop love for their parents is because they satisfy biological and safety needs.
4. Most people with exceptionally high IQs are poorly adjusted in other areas of their life.
5. A person who is innocent of a crime has nothing to fear from a lie detector test.
6. Hypnosis is a reliable method for helping people recover unconscious memories of childhood sexual abuse.
7. People who need help in an emergency are more likely to get it if there are many bystanders present than if there is only one.
8. A schizophrenic is a person who has two distinct personalities, hence the term "split personality."
9. In romantic relationships, opposites usually attract.
10. If ordered to do so by an authority who could not punish disobedience, most people would refuse to perform an act that would harm another.
11. Consistent punishment for misbehavior is the most effective way to make people behave appropriately.
12. People who commit suicide usually have signaled to others their intention to do so.

Note: The first 11 statements have been disproved by psychological research. The last statement is supported by research findings.

consumer of the many claims made in the name of psychology. For one thing, this course will teach you that many widely held beliefs about behavior have no basis in fact. That's important to know for, as the American Revolutionary War general Artemus Ward pointed out, "It ain't so much the things we don't know that get us into trouble. It's the things we know that just ain't so." Table 1.1 presents some widely held popular beliefs that "just ain't so." Perhaps even more important than the facts you learn in your psychology course will be the habits of thought that you acquire. As you develop the skills of critical thinking, you will learn to ask several very important questions when told about a new "fact":

- "What exactly are you asking me to believe?"
- "How do you know? What's the evidence?"
- "Are there other possible explanations?"

We want you to leave your introductory psychology course with improved critical thinking skills, and with the ability to analyze behavior and its causes. These skills will serve you well in many areas of your life.

Psychology as a Basic and Applied Science

As scientists, psychologists employ a variety of research methods for developing and testing theories about behavior and its causes. A distinction is sometimes made between **basic research,** the quest for knowledge purely for its own sake, and **applied research,** which is designed to solve specific practical problems. In psychology, the goals of basic research are to describe how people behave and to identify the factors that influence or cause a particular type of behavior. Such research may be carried out in the laboratory or in real-world settings. Applied research often uses principles discovered through basic research to solve practical problems.

➤ 2. How do the goals of basic research and applied research differ?

Let us consider an example of the link between basic and applied research. In this case a classic research study carried out more than a generation ago inspired a more recent educational strategy designed to reduce interracial conflict and increase learning in multicultural schools.

From Robbers Cave to the Jigsaw Classroom

How does intergroup hostility and prejudice develop, and what can be done to reduce it? In today's multicultural world, where religious and ethnic groups often clash with one another, this question has great societal importance. To provide an answer to it, basic research explores the factors that increase and reduce intergroup hostility.

Psychologists conducted one such study at a summer camp for 11-year-old boys in Robbers Cave, Oklahoma (Sherif et al., 1961). When they arrived at the camp, the boys were divided by the researchers into two groups, which chose to call themselves the Eagles and the Rattlers. The Eagles and Rattlers lived in different cabins, but did all other activities together and got along well until the second week, when the experimenters began to pit them against one another in a series of competitive contests. It wasn't long before strong hostility developed between the groups. Group members discriminated against children from the other group and would not form friendships with them. The researchers then attempted to reduce the escalating conflict, but soon learned that simply increasing contact between the groups only increased the level of hostility and distrust. Was there anything that could be done to restore harmony?

The researchers finally succeeded in reducing the hostility by placing the children in situations in which the two groups were forced to cooperate with each other to accomplish goals that were important to both groups. These activities included repairing the water supply system, pooling their money to rent a movie, and towing a truck to get it started so they could all go into town. In each instance, the Eagles and Rattlers needed each other in order to attain a common goal. Within six days, these cooperative experiences virtually dissolved the boundaries between the groups, and many new friendships developed between Eagles and Rattlers.

The Robbers Cave study showed that competition could breed hostility and that conflict between groups could be decreased by making the groups dependent upon one another so that they would need to cooperate. Could this principle, derived from basic research, be applied to increase harmony and academic achievement in multiracial schools, where different ethnic groups sometimes compete against one another in much the same way the Eagles and Rattlers did? Years later, in the midst of a stormy desegregation of public schools in Texas, psychologist Elliot Aronson and his coworkers applied the Robbers Cave techniques in the form of a classroom procedure called the **jigsaw program** (Aronson et al., 1978). This program requires children to cooperate with one another rather than compete in order for any of them to succeed. It involves creating multiethnic groups of five or six children who are assigned to prepare for an upcoming test on, for example, the life of Abraham Lincoln. Within the groups, each child is given a "piece" of the total knowledge to be learned. Only one child has information about Lincoln's early childhood, another about his political career, a third about his death, and so on. For any of the group members to pass the test, they must fit their knowledge "pieces" together as if they were working on a jigsaw puzzle. Each child must teach the others his or her piece of knowledge. Like the children at Robbers Cave, the students soon learn that the only way they can be successful is to work together and help one another. In so doing, they learn to appreciate one another and to feel appreciated by the other group members (Figure 1.1).

The effects of the jigsaw technique and other "cooperative learning" programs have been carefully evaluated in hundreds of classrooms, and the results are encouraging (Aronson, 1997; Johnson, 2000). Across racial boundaries, children's liking for one another generally increased, prejudice decreased, and self-esteem as well as school achievement improved. In one study, minority children increased their performance by almost one full letter grade after only two weeks of jigsaw participation (Lucker et al., 1977). Measures of school enjoyment also increased for all ethnic groups.

Cooperative learning programs show how basic research like the Robbers Cave experiment can be used as a basis for designing an intervention program.

➤ 3. How do the Robbers Cave experiment and the jigsaw classroom program illustrate the relation between basic and applied science?

FIGURE 1.1 The jigsaw classroom designed by psychologist Elliot Aronson, was inspired by basic research that showed how conditions of mutual dependence and cooperation among hostile groups can reduce intergroup hostility. Aronson's applied research intervention had similar effects within racially integrated classrooms.

We will see many other examples of how basic research provides knowledge that not only satisfies our desire to understand our world, but also can be applied to solve practical problems.

Goals of Psychology

As scientists, psychologists have four basic goals:

1. to *describe* how people and other animals behave
2. to *understand* (explain) the causes of these behaviors
3. to *predict* how people and animals will behave under certain conditions
4. to *control,* or influence, behavior through knowledge and control of its causes

➤ 4. What are the four goals of psychology? How are these goals linked to one another?

As you will learn in Chapter 2, the scientific goals of understanding, prediction, and control are linked in the following manner: If we understand the causes of a behavior and know when the causal factors are present or absent, then we should be able to successfully predict when the behavior will occur. Moreover, if we can control the causes, then we should be able to control the behavior. For scientists, successful prediction and control are the best way for us to know whether we truly understand the causes of a behavior. We should also note, however, that prediction can have important practical uses that do not require a complete understanding of why some behavior occurs. For example, a psychologist might find that scores on a personality test dependably predict school dropout without fully understanding the psychological processes involved.

All of these goals were pursued in the basic and applied research examples described above. At Robbers Cave, the researchers carefully observed the behavior of the boys under certain conditions (description). They believed that competition is one cause of intergroup hostility and discrimination, and that cooperation to achieve common goals could reduce such hostility (understanding). They then tested their understanding by forecasting what would happen if they created conditions that first pitted the Eagles and Rattlers against one another, then forced them to cooperate (prediction). When they imposed these conditions, they first created and then reduced intergroup hostility (control). Later, when Aronson and his coworkers wanted to reduce racial hostility and discrimination within newly integrated schools, they had a scientific basis for predicting what might work, and they were able to successfully apply their understanding in the form of the jigsaw program.

➤ 5. How were the four goals of scientific psychology illustrated in the Robber's Cave study?

These four goals of description, understanding, prediction, and control are not limited to the world of science. They are also important goals of daily life. On a day-to-day basis, we all ask questions such as "What's happening? What am I (or they) doing?" (description); "Why did she do that?" (understanding or explanation); "What will happen if I do it this way?" (prediction); and "What can I do to make sure things turn out the way I want them to?" (control). In daily life, however, we are often satisfied with our "understanding" if we have a logical explanation that is consistent with what happened in the past. We usually don't go the extra mile to test our understanding more systematically through prediction and control, as scientists do.

❯ PERSPECTIVES ON BEHAVIOR: GUIDES TO UNDERSTANDING AND DISCOVERY

On a hot summer evening, a University of Texas student wrote the following letter:

> I don't really understand myself these days. I am supposed to be an average, reasonable, and intelligent young man. However, lately (I can't recall when it started) I have been the victim of many unusual and irrational thoughts. These thoughts constantly recur, and it requires a tremendous mental effort to concentrate on useful and progressive tasks. In March when my parents made a physical break I noticed a great deal of stress. I consulted a Dr. Cochrum at the University Health Center and asked him to recommend someone that I could consult with about some psychiatric disorders I felt I had. I talked with a doctor once for about two hours and tried to convey to him my fears that I felt overcome by overwhelming violent impulses. After one session I never saw the doctor again, and since then I have been fighting my mental turmoil alone, and seemingly to no avail. After my death I wish that an autopsy would be performed on me to see if there is any visible physical disorder. I have had some tremendous headaches in the past and have consumed two large bottles of Excedrin in the past three months.

Later that night Charles Whitman killed his wife and mother. The next morning he went to a tower on the University of Texas campus and opened fire on the crowded campus below with a high-powered hunting rifle. In 90 horrifying minutes he killed 14 people, wounded another 24, and even managed to hit an airplane before he himself was killed by police.

School shootings and other acts of apparently senseless violence are all too common in today's world. After the Whitman incident, the first question asked was a familiar one: What caused this mild-mannered young man (Figure 1.2) to explode into violence? Psychologists sought clues in the letter he wrote. Following up on his reference to intense headaches, a postmortem examination was conducted. It revealed a highly malignant tumor in an area of the brain known to be involved in aggressive behavior. Some experts therefore suggested that Whitman's damaged brain might have predisposed him to violent behavior. Others focused on the "unusual and irrational thoughts" to which he referred and to his "overwhelming violent impulses." Still others sought the answer in Whitman's previous learning experiences and the culture he grew up in. A study of his past revealed a long history of fascination and rewarding experiences with guns, as well as exposure to a brutally abusive father who often beat his mother and siblings. He also lived in a culture that is renowned for its violent solutions to conflict. Perhaps the environment in which he developed had primed him to solve his problems in a violent manner, particularly when he was overwhelmed by the recent life stresses that he described in his letter. The Whitman case thus illustrates how many potential causes, past and present, could contribute to a given behavior. In their attempts to understand Whitman's actions, psychologists considered potential causes at

FIGURE 1.2 Mass murderer Charles Whitman had no previous history of criminal violence. How can we explain such an apparently irrational act?

➤ 6. At what three levels of analysis were possible causes for Charles Whitman's violent outburst explored?

three different *levels of analysis:* biological, psychological, and environmental. We shall return to the levels of analysis concept later in the chapter. First, however, we consider the major psychological perspectives that provide an understanding of the specific causal factors that are studied at each level of analysis.

The Importance of Perspectives

Partly because psychology has its roots in such varied disciplines as philosophy, medicine, and the biological and physical sciences, different ways of viewing people and their behavior make up its intellectual and scientific traditions. These diverse viewpoints, or, as we shall call them, **perspectives,** are vantage points for analyzing behavior and its biological, psychological, and environmental causes (Figure 1.3). Thinking about a behavioral phenomenon from different perspectives can enrich our understanding of its diverse causes.

If you've ever encountered a person who seems to view the world much differently from the way you do, you know that perspectives make a difference. You may have found that he or she had different notions of why things happen and attached great importance to things you barely noticed. Like our own personal viewpoints, psychological perspectives serve as lenses through which the world of behavior is viewed, and they reflect and shape our conception of human nature. They also determine which aspects of behavior we consider important and worthy of study, which questions we ask, and which methods of study we employ. Perspectives on behavior thereby influence the directions in which psychology develops, what it learns about behavior, and the kinds of contributions it makes to improving the human condition.

Six major perspectives characterize contemporary psychological thought. They are the biological, cognitive, psychodynamic, behavioral, humanistic, and sociocultural perspectives (Figure 1.4). Each attempts to address timeless philosophical questions about human nature, and they often build upon insights achieved by other perspectives. The six perspectives also provide us with a historical framework for tracing the intellectual and scientific traditions that have fostered the development of modern-day psychology.

In science, new viewpoints are the lifeblood of progress. Advances occur as existing beliefs are challenged, a debate ensues, and scientists seek new evidence to resolve the debate. Sometimes, the best-supported elements of the contrasting viewpoints are melded into a new viewpoint which, in turn, stimulates new understandings when it is later challenged. Thus, as one scientist notes, "Science consists of organizing controversy or, if need be, generating it" (Murphy 1982).

We first consider each of the perspectives individually, focusing on their conceptions of human nature and their viewpoints about causal factors in behavior. Then, we place their contributions in historical perspective, showing how their influence has contributed to the evolution of psychology.

The Biological Perspective: Brain, Genes, and Behavior

Humans have long sought to understand the role of biological factors in their behavior. At the center of this quest lies a philosophical question that has tested and bested the greatest minds of the ages: the so-called *mind-body problem.* The concept of mind—the inner agent of consciousness and thought—has its roots in antiquity. Yet its very nature has been debated down through the ages. Is it a spiritual entity separate from the body, or is it part of our body's activities?

➤ 7. What are perspectives on behavior? Cite four ways in which they can influence psychological science.

FIGURE 1.3 Youth and beauty? . . . or maturity and wisdom? If you examine this drawing, you will see at various times either a young woman or an old one. The images will alternate as you examine the drawing, particularly if you interpret the dark horizontal line in the lower half of the figure as either a necklace or a mouth. Like many aspects of our experience, what we perceive depends on our perspective at the moment.

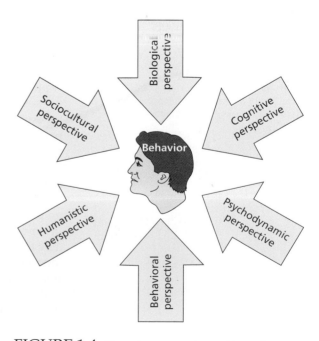

FIGURE 1.4 Six major perspectives guide modern psychology's attempts to understand human behavior.

➤ 8. Contrast the positions of dualism and monism as they apply to the "mind-body" problem.

➤ 9. What three classes of causal factors does the biological perspective focus on?

➤ 10. What was the importance of Galvani's discovery for (a) the body-mind puzzle, and (b) the development of psychology as a science?

The ancient Greeks could not agree on the vital question of how mind and body are related. Pythagoras, Plato, and Hippocrates all believed that the brain is the seat of the mind and the intellect. Aristotle disagreed, believing that the mind is located in the heart. Many of the Greeks as well as other philosophers held a position of **mind-body dualism,** the belief that the mind is a spiritual entity that is not subject to the physical laws that govern the body. This view implies that no amount of research on the body could ever hope to unravel the mysteries of the mind.

An alternative view of mind-body relations is derived from the Greek word *monos,* meaning "one." **Monism** holds that the "mind" is not a separate spiritual entity. Mind and body are one, and mental events are simply a product of physical events. In the modern view, these physical events are electrical and chemical processes occurring in the brain. If this is so, then questions about mental functions *can* be studied scientifically, for we can potentially measure these physical processes. Most modern scientists hold the view that mind and body are one, and many who hold a biological perspective would agree with this somewhat provocative statement by physiological psychologists Richard Thompson and Daniel Robinson:

> . . . answers to the great questions of psychology will ultimately be found in "physiology." Higher organisms, after all, are simply brains with a few minor appendages. All behavior, all experience, all feeling, indeed all the subject matter of psychology, are nothing more than the outcomes of the activity of the nervous system. (Thompson & Robinson, 1979, p. 449)

In the case of Charles Whitman's murderous behavior, a biological perspective would attach great importance to the headaches he reported in his letter and the brain tumor found during his autopsy. The **biological perspective** thus focuses on the physical side of human nature. It emphasizes the role of our highly developed brain; the biochemical processes that underlie our every thought, emotion, and action; and the manner in which genetic factors influence the development and behavior of human organisms.

Discovery of Brain-Behavior Relations

Because the biological perspective focuses on processes that are largely invisible to the naked eye, its development has depended on scientific and technological developments. Perhaps the most important discovery for the future science of psychology concerned the electrical nature of nerve conduction. In a landmark experiment in the late 1700s, the Italian scientist Luigi Galvani discovered that the severed leg of a frog would move if an electrical current was applied to it. Galvani's reports were ridiculed by dualist philosophers who believed that all bodily movements were caused by spiritual forces from the soul, but further experiments confirmed Galvani's findings. Soon many experiments on electrical nerve conduction were under way, borne on a wave of excitement about the discovery of "nervous energy." By 1870, researchers at the University of Berlin were applying electrical stimulation directly to the exposed brains of experimental animals. They discovered that stimulation of specific areas on the surface of the brain resulted in movements of particular muscles in the body. Soon they were able to "map" the areas on the brain's surface that controlled movement in various body regions. During this same period, many clinical reports appeared linking damage in specific areas of the brain with behavioral impairments of various kinds. For example, it was found that damage to a region on the left side of the brain resulted in the loss of the ability to understand or produce language.

As psychology entered the 20th century, the study of brain-behavior relations was still in its infancy. Karl Lashley, perhaps the most important figure in the early development of biological psychology in America, was interested in brain mechanisms in learning. His approach was to create lesions (damage) in specific brain regions and to study their effects on the learning and memory abilities of experimental animals who had been trained to run mazes. Lashley's research inspired many other attempts to study brain-behavior relations experimentally and to map the areas of the brain that are involved in specific psychological functions (Figure 1.5).

In 1929, the invention of the electroencephalogram (EEG) allowed researchers to measure the electrical activity of large areas of the brain through electrodes attached to the scalp. Scientists could now study brain-wave correlates of behaviors and states of consciousness without invading the brain. Yet, the EEG is primitive compared with more recent technical tools. For example, tiny microelectrodes now permit the recording of electrical activities from individual brain cells. The electron microscope has made it possible to study formerly invisible brain structures. New computer-based imaging techniques have provided ways of watching the electrochemical activities that are the bases for thought, emotion, and behavior. Biochemical research has shown that the brain's electrical activity is controlled by chemical substances released by nerve cells. The role of these *neurotransmitter* substances in both normal and abnormal behavior is one of the most important areas of current research. As you will see throughout the text, we are on the threshold of many other revolutionary discoveries of brain-behavior relations.

FIGURE 1.5 Relations between brain functions and behavior have long been a focus of the biological perspective. Here, a scientist has implanted stimulating electrodes in a brain region thought to be involved in fear and is recording the results of brief electrical stimulations as the animals interact.

Evolution and Behavior: From Darwin to Evolutionary Psychology

As thinking and acting organisms, we go back a long way—long before our birth. Our species exists today because of our ancestors' ability to adapt, both biologically and behaviorally, to a changing and often hostile environment. Whereas the study of brain functioning often focuses on biological processes that occur in thousandths of a second, another portion of the biological perspective focuses on processes that may occur over thousands of generations.

➤ 11. What subsequent technical developments were important in the study of brain-behavior relations?

Darwin's evolutionary theory. Charles Darwin (Figure 1.6) casts a giant shadow in the history of scientific thought. In 1859, his book *On the Origin of Species* generated shock waves that are still felt today in the debates between creationists and evolutionists. Darwin was not the first to suggest the possibility of evolution in animals, but his theory was the most plausible and best documented. It was vigorously opposed, however, for it seemed to many a denial of philosophical and religious beliefs about the exalted nature of human beings.

Darwin's theory was stimulated by observations made during a five-year voyage on a British research vessel that explored the coasts of South America, Australia, South Africa, and many South Atlantic and South Pacific islands. Darwin was struck by the many differences between seemingly similar species who lived in different environments. He began to view these differences as ways in which the species had adapted to these environments.

In his theory of evolution, Darwin proposed that species evolve over time in response to environmental conditions through a process called natural selection, or "survival of the fittest." **Natural selection** means that any inheritable characteristic that increases the likelihood of survival will be maintained in the species because individuals having the characteristic will be more likely to survive and reproduce. The underlying principle is that members of a given species differ naturally in many ways. Some possess specific traits to a greater extent than others do. If any of those traits give some members a competitive advantage over others, such as increasing their ability to attract mates, escape danger, and acquire food, these members are more likely to survive and pass their genes on to their offspring. In this way, the presence of adaptive traits will increase within the population over generations. In contrast, characteristics that reduce chances for survival will be eliminated from the species over time because creatures having such characteristics will be less

FIGURE 1.6 Charles Darwin's theory of evolution had a tremendous impact on scientific thought that persists to this day.

➤ 12. What is meant by natural selection? What is its role in physical and behavioral evolution?

FIGURE 1.7 Natural selection pressures result in physical changes. The peppered moth's natural color is that of the lighter insect. However, over many generations, peppered moths who live in polluted urban areas have become darker because darker insects blended into their grimy environment and were more likely to survive predators and pass their "dark" genes on to their progeny. However, a trip into the countryside to visit their light-colored relatives could prove fatal for these urban insects.

➤ 13. According to evolutionary psychology, how do biological and behavioral evolution influence one another?

➤ 14. According to sociobiology, what is the ultimate importance of evolved social behaviors? On what bases has this position been criticized by other theorists?

likely to survive (Figure 1.7). Darwin did not know the exact mechanism for the passing on of characteristics. That mechanism was to become evident later in the 19th century when Gregor Mendel's pioneering work on genetic transmission of characteristics in plants led to the discovery of genes.

The characteristics favored by natural selection are not always positive ones. Sometimes natural selection favors the lesser of two evils. An example is sickle cell disease, a genetically caused blood disorder that is prevalent among people of African descent. Although the long-term effect of the sickle cell gene is to lower life expectancy, it does have one redeeming quality: It offers protection against malaria. Because people having the sickle cell gene were more likely to survive malaria epidemics, the prevalence of sickle cell disorder among African people increased over time (Nascutiu, 1997).

Darwin assumed that the principle of natural selection could be applied to all living things, including human beings. Contrary to a popular misconception, Darwin did *not* propose that humans are the direct descendants of modern apes. Rather, he believed that both human beings and apes branched off from a common ancestor in the distant past.

Modern evolutionary psychology.   Evolutionary psychology is an emerging discipline that focuses on the role of evolution in the development of human behavior. Psychologists in this field stress that an organism's biology determines its behavioral capabilities, and its behavior (including its mental abilities) determines whether or not it will survive. In this manner, successful human behavior evolved along with a changing body (Buss, 1995; Tooby & Cosmides, 1992).

One theory is that when dwindling vegetation in some parts of the world forced apelike animals from the trees and required that they hunt for food, chances for survival were greater for those who were capable of *bipedal locomotion* (walking on two legs) (Pilbeam, 1984). By freeing the hands, bipedalism in turn fostered the development and use of improved tools and weapons, and hunting in groups encouraged social organization. Social organization, in turn, stimulated the development of specialized social roles (such as hunter and protector in the male and caring for children in the female) that exist in most cultures. It also fostered the development of language, which enhanced social communication and the transmission of knowledge.

Tool use and bipedal locomotion put new natural selection pressures on many parts of the body. These included the teeth, the hands, and the pelvis, all of which changed over time in response to the new demands. But the greatest pressure was placed on the brain structures involved in the abilities most critical to the emerging way of life: attention, memory, language, and thought. These mental abilities became important to survival in an environment that required the ability to learn and to solve problems. From the early humanlike creature of 2 million years ago to the Neanderthal of 75,000 years ago, the brain tripled in size, and the most dramatic increase occurred in the parts of the brain that are the seat of the higher mental processes (Figure 1.8). Thus evolved changes in behavior seem to have contributed to the development of the brain, just as the growth of the brain contributed to the development of human behavior.

The notion that evolutionary pressures have stimulated the development of brain mechanisms that allow us to learn, think, reason, and socialize more effectively is generally accepted today. However, one evolutionary theory (and there are many theories) is more controversial. **Sociobiology** (Wilson, 1980) holds that complex social behaviors are also built into the human species as products of evolution. Sociobiologists argue that natural selection favors behaviors that increase the ability to pass on one's genes to the next generation. These social behaviors include aggression, competition, and dominance in males, and cooperative and nurturing tendencies in females. Indeed, one's *genetic* survival (i.e., transmission of one's genes) is more important than one's own physical survival in the eyes of sociobiologists. This principle is even used to explain certain "altruistic" behaviors, includ-

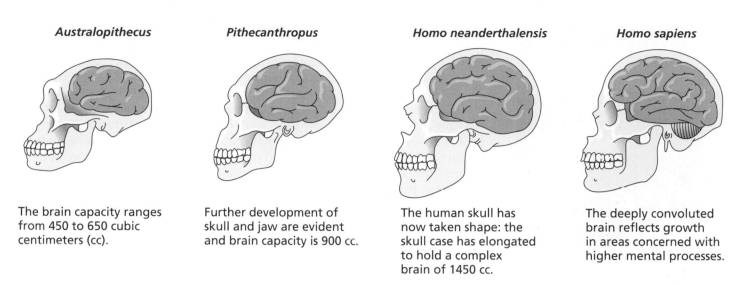

Australopithecus

The brain capacity ranges from 450 to 650 cubic centimeters (cc).

Pithecanthropus

Further development of skull and jaw are evident and brain capacity is 900 cc.

Homo neanderthalensis

The human skull has now taken shape: the skull case has elongated to hold a complex brain of 1450 cc.

Homo sapiens

The deeply convoluted brain reflects growth in areas concerned with higher mental processes.

FIGURE 1.8 The human brain evolved over a period of several million years. The greatest growth occurred in those areas concerned with the higher mental processes, particularly memory, thought, and language.

ing giving up one's life to save children or relatives. Although such behavior is hardly in the survival interests of the individual, it serves a higher purpose: It keeps one's genes alive in the gene pool to live on in our ancestors (Sober & Wilson, 1998).

Many critics believe that sociobiology overemphasizes innate biological factors at the expense of cultural and social learning factors in explaining complex human social behavior (Caporael, 1997; Eagly & Wood, 1999). Evolutionary theorists with a more cultural orientation suggest that the evolved brain structures that underlie psychological mechanisms (such as the ability to use language) developed in order to enhance adaptation to the demands of social and group living rather than to simply further the survival of one's genes (Caporael, 1997).

➤ 15 What methods do behavior geneticists use to investigate the role of genetic factors in animal and human behavior?

Behavior Genetics

Although scientists sometimes disagree about the role of evolution in the development of the human species, there is no question that our development and behavior are affected by the genetic blueprint with which we are born (Efran & Greene, 2000; Turkheimer & Waldron, 2000). Psychologists have had a long-standing interest in **behavior genetics,** the study of how behavioral tendencies are influenced by genetic factors.

Animals can be selectively bred not only for physical traits (Figure 1.9), but also for behavioral traits such as aggression or intelligence. This is done by allowing highly aggressive or very bright males and females to mate with one another over a number of generations. In Thailand, where gambling on fish fights has long been a national pasttime, the selective breeding of winners has produced the highly aggressive Siamese fighting fish. The male of this species will instantly attack his own image in a mirror and can sometimes engage in fierce fighting contests that last up to six hours.

Human behavior also is influenced by genetic factors. Identical twins, who result from the splitting of a fertilized egg and therefore have exactly the same genetic makeup, are far more similar to one another on many behavioral traits than are fraternal twins, who result from two different fertilized eggs and therefore differ genetically. This greater degree of similarity is found even when the identical twins have been reared in different homes and dissimilar environments (Bouchard et al., 1990; Plomin & Caspi, 1999; Tellegen et al., 1988). Genetic factors are also implicated in certain brain dysfunctions that produce disturbed behavior (Gottesman, 1991; Papolos & Lachman, 1994).

FIGURE 1.9 Selective breeding can produce both physical and behavioral characteristics. This tiny horse was produced by selectively breeding very small horses over a number of generations.

➤ 16. What is the conception of human nature advanced by the cognitive perspective?

FIGURE 1.10 The thinking human is the focus of the cognitive perspective.

➤ 17. Compare the goals of structuralism and functionalism.

FIGURE 1.11 Wilhelm Wundt (right) founded the German school of structuralism and established the first laboratory of experimental psychology in 1879 to study the nature of consciousness and the structure of the mind.

The Cognitive Perspective: The Thinking Human

If you were asked what sets humans apart from other species, chances are that you would point to our unique mental capabilities. Indeed, the name we have immodestly given to our own species, *Homo sapiens,* is Latin for "wise man."

A large slice of human nature is captured in our conception of "the thinking human." Derived from the Latin word *cogitare* (to think), the **cognitive perspective** views humans as information processors and problem solvers whose actions are governed by thought and planning (Figure 1.10). Today's cognitive perspective is concerned with ageless questions about how information is perceived and then organized in our minds, as well as how that information is combined with other contents of the mind to create memories, problem-solving strategies, and creative thoughts. The cognitive perspective causes us to ask how mental processes influence our motives, emotions, and behavior.

Origins of the Cognitive Perspective

Psychology has been concerned with mental processes from its very beginning. As it developed from its roots in philosophy and medicine, questions concerning the nature of the mind and its relation to the body were foremost in psychology. In the early years, several important schools of psychological thought developed, each of which had its own way of studying mental processes and each of which contributed to today's cognitive perspective. These schools included structuralism, functionalism, and Gestalt psychology.

Structuralism. Wilhelm Wundt (1832–1920) was a German scientist who wanted to model the study of the mind after the physical and biological sciences. These sciences were analyzing materials with their new scientific tools, such as the microscope and chemical analysis. He therefore founded the first laboratory of experimental psychology at Leipzig in 1879. There he helped train the first generation of scientific psychologists (Figure 1.11). One of his students was Edward Titchener, who later established a psychological laboratory in the United States at Cornell University. Like Wundt, Titchener was a kind of mental chemist. He believed that the mind could be studied by breaking it down into its basic components or structures, as a chemist might do in studying a complex chemical compound. Wundt and Titchener's approach was therefore known as **structuralism,** the analysis of the mind in terms of its basic elements.

The structuralists believed that sensations are the basic elements of consciousness, and they set out to study sensations through the method of **introspection** ("looking within"). Participants in their experiments were exposed to all sorts of sensory stimuli—lights, sounds, tastes—and were trained to describe their inner experiences. Although this method of studying the mind died out after a few decades, the structuralists left an important mark on the infant science of psychology by establishing a scientific tradition for the study of cognition that persists to this day.

Functionalism. In the United States, structuralism eventually gave way to an approach called **functionalism,** which held that psychology should study the *functions*—the whys—of consciousness, rather than its structure—the whats. In part, functionalism was influenced by Darwin's evolutionary theory, which stressed the importance of adaptive behavior in helping organisms to respond successfully to their environment and survive. Much of the early research on the nature of learning and problem solving in humans and animals was done by functionalists. William James, a leader in the movement, was himself a "big-picture" person who concurrently taught courses in physiology, psychology, and philosophy at Harvard University. James's broad functionalist approach helped widen the scope of psychology to include biological processes, mental processes, and behavior. Although it no longer exists as a formal school of thought within psychology, the tradition of functionalism endures in modern-day psychology as an emphasis on how the mind processes information and directs behavior. It also is seen in evolutionary psychology's focus on the origins of adaptive behavior.

Gestalt psychology. In the 1920s, German scientists were again helping to shape psychology through a school of thought known as Gestalt psychology. The word *gestalt* may be translated as "whole" or "organization," and **Gestalt psychology** was concerned with how elements of experience are organized into wholes. The Gestalt approach was the opposite of that taken by the structuralists. Instead of trying to break consciousness down into its basic elements, the Gestalt psychologists argued that our perceptions and other mental processes are organized so that the whole is not only greater than, but also quite different from, the sum of its parts.

As an example, consider the painting in Figure 1.12. When you first looked at it, what did you see? Many people initially perceive it as a weird portrait of a person. You were less likely to immediately perceive it as a mosaic comprised of individual sea creatures. The Gestalt psychologists believed that this tendency to perceive wholes is, like other forms of perceptual organization, built into our nervous system.

Wolfgang Köhler (1887–1967) was one of the leaders of Gestalt psychology. He conducted research with apes and other animals while stranded at a research station in the Canary Islands during World War I. Köhler concluded that the ability to perceive relationships is the essence of what we call intelligence, and he defined **insight** as the sudden perception of a useful relationship or solution to a problem—a kind of "Aha!" experience.

Several examples of insight were demonstrated by Sultan, one of Köhler's chimpanzees. One day, Köhler hung a banana from the top of Sultan's cage, out of the ape's reach. Sultan seemed perplexed at first, but then he looked about his cage, noticed a box in one corner, and placed the box beneath the dangling banana so that he could reach it. Another time, Sultan joined two sticks together to reach a banana that had been placed on the ground outside his cage, a feat that has gone down in history as an act of presumed simian genius (Figure 1.13). Gestalt psychology's demonstrations of insight learning in both animals and humans stimulated new interest in cognitive topics such as perception, problem solving, and intelligence.

➤ 18. What does *gestalt* mean? How does this meaning relate to the goals and findings of Gestalt psychology?

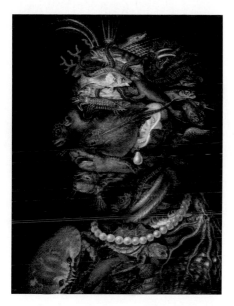

FIGURE 1.12 This painting illustrates the Gestalt principle that the whole is often greater than the sum of its parts. Once you have perceived the organized image of a portrait, you are less likely to perceive the sea creatures as separate elements.

Source: Water by Arcimboldo from Kunsthistorisches Museum, Vienna.

FIGURE 1.13 A modern-day counterpart of Sultan demonstrates insight learning by using a series of shorter sticks to pull in a stick that is long enough to reach the delicacy.

In addition to the schools of structuralism, functionalism, and Gestalt psychology, several other prominent theorists exerted a strong influence on the development of the cognitive perspective. Three of these individuals were Jean Piaget, Albert Ellis, and Aaron Beck.

Piaget: Cognitive development in children.   A zoologist by training, Jean Piaget (1896–1980) spent more than 50 years studying how children think, reason, and solve problems, and he developed a remarkably influential theory of cognitive development. Like the functionalists, Piaget was concerned with how the mind and its development contributes to our ability to adapt to our environment.

> 19. What were the methods used and conclusions reached by Piaget in his studies of cognitive development?

Piaget's primary technique was to carefully observe children as they tried to solve problems. He then tried to imagine how they must have experienced the situation to respond as they did (Figure 1.14). As a result of his systematic observations, Piaget concluded that new and specific stages of cognitive development unfold naturally as children mature and that these abilities cannot be explained by the accumulation of past experiences. Rather, the stages that naturally unfold represent fundamentally different ways of learning about and understanding the world. We consider Piaget's contributions in greater detail in Chapter 12, where we explore cognitive development in children and adults.

Cognitive approaches to psychological disorders.   The cognitive perspective has strongly influenced our understanding not only of adaptive human thinking, but also of human unhappiness and problems in living. Two prominent psychotherapists, Albert Ellis (1962) and Aaron Beck (1976), led early attempts to understand how mental distortions and irrational thought patterns create emotional problems. Recall, for example, Charles Whitman's reference to his "unusual and irrational thoughts" in the letter written before his murderous rampage. By emphasizing the fact that distress and maladaptive behavior are caused not by external situations but by the ways we think about those situations, and by developing ways of helping people to change self-defeating thought habits, Ellis and Beck made notable contributions to the understanding and treatment of clinical disorders.

FIGURE 1.14 Jean Piaget was a master of observation. Many of his conclusions about stages of cognitive development came from watching children solve problems and inferring how they must have thought about them to respond as they did.

> 20. How have Beck and Ellis advanced our understanding of emotional problems?

> 21. What is studied in the cognitive science areas of artificial intelligence and cognitive neuroscience?

Modern Cognitive Science

Today's cognitive science has links with computer science, linguistics, biology, and mathematics (Clark & Toribio, 1998; Wagman, 1998). One area of cognitive science, **artificial intelligence**, develops computer models of complex human thought, reasoning, and problem solving (Wagman, 1997). Artificial intelligence researchers reason that by developing computer models that seem to duplicate natural cognitive processes, they will have a better understanding of how humans think. Moreover, by studying the ways experts think about and solve problems, they can develop computerized "expert" systems to lead others along the same cognitive paths. For example, there are now computerized medical diagnostic systems that are based upon the thought processes of eminent physicians.

Cognitive scientists are also interested in how people produce and recognize speech, how memory operates, and how creative solutions to problems are produced. An important melding of the biological and cognitive perspectives has resulted in a new area called *cognitive neuroscience*, where scientists use sophisticated electrical recording and brain-imaging techniques to eavesdrop on the brain as people engage in mental activities.

Social Constructivism

Social constructivism is a highly influential viewpoint within the cognitive perspective (Gergen, 2000). Its proponents maintain that what we consider "reality" is in large part our own mental creation. According to these theorists, little shared reality exists apart from what groups of people socially construct through the subjective meaning they give to their experiences. Constructivists would maintain, for example, that male and female sex roles are created not by "nature," but by the shared worldview that exists within social groups. Likewise, conflicts between groups of people are a product of differing "realities" that they live. For example, the long-standing conflict between Middle East Jews and Arabs reflects radically different conceptions of God's plan for them, of what is right and what is wrong, and differing historical interpretations and understandings (Rouhana & Bar-Tal, 1998). These two groups, though coexisting in the same places, live in entirely different subjective worlds.

Even highly similar groups from the same culture can be led by their needs and emotions to construct different versions of the same reality. One example is shown in our first *Research Close-Up.*

➤ 22. What do social constructivists say about the nature of "reality"?

RESEARCH CLOSE-UP

The Social Construction of Reality: They Saw a Game

▶ **Background**

Important beginnings of what is now termed the "cognitive revolution" occurred in the late 1940s and early 1950s as research demonstrated how people's motives, values, and beliefs can strongly affect their perceptions. One such demonstration occurred after a football game between Dartmouth and Princeton. From the opening kickoff, it was clear that the heated rivalry between the two schools was going to result in a very rough game. Tempers flared frequently, and the officials had difficulty maintaining control of the game. In the second quarter, Princeton's All-American running back, Dick Kazmaier, was led from the field with a concussion and a broken nose. Later in the game, a Dartmouth player was carried from the field with a broken leg. Several other players on both sides suffered serious injuries.

After the game, the air was filled with accusations. Princeton coaches, officials, and fans accused Dartmouth of deliberately trying to maim Kazmaier. In turn, Dartmouth supporters accused Princeton of flagrantly dirty football. Charges and countercharges were exchanged for several weeks, and the heated controversy attracted national attention.

Fortunately, a few of the people at the two institutions were still talking to one another without snarling. Psychologists Albert Hastorf of Dartmouth and Hadley Cantril of Princeton were struck by the violent disagreements over what had actually occurred during the game. It was almost as if the fans had been in two different stadiums that day. Their curiosity aroused, Hastorf and Cantril decided to collaborate on a study of these perceptions.

▶ **Method**

Dartmouth and Princeton undergraduates participated in the study, which had two phases. In the first phase, 163 Dartmouth students and 161 Princeton students completed a questionnaire concerning their beliefs about what had happened during the game. Next, 48 Dartmouth students and 49 Princeton students were shown a film of the game and were asked to tally any instances of rule infractions, unnecessary roughness, or dirty play that they saw.

▶ **Results**

The first questionnaire reflected the differing opinions of students from the two schools. When asked who started the rough play, 86 percent of the Princeton students but only 36 percent of Dartmouth students said that Dartmouth started it. Fifty-five percent of the Princeton students were convinced that Dartmouth had purposely tried to maim Kazmaier, compared with only 10 percent of the Dartmouth students. Equally striking were the results derived from the viewing of

—Continued

the game film. As shown in Figure 1.15, Dartmouth students saw both teams make about the same number of infractions. Princeton fans, however, saw the Dartmouth team make twice as many infractions as the Princeton team did. Compared with the Dartmouth fans, they also detected twice the number of infractions committed by Dartmouth. Even on the not-so-instant replay, students from the two schools continued to see "different" games.

▶ Critical Discussion

This simple but elegant little study illustrates nicely how people's preconceptions and identification with a particular group can influence perceptions and beliefs. Even in the face of "objective" reality as represented by the game film they watched, Dartmouth and Princeton students mentally constructed differing realities through their own perceptions. The study also shows how phenomena from the "real world" can be brought into a laboratory setting and studied under controlled conditions.

   "They Saw a Game" and other studies comprising what was termed the "new look" in perception research gave impetus to the cognitive revolution that was soon to occur in psychology. They demonstrated that a psychology based only on external stimuli and responses

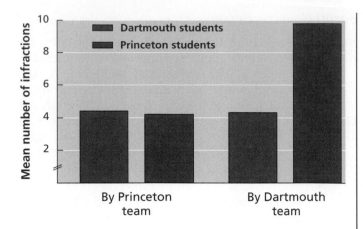

FIGURE 1.15   Average number of infractions detected by Dartmouth and Princeton students while watching the game film. (Data from Hastorf & Cantril, 1954.)

leaves the person who interprets and thinks about those stimuli out of the causal equation. In the cognitive view, people are less what their experiences make them than what they make of their experiences. Thinking clearly matters.

Source: Albert Hastorf and Hadley Cantril (1954). They saw a game: A case study. *Journal of Abnormal and Social Psychology, 49,* 129–134.[1]

[1]The citation system used in psychology lists the authors, year of publication, title, journal or book, volume number of the journal, and page numbers.

The Psychodynamic Perspective: The Forces Within

I don't know why I did it. . . . Often in my life, I have done things I had decided not to do. Something—whatever that may be—goes into action; "it" goes to the woman I don't want to see anymore, "it" makes the remark to the boss that costs me my head, "it" keeps on smoking when I have decided to quit, and then quits smoking just when I've accepted the fact that I'm a smoker and always will be. (Schlink, 1997, p. 20)

   Have you ever felt mystified by why you did something that seemed "out of character"? If so, you are not alone, for each of us is a unique person with an individual pattern of traits, emotions, motives, and inner conflicts.

   The **psychodynamic perspective** searches for the causes of behavior within the workings of our personality, emphasizing the role of unconscious processes and unresolved conflicts from the past. The first and most influential psychodynamic theory was Sigmund Freud's theory of psychoanalysis.

Psychoanalysis: Freud's Great Challenge

Although the shadowy underworld of hidden motives and meanings has enticed thinkers throughout history, humans have traditionally viewed themselves as creatures ruled by reason and conscious thought. But late in the 19th century, as the aftershocks produced by Darwin's evolutionary theory were still being felt throughout the intellectual world, Sigmund Freud (1856–1939) mounted a second and equally shocking assault on the prevailing conception of human beings as rational, civilized creatures. Unlike Darwin, however, Freud emphasized the

➤ 23. What causal factors are the focus of the psychodynamic perspective?

role of complex psychological forces in controlling human behavior (Figure 1.16). He called the theory that he developed psychoanalysis—the analysis of internal psychological forces.

As a young Viennese medical student in the early 1880s, Freud was intensely interested in the workings of the brain (Miller, 1991). He began to focus his attention on the treatment of **hysteria,** a psychological disorder in which physical symptoms such as blindness, pain, or paralysis develop without any apparent organic cause. This disorder was erroneously thought to be specific to women, hence the diagnostic label derived from the Greek word *hystera,* which means "womb." Freud treated hysterical women, first by using hypnosis and later by using a technique called free association, in which the patient was to say whatever came to mind and to let one association lead freely to another, even if the order did not seem logical or rational. To Freud's surprise, his female patients consistently reported and relived painful and long-"forgotten" childhood sexual experiences. After reliving these experiences, Freud reported, the patients' symptoms often showed considerable improvement.

Even though Freud was the product of a Victorian culture that regarded sexuality as a taboo topic, he at first believed the reports of sexual abuse given by his clients. Later, perhaps in response to the cries of outrage from the medical and scientific communities that threatened to ruin his career, he concluded that, in all likelihood, most of these childhood sexual experiences had never actually occurred. Freud was now faced with the problem of explaining how the "reliving" of events that had never actually occurred could abolish the symptoms of hysteria. He became convinced that his patients were prompted to create these fantasies because of a compelling and unsatisfied sexual drive that is a universal aspect of human nature.

Freud also observed that sexual material often emerged in dreams and in slips of the tongue (so-called "Freudian slips"). These observations, plus an intensive period of self-analysis, led Freud to propose that much of human behavior is influenced by forces of which we are unaware. He claimed that we have inborn sexual and aggressive drives, and he believed that our adult personality is strongly influenced by early childhood experiences and by the ways in which we cope with the internal forces that govern our behavior as we grow up.

Freud speculated that because early sexual desires and needs are punished, we learn to fear them and become anxious when we are aware of their presence. Consequently, to cope with our anxiety, we develop psychological techniques called defense mechanisms. One of the most important defense mechanisms is **repression,** which protects us by keeping anxiety-arousing impulses, feelings, and memories in the unconscious depths of the mind. There they remain as sources of energy, continually striving for release. All behavior, whether it is normal or abnormal, is a reflection of the never-ending and largely unconscious internal struggle between the conflicting psychological forces of the impulses and the defenses. This ongoing psychological struggle between conflicting energy forces is dynamic in nature, hence the term *psychodynamic.* To explain Charles Whitman's shooting rampage, Freud would surely point to the "overwhelming violent impulses" to which Whitman referred in his letter, explaining that these impulses exploded into action when the defenses that held them in check finally shattered in the face of unbearable life stresses.

Freud wrote numerous works of great psychological and literary significance, but he was not a conventional scientist. Freud was opposed to any attempts to explore psychoanalytic theory through laboratory research, believing that his clinical observations and personal self-analysis were far more valid "data" (Rosenzweig, 1992). Many contemporary psychologists view Freud's theory as difficult to test. Nevertheless, Freud's ideas have stimulated considerable psychological research on topics as diverse as dreams, the effects of child-rearing practices, memory, aggression, sex roles, moral development, defense mechanisms, psychological

FIGURE 1.16 For more than 50 years, Sigmund Freud probed the hidden recesses of the human mind.

➤ 24. What observations convinced Freud of the importance of unconscious and childhood determinants of adult behavior?

➤ 25. In what sense is the human in continuous internal conflict, according to Freud?

disorders, and psychological treatment. In one scholarly analysis of research based on Freud's ideas, Seymour Fisher and Roger Greenberg (1995) surveyed more than 3,000 studies in the scientific literature. Some of Freud's ideas were supported by subsequent research, whereas others were unsupported or directly contradicted. But even where psychoanalytic theory was not supported, the research it inspired has led to many important discoveries and helped stimulate the development of new theories. Psychoanalytic theory may be the best example of the truism that a theorist doesn't have to be "right" about everything (or even about most things) in order to make a notable scientific contribution.

Current Developments

➤ 26. What influences does Freud's theory have on contemporary psychology?

Psychodynamic concepts derived from Freud's psychoanalytic theory continue to have an influence within both academic and applied psychology. Among clinical psychologists in U.S. academic and applied settings 20 to 30 percent report their orientation as being psychodynamic, and many other practitioners say that they make use of psychodynamic concepts in understanding and treating clinical disorders (Mayne et al., 1994; Norcross et al., 1995). Psychoanalysis continues to be a major force in European psychology, and most major cities in the United States, Canada, and Europe have psychoanalytic training institutes. Some of its methods and concepts are now being integrated with other forms of treatment to provide more effective ways of helping people change maladaptive behavior patterns (Wachtel, 1997).

Links with psychodynamic concepts can be found within other areas of psychological science. For example, scientists working within the biological perspective have identified brain mechanisms that can produce emotional reactions of which we are consciously unaware (LeDoux, 2000). Freud, who was himself trained within the biological perspective, clearly recognized the importance of studying behavior with different methods and from several vantage points when he wrote, "Let the biologists go as far as they can, and let us go as far as we can. One day the two will meet" (Freud, 1900, p. 276).

Some of Freud's ideas about mental events are also helping to stimulate new theoretical advances and research within the cognitive perspective (Bucci, 1997; Erdelyi, 1995). Cognitive scientists have shown that many aspects of information processing occurs outside of our awareness (Wegner, 2000). Moreover, mental events that lie beyond the focus of our awareness, such as our self-concept and social stereotypes, can influence our thoughts, feelings, and behaviors. Thus, while Freud's vision of the unconscious mind as a seething cauldron of painful memories and destructive impulses is not accepted by most contemporary psychological scientists, the concept of a kinder, gentler unconscious endures, as does the notion that many of our behaviors are triggered by subconscious processes (Bargh & Chartrand, 1999; Kirsch & Lynn, 1999; Westen, 1998).

The Behavioral Perspective: The Power of the Environment

➤ 27. What are the important causal factors in behavior within the behavioral perspective? How was this school of thought influenced by British empiricism?

The **behavioral perspective** focuses on the role of the external environment in shaping and governing our actions. From this perspective, people's behavior is jointly determined by learned habits fashioned by their previous life experiences and by stimuli in their immediate environment. Particular emphasis is placed on the effect of rewards and punishment in shaping behavior (Rachlin, 1995).

Origins of the Behavioral Perspective

The behavioral perspective is rooted in a seventeenth-century school of philosophy known as **British empiricism,** which held that all ideas and knowledge are gained empirically—that is, through the senses. According to John Locke (1632–1704), one of the early empiricists, the human mind is initially "white paper void of all characters, without any ideas: How comes it to be furnished? To this I answer, in one word, from experience" (*An Essay Concerning Human Understanding*, 1690). Human beings are born as a *tabula rasa*—a blank tablet—and then shaped by their environment. Empiricism also maintained that observation is a more valid approach to knowledge than is reason. To empiricists, seeing was believing, whereas reasoning was fraught with the potential for error. This idea has been enormously influential in the development of science, whose methods are rooted in empirical observation.

In the early 1900s Ivan Pavlov, a Russian physiologist, reported experiments that demonstrated "involuntary" learning in dogs. Pavlov showed that dogs would learn to salivate to the sound of a "new" stimulus, such as a tone, if that stimulus were paired a number of times with the appearance of food. In the United States, meanwhile, researchers were studying more complex forms of learning in both animals and humans. Learning was to be the medium through which experience made its mark on Locke's "white paper void of all characters."

Behaviorism

In the 1920s, **behaviorism,** a school of thought that emphasizes environmental control of behavior through learning, emerged as an outspoken alternative to the cognitive and psychodynamic perspectives. John B. Watson (1878–1958) was the leader of the new movement (Figure 1.17). Watson strongly opposed the "mentalism" of the structuralists, functionalists, and psychoanalysts. He argued that the proper subject matter of psychology was observable behavior, not unobservable inner consciousness. Human beings, he said, are products of their conditioning experiences, and their behavior can be controlled completely by manipulating their environment. So passionately did Watson hold this position that in 1924 he issued the following challenge:

> Give me a dozen healthy infants, well-formed, and my own specialized world to bring them up in and I'll guarantee you to take any one of them at random and train him to become any type of specialist I might select— doctor, lawyer, artist, merchant-chief and, yes, even beggar-man and thief, regardless of his talents, penchants, tendencies, abilities, vocations, and race of his ancestors. (p. 82)

Clearly, the behaviorists' approach of examining behavior strictly from the "outside" differs a great deal from our usual approach to understanding our inner selves. This approach is spoofed in the tongue-in-cheek story of the radical behaviorist who, after making love, turned to his partner and said, "That was great for you. How was it for me?"

Because of the behaviorists' belief that we are who we are because of what we learn, they devoted their efforts to discovering the laws that govern learning and performance. Behaviorists believed that the same basic principles of learning apply to all organisms, and their research with both humans and animals led to many discoveries and applications of these principles. Many would argue that the discovery of the laws of learning was the greatest contribution made by American psychology in the first half of the 20th century.

The leading modern figure in behaviorism was B. F. Skinner (1904–1990) of Harvard University (Figure 1.18). Although Skinner did not deny that mental events, images, and feelings occur within us, he maintained that these are themselves behaviors and not causes. "No account of what is happening inside the human body, no matter how complete, will explain the origins of human behavior," he insisted (Skinner, 1989, p. 18). For Skinner, there was no room for the "mind" or unobservable "mental events" in a scientific account of the causes of human behavior. Indeed, Skinner believed that a focus on inner factors would lead psychology astray by diverting attention from the real causes of behavior,

FIGURE 1.17 John B. Watson founded the school of behaviorism in the 1920s.

FIGURE 1.18 B. F. Skinner was a major figure in modern behaviorism.

which reside in the outer world. He insisted that "A person does not act upon the world, the world acts upon him" (Skinner, 1971, p. 211).

As expressed eloquently in his novel, *Walden Two* (Skinner, 1948), Skinner believed that the power of the environment could be harnessed for good or for evil. If human beings are to be changed, indeed saved, Skinner maintained, we must manipulate the environment that controls behavior through its pattern of rewards and punishments. Skinner believed that large-scale control over human behavior is possible today but that the chief barrier to creating a better world through "social engineering" is an outmoded conception of people as free agents. Needless to say, this was a highly controversial position. Skinner's view was considered extreme by many psychologists, but he was esteemed for his scientific contributions to the study of learning, for the force of his intellect, and for focusing attention on the power of environmental forces and how they could be used to enhance human welfare. In the 1960s, behaviorism inspired powerful techniques of behavior change that were known collectively as **behavior modification.** These techniques, which continue to be used today, proved to be effective ways to change problem behaviors and increase positive ones by manipulating the environmental factors that control the behavior (Martin & Pear, 1998). Overall, however, the influence of radical behaviorism waned after the 1970s, when it was overtaken by the cognitive revolution (Robins et al., 1999).

Cognitive Behaviorism

How does the behavioristic picture of humans as reactors to the environment square with the cognitive perspective's image of the human as thinker? Are we willing to ignore the mental processes that we ourselves experience, or declare them off limits for scientific purposes because we cannot observe them directly? For many behaviorists, the answer was no. That answer stimulated an important recent development within the behavioral perspective known as cognitive behaviorism. **Cognitive behaviorism** is an attempt to bridge the gap between the behavioral and cognitive perspectives and to combine them into a more comprehensive theory (Cervone & Shoda, 1999).

A leading cognitive behaviorist is Albert Bandura of Stanford University (Figure 1.19), who believes that the environment exerts its effects on behavior not by automatically "stamping in" or "stamping out" behaviors, as Watson or Skinner would maintain, but rather by affecting our thoughts. In this view, learning experiences and the environment affect our behavior by giving us the *information* we need to behave effectively (Bandura, 1969, 1999).

Cognitive behaviorists also stress that we can learn new behaviors by observing the actions of others and storing this information in memory. We can then imitate and reproduce these behaviors when we believe they will work for us. Finally, these theorists maintain that our mental abilities allow us to control our own behavior and thereby influence our environment. Control therefore goes both ways, from environment to person and from person to environment.

The Humanistic Perspective: Freedom and Self-Actualization

As noted earlier, Freud's theory acted as a lightning rod. So did the tenets of radical behaviorism. Many rejected the images of humans being controlled by destructive and unconscious forces or by the external environment, and they offered competing images of human nature. The **humanistic perspective** arose largely out of philosophical schools that emphasize free will, innate tendencies toward growth, and the attempt to find ultimate meaning in one's existence (Moss, 1998). Like psychoanalytic theorists, humanistic theorists emphasize the role of internal personality processes, but in contrast to the psychoanalytic emphasis on uncon-

➤ 28. What is cognitive behaviorism? How does it differ from radical behaviorism?

FIGURE 1.19 Albert Bandura has played a key role in merging the cognitive and behavioral perspectives into cognitive behaviorism.

➤ 29. How does the humanistic conception of human nature and motivation differ from that advanced by psychoanalysis and behaviorism?

scious determinants of behavior, humanists stress the importance of conscious motives, freedom, and choice. Humanistic theorists believe that in every human being there is an active force toward growth and **self-actualization,** the reaching of one's individual potential (Figure 1.20). When the human personality unfolds in a benign and supportive environment that allows these creative forces free rein, the positive inner nature of a person emerges. Human misery and pathology, in contrast, are fostered by environments that frustrate the innate tendencies toward self-actualization. In sharp contrast to the image of humans ruled by unconscious dynamics or external stimuli, humanistic theorists like Rollo May (1961), Carl Rogers (1983), and R. D. Laing (1967) insist that our existence and its meaning are squarely in our own hands, for we alone can decide what our attitudes and behaviors will be.

Although few of the humanistic thinkers were themselves scientists, many important areas of scientific research have been inspired by the humanistic perspective. For example, research on the self-concept has been one of the most active areas of personality research for the past two decades (Brown, 1998). Much of this research combines concepts from the cognitive perspective with formulations of the self derived from Carl Rogers's (1959) humanistic theory of self functioning. Rogers was also a pioneer in the scientific study of psychotherapy. In the 1940s and 1950s, his research group was the first to make audio recordings of counseling sessions and subject the recordings to systematic analysis. This research helped identify important therapeutic processes that led to constructive change in clients (Rogers, 1966).

Questions about the ultimate meaning of life and death are a critically important part of our existence, and of the humanistic perspective. According to **terror management theory,** an innate desire for continued life, combined with the uniquely human awareness of the inevitability of death creates an anxiety called existential terror (Becker, 1973; Kastenbaum, 2000). Current research inspired by this theory addresses how people defend themselves against this anxiety (Greenberg et al., 1997; Pysczynski, et al., 1999; Solomon et al., 1991). To defend their members against the terror, each culture establishes its own "worldview." This cultural construction of reality, which often includes some notion of an afterlife, confers a sense of order, permanence, and stability on life, and it establishes standards for attaining "a sense of personal value and some hope of literally or symbolically transcending death" (Pysczynski et al., 1999 p. 836).

Terror management theorists believe that in order to allay death-related anxiety, people are motivated to support and defend their cultural worldview (often expressed in the form of religious precepts) and to live up to its standards of value. Research inspired by terror management theory has supported two of its most important hypotheses. First, people who see themselves as living up to their culture's values—of living a "good life"— score higher on measures of self-esteem and report lower death anxiety. Second, reminders of their own mortality cause people to be more attracted to people who share and uphold their worldview and to react with increased hostility to those who challenge or disagree with their beliefs and values (Greenberg, 1997; Pysczynski, et al., 1999). Terror management theory is thus a current example of how humanistic ideas continue to stimulate psychological theory and research.

The Sociocultural Perspective: The Embedded Human

Every person has his or her individual learning history, but each of us is also embedded in a larger culture that helps shape who we are. How has your own culture influenced your values, your ways of thinking and behaving, your very conception of reality? Such questions, which psychologists of a generation ago might have left to anthropologists, assume increasing importance as technology

FIGURE 1.20 The humanistic perspective emphasizes the human ability to surmount obstacles in our drive toward self-actualization.

➤ 30. How does terror management theory draw on humanistic concepts? What are some of its major findings?

and emigration shrink the world and our everyday environment becomes increasingly diverse and multicultural. The **sociocultural perspective** focuses on the manner in which culture is transmitted to its members and on the similarities and differences that occur among people from diverse cultures (Valsiner, 2000).

Culture refers to the enduring values, beliefs, behaviors, and traditions that are shared by a large group of people and passed on from one generation to the next (Brislin, 1993). All cultural groups develop their own social norms. **Norms** are rules that specify what is acceptable and expected behavior for members of that group. They may involve rules for how to dress, respond to people higher in status, behave during religious ceremonies, or act as a woman in that culture. The fact that norms can differ widely from culture to culture—and even at different times within the same culture—introduces another environmental factor that must be considered if we are to understand the causes of behavior.

Humans seem to have an inherent need to develop cultures. Cultures introduce order and a particular worldview into a social system, thus creating predictability, guidelines for thought and behavior, and a kind of map for living our lives. As suggested by terror management theory, described earlier, the worldview helps us to "understand" many of the unknowns of our existence and thereby reduces some of the anxieties of human existence (Becker, 1973). Culture also provides an expression of a people's way of being through art, literature, and the development of knowledge.

Cultural Learning and Diversity

In 1935, anthropologist Margaret Mead published an account of three tribes in New Guinea that showed striking differences in "normal" behavior among men and women. Among the Arapesh, both men and women were uncommonly kind, sympathetic, and cooperative. For men to behave aggressively was almost unheard of. The Mundugumor were quite different. Both men and women were expected to be fierce and aggressive, even vicious. A third tribe, the Tchambuli, exhibited a reversal of traditional Western sex roles. The women were boisterous, shaved their heads, and took responsibility for going out and obtaining the tribe's food. The men, in turn, spent their days focusing on their art, their hairstyles, and gossiping about the women (Mead, 1935). Mead's observations provided a graphic illustration of how cultural expectations and learning experiences can affect behavior.

Cultures differ from one another in many ways, but one of the most important differences from a psychological perspective is the extent to which they emphasize individualism versus collectivism (Markus & Kitayama, 1991; Triandis, 1989). Most industrialized cultures of northern Europe and North America promote **individualism,** an emphasis on personal goals and a self-identity based primarily on one's own attributes and achievements. In contrast, many cultures in Asia, Africa, and South America nurture **collectivism,** in which individual goals are subordinated to those of the group and personal identity is defined largely by the ties that bind one to family and other social groups.

Japan and the United States provide examples of cultures that differ significantly on the individualism-collectivism dimension (Kagitcibasi, 1997). The United States is an inherently individualistic culture, whereas Japan's culture is far more collectivist in nature. This difference is created by social learning experiences that begin in childhood and continue thereafter in the form of social customs. For example, observational studies in Japanese and American schools have shown that Japanese children work more often as part of a group having a common assignment, whereas American children are more likely to work alone on individual projects and assignments (White, 1987). Moreover, even when American children are working in groups, American teachers are far more likely than Japanese teach-

➤ 31. Define culture and norms. What functions does a culture serve?

➤ 32. Contrast individualistic and collectivistic societies.

ers to direct their comments to individuals rather than to the group as a whole (Hamilton et al., 1991). Cultural learning experiences like these undoubtedly reflect and also reinforce cultural norms (Lamal, 1991). At many points in this book, we shall discover how the cultural environment can affect the entire spectrum of human behavior. In the *Psychological Frontiers* feature that follows, we discuss current conceptions of how culture and biology combine to influence behavior.

➤ 33. Why is the distinction between originating and present causes important in the nature-nurture focus on evolutionary and cultural factors in behavior?

PSYCHOLOGICAL FRONTIERS

Nature *and* Nurture: Biology, Culture, and Behavior

The behavioral and sociocultural perspectives emphasize the role of the environment on the development of behavior. They tell us that we are molded by our unique learning histories and shaped by the culture into which we are born. Our learning and cultural experiences influence not only our behavior, but also how we view ourselves (i.e., our "cultural identity") and the world. How are we to reconcile this image of human nature with that proposed by the biological perspective, which points to our human brain, our genes, and to human evolutionary history as determinants of behavior? Which is it that determines our behavior: nature (our biological endowment) or nurture (our environment and learning history)? This question has been debated vigorously in relation to everything from racial differences in measured IQ to psychological differences between men and women (Thomas, 2000).

In the early years of the 20th century, the nature emphasis predominated. Many scientists believed that human characteristics are genetically determined. This conviction reached its most extreme form in a movement known as *eugenics,* which promoted the idea of selective breeding of the most desirable people with one another to improve the human race. Eugenics also promoted the more sinister idea of minimizing the influence of the "unfit" in the gene pool, a position that was to have horrible practical consequences during the Nazi regime.

By the 1950s and 1960s, the pendulum had swung toward the nurture position, and it was believed that humans are largely a product of their environment. Child-rearing practices were given special emphasis as a result of the influence wielded by psychoanalysis, humanism, and behaviorism. Within this climate, Dr. Benjamin Spock's *Baby and Child Care* became a must-read for several generations of parents, outselling all books except the Bible. Ambitious social and educational interventions of the 1960s, such as Project Head Start, found fertile soil in the optimistic conviction that wonders could be wrought if only we could find the right ways to arrange the environment (Smith & Woodward, 1996). On the negative side, countless parents blamed themselves for psy-

chological conditions in their children that are now known to be at least partly influenced by genetic factors.

Advances in behavior genetics as well as new discoveries about the brain swung the pendulum back to a balanced position between nature and nurture. The emergence of evolutionary psychology over the past three decades has brought with it new attempts to link complex human behavior to innate biological factors. For example, evolutionary theorists have asked why there are certain behavioral differences between men and women, such as tendencies toward greater aggressiveness in men and greater emotional expressiveness and tenderness in women. Their answer is that these differences result from males' predominant roles of hunter/protector and women's role as caretaker of children. These roles, both of which helped the species survive, have over the course of evolution created genetically based differences in men and women through a process of natural selection that predispose men to be more aggressive and women to be more nurturing and emotionally expressive (Archer, 1996). On the other hand, cultural theorists have attributed the same findings to social and cultural learning experiences in a society that dictates what men and women "should" be like (Eagly & Wood, 1999). One could easily be tempted to take sides and answer the nature *or* nurture question, for there are data to support either view.

But "nature *or* nurture?" is viewed today as the wrong question. In most instances, it is probably nature *and* nurture. Seldom does one or the other operate in isolation, unaffected by the other (Wachs, 2000). Returning to our example of male-female differences, it is possible that both evolutionary and cultural factors could be at work (Valsiner, 2000). The key to understanding this possibility is the distinction between *originating causes* and *present causes.* Although not all scientists would agree, it is possible that the *origin* of a behavioral tendency might lie in our evolutionary history as something that had survival value. We don't know for certain that this is the case, but we certainly should not close the door to that possibility. However, there are

–Continued

also present causes to take into account, such as cultural learning factors, that could determine whether or not the behavior actually appears (Scher, 1999). It is quite possible that an evolutionary tendency originating in the distant past could be overridden by cultural factors in today's world that oppose it. For example, in today's Western society, women who are socialized into competitive athletics are encouraged to be every bit as aggressive as are men in those sports (Figure 1.21). Moreover, the differences in aggression between men and women are actually quite small, and many women score higher on measures of aggression than the average man does (Halpern, 2000). Thus, in many complex ways, nature and nurture can influence one another, as we see repeatedly in the pages to come. The task for psychological science is to discover the ways in which nature *and* nurture combine to influence our behavior.

FIGURE 1.21 Social norms change over time. Today, competitive, even aggressive behavior is seen as appropriate in women's sports. Several generations ago, such behavior would have been seen as highly inconsistent with sex role norms for women.

The Perspectives in Historical Context

Today, psychology stands at a scientific crossroads formed by the six perspectives on behavior. As we have seen, the perspectives provide us with differing conceptions of human nature, they focus on different causes of behavior, and they sometimes use different methods in their attempt to understand these causes. Table 1.2 summarizes these themes.

Having considered the six perspectives on behavior individually, let us pull these diverse threads together and trace their historical impact on the development of today's psychology. As an experimental science, psychology began with a cognitive focus in 1879 as Wilhelm Wundt founded the school of structuralism in Germany and used the method of introspection to study the contents of the mind. Near the end of the 19th century, functionalism began to flourish in the United States as Harvard's William James and other pioneers explored cognitive processes such as thinking, memory, and the self-concept. At about the same time, a very different conception of mental life appeared in the person of Sigmund Freud, and psychology became both a laboratory science and a clinical enterprise dedicated to understanding and treating psychological disorders. The psychodynamic perspective dominated clinical thinking and practice for nearly 50 years before being gradually overtaken by behavioral, humanistic, and cognitive approaches to personality and psychological treatment.

The 1920s were a period of dramatic change for psychology. Sparked by Ivan Pavlov's earlier research on "automatic" learning in dogs and John Watson's stimulus-response analysis of behavior, the new school of behaviorism became a powerful force in American psychology. Its insistence that the only suitable matter for scientific study is externally observable stimuli and responses resonated with many who wanted psychology to model itself on the

TABLE 1.2	COMPARISON OF SIX MAJOR PERSPECTIVES ON HUMAN BEHAVIOR					
	Biological	**Cognitive**	**Psychodynamic**	**Behavioral**	**Humanistic**	**Sociocultural**
Conception of human nature	The human animal	The human as thinker and information processor	The human as controlled by inner forces and conflicts	The human as a reactor to the environment	The human as free agent, seeking self-actualization and personal meaning	The human as a social being embedded in a culture
Major causal factors in behavior	Genetic and evolutionary factors; brain and biochemical processes	Thought, anticipations, planning, perception, and memory processes	Unconscious motives, conflicts, and defenses; early childhood experiences and unresolved conflicts	Past learning experiences and the stimuli and behavioral consequences that exist in the current environment	Free will, choice, and innate drive toward self-actualization; search for personal meaning of existence	Social forces, including norms, social interactions, and group processes in one's culture and social environment
Predominant focus and methods of discovery	Study of brain-behavior relations; role of hormones and biochemical factors on behavior; behavior genetics research	Study of cognitive processes, usually under highly controlled laboratory conditions	Intensive observations of personality processes in clinical settings; some laboratory research on personality processes	Study of learning processes in both laboratory and real-world settings, with an emphasis on precise observation of stimuli and responses	Study of meaning, values, and purpose in life; study of self-concept, and its role in thought, emotion, and behavior	Comparisons of the behaviors and mental processes of people in different cultures; effects of culturally acquired personal characteristics on behavior

physical and biological sciences. Led by B. F. Skinner, behaviorism's emphasis on the objective study of learning remained at the forefront of psychological thought into the 1960s. For many years, mentalistic concepts were considered "soft" and nonscientific, and few psychologists would even dare to use the word "mind" in their scientific writings.

The mid-1960s witnessed the beginning of the so-called "cognitive revolution" and a reawakening of interest in mental events. Studies like "They Saw a Game" (*Research Close-Up*) helped lay the groundwork for a new interest in how people's mental processes and motives influence their constructions of reality. Even behaviorists saw a need to incorporate cognitive concepts into their theories, and cognitive-behavioral theories eventually pushed radical behaviorism into the background. The advent of the computer inspired new models of the mind based on information-processing concepts. By the end of the 20th century, psychology had in many ways come full circle from its cognitive origins, now armed with far more sophisticated methods for investigating mental events. On another front, a new appreciation for the role of culture in thinking and behavior has created the thriving area of cross-cultural psychology and an influential sociocultural perspective.

Biological psychology has always been a prominent part of the field, but its influence has dramatically increased with the development of new tools of discovery, such as computer-based brain-imaging methods. Psychologists no longer need to infer what must be going on inside the brain, as the structuralists had to. They can now "watch" mental events occur as particular brain areas light up during brain-imaging sessions. These advances have resulted in new interactions between the perspectives. One example, described earlier, is cognitive neuroscience, where scientists representing the biological and cognitive perspectives are joining forces to discover the brain processes that underlie many kinds of mental phenomena.

➤ 34. In what sense has psychology come "full circle" from its early focus on mental events?

〉 INTEGRATING THE PERSPECTIVES: THREE LEVELS OF ANALYSIS

One way to simplify what the various perspectives bring to our understanding of human behavior is to realize that behavior always involves a biopsychological person acting within an environment. The behavior that results is a reflection

FIGURE 1.22 Each of the six perspectives on behavior focuses primary attention on one of three levels of analysis, emphasizing the role of biological, psychological, or environmental causal factors.

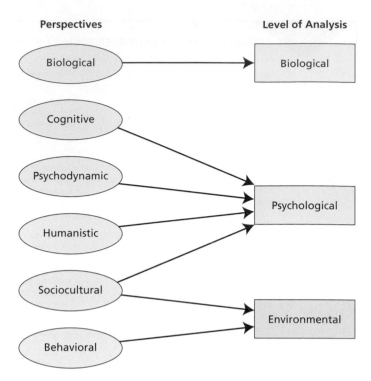

➤ 35. What three levels of analysis allow us to incorporate causal factors suggested by each of the perspectives?

of both the characteristics of the person and the features of the environment. Taking these factors into account provides us with a useful framework for approaching the study of behavior. As noted earlier in the chapter, the various perspectives contribute to three potential **levels of analysis** for describing various aspects of behavior and classifying causal factors: biological, psychological, and environmental (Figure 1.22).

Everything psychological is at the same time biological, reflecting the activities of the physiological processes that underlie behavior. Thus we can analyze behavior and its causes in terms of how brain processes, hormones, and genetic factors contribute to it. This is the *biological level of analysis*. Yet the biological level of analysis cannot tell us everything. To know that certain kinds of thinking and emotions are associated with electrochemical activity in particular brain regions does not tell us what those thoughts and feelings are, how they fit together, and how the person experiences them. To answer such questions, we must move to a different level of analysis, namely, the *psychological level of analysis*. Here, we can take a cognitive perspective and analyze the role of thought, memory, planning, and problem solving in the behavior of interest. The psychodynamic and humanistic perspectives also lead us to the psychological level of analysis, and beckon us to take account of the motivational, emotional, and personality processes that influence how people respond to their environment.

Finally, an understanding of behavior requires that we take account of the environment, past and present, personal and cultural, that helps shape and stimulate our behaviors. Thus the behavioral and sociocultural perspectives focus our attention on a third level of analysis, the *environmental level of analysis*.

The concept of levels of analysis helps simplify matters somewhat, but a full understanding of a behavior may move us back and forth from one level of analysis to another. For example, when we are describing the features of a particular culture, such as the religious values that it conveys to its members, we are operating at the environmental level of analysis. However, once people have been exposed to that culture and taken on those beliefs as their own, they become characteristics of the person and would now be viewed from the psychological level of analysis. Similarly, we might describe a family environment as physically abusive, but the personality traits that result (such as the tendency for a child exposed to that environment to become an aggressive person) will probably move us to the psychological level of analysis. Or, if we're interested in how that child's physiology has been altered by the abusive environment, we may move to a biological level of analysis.

An Example: Understanding Depression

To appreciate how the biological, psychological, and environmental levels of analysis can help us to understand an important behavior, let us briefly summarize what is known about one of the most commonly experienced psychological problems in our culture, namely, depression.

Most of us have probably experienced feelings of sadness, grief, or "the blues" at some time in our lives. These feelings, often accompanied by biological reactions such as loss of appetite and sleep difficulties, are usually normal responses to negative events or meaningful losses that we have experienced. However, when these emotional responses remain intense over a long time period and when they are accompanied by thoughts of hopelessness and an inability to experience pleasure, we have crossed the boundary between a normal reaction and clinical depression (Rubin, 2000).

Depression has sometimes been referred to as the "common cold" of emotional disturbances because it is experienced by so many people. Even if we consider only severe depressive disorders, studies indicate that one in four women and one in eight men in the United States can expect to experience a major depression during their lifetime (Satcher, 1999).

Let's begin at the biological level of analysis. First, genetic factors appear to be involved in at least some cases (Papolos & Lachman, 1994). In one study, relatives of people who had developed a major depression before age 20 were eight times more likely to eventually become depressed than were relatives of nondepressed people (Weissman et al., 1984).

> 36. What does the biological level of analysis tell us about the causes of depression?

Depression is also related to biochemical factors and sleep/wakefulness rhythms in the brain. Of special interest are certain chemicals, known as neurotransmitters, that are involved in the transmission of nerve impulses within the brain. One line of evidence that these substances are important is the fact that the most effective antidepressant drugs seem to operate by restoring a normal balance of these neurotransmitters (Roland, 1997). Also, researchers have found disruptions in biological rhythms that underlie sleep and dreaming in the brain waves of depressed people (Buysse et al., 1997). If the "depressive" brain rhythm is interfered with by waking depressed people up when it is occurring, they feel less depressed afterward (Berger et al., 1997).

Moving from a biological to a psychological level of analysis provides additional understanding of depression and its causes. For example, many studies have shown that depression is associated with a particular thinking style in which the person interprets events in a pessimistic way (Beck, 1976; Seligman & Isaacowitz, 2000). Depressed people can find the black cloud that surrounds every silver lining. They tend to blame themselves for negative things that occur while taking no personal credit for the good things that happen in their lives, and they generally feel that the world, the self, and the future are bleak and hopeless (Beck, 1991).

> 37. What kinds of psychological causal factors have been identified in depression?

Are some personality patterns more prone to depression than others? Many psychodynamic theorists believe that severe losses or rejections in childhood help to create a personality style that causes people to overreact to future losses, setting the stage for later depression. In support of this notion, studies of depressed patients show that they are more likely than nondepressed people to have experienced the loss of a parent through death or separation during childhood (Bowlby, 2000; Brown & Harris, 1978). Depression is also related to childhood histories of abuse, parental rejection, and family discord (Hammen, 1991). People who have

➤ 38. Which causal factors in depression are seen at the environmental level of analysis?

been subjected to severe loss and neglect may develop pessimistic personalities that predispose them to slide into depression in the face of later life stresses.

Finally, the environmental level of analysis reveals several factors that play a major role in depression. According to the behavioral view, depression is a reaction to a nonrewarding environment. A vicious cycle begins when the environment provides fewer rewards for the person. As depression intensifies, such people feel so badly that they to stop doing the things that ordinarily give them pleasure, a pattern that decreases environmental rewards still further. To make things worse, depressed people complain a good deal, seek excessive reassurance and support from others, and generally become less likeable. These behaviors eventually begin to alienate others and cause them to shy away from the depressed person. The net result is a worsening environment with fewer rewards, a reduction in support from others, and the unhappiness and hopeless pessimism that characterize chronic depression (Lewinsohn et al., 1985; Nezlek et al., 2000).

The sociocultural environment also affects depression. Although depression is found in virtually all cultures, both its symptom pattern and its causes may reflect cultural differences. For example, feelings of guilt and personal inadequacy seem to predominate in North American and western European countries, whereas bodily symptoms of fatigue, loss of appetite, and sleep difficulties are more often reported in Latin, Chinese, and African cultures (Brislin, 1993; Lopez & Guarnaccia, 2000). Cross-cultural studies have also shown that in developed countries like the United States, Canada, and other Western nations, women are about twice as likely as men to report feeling depressed, whereas no such sex difference is found in developing countries (Culbertson, 1997; Nolen-Hoeksema, 1990). Why should this be? At present, we do not have the answer, but we must wonder what it is about more technologically advanced cultures that would produce a sex difference that does not show up in developing countries.

➤ 39. What is meant by the interaction of causal factors?

Figure 1.23 summarizes causal factors in depression that are supported by theory and research. Although these causal factors are organized into three classes (biological, psychological, and environmental), we should keep two important points in mind. First, the specific causes of depression can not only differ from case to case, but they can also combine or *interact* with one another in ways that vary according to the person and the situation. **Interaction** means that the presence or strength of one factor can influence the effects of other factors. For example, a person who has a strong biological predisposition for depression may become de-

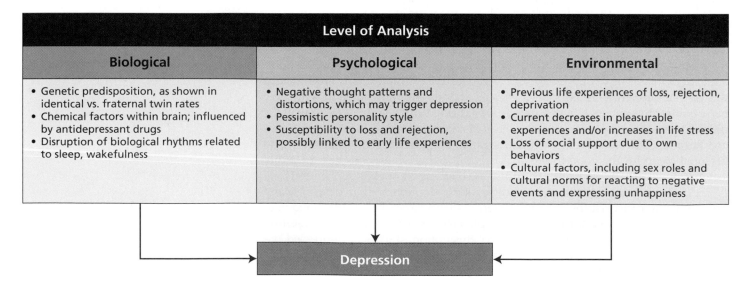

FIGURE 1.23   Understanding the Causes of Behavior: Biological, psychological, and environmental factors in depression.

pressed when faced with a relatively minor setback in life that would barely phase a second person who does not have that predisposition. This second person might require a catastrophic loss in order to become depressed. In this instance, strength of biological predisposition and intensity of life stress would combine, or interact, to influence behavior. Just as boiling water softens celery and hardens an egg, the same environment can affect two different people in very different ways.

Summary of Major Themes

We have now surveyed the six major perspectives that shape psychological thought and the levels of analysis at which behavior is studied. What has our excursion shown us about the science of psychology and its subject matter? The following principles are widely accepted by psychologists and are seen repeatedly as we explore the realm of behavior:

➤ 40. Summarize six important themes in contemporary psychology.

- As a science, *psychology is empirical,* meaning that it favors direct observation over pure intuition or reasoning as a means of attaining knowledge about behavior. In Chapter 2 and throughout the book, we study the empirical methods that are used to observe behavior and identify its causes.

- Though committed to an objective study of behavior, psychologists recognize that *our experience of the world is subjective* and that we respond to a psychological reality created by our own thought processes, motives, and expectations. Many of these influences operate beyond our conscious awareness.

- As our levels of analysis theme shows us, *behavior is determined by multiple causal factors* that can interact with one another in complex ways. This increases the challenge of understanding behavior.

- *Nature and nurture* not only combine to shape our behavior, but also influence one another. Our biological endowment helps determine the kinds of experiences we can have, and biological processes are, in turn, influenced by our experiences.

- Behavior is a means of adapting to environmental demands, and *psychological capacities have evolved* during each species' history because they facilitated adaptation and survival.

- Behavior and mental processes are strongly affected by the *cultural environment* in which they develop. In an increasingly multicultural world, there is a growing need to understand and appreciate the role of cultural factors in behavior.

❯ FIELDS WITHIN PSYCHOLOGY

Modern-day psychology is a sprawling intellectual domain that stretches from the borders of medicine and the biological sciences to those of the social sciences and on into the realm of philosophy. Figure 1.24 shows psychology's position in the family of modern sciences. Because of the enormous breadth of psychology's subject matter, no psychologist can be an expert on all aspects of behavior, just as no physician can be an expert in all areas of medicine. As in other scholarly disciplines, areas of specialization have emerged within psychology. Some of the major specialty areas are described in Table 1.3.

To many people, the term psychologist evokes the image of a "therapist" or "counselor." Many psychologists are, in fact, clinical psychologists who diagnose and treat people

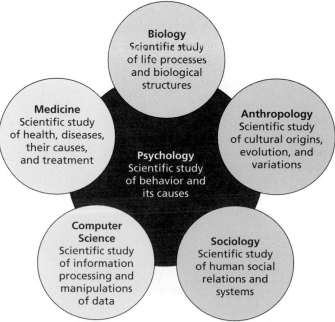

FIGURE 1.24 As the study of behavior and its causes, psychology draws from and overlaps with many other scientific disciplines.

TABLE 1.3	MAJOR SPECIALTY AREAS WITHIN PSYCHOLOGY

Specialty	Major Focus
Clinical	Diagnosis and treatment of emotional disorders; research on personality and abnormal behavior
Counseling	Consultation with clients concerning personal adjustment and vocational and career plans; interest and aptitude testing
Educational	Psychological aspects of the educational process; curriculum and instructional research; teacher training
Experimental	Research on basic psychological processes such as learning, memory, perception, and motivation, much of it conducted in laboratory settings
Industrial	Examination of behavior in work settings; study of factors related to morale and productivity; design of training programs; design of machines and tasks to fit human capabilities
Developmental	Study of physical, mental, emotional, and social development across the entire life span
Social	All aspects of social behavior and the conditions that affect it
Personality	Individual differences in personality and their effects on behavior; factors involved in personality development and change
Physiological	Biological foundations of behavior; brain/behavior relationships, genetic processes, and the functioning of sensory and motor systems
Quantitative	Measurement and data analysis; development of mathematical models of behavior; computer science

with psychological problems in clinics, hospitals, and in private practice. But there are many other types of psychologists who have no connection with therapy in any form. These psychologists work as basic or applied researchers in their chosen subfield. Even within clinical psychology are scientists who spend most of their time doing research on the causes of mental disorders and the effects of various kinds of treatment.

A career in most of the subfields described in Table 1.3 requires a doctoral degree based on four to six years of training beyond the bachelor's degree. Graduate training in psychology includes broad exposure to the theories and body of knowledge in the field, concentrated study in one or more of the subfields, and extensive training in research methods. In some areas, such as clinical, counseling, school, and industrial-organizational psychology, an additional year or more of supervised practical experience in a hospital, clinic, school, or workplace setting is generally required. Please note, however, that psychologists who perform mental-health services are not the same as psychiatrists. Psychiatrists are medical doctors who receive additional specialized training in diagnosing and treating mental disorders.

Besides the fascinating subject matter of psychology, the rich variety of career options and work settings available to the well-trained professional attracts many people to a career in psychology. Figure 1.25 shows some of the major settings in which psychologists work. Many psychologists teach, engage in research, or apply psychological principles and techniques to help solve personal or social problems. Appendix B following Chapter 16 provides more detail about educational and career opportunities in psychology.

Psychologists in all of the areas shown in Table 1.3 engage in basic research and applied work. Some do one or the other, some do both. As we see throughout

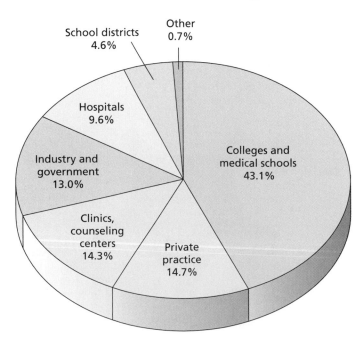

FIGURE 1.25 Work settings of psychologists
Source: American Psychological Association, 2000.

the book, psychological principles discovered through basic psychological research can be applied to many areas of our lives and to the solution of important social problems. For example, research on learning and memory conducted within the areas of educational and experimental psychology has provided practical guidelines that can enhance your academic performance. Our first *Applications of Psychological Science* feature provides some research-based pointers that can help you to be more successful in your coursework.

➤ 41. Describe three important principles of effective time management.

➤ 42. What does educational psychology research tell us about the effects of directed questions on retention of information? Why do they have these effects?

➤ 43. What kinds of strategies are used by testwise students when they take tests?

APPLICATIONS OF PSYCHOLOGICAL SCIENCE

Academic Performance Enhancement Strategies

Four classes of strategies—time management, study skills, test-preparation strategies, and test-taking skills—are particularly useful for increasing your learning and academic performance, both in this course and throughout your educational experience (see Figure 1.26).

❱ Effective Time Management

College life imposes conflicting demands that can challenge even the most organized student. However, if you manage your time efficiently, you can allocate the time needed for study and have a clear conscience when it's time for recreational activities and relaxation.

First, it is essential to develop a written schedule. You have exactly 168 hours in every week, no more, no less. A written schedule forces you to decide how you are going to allocate your time to meet particular course demands and increases your commitment to the plan. Begin your master schedule by writing in all of your class meetings and other responsibilities, such as your job schedule. Then block in definite study times, taking into account how long you can study efficiently at one time and avoiding times when you are likely to be tired. Try to distribute your study times throughout the week. If possible, schedule some of your study times immediately before enjoyable activities so that you can use these as rewards for studying.

Once your study times are set, you are ready to apply the time management principle of *prioritizing* (Lakein, 1973). We all tend to work on routine or simple tasks while putting off the most demanding ones until we "have more time." Unfortunately, this can result in never getting to the major tasks (such as a term paper or a major reading assignment) until it is too late to devote sufficient time to them. Prioritizing means asking yourself weekly or even daily, "What is the most important thing to get done?" Do that task first, then move to the second most important, and so on.

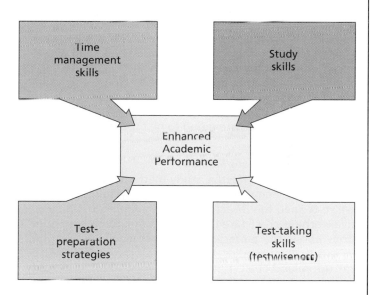

FIGURE 1.26 Academic performance-enhancement methods for students include strategies for managing and allocating time more effectively, study skills, test-preparation strategies, and test-taking skills.

Often the large or important task is too big to complete all at once. Time management experts tell us to break the large task down into smaller ones that can be completed at specific times (Haynes, 1987). Also, define each task in terms of a specific but realistic goal (e.g., number of pages to be read or amount of material to be studied). Achieving these goals is rewarding, and such success strengthens your study skills and increases your feelings of mastery.

—Continued

Like any other skill, time management requires practice. The important tasks are (1) creating written schedules, (2) prioritizing, and (3) constantly monitoring your progress so you can modify your weekly schedule as necessary. The effort put into time management is more than repaid. Working smart can be as important as working hard.

▶ Studying More Effectively

Once you have planned your study time, you will want to use that time most effectively. *Where* you study can make a difference. Choose a place where you can concentrate and where there are no distracting influences. Most students can study better in a quiet library than in front of a TV or in the middle of a Student Union cafeteria. According to a principle of learning that we study in Chapter 6, an excellent practice is to choose a quiet place where you do *nothing* but study. In time, that place will become associated with study behaviors and it will be easier to study there (Watson & Tharp, 1998).

How you study is vital to your academic success. Rather than simply reading material and passively letting it soak in, you must engage in an active learning process to study most effectively. Psychological research confirms the value of an active approach to learning (Glaser & Bassok, 1989). For example, when you read a chapter in a textbook, don't just start reading from the beginning. First, look over the chapter outline. Then go to the end of the chapter and read the chapter summary, which reviews the chapter's main points. You will then have a good idea of the information you are going to be processing.

The Directed Questions Method

One of the most effective study methods we've encountered in our many years of teaching psychology is what we've termed the *Directed Questions Method.* It is an active learning procedure that requires you to prepare questions about the material you are reading. Research has shown that responding to questions promotes better recall (Moreland et al., 1997; Pauk & Fiore, 2000). In a major review of the scientific literature on learning aids, Richard Hamilton (1985) reviewed 35 different experimental studies in which the use of "adjunct questions" was compared with control conditions in which participants simply read textual material. He found that using questions like ours resulted in a superiority of about 20 percent in the retention of material. With our own students over the years, this approach has proven so successful that we chose to make it an integral learning tool in this text in the form of the directed questions found in the margins. These questions cover major facts and concepts you should know. Our directed questions can be supplemented by additional questions of your own. These questions will be an invaluable study aid when you prepare for tests. Here's how the directed questions method works.

As you read the material in a textbook, compose a question about each important point that is made. This forces you to actively identify what is being communicated. Put the number of the question in the margin next to where the answer is found. Do the same thing for your lecture notes. You can now study from your lists of questions and mentally recite the answers to yourself, referring back to your text and lecture notes to make sure that you are answering them correctly. The questions are written in such a way that they serve as a stimulus or prompt for the correct response, resulting in thorough learning.

The directed questions method has two other benefits. Research shows that there is almost no relation between what students think they know and how well they actually perform on tests (Glenberg et al., 1987; Pressley et al., 1987). However, the specific questions that you prepare in the Directed Questions Method allow you to appraise your current level of mastery. Second, the method can reduce test anxiety. You are likely to go into a test more confidently, and such confidence tends to enhance performance (Bandura, 1997). Active learning using a method like directed questions requires more effort than passive reading does, but it results in more facts being absorbed and principles understood (Estes & Vaughn, 1985).

▶ Preparing for Tests

Bunker Hunt, a Texas oil billionaire, was once asked what advice he would give to someone who wanted to be successful. He answered, "First, decide exactly what you want. Second, decide what it's going to take to get it. Third, decide if you're willing to pay the price. Then, pay the price."

Introductory psychology is not an easy course. In fact, it is often a very demanding one because of the sheer amount of material that is covered and the many new concepts that must be mastered. Many students who take the course are relatively new to college and don't realize that the price to be paid for success in college far exceeds the demands that existed in high school. Moreover, many students are not aware of how hard high achievers actually work. In one study, students in an introductory psychology class were asked to record the number of hours outside class that they devoted to the course over a period of several weeks. When the students who were failing the course were compared with those who were getting A grades, the researchers found that the failing students were spending only one-third as many hours studying as were the A students (who were spending about 2 hours of active study for every hour spent in class). Yet the failing students *thought* they were studying as much as anyone else in the class, and many were mystified at why they were not doing as well as their high-achieving peers (Watson & Tharp, 1998).

The time management and study strategies we've discussed can be very helpful when preparing for tests. First, the written study schedule helps you allocate sufficient study time, distribute your learning of the material over time, and it helps avoid the need to cram at the last

—*Continued*

minute. Cramming, or *massed learning,* is a less effective way to study because it is fatiguing and it taxes your memory abilities. Moreover, it often increases test anxiety, which can interfere with both the learning process and with actual test performance (Sarason & Sarason, 1990). The ideal situation as you near an exam is to have a solid familiarity with the material through previous study and to use the time before the test to reinforce and refine what you already know at a more general level. The Directed Questions approach can pay big dividends in the final days before an exam if you've paid the price required to prepare them.

▶ Test-Taking Strategies

Some students are more effective test takers than others. They know how to take advantage of the kind of test they are taking (e.g., multiple-choice or essay format) to maximize their performance. Such skills are called *testwiseness* (Fagley, 1987). Here are some of the strategies that testwise students use (Millman et al., 1965):

1. Because you have a time limit in which to complete the test, use the time wisely. Check your progress occasionally to make sure that you are on track. Answer the questions you know first (and, in the case of essay exams, the ones that count for the most points). Do not get bogged down on a question you find difficult to answer. Mark it and come back to it later.
2. On essay exams, organize your answer before you begin writing. Make a rough outline of the points you want to make. On essay exams, try to cover all of the critical points in enough detail to communicate what you know without needless verbiage.
3. On a test in an introductory psychology course, you are likely to have multiple-choice questions. As you read each multiple choice question, try to answer it without looking at the alternatives. Then look at the answer options. If you find your answer among the alternatives, that alternative is probably the correct one. Nonetheless, read all other alternatives to make sure that you chose the best one.
4. A widely held belief among both professors and students is that one should not change answers on multiple-choice tests because the first guess is most likely to be correct. Psychologists have checked out this belief and have found it to be untrue. Ludy Benjamin and his colleagues (1984) reviewed 20 different studies that investigated the consequences of changing answers. The results are summarized in Figure 1.27. As you can see, changing an answer is far more likely to result in a wrong answer becoming a correct one than vice versa. Another study showed that, on average, 3 points are gained for each point lost because of changing answers (Geiger, 1991). Therefore don't be reluctant to change an answer if you are fairly sure that another alternative is better. At the same time, don't outthink yourself by attaching some esoteric

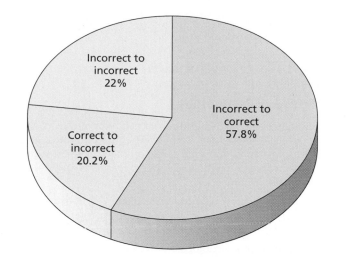

FIGURE 1.27 Combined results of 20 studies on the effects of changing answers on multiple-choice examinations contradict the widespread belief that one's first chosen answer is most likely to be correct and therefore should not be changed. (Data from Benjamin et al., 1984)

meaning to an alternative so that it could *possibly* be correct. Most multiple-choice alternatives are fairly straightforward and not meant to trick you.

5. Many multiple-choice items have one or two alternatives that you can rule out immediately. Eliminate them first, then choose your answer from the remaining alternatives, which are likely to have at least a grain of truth in them.
6. Some questions have "all of the above" as an alternative. If one of the other three or four alternatives is clearly incorrect, eliminate this option; if you are sure at least two of the other alternatives are correct but are not sure about the third, choose "all of the above."

The performance enhancement skills of time management, study skills, test-preparation strategies, and testwiseness can help you improve your academic performance. Remember, however, that such skills are not acquired overnight; they require effort and practice. Psychology is an ideal course in which to acquire or refine them because the subject matter (learning, memory, problem solving, motivation, etc.) often pertains to the very principles you are perfecting. Some of the *Applications of Psychological Science* features in other chapters also may help you enhance your academic performance. These include the following:

- systematic goal-setting strategies (see Chapter 13)
- self-control of behavior (see Chapter 6)
- improving memory (see Chapter 7)
- coping with stress—including test anxiety (see Chapter 10)

▼▼

CHAPTER SUMMARY

The Nature of Psychology

- Psychology is the scientific study of behavior and its causes. Most psychologists use the term *behavior* in its broadest sense to include anything that a human or animal can do, including both observable behavior and inner mental and physiological processes.

- Basic science is the quest for knowledge for its own sake, whereas applied science involves the application of knowledge derived from basic science to solve practical problems.

- The basic goals of psychological research and applications are to describe, understand (explain), predict, and control (influence) behavior.

Perspectives on Behavior

- A number of important perspectives on human behavior have shaped the development of psychology. The perspectives serve as lenses through which the world of behavior is viewed, and they help to determine which aspects of behavior are studied and how. Each perspective provides a different conception of human nature and a focus on different causes of behavior.

The Biological Perspective

- The biological perspective views humans as complex animals and focuses on genetic and physiological influences on behavior. Mental events are seen as the outcomes of physiological processes, and much attention is paid to brain-behavior relations.

- Darwin's theory of evolution popularized the concept of natural selection. Modern evolutionary psychology focuses on the manner in which mental functions and social behaviors may have evolved in humans and how they may affect our behavior today.

- Research in behavior genetics indicates that many complex human behaviors may be influenced by genetic factors.

The Cognitive Perspective

- The cognitive perspective views humans as rational information processors and problem solvers whose higher mental processes allow them to think, judge, imagine, and plan. The roots of the cognitive perspective lie in structuralism, functionalism, and Gestalt psychology. Piaget made great contributions to our understanding of cognitive development in children. Cognitive theorists have made important contributions to the analysis and treatment of self-defeating thought patterns that contribute to psychological disorders. Social constructivists maintain that much of what we call reality is a creation of our own mental processes.

The Psychodynamic Perspective

- The psychodynamic perspective focuses on personality processes, stressing the influence of internal needs, conflicts, and defense mechanisms on behavior.

- Freud's psychoanalytic theory was the earliest and most influential of the psychodynamic theories. He emphasized the role of unconscious impulses and defenses, as well as the importance of early childhood experiences.

- Although many of Freud's ideas have not been supported by research, his theory played an important role in the development of psychology by stimulating research designed to test his theory as well as alternative theories. Even today, biological and cognitive scientists are exploring concepts that relate to Freudian concepts.

The Behavioral Perspective

- The behavioral perspective had its roots in the philosophical tradition of British empiricism. Behaviorists emphasize the role of the external environment and learning in behavior. They deny that humans freely choose how to behave.

- Behaviorists such as Watson and Skinner believed that psychology should restrict itself to the study of observable stimuli and responses. Both felt that control of the environment was the key to bringing about positive social and personal change.

- Cognitive behaviorists such as Bandura have combined the behavioral and cognitive perspectives into a more comprehensive social cognitive theory of behavior that takes into account both mental and environmental factors.

The Humanistic Perspective

- Humanistic theorists rejected many of Freud's notions and emphasized instead the role of self-actualization, freedom, and choice. The humanistic perspective has focused scientifically on the self, motivation, and the process of psychotherapy. Current research in terror management theory is concerned with how people defend themselves against death anxiety.

The Sociocultural Perspective

- Culture refers to the enduring values, beliefs, and traditions that are shared by a large group and passed on from one generation to the next. Cultural factors have strong influences on how people think and behave.

- Individualism and collectivism reflect different orientations to the self in relation to the larger social group. Cultures may be differentiated in terms of their emphasis on individualism and collectivism, and these differences are seen to be the product of cultural learning.

- Today's perspective on the nature-nurture controversy holds that biological and social factors combine in complex ways to influence behavior and that these sets of factors also influence one another.

Integrating the Perspectives: Three Levels of Analysis

- The perspectives provide us with three classes of causal factors: biological; psychological, and environmental factors. The manner in which these three levels of analysis can be used to understand the causes of behavior was illustrated by relating them to depression.

- Biological, psychological, and environmental factors can interact with one another in complex ways to influence a given behavior.

Fields Within Psychology

- Psychologists specialize in numerous subfields and work in many settings. Their professional activities include teaching, research, clinical work, and application of psychological principles to solve personal and social problems.

▼▼

KEY TERMS AND CONCEPTS*

applied research (5)

artificial intelligence (16)

basic research (5)

behavior genetics (13)

behavior modification (22)

behavioral perspective (20)

behaviorism (21)

biological perspective (10)

British empiricism (20)

cognitive behaviorism (22)

cognitive perspective (14)

collectivism (24)

culture (24)

evolutionary psychology (12)

functionalism (14)

Gestalt psychology (15)

humanistic perspective (22)

hysteria (19)

individualism (24)

insight (15)

interaction (30)

introspection (14)

jigsaw program (6)

levels of analysis (28)

mind-body dualism (10)

monism (10)

natural selection (11)

norms (24)

perspective (9)

psychodynamic perspective (18)

psychology (4)

repression (19)

self-actualization (23)

social constructivism (17)

sociobiology (12)

sociocultural perspective (24)

structuralism (14)

terror management theory (23)

* Each term has been boldfaced and defined in the text on the page indicated in parentheses.

▼▼

APPLYING YOUR KNOWLEDGE

These questions allow you to apply your understanding of material in this chapter.

1. Which of the following activities represents basic research?
   a) studying methods for reducing depression after the death of a loved one
   b) studying changes in brain chemistry that are associated with depression
   c) studying how to help AIDS victims cope with their disease
   d) studying the effects of a reading program for disadvantaged children

2. Anna is brought to see a doctor because she woke up one morning unable to move her hands. The doctors can find no medical reason for her paralysis and refer her for a psychological evaluation. A Freudian psychologist would most likely see her problem as
   a) an attempt to avoid responsibilities.
   b) a bid for attention.
   c) a defense against unconscious sexual or aggressive impulses.
   d) an expression of self-actualization.

3. Wayne is doing a psychology experiment in which he compares people's perceptions of a line presented either alone or as part of a larger figure. His hypothesis, that the line will be perceived differently when part of the larger figure than when presented alone is most consistent with which early school of psychology?
   a) functionalism
   b) structuralism
   c) behaviorism
   d) Gestalt psychology

4. Dr. Wu is studying ways in which chimps learn to solve problems in order to obtain food. She believes that her research will provide insights into human problem solving. This belief is based upon the behaviorist assumption that
   a) human beings are too complex to study precisely.
   b) since humans have evolved from apes, they have similar cognitive processes.
   c) at a behavioral level, chimps and humans are pretty much alike.
   d) the same basic laws of learning apply to all organisms.

5. Parents of a 3-year-old child who constantly misbehaves consult with a psychologist, who observes the child in the home situation. The psychologist notices that the mother always pays attention to the child's misbehavior but pays little attention when the child is behaving appropriately. The psychologist advises the mother to pay attention to and praise positive behaviors and to ignore the negative ones. The psychologist is most likely
   a) psychodynamic in orientation.
   b) a humanist.
   c) a behaviorist.
   d) a cognitive therapist.

6. The Russian author Anton Chekhov once wrote, "Man is what he believes." This statement would be most consistent with the tenets of
   a) behaviorism.
   b) psychoanalysis.
   c) social constructivism.
   d) structuralism.

7. Molly's best friend died recently in an auto accident. Molly has been tormented with questions about the meaning of

life, when death can come so suddenly and unjustifiably. You believe that she could profit from counseling. What type of psychotherapist would be most likely to focus on Molly's questions about the meaning of life?

a) Freudian psychoanalyst
b) behaviorist
c) humanistic
d) cognitive

8. Kerry's older brother is constantly arguing with their parents, and constantly being punished for it. Kerry rarely does so. One explanation is that Kerry has learned not to argue with his parents because he has observed what happens to his brother. Which theorist would be most likely to offer this explanation?

a) John Watson
b) Albert Bandura
c) Wilhelm Wundt
d) Carl Rogers

9. Dee confides to her best friend that she is depressed. Trying to cheer her up, her friend tells her that she's a wonderful person with many friends, a loving boyfriend, a happy family, and a major that she loves. Her friend counsels her not to get down on herself because she is not getting good grades in school. Dee is most likely to remember that her friend told her that

a) she is not getting good grades.
b) she is a wonderful person.
c) she has many friends.
d) her boyfriend loves her.

10. Based on the performance enhancement principles discussed in the *Applications* feature of this chapter, which of the following statements represents a good strategy for taking multiple-choice tests?

a) Answer all the questions in order; avoid skipping over some questions and trying to answer them later.
b) After reading the question, try to answer it before looking at the alternatives. If you find your answer among the alternatives, it's probably correct.
c) If you are uncertain about one of your answers, do not go back and change it, for you are more likely to go from being correct to being incorrect.
d) Choose alternative b if you do not know the answer, for that is most often the correct alternative.

Answers

1. b) (page 5); 2. c) (page 19); 3. d) (page 15); 4. d) (page 21); 5. c) (page 21); 6. c) (page 17); 7. c) (page 22); 8. b) (page 22); 9. a) (page 29); 10. b) (page 35).

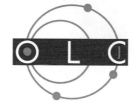

For additional quizzing and a variety of interactive resources, visit the book's Online Learning Center at www.mhhe.com/passer.

STUDYING BEHAVIOR
SCIENTIFICALLY

I have no special talents. I am only passionately curious.
— *Albert Einstein*

2

CHAPTER OUTLINE

▼▼▼▼▼▼▼▼▼▼▼▼▼▼▼▼▼▼▼▼▼▼▼▼▼▼▼▼▼▼▼▼▼▼▼▼▼▼▼

Winter was around the corner, and Teryl's Sunday morning drive to Oregon City was about to take an unexpected twist: The pickup truck in front of her hit a slick spot, veered off the road, and went over the edge. Teryl, who has paralyzed legs and only partial use of her arms, stopped her minivan, lowered herself into her wheelchair, and headed to the crash site. She then got out of her wheelchair, slid down the wet embankment, crawled to reach the bleeding, dazed driver, and administered first aid until the paramedics arrived. Said Teryl, "I think anybody would have done that. You see a car go down a ditch, and I can't imagine not stopping to help" (*Seattle Times*, December 11, 1997). Yet three decades earlier, the unimaginable had occurred.

▼▼▼▼▼▼▼▼▼▼▼▼▼▼▼▼▼▼▼▼▼▼▼▼▼▼▼▼▼▼▼▼▼▼▼▼▼▼▼

In March of 1964 a young woman named Kitty Genovese was stabbed repeatedly and raped by a knife-wielding assailant as she returned from work to her New York City apartment. The 3 A.M. attack lasted about 30 minutes, during which time her screams and pleas for help were heard by 38 of her neighbors. Many went to their windows to find out what was happening. Yet nobody assisted her, and by the time anyone called the police, she had died. The incident drew international attention from a shocked public and commentators expressed outrage over "bystander apathy" and people's refusal to "get involved." In New York City and elsewhere, people reacted with disbelief and even shame to the Kitty Genovese murder.

Science frequently has all the mystery and drama of a detective story. Consider the psychological puzzle of bystander intervention. Ordinary citizens like Teryl often take decisive action to help someone in need. A Long Island man on his way to work rescues a woman trapped inside a burning car (*New York Times*, January 30, 1999). A volunteer school-crossing guard in California uses her body to shield several children from an oncoming automobile (*KIRO News*, January 17, 1998). In Washington, D.C., two pedestrians subdue a gunman who is shooting at the White House with an assault rifle (*Washington Post*, October 30, 1994). But as the Kitty Genovese murder and similar tragedies illustrate, people do not always come to another's aid. Why do bystanders sometimes risk injury and death to assist a complete stranger, yet at other times fail to intervene—even when providing help or calling the police entails little personal risk (Figure 2.1)? We will return to this puzzle shortly.

In this chapter we explore principles and methods that form the foundation of psychological science. Virtually all of what you will learn in your introductory psychology course is a product of these principles and methods. These scientific principles also form the basis for a way of thinking—critical thinking—that can serve you well in many aspects of life well beyond your course.

❯ SCIENTIFIC PRINCIPLES IN PSYCHOLOGY

Science is about discovery. At its core, science simply is an approach to asking and answering questions about the universe around us. Certainly, there are other ways we learn about our world and ourselves: through philosophy, reason and logic, religious faith, art and literature, the teachings of others, and everyday common sense. What distinguishes science from these approaches is a general process guided by certain principles.

(a)   (b)

FIGURE 2.1 What determines whether a bystander will help a victim? (a) In Greece, as a rapidly advancing fire engulfs everything in its path, a man risks his life to help an elderly man who has trouble walking. (b) In 1995, an enraged 19-year-old whose car had been hit by Deletha Word caught up to her in traffic on a Detroit-area bridge. He smashed her car windows, dragged her out, ripped off most of her clothes, and beat her. As in the Kitty Genovese murder, none of the 40 bystanders intervened during this half-hour incident. Overcome with terror, Word escaped, jumped off the bridge, and drowned. Here at the bridge, Deletha's mother and loved ones mourn her death.

Scientific Attitudes

Curiosity, skepticism, and *open-mindedness* are driving forces behind scientific inquiry. Like a child who constantly asks "Why?", the good scientist has an insatiable curiosity. And like a master detective, the good scientist is an incurable skeptic. Each claim is met with the reply "Show me your evidence," and even when a mystery appears to be solved the good scientist asks, "Might there be a better explanation?" Scientists also must remain open-minded to conclusions that are supported by facts, even if those conclusions refute their own beliefs (Figure 2.2).

Following the Kitty Genovese murder, two psychology professors in New York City, John Darley of New York University and Bibb Latané of Columbia University, met for dinner. Like everyone else, they wondered how 38 people could witness a criminal act and not even call the police. But their curiosity was piqued so strongly that they decided to investigate further. Darley and Latané were skeptical of the "bystander apathy" explanation offered by social commentators, and believed it was unlikely that every one of the 38 bystanders could have been apathetic. As social psychologists, they knew that the immediate environment powerfully influences behavior, even though people may be unaware of this influence. They noted that the bystanders could see that other neighbors had turned on their lights and were looking out their windows. Each bystander might have been concerned about Kitty Genovese's plight but assumed that someone else surely would help or call the police.

Darley and Latané reasoned that the presence of multiple bystanders produced a *diffusion of responsibility*, a psychological state in which each person feels decreased personal responsibility for intervening. To test their explanation, they performed several experiments that have become classics in social psychology. However, as Darley and Latané set out to gather evidence, they had to remain open-minded to the possibility that the findings would not support their point of view.

"No doubt about it, Ellington—we've mathematically expressed the purpose of the universe. God, how I love the thrill of scientific discovery!"

FIGURE 2.2 The joy of scientific curiosity, the thrill of discovery, and the importance of being open-minded.

➤ 1. What key scientific attitudes did Darley and Latané display?

Gathering Evidence: Steps in the Scientific Process

➤ 2. How does Darley and Latané's research illustrate the basic steps of the scientific process?

Science involves a continuous interplay between observing and explaining events. Figure 2.3 shows the steps through which the gathering of scientific evidence often proceeds. Curiosity sparks the first step: Scientists observe something noteworthy and ask a question about it. For Darley and Latané, the initial observation was that nobody helped Kitty Genovese, and the question became "Why?"

➤ 3. What is a hypothesis?

Next scientists formulate a testable hypothesis. A **hypothesis** is a tentative explanation or prediction about some phenomenon. To develop a hypothesis, scientists gather clues and logically analyze them. Noting that many bystanders had been present and recognizing that each one probably knew that others were watching, Darley and Latané combined these clues to arrive at a hypothesis: A diffusion of responsibility reduced the likelihood that any one bystander would feel responsible for helping.

Casual observers might stop here, satisfied that they now understand why the bystanders did not help. But the scientist knows that the hypothesis is tentative and must be tested. To do this, the hypothesis is translated into a specific prediction that often takes the form of an "If—Then" statement. Thus the diffusion of responsibility hypothesis becomes the following: IF an emergency occurs, THEN the greater the number of bystanders, the less likely any one bystander will be to intervene."

The third step of scientific inquiry is to test the hypothesis by gathering evidence. Scientists do this by conducting research. Darley and Latané (1968) carefully created an "emergency" in their experimental laboratory and observed people's responses. The participants were undergraduates who were told that they would be discussing "personal problems faced by normal college students." They were informed that to ensure privacy, they would be seated in separate rooms, communicate through an intercom system, and the experimenter would not listen to their conversation. Participants would take turns speaking for several rounds. In each round, a participant would have two minutes to speak, during which time the others would be unable to interrupt or be heard, because their microphones would be turned off.

As the discussion began over the intercom, a speaker described his difficulties adjusting to college life and disclosed that he suffered from seizures. During the next round of conversation, this same speaker began to gasp and stammer, saying: "... Could somebody-er-er—help ... [choking sounds] ... I'm gonna die-er-er—I'm gonna die-er—help ... seizure" [chokes, then silence] (Darley & Latané, 1968, p. 379).

Unbeknownst to the participants, they actually were listening to a tape recording. This ensured that all of them were exposed to the identical "emergency." To test how the number of bystanders influence helping, Darley and Latané manipulated the number of other people that each participant believed to be present and listening over the intercom. On a random basis, some participants were told that they were alone with the victim; in a second condition, participants were led to believe there was another listener present. In a third condition, they believed that four other listeners were present. The participants believed that the seizure was real and serious. But did they help?

At the fourth step of scientific inquiry, researchers analyze the information (called *data*) they collect and draw tentative conclusions. Darley and Latané

1. Initial Observation/Question
Kitty Genovese incident. Why did no one help?
2. Form Hypothesis
IF multiple bystanders are present, THEN a diffusion of responsibility will decrease each bystander's likelihood of intervening.
3. Test Hypothesis (conduct research)
• Create "emergency" in controlled setting. • Manipulate perceived number of bystanders. • Measure helping.
4. Analyze Data
Helping decreases as the perceived number of bystanders increases. The hypothesis is supported. (If data do not support the hypothesis, revise and retest.)
5. Further Research and Theory Building
Additional studies support the hypothesis. A Theory of Social Impact is developed based on these and other findings.
6. New Hypothesis Derived from Theory
The theory is tested directly by deriving new hypothesis and conducting new research.

FIGURE 2.3 This sequence represents one common path to scientific understanding. In other cases, scientists begin with an observation/question and proceed directly to research without testing hypotheses or trying to build theories.

measured the percentage of participants who left their room to go to the victim or find help, and the speed with which they acted. Figure 2.4 shows that 80 percent of the participants who thought they were alone with the victim helped within the first minute of the seizure and 100 percent helped within three minutes. As the number of presumed bystanders increased, the proportion who helped decreased and those who did help took longer to respond. Darley and Latané concluded that the findings supported the diffusion of responsibility hypothesis. Their results also demonstrate how scientific research can contradict commonsense adages such as "There's safety in numbers." As you will see throughout this book, many common-sense beliefs have not survived the cutting edge of psychological research.

We have described four steps of gathering scientific evidence: asking a question, forming a hypothesis, conducting research, and drawing conclusions based on data analysis. However, the process of inquiry doesn't end here.

At the fifth step scientists conduct more research and, as additional evidence comes in, they attempt to build theories. A **theory** is a set of formal statements that explains how and why certain events are related to one another. Theories are broader than hypotheses, and in psychology theories typically specify lawful relations between certain behaviors and their causes. For example, to establish that diffusion of responsibility occurred across a range of situations, researchers conducted nearly 50 additional experiments in laboratories and natural settings, the vast majority of which supported the initial findings (Latané & Nida, 1981). Latané (1981) combined the principle of diffusion of responsibility with other principles of group behavior to develop a Theory of Social Impact, which he then used to explain a variety of human social behaviors.

Finally, at the sixth step, the theory is used to develop new hypotheses, which are then tested by conducting additional research and gathering new evidence. In this manner the scientific process becomes self-correcting. If research consistently supports the hypotheses derived from the theory, our confidence in the theory becomes stronger. If the predictions made by the theory are not supported, then it will need to be modified or, ultimately, discarded.

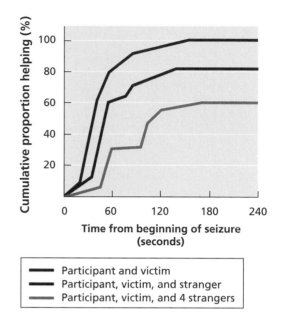

FIGURE 2.4 Some participants believed that they were alone with a student who presumably was having a seizure. Others believed that either one or four more bystanders were present. Participants who believed they were alone with the victim were more likely to intervene, and did so more quickly. Data from Darley & Latané, 1968.

➤ 4. What is a theory? How does it differ from a hypothesis?

Two Approaches to Understanding Behavior

Humans have a strong desire to understand why things happen. To psychologists, such understanding means being able to specify the causes of behavior, the conditions responsible for its occurrence. Why do scientists favor the step-by-step approach to understanding described above over the approach typically involved in everyday common sense: hindsight (after-the-fact) understanding?

Hindsight Understanding

One sometimes hears the statement that psychology is nothing more than common sense. "I knew that all along" is a common response to findings from psychological research. In fact, a *New York Times* book reviewer leveled this criticism some years ago. The report he was reviewing, *The American Soldier* (Stouffer et al., 1949a, 1949b), summarized the results of a large-scale study of the goals, attitudes, and behavior of U.S. soldiers during World War II. The reviewer blasted the government for spending a lot of money to "tell us nothing we don't already know."

Consider the following statements. How would you account for each of them?

1. The motivation to become officers was higher among White soldiers than among Blacks.

2. During basic training, soldiers from rural backgrounds had higher morale and adapted better than soldiers from large cities.

➤ 5. Explain the major drawback of hindsight understanding.

3. During combat, soldiers with higher intelligence were more fearful and more likely to develop "psychosomatic" disorders (emotionally caused physical illnesses) than less intelligent soldiers.

4. Soldiers serving in Europe were more highly motivated to return home while the fighting was going on than they were after the war had ended.

You should have no difficulty arriving at psychological explanations for these results. A typical line of reasoning might be as follows: (1) Because of widespread prejudice, Black soldiers knew that their chances of becoming officers were remote. Why should they torture themselves wanting something that was unattainable? (2) It makes sense that the rigors of basic training would be more tolerable for people from farm settings who were used to working hard and getting up at the crack of dawn. (3) Brighter soldiers were smart enough to realize what might happen to them in combat; hence, they experienced more anxiety. (4) Who in his right mind would not want to go home while bullets were flying and people were dying?

Did your explanations resemble these? If so, they are perfectly reasonable. There is one catch, however. The results you have just explained are the *exact opposite* of the actual findings. In fact, Black soldiers were more highly motivated than Whites to become officers, and city boys had higher morale than farm boys during basic training. Less intelligent soldiers were more anxious and more likely to develop psychosomatic problems in combat. Finally, soldiers were more eager to return home *after* the war ended than they were during the fighting. When told these true results, our students quickly find plausible explanations for them. In short, it is easy to arrive at completely reasonable after-the-fact explanations for almost any result.

In everyday life, after-the-fact ("hindsight") explanation probably is our most common method of trying to understand behavior. In the words of the Danish philosopher Søren Kierkegaard, "Life is lived forwards, but understood backwards." The major limitation of relying solely on hindsight understanding is that past events usually can be explained in many ways, and there is no sure way to determine which—if any—of the alternatives is correct. But despite this drawback, hindsight understanding can provide valuable insights, and is often the foundation on which further scientific inquiry is built. For example, Darley and Latané's diffusion of responsibility explanation initially was based on after-the-fact reasoning about the Kitty Genovese murder.

Understanding Through Prediction, Control, and Theory Building

➤ 6. What approach to understanding do scientists prefer? Why?

Whenever possible, scientists prefer to test their understanding of "what causes what" more directly. If we understand the causes of a given behavior, then we should be able to predict the conditions under which that behavior will occur in the future. Furthermore, if we can control those conditions (e.g., in the laboratory), then we should be able to produce that behavior.

Darley and Latané's research illustrates this approach. To test their causal explanation for why bystanders failed to help Kitty Genovese, Darley and Latané predicted that a greater number of bystanders present during an emergency would reduce individual helping. Next they created a laboratory setting to produce this result. They staged an emergency, controlled participants' beliefs about the number of bystanders present, and carefully structured the environment so that each participant could not tell whether the other "bystanders" were taking action (as was the case in the Kitty Genovese murder). Their prediction was supported. Understanding through prediction and control is a scientific alternative to after-the-fact understanding.

➤ 7. Describe the characteristics of a good theory.

Theory development is the strongest test of scientific understanding because good theories generate an *integrated network of predictions*. A good theory has several important characteristics.

- It incorporates existing facts and observations within a single broad frame-work. In other words, it organizes information in a meaningful way.

- It is testable. It generates new hypotheses—new specific predictions—whose accuracy or inaccuracy can be evaluated by gathering new evidence (Figure 2.5).

- The predictions made by the theory are supported by the findings of new research.

- It conforms to the *law of parsimony*. If two theories can explain and predict the same phenomena equally well, the simpler theory is the preferred one.

Even when a theory is supported by many successful predictions, it is never regarded as an absolute truth. It is always possible that some future observation will contradict it, or that a newer and more accurate theory will take its place. If this happens, scientists do not wring their hands in despair. Disproving established theories frequently opens up exciting new frontiers for investigation. The displacement of old beliefs and theoretical frameworks by new ones is the essence of science (Klahr & Simon, 1999).

Finally, although scientists use prediction as a test of "understanding," this does *not* mean that prediction *requires* understanding. Based on experience, a child can predict that thunder will follow lightning without knowing why it does so. Our primeval ancestors undoubtedly could predict that eating certain plants would make them sick, without understanding principles of human physiology. But prediction based on understanding (i.e., "theory building") has important advantages: It satisfies our curiosity, increases knowledge, and generates principles that can be applied to new situations that we have not yet directly experienced.

Defining and Measuring Variables

Psychologists study variables and the relations among them. A **variable,** quite simply, is any characteristic that can vary. Gender is a variable: Some people are female, others male. People's age, ethnicity, school grades, and typing speed are variables, as are national daily ice cream consumption and stock market prices.

Many variables represent nonmaterial concepts, such as *memory, personality, intelligence, stress, learning, and motivation.* Such terms may have different meanings for different people. Unless two people share a common definition of what "intelligence" or "stress" means, they cannot be sure that they are talking about the same thing when they discuss these concepts. When scientists conduct research, they resolve this problem by operationally defining concepts. An **operational definition** defines a variable in terms of the specific procedures used to produce or measure it. In essence, operational definitions *translate an abstract term into something observable and measurable.*

For example, to examine whether six months of regular exercise reduces stress, we must first decide upon definitions of "regular exercise" and "stress." We could operationally define "regular exercise" in many ways, such as taking a daily two-mile walk or engaging in 30 minutes of vigorous physical activity four times a week. We can operationally define "stress" as people's questionnaire rating of how tense they feel, their level of muscle tension, or frequency of fidgeting (e.g., nail biting, foot tapping). As a researcher, you would use your knowledge about exercise and stress to identify operational definitions that seem most appropriate.

Consider another example. As you may know all too well, taking exams can be stressful. Suppose that we want to study the relation between exam stress and academic performance among college students. How might you operationally define "exam stress" at a biological, psychological, and environmental level of analysis? Think about this, and then see Figure 2.6.

"IT MAY VERY WELL BRING ABOUT IMMORTALITY, BUT IT WILL TAKE FOREVER TO TEST IT."

FIGURE 2.5 Is the scientist's claim of discovering an "eternal life potion" a testable hypothesis? Yes, because it is possible to show the hypothesis to be false. If people drink it but still die, then we have refuted the hypothesis. Therefore it is testable. It is, however, impossible to absolutely prove true. Even after living for a million years, a person who drank the potion could die the next day.

▶ 8. Why are operational definitions important?

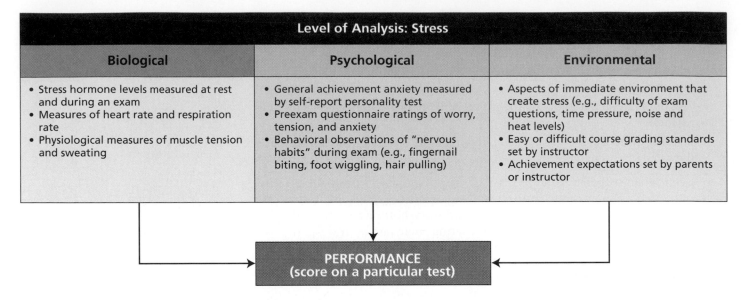

FIGURE 2.6 Understanding the Causes of Behavior: When studying the effects of exam stress on academic performance, the concept of *"exam stress"* can be operationally defined at the biological, psychological, and environmental levels of analysis.

Of course, operational definitions don't solve every problem. Just as you and a friend may disagree about what constitutes a great movie, other scientists may not agree with our definitions of regular exercise and stress. Even so, the key point is that operational definitions let other scientists know exactly what we mean by those terms.

To operationally define a concept, we must be able to measure it. Measurement is challenging because psychologists study incredibly varied and complex processes. Some processes are directly observable, but others are not. Fortunately, psychologists have numerous measurement techniques at their disposal (Figure 2.7).

Self-Report Measures

Self-report measures ask people to report on their own knowledge, beliefs, feelings, experiences, or behavior. This information can be gathered in several ways, such as interviews, questionnaires, or specially designed psychological tests. The accuracy of self-report measures hinges on people's ability and willingness to respond honestly. Especially when research questions focus on sensitive topics, such as sexual habits and drug use, participants' self-reports may be distorted by a *social desirability bias:* the tendency to respond in a socially acceptable manner rather than according to how one truly feels or behaves. Researchers try to minimize this bias by establishing rapport with participants and allowing them to respond confidentially or anonymously. Questionnaires and psychological tests also can be designed to reduce social desirability bias (Nederhof, 1985).

In interviews, the accuracy of self-reports also can be influenced by the interviewer's behavior. Nowhere is this issue more explosive that with regard to child sexual abuse. Over 100,000 substantiated cases a year are reported in the United States alone, and others go unreported (Department of Health and Human Services, 1999). Yet some allegations are found to be false. In most cases there is no clear-cut medical evidence, so the accuracy of the child's testimony becomes paramount (Bruck et al., 1998).

➤ 9. Describe the major ways psychologists measure behavior, and a limitation of each.

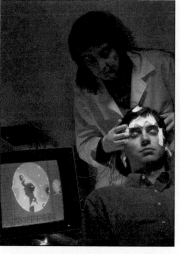

(a)

FIGURE 2.7 Self-report (a), physiological (b), and behavioral (c) measures are important scientific tools for psychologists.

(b)

(c)

Some therapists and police investigators use suggestive interview techniques to "draw out" allegations of sexual abuse from children who initially deny it, but presumably are reluctant to discuss their experience. Unfortunately, research by American and Canadian psychologists shows that suggestive questions can cause some children to falsely report and come to believe that fictitious events are real (Bruck et al., 1995; Ceci & Huffman, 1997). This does not imply that most abuse allegations are false, but it raises a hornet's nest of controversy regarding the optimal way to interview children about potential sexual abuse (Bruck et al., 2000).

Reports by Others

We also can learn about someone's behavior by obtaining reports made by other people. Parents, spouses, and teachers who know a person can provide useful information about him or her. College students might be asked to rate their roommates' personality traits, and job supervisors might be asked to rate a worker's competence and motivation.

As with self-reports, researchers try to maximize participants' honesty in reporting about other people. We also must keep in mind that the people providing these reports may be familiar with the person they are judging only in certain situations (e.g., work), and that this person's behavior may be quite different in other situations.

Physiological Measures

Although psychologists frequently depend on participants' self-reports to measure subjective experiences, there are other ways to measure what is happening "inside" a person. Scientists are able to measure many aspects of physiological functioning, ranging from heart rate, blood pressure, respiration rate, and hormonal secretions, to electrical and biochemical processes in the brain. Physiological measures have long been the mainstay of researchers working within the biological perspective, but these measures have become increasingly important in many areas of psychology.

Physiological responses can have their own interpretive problems, the main one being that we don't always understand what they mean. For example, if a person shows increased heart rate and brain activity in a particular situation, what emotion or thought is being expressed? The links between specific patterns of physiological activity and particular mental events are far from being completely understood.

Behavioral Observations

A fourth measurement approach is to observe people's overt (i.e., directly visible) behaviors in either real-life or laboratory settings. To do so, psychologists often develop coding systems made up of specific behavior categories. Coding systems are used to measure such diverse behaviors as people's facial expressions, parent-child interactions, and marital communications (Ekman & Friesen, 1987). Once a coding system is developed, observers are rigorously trained to use it in exactly the same way so that their measurements will be *reliable,* which means that they are consistent. If two observers watching the same behaviors repeatedly disagree in their coding, then the data are unreliable and of little use.

Psychologists sometimes gather information about people's overt behavior by using **archival measures,** which are already existing records or documents. For example, researchers comparing different programs designed to reduce drunk driving could use police arrest records to measure the frequency of "drunk driving."

➤ 10. What is unobtrusive measurement?

Humans and other animals may behave differently when they know they are being observed, resulting in an unrepresentative (i.e., atypical) sample of behavior. To counter this problem researchers in natural environments may camouflage themselves or use *unobtrusive measures,* which record behavior in a way that keeps participants unaware that they are being observed (Lee, 2000; Webb et al., 1966). For example, researchers from the Centers for Disease Control assessed the effects of a "safer sex" program by counting the number of used condoms that turned up in a Baltimore sewage treatment plant before and after the program (no one promised that science would always be glamorous).

In sum, psychologists can measure behavior in many ways, each with advantages and disadvantages. To gain greater confidence in their findings, researchers may use several types of measures within a single study.

〉 METHODS OF RESEARCH

Like detectives searching for clues to solve a case, psychologists conduct research to gather evidence about behavior and its causes. The research method chosen depends upon the problem being studied, the investigator's objectives, and ethical principles.

Descriptive Research: Recording Events

The most basic goal of science is to describe phenomena. In psychology, **descriptive research** seeks to identify how humans and other animals behave, particularly in natural settings. It provides valuable information about the diversity of behavior, can be used to test hypotheses, and may yield clues about potential cause-effect relations that are later tested experimentally. Case studies, naturalistic observation, and surveys are common descriptive methods.

Case Studies: The Hmong Sudden Death Syndrome

➤ 11. What is a case study? Identify its advantages.

A **case study** is an in-depth analysis of an individual, group, or event. By studying a single case in great detail the researcher typically hopes to discover principles of behavior that are true for people or situations in general. Data may be gathered through observation, interviews, psychological tests, physiological recordings, and task performance. Archival data may be examined when a case study focuses on people or events from the past.

Case studies have several advantages but also significant drawbacks. One advantage is that when a rare phenomenon occurs, the case study method enables scientists to study it intensively and collect a large amount of data. A second advantage is that a case study may challenge the validity of a theory or widely held scientific belief. For example, suppose a theory proposed that, for humans to learn language, they *must* be exposed to a language-rich environment sometime during their childhood. By finding a single contradictory case—a person who was not exposed to language during childhood but later learned to speak normally—this proposition would be shown to be incorrect and the theory would have to be modified.

Perhaps the biggest advantage of case studies is that they can be a vibrant source of new ideas and hypotheses that may subsequently be examined using more controlled research methods. Case studies have provided important insights into such diverse topics as brain functioning, child development, mental disorders, and cultural influences, as illustrated by the following example.

Vang is a former Hmong (Laotian) soldier who resettled in Chicago in 1980 after escaping from the ravages of war in Laos. Vang had traumatic memories of death and destruction as well as severe guilt about leaving his brothers and sisters behind when he fled with his wife and child (Figure 2.8). The culture shock created by moving from his rural Laotian home to Chicago's urban environment increased Vang's stress. According to a mental-health team that reported on Vang's case, he experienced problems almost immediately:

> [He] could not sleep the first night in the apartment, nor the second, nor the third. After three days . . . Vang came to see his resettlement worker, a young bilingual Hmong man named Moua Lee. Vang told Moua that the first night he woke suddenly, short of breath, from a dream in which a cat was sitting on his chest. The second night . . . a figure, like a large black dog, came to his bed and sat on his chest. He could not push the dog off and he grew quickly and dangerously short of breath. The third night, a tall, white-skinned female spirit came into his bedroom . . . and lay on top of him. Her weight made it increasingly difficult for him to breathe, and as he grew frantic and tried to call out he could manage but a whisper. He attempted to turn onto his side, but found he was pinned down. After 15 minutes, the spirit left him and he awoke, screaming. (Tobin & Friedman, 1983, p. 440)

Vang's report may not have attracted scientific interest had it not been for one fact: About 25 Laotian refugees in the United States had died of what was termed the "Hmong sudden death syndrome." The cases were strikingly similar to Vang's: A person in good health died in his or her sleep after exhibiting labored breathing, screams, and frantic movements. The U.S. Centers for Disease Control investigated these mysterious deaths. Unable to find a physical cause, the investigators concluded that the deaths were triggered by a combination of psychological factors: the stress of resettlement, guilt stemming from abandoning family in Laos, and the Hmong's cultural beliefs about angry spirits.

The authors of Vang's case study concluded that he might have been a survivor of the sudden death syndrome. The role of cultural beliefs in this syndrome is suggested by what happened next. Vang went for treatment to a Hmong woman regarded as a shaman (a person, acting as both doctor and priest, who is believed to work with spirits and the supernatural). She told him his problems were caused by unhappy spirits and performed the ceremonies needed to release the spirits. Vang encountered no further problems with nightmares or with his breathing during sleep.

Vang's case study and the Hmong sudden death syndrome suggest that stress and cultural beliefs may have profound effects on physical well-being. This work was followed by other studies of Hmong immigrants in the United States and Canada, and stimulated additional scientific interest in the general relation between cultural beliefs and health (Adler, 1995; Schriever, 1990).

The most important limitation of case studies is that they are a poor method for determining cause-effect relations. Vang's case study cannot prove that the Hmong sudden death syndrome is a fatal stress response produced by

FIGURE 2.8 Many Hmong refugees who escaped the ravages of war in their homeland experienced great stress and guilt when they resettled in North America. This stress, combined with cultural beliefs about angry spirits, may have contributed to the Hmong sudden death syndrome, which eventually claimed more than 40 lives.

► 12. What are the major limitations of case studies?

cultural beliefs. In most case studies explanations of behavior occur after the fact and there is little opportunity to rule out alternative explanations. Thus the fact that Vang's symptoms ended after seeing a shaman could have been pure coincidence: Some other change in Vang's life could have been responsible, or the symptoms may have ended because of the passage of time. We simply cannot determine which explanation is correct.

A second potential drawback concerns the generalizability of the findings: Will the principles uncovered in a case study hold true for other people or in other situations? The question of generalizability pertains to all research methods, but drawing broad conclusions from one or several case studies can be particularly risky. The key issue is the degree to which the case under study is representative of other people or situations. Vang's case and the deaths of other Hmong immigrants may be a rare, atypical phenomenon. They suggest that cultural beliefs may affect health, but the generalizability of this principle must be examined using other research methods and studying a variety of cultural groups.

A third drawback is the possible lack of objectivity in the way the researcher gathers and interprets the data. Although such bias can occur in any type of research, case studies can be particularly worrisome because they are often based largely on the subjective impressions of the researcher. In science a skeptical attitude requires that, whenever possible, claims based on case studies be followed up by more comprehensive research methods before they are accepted. In everyday life we should adopt a similar skeptical view. When encountering claims based on case examples or anecdotes, keep in mind that the case may be atypical, think about whether the person making the claim may be biased or have an ulterior motive, and try to seek out other evidence to support or refute the claim.

Naturalistic Observation: Chimpanzees, Tool Use, and Cultural Learning

➤ 13. What is naturalistic observation, and what is its major advantage?

In **naturalistic observation,** the researcher observes behavior as it occurs in a natural setting. Naturalistic observation is used extensively to study animal behavior (Figure 2.9). British researcher Jane Goodall gained worldwide fame for her extensive observations of African chimpanzees in the wild. Goodall (1986) and other researchers have found that chimpanzees display a variety of behaviors, such as making and using tools, that were formerly believed to lie only within the domain of human capabilities.

Swiss researcher Christophe Boesch (1991, 1995) has observed a "hammer/anvil" tool use technique among wild African chimpanzees. A chimp places a nut on a hard surface (the anvil), and then hammers it several times with a dead branch or stone until it cracks. Some nuts with hard woody shells are tricky to open, and it may take several years for chimps to perfect their hammering. Especially fascinating is Boesch's observation that mothers seem to intentionally teach their young how to use this technique. Consider this interaction between a chimp named Ricci and her 5-year-old daughter Nina:

FIGURE 2.9 Researcher Jane Goodall uses naturalistic observation to study the behavior of wild chimpanzees.

> Nina . . . tried to open nuts with the only available hammer, which was of an irregular shape. As she struggled unsuccessfully . . . Ricci was resting. Eventually . . . Ricci joined her and Nina immediately gave her the hammer. Then, with Nina sitting in front of her, Ricci, in a very deliberate manner, slowly rotated the hammer into the best position with which to pound the nut effectively. As if to emphasize the meaning of this movement, it took her a full minute to perform this simple rotation. With Nina watching her, she then proceeded to use the hammer to crack 10 nuts . . . then Ricci left and Nina resumed cracking. Now, by adopting the same hammer grip as her mother, she succeeded in opening four nuts in 15 min. . . . In this example the mother corrected an error in her daughter's behaviour and Nina seemingly understood this perfectly . . . (Boesch, 1995, p. 532)

For both evolutionary and cultural psychologists, naturalistic observations of animals can provide important clues about the possible origins of human behavior. As in human cultures, these chimpanzees have developed a unique method for using tools and appear to intentionally teach it to their young. These findings support the hypothesis that the mechanisms by which human cultures are formed and maintained—such as the intentional transmission of information across age generations—may have an evolutionary basis (Greenfield, 1997).

The excerpt about Ricci and Nina illustrates how naturalistic observation can provide a rich description of naturally occurring behavior. The researcher may take extensive notes to provide a detailed running account of everything she or he sees. Numerical data, such as the frequency of various behaviors, may be recorded and analyzed. Naturalistic observation also is used to study many types of human behavior. For example, developmental psychologists observe children in natural settings to learn about their cooperative and competitive play, aggression, and problem-solving abilities.

Like case studies, naturalistic observation does not permit clear causal conclusions about the relations between variables. In the real world many variables simultaneously influence behavior and they cannot be disentangled with this research technique. There also is the possibility of bias in the way that researchers interpret the behaviors they observe. Finally, researchers must try to avoid influencing the participants being studied. Even the mere presence of a human observer may disrupt a person's or animal's behavior, at least initially. As time passes, people and other animals adapt and typically ignore the presence of an observer. This adaptation process is called *habituation*, but is not always perfect:

> ➤ 14. What problems can occur when conducting naturalistic observations?

> In Gombe [Tanzania] . . . the fieldworkers sometimes simply go and sit down by the chimpanzees and look on . . . David Bygott writes: '. . . during the period of my study it was not uncommon for the most habituated male chimpanzees briefly to slap, knock down, or drag an observer during the course of a charging display.' These were not, it is true, serious attacks, but even a passing slap from an adult chimpanzee can be a painful experience. (de Waal, 1982, pp. 28–29).

As you can see, some methods of research have unique hazards!

Survey Research: How Well Do You Sleep?

In **survey research,** information about a topic is obtained by administering questionnaires or interviews to many people. Survey questions typically ask about participants' attitudes, opinions, and behaviors. For example, do you sometimes have difficulty falling asleep? Have you ever fallen asleep while driving? The National Sleep Foundation (2000) recently conducted a national survey of American adults' sleep problems. About 60 percent of the participants reported trouble sleeping at one time or another. Astoundingly, one out of every six admitted to falling asleep while driving.

This survey studied 1,154 Americans, aged 18 and over, who were interviewed by telephone. How is it possible to accurately estimate the sleep problems of almost 200 million adults based on these data?

Two key concepts in survey research are "population" and "sample." A **population** consists of all the individuals that we are interested in drawing a conclusion about. Sometimes it is possible to survey every member of the population. If a professor's only interest is to learn about the sleep habits of the 50 students in her Introductory Psychology class, then her students are the population and a questionnaire can be given to every one of them. If we were interested in the sleep habits of American adults, however, it would be impractical to study everyone. Therefore we would administer the survey to a **sample,** which is a subset of individuals drawn from the larger population of interest.

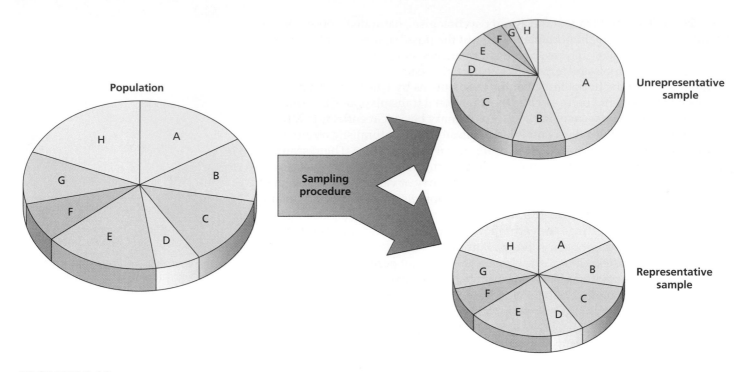

FIGURE 2.10 A representative sample possesses the important characteristics of the population in the same proportions. Data from a representative sample are more likely to generalize to the larger population than data from an unrepresentative sample.

➤ 15. Explain what random sampling is, and why survey researchers use it.

➤ 16. What are some advantages and disadvantages of survey research?

To draw valid conclusions about a population from the results of a single survey, the sample must be representative: A **representative sample** is one that reflects the important characteristics of the population (Figure 2.10). A sample composed of 80 percent males would not be representative of the student body at a college where only 50 percent of the students are men. To obtain a representative sample, survey researchers typically use a procedure called random sampling. In **random sampling,** every member of the population has an equal probability of being chosen to participate in the survey. A common variation of this procedure is first divide the population into subgroups based on characteristics such as gender or ethnic identity. Suppose the population is 55 percent female. In this case, 55 percent of the spaces in the sample would be allocated to women, and 45 percent to men. Random sampling is then used to select the individual women and men who will be in the survey.

When a representative sample is surveyed, we can be confident (though never completely certain) that the findings closely portray the population as a whole. This is the strongest advantage of survey research. Modern political opinion polls use such excellent sampling procedures that, just prior to elections, they can reasonably predict from a sample of one to two thousand people how a national election is going to turn out.

In contrast, unrepresentative samples can produce distorted results. Other things being equal, large samples are better than small ones, but it is better to have a smaller representative sample than a larger, unrepresentative one. In 1936, a mail survey of almost 2 million voters by *Literary Digest* magazine predicted that Republican presidential candidate Alf Landon would easily defeat Democratic candidate Franklin Roosevelt. When the election took place, Roosevelt won in a landslide!

How could a prediction based on 2 million people be wrong? The answer is that the sample selected for the poll was unrepresentative of the population that voted in the election. Names were chosen from telephone directories, automobile registration lists, and magazine subscription lists. In 1936, poorer Americans often did not have telephones or cars, and were less likely to afford magazine subscriptions. Thus the sample underrepresented poorer socioeconomic groups and overrepresented wealthier people. Bad sample. Bad prediction. The magazine went out of business shortly thereafter. In sum, always consider the nature of the sample when interpreting survey results.

Surveys are an efficient method for collecting a large amount of information about people's opinions and lifestyles. Just as political surveys track changes in voter's preferences over the months leading up to an election, surveys can monitor changes in people's beliefs and habits over many years. For example, the 2000 National Sleep Foundation survey found a 13 percent increase in the number of people who reported having sleep problems as compared with a similar survey conducted in 1995.

There are three major drawbacks to surveys. First, unrepresentative samples can lead to faulty generalizations about how an entire population would respond. Second, surveys rely on participants' self-reports, which can be distorted by factors such as social desirability bias, interviewer bias, or people's inaccurate perceptions of their own behavior. Finally, survey data cannot be used to draw conclusions about cause and effect.

Correlational Research: Measuring Associations Between Events

What factors distinguish happily married couples from those headed for divorce? Do firstborn versus later-born children differ in personality? Is monetary wealth related to happiness? These and countless other psychological questions ask about *associations* between naturally occurring events or variables. To examine such relationships scientists typically conduct **correlational research,** which in its simplest form has three components:

> ➤ 17. Explain the main goal of correlational research, and how this is achieved.

1. The researcher *measures one variable* (X), such as monetary wealth.
2. The researcher *measures a second variable* (Y), such as happiness.
3. The researcher *statistically determines whether X and Y are related.*

Keep in mind that correlational research involves measuring variables, *not manipulating them.*

Naturalistic observation and surveys are often used not only to describe events, but also to study associations between variables. For example, Boesch found that the approach used by adult chimps to teach the hammer/anvil technique depended upon the age of the pupil (Boesch, 1991). We might conduct a sleep survey to test hypotheses about how sleep difficulties are associated with people's age and self-reported lifestyle habits. Other types of studies also fall under the correlational umbrella, as the following example illustrates.

A Correlational Study: Parenting Styles and Children's Adjustment

In 1951, Robert Sears, Eleanor Maccoby, and Harry Levin (1957) began a landmark study of parenting styles. At the time, child psychologists and the media advocated strictness and discipline as the preferred approach to raising well-adjusted children. During interviews with 379 mothers of 5-year-old children in the Boston area, Sears and his coworkers asked the mothers how they and their husbands behaved in certain child-rearing situations. The researchers were especially interested in a variable called "parental warmth." Warm parents express affection and positive regard for their children, whereas cold parents tend to be disapproving, emotionless, or punitive. Sears, Maccoby, and Levin also asked questions about the children's behavior, and then examined whether this behavior was related to parental warmth.

➤ 18. Why are we unable to draw causal conclusions from correlational findings?

Warmer parenting
(*X*) ——————— Better-adjusted children
(*Y*)

(a)
Parental Warmth and Children's Adjustment Are Correlated

Does *X* cause *Y*?
Warmer parenting (*X*) ⟶ Better-adjusted children (*Y*)

Does *Y* cause *X*?
Warmer parenting (*X*) ⟵ Better-adjusted children (*Y*)

(b)
Bidirectionality Problem

Warmer parenting (*X*)　　There may be no causal relation between *X* and *Y*　　Better-adjusted children (*Y*)

Shared genetic factors that contribute to personality style (*Z*)

(c)
Third-Variable Problem

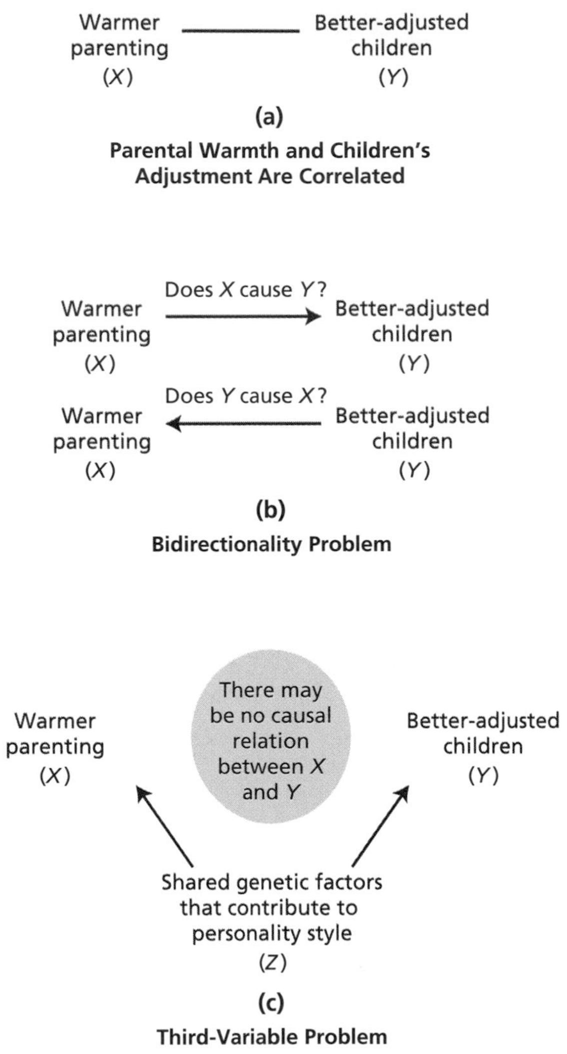

FIGURE 2.11 (a) Parents who act more warmly toward their children have better adjusted children. But why does this association occur? (b) Parental warmth could enhance children's adjustment, or conversely, better-adjusted children may stimulate warmer behaviors from their parents. This is the bidirectional causality problem. (c) There may be no causal relation between parental warmth and children's adjustment. Other variables, such as a genetic predisposition, may be part of the true common origin of both parental warmth and children's adjustment. This is the "third-variable" problem.

Contrary to popular wisdom of that era, the findings suggested that children who had warmer mothers were better adjusted (Figure 2.11a). Maternal coldness was related to a variety of children's problems, including bed-wetting, feeding problems, and aggression. It is tempting to conclude from these findings that parental warmth influences the degree to which children are well adjusted. Unfortunately, correlational research does not allow us to draw such a conclusion.

First, consider the positive relation between parental warmth and children's adjustment when they were 5 years old. As the researchers pointed out, the direction of causality could be just the opposite. Perhaps parents behaved warmly *in response to* the fact that their children were less aggressive, more affectionate and sociable, and generally easier to raise. In other words, children's positive or negative characteristics may have caused the warm or cold parenting style. In correlational research, you must consider the possibility that variable *X* (parental warmth) has caused variable *Y* (children's adjustment), that *Y* has caused *X*, or that both variables have influenced each other. This interpretive problem is called the *bidirectional (two-way) causality problem* (Figure 2.11b).

To make matters worse, we have another problem. Perhaps the relation between parental warmth and childhood adjustment is artificial, or what scientists call "spurious" ("spurious" means "not genuine"). That is, it may look like parental warmth and childhood adjustment are related, but in fact, neither has any causal effect on the other! A third variable, Z, may really be the cause of why some parents are warmer than others, and also be the cause of why some children are better adjusted than others. For example, *Z* might be a "genetic predisposition." Genetic factors that partially determine personality might cause some parents to be more sociable, less irritable, and warmer. The same genetic predispositions are passed on to their children, causing them to become more sociable, less irritable, and better adjusted. Therefore it looks like parental warmth and child adjustment are related, but in reality this is only because a third factor is causing differences in both parental warmth and children's adjustment.

This interpretive problem is called the *"third-variable problem"*: *Z* is responsible for what looks like a relation between *X* and *Y* (Figure 2.11c). As *Z* varies it causes *X* to change. As *Z* varies it also causes *Y* to change. The net result is that *X* and *Y* change in unison, but this is caused by *Z*—not by any direct effect of *X* or *Y* on each other. To test your understanding, identify the third variable (*Z*) that explains the following relation: Nationally, as the amount of ice cream consumed each day (*X*) increases, the number of drownings per day (*Y*) also tends to increase. The answer appears in the margin at the bottom of page 57.

In sum, the major disadvantage of correlational research is that *correlation does not demonstrate causation*. If *X* and *Y* are correlated, this might mean that *X* causes *Y*, *Y* causes *X*, some third factor (*Z*) causes them both, or any combination of the above. In almost every case, the correlational method cannot provide the information needed to determine which of these possibilities is correct. The pages of history are filled with erroneous conclusions about causality drawn on the basis of correlational data. At one time, medical authorities concluded that "general paresis" (a fatal deterioration of the brain actually caused by syphilis) was caused by seawater because this malady occurred so often among sailors. We invite you to speculate on the real causal factor.

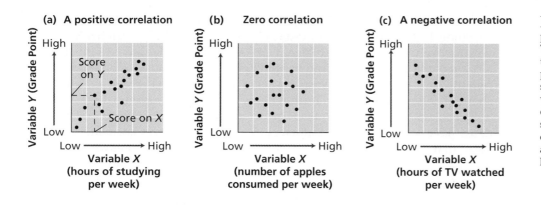

FIGURE 2.12 A scatterplot depicts the correlation between variables. The horizontal axis represents variable X, the vertical axis variable Y. Each data point represents a specific pair of X and Y scores, such as the number of hours a week a student studies (X), and that student's grade point average (Y). The three scatterplots show (a) a strong positive correlation, (b) a zero correlation (0.00), and (c) a strong negative correlation, for hypothetical sets of data.

The Correlation Coefficient

A **correlation coefficient** is a statistic that indicates the direction and strength of the relation between two variables. Variables can be correlated either positively or negatively. A **positive correlation** means that higher scores on one variable are associated with higher scores on a second variable. Thus parental warmth and childhood adjustment are positively correlated: Higher levels of warmth are associated with higher levels of adjustment. People's height is positively correlated with their weight: Overall, taller people tend to weigh more.

A **negative correlation** occurs when higher scores on one variable are associated with lower scores on a second variable. Job turnover and job satisfaction are negatively correlated: Workers who have *higher* rates of turnover (e.g., quitting, being fired) tend to be *less* satisfied with their jobs. For people who suffer from a condition called seasonal affective disorder, depression is negatively correlated with the amount of monthly daylight. These individuals have *more* symptoms of depression in months when there is *less* daylight.

Correlation coefficients range from values of +1.00 to −1.00. The plus or minus sign tells you the *direction* of a correlation (i.e., whether the variables are positively or negatively correlated). The absolute value of the statistic tells you the *strength* of the correlation. The closer the correlation is to +1.00 or −1.00, the more strongly the two variables are related. Therefore a correlation of −.59 indicates a stronger association between X and Y than does a correlation of +.37. A zero correlation means that X and Y are not related statistically: As scores on X increase or decrease, scores on Y do not change in any orderly fashion. Figure 2.12 shows how the correlation between two variables can be depicted on a graph called a **scatterplot**.

Correlation as a Basis for Prediction

You might wonder why scientists conduct correlational research if the data do not permit clear cause-effect conclusions. One benefit is that correlational research identifies associations in real-world contexts that subsequently can be studied under controlled laboratory conditions. Another benefit is that some questions cannot be studied with experiments, but can be examined correlationally. For practical or ethical reasons, we cannot experimentally manipulate how religious people are or how much alcohol pregnant mothers consume. But we can measure these variables and determine if they are associated with other factors, such as helping behavior and fetal brain damage, respectively.

Perhaps the most important benefit is that correlational data allow us to make predictions. If two variables are correlated, either positively or negatively, knowing the score of one variable helps us to predict (within certain limits) the score on the other variable. For example, students who apply to college in North

➤ 19. How do positive and negative correlations differ?

➤ 20. How is a correlation coefficient interpreted?

➤ 21. Explain how correlational research can be used to predict behavior.

Ice cream and drownings. Correlation does not demonstrate causation. It is unlikely that mass national ice cream consumption causes individuals to drown, or that drownings cause the public to eat more ice cream! Rather, as we move from winter into summer and days get hotter, people eat more ice cream. Because more people also go swimming, more drownings occur. Variable Z is average daytime temperature.

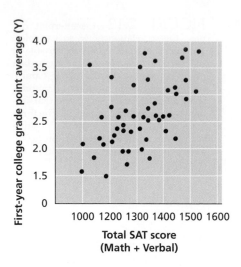

FIGURE 2.13 Data for a hypothetical sample of 50 students. The horizontal axis represents variable *X,* SAT scores. The vertical axis represents variable *Y,* these same students' overall grade point average (GPA) for their first year in college. Variables *X* and *Y* are moderately correlated.

➤ 22. Describe the logic of experimentation.

America typically are asked to take a national test, such as the SAT (Scholastic Aptitude Test). Scores on these tests help admissions officers predict how well you are likely to do in their college, as the scatterplot in Figure 2.13 illustrates.

You can see a clear overall trend: Higher SAT scores are moderately associated with a higher first-year grade point average (GPA). The scatterplot also shows that the correlation is far from perfect. Some students who do well on the SATs end up having only an average or poor GPA, and conversely, some students have low SAT scores but excel in college. A perfect correlation would mean that, for this set of data, if we knew a student's SAT score, we could predict her or his first-year GPA precisely. Nevertheless, even a moderate SAT-GPA correlation is useful to college admissions officers, particularly when SAT scores are used along with other variables—such as high school GPA—that also help predict college performance. Remember, we are *not* saying that SAT scores cause better first-year performance, only that they help predict it.

Business, government, and military organizations spend millions of dollars developing screening tests that correlate with job performance and therefore help predict how well applicants will do on the job. Insurance premiums are based on correlational data. In a sense, your insurance company is betting you that you will not demolish your car, become seriously ill, or die before you are statistically "supposed to," based on how these factors correlate with people's age, marital status, driving history, and so on. Because insurers' predictions are based on sound correlational data, the odds are solidly in their favor. If you doubt this, notice who owns some of the largest and newest buildings in your community.

Experiments: Examining Cause and Effect

In contrast to descriptive and correlational methods, experiments are a powerful tool for examining cause-and-effect relations. For psychologists, experimentation is the most direct method for testing explanations of why phenomena occur.

The Logic of Experimentation

Suppose we want to determine whether noise influences students' ability to learn new information. Each student is placed alone in a room, has 30 minutes to study five pages of textbook material, and then takes a 10-item multiple-choice test. In its simplest form, an **experiment** has three essential characteristics:

1. The researcher *manipulates one variable.* In this case, the researcher manipulates (i.e., controls) the amount of noise in the room. Some students are exposed to a tape recording of street noise, while for others the room is kept quiet. These would represent the groups or "conditions" of the experiment (i.e., noise condition, no noise condition).

2. The researcher *measures whether this manipulation produces changes in a second variable.* In our example, the researcher uses the multiple-choice test to measure whether the amount of learning differs in the noise versus no noise conditions.

3. The researcher *attempts to control for extraneous factors* that might influence the outcome of the experiment. For example, we would not want one group to do better because they had easier textbook material or test questions. So all the participants will read the same textbook pages and take the same test. Similarly, room temperature and lighting will be kept constant, and the researcher will be friendly to everyone.

The logic behind this approach is straightforward: You start out with equivalent groups of people. You treat them equally in all respects except for one variable that is of particular interest (in this case, noise). You isolate this variable and manipulate it (creating the presence or absence of noise). You then measure how the groups respond (in this case, the amount they learn). If the groups respond differently, then the most plausible explanation is that these differences were caused by the variable that you manipulated (Figure 2.14).

Independent and Dependent Variables

The term **independent variable** refers to the factor that is *manipulated* by the experimenter. In our example, noise is the independent variable. The **dependent variable** is the factor that is *measured* by the experimenter and may be influenced by the independent variable. In this experiment, the amount of learning is the dependent variable.

An easy way to keep this distinction clear is to remember that the dependent variable *depends upon* the independent variable. Presumably, students' learning will depend upon whether they were in a noisy or quiet room. The independent variable is the *cause,* and the dependent variable is the *effect.*

We have described the independent and dependent variables at a general level, but recall that when doing research we also must operationally define our variables. "Noise" could mean many things, from the roar of a jet plane to the quiet but annoying drip of a faucet. Learning could mean anything from memorizing a list of words to acquiring the skill to ride a bicycle. In our experiment, we could operationally define our independent and dependent variables as follows:

	Independent Variable (Cause)	Dependent Variable (Effect)
General level	Noise	Learning
Operational level	Listening to a tape of street sounds at 60dB for 30 minutes	Number of multiple-choice questions based on 5 pages of text answered correctly

If asked what the dependent variable in our experiment is, we can state that it is learning, or instead reply that it is the number of multiple-choice questions answered correctly. Both answers are correct. They are just describing the dependent variable at different levels of specificity. Our noise experiment thus far has only one dependent variable, but we could have many. For example, we could measure how quickly participants read the material, how many answers they change, their stress during the task, and so on. In this manner, we gain more knowledge about how people are affected by noise.

To test your understanding, think back to the Darley and Latané experiment on bystander helping in an emergency. Can you identify the independent and dependent variables? The answer appears in the margin on page 60.

Experimental and Control Groups

The terms "experimental group" and "control group" are often used when discussing experiments. An **experimental group** is the group that receives a treatment or an "active level" of the independent variable. A **control group** is not exposed to the treatment; it receives a zero-level of the independent variable. The purpose of the control group is to provide a standard of behavior to which our experimental group can be compared. The participants exposed to noise represent the experimental group (also called the "experimental condition"), and the participants in the quiet room represent the control group (or "control condition").

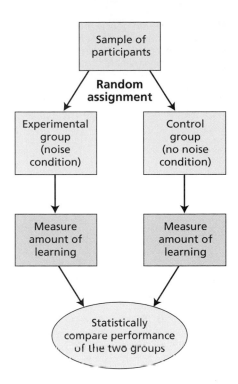

FIGURE 2.14 The logic of designing an experiment. The experimenter manipulates the amount of noise to which participants are exposed, measures their learning, and attempts to treat them equally in every other way. This creates an experimental group and a control group.

➤ 23. What are independent and dependent variables? How are they related?

➤ 24. Why are control groups important?

Helping in an emergency. The independent variable in the Darley and Latané experiment was the number of other bystanders presumed to be present (0, 1, or 4). The dependent variables were the percentage of participants who aided the victim, and the speed of response.

Experiments often include several experimental groups. In our study on noise, we could play the tape of street noise at three different volume levels, creating high noise, moderate noise, and low noise experimental conditions. The no noise condition would still represent the control group (zero-level of noise). In some experiments, however, the concept of a control group does not apply. In a "taste test" experiment in which participants taste and rate how much they like Coca-Cola and Pepsi-Cola, each drink represents an experimental condition and we simply make a direct comparison between them.

Two Basic Ways to Design an Experiment

One common way to design an experiment is to have different participants in each condition. If you participated in the noise experiment, you would be in either the experimental group or the control group, but not both. To draw meaningful conclusions, the different groups of participants must be equivalent at the start of the study.

Suppose that the noise group performs substantially worse on the multiple-choice test than the no noise group. Further, let's assume that the two groups are treated equally in every important way you can think of (e.g., room temperature, experimenter friendliness). Before concluding that the noise caused poorer learning, we must address a key question: How can we be sure that the noise group would not have done worse than the no noise group anyway, even if they had not been exposed to noise? Perhaps the students in the noise group were, on average, less intelligent, poorer readers, or more anxious than the students in the no noise group. Maybe one of these factors—and nothing to do with the noise at all—was the reason why they performed more poorly.

➤ 25. Why do researchers randomly assign participants to the conditions in an experiment?

To deal with this issue researchers typically use **random assignment,** a procedure in which each participant has an equal likelihood of being assigned to any one group within an experiment. Thus you would have a 50 percent chance of being in the noise group, a 50 percent chance of being in the no noise group, and that determination would be made randomly. This procedure does not eliminate the fact that participants differ from one another in important ways. Instead, random assignment *balances* these differences across the various conditions of the experiment. It increases our confidence that, at the start of an experiment, participants in the various conditions are equivalent overall.

A second way to design experiments is to expose each participant to all the conditions. We could measure how much the same people learn when exposed to noise and when the room is quiet. By doing so, factors such as the participants' intelligence, reading ability, and general anxiety are held constant across the no noise and noise conditions, and therefore we can rule them out as alternative explanations for any results we obtain. However, this approach creates problems if not used properly.

➤ 26. In experiments, identify an alternative to using random assignment.

For one thing, it would make little sense to have our participants read the same text material and take the same multiple-choice questions twice. Instead, we would develop two equally difficult reading tasks and participants would perform each task only once. Most importantly, suppose that every participant was exposed to the no noise condition first. If they then learned more poorly in the noise condition, what would be the cause? The noise? Perhaps. But it could be that participants were bored or fatigued by the time they performed the second task. A procedure called *counterbalancing* avoids this problem: The order of conditions is varied so that no condition has an advantage relative to the others. Half the participants would be exposed to the no noise condition first and the noise condition second. For the remaining participants this order would be reversed.

Manipulating One Independent Variable: Effects of Environmental Stimulation on Brain Development

In a Miami hospital, a massage therapist gently strokes a tiny premature baby who was exposed to cocaine while in its mother's womb. This procedure is repeated several times each day. Why is the infant receiving this treatment?

The answer partially lies in landmark experiments by physiological psychologist Mark Rosenzweig (1984) and his coworkers at the University of California, Berkeley. Like many scientific discoveries, this one began accidentally. The researchers were studying a brain chemical thought to be involved in learning and memory. Unexpectedly, they found more brain chemical activity in those rats who had been tested on more difficult and stimulating problems. Curiosity then led to a key question: Could exposure to a stimulating environment early in life actually enhance rats' brain development and behavioral capabilities?

➤ 27. Identify the independent and dependent variables in Rosenzweig's experiment.

To investigate, the researchers experimentally manipulated the degree of environmental stimulation to which the rats were exposed. This independent variable was operationally defined by creating two conditions: an experimental condition in which infant rats (called "pups") lived in a stimulating environment containing toys and other pups with whom they could interact, and a control condition in which pups lived in standard laboratory cages (Figure 2.15). The pups came from several litters, so to create equivalent groups at the outset the researchers randomly assigned some pups from each litter to the enriched and standard environments.

After the rats had lived in these environments for several months, their brain development was measured. This dependent variable was operationally defined by several measures, such as the weight of the rats' brains, the size of brain cells, and the concentrations of brain chemicals involved in learning and memory. The rats raised in the enriched environment were superior on each measure and also performed better on learning tasks than rats raised in the standard environment.

These experiments sparked a wave of research on how the brain is affected by experience. Across Canada, Europe, and the United States, researchers found that enriched environments and other types of stimulation, such as physical touch when animals are handled, enhanced rats' brain development and performance on learning and memory tasks (Escorihuela et al., 1995; Meaney et al., 1991). And this brings us back to the "crack baby" in Miami.

Developmental psychologist Tiffany Field and other University of Miami researchers have found that tactile (touch) stimulation enhances early infant development (Field, 2000). In one experiment they studied premature infants exposed to cocaine by their mothers' drug use during pregnancy (Wheeden et al., 1993). The researchers manipulated one independent variable, randomly assigning infants either to receive massage therapy for 10 days, or to a control group receiving standard care and contact. Results showed that the massaged infants had fewer health complications, less stress, more mature movement patterns, and averaged 28 percent greater weight gain per day (Figure 2.16).

Over the past 20 years this work has revolutionized scientists' thinking about the role of experience in brain development and functioning. It demonstrates how basic scientific research—including animal experiments—can have important human applications. These findings have been used to enhance infant development and promote health among the elderly (Rosenzweig & Bennett,

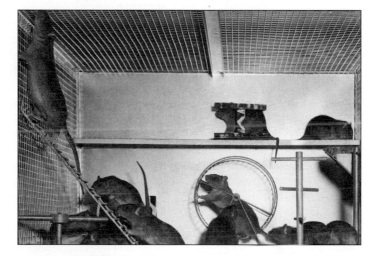

FIGURE 2.15 At birth, rat pups from the same litters were randomly assigned to experimental and control groups. This photo illustrates the "enriched" environment of the experimental group, with toys and playmates. The control group was raised in standard laboratory cages. In this experiment, the difference in the environmental conditions represented the independent variable. Brain development was the main dependent variable.

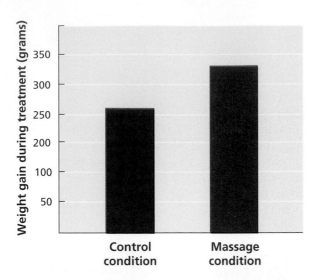

FIGURE 2.16 Daily massage sessions enhanced the development of premature infants, compared to nonmassaged control infants. However, we cannot tell what aspect of the massage sessions produced this benefit. Was it the gentle physical stroking of the massage, the mere touch, or the greater attention infants received? In other research with 1- to 3-month-olds, researchers provided the control group with touch and attention equivalent to the massaged group (Field et al., 1996). Once again, massaged infants showed larger physical and psychological gains.

Data adapted from Wheeden et al., 1993.

➤ 28. Why do researchers manipulate two idependent variables in the same experiment?

1996). They also support the importance of early enrichment programs for children who have special needs or are from disadvantaged environments (Ramey & Ramey, 1998).

Manipulating Two Independent Variables: Effects of Alcohol and Expectations on Sexual Arousal

As noted in Chapter 1, behavior is complex and has multiple causes. To better capture this complexity, researchers often examine several causal factors within a single experiment by manipulating two or more independent variables simultaneously. The separate influence of each variable on behavior can then be examined, and researchers also can determine whether particular combinations of variables produce unique effects.

Consider the widely held belief that alcohol is a sexual stimulant, and that a few drinks can lower sexual inhibitions and increase sexual attraction toward someone else. Many men and women report that alcohol enhances their sexual arousal, and people who have been drinking are viewed by others as more responsive to sexual advances (George et al., 2000; Norris, 1994). Why might alcohol influence sexual arousal? Perhaps its chemical properties directly influence sexual arousal, or maybe the cause is psychological. That is, if people simply *believe* that alcohol will enhance their sexual arousal, then perhaps this expectation by itself can bring about increased sexual responsiveness.

How can a researcher separate the purely physiological effects of drinking from the psychological ones in order to test this possibility? The answer emerged in the form of an ingenious experimental procedure developed several decades ago (Marlatt et al., 1973; Rohsenow & Marlatt, 1981). The researchers created two drinks that people could not tell apart by taste, one with tonic water and a squirt of lime juice, and the other with vodka added to this mix. Then they designed an experiment with two independent variables. The first variable was whether participants received the alcoholic drink or the nonalcoholic drink. The second variable manipulated participants' expectations. They were told either that their drink contained alcohol or that it didn't.

As Figure 2.17a shows, when these two independent variables are combined within the same experiment, four different conditions are created. Condition 1 is *expect alcohol/receive alcohol.* This is the normal state of affairs when people drink; they expect that they are drinking alcohol, and actually are. Changes in sexual arousal that occur in this condition could reflect either the chemical effects of alcohol, psychological expectations, or a combination of both. Condition 2 is *expect no alcohol/receive alcohol.* This condition assesses physiological effects alone. Because participants believe they are not receiving alcohol, changes in sexual arousal presumably would be due to alcohol's chemical effects. Condition 3 is *expect alcohol/receive no alcohol.* Because no alcohol is consumed, changes in sexual arousal would have to be caused by participants' expectations about drinking alcohol. Finally, Condition 4 is *expect no alcohol/receive no alcohol.* This condition creates a control group having neither alcohol nor alcohol expectations.

Participants in the four conditions are then shown identical sexually stimulating materials (e.g., slides or films) or are led to anticipate that they will be viewing such materials. Their sexual arousal is assessed by self-report ratings on questionnaires and by physiological measures.

Most experiments have studied male participants. (In part, this is due to researchers' interest in the issue of alcohol consumption and rape, which overwhelmingly is committed by men. We will examine the findings with women

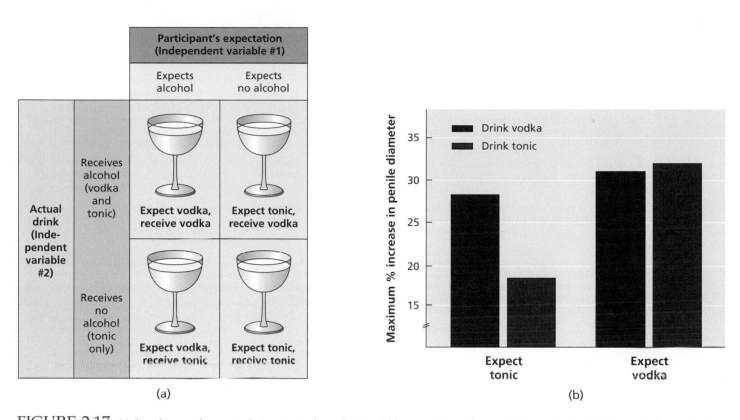

FIGURE 2.17 (a) Simultaneously manipulating two independent variables—participant's expectation and actual drink content—creates four conditions in this design. (b) In one experiment, male participants in these four conditions were shown sexually explicit films. The dependent variable, sexual arousal, was measured by a device that recorded changes in the size of each man's penis. Regardless of what they actually drank, men who *believed* they had consumed alcohol showed more sexual arousal than men who believed they had not consumed alcohol. Among men who believed they drank alcohol, those who drank only tonic were just as aroused as those who actually drank alcohol.
Data adapted from Wilson & Lawson, 1976.

shortly.) In which conditions shown in Figure 2.17a would you predict that men would be most aroused when exposed to sexual stimuli? Overall, as Figure 2.17b shows, participants who are led to believe that they have consumed low to moderate doses of alcohol—regardless of whether they actually drink alcohol—feel more aroused and show greater physiological arousal to sexual stimuli than participants who believe that they have consumed only tonic water (Crowe and George, 1989; Seto & Barbaree, 1995). Among men, the mere expectation that one is drinking alcohol also produces more intense sexual fantasies, lower sexual inhibitions, and greater interest in viewing scenes of sexual violence.

Thus at low to moderate doses that produce blood alcohol levels of about .04 or less, men's expectations and beliefs about alcohol contribute significantly to the enhanced sexual arousal that they experience. At higher doses, the chemical effects of alcohol take over and decrease—yes, decrease—men's sexual arousal (Kelly, 2001). This occurs because alcohol is a depressant drug; it suppresses neural activity. As blood alcohol levels increase, men typically take longer to reach orgasm, report that orgasms are less intense and less pleasurable, and may be unable to reach orgasm.

This research illustrates how studying several independent variables simultaneously can help unravel some of the complexity of behavior. It also reinforces one of our main themes: Behavior (in this case, sexual arousal) results from an interplay of factors that are psychological (beliefs and expectations), environmental (the presence of sexual stimuli), and physiological (chemical effects of alcohol at certain doses).

| TABLE 2.1 | AN OVERVIEW OF RESEARCH METHODS | | |

Method	Primary Feature	Main Advantages	Main Disadvantages
Case studies	An individual, group, or event is examined in detail, often using several techniques (observations, interviews, psychological tests).	Provides rich descriptive information, often suggesting hypotheses for further study. Can study rare phenomena in depth.	Poor method for establishing cause-effect relations. The person or event may not be representative. Often relies heavily on the researcher's subjective interpretations.
Naturalistic observation	Behavior is observed in the setting where it naturally occurs.	Can provide detailed information about the nature, frequency, and context of naturally occurring behaviors.	Poor method for establishing cause-effect relations. Observer's presence, if known, may influence participants' behavior.
Surveys	Questions or tests are administered to a sample drawn from a larger population.	A properly selected, representative sample typically yields accurate information about the broader population.	Unrepresentative samples can provide misleading information about the population. Interviewer bias and social desirability bias can distort the findings.
Correlational studies	Variables are measured and the strength of the association between them is calculated. Naturalistic observation and surveys also are often used to examine associations between variables.	Correlation allows prediction. May help establish how well findings from experiments generalize to more natural settings. Can examine issues that cannot be studied ethically or practically in experiments.	Correlation does not imply causation, due to bidirectionality problem and third-variable problem.
Experiments	Independent variables are manipulated and their effects on dependent variables are measured.	Optimal method for examining cause-effect relations. Ability to control extraneous factors helps rule out alternative explanations.	As described in the text below, confounding of variables, demand characteristics, placebo effects, and experimenter expectancies can threaten the validity of causal conclusions.

Experimental Versus Descriptive/ Correlational Approaches

> 29. What are three major differences between the experimental and descriptive/correlational approaches?

You can see that there are three major ways in which experiments differ from the descriptive and correlational approaches. First, in an experiment the researcher *manipulates* one or more (independent) variables and measures their effect on other (dependent) variables; in descriptive/correlational research all variables are *measured*. Second, whereas most experiments take place in the laboratory, descriptive and correlational research typically examine more natural contexts. Third, descriptive and correlational researchers are not able to keep extraneous factors constant in the way that experimenters can.

The net result is that the descriptive and correlational approaches are not well suited for examining cause-effect relations, which is a serious limitation. Nevertheless, these methods shine in uncovering exciting new phenomena and in stimulating hypotheses for further research (Klahr & Simon, 1999). And like experiments, they are used to test hypotheses, build new theories, and help confirm or refute existing theories. Table 2.1 summarizes the key features, advantages, and disadvantages of these various research methods.

❯ THREATS TO THE VALIDITY OF RESEARCH

Although the experimental approach is a powerful tool for examining causality, it is not infallible. Researchers must avoid several sources of error that can lead to erroneous conclusions. **Internal validity** represents the degree to which an experiment supports clear causal conclusions. If an experiment is well designed and properly conducted, we can be confident that the independent variable really was the cause of differences in the dependent variable. Such an experiment would have "high internal validity." For example, because Darley and Latané's bystander experiment was conducted carefully and had proper controls, it had high internal validity. We can be confident that it was the presence of multiple bystanders (and not some other factor) that caused participants to help the seizure victim less often and more slowly. But if an experiment contains important flaws—such as those described below—we can no longer be sure what caused the differences in the dependent variable. In this event, an experiment would have "low internal validity."

Confounding of Variables

To introduce the concept of "confounding," consider the following experiment. Dr. Starr conducts an experiment to examine how listening to different types of music influences people's feelings of relaxation. The independent variable is the type of music: classical, country, or rock. A total of 30 college students participate, with each student randomly assigned to one of the three experimental groups. The experiment is conducted with one student at a time. Each participant sits in the same room, in the same chair, and listens to one type of music for 20 minutes. Afterward, participants rate how relaxed they feel on a questionnaire.

> 30. Explain why confounding decreases the internal validity of experiments.

Dr. Starr believes that the experiment will be more realistic to the students if the classical music is played at a low volume, the country music at a moderate volume, and the rock music at a loud volume. The results show that students who listened to the classical music feel most relaxed, while those who listened to the rock music feel least relaxed. Dr. Starr concludes that, of the three types of music tested, classical music is the most relaxing.

What is wrong with Dr. Starr's conclusion that the type of music caused the differences in how relaxed students felt? Stated differently, can you identify another major factor that could have produced these results? Perhaps the reason students who listened to classical music felt most relaxed was because their music was played at the lowest, most soothing volume. Had they listened to it at a high volume, maybe they would have been no more relaxed than the students who listed to rock music. We now have two variables that, like the strands of a rope, are intertwined or linked together: the independent variable (type of music) that Dr. Starr really was interested in and a second variable (volume level) that Dr. Starr was not interested in, but foolishly did not keep constant.

Confounding of variables means that two variables are intertwined in such a way that we cannot determine which one has influenced a dependent variable. In this experiment the volume level of music would be called a "confound" or a "confounding variable."

	Group 1	Group 2	Group 3
Independent variable (type of music)	Classical	Country	Rock
Confounding variable (volume level)	Low	Medium	High

An essential point to remember is that this confounding of variables prevents Dr. Starr from drawing clear causal conclusions, and therefore it has ruined the internal validity of the experiment. The simplest way to eliminate this problem is keep the volume level constant across the three music conditions.

Confounding is a key reason why causal conclusions cannot be drawn from correlational research. Earlier we described the "third-variable problem." When variables X and Y (e.g., parental warmth and children's adjustment) are correlated, many other Z variables (e.g., genetic or environmental factors) may be mixed up with either X or Y, so we cannot tell what has caused what. Thus the "third variable," Z, really is just another type of confounding variable.

Demand Characteristics

➤ 31. What are demand characteristics? Why do they lower the internal validity of experiments?

"WHAT IT COMES DOWN TO IS YOU HAVE TO FIND OUT WHAT REACTION THEY'RE LOOKING FOR, AND YOU GIVE THEM THAT REACTION."

FIGURE 2.18 Demand characteristics provide participants with clues about how they "should" behave during a study. This may cause participants to alter their natural responses, thereby ruining the internal validity of the experiment.

When we enter unfamiliar situations, it is natural for us to search for clues about how we are expected to act. **Demand characteristics** are cues that participants pick up about the hypothesis of a study or about how they are supposed to behave (Orne, 1962). Consider the experiments on alcohol and sexual arousal discussed earlier. In one condition participants are told that they are drinking alcohol, but in reality are given nonalcoholic drinks. Suppose that after a few drinks a participant does not feel intoxicated and concludes that the drinks were nonalcoholic. The participant might think, "Hmm. They told me the drinks were alcoholic, yet I don't feel a thing. Now they're showing me a sex film. Maybe they're just trying to make me think I drank alcohol, to see if I'll be more aroused."

At this point the film, the researchers' statement that the drinks were alcoholic, and the participant's feeling of not being intoxicated have become cues— demand characteristics—that have tipped off the participant about the hypothesis being tested. This damages the internal validity of the experiment because it can distort participants' true response tendencies (Orne, 1962). In some cases participants may intentionally attempt to foil the experimenter's hypothesis, but most people are eager to be "good participants" and may try to give the experimenter the results they think she or he wants (Figure 2.18). In either case, the participant is no longer behaving naturally.

Skilled researchers try to anticipate demand characteristics and design studies to avoid them. For example, if careful procedures are used, participants given nonalcoholic drinks can be convinced that they have consumed moderate to high amounts of alcohol (MacDonald et al., 2000). Most people who actually have consumed alcohol, however, can be led to believe that they haven't only when lower doses are involved (Lyvers & Maltzman, 1991; Seto & Barbaree, 1995). After a few alcoholic drinks people feel intoxicated and the experimenter's statement that they have not had alcohol no longer is credible. Thus to avoid demand characteristics, a researcher would design this type of experiment to involve low alcohol doses.

Placebo Effects

➤ 32. Explain how the "placebo effect" can cloud the interpretation of research results.

FIGURE 2.19 Throughout history, placebo effects have fostered the commercial success of many products that had no proven physiological benefit. Herbal medicines are one of today's "health crazes." Do they really work? If so, is it because of placebo effects or the herbs' chemical properties? The best way to answer this question is through experiments that include placebo control groups.

In medical research, the term **placebo** refers to an inactive or inert substance. In experiments testing the effectiveness of new drugs for treating diseases, one group of patients—the treatment group—receives pills containing the actual drug being investigated. A second group of patients, called a placebo control group, receives pills that do not contain the drug; they contain only inactive or inert substances that will not alter the body's physiology. Typically, patients who volunteer for this research are informed that their pills may either contain the true drug or a placebo, but they are not told specifically which type of pill they are receiving.

The rationale for this procedure is simple. Physicians have known for decades that patients' symptoms may improve solely because they *expect* that the drug will help them. Thus if 40 percent of patients receiving the actual drug improve, but 37 percent of the placebo-control patients show similar improvement, then we have evidence of a strong **placebo effect:** People receiving a treatment show a change in behavior because of their expectations, not because the treatment itself had any specific benefit (Ray, 2000; Figure 2.19).

Placebo effects decrease internal validity by providing an alternative explanation for why responses change after exposure to an independent variable. For example, if patients improve after undergoing psychotherapy, is this due to the therapy itself, or might it be a placebo effect? In Vang's case study (Hmong sudden death syndrome), the fact that his symptoms disappeared after visiting a shaman could represent a placebo effect. Similarly, suppose that business managers feel more confident after taking a leadership training program, or that anxious people become more relaxed after learning how to meditate. By carefully designing experiments to include placebo control conditions, researchers can determine whether behavior change is truly caused by the various interventions, or whether a placebo effect might have played a role.

Experimenter Expectancy Effects

Participants are not the only ones who develop expectations about how an experiment is supposed to come out. Researchers typically have a strong commitment to the hypothesis they are testing. In psychology, the term **experimenter expectancy effects** refers to subtle and unintentional ways in which experimenters influence their participants to respond in a manner that is consistent with the experimenter's hypothesis. Although this type of bias historically is called "experimenter" expectancy effects, it also can occur in correlational and descriptive research where hypotheses are being tested.

Hundreds of studies demonstrate that, in both human and animal research, if people expect to obtain certain results they are more likely to do so (Rosenthal, 1994). Scientists can take several steps to avoid experimenter expectancy effects. For example, researchers who interact with participants in a study are often "kept *blind* to" (i.e., not told about) the hypothesis or the specific condition to which a participant has been assigned. This makes it less likely that these researchers will develop expectations about how participants "should" behave.

In experiments, the **double-blind procedure** is a powerful technique for simultaneously minimizing participant placebo effects and experimenter expectancy effects. Both the participant and experimenter are kept "blind" as to which experimental condition the participant is in. This procedure is almost always used in research testing drug effects. Each participant receives either a real drug or a placebo, but does not know which. People who interact with participants (e.g., who dispense the drugs or measure participants' behavior) also are kept unaware of which participants received the drug or placebo. This minimizes the likelihood that experimenters will react differently to the two groups of participants, and also reduces the chance that participants' own expectations will influence the outcome of the experiment (Figure 2.20).

Replicating and Generalizing the Findings

Let's return for a moment to our hypothetical experiment on noise and learning. Suppose we find that college students perform more poorly when learning a task in a noisy room than in a quiet room. Assume that we have designed our experiment properly, eliminated potential flaws, and achieved high internal validity. Thus we are reasonably confident that it was the noise, and not some other factor, that caused the poorer performance.

There remains, however, another important set of questions that we must ask. If this experiment were repeated in other laboratories, would we obtain the same finding? What if the participants were children, or full-time working adults not in college? Would noise impair learning and performance in real-world settings, such as schools, factories, and businesses? Would the results be the same if we examined other types of noise and used other types of learning tasks?

These questions all focus on another important type of validity, known as external validity. **External validity** is the degree to which the results of a study can be generalized to other people, settings, and conditions. It is important to remember that in experiments and most other research, judgments about external validity do not focus on the exact responses of the participants. For example, in our noise experiment, the fact that students in the noisy versus quiet rooms might have answered exactly 48 percent versus 83 percent of the questions correctly is not the issue. Rather, what we are concerned about is the external validity of the basic *underlying principle of behavior:* Does noise decrease learning?

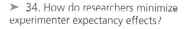

➤ 33. Why do experimenter expectancy effects lower the internal validity of experiments?

➤ 34. How do researchers minimize experimenter expectancy effects?

© 2000 by Sidney Harris

"IT WAS MORE OF A 'TRIPLE-BLIND' TEST. THE PATIENTS DIDN'T KNOW WHICH ONES WERE GETTING THE REAL DRUG, THE DOCTORS DIDN'T KNOW, AND I'M AFRAID, NOBODY KNEW"

FIGURE 2.20 Although the double-blind technique is a powerful tool for controlling participants' and researchers' expectations, scientists try to avoid the infamous "triple-blind procedure."

➤ 35. How does external validity differ from internal validity?

Ultimately, to determine whether our tentative conclusion that noise impairs learning has external validity, either we or other scientists will need to replicate our experiment. **Replication** is the process of repeating a study to determine whether the original findings can be duplicated. If our findings are successfully replicated by other scientists, we become more confident in our original conclusion that noise impairs learning. There is just one problem. If every replication uses the same type of participants (i.e., college students), same type of noise (i.e., street noise), and measures learning in the same way (i.e., reading comprehension), we still won't know whether the noise-learning relation would hold true in different types of situations. Thus attempts to replicate original findings are particularly valuable when the researcher adds something new to the equation.

For example, researchers in Canada, Israel, Japan, and the United States attempted to replicate Darley and Latané's (1968) findings on bystander helping behavior. Some experiments were performed in laboratories with college students and others took place in real-life settings such as subways, liquor stores, and the workplace. The number of bystanders who were present varied across different experiments, and different types of helping behavior were measured. Women and men were studied. Over a few dozen replications, the vast majority confirmed the original finding (Latané and Nida, 1981).

What happens when research findings fail to replicate? On the one hand, such failures often lead to important discoveries. For example, we have seen that men's belief that they have consumed a few alcoholic drinks (even if the drinks are nonalcoholic) increases their sexual arousal to explicit sexual materials. But replications with women yield a different finding. Women's expectation of having consumed a few alcoholic drinks does *not* increase their sexual responsiveness (Crowe & George, 1989; Norris, 1994). Scientists currently are exploring why this gender difference occurs.

On the other hand, when new studies consistently fail to replicate the original results of earlier research, this suggests that the original study may have been flawed or that the finding was a fluke. If so, the scientific process has done its job and prevented us from getting caught in a blind alley. Our *Psychological Frontiers* feature highlights why replication is such an important component of the scientific process.

PSYCHOLOGICAL FRONTIERS

Science and the Paranormal

Natural phenomena offer scientists an endless supply of fascinating questions. Yet for many people the most exciting questions are those that seem to defy explanation in terms of normal causes. Half of American adults believe in psychic or paranormal phenomena (Gallup & Newport, 1991). Surveys of college students and other adults in Brazil, Great Britain, India, New Zealand, Sweden, and western Europe also reveal widespread belief in the paranormal (Duncan et al., 1992; Zangari & Machado,

1996; Figure 2.21). These phenomena include *mental telepathy* (transmission of thoughts between individuals), *precognition* (foretelling of the future), *clairvoyance* (perception of remote objects or events, such as "sensing" that a friend is in trouble right now), and *psychokinesis* ("mind over matter," such as "mentally" bending metal keys).

Do you believe in such phenomena? How should you, and how should a science of psychology, approach claims of

–Continued

FIGURE 2.21 Many people believe in the paranormal despite an overwhelming lack of reliable scientific evidence. "Psychic readings," "psychic hotlines," and popular TV shows and movies such as *The X-Files* and *The Sixth Sense* illustrate the public's fascination.

paranormal events? Adopting a scientific attitude means that we should approach this issue with open-minded skepticism. We should not reject paranormal claims merely because they seem "impossible" in terms of our present conceptions of reality. Rather, skepticism means that we apply the same rigorous standards of proof that we do to all phenomena—no more, no less (Cardeña et al., 2000). The ability of independent investigators to replicate initial research findings is one of those standards.

In 1976, the Committee for the Scientific Investigation of Claims of the Paranormal was formed to begin this task (Frazier, 1986). It consists of leading psychologists and other scientists, philosophers, and magicians expert in the art of fakery. To conclude that a phenomenon is "psychic" the committee requires that presently known "natural" physical or psychological explanations be ruled out. It publishes a fascinating journal called *The Skeptical Inquirer*, which is found in many college libraries.

We might like to believe otherwise, but at present there is no generally accepted scientific evidence to support the existence of paranormal phenomena. Instead, we have a mountain of poorly designed experiments and findings that fail to replicate. Tallies of "psychic predictions" also yield dismal results. A check of 550 predictions made by 36 leading psychics in national newspapers yielded only 24 (4 percent) correct predictions, and another tally of 425 predictions made by the *National Enquirer's* leading psychics found that only 2 (1/2 of 1 percent) were correct (Blodgett, 1986; Strentz, 1984).

What about "paranormal demonstrations" by self-proclaimed psychics? James Randi, a magician and expert in the art of psychic fraud, has had a standing offer for more than 20 years of $10,000 to anyone who can demonstrate paranormal ability under his scrutiny. To date, no one has collected, and not a single psychic has been found who could demonstrate paranormal powers to the satisfaction of impartial scientists.

As paranormal research becomes better designed, results become more discouraging. Consider claims of *dermo-optical perception (DOP)*, which refers to the ability to use the skin (mainly on the forehead) as a visual sensor and therefore to be able to see while blindfolded. Many people who claimed this ability decades ago were discovered to be peeking through their blindfolds, but in 1996 medical researchers from two respected laboratories in Paris seemingly obtained evidence to support the existence of DOP. Yet when a subsequent team of French scientists (including psychologists and physicists) employed more rigorous procedures, they found no evidence of DOP (Benski et al., 1998).

Several years ago a report in a major scientific journal presented evidence of mental telepathy from 11 studies using the *ganzfeld procedure* (Bem & Honorton, 1994). In this approach, one participant (the "receiver") listens to a hissing sound played through earphones, and sees red light through translucent goggles. This procedure is thought by parapsychologists to make the receiver more sensitive to mental telepathy signals. In another shielded room, the "sender" concentrates on four different visual forms presented in random order. In these studies, the receivers reported the correct form on 32 percent of the trials, a statistically significant increase above the chance level of 25 percent.

Does the ganzfeld procedure—which involves many rigorous controls—provide the first solid evidence of a psychic phenomenon? Some scientists suggest that the original ganzfeld studies may not have fully prevented the receivers from detecting extremely subtle cues that could have influenced their responses (Hyman, 1994; Wiseman et al., 1996). Although several parapsychology researchers have reported successful replications (Parker, 2000), psychologists Julie Milton and Richard Wiseman (1999) recently analyzed 30 ganzfeld studies conducted by seven independent laboratories. They concluded that "the ganzfeld technique does *not* at present offer a replicable method for producing ESP in the laboratory" (p. 387, italics added).

Perhaps the most interesting psychological question is why beliefs in the paranormal persist despite overwhelming contrary evidence. One answer is that many people *want* to believe in the paranormal. They welcome the notion that cosmic forces shape their lives and that there are psychics who can help them discover their destinies. The paranormal also appeals to our sense of wonder about the unknown. And ironically, the very institution—science—that is so skeptical of the paranormal helps to promote our belief in it. The dizzying pace of scientific discovery reinforces the belief that almost anything is possible ('T Hooft, 2000). In many ways, what was science fiction yesterday is fact today.

Should psychology close the book on the paranormal? Critical thinking requires us to have a reasoned skepticism that demands solid scientific proof, but not a blind skepticism that rejects the unknown as impossible. We should not be like the Italian philosophers who refused to look through Galileo's telescope because they already knew that the moons of Jupiter did not exist. The burden of proof lies with those who believe in the paranormal, but evaluations of their claims should be based on scientific evidence and not on blind prejudice.

Meta-Analysis: Combining the Results of Many Studies

➤ 36. Describe the purpose of meta-analysis.

As research on a topic accumulates, scientists must reach overall conclusions about how variables are related. Often experts on a topic will examine the number and quality of studies that support or fail to support a particular relation, and then draw conclusions that they believe are best supported by the facts.

Increasingly, an approach called meta-analysis is being used to supplement these expert reviews. **Meta-analysis** is a statistical procedure for combining the results of different studies that examine the same topic. In an individual study, the responses of each participant are analyzed. In a meta-analysis, each *study* is treated as a "single participant," and its overall results are analyzed with those of other studies. A meta-analysis will tell researchers about the direction and statistical strength of the relation between two variables.

Given that many people feel they have sleep problems (as indicated earlier by the National Sleep Foundation survey), let's consider whether exercising might help. Do you believe that exercising during the day helps people sleep better at night? A recent meta-analysis combined the results of 38 studies on this topic and concluded that the overall relation is weak (Youngstedt et al., 1997). On average, people slept about ten minutes longer when they had exercised that day, but they fell asleep only about one minute faster. If they awakened during the night, they did not fall back asleep any sooner.

Although meta-analysis is a statistical procedure, the researcher must decide which studies to include and point out limitations common to those studies. The authors of the meta-analysis on exercise and sleep cautioned that most studies examined young adults who slept well and did not focus on people with insomnia (Youngstedt et al., 1997). When properly used, many researchers consider meta-analysis to be the most objective way to integrate the findings of various studies and reach overall conclusions about behavior.

❯ ETHICAL PRINCIPLES IN HUMAN AND ANIMAL RESEARCH

Psychologists sometimes walk an ethical tightrope when they study important problems, weighing the knowledge and possible applications to be gained against potential risks to which research participants may be exposed. Investigators are obligated to adhere to a set of ethical standards based on government regulations and guidelines developed by national psychological organizations.

To safeguard the rights of human and animal participants, academic and research institutions have created scientific committees that review the ethical issues involved in every research proposal (Figure 2.22). If a proposed study is considered ethically questionable, or if the rights of participants are not sufficiently protected, the methods must be modified or the research cannot be conducted.

Ethical Standards in Human Research

➤ 37. Describe the major ethical issues in human research and how participants' rights are protected.

According to the American Psychological Association (APA) guideline of **informed consent,** research participants should be:

- given a full description of the procedures to be followed,
- informed about any risks that might be involved, and
- told that they are free to withdraw from a study at any time without penalty.

When children, seriously disturbed mental patients, or others who are not able to give true informed consent are involved, consent must be obtained from their parents or guardians.

FIGURE 2.22 Ethical standards are designed to protect the welfare of both human and animal subjects in psychological research.

To safeguard a participant's *right to privacy*, researchers consider the setting in which behavior will be studied (public or private) and the manner in which information will be recorded and released (e.g., will the person's identity be anonymous, and if not, what steps will be taken to ensure confidentiality). Two other considerations are *psychological risk*, which represents the degree to which the research procedures may expose someone to significant mental or emotional stress, and *social risk*, which asks whether information recorded about individual participants could become known to others and, if so, would negative consequences for the participant result.

Deception, which occurs when participants are misled about the nature of a study, is highly controversial. Consider the Darley and Latané (1968) bystander experiment. Participants were not told that the study was going to examine how they would respond to an emergency, nor were they informed that the procedures (someone presumably having a seizure) might cause them stress. Instead, they were misled to expect a group discussion about the problems of college students. Proponents of deception research argue that, when studying certain types of behaviors, deception is the only way to obtain natural, spontaneous responses from participants. In other words, Darley and Latané's participants had to believe that the emergency was significant and real.

Deception, however, violates the principle of informed consent. Guidelines currently permit deception under limited circumstances and only when no other feasible alternative is available. The study must have scientific, educational, or applied benefits that clearly outweigh the ethical costs of deceiving participants. When deception is used the true purpose of the study should be explained to participants after it is over. The vast majority of psychological studies do not involve deception, and deception research has decreased in recent decades (Nicks et al., 1997). Still many scientists oppose the use of deception under any circumstance, and the debate continues (Kron, 1998; Ortmann & Hertwig, 1997). Overall, most students (93 percent in a survey we conducted among several thousand introductory psychology students at our university) report that their experiences as research participants are pleasant and informative.

> 38. Why does some research involve deception? What ethical principle does deception violate?

Ethical Standards in Animal Research

As in medical research, animals frequently are subjects in psychological studies considered too hazardous for humans. APA and federal government guidelines require that animals be treated humanely and that the risks to which they are exposed be

> 39. What are the justifications for, and criticisms of, research in which animals are harmed?

FIGURE 2.23 The debate on animal research highlights the challenging task researchers face in attempting to protect the welfare of animals while ensuring that society continues to receive the benefits that animal research provides. The "20.8 years longer" mentioned in the photo (*right*) refers to a U.S. Department of Health and Human Services estimate of increased human life expectancy due to animal research.

justified by the potential importance of the research. This determination, however, is not always easy to make. For example, should researchers be allowed to inject a chemical into an animal's brain in order to learn whether a specific chemical imbalance ultimately might impair memory in humans? People of good will can disagree. As noted earlier, before animal research can be conducted it must reviewed and approved, often by panels that include nonscientists from the community.

Animal research is hotly debated, both outside and within the psychological community (Baldwin, 1993; Vonk, 1997). National surveys find that the overwhelming majority of practicing psychologists and college psychology majors believe that animal research is necessary for scientific progress in psychology (Plous, 1996a, 1996b). However, most psychologists oppose animal research involving pain or death.

Psychologists agree that it is morally wrong to subject animals to needless suffering. Many scientists, however, do not agree with the head of the American Anti-Vivisection Society, who maintained that animals should never be used in research "which is not for the benefit of the animals involved" (Goodman, 1982, p. 61). They point to important medical and psychological advances made possible by animal research (Baldwin, 1993). For example, had Pasteur not subjected some dogs to suffering, he could not have developed the rabies vaccine, which has saved the lives of countless animals as well as humans. They ask, "Does the prospect of finding a cure for cancer or identifying the causes of psychological disorders justify exposing some animals to harm" (Figure 2.23)?

Although animal research has declined slightly in recent years, the ethical questions remain as vexing as ever (Petrinovich, 1999; Plous, 1996a). What is most encouraging is that the welfare of animals in research is receiving the careful attention it deserves.

❭ CRITICAL THINKING IN SCIENCE AND EVERYDAY LIFE

In today's world we are exposed to a great deal of scientific information, not just in school, but also in the popular media. To be an informed consumer you must be able to critically evaluate research and identify features that limit the validity of conclusions. Critical thinking skills can also help you avoid being misled by claims made in everyday life, such as those in advertisements. Thus enhancing your critical thinking skills may be one of the most important benefits you will derive from your psychology course. That is why these first two chapters have focused on how psychologists think about and study behavior.

As critical thinkers, we must be open-minded and able to tolerate uncertainty. It may be comforting to have the conviction that we possess "truth," but a stubborn refusal to consider other viewpoints or evidence will not serve us well in the long run. At the same time, we should recognize that our beliefs and emotions can act as psychological blinders that allow us to uncritically accept inadequate evidence, especially when this evidence supports our current views. This does not mean that we should be so skeptical of everything that we believe nothing. Rather, we need to balance open-mindedness with a healthy skepticism, and evaluate evidence for what it is worth.

➤ 40. As a critical thinker, what questions should you ask when someone makes a claim or assertion?

You can assume that stimulating the caudate nucleus caused the bull to stop charging. But does this demonstrate that the caudate nucleus is an aggressive-off center? Write down your criticisms and check your critical thinking against the points raised at the end of this feature. (For a hint, read on. Perhaps stimulating the caudate nucleus produced intense pain, and that is why the bull ended its attack. What other bodily functions might the caudate nucleus help regulate that would cause the bull to stop charging?)

▶ Example 2: Vacations and Burglaries.

A newspaper advertisement appeared many times in several American cities. The headline "While You're on Vacation, Burglars go to Work" is followed by this statement: "According to FBI statistics, over 26 percent of home burglaries take place between Memorial Day and Labor Day" (U.S. holidays in late May and early September). The ad then offers a special summer sale price for installation of a home security system. In sum, the ad implies that burglaries are particularly likely to occur while people are away on summer vacation. How do you feel about this claim and its supporting evidence?

▶ Example 3: Will Staying Up Late Cause You to Forget What You Have Studied?

The headline of a newspaper article reads: "Best Way to Retain Complex Information? Sleep On It, Researcher Says." The article begins: "Students who study hard Monday through Friday and then party all night on weekends may lose much of what they learned during the week, according to a sleep researcher." The researcher is then quoted as saying: "It appears skewing the sleep cycle by just two hours can have this effect. Watching a long, late movie the night following a class and then sleeping in the next morning will make it so you're not learning what you thought. You'll not lose it all—just about 30 percent."

Next the experiment is described. Participants were college students who were taught a complex logic game. Afterward they were assigned to one of four sleep conditions for the night: Students in the control condition were allowed to have a normal night's sleep. Those in Condition 2 were not allowed to have any sleep. In Conditions 3 and 4, students were awakened only when they went into a particular stage (phase) of sleep (we'll learn about sleep

stages in Chapter 5). A week later everyone was tested again. Participants in Conditions 3 and 4 performed 30 percent worse than the other two groups.

Think about the claims reported in the first paragraph above. Then examine the experimental conditions. Does anything seem wrong to you?

▶ Critical Analyses of the Studies

Analysis 1: A Lot of Bull

Perhaps the caudate nucleus plays a role in vision, memory, or movement, and stimulating it momentarily caused the bull either to become blind, to forget what it was doing, or to alter its movement. Perhaps the bull simply became dizzy. These are all possible explanations for why the bull stopped charging. In fact, the caudate nucleus helps to regulate movement; it is *not* an aggression-off center in the brain.

Analysis 2: Vacations and Burglaries

First, how much is "over 26 percent"? We don't know for sure, but can assume that it is less than 27 percent, because it would be to the advertiser's advantage to state the highest number possible. The key problem is the Memorial Day to Labor Day time period, which typically represents between 26 and 29 percent of the days of the year. Therefore about 26 percent of burglaries occur during about 26 percent of the year. Wow! Technically the ad is correct: Burglars do go to work in the summer while you're on vacation. But the ad also may mislead people. Burglars seem to be just as busy at other times of the year.

Analysis 3: Staying Up Late

It could be true that going to bed and waking up later than usual might cause you to forget more of what you study. However, the article does not provide evidence for this claim. Look at the four experimental conditions carefully. Not one involved participants' getting a normal *amount* of sleep, but merely delaying when they went to bed and got up. The conditions examined only the effects of getting no sleep or losing certain types of sleep. When reading newspaper or magazine articles, look beyond the headlines and think about whether the claims are truly supported by the evidence.

Were you able to pick out some flaws? Critical thinking requires practice and you will get better at it if you keep asking the five critical thinking questions listed earlier.

CHAPTER SUMMARY

Scientific Principles in Psychology

- Curiosity, skepticism, and open-mindedness are key scientific attitudes. The scientific process proceeds through several steps: (1) asking questions based on some type of observation; (2) formulating a hypothesis; (3) conducting research to test the hypothesis; (4) analyzing the data and drawing a tentative conclusion; (5) building theories; and (6) using the theory to generate new hypotheses, which are then tested by more research.

- In everyday life we typically use hindsight (after-the-fact) understanding to explain behavior. This approach is limited because there may be countless possible explanations and no way to ascertain which is correct. Psychologists prefer to test their understanding through prediction, control, and building theories about the causes of behavior.

- A good theory organizes known facts, gives rise to additional hypotheses that are testable, is supported by the findings of new research, and is parsimonious.

- Psychologists use operational definitions to clearly define the concepts they study. To "operationally define" a concept or variable, you define it in terms of the specific procedures used to produce or measure it.

- Psychologists measure behavior by obtaining participants' self-reports, gathering reports from others who know the participants, measuring physiological responses, and directly observing behavior. When possible, behavioral observations are made unobtrusively, which means that the participants are not aware that their behavior is being recorded.

Methods of Research: Descriptive/Correlational

- The goal of descriptive research is to carefully identify how organisms behave, especially in natural settings.

- Case studies involve the detailed study of a person, group, or event. Although causal conclusions are difficult to establish, case studies often suggest important ideas for further research. In some instances they can demonstrate that a theory is invalid.

- Naturalistic observation is used to gather information about animal and human behavior in real-life settings. Rich descriptions of behavior are often provided, and relations between variables also can be examined. Researchers must be careful to interpret their observations in an objective manner and avoid influencing the participants being observed.

- Surveys involved administering questionnaires or interviews to many people. Most surveys study a subset of people, called a sample, which is randomly drawn from the larger population of people the researcher is interested in. The goal is to produce a representative sample that reflects the characteristics of the larger population.

- A major advantage of surveys is that representative samples allow for reasonably accurate estimates of the opinions or behaviors of the population. Unrepresentative samples can lead to inaccurate estimates. Survey results also can be distorted by interviewer bias or biases in the way participants report about themselves.

- Correlational research measures the relation between naturally occurring variables. Two variables are positively correlated when increases in variable X correspond to increases in variable Y. A negative correlation occurs when increases in variable X correspond to decreases in variable Y.

- Causal conclusions cannot be drawn from correlational data. Variable X may cause Y, Y may cause X, or some third variable (Z) may be the true cause of both X and Y. Nevertheless, if two variables are correlated, then knowing the scores of one variable will help you predict the scores of the other.

Methods of Research: Experiments

- Experiments examine cause-effect relations. They have three essential characteristics: (1) one or more variables are manipulated; (2) their effects on other variables are measured; and (3) an attempt is made to hold extraneous factors constant so that cause-and-effect conclusions can be drawn.

- Each variable manipulated by the experimenter is called an independent variable. Variables that are measured are called dependent variables. The independent variable is viewed as the cause, the dependent variable as the effect.

- The experimental group receives a treatment or an active level of the independent variable, whereas the control group does not. The behavior of the control group sets a standard to which the behavior of the experimental group can be compared.

- Some experimenters randomly assign different participants to each condition, creating experimental and control groups that are equivalent at the start of the study. Other experimenters expose each participant to all the conditions and counterbalance the order in which the conditions are presented.

- Descriptive and correlational research differ from experiments in three key ways: (1) no variables are manipulated, they are only measured; (2) data typically are gathered in more natural settings, as opposed to laboratories; and (3) extraneous variables cannot be controlled in the precise manner possible with experiments.

Threats to the Validity of Research

- An experiment has high internal validity when it is designed well and permits clear causal conclusions. Confounding of variables occurs when the independent variable becomes mixed up with an uncontrolled variable. This ruins internal validity because we can no longer tell which variable has produced the changes in the dependent variable.

- Internal validity is weakened by (1) demand characteristics, which are cues that tip off to participants how they should behave; (2) placebo effects, in which the mere expectation of receiving a treatment produces a change in behavior; and (3) experimenter expectancy effects, which refer to subtle ways in which a researcher's behavior influences participants to behave in a manner consistent with the hypothesis being tested. The double-blind procedure prevents placebo effects and experimenter expectancy effects from biasing research results.

- External validity is the degree to which the findings of a study can be generalized to other people, settings, and conditions. By replicating (repeating) a study under both similar and dissimilar circumstances, its external validity can be examined.

- There is no generally accepted, replicable scientific evidence to support the existence of paranormal phenomena. Even the ganzfeld procedure, initially supported by several highly controlled experiments, has often failed to replicate. Despite the negative evidence, many people continue to believe in the paranormal.

- Meta-analysis statistically combines the results of many studies that examine the same variables and calculates the strength of the overall relation between two variables.

Ethical Principles in Human and Animal Research

- Psychological research follows extensive ethical guidelines. In human research, key issues are the use of informed consent, the participants' right to privacy, the degree of psychological and social risk, and the use of deception.

- Ethical guidelines require that animals be treated humanely and that risks to which they are exposed be justified by the potential importance of the research. Animal research involving pain and death is controversial.

Critical Thinking in Science and Everyday Life

- Critical thinking is an important life skill. It can prevent us from developing false impressions about how the world operates and from being duped in everyday life by unsubstantiated claims. However, we should also be open-minded to ideas that are supported by solid evidence, even when they conflict with our preconceptions.

KEY TERMS AND CONCEPTS*

archival measures (50)

case study (50)

confounding of variables (65)

control group (59)

correlation coefficient (57)

correlational research (55)

demand characteristics (66)

dependent variable (59)

descriptive research (50)

double-blind procedure (67)

experiment (58)

experimental group (59)

experimenter expectancy effects (67)

external validity (67)

hypothesis (44)

independent variable (59)

informed consent (70)

internal validity (64)

meta-analysis (70)

naturalistic observation (52)

negative correlation (57)

operational definition (47)

placebo (66)

placebo effect (66)

population (53)

positive correlation (57)

random assignment (60)

random sampling (54)

replication (68)

representative sample (54)

sample (53)

scatterplot (57)

survey research (53)

theory (45)

variable (47)

* Each term has been boldfaced in the text on the page indicated in parentheses.

APPLYING YOUR KNOWLEDGE

These questions allow you to apply your understanding of the material in this chapter.

1. You tell a friend, "A bystander is *more* likely to help a victim if other bystanders are present." "That's obvious," he says, "because each bystander feels safer if others are present." Then you tell another friend, "A bystander is *less* likely to help a victim if other bystanders are present." "That's obvious," she says, "because each bystander figures someone else will help." This example best illustrates
   a) how demand characteristics influence behavior.
   b) the importance of random sampling when conducting research.
   c) a limitation of after-the-fact explanations.
   d) that describing events is the major goal of psychological research.

2. According to our new theory, a small creature—called a Floobah—sits on the left shoulder of every human. You cannot see, hear, smell, touch, or detect Floobahs in any way, but we know they are there. Every action you take is controlled by your Floobah. Your most appropriate response would be, "Professors, this is a poor theory because"
   a) it challenges existing beliefs about behavior.
   b) no possible evidence can disconfirm it, and therefore it cannot be tested.
   c) it is too simple to account for the diversity of human behavior.
   d) the Floobah said so.

3. Dr. Gonzalez surveys how the 8,000 students on her campus feel about a proposed tuition increase. She selects 600 students for the survey. These 600 students represent the _____, and the 8,000 students represent the _____.
   a) experimental group; control group
   b) sample; control group
   c) experimental group; population
   d) sample; population

4. Dr. Peters wants to identify the characteristics of "corporate success," so he studies an extremely successful company for six months. He reads corporate documents, interviews employees, gives managers psychological tests to identify their leadership style, and observes people performing their jobs. Overall, Dr. Peters study best represents
   a) a case study.
   b) naturalistic observation.
   c) a survey.
   d) an experiment.

5. If you were to conduct a survey, you would want to use _____ to select the participants. If you were to conduct an experiment, you would use _____ to determine which participants were exposed to each particular condition.
   a) random assignment; random sampling
   b) random assignment; random assignment
   c) random sampling; random assignment
   d) random sampling; random sampling

6. You study 100 children for a month, measuring how much TV they watch and how many aggressive acts they perform. You find that TV watching and aggression are highly and positively correlated. Based on this study, you
   a) can conclude that watching TV causes children to behave more aggressively.
   b) can conclude that an aggressive personality causes children to watch more TV.
   c) can conclude that TV watching and aggression are causally related, although we cannot tell which causes which.
   d) cannot draw any causal conclusions about the relation between TV watching and aggression.

7. Dr. Nguyen conducts an experiment. In one condition, participants perform a physical task in a room, alone. In a second condition, participants perform the same task, but do so in front of an audience of five people. Dr. Nguyen then measures how well each participant performs. In this experiment, task performance represents
   a) a confounding variable.
   b) the dependent variable.
   c) the independent variable.
   d) a demand characteristic.

8. In Dr. Nguyen's experiment, the fact that each participant is either alone or in front of an audience represents
   a) a confounding variable.
   b) the dependent variable.
   c) the independent variable.
   d) a demand characteristic.

9. If you were conducting an experiment, you would use a double-blind procedure to
   a) prevent people from realizing that they were participating in an experiment.
   b) select participants so that they would be representative of people in general.
   c) ensure that people who know each other do not participate in the same condition.
   d) prevent the experimenter's and participant's expectations from influencing the results.

10. You want to conduct a study for your honor's project in psychology. The participants will be college students. In order to fully follow the ethical principle of informed consent, your study must involve
    a) no social risk to the participants.
    b) no psychological risk.
    c) no deception.
    d) no social risk, no psychological risk, and no deception.

Answers

1. c) (page 45); 2. b) (page 46); 3. d) (page 53); 4. a) (page 50); 5. c) (page 54); 6. d) (page 56); 7. b) (page 59); 8. c) (page 59); 9. d) (page 67); 10. c) (page 70)

For additional quizzing and a variety of interactive resources, visit the book's Online Learning Center at www.mhhe.com/passer.

BIOLOGICAL FOUNDATIONS OF BEHAVIOR

The brain is the last and grandest biological frontier, the most complex thing we have yet discovered in our universe. It contains hundreds of billions of cells interlinked through trillions of connections. The brain boggles the mind.

— *James Watson*

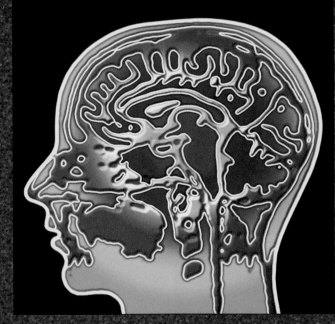

3

CHAPTER OUTLINE

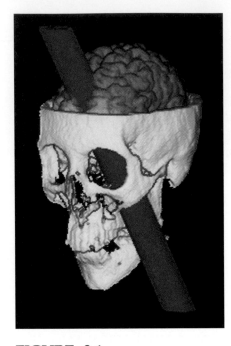

FIGURE 3.1 The brain damage suffered by Phineas Gage seemed to change him into a new person.

The year was 1848. As the Vermont winter approached, a railroad construction crew hurried to complete its work on a new track. They could not know that they were about to witness one of the most celebrated incidents in the annals of neuroscience.

As a blasting crew prepared its charges, the dynamite accidentally exploded. A spike more than 3 feet long and weighing 13 pounds was propelled through the face and head of Phineas Gage, a 25-year-old foreman. The spike entered through the left cheek, passed through the brain, and emerged through the top of the skull (Figure 3.1). Dr. J. M. Harlow, who treated Gage, described the incident:

> The patient was thrown upon his back by the explosion, and gave a few convulsive motions of the extremities, but spoke in a few minutes. He . . . seemed perfectly conscious, but was becoming exhausted from the hemorrhage, . . . the blood pouring from the top of his head. . . . He bore his sufferings with firmness, and directed my attention to the hole in his cheek, saying, "the iron entered there and passed through my head." (Harlow, 1868, pp. 330–332)

Miraculously, Gage survived. Or did he?

> His physical health is good, and I am inclined to say that he has recovered. Has no pain in his head, but says it has a queer feeling that he is not able to describe. . . . His contractors, who regarded him as the most efficient and capable foreman in their employ previous to his injury, considered the change in his mind so marked that they could not give him his place again. The equilibrium or balance, so to speak, between his intellectual faculties and animal propensities, seems to have been destroyed. He is fitful, irreverent, indulging at times in the grossest profanity (which was not previously his custom), manifesting but little deference for his fellows, impatient of restraint or advice when it conflicts with his desires . . . devising many plans of future operations, which are no sooner arranged than they are abandoned in turn for others. . . . His mind is radically changed, so decidedly that his friends and acquaintances say that he is "no longer Gage." (Harlow, 1868, pp. 339–340)

A young woman appeared in the emergency room of Baltimore City Hospital three days before her 23rd birthday, pleading for help. The story she told was a strange one indeed.

She and two other girls had been delivered by the same midwife in Georgia's Okefenokee Swamp on a Friday the 13th. The midwife, a member of a voodoo cult had, for reasons known only to herself, placed a curse on all three babies. She proclaimed that one would die before her 16th birthday, another before her 21st birthday, and the third (the patient) before her 23rd birthday.

True to the midwife's prediction, the girl who was to die before her 16th birthday was killed in an auto accident when she was 15 years old. The second young woman was killed by a stray bullet during a shooting in a night club where she was celebrating her 21st birthday. Now, the third woman waited in terror for her own death.

The emergency room psychiatrist reassured the terrified woman that no harm would come to her in the hospital and reluctantly admitted her for observation. Despite the doctor's reassurance, the woman remained convinced that she was doomed. The next morning, two days before her 23rd birthday, she was found dead in her hospital bed. Doctors were unable to determine a physical cause for her death. (Seligman, 1975)

As the tragic accident to Phineas Gage and the young woman's sudden death show us, biological and psychological processes are intimately related. In one case, physical damage to Gage's brain changed his thinking and behavior so radically that a psychologically different person emerged. The death of the young woman suggests the possibility that her psychological belief that she was doomed brought about biological changes so profound that they killed her.

In this chapter we explore three interrelated biological systems. The nervous system is the master control network of nerve cells whose activities underlie your every thought, feeling, and behavior. The endocrine system of glands influences many behaviors through the activities of hormones. The immune system, the body's defense network, is the site of some of the most profound recent discoveries of so-called psychological-biological interactions. We also examine genetic processes that help determine who you are, how you behave, and what you are capable of becoming.

❯ THE NEURAL BASES OF BEHAVIOR

The brain is a grapefruit-size mass of tissue that feels like jelly and looks like a grayish gnarled walnut. One of the true marvels of nature, it has been termed "our three-pound universe" (Hooper & Teresi, 1986). To understand how the brain controls our experience and behavior, we must first understand how its individual cells function and how they communicate with one another.

Neurons

Specialized cells called **neurons** are the basic building blocks of the nervous system. These nerve cells are linked together in circuits, not unlike the electrical circuits in a computer. At birth your brain contained about 100 billion neurons (Bloom, 2000; Kolb & Whishaw, 1989). To put this number in perspective, if each neuron were an inch long and they were placed end to end, the resulting chain would circle the earth more than 63 times. It is fortunate that humans have this many neurons, for it is estimated that through the normal process of cell death that accompanies aging, about 10,000 of them are lost each day of our lives (Filogamo, 1998).

Each neuron has three main parts: a cell body, dendrites, and an axon (Figure 3.2). The cell body or *soma,* contains the biochemical structures needed to keep the neuron alive, and its nucleus carries the genetic information that determines how the cell develops and functions. Emerging from the cell body are branchlike fibers called **dendrites** (from the Greek word meaning "tree"). These specialized receiving units are like antennas that collect messages from neighboring neurons and send them on to the cell body. There the incoming information is combined and processed. The many branches of the dendrites can receive input from 1,000 or more neighboring neurons. The surface of the cell body also has receptor areas that can be directly stimulated by other neurons. Extending from one side of the cell body is a single **axon,** which conducts electrical impulses away from the cell body to other neurons, muscles, or

➤ 1. Name the three main parts of the neuron and describe their functions.

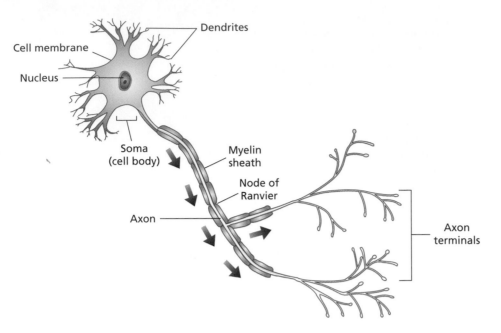

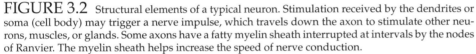

FIGURE 3.2 Structural elements of a typical neuron. Stimulation received by the dendrites or soma (cell body) may trigger a nerve impulse, which travels down the axon to stimulate other neurons, muscles, or glands. Some axons have a fatty myelin sheath interrupted at intervals by the nodes of Ranvier. The myelin sheath helps increase the speed of nerve conduction.

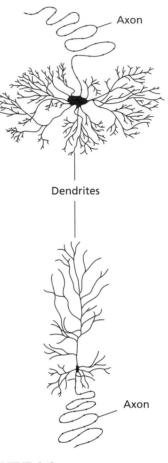

FIGURE 3.3 Neurons' structural characteristics can vary widely. Despite these differences, all neurons have only one cell body and one axon.

➤ 2. Which structural characteristics permit the many possible interconnections among neurons?

➤ 3. How do glial cells differ from neurons? What three functions do they have in the nervous system?

glands. The axon branches out at its end to form a number of *axon terminals*—as many as several hundred in some cases. Each axon terminal may connect with dendritic branches from numerous neurons, making it possible for a single neuron to pass messages to as many as 50,000 other neurons (Fain, 1999; Shepherd, 1997). Given the structure of the dendrites and axons, it is easy to see how there can be trillions of interconnections in the brain, making it capable of performing the complex psychological activities that are of interest to psychologists.

Neurons can vary greatly in size and shape (Figure 3.3). More than 200 different types of neurons have been viewed through electron microscopes (Nolte, 1998). A neuron with its cell body in your spinal cord may have an axon that extends several feet to one of your fingertips, equivalent in scale to a basketball attached to a cord 4 miles long; a neuron in your brain may be no more than a thousandth of an inch long. Regardless of their shape or size, neurons have been exquisitely sculpted by nature to perform their function of receiving, processing, and sending messages.

Neurons are supported in their functions by *glial cells*, (from the Greek word for *glue*). Glial cells do not send or receive nerve impulses, but they surround neurons and hold them in place. The glial cells also manufacture nutrient chemicals that neurons need, and they absorb toxins and waste materials that might damage neurons. During prenatal brain development, as new neurons are being formed through cell division, glial cells send out long fibers that guide newly divided neurons to their targeted place in the brain (Filogamo, 1998). Within the nervous system, glial cells outnumber neurons about ten to one.

Nerve Conduction: An Electrochemical Process

Neurons do two important things: They generate electricity and they release chemicals. Nerve conduction is thus an electrochemical process. The electrical properties of neurons have been known for more than a century, but we have only recently begun to understand the chemical processes involved in neural activity. An understanding of how neurons generate electricity requires a brief excursion into chemistry.

Neurons function a bit like batteries in that their own chemical substances are a source of energy. Like other cells, the neuron is surrounded by a cell membrane. This membrane not only protects the inner structures but also operates as a kind of selective filter that allows certain particles in the body fluid around the cell to pass through while refusing passage to other substances.

➤ 4. What causes the negative resting potential of neurons? When is a neuron said to be in a state of polarization?

Neurons are surrounded by a salty liquid environment. This environment's high concentration of sodium carries a positive atomic charge, that is, it has a high concentration of positively charged particles, or ions. Although the inside of the neuron has some positively charged potassium ions, it contains many other ions that carry a negative charge. As a result, the inside of the neuron is electrically negative in relation to the outside, producing an electrical *resting potential* of about −70 millivolts, or −70/1,000 of a volt, across the membrane. When in this resting state, the neuron is said to be *polarized.*

All cells in the body have a similar resting voltage. In some animals, specialized organs can combine this tiny voltage to generate very high voltages. For example, electric eels can generate 600 to 700 volts because their muscle tissue cell membranes are arranged so that the small individual cell voltages can be combined to produce one big jolt.

The Action Potential

Neurons, like muscle cells, have a unique property among body cells: Sudden and extreme changes can occur in their resting potential voltage. An **action potential,** or nerve impulse, is a sudden reversal in the neuron's membrane voltage, during which the membrane voltage momentarily moves from −70 millivolts (inside) to +40 millivolts (Figure 3.4). This shift from negative toward positive voltage is called **depolarization.**

To understand how this depolarization process occurs, we might liken the release of an action potential to the firing of a gun. When the dendrites or the cell body of a neuron are stimulated by axons from other neurons, small shifts occur in the cell membrane's electrical potential. These changes, called **graded potentials,** are proportional to the amount of incoming stimulation. If the graded potential is not strong enough, the neuron will be partially depolarized, but not enough to fire off an action potential. In this sense, a graded potential is like light pressure on the trigger of a gun that is not sufficient to activate its hammer. But if the graded potential is large enough to reach the **action potential threshold,** the required level of intensity needed to fire the neuron, the neuron discharges with an action potential. Unlike the graded potential, which varies in proportion to the intensity of stimulation, the action potential obeys the **all-or-none law;** it either occurs with maximum intensity or it does not occur at all. It is in this sense that triggering an action potential is like firing a gun. Unless enough energy is

➤ 5. What chemical changes cause the process of depolarization that creates graded and action potentials? How do these potentials differ?

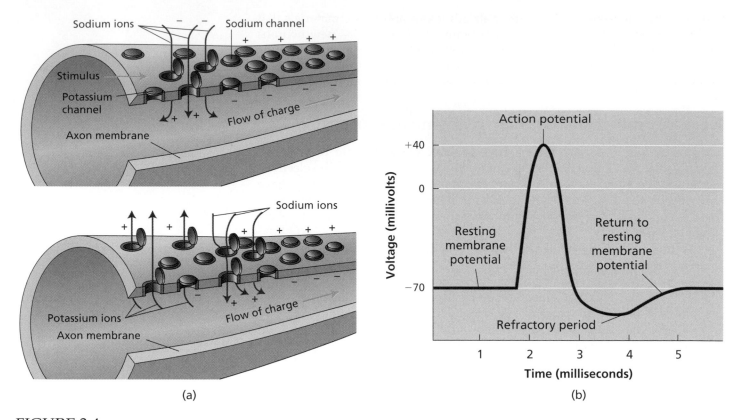

FIGURE 3.4 The nerve impulse is a change in electrical potential resulting from depolarization of the cell membrane. The movement of a nerve impulse along an axon involves the opening of sodium ion channels that allow many positively charged sodium ions to flow into the cell (a) while a smaller number of potassium ions flow out (b). The net effect is a reversal of the membrane polarity from about −70 millivolts (resting potential) to about +40 millivolts (action potential). An instant later the sodium ion channels close and the sodium ions are pumped back out of the cell and the potassium ions flow back in, restoring the negative resting potential. After a brief refractory period, another impulse can follow.

applied to the trigger, the gun will not fire. But once it does fire, the velocity of the bullet bears no relation to how hard the trigger was pulled.

What causes the depolarization of the neuron membrane that may result in an action potential? Through a series of sophisticated experiments that won them the 1963 Nobel Prize, British scientists Alan Hodgkin and Andrew Huxley provided the answer. Recall that when the cell is resting, positively charged sodium ions in the salty liquid environment are kept outside the cell. When a neuron is stimulated, however, tiny protein structures on the cell membrane called **ion channels** are activated. Each channel can allow specific ions back and forth across the cell membrane. Sodium ion channels in the cell membrane open for an instant, and positively charged sodium ions flow into the interior of the cell, attracted by the negative electrical force inside the neuron. The influx of sodium ions causes the interior of the cell to become less negative than it was, creating a state of partial depolarization that may reach the action potential threshold (which is at about −.55 millivolts in most neurons—a decrease of only .15 millivolts from the resting potential). If that occurs, the inside of the neuron responds by becoming more positively charged than the outside for an instant, producing the state of complete depolarization that constitutes the action potential. In a reflex action to restore the resting polarity, the cell quickly closes the sodium ion channels and opens potassium channels through which positive potassium ions can flow out of the cell. In this way, the cell's negatively charged resting potential is restored (Fain, 1999). In less than 1/1,000 of a second, the process is over at any given point on the membrane, but the action potential has started a chain reaction "wave" that flows down the membrane as succeeding sodium gates open and the process is repeated. After a brief instant, the sodium ions inside the membrane are pumped back outside and the potassium ions flow back inside the membrane, restoring the normal ion distribution. Figure 3.4 shows this sequence of events.

The wavelike quality of the action potential as it moves down the length of the axon is not unlike the human "wave" that occurs in sports stadiums as fans in adjacent seats successively stand up, cheer, and raise their arms, then sit back down. Nobody actually changes position, but the visual (and auditory) effect is of a "wave" that moves around the stadium.

Immediately after an impulse passes any given point along the axon, there occurs a *refractory period,* a time period during which the membrane is not excitable and cannot discharge another action potential. This refractory period, lasting one or two thousandths of a second, limits the rate at which action potentials can be triggered in a neuron. In humans the limit seems to be about 300 nerve impulses per second (Roland, 1997).

If action potentials are always identical to one another, how does the nervous system tell the difference between, for example, a dim light and a bright light, or between a light touch and a hard rub? Such information is communicated in a number of ways. For example, a strong stimulus may increase the *rate* of firing of the individual neuron. Or it may increase the *number* of neurons that fire by stimulating additional neurons that fire only in response to high-intensity stimulation. In such ways, information is provided concerning the nature of the stimulus.

The Myelin Sheath

Many axons that transmit information throughout the brain and spinal cord are covered by a tubelike **myelin sheath,** a fatty whitish insulation layer derived from glial cells during development. The myelin sheath is interrupted at regular intervals by the *nodes of Ranvier,* where the myelin is either extremely thin or absent). The nodes make the myelin sheath look a bit like sausages placed end to end (see Figure 3.2). In unmyelinated axons, the action potential travels down the axon length like a burning fuse. In myelinated axons, electrical conduction can skip from node to node, and these "great leaps" from one gap to another account for high conduction speeds of more than 200 miles per hour. But even these high-speed fibers are 3 million times slower than the speed at which electricity courses through an electric wire. This is why your brain, though vastly more complex than any computer, cannot begin to match it in speed of operation.

The myelin sheath is most commonly found in the nervous systems of higher animals. In many nerve fibers, the myelin sheath is not completely formed until some time after birth. The increased efficiency of neural transmission that results is partly responsible for the gains that infants exhibit in muscular coordination as they grow older (Weyhenmeyer et al., 2000).

The tragic effects of damage to the myelin coating can be seen in people who suffer from *multiple sclerosis.* This progressive disease occurs when the person's own immune system attacks the myelin sheath. Damage to the myelin sheath disrupts the delicate timing of nerve impulses, resulting in jerky, uncoordinated movements and, in the final stages, paralysis.

➤ 6. What is the nature and importance of the myelin sheath? Which disorder results from inadequate myelinization?

How Neurons Communicate: Synaptic Transmission

The nervous system operates as a giant communications network, and its action requires the transmission of nerve impulses from one neuron to another. Early in the history of brain research, scientists thought that the tip of the axon made physical contact with the dendrites or cell bodies of other neurons, passing electricity directly from one neuron to the next. With the advent of the electron microscope, however, researchers discovered that there is actually a **synapse,** a tiny gap between the axon terminal and the next neuron. This discovery raised new and perplexing questions: If neurons do not physically touch the other neurons to which they send signals, how does communication occur? If the action potential does not cross the synapse, what does? What carries the message?

Neurotransmitters

We now know that in addition to generating electricity, neurons produce **neurotransmitters,** chemical substances that carry messages across the synapse to either excite other neurons or inhibit their firing. This process of chemical communication involves five steps: synthesis, storage, release, binding, and deactivation. In the *synthesis* stage, the chemical molecules are formed inside the neuron. The molecules are then *stored* in chambers called **synaptic vesicles** within the axon terminals. When an action potential comes down the axon, these vesicles move to the surface of the axon terminal and the molecules are *released* into the fluid-filled space between the axon of the sending (presynaptic) neuron and the membrane of the receiving (postsynaptic) neuron. The molecules cross the synaptic space and *bind* (attach themselves) to **receptor sites**—large protein molecules embedded in the receiving neuron's cell membrane. These receptor sites, which look a bit like lily pads when viewed through an electron microscope, have a specially shaped surface that fits a specific transmitter molecule much like a lock accommodates a single key (Figure 3.5).

Excitation, Inhibition, and Deactivation

➤ 7. How do neurotransmitters achieve the processes of excitation and inhibition of postsynaptic neurons?

The binding of transmitter molecule to the receptor site produces a chemical reaction that can have one of two effects on the postsynaptic neuron. In some cases, the reaction will depolarize (excite) the postsynaptic cell membrane by stimulating the inflow of sodium ions. Neurotransmitters that create depolarization are called *excitatory* transmitters. This stimulation, alone or in combination with activity at other excitatory synapses on the dendrites or cell body, may exceed the action potential threshold and cause the postsynaptic neuron to fire an action potential.

In other cases, the chemical reaction created by the docking of a neurotransmitter at its receptor site will *hyperpolarize* the postsynaptic membrane by stimulating ion channels that allow positively charged potassium ions to flow out of the neuron and thereby make its resting potential even more negative (e.g., increasing it from −70 millivolts to −72 millivolts). Hyperpolarization makes it more difficult for excitatory transmitters at other receptor sites to depolarize the neuron to its action potential threshold of −.65. Transmitters that create hyperpolarization are thus *inhibitory* in their function (Figure 3.6). A given neurotransmitter can have an excitatory effect on some neurons and an inhibitory influence on others.

Every neuron is constantly bombarded with excitatory and inhibitory neurotransmitters from other neurons, and the interplay of these influences determines whether or not the cell fires an action potential. The action of an inhibitory transmitter from one presynaptic neuron may prevent the postsynaptic neuron from reaching the action potential threshold even if it is receiving excitatory stimulation from several other neurons at the same time. An exquisite balance between excitatory and inhibitory processes must be maintained if the nervous system is to function properly. The process of inhibition allows a fine-tuning of neural activity and prevents an uncoordinated discharge of the nervous system, as occurs in a seizure, when large numbers of neurons fire off action potentials in a runaway fashion.

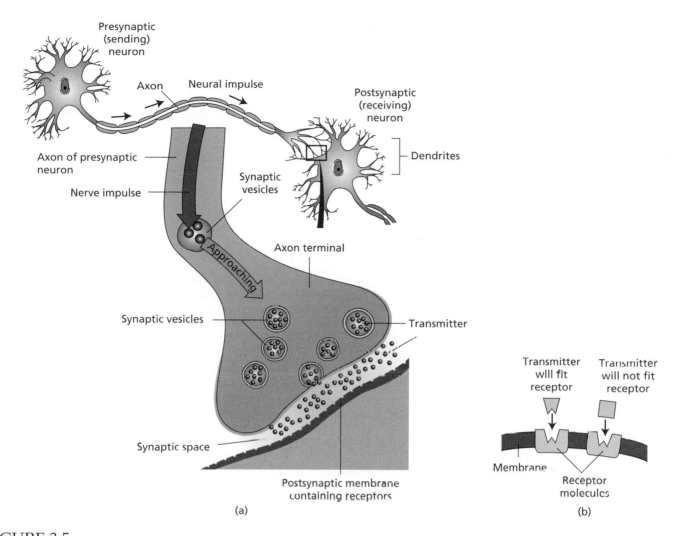

FIGURE 3.5 A synapse between two neurons. The action potential travels to the axon terminals, where it stimulates the release of transmitter molecules from the synaptic vesicles. These molecules travel across the synapse and bind to specially keyed receptor sites on the dendrite of the postsynaptic neuron (a). The lock-and key nature of neurotransmitters and receptor sites is shown in (b). Only transmitters that fit the receptor will influence membrane potentials.

FIGURE 3.6 Neurotransmitters have either excitatory or inhibitory effects on postsynaptic neurons. Excitatory transmitters depolarize the postsynaptic neuron's cell membrane, making it less negative and thereby moving it toward the action potential threshold. Inhibitory neurons hyperpolarize the membrane, making it more negative and therefore more difficult to excite to an action potential.

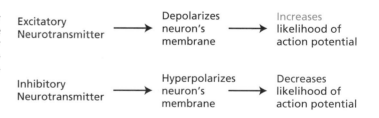

Once a neurotransmitter molecule binds to its receptor, it continues to activate or inhibit the neuron until it is shut off, or *deactivated.* This occurs in two major ways (Fain, 1999). Some transmitter molecules are deactivated by other chemicals located in the synaptic space that break them down into their chemical components. In other instances, the deactivation mechanism is **reuptake,** in which the transmitter molecules are reabsorbed into the presynaptic axon terminal. When the receptor molecule is vacant, the postsynaptic neuron returns to its former resting state, awaiting the next chemical stimulation.

➤ 8. Describe two methods by which neurotransmitter molecules are deactivated at the synapse.

	TABLE 3.1 SOME NEUROTRANSMITTERS AND THEIR EFFECTS		

Neurotransmitter	Major Function	Disorders Associated with Malfunctioning
Acetylcholine (ACh)	Excitatory at synapses involved in muscular movement and memory	Undersupply produces memory loss in Alzheimer's disease.
Norepinephrine	Excitatory and inhibitory functions at various sites. Involved in neural circuits controlling learning, memory, wakefulness, and eating.	Depression (undersupply)
Serotonin	Inhibitory at most sites. Involved in mood, sleep, eating, and arousal, and may be an important transmitter underlying pleasure and pain.	Depression, sleeping, and eating disorders (undersupply)
Dopamine	Excitatory. Involved in voluntary movement, emotional arousal, learning, memory, and experiencing of pleasure or pain.	Parkinson's disease and depression (undersupply) Schizophrenia (oversupply)
GABA	Inhibitory transmitter in motor system	Destruction of GABA-producing neurons in Huntington's disease produces tremors and loss of motor control, as well as personality changes.

Specialized Transmitter Systems

Through the use of chemical transmitters, nature has found an ingenious way of dividing up the brain into systems that are uniquely sensitive to certain messages. There is only one kind of electricity, but there are many shapes that can be assumed by transmitter molecules. Because the various systems in the brain recognize only certain chemical messengers, they are immune to "cross talk" from other systems. At present, 100 to 150 different substances are known or suspected transmitters in the brain, but there may be hundreds more (Fain, 1999; Wayne & Morris, 1999). Each substance has a specific excitatory or inhibitory effect on certain neurons. Table 3.1 lists several of the more important neurotransmitters that have been linked to psychological phenomena.

➤ 9. Describe the roles of (a) acetylcholine, (b) dopamine, (c) serotonin, and (d) endorphins in psychological functions.

Perhaps the best understood neurotransmitter is **acetylcholine (ACh),** which is involved in memory and in muscle activity. Underproduction of acetylcholine is thought to be an important factor in *Alzheimer's disease,* a degenerative brain disorder involving profound memory impairments that afflicts between 5 and 10 percent of all people over 65 years of age (Ron & David, 1997). Reductions in ACh weaken or deactivate neural circuitry that stores memories.

Acetylcholine is also an excitatory transmitter at the synapses where neurons activate muscle cells (Sherwood, 1991). Drugs that block the action of ACh can therefore prevent muscle activation, resulting in muscular paralysis. One example occurs in *botulism,* a serious type of food poisoning that can result from improperly canned food. The toxin formed by the botulinum bacteria blocks the release of ACh from the axon terminal, resulting in a potentially fatal paralysis of the muscles, including those of the respiratory system. The opposite effect on ACh occurs with the bite of the black widow spider. The spider's venom produces a torrent of ACh, resulting in violent muscle contractions, convulsions, and possible death. Thus although botulism and black widow venom affect ACh synapses in different ways, they can have equally fatal effects.

The treatment of emotionally disturbed people has been revolutionized by the development of psychoactive drugs that affect experience and behavior. Like the poisons described above, these drugs operate by either enhancing or inhibiting the actions of certain transmitters at the synapse. For example, abnormally high concentrations of **dopamine,** an excitatory transmitter, have been found in the brains of patients suffering from schizophrenia, a severe disorder of thought, emotion, and behavior (Depue, 1991). Researchers speculate that one factor in schizophrenia may be overactivity in the brain's dopamine transmitter system, producing disordered thinking, hallucinations, and other psychotic symptoms. Certain *antipsychotic drugs* fit like keys into the receptor "locks" meant for dopamine, thus blocking dopamine from overstimulating neurons and producing the symptoms (LeMoal, 1999; Robinson, 1997).

Quite a different mechanism occurs in the treatment of depression. Depression involves an underactivity of **serotonin,** a neurotransmitter that enhances mood, eating, sleep, and sexual behavior. Antidepressant drugs increase serotonin activity in several ways. The drug Prozac blocks the reuptake of serotonin from the synaptic space, allowing serotonin molecules to remain active and exert their mood-elevating effects on depressed patients. Other antidepressant drugs work on a different deactivating mechanism. They inhibit the activity of enzymes in the synaptic space that deactivate serotonin by breaking it down into simpler chemicals. In so doing, they prolong serotonin activity at the synapse.

Endorphins are another important family of neurotransmitters. **Endorphins** reduce pain and increase feelings of well-being. They bind to the same receptors as the ones activated by opiate drugs, such as opium and morphine, which produce similar psychological effects. We discuss the endorphins in greater detail in Chapter 4.

Most neurotransmitters have their excitatory or inhibitory effects only on specific neurons that have receptors for them. Others, called **neuromodulators,** have a more widespread and generalized influence on synaptic transmission. These substances circulate through the brain and either increase or decrease (i.e., modulate) the sensitivity of thousands, perhaps millions, of neurons to their specific transmitters. The best-known neuromodulator is the endorphins, which travel through the brain's circulatory system and inhibit pain transmission while enhancing neural activity that produces pleasurable feelings. Other neuromodulators play important roles in functions such as eating, sleep, and stress. Thus some neurotransmitters have very specific effects, whereas others have more general effects on neural activity.

❯ THE NERVOUS SYSTEM

The nervous system is the body's master control center. Three major types of neurons carry out the system's input, output, and integration functions. **Sensory neurons** carry input messages from the sense organs to the spinal cord and brain. **Motor neurons** transmit output impulses from the brain and spinal cord to the body's muscles and organs. Finally, there are neurons that link the input and output functions. **Interneurons**, which far outnumber sensory and motor neurons, perform connective or associative functions within the nervous system. For example, interneurons would allow us to recognize a tune by linking the sensory input from the song we're hearing with the memory of that song stored elsewhere in the brain. The activity of interneurons makes possible the complexity of our higher mental functions, emotions, and behavioral capabilities.

➤ 10. What are the three major types of neurons? What are their functions?

The nervous system can be broken down into several interrelated subsystems (Figure 3.7). The two major divisions are the **central nervous system,** consisting of all the neurons in the brain and spinal cord, and the **peripheral nervous system,** comprising all the neurons that connect the central nervous system with the muscles, glands, and sensory receptors.

➤ 11. Differentiate between the central nervous system and the peripheral nervous system. What are the two divisions of the peripheral nervous system?

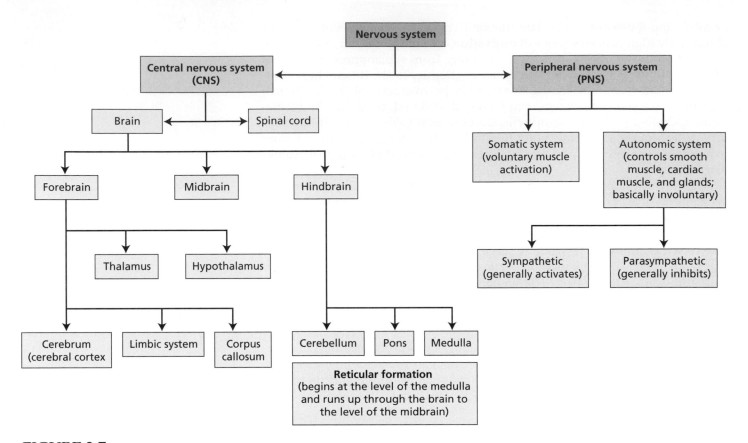

FIGURE 3.7   Structural organization of the nervous system.

The Peripheral Nervous System

The peripheral nervous system contains all the neural structures that lie outside of the brain and spinal cord. Its specialized neurons help carry out the input and output functions that are necessary for us to sense what is going on inside and outside our bodies and to respond with our muscles and glands. The peripheral nervous system has two major divisions, the somatic nervous system and the autonomic nervous system.

The Somatic Nervous System

The **somatic nervous system** consists of the *sensory neurons* that are specialized to transmit messages from the eyes, ears, and other sensory receptors, and the *motor neurons* that send messages from the brain and spinal cord to the muscles that control our voluntary movements. The axons of sensory neurons group together like the many strands of a rope to form *sensory nerves,* and motor neuron axons combine to form *motor nerves.* (Inside the brain and spinal cord, nerves are called *tracts.*) As you read this page, sensory neurons located in your eyes are sending impulses into a complex network of specialized visual tracts that course through your brain. At the same time, motor neurons are stimulating the eye movements that allow you to scan the lines of type and turn the pages. The somatic system thus allows you to sense and respond to your environment.

The Autonomic Nervous System

The body's internal environment is regulated largely through the activities of the **autonomic nervous system,** which controls the glands and the smooth

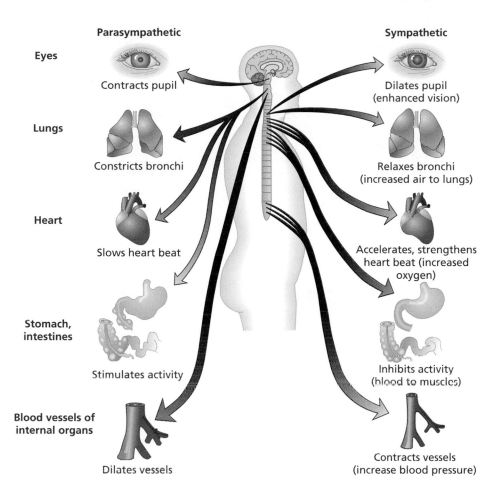

Parasympathetic   **Sympathetic**

Eyes

Contracts pupil   Dilates pupil
                                        (enhanced vision)

Lungs

Constricts bronchi   Relaxes bronchi
                                        (increased air to lungs)

Heart

Slows heart beat   Accelerates, strengthens
                                        heart beat (increased
                                        oxygen)

**Stomach,
intestines**

Stimulates activity   Inhibits activity
                                        (blood to muscles)

**Blood vessels of
internal organs**

Dilates vessels   Contracts vessels
                                        (increase blood pressure)

FIGURE 3.8 The sympathetic branch of the autonomic nervous system arouses the body and speeds up its vital processes, whereas the parasympathetic division slows down body processes. The two divisions work together to maintain an equilibrium within the body.

(involuntary) muscles that form the heart, the blood vessels, and the lining of the stomach and intestines. The autonomic system is largely concerned with involuntary functions, such as respiration, circulation, and digestion, and it is also involved in many aspects of motivation, emotional behavior, and stress responses. It consists of two subdivisions, the sympathetic nervous system and the parasympathetic nervous system (Figure 3.8). Typically, these two divisions affect the same organ or gland in opposing ways.

The **sympathetic nervous system** has an activation or arousal function, and it tends to act as a total unit. For example, when you encounter a stressful situation, your sympathetic nervous system simultaneously speeds your heart rate so it can pump more blood to your muscles, dilates your pupils so more light can enter the eye and improve your vision, slows down your digestive system so that blood can be transferred to the muscles, increases your rate of respiration so your body can get more oxygen, and, in general, mobilizes your body to confront the stressor. This is sometimes called the *fight-or-flight response*.

Compared with the sympathetic branch, which tends to act as a unit, the parasympathetic system is far more specific in its opposing actions, affecting one or a few organs at a time. The **parasympathetic nervous system** slows down body processes and maintains a state of tranquility. Thus your sympathetic system speeds up your heart rate; your parasympathetic system slows it down. By working together to maintain equilibrium in our internal organs, the two divisions can maintain *homeostasis*, a delicately balanced or constant internal state. Some acts also require a coordinated sequence of sympathetic and parasympathetic activities. For example, sexual function in the male involves penile erection (through parasympathetic dilation of blood vessels) followed by ejaculation (a primarily sympathetic function) (Masters et al., 1988).

➤ 12. Describe the two divisions of the autonomic nervous system, as well as their roles in maintaining homeostasis.

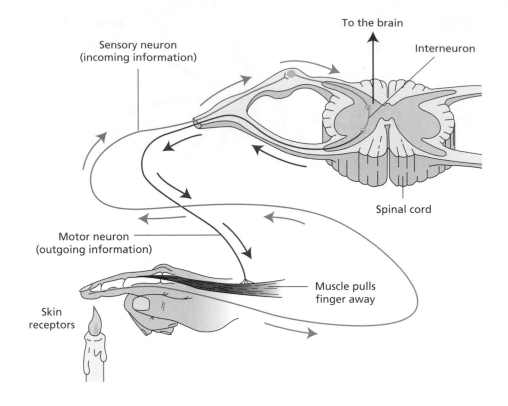

FIGURE 3.9 A cross section of the spinal cord shows the organization of sensory and motor nerves. Sensory and motor nerves enter and exit the spinal cord on both sides of the spinal column. Interneurons within the H-shaped spinal gray matter can serve a connective function, as shown here, but in many cases, sensory neurons can also synapse directly with motor neurons. At this level of the nervous system, reflex activity is possible without involving the brain.

The Central Nervous System

More than any other system in our body, the central nervous system distinguishes us from other creatures. This system contains the spinal cord, which connects most parts of the peripheral nervous system with the brain, and the brain itself.

The Spinal Cord

Most nerves enter and leave the central nervous system by way of the spinal cord, a structure that in a human adult is 16 to 18 inches long and about one inch in diameter. The spinal cord's neurons are protected by the vertebrae (bones of the spine). When the spinal cord is viewed in cross section (Figure 3.9), its central portion resembles an H, or a butterfly. The H-shaped portion consists largely of gray-colored neuron cell bodies and their interconnections. Surrounding the gray matter are white-colored myelinated axons that connect various levels of the spinal cord with each other and with the higher centers of the brain. Entering the back side of the spinal cord along its length are sensory nerves. Motor nerves exit the spinal cord's front side.

> ➤ 13. How do spinal reflexes occur?

Some simple stimulus-response sequences, known as *spinal reflexes,* can be triggered at the level of the spinal cord without any involvement of the brain. For example, if you touch something hot, sensory receptors in your skin trigger nerve impulses in sensory nerves that flash into your spinal cord and synapse inside with interneurons. The interneurons then excite motor neurons that send impulses to your hand, so that it pulls away. Other interneurons simultaneously carry the "Hot!" message up the spinal cord to your brain, but it is a good thing that you don't have to wait for the brain to tell you what to do in such emergencies. Getting messages to and from the brain takes slightly longer, so the spinal cord reflex system significantly reduces reaction time, and, in this case, potential tissue damage.

The Brain

The three pounds of protein, fat, and fluid that you carry around inside your skull is the real "you." It is also the most complex structure in the known universe and the only one that can wonder about itself. As befits this biological marvel, your brain is the most active energy consumer of all your body organs. Although the brain accounts for only about 2 percent of your total body weight, your brain consumes about 20 percent of the oxygen you use in a resting state (Robinson, 1997). Moreover, the brain never rests; its rate of energy metabolism is relatively constant day and night. In fact, when you dream, the brain's metabolic rate actually increases slightly (Hobson, 1996).

How can this rather nondescript blob of grayish tissue discover the principle of relativity, build the Hubble Telescope, and produce great works of art, music, and literature? Answering such questions requires the ability to study the brain and how it functions. To do so, neuroscientists use a diverse set of tools and procedures.

Unlocking the Secrets of the Brain

More has been learned in the past three decades about the brain and its role in behavior than was known in all the preceding ages. This knowledge explosion is due in large part to revolutionary technical advances that have provided scientists with new research tools, as well as to the contributions of psychological research on brain-behavior relations. Investigators can use a variety of methods to study the brain's structures and activities.

Neuropsychological tests.   Psychologists have developed a variety of *neuropsychological tests* to measure verbal and nonverbal behaviors that are known to be affected by particular types of brain damage (Lezak, 1995). These tests are used in clinical evaluations of people who may have suffered brain damage through accident or disease. They are also important research tools. For example, Figure 3.10 shows a portion of a Trail Making Test, used to test memory and planning. Scores on the test give an indication of the type and severity of damage the person may have. Neuropsychological tests of this kind have provided much information about brain-behavior relations.

Destruction and stimulation techniques.   Experimental studies are another useful method of learning about the brain. Researchers can produce brain damage (lesions) under carefully controlled conditions in which specific nervous tissue is destroyed with electricity, with cold or heat, or with chemicals. They can also surgically remove some portion of the brain and study the consequences. Most experiments of this kind are performed on animals, but humans can also be studied when accident or disease produces a specific lesion or when abnormal brain tissue must be surgically removed.

An alternative to destroying neurons is stimulating them, which typically produces opposite effects. A specific region of the brain can be stimulated by a mild electric current or by chemicals that excite neurons. Electrodes can be permanently implanted so that the region of interest can be stimulated repeatedly. Some of these electrodes are so tiny that they can stimulate individual neurons. In chemical stimulation studies, a tiny tube is inserted into the brain so that a small amount of the chemical can be delivered directly to the area to be studied. Again, most of these techniques are used with animals, but in many respects, animal and human brains are similar enough in structure and functions that results with animals can often be generalized to humans.

Electrical recording.   Because electrodes can record brain activity as well as stimulate it, it is also possible to "eavesdrop" on the electrical conversations occurring within the brain. Neurons' electrical activity can be measured by inserting small electrodes in particular areas of the brain or even in individual neurons.

➤ 14. Describe four methods used to study brain-behavior relations.

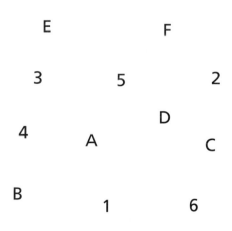

FIGURE 3.10 The Trail Making Test consists of a randomly scattered set of numbers and letters. On this timed test, the patient must connect the numbers and letters consecutively with a continuous line, or "trail" (i.e., A to 1 to B to 2 to C to 3, and so on). People with certain kinds of brain damage have trouble alternating between the numbers and letters because they cannot retain a plan in memory long enough, and poor test performance picks up this deficit.

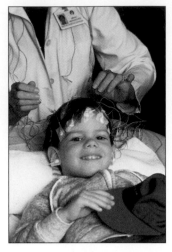

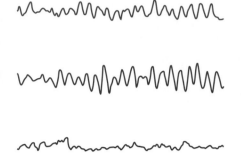

(a)

(b)

(c)

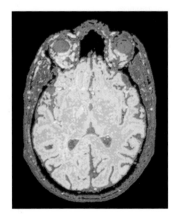

(d)

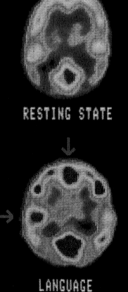

(e)

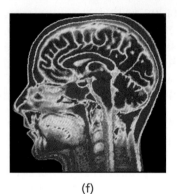

(f)

FIGURE 3.11 The electroencephalogram (EEG), shown in (a) records the electrical activity of large groups of neurons in the brain by means of electrodes attached to the scalp. An EEG readout is shown in (b). Various brain scanning machines, such as the one shown in (c), produce different types of images. The CT scan uses narrow beams of X-rays to construct a composite picture of brain structures (d). PET scans (e) record the amount of radioactive substance that collects in various brain regions to assess brain activity. MRI scanners produce vivid pictures of brain structures (f). Functional MRI procedures take images in rapid succession, showing neural activity as it occurs.

In addition to measuring individual voices, scientists can tune in to "crowd noise" by placing larger electrodes on the scalp to measure the activity of large groups of neurons with the **electroencephalogram (EEG)** (Figure 3.11*a, b*). Although the EEG is a rather gross measure that taps the electrical activity of thousands of neurons in many parts of the brain, specific EEG patterns correspond to certain states of consciousness, such as wakefulness and sleep. Clinicians also use the EEG to detect abnormal electrical patterns that signal the presence of brain disorders.

Brain imaging. The newest tools of discovery are imaging techniques that permit neuroscientists to peer into the living brain (Figure 3.11*c*). The most important of these technological "windows" are CT scans, PET scans, and magnetic resonance imaging (MRI).

Developed in the 1970s, **computerized axial tomography (CT)** scans use X-ray technology to study brain structures (Peyster, 2000). A highly focused beam of X rays takes pictures of narrow slices of the brain. A computer analyzes

➤ 15. How are CT scans, PET scans, and MRIs produced, and how is each used in brain research?

the X-rayed slices and creates pictures of the brain's interior from many different angles (Figure 3.11d). Pinpointing where injuries or deterioration have occurred helps clarify relations between brain damage and psychological functioning. CT scans are 100 times more sensitive than standard X-ray procedures, and the technological advance was so dramatic that its developers, Allan Cormack and Godfrey Hounsfield, were awarded the 1979 Nobel Prize for Medicine.

Whereas CT scans provide pictures of brain structures, **positron emission tomography (PET)** scans measure brain activity, including metabolism, blood flow, and neurotransmitter activity (Hornak, 2000; Ron & David, 1997). PET is based on the fact that glucose, a natural sugar, is the major nutrient of neurons. Thus when neurons are active, they consume more glucose. To prepare a patient for a PET scan, a harmless form of radioactive glucose is injected into the bloodstream and travels to the brain, where it circulates in the blood supply. The energy emitted by the radioactive substance is measured by the PET scan, and the data are fed into a computer that uses the readings to produce a color picture of the brain on a display screen (Figure 3.11c, e). Researchers can tell how active particular neurons are by using the PET scan to measure the amount of radioactive glucose that accumulates in them. If a person is performing a mental reasoning task, for example, a researcher can tell by the glucose concentration pattern which parts of the brain were activated by the task (Raichle, 1994). Using the PET scan, brain activity can be studied in relation to cognitive processes, behavior, and even forms of mental illness.

Magnetic resonance imaging (MRI) combines features of CT and PET scans and can be used to study both brain structures and brain activity (Chakeres, 2000). MRI creates images based on how atoms in living tissue respond to a magnetic pulse delivered by the device. MRI can make out details one-tenth the size that can be detected by CT scans, and it distinguishes much better among different types of brain tissue (Leondes, 1997). To obtain an MRI, the part of the body to be studied is placed in the hollow core of a long magnetic cylinder and the atoms in the subject's body are exposed to a uniform magnetic field. The field is then altered, and when the magnetic field is shut off, the magnetic energy absorbed by the atoms in the tissue emits a small electrical voltage. The voltage is picked up by detectors and relayed to a computer for analysis. In addition to providing color images of the tissue, MRI can also tell researchers which chemicals (such as neurotransmitters) are active in the tissue (Figure 3.11f).

The conventional MRI yields pictures taken several minutes apart. A recent advance in MRI technology is *functional MRI (FMRI)*, which can produce pictures of blood flow in the brain taken less than a second apart (Baert et al., 1999). Researchers can now, quite literally, watch "live" presentations as different regions of the brain "light up" when subjects are given various types of tasks to perform. Researchers can thereby identify brain regions involved in specific psychological functions. In this chapter's *Research Close-up*, we will see FMRI's value in providing new information about differences between men and women in language-related brain activity.

Advances in brain research have made this area one of the most exciting frontiers of psychology. Driven by its intense desire to "know thyself," the brain is beginning to yield its many secrets. Yet many important questions remain. This should not surprise us for, as one observer noted, "If the brain were so simple that we could understand it, we would be so simple that we couldn't" (Pugh, 1977).

The Hierarchical Brain: Structures and Behavioral Functions

In an evolutionary sense, your brain is far older than you are, for it represents perhaps 500 million years of evolutionary development and fine tuning (Roth, 2000). The human brain can be likened to a living archaeological site, with the

➤ 16. In what sense might the structure of the human brain mirror evolutionary development?

more recently developed structures built atop structures from the distant evolutionary past. The structures at the brain's core govern the basic physiological functions, such as breathing and heart rate, that keep us alive. These we share with all other vertebrates (animals having backbones). Built upon these basic structures are newer systems that involve progressively more complex functions—sensing, emoting, wanting, thinking, reasoning. Evolutionary theorists believe that as genetic variation and recombination sculpted these newer structures over time, natural selection favored their retention because animals who had them were more likely to survive in changing environments. The crowning feature of brain development is the cerebrum, the biological seat of Einstein's scientific genius, Mozart's creativity, Mother Teresa's compassion, and that which makes you a unique human being.

The major structures of the human brain, together with their psychological functions, are shown in Figure 3.12. The brain has traditionally been divided into three major subdivisions: the hindbrain, which is the lowest and most primitive level of the brain; the midbrain, which lies above the hindbrain; and the forebrain.

The Hindbrain

> 17. Which behavioral functions are controlled by the hindbrain structures, namely, the medulla, the pons, and the cerebellum? What occurs with damage to these structures?

As the spinal cord enters the brain, it enlarges to form the structures that compose the stalklike **brain stem.** Attached to the brain stem is the other major portion of the hindbrain, the cerebellum.

The brain stem: life support systems.   The medulla is the first structure encountered after leaving the spinal cord. Well developed at birth, the 1.5 inch-long **medulla** plays an important role in vital body functions such as heart rate and respiration. Because of your medulla, these functions occur automatically. Damage to the medulla usually results in death or, at best, the need to be maintained on life support systems. Suppression of medulla activity can occur at high levels of alcohol intoxication, resulting in death by heart or respiratory failure (Blessing, 1997).

The medulla is also a two-way thoroughfare for all the sensory and motor nerve tracts coming up from the spinal cord and descending from the brain. Most of these tracts cross over within the medulla, so the left side of the brain receives sensory input from and exerts motor control over the right side of the body, and the right side of the brain serves the left side of the body. Why this crossover occurs is one of the unsolved mysteries of brain function.

The **pons** (meaning *bridge* in Latin) lies just above the medulla, and it indeed serves as a bridge carrying nerve impulses between higher and lower levels of the nervous system. The pons also has clusters of neurons that help regulate sleep and are involved in dreaming, and it contains motor neurons that control the muscles and glands of the face and neck. Like the medulla, the pons helps to control vital functions, especially respiration, and damage to it can produce death.

The cerebellum: motor coordination center.   The cerebellum ("little brain" in Latin) does indeed look like a miniature brain attached to the rear of the brain stem directly above the pons. Its wrinkled cortex, or covering, consists mainly of gray cell bodies (gray matter). The **cerebellum** is concerned primarily with muscular movement coordination, but it also plays a role in certain types of learning and memory.

Specific motor movements are initiated in higher brain centers, but their timing and coordination depend on the cerebellum (Thatch et al., 1992). The cerebellum regulates complex, rapidly changing movements that require exquisite timing, such as those of a ballet dancer or a competitive diver. Within the animal kingdom, cats have an especially well-developed cerebellum, helping to account for their graceful movement abilities (Altman & Bayer, 1996).

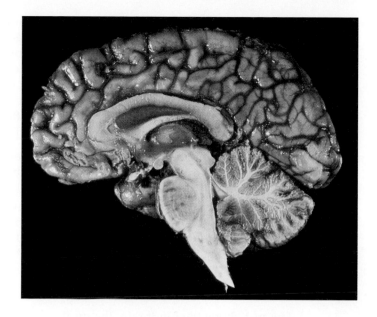

Corpus callosum
Bridge of fibers passing
information between the
two cerebral hemispheres

Thalamus
Relay center for
incoming sensory
information

Hypothalamus
Regulates basic biological
needs: hunger, thirst,
temperature control

Pituitary gland
"Master" gland that regulates
other endocrine glands

Hippocampus
Limbic system structure involved
in learning and memory

Pons
Involved in sleep
and arousal

Medulla
Regulates vital functions
such as breathing and
circulation

Reticular formation
Group of fibers that
carry stimulation
related to sleep and
arousal through
brainstem

Spinal cord
Transmits information
between brain and
rest of body; handles
simple reflexes

Cerebrum
Sensing, thinking,
learning, emotion,
consciousness, and
voluntary movement

Amygdala
Limbic system
structure
involved in
emotion and
aggression

Cerebellum
Coordinates fine
muscle movement,
balance

Brainstem

FIGURE 3.12 The major structures of the brain and their functions are shown as they would appear if the brain was sectioned at its midline, as in the photo.

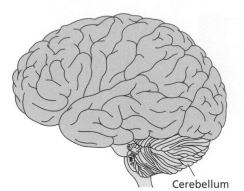

FIGURE 3.13 The movement-control functions of the cerebellum are easily disrupted by alcohol, providing the neural basis for the sobriety tests administered by police.

➤ 18. Describe the roles played by the ascending and descending reticular formation. Why is it called the "brain's gatekeeper"?

The motor control functions of the cerebellum are easily disrupted by alcohol, producing the coordination difficulties that police look for in their roadside tests of sobriety (Ito, 1984). Intoxicated people may be unable to walk a straight line or touch their nose with their index finger (Figure 3.13). Physical damage to the cerebellum results in severe motor disturbances characterized by jerky, uncoordinated movements, as well as an inability to perform habitual movements such as walking. The behavioral effects of a rapidly developing cerebellar tumor are apparent in the following clinical case:

> Ed could no longer walk a straight line. His gait involved wide separation of his legs. The timing of his steps was jerky and irregular, causing him to lurch from side to side. . . . By the fifth day he could no longer stand without assistance, and he began to display rapid and jerky eye movements. Ed was admitted to a hospital, where imaging techniques revealed a cerebellar tumor. Surgical removal of the tumor resulted in a marked improvement in his motor coordination. (Gazzaniga et al., 1979)

The Midbrain

Lying just above the hindbrain, the **midbrain** contains clusters of sensory and motor neurons, as well as many sensory and motor fiber tracts that connect higher and lower portions of the nervous system. The sensory portion of the midbrain contains important relay centers for the visual and auditory systems. Here, nerve impulses from the eyes and ears are organized and sent to forebrain structures involved in visual and auditory perception (Nolte, 1998). The midbrain also contains motor neurons that control eye movements. For example, if you see movement out of the corner of your eye, midbrain activity causes your eyes to swing toward the source of the movement in order to identify it.

The reticular formation: the brain's gatekeeper. Buried within the midbrain is a finger-shaped structure that extends from the hindbrain up into the lower portions of the forebrain. This structure receives its name from its resemblance under a microscope to a *reticulum,* or net. The **reticular formation** acts as a kind of sentry, both alerting higher centers of the brain that messages are coming and then either blocking those messages or allowing them to go forward. The reticular formation has an *ascending* part, which sends input to higher regions of the brain to alert it, and a *descending* portion, through which higher brain centers can either admit or block out sensory input.

The reticular formation has attracted a great deal of interest from psychologists because of its central role in consciousness, sleep, and attention. The ascending reticular formation rouses higher centers in the brain, preparing them to receive input from our sense organs. Without reticular stimulation of higher brain regions, sensory messages do not register in conscious awareness even though the nerve impulses may reach the appropriate higher areas of the brain. It is as if the brain is not "awake" enough to notice them. In fact, some general anesthetics work by deactivating neurons of the ascending reticular formation, producing a state of unconsciousness in which the sensory impulses that ordinarily would be experienced as pain never "register" in the sensory areas of the brain involved in pain perception (Derogatis, 1986).

Sleep, wakefulness, and attention are also affected by the reticular formation. In a classic series of experiments in the late 1940s, researchers discovered that electrical stimulation of different portions of the reticular formation can produce instant sleep in a wakeful cat and sudden wakefulness in a sleeping animal (Moruzzi & Magoun, 1949; Marshall & Magoun, 1997). As you might expect, severe damage to the reticular formation can produce a permanent coma (Roland, 1997).

Attention is an active process in which only important or meaningful sensory inputs get through to our consciousness. Other inputs have to be toned down or completely blocked out or we'd be overwhelmed by stimulation. The descending reticular formation plays an important part in this process, serving as a kind of "gate" through which some inputs are admitted while others are blocked out by signals coming down from higher brain centers (Van Zomeren & Brouwer, 1994). We hope it is operating for you right now, as you focus on these words and "block out" other sights, sounds, and body sensations that could distract you from our messages.

The Forebrain

The most profound biological difference between your brain and that of a lower animal is the size and complexity of your forebrain, or *cerebrum*. The **forebrain** consists of two large cerebral hemispheres, a left side and a right side, that wrap around the brain stem like the two halves of a cut grapefruit might wrap around a spoon. The outer portion of the forebrain has a thin covering, or cortex, and there are a number of important structures buried in the central regions of the hemispheres.

The thalamus: the brain's sensory switchboard. The thalamus is located above the midbrain. It resembles two small footballs, one within each cerebral hemisphere. The **thalamus** is an important sensory relay station and has sometimes been likened to a switchboard that organizes input from sense organs and routes them to the appropriate areas of the brain. The visual, auditory, and body senses (balance and equilibrium) all have major relay stations in the thalamus. In each case, nerve tracts from the sensory receptors (e.g., the eyes or the ears) are sent to specific areas of the thalamus. There they synapse with neurons that send the messages on their way to the higher brain regions that create our perceptions (Jones et al., 1997).

➤ 19. What is the role of the thalamus in sensory input, and possibly in thought and perceptual disorders?

Because the thalamus plays such a key role in routing sensory information to higher brain regions, disrupted thalamic functioning can produce a highly confusing world for its victims. In research at the National Institute of Mental Health (NIMH) carried out by Nancy Andreason and her coworkers (1994), MRIs from 39 schizophrenic men were compared with those of 47 normal male volunteers. The brain images showed specific abnormalities in the thalamus of the "schizophrenic" brains. The researchers suggested that malfunctioning in this structure could help account for the confused thinking and disordered attention that characterize schizophrenic behavior. Perhaps the thalamus is sending garbled sensory information to the higher regions of the brain. If substantiated by future research, the NIMH discovery may provide increased understanding of this baffling mental disorder.

The hypothalamus: motivation and emotion. The hypothalamus (literally, "under the thalamus") consists of tiny groups of neuron cell bodies that lie at the base of the brain, above the roof of the mouth. The **hypothalamus** plays a major role in many aspects of motivational and emotional behavior, including sexual behavior, temperature regulation, sleeping, eating, drinking, aggression, and the expression of emotion. Damage to the hypothalamus can disrupt all of these behaviors. For example, destruction of one area of a male's hypothalamus results in a complete loss of sex drive; damage to another portion produces an overwhelming urge to eat that results in extreme obesity. Recently, neuroscientists at the University of Texas Southwestern Medical School found that certain neurons in the hypothalamus manufacture a substance which they called *orexins* (after the Greek word for hunger) that stimulates eating. When they gave orexin to laboratory rats, they ate 8 to 10 times more food than they ordinarily would over a period of hours (Yanagisawa et al., 1998). This discovery holds out the hope that it might be possible to control both undereating (as occurs in some cancer patients) and obesity by producing medicines that either enhance or inhibit orexin activity at the synapses where eating is controlled.

➤ 20. What role does the hypothalamus have in motivated behavior, hunger, pleasure-pain, and hormonal functions?

The hypothalamus has important connections with the endocrine system, the body's collection of hormone-producing glands. Through its connection with the pituitary gland (the master gland that exerts control over the other glands of the endocrine system), the hypothalamus directly controls many hormonal secretions that regulate sexual development and behavior, metabolism, and reactions to stress.

The hypothalamus is also involved in our experiences of pleasure and displeasure. The discovery of this fact occurred quite by accident. In 1953, psychologist James Olds was conducting an experiment to study the effects of electrical stimulation in a rat's midbrain reticular formation. One of the electrodes missed the target and was mistakenly implanted in the hypothalamus. The investigators noticed that whenever this rat was stimulated, it repeated whatever it had just done, as if it had been rewarded for that behavior. In a variety of learning situations, other animals with similarly implanted electrodes also learned and performed behaviors in order to receive what was clearly an electrical reward. Some of the rats pressed a pedal up to 5,000 times in an hour in order to receive their electrical reward until they dropped from exhaustion. Stimulation of other nearby areas produced just the opposite effect—a tendency to stop performing any behavior that was followed by stimulation, as if the animal had been punished. The investigators concluded that they had discovered what they called "reward and punishment centers" in the brain, some of which were in the hypothalamus (Olds, 1958; White & Milner, 1992; Wise & Rompre, 1989).

Humans who have had electrodes implanted in their brains to search for abnormal brain tissue have reported experiencing pleasure when electrically stimulated in these regions of the brain (Heath, 1972). One patient reportedly proposed marriage to the experimenter while being so stimulated. Thus a misplaced electrode led to a discovery that neural events occurring in the hypothalamus and adjacent areas have important roles in motivation.

The limbic system: memory and goal-directed behavior.   As we continue our journey up through the brain, we come to the limbic system, a set of structures lying deep within the cerebral hemispheres. These structures, which are shaped like a wishbone, have an important partnership with the hypothalamus. The **limbic system** helps to coordinate behaviors needed to satisfy motivational and emotional urges that arise in the hypothalamus, and it is also involved in memory. Many instinctive activities in lower animals, such as mating, attacking, feeding, and fleeing from danger appear to be organized by the limbic system (Davis, 1992). Human behaviors are similarly organized into goal-directed sequences. If certain parts of your limbic system were injured, you would be unable to carry out organized sequences of actions to satisfy your needs. A small distraction would make you forget what you had set out to do.

Two key structures in the limbic system are the hippocampus and the amygdala. The **hippocampus** is involved in forming and retrieving memories. Damage there can result in severe memory impairment for recent events (Schacter, 2000; Squire, 1992). The **amygdala** organizes emotional response patterns, particularly those linked to aggression and fear (LeDoux, 1998). Electrically stimulating certain areas of the amygdala causes animals to snarl and assume aggressive postures (Figure 3.14), whereas stimulation of other areas results in a fearful inability to respond aggressively, even in self-defense. For example, a normally aggressive and hungry cat will cower in fear from a tiny mouse placed in its cage. The amygdala is a key part of a larger control system for anger and fear that also involves other brain regions (Borod, 2000).

An interesting feature of the amygdala is that it can produce emotional responses without the higher centers of the brain "knowing" that we are emotionally aroused. This may provide a possible explanation of clinicians' observations of "unconscious" emotional responses (LeDoux, 1998).

➤ 21. What is the possible relation between the hypothalamus and the limbic system in relation to emotion and motivation? What roles do the hippocampus and amygdala play in psychological functions?

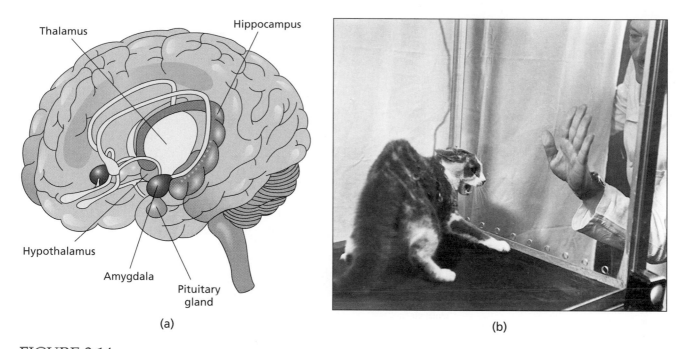

Thalamus

Hippocampus

Hypothalamus

Amygdala

Pituitary
gland

(a)

(b)

FIGURE 3.14 The limbic system structures are shown in (a). Electrical stimulation of the amygdala, as in (b) can produce an immediate aggressive response.

Finally, like the hypothalamus, the limbic system contains "reward" and "punishment" areas that have important motivational functions. Certain drugs, such as cocaine and marijuana, seem to induce pleasure by stimulating limbic reward areas that use dopamine as their neurotransmitter (Holloway, 1991; LeMoal, 1999). As noted earlier, lowered dopamine activity is found in people who are depressed (Depue & Iacono, 1989). These observations may provide important clues to understanding how the amygdala is involved in the creation of pleasure and pain.

The Cerebral Cortex: Crown of the Brain

The **cerebral cortex**, a 1/4-inch-thick sheet of gray (unmyelinated) cells that form the outermost layer of the human brain, is the crowning achievement of brain evolution. Fish and amphibians have no cerebral cortex, and the progression from more primitive to more advanced mammals is marked by a dramatic increase in the proportion of cortical tissue. In humans, the cortex constitutes fully 80 percent of brain tissue (Nolte, 1998).

The cerebral cortex is not essential for physical survival in the way that the brain stem structures are, but it is essential for a human quality of living. How much so is evident in this description of patients who, as a result of an accident during prenatal development, were born without a cerebral cortex:

> Some of these individuals may survive for years, in one case of mine for twenty years. From these cases, it appears that the human [lacking a cortex] sleeps and wakes; . . . reacts to hunger, loud sounds, and crude visual stimuli by movement of eyes, eyelids, and facial muscles; . . . may see and hear, . . . may be able to taste and smell, to reject the unpalatable and accept such food as it likes. . . . [They can] utter crude sounds, can cry and smile, showing displeasure when hungry and pleasure, in a babyish way, when being sung to; [they] may be able to perform spontaneously crude [limb] movements. (Cairns, 1952, p. 109)

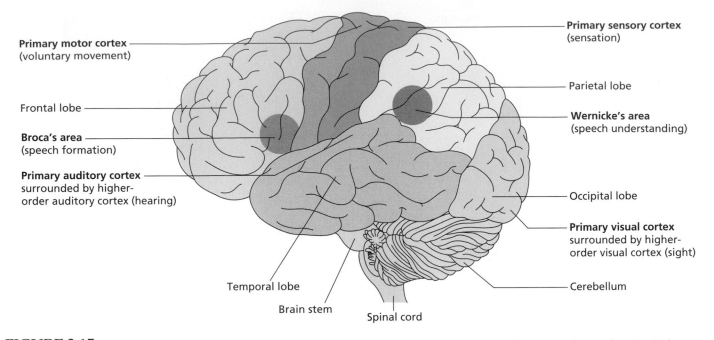

FIGURE 3.15 Division of the brain into frontal, parietal, occipital, and temporal lobes, and localization of sensory and motor functions in the cortex. The remainder is primarily association cortex, consisting of interneurons involved in complex psychological functions, such as perception and reasoning.

Because the cortex is wrinkled and convoluted, like a wadded-up piece of paper, a great amount of cortical tissue is compressed into a relatively small space inside the skull. Perhaps 75 percent of the cortex's total surface area lies within its *fissures,* or canyonlike folds. Three of these fissures are important landmarks. One large fissure runs up the front and along the top of the brain, dividing it into right and left hemispheres. Another major fissure within each hemisphere divides the cerebrum into front and rear halves, and the third fissure runs from front to rear along the side of the brain. On the basis of these landmarks, neurologists have divided each hemisphere into four lobes: **frontal, parietal, occipital,** and **temporal** (Figure 3.15).

Each of the four cerebral lobes is associated with particular sensory and motor functions (also shown in Figure 3.15). Speech and skeletal motor functions are localized in the frontal lobe. The area governing body sensations is located in the parietal lobe immediately behind the *central fissure,* which separates the frontal and parietal lobes. The brain's visual area is located in the occipital lobe at the back of the brain. Finally, messages from the auditory system are sent to a region in the top of the temporal lobe (Robinson, 1997). The large areas in Figure 3.16 that are not associated with sensory or motor functions (about three-fourths of the cortex) are *association cortex* involved in mental processes such as thought, memory, and perception.

Most sensory systems send information to specific regions of the cerebral cortex. Motor systems that control the activity of skeletal muscles are situated in other cortical regions. The basic organization of the cortex's sensory and motor areas is quite similar from rats to humans. Let us explore these regions more closely.

The motor cortex.   The **motor cortex,** which controls the 600 or more muscles involved in voluntary body movements, lies at the rear of the frontal lobe adjacent to the central fissure. Each hemisphere governs movement on the opposite side of the body. Thus severe damage to the right motor cortex would produce paralysis in the left side of the body. The left side of Figure 3.16 shows the relative organization of function within the motor cortex. As you can see, specific body areas are represented in different parts of the motor cortex, and the amount of cortex

➤ 22. What are the four lobes of the brain, and where are they located?

➤ 23. Differentiate between sensory, motor, and association cortex.

➤ 24. How are the somatic sensory and motor cortexes organized?

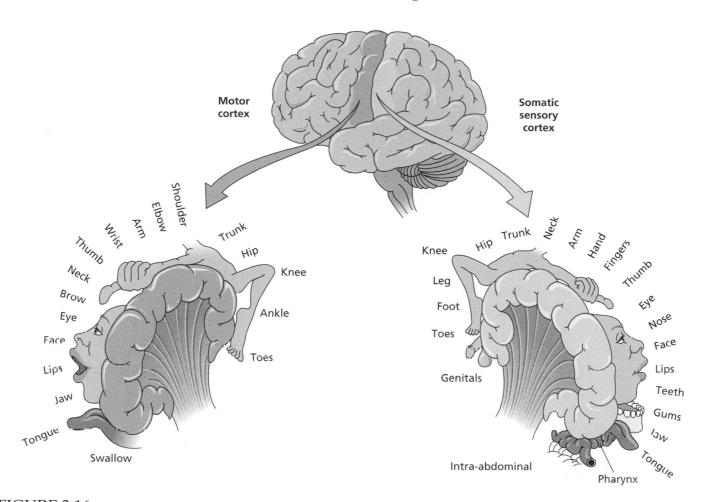

FIGURE 3.16 Both the somatic sensory and the motor cortex are highly specialized so that every site is associated with a particular part of the body. The amount of cortex devoted to each body part is proportional to the sensitivity of that area's motor or sensory functions. Both the sensory and motor cortex are arranged in an upside-down fashion and serve the opposite side of the body.

devoted to each area depends on the complexity of the movements that are carried out by the body part. Note, for example, that the amount of cortical tissue devoted to your fingers is far greater than that devoted to your torso, even though your torso is much larger. If we electrically stimulate a particular point on the motor cortex, movements occur in the muscles governed by that part of the cortex.

The sensory cortex. Specific areas of the cortex receive input from our sensory receptors. With the exception of taste and smell, at least one specific area in the cortex has been identified for each of the senses.

The **somatic sensory cortex** receives sensory input that gives rise to our sensations of heat, touch, cold, and our senses of balance and body movement (kinesthesis). It lies in the parietal lobe just behind the motor cortex, separated from it by the large fissure that divides the frontal lobe from the parietal lobe. As in the case of the motor system, each side of the body sends sensory input to the opposite hemisphere. Like the motor area next to it, the somatic sensory area is basically organized in an upside-down fashion, with the feet being represented near the top of the brain. Likewise, the amount of cortex devoted to each body area is directly proportional to that region's sensory sensitivity. The organization of the sensory cortex is shown on the right side of Figure 3.16, as is the proportion of cortex devoted to each body area. As far as your sensory cortex is concerned, you are mainly fingers, lips, and tongue. Notice also that the organization of the sensory cortex is such that the body structures it serves lie side by side with those in the motor cortex, an arrangement that enhances sensory-motor interactions in the same body area.

The senses of hearing and sight are well represented in the cortex. The auditory area lies on the surface of the temporal lobe at the side of each hemisphere. Each ear sends messages to the auditory areas of both hemispheres, so the loss of one temporal lobe has little effect on hearing. The major sensory area for vision lies at the rear of the occipital lobe. Here messages from the visual receptors are analyzed, integrated, and translated into sight. As in the auditory system, each eye sends input to both hemispheres.

Within each sensory area, neurons respond to particular aspects of the sensory stimulus; they are tuned in to specific aspects of the environment. Thus certain cells in the visual cortex fire only when we look at a particular kind of stimulus, such as a vertical line or a corner (Hubel & Wiesel, 1979). In the auditory cortex, some neurons fire only in response to high tones, whereas others respond only to tones having some other specific frequency. Many of these single-cell responses are present at birth, suggesting that we are "prewired" to perceive many aspects of our sensory environment (Shair et al., 1991). Nonetheless, the sensory cortex, like other parts of the brain, is also sensitive to experience. For example, when people learn to read Braille, the area in the sensory cortex that receives input from the fingertips increases in size, making the person more sensitive to the tiny sets of raised dots (Pool, 1994).

Speech comprehension and production.   Two specific areas that govern the understanding and production of speech are also located in the cortex (Figure 3.17).

➤ 25. Where are Wernicke's and Broca's areas? How are they involved in speech?

Wernicke's area in the temporal lobe is involved in speech comprehension. The area is named for Carl Wernicke, who in 1874 discovered that damage to this cortical region left patients unable to understand written or spoken speech. **Broca's area** in the frontal lobe is involved in the production of speech through its connections with the motor cortex region that controls the muscles used in speech. Its discoverer, Paul Broca, found that damage to this frontal area left patients with the ability to comprehend speech but not to express themselves in words or sentences. These two speech areas normally work in concert when you are conversing with another person. They allow you to comprehend what the other person is saying and to express your own thoughts (Werker & Tees, 1992). In this example, input is sent from the ears to the auditory cortex and is routed to Wernicke's area for comprehension. When you decide to reply, nerve impulses are sent from Wernicke's area to Broca's area, and impulses passed on from Broca's area to the motor cortex result in the mouthing of a verbal response. This sequence illustrates a key action principle of brain functioning: even relatively simple acts usually involve the coordinated action of several brain regions.

Broca's area
Formulates a speech response and stimulates motor cortex

Motor cortex
Stimulates muscles that produce speech

Wernicke's area
Processes incoming speech and comprehends it

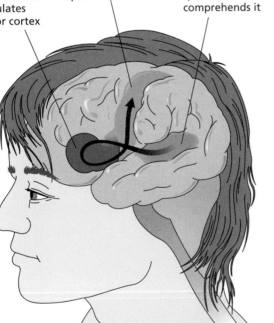

FIGURE 3.17 Cortical areas involved in language. Wernicke's area is important in the comprehension of spoken or written speech. Broca's area is involved in the production of speech, and the motor cortex stimulates the speech production muscles.

➤ 26. What is the role of association cortex, the "silent areas"?

Association cortex.   The **association cortex** is critically involved in the highest level of mental functions, including perception, language, and thought. These areas are sometimes referred to as "silent areas" because electrically stimulating them does not give rise to either sensory experiences or motor responses. This fact has probably helped promote the widely cited myth that most humans use only 10 percent of their brain power. Nothing could be farther from the truth.

Damage to specific parts of the association cortex causes disruption or loss of functions such as speech, understanding, thinking, and problem solving. As we might expect if the association cortex is involved in higher mental processes, the amount of association cortex increases dramatically as we move up the brain ladder from lower animals to human beings. It constitutes about 75 percent of the human cerebral cortex and accounts for people's superior cognitive abilities. Our mass of association cortex has been described by one scientist as "evolution's missing link" (Skoyles, 1997). He suggests that its mental flexibility and learning capacity has allowed us to upgrade our cognitive skills and to acquire new mental skills specific to our human way of life, such as reading and mathematics, more quickly than could have occurred through natural selection alone.

The importance of association cortex is demonstrated in people who suffer from *agnosia,* the inability to identify familiar objects. One such case is described by the neurologist Oliver Sacks (1985).

> Dr. P. was a talented and accomplished musician whose behavior was quite normal except for one glaring exception: Although his vision was perfect, he often had difficulty recognizing familiar people and objects. Thus, he would chat with pieces of furniture and wonder why they did not reply, or pat the tops of fire hydrants, thinking they were children. One day, while visiting Sack's office for an examination, Dr. P. looked for his hat as he was ready to depart. He suddenly reached out and grabbed his wife's head, trying to lift it. He had mistaken his wife for his hat! His wife smiled tolerantly; she had become accustomed to such actions on his part.

Dr. P. had suffered brain damage that left him unable to relate the information sent to the visual cortex with information stored in other cortical areas that concerned the nature of objects. The associative neurons responsible for linking the two types of information no longer served him.

The frontal lobes: the human difference. Some neuroscientists have suggested that the entire period of human evolutionary existence could well be termed the "age of the frontal lobe" (Krasnegor et al., 1997). This mass of cortex residing behind our eyes and forehead hardly exists in mammals such as mice and rats. The frontal lobes comprise about 3.5 percent of the cerebral cortex in the cat, 7 percent in the dog, and 17 percent in the chimpanzee. In a human, the frontal lobes constitute 29 percent of the cortex. The site of such human qualities as self-awareness, planning, initiative, and responsibility, the frontal lobes are in some respects the most mysterious and least understood part of the brain.

➤ 27. Describe the role of the frontal cortex in higher mental (including "executive") functions.

Much of what we know about the frontal lobes comes from detailed studies of patients who have experienced brain damage. Frontal lobe damage results not so much in a loss of intellectual abilities as in an inability to plan and carry out a sequence of actions, even when patients can verbalize what they should do. This can result in an inability to correct actions that are clearly erroneous and self-defeating (Shallice & Burgess, 1991).

The frontal cortex is also involved in emotional experience. In people with normal brains, PET scans show increased activity in the frontal cortex when people are experiencing feelings of happiness, sadness, or disgust (Lane et al., 1997). In contrast, patients with frontal lobe damage often exhibit attitudes of apathy and lack of concern. They literally don't seem to care about anything.

A region of the frontal lobe known as the prefrontal cortex has received increasing attention in recent years. The **prefrontal cortex**, located just behind the forehead, is the seat of the so-called executive functions. *Executive functions,* mental abilities involving goal setting, judgment, strategic planning, and impulse control, allow people to direct their behavior in an adaptive fashion. Deficits in executive functions seem to underlie a number of problem behaviors. People with prefrontal cortex disorders seem oblivious to the future consequences of their actions and seem to be governed only by immediate consequences (Bechara et al., 1994). As you may have guessed by now, Phineas Gage, the railroad foreman described in our chapter-opening case, suffered massive frontal lobe damage when the spike tore through his brain (see Figure 3.1).

Thereafter he exhibited classic symptoms of disturbed executive functions, becoming behaviorally impulsive and losing his capacity for future planning.

A more ominous manifestation of prefrontal dysfunction was discovered by Adrian Raine and his coworkers (1997). Using brain-imaging techniques, the researchers studied 41 violent murderers who had pleaded not guilty by reason of insanity. The murderers' PET scans showed clear evidence of reduced activity in the prefrontal cortex. Their murderous acts, which were often random and impulsive in nature, showed parallel evidence of failure in executive functions such as judgment, foresight, and impulse control. Raine suggested that people with similar prefrontal dysfunction may have a neural predisposition to impulsive violence.

During the 1940s and 1950s many thousands of psychiatric patients who suffered from disturbed and violently emotional behavior were subjected to operations called *prefrontal lobotomies* (Shorter, 1998). The operation was performed by inserting an instrument with sharp edges into the brain, then wiggling it back and forth to sever the nerve tracts that connected the the frontal lobes with the subcortical regions connected with emotion. The calming effect was so dramatic that Egas Moniz, the developer of the technique, was awarded a Nobel Prize. However, the devastating side effects on mental functions that occurred as the executive functions were destroyed were equally dramatic, and the development of antipsychotic drugs resulted in an abandonment of this form of "treatment."

Hemispheric Lateralization: The Left and Right Brains

The left and right cerebral hemispheres are connected by a broad white band of myelinated nerve fibers. The **corpus callosum** is a neural bridge that acts as a major communication link between the two hemispheres and allows them to function as a single unit. Despite the fact that they normally act in concert, however, there are important differences between the psychological functions that are represented in the two cerebral hemispheres. **Lateralization** refers to the relatively greater localization of a function in one hemisphere or the other.

Medical studies of patients who suffered various types of brain damage provided the first clues that certain complex psychological functions were lateralized on one side of the brain or the other. The deficits observed in people with damage to either the left or right hemisphere suggested that for most people, verbal abilities and speech are localized in the left hemisphere, as are mathematical and logical abilities (Springer, 1997).

When Broca's or Wernicke's speech areas are damaged, the result is **aphasia,** the partial or total loss of the ability to communicate. Depending on the location of the damage, the problem may lie in recognizing the meaning of words, in communicating verbally with others, or in both functions. C. Scott Moss, a clinical psychologist who became aphasic in both ways for a time as a result of a left hemisphere stroke, described what it was like for him.

> I recollect trying to read the headlines of the *Chicago Tribune* but they didn't make any sense to me at all. I didn't have any difficulty focusing; it was simply that the words, individually or in combination, didn't have meaning, and even more amazing, I was only a trifle bothered by that fact. . . . I think part of the explanation was that I had [also] lost the ability to engage in self-talk. In other words, I didn't have the ability to think about the future—to worry, or anticipate or perceive it—at least not with words. (Moss, 1972, pp. 4–5)

When the right hemisphere is damaged, the clinical picture is quite different. Language functions are not ordinarily affected, but the person has great difficulty in performing tasks that demand the ability to perceive spatial relations. A patient may have a hard time recognizing faces and may even forget a well-

► 28. What is hemispheric lateralization and what do we know about the functions that are concentrated in the left and right hemispheres?

traveled route or, as in the case of Dr. P., mistake his wife for a hat (Sacks, 1985). It appears that mental imagery, musical and artistic abilities, and the ability to perceive and understand spatial relationships are primarily right-hemisphere functions (Ornstein, 1997).

The two hemispheres differ not only in the cognitive functions that reside there, but also in their links with particular types of emotions. EEG studies have shown that the right hemisphere is relatively more active when negative emotions such as sadness and anger are being experienced. Positive emotions such as joy and happiness are accompanied by relatively greater left-hemisphere activation (Fox & Davidson, 1991; Tomarken et al., 1992).

The split brain: two minds in one body?   Despite the lateralization of specific functions in the two cerebral hemispheres, the brain normally functions as a unified whole because the two hemispheres communicate with one another through the corpus callosum. But what would happen if this communication link between the two hemispheres were cut? Would we, in effect, produce two different and largely independent minds in the same person? A series of Nobel Prize–winning studies by Roger Sperry (1970) and his associates addressed this question.

Like many scientific advances, this discovery resulted from natural human misfortune. Some patients suffer from a form of epilepsy in which a seizure that begins as an uncontrolled electrical discharge of neurons on one side of the brain spreads to the other hemisphere. Years ago, neurosurgeons found that by cutting the nerve fibers of the corpus callosum, they could prevent the seizure from spreading to the other hemisphere. Moreover, the operation did not seem to disrupt other major psychological functions. Sperry's studies of patients who had had such operations involved some ingenious ways to test the functions of the two hemispheres after the corpus callosum was cut.

Split-brain research was made possible by the way in which our visual input to the brain is "wired." To illustrate, extend your two hands straight out in front of you, separated by about one foot. Now focus on the point between them. You'll find that you can still see both hands in your peripheral division, and that you have a unified view of the scene. It therefore might surprise you to know that your left hand is being "seen" only by your right hemisphere and your right hand only by your left hemisphere. To see how this occurs, examine Figure 3.18, which shows that some of the fibers of the optic nerve from each eye cross over at the *optic chiasma* and travel to the opposite brain hemisphere. Fibers that transmit messages from the right side of the visual field project to the left hemisphere; fibers from the visual field's left half project to the right hemisphere. Despite this arrangement, we experience a unified visual world (as you did when you looked at your hands) rather than two half-worlds because the hemispheres' visual areas are normally connected by the corpus callosum. When the corpus callosum is cut, however, visual input to one hemisphere can be restricted by projecting the stimulus to either the right side of the visual field (in which case the image goes only to the left hemisphere) or to the left side of the visual field, which sends it to the right hemisphere.

In Sperry's experiments, split-brain patients basically did what you did with your hands: They focused on a fixation point, a dot on the center of a screen, while slides containing visual stimuli

> 29. What roles have (a) the corpus collosum and (b) the optic chiasma played in "split-brain" research? Is it reasonable to speak of separate "right" and "left" brains in normal people?

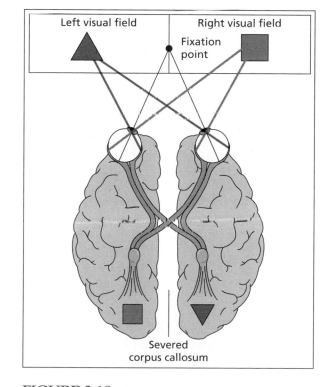

FIGURE 3.18   The visual system's anatomy made studies of split-brain subjects possible. Images entering the eye are reversed by the lens. Optic nerve fibers from the inner portion of the retina (toward the nose) cross over at the optic chiasma, whereas the fibers from the outer portion of the retina do not. As a result, the right side of each eye's visual field projects to the visual cortex of the left hemisphere, whereas the left visual field projects to the right hemisphere. When the corpus callosum is cut, the two hemispheres no longer communicate with each other. By presenting stimuli to either side of the visual fixation point, researchers can control which hemisphere receives the information.

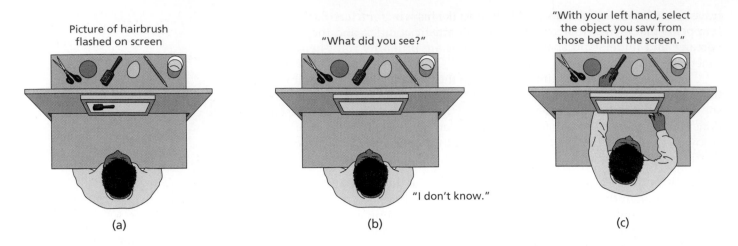

Picture of hairbrush flashed on screen

"What did you see?"

"With your left hand, select the object you saw from those behind the screen."

"I don't know."

(a)　　　　　　　　(b)　　　　　　　　(c)

FIGURE 3.19 A split-brain patient focuses on the fixation point in the center of the screen. In (a), a picture of a hairbrush is briefly projected to the left side of the visual field, thus sending the information to the right hemisphere. In (b), the patient is asked to state verbally what she saw. She cannot name the object. In (c), she is asked to select the object she saw, and is able to find it with her left hand. If the object were transferred to her right hand or if the word were flashed to the right side of the visual field, the information would be sent to the language-rich left hemisphere, and she would be able to name the object.

(words, pictures, and so on) were flashed to the right or left side of the fixation point (Figure 3.19).

Sperry found that when words were flashed to the right side of the visual field, resulting in their being sent to the language-rich left hemisphere, subjects could verbally describe what they had seen. They could also write what they had seen with their right hand (which is controlled by the left hemisphere). However, if words were flashed to the left side of the visual field and sent on to the right hemisphere, the subjects could not describe what they had read on the screen. This pattern of findings indicated that the right hemisphere does not have well-developed language abilities.

The inability to describe stimuli verbally did not mean, however, that the right hemisphere was incapable of recognizing them. If a picture of an object (e.g., a hairbrush) was flashed to the right hemisphere and the left hand (controlled by the right hemisphere) was allowed to feel many different objects behind the screen, the person's hand would immediately select the brush and hold it up (Figure 3.19c). As long as the person continued to hold the brush in the left hand, sending sensory input about the object to the "nonverbal" right hemisphere, the person was unable to name it. However, if the brush was transferred to the right hand, the person could immediately name it. In other words, until the object was transferred to the right hand, the left hemisphere had no knowledge of what the right hemisphere was experiencing.

Later research showed the right hemisphere's definite superiority over the left in the recognition of patterns. In one study, three split-brain patients were presented with photographs of similar-looking faces projected in either the left or right visual fields. On each trial, they were asked to select the photo they had just seen from a set of 10 cards. On this task, the spatially oriented right hemisphere was far more accurate than the linguistic left hemisphere in correctly identifying the photos (Figure 3.20). Apparently, the faces were too similar to one another to be differentiated very easily by left-hemisphere verbal descriptions, but the spatial abilities of the right hemisphere could differentiate among them (Gazzaniga & Smylie, 1983).

Some psychologists have suggested that what we call the conscious self resides in the left hemisphere, because consciousness is based on our ability to verbalize about the past and present. Is the right hemisphere, then, an unconscious (nonverbal) mind? Yes, these psychologists answer, except when it communicates with the left hemisphere across the corpus callosum (Ornstein, 1997).

But when the connections between the two hemispheres are cut, each hemisphere, in a sense, can have a "mind of its own," as this example shows.

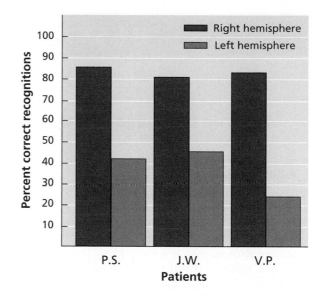

One split-brain patient learned to use Scrabble letters to communicate from his right hemisphere using his left hand. To test the dual-mind hypothesis, researchers asked the two hemispheres the same questions—and found that the answers often disagreed. For example, when asked what occupation he would prefer, the left hemisphere responded verbally, "a draftsman." But the right hemisphere used the Scrabble pieces to spell out, "race car driver." (LeDoux and others, 1977)

Keep in mind that in daily life, the split-brain patients could function adequately because they had learned to compensate for their disconnected hemispheres. For example, they could scan the visual environment so that visual input from both the left and right visual fields got into both hemispheres. The "split-mind" phenomena shown in the laboratory appeared because the patients were tested under experimental conditions that were specifically designed to isolate the functions of the two hemispheres. Nonetheless, the results of split-brain research were so dramatic that they led some people (and even some scientists) to promote a conception of brain functions as being highly localized and restricted to one hemisphere or the other. Even today, we hear about "right brain" education programs and the untapped potentials that they can release. Certainly, there is some degree of localization of brain functions, but a far more important principle is that in the normal brain, most functions involve many areas of the brain working together. The brain is an exquisitely integrated system, not a collection of localized functions.

FIGURE 3.20 Facial recognition accuracy by the left and right hemispheres of three split-brain patients, showing greater accuracy when information is flashed to the right hemisphere, which has stronger pattern-recognition abilities. Data from Gazzaniga & Smylie, 1983

Hemispheric lateralization of language. For many years, scientists have known that for most people language is primarily a left-hemisphere function. Why language tends to be localized in the left hemisphere is not clear, but it may have some undiscovered evolutionary significance. The brain of the chimpanzee, our genetically closest relative in the animal kingdom, also has a larger left hemisphere in the region that corresponds with Wernicke's speech comprehension area in the human brain (Gannon et al., 1998).

About 90 percent of people are right-handed, and among this majority, 95 percent have left hemisphere language dominance. Among left-handers, half have language in the left hemisphere, 25 percent have it localized in the right hemisphere, and the rest have language functions in both hemispheres. Those who use both hemispheres for language functions have a larger corpus callosum, perhaps because more interhemispheric communication is required (Springer, 1998).

Left-hemisphere lateralization is the case not only for spoken and written language, but also for nonverbal kinds of language, such as sign language. PET scans of neural activity show that just as hearing people process speech with their left hemisphere, deaf people use the left hemisphere to decipher sign language. Likewise, a left-hemisphere stroke affects their ability to understand or produce sign language (Corina et al., 1992).

Realize, however, that even if your left hemisphere is dominant for language, this does not mean that your right hemisphere lacks language ability. PET scan studies measuring cerebral blood flow in the brains of normal people indicate that both hemispheres are involved in speaking, reading, and listening (Leondes, 1997; Raichle, 1994). One notable finding, however, is that males and females may differ in the extent to which certain language functions are lateralized, or located, on one side of the brain. This chapter's *Research Close-Up* describes the use of brain imaging to study possible sex differences in the brain's language capabilities.

> 30. How is language lateralized in the brain? Are there sex differences?

RESEARCH ✷ CLOSE-UP

Are Language Functions Localized Differently in Men and Women?

▶ Background

There have been tantalizing hints that the brains of men and women may differ in the extent to which language is localized in the left hemisphere. For example, clinicians have observed that among people who suffer left-hemisphere strokes, men are more likely than women to show severe aphasic symptoms. This suggests that more of women's language function is shared with the right hemisphere. What has been lacking, however, is direct comparisons of the functioning brains of men and women. This classic study, performed by Bennett and Sally Shaywitz and coworkers, was the first to use modern brain-imaging techniques to explore the hypothesis of greater male lateralization

▶ Method

The sample consisted of 19 males and 19 females averaging 26 years of age. All participants were right-handed and neurologically normal. The participants performed several language tasks while functional magnetic resonance imaging (FMRI) recordings were made of changes in patterns of cerebral blood flow within the left and right hemispheres. This procedure allowed the researchers to identify brain regions where levels of neural activity increased in response to four different mental tasks. The critical task was a language task that required participants to view sets of randomly arranged vowels and consonants and decide whether or not the two "nonsense" words rhymed with each other. This task was chosen because it required the subjects to "sound out" the words in their minds to form a representation of the word sounds, a function that is critical in understanding language.

▶ Results

The FMRIs allowed the researchers to compare the cerebral blood flow responses of males and females as they responded to the experimental tasks. Their analyses revealed that the rhyming task produced increased cortical activity in a region of the left hemisphere that is known to be involved in language. For males, this neural activity was restricted to the left hemisphere, but for females, the activity was represented in the corresponding areas of both hemispheres (Figure 3.21).

▶ Critical Analysis

This study provided the first direct evidence through brain imaging of a gender difference in language organization within the normal brain. It also demonstrates the tremendous value of FMRI technology (Rugg, 1995). Greater left-hemisphere lateralization of language in males may help to

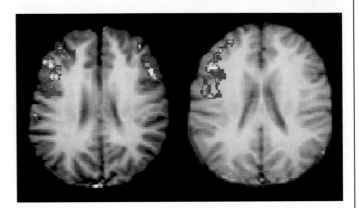

FIGURE 3.21 Functional MRI recordings of brain activity in men and women as they performed a language task showed greater left hemisphere lateralization in men (right image). Women showed activity in both hemispheres.
Shaywitz & others, 1995

account for the aphasia differences that have been observed between brain-damaged men and women, showing how clinical and experimental observations can complement one another. More importantly, the results of this landmark study add to a growing body of evidence that differences between the brains of men and women may help account for emotional, cognitive, and behavioral differences between the sexes (Halpern, 1992; Kimura & Hampson, 1994). For example, in a finding that may shed light on the results of this study, Laura Allen and Roger Gorski (1991) discovered through postmortem examinations of 100 age-matched men and women that the corpus callosum and other tracts that connect the two hemispheres were significantly larger in females than in males, suggesting the potential for greater communication between the hemispheres in women.

Before concluding that women's brains are more "holistic" than men's, however, we should note that several important questions remain unanswered:

- Can these findings be replicated by other researchers and with other language tasks?
- The fact that the right hemisphere of women was active during the language task was clearly evident in the data, but what we have so far is a correlation between task performance and biological activity. Does this activity play a causal role in task performance? Is it essential for task performance? We simply don't know at this point.

—Continued

- If there is a real gender difference, what causes it—innate biological differences or differences in experience that affect thinking and brain development? Or both?

  A related question is whether language in women requires greater right-hemisphere activation. One thing we do know is that women with right- hemisphere dam-

age are *not* more likely than men to become aphasic (Rugg, 1995). If the right hemisphere were essential for language in women, we might expect to find more aphasia in women with damage in that hemisphere. Perhaps women utilize both hemispheres for the performance of some language functions, but can fall back on one if damage occurs to the other. Future research will provide answers to these important questions.

Source: Bennett Shaywitz, Sally Shaywitz, Kenneth Pugh et al. (1995). Sex differences in the functional organization of the brain for language. *Nature, 373,* 607–609.

Plasticity in the Brain: The Role of Experience and the Recovery of Function

Learn to walk, acquire speech, begin to read, fall in love, and your brain changes in a way that makes you a different person than you were before. Learning and practicing a mental or physical skill may change the size or number of brain areas involved and alter the neural pathways used in the skill (Posner et al., 1997). This process of brain alteration begins in the womb and continues throughout life. It is governed in important ways by genetic factors, but also is strongly influenced by the environment.

Neural plasticity refers to the ability of neurons to change in structure and function (Kolb & Whishaw, 1998). Two aspects of neural plasticity—the effects of early experience on brain development and recovery from brain damage—are at the forefront of current research.

➤ 31. What is neural plasticity? How do age, environment, and behavior affect plasticity?

The role of early experience.   Brain development is programmed by complex commands from our genes, but how these genetic commands express themselves can be powerfully affected by the environment in which we develop, including the environment we are exposed to in the womb (Filogamo, 1998). Consider the following research findings:

- For the fetus in the womb, exposure to high levels of alcohol ingested by the pregnant mother can disrupt brain development and produce the lifelong mental and behavioral damage seen in fetal alcohol syndrome (Streissguth et al., 1990).

- The brains of rat pups raised in a stimulating early environment containing lots of playmates and toys weighed more, had larger neurons and more dendritic branches, and greater concentrations of acetylcholine, the neurotransmitter involved in motor control and in memory (Rosenzweig, 1984).

- Prematurely born human infants who were caressed and massaged on a regular basis showed faster neurological development than did those given normal care and human contact (Field et al., 1986).

- MRI recordings revealed that experienced string musicians who do elaborate movements on the strings with their left hands had a larger right-hemisphere somatosensory area devoted to these fingers than did nonmusicians. The corresponding left-hemisphere (right-hand) cortical areas of the musicians and nonmusicians did not differ. The earlier in life the musicians had started playing their instruments, the more cortical change had occurred (Ebert et al., 1995).

- Cultural factors may affect brain development as well. For example, the Chinese language uses complex pictorial images (rather than words) to represent objects or concepts. Because pictorial stimuli are processed in the right hemisphere, we might expect less left-hemisphere lateralization of language among speakers of Chinese than among people who speak English or other alphabet-based languages. There is evidence to support this hypothesis in the areas of reading and writing (Tzeng et al., 1979).

In a sense, your brain goes through its own personal "evolutionary" process as it adapts to and is molded by your individual environment during the course of your life. Once again we can see why the nature-nurture debate described in Chapter 1 has given way to an appreciation for the many ways in which biology and experience continually interact.

Recovery of function after injury.   When an injury results in the destruction of brain tissue, other neurons must take over the lost functions of the dead neurons if recovery is to occur. At times the brain shows an amazing plasticity and recovery of function, as the following case illustrates:

> Jimmy was a healthy and normal 5-year-old child who awoke one day unable to speak and slightly paralyzed on the right side of his body. A blood vessel in his left temporal lobe had ruptured and an area of the brain "downstream" from the site of the stroke had died when its blood supply was cut off. For Jimmy's father, it was like reliving a nightmare. His own grandfather had also suffered a left hemisphere stroke late in life. The elderly man never recovered his speech and he remained partially paralyzed until his eventual death. But for Jimmy, the story had a happier ending. Within three months, Jimmy was again speaking normally, and his paralysis had disappeared completely. He was ready to resume the life of a normal 5-year-old. All that remained of his ordeal was a frightening memory. (Gazzaniga et al., 1979)

Neural reorganization had occurred in Jimmy's brain, allowing other neurons to take over the functions of those that had died. The outcomes for Jimmy and his grandfather also illustrate an important general principle: Brain damage suffered early in life is less devastating than damage suffered as an adult (Blosser, 2000).

The brain is clearly capable of greater plasticity early in life. In one study, researchers took neurons from the visual cortex of cats and then raised the neurons in a culture containing the nutrients needed for survival. They found that the neurons could survive and create new synapses with other neurons in the culture quite well if they were taken from kittens who were 2 to 4 weeks old, but not if they were obtained from older animals (Schoop et al., 1997).

► 32. Why do children typically show better recovery of function after brain injury?

Studies using the electron microscope may explain why such plasticity is possible early in life. The 1- to 2-year-old child has about 50 percent more brain synapses than mature adults do (Huttenlocher, 1979). This greater availability of synapses may help to explain why children can recover from brain damage more quickly and completely than adults. But sadly the days of synaptic riches don't last forever. Unused or weaker synapses deteriorate with age so that the brain loses some of its plasticity (Filogamo, 1998). Moreover, cell death is programmed into every neuron by its genes, and what some neuroscientists refer to as the neuron's "suicide apparatus" is activated by a lack of stimulation from other neurons and by many other unknown factors (Milligan & Schwartz, 1997). As a result, adults actually have fewer synapses in the brain than do children, despite their more advanced cognitive and motor capabilities.

Yet even adults can maintain or recover some functions after neuron death (Varney & Roberts, 1999). When nerve tissue is destroyed or neurons die as part of the aging process, surviving neurons can restore functioning by modifying themselves either structurally or biochemically. They can alter their structure by sprouting enlarged networks of dendrites or by extending axons from surviving neurons to form new synapses (Shepherd, 1997). Surviving neurons may also make up for the loss by increasing the volume of neurotransmitters they release (Robinson, 1997). Finally, recent research findings have begun to challenge the long-standing assumption of brain scientists that dead neurons cannot be replaced in the mature brain (McMillan et al., 1999). The development of new cells (*neurogenesis*) has been demonstrated in the brains of rodents and primates within the hippocampus, which is involved in memory. In 1998, evidence for the birth of new cells in the human adult hippocampus appeared (Eriksson et al., 1998). Then in what could be a landmark scientific discovery, psychologist Elizabeth Gould and her Princeton coworkers (1999) provided the first evidence of neurogenesis in the cerebral cortex of a primate. Using complex chemical and microscopic analysis techniques with adult macaque monkeys, Gould's team tracked newly developed neurons from their birthplace in subcortical tissue. The immature neurons migrated upward along myelinated nerve tracts into the association areas of the cerebral cortex, where they sprouted axons and extended them toward existing neurons. The researchers speculated that these new neurons may be involved in higher-order mental functions, such as complex learning and memory. If similar results are found in humans, whose brain structures and functions are similar to those of primates, new light could be shed on brain mechanisms of information storage and plasticity. It is even possible that degenerative mental disorders such as Alzheimer's disease represent a failure or decline in a previously unknown process of neuron regeneration in the mature brain.

Behavioral and lifestyle measures can also help preserve brain functioning. In elderly people, for example, continued intellectual stimulation and activity seems to preserve synapses and their resulting cognitive functions, adding support to physiological psychologist David Krech's statement that "Those who live by their wits die with their wits" (Krech, 1978).

Basic research on naturally occurring recovery processes is leading to new ways to help the brain heal itself. These efforts are the focus of this chapter's *Applications of Psychological Science.*

➤33. How are axon repair, brain grafts, and neural stem cell injections being used to improve the functioning of damaged brains? What kinds of ethical issues arise in the use of these procedures?

APPLICATIONS OF PSYCHOLOGICAL SCIENCE

Healing the Nervous System

Neurological disorders take a frightening psychological toll on their victims, who often lose basic cognitive, sensory, and motor functions and can suffer devastating emotional and social consequences. Although severed fingers and toes can be reattached and regain their functions, the same has not been true in the damaged spinal cord and brain. Until recently, it was thought that dead neurons were impossible to replace. Now, however, hope for victims of neurological disease or injuries has been rekindled by the discovery that damaged neurons can be repaired (Solso, 1999).

Until recently, paralyzed individuals with spinal injuries have had little hope of recovering lost motor and sensory functions. Such injuries usually involve severed axons, resulting in a loss of nerve transmission to neighboring neurons. But in several experiments involving rats, axons in the spinal cord have been severed, and the neurons from which the axons originated placed under a weak electrical current. This current stimulated regrowth of axons out of the cell bodies. The axons grew over the injury to seek their predamage positions on the other side of the cut. Other studies have used chemical methods to stimu-

late axon development, including the implantation of cells that produce *nerve growth factor*, a substance that helps stimulate and guide the growth of axons. In many cases, surviving neurons responded by sprouting axons that grew toward the graft and repaired the damaged tract (Joosten, 1997). The positive results obtained in animal research on neural regrowth following injury gives scientists hope that they may one day be able to fix what has long been irreparable—the severed spinal cord.

Parkinson's disease is a progressive brain disorder that produces uncontrollable tremors, difficulties in movement, and body rigidity that can eventually border on paralysis. Psychological problems such as memory loss, concentration difficulties, and depression are also commonly experienced. The disease is caused by the chemical destruction of dopamine-producing cells within a small midbrain structure. Victims of Parkinson's can obtain some relief with *L-DOPA*, a drug that helps restore missing dopamine and helps alleviate the movement problems. Unfortunately, after 5 to 10 years of using the drug, many patients must stop taking it because of serious side effects, whereupon their symptoms return

—Continued

and become progressively worse (Ron & David, 1997). Thus the long-term prognosis for Parkinson's disease patients has been rather grim.

Might it be possible to transplant healthy neural tissue into diseased areas of the brain so as to produce the missing dopamine and restore neurological function? Successes with animal implants have stimulated experiments with human patients. Scientists have taken advantage of the fact that one of the substances produced by the adrenal glands is dopamine. They have therefore taken dopamine-producing cells from patients' own adrenal glands (to avoid rejection of the transplant) and implanted them into the subcortical brain region affected by Parkinson's disease. So far the results have been variable, with dramatic improvement occurring in some cases and no improvement at all in others. In one of the successes reported by a team of Mexican scientists, a patient who had been confined to a wheelchair was out playing soccer with his son 10 months after the surgery (Madrazo et al., 1987).

Dopamine-producing human fetal tissue seems to be even better for transplants than a patient's own adrenal tissue, because fetal tissue tends to secrete more dopamine and is more likely to survive and "take hold" in the damaged area. Such tissue is sometimes available as a result of miscarriages. In one study, 6 patients who had received fetal tissue transplants were followed up for periods of up to 6 years. After 8 to 12 months, PET scans showed that the transplanted tissue had survived and was producing significant amounts of dopamine. As a result, the patients required less L-DOPA over time, and one patient was able to be taken off the drug altogether after 32 months. Significant improvement in motor function was observed in 4 of the 6 patients (Wenning et al., 1997). These results are encouraging, but before the new treatment will be ready for widespread clinical use, researchers must increase the survival and growth of the transplanted fetal tissue. Meanwhile researchers working with laboratory animals have reported success in using neural transplants to treat epilepsy and even strokes (Blank, 1999). This is an example of the important role that animal research can play in developing the knowledge and techniques needed for human interventions.

As brain grafting takes us into a new era in which we may be able to physically modify the brain, new ethical and legal questions have become topics for debate (Gold, 1997; Sauer, 1998). What do you think about the following issues?

- Is it possible that increased demand for fetal tissue may provide a profitable market for the "harvesting" of needlessly aborted fetuses? Could the prospect of financial gain encourage some women to become pregnant with the intention of aborting the fetus and selling the tissue? Is it the parents' tissue to sell? (Gold, 1998)
- Suppose the daughter of a Parkinson's patient asked to be artificially inseminated with her father's sperm so that she could later have an abortion, thereby producing a supply of fetal tissue for implantation in his brain with a reduced likelihood of tissue rejection because of genetic similarity. Aside from the moral issue concerning the premeditated abortion, would the insemination constitute incest?

- Suppose a brain graft from another person results in a genetically based change in personality and a penchant for antisocial behavior. Is the person legally responsible for his or her subsequent acts? In fact, because of the genetic change, is he or she still the same person?

Such issues are now being debated by medical ethicists. Meanwhile practical steps are being taken in anticipation of future advances in brain grafting and other interventions. For example, scientists at the National Institutes of Health in the United States are attempting to grow tissue cultures of human fetal cells that could be used in future transplants as an alternative to actual fetal tissue. Other interventions currently being developed include the implanting of genetically altered cells into the brain, where they could directly change cellular processes, such as the production of neurotransmitters (Horellou et al., 1997; Wood, 1997).

One revolutionary technique involves the transplantation into the brain of **neural stem cells,** immature "uncommitted" cells that can mature into any type of neuron or glial cell needed by the brain (Gage & Christen, 1997). These cells, found in both the developing and adult nervous system, can be put into a liquid medium and injected directly into the brain. Once in the brain, they can travel to any of its regions, especially developing or degenerating areas. There they can detect defective or genetically impaired cells and somehow convert themselves into healthy forms of the defective cells.

Researchers at Harvard Medical School demonstrated the potential value of stem cell transplantation (Yandava et al., 1999). They worked with a strain of mice called "shiverers" who have a genetic defect that prevents their glial cells from producing the insulating myelin sheath on axons. Within 3 weeks after birth, the animals begin to develop severe tremors similar to those seen in multiple sclerosis, a human disease produced by insufficient myelin. Using a neural stem cell culture grown from cells removed 13 years ago from the brain of a newborn mouse, the researchers injected stem cells directly into the brains of randomly selected shiverers. A control group of shiverers did not receive the cells. In the injected rats, the stem cells apparently detected the defective gene and converted themselves into the myelin-producing cells. They then began to produce the missing myelin throughout the brain, and some of the mice developed myelin sheaths that could not be distinguished from those of normal mice. About 60 percent of the experimental group mice appeared to behave like normal mice, showing no signs of the motor disturbances that accompany insufficient myelinization. Others showed greatly reduced motor symptoms. All of the control animals became shiverers.

The fact that transplanted stem cells can apparently go anywhere in the brain and become any kind of cell suggests the possibility of revolutionary treatments for diseases involving widespread neural degeneration and dysfunction, such as Alzheimer's, multiple sclerosis, strokes, mental disorders, and genetically based birth defects, all of which have serious psychological consequences. Much more research is needed, but at long last we may be on the threshold of being able to heal the damaged brain and restore lost psychological functions.

❭ NERVOUS SYSTEM INTERACTIONS WITH THE ENDOCRINE AND IMMUNE SYSTEMS

The nervous system interacts with two other communication systems within the body, namely, the endocrine and immune systems. These interactions have major influences on behavior and on psychological and physical well-being.

Interactions with the Endocrine System

The **endocrine system** consists of numerous glands distributed throughout the body. The locations of the endocrine glands within the human body and a list of their functions are presented in Figure 3.22.

    Like the nervous system, the endocrine system's function is to convey information from one area of the body to another. Rather than using nerve impulses, however, the endocrine system conveys information in the form of **hormones,** chemical messengers that are secreted from its glands into the bloodstream. Just as neurons have receptors for certain neurotransmitters, cells in the body (including neurons) have receptor molecules that respond to specific hormones from the endocrine glands. Many of the hormones secreted by these glands affect psychological development and functioning (Becker et al., 1992). For example, the genetically programmed secretion of sex hormones within the human fetus during the early months following conception affects not only the development of male or female sex organs, but also the development of sex differences in the brain that influence behavioral functions throughout life (Schmidt & Rubinow, 1997). One example may be the sex differences in lateralization of language described earlier.

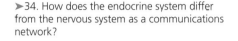
➤34. How does the endocrine system differ from the nervous system as a communications network?

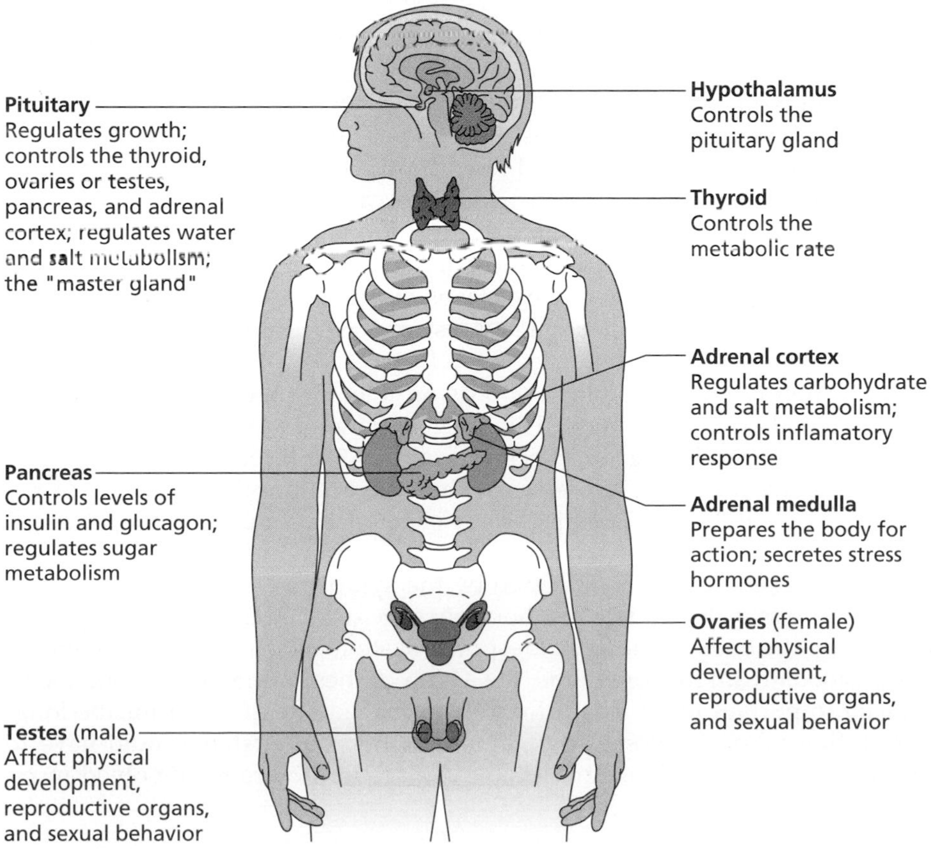

Pituitary
Regulates growth; controls the thyroid, ovaries or testes, pancreas, and adrenal cortex; regulates water and **salt** metabolism; the "master gland"

Hypothalamus
Controls the pituitary gland

Thyroid
Controls the metabolic rate

Adrenal cortex
Regulates carbohydrate and salt metabolism; controls inflamatory response

Pancreas
Controls levels of insulin and glucagon; regulates sugar metabolism

Adrenal medulla
Prepares the body for action; secretes stress hormones

Ovaries (female)
Affect physical development, reproductive organs, and sexual behavior

Testes (male)
Affect physical development, reproductive organs, and sexual behavior

FIGURE 3.22 The glands that comprise the endocrine system and the effects of their hormones on bodily functions. The hypothalamus affects the endocrine system by stimulating the pituitary gland.

➤35. What are some ways in which the nervous and endocrine systems affect one another?

Endocrine messages can affect the nervous system, and mental processes within the brain can, in turn, affect endocrine functioning. For example, negative thoughts about a stressful situation can quickly trigger the secretion of stress hormones within the body (Borod, 2000). Consider in this light the "voodoo death" of the young woman described at the beginning of the chapter. How are we to account for such events without invoking supernatural forces? One possibility is through the interaction of the brain and the endocrine system. Many years ago, the physiologist Walter Cannon (1942) suggested a possible mechanism, drawing upon his own research on severe stress responses in animals and quoting eyewitness reports by cultural anthropologists of deaths by "black magic." One such account involved the practice of placing a death curse on another by pointing a sacred bone at the victim.

> The man who discovers that he is being boned by any enemy is, indeed, a pitiable sight. He stands aghast, with his eyes staring at the treacherous pointer, and with his hands lifted as though to ward off the lethal medium, which he imagines is pouring into his body. . . . Unless help is forthcoming in the shape of a countercharm administered by the hands of the Nangarri, or medicine-man, his death is only a matter of a comparatively short time. (Basedow, quoted in Cannon, 1942, p. 172)

➤36. What physiological explanation did Cannon offer for death by "black magic"?

Cannon noted that in cases of death by "black magic," the victim of the curse invariably believed (as did family, friends, and enemies) that he or she was doomed, a conviction that was unquestioned within the victim's culture. He speculated that the victim's beliefs triggered a profound stress response that included a torrent of stress hormones released by the endocrine system, sending the victim into physiological shock. Cannon's research had shown that one aspect of such shock is a rapid and often fatal drop in blood pressure as the stress hormones allow fluid to leak out of veins and capillaries. He noted that normal autopsy procedures would not detect this mechanism of death, making it appear, as in the case of the young woman, that there was no natural cause. Cannon's hypothesis is a plausible alternative to supernatural explanations, and it is consistent with the results of stress research.

The nervous system transmits information rapidly, with the speed of nerve impulses. The endocrine system is much slower because delivery of its messages depends on the rate of blood flow. On the other hand, hormones travel throughout the body in the bloodstream and can reach billions of individual cells. Thus when the brain has important information to transmit, it has the choice of sending it directly in the form of nerve impulses to a relatively small number of neurons or indirectly by means of hormones to a large number of cells. Often both communication networks are used, resulting in both immediate and prolonged stimulation.

Of special interest to psychologists are the **adrenal glands,** twin structures perched atop the kidneys. The adrenal glands are, quite literally, a hormone factory, producing and secreting about 50 different hormones that regulate many metabolic processes within the brain and other parts of the body. As we have seen, dopamine is one substance produced in the adrenals. Also produced there are several stress hormones cited by Cannon. In an emergency, the adrenal gland is activated by the sympathetic branch of the autonomic nervous system, and stress hormones are secreted into the bloodstream, mobilizing the body's emergency response system. Because hormones remain in the bloodstream for some time, the action of these adrenal hormones is especially important under conditions of prolonged stress. If not for the long-term influence of hormones, the autonomic nervous system would have to produce a constant barrage of nerve impulses to the organs involved in responding to stress.

Interactions Involving the Immune System

The nervous and endocrine systems interact not only with one another, but also with the immune system. A normal, healthy immune system is a wonder of nature. At this moment, microscopic soldiers patrol every part of your body, including your brain. They are on a search-and-destroy mission, seeking out biological invaders that could disable or kill you. Programmed into this legion of tiny defenders is an innate ability to recognize which substances belong to the body and which are foreigners that must be destroyed. Such recognition occurs because foreign substances known as **antigens** (meaning *anti*body *gen*erators) trigger a biochemical response from the immune system. Bacteria, viruses, abnormal cells, and many chemical molecules with antigenic properties start the wars that rage inside our bodies every moment of every day (Figure 3.23).

The immune system has a remarkable memory. Once it has encountered one of the millions of different antigens that enter the body, it will recognize the antigen immediately in the future and will produce the biochemical weapons, or antibodies, needed to destroy it (Nossal & Hall, 1995). This is why we can develop vaccines to protect animals and people from some diseases, and why we normally catch diseases like mumps and chicken pox only once in our lives. Unfortunately, though the memory may be perfect, our body's defenses may not be. Some bacteria and viruses evolve so rapidly that they can change just enough over time to slip past the sentinels in our immune system and give us this year's cold or flu.

Antigens can originate externally (a flu virus or a pollen) or internally (a cancerous tumor). Problems arise when the immune system has either an underactive or an overactive response (Figure 3.24). An *underactive* immune system response to external antigens is dramatically illustrated in acquired immune deficiency syndrome (AIDS). One class of immune cells, *helper T cells*, issue "calls to action," mobilizing antigen-killing cells in the immune system. The human immunodeficiency virus (HIV) attacks the helper T cells and disables them. As a result, the individual's immune system doesn't get the order to attack and kill invaders. This leaves the body defenseless against virtually anything that can infect humans: bacteria, viruses of all kinds, fungi, and protozoa. Underreaction can also occur to an internal antigen. This is what occurs in cancer. Abnormal body cells are allowed to proliferate, resulting in the formation of tumors.

An *overactive* response to an external antigen presents problems in the form of an allergy. For example, in its violent reaction to an allergen, an asthmatic's immune system releases a torrent of histamine, a chemical that causes critical breathing muscles around the bronchial tubes to contract, leaving the asthmatic person wheezing and gasping for air.

Another type of overactive response, an **autoimmune reaction,** results when the immune system mistakenly identifies part of the body as an enemy and attacks it. For example, in rheumatoid arthritis, the immune system attacks connective tissue in the joints, causing inflammation, pain, and loss of flexibility. In diabetes, immune cells attack cells in the pancreas that produce the hormone insulin, which regulates blood sugar level. As a result the diabetic person may experience abnormally high blood sugar that can damage other organs, or drops in blood sugar that can result in a coma.

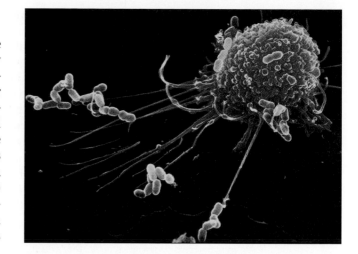

FIGURE 3.23 An immune system cell reaches out to capture bacteria, shown here in green. The bacteria that have already been pulled to the surface of the cell will be engulfed and devoured.

➤37. In what ways does the immune system have sensory, response, and memory capabilities?

➤38. How do under- or overreactivity to internal or external antigens give rise to four varieties of immune dysfunction?

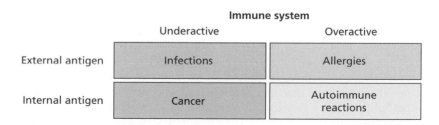

	Immune system	
	Underactive	Overactive
External antigen	Infections	Allergies
Internal antigen	Cancer	Autoimmune reactions

FIGURE 3.24 Disorders of the immune system created by under- or overreaction to either internal or external antigens.

The immune system, like the nervous system, thus has an exquisite capacity to receive, interpret, and respond to specific forms of stimulation. It senses, learns, remembers, and reacts; in other words, it behaves. Despite these similarities, research on the nervous and immune systems proceeded along independent paths for many years, with only a few visionaries suggesting that the two systems might be able to communicate and influence each others' activities. They were right. We now know that the nervous, endocrine, and immune systems are all parts of a communication network that so completely underlies our every mental, emotional, and physical action that neuroscientist Candace Pert, one of the pioneers in this area of research, has dubbed this network "bodymind" (Pert, 1986).

Pieces of this communication puzzle began to fall into place with several key discoveries. The first was that selective electrical stimulation or destruction of certain areas of the hypothalamus and cerebral cortex resulted in almost instantaneous increases or decreases in immune-system activity. Conversely, activation of the immune system by injecting antigens into the body resulted in increased electrical activity in several brain regions (Saphier, 1992). Clearly, the nervous and immune systems were communicating with and influencing one another.

➤39. What evidence exists that the immune and nervous system communicate with and affect one another?

Later research showed that the nervous and immune systems are chemically connected as well. Immune system cells contain receptors keyed to specific neurotransmitter substances, meaning that the action of immune cells can be directly influenced by chemical messengers from the brain (Maier & Watkins, 1999). An equally startling discovery was that immune cells can actually produce hormones and neurotransmitters, allowing them to directly influence the brain and endocrine system glands. The immune system is therefore not only a response system, but also a giant sensory system. It responds to antigens by sending chemical messengers that affect neurotransmitter activity in the brain and the autonomic nervous system. The brain, in turn, responds with a cascade of chemical and neural signals to both the immune cells and to the endocrine glands and organs of the body (Felton & Maida, 2000). In sum, the brain, endocrine glands, and immune system form a complete communication loop, with each influencing and being influenced by one another (Figure 3.25). Implications of these linkages are discussed in our *Psychological Frontiers* feature.

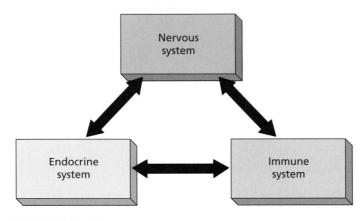

FIGURE 3.25 The nervous, endocrine, and immune systems are part of a complex communication system in which each can affect and be affected by the others. This fact accounts for many of the so-called "body-mind" interactions that are the focus of current interest in psychology.

➤40. Which psychosocial factors have been shown to influence immune functioning?

➤41. What can be done to enhance immune functioning?

PSYCHOLOGICAL FRONTIERS

How Psychological Factors Affect the Immune System

In an effort to understand how psychological factors affect health and illness, psychologists have teamed with immunologists to form a new discipline known as **psychoneuroimmunology (PNI** for short). Their research has shown that psychosocial factors such as stress, depression, social support, and personality factors have significant effects on immune system functioning, and thereby on health and illness (Ader et al., 1995; Maier & Watkins, 1998; Marsland et al., 2000).

Stress makes many people more susceptible to illness (Dougall & Baum, 2000). Research by Ronald Glaser, Janet Kiecolt-Glaser, and their coworkers at Ohio State University has shown that one possible reason is reduced immune sys-

—Continued

tem effectiveness (Glaser & Glaser, 1995). In one study, medical students were followed closely over a one-year period. Blood samples collected during three stressful academic examination periods were used to measure immune cell activity. The researchers found that immune system effectiveness was reduced during the stressful exam periods and that this reduction was linked to the likelihood of becoming ill. Other studies showed that stress hormones released into the bloodstream by the adrenal glands as part of the stress response can suppress the activity of specific immune system cells, increasing the likelihood of illness (Cohen & Herbert, 1996; Maier & Watkins, 1999; Sapse, 1997).

School examinations are stressful, but they pale in comparison with some other life stressors, such as the death of a loved one. Within one year after the death of their spouse, about two-thirds of bereaved people decline in health (Ader, 1995; Irwin et al., 1987). An increased rate of mortality is also found, particularly in widowers. To study the impact of bereavement on immune system functioning, Michael Irwin and his associates (1987) monitored the immune cell activity of women before and after the death of their husbands. They found a decrease in immune cell activity, but only in women who reacted to the death of their husband with depressive symptoms. Depression thus appears to be an active ingredient in weakening the immune system. So is a high level of general distress. A study involving people who were followed over four months following the 1994 Northridge, California, earthquake revealed that those who reacted with the highest levels of distress showed poorer immune function than did those who reacted with less distress (Solomon et al., 1997). A reduction in immune functioning caused by distress or depression can increase the body's vulnerability to viral diseases and, possibly, to cancer cells (Chiapelli, 2000; Lewis et al., 1995).

Personality and environmental factors have been implicated in other ways as well. David McClelland and his coworkers reported that people who had a strong need for power showed decreased immune system functioning when they experienced stressful situations that frustrated their power needs (Jemmott et al., 1988; McClelland, 1989). Bottling up negative feelings may also take a toll on immune functioning. In a long-term European study, people who were experiencing high levels of stress but were too emotionally restrained to express negative feelings had a significantly higher likelihood of developing cancer than did highly stressed people who were not so emotionally restrained (Eysenck, 1994). Thus persons with certain personality patterns appear to be at increased risk for illness when they are subjected to stress.

Many cancer specialists are convinced that an aggressive and determined attitude and a will to live characterize cancer survivors, whereas patients who resign themselves to their fate are less likely to survive (Greer et al., 1979; Lewis et al., 1995). High levels of social support from the environment can also increase immune system functioning (Hall & O'Grady, 1990). One review of 81 published studies revealed that level of social support available to people was reliably related to beneficial endocrine and immune system responses to stress (Uchino et al., 1996). Finally, a good sense of humor can also help. A series of studies carried out at

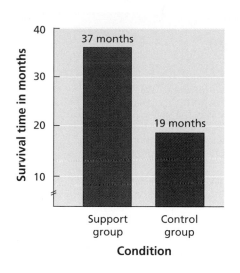

FIGURE 3.26 Mean survival time in breast cancer patients who received a coping skills and social support intervention compared with control patients who received normal cancer treatment. Data from Spiegel et al., 1989

Boston University showed that watching a humorous movie increased immune activity, whereas a control movie did not. Moreover, people who had a good sense of humor as measured by a psychological test had stronger immune responses overall. A sense of humor may cause one to appraise some potentially stressful situations in a more benign fashion by seeing humor in them (McClelland & Cheriff, 1997).

Can psychological interventions enhance people's immune functioning? Psychological training techniques involving imagery, relaxation, and stress management training have produced promising results. In Europe, a treatment program was designed to help stress-ridden but emotionally constrained people who had not yet developed cancer, but were considered to be at risk for the disease because of their personality style. The program focused on building stress-coping skills and on helping the people learn how to express their emotions in an adaptive fashion. A control group of similar people did not receive the training. Thirteen years later, a follow-up study revealed that 90 percent of the trained people subjects were still alive, compared with only 38 percent of the untreated control group (Eysenck, 1994; Eysenck & Grossarth-Maticek, 1991). In another study involving 86 women undergoing breast cancer treatment at Stanford Medical School, women were randomly assigned to either a weekly therapy group designed to strengthen their coping skills and social support or to a no-treatment control group. As shown in Figure 3.26, those in the therapy groups survived nearly twice as long as did the controls (Spiegel et al., 1989).

Obviously, the immune system does not "know" that a feared examination is at hand, that a spouse has died, an earthquake has occurred, or that social support is available. But the brain knows, and there is increasing evidence that what the brain knows and does can affect how well the immune system protects us. The implications are attracting an increasing number of psychologists to the frontiers of psychoneuroimmunology.

Level of Analysis		
Biological	**Psychological**	**Environmental**
• Antigens within body, which trigger immune response • Nerve impulses and hormonal messages from the brain and endocrine system that affect immune functioning • Strength of immune responses	• Cognitive factors, including optimistic and pessimistic thinking • Feelings of helplessness and hopelessness, which depress functioning • Personality factors, including emotionally restrained personality style and sense of humor • Stress management coping skills that help prevent negative effects of stress	• Environmental stressors and significant losses decrease immune functioning • Social support when stressed enhances immune function

IMMUNE FUNCTIONING

FIGURE 3.27 Understanding the Causes of Behavior: Factors influencing immune functions.

The immune system is clearly affected by a host of factors. As shown in Figure 3.27, these factors can be examined at biological, psychological, and environmental levels of analysis.

〉 GENETIC INFLUENCES ON BEHAVIOR

Our physical development, including the development of the nervous system, is in large part directed by an elaborate genetic blueprint passed on to us by our parents. These biological characteristics set limits on our behavioral capabilities. However, our genetic endowment combines with environmental forces to determine our behavior. Modern scientists realize that asking whether a particular behavior is caused by genetic or environmental factors makes no more sense than asking if a triangle is formed by its sides or its corners. Instead, psychologists working in the field of behavior genetics study the ways in which favorable or unfavorable environmental conditions can affect the genetically inherited potential of an organism.

Chromosomes and Genes

How are physical characteristics passed on from parents to their offspring? This question originated in antiquity, and the ancient Greek physician Hippocrates was one of the first to provide a semi-correct answer. Hippocrates suggested that semen contains not body parts, but rather some sort of design for the formation of the offspring. It was not until 22 centuries later that the wisdom of Hippocrates's answer was confirmed by Gregor Mendel, a monk whose research with garden peas in the 1860s marked the beginning of modern genetic theory.

Mendel showed that heredity involves the passing on of specific organic factors, not a simple blending of the parents' characteristics. These specific factors might produce visible characteristics in the offspring, or they might simply be carried for possible transmission to another generation. In any case, the offspring of one set of parents did not all inherit the same traits, as is evident in the differences we see between brothers and sisters.

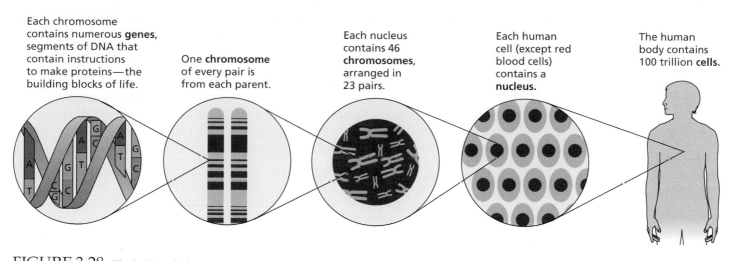

Each chromosome contains numerous **genes**, segments of DNA that contain instructions to make proteins—the building blocks of life.

One **chromosome** of every pair is from each parent.

Each nucleus contains 46 **chromosomes**, arranged in 23 pairs.

Each human cell (except red blood cells) contains a **nucleus.**

The human body contains 100 trillion **cells.**

FIGURE 3.28 The ladder of life. Chromosomes consist of two long, twisted strands of DNA, the chemical that carries genetic information in the form of specific sequences of the substances adenine, thymine, guanine, and cytosine (A, T, G, and C). Every cell in the body (with the exception of red blood cells) carries within its nucleus 23 pairs of chromosomes, each containing numerous genes that regulate every aspect of cellular functioning.

Early in the 20th century, geneticists made the important distinction between **genotype,** the specific genetic makeup of the individual, and **phenotype,** the observable characteristics produced by that genetic endowment. A person's genotype is like the commands in a computer software program. Some of the directives are used on one occasion, some on another. Some are never used at all, either because they are contradicted by other genetic directives or because the environment never calls them forth. Thus genotypes are present from conception and never change, but phenotypes can be affected by other genes and by the environment. For example, geneticists have discovered that chickens have retained the genetic code for teeth (Kollar & Fischer, 1980). Yet because the code is prevented from being expressed, "hens' teeth" remains a cliche for scarcity.

The union of two cells, the egg from the mother and the sperm from the father, is the beginning of a new individual. Like all other cells in the body, the egg and sperm carry within them the material of heredity in the form of rodlike units called chromosomes. A **chromosome** is a tightly coiled molecule of *deoxyribonucleic acid (DNA)* that is partly covered by protein. The DNA portion of the chromosome carries the hereditary blueprint in units called **genes** (Figure 3.28). The many or so genes carried on each chromosome are like a giant computer file of information about your characteristics, potentials, and limitations. Every moment of every day, the strands of DNA silently transmit their detailed instructions for cellular functioning.

In humans, every cell in the body except one type has 46 chromosomes. The exception is the sex cell (the egg or sperm), which has only 23. At conception, the 23 chromosomes from the egg combine with the 23 from the sperm to form a new cell containing 46 chromosomes. The genes within each chromosome also occur in pairs, so that the offspring receives one of each gene pair from each parent. It is estimated that the union of sperm and egg can result in about 70 trillion potential genotypes, accounting for the great diversity in characteristics even in siblings.

Dominant, Recessive, and Polygenic Effects

Genotype and phenotype are not identical because some genes are dominant and some are recessive. If a gene in the pair received from the mother and father is **dominant,** the particular characteristic that it controls will be displayed; if the gene is **recessive,** the characteristic will not show up *unless* the partner gene inherited from the other parent is also recessive. In humans, for example,

➤42. Differentiate between genotype and phenotype.

➤43. How does genetic transmission occur from parents to offspring?

➤44. Compare dominant, recessive, and polygenic influences on phenotypic characteristics.

brown eyes and dark hair are dominant over blue eyes and light hair. Thus a child will have blue eyes only if both parents have contributed genes for blue eyes. Even if their traits remain hidden, however, recessive genes can be passed on to offspring.

In a great many instances, a number of gene pairs combine their influences to create a single phenotypic trait. This is known as **polygenic transmission,** and it complicates the straightforward picture that would occur if all characteristics were determined by one pair of genes. It also magnifies the number of possible variations in a trait that can occur.

Mapping the Genetic Code

At present, our knowledge of phenotypes of traits and disorders greatly exceeds our understanding of the underlying genotype, but that may soon change. In 1990, geneticists began the *Human Genome Project,* a coordinated effort to map all the genes of the human organism. The genetic structure in every one of the 23 chromosome pairs has now been mapped by methods that allow the investigators to literally disassemble the genes on each chromosome and study the specific sequence of substances (A,T,G, and C; Figure 3.28) that occur in each gene. The 3.5 billion letters in the entire human genome would fill 152,000 newspaper pages if printed consecutively. We shall soon have greater knowledge of which specific genes or gene combinations are involved in normal and abnormal characteristics. To date, the location and structure of more than 75 genes that contribute to hereditary diseases have been identified through gene mapping (Wahlsten, 1999).

Genetic Engineering: The Edge of Creation

➤ 45. Describe the methods used in recombinant DNA research.

Advances in molecular biology enable scientists not only to map the human genome, but also to duplicate and modify the structures of genes themselves (Aldridge, 1998). In **recombinant DNA procedures,** researchers use certain enzymes to cut the long threadlike molecules of genetic DNA into pieces, combine it with DNA from another organism, and insert it into a host organism, such as a bacterium. Inside the host, the new DNA combination continues to divide and produce many copies of itself.

This procedure has been used to produce *human growth hormone,* which is very difficult to obtain naturally in large enough quantities to use for therapeutic purposes. In one study, the availability of growth hormone produced through recombinant procedures made it possible to treat 121 children of abnormally short stature who were deficient in the hormone. As a result of their treatment, the children achieved adolescent heights that were only slightly below average, and far beyond what would have been possible without the treatment (Blethen et al., 1997). The positive social and psychological consequences that could occur for the children who received such treatments have interested many psychologists in the application of recombinant technology.

➤ 46. What is the knockout procedure and how is it used by psychologists to study behavior?

Molecular biologists have developed methods for inserting new genetic material into viruses that can infiltrate neurons and modify their genetic structure. These methods are now becoming part of the tool kit of physiological psychologists who wish to study genetic influences on behavior. Recent gene-modification research by psychologists has focused on processes such as learning, memory, emotion, and motivation (Wahlsten, 1999). One procedure done with animals (typically, mice) is to alter a specific gene in a way that prevents it from carrying out its normal function. This is called a *knockout* procedure because that particular function of the gene is eliminated. The effects on behavior are then observed. For example, psychologists can insert genetic material that will prevent neurons from responding to a particular neurotransmitter, then measure whether the animal's ability to learn or remember is affected. This can help psychologists determine the importance of particular transmitter substances in relation to the behaviors of interest (Thomas & Palmiter, 1997). Gene-modification techniques may one day enable us to alter genes that contribute to psychological disorders, such as schizophrenia.

Genetic engineering gives humans potential control over the processes of heredity and evolution. But these revolutionary techniques also give birth to a host of ethical and moral issues (Reiss & Straughan, 1998; Stephenson, 1998). How and when, if ever, should these techniques be used? To prevent genetic disorders? To propogate desirable human characteristics? To duplicate or clone exceptional people? What are the social and environmental consequences of using genetic engineering to greatly extend the healthy life span of people? Questions like these are already the topic of intense discussion as scientific and technological advances carry us toward uncharted genetic frontiers.

Behavior Genetics Techniques

Knowledge of the principles of genetic transmission tell us how genetically similar people are, depending on their degree of relatedness to one another. Recall that children get half of their genetic material from each parent. Thus the probability of sharing any particular gene with one of your parents is 50%, or .50. Brothers and sisters also have a probability of .50 of sharing the same gene with one another, since they get their genetic material from the same parents. And what about grandparents? Here, the probability of a shared gene is .25 because, for example, your maternal grandmother passed half of her genes on to your mother, who passed half of hers on to you. Thus the likelihood that you inherited one of your grandmother's genes is .50 × .50, or .25. The probability of sharing a gene is also .25 for half siblings, who share half their genes with their biological parent, but none with the other parent. An adopted child has no genes in common with his or her adoptive parents, nor do unrelated people share genes in common.

Behavior geneticists are interested in studying how hereditary and environmental factors combine to influence psychological characteristics. One important question is the potential role of genetic factors in accounting for differences among people. The extent to which the degree of variation among a group of people in a particular characteristic can be attributed to genetic factors is estimated by means of a *heritability coefficient*. For example, a heritability coefficient of .50 for intelligence indicates that half of the variation in IQ scores among the people in that group can be attributed to genetic differences. It does *not* mean that for any given individual in that group, 50 percent of the person's intelligence is due to genetic factors and the rest to the environment. Heritability applies only to differences within groups, not to the contribution of genetic factors to any individual within that group. This point is widely misunderstood and misreported in the popular media.

Knowing the level of genetic similarity in family members and relatives provides a basis for estimating the relative contributions of heredity and environment to a physical or psychological characteristic (Plomin, 1997). If a characteristic has higher **concordance,** or co-occurrence, in people who are more highly related to one another, this points to a possible genetic contribution, particularly if the people have lived in different environments.

One research method based on this principle is the **adoption study,** in which a person who was adopted early in life is compared on some characteristic with both the biological parents, with whom the person shares genetic endowment, and with the adoptive parents, with whom no genes are shared. If the adopted person is more similar to the biological parents than to the adoptive parents, a genetic influence is suggested. If greater similarity is shown with the adoptive parents, environmental factors are probably more important. In one study of genetic factors in schizophrenia, Seymour Kety and coworkers (1978) identified formerly adopted children who were diagnosed with the disorder later in life. They then examined the backgrounds of the biological and adoptive

➤47. What is the percentage of genetic resemblance between parents and children, identical and fraternal twins, brothers and sisters, and grandparents and grandchildren?

➤48. How are adoption and twin studies used to achieve heritability estimates? What have such studies shown?

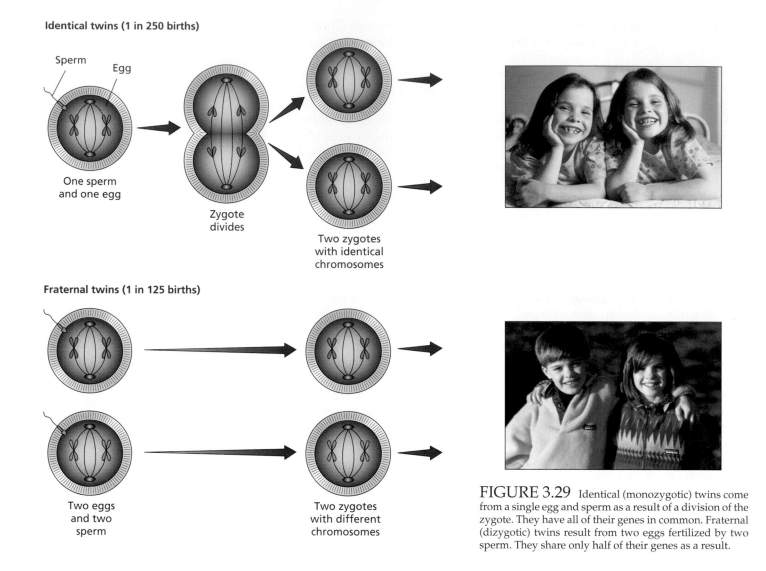

Identical twins (1 in 250 births)

Sperm

Egg

One sperm
and one egg

Zygote
divides

Two zygotes
with identical
chromosomes

Fraternal twins (1 in 125 births)

Two eggs
and two
sperm

Two zygotes
with different
chromosomes

FIGURE 3.29 Identical (monozygotic) twins come from a single egg and sperm as a result of a division of the zygote. They have all of their genes in common. Fraternal (dizygotic) twins result from two eggs fertilized by two sperm. They share only half of their genes as a result.

parents and relatives to determine the rate of schizophrenia in the two sets of families. The researchers found that 12 percent of biological family members had also been diagnosed with schizophrenia, compared with a concordance rate of only 3 percent of adoptive family members, suggesting a hereditary link.

Twin studies are one of the more powerful techniques used in behavior genetics. *Monozygotic*, or identical, twins develop from the same fertilized egg, so they are genetically identical (Figure 3.29). Approximately 1 in 250 births produces identical twins. *Dizygotic*, or fraternal, twins develop from two fertilized eggs, so they share 50 percent of their genetic endowment, like any other set of brothers and sisters. They occur once in 125 births.

Twins are usually raised in the same familial environment. Thus we can compare concordance rates or behavioral similarity in samples of identical and fraternal twins with the idea that if the identical twins are far more similar to one another than are the fraternal twins, a genetic factor is likely to be involved. Of course, it is always possible that because identical twins are more similar to one another in appearance than fraternal twins are, they are treated more alike and therefore share a more similar environment. This environmental factor could partially account for greater behavioral similarity in identical twins. To rule out this environmental explanation for greater psychological similarity, behavior

➤49. Why are studies of twins raised together and apart especially informative? What findings have occurred in such studies?

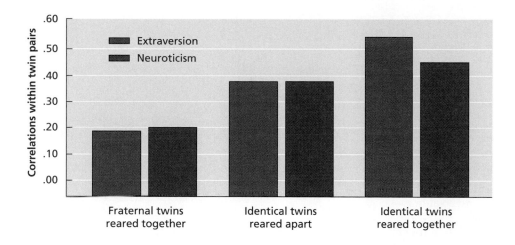

FIGURE 3.30 Degree of similarity on personality measures of extraversion and neuroticism of 24,000 pairs of twins who were reared together and apart.
Data from Loehlin, 1992.

geneticists have adopted an even more elegant research method. Sometimes they are able to find and compare sets of identical and fraternal twins who were separated very early in life and raised in *different* environments (Bouchard et al., 1990). This design permits a better basis for evaluating the respective contributions of genes and environment.

Both adoption and twin studies have led behavioral geneticists to conclude that many psychological characteristics, including intelligence, personality traits, and certain psychological disorders have a notable genetic contribution. Adoptive children are frequently found to be more similar to their biological parents than to their adoptive parents, and identical twins tend to be more similar to one another on many traits than are fraternal twins, even when they have been reared in different environments (Loehlin, 1992; Lykken et al., 1992; Plomin, 1997). Figure 3.30 shows the results of one such comparison. Three groups of twins—identical twins reared together and apart and fraternal twins reared together—completed personality tests of extraversion (sociability, liveliness, impulsiveness) and neuroticism (moodiness, anxiousness, and irritability). The higher correlation coefficients reveal that the identical twins are more similar to one another than are the fraternal twins, and that the degree of similarity in identical twins on the trait of neuroticism is almost as great when they are reared in different environments as when they are reared together (Loehlin, 1992).

On the other hand, heritability studies have also demonstrated that environmental factors interact with genetic endowment in important ways. For example, one adoption study compared the criminal records of men who were adopted at an early age with the criminal records of their biological fathers and their adoptive fathers. A low incidence of criminal behavior was found in the sons whose biological fathers had no criminal record, even if the adoptive fathers who reared them had criminal records. In contrast, the criminal behavior of sons whose biological fathers had criminal records was very high, even if their adoptive fathers had no criminal records. This pattern clearly points to a genetic component in criminality. But one additional finding deserves our attention: The level of criminality was highest of all for those sons whose biological and adoptive fathers *both* had criminal records, suggesting a combined impact of genetic and environmental factors (Cloninger & Gottesman, 1987). In this case, heredity and environment combined to create a double-whammy for society. This finding underscores the conclusion reached when we discussed the nature-nurture issue in Chapter 1: Genetic and environmental factors almost always interact with one another to influence behavior. In the chapters to follow, we focus in more detail on the methods and findings of behavior genetics in relation to many aspects of development and behavior.

CHAPTER SUMMARY

The Neural Bases of Behavior

- Each neuron has dendrites, which receive nerve impulses from other neurons; a cell body (soma), which controls the vital processes of the cell; and an axon, which conducts nerve impulses to adjacent neurons, muscles, and glands.

- Neural transmission is an electrochemical process. The nerve impulse, or action potential, is a brief reversal in the electrical potential of the cell membrane as sodium ions from the surrounding fluid flow into the cell through sodium ion channels, depolarizing the axon's membrane. Graded potentials are proportional to the amount of stimulation being received, whereas action potentials obey the all-or-none law and occur at full intensity if the action potential threshold of stimulation is reached. The myelin sheath increases the speed of neural transmission.

- Passage of the impulse across the synapse is mediated by chemical transmitter substances. Neurons are selective in the neurotransmitters that can stimulate them. Some neurotransmitters excite neurons, whereas others inhibit firing of the postsynaptic neuron.

The Nervous System

- The nervous system is comprised of sensory neurons, motor neurons, and interneurons (associative neurons). Its two major divisions are the central nervous system, consisting of the brain and spinal cord, and the peripheral nervous system. The latter is divided into the somatic system, which has sensory and motor functions, and the autonomic nervous system, which directs the activity of the body's internal organs and glands.

- The spinal cord contains sensory neurons and motor neurons. Interneurons inside the spinal cord serve a connective function between the two. Simple stimulus-response connections can occur as spinal reflexes.

- The autonomic nervous system consists of sympathetic and parasympathetic divisions. The sympathetic system has an arousal function and tends to act as a unit. The parasympathetic system slows down body processes and is more specific in its actions. Together, the two divisions maintain a state of internal balance, or homeostasis.

- Discoveries about brain-behavior relations are made using techniques such as neuropsychological tests, lesioning and surgical ablation, electrical and chemical stimulation of the brain, electrical recording, and brain-imaging techniques. Recently developed methods for producing computer-generated pictures of structures and processes within the living brain include CT and PET scans and magnetic resonance imaging (MRI).

The Hierarchical Brain: Structures and Behavioral Functions

- The human brain consists of the hindbrain, the midbrain, and the forebrain, an organization that reflects the evolution of increasingly more complex brain structures related to behavioral capabilities.

- Major structures within the hindbrain include the medulla, which monitors and controls vital body functions; the pons, which contains important groups of sensory and motor neurons; and the cerebellum, which is concerned with motor coordination.

- The midbrain contains important sensory and motor neurons, as well as many sensory and motor tracts connecting higher and lower parts of the nervous system. The reticular formation plays a vital role in consciousness, attention, and sleep. Activity of the ascending reticular formation excites higher areas of the brain and prepares them to respond to stimulation. The descending reticular formation acts as a gate, determining which stimuli get through to enter into consciousness.

- The forebrain consists of two cerebral hemispheres and a number of subcortical structures. The cerebral hemispheres are connected by the corpus callosum.

- The thalamus acts as a switchboard through which impulses originating in sense organs are routed to the appropriate sensory projection areas. The hypothalamus plays a major role in many aspects of motivational and emotional behavior. The limbic system seems to be involved in organizing the behaviors involved in motivation and emotion.

- The cerebral cortex is divided into frontal, parietal, occipital, and temporal lobes. Some areas of the cerebral cortex receive sensory input, some control motor functions, and others (the association cortex) are involved in higher mental processes in humans. The frontal lobes are particularly important in such executive functions as planning, voluntary behavior, and self-awareness.

- Although the two cerebral hemispheres ordinarily work in coordination with one another, they appear to have different functions and abilities. Studies of split-brain patients who have had the corpus callosum cut indicate that the left hemisphere commands language and mathematical abilities, whereas the right hemisphere has well-developed spatial abilities but a generally limited ability to communicate through speech. However, recent findings indicate that language functions are less lateralized in women than in men. Positive emotions are believed to be linked to relatively greater left-hemisphere activation and negative ones to relatively greater right-hemisphere involvement. Despite hemispheric localization, however, most behaviors involve interactions between both hemispheres; the brain operates as a system.

Plasticity in the Brain

- Neural plasticity refers to the ability of neurons to change in structure and functions. Environmental factors, particularly early in life, have notable effects on brain development.

- A person's ability to recover from brain damage depends on several factors. Other things being equal, recovery is greatest early in life and declines with age.

- When neurons die, surviving neurons can sprout enlarged dendritic networks and extend axons to form new synapses. Neurons can also increase the amount of neurotransmitter substance they release so that they are more sensitive to stimulation. Recent findings suggest that the brains of mature primates and humans are capable of producing new neurons.

- Current advances in the treatment of neurological disorders include experiments on neuron regeneration, the grafting of nerve tissue that produces dopamine into the brains of Parkinson's disease patients, and the injection of neural stem cells into the brain, where they find and replace diseased or dead neurons.

Nervous System Interactions with the Endocrine and Immune Systems

- The nervous, endocrine, and immune systems have extensive neural and chemical means of communication, and each is capable of affecting and being affected by the others.

- The endocrine system secretes hormones into the bloodstream. These chemical messengers affect many body processes, including the activities of the central and autonomic nervous systems. Hormonal effects in the womb may produce brain differences in males and females that influence sex differences in certain psychological functions.

- As a behaving entity, the immune system has the capacity to sense, to interpret, and to respond to specific forms of stimulation. Immune system disorders can occur because of either an underactive or an overactive immune system. Allergic reactions and autoimmune conditions are caused by overactivity; cancer and AIDS result from underactivity.

- The new field of psychoneuroimmunology studies relations between psychological factors and immune system functioning. Messages from the nervous and endocrine systems can affect the functioning of the immune system, making it susceptible to a variety of psychosocial influences. These include stress, cognitive processes, personality factors, and social support.

Genetic Influences on Behavior

- Hereditary potential is carried within the DNA portion of the 23 pairs of chromosomes in units called genes. Genotype and phenotype are not identical because some genes are dominant while others are recessive. Many characteristics are polygenic in origin, influenced by the interactions of multiple genes.

- Genetic engineering allows scientists to duplicate and alter genetic material or, potentially, to repair dysfunctional genes.

- The field of behavior genetics studies the contributions of genetic and environmental factors in psychological traits and behaviors. The major research methods used in an attempt to disentangle hereditary and environmental factors are adoption and twin studies. The most useful research strategy in this regard is the study of identical and fraternal twins who were separated early in life and raised in different environments.

▼▼

KEY TERMS AND CONCEPTS*

acetylcholine (ACh) (88)

action potential (83)

action potential threshold (83)

adoption studies (123)

adrenal glands (116)

all-or-none law (83)

amygdala (100)

aphasia (106)

association cortex (104)

autoimmune reactions (117)

autonomic nervous system (90)

axon (81)

brain stem (96)

Broca's area (104)

central nervous system (89)

cerebellum (96)

cerebral cortex (101)

chromosomes (121)

computerized axial tomography (CT) scan (94)

concordance (123)

corpus callosum (106)

dendrites (81)

depolarization (83)

dominant gene (121)

dopamine (89)

electroencephalogram (EEG) (94)

endocrine system (115)

endorphins (89)

forebrain (99)

frontal lobe (102)

genes (121)

genotype (121)

graded potential (83)

hippocampus (100)

hormones (115)

hypothalamus (99)

interneurons(89)

ion channels (84)

lateralization (106)

limbic system (100)

magnetic resonance imaging (MRI) (95)

medulla (96)

midbrain (98)

motor cortex (102)

motor neuron (89)

myelin sheath (85)

neural stem cells (114)

neural plasticity (111)

neuromodulators (89)

neurons (81)

neurotransmitter (86)

occipital lobe (102)

parasympathetic nervous system (91)

parietal lobe (102)

peripheral nervous system (89)

phenotype (121)

polygenic transmission (122)

pons (96)

positron emission tomography (PET) scan (95)

prefrontal cortex (105)

psychoneuroimmunology (PNI) (118)

receptor sites (86)

recessive gene (121)

recombinant DNA procedures (122)

reticular formation (98)

reuptake (87)

sensory neurons (89)

serotonin (89)

somatic nervous system (90)

somatic sensory cortex (103)

sympathetic nervous system (91)

synapse (86)

synaptic vesicles (86)

temporal lobe (102)

thalamus (99)

twin studies (124)

Wernicke's area (104)

* Each term has been boldfaced in the text on the page indicated in parentheses.

▼▼▼

APPLYING YOUR KNOWLEDGE

These questions allow you to apply your understanding of material in this chapter.

1. In a class report, you wish to summarize the relationship between psychology and biology from the perspective of a neuroscientist. Which of the following statements would you choose?
   a) All psychological processes result from the functioning of biological systems.
   b) Mind is spiritual in nature; brain is biological. The two interact with one another.
   c) Psychological process involve, but do not result from, biological processes.
   d) The biological level of analysis is the only useful one for understanding behavior.

2. Molly suffers from multiple sclerosis, and her movements are jerky and uncoordinated. Which part of the neuron has been damaged by this disease?
   a) the dendrites
   b) the axon
   c) the myelin sheath
   d) the synaptic vessicles

3. Curare is a poisonous plant extract into which native hunters of South America dip their arrows. It paralyzes the muscles of their prey. Based on your knowledge, which neurotransmitter is affected by this poison?
   a) dopamine
   b) acetylcholine
   c) serotonin
   d) endorphins

4. Jason is suffering from schizophrenia. His doctor prescribes a drug that dramatically reduces his thought disorder and hallucinations. The drug most likely helps Jason by
   a) reducing dopamine activity at synapses within the brain.
   b) increasing serotonin activity in the brain.
   c) reducing the activity of the sympathetic nervous system.
   d) inhibiting neurons that are activated by acetylcholine.

5. You are a physiological psychologist who wishes to record changes in neural activity within specific brain areas while humans perform a learning task. Which brain scan

method would you find most useful to record ongoing changes?

a) EEG

b) PET scan

c) CT scan

d) functional magnetic resonance imaging (FMRI)

6. After being knocked out and striking the back of his head on the canvas, a boxer lapses into a permanent coma. Which part of his brain has most likely been damaged?

a) the thalamus

b) the hypothalamus

c) the cerebellum

d) the reticular formation

7. After an automobile accident, Lynn is unable to form memories of recent events. The brain structure most likely damaged is the

a) amygdala.

b) hypothalamus.

c) hippocampus.

d) medulla.

8. Martin has a history of poorly planned and impulsive criminal behavior resulting from a tendency to ignore future consequences and failure to make meaningful plans. As a neuropsychologist, which cortical area would you see as most likely being dysfunctional in him?

a) frontal

b) parietal

c) occipital

d) temporal

9. Two people, Chris A. and Chris B., suffer similar strokes in the left hemisphere. Chris A. exhibits severe aphasia as a result, whereas Chris B.'s language functions are less severely affected. Based on current knowledge of language lateralization, Chris A. and Chris B. are likely to be, respectively, a(n) _____ and a(n) _____.

a) young woman; old woman

b) man; woman

c) child; adult

d) woman; man

10. As you enter the classroom for the course examination on this material, you find yourself experiencing anxiety in the form of increased heart rate, muscle tension, and wet underarms. These symptoms are most likely produced by your

a) somatic nervous system.

b) immune system.

c) parasympathetic nervous system.

d) sympathetic nervous system.

Answers

1. a) (page 81); 2. c) (page 85); 3. b) (page 88); 4. a) (page 89); 5. d) (page 95); 6. d) (page 98); 7. c) (page 100); 8. a) (page 105); 9. b) (page 110); 10. d) (page 91).

For additional quizzing and a variety of interactive resources, visit the book's Online Learning Center at www.mhhe.com/passer.

SENSATION AND PERCEPTION

All our knowledge has its origins in our perceptions.
—Leonardo da Vinci

4

CHAPTER 4 OUTLINE

Helen Keller (*left*) "hears" her teacher Anne Sullivan by reading Sullivan's lips with her fingers.

Source: AP/Wide World Photos Helen Keller/Anne Sullivan

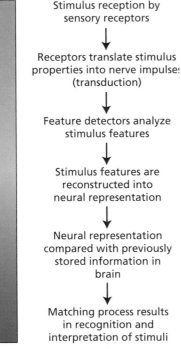

Sensation

Stimulus reception by sensory receptors

↓

Receptors translate stimulus properties into nerve impulses (transduction)

↓

Feature detectors analyze stimulus features

↓

Stimulus features are reconstructed into neural representation

↓

Neural representation compared with previously stored information in brain

↓

Matching process results in recognition and interpretation of stimuli

Perception

FIGURE 4.1 Sensory and perceptual processes proceed from the reception and translation of physical energies into nerve impulses to the active process by which the brain receives the nerve impulses, organizes and confers meaning on them, and constructs a perceptual experience.

➤ 1. Describe the five stages that comprise the process of sensory processing and perception of information.

Sometimes, it is true, a sense of isolation enfolds me like a cold mist as I sit alone and wait at life's shut gate. Beyond, there is light, and music, and sweet companionship; but I may not enter. Fate, silent, pitiless, bars the way. . . . Silence sits immense upon my soul. (Keller, 1955, p. 62)

So wrote Helen Keller, deprived of both vision and hearing by an acute illness suffered when she was 19 months old. For those of us who enjoy and take for granted the use of these senses, it is hard to imagine what it would be like to sink into a dark and silent universe, cut off from all sight and sound. Helen Keller was saved from this abyss by her teacher, Anne Sullivan, who taught and communicated with her by tapping signs onto the little girl's palm. One day, Sullivan tapped "water" onto Helen's palm as she placed the child's hand under the gushing spout of a pump.

That living word awakened my soul, gave it light, hope, joy, set it free! That was because I saw everything with a strange new sight that had come to me. . . . It would have been difficult to find a happier child than I was. (p. 103)

Helen Keller went on to write her celebrated book, *The Story of My Life*, while an undergraduate at Radcliffe College, and she became an inspiration and advocate for people with disabilities.

Nature gives us a marvelous set of sensory contacts with our world. If our sense organs are not defective, we experience light waves as brightnesses and colors, air vibrations as sounds, chemical substances as odors or tastes, and so on. However, such is not the case for people with a rare and mysterious condition called **synesthesia,** which means, quite literally, "mixing of the senses" (Cytowic, 1989; Harrison & Baron-Cohen, 1997). They may experience sounds as colors or tastes as touch sensations that have different shapes.

The Russian psychologist A. R. Luria (1968) studied a highly successful writer and musician whose life was a perpetual stream of mixed-up sensations. On one occasion, Luria asked him to report on his experiences while listening to electronically generated musical tones. To a medium-pitch tone, the man experienced a brown strip with red edges, together with a sweet and sour flavor. A very high-pitched tone evoked the following sensation: "It looks something like a fireworks tinged with a pink-red hue. The strip of color feels rough and unpleasant, and it has an ugly taste—rather like that of a briny pickle. . . . You could hurt your hand on this." Mixed-up sensations like these also occurred in the man's daily life, and sometimes they were disconcerting. On one occasion, the man asked an ice cream vendor what flavors she sold. "But she answered in such a tone that a whole pile of coals, of black cinders, came bursting out of her mouth, and I couldn't bring myself to buy any ice cream after she answered that way."

Sensory-impaired people like Helen Keller and those who experience synesthesia provide glimpses into different aspects of how we "sense" and "understand" our world. These processes, previewed in Figure 4.1, begin when specific types of stimuli activate specialized sensory receptors. Whether the stimulus is light, sound waves, a chemical molecule, or pressure, your sensory receptors must translate this information into the only language your nervous system understands—the language of nerve impulses. Once this translation occurs, specialized neurons break down and analyze the specific features of the stimuli. At the next stage, these numerous stimulus "pieces" are reconstructed into a neural representation that is then compared with previously stored information, such as our knowledge of what particular objects look, smell, or feel like. This matching of a new stimulus with our internal storehouse of knowledge allows us to recognize the stimulus and give it meaning. We then consciously experience a perception.

Helen Keller could not detect light waves or sound waves, the stimuli for sight and hearing. But for her, the sense of touch helped make up for this deficit, giving her a substitute window to her world. In the mysterious condition of synesthesia, something goes wrong at the level of either feature detection or the recombining of the elements of a stimulus so that light waves might give rise to an experience of a sound or texture (Harrison & Baron-Cohen, 1997).

In some ways, sensation and perception blend together so completely that they are difficult to separate, for the stimulation we receive through our sense organs is instantaneously organized and transformed into the experiences that we refer to as perceptions. Nevertheless, psychologists do distinguish between them. **Sensation** is the stimulus-detection process by which our sense organs respond to and translate environmental stimuli into nerve impulses that are sent to the brain. **Perception**—making "sense" of what our senses tell us—is the active process of organizing this stimulus input and giving it meaning (Banks & Krajicek, 1991).

Because perception is an active and creative process, the same sensory input may be perceived in different ways at different times. For example, read the two sets of symbols in Figure 4.2. The middle symbols in both sets of curved lines are exactly the same and they sent identical input to your brain, but you probably perceived them differently. Your interpretation, or perception, of the characters was influenced by their *context*—that is, by the characters that preceded and followed them, and by your learned expectation of what normally follows the letter A and the number 12. This is a simple illustration of how perception takes us a step beyond sensation.

➤ 2. How do psychologists differentiate between sensation and perception?

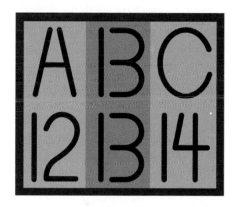

FIGURE 4.2 Quickly read these two lines of symbols out loud. Did your perception of the middle symbol in each line depend on the symbols that surrounded it?

❭ SENSORY PROCESSES

Locked within the silent, dark recesses of your skull, your brain cannot "understand" light waves, sound waves, or the other forms of energy that make up the language of the environment. Contact with the outer world is possible only because certain neurons have developed into specialized sensory receptors that can transform these energy forms into the code language of nerve impulses.

As a starting point, we might ask: How many senses are there? Certainly there appear to be more than the five classical senses with which we are familiar: vision, audition (hearing), touch, gustation (taste), and olfaction (smell). For example, there are senses that provide information about balance and body position. Also, the sense of touch can be subdivided into separate senses of pressure, pain, and temperature. Receptors deep within the brain monitor the chemical composition of our blood. The immune system also has sensory functions that allow it to detect foreign invaders and to receive stimulation from the brain (Nossal & Hall, 1995).

Like those of other organisms, human sensory systems are designed to extract from the environment the information that we need to function and survive. Although our survival does not depend upon having eyes like eagles or owls, noses like bloodhounds, or ears as sensitive as those of the worm-hunting

TABLE 4.1	SOME APPROXIMATE ABSOLUTE THRESHOLDS FOR VARIOUS SENSES
Sense Modality	Absolute Threshold
Vision	Candle flame seen at 30 miles on a clear, dark night
Hearing	Tick of a watch under quiet conditions at 20 feet
Taste	1 teaspoon of sugar in 2 gallons of water
Smell	1 drop of perfume diffused into the entire volume of a large apartment
Touch	Wing of a fly or bee falling on your cheek from a distance of 1 cm

Source: Based on Galanter, 1962.

➤ 3. What two kinds of sensory capabilities are studied by psychophysics researchers?

robin, we do have specialized sensors that can detect many different kinds of stimuli with considerable sensitivity. The scientific area of **psychophysics,** which studies relations between the physical characteristics of stimuli and sensory capabilities, is concerned with two kinds of sensitivity. The first concerns the absolute limits of sensitivity. For example, what is the dimmest light, the softest sound, or the weakest salt solution that humans can detect? The second kind of sensitivity has to do with differences between stimuli. What is the smallest difference in brightness that we can detect? How much difference must there be in two tones before we can tell that they are not identical?

Stimulus Detection: The Absolute Threshold

➤ 4. What is the absolute threshold, and how is it technically defined and measured?

How intense must a stimulus be before we can detect its presence? Researchers answer this question by systematically presenting stimuli of varying intensities and asking people whether they can detect them. Because we are often unsure of whether we have actually sensed very faint stimuli, researchers designate the **absolute threshold** as the lowest intensity at which a stimulus can be detected 50 percent of the time. Thus the *lower* the absolute threshold, the *greater* the sensitivity. From studies of absolute thresholds, the general limits of human sensitivity for the five major senses can be estimated. Some examples are presented in Table 4.1. As you can see, many of our senses are surprisingly sensitive. Yet some other species have absolute thresholds that seem incredible by comparison. For example, a female silkworm moth who is ready to mate needs to release only a billionth of an ounce of an attractant chemical molecule per second to attract every male silkworm moth within a radius of a mile.

Signal Detection Theory

I can remember lying in bed as a child after seeing a horror movie, straining my ears to detect any unusual sound that might signal the presence of a monster in the house. My vigilance caused me to detect faint and ominous sounds that would have probably gone unnoticed had I seen a comedy or a western earlier in the evening. Perhaps you have had a similar experience.

➤ 5. Why do signal detection theorists view stimulus detection as a decision? What are the four possible outcomes of such a decision?

At one time it was assumed that each person had a more or less fixed level of sensitivity for each sense. But psychologists who study stimulus detection found that people's apparent sensitivity can fluctuate quite a bit. They concluded that the concept of a fixed absolute threshold is inaccurate because there is no single point on the intensity scale that separates nondetection from detection of a stimulus. There is instead a range of uncertainty, and people set their own **decision criterion,** a standard of how certain they must be that a stimulus is present before they will say they detect it. The decision criterion can also change from time to time, depending on such factors as fatigue, expectation, and the potential significance of the stimulus. **Signal detection theory** is concerned with the factors that influence sensory judgments.

In a typical signal detection experiment, participants are told that after a warning light appears, a barely perceptible tone may or may not be presented. Their task is to tell the experimenter whether they heard the tone. Under these conditions, there are four possible outcomes, as shown in Figure 4.3. When the tone is in fact presented, the participant may say "yes" (a hit) or "no" (a miss). When no tone is presented, the participant may also say "yes" (a false alarm) or "no" (a correct rejection).

At low stimulus intensities, both the participant's and the situation's characteristics influence the decision criterion (Methot & Huitema, 1998; Pitz & Sachs, 1984). Bold participants who frequently say "yes" have more hits, but they also have more false alarms than do conservative participants. Participants can also be influenced to become bolder or more conservative by manipulating the rewards and costs for giving correct or incorrect responses. Increasing the rewards for hits or the costs for misses results in lower detection thresholds (more "yes" responses at low intensities). Thus a Navy radar operator may be more likely to notice a faint blip on her screen during a wartime mission, where a miss might have disastrous consequences, than during a peacetime voyage. Conversely, like physicians who will not perform a risky medical procedure without strong evidence to support their diagnosis, participants become more conservative in their "yes" responses as costs for false alarms are increased, resulting in higher detection thresholds (Irwin & McCarthy, 1998). Signal detection research shows us that perception is, in part, a decision.

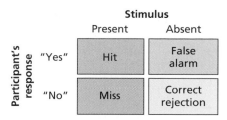

FIGURE 4.3 This matrix shows the four possible outcomes in a signal detection experiment in which participants decide whether a stimulus has been presented or not presented. The percentages of responses that fall wihin each category can be affected by both characteristics of the participants and the nature of the situation.

➤ 6. What kinds of personal and situational factors influence signal detection decision criteria?

Subliminal Stimuli: Can They Affect Behavior?

A **subliminal stimulus** is one that is so weak or brief that although it is received by the senses, it cannot be perceived consciously. There is little question that subliminal stimuli can register in the nervous system (Kihlstrom, 1990; MacLeod, 1998; Merickle & Daneman, 1998). But can such stimuli affect attitudes and behavior without our knowing it? The answer appears to be yes—to a limited extent.

In the late 1950s, James Vicary, a public-relations executive, arranged to have subliminal messages flashed on a theater screen during a movie. The messages urged the audience to "drink Coca-Cola" and "eat popcorn." Vicary's claim that the subliminal messages increased popcorn sales by 50 percent and soft drink sales by 18 percent aroused a public furor. Consumers and scientists feared possible abuse of subliminal messages to covertly influence the buying habits of consumers, and even for mind control and brainwashing purposes. The National Association of Broadcasters reacted by outlawing subliminal messages on American television.

The outcries were, in large part, false alarms. Several attempts to reproduce Vicary's results under controlled conditions failed, and many other studies conducted in laboratory settings, on television and radio, and in movie theaters indicated that there is little reason to be seriously concerned about significant or widespread control of consumer behavior through subliminal stimulation (Dixon, 1981; Drukin, 1998). Ironically, Vicary admitted years later that his study was a hoax designed to revive his floundering advertising agency. Nonetheless, his false report stimulated a great deal of useful research on the power of subliminal stimuli to influence behavior. Where consumer behavior is concerned, the conclusion is that persuasive stimuli above the perceptual threshold are far more influential than subliminal attempts to sneak into our subconscious mind, perhaps because we are more certain to "get the message."

➤ 7. According to research results, what effects do subliminal stimuli have on consumer behavior, attitudes, and self-improvement outcomes?

Though consumer behavior cannot be controlled subliminally, can such stimuli affect more subtle phenomena, such as attitudes? Here the effects are stronger (Arndt et al., 1997; Greenwald & Benaji, 1995). In one study, Jon Krosnick (1992) showed participants nine slides of a particular person and then measured their attitudes toward the target person. For half of the participants, each photograph was immediately preceded by an unpleasant picture (e.g., a face on fire) that was presented subliminally. The remaining participants were shown pleasant subliminal stimuli, such as smiling babies. Participants shown the associated unpleasant subliminal stimuli expressed somewhat negative attitudes toward the person, indicating a process of subconscious attitude conditioning, whereas those who saw the positive subliminal stimuli did not.

Most commonly, subliminal materials are used by people who are trying to change themselves. Each year, consumers spend many millions of dollars on subliminal tapes in the hope that they can lose weight, gain self-confidence, stop smoking, make friends, conquer fears, and reach other personal-improvement goals by using subthreshold stimulation to program the subconscious mind (Pratkanis et al., 1994). How effective is this approach to personal enhancement? Anthony Greenwald and his coworkers (1991) conducted an experimental test of commercially produced tapes purporting either to increase self-esteem or improve memory. Through newspaper advertisements, the researchers recruited participants who wanted to improve in these areas and pretested them for their level of self-esteem and their memory abilities. They then gave the participants a subliminal tape to use daily for a month. At the end of the month, the participants were retested for self-esteem and memory improvement.

The experimental manipulation, or independent variable, was the label on the tape. Half of the participants who were given the tape labeled "self-esteem improvement" actually received the memory-improvement tape, and half of those who were given the tape labeled "memory improvement" actually got the self-esteem tape. The researchers reasoned that if the subliminal tapes were effective, the participants should show improvement in the area that was targeted by the tape they actually received. On the other hand, if improvement was based solely on the participants' expectations that the tape would help them, they should show greater change in the area they thought they were improving with the tape.

Overall, the participants improved significantly in both self-esteem and memory. But as Figure 4.4 shows, the participants who thought they were listening to a self-esteem improvement tape but were actually given the memory improvement tape showed a larger increase in self-esteem than did participants who actually listened to the self-esteem tape. In the case of memory improvement, those who listened to the self-esteem tape did slightly better than those actually given the memory tape. Thus the positive changes in self-esteem and memory that did occur seem attributable to a general expectancy or placebo effect that had nothing to do with the actual content of the subliminal tape. Apparently, the power of belief is greater than the power of subliminal self-improvement messages.

The Difference Threshold

Distinguishing between stimuli can sometimes be as important as detecting stimuli in the first place. When we try to match the colors of paints or clothing, very subtle differences can be quite important. Likewise, a slight variation in taste might signal that food is tainted or spoiled. Professional wine tasters and piano tuners make their livings by being able to make very slight discriminations between stimuli.

The **difference threshold** is defined as the smallest difference between two stimuli that people can perceive 50 percent of the time. The difference threshold is sometimes called the *just noticeable difference (jnd)*. Fortunately, as the German

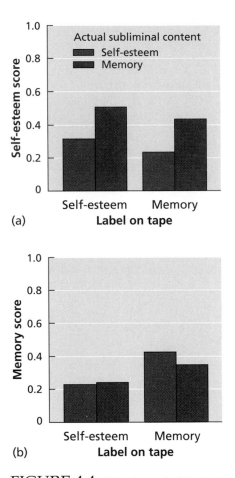

FIGURE 4.4 The effects of subliminal self-help tapes on self-esteem and memory are shown. Participants who were given a tape labeled as either self-esteem or memory improvement, but who actually received the opposite tape, improved as much or more than participants whose subliminal tape actually corresponded to the label.

➤ 8. What is the technical definition of a difference threshold? How does Weber's law help us compare jnd sensitivities in the various senses?

TABLE 4.2	WEBER FRACTIONS FOR VARIOUS SENSORY MODALITIES

Sensory Modality	Weber Fraction
Audition (tonal pitch)	1/333
Vision (brightness, white light)	1/60
Kinesthesis (lifted weights)	1/50
Pain (heat produced)	1/30
Audition (loudness)	1/20
Touch (pressure applied to skin)	1/7
Smell (India rubber)	1/4
Taste (salt concentration)	1/3

Sources: Geldard, 1962; Teghtsoonian, 1971.

physiologist Ernst Weber discovered in the 1830s, there is some degree of lawfulness in the range of sensitivities within our sensory systems. **Weber's law** states that the difference threshold, or jnd, is directly proportional to the magnitude of the stimulus with which the comparison is being made and can be expressed as a *Weber fraction.* For example, the jnd value for weights is a Weber fraction of approximately 1/50 (Teghtsoonian, 1971). This means that if you lift a weight of 50 grams, a comparison weight must weigh at least 51 grams in order for you to be able to judge it as heavier. If the weight were 500 grams, a second weight must weigh at least 510 grams (i.e., 1/50 = 10 g/500 g) for you to discriminate between them.

Although Weber's law breaks down at extremely high and low intensities of stimulation, it holds up reasonably well within the most frequently encountered range, therefore providing a reasonable barometer of our abilities to discern differences in the various sensory modalities. Table 4.2 lists Weber fractions for the various senses. The smaller the fraction, the greater the sensitivity to differences. As highly visual creatures, humans show greater sensitivity in their visual sense than they do in, for example, their sense of smell. Undoubtedly many creatures who depend upon their sense of smell to track their prey would show quite a different order of sensitivity. Weber fractions also show that humans are highly sensitive to differences in the pitch of sounds, but far less sensitive to loudness differences.

Sensory Adaptation

Because changes in our environment are often most newsworthy, sensory systems are finely attuned to *changes* in stimulation. Sensory neurons are engineered to respond to a constant stimulus by *decreasing* their activity, and the diminishing sensitivity to an unchanging stimulus is called **sensory adaptation.**

Adaptation (sometimes called *habituation*) is a part of everyday experience. After a while, monotonous background sounds are largely unheard. The feel of your wristwatch against your skin recedes from awareness. If you dive into a swimming pool, the water may feel cold at first because your body's temperature sensors respond to the change in temperature. With time, however, you become used to the water temperature.

Adaptation occurs in all sensory modalities, including vision. Indeed, were it not for tiny involuntary eye movements that keep images moving about the retina, stationary objects would simply fade from sight if we stared at them. In an ingenious demonstration of this variety of adaptation, R. M. Pritchard

➤ 9. What accounts for sensory adaptation? Of what survival value is adaptation?

(1961) attached a tiny projector to a contact lens worn by the participant (Figure 4.5*a*). This procedure guaranteed that visual images presented through the projector would maintain a constant position on the retina, even when the eye moved. When a stabilized image was projected through the lens onto the retina, participants reported that the image appeared in its entirety for a time, then began to vanish and reappear as parts of the original stimulus (Figure 4.5*b*).

Although sensory adaptation may reduce our overall sensitivity, it is adaptive, for it frees our senses from the constant and the mundane to pick up informative changes in the environment. Such changes may turn out to be important to our well-being or survival.

❯ THE SENSORY SYSTEMS

Vision

The normal stimulus for vision is electromagnetic energy, or light waves, which are measured in *nanometers* (nm, or one billionth of a meter). In addition to that tiny portion that humans can perceive, the electromagnetic spectrum includes X rays, television and radio signals, and infrared and ultraviolet rays (Figure 4.6). Bees are able to "see" ultraviolet light, and rattlesnakes can detect infrared energy. Our visual system is sensitive only to wavelengths extending from about 700 nm (red) down to about 400 nm (blue-violet). (You can remember the order of the spectrum, from higher wavelengths to lower ones, with the name ROY G. BIV—red, orange, yellow, green, blue, indigo, and violet.)

The Human Eye

Light waves enter the eye through the *cornea*, a transparent protective structure at the front of the eye (Figure 4.7). Behind the cornea is the *pupil*, an adjustable opening that can dilate or constrict to control the amount of light that enters the eye. The pupil's size is controlled by muscles in the colored *iris* that surrounds the pupil. Low levels of illumination cause the pupil to dilate, letting more light into the eye to improve optical clarity; bright light triggers constriction of the pupil.

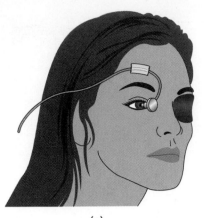

(a)

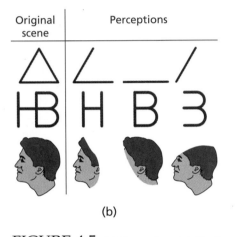

(b)

FIGURE 4.5 (a) To create a stabilized retinal image, a person wears a contact lens to which a tiny projector has been attached. Despite eye movements, images will be cast on the same region of the retina. (b) Under these conditions, the stabilized image is clear at first, then begins to fade and reappear in meaningful segments as the receptors fatigue and recover.

Adapted from Pritchard, 1961.

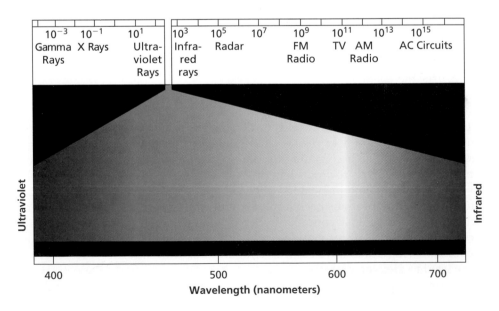

FIGURE 4.6 The full spectrum of electromagnetic radiation. Only the narrow band between 400 and 700 nanometers (nm) is visible to the human eye. One nanometer = 1,000,000,000th of a meter.

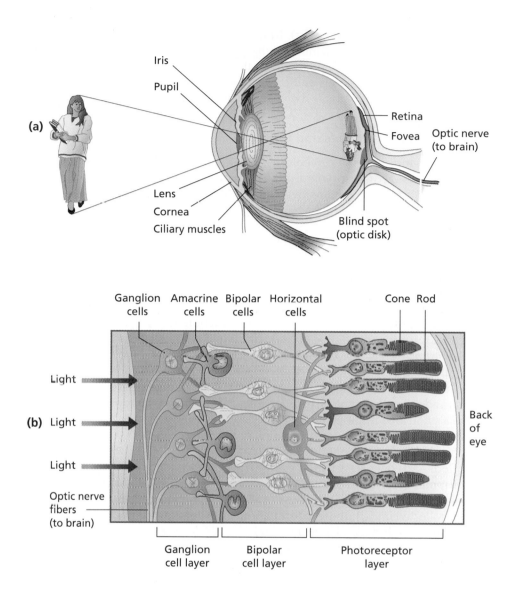

FIGURE 4.7 (a) This cross section shows the major parts of the human eye. The iris regulates the size of the pupil. The ciliary muscles regulate the shape of the lens. The image entering the eye is reversed by the lens and cast on the retina, which contains the photoreceptor cells. The optic disk, where the optic nerve exits the eye, has no receptors and produces a "blind spot" as demonstrated in Figure 4.8. (b) Photoreceptor connections in the retina. The rods and cones synapse with bipolar cells, which in turn synapse with ganglion cells, whose axons form the optic nerve. The horizontal and amacrine cells allow sideways integration of retinal activity across areas of the retina.

Behind the pupil is the **lens,** an elastic structure that becomes thinner to focus on distant objects and thicker to focus on nearby objects. Just as the lens of a camera focuses an image on a photosensitive material (film), so the lens of the eye focuses the visual image on the light-sensitive **retina,** a multilayered tissue at the rear of the fluid-filled eyeball. As seen in Figure 4.7, the lens reverses the image from right to left and top to bottom when it is projected upon the retina, but the brain reconstructs the visual input into the image that we perceive.

The ability to see clearly depends on the lens's ability to focus the image directly onto the retina (Pedrotti & Pedrotti, 1997). If you have good vision for nearby objects but have difficulty seeing faraway objects, you probably suffer from **myopia** (nearsightedness). In nearsighted people, the lens focuses the visual image *in front of* the retina (or too near the lens), resulting in a blurred image for faraway objects. This condition generally occurs becase the eyeball is longer (front to back) than normal. In contrast, some people have excellent distance vision but have difficulty seeing close-up objects clearly. **Hyperopia** (farsightedness) occurs when the lens does not thicken enough and the image is therefore focused on a point *behind* the retina (or too far from the lens). The aging process typically causes the eyeball to become shorter over time, contributing to the development of hyperopia and the need for many middle-aged people to acquire reading glasses (after complaining that their arms are not long enough to read

➤ 10. How does the lens affect visual acuity, and how does its dysfunction cause the visual problems of myopia and hyperopia?

newspapers and telephone books). Ironically, this age-related shortening of the eyeball often improves the vision of myopic people, for as the retina moves closer to the lens, it approaches the point where the "nearsighted" lens is projecting the image (Orr, 1998). Eyeglasses and contact lenses are designed to correct for the natural lens's inability to focus the visual image directly onto the retina.

Photoreceptors: The Rods and Cones

The retina, a multilayered screen that lines the back surface of the eyeball and contains specialized sensory neurons, is actually an extension of the brain (Gregory, 1990). The retina contains two types of light-sensitive receptor cells, called rods and cones because of their shapes (Figure 4.7b). There are about 120 million rods and 6 million cones in the human eye.

> ➤ 11. How are the rods and cones distributed in the retina, and how do they contribute to brightness perception, color vision, and visual acuity?

The **rods,** which function best in dim light, are primarily black-and-white brightness receptors. They are about 500 times more sensitive to light than are the cones, but they do not give rise to color sensations. The retinas of some night creatures, such as the owl, contain only rods, so they have exceptional vision in very dim light but no color vision during the day (Dossenbach & Dossenbach, 1998). The **cones,** which are color receptors, function best in bright illumination. Some creatures that are active only during the day, such as the the pigeon and the chipmunk, have only cones in their retinas, so they see the world in living color but have very poor night vision (Dossenbach & Dossenbach, 1998). Animals that are active during both day and night, as humans are, have a mixture of rods and cones. In humans, rods are found throughout the retina except in the **fovea,** a small area in the center of the retina that contains only cones. Cones decrease in concentration as one moves away from the center of the retina, and the periphery of the retina contains mainly rods.

Rods and cones send their messages to the brain via two additional layers of cells. **Bipolar cells** have synaptic connections with the rods and cones. The bipolar cells, in turn, synapse with a layer of about 1 million **ganglion cells,** whose axons are collected into a bundle to form the **optic nerve.** Thus input from more than 126 million rods and cones is eventually funnelled into only 1 million traffic lanes leading out of the retina toward higher visual centers. Figure 4.7*b* shows how the rods and cones are connected to the bipolar and ganglion cells. One interesting aspect of these connections is the fact that the rods and cones not only form the *rear* layer of the retina, but their light-sensitive ends actually point *away from* the direction of the entering light so that they receive only a fraction of the light energy that enters the eye. Further, the manner in which the rods and cones are connected to the bipolar cells account for both the greater importance of rods in dim light and our greater ability to see fine detail in bright illumination, when the cones are most active. Typically, many rods are connected to the same bipolar cell. They can therefore combine or "funnel" their individual electrical messages to the bipolar cell, where the additive effect of the many signals may be enough to fire it. That is why we can more easily detect a faint stimulus, such as a dim star, if we look slightly to one side so that its image falls not on the fovea but on the peripheral portion of the retina, where the rods are packed most densely.

Like the rods, the cones that lie in the periphery of the retina also share bipolar cells. In the fovea, however, the densely packed cones each have their own "private line" to a single bipolar cell. As a result, our **visual acuity,** or ability to see fine detail, is greatest when the visual image projects directly onto the fovea. Such focusing results in the firing of a large number of cones and their private-line bipolar cells.

The optic nerve formed by the axons of the ganglion cells exits through the back of the eye not far from the fovea, producing a *blind spot,* where there are no photoreceptors. You can demonstrate the existence of your blind spot by following the directions for the demonstration in Figure 4.8. Ordinarily, we are

FIGURE 4.8 Close your left eye and from a distance of about 12 inches, focus steadily on the dot with your right eye as you slowly move the book toward your face. At some point the image of the X will cross your optic disk (blind spot) and disappear. It will reappear after it crosses the blind spot. Note how the checkerboard remains wholly visible even though part of it falls on the blind spot. Your perceptual system "fills in" the missing information.

unaware of the blind spot because our perceptual system "fills in" the missing part of the visual field.

Visual Transduction: From Light to Nerve Impulses

The process whereby the characteristics of a stimulus are converted into nerve impulses is called **transduction.** Rods and cones translate light waves into nerve impulses through the action of protein molecules called **photopigments** (Stryer, 1987; Wolken, 1995). The absorption of light by these molecules produces a chemical reaction that changes the rate of neurotransmitter release at the receptor's synapse with the bipolar cells. The greater the change in transmitter release, the stronger the signal passed on to the bipolar cell and, in turn, to the ganglion cells whose axons form the optic nerve. If nerve responses are triggered at each of the three levels (rod or cone, bipolar cell, and ganglion cell), the message is instantaneously on its way to the visual relay station in the thalamus, and then on to the visual cortex of the brain.

Brightness Vision and Dark Adaptation

As noted earlier, rods are far more sensitive than cones under conditions of low illumination. Nonetheless, the brightness sensitivity of both the rods and the cones depends in part on the wavelength of the light. Research has shown that rods have a much greater brightness sensitivity than cones throughout the color spectrum *except* at the red end, where rods are relatively insensitive. Cones are most sensitive to low illumination in the greenish-yellow range of the spectrum. These findings have prompted many cities to change the color of their fire engines from the traditional red (which rods are insensitive to) to yellow-green in order to increase the vehicles' visibility to both rods and cones in dim lighting. Similarly, airport landing lights are often blue because this wavelength is picked up particularly well by the rods during night vision, when the cones are relatively inoperative.

Although the rods are by nature sensitive to low illumination, they are not always ready to fulfill their function. Perhaps you have had the embarrassing experience of entering a movie theater from bright sunlight, groping around in the darkness, and finally sitting down in someone's lap. Although one can meet interesting people this way, most of us prefer to stand in the rear of the theater until our eyes adapt to the dimly lit interior.

Dark adaptation is the progressive improvement in brightness sensitivity that occurs over time under conditions of low illumination. After absorbing light, a photoreceptor is depleted of its pigment molecules for a period of time. If the eye has been exposed to conditions of high illumination, such as bright sunlight, a substantial amount of photopigment will be depleted. During the process of dark adaptation, the photopigment molecules are regenerated, and the receptor's sensitivity increases greatly.

Vision researchers have plotted the course of dark adaptation as people move from conditions of bright light into darkness (Carpenter & Robson, 1999). By focusing light flashes of varying wavelengths and brightness on the fovea, which contains only cones, or on the periphery of the retina, where rods reside, they discovered the two-part curve shown in Figure 4.9. The first part of the curve is due to dark adaptation of the cones. As you can see, the cones gradually become sensitive to fainter lights as time passes, but after about 5 to 10 minutes in the dark, their sensitivity has reached its maximum. The rods, whose photopigments regenerate more slowly, do not reach their maximum sensitivity for about half an hour. It is estimated that after complete adaptation, rods are able to detect light intensities only 1/10,000 as great as those that could be detected before dark adaptation began (Stryer, 1987).

➤ 12. What is transduction, and how does this process occur in the photoreceptors of the eye?

➤ 13. How is brightness sensitivity in rods and cones affected by the color spectrum?

➤ 14. What is the physiological basis for dark adaptation? What are the two components of the dark adaptation curve?

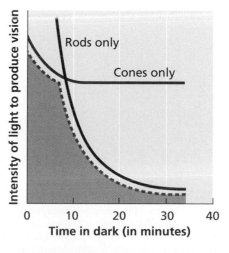

FIGURE 4.9 The course of dark adaptation is graphed over time. The curve has two parts, one for the cones and one for the rods. The cones adapt completely in about 10 minutes, whereas the rods continue to increase their sensitivity for another 20 minutes.

FIGURE 4.10 Working in red light keeps the rods in a state of dark adaptation because rods are quite insensitive to that wavelength. Therefore they retain high levels of photopigment and remain sensitive to low illumination.

➤ 15. Describe the Young-Helmholtz trichromatic theory of color vision. What kinds of evidence support this theory, and what two phenomena challenge it?

➤ 16. Describe the opponent-process theory. What evidence supports it?

➤ 17. How does the dual-process theory of color vision combine the trichromatic and opponent-process theories?

During World War II, psychologists familiar with the facts about dark adaptation provided a method for enhancing night vision in pilots who needed to take off on a moment's notice and see their targets under conditions of low illumination. Knowing that the rods are important in night vision and relatively insensitive to red wavelengths, they suggested that fighter pilots either wear goggles with red lenses or work in rooms lit only by red lights while waiting to be called for a mission. Because red light stimulates only the cones, the rods remain in a state of dark adaptation, ready for immediate service in the dark. That highly practical principle continues to be useful to this day (Figure 4.10).

Color Vision

We are blessed with a world rich in color. The majesty of a glowing sunset, the rich blues and greens of a tropical bay, the brilliant colors of fall foliage all produce visual delights for us. Human vision is finely attuned to color; our difference thresholds for light wavelengths are so small that we are able to distinguish an estimated 7.5 million hue variations (Backhaus et al., 1998). Historically, two different theories of color vision have tried to explain how this occurs.

The trichromatic theory.   Around 1800, it was discovered that any color in the visible spectrum can be produced by some combination of the wavelengths that correspond to the colors blue, green, and red in what is known as *additive color mixture* (Figure 4.11*a*). This fact was the basis of an important trichromatic (three-color) theory of color vision advanced by Thomas Young, an English physicist, and Hermann von Helmholtz, a German physiologist. According to the **Young-Helmholtz trichromatic theory,** there are three types of color receptors in the retina. Although all cones can be stimulated by most wavelengths to varying degrees, individual cones are most sensitive to wavelengths that correspond to either blue, green, or red (Figure 4.12). Presumably, each of these receptor classes sends messages to the brain, based on the extent to which they are activated by the light energy's wavelength. The visual system then combines the signals to recreate the original hue. If all three cones are equally activated, a pure white color is produced.

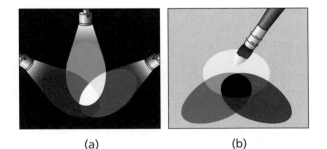

(a)   (b)

FIGURE 4.11 Additive and subtractive color mixture are different processes. (a) Additive color mixture. A beam of light of a specific wavelength directed onto a white surface is perceived as the color that corresponds to that wavelength on the visible spectrum. If beams of light that fall at certain points within the red, green, or blue color range are directed together onto the surface in the correct proportions, a combined or additive mixture of wavelengths will result and any color in the visible spectrum can be produced (including white at the point where all three colors intersect). The Young-Helmholtz trichromatic theory of color vision assumes that color perception results from the additive mixture of impulses from cones that are sensitive to red, blue, and green (see text). (b) Subtractive color mixture. Mixing pigments or paints produces new colors by subtraction—that is, by removing (i.e., absorbing) other wavelengths. Paints absorb (subtract) colors different from themselves while reflecting their own color. For example, blue paint mainly absorbs wavelengths that correspond to nonblue hues. Mixing blue paint with yellow paint (which absorbs wavelengths other than yellow) will produce a subtractive mixture that emits wavelengths between yellow and blue (i.e., green). Theoretically, certain wavelengths of the three primary colors of red, yellow (not green, as in additive mixture), and blue can produce the whole spectrum of colors by subtractive mixture. Thus in additive color mixture, the primary colors are red, blue and green; in subtractive color mixture, they are red, yellow, and blue.

Although the Young-Helmholtz theory was consistent with the laws of additive color mixture, there are several facts that did not fit the theory. For example, according to the theory, yellow is produced by activity of red and green receptors. Yet certain people with red-green color blindness are able to experience yellow. This finding suggested to other scientists that there must be a different means for perceiving yellow. A second phenomenon that posed problems for the trichromatic theory was the color *afterimage,* in which an image in a different color appears after a color stimulus has been viewed steadily and then withdrawn. To experience one yourself, stare steadily at the object in Figure 4.13 for a full minute, then shift your gaze to the blank white space. Trichromatic theory cannot account for what you'll see.

Opponent-process theory.   A second influential color theory, formulated by Ewald Hering in 1870, also assumed that there are three types of cones. Hering's **opponent-process theory** proposed that each of the three cone types responds to *two* different wavelengths. One type responds to red *or* green, another to blue *or* yellow, and a third to black *or* white. For example, a red-green cone responds with one chemical reaction to a green stimulus and with its other chemical reaction (opponent process) to a red stimulus (Figure 4.12). You have experienced one of the phenomena that supports the existence of opponent processes if you did the exercise in Figure 4.13. The color afterimage that you saw in the blank space contains the colors specified by opponent-process theory: The black portion of the flag appeared as white, the green portion "turned" red, and yellow "became" blue. According to opponent-process theory, as you stared at the green, black, and yellow colors, the neural processes that register these colors became fatigued. Then when you cast your gaze upon the white surface, which reflects all wavelengths, a "rebound" opponent reaction occurred as each receptor responded with its opposing red, white, or blue reactions.

Dual processes in color transduction.   Which theory—the trichromatic theory or the opponent-process theory—is correct? Two centuries of research have yielded a win-win verdict for both sets of theorists. Today's **dual-process theory** combines the trichromatic and opponent-process theories to account for the color transduction process (Backhaus et al., 1998).

Trichromatic theorists like Young and Helmholtz were right about the cones. The cones do indeed contain one of three different protein photopigments that are most sensitive to wavelengths roughly corresponding to the colors blue, red, and green (Abramov & Gordon, 1994). Different ratios of activity in the red-, blue-, and green-sensitive cones can produce a pattern of neural activity that corresponds to any hue in the spectrum (Backhaus et al., 1998). This process is similar to that which occurs on your television screen, where color pictures (including white hues) are produced by activating combinations of tiny red, green, and blue dots in a process of additive color mixture.

Hering's opponent-process theory was also partly correct, but opponent processes do not occur at the level of the cones, as he maintained. When researchers began to use microelectrodes to record from single cells in the visual system, they discovered that certain ganglion cells in the retina, as well as some neurons in visual relay stations and the visual cortex, respond in an opponent-process

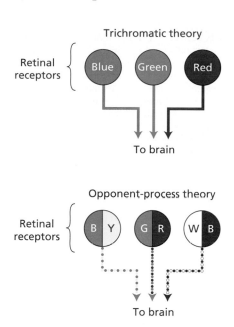

Trichromatic theory

Opponent-process theory

FIGURE 4.12 Two classic theories of color vision. The Young-Helmholtz trichromatic theory proposed three different receptors, one for blue, one for red, and one for green. The ratio of activity in the three types of cones in response to a stimulus yields our experience of color. Hering's opponent-process theory also assumed that there are three different receptors: one for yellow-blue, one for red-green, and one for black-white. Each of the receptors can function in two possible ways, depending on the wavelength of the stimulus. Again, the pattern of activity in the receptors yields our perception of the hue.

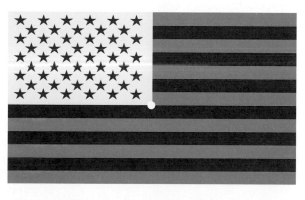

FIGURE 4.13 Negative color afterimages demonstrate opponent processes occurring somewhere in the visual system. Stare steadily at the white dot in the center of the flag for about a minute, then shift your gaze to the black dot in the blank space. The opponent colors should appear.

FIGURE 4.14 Color vision involves both trichromatic and opponent processes that occur at different places in the visual system. Consistent with trichromatic theory, three types of cones are maximally sensitive to short (blue), medium (green), and long (red) wavelengths, respectively. However, opponent processes occur further along in the visual system, as opponent cells in the retina, visual relay stations, and the visual cortex respond differentially to red versus green, blue versus yellow, and black versus white stimuli. Shown here are the inputs from the cones that produce the red-green and blue-yellow opponent processes.

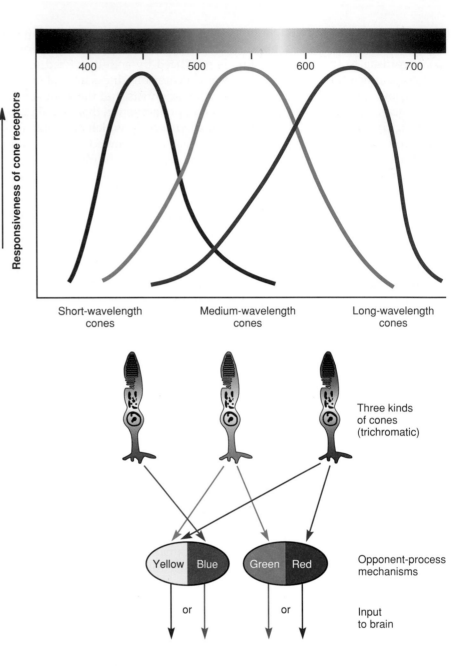

fashion by altering their rate of firing (DeValois & DeValois, 1993). For example, if a red light is shined on the retina, an opponent-process ganglion cell may respond with a high rate of firing, but a green light will cause the same cell to fire at a very low rate. Other neurons respond in a similar opponent fashion to blue and yellow stimuli. The red-green opponent processes are triggered directly by input from the red- or green-sensitive cones in the retina (Figure 4.14). The blue-yellow opponent process is a bit more complex. Activity of blue-sensitive cones directly stimulates the "blue" process farther along in the visual system. And yellow? The yellow opponent process is triggered not by a "yellow-sensitive" cone, as Hering proposed, but rather by simultaneous input from the red- and green-sensitive cones (Abramov & Gordon, 1994).

Color-deficient vision.   People with normal color vision are referred to as *trichromats.* They are sensitive to all three systems: red-green, yellow-blue, and black-white. However, about 7 percent of the male population and 1 percent of the female population have a deficiency in the red-green system, the yellow-blue

➤ 18. What are the two major types of color blindness? How are they tested?

system, or both. This deficiency is caused by an absence of hue-sensitive photopigment in certain cone types. A *dichromat* is a person who is color-blind in only one of the systems (red-green or yellow-blue). A *monochromat* is sensitive only to the black-white system and is totally color-blind. Most color-deficient people are dichromats and have their deficiency in the red-green system. Tests of color blindness typically contain sets of colored dots such as those in Figure 4.15. Depending on the type of deficit, a color-blind person cannot discern certain numbers embedded in the circles.

Analysis and Reconstruction of Visual Scenes

Once the transformation of light energy to nerve impulses occurs, the process of combining the messages received from the photoreceptors into the perception of a visual scene begins. As you read this page, nerve impulses from countless neurons are being analyzed and the visual image that you perceive is being reconstructed. Moreover, you know what these black squiggles on the page "mean." How does this occur?

Feature detectors. From the retina, the optic nerve sends nerve impulses to a visual relay station in the thalamus, the brain's sensory switchboard. From there, the input is routed to various parts of the cortex, particularly the **primary visual cortex** in the occipital lobe at the rear of the brain. Microelectrode studies have shown that there is a point-to-point correspondence between tiny regions of the retina and groups of neurons in the visual cortex. As you might expect, the fovea, where the one-to-one synapses of cones with bipolar cells produces high visual acuity, is represented by a disproportionately large area of the visual cortex. Somewhat more surprising is the fact that there is more than one cortical "map" of the retina; there are at least 10 duplicate mappings. Perhaps this is nature's insurance policy against damage to any one of them, or perhaps the duplicate maps are somehow involved in the integration of visual input.

Groups of neurons within the primary visual cortex are organized to receive and integrate sensory nerve impulses originating in specific regions of the retina. Some of these cells are known as **feature detectors.** They fire selectively in response to stimuli that have specific characteristics (Kanwisher, 1998). Discovery of these feature detectors won David Hubel and Torsten Wiesel of Harvard University the 1981 Nobel Prize. Using tiny electrodes to record the activity of individual cells of the visual cortex of animals (Figure 4.16), Hubel and Wiesel found that certain neurons fired most frequently when lines of certain orientations were presented. One neuron might fire most frequently when a horizontal line was presented; another neuron would fire most frequently to a line of a slightly different orientation, and so on "around the clock." For example, a letter "A" could be constructed from the response of feature detectors that responded to three different line orientations: /, \, and —.

The discovery of feature detectors revolutionized vision research. Since then, scientists have found cells that respond most strongly to bars, slits, and edges in certain positions. Within the cortex, this information is integrated and analyzed by successively more

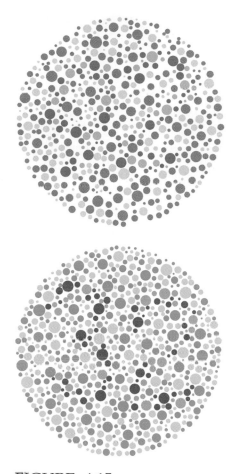

FIGURE 4.15 These dotted figures are used to test for color-deficient vision. The upper one tests for yellow-blue color blindness, the lower one for red-green color blindness. Because the dots in the picture are of equal brightness, color is the only available cue for perceiving the numbers in the chips.

➤ 19. What kinds of feature detectors exist in the visual system? What is meant by parallel processing of sensory information?

FIGURE 4.16 A partially anesthetized monkey views an image projected on the screen while an electrode embedded in its visual cortex records the activity of a single neuron. This research by Hubel and Wiesel led to the discovery of feature detectors that analyze visual stimulus features such as contours and shapes, movement, and color.

FIGURE 4.17 Is the white triangle "real"? It appears to be because feature detectors that analyze the contours of the pie-shaped circles analyze the corners, and the brain fills in the "missing" lines. The contours are illusory, but they appear real. See what happens to the triangle if you cover up one or two of the circles.

➤ 20. What are the two physical characteristics of sound waves, and which auditory qualities do these characteristics produce?

complex feature detector systems to produce our perception of objects. This process is illustrated by the illusion shown in Figure 4.17.

Other classes of feature detectors respond to color, to depth, or to movement (Livingstone & Hubel, 1994; Smith & Snowden, 1995). These feature detector "modules" subdivide a visual scene into its component dimensions and process them simultaneously. Thus as a red, white, and green beach ball sails toward you, separate but overlapping modules within the brain are simultaneously analyzing its colors, shape, distance, and movement by engaging in **parallel processing** of the information and constructing a unified image of its properties (Kanwisher, 1998).

Visual association processes. The final stages in the process of constructing a visual representation occur when the information analyzed and recombined by the primary visual cortex is routed to other cortical regions known as **visual association cortex.** Here successively more complex features of the visual scene are combined and interpreted in light of our memories and knowledge. If all goes correctly, a process that began with nerve impulses from the rods and cones now ends with us "recognizing" the beach ball for what it "is" and catching it. Quite another conscious experience and response would probably occur if we interpreted the oncoming object as a water balloon.

Audition

The stimuli for our sense of hearing are sound waves, a form of mechanical energy. What we call sound is actually pressure waves in air, water, or some other conducting medium. When a stereo's volume is high enough, you can actually see cloth speaker covers moving in and out. The resulting vibrations cause successive waves of compression and expansion among the air molecules surrounding the source of the sound. These sound waves have two characteristics: frequency and amplitude (Figure 4.18).

Frequency is the number of sound waves, or cycles, per second. The **hertz (Hz)** is the technical measure of cycles per second; 1 Hz equals one cycle per second. The sound waves' frequency is related to the pitch that we perceive; the higher the frequency (Hz), the higher the perceived pitch. Humans are capable of detecting sound frequencies from 20 Hz up to 20,000 Hz (about 12,000 Hz in

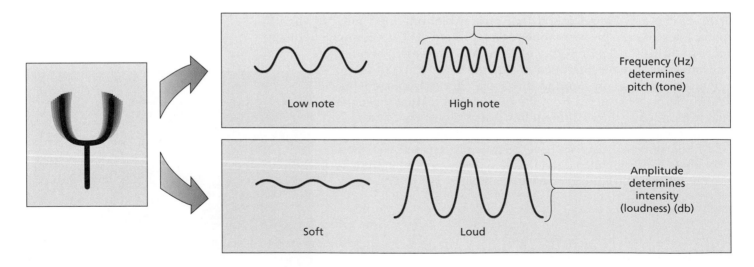

FIGURE 4.18 Sound waves are a form of mechanical energy. As the tuning fork vibrates, it produces successive waves of compression and expansion of air molecules. The number of maximum compressions per second (cycles per second) is its frequency, measured in hertz (Hz). The height of the wave above zero air pressure represents the sound's amplitude. Frequency determines pitch; amplitude determines loudness, measured in decibels (db).

TABLE 4.3	DECIBEL SCALING OF COMMON SOUNDS	

Level in Decibels (db)	Common Sounds	Threshold Levels
140	50 hp siren at a distance of 100 feet; jet fighter taking off at 80 feet from	Potential damage to auditory system
130	plane	
	Boiler shop	
120	Air hammer at position of operator	Human pain threshold
	Rock and roll band	
	Jet aircraft at 500 feet overhead	
110	Trumpet automobile horn at 3 feet	
100	Crosscut saw at position of operator	
90	Inside subway car	Hearing damage with prolonged exposure
	Train whistle at 500 feet	
80		
70	Inside automobile in city	
60	Downtown city street (Chicago)	
	Average traffic	
50	Restaurant	
	Business office	
40	Classroom	
	Church	
30	Hospital room	
	Quiet bedroom	
20	Recording studio	Threshold of hearing (young men)
10		
0		Minimum threshold of hearing

The decibel scale relates a physical quantity—sound intensity—to the human perception of that quantity—sound loudness. It is a logarithmic scale—that is, each increment of 10 db represents a tenfold increase in loudness. The table indicates the decibel ranges of some common sounds as well as thresholds for hearing, hearing damage, and pain. Prolonged exposure at 150 db causes death in laboratory rats.

older people). Most common sounds are in the lower frequencies. Among musical instruments, the piano can play the widest range of frequencies, from 27.5 Hz at the low end of the keyboard to 4,186 Hz at the high end. An operatic soprano's voice, in comparison, has a range of only 250 Hz to 1,100 Hz (Aiello, 1994).

Amplitude refers to the vertical size of the sound waves—that is, to the amount of compression and expansion of the molecules in the conducting medium. The sound wave's amplitude is the primary determinant of the sound's perceived loudness. Differences in amplitude are expressed as **decibels (db)**, a measure of the physical pressures that occur at the eardrum. The absolute threshold for hearing is arbitrarily designated as 0 db, and each increase of 10 db represents a tenfold increase in loudness. Table 4.3 shows various common sounds scaled in decibels.

Auditory Transduction: From Pressure Waves to Nerve Impulses

The transduction system of the ear is made up of tiny bones, membranes, and liquid-filled tubes designed to translate pressure waves into nerve impulses (Figure 4.19). Sound waves travel into an auditory canal leading to the eardrum, a movable membrane that vibrates in response to the sound waves. Beyond the eardrum is the middle ear, a cavity housing three tiny bones (the smallest in the body, in fact). The vibrating activity of these bones—the *hammer* (malleus), *anvil* (incus), and *stirrup* (stapes)—amplifies the sound waves more than 30 times. The first bone, the hammer, is attached firmly to the eardrum, and the stirrup is attached to another membrane, the *oval window*, which forms the boundary between the middle ear and the inner ear. The inner ear contains the **cochlea,** a coiled, snail-shaped tube about 3.5 cm (1.4 in.) in length that is filled with fluid and contains the **basilar membrane,** a sheet of tissue that runs its length. Resting on the basilar membrane is the **organ of Corti,**

➤ 21. Describe how the middle and inner ear structures are involved in the auditory transduction process.

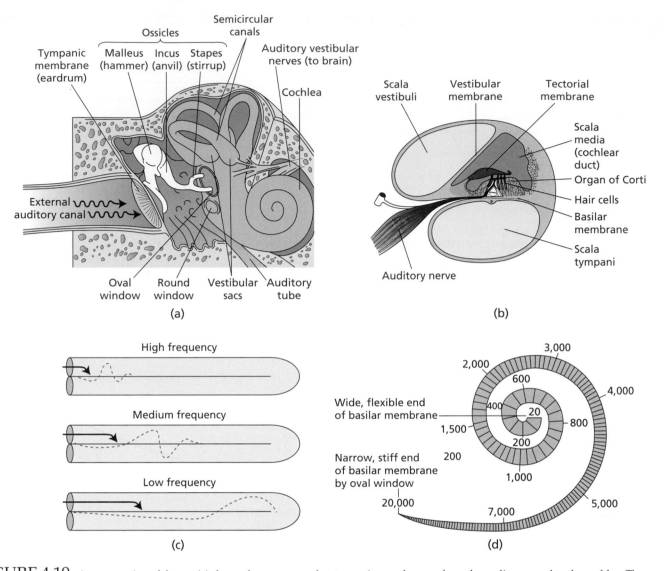

FIGURE 4.19 A cross section of the ear (a) shows the structures that transmit sound waves from the auditory canal to the cochlea. There sound waves are translated into fluid waves that stimulate hair cells in the organ of Corti (b). The resulting nerve impulses reach the brain via the auditory nerve. The semicircular and vestibular sacs of the inner ear contain sense organs for equilibrium. In (c), the fluid waves created by different sound frequencies are shown, and (d) shows the frequencies that maximally stimulate different areas of the basilar membrane. High-frequency waves peak quickly and stimulate the membrane close to the oval window.

which contains thousands of tiny hair cells that are the actual sound receptors. The tips of the hair cells are attached to another membrane that overhangs the basilar membrane along the entire length of the cochlea. The hair cells synapse with the neurons of the auditory nerve which, in turn, sends impulses via an auditory relay station in the thalamus to the auditory cortex, which is located in the temporal lobe.

When sound waves strike the eardrum, pressure created at the oval window by the hammer, anvil, and stirrup of the middle ear sets the fluid inside the cochlea into motion. The fluid waves that result vibrate the basilar membrane and the membrane above it, causing a bending of the hair cells in the organ of Corti (Figure 4.19*b*). This bending of the hair cells triggers a release of neurotransmitter substance into the synaptic space between the hair cells and the neurons of the auditory nerve, resulting in nerve impulses that are sent to the brain. Within the auditory cortex, located in the temporal lobe, are feature detector neurons that respond to specific kinds of auditory input, much as occurs in the visual system (Goldstein, 1998).

Coding of Pitch and Loudness

The auditory system transforms the sensory qualities of loudness and pitch into the language of nerve impulses. In the case of loudness, high-amplitude sound waves cause the hair cells to bend more and release more neurotransmitter substance at the point where they synapse with auditory nerve cells, resulting in a higher rate of firing within the auditory nerve. Second, certain receptor neurons have higher thresholds than others, so that they will fire only when considerable bending of the hair cells occurs in response to an intense sound. Thus loudness is coded in terms of both the rate of firing in the axons of the auditory nerve and in terms of which specific hair cells are sending messages.

The coding of pitch also involves two different processes, one for frequencies below about 1,000 Hz (approximately the midpoint of the piano keyboard) and another for higher frequencies. Historically, as in the case of color vision, two competing theories were advanced to account for pitch perception. According to the **frequency theory** of pitch perception, nerve impulses sent to the brain match the frequency of the sound wave. Thus a 30 Hz (cycles per second) sound wave from a piano should send 30 volleys of nerve impulses per second to the brain. Unfortunately, frequency theory encounters a major problem. Because neurons are limited in their rate of firing, individual impulses or volleys of impulses fired by groups of neurons cannot produce high enough frequencies of firing to match sound wave frequencies above 1,000 Hz. How then do we perceive higher frequencies, such as a 4,000 Hz note from the same piano?

Experiments conducted by Georg von Bekesy (1957) uncovered a second mechanism for coding pitch and earned him the 1961 Nobel Prize. Bekesy cut tiny holes in the cochleas of guinea pigs and human cadavers and observed through a microscope what happened inside the fluid-filled cochlea when he stimulated the eardrum with tones of varying frequencies. He found that high-frequency sounds produced an abrupt wave that peaked close to the oval window, whereas lower-frequency vibrations produced a slower fluid wave that peaked farther down the cochlear canal (Figure 4.19c). Bekesy's observations supported a **place theory** of pitch perception, suggesting that the specific point in the cochlea where the fluid wave peaks and most strongly bends the hair cells serves as a frequency coding cue (Figure 4.19d). Later it was found that similar to the manner in which the retina is "mapped" onto the visual cortex, the auditory cortex has a tonal frequency "map" that corresponds to specific areas of the cochlea. By analyzing the specific location of the cochlea from which auditory nerve impulses are being received, the brain can code pitches like our 4,000 Hz piano note (Goldstein, 1998).

Thus, like trichromatic and opponent-process theories of color vision, which were once thought to contradict one another, frequency and place theories of pitch transduction have both proved to be applicable in their own ways. At low frequencies, frequency theory holds true; at higher frequencies, place theory provides the mechanism for coding the pitch of a sound.

Sound Localization

Have you ever wondered why you have two ears, one located on each side of your head? As is usually the case in nature's designs, there is a good reason. Our very survival can depend upon our ability to locate objects that emit sounds. The two ears play a crucial role in *sound localization*. The nervous system uses information concerning the time and intensity differences of sounds arriving at the two ears to locate the source of sounds in space (Middlebrooks & Green, 1991).

➤ 22. Describe the frequency and place theories of pitch perception. In what sense are both theories correct?

➤ 23. How does the structure of the auditory system permit humans to localize sounds? What sensory information is used by the brain in localization?

PROFESSOR MAYER'S TOPOPHONE.

FIGURE 4.20 This device, used in the late 1800s by sailors to increase their ability to locate sounds while navigating in thick fog, assisted in two ways. First, because the two ear receptors were much larger than human ears, they could capture more sound waves. More importantly, the wide spacing between the receptors increased the time difference between the sound's arrival at the two human ears, thus increasing directional sensitivity.

➤ 24. What are the two varieties of deafness, and how do they differ in their physical bases and in possible treatment?

➤ 25. Describe the sensory principles that are applied to create sensory prosthetics for visually and hearing impaired people.

Sounds arrive first and loudest at the ear closest to the sound. When the source of the sound is directly in front of us, the sound wave reaches both ears at the same time and at the same intensity, so the source is perceived as being straight ahead. Our binaural (two-eared) ability to localize sounds is amazingly sensitive. For example, a sound 3 degrees to the right arrives at the right ear only 300 millionths of a second before it arrives at the left ear, and yet we can tell which direction the sound is coming from (Yin & Kuwada, 1984). But, as Figure 4.20 shows, there is always room for improvement.

Nature's design often bests even human ingenuity. For example, the barn owl comes equipped with ears that are exquisitely tailored for pinpoint localization of its prey during night hunting. Its right ear is directed slightly upward, its left ear slightly downward. This allows it to localize sounds precisely in both the vertical and horizontal planes, and thereby to zero in on its prey with deadly accuracy.

Hearing Loss

If you had to make the unwelcome choice of being blind or being deaf, which impairment would you choose? When asked this question, most of our students say that they would rather be deaf. Yet hearing loss can have more devastating social consequences than blindness does (Fletcher, 1995). Helen Keller, who was both blind and deaf, considered deafness to be more socially debilitating. She wrote, "Blindness cuts people off from things. Deafness cuts people off from people."

In the United States alone, more than 20 million people suffer from impaired hearing. Of these, 90 percent were born with normal hearing (Fletcher, 1995). They suffer from two major types of hearing loss. **Conduction deafness** is caused by problems involving the mechanical system that transmits sound waves to the cochlea. For example, a punctured eardrum or a loss of function in the tiny bones of the middle ear can reduce the ear's capacity to transmit vibrations. Use of a hearing aid, which amplifies the sounds entering the ear, may correct many cases of conduction deafness.

Nerve deafness is an entirely different matter. It is caused by damaged receptors within the inner ear or damage to the auditory nerve itself, and it cannot be helped by a hearing aid. Although aging and disease can produce nerve deafness, exposure to loud sounds is a leading cause of nerve deafness. Repeated exposure to loud sounds of a particular frequency (as might be produced by a machine in a factory) can eventually cause workers to lose hair cells at a particular point on the basilar membrane, thereby causing hearing loss for that frequency.

Extremely loud music can take a serious toll on young people's hearing (West & Evans, 1990). Figure 4.21 shows the devastating results of a guinea pig's exposure to a sound level approximating that of loud rock music heard through earphones. As Table 4.3 shows, even brief exposure to sounds exceeding 140 db can cause irreversible damage to the transducers in the middle and inner ears, and so can more continuous sounds at lower decibel levels. In 1986, the music at a rock concert conducted by The Who reached 120 db at a distance of 164 feet from the speakers. This earned The Who a place in the *Guinness Book of Records* for the all-time loudest concert, but inflicted severe and permanent damage to many of the concert's spectators (Troufexis, 1990). The Who's guitarist, Pete Townshend, eventually suffered severe hearing loss from this prolonged noise exposure.

Although hearing aids can do little to remedy such problems, measures can be taken to prevent damage in people who are exposed to hazardous noise in the workplace. Figure 4.22 shows one high-tech "antinoise" solution.

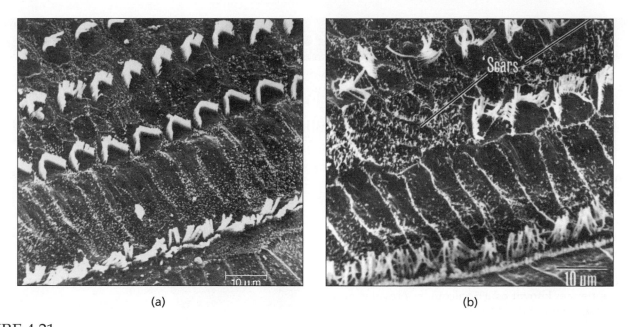

(a)   (b)

FIGURE 4.21 Exposure to loud sounds can destroy auditory receptors in the inner ear. These pictures, taken through an electron microscope, show the hair cells of a guinea pig before (a) and after (b) exposure to 24 hours of noise comparable to that of a loud rock concert. Micrographs by Robert E. Preston, courtesy of Professor J. E. Hawkins, Kresge Hearing Research Institute, University of Michigan.

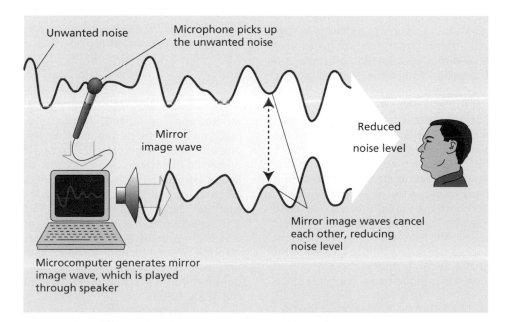

FIGURE 4.22 Recently developed antinoise devices contain a microphone that detects the unwanted sound waves and a microcomputer that analyzes the offending wave's frequency and amplitude and generates an identical waveform that is 180 degrees out of phase. The opposing sound waves cancel each other out, deadening the hazardous noise.

APPLICATIONS OF PSYCHOLOGICAL SCIENCE

Sensory Prosthetics: "Eyes" for the Blind, "Ears" for the Hearing Impaired

Millions of people suffer from blindness and deafness, living in sightless or soundless worlds. Psychological research on the workings of the sensory systems, coupled with technical advances in bioengineering, is being used to produce *sensory prosthetic devices.* These devices produce sensory input that can, to some extent, substitute for what cannot be provided by the normal sensory receptors.

One device, known as a Sonicguide, provides new "eyes" by applying principles of auditory localization (Kay, 1982). The Sonicguide (Figure 4.23) works on the same principle as echolocation, the sensory tool used by bats to navigate in total darkness. The headset contains a transmitter that emits high-frequency sound waves beyond the range of human hearing. These waves bounce back from objects in the environment and are transformed by the Sonicguide into sounds that can be heard through the earphones. Different sound qualities match specific features of external objects, and the wearer must learn to interpret the sonic messages. For example, the sound's pitch tells the person how far away the object is; a low pitch signals a nearby object and the pitch becomes higher with increasing distance. The loudness of the sound tells how large the object is, and the clarity of the sound (ranging from a staticlike sound to a clear tone) signals the texture of the object, from very rough to very smooth. Finally, the auditory localization principle described earlier tells the person where the object is located in the environment by means of differences in the time at which sounds arrive at the two ears.

In the first laboratory tests of the Sonicguide, psychologists Stuart Aitken and T. G. R. Bower (1982) used the apparatus with six blind babies who ranged in age from 5 to 16 months. In his first Sonicguide session with the youngest baby, Bower swung an object on a string until it lightly tapped the baby's nose. After only two presentations, the baby rotated both eyes inward toward his nose as the object approached, and outward as the object swung away. On the seventh trial, the baby reached out with his hand and blocked the object before it reached his face. The blind infant also began to follow the object with his eyes and head when it was moved on a right-left plane in front of him.

Within hours or days, all of the babies using the Sonicguide could reach for objects, walk or crawl through doorways, and listen to the movement of their hands and arms as they moved them about. Moreover, abilities such

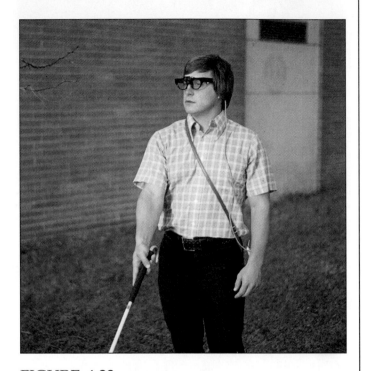

FIGURE 4.23 The Sonicguide allows a blind person to perceive the size, movement, shape, and texture of objects through sound waves that represent the visual features of objects.

as reaching for objects, recognizing favorite toys, and reaching out to be picked up when mother (but not someone else) approached seemed to occur on the same developmental timetable as in sighted children. Aitken and Bower concluded that blind infants can extract the same information from sonic cues as sighted babies do from visual cues. Older children trained with the device can easily find objects, such as water fountains and specific toys with which they want to play. They can thread their way through crowded school corridors and can even play hide-and-seek. The Sonicguide is now being used by visually impaired children in schools and other natural settings (e.g., Hill et al., 1995).

Sonicguide research provides clues for understanding sensory development (Hill et al., 1995; Sampaio, 1989). Older children and adults can learn to use the device, but not as easily as babies can. For very young children, auditory and

—Continued

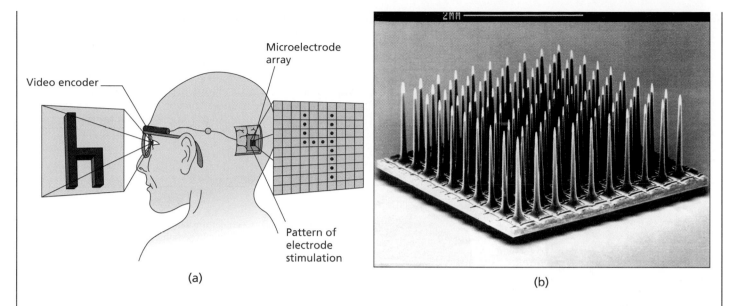

(a)

(b)

FIGURE 4.24 Artificial vision for the blind is produced by direct stimulation of cells in the visual cortex to produce patterns of phosphenes that correspond to the visual scene onserved through the video camera and encoder. The Utah Intracortical Electrode Array is shown in the right photo, taken through an electron microscope. Each of the tiny electrodes can stimulate a single visual neuron. Note how the "image" is reversed as in normal visual input.

visual information seems to be essentially interchangeable information about their world. But by the time children are a year old, they have already learned to differentiate between their senses. They therefore treat the sound as a property of the object rather than as raw information about the object's location and characteristics. For example, older children sometimes hold the objects up to their ears to "listen" to them.

A different approach to a visual prosthesis is being perfected at the University of Utah, where researchers have developed a device to stimulate the visual cortex directly (Normann, 1995). When cells in the visual cortex are stimulated electrically, discrete flashes of light called *phosphenes* are experienced by both sighted and blind people. Because sensory neurons in the visual cortex are arranged in a manner that corresponds to the organization of the retina, a specific pattern of stimulation applied to individual neurons in the cortex can form a phosphene pattern that conforms to the shapes of letters or objects. The detail or acuity of the pattern depends on the area of the visual cortex that is stimulated (the portion receiving input from the densely packed fovea produces greatest acuity) and on the number of stimulating electrodes in the array.

Building on this approach, researchers have developed the device shown in Figure 4.24. The Utah Intracortical Electrode Array consists of a silicon strip containing thousands of tiny stimulating electrodes that penetrate directly into individual neurons in the visual cortex, where they can stimulate phosphene patterns. Eventually, a tiny television camera mounted in specially de-

signed eyeglasses will provide visual information to a microcomputer that will analyze the scene and then send the appropriate patterns of electrical stimulation through the implanted electrodes to produce corresponding phosphene patterns in the visual cortex. The researchers have already shown that sighted participants who wore darkened goggles that produce phosphenelike patterns of light flashes could quickly learn to navigate through complex environments and were able to read text at about two thirds their normal rate (Normann et al., 1996, 1998). Blind people who had the stimulating electrodes implanted in their visual cortex have also been able to learn a kind of "cortical braille" for reading purposes. Although still experimental, a commercially available intracortical prosthetic device should be available in the near future (Normann et al., 1998).

The hearing impaired have also been assisted by the development of prosthetic devices. Many have been helped by the *cochlear implant,* a device that can restore hearing in people suffering from nerve deafness. The cochlear implant does not amplify sound like a conventional hearing aid, for people with nerve deafness cannot be helped by mere sound amplification. Instead, the device sorts out useful sounds and converts them into electrical impulses, bypassing the disabled hair cells in the cochlea and stimulating the auditory nerve directly (Figure 4.25). With a cochlear implant, patients can hear everyday sounds like sirens, and many of them can understand speech (Meyer et al., 1998; Parkinson et al., 1998). Nonetheless, sounds tend to be muffled, and people who expect currently developed cochlear implants to restore normal hearing are invariably disappointed.

—Continued

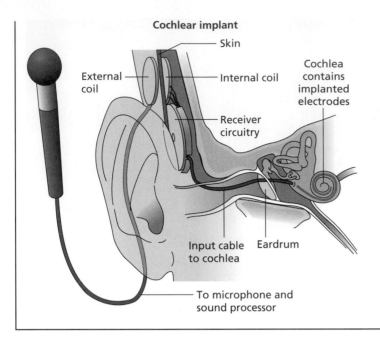

Cochlear implant

Skin

External coil

Internal coil

Cochlea contains implanted electrodes

Receiver circuitry

Input cable to cochlea

Eardrum

To microphone and sound processor

Sensory prosthetics illustrate the ways in which knowledge about sensory phenomena such as phosphenes, the organization of the visual cortex, auditory localization, and the place theory of frequency coding can provide the information needed to take advantage of new technological advances. Yet even with all our present ingenuity, prosthetic devices are not substitutes for our normal sensory systems, a fact that should increase our appreciation for what nature has given us.

FIGURE 4.25 Cochlear implants provide direct stimulation of the auditory nerve in people whose hair cells are too damaged to respond to fluid waves in the cochlea. Sounds enter a microphone worn by the person and are sent to a processor that breaks the sound down into its principal frequencies and sends electrical signals to external and internal coils. The receiver circuitry stimulates electrodes implanted in cochlear areas associated with particular frequencies.

Taste and Smell: The Chemical Senses

➤ 26. Describe the stimuli and the receptors involved in gustation and olfaction. Why do researchers sometimes refer to a "common chemical sense"?

Gustation (taste) and **olfaction** (smell) are chemical senses because their receptors are sensitive to chemical molecules rather than some form of energy. These senses are so intertwined that some scientists refer to a "common chemical sense" (Beauchamp & Bartoshuk, 1997). Enjoying a good meal usually depends on the simultaneous activity of taste and odor receptors, as becomes apparent when we have a stuffy nose and our food tastes bland. People who lose their sense of smell typically believe they have lost their sense of taste as well (Bartoshuk, 1993).

Gustation: The Sense of Taste

People who fancy themselves as gourmets are frequently surprised to learn that their sense of taste responds to only four qualities: sweet, sour, salty, and bitter. Every other taste experience combines these qualities and those of other senses, such as smell, temperature, and touch. For example, part of the "taste" of popcorn includes its texture, its crunchiness, and its odor.

Taste buds are receptors concentrated along the edges and back surface of the tongue. Humans have about 9,000 taste buds, each one consisting of several receptor cells arranged like the segments of an orange (Figure 4.26). A small number of receptors are also found in the roof and back of the mouth, so that even people without a tongue can taste substances. Hairlike structures project from the top of each cell into the taste pore, an opening to the outside surface of the tongue. When a substance is taken into the mouth, it interacts with saliva to form a chemical solution that flows into the taste pore and stimulates the receptor cells. A "taste" results from complex patterns of neural activity produced by the four types of taste receptors (Bartoshuk, 1998).

The sense of taste not only provides us with pleasure, but also has adaptive significance in discriminating between nutrients and toxins (Scott, 1992). Our response to some taste qualities is innate. For example, newborn infants respond positively to sugar water placed on the tongue and negatively to bitter substances such as quinine (Davidson & Fox, 1988). Many poisonous substances in nature have bitter tastes, so this emotional response seems to be "hardwired" into our physiology (Hoebel, 1997). In nature, sweet substances are more likely to occur in nutritious foods. Unfortunately, many humans now live in an environment that is different from the food-scarce environment in which preferences for sweet substances may have evolved (Scott & Giza, 1993). As a result, people in affluent countries overconsume sweet foods that are good for us only in small quantities.

Olfaction: The Sense of Smell

Humans are visually oriented creatures, but the sense of smell (olfaction) is of great importance for many species. Bloodhounds, for example, have poor eyesight but an exquisitely developed olfactory sense that is about 2 million times more sensitive than ours (Thomas, 1974). A bloodhound can detect a person's scent in a footprint that is 4 days old, something no human could do. Yet people who are deprived of other senses often develop a highly sensitive olfactory sense. Helen Keller, though blind and deaf, exhibited a remarkable ability to "smell" her environment. With uncanny accuracy, she could tell when a storm was brewing by detecting subtle odor changes in the air. She could also identify people (even those who bathed regularly and did not wear perfumes or colognes) by their distinctive odors (Keller, 1955).

The receptors for smell are long cells that project through the lining of the upper part of the nasal cavity and into the mucous membrane. Humans have about 40 million olfactory receptors, dogs about 1 billion. Unfortunately, our ability to discriminate among different odors is not well understood. The most popular current theory is that olfactory receptors recognize diverse odors individually rather than by mixing the activity of a smaller number of basic receptors, as occurs in taste (Bartoshuk & Beauchamp, 1994). Olfactory receptors have receptor structures that resemble neurotransmitter binding sites on neurons. Any of the thousands of potential odor molecules can lock into sites that are tailored to fit them (Buck & Axel, 1991).

The social and sexual behavior of animals is more strongly regulated by olfaction than is human behavior (Doty & Muller-Schwarze, 1992). For example, most of us find other ways to mark our territories, such as by erecting fences or spreading belongings over the table we are using in the library. Nonetheless, like animals, humans have special receptors in the nose that send impulses to a separate olfactory area in the brain that connects with brain structures involved in social and reproductive behavior. Some researchers believe that **pheromones,** chemical signals found in natural body scents, may affect human behavior in subtle ways (Bartoshuk & Beauchamp, 1994; Monti-Bloch & Grosser, 1991). One interesting but puzzling observation, known as **menstrual synchrony,** is the tendency of women who live together or are close friends to become more similar in their menstrual cycles. Psychologist Martha McClintock (1971) tested 135 college women and found that during the course of an academic year, roommates moved from a mean of 8.5 days apart in their periods to 4.9 days apart. Another study of 51 women who worked together showed that close friends had menstrual onsets averaging 3.5 to 4.3 days apart, whereas those who were not close friends had onsets that averaged 8 to 9 days apart (Weller et al., 1999). Are pheromones responsible for synchrony? In experiments conducted at the Monell Chemical Senses Center in Philadelphia, 10 women with regular cycles were daubed under the nose every few days with underarm secretions collected from other women. After three months, the participants' cycles began to coincide with the sweat donors' cycles. A control group of women who were daubed with an

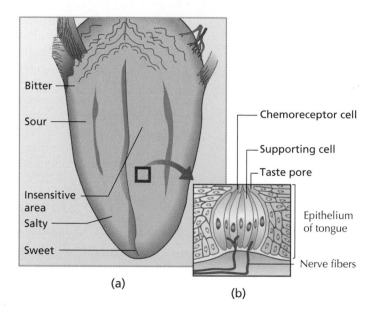

FIGURE 4.26 The receptors for taste are specialized cells located in the tongue's taste buds. The tongue's 9,000 taste buds are grouped in different areas according to the taste sensation they produce. The center of the tongue is relatively insensitive to the chemical molecules that constitute gustatory stimuli.

➤ 27. What is menstrual synchrony, and what evidence is there that pheromones are involved?

alcohol solution rather than sweat showed no menstrual synchrony with a partner (Preti et al., 1986). In other studies, however, menstrual synchrony was not found for cohabitating lesbian couples or for Bedouin women who spent most of their time together, indicating that prolonged and very intensive contact may not be conducive to menstrual synchrony (Weller & Weller, 1997, 1998).

As anyone who has owned a dog or cat in heat could attest, odors strongly affect the sexual attractiveness of animals. On the other hand, there is no solid evidence to justify the recent rise in commercial sales of "pheromone substances" to humans who wish to become sexually irresistible. At this point, we would conclude that a good personality is a better bet than a good pheromone.

The Skin and Body Senses

The skin and body senses include the senses of touch, kinesthesis (muscle movement), and equilibrium. The last two are called body senses because they inform us of the body's position and movement. They tell us, for example, if we are running or standing still, lying down or sitting up.

The Tactile Senses

Touch is important to us in many ways. Sensitivity to extreme temperatures and pain enables us to avoid external danger and alerts us to disorders within our bodies. Tactile sensations are also a source of many of life's pleasures, including sexual orgasm. A lack of tactual contact with a caretaking adult retards physical, social, and emotional development (Harlow, 1958), and physically massaging newborn babies enhances their development (Cigales et al., 1997; Field et al., 1996).

▶ 28. What four tactile sensations are humans sensitive to? How are these sensations localized, and how are phantom limb sensations produced?

Humans are sensitive to at least four tactile sensations: pressure (touch), pain, warmth, and cold. These sensations are conveyed by receptors in the skin and in our internal organs. Mixtures of these four sensations form the basis for all other common skin sensations, such as itch.

Considering the importance of our skin senses, surprisingly little is known about how they work. The skin, a multilayered elastic structure that covers two square yards and weighs between 6 and 10 pounds, is the largest organ in our body. It contains a variety of receptor structures, but their role in specific sensations is less clear than for the other senses. Many sensations probably depend upon specific patterns of activity in the various receptors (Goldstein, 1998). We do know that primary receptors for pain and temperature are *free nerve endings,* simple nerve cells beneath the skin's surface that resemble the bare branches of a tree in winter. Nerve fibers situated at the base of hair follicles are receptors for touch and light pressure (Heller & Schiff, 1991).

The brain can locate sensations because skin receptors send their messages to the point in the somatosensory cortex that corresponds to the area of the body where the receptor is located. The amount of cortex devoted to each area of the body is related to that part's sensitivity. Our fingers, lips, and tongue are well represented, accounting for their extreme sensitivity to stimulation.

Sometimes the brain "locates" sensations that cannot possibly be present. This occurs in the puzzling *phantom limb* phenomenon, in which amputees experience vivid sensations coming from the missing limb (Warga, 1987). Apparently, an irritation of the nerves that used to originate in the limb fools the brain into interpreting the resulting nerve impulses as real sensations. Joel Katz and Ronald Melzack (1990) studied 68 amputees who insisted that they experienced pain from the amputated limb that was as vivid and "real" as any pain they had ever experienced. This pain was not merely a recollection of what pain used to feel like in the phantom limb; it was actually experienced in the present. The phantom limb phenomenon can be quite maddening: Imagine having an intense itch that you never can scratch, or an ache you cannot rub.

The Body Senses

We would be totally unable to coordinate our body movements were it not for the sense of **kinesthesis,** which provides us with feedback about our muscles' and joints' positions and movements. The receptors are nerve endings in the muscles, tendons, and joints. The information this sense gives us is the basis for making coordinated movements. Cooperating with kinesthesis is the **vestibular sense,** the sense of body orientation or equilibrium (Figure 4.27). The vestibular receptors are located in the *vestibular apparatus* of the inner ear (see Figure 4.19). One part of the equilibrium system consists of three *semicircular canals,* which contain the receptors for head movement. Each canal lies in a different plane: left/right, backward/forward, or up/down. These canals are filled with fluid and lined with hairlike cells that function as receptors. When the head moves, the fluid in the appropriate canal shifts, stimulating the hair cells and sending messages to the brain. The semicircular canals respond only to acceleration and deceleration; when a constant speed is reached (no matter how high), the fluid and the hair cells return to their normal resting state. That's why takeoffs and landings give a sense of movement, whereas flying at 500 mph on a cruising airliner does not. Located at the base of the semicircular canals, the *vestibular sacs* also contain hair cells that respond to the position of the body and tell us whether we are upright or tilted at an angle. These structures comprise the second part of the body-sense system.

FIGURE 4.27 Kinesthesis and the vestibular sense are especially well developed in some people, and essential for performing feats like this one.

❯ PERCEPTION: THE CREATION OF EXPERIENCE

Sensory systems provide the raw materials from which experiences are formed. Our sense organs do not select what we will be aware of or how we will experience it; they merely transmit as much information as they can through our nervous system. Yet our experiences are not simply a one-to-one reflection of what is "out there." Different people may experience the same sensory information in radically different ways because perception is an active, creative process in which raw sensory data are organized and given meaning.

To create our perceptions, the brain carries out two different kinds of processing functions (Figure 4.28). In **bottom-up processing,** the system takes in individual elements of the stimulus and then combines them into a unified perception. Your visual system operates in a bottom-up fashion as you read; its feature detectors analyze the elements in each letter of every word, then recombine them into your visual perception of the letters and words. In **top-down processing,** sensory information is interpreted in the light of existing knowledge, concepts, ideas, and expectations. Top-down processing is occurring as you interpret the words and sentences constructed by the bottom-up process. Here you make use of "higher-order" knowledge, including what you have learned about the meaning of words and sentence construction. Indeed, a given sentence may even convey a different personal meaning to you than to another person if you relate its content to some unique personal experiences. Top-down processing accounts for many psychological influences on perception, such as the roles played by our motives, expectations, previous experiences, and cultural learning.

➤ 29. Differentiate between bottom-up and top-down processing of sensory information.

Perception Is Selective: The Role of Attention

As you read these words, 100 million sensory messages may be clamoring for your attention. Only a few of these messages register in awareness; the rest you perceive either dimly or not at all. But you can shift your attention to one of those "unregistered" stimuli at any

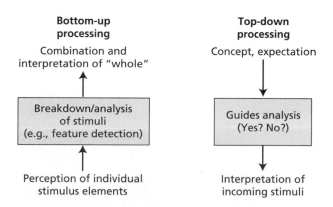

FIGURE 4.28 Bottom-up perceptual processing builds from an analysis of individual stimulus features to a unified perception. Top-down processing begins with a perceptual whole, such as an expectation or an image of an object, then determines the degree of "fit" with the stimulus features.

➤ 30. What two complementary processes occur in attention?

➤ 31. Describe the results of shadowing experiments in relation to attentional capabilities.

time. (For example, how does the big toe of your right foot feel right now?) Attention, then, involves two processes of selection: (1) focusing on certain stimuli and (2) filtering out other incoming information (van der Heijden, 1991).

These processes have been studied experimentally through a technique called **shadowing.** Participants wear earphones and listen simultaneously to two messages, one sent through each earphone. They are asked to repeat (or "shadow") one of the messages word for word as they listen. Most participants can do this quite successfully, but only at the cost of not remembering what the other message was about. Shadowing experiments demonstrate that we *cannot* attend completely to more than one thing at a time. But we can shift our attention rapidly back and forth between the two messages, drawing on our general knowledge to fill in the gaps (Bonnel & Hafter, 1998; Sperling, 1984).

Environmental and Personal Factors in Attention

➤ 32. What stimulus and personal characteristics influence attention?

Attention is strongly affected by both the nature of the stimulus and by personal factors. Stimulus characteristics that attract our attention include intensity, novelty, movement, contrast, and repetition. Advertisers use these properties in their commercials and packaging (Figure 4.29).

Internal factors, such as our motives and interests, act as powerful filters and influence which stimuli in our environment we will notice. For example, when we are hungry, we are especially sensitive to food-related cues. A botanist walking through a park is especially attentive to the plants; a landscape architect attends primarily to the layout of the park.

People are especially attentive to stimuli that might represent a threat to their well-being, a tendency that would clearly have biological survival value (Bargh, 1984; Izard, 1989). Christine and Ranald Hansen (1988) presented slides showing groups of nine people. In half of the pictures, all of the people looked either angry or happy. In the other half, there was one discrepant face, either an angry face in a happy crowd or a happy face in an angry crowd. Participants were asked to judge as quickly as possible whether there was a discrepant face in the crowd, then press "yes" or "no" buttons attached to electrical timers. The dependent variable was the length of time required to make this judgment, measured in milliseconds (thousandths of a second). The results, summarized in Figure 4.30, showed that participants were much faster at detecting a single angry face in an otherwise happy crowd than at finding a happy face in an angry crowd. It was as if the angry face, which the experimenters assumed to have threat value, "jumped out" of the crowd when the stimuli were scanned.

FIGURE 4.29 Advertisers are adept at using attention-attracting stimulus characteristics in their advertisements. Personal characteristics are also important. What kinds of individuals do you suppose would be most attentive to these ads?

Swedish psychologist Ulf Dimberg (1997) believes that humans are biologically programmed to detect threatening faces, and he has shown via high-speed photography that emotional facial responses to such stimuli occur in observers within one third of a second. Attentional processes are thus based both on innate biological factors and on past experiences that make certain stimuli important or meaningful to us.

Perceptions Have Organization and Structure

Have you ever stopped to wonder why we perceive the visual world as being composed of distinct objects? After all, the information sent by the retina reflects nothing but an array of varying intensities and frequencies of light energy. The light rays reflected from different parts of a single object have no more natural "belongingness" to one another than those coming from two different objects. Yet we perceive scenes as involving separate objects, such as trees, buildings, and people. These perceptions must be a product of an organization imposed by our nervous system. This top-down process of perceptual organization occurs so automatically that we take it for granted. But Dr. Richard, a prominent psychologist who suffered brain damage in an accident, no longer does.

> There was nothing wrong with his eyes, yet the input he received from them was not put together correctly. Dr. Richard reported that if he saw a person, he sometimes would perceive the separate parts of the person as not belonging together in a single body. But if all the parts moved in the same direction, Dr. Richard then saw them as one complete person. At other times, he would perceive people in crowds wearing the same color clothes as "going together" rather than as separate people. He also had difficulty putting sights and sounds together. Sometimes, the movement of the lips did not correspond to the sounds he heard, as if he were watching a badly dubbed foreign movie. Dr. Richard's experience of his environment was thus disjointed and fragmented. . . . (Sacks, 1986, p. 76)

Synesthesia, in which stimuli in one sensory modality give rise to perceptions in other modalities, is an even more radical departure from ordinary perceptual experience. What, then, are the processes whereby sensory nonsense becomes perceptual sense?

Gestalt Principles of Perceptual Organization

Early in the 20th century, psychologists from the German school of Gestalt psychology set out to discover how we organize the separate parts of our perceptual field into a unified and meaningful whole. *Gestalt* is the German term for "pattern," "shape," or "form." Gestalt theorists were early champions of top-down processing, arguing that the wholes we perceive are often more than (and frequently different from) the sum of their parts. Thus your perception of the photo in Figure 4.31 is likely to be more than "lots of people."

The Gestalt theorists emphasized the importance of **figure-ground relations.** We tend to organize stimuli into a central or foreground figure and a background. In vision, the central figure is usually in front of or on top of what we perceive as background. It has a distinct shape and is more striking in our perceptions and memory than the background. We perceive borders or contours wherever there is a distinct change in the color or brightness of a visual scene, but we interpret these contours as part of the figure rather than background. Likewise, instrumental music is heard as

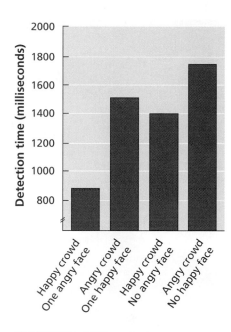

FIGURE 4.30 Perceptual vigilance to threatening stimuli is shown in the finding that people required less time to detect an angry face in a happy crowd than to detect a happy face in an angry crowd or to determine if there was any discrepant face in a happy or an angry crowd.

Data from Hansen & Hansen, 1988.

FIGURE 4.31 As Gestalt psychologists emphasized, what we perceive (i.e., "Ohio") is more than simply the sum of its individual parts.

➤ 33. How does our tendency to separate figure and ground contribute to perception?

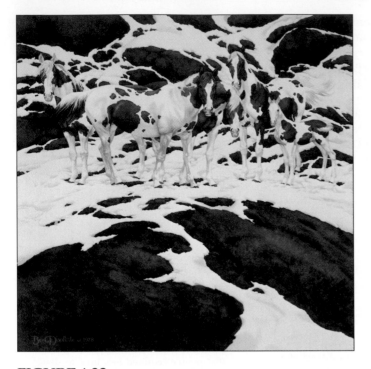

FIGURE 4.32 Figure-ground relations are important in perceptual organization. Here the artist Bev Doolittle has created great similarity between figure and ground in this representation of natural camouflage, yet enough figural cues remain to permit most people to detect the ponies.
Source: Pintos, Bev Doolittle, 1979. The Greenwich Workshop, Trumbull, Conn.

➤ 34. Define and give examples of the four Gestalt laws of perceptual organization.

FIGURE 4.33 This reversible figure illustrates alternating figure-ground relations. It can be seen as a vase or as two people facing one another. Whichever percept exists at the moment is seen as figure against background.

a melody (figure) surrounded by other chords or harmonies (ground).

At times, separating figure from ground can be a challenging task (Figure 4.32), yet our perceptual systems are usually equal to the task. At times, however, what's figure and what's ground is not completely obvious, and the same stimulus can give rise to two different perceptions. Consider Figure 4.33, for example. If you examine it for a while, two alternating but equally plausible perceptions will emerge, one based on the inner portion and the other formed by the two outer portions. When the alternative perception (figure) occurs, what was previously the figure becomes the background.

In addition to figure-ground relations, the Gestalt psychologists were interested in how separate stimuli come to be perceived as parts of larger wholes. They suggested that people group and interpret stimuli in accordance with four **Gestalt laws of perceptual organization:** similarity, proximity, closure, and continuity. These organizing principles are illustrated in Figure 4.34.

What was your perception of Figure 4.34a? Did you perceive 15 unrelated dots, or did you view the stimulus as two triangles formed by different-sized dots? If you saw triangles, your perception obeyed the Gestalt *law of similarity*, which says that when parts of a configuration are perceived as similar, they will be perceived as belonging together. The *law of proximity* says that elements that are near each other are likely to be perceived as part of the same configuration. Thus most people perceive Figure 4.34b as three sets of lines rather than as six separate lines. Illustrated in Figure 4.34c is the *law of closure,* which states that people tend to close the open edges of a figure or fill in gaps in an incomplete figure, so that their identification of the form (in this case, a circle) is more complete than what is actually there. Finally, the *law of continuity* holds that people link individual elements together so they form a continuous line or pattern that makes sense. Thus Figure 4.34d is far more likely to be seen as combining components (ab and cd) than (ad and cb), which have poor continuity. Or consider Fraser's spiral, shown in Figure 4.35, which is not really a spiral at all! (To demonstrate, trace one of the circles with a pencil.) We perceive the concentric circles as a spiral because, to our nervous system, a spiral gives better continuity between individual elements than does a set of circles. The spiral is created by us, not by the stimulus.

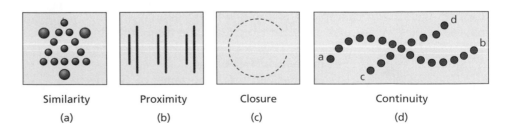

| Similarity | Proximity | Closure | Continuity |
| (a) | (b) | (c) | (d) |

FIGURE 4.34 Among the Gestalt principles for perceptual organization are the laws of similarity (a), proximity (b), closure (c), and continuity (d). Each principle causes us to organize stimuli into "wholes" that are greater than the sums of their parts.

Perception Involves Hypothesis Testing

"Recognizing" a stimulus implies that we have a **perceptual schema**—a mental representation or image—to compare it with. Our schemas contain the critical features of objects, events, and other perceptual phenomena (Wade & Swanston, 1991). They allow us to classify and identify sensory input in a top-down fashion.

Imagine, for example, that a person approaches you and calls out your name. Who is this person? If the stimuli match your inner representation of your best friend's appearance and voice closely enough, you identify the person as your friend. Many political cartoonists have an uncanny ability to capture the most noteworthy facial features of famous people, so that we can easily recognize the person represented by even the simplest line sketch.

Perception is, in this sense, an attempt to make sense of stimulus input, to search for the "best" interpretation of sensory information we can arrive at based on our knowledge and experience. Likening the process to the scientific enterprise described in Chapter 2, Richard L. Gregory (1966) suggested that each of our perceptions is essentially a hypothesis about the nature of the object or, more generally, the meaning of the sensory information. The perceptual system actively searches its gigantic library of internal schemas for the interpretation that best fits the sensory data.

An example of how effortlessly our perceptual systems build up descriptions or hypotheses that best fit the available evidence is found in the comic strips created by Gustave Verbeek in the early 1900s. The Sunday *New York Herald* told Verbeek that his comic strip had to be restricted to 6 panels. Verbeek wanted 12 panels, so he ingeniously created 12-panel cartoons in only 6 panels by drawing pictures like that shown in Figure 4.36*a*. The reader viewed the first 6 panels, then turned the newspaper upside down. Try this yourself, and you will find that a bird story becomes a fish story! The point is that you do not simply see an upside-down bird, even though the physical stimuli remain exactly the same. You see a radically different picture because the new stimulus closely matches another of your perceptual schemas.

In some instances, sensory information fits two different internal representations, and there is not enough information to permanently rule out one of

FIGURE 4.35 Fraser's spiral illustrates the Gestalt law of continuity. If you follow any part of the "spiral" with your finger, you will find that it is not a spiral at all but a series of concentric circles. The "spiral" is created by your nervous system because that perception is more consistent with continuity of the individual elements.

➤ 35. In what sense is perception a kind of hypothesis testing? What is the role of perceptual schemas in this process?

(a)

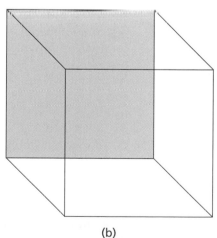

(b)

FIGURE 4.36 Two examples of how the same stimulus can give rise to different perceptions are found in the comic strips of Gustave Verbeek (a) and the Necker cube (b). To produce the reversals, turn the comic strip panel upside down and stare at the cube. The front of the cube will suddenly become the back, and it will appear that the cube is being viewed from a different angle.

them in favor of the other. For example, examine the Necker cube, shown in Figure 4.36*b*. If you stare at the cube for a while, you will find that it changes before your eyes as your nervous system "tries out" a new perceptual hypothesis.

Perception is Influenced by Expectations: Perceptual Sets

On July 3, 1988, the warship USS *Vincennes* was engaged in a pitched battle with several speedy Iranian gunboats. Suddenly, the *Vincennes*'s advanced radar system detected an aircraft taking off from a military/civilian airfield in Iran and heading straight toward the American vessel. Radar operators identified the plane as an Iranian F-14 fighter, known to carry lethal air-to-surface missiles used earlier in a damaging attack on another U.S. warship. Repeated requests to the plane to identify itself yielded no response. The plane was now only 10 miles from the ship and, according to the crewmen watching on radar, descending toward the *Vincennes* on an attack course. A final warning evoked no response, and the *Vincennes*'s captain gave the command to fire on the plane. Two surface-to-air missiles streaked into the sky. Moments later, all that remained of the plane was a shower of flaming debris.

The jubilation and relief of the *Vincennes*'s crew was short-lived. Soon the awful truth was known: The plane they had shot down was not an attacking F-14 warplane. Instead, it was a commercial airliner carrying 290 passengers, all of whom died when the aircraft was destroyed. Moreover, videotape recordings of the electronic information that the crew had used to identify the plane and its flight pattern showed conclusively that the aircraft was not an F-14 and that it had actually been climbing rather than descending toward the ship.

How could such a tragic error have been made by a well-trained and experienced crew with access to the world's most sophisticated radar equipment? At a Congressional hearing on the incident, several prominent perception researchers reconstructed the psychological environment that could have caused the radar operators' eyes to "lie."

Clearly, the situation was stressful and dangerous. The *Vincennes* was already under attack by Iranian gunboats, and other attacks could be expected. It was easy for the radar operators, observing a plane taking off from a military field and heading toward the ship, to interpret this as the possible prelude to an air attack. The *Vincennes*'s crew was determined to avoid the fate of the other American warship, producing a high level of vigilance to any stimuli that suggested an impending attack. Fear and expectation thus created a psychological context within which the sensory input from the computer system was interpreted in a top-down fashion. The perception that the aircraft was a warplane and that it was descending toward the ship fit the crew's expectations and fears, and it became the "reality" that they experienced. They had a **perceptual set**—a readiness to perceive stimuli in a particular way. Sometimes believing is seeing.

Perceptual sets influence our social perceptions as well, as psychologist Harold Kelly (1950) demonstrated the day he invited a guest lecturer into his class. Half of the students in the class were given a set of introductory notes that described the guest as "industrious, critical, practical, determined and a rather *cold* person" (italics ours). The other half were given notes that described the visitor as "industrious, critical, practical, determined and a rather *warm* person." After the class, the students rated the guest lecturer and his presentation. Those who received the *cold* description interacted very little with him and later rated the guest lecturer as unhappy and irritable during the lecture. But those who got the *warm* description rated him as happy and good natured during the lecture, and they actively took part in the class discussion. They also rated his presentation more favorably. Now all of the students had seen and heard the *same lecturer,* or had they? It seems as if they perceived what they expected to.

> 36. What is a perceptual set? What factors can create such sets? How did the *Vincennes* incident illustrate this concept? How is it involved in perceiving people?

Stimuli Are Recognizable Under Changing Conditions: Perceptual Constancies

When a door swings open, it casts a different image on our retina, but we still perceive it as the door. Our perceptual hypothesis remains the same. Were it not for **perceptual constancies** that allow us to recognize familiar stimuli under varying conditions, we would have to literally rediscover what something is each time it appeared under different conditions. Thus you can recognize a tune even if it is played in a different octave, as long as the relations among its notes are maintained. You can detect the flavor of a particular spice even when it occurs in foods having very different tastes.

In vision, several constancies are important. *Shape constancy* allows us to recognize people and other objects from many different angles, as in the case of the swinging door. Perhaps you have had the experience of sitting up front and off to one side of the screen in a crowded movie theater. At first, the picture probably looked distorted, but after a while your visual system corrected for the distortion, and objects on the screen looked normal again.

Because of *brightness constancy,* the relative brightness of objects remains the same under different conditions of illumination, such as full sunlight and shade. Brightness constancy occurs because the ratio of light intensity between an object and its surroundings is usually constant. The actual brightness of the light that illuminates the objects does not matter, as long as the same light intensity illuminates both an object and its surroundings.

When we take off in an airplane, we know that the cars on the highway below are not shrinking and becoming the size of ants. *Size constancy* is the perception that the size of objects remains relatively constant even though images on our retina change in size with variations in distance. Thus a man who is judged to be 6 feet tall when standing 5 feet away is not perceived to be 3 feet tall at a distance of 10 feet, even though the size of his image on the retina is reduced to half its original size (Figure 4.37).

➤ 37. What is the nature and adaptive value of perceptual constancies?

FIGURE 4.37   Size constancy based on distance cues causes us to perceive the person in the background as being a normal size. When the same stimulus is seen in the absence of the distance cues, size constancy breaks down.

FIGURE 4.38 The demands faced by a batter in judging the speed, distance, and movements of a pitched baseball within thousandths of a second underscores the capabilities of the visual perceptual system.

> ➤ 38. Identify eight monocular cues for distance and depth.

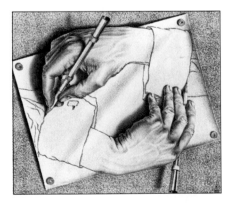

FIGURE 4.39 Patterns of light and shadow can serve as monocular depth cues, as shown in *Drawing Hands* by M. C. Escher.

❭ PERCEPTION OF DEPTH, DISTANCE, AND MOVEMENT

The ability to adapt to a spatial world requires that we make fine distinctions involving distances and the movement of objects within the environment. Humans are capable of great precision in making such judgments. Consider, for example, the perceptual task faced by a batter in the sport of baseball (Figure 4.38). A fast ball thrown by the pitcher at 90 mph from 60 feet will reach the batter who is trying to hit it in about 42/100 of a second. A curve ball thrown at 80 mph will reach the hitting zone in 47/100 of a second, a difference of only 5/100 of a second (but a world of difference for timing and hitting the pitch). Within the first 6 to 8 feet of a ball's flight from the pitcher's hand (an interval of about 25/1,000 of a second), the batter must correctly judge the speed, type, and location of the pitch. If any of the judgments is in error, the hitter will be unable to hit a fair ball (Adair, 1990). The perceptual demands of such a task are imposing indeed (as are the salaries earned by those who can perform this task consistently). How does the visual perception system make such judgments?

Depth and Distance Perception

One of the more intriguing aspects of visual perception is our ability to perceive depth. The retina receives information in only two dimensions (length and width), but the brain translates these cues into three-dimensional perceptions. It does this by using both **monocular cues** (which require only one eye) and **binocular cues** (which require both eyes).

Monocular Depth Cues

Judging the relative distances of objects is one important key to perceiving depth. Because artists paint their portraits on a flat canvas, they depend upon a variety of monocular cues to create perceptions of depth in their pictures. One such cue is patterns of *light and shadow*. The Dutch artist M. C. Escher skillfully used light and shadow to create the three-dimensional effect shown in Figure 4.39. The depth effect is as powerful if you close one eye as it is when you use both. Another, *linear perspective*, refers to the perception that parallel lines converge or angle toward one another as they recede into the distance. Thus if you look down railroad tracks, they appear to angle toward one another with increased distance, and we use this a depth cue. The same occurs with the edges of a highway or the sides of an elevator shaft. *Interposition*, in which objects closer to us may cut off part of our view of more distant objects, provides another cue for distance and depth.

An object's *height in the horizontal plane* provides another source of information. For example, a ship five miles offshore appears in a higher plane and closer to the horizon than does one that is only one mile from shore. *Texture* is a fifth cue, because the texture or grain of an object appears finer as distance increases. Likewise, *clarity* can be an important cue for judging distance; we can see nearby hills more clearly than ones that are far away, especially on hazy days. *Relative size* is yet another basis for distance judgments. If we see two objects that we know to be of similar size, then the one that looks smaller will be judged to be farther away. A final monocular cue is *motion parallax*, which tells us that if we are moving, nearby objects appear to move faster in the opposite direction than do far-away ones. All of these cues provide us with information that we can use to make judgments about distance and therefore about depth.

The artist Raphael Sanzio was a master at using monocular depth and distance cues. *The School of Athens*, shown in Figure 4.40, illustrates seven of the monocular cues described above.

Binocular Disparity

The most dramatic perceptions of depth arise with binocular depth cues, which require the use of both eyes. For an interesting binocular effect, hold your two index fingers about 6 in. in front of your eyes with their tips about an inch apart. Focus on your fingers first, then focus beyond them across the room. The two different views will produce a "third" finger between the other two. This "finger sausage" will disappear if you close either eye.

Most of us are familiar with the delightful depth experiences provided by View Master slides and 3-D movies watched through special glasses. These devices make use of the principle of **binocular disparity**, in which each eye sees a slightly different image. Within the brain, the visual input from the two eyes is analyzed by feature detectors that are attuned to depth (Howard & Rogers, 1995; Livingstone & Hubel, 1994). Some of the feature detectors respond only to stimuli that are either in front of or behind the point we are fixing our gaze upon. The responses of these depth-sensitive neurons are integrated to produce our perception of depth (Goldstein, 1998).

A second binocular distance cue, **convergence,** is produced by feedback from the muscles that turn your eyes inward to view a near object. You can experience this cue by holding a finger about a foot in front of your face, then moving it slowly toward you. Messages sent to your brain by the eye muscles provide it with a depth cue.

FIGURE 4.40 *The School of Athens,* by Raphael Sanzio, illustrates seven monocular depth cues. (1) Linear perspective is produced by the converging lines of the corridor in the background. (2) The arches and the people in the background are smaller than those in front (relative size). (3) The back of the floor is in a higher horizontal plane than the foreground. (4, 5) The objects in the background are less detailed than the closer ones (texture and clarity). (6) Light and shadow are used to create depth. (7) The arches and people in the front of the painting cut off parts of the corridor behind them (interposition).

Perception of Movement

The perception of movement is a complex process that requires the brain to integrate information from several different senses. Try this demonstration: Hold your pen in front of your face. Now while holding your head still, move the pen back and forth. You will perceive the pen moving. Now hold the pen still and move your head back and forth at the same rate of speed. In both cases, the image of the pen moved across your retina in about the same way. But when you moved your head, your brain took into account input from your kinesthetic and vestibular systems and "concluded" that you were moving but the pen was not.

➤ 39. Describe two binocular depth cues.

The primary cue for perceiving motion is the movement of the stimulus across the retina. Under optimal conditions, a retinal image need move only about one fifth the diameter of a single cone for us to detect movement (Nakayama & Tyler, 1981). The relative movement of an object against a structured background is also a movement cue (Gibson, 1979). For example, if you fixate on a bird in flight, the relative motion of the bird against its background is a strong cue for perceived speed of movement.

The illusion of smooth motion can be produced if we arrange for the sequential appearance of two or more stimuli. Gestalt psychologist Max Wertheimer (1912) demonstrated this in his studies of **stroboscopic movement,** illusory movement produced when a light was briefly flashed in darkness and then, a few milliseconds later, another light was flashed nearby. If the timing was just right, the first light seemed to move from one place to the other in a manner indistinguishable from real movement.

➤ 40. What is the primary cue for motion perception? How is stroboscopic movement used in motion pictures and television?

Stroboscopic movement (termed the *phi phenomenon* by Wertheimer) has been used commercially in numerous ways. For example, we have all seen the strings of successively illuminated lights on theater marquees that seem to move endlessly around the border or that spell out messages in a "moving" script.

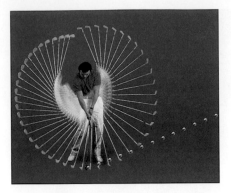

FIGURE 4.41 Stroboscopic movement is produced in moving pictures as a series of still photographs projected at a rate of 24 per second.

➤ 41. In what sense is an illusion a false perceptual hypothesis? In what ways are constancies and context involved in producing visual illusions?

(a)

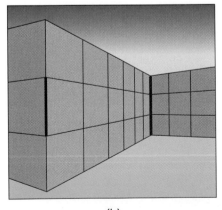

(b)

FIGURE 4.42 The Ponzo illusion. Which lines in (a) and (b) are longer? Measure them and see. The distance cues provided by the converging railroad tracks and walls affect size perception and disrupt size constancy.

Stroboscopic movement is also the principle behind motion pictures, which consist of a series of still photographs, or frames, that are projected on a screen in rapid succession with dark intervals in between (Figure 4.41). The rate at which the frames are projected is critical to our perception of smooth movement. Early movies, such as the "silent" films of the 1920s, projected the "stills" at only 16 frames per second, and the movements appeared fast and jerky. Today the usual speed is 24 frames per second, which more perfectly produces an illusion of smooth movement.

❯ ILLUSIONS: FALSE PERCEPTUAL HYPOTHESES

Our knowledge of perceptual schemas, hypotheses, sets, and constancies allows us to understand some interesting perceptual experiences known as illusions. **Illusions** are compelling but incorrect perceptions. They can be understood as erroneous perceptual hypotheses about the nature of the stimulus. Illusions are not only intriguing and sometimes delightful visual experiences, but they also provide important information about how our perceptual processes work under normal conditions.

Ironically, most visual illusions can be attributed to perceptual constancies that ordinarily help us to perceive more accurately (Frisby, 1980). For example, size constancy results in part from our ability to use distance cues to judge the size of objects. But distance cues can sometimes fool us. In the *Ponzo illusion*, shown in Figure 4.42, the depth cues of linear perspective (the tracks converging) and height in the horizontal plane provide distance cues that make the upper bar appear farther away than the lower bar. Because it seems farther away, the perceptual system concludes that the bar in the background must be larger than the bar in the foreground, despite the fact that the two bars cast retinal images of the same size. The same occurs in the vertical arrangement seen in Figure 4.42b.

Distance cues can be manipulated to create other size illusions. One occurs in a room constructed by Adelbert Ames. Viewed through a peephole with one eye, the scene presents a startling size reversal (Figure 4.43a). Our perceptual system assumes that the room has a normal rectangular shape because, in fact, most rooms do. Monocular depth cues do not allow us to see that in reality, the left corner of the room is twice as far away as the right corner (Figure 4.43b). As a result, size constancy breaks down, and we base our judgment of size on the sizes of the retinal images cast by the two people.

The study of perceptual constancies shows that our perceptual hypotheses are strongly influenced by the *context*, or surroundings, in which a stimulus occurs. Figure 4.44 shows some examples of how context can produce illusory perceptions.

Some of the most intriguing perceptual distortions are produced when monocular depth cues are manipulated to produce a figure or scene whose individual parts make sense but whose overall organization is "impossible" in terms of our existing perceptual schemas. Figure 4.45 shows three impossible figures. In each case, our brains extract information about depth from the individual features of the objects, but when this information is put together and matched with our existing schemas, the percept that results simply doesn't make sense. The "devil's tuning fork," for example, could not exist in our universe. It is a two-dimensional image containing paradoxical depth cues. Your brain, however, automatically interprets it as a three-dimensional object and matches it with its internal schema of a fork, a bad fit indeed. The never-ending staircase provides another compelling example of an impossible scene that seems perfectly reasonable when we focus only on its individual elements.

Illusions are not only personally and scientifically interesting, but they can have important real-life implications. Our *Research Close-up* describes one scientist's search for an illusion having life-and-death implications.

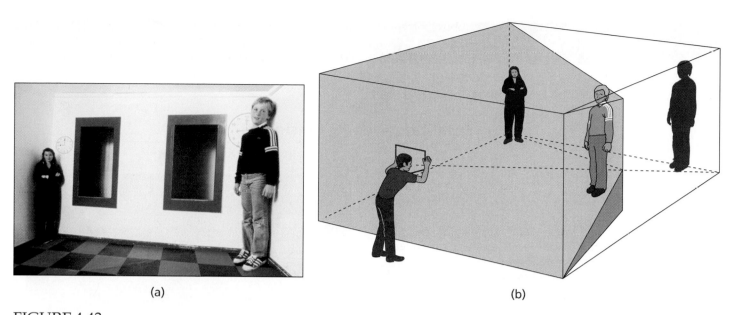

(a)

(b)

FIGURE 4.43 The Ames Room (a) produces a striking size perception because it is designed to appear rectangular. However, as (b) shows, the room is actually trapezoidal in shape, and the figure on the left is actually much farther away from the viewer than the one on the right, making it appear smaller.

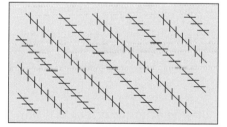

The long lines are actually parallel, but the small lines make them appear crooked.

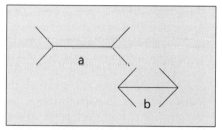

Which inner circle is larger? Check and see.

The Müller-Lyer illusion. Which line, a or b, is longer? Compare them with a ruler.

FIGURE 4.44 Context-produced geometric illusions.

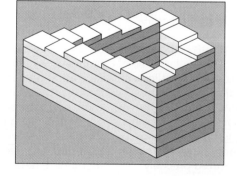

FIGURE 4.45 Monocular depth cues are cleverly manipulated to produce an impossible triangle, a never-ending staircase, and the "devil's tuning fork."

RESEARCH   CLOSE-UP

Stalking a Deadly Illusion

▶ Background

When the Boeing Company introduced the 727 jet airliner in the mid-1960s, it was the latest word in aviation technology. The plane performed well in test flights, but four fatal crashes soon after it was placed in service raised fears that there might be some fatal flaw in its design.

The first accident occurred as a 727 made its approach to Chicago over Lake Michigan on a clear night. The plane plunged into the lake 19 miles offshore. About a month later, another 727 glided in over the Ohio River to land in Cincinnati. Unaccountably, it struck the ground about 12 feet below the runway elevation and burst into flames. The third accident occurred as an aircraft approached Salt Lake City over dark land. The lights of the city twinkled in the distance, but the plane made too rapid a descent and crashed short of the runway. Months later, a Japanese airliner approached Tokyo at night. The flight ended tragically as the plane, its landing gear not yet lowered, struck the waters of Tokyo Bay 6 miles from the runway.

Analysis of these four accidents, as well as others, suggested a common pattern. All occurred at night under clear weather conditions, so that the pilots were operating under visual flight rules rather than performing instrument landings. In each instance, the plane was approaching city lights over dark areas of water or land. In all cases, the lights in the background sloped upward to varying degrees. Finally, all of the planes crashed short of the runway. These observations led a Boeing psychologist, Conrad L. Kraft, to suspect that the cause of the crashes might be pilot error based on some sort of visual illusion.

▶ Method

To test this possibility, Boeing engineers constructed an apparatus to simulate night landings (Figure 4.46). It consisted of a cockpit and a miniature lighted "city" named Nightertown. The city moved toward the cockpit on computer-controlled rollers, and it could be tilted to simulate various terrain slopes. The pilot could control simulated air speed and rate of climb and descent, and the Nightertown scene was controlled by the pilot's responses just as a true visual scene would be.

The participants were 12 experienced Boeing flight instructors who made virtual reality "landings" at Nightertown under systematically varied conditions created by the computerized simulator. All of their landings were visual landings so as to be able to test whether a visual illusion was occurring. Every aspect of their approach and the manner in which they controlled the aircraft was measured precisely.

FIGURE 4.46 Conrad Kraft, a Boeing psychologist, created an apparatus to study how visual cues can affect the simulated landings of airline pilots. Pilots approached Nightertown in a simulated cockpit. The computer-controlled city could be tilted to reproduce the illusion thought to be responsible for fatal air crashes.

▶ Results

The landings made by the flight instructors were nearly flawless until Kraft duplicated the conditions of the fatal crashes by having the pilots approach an upward-sloping distant city over a dark area. When this occurred, the pilots were unable to detect the upward slope, assumed that the background city was flat, and consistently overestimated their altitude. On a normal landing, the preferred altitude at 4.5 miles from the runway is about 1,240 feet. As Figure 4.47 shows, the pilots approached at about this altitude when the simulated city was in a flat position. But when it was sloped upward, 11 of the 12 experienced pilot instructors crashed about 4.5 miles short of the runway.

▶ Critical Analysis

This study shows the value of being able to study behavior under highly controlled conditions and with precise measurements. By simulating the conditions under which the fatal crashes had occurred, Kraft identified the visual illusion that was the source of pilot error. He showed that the perceptual hypotheses of the flight instructors, like those of the pilots involved in the real crashes, were tragically incorrect. It would have been ironic if one of the finest jet liners ever built had been removed from service because of presumed mechanical defects while other aircraft remained at risk.

—Continued

Kraft's research not only saved the 727 from months, and perhaps years, of needless mechanical analysis but, more importantly, it identified a potentially deadly illusion and the precise conditions under which it occurred. On the basis of Kraft's findings, Boeing recommended that pilots attend carefully to their instruments when landing at night, even under perfect weather conditions. Today commercial airline pilots are required to make instrument landings not only at night, but also during the day.

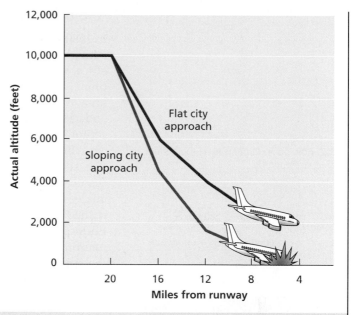

FIGURE 4.47 The illusion caused by upward-sloping city lights caused even highly experienced pilots to overestimate their altitude, and 11 of the 12 flight instructors "crashed" short of the runway. When the lights were flat, all the pilots made perfect approaches. Data from Kraft, 1978.

Source: Conrad L. Kraft (1978). A psychophysical contribution to air safety: Simulator studies of illusions in night visual approaches. In H. L. Pick, Jr., H. W. Leibowitz, J. E. Singer, A. Steinschneider, & H. W. Stevenson (Eds.), *Psychology: From research to practice.* New York: Plenum.

❭ PERCEPTION AS A PSYCHOBIOLOGICAL PROCESS: UNDERSTANDING PAIN

Physical pain is surely one of the most unpleasant realities of life, and most of us do our best to avoid it. Yet pain also has important survival functions. It serves as a warning signal when the body is being threatened or damaged, and it can trigger a variety of behavioral reactions that help us cope with the threat, such as jerking back from a hot skillet or going to see a doctor.

Pain is more than just a sensory phenomenon; it is a complex perception that reflects the operation of numerous psychological processes. For example, it is possible for people to experience excruciating pain in the absence of tissue damage (Melzack, 1998). Conversely, people may experience physical damage and yet experience no pain, as has occurred in soldiers engaged in combat who were unaware for several hours that they had been wounded (Fordyce, 1988). Thus both biological and psychological factors influence the perception of pain.

Biological Mechanisms of Pain

Pain receptors are found in all body tissues with the exception of the brain, bones, hair, nails, and nonliving parts of the teeth. Free nerve endings in the skin and internal organs respond to intense mechanical, thermal, or chemical stimulation, then send nerve impulses into the spinal cord, where sensory tracts carry pain information to the brain. Once in the brain, the sensory information about pain intensity and location is relayed by the thalamus to the somatosensory and frontal areas of the cerebral cortex (Davis et al., 1998). Other tracts from the thalamus direct nerve impulses to the limbic system, which is involved in motivation and emotion. These tracts seem to control the emotional component of pain (Melzack, 1998). Thus pain has both a sensory and an emotional component. Suffering occurs when the emotional component is present (Fordyce, 1988).

Natural Opiates Within the Body

In 1680 an English physician wrote, "Among the remedies which it has pleased Almighty God to give man to relieve his suffering, none is so universal and so efficacious as opium" (quoted in Snyder, 1978). Opiates (such as opium, morphine, and heroin) have been used to relieve pain for centuries, and they were known to strongly affect the brain's pain and pleasure systems. In the 1970s, scientists discovered that opiates produce their effects by locking into specific receptor sites in brain regions to which pain receptors send nerve impulses.

But why would the brain have built-in receptors for opiates unless there was some natural chemical in the brain for the receptor to receive? Later research disclosed what had to be true: The nervous system has its own built-in analgesics (painkillers) with opiatelike properties. These natural opiates were named **endorphins** (meaning *endo*genous, or internally produced, m*orphin*es). Endorphins exert some of their pain-killing effects by inhibiting the release of neurotransmitters involved in the synaptic transmission of pain impulses from the spinal cord to the brain (Fessler, 1989). Some of the endorphins are enormously potent: One brain endorphin isolated by scientists is more than 200 times more powerful than morphine (Franklin, 1987).

Endorphins and Pain Reduction

Behavioral researchers study the effects of endorphins in two major ways. One method is to inject endorphins into participants who are experiencing pain and measure analgesic (pain-reducing) effects. The other is to inject *naloxone*, a drug that blocks the action of endorphins, and observe the consequences. If a procedure produces pain relief when naloxone is not used, but no longer does so if naloxone is present, we have indirect evidence that endorphins are responsible for the pain-reducing effects of the procedure. Endorphins are of great interest to psychologists because they could help explain how psychological factors "in the head" can have such strong effects on pain and suffering.

Acupuncture is a pain-reduction technique that may ultimately be understood in terms of endorphin mechanisms (Figure 4.48). Research in China has shown that injections of naloxone greatly reduce the analgesic effects of acupuncture (Fang et al., 1993; Zhu et al., 1993). Another phenomenon attributable to endorphins is **stress-induced analgesia,** a reduction in perceived pain that occurs under stressful conditions. For example, research has shown that about 65 percent of soldiers wounded during combat report having felt no pain at the time (Warga, 1987). Likewise, people involved in accidents are sometimes unaware of serious injuries until the crisis is over. This analgesic response could be highly adaptive. In a life-threatening situation, defensive behavior must be given immediate priority over normal responses to pain, which typically involve immobility. By reducing or preventing pain sensations through the mechanism of endorphin release, stress-induced analgesia helps suppress these pain-related behaviors so that the person or animal can get on with the actions that are needed for immediate survival, such as fleeing, fighting, or getting help. Stress-induced analgesia seems to be produced at least in part by the release of endorphins as part of an adaptive survival mechanism, for naloxone can sharply reduce pain analgesia under stressful conditions (Fanselow, 1991).

The release of endorphins seems to be part of the body's natural response to stress, but we may pay a price for this temporary relief from pain. It now appears that chronically high levels of endorphin release help block the activity of immune system cells that recognize and selectively kill tumor cells. This may be one way in which stress makes us more susceptible to serious illnesses, such as cancer (Shavit, 1990).

Pain perception is influenced not only by the nature of the painful stimulation, but also by psychological and cultural factors. The *Psychological Frontiers* feature focuses on these determinants of pain.

➤ 42. How do endorphins exert their effects on pain perception?

➤ 43. How do researchers determine whether endorphins underlie the analgesic effects of a procedure, such as acupuncture or hypnosis?

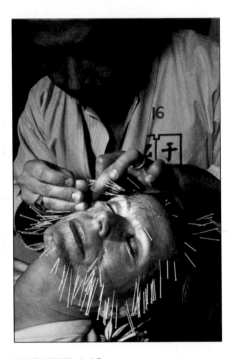

FIGURE 4.48 Acupuncture treatments can reduce pain. The needles may produce an analgesic effect by stimulating the release of endorphins.

➤ 44. What is stress-induced analgesia, and what is its adaptive value? How do we know if endorphins play a role in it?

➤ 45. Can endorphins have negative effects on the body?

➤ 46. What evidence is there that cultural learning, beliefs, and personality factors influence pain perception?

PSYCHOLOGICAL FRONTIERS

Cultural and Psychological Influences on Pain

Our interpretation of pain impulses sent to the brain depends in part on our experiences and beliefs, and both of these factors are influenced by the culture in which we develop (Rollman, 1998). Consider childbirth, for example. This event is a painful ordeal for many mothers in Western cultures, and many women express considerable anxiety about going through it (Blechman & Brownell, 1998). Yet in certain cultures women show virtually no distress during childbirth. Indeed, in one culture studied by anthropologists, it was customary for the woman's husband to get into bed and groan as if he were in great pain, while the woman calmly gave birth to the child. The husband stayed in bed with the baby to recover from his terrible ordeal while the mother returned to work in the fields almost immediately (Kroeber, 1948).

In certain parts of India, people practice an unusual hook-hanging ritual. A holy person is chosen to bless the children and crops in a number of neighboring villages. Large steel hooks attached by ropes to the top of a special ceremonial cart are then shoved under the skin and muscles on each side of his back, and he travels on the cart from village to village. At the climax of a ceremony in each village, the celebrant leaps from the cart and swings free, hanging only by the hooks embedded in his back (Figure 4.49). Incredibly, though impaled on the hooks with his entire body weight, the celebrant shows no evidence of pain during the ritual; on the contrary, he appears to be in a state of ecstasy. When the hooks are removed, the wounds heal rapidly and are scarcely visible within two weeks (Kosambi, 1967).

Although ethnic groups do not appear to differ in their ability to discriminate among pain stimuli, members of different cultural groups may differ greatly in their interpretation of pain and the amount of suffering they experience (Rollman, 1998; Zatzick & Dimsdale, 1990). In the Indian hook-hanging ceremony, for example, the religious meanings attached to the act seem to transform the interpretations and meaning of the sensory input from the hooks as well. The role of cultural factors in pain is found even within modern Western subcultures. In a study done in the Worcester, Massachusetts, area, researchers studied pain perception in 372 medical patients who represented six different ethnic groups: Old Americans (at least third-generation U.S.-born Caucasians who identified with no ethnic group except Americans), Hispanics, Italians, Irish, French Canadians, and Polish. All of the patients suffered from chronic pain conditions that had persisted for at least three months and were beyond the point of healing. The patients completed self-report measures about their pain experiences.

The ethnic groups did not differ overall in type of physical affliction, how long they had had it, or the kinds

FIGURE 4.49 A hook-swinging ceremony practiced in remote villages in India illustrates the importance of the meaning attributed to pain stimuli. After blessing all the children and farm fields in a village, the celebrant leaps from the cart and hangs suspended by the hooks in a state of ecstasy, showing no sign of pain.
Adapted from Kosambi, 1967.

of treatments and medications they were receiving. They did differ, however, in the pain levels they reported, and these differences were associated with different attitudes and beliefs about their pain. The Hispanic and Italian patients believed most strongly that they had no control over their pain, reported feeling worried and angry about it, and believed that they would be unhappy as long as they experienced it. They also believed that it is appropriate to express one's pain openly. These two ethnic groups reported the highest levels of pain and suffering. In contrast, the Old American and Polish patients felt it best to suppress the outward expression of pain, reported feeling less upset about their pain sensations, and believed that they had greater personal control over their lives. These attitudinal differences were associated with much lower levels of reported suffering (Bates et al., 1993).

Differences exist not only between cultural groups but also within them, as the physician Henry Beecher (1959) observed while working at Anzio Beachhead in World War II and later at Massachusetts General Hospital. Beecher found that only about 25 percent of the severely wounded

–Continued

soldiers he observed required pain medication, compared with 80 percent of civilian men who had received similarly serious "wounds" from surgeons at Massachusetts General. Why the difference? Beecher concluded that for the soldiers, the wounds had a fundamentally positive meaning: They spelled evacuation from the war zone and a "ticket back home" to their loved ones. For the civilian surgical patients, on the other hand, the operations meant a major life disruption. The different meanings attributed to the pain stimuli resulted in very different levels of suffering and, consequently, different needs for pain relief.

Nowhere is the influence of belief on pain perception more evident than in the effects of placebos. In one study, either a placebo or a morphine injection was given to 122 surgical patients who were suffering postoperative pain. All were told they were receiving pain medication. Of those who received morphine, 67 percent reported relief, but 42 percent of those given placebos reported equal relief (Beecher, 1959). More recent medical studies of placebo effects have yielded even higher rates of pain relief, some as high as 100 percent (Turner et al., 1994). However, it is also clear that placebos work only if people *believe* they are going to work. Given that positive belief, the brain sends messages that result in the release of endorphins to reduce pain (ter Reit et al., 1998).

Where pain is concerned, the statement "I can control it" may be more than an idle boast or a reassuring phrase. In one experiment, patients suffering from the prolonged pain of a bone-marrow transplant were randomly assigned to one of two conditions. One group was allowed to directly control the amount of pain medication that they received intravenously. The other patients were given prescribed amounts of the same medication by the hospital staff (and told they could request additional medication if needed). The patients who had direct control over their medication not only rated their pain as less intense, but also gave themselves less pain medication (Zucker et al., 1998). As with placebo effects, beliefs about

personal control apparently exert their effects by increasing endorphin release, for naloxone injections sharply reduce the ability of people with high confidence in their pain tolerance to endure intensely painful stimuli (Bandura et al., 1987).

Beginning with Sigmund Freud, personality theorists have suggested that emotional and personality factors can play a role in experiencing and responding to pain. Pain and suffering can be a way of attaining certain goals. For some bitter and deprived people, pain can be a way of dramatizing their unhappiness, eliciting caring, sympathy, or guilt from others, or gaining favors from them. Pain may also be a way of escaping from or avoiding threatening situations. For example, an athlete who dreads the possibility of failing may avoid the feared competitive situation by experiencing severe pain that prevents a return to action. This coping process can occur at a subconscious level that is different from simply "faking" being hurt (May & Sieb, 1987).

People who have the personality trait of *neuroticism,* the tendency to experience negative emotions such as anxiety and depression, report higher levels of physical pain, both in relation to medical conditions and in controlled laboratory administrations of painful stimuli such as heat, cold, electrical shock, or pressure (Jess & Bech, 1994; Lehofer et al., 1998; Sist et al., 1998). In contrast, personality styles that include optimism and a sense of personal control over one's life are associated with lower pain perception and less suffering (Pellino & Ward, 1998). Moreover, patients with chronic pain conditions who are able to simply accept the pain rather than bemoaning their fate and responding emotionally to it have less disability, better social adjustment, and higher work performance (McCracken, 1998). Thus it seems clear that psychological factors play important roles in pain perception and adaptation. As shown in Figure 4.50, they add to the biological and environmental levels of analysis important pieces to the puzzle of pain.

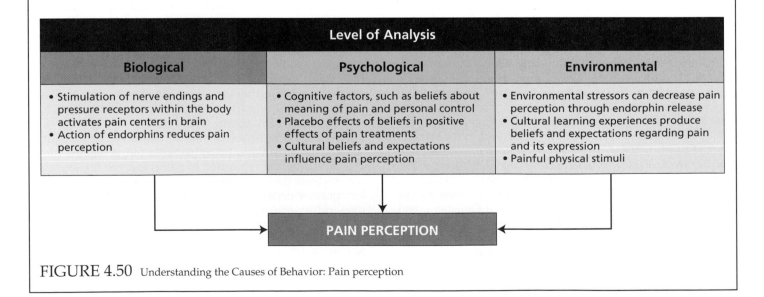

FIGURE 4.50   Understanding the Causes of Behavior: Pain perception

❯ EXPERIENCE, CRITICAL PERIODS, AND PERCEPTUAL DEVELOPMENT

Development of sensory and perceptual systems results from the interplay of biological and experiential factors. Genes program biological development, but this development is also influenced by environmental experiences. For example, if you were to be blinded in an accident and later learned to read braille, the area of the somatosensory cortex that is devoted to the fingertips would enlarge over time as it "borrowed" other neurons to increase its sensitivity (Pool, 1994). By the time they are old enough to crawl, children placed on a *visual cliff* formed by a glass-covered table that suddenly drops off beneath the glass will not ordinarily venture "over the edge" (Figure 4.51). This aversion may result from the interaction of innate depth perception abilities and previous experience (Gibson & Walk, 1960).

What might a lifetime of experience in a limited environment do to perceptual abilities that seem innate? The Ba Mbuti pygmies, who live in the rain forests of central Africa, spend their lives in a closed-in green world of densely packed trees without open spaces. The anthropologist C. M. Turnbull (1961) once brought a man named Kenge out of the forest to the edge of a vast plain. A herd of buffalo grazed in the distance. To Turnbull's surprise, Kenge remarked that he had never seen insects of that kind. When told that they were buffalo, not insects, he was deeply offended and felt that Turnbull was insulting his intelligence. To prove his point, Turnbull drove Kenge in his jeep toward the animals. Kenge's eyes widened in amazement as the "insects" grew into buffalo before his eyes. To explain his perceptual experience to himself, he concluded that witchcraft was being used to fool him. Kenge's misperception occurred as a failure in size constancy. Having lived in an environment without open spaces, he had no experience in judging the size of objects at great distances.

As noted earlier, when light passes through the lens of the eye, the image projected on the retina is reversed, so that right is left and up is down. What would happen if you were to wear a special set of of glasses that undid this natural reversal of the visual image and created a world like that in Figure 4.52? In 1896, perception researcher George Stratton did just that, possibly becoming the first human ever to have a right-side-up image on his retina while standing upright. Reversing how nature and a lifetime of experience had fashioned his perceptual system disoriented Stratton at first. The ground and his feet were now "up" and he had to put on his hat on from the bottom up. He had to reach to his left to touch something he saw on his right. Stratton suffered from nausea and couldn't eat or get around for several days. Gradually, however, he adapted to his inverted world and by the end of eight days, he was able to successfully reach for objects and walk around. Years later, people who wore inverting lenses for longer periods of time did the same. Some were able to ski down mountain slopes or ride motorcycles while wearing the lenses, even though their visual world remained "upside down" and never became normal for them. When they removed the inverting lenses, they had some initial problems, but soon readapted to the normal visual world (Dolezal, 1982).

Cross-Cultural Research on Perception

As far as we know, humans normally come into the world with the same perceptual abilities. However, from that point, the culture one grows up in helps determine the kinds of perceptual learning experiences people have. Cross-cultural research can help identify which aspects of perception occur in all people, regardless of their culture, as well as perceptual differences that result from cultural experiences (Deregowski & Kinnear, 1997). Athough there are far more perceptual similarities than differences in the peoples of the world, the differences that do exist show us that perception can indeed be influenced by experience.

FIGURE 4.51 Eleanor Gibson and Richard Walk constructed this "visual cliff" with a glass-covered drop-off to determine whether crawling infants and newborn animals can perceive depth. Even when coaxed by their mothers, infants refuse to venture onto the glass over the cliff. Newborn animals also avoid the cliff.

FIGURE 4.52 Inverted vision would create a world that looks like this. Adaptation to such a world is possible, but challenging.

➤ 47. What evidence is there that cultural factors can influence picture interpretations, constancies, and susceptibility to illusions?

(a)

(b)

FIGURE 4.53   (a) What is the object above the woman's head? East Africans had a far different answer than did North Americans. (b) Cultural differences also occurred when people were asked which animal the archer was about to shoot.

(*a*) Adapted from Gregory & Gombrich, 1973; (*b*) Adapted from Hudson, 1960.

➤ 48. How do animal studies of restricted stimulation and human studies of restored vision illustrate the important role of critical periods for perceptual development?

Consider the perception of a picture, which depends on both the nature of the picture and characteristics of the perceiver. In Figure 4.53*a*, what is the object above the woman's head? Most North Americans and Europeans reply instantly, "A window." They also tend to see the family sitting inside a dwelling. But when the same picture was shown to East Africans, nearly all perceive the object as a basket or box that the woman is balancing on her head. To them, the family is also outside, sitting under a tree (Gregory & Gombrich, 1973). These interpretations are more consistent with their cultural experiences.

In our earlier discussion of monocular depth cues, we used paintings such as those in Figure 4.40 to illustrate monocular depth perception. In Western culture, we have constant exposure to two-dimensional pictures that our perceptual system effortlessly turns into three-dimensional perceptions. Do people who grow up in cultures where they are not exposed to pictures have the same perceptions? When presented with the picture in Figure 4.53*b* and asked which animal the hunter was about to shoot, tribal African people answered that he was about to kill the "baby elephant." They did not use the monocular cues that cause Westerners to perceive the man as hunting the antelope and to view the elephant as an adult animal in the distance (Hudson, 1960).

Illusions occur when one of our common perceptual hypotheses is in error. Earlier, we showed you the Müller-Lyer illusion (see Figure 4.44) in which a line appears longer when the V-shaped lines at its ends radiate outward than when they face inward. Westerners are very susceptible to this illusion. They have learned that in their "carpentered" environment, which has many corners and square shapes, inward-facing lines occur when corners are closer, outward-facing lines when they are farther away (Figure 4.54). But when people from other cultures who live in more rounded environments are shown the Müller-Lyer stimuli, they are more likely to correctly perceive the lines as equal in length (Segall et al., 1966). They do not fall prey to a perceptual hypothesis that normally is correct in an environment like ours that is filled with sharp corners, but is wrong when applied to the lines in the Müller-Lyer illusion (Deregowski & Kinnear, 1997).

Cultural learning affects perceptions in other modalities as well. Our perceptions of tastes, odors, and textures are strongly influenced by our cultural experiences. A taste that might produce nausea in one culture may be considered delicious in another. The taste and gritty texture experienced as you chew a large raw insect or the rubbery texture of a fish eye may appeal far less to you than it would to a person from a culture in which that is a food staple.

Critical Periods: The Role of Early Experience

These examples suggest that experience is critical to the development of perceptual abilities. For some aspects of perception, there are also **critical periods** during which certain kinds of experiences must occur if perceptual abilities and the brain mechanisms that underlie them are to develop normally. If the critical period passes without the experience occurring, it is too late to undo the deficit that results.

Earlier, we saw that the visual cortex has feature detectors composed of neurons that respond only to lines at particular angles. What would happen if newborn animals grew up in a world in which they saw some angles but not others? British researchers Colin Blakemore and Grahame Cooper (1970) created such a world for newborn kittens. The animals were raised in the dark except for a 5-hour period each day during which they were placed in round chambers that had either vertical or horizonal stripes on the walls. Figure 4.55*a* shows one of the kittens in a vertically striped chamber. A special collar prevented the kittens from seeing their own bodies while they were in the chamber, guaranteeing that they saw nothing but stripes.

When the kittens were 5 months of age, Blakemore and Cooper presented bars of light at differing angles to them and used microelectrodes to test the electrical responses of individual feature detector cells in their visual cortex. The results for animals raised in the vertically striped environment are shown in Figure 4.55*b*. As you can see, the kittens had no cells that fired in response to horizontal stimuli, resulting in visual impairments. They also acted as if they could not see a pencil when it was held in a horizontal position and moved up and down in front of them. However, as soon as the pencil was rotated to a vertical position, the animals began to follow it with their eyes as it was moved back and forth.

As you might expect, the animals raised in the horizontally striped environment showed the opposite effects. They had no feature detectors for vertical stimuli and did not seem to see them. Thus the cortical neurons of both groups of kittens developed in accordance with the stimulus features of their environments.

Some perceptual abilities are influenced more than others by restricted stimulation. For example, monkeys, chimpanzees, and kittens have been raised in an environment devoid of shapes. Such animals distinguish differences in size, brightness, and color almost as well as normally reared animals do. On the other hand, for the rest of their lives they perform poorly on more complex tasks, such as distinguishing different types of objects and geometric shapes (Riesen, 1965).

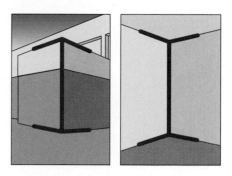

FIGURE 4.54 Perceptual experiences within our "carpentered" environment makes us susceptible to the Müller-Lyer illusion, which appears here in vertical form. Again, the vertical lines are the same physical length.

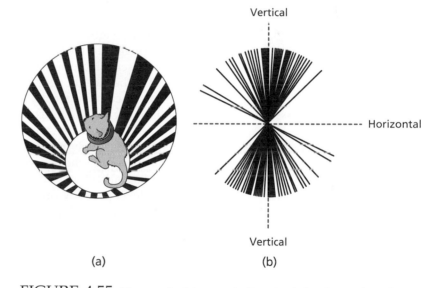

(a) (b)

FIGURE 4.55 Kittens raised in a vertically striped chamber such as the one shown in (a) lacked cortical cells that fired in response to horizontal stimuli. The perceptual "holes" are easily seen in (b), which shows the orientation angles that resulted in evoked potentials from feature detectors.

Adapted from Blakemore & Cooper, 1970.

Restored Sensory Capacity

Suppose it had been possible to restore Helen Keller's vision when she reached adulthood. What would she have seen? Could she have perceived visually the things that she had learned to identify through her other senses?

Unfortunately, it was not possible to provide Helen Keller with the miracle of restored vision. However, scientists have studied the experiences of other visually impaired people who acquired the ability to see later in life. For example, people born with cataracts grow up in a visual world without form. The clouded lenses of their eyes permit them to perceive light, but not patterns or shapes. One such person was Virgil, who had been almost totally blind since childhood. He read braille, enjoyed listening to sports on the radio and conversing with other people, and had adjusted quite well to his disability. At the urging of his fiancée, Virgil agreed to undergo surgery to remove his thick cataracts. The day after the surgery, his bandages were removed. Neurologist Oliver Sacks recounts what happened next.

There was light, there was color, all mixed up, meaningless, a blur. Then out of the blur came a voice that said, "Well?" Then, and only then . . . did he finally realize that this chaos of light and shadow was a face—and, indeed, the face of his surgeon. . . . His retina and optic nerve were active, transmitting impulses, but his brain could make no sense of them. (Sacks, 1993, p. 62)

Virgil was never able to adjust to his new visual world. He had to touch objects in order to identify them. He had to be led through his own house and would quickly become disoriented if he deviated from his path. Eventually, Virgil lost his sight once again. This time, however, he regarded his blindness as a gift, a release from a sighted world that had become bewildering to him.

Virgil's experiences are characteristic of people who have their vision restored later in life. A German physician, von Senden (1960), compiled data on patients born with cataracts who were tested soon after their cataracts were surgically removed in adulthood. These people were immediately able to perceive figure-ground relations, to scan objects visually, and to follow moving targets with their eyes, indicating that such abilities are innate. However, they could not visually identify objects, such as eating utensils, that they were familiar with through touch, nor were they able to distinguish simple geometric figures without counting the corners or tracing the figures with their fingers.

After several weeks of training, the patients were able to identify simple objects by sight, but their perceptual constancies were very poor. Often they were unable to recognize the same shape in another color, even though they could discriminate between colors. Years later, some patients could identify only a few of the faces of people they knew well. Many also had great difficulty judging distances. Apparently, no amount of subsequent experience could make up for their lack of visual experience during the critical period of childhood.

All of these lines of evidence—cross-cultural perceptual differences, animal studies involving visual deprivation, and observations of congenitally impaired people whose vision has been restored—suggest that biological and experiential factors interact in complex ways. Some of our perceptual abilities are at least partially present at birth, but experience plays an important role in their normal development. How innate and experiential factors interact promises to be a continued focus of perception research.

▼▼

CHAPTER SUMMARY

Sensation and Perception

- Although sensation and perception are interrelated, sensation refers to the activities by which our sense organs receive and transmit information, whereas perception involves the brain's processing and interpretation of the information.

Sensory Processes

- Psychophysics is the scientific study of how the physical properties of stimuli are related to sensory experiences. Sensory sensitivity is concerned in part with the limits of stimulus detectability (absolute threshold) and the ability to discriminate between stimuli (difference threshold). The absolute threshold is the intensity at which a stimulus is de-

tected 50 percent of the time. Signal detection theory studies factors that influence decisions about whether or not a stimulus is present.

- Research indicates that subliminal stimuli, which are not consciously perceived, can influence behavior in subtle ways, but not strongly enough to justify concerns about subconscious control of behavior through subliminal messages. There is some evidence that attitudes can be affected. Use of subliminal self-help materials sometimes results in positive behavior changes, but such changes may be produced by expectancy factors rather than by the subliminal messages.

- The difference threshold (just noticeable difference, or jnd) is the amount by which two stimuli must differ for them to be perceived as different. Studies of the jnd led to Weber's law, which states that the jnd is proportional to the intensity of the original stimulus and is constant within a given sense modality.

- Sensory systems are particularly responsive to changes in stimulation, and adaptation occurs in response to unchanging stimuli.

The Sensory Systems

- The senses may be classified in terms of the energy to which they respond. Through the process of transduction, these energy forms are transformed into the common language of nerve impulses.

- The normal stimulus for vision is electromagnetic energy, or light waves. Light-sensitive visual receptor cells are located in the retina. The rods are brightness receptors and the less numerous cones are color receptors. Light energy striking the retina is converted into nerve impulses by chemical reactions in the photopigments of the rods and cones. Dark adaptation involves the gradual regeneration of photopigments that have been depleted by brighter illumination.

- The two classical color vision theories are the Young-Helmholtz trichromatic theory and Hering's opponent-process theory. Color vision appears to be a two-stage process involving both trichromatic and opponent-process components. The first stage involves the reactions of cones that are maximally sensitive to red, green, and blue wavelengths. In the second stage, color information from the cones is coded through an opponent-process mechanism farther along in the visual system.

- Visual stimuli are analyzed by feature detectors in the primary visual cortex, and the stimulus elements are reconstructed and interpreted in light of input from the visual association cortex.

- Sound waves, the stimuli for audition, have two characteristics: frequency, measured in terms of cycles per second or hertz (Hz), and amplitude, measured in terms of decibels (db). Frequency is related to pitch, amplitude to loudness. The receptors for hearing are hair cells in the organ of Corti of the inner ear.

- Loudness is coded in terms of the number and types of auditory nerve fibers that fire. Pitch is coded in two ways. Low-frequency tones are coded in terms of corresponding numbers of nerve impulses in individual receptors or of volleys of impulses from a number of receptors. Frequencies above 4,000 Hz are coded according to the region of the basilar membrane that is displaced most by the fluid wave in the cochlear canal.

- Hearing loss may result from conduction deafness, produced by problems involving the structures of the inner ear that transmit vibrations to the cochlea, or nerve deafness, in which the receptors of the inner ear or the auditory nerve are damaged.

- Principles derived from the study of sensory processes have been applied in developing sensory prosthetics for the blind and the hearing impaired. Examples include the Sonicguide, the Utah Intracortical Electrode Array, and cochlear inplants.

- The receptors for taste and smell respond to chemical molecules. Taste buds are responsive to four basic qualities: sweet, sour, salty, and bitter. The receptors for smell (olfaction) are long cells in the upper nasal cavity. Natural body odors produced by pheromones appear to account for menstrual synchrony that sometimes occurs among women who are in frequent contact.

- The skin and body senses include touch, kinesthesis, and equilibrium. Receptors in the skin and body tissues are sensitive to touch, pain, warmth, and cold. These receptors send their messages to particular areas of the sensory cortex. Kinesthesis functions by means of nerve endings in the muscles, tendons, and joints. The sense organs for equilibrium are in the vestibular apparatus of the inner ear.

Perception

- Perception is selective. Attention is an active process in which we focus on certain stimuli while blocking out other stimuli. We cannot attend completely to more than one thing at a time, but we are capable of rapid attentional shifts. Attentional processes are affected by the nature of the stimulus as well as by personal factors such as motives and interests. The perceptual system appears to be especially vigilant to stimuli that denote threat or danger.

- Perception is an active process that confers organization and structure on stimuli. Perception involves both bottom-up processing, in which individual stimulus fragments are combined into a perception, and top-down processing, in which existing knowledge and perceptual schemas are applied to interpret stimuli.

- The Gestalt psychologists identified a number of principles of perceptual organization, including figure-ground relations and the laws of similarity, proximity, closure, and continuity. R. L. Gregory suggested that perception is essentially a hypothesis about what a stimulus is, based on previous experience and the nature of the stimulus.

- Perceptual sets involve a readiness to perceive stimuli in certain ways, based on our expectations, assumptions, motivations, and current emotional state.

- Perceptual constancies allow us to recognize familiar stimuli under changing conditions. In the visual realm, there are three constancies: shape, brightness, and size.

Perception of Depth, Distance, and Movement

- Several monocular cues help us to judge distance. These include linear perspective, relative size, height in the horizontal plane, texture, and clarity. These distance cues also help us to judge depth. Depth perception also occurs through the monocular cues of light and shadow patterns, motion parallax, and interposition.

- Binocular disparity is the basis for the perception of depth that results from the use of both eyes as slightly different images are viewed by each eye and acted upon by feature detectors for depth. Convergence of the eyes provides a second binocular cue.

- The stimulus for perception of movement is absolute movement of a stimulus across the retina or relative movement of an object in relation to its background. Stroboscopic movement is illusory.

Illusions

- Illusions are erroneous perceptions. They may be regarded as incorrect perceptual hypotheses. Perceptual constancies help produce many illusions.

Pain Perception

- The major pain receptors appear to be free nerve endings. The nervous system contains endorphins, which play a major role in pain reduction. Endorphins released in response to stress produce analgesia and thus increase pain tolerance.

- Psychological factors strongly influence responses to painful stimuli. Placebos can markedly reduce pain. Cultural factors also influence the manner in which painful stimuli are appraised and responded to, as do personal control beliefs. Negative emotional states increase the unpleasantness of pain and decrease pain tolerance.

Experience, Critical Periods, and Perceptual Development

- Perceptual development involves both physical maturation and learning. Certain perceptual abilities are innate or develop shortly after birth, whereas others require particular experiences in order to develop.

- Cultural factors can influence certain aspects of perception, including picture perception and susceptibility to illusions. However, many aspects of perception seem constant across cultures.

- Visual deprivation studies, manipulation of visual input, and studies of restored vision have shown that the normal biological development of the perceptual system depends on certain sensory experiences at early periods of development.

▼▼

KEY TERMS AND CONCEPTS*

absolute threshold (134)

amplitude (147)

basilar membrane (147)

binocular cues (164)

binocular disparity (165)

bipolar cells (140)

bottom-up processing (157)

cochlea (147)

conduction deafness (150)

cones (140)

convergence (165)

critical periods (174)

dark adaptation (141)

decibels (db) (147)

decision criterion (134)

difference threshold (136)

dual-process theory (143)

endorphins (170)

feature detectors (145)

figure-ground relations (159)

fovea (140)

frequency (146)

frequency theory (149)

ganglion cells (140)

Gestalt laws (160)

gustation (154)

hertz (Hz) (146)

hyperopia (139)

illusion (166)

kinesthesis (157)

lens (139)

menstrual synchrony (155)

monocular cues (164)

myopia (139)

nerve deafness (150)

olfaction (154)

opponent-process theory (143)

optic nerve (140)

organ of Corti (147)

parallel process (146)

perception (133)

perceptual constancies (163)

perceptual schemas (161)

perceptual set (162)

pheromones (155)

photopigments (141)

place theory (149)

primary visual cortex (145)

psychophysics (134)

retina (139)

rods (140)

sensation (133)

sensory adaptation (137)

shadowing (158)

signal detection theory (135)

stress-induced analgesia (170)

stroboscopic movement (166)

subliminal stimuli (135)

synesthesia (132)

taste buds (154)

top-down processing (157)

transduction (141)

trichromatic theory (142)

vestibular sense (157)

visual acuity (140)

visual association cortex (146)

Weber's law (137)

* Each term has been boldfaced in the text on the page indicated in parentheses.

APPLYING YOUR KNOWLEDGE

These questions allow you to apply your understanding of the material.

1. You are looking at a very blurry photograph. At first, all you can see is a vague red circle, but after studying the picture for a few minutes, you finally see that it is an apple. You have moved from
   a) perception to sensation.
   b) sensation to perception.
   c) perception to adaptation.
   d) sensation to synesthesia.

2. Adam and Mark are hunting when they suddenly see a vague shape in the underbrush. "There's a deer," whispers Mark, raising his rifle to fire. "Don't shoot," whispers Adam. "I'm not sure it is." From a signal detection standpoint, Adam has a more _____ decision criterion and wants to avoid a _____.
   a) conservative; false alarm
   b) liberal; hit
   c) optimistic; miss
   d) conservative; hit

3. You climb into a hot tub and find the water to be very hot, but in a few minutes the water becomes comfortable and you begin to enjoy it. Physiologically, the temperature receptors in your skin
   a) are being deactivated by endorphin release.
   b) have greatly reduced their rate of firing.
   c) are now sending "cold" signals.
   d) have increased the strength of their action potentials.

4. We cannot see colors on a dark night because
   a) color information is carried only by high-intensity light.
   b) the rods do not function well at low levels of illumination.
   c) the cones do not function well in dim light.
   d) bipolar cells are inactive in dim light.

5. Which of the following could cause you to experience conduction deafness?
   a) injured hair cells in the cochlea
   b) a punctured eardrum
   c) damage to the auditory nerve
   d) a tumor in the auditory cortex

6. Valerie is amazingly quick to interpret others' behavior as indicating that they do not think highly of her. This best illustrates
   a) subliminal perception.
   b) synesthesia.
   c) bottom-up processing.
   d) perceptual set.

7. You are reading a photocopy of an article. The last word or two on the right side of each page did not copy well and is blurry. If these blurry words are the last words of a sentence, you can decipher them more easily than if they are the first words of a sentence. This is probably due to
   a) the Gestalt law of proximity.
   b) top-down processing.
   c) enhanced feature detection.
   d) bottom-up processing.

8. On her way home from the library late at night, Leila is physically assaulted. After a brief but fierce struggle, Leila manages to escape and runs home, terrified. Only after arriving home does she realize that her wrist has probably been broken. Her pain-free interval is probably a case of _____ and is due to the action of _____.
   a) neuroticism; naloxone
   b) stress-induced analgesia; endorphins
   c) personal control beliefs; endorphins
   d) placebo pain control; endorphins

9. Long-term intense stress appears to make people more susceptible to cancer. One reason may be that
   a) stress reduces endorphin activity.
   b) stressful events cause increases in neuroticism.
   c) chronically high levels of endorphins block the activity of tumor-killing immune cells.
   d) stress-induced analgesia strengthens the immune system.

10. Matthew, age 19, has been blind since birth, but a newly developed surgical procedure allows him to see for the first time in his life. Which of the following perceptual abilities is he likely to have?
    a) perception of figure-ground relationships
    b) ability to discriminate among faces
    c) visually recognize objects he previously identified through touch
    d) all of the above

Answers

1. b) (page 133); 2. a) (page 135); 3. b) (page 137); 4. c) (page 140); 5. b) (page 150); 6. d) (page 162); 7. b) (page 157); 8. b) (page 170); 9. c) (page 170); 10. a) (page 176).

For additional quizzing and a variety of interactive resources, visit the book's Online Learning Center at www.mhhe.com/passer.

STATES OF CONSCIOUSNESS

The mind, of course, is just what the brain does for a living.
—Sharon Begley

5

CHAPTER OUTLINE

One autumn afternoon in 1943, Swiss chemist Albert Hofmann became unable to concentrate and noticed that his laboratory assistants were changing shape. He went home to bed, experiencing vivid dreams with intense colors. The next day, Hofmann concluded that a chemical he synthesized had been absorbed through his skin. Curious, he put a tiny bit on his tongue and soon felt like he was splitting into two people. Hofmann's alarmed assistants took him home, where his strange experiences continued:

> The dizziness . . . became so strong at times that I . . . had to lie down on a sofa. . . . Everything in the room spun around and the familiar objects and pieces of furniture assumed grotesque, mostly threatening forms. . . . The neighbor woman who brought me milk . . . She was no longer Mrs. R., but rather a malevolent insidious witch with a colored mask. Even worse . . . were the alterations that I perceived in myself, in my inner being. . . . A demon had invaded me and had taken possession of my body, mind and soul. (Hofmann, 1980, p. 58)

So it was that Albert Hofmann accidentally discovered the striking alterations in consciousness that can be produced by a dose of lysergic acid diethylamide (LSD) no larger than the tip of a pin.

Billy Milligan was a most unusual person. In fact, he may have been 24 unusual people. After Milligan was arrested for kidnapping and rape, a psychologist began a jailhouse interview by asking him if he was William Milligan. "Billy's asleep" came the reply; "I'm David." Intensive psychological study suggested the possibility that Milligan's consciousness had become dramatically divided. Two dozen identities seemed to emerge over time, including Christene, a loving 3-year-old girl who drew flowers; Tommy, an escape artist who slithered out of a straitjacket in less than 10 seconds; and Adalana, a lonely and shy lesbian (Keyes, 1982). Most identities were unaware of the others, and on intelligence tests they obtained IQs ranging from 68 to over 130.

Although Albert Hofmann and Billy Milligan's experiences are unusual, they are not as far removed from our normal existence as we might think. We all drift into and out of various states of consciousness. While daydreaming or passing from wakefulness to sleep we may experience vivid images that rival Hofmann's hallucinations, and our nighttime dreams can seem just as real and emotionally charged as his drug-induced perceptions.

We also experience divisions of awareness, though thankfully less extreme than Milligan's multiple selves. Consider this: Why don't you fall out of bed at night? You are not consciously aware of major postural shifts while soundly asleep, yet a part of you somehow knows where the edge of the bed is. Similarly, have you ever "spaced out" while driving, deeply engrossed in thought? Suddenly you snap out of it, with no memory of the miles just driven. While you were consciously focused inward, some part of you kept track of the road and controlled your responses at the wheel.

Philosopher David Chalmers (1995) notes that "Conscious experience is at once the most familiar thing in the world and the most mysterious." As we shall see, its mysteries span a range from normal waking states to sleep and dreams, drug-induced experiences, hypnosis, and beyond. When psychology was founded in the late 1800s, its "Great Project" was to scientifically unravel some of the puzzles of consciousness (Natsoulas, 1999). This interest waned during behaviorism's dominance in the mid-20th century, but resurgence of the cognitive and biological perspectives has sparked new research, forcing us to rethink long-standing conceptions about the mind (Figure 5.1).

❭ THE PUZZLE OF CONSCIOUSNESS

What is consciousness, and how does it arise? In psychology, **consciousness** often is defined as our moment-to-moment awareness of ourselves and our environment. Among its characteristics, consciousness is

- *subjective and private.* Other people cannot directly know what reality is for you, nor can you enter directly into their experience. As the author Charles Dickens observed, "Every human creature is constituted to be that profound secret and mystery to every other."

- *dynamic (ever-changing).* We drift in and out of various states throughout each day. Although the stimuli of which we are aware constantly change, we typically experience consciousness as a continuously flowing "stream" of mental activity, rather than as disjointed perceptions and thoughts (James, 1890/1950).

- *self-reflective and central to our sense of self.* The mind is aware of its own consciousness. Thus no matter what your awareness is focused on—a lovely sunset or an itch on your back—you can reflect upon the fact that "*you*" are the one who is conscious of it.

Finally, consciousness is *intimately connected with the process of selective attention,* discussed in Chapter 4. William James noted that ". . . the mind is at every stage a theatre of simultaneous possibilities. Consciousness consists in . . . the selection of some, and the suppression of the rest by the . . . agency of Attention" (1879, p. 13). Selective attention focuses conscious awareness on some stimuli to the exclusion of others. If the mind is a theater of mental activity, then consciousness reflects whatever is illuminated at the moment—the "bright spot on the stage"—and selective attention is the "spotlight" or mechanism behind it (Baars, 1997).

Measuring States of Consciousness

Scientists who study consciousness must find ways to operationally define private inner states in terms of measurable responses. The most common measure is *self-report,* in which people describe their inner experiences. Self-reports offer the most direct insight into a person's subjective experiences, but they are not always verifiable. In contrast, *physiological measures* establish the correspondence between bodily states and mental processes. For example, EEG recordings of brain activity help identify different stages of sleep throughout the night. Physiological measures are objective, but cannot tell us what a person is experiencing subjectively. *Behavioral measures* are also used, including performance on special tasks such as the *rouge test* (Figure 5.2). Behavioral measures are objective, but we still must infer the person's (or chimp's) state of mind.

The challenge of measuring consciousness also has practical implications. For example, did Billy Milligan's multiple identities—called *dissociative identity disorder*—really exist, or was he cleverly faking them to avoid a prison sentence? Even if multiple identities are not intentionally faked, how can we be sure that they truly represent unique, altered states of consciousness (Lilienfeld et al., 1999; Spanos, 1994)?

FIGURE 5.1 The mysteries of consciousness have intrigued scholars for ages.

➤ 1. Describe some basic characteristics of consciousness.

➤ 2. How do psychologists measure states of consciousness?

FIGURE 5.2 Gordon Gallup (1970) exposed 4 chimps to a mirror. By day 3 they used it to inspect hard-to-see parts of their own bodies and began making odd faces at themselves in the mirror. To further test whether the chimps knew the mirror image was their own reflection, Gordon anesthetized them and put a red mark on their faces. Later, with no mirror, the chimps rarely touched the red mark. But upon seeing it when a mirror was introduced, they touched the red spot on their face almost 30 times in 30 minutes, suggesting that the chimps had some self-awareness. Using a similar test in which a red rouge mark is placed on the tip of the infant's nose, researchers find that infants begin to recognize themselves in a mirror around 18 months of age.

Levels of Consciousness:
Psychodynamic and Cognitive Perspectives

➤ 3. Explain Freud's three-level model of consciousness.

A century ago Sigmund Freud (1900/1953) proposed that the human mind consists of three levels of awareness. The *conscious* mind contains thoughts, perceptions, and other mental events of which we are currently aware. *Preconscious* mental events are outside current awareness, but can easily be recalled under certain conditions. For instance, you may not have thought about a childhood friend for years, but when someone mentions your friend's name, you become aware of pleasant memories. *Unconscious* events cannot be brought into conscious awareness under ordinary circumstances. Some unconscious content—such as unacceptable urges and desires stemming from instinctive sexual and aggressive drives, traumatic memories, and threatening emotional conflicts—is kept out of conscious awareness because it would arouse anxiety, guilt, or other negative emotions.

Behaviorists roundly criticized Freud's model. After all, they sought to explain behavior without invoking *conscious* mental processes, much less unconscious ones. Cognitive psychologists and many contemporary psychodynamic psychologists also take issue with specific aspects of Freud's model, which we describe more fully in Chapter 13. As psychodynamic psychologist Drew Westen (1998, p. 333) notes, "Many aspects of Freudian theory are indeed out of date, and they should be. Freud died in 1939, and he has been slow to undertake further revisions."

On a broad level, however, research strongly supports Freud's general premise: Nonconscious processes influence behavior (Dimberg et al., 2000; Westen, 1998). Studies of *placebo effects* (see Chapter 2), *split-brain patients* (see Chapter 3), *subliminal perception* (see Chapter 4), and phenomena that you will encounter in upcoming chapters all indicate that mental processes can affect our behavior without conscious awareness (Kirsch & Lynn, 1999).

The Cognitive Unconscious

➤ 4. How do cognitive psychologists view the unconscious?

Cognitive psychologists reject the notion of an unconscious mind driven by instinctive urges and repressed conflicts. Rather, they view conscious and unconscious mental life as complementary forms of information processing. As Daniel Reisberg (1997, p. 601) notes, unconscious mental activity is "not an adversary to the conscious mind. Instead, the cognitive unconscious functions as a sophisticated support service, working in harmony with our conscious thoughts." To illustrate, consider how we perform everyday tasks.

➤ 5. What is automatic processing, and why is it important?

Controlled versus automatic processing.   Many activities, such as planning a vacation or studying, involve **controlled (effortful) processing**, the voluntary use of attention and conscious effort. Other activities involve **automatic processing** and can be performed with little or no conscious effort. Automatic processing occurs most often when we carry out routine actions or well-learned tasks, particularly under constant or familiar circumstances (Ouellette & Wood, 1998). Learning to type, drive, and eat with utensils all involve controlled processing; you have to pay a lot of attention to what you are doing. With practice, they become more automatic. Through years of practice, typists, athletes, and musicians program themselves to execute highly complex skills with a minimum of conscious thought.

Ellen Langer (1989) points out that automatic processing has a key disadvantage: It can reduce our chances of finding new ways to approach problems. Controlled processing requires effort and therefore is slower than automatic processing, but it is more flexible and open to change. Still, automatic processing offers speed and economy of effort, and in everyday life most actions may be processed this way (Bargh & Chartrand, 1999). In fact, many well-learned behaviors seem performed best when our mind is on "autopilot," with controlled processing taking a backseat. The famous baseball player, Yogi Berra, captured this idea in his classic statement that "You can't think and hit at the same time."

At tasks ranging from golf putting to video games, experiments suggest that too much self-focused thinking can hurt task performance and cause people to "choke" under pressure (Baumeister, 1984; Lewis & Linder, 1997).

Divided attention.   Automatic processing also facilitates **divided attention,** the ability to perform more than one activity at the same time. We can talk while we walk, type as we read, eat while watching TV, and so on. Without the capacity to divide attention, every act would require our full attention and quickly overwhelm our mental capacity. Yet divided attention has limits, and is more difficult when tasks require similar mental resources (Reisberg, 1997). For example, the shadowing experiments described in Chapter 4 indicate that we cannot fully attend to separate messages delivered simultaneously through two earphones.

Although divided attention is wonderfully adaptive most of the time, it can have serious negative consequences in certain situations (Figure 5.3). For example, some studies have found that collision rates triple or quadruple when people talk on the telephone while driving; they are more likely to speed, drive on the wrong side of the road, run off the road, hit fixed objects, and overturn their cars (Redelmeier & Tibshirani, 1997; Violanti & Marshall, 1996). Driving simulator and actual on-road experiments also indicate that using an automobile cell phone slows drivers' reaction times to traffic hazards (Alm & Nilsson, 1995; Lamble et al., 1999).

FIGURE 5.3 Several countries have banned the use of hand-held mobile phones while driving. Brooklyn, Ohio, was the first U.S. municipality to take a similar action, and others are considering a similar ban. According to some researchers, even hands-free phone conversations are associated with impaired attention while driving and an increased risk of accidents.

The Emotional Unconscious

Some modern psychodynamic views incorporate information-processing concepts from cognitive psychology, but strongly emphasize that emotional and motivational processes also operate unconsciously and influence behavior (Gillett, 1997; Westen, 1998). At times, these hidden processes can cause us to feel and act in ways that mystify us or that we cannot explain. Consider the famous case of a 47-year-old amnesia patient who could not remember new personal experiences. One day, as Swiss psychologist Edouard Claparède (1911) shook this woman's hand, he intentionally pricked her hand with a pin hidden between his fingers. Later, Claparède extended his hand toward hers again. The woman could not consciously remember the pinprick, but despite her amnesia, she suddenly withdrew her hand. Apparently, a nonconscious memory of her painful past experience influenced her behavior.

In the past 15 years an explosion of research—much of it by cognitive, social, physiological, and clinical psychologists—has strengthened the view that unconscious processes can have an emotional and motivational flavor (Epstein, 1994; LeDoux, 2000; Westen, 1998). For example, have you ever been in a bad or good mood, and unsure of why you were feeling that way? Perhaps, as John Bargh and Tanya Chartrand (1999) propose, it is because you were influenced by events in your environment of which you were not consciously aware.

In one study, Chartrand and Bargh (2000) *subliminally* presented college students with nouns that were either strongly negative (e.g., cancer, cockroach), mildly negative (e.g., Monday, worm), mildly positive (e.g., parade, clown), or strongly positive (e.g., friends, music). Later, students rated their mood on standard psychological inventories. Although they were not consciously aware of seeing the nouns, those shown the strongly negative words displayed the saddest mood, whereas those who had seen the strongly positive words reported the happiest mood. In Chapter 10 we explore other aspects of the modern "emotional unconscious."

➤ 6. Can nonconscious processes influence emotional responses?

The Modular Mind

Given these findings, how shall we view the human mind? Freud's theory challenged the traditional view that the mind is a single "entity" or process. Today a growing number of models also challenge this traditional view and propose that the mind is a collection of largely separate but interacting *modules* (Epstein, 1999; Estes, 1991; Gazzaniga, 1985). These modules are information-processing

➤ 7. Based on the modular model of mind, how does consciousness arise?

subsystems or "networks" within the brain that perform tasks related to sensation, perception, memory, problem solving, emotion, motor behavior, and so on. The various modules process information in parallel—that is, simultaneously and largely independently. However, the output from one module can provide input for another, as when information recalled from memory becomes input to the problem-solving and motor modules that allow you to write down answers during a math exam.

According to this perspective our subjective experience of consciousness arises from the integrated activity of the various modules, somewhat akin to listening to a choir sing. We are aware of the integrated, harmonious sound of the choir rather than the voice of each individual member. As we now see, many factors can influence the activity of these modules and, in so doing, alter our state of consciousness.

❭ CIRCADIAN RHYTHMS: OUR DAILY BIOLOGICAL CLOCKS

Like other animals, humans have adapted to a world with a 24-hour day-night cycle. Every 24 hours our body temperature, certain hormonal secretions, and other bodily functions undergo a rhythmic change that affects our mental alertness and readies our passage back and forth between states of wakefulness and sleep (Figure 5.4). These daily biological cycles are called **circadian rhythms** (from the Latin *circa*, "around," and *dia*, "day").

Keeping Time: Brain and Environment

➤ 8. How do the brain and environment regulate circadian rhythms?

As Figure 5.5 shows, most circadian rhythms are regulated by the brain's **suprachiasmatic nuclei (SCN),** located in the hypothalamus (Miller et al., 1996). SCN neurons have a genetically programmed cycle of activity and inactivity, functioning like a "biological clock." They link to the tiny pineal gland, which secretes **melatonin,** a hormone that has a relaxing effect on the body. SCN neu-

FIGURE 5.4 Changes in our core body temperature, levels of melatonin in our blood, and degree of alertness/sleepiness follow a cyclical 24-hour pattern called a *circadian rhythm*. Humans also have longer and shorter biological cycles, such as the 28-day female menstrual cycle and a roughly 90-minute brain activity cycle during sleep.

Adapted from Monk et al., 1996.

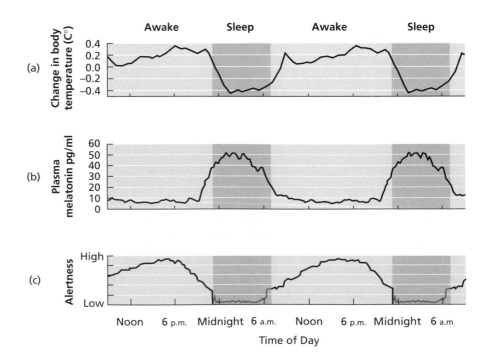

rons become active during daytime and reduce the pineal gland's secretion of melatonin, raising your body temperature and heightening alertness. At night SCN neurons are inactive, allowing melatonin levels to increase and promoting relaxation and sleepiness (Zhdanova et al., 1997).

Our circadian clock is biological, but environmental factors such as the day-night cycle help keep SCN neurons on a 24-hour schedule (Lewy et al., 1998; Wever, 1979). Your eyes have neural connections to the SCN. After a night's sleep, the light of day increases SCN activity and helps reset your 24-hour biological clock. What would happen if you lived in the dark, or in a laboratory or underground cave without clocks, and could not tell whether it was day or night outside? Most people drift into a longer "natural" cycle of about 24.2 to 24.8 hours, called a *free-running circadian rhythm* (Hillman et al., 1994; Shanahan et al., 1999; Wever, 1989). Amazingly, SCN neurons exhibit this longer cycle of firing even when they are surgically removed from the brain and kept alive in a dish containing nutrients (Gillette, 1986).

Because their free-running circadian rhythm is desynchronized (out of sync) with the 24-hour day-night cycle, participants in these "isolation studies" tend to go to bed and wake up later each day (Figure 5.6). They do not realize it, but within a few weeks they may be going to bed at noon and awakening at midnight. Blind children and adults whose eyes are completely insensitive to light also may experience free-running circadian rhythms (Sack & Lewy, 1997). When they try to force their sleep-wake cycle into the 24-hour world by going to bed at fixed times, blind people often experience insomnia, other sleep problems, and daytime fatigue.

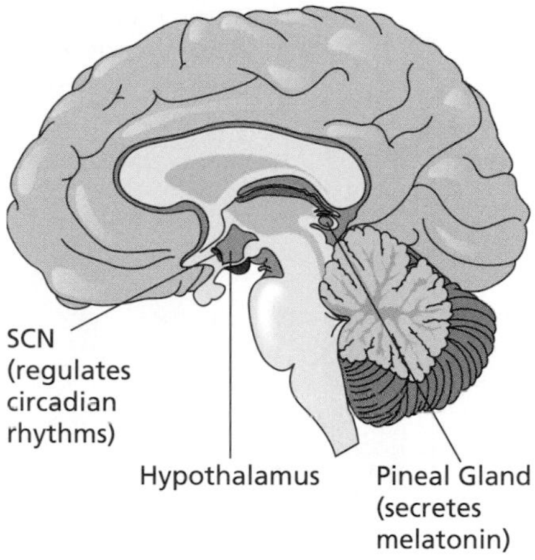

Early Birds And Night Owls

Circadian rhythms influence our tendency to be a "morning person" or a "night person." Compared to night people, morning people go to bed and rise earlier,

FIGURE 5.5 The suprachiasmatic nuclei (SCN) are the brain's master circadian clock. Neurons in the SCN have a genetically programmed cycle of activity and inactivity, but daylight and darkness help regulate this cycle. The optic nerve links our eyes to the SCN, and SCN activity affects the pineal gland's secretion of melatonin. In turn, melatonin influences other brain systems governing alertness and sleepiness.

➤ 9. What are free-running circadian rhythms?

(a)

(b)

FIGURE 5.6 (a) On May 23, 1989, an elated Stefania Follini emerged from the New Mexico cave that she called home for 4 months. (b) Follini was isolated from daylight and all time cues. A computer provided her only link to the outside world. Her "daily" wake-sleep pattern extended to 25 hours, and eventually to over 40 hours. When she emerged she thought only 2 months had passed (Toufexis, 1989).

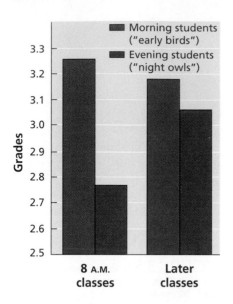

FIGURE 5.7 In a study of 454 University of Kansas students, "night owls" struggled in their 8 A.M. classes, as compared with "early birds." In later classes the two groups performed more similarly. Stated differently, early birds did slightly better in their earliest class than in later classes, whereas night owls did better in their later rather than earliest classes. Data from Guthrie et al., 1995.

➤ 10. Explain how SAD, jet lag, and night shiftwork involve circadian disruptions.

and their body temperature, blood pressure, and alertness peak earlier in the day. Studies around the globe indicate that "morningness" is more common among older adults, whereas more night people are found among 18- to 30-year-olds (Ishikara et al., 1992).

In college, morning people are more likely to take very early classes than are night persons and, as Figure 5.7 shows, they perform better than night people in early morning (8 A.M.) classes. Experiments also find that early birds tend to perform best on some mental tasks in the morning, whereas night owls perform best in the late afternoon or evening (Gordon, 1997; Natale & Lorenzetti, 1997).

Environmental Disruptions of Circadian Rhythms

Gradual and sudden environmental changes can disrupt our circadian rhythms. **Seasonal affective disorder (SAD)** is a cyclic tendency to become psychologically depressed during certain months of the year. Symptoms typically begin in fall or winter, which usher in shorter periods of daylight, and then lift in spring (Rosenthal & Wehr, 1987). Many experts believe that the circadian rhythms of SAD sufferers may be particularly sensitive to light, so as sunrises occur later in winter, the daily "onset" time of their circadian clocks may be pushed back to an unusual degree (Avery et al., 1997; Teicher et al., 1997). In late fall and winter, when many people must arise for work and school in darkness, SAD sufferers are still in "sleepiness" mode long after the morning alarm clock sounds (Figure 5.8).

Jet lag is a sudden circadian disruption caused by flying across several time zones in one day. Flying east, you "lose" hours from the day; flying west, the travel day becomes longer than 24 hours. Jet lag often causes insomnia, decreased alertness, and poorer performance until the body readjusts. It is a significant concern for businesspeople, athletes, airline crews, and others who frequently travel across many time zones (Criglington, 1998). The body naturally adjusts about one hour or less per day to time zone changes. Typically, people adjust faster when flying west, presumably because lengthening the travel day is more compatible with our natural free-running circadian cycle (Kimble, 1992).

The most problematic circadian disruption for society is caused by *night shiftwork*. In the United States alone, about 9 million full-time workers perform night duty (U.S. Department of Labor, 1998). Adjusting to an inverted night-day world can be difficult. Night shiftworkers often drive home in morning daylight, making it harder to reset their biological clocks. On days off they often fall back into a day-night schedule to spend daytime with family, which disrupts their hard-earned circadian adjustments.

Our biological clocks promote sleepiness in the early morning hours (Akerstedt, 1988). Combined with fatigue from poor daytime sleep, this can be a recipe for disaster. Job performance errors, fatal traffic accidents, and engineering and industrial disasters peak between midnight and 6:00 A.M. (Mitler et al., 1988; Monk et al., 1996). Major nuclear accidents at Chernobyl, Three Mile Island, and several other plants occurred between 1 A.M. and 5 A.M., and in some cases night operators at nuclear power plants have been found asleep at the controls. On-the-job sleepiness is a major concern among nighttime long-distance truck and bus drivers, locomotive engineers, airline crews, and medical doctors and nurses (Quera-Salva et al., 1997).

Some people adjust to night work, but others never do. They become fatigued, stressed, and more accident prone on and off the job. You can see in Figure 5.9 that, overall, nightworkers who try to go to bed during the middle of the day get frightfully little sleep.

➤ 11. How is exposure to light used to treat circadian disruptions?

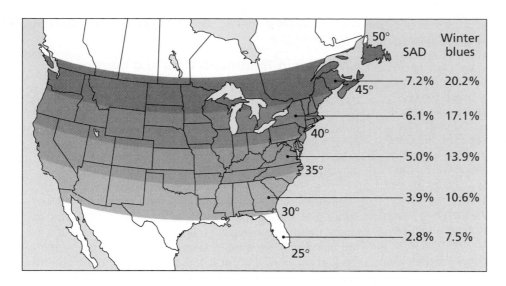

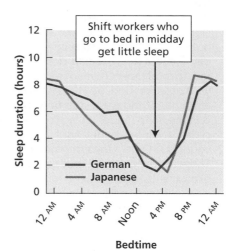

FIGURE 5.8 The latitude puzzle. In North America, the prevalence of winter SAD and milder depression ("winter blues") increases at more northerly latitudes, where the hours of daylight diminish more severely in late fall and winter. SAD and "winter blues" rates of 9.2% and 19.1 %, respectively, have been found in Fairbanks, Alaska (64° latitude). Yet European studies report lower winter SAD rates and a weaker SAD–latitude relation. In fact, most studies in Sweden, Norway, Finland, and Iceland (roughly 55° to 70° latitude) report winter SAD rates similar to those in the southern United States (Mersch et al., 1999). At present, the reason for this discrepancy is debated.

FIGURE 5.9 When night workers try to go to bed in midday, they get little sleep. These data are based on 2,322 German shiftworkers (red line) and 3,240 Japanese shiftworkers (brown line) who recorded their bedtimes and length of sleep.

(From Monk et al., 1996.)

APPLICATIONS OF PSYCHOLOGICAL SCIENCE

Combating Winter Depression, Jet Lag, and Night Shiftwork Disruptions

Circadian research has provided important insights on the nature of consciousness. It also has led to several treatments for circadian disruptions affecting millions of people.

▶ Controlling Exposure to Light

Treating SAD

Many experts believe that *phototherapy,* which involves properly timed exposure to bright artificial lights, is the best treatment for SAD (Lewy et al., 1998b). Several hours of daily phototherapy can shift circadian rhythms by as much as 2 or 3 hours per day (Shanahan et al., 1999). Timo Partonen (1994) found that, during Finland's short winter days, phototherapy for just one hour a day over two weeks significantly reduced SAD sufferers' depression. In *dawn simulation,* artificial lights gradually intensify to normal light levels over the course of one to two hours in the early morning, which helps to reset the circadian clock to an earlier time. The fact that phototherapy effectively treats SAD is the strongest evidence that SAD is triggered by winter's lack of sunlight, rather than its colder temperatures (Figure 5.10).

FIGURE 5.10 For many people, the depression accompanying seasonal affective disorder can be reduced by daily exposure to bright fluorescent lights.

—*Continued*

Reducing Jet Lag

When you fly east across time zones, your body's internal clock "falls behind" the time at your destination. Exposure to outdoor light *in the morning*—and avoiding light late in the day—moves the circadian clock forward and helps it "catch up" to local time. (Think of morning light as "jump starting" your circadian clock at a time when you would be asleep back at home.) Flying west, your body clock moves "ahead" of local time, so to reduce jet lag you want to delay your circadian cycles. Avoiding bright light in the morning and exposing yourself to light *in the afternoon or early evening* will do this. These are general rules, but the specific timing and length of exposure to light depend on the number of time zones crossed (Houpt et al., 1996). For jet travelers, spending time outside (even on cloudy days) is the easiest way to get the needed exposure to light. However, several hotels now offer rooms equipped with phototherapy systems to speed up their guests' recovery from jet lag.

Adjusting to Nightwork

Many night employees work indoors, where the artificial light is too weak to shift their circadian rhythms toward a night-day schedule. Circadian adjustment can be increased by having very bright indoor lighting at the workplace, keeping bedrooms dark and quiet to foster daytime sleep, and maintaining a schedule of daytime sleep even during days off (Boulos, 1998).

Phototherapy in the 21st Century

Amazingly, Scott Campbell and Patricia Murphy (1998) of Cornell University have shifted people's circadian rhythms by exposing them to bright artificial light from a special optic pad—secured to the back of their knee! This light did not reach participants' eyes, nor did it heat their skin. Presumably, the intense light reached blood vessels beneath the skin. Some researchers speculate that chemicals in human blood are sensitive to light and may influence the timing of circadian rhythms (Oren & Terman, 1998).

If other experiments replicate these findings they could have enormous application. The optic pad system could deliver light to the skin of SAD patients or jet-lagged travelers while they sleep at night in their darkened bedroom. This system also could help treat the circadian disruptions of blind people, resulting in better sleep and less daytime fatigue.

▶ Melatonin Treatment: Uses and Cautions

Melatonin levels in the brain can be manipulated directly by oral doses. Depending on when it is taken, oral melatonin can shift some circadian cycles forward or backward by as much as 30 to 60 minutes per day of use (Zhdanova et al., 1997). Melatonin treatment has been used with some success to alleviate SAD, decrease jet lag, and help employees adapt to night shiftwork (Arendt et al., 1997).

Melatonin is a prescription drug in some countries and is not made available to the public in others. But in the United States it is a nonprescription "dietary supplement." Tablet doses are often 3 milligrams, producing melatonin levels in the blood that are over 10 times the normal concentration (Sack et al., 1997). In contrast, doses of 0.1 to 0.5 milligrams used in research produce blood concentrations more typical of normal levels and are sufficient to produce circadian shifts.

In research, melatonin use is supervised. Taking melatonin at the wrong time can backfire and make circadian adjustments more difficult. Daytime use may decrease alertness. Experts are also concerned that millions of people are using melatonin tablets as a nightly sleeping aid, even though possible side effects of long-term use have not been adequately studied (Sack et al., 1998; Zhdanova et al., 1997).

▶ Regulating Activity Schedules

Some animal and human studies suggest that properly timed physical exercise can help shift the circadian clock (Eastman et al., 1995; Sinclair & Mistlberger, 1997). To reduce jet lag, you can also begin resynchronizing your biological clock to the new time zone in advance. To do so, adjust your sleep and eating schedules one hour per day, starting several days before you leave. Schedule management also applies to night shiftwork. For workers on rotating shifts, circadian disruptions can be reduced significantly by a *forward rotating shift schedule*—moving from day to evening to night shifts—rather than a schedule that rotates backward from day to night to evening shifts (Czeisler et al., 1982; Knauth, 1996). Can you hypothesize why this is the case? For the answer, see the margin note on page 192.

❯ SLEEP AND DREAMING

Our circadian rhythms do not regulate sleep directly. Rather, by decreasing nighttime alertness they promote a readiness for sleep and help determine the optimal time period when we can sleep most soundly (Sack et al., 1998). We spend approximately one third of our lives asleep and it is easy to understand why this state of altered consciousness has mystified humans for ages. Each night we seem to relinquish conscious control of our thoughts and actions, enter a world of dreams, toss about and possibly mutter or talk, but remember so little of it upon awakening. Yet sleep is a behavior that, like others, can be studied scientifically at biological, psychological, and environmental levels.

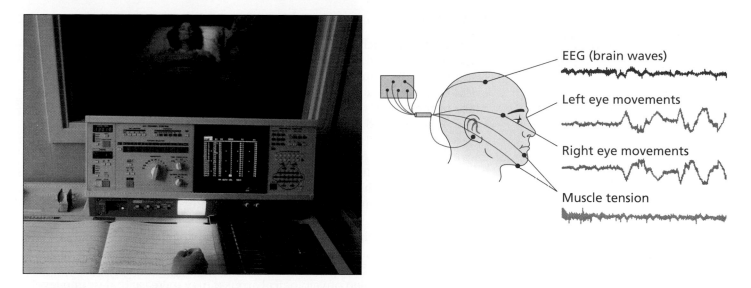

FIGURE 5.11 In a modern sleep laboratory, people sleep while their physiological responses are monitored. Electrodes attached to the scalp area record the person's EEG brain-wave patterns. Electrodes attached beside the eyes record eye movements during sleep. Muscle tension is recorded, and a neutral electrode is attached to the ear.

Stages of Sleep

Just as waking consciousness involves different states of alertness and awareness, so does sleep. Approximately every 90 minutes while asleep, we cycle through different stages in which our brain activity and other physiological responses change in a generally predictable way (Kleitman, 1963; Dement, 1974).

As Figure 5.11 shows, sleep research is often carried out in specially equipped laboratories where sleepers' physiological responses are recorded. EEG recordings of your brain's electrical activity would show a pattern of **beta waves** when you are awake and alert. Beta waves have a high frequency (of about 15 to 30 cycles per second, or *cps*) but a low "amplitude" or height (Figure 5.12). As you close your eyes, feeling relaxed and drowsy, your brain waves slow down and **alpha waves** occur at about 8 to 12 cps.

Stage 1 Through Stage 4

As sleep begins your brain-wave pattern becomes more irregular, and slower *theta waves* (3.5 to 7.5 cps) increase. You are now in *stage 1*, a form of light sleep from which you can easily be awakened. You'll probably spend just a few minutes in stage 1, during which time some people experience dreams, vivid images, and sudden body jerks. As sleep becomes deeper, *sleep spindles*—periodic 1- to 2-second bursts of rapid brain-wave activity (12 to 15 cps)—begin to appear. Sleep spindles indicate that you are now in *stage 2* (Figure 5.12). Your muscles are more relaxed, breathing and heart rate are slower, dreams may occur, and you are harder to awaken.

Sleep deepens as you move into *stage 3*, marked by the regular appearance of very slow (0.5 to 2 cps) and large **delta waves**. As time passes, they occur more often, and when delta waves *dominate* the EEG pattern this indicates that you have reached *stage 4*. Together, stage 3 and stage 4 are often referred to as **slow-wave sleep.** Your body is relaxed, activity in various parts of your brain has decreased, you are hard to awaken, and you may have dreams. After 20 to 30 minutes of stage 4 sleep, your EEG pattern changes as you go "back through" stages 3 and 2, spending a little time in each. Overall, within 60 to 90 minutes of going to sleep, you have completed a cycle of stages 1-2-3-4-3-2. At this point, a remarkably different sleep stage ensues.

➤ 12. What brain-wave patterns distinguish the first four stages of sleep?

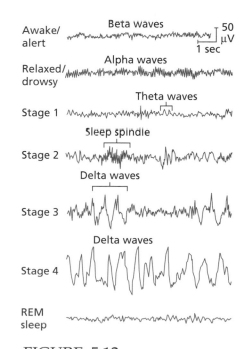

FIGURE 5.12 Changing patterns of brain-wave activity help define the various stages of sleep. Note that brain waves become slower and larger as sleep deepens, and that the general pattern of REM sleep is similar to that of stage 1.

(Adapted from Dement, 1978; Hauri, 1982.)

➤ 13. Describe some major characteristics of REM sleep.

Rotating shiftwork   A forward rotating schedule takes advantage of the body's free-running circadian rhythms. When work shifts change, it is easier to extend the "waking day" than to compress it.

REM Sleep

In 1953, sleep researchers Eugene Aserinsky and Nathaniel Kleitman of the University of Chicago struck scientific gold: They identified a sleep stage unlike the rest. Every half minute or so, bursts of muscular activity caused the sleepers' eyeballs to vigorously move back and forth beneath their closed eyelids. Because of these *rapid eye movements* (REMs), this stage was called **REM sleep.** When Aserinsky and Kleitman awakened sleepers from REM periods, they discovered that a dream was almost always reported. Even people who swore they "never had dreams" recalled them when awakened during REM. At last, science had a window through which to examine dreaming more closely. Wait for a REM period, awaken the sleeper, and catch a dream.

REM sleep often is portrayed in scientific and popular writings as *the* stage in which we dream. But this is not correct. We also dream during non-REM (NREM) stages, albeit less often. There is one striking difference between REM and NREM dreams, however: In almost all instances, our REM dreams are longer (Antrobus, 1983; Stickgold et al., 1994).

During REM sleep physiological arousal may increase to daytime levels. Heart rate quickens, breathing becomes more rapid and irregular, and brainwave activity resembles that of active wakefulness. Men have penile erections and women experience vaginal lubrication. Because most dreams do not have sexual content, this REM-induced genital arousal is *not* a response to sexual imagery.

The brain also sends signals making it more difficult for voluntary muscles to contract. As a result, muscles in the arms, legs, and torso lose tone and become relaxed. These muscles may twitch, but in effect you are "paralyzed" and unable to move. This state is called *REM sleep paralysis*, and because of it REM sleep is sometimes called *paradoxical sleep:* Your body is highly aroused, yet it looks like you are sleeping peacefully because there is so little movement.

Each cycle through the sleep stages takes about 90 minutes. Figure 5.13 shows that as the hours pass, stage 4 and stage 3 drop out and REM periods become longer.

FIGURE 5.13 This graph shows a record of a night's sleep. The REM stages are shown in blue. People typically average four to five REM periods during the night, and these tend to become longer as the night wears on.

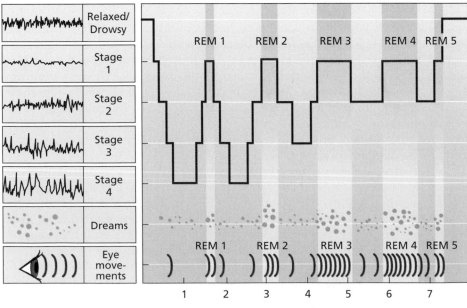

Getting a Night's Sleep: Brain and Environment

The brain steers our nightly passage into and through sleep, but it does not contain a single "sleep center." Different aspects of the sleep cycle, such as falling asleep, REM sleep, and slow-wave sleep, are controlled by different brain mechanisms. Moreover, falling asleep is not just a matter of "turning off" the brain systems that regulate wakefulness. There are separate systems that "turn on" and actively promote sleep.

Areas at the base of the forebrain (called the *basal forebrain*) and within the brain stem are particularly important in regulating our falling asleep (McGinty & Sterman, 1968; Szymusiak, 1995). A different brain stem area—where the reticular formation passes through the pons—plays a key role in initiating REM sleep (Hobson et al., 1998). This region contains "REM-sleep On" neurons that periodically activate other brain systems, each of which controls a different aspect of REM sleep, such as the eye movements, muscular paralysis, and genital arousal.

Sleep is biologically regulated, but the environment plays a role as well. The change of seasons affects sleep; in fall and winter, most people sleep about 15 to 60 minutes longer per night (Campbell, 1993). Shiftwork, jet lag, stress at work and school, and nighttime noise can decrease sleep quality (Bronzaft et al., 1998). In fact, although many people report sleeping well in noisy environments, experiments reveal that noise affects us even while we sleep through it. Noise may increase our arousal and heart rate, decrease time in deep slow-wave sleep, and increase our time in less restful light sleep (Pollak, 1991).

How Much Do We Sleep?

The question seems simple enough, as does the answer for many of us: not enough! In reality, the issue is complex. First, Figure 5.14 reveals that there are substantial differences in how much people sleep at various ages. Newborn infants average 16 hours of sleep a day and almost half of their sleep time is in REM. But as we age, three important changes occur:

- We sleep less. On average, 19- to 30-year-olds average slightly less than 8 hours of sleep per day, and elderly adults average just under 6 hours.

➤ 14. What brain areas help regulate sleep onset and REM sleep?

➤ 15. How do sleep patterns change as we age?

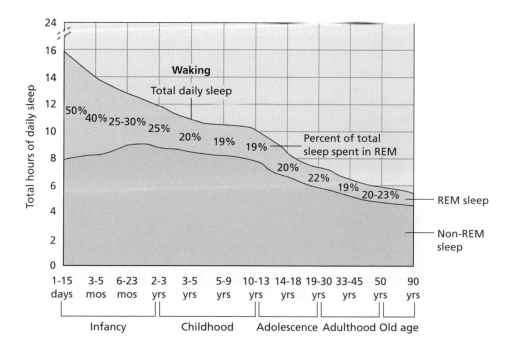

FIGURE 5.14 The percentage of sleep time in REM and NREM sleep changes with age. Average daily sleep time decreases over the lifespan, and most of the decrease in NREM sleep is due to decreasing delta sleep (stages 3 and 4). REM sleep time decreases throughout childhood and then is relatively stable through adulthood.
Data from Hartmann, 1977.

- REM sleep decreases dramatically during infancy and early childhood, but remains relatively stable thereafter.
- Time spent in stages 3 and 4 declines. By late adulthood we get relatively little slow-wave sleep.

Second, there are wide individual differences within each age range. Based on various surveys, including a study of over 1 million Americans and another of 30,000 people in eleven countries, Wilse Webb (1992) of the University of Florida estimates that two thirds of young adults sleep between 6.5 to 8.5 hours a night. About 1 percent sleep more than 10 hours per night and 1 percent less than 5.

Short- and Long-Sleepers

Sleep surveys describe how much sleep people believe they "get," not how much they "need." Still, it appears that the old adage that "everyone needs 8 hours of sleep a night" is not true. Some of us need more sleep, others less. British Prime Ministers Winston Churchill and Margaret Thatcher, U.S. President John F. Kennedy, and Napoleon Bonaparte all reportedly slept between 3 to 5.5 hours a night (Sharkey, 1993). Some nighttime short-sleepers take a daytime nap, as Kennedy often did.

Laboratory studies confirm that a few people function well on little sleep (Stuss & Broughton, 1978). Researchers in London examined a healthy, energetic 70-year-old woman who claimed to sleep less than 1 hour a night (Meddis et al., 1973). In 5 consecutive nights at the sleep lab she averaged 67 minutes of sleep a night and showed no ill effects. During another observation period she stayed awake for 56 hours and recovered by sleeping only 99 minutes the next night! Beyond how much they sleep, short- and long-sleepers do not differ consistently in other personal characteristics.

From Genes to Lifestyles

➤ 16. What evidence indicates that genetic factors partly account for differences in people's sleep behaviors?

What accounts for differences in how much we sleep? Using selective breeding, researchers have developed some genetic strains of mice that are long- versus short-sleepers, other strains that spend more or less time in REM, and still others that spend more or less time in slow-wave sleep (Toth & Williams, 1999).

In humans, surveys of nearly 7,000 pairs of twins in Finland and of almost 4,000 Australian twin pairs reveal that identical twins have more similar sleep length, bedtimes, and sleep patterns than do fraternal twins (Heath, 1990; Partinen et al., 1983). Sleep laboratory EEG recordings of identical and fraternal twins also find more similar sleep behavior among identical twins (Webb & Campbell, 1983).

These twin studies indicate that differences between people in sleep length and sleep patterns are also affected by nongenetic factors (Heath, 1990; Partinen et al., 1983). Working day versus night jobs, having high-pressure versus low-key lifestyles, and sleeping in noisy versus quiet environments are among many factors contributing to the variability in people's sleep. In some countries, particularly those in the tropical climates of Central and South America and the Mediterranean, many people enjoy the traditional ritual of a one- to two-hour midday nap (often taken after lunch), and reduce the length of nighttime sleep (Kribbs, 1993).

Sleep Deprivation

➤ 17. How do different types of sleep deprivation affect mood and performance?

Sleep deprivation is a way of life for many college students, and they are not alone. Almost half of Americans sacrifice some sleep to accomplish more work (National Sleep Foundation, 2000). Millions more lose sleep due to disorders.

Psychologists study sleep deprivation for its practical significance and to gain insights into why we need to sleep. June Pilcher and Allen Huffcutt (1996) of Bradley University meta-analyzed 19 sleep deprivation studies in which participants underwent either *short-term total sleep deprivation* (up to 45 hours without sleep), *long-term total sleep deprivation* (more than 45 hours without sleep), or *partial deprivation* (being allowed to sleep no more than 5 hours per night for 1 or more consecutive nights). Participants' self-reported mood (e.g., ability to concentrate, irritability, disorientation) and responses on mental tasks (e.g., logical reasoning, word memory) and physical tasks (e.g., manual dexterity, treadmill walking) were measured.

What would you predict? Would all types of deprivation affect behavior, and which behaviors would be affected the most? Combining across the different types of deprivation and behavior, the results were remarkable: The "average" sleep-deprived person functioned only as well as someone in the bottom 9 percent of nondeprived participants. All three types of sleep deprivation had a large, negative impact on functioning. Mood suffered most, followed by cognitive and then physical performance, although *all three* behaviors showed significant impairments from sleep loss.

What about students who pull all-nighters or drastically cut back their sleep, and claim they still perform as well as ever? Pilcher & Walters (1997) found that college students deprived of one night's sleep performed more poorly on a critical-thinking task than students allowed to sleep. Yet sleep-deprived students incorrectly perceived that they performed better and felt that they concentrated and tried harder. The authors concluded that students underestimate the negative effects of sleep loss on performance.

Most total sleep deprivation studies with humans last less than 5 days, but 17-year-old Randy Gardner set a world record (since broken) of staying awake for 11 days as his project for a 1964 high school science fair in San Diego. Grateful sleep researchers received permission to study him (Gulevisch et al., 1966). At times during the first few days Randy became irritable, forgetful, nauseous, and intensely tired. By day 5 he had periods of disorientation, distorted thinking, and mild hallucinations. In the last four days he developed finger tremors and slurred speech. Still, in his final day without sleep he beat sleep researcher William Dement 100 consecutive times at a pinball-type game.

When Randy finally went to bed, he slept almost 15 hours the first night and returned to his normal amount of sleep within a week. In general, it takes several nights to recover from extended total sleep deprivation, and we do not make up all the sleep time that we have lost.

Why Do We Sleep?

Given that we spend almost a third of our lives sleeping, it must serve an important purpose. According to the **restoration model,** sleep recharges our run-down bodies and allows us to recover from physical and mental fatigue (Hess, 1965). Sleep deprivation and night shiftwork studies strongly support this view: We need sleep to function at our emotional, mental and physical best. In fact, we may need sleep to live. Laboratory rats deprived of all sleep usually die within a few weeks, and scientists are trying to pinpoint the physiological causes (Constantine et al., 1996; Cirelli et al., 1999).

If the restoration model is correct, activities that increase daily wear on the body should increase sleep. Evidence is mildly supportive. A study of 18- to 26-year-old ultramarathon runners found that they slept much longer and spent a greater percentage of time in slow-wave sleep on the two nights following their 57-mile run (Shapiro et al., 1981). For the rest of us mere mortals, a meta-analysis of 38 studies found that we tend to sleep longer by only about 10 minutes on days we have exercised (Youngstedt et al., 1997).

The biggest challenge is determining exactly what it is that "gets restored" in our bodies while we sleep. Are vital chemicals depleted during the day and replenished at night? Does waking activity produce toxins that are purged during

➤ 18. Explain the restoration and evolutionary theories of sleep.

sleep? If so, how do these chemical changes regulate sleep? We do not have precise answers, but some researchers believe that a cellular waste product called *adenosine* may play a role (Mendelson, 2000; Rail, 1980). Like a car's exhaust emissions, adenosine is produced as cells consume fuel. As adenosine accumulates, it influences brain systems that decrease alertness and promote sleep, signaling the body to slow down because too much cellular fuel has been burned. Interestingly, caffeine has a molecular structure similar to adenosine's. It fits into adenosine receptor sites but doesn't stimulate them. This blocks the action of adenosine, prevents it from signaling the brain to "slow down," and increases alertness.

Evolutionary/circadian sleep models emphasize that sleep's main purpose is to increase a species' chances of survival in relation to its environmental demands (Webb, 1974). Our prehistoric ancestors had little to gain and much to lose by being active at night. Hunting, food gathering, and traveling were accomplished more easily and safely during daylight. Leaving the protection of one's shelter at night would have served little purpose other than to become dinner for nighttime predators.

In the course of evolution each species developed a circadian sleep-wake pattern that was adaptive in terms of whether it was predator or prey, its food requirements, and its methods of defense from attack. For small prey animals such as mice and squirrels, who reside in burrows or trees safely away from predators, spending a lot of time asleep is adaptive. For large prey animals such as horses, deer, and zebras, who sleep in relatively exposed environments and whose safety from predators depends on running away, spending a lot of time asleep would be hazardous. Sleep also may have evolved as a mechanism for conserving energy (Berger & Phillips, 1995; Horne, 1977). Our body's overall metabolic rate during sleep is about 10 to 25 percent slower than during waking rest (McGinty, 1993). The restoration and evolutionary theories highlight complementary functions of sleep, and both contribute to a two-factor model of why we sleep (Borbely, 1984; Webb, 1994).

Do specific sleep stages have special functions? To answer this question, imagine volunteering for a sleep deprivation study in which we awaken you only when you enter REM sleep; you can sleep through the other sleep stages. In this situation, two things will happen (beyond any unpleasant looks you may give us). First, on successive nights, we will have to awaken you more often, because your brain will be fighting back to get REM sleep (Figure 5.15a). Second, when the study ends, for the first few nights you probably will experience a *REM-rebound effect,* a tendency to increase the amount of REM sleep after being deprived of it (Figure 5.15b). REM-rebound occurs in rats as well as humans (Rechtschaffen et al., 1999).

This suggests that the body needs REM sleep (similar effects are found for slow-wave sleep). But for what purpose? Several theories propose that REM sleep is vital for mental functioning (Crick & Mitchison 1983; Winson, 1990). For example, the high levels of brain activity produced in REM sleep may strengthen the neural circuits involved in remembering important information that we learned during the day, a process called *memory consolidation* (Winson, 1990). Unfortunately, studies examining whether REM-sleep deprivation is *more* disruptive to cognitive functioning than NREM-sleep deprivation yield mixed findings. Further, many antidepressant drugs greatly suppress REM sleep, yet patients taking these drugs for long periods of time do not show cognitive impairments. At present, the unique functions of REM and other sleep stages are still debated.

Sleep Disorders

The mechanisms involved in sleep are complex and can go wrong in a variety of ways. A staggering one half to two thirds of American adults feel that they have some type of sleep problem (National Sleep Foundation, 2000).

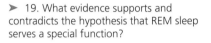

➤ 19. What evidence supports and contradicts the hypothesis that REM sleep serves a special function?

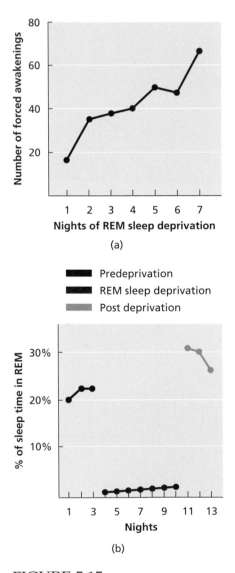

FIGURE 5.15 (a) In REM-sleep deprivation studies, participants start to go into REM periods more times with each passing night, as the brain tries to get REM sleep. (b) After REM deprivation ends, the sleeper spends more time than usual in REM sleep for a few nights. This is the REM-rebound effect. Data from Agnew & Webb, 1967.

Insomnia

True or False: Someone who falls asleep easily can still have insomnia? The statement is true because **insomnia** refers to chronic difficulty in falling asleep, staying asleep, or experiencing restful sleep. Trouble falling asleep is most common among young adults, and difficulty staying asleep is most common among older adults. If you occasionally have trouble getting a good night's sleep, don't worry: almost everyone does. True insomniacs' sleep troubles are frequent and persistent.

➤ 20. What is insomnia and how is it treated?

Insomnia is the most common sleep disorder, experienced by approximately 10 to 40 percent of the population of various countries. Many insomniacs overestimate how much sleep they lose and how long it takes them to fall asleep: 20 minutes may seem like an hour. Certain people, called *pseudoinsomniacs*, complain of insomnia but sleep normally when examined in the laboratory (Schneider, 1985). Despite a sound night of sleep, some pseudoinsomniacs awaken in the morning and claim that their insomnia was so bad that they didn't get any sleep at all (McCall & Edinger, 1992)!

Insomnia has biological, psychological, and environmental causes. Some people are genetically predisposed toward insomnia, and medical conditions, mental disorders such as anxiety and depression, and many drugs can disrupt sleep (Lydic & Biebuyck, 1989). So can general worrying, stress at home and work, poor lifestyle habits, and circadian disruptions such as jet lag and night shiftwork.

Psychologists have pioneered many nondrug treatments to reduce insomnia and improve sleep quality (Bootzin, 1979; Haynes et al., 1975; Lacks, 1983). One treatment, called *stimulus control*, is based on learning principles. It involves conditioning your body to associate the stimuli in your sleep environment (such as your bed) with sleep, rather than with waking activities and sleeplessness. For example, if you are having sleep difficulties, do not study, do homework, watch TV, or snack in your bedroom. Use your bed only for sleeping. If you cannot fall asleep within 10 minutes, get up and leave the bedroom for a period of time. Do something relaxing until you feel sleepy, then return to bed. Table 5.1 contains additional guidelines from sleep experts for reducing insomnia and achieving better sleep (Bootzin & Rider, 1997; Hryshko et al., 2000).

TABLE 5.1	HOW TO IMPROVE THE QUALITY OF YOUR SLEEP

- Maintain a regular sleep-wake pattern to establish a stable circadian rhythm.
- Get the amount of sleep you need during the week and avoid sleeping in on weekends, as doing so will disrupt your sleep rhythm. Even if you sleep poorly or not at all on one night, try to maintain your regular schedule the next.
- If you have trouble falling asleep at night, then avoid napping if possible. Evening naps should be especially avoided because they will make you less sleepy when you go to bed.
- Do not eat a lot before going to sleep. If you must eat something, have a light snack, and preferably one that contains L-tryptophan. L-tryptophan is an amino acid that helps the brain produce serotonin, and it can have a sedating effect. It is found in milk and other dairy foods.
- Avoid stimulants. This includes not just tobacco products and coffee, but also soft drinks and chocolate (sorry), both of which contain caffeine. It can take the body 4–5 hours to reduce the amount of caffeine in the bloodstream by 50%.
- Avoid alcohol and sleeping pills. As a depressant, alcohol may make it easier to go to sleep, but it disrupts the sleep cycle and interferes with REM sleep. Sleeping pills also impair REM sleep and constant use can lead to dependence and insomnia.
- Try to go to bed in a relaxed state. Muscular relaxation techniques and meditation can reduce tension, remove worrisome thoughts, and help induce sleep.
- Avoid physical exercise before bedtime because it is too stimulating. If you are unable to fall asleep, do not use exercise to try and wear yourself out.
- If you are having sleep difficulties, then avoid performing nonsleep activities in your bedroom. This will condition your body to associate bedroom stimuli with sleep.

Sleep experts recommend a variety of procedures to reduce insomnia and improve the general quality of sleep (Bootzin & Rider, 1997; Hauri, 1997; Hryshko et al., 2000; Lundh, 1998).

➤ 21. Describe the major symptoms of narcolepsy and REM-BD.

Narcolepsy

Some people suffer not from an inability to sleep, but from an inability to stay awake. **Narcolepsy** involves extreme daytime sleepiness and sudden, uncontrollable sleep attacks that may last from less than a minute to an hour. No matter how much narcoleptics rest at night, sleep attacks may occur at any time. About 1 out of every 1,000 people is narcoleptic (Mignot, 1998).

When a sleep attacks occurs, narcoleptics may go right into a REM stage, and some have intense, dreamlike visual images and sounds (Parkes et al., 1995). Narcoleptics also may experience attacks of *cataplexy,* a sudden loss of muscle tone often triggered by laughter, excitement, and other strong emotions. In severe cases, the knees buckle and the person collapses, conscious but unable to move for anywhere from a few seconds to a few minutes. Cataplexy is an abnormal version of the normal muscular paralysis that takes place during nighttime REM sleep, and many experts view narcolepsy as a disorder in which REM sleep intrudes into waking consciousness.

Narcolepsy can be devastating. Narcoleptics may be discriminated against when seeking jobs and mistakenly viewed as lazy at work (Douglas, 1998). They report a lowered quality of life and are more prone to accidents. In a large study, 75 percent of narcoleptics reported falling asleep while driving, in contrast to 12 percent of the non-narcoleptic comparison group (Cohen et al., 1992).

What causes narcolepsy? In humans, if one identical twin is narcoleptic, the other twin has a 30 percent chance of developing it (Mignot, 1998). Narcolepsy also can be selectively bred in dogs (Figure 5.16). Thus experts believe that a genetic predisposition combines with still unknown environmental factors to cause narcolepsy (Stanford Center for Narcolepsy, 2000). At present there is no cure, but stimulant drugs often reduce daytime sleepiness, and antidepressant drugs (which suppress REM sleep) can decrease attacks of cataplexy (Fry, 1998). Daytime naps help some narcoleptics feel more alert, but their positive effects last for only a few hours.

REM-Sleep Behavior Disorder

Kaku Kimura and his colleagues in Japan (1997) report the case of a 72-year-old woman who, during a night's observation in a sleep laboratory, repeatedly talked, sang, and moved her hands and legs during REM sleep. One singing episode lasted 3 minutes. She was experiencing **REM-sleep behavior disorder (RBD),** in which the loss of muscle tone that causes normal REM sleep paralysis is absent (Olson et al., 2000). If awakened, RBD patients often report dream content that matches their behavior, as if they were acting out their dreams (Dyken et al., 1995). Unfortunately, the consequences of RBD can be severe:

> . . . a 67-year-old man . . . was awakened one night by his wife's yelling as he was choking her. He was dreaming of breaking the neck of a deer he had just knocked down. This patient had tied himself to his bed with a rope at night for 6 years as a protective measure, owing to repeated episodes of jumping from the bed and colliding with furniture and walls. (Schenck et al., 1989, p. 1169)

RBD sleepers may kick violently, throw punches, or get out of bed and move about wildly, leaving the bedroom in shambles. Many RBD patients seen in sleep clinics have injured themselves while sleeping, and almost half have injured their sleeping partners (Schenck, 1993). Some researchers propose that brain abnormalities may prevent signals that normally inhibit movement during REM from being sent, but at present the causes of RBD are unknown (Olson et al., 2000).

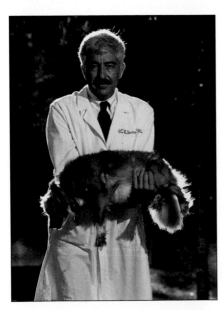

FIGURE 5.16 This dog lapses suddenly from alert wakefulness into a limp sleep while being held by sleep researcher William Dement. Narcolepsy occurs naturally in some dogs, and using selective breeding researchers at Stanford's Sleep Disorders Center have established a colony of narcoleptic canines.

Sleep Apnea

People with **sleep apnea** repeatedly stop and restart breathing during sleep. Stoppages usually last 20 to 40 seconds, but can be a minute or two. In severe cases they occur 400 to 500 times a night. Sleep apnea is most commonly caused by an obstruction in the upper airways, such as from sagging tissue as muscles lose tone during sleep (Guilleminault, 1987). The chest and abdomen keep moving, but no air gets through to the lungs. Finally, reflexes kick in and the person gasps or produces a loud, startling snore, followed by a several-second awakening.

About 1 to 5 percent of the world's population has sleep apnea, and the obstructive type is most common among overweight, middle-aged males (Ip et al., 1998). Surgery may be performed to remove the obstruction blocking the airways, and sleep apnea sometimes is treated by having the sleeper wear a mask that continuously pumps air, keeping the air passages open. Sleep apnea stresses the heart and contributes to hypertension, excessive daytime sleepiness, and increased automobile accident rates (Guilleminault, 1987; Ichimaru & Miyamoto, 1998). The partners of people with sleep apnea, repeatedly awakened by the gasps, loud snores, and jerking body movements, often end up sleeping in another room.

Sleepwalking

Sleepwalking typically occurs during a stage 3 or stage 4 period of slow-wave sleep (Horne, 1992; Kales & Kales, 1975). Sleepwalkers often have blank stares, are unresponsive to other people, but seem vaguely conscious of the environment as they navigate around furniture, go to the bathroom, or find something to eat. Sleepwalkers often return to bed and awaken in the morning with no memory of the event. About 10 to 30 percent of children sleepwalk at least once, but less than 5 percent of adults do. If you did not sleepwalk as a child, the odds are less than 1 percent that you will do so as an adult (Hublin et al., 1997). Sleepwalkers can injure themselves accidentally, such as by falling down stairs or wandering out of their home.

A tendency to sleepwalk may be inherited, and daytime stress, alcohol, and certain illnesses and medications also increase sleepwalking (Berlin & Qayyum, 1986). Various treatments may be used, including psychotherapy, hypnosis, drugs, and routinely awakening children before the time they typically sleepwalk (Frank et al., 1997). But the most common "treatment" simply is to wait for children to outgrow it while creating a safe home environment so that the sleepwalker will not get injured. Contrary to common belief, awakening sleepwalkers is not harmful, although they may be confused for a few minutes.

Nightmares and Night Terrors

Nightmares are frightening dreams and virtually everyone has them. Like all dreams, they occur more often during REM sleep and in the hours before we arise. Physiological arousal during nightmares is similar to levels experienced during pleasant dreams.

Night terrors (also called "sleep terrors") are more intense than nightmares. The sleeper, usually a child, suddenly sits up and seems to awaken, letting out a blood-curdling scream. Terrified and aroused to a near-panic state, the person might thrash about in bed or flee to another room, as if trying to escape from something. Come morning, the person often has no memory of the episode. If brought to full consciousness during an episode—which is hard to do—the person may report images or a vague sense of having being choked, crushed, attacked, or exposed to some other type of danger (Fisher et al., 1974).

Unlike nightmares, night terrors are most common during slow-wave sleep (stages 3 and 4) and involve greatly elevated physiological arousal; heart rate may double or triple. Up to 6 percent of children, but only 1 or 2 percent of adults,

➤ 22. Identify the major differences between nightmares and night terrors.

FIGURE 5.17 The *Wizard of Oz* is one of the most famous movies in history, and almost all of it focuses on the dream sequence of a girl named Dorothy. Her dream includes witches, an army of flying monkeys, and of course, the Scarecrow, Cowardly Lion, and Tin Man—who talk and act like humans. Are most of our dreams this bizarre?

➤ 23. When do we dream the most? Why?

experience night terrors (Ohayon et al., 1999). In most childhood cases, treatment is simply to wait for the night terrors to diminish with age.

The Nature of Dreams

Traditional aboriginal peoples of Australia speak of The Dreaming. They view dreaming as a "parallel reality" connecting them to the spiritual world and a collective unconscious linked to their ancestral past (Dawson, 1993). The Dreaming involves stories of creation and beliefs that are passed on orally to educate each successive generation, and it defines their personal and cultural identities. Dreams also are a central guiding force in other cultures, such as the Senoi of Malaysia, who believe that events in dreaming and waking life influence one another (Greenleaf, 1973).

Although Western societies attach less importance to dreams than do many cultures, dreams remain a source of endless curiosity. Some Westerners view them as symbolic and informative, and dreams have long been the subject of art, literature, theater, and cinema (Figure 5.17). Psychologists study dreaming not only to learn about consciousness, but also because dreaming is a universal mental activity among humans (Foulkes, 1996).

When Do We Dream?

Mental activity occurs throughout the sleep cycle. When Jason Rowley and his colleagues (1998) awakened sleepers merely 45 seconds after sleep onset, participants reported visual images about 25 percent of the time. As this *hypnagogic state* (the transitional state from wakefulness through early stage 2 sleep) continued, mental activity became more dreamlike (Figure 5.18). In general, between 15 to 40 percent of sleepers report dreamlike activity when awakened within six minutes of falling asleep.

Research shows that we dream most when the brain is most active (Antrobus, 1991, 1995). Brain activity is higher during REM sleep than NREM sleep, and we dream more during REM. When awakened from REM and NREM sleep, people report a dream about 80 percent versus 15 to 50 percent of the time, respectively (Dement, 1978; Foulkes, 1962; Rowley et al., 1998). Brain activity also is higher in the final hours of sleep than it is during the earlier hours, thanks to our circadian sleep-wake cycle preparing us to rise for a new day. Thus we dream more in the last few hours of both REM and NREM sleep than during the same stages earlier in the night.

FIGURE 5.18 The mental activity of 11 male and female undergraduates was measured by self-report while awake and 15, 45, 75, 120, and 300 seconds after sleep onset. Students slept at home, were awakened by computer, and the time of awakenings varied across different nights. In total, 477 reports of mental activity were collected. In general, after sleep onset normal "waking-type" thoughts decreased, unusual thoughts and visual hallucinations (images that seemed "real") increased, and mental activity was more "dreamy." Unlike many REM dreams, however, mental activity after sleep onset rarely had a plot (e.g., a "storyline").
Adapted from Rowley et al., 1998.

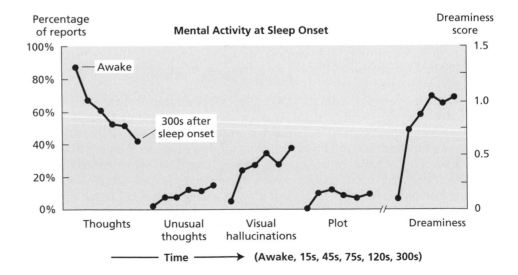

What Do We Dream About?

Much of our knowledge about dream content derives from 35 years of research using a coding system developed by Calvin Hall and Robert Van de Castle (1966). Analyzing 1,000 dream reports (mostly from college students), they found that dreams are not nearly as strange as they are stereotyped to be. Most take place in familiar settings and often involve people we know. Certainly, some dreams are highly bizarre, but they often make a lasting impression that biases our perception of what most dreams are like. As a case in point, have you ever dreamt that you were flying (under your own power, without a plane!)? Between a third and a half of college students say they have. Yet a study of 635 actual dream reports found only one dream that included flying (Snyder, 1970). This suggests that dreams about flying are quite *un*common, but because they are so striking many people can recall having such a dream at least once.

Given the stereotype of "blissful dreaming," it may surprise you that most dreams contain some negative content (Domhoff, 1999). Hall and Van de Castle (1966) found that 80 percent of dream reports involved negative emotions, almost half contained aggressive acts, and a third involved some type of misfortune. They also found that women dreamt almost equally about male and female characters, whereas about two thirds of men's dream characters were male. Although the reason for this gender difference is not clear, a similar pattern has been found across several cultures and among teenagers and preadolescents (Avila-White et al., 1999; Hall, 1984).

Our cultural background, life experiences, and current concerns shape dream content. For example, Palestinian children living in violent regions of the Gaza Strip dream about persecution and aggression more often than do their peers living in nonviolent areas (Punamaeki & Joustie, 1998). Pregnant women have dreams with many pregnancy themes, and in the three weeks following a severe 1989 earthquake in the San Francisco area, local college students reported twice as many nightmares compared with students in Arizona (Van de Castle & Kinder, 1968; Wood et al., 1992). Moreover, 40 percent of their nightmares were about earthquakes, compared with only 5 percent for the Arizona students. What about more typical day-to-day events? Overall, it appears that up to 50 percent of our dreams contain some content reflecting the experiences of our most recent day (Botman & Crovitz, 1992; Harlow & Roll, 1992).

Why Do We Dream?

Speculations about why we dream and whether dreams have special meaning have intrigued humankind for ages. Most scientific dream theories arise from the psychoanalytic, physiological, and cognitive perspectives.

> 24. According to the Freudian and activation-synthesis theories, why do we dream?

Freud's psychoanalytic theory. Sigmund Freud (1900/1953) believed that the main purpose of dreaming is **wish fulfillment,** the gratification of our unconscious desires and needs. These desires include sexual and aggressive urges that are too unacceptable to be consciously acknowledged and fulfilled in real life. Freud distinguished between a dream's *manifest content*—the "surface" story that the dreamer reports—and its *latent content*, which is its disguised psychological meaning. Thus a dream about being with a stranger on a train that goes through a tunnel (manifest content) might represent a hidden desire for sexual intercourse with a "forbidden" partner (latent content). *Dream work* was Freud's term for the process by which the dream's latent content is transformed into the manifest content. This occurs through symbols (e.g., train = penis; tunnel = vagina), and by creating individual characters who combine the features of several people in real life. In this way, unconscious needs can be fulfilled and, because they are disguised within the dream, the sleeper does not become anxious and can sleep peacefully.

Freud sparked great interest in dreams and laid the groundwork for other dream theories. As we saw above, research on dream content supports Freud's insight that dreams can reflect ongoing emotional concerns and conflicts (Epstein, 1999). Yet many contemporary researchers reject the more specific postulates of his theory. They conclude, for example, that there is little evidence that dreams have disguised meaning or that their general purpose is to satisfy forbidden, unconscious needs and conflicts (Domhoff, 1999; Fisher & Greenberg, 1996). Dream analysis has been criticized as highly subjective: The same dream can be interpreted differently to fit the particular analyst's point of view.

Activation-synthesis theory.   Is it possible that dreams serve no special purpose? In 1977, J. Allan Hobson and Robert McCarley proposed a physiological theory of dreaming. When we are awake, neural circuits in our brain are activated by sensory input—sights, sounds, tastes, and so on. The cerebral cortex interprets these patterns of neural activation, producing meaningful perceptions. According to the **activation-synthesis theory,** during REM sleep the brain stem bombards our higher brain centers with random neural activity (the *activation* component). Because we are asleep, this neural activity does not match any external sensory events, but our cerebral cortex continues to perform its job of interpretation. It does this by creating a dream that provides the "best fit" to the particular pattern of activation that exists at any particular moment (the *synthesis* component). This accounts for the bizarreness of dreams: the brain is trying to "make sense" out of *random* neural activity. Our memories and experiences can influence the stories that our brain develops, and therefore dream content may reflect themes pertaining to our lives. In this limited sense, dreams can have meaning (Hobson, 1988; McCarley, 1998). However, dreaming does not serve any particular *function*—it is merely *a by-product of REM neural activity.*

Critics claim that the activation-synthesis theory overestimates the bizarreness of dreams. It also assumes that unique REM brain activity causes dreaming, ignoring the fact that dreaming occurs during NREM sleep (Domhoff, 1999; Vogel, 1978). Nevertheless, the theory has supporters and helped revolutionize dream research by calling attention to a physiological basis for dreaming.

➤ 25. Describe the main assumption of cognitive-process dream theory. What evidence supports it?

Cognitive approaches.   According to **problem-solving models,** dreams can help us find creative solutions to our problems and conflicts because they are not constrained by reality (Cartwright et al., 1977). Based on research with men and women undergoing divorce, Rosalind Cartwright (1991, p. 3) notes that those who dream ". . . with strong feelings, and who incorporate the stressor directly into their dreams, appear to 'work through' their depression more successfully than those who do not." But critics note that just because a problem shows up in a dream, this does not mean that the dream involved an attempt to solve it. We also may think about our dreams after awakening and obtain new insights, but this also is not the same as solving problems *while* dreaming (Squier & Domhoff, 1998).

Cognitive-process dream theories focus on the *process* of how we dream (Antrobus, 1991; Foulkes, 1982). Based on the modular model of consciousness, these theories propose that dreaming and waking thought are produced by the same mental systems in the brain. Consider that when 3- and 4-year-old children are awakened from REM sleep, they rarely report dreams, whereas 8- and 9-year-olds display some features of adult dreaming (Foulkes, 1982). Why should this be? According to David Foulkes (1999), it is because dreaming requires imagery skills and other cognitive abilities that young children have not yet developed sufficiently in waking life. As children's mental abilities develop with age, so does their ability to dream.

Research indicates far greater similarity between dreaming and waking mental activity than traditionally believed (Domhoff, 1999). Consider that one reason many dreams appear bizarre is because their content shifts rapidly

(Antrobus, 1991). "I was dreaming about an exam *and all of a sudden,* the next thing I knew, I was in Hawaii on the beach." (Don't we wish.) Yet if you reflect on the contents of your waking thoughts—your stream of consciousness—you will realize they also shift suddenly. In fact, about half of REM dream reports involve rapid content shifts. But when people are awake and placed in the same environmental conditions as sleepers (a dark, quiet room), about 90 percent of their reports involve rapid content shifts (Antrobus, 1991). Thus rapid shifting of attention is a *process* common to dreaming and waking mental activity.

Toward integration.   Although there presently is no agreed-upon model of dreaming, some theorists have begun to integrate concepts from cognitive, biological, and modern psychodynamic perspectives. For example, John Antrobus (1991) has developed a model to explain how our sleeping brain creates dreams. As Figure 5.19 shows, it incorporates findings on sleep physiology with the cognitive principle of modular consciousness.

Seymour Epstein (1999) also views the unconscious mind as an information processor that weaves input from different brain modules into a coherent story while we dream. He deemphasizes Freud's notion of wish fulfillment, but adopts the psychodynamic view that the unconscious mind involves emotional and motivational processes as well as cognitive ones. As Epstein (1999, p. 76) notes, in dreams these emotional themes may simply be ". . . extensions of everyday waking thought, rather than disguised expressions of . . . unconscious conflict." Thus dreams are woven together by an unconscious mind that, in part, is emotionally driven. Notice that Antrobus's model in Figure 5.19 includes emotional modules.

Though in need of more testing, these integrative models may signal the future of dream theorizing. As we described earlier, evidence is rapidly growing that unconscious cognitive, emotional, and motivational processes influence our waking life. These models extend this view to sleeping mental life.

Daydreams and Waking Fantasies

Our dreams and fantasy lives are not restricted to the nocturnal realm. Daydreams are a significant part of waking consciousness, providing stimulation during periods of boredom and letting us experience positive emotions (Singer, 1997). In *The*

➤ 26. Does daydreaming serve any function? How similar are daydreams and night dreams?

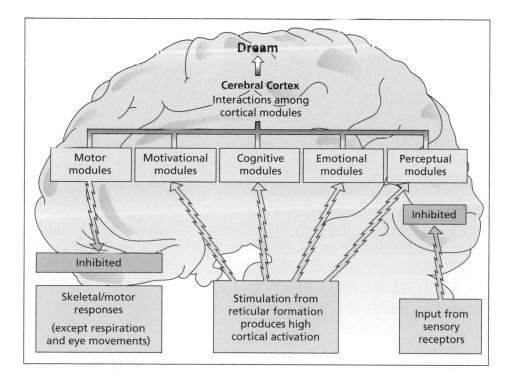

FIGURE 5.19 Antrobus's (1991) theory proposes that during REM sleep, the reticular formation stimulates various modules in the cortex. These modules interact, as they do during waking mental activity. The perceptual modules produce images that are then interpreted by the cognitive modules. Emotional modules may overlay an "emotional theme" to the dream, which stimulates the perceptual modules to produce additional images consistent with the theme. Because external sensory input is restricted, the brain attempts to provide the "best fit" interpretations of these internally generated images. Motor modules are active, but their output is blocked by REM muscular paralysis. This theory places greater emphasis than activation-synthesis theory on interactions between brain modules and proposes other mechanisms for NREM dreams.

Secret Life of Walter Mitty, author James Thurber portrayed the main character of Walter Mitty as a person who transformed his humdrum existence into an exhilarating fantasy world of adventure and personal fulfillment. Like the fictional Mitty, people who have a **fantasy-prone personality** often live in a vivid, rich fantasy world that they control. They comprise about 2 to 4 percent of the population, and most are female. In one study, about three quarters of fantasy-prone people were able to achieve sexual orgasm merely by fantasizing about sexual activity, and all could experience fantasies "as real as real" in each of the five senses (Wilson & Barber 1984).

Daydreams typically involve greater visual imagery than other forms of waking mental activity, but tend to be less vivid, emotional, and bizarre than nighttime dreams (Antonietti & Colombo, 1997; Kunzendorf et al., 1997). Their content often reflects personal concerns. In one study, college students listed their major daily issues and kept a daydream diary for 2 weeks. Nearly two-thirds of their daydreams focused on current concerns (Gold & Reilly, 1985–1986). There also is a surprising degree of similarity in the themes of day-dreams and nighttime dreams, suggesting once again that nocturnal dreams may be an extension of daytime mental activity, sometimes reflecting current concerns in the person's life (Klinger, 1990; Singer, 1988).

❭ DRUGS AND ALTERED CONSCIOUSNESS

Like sleep and dreaming, drug-induced states have mystified humans for ages. Three millennia ago the Aztecs considered hallucinogenic mushrooms to be a sacred substance for communicating with the spirit world (Diaz, 1997). Ancient peoples also attributed "magical" healing powers to drugs and used them recreationally for their mind-altering effects. Today drugs are a corner-stone of medical practice and, as Figure 5.20 shows, a pervasive part of social life. They alter consciousness by modifying brain chemistry, but drug effects are also influenced by psychological, environmental, and cultural factors (Diaz, 1997; Weil, 1996).

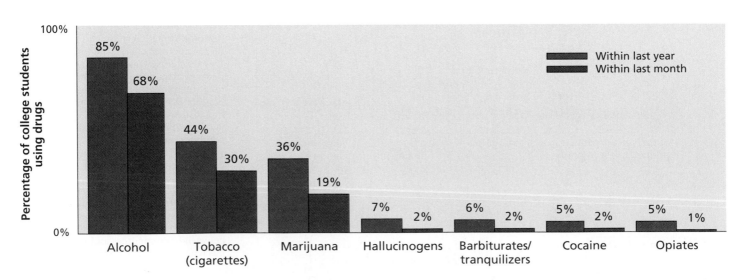

FIGURE 5.20 Nonmedical drug use among American college students. These data are based on a nationally representative survey of 1,440 students. Compared with college students over the past 12 months, "young adults" in general are less likely to use marijuana (27%), but show similar levels of other drug use.

Adapted from Johnston et al., 1999.

Drugs and the Brain

Like any cell, a neuron essentially is a fragile bag of chemicals, and it takes a delicate chemical balancing act for neurons to function properly. Drugs work their way into the bloodstream and are carried throughout the brain by an extensive network of small blood vessels, called *capillaries*. These capillaries contain a **blood-brain barrier,** a special lining of tightly packed cells that lets vital nutrients pass through so neurons can function. The blood-brain barrier screens out many foreign substances, but some, including a variety of drugs, manage to pass through. Once inside, they alter consciousness by facilitating or inhibiting synaptic transmission (Heckers & Konradi, 2000; Julien, 1991).

How Drugs Facilitate Synaptic Transmission

Recall from Chapter 3 that synaptic transmission involves several basic steps. First, neurotransmitters are synthesized inside the presynaptic (sending) neuron and stored in vesicles. Next, neurotransmitters are released into the synapse, where they bind with and stimulate receptor sites on the postsynaptic (receiving) neuron. Finally, neurotransmitter molecules are deactivated by enzymes or by reuptake.

An *agonist* is a drug that increases the activity of a neurotransmitter. Figure 5.21 shows that agonists may

- enhance a neuron's ability to synthesize, store, or release neurotransmitters;
- bind with and stimulate postsynaptic receptor sites (or make it easier for neurotransmitters to stimulate these sites); and
- make it more difficult for neurotransmitters to be deactivated, such as by inhibiting reputake.

Consider two examples. Opiates (such as morphine and codeine) are effective pain relievers. Recall that the brain contains its own chemicals, the endorphins, which play a major role in pain relief. Opiates have a molecular structure similar to the endorphins: They bind to and activate receptor sites that receive endorphins. To draw an analogy, think of trying to open a lock with a key. Normally, an endorphin molecule acts as the key, but due to their similar shape, opiates can fit into the lock and open it.

Amphetamines are stimulant drugs that boost arousal and mood by increasing the activity of two neurotransmitters: dopamine and norepinephrine. They do so in two major ways. First, they cause firing neurons to release greater amounts of these neurotransmitters. Second, they inhibit reuptake. During reuptake, dopamine and norepinephrine molecules in the synapse normally are sucked back into the presynaptic neuron through special openings. Similar to Figure 5.21c, amphetamine molecules "block" this process. This allows dopamine and norepinephrine to remain in the synapse longer and keep stimulating postsynaptic neurons (Diaz, 1997).

How Drugs Inhibit Synaptic Transmission

A drug that inhibits or decreases the action of a neurotransmitter is called an *antagonist.* As Figure 5.21 shows, an antagonist may

- reduce a neuron's ability to synthesize, store, or release neurotransmitters; or
- prevent a neurotransmitter from binding with the postsynaptic neuron, such as by fitting into and blocking the receptor sites on the postsynaptic neuron.

As an example, consider the action of so-called "antipsychotic" drugs used to treat schizophrenia, a severe psychological disorder whose symptoms may include incoherent speech, hallucinations (e.g., hearing voices) and delusions (clearly false beliefs, such as believing you are Albert Einstein). These symptoms

➤ 27. How do drugs increase and decrease synaptic transmission?

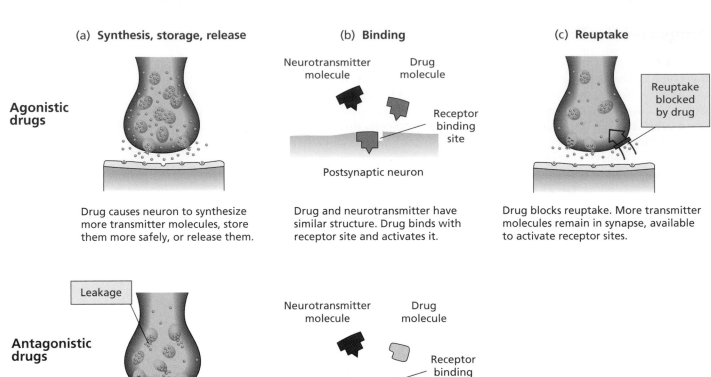

FIGURE 5.21 (a) Agonists cause neurons to synthesize more neurotransmitter molecules, store them more safely, or release them. In contrast, antagonists impair neurons' ability to synthesize, store, or release neurotransmitters. (b) Agonist and neurotransmitter have similar molecular structure. Drug binds with receptor site and activates it. In contrast, antagonist binds with receptor site but is not similar enough to neurotransmitter to activate the site. This prevents the real neurotransmitter from binding with and activating the site. (c) Agonist blocks reuptake of neurotransmitter into the presynaptic neuron. More neurotransmitter molecules remain in the synapse, available to activate the postsynaptic neuron.

are often associated with abnormal overactivity of the dopamine neurotransmitter system. To bring dopamine activity back down to more normal levels, pharmaceutical companies have developed drugs with a molecular structure similar enough to dopamine to fit into the receptor sites that are shaped for receiving dopamine, but not so similar that they actually activate those receptor sites.

To return to the lock-and-key analogy, imagine finding a key that fits into the lock, but it won't turn. The key's shape was close enough to the real key to get in, but not to open the lock. Similarly, antipsychotic drugs fit into receptor sites, but not well enough to stimulate them. While they occupy the sites, dopamine released by presynaptic neurons is blocked and cannot get in, and the schizophrenic symptoms usually decrease.

Tolerance and Withdrawal

> 28. What is the relation between tolerance, compensatory responses, and withdrawal?

When a drug is used repeatedly, the intensity of effects produced by the same dosage level may decrease over time. This decreasing responsivity to a drug is called **tolerance.** As it develops, the person must take increasingly larger doses to achieve the same physical and psychological effects. Tolerance stems from the body's attempt to maintain a state of optimal physiological balance, called *homeostasis.* If a drug changes bodily functioning in a certain way, say by increasing heart rate, the brain will try to adjust for this imbalance by producing **compensatory**

responses, which are reactions opposite to that of the drug (e.g., reactions that decrease heart rate). In effect, compensatory responses represent the body's way of fighting the invasion of drugs.

What happens when drug tolerance develops and the person suddenly stops using the drug? The body's compensatory responses may continue and, no longer balanced out by the drug's effects, the person can experience strong reactions opposite to those produced by the drug. This occurrence of compensatory responses after discontinued drug use is known as **withdrawal** (Diaz, 1997). For example, in the absence of alcohol's sedating and relaxing effects, the chronic drinker may experience increased heart rate, anxiety, and hypertension.

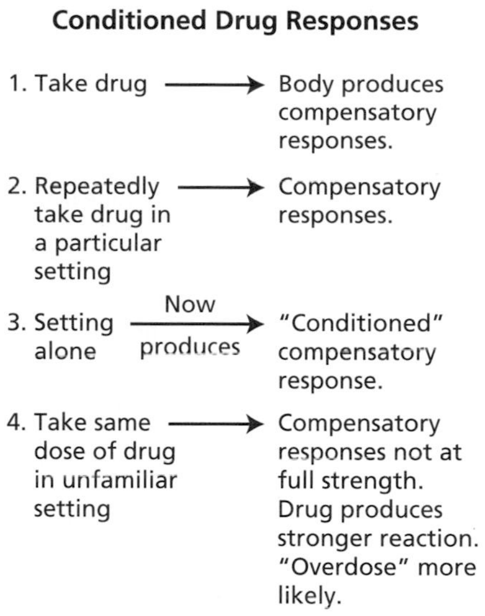

Learning, Drug Tolerance, and Overdose

Experiments show that tolerance for various drugs partly depends on the familiarity of the drug setting (Larson & Siegel, 1998; Siegel, 1984). Figure 5.22 illustrates how environmental stimuli associated with drug use begin to elicit compensatory responses through a learning process called *classical conditioning.* As drug use continues, the physical setting triggers progressively stronger compensatory responses, increasing the user's tolerance. This helps to explain why addicts often experience increased cravings when they enter a setting associated with drug use. The environmental stimuli trigger compensatory responses, which, without drugs to mask their effect, cause the user to feel withdrawal symptoms (Pilla et al., 1999).

There is a hidden danger in this process, particularly for experienced drug users. Compensatory responses serve a protective function by physiologically countering part of the drug's effects. If a user takes his or her usual high dose in a familiar environment, the body's compensatory responses are at full strength—a combination of compensatory reactions directly to the drug and also to the conditioned environmental stimuli. But in an *unfamiliar* environment, the conditioned compensatory responses are weaker, and the drug has a stronger physiological net effect than usual.

Shepard Siegel (1984) of McMaster University interviewed heroin addicts who experienced near-fatal overdoses. He found that in most cases they *had not* taken a dose larger than their customary one. However, in 70 percent of the cases they *had* injected themselves in unfamiliar environments. Siegel concluded that the addicts were not protected by their usual compensatory responses, resulting in an "overdose" reaction.

Myths About Drug Addiction and Dependence

Drug addiction, which is formally called **substance dependence,** represents a maladaptive pattern of substance use that causes a person significant distress or substantially impairs that person's life. Substance dependence is diagnosed as occurring with *physiological dependence* if drug tolerance or withdrawal symptoms have developed. You probably have heard the term *psychological dependence* used to describe situations where people strongly crave a drug because of its pleasurable effects, even if they are not physiologically dependent. However, this is not a diagnostic term, and many drug experts feel it is misleading. They note that such cravings do have a physical basis because they are rooted in patterns of brain activity (Diaz, 1997).

Several misconceptions surround the issue of substance dependence:

Myth 1: Drug tolerance always leads to significant withdrawal. It often does, but not always. Tolerance develops to marijuana and hallucinogens, such as LSD, yet at typical doses withdrawal symptoms are mild (O'Brien, 1997).

Myth 2: If a drug does not produce tolerance or withdrawal, you cannot become dependent on it. Neither tolerance nor withdrawal is needed for a diagnosis of substance dependence (Nathan, 1997).

Conditioned Drug Responses

1. Take drug $\longrightarrow$ Body produces compensatory responses.

2. Repeatedly take drug in a particular setting $\longrightarrow$ Compensatory responses.

3. Setting alone $\xrightarrow{\text{Now produces}}$ "Conditioned" compensatory response.

4. Take same dose of drug in unfamiliar setting $\longrightarrow$ Compensatory responses not at full strength. Drug produces stronger reaction. "Overdose" more likely.

FIGURE 5.22 Environmental stimuli that are repeatedly paired with the use of a drug can acquire the ability to trigger compensatory responses on their own.

➤ 29. Describe some myths about drug dependence.

➤ 30. Explain how alcohol affects the brain.

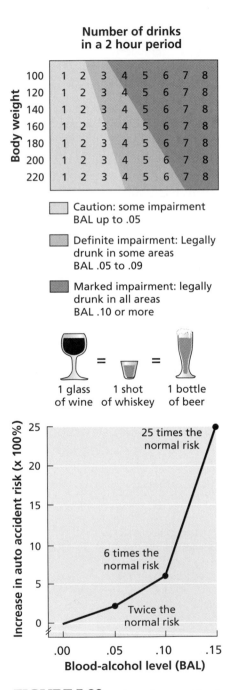

Number of drinks in a 2 hour period

Caution: some impairment
BAL up to .05

Definite impairment: Legally
drunk in some areas
BAL .05 to .09

Marked impairment: legally
drunk in all areas
BAL .10 or more

1 glass   1 shot   1 bottle
of wine   of whiskey   of beer

FIGURE 5.23 Relation between blood-alcohol level and risk of having an auto accident. At .08 to 0.10, the legal definition of intoxication in most American states and Canadian provinces, the risk is 6 times greater than at 0.00, and the risk climbs to 25 times higher at a BAL of 0.15.

Based on National Safety Council, 1992.

Myth 3: Physiological dependence is the major cause of drug addiction. The image of a shaking alcoholic or "heroin junkie" desperately searching for a drink or "fix" contributes to the perception that the motivation to avoid or end withdrawal symptoms is the primary cause of addiction. Certainly, this contributes to drug dependence. But consider these points:

- People become highly dependent on some drugs, like cocaine, that produce only mild withdrawal (Diaz, 1997). The pleasurable effects of these drugs—often produced by boosting *dopamine* activity—play a powerful role in drug dependence (Everitt et al., 1999).

- Many drug users who quit and make it through withdrawal eventually start using again, even though they are no longer physiologically dependent.

- Drug dependence is influenced by many factors beyond a drug's chemical effects, including genetic predispositions, personality traits, religious beliefs, peer influences, and cultural norms (Marlatt & VandenBos, 1997).

Depressants

Depressants decrease nervous system activity. In moderate doses, they reduce feelings of tension and anxiety, and produce a state of relaxed euphoria. In extremely high doses, depressants can slow down vital life processes to the point of death.

Alcohol

Alcohol is the most widely used recreational drug in numerous countries. A national survey of 51,000 American college students found that they averaged 4 drinks per week, with 36 percent bingeing (5 or more drinks at one time) in a 2-week period (Leichliter et al., 1998). Tolerance develops gradually and can lead to physiological dependence. About 1 in 7 Americans has been or is currently addicted to alcohol (Anthony et al., 1997).

Alcohol increases the activity of gamma-aminobutyric acid (GABA), the main inhibitory neurotransmitter in the brain (Korpi, 1994). By increasing the action of an *inhibitory* neurotransmitter, alcohol dampens down neural firing. Alcohol also decreases the activity of glutamate, a major *excitatory* neurotransmitter (Gonzales & Jaworski, 1997). This further depresses neural firing. Why then do many people report getting a "high" from alcohol and initially seem livelier? The answer is that the neural slowdown depresses the action of inhibitory control centers in the cerebral cortex, so the person literally becomes "less inhibited" and feels euphoric. At higher doses, the brain's control centers become increasingly disrupted, thinking and physical coordination become disorganized, and fatigue and psychological depression may occur (Table 5.2).

Thus alcohol's subjective effects seem to have an initial "upper" phase from the release of inhibitions, followed by a "downer" phase as brain centers become increasingly depressed (Marlatt, 1987). But both phases result from alcohol's action as a nervous system *depressant.* Unfortunately, some people respond to the "downer" phase by drinking even more alcohol in the hope that it will make them feel "high" again, a self-defeating strategy if ever there was one.

The *blood-alcohol level (BAL)* is a measure of alcohol concentration in the body. Elevated BAL is linked to risky and harmful behaviors, such as having unprotected sex (Leigh & Stall, 1993). About 40 percent of American and Canadian traffic accident deaths involve alcohol (National Highway Traffic Safety Administration, 2000). As the BAL increases, reaction time, eye-hand coordination, and decision making are impaired (Figure 5.23).

	TABLE 5.2	BEHAVIORAL EFFECTS OF ALCOHOL	

BAL	Hours to Leave Body	Behavioral Effects
.03	1	Decreased alertness, impaired reaction time in some people
.05	2	Decreased alertness, impaired judgment and reaction time, feeling of relaxation, release of inhibitions
.10	4	Severely impaired reaction time, motor function, and judgment; less caution
.15	10	Gross intoxication; impairments worsen
.25	?	Extreme sensory and motor impairment, staggering
.30	?	Stuporous but conscious, cannot comprehend immediate environment
.40	?	Lethal in over 50% of cases

Why do intoxicated people often act in risky ways that they wouldn't when sober? It is not simply a matter of lowered inhibitions; alcohol also reduces cognitive capacity. Intoxicated people display what Claude Steele and Robert Josephs (1990) termed **alcohol myopia,** a "shortsightedness" in thinking caused by the inability to pay attention to as much information as sober people. Drinkers start to concentrate only on those aspects of the situation (called *cues*) that stand out. As a result, in the absence of strong cautionary cues (such as warnings) to inhibit risky behavior, drinkers do not think about the long-term consequences of their actions as carefully as when they are sober (MacDonald et al., 2000). Our *Research Close-Up* illustrates this effect.

➤ 31. How does being intoxicated affect decisions about drinking and driving?

RESEARCH ▼ CLOSE-UP

Drinking and Driving: Decision Making in Altered States

▶ Background

Most people have very negative attitudes about drunk driving and say they would not do it. They realize that the cons (e.g., risk of accident, injury, death, and police arrest) far outweigh the pros (e.g., avoiding cab fare, not leaving one's car behind). Why then do so many people decide to drive after they become intoxicated?

Tara MacDonald and her colleagues examined how alcohol myopia affects decisions about drinking and driving. The authors reasoned that when intoxicated people decide whether to drive, they may focus on the pros or the cons, but do not have the capacity to focus on both. If some aspect of the situation that favors driving (a "facilitating cue") is made salient and captures the intoxicated person's attention (e.g., "It will only be for a short distance"), she or he will latch on to it and fail to consider the cons. But in general situations that do not contain facilitating cues, intoxicated people's feelings about driving should remain as negative as when they were sober.

Based on alcohol myopia principles, the authors made two predictions. First, intoxicated and sober people will have *equally* negative *general* attitudes and intentions toward drinking and driving. Second, intoxicated people will have less negative attitudes and greater intentions to drive than sober people in situations where a facilitating cue or special circumstance is made salient.

▶ Method

Laboratory Experiment

Fifty-seven male introductory psychology students, all regular drinkers who owned cars, participated. They were randomly assigned to either the sober condition, in which

—Continued

they received no alcohol, or the alcohol condition, in which they received 3 alcoholic drinks within an hour (the average BAL was .074 percent, just below the .08 percent legal driving limit in Ontario, Canada).

Participants then completed a "drinking and driving questionnaire." Some items asked about *general* attitudes and intentions (e.g., "I will drink and drive the next time that I am out at a party or bar with friends"). Other items contained a *facilitating cue*, a special circumstance that suggested a possible reason for drinking and driving ("If I only had a short distance to drive home . . . / If my friends tried to persuade me to drink and drive . . . I would drive while intoxicated"). Participants rated each item on a 9-point scale (1 = strongly disagree; 9 = strongly agree).

Party/Bar Diary Study

Fifty-one male and female college students recorded a telephone diary while at a party or bar where they were going to drink alcohol. Some were randomly assigned to record the diary when they first arrived, and others recorded it just before they left. To record the diary, participants opened up a packet containing the same drinking and driving questionnaire described above, called a number on the packet, and recorded their responses on the researchers' answering machine. Based on participants' descriptions of how much alcohol they had consumed, the researchers estimated their BAL and identified two groups: sober participants (average BAL = .01), and intoxicated participants (average BAL = .11).

▶ Results

The findings from both studies supported the predictions. Sober participants and intoxicated participants both expressed negative general attitudes about drinking and driving, and indicated they would not drive when intoxicated. But when the questions presented a facilitating cue, intoxicated participants expressed more favorable attitudes and a greater intention to drive than sober participants (Figure 5.24).

▶ Critical Analysis

This study nicely illustrates how a person's physiological state (sober vs. intoxicated) and an environmental factor (general situation vs. special circumstance) interact to influence psychological functioning (attitudes and decision making). However, before accepting the researchers' claim that alcohol myopia caused the changes in intoxicated participants' responses, we need to think critically about other possible explanations for the results. The authors' anticipated two other reasons for why people might drive when drunk. First,

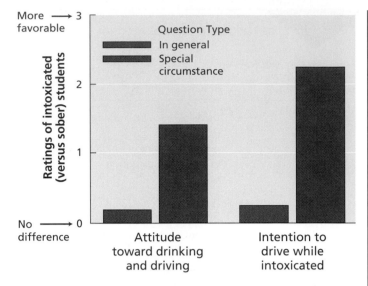

FIGURE 5.24 When general attitudes and intentions toward drinking and driving are measured, intoxicated and sober participants have similarly negative reactions. But when situations involving special circumstances (facilitating cues) are presented, intoxicated participants have less negative attitudes and intentions about drinking and driving than do sober participants.

From MacDonald et al., 1995.

perhaps drinkers do not realize how intoxicated they are. Second, perhaps intoxicated people overestimate their driving ability, a belief called *drunken invincibility.*

The authors tested and ruled out these explanations. Intoxicated participants believed they were *more* intoxicated than they actually were and estimated that they would drive *more poorly* than the average person. The authors also conducted a placebo control experiment in which some participants were convincingly misled to believe they were intoxicated. Results showed that the alcohol myopia effect occurred only for participants who truly had consumed alcohol, and was not caused by participants' expectations.

The party/bar study examined decision making in a real-life but uncontrolled drinking situation, and therefore we cannot draw clear causal conclusions from it. The laboratory experiment examined behavior in an artificial but controlled setting, permitting clearer causal conclusions. Because the authors conducted both types of research and obtained consistent findings, we can be more confident in their conclusions and the external validity (generalizability) of the findings.

Source: Tara K. MacDonald, Mark P. Zanna, & Geoffrey T. Fong, (1995). Decision making in altered states: Effects of alcohol on attitudes toward drinking and driving. *Journal of Personality and Social Psychology, 68,* 973–985.

Barbiturates and Tranquilizers

Physicians frequently prescribe barbiturates ("sleeping pills") and tranquilizers (antianxiety drugs, such as Valium) as sedatives and relaxants. Like alcohol, the vast majority of these drugs depress the nervous system by increasing the activity of the inhibitory neurotransmitter, GABA (Diaz, 1997; Ito et al., 1996).

Mild doses of barbiturates are effective as sleeping pills, but they are highly addictive. As tolerance builds, addicts may take as many as 50 sleeping pills a day. At high doses barbiturates trigger initial excitation, followed by slurred speech, loss of coordination, depression, and severe memory impairment. Overdoses, particularly when taken with alcohol, may cause unconsciousness, coma, and death. Sudden withdrawal after heavy use can cause death, so several months of gradual withdrawal may be needed before addicts lose their physiological dependence.

Barbiturates and tranquilizers are widely overused, and nearly 90 million tranquilizer prescriptions are filled each year (Anthony et al., 1997). Many people mistakenly regard Valium as harmless, but it is not. Tolerance and physiological dependence can occur. Users often don't recognize that they have become dependent until they try to stop and experience serious withdrawal symptoms, such as anxiety, insomnia, and possibly seizures.

Stimulants

Stimulants increase neural firing and arouse the nervous system. They increase blood pressure, respiration, heart rate, and overall alertness. They also can boost mood, produce euphoria, and heighten irritability.

➤ 32. How do stimulants affect brain functioning? Why does heavy use lead to a "crash"?

Amphetamines

Amphetamines—popularly known as speed, uppers, and bennies—are powerful stimulants. They are prescribed to reduce appetite and fatigue, decrease the need for sleep, and sometimes, to reduce depression. Unfortunately, they are widely overused to boost energy and mood (Anthony et al., 1997).

Amphetamines increase dopamine and norepinephrine activity. Tolerance develops and users may crave their pleasurable effects. Eventually, many heavy users start injecting large quantities, producing a sudden surge of energy and rush of intense pleasure. With frequent injections they may remain awake continuously for as long as a week, their bodily systems racing at breakneck speed. Injecting amphetamines greatly increases blood pressure and can lead to heart failure and cerebral hemorrhage (stroke); repeated high doses may cause brain damage (Diaz, 1997).

Recall that in schizophrenia, hallucinations and delusions are associated with excess dopamine activity. Imagine what happens when the brain's dopamine activity is artificially increased well beyond normal levels by continuous, heavy amphetamine use: It can cause schizophrenia-like hallucinations and paranoid delusions, a reaction called **amphetamine psychosis** (Lynn, 1971). There is an inevitable "crash" when heavy users stop taking the drug. They may sleep for one or two days, waking up depressed, exhausted, and irritable. This crash occurs because neurons' norepinephrine and dopamine supplies have become depleted. Amphetamines tax the body heavily, and addicts have a short life expectancy. This kind of speed kills, too.

Cocaine

Cocaine is a powder derived from the coca plant, which grows mainly in western South America. Usually inhaled or injected, it produces excitation, a sense of increased muscular strength, and euphoria. Like amphetamines, cocaine increases the activity of norepinephrine and dopamine, but it does so in only one major way: It blocks their reuptake.

At various times in history, cocaine has been hailed as a wonder drug and branded as a menace. It was once widely used as a local anesthetic in eye, nose, and throat surgery. Novocain, a synthetic form of cocaine, is still used in dentistry as an anesthetic. Due to its stimulating effects, cocaine found its way into

FIGURE 5.25 When Coca-Cola was first produced there was a clear reason why it was "vigorously good." It contained cocaine.

➤ 33. Describe the two effects of opiates.

➤ 34. What is the greatest danger of hallucinogens?

FIGURE 5.26 In some cultures, powerful hallucinogenic drugs are thought to have spiritual powers. Under the influence of peyote, this modern Indian shaman prepares to conduct a religious ceremony.

potions and tonics sold to the public to enhance health and emotional well-being. In 1885, John Pemberton mixed cocaine with the kola nut and syrup and developed a soda fountain drink that has become one of the icons of American beverages (Figure 5.25).

In large doses cocaine can produce fever, vomiting, convulsions, hallucinations, and paranoid delusions. A severe depressive crash may occur after a cocaine high, particularly with repeated doses. *Crack* is a chemically converted form of cocaine that can be smoked, and its effects are faster, more intense, and more dangerous. Overdoses of crack cocaine can cause sudden death from cardiorespiratory arrest (Ruttenber et al., 1997).

Tolerance develops to many of cocaine's effects, but withdrawal symptoms are mild and the potential for physiological dependence is low. However, cocaine users often develop strong cravings for the drug. At present, about 32 million Americans have used cocaine at least once, and about 6 million have developed cocaine dependence (Anthony et al., 1997).

Opiates

Opium is a product of the opium poppy, a plant grown in hot, dry climates. Opium and drugs derived from it, such as morphine, codeine, and heroin, are called **opiates.** Opiates have two major effects. First, they provide pain relief. Second, they cause mood changes, which may include intense euphoria. Opiates bind to and stimulate receptors normally activated by endorphins, thereby producing pain relief. Opiates also increase dopamine activity, which may be one reason they induce euphoria (Bardo, 1998).

Opiates are indispensable in medicine because they are the most effective agents known for relieving intense pain. Heroin was developed in 1889 to be a nonaddictive painkiller. Who developed it? The Bayer Company (which today produces aspirin). Unfortunately, tolerance to heroin develops rapidly, and like other opiates it proved to be highly addictive. In the 1920s, it was made illegal in the United States.

Experienced heroin users feel an intense, pleasurable "rush" within several minutes of an injection. For a time, users feel peaceful and nonaggressive, as if they are "on top of the world" with no concerns. Heroin users, however, often pay a substantial price for these transient pleasures. High doses can greatly reduce a person's breathing rate and may lead to coma. Overdoses can cause death. Only 2 percent of Americans have used heroin, but nearly 25% of those who use it become addicted to it (Anthony et al., 1997). Withdrawal symptoms are traumatic, as illustrated by the following description from a former addict:

> It's like a terrible case of flu. Your joints move involuntarily. That's where the phrase "kick the habit" comes from. You jerk and twitch and you just can't control it. You throw up. You can't control your bowels either and this goes on for four or five days afterwards. You can't sleep and you cough up blood, because . . . you can't eat and that's all there is to cough up.

Hallucinogens

Hallucinogens are powerful mind-altering drugs that produce hallucinations. Many are derived from natural sources; mescaline comes from the peyote cactus and psilocybin from mushrooms. Natural hallucinogens have been considered sacred in many tribal cultures because of their ability to produce "unearthly" states of consciousness and contact with spiritual forces (Figure 5.26). Other hallucinogens, such as LSD and phencyclidine ("Angel Dust") are synthetic.

About 10 percent of Americans have used hallucinogenic drugs (Anthony et al., 1997). Hallucinogens usually distort or intensify sensory experience and can blur the boundaries between reality and fantasy. Users may speak of seeing sounds and hearing colors, of mystical experiences and insights, and of feeling exhilarated. They also may have violent outbursts, experience paranoia and panic, and have flashbacks after the "trip" has ended. The mental effects of hallucinogens are always unpredictable, even if they are taken repeatedly. This unpredictability constitutes their greatest danger.

Lysergic acid diethylamide (LSD) is a powerful hallucinogen. Also known as "acid," LSD causes a flooding of excitation in the nervous system. A dose of pure LSD no larger than the tip of a pin can affect a user for 8 to 16 hours. Tolerance develops rapidly, but decreases quickly. Although chronic use does not appear to produce withdrawal symptoms, about 5 percent of Americans have developed a dependence on LSD or other hallucinogens (Anthony et al., 1997).

We do not know how LSD produces hallucinations. Part of the LSD molecule has a shape similar to serotonin and, overall, it decreases serotonin activity. During normal sleep, decreased serotonin activity in parts of the brain stem allows REM-On neurons to become active and initiate REM sleep, with its high level of dreaming. For decades, researchers have speculated that LSD's inhibiting action on serotonin allows dreamlike altered perceptions and hallucinations to emerge (Trulson & Jacobs, 1979).

Marijuana

Marijuana is a product of the hemp plant (*Cannabis sativa*). Some experts classify it as a hallucinogen, others as a sedative, and some feel it belongs in its own category (Diaz, 1997). Marijuana is the most widely used illegal drug in the United States. About 46 percent of adults have used it at least once (Anthony et al., 1997).

THC (tetrahydrocannabinol) is marijuana's major active ingredient, and it binds to receptors on neurons throughout the brain. You might wonder, as scientists have, why the brain would have specific receptor sites for a "foreign" substance like marijuana? The answer is that the brain produces its own THC-like substances, called *cannabinoids* (Devane et al., 1992; Stella et al., 1997). With chronic use, THC may increase GABA activity, which slows down neural activity and produces relaxing effects (Diaz, 1997). THC also increases dopamine activity, which may account for some of its pleasurable subjective effects (Ameri, 1999). Recent attempts to legalize marijuana use for medical purposes have stirred up waves of political controversy (Gottfried, 2000) (Figure 5.27).

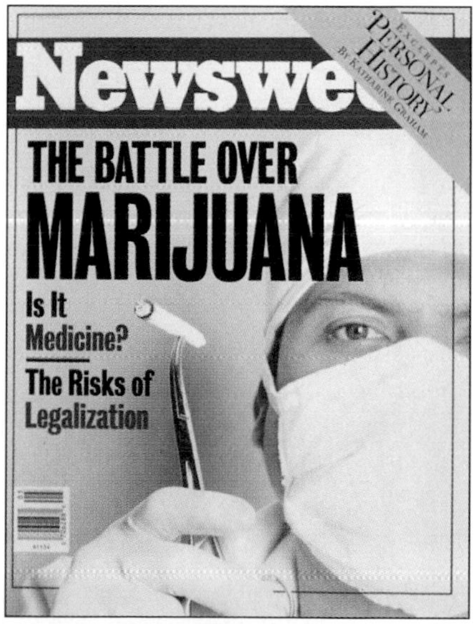

Certain myths exist about marijuana. One is that chronic use causes people to become unmotivated and apathetic toward everything, a condition called *amotivational syndrome.* Another myth is that marijuana causes people to start using more dangerous drugs. Neither statement is supported by good scientific evidence (Diaz, 1997). A third myth is that using marijuana has no significant dangers. This also is untrue. Marijuana smoke contains more cancer-causing substances than does tobacco smoke. At high doses, users may experience negative changes in mood, sensory distortions, and feelings of panic and anxiety. Marijuana can impair reaction time, thinking, memory, and learning (Smiley, 1986). Research clearly shows that driving under the influence of marijuana (even "social doses") can be hazardous (Robbe, 1998).

Repeated marijuana use produces tolerance. At typical doses, some chronic users may experience mild withdrawal symptoms, such as restlessness. But users of chronically high doses who suddenly stop may experience nausea and vomiting, sleep disruptions, and irritability. About 10 percent of marijuana users develop dependence (Anthony et al., 1997). One team of researchers studied 37 Americans who had smoked marijuana 5,000 or more times over a span of 20 to 30 years (Gruber et al., 1997). Many participants reported using marijuana chronically because it reduced their anxiety, depression, and other unpleasant feelings.

➤ 35. Explain three myths about marijuana.

FIGURE 5.27 Marijuana is an illegal drug in the United States at the federal level. However, in some jurisdictions voters have legalized marijuana use for certain medical purposes, such as in helping cancer patients reduce some of the negative side effects (e.g., nausea) of chemotherapy. The medical legalization of marijuana is hotly debated.

TABLE 5.3	EFFECTS OF SOME MAJOR DRUGS	
Class	**Typical Effects**	**Overdose Effects**
DEPRESSANTS		
Alcohol	Relaxation, lowered inhibition, depressed/impaired physical and psychological functioning	Disorientation, unconsciousness, possible death at extreme doses
Barbiturates/ Tranquilizers	Tension reduction, depressed reflexes and impaired motor functioning, induce sleep	Shallow breathing, clammy skin, weak and rapid pulse, coma, possible death
STIMULANTS		
Amphetamines Cocaine	Increased alertness, pulse, and blood pressure; elevated mood, suppressed appetite, sleeplessness	Agitation, hallucinations, paranoid delusions, convulsions, possible death
OPIATES		
Opium Morphine Heroin	Euphoria, pain relief, drowsiness, impaired motor and psychological functioning	Shallow breathing, convulsions, coma, possible death
HALLUCINOGENS		
LSD Mescaline Psilocybin	Hallucinations and "visions," distorted time perception, loss of reality contact, nausea, restlessness, risk of panic	Psychotic reactions (delusions, paranoia), panic, that may lead to behavior causing injury
MARIJUANA	Mild euphoria, relaxation, enhanced sensory experience, increased appetite, impaired memory and reaction time	Fatigue, anxiety, disorientation, sensory distortions and possible psychotic reactions

From Genes to Culture: Determinants of Drug Effects

➤ 36. What evidence supports the hypothesis that genetic factors influence drug reactions?

Table 5.3 summarizes some typical drug effects, but a user's reaction depends on more than the drug's chemical structure. Other biological, psychological, and environmental factors can influence the drug experience.

At the biological level, animal research indicates that genetic factors influence sensitivity and tolerance to drugs effects. This has been examined most extensively with alcohol. Rats and mice can be genetically bred to inherit a strong preference for drinking alcohol instead of water (He et al., 1997; Whitney et al., 1970). Even in their first exposure to alcohol, these rats show greater tolerance than normal rats (Gattoet al., 1986). The degree to which mice experience seizures during alcohol withdrawal also can be increased or decreased through genetic breeding (Crabbe et al., 1986).

In human research, three types of correlational evidence are intriguing. First, identical twins have a higher concordance rate for alcoholism than do fraternal twins (Heath et al., 1997). Second, scientists have identified a particular gene that is found more often among alcoholics and their children than among nonalcoholics and their offspring (Hill et al., 1998; Noble, 1998). No one is proposing that this gene "causes" alcoholism. Rather, it may influence how the brain responds to alcohol.

Third, people who grow up with alcoholic versus nonalcoholic parents respond differently to drinking alcohol under laboratory conditions. Offspring of alcoholic parents typically display faster hormonal and psychological reactions as blood-alcohol level rises, but these responses drop off more quickly as blood-alcohol levels decrease (Newlin & Thomson, 1997). Compared with other people, they must drink more alcohol over the course of a few hours to maintain their feeling of intoxication. Overall, many scientists find compelling evidence for a genetic role in determining responsiveness to alcohol (Li, 2000).

➤ 37. Describe how environmental and psychological factors influence drug reactions.

At the environmental level, the physical and social setting in which a drug is taken can strongly influence a user's reactions. As noted earlier, compensatory physiological responses to a drug can become associated with, and ultimately triggered by, environmental stimuli in the drug setting. The behavior of other people who are sharing the drug experience provides important cues for how to respond, and a hostile environment may increase the chances of a "bad trip" with drugs such as LSD (Palfai & Jankiewicz, 1991).

Cultural learning also affects how people respond to a drug (Weil, 1986). In many Western cultures, increased aggressiveness and sexual promiscuity are commonly associated with drunken excess. In contrast, members of the Camba culture of Bolivia customarily drink large quantities of a 178-proof beverage, remaining cordial and nonaggressive between episodes of passing out (MacAndrew & Edgerton, 1969). In the 1700s, Tahitians introduced to alcohol by European sailors reacted at first with pleasant relaxation when intoxicated, but after witnessing the violent aggressiveness exhibited by drunken sailors, they too began behaving aggressively (MacAndrew & Edgerton, 1969).

Cultural factors also affect drug consumption. Traditionally, American Navajo Indians do not consider drinking any amount of alcohol to be normal, whereas drinking wine or beer is central to social life and cultural identity in some parts of the world (Tanaka-Matsumi & Draguns, 1997). In some cultures, hallucinogenic drugs are feared and outlawed, whereas in others they are used in medicinal or religious contexts to provide new types of awareness and seek advice from spirits (Beardsley & Pedersen, 1997). In many countries, drug use varies across ethnic groups. Black and Hispanic Americans, for example, are less likely to have ever used alcohol, cocaine, marijuana, and hallucinogens than their White peers (Department of Health and Human Services, 1998).

Finally, at the psychological level, people's beliefs and expectancies can influence drug reactions (George et al., 2000). Experiments show that people may behave as if "drunk" if they simply think they have consumed alcohol, but actually have not (Marlatt & Rohsenow, 1980). If a person's fellow drinkers are happy and gregarious, he or she may expect to respond the same way. The cultural norm that a hallucinogen will enable contact with spirits provides the user with a powerful belief system and expectation that can shape the nature of the hallucinations and overall emotional reaction to the experience.

Personality factors also influence drug reactions and usage. People who have difficulty adjusting to life's demands or whose contact with reality is marginal may be particularly vulnerable to severe and negative drug reactions and to drug addiction (Ray & Ksir, 1987). Chronic drug use among young people often is associated with a sense of meaninglessness and lack of direction in life (Newcomb & Harlow, 1986). Figure 5.28 illustrates some of the biological, environmental, and psychological factors that may determine drug experiences.

〉 HYPNOSIS

In 18th-century Vienna, physician Anton Mesmer gained fame for using magnetized objects to cure physical and psychological afflictions. He claimed that illness was caused by blockages of an invisible bodily fluid that obeyed the laws of magnetism, and that his technique of *animal magnetism* (later named *mesmerism* in his honor) would restore the fluid's normal flow. A scientific commission discredited mesmerism, but its use continued. Decades later, Scottish surgeon James Braid investigated the fact that mesmerized patients often went into a "trance" in which they seemed oblivious to their surroundings (Figure 5.29). He concluded that mesmerism was a state of "nervous sleep" produced by concentrated attention, and renamed it "hypnosis," after Hypnos, the Greek god of sleep.

The Scientific Study of Hypnosis

Hypnosis is a state of heightened suggestibility in which some people are able to experience imagined test suggestions as if they were real. Hypnosis draws great interest because many therapists use it in treating mental disorders. In the United States, about 25 percent of psychology Ph.D. programs offer a course in hypnosis

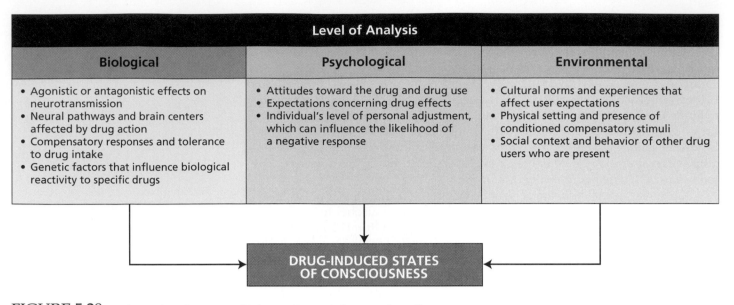

Level of Analysis		
Biological	**Psychological**	**Environmental**
• Agonistic or antagonistic effects on neurotransmission • Neural pathways and brain centers affected by drug action • Compensatory responses and tolerance to drug intake • Genetic factors that influence biological reactivity to specific drugs	• Attitudes toward the drug and drug use • Expectations concerning drug effects • Individual's level of personal adjustment, which can influence the likelihood of a negative response	• Cultural norms and experiences that affect user expectations • Physical setting and presence of conditioned compensatory stimuli • Social context and behavior of other drug users who are present

DRUG-INDUCED STATES OF CONSCIOUSNESS

FIGURE 5.28   Understanding the Causes of Behavior: Factors influencing drug effects.

FIGURE 5.29   A 19th-century "animal magnetizer" places his patient into a trance.

(Walling et al., 1998). Basic scientists explore hypnosis to determine its nature, assess whether it is a unique state of altered consciousness, and put its claims to rigorous experimental test (Hull, 1933; Kirsch, 1999).

Hypnotic induction is the process by which one person (a researcher or hypnotist) leads another person (the subject) into hypnosis. A hypnotist may invite the subject to sit down, relax, gaze at an object on the wall, and then in a quiet voice suggest that the subject's eyes are becoming heavy and tired. The goal is to relax the subject and increase her or his concentration. Contrary to popular belief, people cannot be hypnotized against their will. Even when people want to be hypnotized, they differ in how "susceptible" (i.e., responsive) they are to hypnotic suggestions. **Hypnotic susceptibility scales** contain a standard series of pass/fail suggestions that are read to a subject after a hypnotic induction (Table 5.4). The subject's score is based on the number of "passes." About 10 percent of subjects are completely nonresponsive, 10 percent pass all or nearly all of the items, and the rest fall in between (Hilgard, 1977).

Hypnotic susceptibility is a stable characteristic. In one study, Stanford students differed by no more than 1 point on a 12-item scale when tested 25 years later (Piccione et al., 1989). Hypnotic susceptibility can be enhanced by increasing people's expectation that they have the ability to be hypnotized (Spanos et al., 1991; Vickery & Kirsch, 1991).

Hypnotic Behaviors and Experiences

It is widely claimed that hypnotized people experience substantial alterations in psychological functioning and behavior. Let's examine some of these claims.

TABLE 5.4	SAMPLE TEST ITEMS FROM THE STANFORD HYPNOTIC SUSCEPTIBILITY SCALE, FORM C	
Item	Suggested Behavior	Criterion for Passing
Arm lowering	Right arm is held out; subject is told arm will become heavy and drop.	Arm is lowered at least 6 inches in 10 seconds.
Moving hands apart	With hands extended and close together, subject is asked to imagine a force pushing them apart.	Hands are 6 or more inches apart in 10 seconds.
Mosquito hallucination	It is suggested that a mosquito is buzzing nearby and lands on the subject.	Any grimace or acknowledgment of the mosquito.
Posthypnotic amnesia	Subject is awakened and asked to recall suggestions after being told under hypnosis that they will not remember.	Three or fewer items recalled before subject is told, "Now you can remember everything."

Involuntary Control and Behaving Against One's Will

Hypnotized people *subjectively experience* their actions to be involuntary (Kirsch & Lynn, 1998; Woody & Sadler, 1998). For example, look at the second test item in Table 5.4. To hypnotized subjects, it will really feel like their hands *are* being pushed apart by some mysterious force, rather than by any conscious control of bodily movements.

If behavior seems involuntary under hypnosis, then can a hypnotist make people perform acts that are harmful to themselves or others? Martin Orne and Frederick Evans (1965) found that hypnotized subjects could be induced to dip their hands briefly in a foaming solution they were told was acid and then throw the "acid" in another person's face. This might appear to be a striking example of the power of hypnosis to get people to act "against their will." However, Orne and Evans tested a control group of subjects who were asked to simply pretend that they were hypnotized. These subjects were just as likely as hypnotized subjects to put their hand in the acid or throw it at someone.

In Chapter 12 you will learn about experiments in which researchers induced hundreds of "normal" adults to keep giving what they believed were extremely painful electric shocks to an innocent man with a heart condition who begged them to stop (Milgram, 1974). Not a single one of these participants was hypnotized; they were simply following the researcher's orders. Hypnosis does not involve any unique power to get people to behave "against their will." An authority figure in a legitimate context can induce people to commit highly "out of character" and dangerous acts, whether they are hypnotized or not.

Physiological Effects and Physical Feats

Hypnosis can have striking physiological effects. Consider a classic experiment involving 13 people who were strongly allergic to the toxic leaves of a certain tree (Ikemi & Nakagawa, 1962). Five of them were hypnotized, blindfolded, and told that a leaf from a harmless tree to which they were not allergic was touching one of their arms. In fact, the leaf really was toxic, but 4 out of the 5 hypnotized people had no allergic reaction! Next, the other arm of each hypnotized person was rubbed with a leaf from a harmless tree, but he or she was falsely told that the leaf was toxic. All 5 people responded to the harmless leaf with allergic reactions!

These findings are impressive, but we must also consider the reactions of the 8 nonhypnotized control participants. When blindfolded and exposed to a toxic leaf, but misled to believe that it was harmless, 7 out of the 8 nonhypnotized

> 38. In what sense is hypnotic behavior "involuntary"? Does hypnosis have a unique power to coerce people against their will?

> 39. Can nonhypnotized people produce the same physiological reactions and feats displayed by hypnotized people?

FIGURE 5.30 The "human plank" demonstration, a favorite of stage hypnotists, seems to demonstrate the power of the hypnotic trance. Most of the audience is unaware that the average man suspended in this manner can support a person on his chest without hypnosis. In the photo, The Amazing Kreskin, a professional magician, demonstrates this fact with nonhypnotized men.

➤ 40. Does hypnosis produce pain relief? Is this a placebo effect?

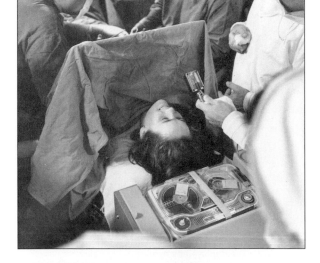

FIGURE 5.31 This patient is having her appendix removed with hypnosis as the sole anesthetic. Her verbal reports that she feels no pain are being tape recorded.

➤ 41. Explain the two major scientific concerns about the use of forensic hypnosis.

persons did not show an allergic response. Conversely, when their arm was rubbed with a harmless leaf but they were falsely told it was toxic, every one of them had an allergic reaction. In short, the nonhypnotized people responded the same way as the hypnotized subjects.

Under hypnosis, nearsighted people can see more clearly, warts can be cured, and stomach acidity can be increased. However, well-controlled studies show that nonhypnotized subjects can exhibit these same responses (Spanos & Chaves, 1988). As we saw when discussing placebo effects in Chapter 2, beliefs and expectations can produce real physiological effects.

Stage hypnotists often get an audience member to perform an amazing physical feat, such as the "human plank" (Figure 5.30). A subject, usually male, is hypnotized and lies outstretched between two chairs. He is told that his body is rigid, and another person stands on his chest. The audience attributes this feat to the "hypnotic trance." What they don't know is that an average man suspended in this manner can support at least 300 pounds on his chest with little discomfort and no need of a hypnotic trance.

Pain Tolerance

Scottish surgeon James Esdaile performed more than 300 major operations in the mid-1800s using hypnosis as the sole anesthetic (Figure 5.31). Joseph Barber (1977), a noted hypnotherapist, needed an average of only 11 minutes to hypnotically produce *analgesia* (an absence of pain) in 99 out of 100 dental patients. Experiments confirm that hypnosis often increases pain tolerance, and that this is not due to a placebo effect (Farthing et al., 1997; Spanos & Katsanis, 1989). For patients who experience chronic pain, hypnosis can produce relief that persists for months or even years (Barber, 1998). But research also shows that nonhypnotic psychological techniques, such as mental imagery, also can reduce pain (Weisenberg, 1998).

We do not know exactly how hypnosis produces its pain-killing effects. It may influence the release of endorphins, decrease patients' fear and anxiety about pain, produce muscular relaxation, distract patients from their pain, or somehow help them separate the pain from conscious experience (Barber, 1998; Chaves, 1994).

Hypnosis and Memory

You may have seen TV shows or movies in which hypnotized people are given a suggestion that they will not remember something, either during the session itself (*hypnotic amnesia*), or after "coming out" of hypnosis (*posthypnotic amnesia*). A "reversal cue" also is given, such as a phrase ("You will now remember everything") that ends the amnesia once the person hears it. Is this Hollywood fiction?

In one interesting case, a math teacher was given a hypnotic suggestion that he would be unable to recall the number 6 during the session. The teacher mistakenly interpreted the suggestion as including *post*hypnotic amnesia. Can you imagine someone trying to teach math while being unable to recall the number 6! Indeed, it proved difficult, until the hypnotist reversed the amnesia suggestion at a later session.

More extensive research indicates that about 25 percent of hypnotized college students can be led to experience amnesia (Kirsch & Lynn, 1998). Though researchers agree that hypnotic and posthypnotic amnesia occur, they dispute the causes. Some feel it results from voluntary attempts to avoid thinking about certain information, and others believe it is caused by an altered state of consciousness or weakening of normal memory systems (Kihlstrom, 1985, 1998, Spanos, 1986).

PSYCHOLOGICAL FRONTIERS

Does Forensic Hypnosis Improve Eyewitness Memory?

Some experts claim that, in contrast to producing forgetting, hypnosis can help people recall information they otherwise cannot remember. Law enforcement agencies and attorneys sometimes use forensic hypnosis to aid the recall of eyewitnesses to crimes. In a celebrated 1977 case in California, a bus carrying 26 children and its driver disappeared without a trace. The victims were later found alive, buried six feet underground in an abandoned trailer truck where they had been imprisoned by three gunmen who demanded a large ransom. After their rescue, a police expert hypnotized the bus driver and asked him to relive the experience in his mind. Under hypnosis, the driver formed a vivid image of the white van used by the kidnappers and could "read" all but one digit on the van's license plate. This information allowed the police to track down and arrest the kidnappers.

Reports like this seem to offer vivid evidence of memory enhancement via hypnosis. Unfortunately, science raises two important concerns. First, controlled experiments find that hypnosis does not reliably improve eyewitness memory. In some experiments, participants watch videotapes of simulated bank robberies or other crimes. They are then questioned—while hypnotized or unhypnotized—by actual police investigators or criminal lawyers. In other experiments, participants are shown drawings of objects or other visual stimuli, and are asked to recall them while hypnotized or unhypnotized. In both types of experiments, memory may be tested immediately or days later.

Findings are mixed (Geiselman et al., 1985; Ready et al., 1997). In some studies, hypnotized and unhypnotized participants recall information with equal accuracy. In others, hypnotized people perform better than unhypnotized controls, though usually not better than unhypnotized people who are asked to use imagery or other memory tricks to aid their recall. And in other experiments, hypnotized participants perform worse than unhypnotized controls: They recall more information, but much of that "extra recall" is inaccurate (Burgess & Kirsch, 1999).

The second scientific concern is more disturbing. It is possible that some "memories" recalled under hypnosis are actually *pseudomemories*, false memories *created* during the hypnosis session by leading suggestions or statements made by the examiner. In one study, Australian researchers identified college students who were high or low in hypnotic susceptibility and randomly divided each group into hypnosis and nonhypnosis conditions (Sheehan et al., 1992). Each student then watched a 43-second videotape in which an unmasked man with a pistol entered a bank from the left door, robbed the bank, but didn't swear.

Students in the experimental group were then hypnotized and told that their subconscious mind had recorded everything they had seen, including details that their conscious mind had forgotten. To test whether they could implant a false memory, the researchers described the robbery and inaccurately stated that the robber had worn a mask, entered from the right, and swore. Students in the experimental group were brought out of hypnosis and both they and the nonhypnotized participants were introduced to a second experimenter who asked them to describe the robbery.

The results showed that nonhypnotized students accurately reported the robbery virtually all the time, and hypnotized students with low susceptibility were almost as accurate. However, on average, highly suggestible students who had been hypnotized typically misreported one or sometimes two of the three key events. Equally disturbing was the fact that they were highly confident that their false memories were accurate.

In sum, forensic hypnosis may have hidden dangers. Even when hypnotized people's memory is tested in a straightforward way and no leading questions are asked, evidence does not consistently show that hypnosis improves memory. Further, the increased suggestibility of hypnotized people makes them particularly susceptible to memory distortion. If the examiner asks leading questions and provides information about the event, such information may be incorporated into the person's memory of what actually happened. Afterward, during court testimony, an eyewitness may report "facts" that never occurred, but which the eyewitness truly believes to be a part of the memory for that event.

Similarly, if a therapist suspects that a patient has repressed memories of sexual abuse and helps the patient "recover" these memories under hypnosis, what shall we conclude? As we explore in Chapter 7, are the horrible memories real or are they pseudomemories prompted by cues from the therapist (Loftus, 2000)? Many experts urge caution when hypnosis is used to enhance memory during therapy (Gow, 1999).

In the meantime, forensic psychologists and the legal system struggle with the issues raised by research on forensic hypnosis (Scheflin et al., 1999; Wagstaff, 1999). Many courts have banned or limited testimony obtained under hypnosis, though some experts believe that the legal system has overreacted to the scientific evidence. Nevertheless, those who believe in the value of forensic hypnosis must devise ways of using hypnosis that do not pose a danger to the cause of justice.

Theories of Hypnosis

Hypnos may have been the Greek god of sleep, but hypnosis definitely is *not* sleep. Moreover, experts still debate whether hypnosis produces a unique pattern of physiological activity (Bauer & McCanne, 1980; Dixon & Laurence, 1992; Woody & Sadler, 1998). What then is hypnosis, and how does it produce its effects?

Dissociation Theories: Hypnosis as Divided Consciousness

➤ 42. According to the dissociation theory of hypnosis, why do hypnotic behaviors seem involuntary?

Several influential researchers propose **dissociation theories** that view hypnosis as an altered state involving a division ("dissociation") of consciousness (Bowers, 1992; Kihlstrom, 1984). For example, Ernest Hilgard of Stanford University (1977, 1991) proposes that hypnosis creates a *division of awareness* in which the person simultaneously experiences two streams of consciousness that are cut off from one another. One stream responds to the hypnotist's suggestions, while the second stream—the part of consciousness that monitors behavior—remains in the background but is aware of everything that goes on. Metaphorically, Hilgard refers to this second "part" of consciousness as the *hidden observer.*

Suppose a hypnotized subject is given a suggestion that she will not feel pain. Her arm is lowered into a tub of ice-cold water for 45 seconds and every few seconds she reports the amount of pain. In contrast to unhypnotized subjects, who find this experience moderately painful, she probably will report feeling little pain. But suppose the procedure is done differently. Before lowering the subject's arm, the hypnotist says, "Perhaps there is another part of you that is more aware than your hypnotized part. If so, would that part of you report the amount of pain." In this case, the subject's other stream of consciousness, the "hidden observer," will report a higher level of pain (Figure 5.32).

For Hilgard, this dissociation explains why behaviors that occur under hypnosis seem involuntary or automatic. Given the suggestion that "your arm will start to feel lighter and will begin to rise," the subject intentionally raises the arm, but only the hidden observer is aware of this. The main stream of consciousness that responds to the command is blocked from this awareness, and thus perceives that the arm is rising all by itself.

FIGURE 5.32 (a) This hypnotized subject's hand is immersed in painfully cold ice water. Placing his hand on her shoulder, Ernest Hilgard contacts her dissociated "hidden observer." (b) Pain intensity ratings given by a subject when she is not hypnotized, by the subject under hypnosis, and by the hidden observer in the same hypnotic state. The hidden observer reports more pain than the hypnotized subject but less than the subject when she is not hypnotized.

Data from Hilgard, 1977.

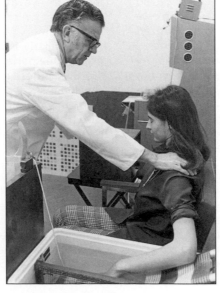

(a)

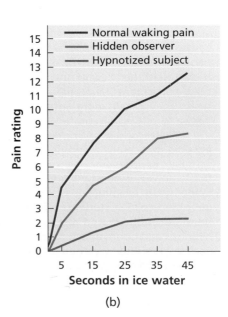

(b)

Social Cognitive Theories: Roles and Expectations

To other theorists, hypnosis does not represent a special state of dissociated consciousness (Kirsch & Lynn, 1998; Sarbin & Coe, 1972; Spanos, 1991). In general, **social cognitive theories** propose that hypnotic experiences result from expectations of people who are motivated to take on the role of being "hypnotized." Most people believe that hypnosis involves a trancelike appearance, responsiveness to suggestions, and a loss of self-consciousness. People motivated to conform to this role and who expect to succeed in it develop a perceptual set—a readiness to respond to the hypnotist's suggestions and to perceive hypnotic experiences as real and "involuntary".

In a classic study, Martin Orne (1959) of the University of Pennsylvania illustrated the importance of expectations about hypnosis. During a classroom demonstration, college students were told that hypnotized people frequently exhibit spontaneous stiffening of the muscles in the dominant hand. Actually, this rarely occurs. An accomplice of the lecturer pretended to be hypnotized and, sure enough, he "spontaneously" exhibited hand stiffness. When students who had seen the demonstration were later hypnotized, 55 percent of them exhibited stiffening of the hand without any suggestion from the hypnotist. Control group participants saw a demonstration that did not mention or display hand stiffening. Not one of these students exhibited hand stiffening when they were hypnotized.

Does social cognitive theory imply that people are faking or playacting when they are hypnotized? Not at all. Role theorists emphasize that when people immerse themselves in the hypnotic role, their responses are completely "real." Recall from the chapter on perception that perceptual sets strongly influence how the brain organizes sensory information. Often we literally "see" what we expect to see. According to social cognitive theory, many of the effects of hypnosis represent an extension of this basic principle. The hypnotized subject whose arm "automatically" rises in response to a suggestion genuinely perceives the behavior to be involuntary because this is what the subject expects, and because attention is focused externally on the hypnotist and hypnotic suggestion.

Can the debate about hypnosis be resolved? Some psychologists believe the dissociation and social cognitive viewpoints can be integrated into a comprehensive theory (Kihlstrom, 1998; Woody & Sadler, 1998). Others disagree, saying it is time to discard some ideas of dissociation theory (Kirsch & Lynn, 1998). The only sure bet is that hypnosis will remain a controversial topic for some time to come.

> ➤ 43. According to the social cognitive theories of hypnosis, why do hypnotic behaviors seem involuntary?

〉 SOME FINAL THOUGHTS

We have seen that consciousness can be studied scientifically at biological, psychological, and environmental levels. In so doing, we have learned that altered states are not as divorced from "normal" waking consciousness as has previously been thought. In a way, we all experience dissociated consciousness in the form of divided attention, and dreaming shares much in common with waking thought processes. As you learned in Chapter 4, expectations powerfully affect everyday waking perception. Now we see that our expectations and beliefs influence hypnotic and drug-induced experiences.

Consider the behavior of the following participant in the *Research Close-Up* experiment on drinking and driving. This college student consumed 3 nonalcoholic drinks, but through taste and smell cues was convincingly led to believe that they were alcoholic. Prior to taking a Breathalyzer test, he estimated his blood-alcohol level to be .07, just below the .08 legal driving limit where he lived. He felt he was almost drunk! When told the drinks were nonalcoholic, he argued that there had to be a mistake. When shown his true Breathalyzer result of .000, he claimed it was rigged and refused to drive home until the effects of his "drinks" wore off (MacDonald et al., 1995)!

Clearly, we have a remarkable capacity to alter our own state of consciousness without being aware that "we" are responsible for causing the change. In fact, returning to our opening case of Billy Milligan, might this capacity to alter consciousness underlie dissociative identity disorder (DID)? Social-cognitive theorists propose that, as with hypnosis, DID is a state in which people become deeply enmeshed in a role and sincerely come to perceive themselves as having multiple identities (Lilienfeld et al, 1999; Spanos, 1991). In contrast, dissociation theorists believe that DID represents a state of divided consciousness that usually develops as a protective reaction to extreme childhood trauma, such as prolonged sexual abuse (Gleaves, 1996; Putnam, 1998). Add to this mix the fact that some people intentionally fake DID, and you have an intriguing controversy that we explore in Chapter 14.

Along with the study of perception, probing the mysteries of conscious experience goes to the heart of understanding the subjective nature of "reality." On this matter, the century-old words of William James remain pertinent today:

> Our normal waking consciousness is but one special type of consciousness, whilst all about it, parted from it by the filmiest of screens, there lie potential forms of consciousness entirely different. . . . No account of the universe in its totality can be final which leaves these other forms of consciousness quite disregarded." (James, 1902, p. 298)

CHAPTER SUMMARY

The Puzzle of Consciousness

- Consciousness refers to our moment-to-moment awareness of ourselves and the environment. It is subjective, dynamic, self-reflective, and central to our sense of identity. Selective attention focuses conscious awareness on some stimuli, to the exclusion of others.

- Scientists use self-report, physiological, and behavioral measures to operationally define states of consciousness.

- Freud believed that the mind has conscious, preconscious, and unconscious levels. He viewed the unconscious as a reservoir of unacceptable desires and repressed experiences. Cognitive psychologists view the unconscious as an information-processing system.

- Controlled processing typically is required for learning new tasks. Automatic processing makes divided attention possible, enabling us to perform several tasks at once. Research on subliminal perception and other topics suggests that emotional and motivational processes also can operate nonconsciously and influence behavior.

- Many theorists propose that the mind consists of separate but interacting information processing modules. Our subjective experience of "unitary" consciousness arises from the integrated output of these modules.

Circadian Rhythms: Our Daily Biological Clocks

- Circadian rhythms are 24-hour biological cycles that help regulate many bodily processes. The suprachiasmatic nuclei (SCN) are the brain's master circadian clock. Environmental factors, such as the day-night cycle, help to reset our daily clocks to a 24-hour schedule.

- Circadian rhythms influence whether we are a "morning person" or a "night person."

- Seasonal affective disorder (SAD), jet lag, and night shiftwork involve environmental disruptions of circadian rhythms. Treatments for circadian disruptions include controlling exposure to light, oral melatonin, and regulating daily activity schedules.

Sleep and Dreaming

- EEG measurements of brain activity indicate 5 main stages of sleep. Stages 1 and 2 are lighter sleep, and stages 3 and 4 are deeper, slow-wave sleep. High physiological arousal and periods of rapid eye movements characterize the fifth stage, REM sleep. Several brain regions, including the brain stem, regulate sleep.

- The amount we sleep nightly changes as we age. Genetic, psychological, and environmental factors affect our sleep patterns and sleep length.

- Sleep deprivation negatively affects mood, mental performance, and physical performance. The restoration model proposes that we sleep to recover from accumulated physical and mental fatigue. Evolutionary/circadian models state that species evolved unique waking-sleeping cycles that maximized their chances of survival.

- Insomnia is the most common sleep disorder, but less common disorders such as narcolepsy, REM-sleep behavior disorder, and sleep apnea can have extremely serious consequences. Sleepwalking typically occurs during slow-wave sleep, whereas nightmares most often occur during REM sleep. Night terrors create a near-panic state of arousal, typically occur in slow-wave sleep, and are most common among children.

- Dreams occur throughout sleep but are most common during REM periods. Unpleasant dreams are common, and there are gender differences in dream content. Our cultural background, current concerns, and recent events influence what we dream about.

- Freud proposed that dreams fulfill unconscious wishes that show up in disguised form within our dreams. Activation-synthesis theory regards dreaming as the brain's attempt to "fit" a story to random neural activity. Cognitive-process theories emphasize that dreaming and waking thought are produced by the same mental systems.

- Daydreams and nocturnal dreams often share similar themes. People with fantasy-prone personalities have especially vivid daydreams.

Drugs and Altered Consciousness

- Drugs alter consciousness by modifying neurotransmitter activity. Agonists increase such activity, whereas antagonists decrease it.

- Tolerance develops when the body produces compensatory responses to counteract a drug's effects. When drug use is stopped, compensatory responses continue and produce withdrawal symptoms. Substance dependence represents a maladaptive pattern of substance use that causes a person significant distress or substantially impairs that person's life. It can occur with or without physiological dependence.

- Depressants decrease neural activity. The subjective "high" and liveliness associated with low alcohol doses occurs because alcohol depresses the activity of inhibitory brain centers. Drinking contributes to poor decision making.

- Stimulants increase arousal and boost mood by enhancing dopamine and norepinephrine activity. Repeated use depletes these neurotransmitters and can cause a severe depressive "crash" after the drug wears off.

- Opiates increase endorphin activity, producing pain relief and mood changes that may include euphoria. Opiates are important in medicine but are highly addictive.

- Hallucinogens, such as LSD, powerfully distort sensory experience and can blur the line between reality and fantasy. The effects of hallucinogens are always unpredictable.

- THC, the main active ingredient in marijuana, produces relaxation and a sense of well-being at low doses, but can cause anxiety and sensory distortions at higher doses. Marijuana can impair thinking and reflexes, and its smoke contains carcinogens.

- A drug's effect depends on its chemical actions, the physical and social setting, cultural norms, learning, and the user's genetic predispositions, expectations, and personality.

Hypnosis

- Hypnosis involves an increased receptiveness to suggestions. Hypnotic susceptibility scales measure people's responsiveness to hypnosis.

- Hypnotized people subjectively experience their actions to be involuntary, but hypnosis has no unique power to make people behave "against their will." In experiments, hypnotized and nonhypnotized people are equally likely to show striking physiological reactions and perform "amazing" physical feats. Hypnosis increases pain tolerance, but other psychological techniques also can reduce pain.

- Some people can be led to experience hypnotic and posthypnotic amnesia. The use of hypnosis to *improve* memory, as in cases of eyewitness testimony, is controversial. Hypnosis does not consistently improve people's ability to recall information, but it increases the danger that they will develop false memories about events in response to leading questions asked by the hypnotist or examiner.

- Dissociation theories view hypnosis as an altered state of divided consciousness. Hilgard proposes that one stream of consciousness responds to the hypnotist's suggestions, while another stream (the hidden observer) stays in the background and is fully aware of everything going on. Social cognitive role theories state that hypnotic experiences occur because people have strong beliefs and expectations about hypnosis and are highly motivated to enter a hypnotized "role." People's actions are sincere, but not the result of divided consciousness.

KEY TERMS AND CONCEPTS*

activation-synthesis theory (202)

alcohol myopia (209)

alpha waves (191)

amphetamine psychosis (211)

automatic processing (184)

beta waves (191)

blood-brain barrier (205)

circadian rhythms (186)

cognitive-process dream theory (202)

compensatory responses (206)

consciousness (183)

controlled (effortful) processing (184)

delta waves (191)

depressants (208)

dissociation theory (of hypnosis) (220)

divided attention (185)

evolutionary/circadian sleep models (196)

fantasy-prone personalities (204)

hallucinogens (212)

hypnosis (215)

hypnotic susceptibility scale (216)

insomnia (197)

melatonin (186)

narcolepsy (198)

night terrors (199)

opiates (212)

problem-solving dream model (202)

REM sleep (192)

REM sleep behavior disorder (RBD) (198)

restoration model (195)

seasonal affective disorder (SAD) (188)

sleep apnea (199)

slow-wave sleep (191)

social cognitive theory (of hypnosis) (221)

stimulants (211)

substance dependence (207)

suprachiasmatic nuclei (SCN) (186)

THC (tetrahydrocannabinol) (213)

tolerance (206)

wish fulfillment (201)

withdrawal (207)

* Each term has been boldfaced in the text on the page indicated in parentheses.

APPLYING YOUR KNOWLEDGE

These questions allow you to apply your understanding of the material in this chapter.

1. Terry has not thought about her favorite uncle for years, but when a friend asks her about "Uncle Joe," Terry talks happily about the good times she and Uncle Joe had together. According to Freud, prior to meeting her friend, Terry's memories of Uncle Joe were at a _____ level of awareness.
   a) conscious
   b) preconscious
   c) unconscious
   d) fragmented

2. You are driving down the highway, lost in your own thoughts instead of focusing on the road. The fact that you do not crash while doing this best illustrates the adaptive value of
   a) automatic processing.
   b) effortful processing.
   c) selective attention.
   d) daydreaming.

3. Your intense curiosity leads you to volunteer for an experiment in which you live in a special underground apartment for a month. There are no windows, clocks, or other cues by which you can tell the time, and you have only artificial lights. As the days progress, it is most likely that your bedtime naturally
   a) will become later and later each day.
   b) will become earlier and earlier each day.
   c) will remain very close to your normal bedtime.
   d) will become later each day for a week or two, and then rebound back toward your normal bedtime.

4. After flying eastward from North America to Europe, you are feeling badly jet lagged. To speed up your adjustment to the new local time zone, for the first few days you should
   a) avoid going outside at any time.
   b) try to remain outside from sunrise to sunset.
   c) avoid early morning daylight but spend the late afternoon outside.
   d) spend early morning outside and avoid late afternoon daylight.

5. Julius is participating in a sleep experiment. At this moment, the EEG shows that his brain-wave pattern consists almost entirely of delta waves. Therefore it is most likely that Julius is in _____ sleep.
   a) stage 1
   b) stage 2
   c) stage 4
   d) REM

6. Lavonne, a college sophomore, has just gone to sleep and will sleep for about 8 hours. As the hours asleep pass, her
   a) REM periods will become shorter and less frequent.
   b) stage 3 periods will become longer and more frequent.
   c) stage 4 periods eventually will stop occurring.
   d) sleep stages will start to occur in a random order.

7. Brian has sudden and uncontrollable sleep attacks several times a day, and sometimes experiences a loss of muscle tone that causes him to collapse to the ground. It is most likely that Brian
   a) has REM-sleep behavior disorder.
   b) has narcolepsy.
   c) has severe insomnia.
   d) is experiencing free-running circadian rhythms.

8. A heroin addict is about to "shoot up" in an unfamiliar setting. Even though he takes his normal dose, his physiological reaction to the drug will likely be _____ than usual because the setting _____ conditioned compensatory responses.
   a) stronger; increases
   b) stronger; fails to trigger
   c) weaker; increases
   d) weaker; fails to trigger

9. When you have a few drinks of alcohol, this increases the activity of _____ and acts as a central nervous system _____ .
   a) norepinephrine; stimulant
   b) norepinephrine; depressant
   c) GABA; stimulant
   d) GABA; depressant

10. Francine has just been hypnotized. When the hypnotist suggests that her arm is feeling "lighter and lighter . . . lighter than air," Francine's arm starts to rise. According to dissociation theories of hypnosis, this response occurs because Francine
   a) is intentionally faking her behavior to please the hypnotist.
   b) is deeply immersed in the "role" of being hypnotized.
   c) has a fantasy-prone personality.
   d) is in an altered state of consciousness.

Answers

1. b) (page 184); 2. a) (page 184); 3. a) (page 187);
4. d) (page 190); 5. c) (page 191); 6. c) (page 192);
7. b) (page 198); 8. b) (page 207); 9. d) (page 208);
10. d) (page 220).

For additional quizzing and a variety of interactive resources, visit the book's Online Learning Center at www.mhhe.com/passer.

LEARNING AND ADAPTATION: THE ROLE OF EXPERIENCE

A man who carries a cat by the tail learns something
he can learn in no other way.

— Mark Twain

6

CHAPTER OUTLINE

▼▼

Thanks to six sessions of psychotherapy, Carol's life is normal again. She is now free from the intense fear of something most of us take for granted: riding in a car. Carol was severely injured in a car crash and hospitalized for months. A year later, she described to a therapist how the fear began when her husband came to take her home from the hospital:

> As we walked toward the new car he had bought, I began to feel uneasy. I felt nervous all the way home. It started to get worse after that. I found myself avoiding riding in the car, and couldn't drive it at all. I stopped visiting friends and tried to get them to come to our house. . . . After a while, even the sight of a car started to make me nervous. . . . You know, this is the first time I've left the house in about four months.

To help Carol, the therapist used a highly successful procedure based, in part, upon century-old principles of behavior discovered in laboratory investigations of salivating dogs.

▼▼

Outside a Las Vegas casino, a woman volunteers her time soliciting donations for a local charity. Though hot and tired, she remains upbeat and thanks each person who drops money in her collection can. Inside, exhausted and down to his last dollar, a man has been playing the slot machines for 36 hours. A casino guard mutters to a cocktail waitress, "I'll never understand what keeps these guys going."

▼▼

A judge in New York City prohibited two teenage brothers from watching professional wrestling on television because they were becoming too violent. The boys vigorously practiced body slams and choke-holds, repeatedly injuring one another. Their frightened mother reported that her 13-year-old son tried to apply a "sleeper hold" on her as she was cooking in the kitchen. Fortunately, she broke free before losing consciousness. The judge told the mother to prohibit the boys from watching wrestling, or he would have the family's TV set removed and might place the boys in foster homes (*The Sporting News*, August 19, 1985).

Though vastly different, the behaviors in these examples share an important characteristic: They are all learned. Our genetic endowment creates the potential for these behaviors to occur, but we are not biologically programmed to fear cars, solicit donations, pull slot machines, or wrestle people by applying "sleeper holds."

Reflect for a moment on how much of your behavior is learned: telling time, getting dressed, driving, reading, using money, playing sports, and so on. Beyond such skills, learning affects our emotional reactions, perceptions, and physiological responses. Through experience, we learn to think, act, and feel in ways that contribute richly to our individual identity.

Learning is a process by which experience produces a relatively enduring change in an organism's behavior or capabilities. The term *capabilities* highlights a distinction made by many theorists: "knowing how" versus "doing." For example, experience may provide us with immediate knowledge (e.g., the boys "learned" how to apply a choke-hold when they watched TV on Sunday), but in science we must *measure* learning by actual changes in performance (e.g., two days later, they began applying choke-holds to each other).

❯ ADAPTING TO THE ENVIRONMENT

We encounter changing environments from the moment we are born, each with its unique challenges. Some challenges affect survival, such as acquiring food and shelter. Others do not, such as deciding where to go on a date. But no matter the challenge, learning makes it possible for us to adapt to it. In fact, we can view learning as a process of *personal adaptation* to the ever-changing circumstances of our lives.

How Do We Learn? The Search for Mechanisms

For a long time, the study of learning proceeded along two largely separate paths, guided by two different perspectives on behavior: behaviorism and ethology (Bolles & Beecher, 1988). Within psychology, behaviorists focused on *how* organisms learn, examining the processes by which experience influences behavior. Behaviorists assumed that there are laws of learning that apply to virtually all organisms. For example, each species they studied—whether birds, reptiles, rats, monkeys, or humans—responded in predictable ways to patterns of reward or punishment.

Behaviorists treated the organism as a *tabula rasa*, or blank tablet, upon which learning experiences were inscribed. Most of their research was conducted with nonhuman species in controlled laboratory settings. Behaviorists explained learning solely in terms of directly observable events and avoided speculating about an organism's unobservable "mental state."

Why Do We Learn? The Search for Functions

While behaviorism flourished in America, a specialty area called ethology arose in Europe within the discipline of biology (Lorenz, 1937; Tinbergen,1951). *Ethology* focused on animal behavior within the natural environment. Ethologists viewed the organism as anything but a blank tablet, arguing that because of evolution every species comes into the world biologically prepared to act in certain ways. They focused on the *functions* of behavior, particularly its **adaptive significance:** How does a behavior influence an organism's chances of survival and reproduction in its natural environment?

Consider how newly hatched herring gulls "beg" for food by pecking at a red mark on their parents' bills. Parents respond by regurgitating food, which the chick ingests. Seeing the red mark and long shape of the parent's bill automatically triggers the chick's pecking. This behavior is so strongly "prewired" that chicks will peck just as much at long inanimate models or objects with red dots or stripes (Figure 6.1). Ethologists call this instinctive behavior a **fixed action pattern:** an unlearned response automatically triggered by a particular stimulus.

As ethological research grew, two things soon became clear. First, some fixed action patterns could be modified by experience. Unlike newly hatched chicks, older chicks have learned what an adult gull looks like and will not peck at inanimate objects unless they resemble the head of an adult (Hailman, 1967). Second, in many cases what appeared to be "instinctive" behavior actually involved learning. Ethologists noted striking differences among species, not so much in how they learned, but in what they learned in order to survive.

❯ 1. Historically, how have behaviorists and ethologists differed in their study of learning?

❯ 2. Explain the concept of adaptive significance.

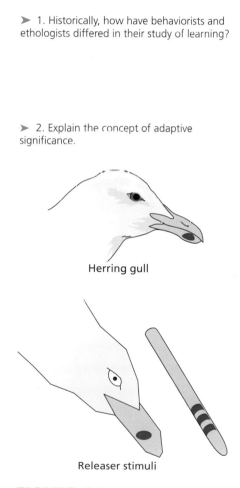

Herring gull

Releaser stimuli

FIGURE 6.1 A newborn herring gull chick will peck most frequently at objects that are long and have red markings, even if they are inanimate models or do not look like an adult gull. This fixed action pattern is present from birth and does not require learning. The stimuli that trigger a fixed action pattern are called "releaser stimuli." Based on Hailman, 1967.

Consider the indigo bunting, a beautiful songbird that migrates during autumn nights from eastern North America to Central America. It navigates by flying "away from" the North Star, which by virtue of being directly over the North Pole, is the only star in the Northern Hemisphere that maintains a fixed compass position as the earth rotates on its axis. In spring the bunting migrates north at night by flying "toward" the North Star. Were the bird to navigate by any other star, it would fly increasingly off course because all other stars move across the night sky.

Navigating by the North Star would seem to be a fixed action pattern, as if birds instinctively know where "north" is. To test this idea, Stephen Emlen (1975) raised indigo buntings in a planetarium with either a true sky (with the North Star as the stationary star) or a false sky (in which a star in a different portion of the sky was the only one that remained stationary). In the fall, the birds became restless in their cages because it was time to migrate. As expected, the buntings raised with a true sky moved away from the North Star. But the other group moved away from the "false" stationary star, indicating that environmental changes could modify the bunting's navigational behavior. Emlen concluded that the bunting is genetically prewired to navigate by a fixed star, but it has to learn which specific star is stationary through observation and experience.

Crossroads of Learning: Biology, Cognition, and Culture

➤ 3. What role does the environment play in *personal* and *species* adaptation?

The separate paths of behaviorism and ethology have increasingly converged in recent decades, reminding us that the environment shapes behavior in two fundamental ways: through *personal adaptation* and through *species adaptation*. Personal adaptation occurs through the laws of learning that the behaviorists examined, and it results from our interactions with immediate and past environments (Dukas, 1998; Hollis, 1997). When you drive or go out on a date, your behavior is influenced by the immediate environment (traffic, your date's smiles) and by capabilities you have acquired through experience (driving skills and social skills).

The environment also plays a role in species adaptation. Through the process of evolution, environmental conditions faced by each species help shape its biology. This does not occur directly—learning, for example, does *not* modify an organism's genes—and therefore learned behaviors are not passed down genetically from one generation to the next. But through natural selection, genetically based features that enhance a species' ability to adapt to the environment, and thus to survive and reproduce, are more likely to be passed on to the next generation. Eventually, as characteristics influenced by those genes become more common, they become a part of a species' very "nature."

Theorists propose that in response to environmental demands faced by our ancestors over millions of years, the human brain acquired the capacity to perform psychological functions that have adaptive value and enable us to learn (Cosmides & Tooby, 1995; Flinn, 1997). In essence, we have become prewired to learn. Of course, to varying degrees, so have other species. Because all organisms face some common adaptive challenges, we might expect some similarity in their "library" of learning mechanisms (Roitblat & von Ferson, 1992). What are these common adaptive challenges? Every organism's environment is full of events, and the organism must learn

- which events are, or are not, important to its survival and well-being;
- which stimuli signal that an important event is about to occur; and
- whether its responses will produce positive or negative consequences.

As we will see, each learning mechanism examined in this chapter helps us respond to one or more of these adaptive challenges.

The resurgence of the *cognitive perspective* and emergence of *cross-cultural psychology* also have expanded our understanding of learning. Cognitive psychologists have continued to challenge the behaviorist assumption that learning does not involve mental processes (Bandura, 1965; Dickinson, 1997). And as we have seen and will continue to explore in upcoming chapters, cross-cultural research highlights the vast impact of culture on what we learn—from social customs (*norms*) and beliefs to our most basic perceptions of the world and ourselves (Figure 6.2; Super & Harkness, 1997). This is not surprising, given that learning represents adaptation to the environment, and culture is the human-made part of our environment (Herskovits, 1948). Yet the learning mechanisms that foster this adaptation are universal among humans and, in some cases, occur across countless species.

Habituation

Imagine that you are sitting alone in a quiet laboratory room. Suddenly, a loud sound occurs and you instantly become startled. Your body jerks slightly, you become aroused, and you look toward the source of the sound. Over time, as the sound occurs again and again, your startle response diminishes and eventually you ignore it. Similarly, studying at the library you initially may be distracted by a student who is coughing frequently or tapping a pen. As time passes, you no longer notice it.

Habituation is a decrease in the strength of response to a repeated stimulus. It may be the simplest form of learning and occurs across species ranging from humans to dragonflies and sea snails (Carew & Kandel, 1973; Manning, 1967). Touch the skin of a sea snail in a certain location, and it will reflexively contract its gill. With repeated touches, this response habituates. Habituation serves a key adaptive function. If an organism responded to every stimulus in its environment, it would rapidly become overwhelmed and exhausted. By learning not to respond to uneventful familiar stimuli, organisms conserve energy and can attend to other stimuli that are important. As Figure 6.3 explains, habituation also plays an important role in enabling scientists to study behavior.

❭ CLASSICAL CONDITIONING: ASSOCIATING ONE STIMULUS WITH ANOTHER

Life is full of interesting associations. Do you ever hear songs on the radio, or find yourself in places, that instantly make you feel good because they're connected to special times you've had? When you smell the aroma of popcorn or freshly baked cookies, does it make your mouth water or stomach growl? These examples illustrate a learning process called **classical conditioning,** in which an organism learns to associate two stimuli (e.g., a song and a pleasant event), such that one stimulus (the song) comes to produce a response (feeling happy) that originally was produced only by the other stimulus (the pleasurable event).

Like habituation, classical conditioning is a basic form of learning that occurs in mammals, birds, reptiles, fish, and even sea snails (Kandel & Hawkins, 1992). But unlike habituation, classical conditioning involves *learning an association* between stimuli. Its discovery dates back to the late 1800s and an odd twist of fate.

Pavlov's Pioneering Research

In the 1860s, Ivan Pavlov was studying theology in a Russian seminary and preparing for the priesthood when his career plans unexpectedly changed. A new government policy allowed the translation of Western scientific publications into Russian. Before long, Pavlov read Darwin's theory of evolution and

FIGURE 6.2 People in different cultures learn different behaviors in order to adapt to their environment. The skills that most urbanized people have learned to acquire food—navigating around a supermarket and using money—would have little adaptive value in some cultures.

➤ 4. What is habituation, and what is its adaptive significance?

March 5, 1984: After several months, I now feel that these strange little rodents have finally accepted me as one of their own.

FIGURE 6.3 Before collecting data, scientists often allow the people or animals that they are studying to habituate to the observer's presence.

(a)   (b)

FIGURE 6.4 (a) Ivan Pavlov (the man with the white beard) is shown here with colleagues and one of his canine subjects. (b) In his early research, Pavlov measured salivation using a simple device similar to the one shown here. In later research, a collection tube was inserted directly into the salivary gland.

other works, sparking a strong interest in the sciences (Windholz, 1997). Pavlov became a renowned physiologist, conducting research on digestion in dogs that won him the Nobel Prize in 1904.

To study digestion, Pavlov presented various types of food to dogs and measured their natural salivary response (Figure 6.4). But as often occurs in science, Pavlov was about to make an accidental but important discovery through astute observation. He noticed that with repeated testing, the dogs began to salivate *before* the food was presented, such as when they heard the footsteps of the approaching experimenter.

Further study confirmed Pavlov's observation. Dogs have a natural reflex to salivate to food, but not to tones. Yet when a tone or other stimulus that ordinarily did not cause salivation was presented just before food powder was squirted directly into a dog's mouth, the sound of the tone alone soon made the dog salivate. Pavlov's (1923/1928) research team rigorously studied this process for decades, and this type of learning by association came to be called *classical* or *Pavlovian* conditioning. Many psychologists regard Pavlov's discovery as "among the most important in the history of psychology" (Dewsbury, 1997). But why all the fuss about dogs salivating to tones?

This question raises a widely misunderstood point about basic scientific research. As noted in Chapter 2, *what is paramount is the underlying principle being demonstrated, not the specific findings.* Even Pavlov (1897/1902) viewed the salivary glands as relatively insignificant organs, but he recognized his discovery. Here was a basic learning process that performs a key adaptive function; classical conditioning alerts organisms to stimuli that signal the impending arrival of an important event. And, Pavlov noted, if salivation could be conditioned, so might other bodily processes, including those affecting susceptibility to disease and mental disorders.

Basic Principles

What factors influence the acquisition and persistence of conditioned responses? Let us examine some basic principles of conditioning.

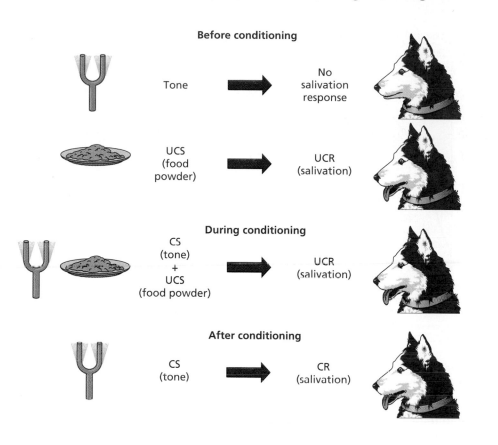

Before conditioning

Tone ➡ No salivation response

UCS (food powder) ➡ UCR (salivation)

During conditioning

CS (tone) + UCS (food powder) ➡ UCR (salivation)

After conditioning

CS (tone) ➡ CR (salivation)

FIGURE 6.5 In classical conditioning, after a neutral stimulus such as a tone is repeatedly associated with food (unconditioned stimulus), the tone becomes capable of eliciting a salivation response.

Acquisition

Acquisition refers to the period during which a response is being learned. Suppose we wish to condition a dog to salivate to a tone. Sounding the tone initially may cause the dog to perk up its ears and stare at us oddly, but not to salivate. At this time, the tone is a *neutral stimulus* because it does not elicit (i.e., trigger) the salivation response (Figure 6.5). Now if we place food in the dog's mouth, the dog will salivate. This salivation response to food is reflexive—it's what dogs do by nature. Because no learning is required for the food to produce salivation, the food is called an **unconditioned stimulus (UCS)** and salivation is an **unconditioned response (UCR).** Next the tone and the food are paired—each pairing is called a *learning trial*—and the dog salivates. After several learning trials, if the tone is presented by itself, the dog salivates even though there is no food. Through association, the tone has become a **conditioned stimulus (CS)** and salivation has become a **conditioned response (CR).**

Notice that we have two terms for salivation: UCR and CR. When the dog salivates to food, this UCR is a *natural, unlearned (unconditioned) reflex.* But when it salivates to a tone, this CR represents a *learned (conditioned) response.*

During acquisition, a CS typically must be paired multiple times with a UCS to establish a strong CR (Figure 6.6). Pavlov also found that a tone became a CS more rapidly when it was followed by greater amounts of food. Indeed, when the UCS is intense and aversive—such as an electric shock or a traumatic event—conditioning may require only one CS-UCS pairing (Richard et al., 2000; Mahoney & Ayres, 1976). Carol's car phobia illustrates

➤ 5. How do you create a conditioned salivation response in a dog?

➤ 6. Under what circumstances are CRs typically acquired most quickly?

FIGURE 6.6 The strength of the CR (salivation) increases during the acquisition phase as the CS (tone) and the UCS (food) are paired on each trial. During the extinction phase, only the CS is presented, and the strength of the CR decreases and finally disappears. After a rest period following extinction, presentation of the CS elicits a weaker CR (spontaneous recovery) that extinguishes more quickly than before.

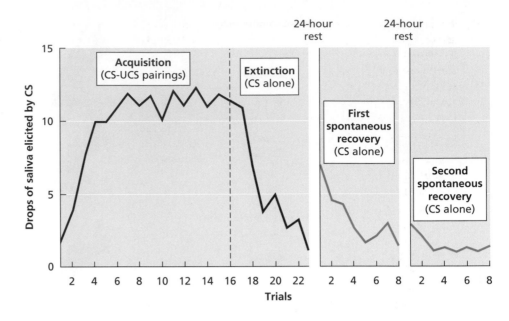

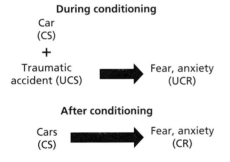

FIGURE 6.7 It is likely that Carol's phobia of cars was acquired through classical conditioning.

➤ 7. Explain the key factor in producing extinction of a CR.

this *one-trial (single-trial) learning.* As she explains to the therapist, her automobile accident was very traumatic:

> My car went out of control. It crashed into a light pole, rolled over, and began to burn. I . . . couldn't get out . . . I'm sorry, doctor, but even thinking about it is horrible. I had a broken pelvis and third-degree burns over half my body.

In Carol's example, a stimulus (riding in or seeing a car) became a CS after only one pairing with an intense UCS (an extremely painful crash). Fear was the UCR, and it became a CR triggered by the sight of cars (Figure 6.7).

The sequence and time interval of the CS—UCS pairing also affect conditioning. Learning usually occurs most quickly with *forward short-delay pairing:* The CS (tone) appears first and is still present when the UCS (food) appears. In *forward trace pairing,* the tone would come on and off, and afterward the food would be presented. In forward pairing, it is often optimal for the CS to appear no more than two or three seconds before the UCS (Klein & Mowrer, 1989). Forward pairing has adaptive value because the CS signals the impending arrival of the UCS. Typically, presenting the CS and UCS at the same time (*simultaneous pairing*) produces less rapid conditioning, and learning is slowest when the CS is presented after the UCS (*backward pairing*).

To summarize, classical conditioning usually is strongest when there are repeated CS-UCS pairings, the UCS is more intense, the sequence involves forward pairing, and the time interval between the CS and UCS is short.

Extinction and Spontaneous Recovery

If the function of classical conditioning is to help organisms adapt to their environment, there must be a way of eliminating the CR when it is no longer appropriate. Fortunately, there is. If the CS is presented repeatedly in the absence of the UCS, the CR weakens and eventually disappears. This process is called **extinction,** and each presentation of the CS without the UCS is called an *extinction trial.* When Pavlov repeatedly presented the tone without the food, the dogs eventually stopped salivating to the tone (Figure 6.6). Occasional re-pairings of the CS (e.g., tone) and the UCS (e.g., food) usually are required to maintain a CR.

In some situations, a CR seems to persist for a long time without such CS-UCS "booster" sessions (Edwards, 1962). For example, Carol's fear of cars persisted for months despite the fact she was in no further crashes, and may have lasted permanently had she not sought therapy. We cannot know for sure why her fear failed to extinguish, but a strong possibility is that her fear was not exposed to sufficient extinction trials. If Carol avoided cars after her accident, there was little opportunity for the CS (being in a car) to occur without the presence of the UCS (an accident). In short, the *key ingredient to extinction is not the mere passage of time, but repeated presentation of the CS without the UCS.* Without exposure to the CS, the CR will be difficult to extinguish.

Even when a CR extinguishes, this does not mean that all traces of it are erased. Suppose we condition a dog to salivate to a tone. Then we repeatedly present the tone without food, and the dog eventually stops salivating to the tone. Later, if we present the tone alone, the dog may salivate once again. This is called **spontaneous recovery,** which is defined as the reappearance of a previously extinguished CR after a rest period, and without new learning trials. As Figure 6.6 shows, the spontaneously recovered CR usually is weaker than the initial CR and extinguishes more rapidly in the absence of the UCS.

Generalization and Discrimination

Thus far we have explained Carol's car phobia as a case of one-trial conditioning in which being in a car was paired with a traumatic experience. But why would Carol fear other cars when it was her old car—now long gone—that was in the accident?

Pavlov found that once a CR is acquired, the organism often responds not only to the original CS, but also to stimuli that are similar to it. The greater the stimulus similarity, the greater the chance that a CR will occur. A dog that salivates to a medium-pitched tone is more likely to salivate to a new tone slightly different in pitch, than to a low- or high-pitched tone. Learning theorists call this **stimulus generalization:** Stimuli similar to the initial CS elicit a CR (Figure 6.8).

Stimulus generalization serves critical adaptive functions. An animal that ignores the sound of rustling bushes and then is attacked by a hidden predator will become alarmed by the sound of a rustling bush in the future (assuming it escapes). If stimulus generalization did not occur, then the next time the animal hears rustling it would become alarmed only if the sound was identical to that preceding the earlier attack. This has little value to the animal's survival. Through stimulus generalization, the animal develops an alarm response to a range of rustling sounds. Some will be false alarms, but safe is better than sorry.

Unfortunately, maladaptive responses can occur when generalization spreads too far. The car involved in Carol's crash was gone, but after leaving the hospital her fear immediately generalized to their new car. Over time, stimulus generalization continued, though the fear was weaker:

Carol: After a while, even the sight of a car started to make me nervous.
Therapist: As nervous as riding in one?
Carol: No, but still nervous. It's so stupid. I'd even turn off the TV during scenes involving car crashes.

To prevent stimulus generalization from running amok, organisms must be able to *discriminate* (i.e., detect) differences among stimuli. An animal that becomes alarmed at every sound it hears would exhaust itself from stress. It must learn to distinguish irrelevant sounds from those that may signal danger. In classical conditioning, **discrimination** is demonstrated when a CR (such as an alarm reaction) occurs to one stimulus (a sound) but not to others. Carol's fear of cars was widespread, but it did not occur when she saw bicycles, trains, or airplanes.

As another example, when my mother was a girl a large, rabid dog bit her several times. From that painful moment on, she was extremely afraid of dogs. Many years later, when my brother wanted a dog, my mother would have none of it. But he pleaded endlessly. How could we satisfy my brother's wish, yet not

> 8. Explain the adaptive significance of stimulus generalization and discrimination.

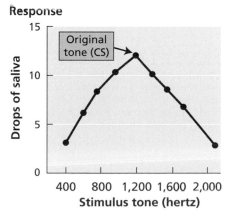

FIGURE 6.8 A stimulus generalization curve. An animal will salivate most strongly to the CS that was originally paired with the UCS. Progressively weaker conditioned responses occur as stimuli become less similar to the CS, as seen here with tones of lower or higher frequencies (pitch).

trigger my mother's fear? The solution was to get a dog as dissimilar as possible to the large dog that bit her, in hopes that my mother's fear would display stimulus discrimination. So we adopted a tiny Chihuahua puppy—and the plan was half-successful. My mother was not afraid, and adored the dog. But my brother's fondness for big dogs failed to generalize to Chihuahuas, and he was repeatedly observed muttering something like "yippity oversized rat."

Higher-Order Conditioning

Imagine that we have exposed a dog to repeated tone-food pairings, and the tone is now a well-established CS that elicits a strong salivation response. Next, suppose that we present a neutral stimulus, such as a black square, and the dog does not salivate. Now we present the black square just prior to sounding the tone, but do not present any food. After repeated square-tone pairings, the square will become a CS and elicit salivation by itself (Figure 6.9). This process, discovered by Pavlov, is called **higher-order conditioning:** a neutral stimulus becomes a CS after being paired with an already established CS. Typically, a higher-order CS produces a CR that is weaker and extinguishes more rapidly than the original CR. The dog will salivate less to the black square than to the tone, and its response to the square will extinguish sooner.

Higher-order conditioning greatly expands the influence of conditioned stimuli and can affect what we come to value, like, fear, or dislike (Gerwitz & Davis, 1998; Mowrer et al., 1988). For example, political candidates try to get us to like them by associating themselves with patriotic symbols, cuddly babies, admired athletes and civic leaders, and other conditioned stimuli that already trigger positive emotional reactions among voters.

Applications of Classical Conditioning

Pavlov's belief that salivation was merely the tip of the classical conditioning iceberg has proven correct. Conditioning principles discovered in laboratory research—much of it with nonhuman species—help us understand diverse human behaviors and problems.

Acquiring and Overcoming Fear

Pavlov's discoveries enabled early American behaviorists to challenge Freud's psychoanalytic view of the causes of anxiety disorders, such as phobias. To explain Carol's car phobia (back then, it might have been a horse-and-buggy phobia), no Freudian assumptions about hidden unconscious conflicts or repressed traumas are needed. Instead, the behaviorist view is that cars have become a fear-triggering CS due to one-trial pairing with the UCS (crash) and stimulus generalization.

Does this explanation seem reasonable? It may, but it suffers from a serious limitation: Almost any explanation can seem plausible when it is provided *after* some event occurs. So behaviorists John B. Watson and Rosalie Rayner (1920) set out to obtain stronger evidence that fear could be conditioned. They studied an 11-month-old infant named Albert. One day, as Albert played in a hospital room, Watson and Rayner showed him a white rat. Albert displayed no sign of fear. Later, knowing that Albert *was* afraid of loud noises, they hit a steel bar with a hammer, making a loud noise as they showed Albert the rat. The noise scared Albert and made him cry. After several rat-noise pairings, the sight of the white rat alone made Albert cry.

To examine stimulus discrimination and generalization, Watson and Rayner exposed Albert to other test stimuli several days later. Albert displayed no fear when shown colored blocks, but furry white or gray objects, such as a rabbit and a bearded Santa Claus mask, made him cry (Figure 6.10). By the time Albert's mother took him from the hospital, he had not been exposed to any treatment designed to extinguish his fear. Unfortunately, we do not know what became of Albert after that.

▶ 9. Explain the process of higher-order conditioning.

1. Before higher-order conditioning

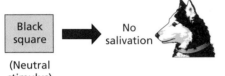

Black square → No salivation

(Neutral stimulus)

2. During higher-order conditioning

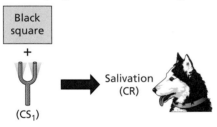

Black square

+

(CS₁) → Salivation (CR)

3. After higher-order conditioning

Black square (CS₂) → Salivation (CR)

FIGURE 6.9 Once a tone has become a conditioned stimulus that triggers salivation, we can now use it to condition a salivation response to a new neutral stimulus—a black square. The tone is the CS₁. The black square becomes the CS₂.

▶ 10. How does classical conditioning explain fear acquisition?

(Had ethics review boards been in existence in the 1920s—they were not—would you have approved this study, and if so, under what conditions or precautions?)

Two other sources of evidence suggest that at least some fears are conditioned. Laboratory experiments convincingly show that animals become afraid of neutral stimuli that are paired with electric shock (Ayres, 1998; Monti & Smith, 1976). In humans, behavioral treatments partially based on classical conditioning principles are among the most effective psychotherapies for phobias (Wolpe, 1997). The key assumption is that if phobias are learned, they can be "unlearned."

In 1924, psychologist Mary Cover Jones successfully treated a boy named Peter, who had a strong fear of rabbits. Jones, who acknowledged Watson and Rayner's work, gradually extinguished Peter's fear using the procedure shown in Table 6.1. Her approach was a forerunner of current behavior therapies, discussed in Chapter 15. In a nutshell, they are called **exposure therapies** because their basic goal is to expose the phobic patient to the feared stimulus (CS) without any UCS, allowing extinction to occur.

Mental imagery, real-life situations, or both can be used to present the phobic stimulus. In one approach, called *systematic desensitization*, the patient learns muscular relaxation techniques and then is gradually exposed to the fear-provoking stimulus (Wolpe, 1958, 1997). Another approach, sometimes called *flooding*, immediately exposes the person to the phobic stimulus (Spiegler & Guevremont, 1998; Nesbitt, 1973). In Carol's case, her therapist extinguished the car phobia in six sessions of flooding. He asked her to imagine vivid scenes in which she drove in freeway traffic and traveled at high speeds on narrow mountain roads. As Carol's initially strong anxiety decreased, she was able to sit in her car and eventually drive it. Exposure therapies are highly effective and represent one of behaviorism's important applied legacies.

Conditioned Attraction and Aversion

Much of what attracts and pleasurably arouses us is influenced by classical conditioning. Consider sexual arousal. The comment, "It really turns me on when you wear that," reflects how a clothing outfit or scent of a partner's cologne can become a conditioned stimulus for arousal. Experiments show that pairing a neutral odor with pleasing physical massage increases people's attraction to that smell (Baeyens et al., 1996), and that people become more sexually aroused to various stimuli—including a photograph of knee-high boots—after those CSs have been paired with sexually arousing UCSs (Rachman & Hodgson, 1968).

FIGURE 6.10 John Watson and Rosalie Rayner examine how little Albert reacts to a furry mask.

➤ 11. How is classical conditioning used in society to increase and decrease our arousal/attraction to stimuli?

TABLE 6.1	USING EXPOSURE TRAINING TO REDUCE FEAR

This table lists 10 of the 17 steps used by Mary Cover Jones to eliminate Peter's fear of rabbits.

Step No.	Peter's Progress
1	Rabbit anywhere in room triggers fear
2	Rabbit 12 feet away tolerated.
4	Rabbit 3 feet away tolerated
5	Rabbit close in cage tolerated
6	Rabbit free in room tolerated
8	Rabbit touched when free in room
10	Rabbit allowed on tray of high chair
12	Holds rabbit on lap
16	Fondles rabbit affectionately
17	Lets rabbit nibble his fingers

Adapted from Jones (1924).

FIGURE 6.11 Advertisers attempt to classically condition favorable consumer attitudes to products by associating products with other positive stimuli, such as physically attractive models.

➤ 12. What is ANV and how does it develop?

➤ 13. How can classical conditioning boost immune system functioning?

Experiments with fish, birds, and rats confirm that originally neutral stimuli can trigger sexual arousal after they have been paired with a naturally arousing UCS (Domjan et al., 1989; Hollis, 1997).

Classical conditioning also can decrease our arousal and attraction to stimuli. This principle is used in **aversion therapy,** which attempts to condition an aversion (a repulsion) to a stimulus that triggers unwanted behavior by pairing it with a noxious UCS. To treat pedophiles (child molesters), pictures of children are paired with strong electric shock (Sandler, 1986). To reduce an alcoholic's attraction to alcohol, the patient is given a drug that induces severe nausea when alcohol is consumed (Nathan, 1985). Aversion therapies yield mixed results, often producing short-term changes that extinguish over time.

Conditioned attraction and aversion also play a role in attitude formation (Olson & Zanna, 1991). Neutral stimuli acquire favorable or unfavorable meaning (they become attractive or unattractive) by being paired with other stimuli that already elicit positive or negative attitudes. Advertising executives are keenly aware of classical conditioning's power. They carefully link products to cute animals, attractive and famous people, humor, "fuzzy-warm" family images, and most of all, to pleasurable interactions with the opposite sex (Figure 6.11). Marketing experiments show that this approach creates favorable attitudes toward novel products (Grossman & Till, 1998; Kim et al., 1998).

Conditioning also can create unfavorable attitudes toward a CS. This is accomplished by pairing the CS with a negative or unpleasant UCS. At times, this principle can have beneficial effects. In a study with fourth- and ninth-grade schoolchildren, Laura Moore and her colleagues at Bucknell University (1982) paired the concepts of smoking, drinking, and drug use with words having negative connotations. Experimental group children exposed to the pairings developed more negative attitudes toward these activities than did control group children who were not exposed.

Beyond influencing fear, attraction, and aversion, classical conditioning also can affect our physical health. We examine this issue in our *Psychological Frontiers* feature.

PSYCHOLOGICAL FRONTIERS

Can Classical Conditioning Make Us Sick—And Healthy Again?

The environment affects our health in many ways. We catch the flu, sneeze from pollen, and become ill from eating tainted food. Our bodily systems also can "learn" to respond in ways that positively or negatively affect our physical health.

▶ Improving the Well-Being of Cancer Patients

Chemotherapy and radiation therapy save countless lives in the fight against cancer, but their toxic effects often induce nausea and vomiting after treatment sessions. About 20 to 50 percent of patients also develop **anticipatory nausea and vomiting (ANV):** They become nauseous and may vomit anywhere from minutes to hours *before* therapy (Morrow et al., 1998; Tyc et al., 1997).

ANV is a classically conditioned response (Tyc et al., 1997). Initially neutral stimuli, such as the sight of hypodermic needles or the treatment room, are associated with the "sickness" produced by the treatment (the UCS), and become CSs that trigger nausea and vomiting (CRs). Claire, a 21-year-old undergoing chemotherapy for leukemia, experienced a progression of ANV symptoms. First, stimuli immediately associated with her treatment—such as the poke of the needle—triggered nausea and gagging. Later on, just entering the hospital and then the mere sight of the hospital began to trigger her nausea.

ANV symptoms often respond poorly to antinausea drugs (Morrow et al., 1998). But like conditioned fear, if

–Continued

ANV is learned, then patients should be able to unlearn it. Psychological treatments have helped patients like Claire reduce ANV (Hailey & White, 1983; King, 1997). The patient may first be taught how to physically relax, and then the conditioned stimuli that trigger ANV are paired with relaxation and pleasant mental imagery.

▶ Training the Immune System

In 1974, University of Rochester psychologist Robert Ader made a landmark discovery that the immune system can be classically conditioned. Ader was studying how rats learned taste aversions. If you ever have been sick to your stomach after eating a certain food, and then developed an aversion to that food, you've had firsthand experience with this topic. Ader's rats drank sweetened water, and were later injected with a nausea-inducing drug that made them ill. Often illustrating one-trial learning, the rats quickly learned the taste-illness association, and subsequently avoided the sweetened water. To examine whether the aversion would extinguish, Ader restricted the rats to drinking sweet water (without further drug injections). To his surprise, many rats became sick and died. The breakthrough came when Ader learned that the drug he used to create nausea also suppressed the immune system. Ader realized that by pairing sweet water with this drug, the taste had acquired the drug's ability to suppress immune functions, making the animals more susceptible to disease and death.

Further experiments confirmed this finding (Ader & Cohen, 1990). In one study, rats in an experimental group drank sweetened water paired with an injection of an immune suppressant drug, while placebo control rats drank sweetened water paired with an injection of saline solution (McCoy et al., 1986). Later all the rats were exposed to an antigen (a foreign substance) designed to trigger an immune response. The rats then drank sweetened water for the next six days and their immune response to the antigen was measured. The results were clear. The experimental group produced fewer antibodies (specialized proteins) to combat the antigen, indicating a weaker immune response (Figure 6.12).

Research suggests that classical conditioning also can increase immune functioning (DeMoranville et al., 2000). At the University of Trier in Germany, Angelika Buske-Kirschbaum and her colleagues (1992; 1994) gave sweet sherbet to experimental group volunteers, along with an injection of epinephrine (i.e., adrenaline), which increases the activity of immune system cells that attack tumors. Compared with several control groups, people receiving the sherbet-epinephrine pairings subsequently reacted to the sherbet with a stronger immune response.

Can these findings be applied to alter immune functioning in people fighting cancer, AIDS, and other diseases? One of Ader's experiments (Ader & Cohen's, 1982) involved

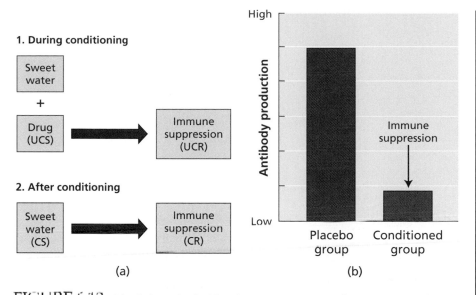

FIGURE 6.12 After being paired with an immune-suppressant drug, sweet water became a CS that triggered a reduced immune response.

Data in (b) from McCoy et al., 1986.

rats who had a normally fatal disease that caused their immune system to attack their own bodies. By classically conditioning a sweet taste (CS) to trigger immune suppression (CR), the researchers boosted the effectiveness of an immune suppressant drug and reduced the rats' mortality rate. A decade later, this procedure was used with an 11-year-old-girl who had a similar life-threatening disease in which her immune system was overactive. To reduce immune system activity, cod liver oil (a distinct taste!) was paired with an immune suppressant drug. Then over the next 12 months, she was given 6 treatments with the immune suppressant drug interspersed with 6 treatments using only cod liver oil (rather than the normal 12 drug treatments). The patient improved and was still doing well after a 5-year follow-up (Olness & Ader, 1992).

▶ Conditioned Allergic and Asthmatic Reactions

Allergic responses occur when the immune system overreacts and releases too many antibodies to combat pollen, dust, or other foreign substances (called *allergens*). When a neutral stimulus (such as a distinct odor) is repeatedly paired with a natural allergen (the UCS), it may become a CS that triggers an allergic CR (Gauci et al., 1994; Russell, 1984). Asthma patients' wheezing attacks also can be triggered by conditioned stimuli, in some cases remarkably so.

> Patient L had told us that she got an asthmatic attack from looking at a goldfish . . . a goldfish in a bowl was brought into the room. . . . Under our eyes she developed a severe asthmatic attack with loud wheezing. . . . During the next experiment the goldfish was replaced by a plastic toy fish which was easily recognized as such . . . but a fierce attack resulted. (Dekker and Groen, 1956, p. 62)

Conditioned allergic reactions can be reduced through extinction trials in which the CS is presented without the UCS (Dark et al., 1987; Khan & Olson, 1977). But at times, the most direct approach may simply be to avoid the goldfish (or other CS)!

❯ OPERANT CONDITIONING: LEARNING THROUGH CONSEQUENCES

For all its power to affect our emotions, attitudes, physiology, and health, classical conditioning cannot explain how a dog learns to sit upon command. Nor can it account for how we learn to drive cars, use computers, make friends, or be good citizens. Unlike salivating to a tone, these are not *elicited responses* automatically triggered by some stimulus. Rather, they are *emitted (voluntary) responses,* and they are learned in a different way.

Thorndike's Law of Effect

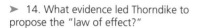 14. What evidence led Thorndike to propose the "law of effect?"

While Pavlov was studying classical conditioning, American psychology student Edward L. Thorndike (1898) was exploring how animals learn to solve problems. He built a special cage, called a *puzzle box,* that could be opened from the inside by pulling a string or stepping on a lever (Figure 6.13). Thorndike placed a hungry animal, such as a cat, inside the box. Food was put outside, and to get it the animal had to learn how to open the box. The cat scratched and pushed the bars, paced, and tried to dig through the floor. By chance, it eventually stepped on the lever, opening the door. Performance slowly improved with repeated trials, and over time the cat learned to press the lever soon after the door was shut.

Because performance improved slowly, Thorndike concluded that the animals did not attain "insight" into the solution. Rather, with trial-and-error, they gradually eliminated responses that failed to open the door, and became more likely to perform actions that worked. Thorndike (1911) called this process *instrumental learning* because an organism's behavior is instrumental in bringing about certain outcomes. He also proposed the **law of effect,** which stated that in a given situation, a response followed by a "satisfying" consequence will become more likely to occur, and a response followed by an unsatisfying outcome will become less likely to occur. The law of effect became the foundation for the school of behaviorism.

Skinner's Analysis of Operant Conditioning

Harvard psychologist B. F. Skinner was America's leading proponent of behaviorism throughout most of the 20th century. Skinner coined the term *operant behavior,* meaning that an organism *operates* on its environment in some way; it emits responses that produce certain consequences. **Operant conditioning** (akin to Thorndike's instrumental learning) is a type of learning in which behavior is influenced by its consequences (Skinner, 1938, 1953). Responses that produce favorable consequences tend to be repeated, whereas responses that produce unfavorable consequences become less likely to occur.

Following Darwin's notion of natural selection, which applies to species adaptation, Skinner viewed operant conditioning as a type of "natural selection" that facilitates an organism's *personal adaptation* to the environment. Through operant conditioning, organisms generally learn to increase behaviors that benefit them and reduce behaviors that harm them.

Skinner designed a special chamber, called a **Skinner box,** to study operant conditioning experimentally. A lever on one wall is positioned above a small cup, and a food pellet automatically drops into the cup whenever a rat presses the lever (Figure 6.14). A hungry rat is put into the chamber and, as it moves about, it accidentally presses the lever. A food pellet clinks into the cup and the rat eats it quickly. We record the rat's behavior on a *cumulative recorder,* and find that it presses the bar more and more frequently over time.

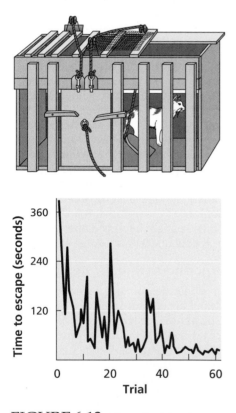

FIGURE 6.13 Through trial and error, cats eventually learned to open Thorndike's puzzle boxes in order to obtain food.
After Thorndike, 1898, 1911.

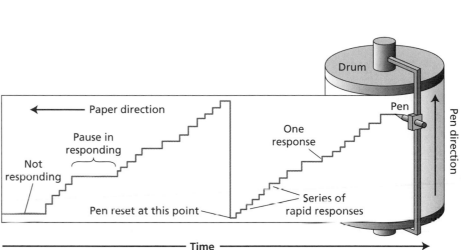

FIGURE 6.14 With B. F. Skinner watching, a rat raises up and presses a lever in an operant experimental chamber (Skinner box). This turns on a light inside the chamber (notice the lever just below and to the right of the light). A food reinforcer is automatically delivered by the apparatus to the left of the box, and the rat's performance is displayed on a cumulative recorder.

Skinner identified several important types of consequences. For now, we focus on two: reinforcement and punishment. With **reinforcement,** a response is *strengthened* by an outcome that follows it. Typically, "strengthened" is operationally defined as an increase in the frequency of a response. The outcome (a stimulus or event) that increases the frequency of a response is a called a *reinforcer.* Food pellets are reinforcers because they increase the rat's frequency of lever pressing. Once a response becomes established, reinforcers maintain it: The rat keeps pressing the lever because it continues to receive food.

Punishment is the opposite of reinforcement; it occurs when a response is *weakened* by outcomes that follow it. Take our lever-pressing rat. Suppose we change things so that pressing the lever delivers a one-second electric shock, rather than food. If lever-pressing decreases (which it will), then the electric shock represents a *punisher:* a consequence that weakens the behavior. Notice that reinforcers and punishers are defined in terms of their observable effects on behavior. If the food doesn't increase lever pressing, then for this particular rat it is not a reinforcer.

ABCs of Operant Conditioning

Skinner's analysis of operant behavior involves three kinds of events: *antecedents* (A), which are stimuli that are present before a behavior occurs; *behaviors* (B) that the organism emits; and *consequences* (C) that follow the behaviors. Thus:

IF *antecedent stimuli* (A) are present IF I say "Sit"

AND *behavior* (B) is emitted, AND my dog Jessie sits,

THEN *consequence* (C) will occur. THEN she gets a tasty treat.

The relations between A and B, and between B and C, are called *contingencies.* Jessie's behavior of sitting is contingent upon my saying "Sit." The consequence of receiving food is then contingent upon her response of sitting.

➤ 15. Identify two key differences between classical and operant conditioning.

Before exploring operant conditioning more closely, we wish to emphasize two points. First, keep in mind the key differences between classical and operant conditioning:

- In classical conditioning the organism learns an *association between two stimuli*—the CS and UCS (e.g., a tone and food)—that occurs *before* the behavior (e.g., salivation). In operant conditioning, the organism learns an *association between behavior and its consequences.* Behavior changes because of events that occur *after* it.

- Classical conditioning focuses on *elicited* behaviors. The conditioned response is triggered involuntarily, almost like a reflex, by a stimulus that precedes it. Operant conditioning focuses on *emitted* behaviors: In a given situation, the organism generates responses (e.g., pressing a lever) that are under its physical control.

Second, although classical and operant conditioning are different processes, many learning situations involve both. Have you ever had a teacher who "squeaked" chalk when writing on a blackboard? One of my high school teachers was a pro. Soon the mere sight of him raising the chalk to the board became a CS that automatically triggered a CR of "shivers up my spine." It also was a signal for me to put my fingers in my ears (an operant response), which was reinforced by the desirable consequence of reducing the squeaking sound. Thus one stimulus (raising the chalk) can have classical as well as operant functions, which appear to be processed through different neural pathways in the brain (Schmajuk et al., 1998).

Antecedent Conditions: Identifying When to Respond

➤ 16. Why are antecedent stimuli important in operant conditioning?

In operant conditioning the antecedent may be a general situation or specific stimulus. Let's return to our lever-pressing rat. At present, simply being in the Skinner box is the antecedent condition. In this situation, the rat will press the lever. Suppose we place a light on the wall above the lever. When the light is on, pressing the lever dispenses food, but when the light is off, no food is given. The rat will soon learn to press the lever only when the light is on. The light becomes a **discriminative stimulus,** a signal that a particular response will now produce certain consequences. Discriminative stimuli "set the occasion" for operant responses. The sight of my high school teacher raising chalk to the blackboard was—in operant conditioning terms—a discriminative stimulus signaling it was time to put my fingers in my ears.

Discriminative stimuli guide much of our everyday behavior. If you are hungry, food on your plate is a discriminative stimulus to start eating. Classroom bells, the words people speak to us, and the sight of a friend's face are all discriminative stimuli that set the occasion for us to make certain responses.

Consequences: Determining How to Respond

Behavior is governed by its consequences. Two major types of reinforcement strengthen responses and two major types of punishment weaken them. Operant behavior also is weakened by extinction. Figure 6.15 shows these processes.

Positive Reinforcement

Behavior is reinforced by desirable outcomes. Being *presented with* a stimulus we find pleasing represents a desirable outcome. A rat receives food for pressing a lever. We receive praise for a job well done. This is called **positive reinforcement:** A response is strengthened by the subsequent *presentation* of a stimulus. The stimulus that follows and strengthens the response is called a *positive reinforcer.* Food, drink, comforting physical contact, attention, praise, and money are common positive reinforcers. In our chapter-opening vignette, the volunteer's

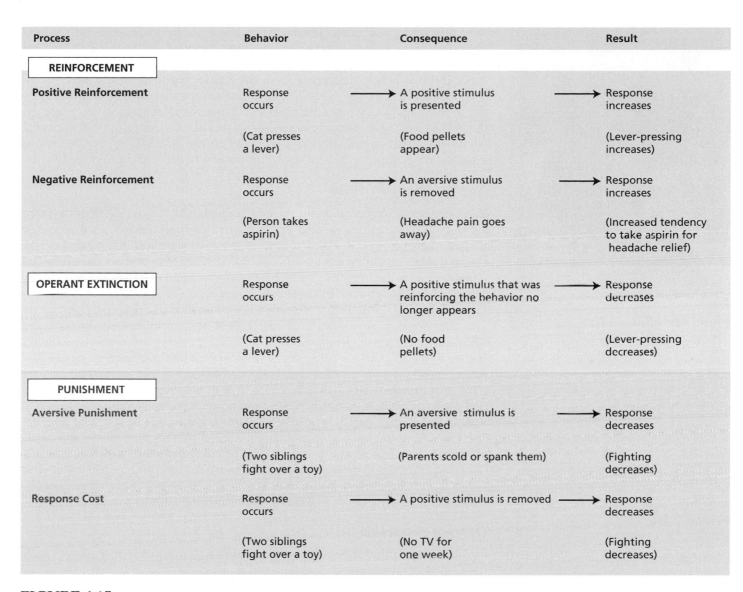

Process	Behavior	Consequence	Result
REINFORCEMENT			
Positive Reinforcement	Response occurs	→ A positive stimulus is presented	→ Response increases
	(Cat presses a lever)	(Food pellets appear)	(Lever-pressing increases)
Negative Reinforcement	Response occurs	→ An aversive stimulus is removed	→ Response increases
	(Person takes aspirin)	(Headache pain goes away)	(Increased tendency to take aspirin for headache relief)
OPERANT EXTINCTION	Response occurs	→ A positive stimulus that was reinforcing the behavior no longer appears	→ Response decreases
	(Cat presses a lever)	(No food pellets)	(Lever-pressing decreases)
PUNISHMENT			
Aversive Punishment	Response occurs	→ An aversive stimulus is presented	→ Response decreases
	(Two siblings fight over a toy)	(Parents scold or spank them)	(Fighting decreases)
Response Cost	Response occurs	→ A positive stimulus is removed	→ Response decreases
	(Two siblings fight over a toy)	(No TV for one week)	(Fighting decreases)

FIGURE 6.15 Five major operant processes.

behavior of soliciting money for charity is positively reinforced by each donation, by the praise of fellow workers at the charity, and by her feeling of pride in helping people.

The term *reward* is often used as if it were synonymous with positive reinforcement. Behaviorists prefer the term *positive reinforcement* because it describes how consequences affect behavior. In many instances "rewards" do not function as positive reinforcers. Parents may "reward" a child with a new toy for cleaning her room, but if the child does not clean her room again, then the toy was not a positive reinforcer for that behavior.

Primary and secondary reinforcers. Psychologists distinguish between two broad types of positive reinforcers. **Primary reinforcers** are stimuli, such as food and water, that an organism naturally finds reinforcing because they satisfy biological needs. Through their association with primary reinforcers, other stimuli can become **secondary**, or **conditioned, reinforcers.** Money is a conditioned reinforcer. In similar fashion, chimpanzees will learn to value and work for (and even to hoard) tokens they can place into a vending machine to obtain raisins. Secondary reinforcers, including praise, performance feedback, and grades are crucial in everyday life (Figure 6.16).

➤ 17. How do secondary reinforcers become "reinforcers"?

FIGURE 6.16 Attention and praise can be powerful secondary reinforcers. Comforting physical contact with a caretaker, some research suggests, may be a primary reinforcer.

➤ 18. How does negative reinforcement differ from positive reinforcement and from punishment?

➤ 19. Explain how operant extinction, aversive punishment, and response cost differ.

Secondary reinforcers illustrate how behavior often depends on a combination of classical and operant conditioning. Consider dog training. Correct responses, such as sitting upon command, initially are operantly reinforced with food. But just before delivering food, the trainer enthusiastically says "Good Dog." At first the words "Good Dog" are just sounds that mean absolutely nothing to the dog. But by repeatedly pairing "Good Dog" with food each time the dog sits, "Good Dog" becomes a classically conditioned stimulus that elicits excitement (salivation, tail wagging). Now the phrase "Good Dog" can be used as a secondary reinforcer, instead of always having to carry and provide food.

Negative Reinforcement

Receiving something pleasurable is a good outcome, but it's only half of the story. Getting rid of something we find aversive—or avoiding something we anticipate will be aversive—also is a good outcome. We take aspirin to relieve headaches, children clean up their room to stop their parents' nagging, and we use umbrellas when it rains to avoid getting wet. This process is called **negative reinforcement:** A response is strengthened by the subsequent *removal or avoidance* of a stimulus (see Figure 6.15) The stimulus that is removed or avoided is called a *negative reinforcer.*

Do not confuse negative reinforcement with punishment. Punishment weakens a response. *Reinforcement*—whether positive or negative—always means that a response is being *strengthened* (or maintained once it has reached full strength).

Negative reinforcement plays a key role in helping us learn to escape from and avoid aversive situations. While showering, have you ever heard someone flush a toilet, only to have your shower turn scalding hot or ice cold? Your response of jumping back is negatively reinforced—strengthened—by the desirable outcome of no longer being scalded or cold. Soon the mere sound of the flush becomes a signal—a discriminative stimulus—for you to back away. You successfully avoid the scalding or cold water, which negatively *reinforces* your response of backing away as soon as you hear the flush.

Operant Extinction

Operant **extinction** is the weakening and eventual disappearance of a response because it is no longer reinforced. When previously reinforced behaviors no longer pay off, we are likely to abandon and replace them with more successful ones. If pressing a lever no longer results in food pellets, the rat eventually will stop making this response.

The degree to which nonreinforced responses persist is called *resistance to extinction.* Nonreinforced responses may stop quickly (low resistance), but they may keep occurring hundreds or thousands of times (high resistance). People who solicit charitable donations, like the woman in Las Vegas, do not stop just because 100 passersby in a row fail to give money. As we examine later, resistance to extinction is strongly influenced by the pattern of reinforcement that has previously maintained the behavior.

Operant extinction often provides a good alternative to punishment as a method for reducing undesirable behaviors (O'Leary & Wilson, 1987). Consider the case of "Pascal the Rascal."

> Mrs. Adams sought help at a child guidance clinic because her 4-year-old son, Pascal, delighted in misbehaving. She had tried to reason with him. Then she resorted to yelling. When that failed, Mrs. Adams began using physical punishment. Even that did not work.

The intended "punishments" failed because they actually reinforced Pascal with what he wanted most: attention. The psychologist instructed Mrs. Adams to use a procedure called *time out,* which is short for "time out from positive reinforcement." When Pascal misbehaved, Mrs. Adams deprived him of attention, either by ignoring him or placing him in another room for a specific period of time. She also began to reinforce Pascal's desirable behaviors by paying attention to him. Soon thereafter, Pascal was no longer a rascal.

Aversive Punishment

Like reinforcement, punishment comes in two forms. One involves actively *applying* aversive stimuli, such as painful slaps, electric shock, and verbal reprimands. This is called **aversive punishment:** a response is *weakened* by the subsequent *presentation* of a stimulus. Spanking or scolding a child for misbehaving are obvious examples, but so is a child's touching a hot stovetop burner. The pain delivered by the burner makes it less likely that the child will touch it in the future. Aversive punishment often is subtle. A teenager wears a new blouse, her close friends halfheartedly say "Uh-huh, nice" but their facial expressions betray dislike and the student stops wearing the outfit.

Aversive punishment often produces rapid results, an important consideration when it is necessary to stop a particularly dangerous behavior, such as an animal or person attacking someone. Sometimes electric shocks are applied to stop the self-destructive behaviors of profoundly disturbed children who injure themselves by banging their heads on sharp objects or biting themselves (Matson & Gardner, 1991). The shock is presented immediately after each self-injurious response begins. In one case, a severely disturbed girl with a 6-year history of banging her head against sharp objects stopped after she received only 15 shocks (Lovaas, 1977).

Though aversive punishment often works, it has important limitations. Punishment suppresses behavior, but does not cause the organism to forget how to make the response. Moreover, this suppression may not generalize to other relevant situations, as when scolded children refrain from using "bad language" only when their parents are present. (Analogously, reinforced behaviors also may fail to generalize, as when a child reinforced for saying "thank you" does so only when a parent is present.)

Unlike reinforcement, punishment arouses negative emotions, such as fear and anger, that can produce dislike and avoidance of the person delivering the punishment. Aversive physical punishment also may set a bad example. It amounts to control by aggression and can send a message to the recipient that such aggression is appropriate and effective.

Do physically punished children learn such a lesson? Correlational research finds that toddlers and children whose parents use physical punishment display more aggression in day care centers and at school than do otherwise similar children who are not physically punished (George & Main, 1979; Hart et al., 1998; Stormshak et al., 2000). Although correlation does not demonstrate causation, controlled experiments indicate that children can learn aggressive behaviors by watching adult models (Bandura, 1965). In sum, aversive punishment has its place, but many psychologists recommend against this form of behavior control unless other alternatives are not feasible.

➤ 20. Describe some disadvantages of using aversive punishment to control behavior.

Response Cost

The legendary baseball umpire Bill Klem once called a batter out on a close third strike. The enraged batter flung his bat high into the air and whirled around to argue the call. Klem whipped off his mask, stared at the batter, and said, "If that bat comes down, it'll cost you 100 bucks."

Monetary fines, loss of privileges, and "groundings" represent attempts to punish behavior by taking away something that an organism desires or finds satisfying ("that'll cost you"). In **response cost,** a response is *weakened* by the subsequent *removal* of a stimulus (see Figure 6.15).

Response cost may seem similar to "time out" (operant extinction) because both processes weaken behavior by depriving the individual of something he or she desires. But there is a key difference. If you recall Pascal the Rascal, "time out" meant depriving him of the specific stimulus (attention) that was reinforcing his misbehavior in the first place. Response cost would have involved depriving him of other stimuli that he desired (perhaps "no TV"), but which did not cause him to act out in the first place.

Response cost has two distinct advantages over aversive punishment. First, although it may arouse temporary frustration or anger, response cost is less likely to create the strong fear or even hatred of the punishing agent (Pazulinec et al., 1983). Second, the punishing agent is not modeling physical aggression, so that there is less opportunity for learning of aggression through imitation.

When parents use response cost to punish children's behavior, the withheld reinforcer should be some prized object or activity, rather than love. Withholding love and rejecting the child can damage the child's self-concept (Brown, 1998). The same principle applies to using aversive punishment. Communicate dislike for the *behavior,* not for the child. Finally, punishment teaches the recipient what *not* to do, but does not guarantee that desirable behavior will appear in its place. Desirable alternative responses should be strengthened directly through positive reinforcement.

Immediate Versus Delayed Consequences

In general, reinforcement or punishment that occurs immediately after a behavior has a stronger effect than when it is delayed (Commons et al., 1984). Training animals typically requires very quick reinforcement so that they associate the correct response—rather than some subsequent behavior—with the satisfying outcome.

The timing of consequences often has less influence on human behavior because we are able to imagine future consequences and weigh them against more immediate ones. This often confronts us with interesting dilemmas. If you could have $100 right now, or $200 a year from now, which would you choose? This decision involves **delay of gratification,** the ability to forego an immediate but smaller reward for a delayed but more satisfying outcome (Mischel et al., 1972, 1989). Do I spend my income as I get it, buying things I want right now? Or, do I save up to buy a special item I want very much?

Individuals vary in their ability to delay gratification, a capacity that typically develops in the preschool years (Metcalfe & Mischel, 1999). Interestingly, young children who display less ability to delay gratification show poorer adjustment and have more difficulty coping with stress and frustration when they become adolescents. The inability to delay gratification also may play a role in behaviors such as chronic drinking, smoking, and even criminal acts (Brown, 1998).

Chronic drug use, for example, is difficult for many people to overcome because the immediate gratifying consequences override the delayed benefits of *not* performing the behavior (e.g., being healthier, living longer). With some drugs, such as cocaine, use is positively reinforced by feelings of pleasure that seem to result from enhanced dopamine activity (Pilla et al., 1999). With other drugs, powerful negative reinforcers play a key role. Chronic cigarette smokers experience increased tension as the level of nicotine in their blood drops after their last cigarette. When they smoke again, tension is reduced. Thus smoking is negatively reinforced by removal of unpleasant tension. Given that the typical chronic smoker inhales about 60,000 cigarette puffs a year (Parrott, 1999), this adds up to a lot of negative reinforcement.

Shaping and Chaining: Taking One Step at a Time

21. How might you shape a child who never cleans up his room to do so?

Mark is a 4-year-old preschooler. He doesn't play much with other children, rarely engages in physical activity, and during outdoor recess spends most of his time sitting in the sandbox. His teachers and parents would like him to be more active, so how can we use operant conditioning to change Mark's behavior?

First, we need to operationally define our goal. What exactly do we mean by "being active"? For starters, let's define it as "playing on the monkey bars." Second, we need to select a positive reinforcer, which in Mark's case will be "attention." Finally, all we need to do is reinforce Mark when he is playing on the monkey bars. The problem is, we will be waiting a long time, because he rarely displays such behavior.

Fortunately, Skinner developed a powerful procedure, called *shaping,* for overcoming this problem. We begin by reinforcing Mark with attention every time he stands up in the sandbox. This is the *first approximation* toward our final goal. Once this response is established, we now reinforce him only if he stands up and walks out of the sandbox toward the monkey bars. This is the *second approximation.* Then we might reinforce him only when he stands next to the bars, and finally only when he is on the bars and moving. This process, called **shaping,** involves reinforcing successive approximations toward a final response. This technique also is called the *method of successive approximations.* Using a shaping procedure similar to the one just described, it took researchers little time to start Mark playing on monkey bars (Johnston et al., 1966).

Even when behaviors might reasonably be learned through trial and error—such as a rat learning to press a lever for food—shaping speeds up the process. By reinforcing successive approximations, such as standing near the lever, raising a front paw, touching the lever, and finally depressing the lever, acquisition time is drastically reduced.

Another procedure, **chaining,** is used to develop a *sequence* (chain) of responses by reinforcing each response with the opportunity to perform the next response. For example, suppose that a rat has learned to press a lever when a light is on to receive food. Next we place a bell nearby. By accident, the rat eventually bumps into and rings the bell, which turns on the light. Seeing the light, the rat runs to and presses the lever. Over time, the rat will learn to ring the bell because this response is reinforced by turning on the light, which provides the opportunity to press the lever for food. As in this example, chaining usually begins with the final response in the sequence and works backward toward the first response (Catania, 1998). Figure 6.17 shows another example.

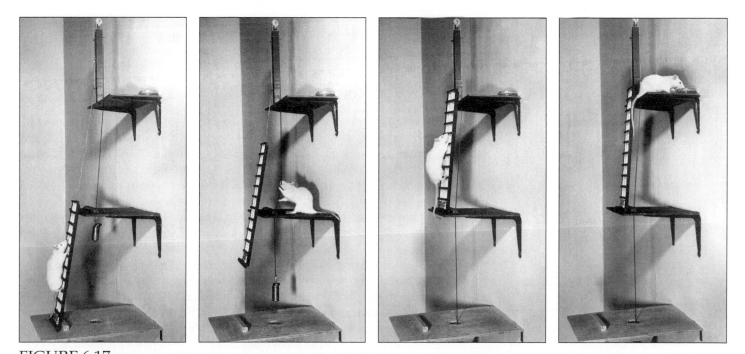

FIGURE 6.17 Through chaining, this rat has learned to climb a ladder to reach a string, pull on the string to raise the ladder, then climb the ladder again to reach food at the top. Typically, you begin this training with the last step in the chain. Then, working backward, each prior step in the chain is reinforced by the opportunity to perform the next step.

FIGURE 6.18 Contrary to some rumors, waterskiing is not an instinctive behavior for squirrels. This response was operantly shaped.

➤ 22. What are some examples of discriminative stimuli in your own life?

➤ 23. Describe four major schedules of partial reinforcement and their effects on behavior.

The amazing feats you see animals perform on TV, in the movies, or at circuses and theme parks, are developed through shaping and chaining (Figure 6.18). So is the behavior of animals who assist people with disabilities. Humans learn many complex behaviors this way. For example, specific musical, athletic, and academic skills are often shaped by starting with a basic, simplified operation and reinforcing progressively closer approximations to the final response.

Generalization and Discrimination

As in classical conditioning, operant responses may generalize to similar antecedent situations. A dog taught to "Sit" by its owner will likely start sitting when other people give the command. A young child who touches a hot stovetop burner learns to avoid touching not only that burner, but other hot burners as well. Thus in **operant generalization,** an operant response occurs to a new antecedent stimulus or situation that is similar to the original one.

Through experience, we also learn to discriminate between antecedent conditions. Children learn to raid the cookie jar only when the parents are not in the kitchen. We learn to board busses and trains marked by specific symbols (79: Express) and avoid otherwise identical vehicles with different symbols (78: Local). **Operant discrimination** means that an operant response will occur to one antecedent stimulus but not to another. As already discussed, these antecedent stimuli—parent's presence or absence, bus markings—are called *discriminative stimuli.* When discriminative stimuli influence a behavior, that behavior is said to be under *stimulus control.* For example, the sight of a police car exerts stimulus control over most people's driving behavior.

The concept of operant discrimination gives science a powerful tool for examining the perceptual and cognitive abilities of infants and nonhuman species (Berg & Boswell, 1998; Lashley, 1930). We can't ask infants and animals to tell us if they can distinguish between different colors, sounds, shapes, faces, and so on. But by using a procedure called *operant discrimination training,* we can teach an organism that making a response (e.g., pressing a lever) when a discriminative stimulus is present (e.g., a red light is on) produces food or some other positive consequence. Now all we have to do is change the color of the light and not reinforce any response when that light is on. If the organism learns to respond to one color and not the other, we infer that it can discriminate between them.

Schedules of Reinforcement

In daily life reinforcement comes in different patterns and frequencies. These patterns, called *schedules of reinforcement*, have strong and predictable effects on learning, extinction, and performance (Ferster & Skinner, 1957). The most basic distinction is between continuous and partial reinforcement. On a **continuous reinforcement** schedule, every response of a particular type is reinforced. Every press of the lever results in food pellets. Every 75-cent deposit in the soda machine results in a can of cool bubbly drink (at least, we hope so). With **partial reinforcement,** also called *intermittent reinforcement*, only some responses are reinforced.

Partial reinforcement schedules can be categorized along two important dimensions. The first is ratio versus interval schedules. On *ratio schedules,* a certain percentage of responses are reinforced. For example, we might decide to reinforce only 50 percent of the rat's lever presses with food. The key factor is that ratio schedules are based on the number of correct responses. More responses . . . more reinforcement. (In the workplace, this is called *pay for performance.*) On *interval schedules,* a certain amount of time must elapse between reinforcements, regardless of how many correct responses might occur during that interval. We might reinforce lever pressing only once per minute, no matter whether the rat presses the lever 5, 10, or 60 times. The key factor is that interval schedules are based on the passage of time.

The second dimension is fixed versus variable schedules. With a *fixed schedule,* reinforcement always occurs after a fixed number of responses or after a fixed time interval. With a *variable schedule,* the required number of responses or the time interval varies at random around an average. Combining these two dimensions creates four types of reinforcement schedules.

Fixed-Ratio Schedule

On a **fixed-ratio (FR) schedule,** reinforcement is given after a fixed number of responses. For example, FR-3 means that reinforcement occurs after every third response, regardless of how long it takes for those responses to occur.

If I told you that you would receive $1 every three times you pressed a lever, would you work hard? Skinner found that fixed-ratio schedules produce high rates of responding. That is one reason why some businesses prefer paying employees' wages based on a set number of items produced. Experiments conducted with several types of tasks confirm that such fixed-ratio "piecework" schedules result in greater work output than hourly wages (Pritchard et al., 1980). If the ratio is gradually increased over time, many responses can be obtained with relatively few reinforcements. Pigeons in a Skinner box have been known to wear down their beaks pecking a disc on an FR-20,000 schedule (one reinforcer per 20,000 responses). Some labor unions fight against the use of piecework wage systems, believing that they tempt employees to work to exhaustion.

FR schedules have a second characteristic effect. As shown in Figure 6.19, the organism often pauses briefly after each reinforcement, perhaps because the next response (or responses) is never reinforced. This pause is called a *scallop.*

Variable-Ratio Schedule

On a **variable-ratio (VR) schedule,** reinforcement is given after a variable number of correct responses, all centered around an average. A VR-3 schedule means that, *on the average,* 3 responses are required for reinforcement. For example, for the first 12 responses, reinforcement might occur after responses 2, 3, 6, and 11.

VR schedules, like FR schedules, produce a high rate of responding. But because the occurrence of reinforcement is less predictable on a VR schedule, there is less pausing after reinforcement. After all, the next response *might* be reinforced. Instead, there is a relatively high, steady rate of responding, as shown in Figure 6.19. VR schedules also are highly resistant to extinction because the organism learns that long periods of no-payoff will eventually be followed by reinforcement. Thus VR schedules can be physically taxing, and both humans and other species may continue to respond to the point of exhaustion.

Gambling activities are maintained by VR schedules (Figure 6.20). Take the slot-machine gambler from our opening vignette. He plays a slot machine programmed to pay off an *average* of every 20 pulls (VR-20). After eight pulls he receives a 10-coin jackpot. After five more attempts, he hits a 15-coin jackpot. But then, after 40 more attempts—nothing. He's frustrated but "hooked" by the VR schedule. That next attempt just might be the one that pays off, so he plays again . . . and again.

Fixed-Interval Schedule

On a **fixed-interval (FI) schedule,** the first correct response that occurs after a fixed time interval is reinforced. Suppose a rat is pressing a lever on an FI-3

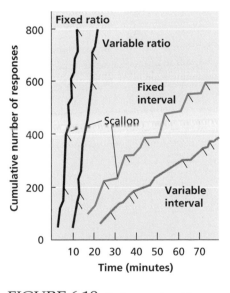

FIGURE 6.19 Each type of positive reinforcement schedule produces a typical cumulative response curve. The hash marks indicate the delivery of a reinforcer. Ratio schedules produce a high rate of responding, as shown in the steep slopes of the curves. Variable schedules produce a steadier rate of responding. Notice the prominent scallops in the fixed interval schedule; the subject learns to stop responding until the time interval for the next reinforcement approaches.

FIGURE 6.20 Gambling is reinforced on a variable-ratio schedule. It is ratio, because the frequency of reinforcement is based on the amount of performance. On average, you will receive more payoffs when you pull the slot machine 100 times than when you play only 10 times. It is variable, because you never know when the next jackpot might occur.

➤ 24. Are variable or fixed schedules more resistant to extinction? Why?

(minute) schedule. After a lever press is reinforced, for the next 3 minutes it makes no difference how many more times the rat responds. There will be no further reinforcement. Once these 3 minutes elapse, the next lever-press is reinforced. The FI schedule's characteristic response pattern is shown in Figure 6.19. After each reinforcement, you see a substantial scallop, followed by increased responding as the time interval passes.

You probably encounter FI schedules in college. Many instructors give exams at equal (or nearly equal) intervals, perhaps one exam every two, three, or four weeks. If you are like many students, your study behavior may resemble the pattern shown in Figure 6.19, reflecting relatively little studying during the period immediately following each exam, and a great deal of "cramming" just before the test. This uneven performance rate is typical of FI schedules.

Variable-Interval Schedule

On a **variable-interval (VI) schedule,** reinforcement is given for the first response that occurs after a variable time interval. A VI-3 schedule means that, *on average,* there is a 3-minute interval between opportunities to obtain reinforcement. Sometimes, responses only a few seconds apart may be reinforced; at other times the interval may be many minutes. As Figure 6.19 shows, because the availability of reinforcement is less predictable than an FI schedule, the VI schedule produces a steadier response rate.

"Pop quizzes" represent a VI schedule. A course might average a quiz every one or two weeks, but their unpredictable timing will likely produce a steadier approach to studying than regularly scheduled quizzes. Other examples of VI schedules include random drug testing of athletes and roadside speed traps. These activities reinforce desired behaviors (staying drug-free, driving within the speed limit) by appearing at unpredictable intervals. Of course, they also punish undesired behaviors with suspensions and fines!

Partial Reinforcement, Learning, and Extinction

Reinforcement schedules significantly influence the rate of learning and extinction. Continuous reinforcement produces more rapid learning than partial reinforcement because the association between behavior and its consequences is easier to perceive. However, continuously reinforced responses also extinguish more rapidly, because the shift to no reinforcement is sudden and easier to perceive.

Partial reinforcement produces behavior that is learned more slowly but is more resistant to extinction, especially if the behavior was reinforced on a *variable* schedule. If reinforcement has been unpredictable in the past, it takes longer to learn that it is gone forever. Most people do not continue to drop coins into a candy or soda machine that doesn't deliver, because vending machines are supposed to operate on a continuous schedule. But it would take many pulls of a slot machine to recognize that it had stopped paying off completely. Similarly, when the response of pecking a key is reinforced on a VR schedule, a pigeon may continue to peck over 100,000 times after reinforcement has ended (Skinner, 1953).

To sum up, the best way to promote fast learning and high resistance to extinction is to begin reinforcing the desired behavior on a continuous schedule until the behavior is well established. Then shift to a partial (preferably variable) schedule that is gradually made more demanding. This is what was done with 4-year-old Mark. Reinforcement for playing on the monkey bars gradually was reduced so that, eventually, maintaining his behavior required only occasional attention from his teachers (Johnston et al., 1966). Once partial reinforcement is used, variable schedules generally produce *steadier* rates of responding than fixed schedules, and ratio schedules typically produce *higher* rates of responding than interval schedules (Ferster & Skinner, 1957).

Escape and Avoidance Conditioning

Behavior often involves escaping from or avoiding unpleasant situations. Simple escape situations include taking medications to relieve pain and putting on more clothes when we are cold. Examples of avoidance include putting on lotion to avoid sunburn and obeying traffic laws to avoid tickets. The examples are endless.

In **escape conditioning,** organisms learn a response to terminate an aversive stimulus. Escape behaviors are acquired and maintained through negative reinforcement. Putting on a sweater is negatively *reinforced* by the desirable consequence that I no longer shiver. Taking two aspirin is negatively *reinforced* by the reduction of headache pain. In **avoidance conditioning,** the organism learns a response to avoid an aversive stimulus. We learn to dress warmly before going outside to avoid feeling cold.

Escape and avoidance conditioning can be demonstrated experimentally (Zhulkov et al., 1999; Solomon & Wynne, 1953). For example, an animal is placed in a shuttlebox, a rectangular chamber divided into two compartments and connected by a doorway (Figure 6.21). The floor is a grid through which electric shock can be delivered to either compartment. When shock is turned on in the animal's compartment, it attempts to escape. Eventually, it runs through the door and into the other compartment. When shock is delivered to that compartment, it can escape by running back to the original side. Running through the door removes the shock, which negatively *reinforces* this escape behavior. Over a few trials, the animal learns to escape as soon as the shock is administered.

To experimentally study avoidance conditioning, researchers introduce a warning signal, such as a light, that precedes the shock by a few seconds. After a few trials, the animal learns that the light signals impending shock. It runs to the other compartment as soon as it sees the light, and thereby avoids being shocked.

Once this avoidance response is learned, it often is hard to extinguish. This is puzzling, because the animal no longer experiences any shock after the light is turned on. We saw the same situation with Carol's car phobia. She continued to avoid cars even though the intense pain from her accident was no longer experienced. What makes avoidance so resistant to extinction?

According to one model, the **two-factor theory of avoidance learning,** classical *and* operant conditioning are involved in avoidance learning (Mowrer, 1947; Rescorla & Solomon, 1967). For our rat, the warning light initially is a neutral stimulus paired with shock (UCS). Through classical conditioning, the light becomes a CS that elicits fear. Now operant conditioning takes over. Fleeing from the light is *negatively reinforced* by the termination of fear. This strengthens and maintains the avoidance response. Now if we permanently turn off the shock, the avoidance response prevents extinction from taking place. Seeing the light come on, the animal will not "hang around" long enough to learn that the shock no longer occurs.

In similar fashion, Carol's fear of cars was classically conditioned. The mere sight of a car (like the light for the rat) elicits fear and she flees, thereby avoiding riding in or driving the car. This avoidance is negatively reinforced by fear reduction, so it remains strong (Figure 6.22). Extinction is difficult because Carol doesn't give herself the opportunity to be in the car without experiencing physical pain and trauma. This is why exposure therapies for phobias are so effective. By preventing avoidance responses, they provide the key ingredient for extinction: exposure to the CS in the absence of the UCS.

➤ 25. Describe the role of negative reinforcement in escape and avoidance conditioning.

FIGURE 6.21 The shuttlebox is used to study escape and avoidance learning.

Factor 1: Classical conditioning of fear

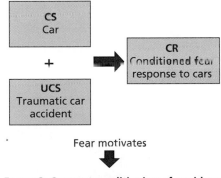

Fear motivates

Factor 2: Operant conditioning of avoidance

FIGURE 6.22 The two-factor theory of avoidance learning would account for Carol's car phobia in terms of two sets of learning processes: classical conditioning of a fear response, and the negative *reinforcement* of avoidance of cars through fear reduction.

Two-factor theory helps us understand how many avoidance behaviors develop (Levis, 1989; Plaud & Plaud, 1998). However, it has trouble explaining some aspects of avoidance, such as why people and other animals develop phobic avoidance to some stimuli (e.g., snakes) much more easily than to others (e.g., squirrels). Modern research shows that our biological predispositions, thinking patterns, and ability to learn through observation also regulate our avoidance responses (Mineka & Zinbarg, 1998).

Applications of Operant Conditioning

Skinner was passionate about applying operant principles to enhance human welfare. In his best-selling books *Walden Two* (1948) and *Beyond Freedom and Dignity* (1971), Skinner set forth his utopian vision of how a "technology of behavior" based on positive reinforcement could put an end to war, deteriorating education, and other social problems. To his critics, Skinner's ideas conjured up images of people manipulated like rats, of "Big Brother" (government) controlling its citizens. But Skinner's point was that social influence is a natural part of human existence. Parents and children influence each other, as do employees and employers, teachers and students, friends, roommates, and romantic partners. We smile and say "please" to influence the chance someone will do us a favor. In Skinner's view, individual and societal problems are created by the all-too-common *haphazard* use of reinforcement and overreliance on punishment.

Training Animals

▶ 26. How has operant animal training helped humans?

Through shaping and chaining, animals can learn to perform some truly remarkable behaviors. Some are trained to be television, movie, or circus performers, whereas others learn to assist people who are blind or have other disabilities (Figure 6.23). Law enforcement and military organizations also rely on operantly trained animals. Police dogs assist officers on routine patrol, and other dogs learn to use their sense of smell to help locate hidden bombs, illegal drugs, and missing persons. The U.S. Navy trains sea lions to dive and retrieve sunken test weapons, and dolphins learn to patrol waters around nuclear submarine bases and search for underwater intruders (Morrison, 1988). Operantly trained dolphins also patrolled the waters around some U.S. ships during the Vietnam and Persian Gulf wars.

Some applications push the boundaries of ingenuity, such as using pigeons to assist in air-sea rescue. Pigeons have sharp long-distance visual acuity and a wide field of vision. Years ago, the U.S. Coast Guard put these abilities to good use by training pigeons to peck a key whenever they saw an orange object (Simmons, 1981). Orange, of course, is the international color of life jackets. Three trained pigeons were then placed in a glass dome mounted underneath the search-and-rescue helicopter. Each pigeon had a different view outside, but together, they covered the entire 360° visual field. When a pigeon spotted an orange object in the ocean, it pecked a key connected to a particular directional signal in the cockpit. Depending on which pigeon was pecking at any moment, the pilot maintained or altered course and was guided to the victim's location!

All of these applications involve training animals to enhance human welfare, but operant conditioning also benefits animals' lives. It is the cornerstone of formal pet training, which with dogs typically includes numerous commands (e.g., "Heel," "Stay") that help keep them away from traffic and other hazards. As Figure 6.24 explains, shaping was also used to aid Keiko, the orca whale who starred in the movie *Free Willy*, but who in reality was far from "free."

FIGURE 6.23 Because of injuries suffered in an accident, this man cannot move his arms or legs. The monkey has been operantly trained to assist him with basic chores, such as eating.

Human Applications: Education, the Workplace, and Beyond

Walk into your local computer store and you likely will find shelves of educational software, teaching everything from geography and math to foreign languages. The effectiveness of such computerized instruction rests on two key principles championed by Skinner: *immediate performance feedback* and *self-paced learning.*

Skinner was deeply concerned about the inefficiency of traditional instructional methods (1961, 1989). Decades ago, long before the advent of personal computers, he developed mechanical teaching machines. Each machine presented material, quizzed the student, and provided immediate feedback. Students who did not learn the material the first time could repeat steps. Those who did could advance their machine to the next set of information. Today personal computers are helping Skinner's vision become an educational reality. *Computer-assisted instruction (CAI)* also is found in business, industry, and the military (Parchman et al., 2000).

Skinner's work also heightened societal attention to the broad issue of "motivation" and reinforcing desired behavior. A key behaviorist assumption is that poor performance should not be attributed to "laziness" or a "bad attitude." Instead, we should assume that the *environment* is not providing the proper consequences to reinforce the desired behavior. Incentive systems—from stock options to bonuses for meeting performance goals—are now common in business and professional sports. **Token economies,** in which desirable behaviors are quickly reinforced with "tokens" (e.g., points, gold stars) that are later turned in for tangible rewards (e.g., prizes, recreational time), have been used to enhance academic and work performance. In one study, a token economy reduced the number of work injuries among open-pit mine workers (Fox et al., 1987). Miners received stamp awards for making safety suggestions and avoiding injuries, and they lost stamps for unsafe behaviors. Stamps were later traded in for tangible reinforcers. The program cost money, but far less that the cost of worker absenteeism due to accidents.

At work, motivating employees is a key managerial function, and many major companies invest heavily in training programs designed to enhance managers' effectiveness in reinforcing desired worker behavior (Saari et al., 1988). Similarly, numerous youth sport organizations require coaches to take training programs that teach how to reinforce young athletes effectively (Smith & Smoll, 1997).

Finally, Skinner's work gave rise to a field called **applied behavior analysis** (also known as *behavior modification*), which combines a behavioral approach with the scientific method to solve individual and societal problems (Kazdin, 1975; Pierce & Epling, 1999). Essentially, a program (usually based on positive reinforcement) is designed and implemented to change behavior, and its effectiveness is objectively measured by gathering data before and after the program is in place.

Applied behavior analysis has been used to reduce an array of behavior problems, from chronic hair pulling to drivers' failure to use seat belts. It has improved students' academic performance and social skills, enhanced elite athletes' performance, and reduced unsportworthy behavior (Hughes et al., 1998). Workplace applications include increasing employee productivity, reducing injuries and accidents, enhancing the job interview skills of unemployed adults, and increasing energy conservation (Staats et al., 2000).

Operant conditioning demonstrates the environment's power in shaping who we are. But this does not mean we are at its mercy. As the following *Applications of Psychological Science* feature shows, we can use our knowledge of learning principles to gain greater control over our own behavior.

FIGURE 6.24 With the long-term goal of releasing Keiko back into the wild, Keiko was moved in 1996 from a small Mexican aquarium to a larger pool at the Oregon Coast Aquarium. Because Keiko lived in pools for most of his life and was fed by humans, he did not hunt fish. To shape this behavior, Keiko's handlers first exposed him to dead fish floating in his pool, then to stunned fish that flapped but didn't swim, and finally to live salmon and cod. In 1998, Keiko was moved to a larger open sea pen in Iceland, where this shaping continued.

➤ 27. In what broad ways has operant conditioning directly enhanced human welfare?

➤ 28. What is the purpose of each of the five major steps in a self-regulation program?

APPLICATIONS OF PSYCHOLOGICAL SCIENCE

Using Operant Principles to Modify Your Behavior

People often blame the inability to overcome bad habits or maladaptive behaviors on vague concepts like poor "will power" and lack of "self-control." Behaviorists prefer the more optimistic assumption that we can acquire **self-regulation,** which means putting on a scientist's "hat" and using learning principles to change our behavior (Kanfer, 1991). This approach has helped people overcome addictions, reduce heart disease, enhance school performance, and improve their lives in many other ways. Let's examine how a college student could use self-regulation principles to increase the amount and effectiveness of studying.

▶ Step 1: Specify the Problem

The first step in a self-regulation program is to pinpoint the behaviors you want to change (Watson & Tharp, 1997). This may be more challenging than it sounds, because we often use vague words to describe our problems. One of our students described her study problem by saying, "I'm just not motivated to study hard." With a little help, she redefined her problem in more specific behavioral terms as follows: "Between 7 P.M. and 10 P.M. I don't spend enough time at my desk reading and outlining my textbook."

Whenever possible, design your program to positively reinforce desirable behaviors (i.e., studying) rather than punish undesirable ones (i.e., not studying). Therefore we define our student's **target behavior** (the specific goal) as follows: "Four nights a week, between 7 and 10 P.M., spend two and a half hours studying."

▶ Step 2: Collect Baseline Data

The next step is to collect *baseline (preintervention) data* on your behavior. Baseline data provide information about how frequently the target behavior currently occurs. Without it, you have no way of measuring how much you change after starting your program. The most effective approach is to plot data on a graph. Figure 6.25 shows data collected by one of our students.

▶ Step 3: Identify Antecedents and Consequences

While you collect baseline data, try to identify *antecedent* factors that disrupt study behavior, such as friends calling or stopping by (Watson & Tharp, 1989). Also focus on the *consequences* of your behavior. Does studying produce outcomes that are satisfying?

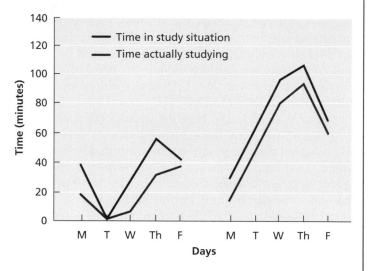

FIGURE 6.25 This student graphed the amount of time he spent in the study environment and the time actually spent studying. Study time increased when he began to self-reinforce study behavior in the second week.

▶ Step 4: Develop a Plan to Modify the Antecedents and Consequences

Once you have identified key antecedents and consequences, you are in position to modify either or both.

Altering the Antecedents
You can modify the environment so that different stimuli start to control your behavior. To increase studying, select a specific place where you do nothing but study. If your attention wanders, get up and leave the study area. Your objective is to condition yourself to study in response to the stimuli present in the study area. B. F. Skinner used this technique throughout his own career: He did all of his writing at a particular desk and did nothing else there.

Altering the Consequences
Consequences determine whether behavior is repeated. Fortunately, we have the power to arrange many of our own consequences. Self-administered *positive reinforcement* should be the cornerstone of most programs. Find an effective reinforcer that you can control and make it available only if you engage in the desired behavior. Almost any activity you enjoy or object you like having can serve as a reinforcer, but it must be potent enough to maintain the

–Continued

desired behavior. Awarding yourself a penny for each hour of study time is unlikely to modify your behavior, whereas a "30-minute credit" toward a recreational activity might be very effective. After selecting a reinforcer, decide how to use it. Draw up and sign a contract with yourself. The contract should precisely state

- how often or how long you must perform the target behavior (or not perform it, if the goal is to reduce an undesirable behavior); and
- the kind and amount of reinforcement you will receive for specific achievements.

Use Reinforcers Effectively

Immediately reinforce the target behavior whenever possible. If your reinforcer cannot be available immediately, use *tokens* that can later be converted into a reinforcer. One student who wanted to increase her study time awarded herself one point per 15 minutes of study time. Points were redeemed for consequences that varied in their reinforcement value. For example, one point was worth 15 minutes of TV viewing, but 15 points earned the right to "do anything I want to, all day." Token economies have been used successfully with workers, children, patients in mental hospitals, prison inmates, and other groups (Swain & McLaughlin, 1998). If it works for them, it can work for you.

Use Shaping

If you collect good baseline data, you will know the level at which you currently perform your target behavior. Begin at this level or *slightly* beyond it and move *slowly* toward your final goal, reinforcing yourself at each step. For example, begin by reinforcing yourself for each 10-minute increase in study time. If you have trouble, reduce the size of your steps. Attaining each small goal along the way can be reinforcing and provides motivation to continue (Locke & Latham, 1994). The goal is to bring about gradual change while enjoying plenty of reinforcers and satisfaction from increasing self-mastery. *The way you arrange reinforcement contingencies is the most critical determinant of whether your goal will be achieved.*

▶ Step 5: Implement the Program and Keep Measuring Behavior

Most people experience occasional setbacks or plateaus where progress seems to stop. If this happens repeatedly, it is not a sign of "weak willpower," but rather, that the program needs to be modified. Yes, self-regulation programs can fail, but this calls for resourcefulness rather than despair. If need be, change the terms of your contract, but always operate under a specific contract. Keep recording and graphing the target behavior. This is only way to accurately identify your progress.

This five-step process is one of several behavioral approaches to gaining greater control of our lives (Azrin & Nunn, 1973; Miltenberger et al., 1998). Psychologists continue to design and test methods to increase self-regulation, adding new meaning to the phrase, "Power to the people."

〉 BIOLOGY AND LEARNING

Behaviorists never suggested that a rat could learn to fly, but for decades they assumed that they could condition virtually any behavior an organism was physically capable of performing. Yet evidence mounted that "conditioned" animals did not always respond as they were supposed to. The behaviorist assumption was wrong because it ignored a key principle discussed at the outset of this chapter: Behavior is influenced by an organism's evolutionary history (Crawford & Anderson, 1989).

Martin Seligman's (1970) concept of "preparedness" captures this idea. **Preparedness** means that, through evolution, animals are biologically "prewired" to easily learn behaviors related to their survival as a species. Behaviors contrary to an organism's natural tendencies are learned slowly, if at all. Let's consider some examples.

Constraints on Classical Conditioning: Learned Taste Aversions

Imagine eating or drinking something, then becoming sick to your stomach and throwing up. Perhaps it is food poisoning. Or perhaps, like cancer patients, it is chemotherapy that makes you ill. Pairing the food (CS) with stomach illness (in this case, the UCS) can produce a CR called a **conditioned taste aversion:** The taste (and sometimes the sight and smell) of the food now disgusts and repulses us (Garcia et al., 1985). It may even make us feel queasy, and we learn to avoid

➤ 29. How do learned taste aversions illustrate the concept of preparedness?

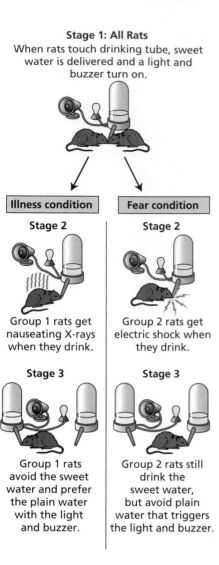

Stage 1: All Rats
When rats touch drinking tube, sweet water is delivered and a light and buzzer turn on.

Illness condition

Stage 2

Group 1 rats get nauseating X-rays when they drink.

Stage 3

Group 1 rats avoid the sweet water and prefer the plain water with the light and buzzer.

Fear condition

Stage 2

Group 2 rats get electric shock when they drink.

Stage 3

Group 2 rats still drink the sweet water, but avoid plain water that triggers the light and buzzer.

FIGURE 6.26 Biological preparedness in classical conditioning. This figure illustrates the design and main results of Garcia and Koelling's (1966) aversion experiment.

➤ 30. How has knowledge of learned taste aversions been applied to help animals?

it. Cancer patients may develop aversions to foods they eat before treatment even though they know that the food did not cause their posttreatment stomach illness. Involuntarily, pairing food with nausea creates an aversion.

Psychologist John Garcia pioneered numerous taste aversion experiments that challenged two basic assumptions of classical conditioning. First, behaviorists had assumed that the CS-UCS time interval had to be relatively short, usually within a few seconds. Garcia showed that animals learned taste aversions even though the food (CS) was consumed up to several hours—or even a day—before they became ill (UCS).

Second, in a classic experiment, Garcia illustrated how biological preparedness influences learned aversions (Garcia & Koelling, 1966). Whenever rats licked a drinking tube they were simultaneously exposed to three neutral stimuli: sweet-tasting water, a bright light, and a buzzer (Figure 6.26). In one condition, half the rats were exposed to X rays upon drinking the water, which later made them ill (UCS). Would the rats develop an aversion to all three neutral stimuli? No, they avoided the sweet water, but not the light or buzzer. Why did only the sweet taste become a CS? Because rats are biologically primed to form taste-illness associations, which means that in nature they most easily identify poisonous or "bad" food by its taste (or smell). Sounds and lights in nature don't make rats sick.

When rats in a second condition licked the tube, the light, buzzer, and sweet taste were all paired with an electric shock. Would the rats learn to fear all three neutral stimuli? No, they avoided the light and buzzer, but kept drinking the sweet water. This also makes adaptive sense. In nature, sights and sounds—but not how food and drink taste—signal fear-provoking situations (e.g., a cat about to pounce). The same principle applies in humans. When a food makes us violently sick, we may develop an aversion to it, but not to the friends we ate with. Further, seeing the food again may repulse us, but not make us afraid.

Psychologists have applied their knowledge about conditioned aversions to save animals' lives. To prevent coyotes from killing ranchers' sheep, Carl Gustavson and his colleagues laced pieces of meat with lithium chloride, a nausea-inducing drug (Gustavson et al., 1974). The meat was wrapped in sheep hide and left out for coyotes to eat. The coyotes ate it, became ill, developed an aversion to the meat, and became less likely to kill sheep. This saved the lives of sheep and also of the coyotes who otherwise would have been shot by ranchers. As part of wildlife management, researchers also have created conditioned aversions to various foods in other species, such as raccoons, wolves, and baboons (Gustavson & Gustavson, 1985). For an intriguing example of nature's own "wildlife management" based on learned taste aversions, see Figure 6.27.

In human research, Darla Broberg and Ilene Bernstein (1987) gave child cancer patients unusual-tasting candy before their chemotherapy treatments. The candy became a conditioned "scapegoat" for the children's taste aversions, protecting them from developing aversions to their normal foods.

Be aware that biological preparedness also influences emotionally "positive" responses. Male Japanese quail become sexually aroused to a stuffed female quail model—but not to a toy model dog—after those models (CS) have been paired with the opportunity to copulate with a live, receptive female (UCS) (Domjan et al., 1988). Experience may affect what "turns us on," but even for quail, conditioned lust apparently has limits.

Are We Biologically Prepared to Fear Certain Things?

Seligman (1971) proposes that, like other animals, humans are biologically prepared to acquire certain fears more readily than others. Case studies of phobic patients support this idea. British therapist Isaac Marks (1977) tells of a 4-year-old girl who saw a snake while walking through a park. She found the snake interesting and didn't fear it. Soon she returned to the family car, and her hand was smashed when the car door closed. She developed a lifelong phobia, not of car doors or automobiles, but of snakes!

Numerous experiments by Arne Öhman and his Swedish research team provide evidence of preparedness (Öhman et al., 1978; Öhman & Soares, 1998). In this research, various CSs were paired with electric shock (UCS), and participants' physiological responses were measured when the CSs were subsequently presented alone. People who received shocks each time pictures of snakes, spiders, or angry faces were flashed on a screen quickly acquired conditioned fear responses to these stimuli, even when the pictures were displayed too briefly to be consciously perceived. But participants who received shocks while looking at slides of flowers, houses, berries, or happy faces displayed much weaker fear conditioning.

Humans develop phobias to many stimuli, but most often we fear things that seem to have greater evolutionary significance: snakes, spiders, other animals, and dangerous places. Is this the result of evolution-based preparedness, or might it be due to learning experiences within our own lifetime? Through cultural transmission of knowledge, perhaps we come to expect that some stimuli can be dangerous, making us "cognitively" rather than "biologically" prepared to acquire certain fears. The role of cognitive factors in human fear conditioning continues to be examined (Davey, 1995), but one thing is clear: As with taste aversions and sexual arousal, fear can be conditioned much more easily to some stimuli than others.

Constraints on Operant Conditioning: Animals That "Won't Shape Up"

Two of B. F. Skinner's students, Keller and Marian Breland, became renowned animal trainers. They used shaping and chaining to train thousands of animals for circuses, advertising agencies, television, and the movies. Training usually was successful, but not always. Sometimes the animals simply refused to behave according to the "laws" of operant conditioning (Breland & Breland, 1961, 1966).

On one occasion, the Brelands tried to train a chicken to play baseball. The game was arranged so that a small ball would roll toward home plate and the chicken would pull a chain to swing a small metal bat. If the ball was hit, a bell would ring and the chicken would run to first base to get its food. The Brelands easily trained the chicken to pull the chain that swung the bat, and to run to first base when it heard the bell. But when the ball was introduced into the game, utter chaos occurred. Whenever the chicken hit the ball, instead of running to first base to collect its food reinforcement, it chased the ball all over the playing field, pecking furiously at it, and flapping its wings. Try as they might, the Brelands could not extinguish these behaviors. End of training and end of the chicken's baseball career. In this and many other examples, animals simply refused to "shape up."

The Brelands found that once a particular stimulus came to represent food, animals began to act as if it *were* food. The chicken pecked at the ball as if it were something to eat. In another example, raccoons kept on rubbing their tokens as if they were "washing" real food. In the raccoon's case, they had successfully performed the conditioned response of dropping a token in a box several times, but their "washing behavior" was so deeply rooted in their evolutionary history that it simply overrode the conditioning procedure. The Brelands called this **instinctive drift:** a conditioned response "drifts back" toward instinctive behavior. People who adopt wild animals as pets, or who train them for circuses, face some personal risk no matter how hard they try to domesticate these animals. An acquaintance of ours once rescued a cuddly baby raccoon and raised it lovingly for nearly a year, at which time the raccoon unexpectedly reverted to its

FIGURE 6.27 This blue jay has never eaten a monarch butterfly before, and doesn't pass up an easy meal. Soon toxins in the butterfly cause food poisoning. The jay feels discomfort, vomits, and develops a conditioned aversion triggered by the sight of the monarch's brightly patterned wings. From now on, it will leave monarchs alone.
Photos courtesy of Lincoln P. Brower.

➤ 31. What evidence led the Brelands' to propose the concept of instinctive drift?

more instinctive, aggressive behavior. Our friend, now known as "Ole Three-Fingers," returned his pet to the wild.

Experiments confirm that operant learning is constrained by biology. It is relatively easy to train a pigeon to peck a novel object (such as a disc on a wall) for food reinforcers, because pigeons come into the world biologically primed to peck for food. Training a pigeon to peck an object to escape from electric shock is more difficult, because in their natural environment pigeons do not escape from danger by pecking. They fly away. As another example, wild rats trained to press a lever for food will often drift back to instinctive behaviors of scratching and biting the lever (Powell & Curley, 1976).

Learning and the Brain

➤ 32. How do biology and learning influence each other?

Biology and learning are deeply intertwined. Clearly, biology determines our ability to learn. The concepts of preparedness and instinctive drift illustrate how organisms are biologically predisposed to learn some associations more easily than others. Neuroscientists have found that certain brain regions, such as the hypothalamus, and certain neurotransmitters, such as dopamine, play a key role in regulating the ability to experience reward (Olds, 1958; Rolls, 2000). Human medical patients report pleasure when specific areas of their hypothalamus are electrically stimulated, and rats will repeatedly press a lever to receive a similar electrical reward.

Yet, no single part of the brain "controls" learning. For example, the cerebellum plays an important role in acquiring classically conditioned movements—such as conditioned eyeblink responses—whereas the amygdala is centrally involved in acquiring classically conditioned fears (Gabrieli, 1998; LeDoux, 1992; Thompson, 1985). We examine the brain mechanisms underlying learning more closely when discussing memory in the next chapter (without memory, we could not learn from experience).

Biology affects learning, but experiences and learning environments also influence our biological functioning (Wachs, 2000). Compared to their littermates who grow up in standard cages, young animals who are exposed to enriched environments—with toys and greater opportunities to learn—develop heavier brains with more dendrites and synapses, and with greater concentrations of various neurotransmitters (Rosenzweig, 1984). In turn, this increased brain development subsequently enables animals to perform better on learning and cognitive tasks (Meaney et al., 1991). Experiments with humans find that infants who regularly receive stimulating "touch sessions" develop more mature movement patterns, are less stressed, and perform better on cognitive tests than infants who do not receive these sessions (Field, 2000).

In late adulthood, continued exposure to stimulating environments seems to slow down declines in human brain functioning, as measured by better performance on intellectual and perceptual tasks (Goldstein et al, 1997; Schaie, 1998). In a sense then, every day you are alive your brain continues its own "personal evolution," its neural networks and patterns of activity affected not only by your genetic endowment, but as Figure 6.28 shows, by your experiences as well.

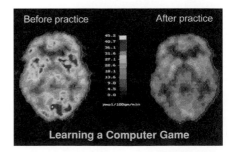

FIGURE 6.28 While learning a computer game, the brain of a novice player is highly active and uses a lot of energy, as indicated by the large yellow and red areas in the left PET scan. As the right scan shows, energy consumption decreases with experience.

❭ COGNITION AND LEARNING

Early behaviorists believed that learning involves the relatively automatic formation of bonds between stimuli and responses. In classical conditioning, the CS elicits the CR: tone→salivation. In operant conditioning, a discriminative stimulus leads to an emitted response: Light comes on→a hungry rat presses the lever to obtain food. This behaviorist orientation came to be known as *S-R (stimulus-response) psychology.* Behaviorists opposed explanations of learning

FIGURE 6.29 Sultan seemed to study the hanging bananas that were out reach. After looking around, he suddenly grabbed some crates, stacked them, and obtained his tasty reward.

that went beyond observable stimuli and responses. They did not deny that people had thoughts and feelings, but argued that behavior could be explained without referring to such mentalistic concepts (Skinner, 1953, 1990).

Behaviorism guided much learning research from the early 1900s through the 1960s, and it remains influential today (Reid & Staddon, 1998; Leighland, 2000). But even in psychology's early days, some learning theorists argued that in between stimulus (S) and response (R) there was something else: the organism's (O) mental representation of the world. This came to be known as the *S-O-R*, or *cognitive model* of learning. Today the cognitive perspective represents an important force in learning theory (Hollis, 1997).

Insight and Cognitive Maps

In the 1920s, German psychologist Wolfgang Köhler (1925) challenged Thorndike's behaviorist assumption that animals learn to perform tasks only by trial-and-error learning. Köhler exposed chimpanzees to novel learning tasks and concluded that they were able to learn by **insight,** the sudden perception of a useful relationship that helps to solve a problem. Figure 6.29 shows how one of his apes solved the problem of how to reach bananas that were dangling beyond reach. Köhler emphasized that the apes often spent time staring at the bananas and available tools, as if they were contemplating the problem, after which the solution suddenly appeared.

Behaviorists argued that such "insight" was merely a combination of previously reinforced and shaped responses (Epstein, 1984). To make their point, they trained pigeons to perform supposedly "insightful" behaviors, such as pushing a platform under some tiny toy bananas, then standing on the platform to peck at the bananas. But just because pigeons must be shaped, does this imply that shaping was responsible for the apes' solutions? Although the debate over animal insight continues, Köhler's work helped place the cognitive learning viewpoint on the map.

Another cognitive pioneer, learning theorist Edward Tolman of the University of California, Berkeley, studied spatial learning in rats. Look at the maze in Figure 6.30a. A rat runs to an open circular table, continues across, and follows the only path available to a goal box containing food. After 12 trials, the rat easily negotiates the maze. Next, the maze is changed. The rat runs its usual route and reaches a dead-end (Figure 6.30b). What will the rat do?

➤ 33. How do the concepts of "insight" and "cognitive maps" challenge the behaviorist view of learning?

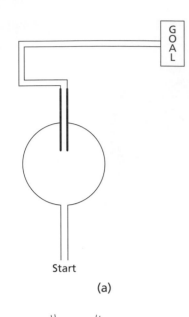

Start

(a)

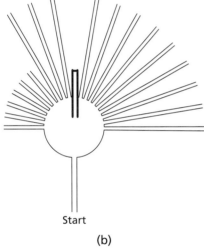

Start

(b)

FIGURE 6.30   Rats first learned to run the simple maze shown in (a). When the maze was switched (b), many rats chose the fourth path to the right of the original route. Tolman proposed that the rats had developed a cognitive map of the maze.

Adapted from Tolman, 1948.

➤ 34. Explain some evidence that supports the "expectancy model" of classical conditioning.

Tolman found that rats returned to the table, briefly explored most of the 18 new paths for just a few inches, and then chose one. By far, the largest number— 36 percent—chose the fourth path to the right of their original route, which took them to about 4 inches in front of where the goal box had been. In short, the rats behaved as you would, given your advantage of seeing the maps in Figure 6.30.

Tolman (1948) argued that reinforcement theory could not explain this behavior, but that he could: The rats had developed a mental representation of the maze layout—a **cognitive map.** The concept of cognitive maps supported Tolman's belief that learning does not merely "stamp in" stimulus-response connections. Rather, learning provides *knowledge,* and based on their knowledge organisms develop an *expectancy,* a cognitive representation of "what leads to what."

Behaviorists disagreed with Tolman's interpretations and developed noncognitive models to explain how organisms learn their way around (Hull, 1943; Reid & Staddon, 1998). Still, an explosion of research on spatial learning offers much support for the concept of cognitive maps in humans and other animals (Jacobs et al., 1998). Most importantly, Tolman's concept of expectancy remains a cornerstone of today's cognitive approaches to both classical and operant conditioning.

Cognition in Classical Conditioning

Early American behaviorists believed that classical conditioning created a direct reflexlike connection between the CS (tone) and CR (salivation). Interestingly, Pavlov held a different view, proposing that a neural bond is formed between the CS and the UCS. Thus the tone triggers an association with meat, which then triggers the reflexive salivation response.

Cognitive learning theorists also believe that classical conditioning forms a CS-UCS link. In cognitive terminology, the link is an expectancy that the CS will be followed by the UCS (Bolles, 1979; Hollis, 1997). This *expectancy model* states that the most important factor in classical conditioning is *not* how often the CS and the UCS are paired, but *how well the CS predicts (i.e., signals) the appearance of the UCS* (Rescorla & Wagner, 1972).

Robert Rescorla (1968) of Yale University demonstrated this principle in an experiment on fear conditioning. Rats in one condition received electric shocks (UCS), and each shock was preceded by a tone. As usual, the tone soon became a CS that elicited a fear response when presented alone. In a second condition, rats received the same number of tone-shock pairings as the first group, but they also received as many shocks that were not preceded by the tone. Would the tone become a CS for fear? According to traditional learning theory, the answer should be "yes," because the number of tone-shock pairings was the same as in the first group. But the expectancy model predicts "no," because the tone does not reliably predict when the shock will occur. The results supported Rescorla's hypothesis: The tone did not elicit a fear response for the second group.

CS-UCS inconsistency also explains why we don't become conditioned to all the neutral stimuli that are present just before a UCS appears. For example, when Pavlov's dogs were presented with tone-food pairings, there was light in the room. Why didn't the dogs learn to salivate whenever they saw light? Or imagine a doctor testing your "knee-jerk reflex." Many of us jerk slightly at the mere sight of that little rubber mallet moving toward our knee. Why doesn't this response occur to other stimuli that are present just before the hammer strikes, such as the sight of a physician sitting on a stool?

The key is that when Pavlov's dogs' room was lit, they often were not receiving food. And most of the time physicians sit on stools, they are not about to tap our knees. From a cognitive viewpoint, these neutral stimuli do not consistently predict the arrival of the UCS, dramatically reducing the chance that they will become a CS. This is highly adaptive; if it were not the case, you and I (along with Pavlov's dogs) would be twitching, salivating, blinking, and exhibiting all sorts of embarrassing reflexive responses to so many stimuli that it would be difficult to function.

Other types of evidence support this cognitive model over a simple CS-UCS pairing model. For example, recall that *forward pairing* (CS followed by UCS) typically produces the strongest learning, *simultaneous pairing* produces weaker learning, and *backward pairing* (UCS followed by CS) produces the weakest or no learning. This makes sense based on the expectancy model. In forward tone-food pairing, the tone predicts the imminent arrival of the UCS; it is a signal that something meaningful is about happen. With simultaneous pairing, the tone has less value as a signal because the food arrives at the same time. And in backward pairing, the tone has no predictive value because the food has already arrived.

Learning theorists continue to test other models of classical conditioning (Schmajuk & Nestor, 1998), but the expectancy model has been highly influential (Siegel & Allan, 1996). In sum, there is good evidence that cognition plays a role in classical conditioning.

Cognition in Operant Conditioning

Cognitive theorists point to a variety of evidence to support their claim that mental processes also play a key role in operant conditioning. We'll examine three issues here.

The Role of Awareness

Cognitive theorists emphasize that organisms develop an *awareness* or *expectancy* of the relations between their responses and probable consequences. Many of Tolman's rats acted as if they were aware that running through one alternate path or the other would produce the best consequence, once they learned that their primary route was blocked. Similarly, suppose you are in an experiment where your task is to make up a sentence and tell it to me. As you speak, I say "good" or "mmm-hmm" every time your sentence contains a noun that refers to humans (e.g., boy, woman, people). We go through this process for 10 sentences, and I measure whether your usage of human nouns changes. In the actual experiment, only those participants who received praise *and* who became aware of the reinforcement contingency increased their usage of human nouns (Spielberger & DeNike, 1966). Those who received praise but remained unaware of why it was given performed no differently than a control group receiving no praise.

From a cognitive perspective, the concept of "awareness" implies that the best predictor of behavior is the *perceived* contingency, not the actual one (Figure 6.31). In many instances the two are identical, but sometimes people perceive contingencies that do not actually exist. One example is superstitious behavior. In cognitive terms, the organism misperceives that a specific behavior (e.g., not walking under ladders, holding on to a "good luck" charm) produces good consequences or helps avoid bad ones.

Another example of a misperceived contingency sometimes occurs with punishment. As the following tongue-in-cheek anecdote illustrates, the person delivering punishment may be attempting to suppress one behavior, but the recipient perceives that the punishment is directed at another behavior:

> A psychologist reported that a frustrated mother once contacted him for assistance in the reduction of swearing behavior on the part of her two young sons. A behavior therapist, the psychologist recommended that she use punishment techniques. He told her that it was important to use immediate and severe punishment

➤ 35. What role does awareness play in operant conditioning?

Reprinted with permission of Jester of Columbia.

"Boy, have I got this guy conditioned! Every time I press the bar down, he drops in a piece of food."

FIGURE 6.31 Perception versus reality.

each and every time the swearing occurred. To maximize the impact of that punishment, he also recommended that she try to use each child as an example for the other—that is, punish him in front of his brother.

Enthusiastic over this advice, the mother returned home. At breakfast the next morning, she sat down ready and raring to modify behavior. The older son opened the conversation by requesting that she "pass the [expletive deleted] Cheerios." With lightning fury, the mother lunged across the table and hit her son—sent both him and his chair sprawling to the floor. Pleased with her skillful execution of behavioral principles, the mother turned to her somewhat bewildered younger son. "Well, what will you have?" He paused a moment, glanced at his supine brother, and answered, "You can bet your sweet ass it isn't Cheerios!" (Mahoney, 1980, pp. 136–137)

Latent Learning

> ➤ 36. How does latent learning challenge the behaviorist view of learning?

Tolman's research, described in Figure 6.30, suggested that rats developed cognitive maps when they were reinforced with food for running the maze. Tolman also believed that cognitive maps could be learned without reinforcement, posing an even greater challenge to the behaviorist viewpoint. In one experiment, three groups of rats were run in a complex maze (Tolman & Honzik, 1930). Rats in Group 1 found food each time they reached the goal box. Rats in Group 2 found the goal box empty each time they reached it. The third group of rats found no food at the end of the maze for the first 10 days, but did find food in the goal box starting on the 11th day.

The results are shown in Figure 6.32, and the key finding is this: On Day 11, the rats in Group 3 discovered food in the goal box for the first time. By the very next day, they were performing just as well as the Group 1 rats who had been reinforced all along. What could explain this large, sudden performance improvement? According to Tolman, during Days 1 to 10, the Group 3 rats were learning the spatial layout of the maze as they wandered about. They were not being reinforced by food, but they gained knowledge and developed their cognitive maps. This learning remained "latent" (hidden) until the rats discovered a good reason on Day 11 to get to the goal box quickly, and then it immediately was manifested in performance the next day. Tolman's experiments supported the concept of **latent learning,** which refers to learning that occurs but is not demonstrated until there is an incentive to perform (Blodgett, 1929). In short, like Tolman's rats, we may "learn how" to do something (gain knowledge), but not display that knowledge outwardly (performance) until some future time.

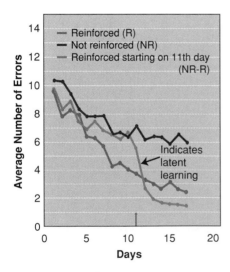

FIGURE 6.32 Tolman's demonstration of latent learning. Rats had one trial in the maze per day. Group NR received no reinforcement in the maze at any time. Group R was reinforced with food every time they reached the end of the maze. The critical group (NR-R) had food reward introduced on the 11th day. Their immediate performance improvement suggested that they had learned the maze prior to the introduction of reinforcement.

(Tolman & Honzik, 1930)

Self-Evaluations as Reinforcers and Punishers

Students called him "Holy Hubert," and he visited my campus for over 10 years. His fire-and-brimstone exhortations to repent and avoid damnation often evoked amused smiles, loud insults, and ridicule. One could hardly imagine less positive consequences for an evangelist. One day, I asked Hubert why he continued to preach when students' responses were so negative. He answered, "I don't care what they say. When I know I'm doing the Lord's work, I feel so good that they could hang me for all I care."

Hubert's persistence in the face of adversity illustrates that external reinforcement and punishment are not the only consequences controlling behavior. If they were, how could we account for the actions of people who resist temptation when there is no chance of discovery and punishment? We often feel pride for doing something, even if others do not know or approve of our deeds. In this sense, virtue is indeed its own reward. We also may disapprove of ourselves for failing to live up to our own standards. These *cognitive self-evaluations* represent important internal reinforcers and punishers (Bandura, 1986; Cervone, 1992).

Our internal standards develop in many ways. As part of our *socialization* into society, parents, teachers, and other people set standards for our behavior, reinforcing us when we meet their expectations and disapproving of us when we don't. Eventually we may adopt (i.e., internalize) their standards. Once we develop self-evaluative standards, our actions can be influenced by external *and* internal consequences. Thinking back to the woman soliciting charitable donations, her strong belief that she is doing something valuable may be all the positive reinforcement she needs.

❯ OBSERVATIONAL LEARNING: WHEN OTHERS PAVE THE WAY

How did you learn to write, drive a car, and make a peanut butter and jelly sandwich? Reinforcement certainly was involved, but so was **observational learning,** the learning that occurs by observing the behavior of a model. Teachers, parents, and peers help us learn by modeling academic skills. Coaches and music teachers demonstrate motor skills. Through observation, we learn that peanut butter is spread across a piece of bread, rather than piled up in the center. In the time-honored apprenticeship system, a novice watches and learns from a master.

> ➤ 37. What is the adaptive significance of observational learning?

Observational learning can be highly adaptive. By observing others, an organism can learn which events are important, which stimuli signal that such events are about to occur, and which responses are likely to produce positive or negative consequences. For example, juvenile canaries learn to recognize seeds in part by watching their parents eat, and jays and nutcrackers seem to learn where food is by observing their feathered friends hide it (Bednekoff & Balda, 1996; Cadieu & Cadieu, 1998). Hens may learn who they can reasonably pick a fight with, and who they should avoid, by observing who emerges the victor and loser in battles between other hens (Hogue et al., 1996). And monkeys may learn adaptive fears—such as a fear of snakes—by observing other monkeys' reactions (Mineka & Hamida, 1998).

Our capacity to learn by observation, which is also called *modeling,* far outstrips that of other creatures. It saves us enormous time and effort, and helps us bypass the potentially time-consuming and dangerous process of trial and error. We do not want each new generation of medical surgeons, airline pilots, and firefighters to learn their craft only through trial and error. Beyond such skill acquisition, what makes observational learning so important is that we also learn fears, prejudices, likes and dislikes, and social behaviors by watching others (Bandura, 1977; Hendy & Raudenbush, 2000). Highly successful models can inspire us and boost our self-image when we view their achievements as attainable and relevant (Lockwood & Kunda, 1997). Through observation we may learn desirable and adaptive responses, or, like the two boys in our opening vignette who overzealously emulated their TV wrestling heroes, we may acquire undesirable behaviors.

Models, of course, differ in many ways. We are more likely to imitate those who are competent, likable, and have higher status or social power (Brewer & Wann, 1998; Brody & Stoneman, 1985). Our reasons for observing behavior also differ. Imagine observing a model, knowing that you will be trying to imitate the behavior later on. Now imagine observing a model, knowing that you will not be asked to imitate the behavior. An experiment using PET scans suggests that brain regions involved in planning are more active when we watch models with the intent of imitating their behavior (Decety et al., 1997).

The Modeling Process

Psychologist Albert Bandura (1977), who helped pioneer the scientific study of observational learning, views it as a cognitive process involving four basic steps: *attention, retention, reproduction,* and *motivation.* First, we must pay attention to

> ➤ 38. Explain how Bandura's experiment illustrates the distinction between learning and performance.

the model's behavior. Second, we must retain that information in memory so that it can be recalled at a later time. Third, we must be physically capable of reproducing the model's behavior, or something similar to it. And fourth, we must be motivated to display the behavior.

The fourth step, motivation, highlights the important distinction between *learning* and *performance*. Recall that we defined learning as a change in an organism's behavior *or capabilities* based on experience. Research shows that observation alone is enough to learn a behavior, but future performance depends on the consequences that we expect (Bandura, 1989). Tolman's work on latent learning and Bandura's research on modeling demonstrate that knowledge and the capability to perform a behavior can be acquired at one time, but not be displayed until a later time.

Bandura (1965) demonstrated this point in a classic experiment. Children watched a film in which a model acted aggressively toward a "Bobo doll" (a plastic, inflatable clown), punching, kicking, and hitting it with a mallet. One group saw the model rewarded with praise and candy, a second group saw the model reprimanded for aggression, and a third group saw no consequences for the model. After the film, each child was placed in a room with various toys, including a Bobo doll (Figure 6.33).

Children who saw the model punished performed fewer aggressive actions toward Bobo than did children in the other two groups. Does this mean that the first group failed to learn how to respond aggressively? To find out, the experimenter later offered the children attractive prizes if they could do what the model had done. All of the children quickly reproduced the model's aggressive responses.

Do these findings generalize to the real world? This research helped stir a societal controversy that was brewing in the 1960s and which continues to this day: What effect does viewing media violence have on our attitudes and behavior? We discuss this issue more fully in Chapter 12. In brief, despite some scientific disagreement, the weight of laboratory experiments and real-world correlational studies strongly suggests that viewing media violence has these effects (Eron, 2000; Huesmman, 1997; Smith & Donnerstein, 1998):

➤ 39. Evaluate the internal and external validity of the *Lassie* experiment.

- it decreases concerns about the suffering of victims,
- it habituates us (reduces our sensitivity) to the sight of violence, and
- it provides aggressive models that increase the likelihood of aggression.

If watching aggressive models on television can enhance our aggression, can watching "prosocial" models (models who do good deeds) increase our tendency to help others? The following *Research Close-Up* examines this question.

FIGURE 6.33 In Bandura's experiment, most children who watched an aggressive model attack a Bobo model later imitated that behavior. These photos show only one of several specific actions that the children spontaneously imitated.

RESEARCH   CLOSE-UP

Lessons From *Lassie:* Can Watching TV Increase Helping Behavior?

▶ **Background**

This experiment by Joyce Sprafkin and her colleagues represents one of the earliest attempts to examine whether children behave more helpfully after watching prosocial models on TV. It is the first controlled experiment to do so using a general "entertainment" program from the major TV networks. The authors also examined whether a specific act of helping had to be modeled *during* the TV program to enhance children's prosocial behavior, or whether merely watching a highly popular, prosocial "action hero" (the dog, Lassie) would produce the same effect. Children's prosocial behavior was measured in a unique conflict-of-interest situation, where a decision to help meant reducing their own chances to obtain a very attractive prize.

▶ **Method**

With their parents' permission, 15 girls and 15 boys were randomly selected from first grade at a suburban school in Long Island, New York. Each child watched a half-hour TV program to pass the time while a special game "was being set up in another room." Children were randomly assigned to one of three TV programs, representing the *independent variable.* In the experimental condition (prosocial Lassie), a puppy fell into a mine shaft, Lassie ran to get her young master, led him back to the mine, and he risked his life to save the puppy. In one control condition (neutral Lassie) the show portrayed a Lassie adventure that did not involve a human helping a dog. In a second control condition, a Brady Bunch episode portraying positive family interactions (but no dogs) was shown. *Lassie* and *The Brady Bunch* were both popular shows at the time.

A second experimenter, blind to the child's TV condition, led the child to a "Point Game" room containing prizes that ranged in size and attractiveness. Nicer prizes cost more points, earned by pressing a button that lit a bulb as fast as possible. Points were automatically recorded and displayed, so the child could watch them accrue. Before leaving the child to play alone, the experimenter said:

> I'm in charge of a dog kennel . . . a place that we keep puppies until a home can be found for them. I had to leave the puppies alone so that I could come here today, but I know whether the dogs are safe or not by listening through these earphones . . . connected to the kennel. When I don't hear any noises

. . . I know the dogs are O.K. . . . but if I hear them barking, I know . . . that they are in trouble and need help. If I hear barking, I press this button [a Help Button] which signals my helper . . . he goes over . . . to make sure nothing bad happened to the dogs.

The children were asked to wear the headphones while playing the Point Game and press the Help Button if the puppies barked. They were reminded that nicer prizes cost more points, to try to get as many points as possible, and that if the dogs barked the child would have to choose what to do, because it was impossible to play the Point Game and signal for help at the same time.

The experimenter left, turned on a tape recorder, and played the same tape for each child: It began with 30 seconds of silence, then 120 seconds of escalating barking. Two *dependent variables* were recorded: the amount of time each child pressed the Help Button during the barking, and the speed with which they intervened once barking began.

▶ **Results**

During the 120-second barking period, children in the prosocial Lassie, neutral Lassie, and Brady Bunch conditions spent 77 percent, 43 percent, and 31 percent of their time pressing the Help Button, respectively. Children's gender did not influence the results. In addition to helping more, the prosocial Lassie children were faster to respond. On average, they began helping 25 seconds after the barking began, compared to 36 seconds and 55 seconds for the other groups.

▶ **Critical Analysis**

This study examined a socially important question under controlled conditions. However, before we can accept the authors' conclusion that the prosocial behavior modeled in *Lassie* was the likely cause of why children helped more, we must ask whether any other factors internal to the experiment could have caused these findings. In other words, did the experiment have high *internal* validity?

The experimenters did many things to reduce alternative explanations. Children were randomly assigned to the TV condition and treated as similarly as possible except for the film they viewed. To minimize the potential for experimenter bias, the researcher who interacted with the children during the Point Game and measured their behavior did not know (was blind to) which TV program the child had watched.

–Continued

Using two control groups was a positive feature, as was the fact that the neutral Lassie and prosocial Lassie programs involved the same main characters, setting, and general dramatic style. However, the authors did not specify whether the neutral Lassie film also involved a puppy (one who didn't have to be rescued). If it didn't, can you see why this might be a problem? Is it *possible* that simply seeing a cute puppy on TV for much of the program increased children's sensitivity or empathy for the barking puppies in the "kennel," and per- haps this is why they helped more. If the "neutral" program had a puppy, this concern would be eliminated.

Finally, there is the question of *external* validity. Do the results generalize to other settings, including "real-world" ones? The answer appears to be yes. A survey of nearly 200 studies examining the effects of prosocial TV within and out- side the laboratory indicates that such programs positively affect children's behavior (Hearold, 1986). The implications for TV programming seem clear: Lassie, come home.

Source: Joyce N. Sprafkin, Robert M. Liebert, and Rita Wicks Poulous (1975). Effects of a prosocial televised example on children's helping. *Journal of Experimental Child Psychology, 20,* 119–129.

❯ THE ROLE OF LANGUAGE

➤ 40. How does language make learning more efficient?

The story is told of an operant conditioning demonstration that occurred in an introductory psychology class. The instructor sent one student out of the room and instructed another student in how to shape the response of flicking the light switch on and off, using M&M's as the reinforcer. When the naive student re- turned, he was reinforced first for looking at the wall that held the light switch, then for approaching the wall, and so on, until, 25 minutes later, he was happily flicking the switch and chomping one M&M after another.

At this point, another student asked if she could serve as experimenter. A new participant left the room while the class decided that he should be shaped to erase the blackboard. When the student reentered the classroom, the new experimenter said, "John, if you'll erase the blackboard immediately, I'll give you this whole bag of M&M's." This time, it took all of 5 seconds to produce the desired behavior.

As this example illustrates, language can be an extremely efficient learn- ing mechanism. Like modeling, language frees us from trial-and-error learn- ing and plays a critical role in teaching us *how* to perform various actions. To get to a friend's house or a hospital for the first time, you do not have to de- velop a cognitive map by driving all around town. You get verbal directions. Language enables us to learn which events are important ("Be sure to turn right at the stop sign"), which stimuli signal their impending occurrence ("There will be a small grocery store 100 yards before the stop sign"), and what the likely consequences of behavior will be ("If you miss the turn, you will end up back at the highway"). Language can convey a vastly wider array of infor- mation than observational learning, including abstract concepts and informa- tion about the past and future.

Language is a cognitive learning mechanism, but it also is a social one. Over the course of evolution, humans adopted a more socially oriented lifestyle that helped them survive and reproduce (Flinn, 1997). As the social en- vironment became more complex, new real-life problems emerged: forming co- operative social systems, developing social customs, communicating one's thoughts to others, creating divisions of labor, and passing on knowledge and wisdom (Kottak, 1999). All of these tasks were made easier by the development of language. Language not only facilitates knowledge transmission, it also helps to build strong social bonds between people, and it is the foundation on which human cultures are built (Skinner, 1986). As we shall see in Chapter 8, no other species has the well-developed language capacity of humans.

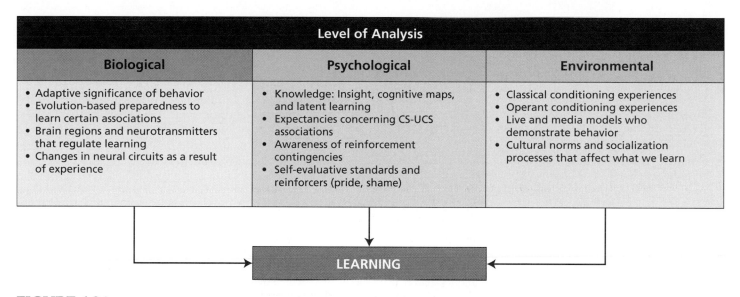

FIGURE 6.34 Understanding the Causes of Behavior: Factors that influence learning.

〉 SOME FINAL THOUGHTS

Advances in the understanding of learning principles are considered by many to be one of the greatest contributions of psychological science. Early in the history of behaviorism, a stimulus-response model dominated learning and emphasized control of behavior by the external environment. Over time, other perspectives have broadened our understanding of learning. Figure 6.34 summarizes how learning, like other aspects of behavior, can be examined at several levels of analysis.

CHAPTER SUMMARY

- Learning is a process by which experience produces a relatively enduring change in an organism's behavior or capabilities. Learning is measured by changes in performance.

Adapting to the Environment

- Learning involves adapting to the environment. Historically, behaviorists focused on the processes by which organisms learn, and ethologists focused on the adaptive significance of learning. Today these two perspectives have crossed paths, and more attention also is paid to how mental processes and cultural environments influence learning.

Habituation

- Habituation is a decrease in the strength of a response to a repeated stimulus. It may be the simplest form of learning.

- Habituation allows organisms to attend to other stimuli that are more important.

Classical Conditioning: Associating One Stimulus With Another

- Classical conditioning involves pairing a neutral stimulus with an unconditioned stimulus (UCS) that elicits an unconditioned response (UCR). Through repeated pairing, the neutral stimulus becomes a conditioned stimulus (CS) that evokes a conditioned response (CR) similar to the original UCR.

- The acquisition phase involves pairing the CS with the UCS. Extinction, the disappearance of the CR, occurs when the CS is presented repeatedly in the absence of the UCS. Sometimes, spontaneous recovery occurs after a rest period and the CS will temporarily evoke a response even after extinction has taken place.

- Stimulus generalization occurs when a CR is evoked by a stimulus similar to the original CS. Discrimination occurs when a CR occurs to one stimulus but not another.

- Once a stimulus (e.g., a tone) becomes a CS, it can now be used in place of the original UCS (food) to condition other neutral stimuli. This is called higher-order conditioning.

- A wide range of bodily and psychological responses can be classically conditioned, including fears, sexual attraction, and positive and negative attitudes. Techniques based on classical conditioning are highly successful in treating fears and phobias.

- Cancer patients may develop anticipatory nausea or vomiting (ANV) to stimuli that are paired with their chemotherapy. ANV is a classically conditioned response. Classical conditioning also can increase or decrease immune system responses.

Operant Conditioning: Learning Through Consequences

- Thorndike's law of effect states that responses followed by satisfying consequences will be strengthened, whereas those followed by unsatisfying consequences will be weakened.

- B. F. Skinner analyzed operant conditioning in terms of relations between antecedents, behaviors, and consequences. Antecedents that signal the likely consequences of particular behaviors in a given situation are called discriminative stimuli.

- Operant behaviors are emitted (under voluntary control), whereas classically conditioned responses are elicited (reflexive). Classically conditioned responses are influenced by what happens before the behavior (i.e., by the CS-UCS pairing), whereas operant behaviors are influenced by consequences that occur after the behavior.

- Reinforcement occurs when a response is strengthened by an outcome (a reinforcer) that follows it. With positive reinforcement, a response is followed by the presentation of a positive stimulus, so the response becomes stronger. With negative reinforcement, a response is followed by the removal of an aversive stimulus, so again, the response becomes stronger.

- Operant extinction is the weakening and eventual disappearance of a response because it no longer is reinforced.

- Punishment occurs when a response is weakened by an outcome (a punisher) that follows it. With aversive punishment, a behavior is followed by the presentation of an aversive stimulus, and the behavior becomes weaker. With response cost, a behavior is followed by the removal of a positive stimulus, and the behavior becomes weaker.

- Shaping, which uses the method of successive approximations, involves the reinforcement of behaviors that increasingly resemble the final desired behavior.

- When behavior changes in one situation due to reinforcement or punishment, and then this new response carries over to similar situations, this is called operant generalization. In contrast, when an operant response is made to one discriminative stimulus but not to another, this is called operant discrimination.

- On a continuous reinforcement schedule every response is reinforced. Partial reinforcement may occur on a ratio schedule, in which a certain percentage of responses are reinforced, or on an interval schedule, in which a certain amount of time must pass before a response gets reinforced. In general, ratio schedules produce higher rates of performance than interval schedules.

- On fixed ratio and interval schedules, reinforcement always occurs after a fixed number of correct responses or a fixed time interval. On variable schedules, the required number of responses or interval of time varies around some average.

- Learning occurs most rapidly under continuous reinforcement, but partial schedules produce behaviors that are more resistant to extinction.

- Escape and avoidance conditioning result from negative reinforcement. According to two-factor theory, fear is created through classical conditioning. This fear motivates escape and avoidance, which is then negatively reinforced by fear reduction.

- Animals are operantly trained to perform in entertainment industries and to assist disabled people, the police, and the military. Human applications include teaching machines, computerized instruction, token economies, and applied behavior analysis.

Biology and Learning

- An animal's evolutionary history prepares it to learn certain associations more easily than others. This principle is called biological preparedness, and it illustrates that there are biological constraints on learning.

- Humans show faster fear conditioning to CSs that have evolutionary significance, suggesting that we are biologically prepared to acquire specific kinds of phobias.

- It is difficult to operantly condition animals to perform behaviors that are contrary to their evolved natural tendencies. Such conditioned behaviors are often abandoned in favor of a more natural response, a concept called instinctive drift.

- Various brain regions and chemicals regulate learning. Environmental experiences affect brain development and functioning, which in turn influences our future ability to learn.

Cognition and Learning

- Köhler's early research on animal insight and Tolman's pioneering research on cognitive maps indicated that cognitive factors play a role in learning. Tolman emphasized that learning is based on knowledge and an expectation of "what leads to what."

- Cognitive interpretations of classical conditioning propose that what is learned is an expectancy that the CS will be followed by the UCS.

- Cognitive theorists view operant conditioning as the development of an expectancy that certain behaviors will produce certain consequences under certain conditions. Tolman's research on latent learning indicates that "knowledge" and "performance" are conceptually distinct, and that learning can occur without reinforcement.

- In humans, internal self-evaluations (e.g., pride and shame) can function as reinforcers and punishers.

Observational Learning: When Others Pave the Way

- Many behaviors are learned through mere observation. The behavior may not be displayed immediately, but instead may appear later when incentive conditions change.

- Emotional responses, aggression, and prosocial behaviors can be learned through observation.

The Role of Language

- For humans, language brings a flexibility and efficiency to learning far beyond that reached by other species. Language facilities the cultural transmission of knowledge from one generation to the next.

▼▼

KEY TERMS AND CONCEPTS*

adaptive significance (229)

anticipatory nausea and vomiting (ANV) (238)

applied behavior analysis (253)

aversive punishment (245)

aversion therapy (238)

avoidance conditioning (251)

chaining (247)

classical conditioning (231)

cognitive map (260)

conditioned response (CR) (233)

conditioned stimulus (CS) (233)

continuous reinforcement (248)

conditioned taste aversion (255)

delay of gratification (246)

discrimination (classical conditioning) (235)

discriminative stimulus (242)

escape conditioning (251)

exposure therapies (237)

extinction (classical conditioning) (234)

extinction (operant conditioning) (244)

fixed action pattern (229)

fixed-interval (FI) schedule (249)

fixed-ratio (FR) schedule (249)

habituation (231)

higher-order conditioning (236)

insight (259)

instinctive drift (257)

latent learning (262)

law of effect (240)

learning (228)

negative reinforcement (244)

observational learning (263)

operant conditioning (240)

operant discrimination (248)

operant generalization (248)

partial reinforcement (248)

positive reinforcement (242)

preparedness (255)

primary reinforcer (243)

punishment (241)

reinforcement (241)

response cost (245)

secondary (conditioned) reinforcer (243)

shaping (247)

Skinner box (240)

spontaneous recovery (235)

stimulus generalization (235)

target behavior (254)

token economy (253)

two-factor theory of avoidance learning (251)

unconditioned response (UCR) (233)

unconditioned stimulus (UCS) (233)

variable-interval (VI) schedule (250)

variable-ratio (VR) schedule (249)

* Each term has been boldfaced in the text on the page indicated in parentheses.

▼▼

APPLYING YOUR KNOWLEDGE

These questions allow you to apply your understanding of material in this chapter.

1. Dr. Martinez is an ethologist, and tomorrow she will present a guest lecture on the topic of learning to your introductory psychology class. Knowing that she is an ethologist, you should expect that her lecture will focus most strongly on
   a) how different schedules of reinforcement influence laboratory animals' behavior.
   b) the adaptive significance of animals' behavior in natural environments.
   c) the role of cognitive factors in human and animal learning.
   d) practical applications of classical conditioning in modifying human behavior.

2. A green light is turned on and Kathy does not blink. Then a puff of air is blown into Kathy's eye, and she blinks. Next the green light is turned on just before the puff of air is presented, and this pairing is repeated several times. Shortly, Kathy starts blinking as soon as she sees the green light. At this point in time (at the end of this procedure), the green light represents
   a) a conditioned stimulus.
   b) an unconditioned stimulus.
   c) a conditioned response.
   d) an unconditioned response.

3. During his first horse-riding lesson, 10-year-old Ken was thrown from a horse named Buster. He became afraid of Buster and would not get back on. A week later, when it was time for his next ride, he was still afraid of Buster, but he was not afraid to get on a much smaller horse, Buttercup. The fact that Ken was *not* afraid of Buttercup best illustrates which of the following learning principles?
   a) spontaneous recovery
   b) higher-order conditioning
   c) stimulus generalization
   d) discrimination

4. Rolfe goes to the supermarket to buy some new batteries for his portable cassette player. There are several brands to choose from, and their products are equally good. But Rolfe has seen dozens of commercials for EverReady Energizer batteries, featuring a cute mechanical bunny in humorous situations. He just "feels good" about Energizer batteries, and buys them. Rolfe's positive feeling about the Energizer batteries is most likely the result of
   a) observational learning.
   b) positive reinforcement.
   c) negative reinforcement.
   d) classical conditioning.

5. Claudia is driving on the highway and exceeding the speed limit. She sees a State Patrol car ahead and immediately slows down. In this example, the State Patrol car represents
   a) an unconditioned stimulus.
   b) a discriminative stimulus.
   c) a positive reinforcer.
   d) a negative reinforcer.

6. Professor Miyamoto tells his new class, "You can earn extra credit by identifying articles in the newspaper. For each article, write a one-page paper relating it to the course content. For every 3 acceptable papers you write, 0.1 grade points will be added to your grade (e.g., a 3.0 becomes a 3.1). You don't have to do any papers, but the maximum number you can write is 15 papers." This extra credit system best represents a
   a) fixed-ratio schedule of reinforcement.
   b) variable-ratio schedule of reinforcement.
   c) fixed-interval schedule of reinforcement.
   d) variable-interval schedule of reinforcement.

7. One day Shirley comes home from work with mild back pain. Her husband suggests that she take a hot bath. Shirley doesn't like baths (she likes showers), but she gives the bath a try. After 15 minutes, her back pain is completely gone. From that point on, whenever Shirley comes home with back pain, she immediately takes a hot bath. Which of the following principles best accounts for this change in bath-taking behavior?
   a) positive reinforcement
   b) negative reinforcement
   c) punishment
   d) classical conditioning

8. Harold feels that he has poor eating habits. He wants to develop a self-regulation program to change this situation. The first two steps in his program should be to
   a) identify the antecedents and consequences of his poor eating habits.
   b) identify the antecedents and collect baseline data.
   c) specify the target behavior and develop a plan to modify his poor eating habits.
   d) specify the target behavior and collect baseline data.

9. As a cognitive learning theorist, Dr. Robertson is most likely to believe that the key factor in classical conditioning is
   a) the strength or intensity of the CS.
   b) the strength or intensity of the UCS.
   c) how predictably the UCS follows the CS.
   d) how often the CS and UCS appear together.

10. One day, 6-year-old Kelley asks her father if she can play a video game on the home computer. Kelley has never played it, but has watched her parents play it many times. To her parents' surprise, Kelley is able to start the program and operate the controls without any help. This example best illustrates the concept of
    a) instinctive drift.
    b) response cost.
    c) latent learning.
    d) spontaneous recovery.

Answers

1. b) (page 229); 2. a) (page 233); 3. d) (page 235); 4. d) (page 238); 5. b) (page 242); 6. a) (page 249); 7. b) (page 244); 8. d) (page 254); 9. c) (page 260); 10. c) (page 262)

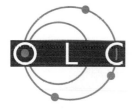

For additional quizzing and a variety of interactive resources, visit the book's Online Learning Center at www.mhhe.com/passer.

MEMORY

The charm, one might say, the genius of memory
is that it is choosy, chancy, and temperamental.
— *Elizabeth Boren*

7

273

▼▼▼▼▼▼▼▼▼▼▼▼▼▼▼▼▼▼▼▼▼▼▼▼▼▼▼▼▼▼▼▼▼▼▼▼▼▼▼

You are about to meet H. M., a 27-year-old man who recently had most of his hippocampus and surrounding brain tissue surgically removed to reduce his severe epileptic seizures. The operation succeeded, but it has unexpectedly left H. M. with *amnesia,* or memory loss.

When you first meet H. M. he might appear normal, for he is bright and has retained good language and social skills. Perhaps to your surprise, he can discuss his childhood, teens, and early twenties, for those memories are intact. H. M. has forgotten some events that occurred within the two years prior to surgery, but for the most part, his amnesia has not robbed him of his past. Rather, as of age 27, it is about to rob him of his future.

H. M. has lost the ability to form new memories that he can consciously recall. Typically, once an experience or fact leaves his immediate train of thought, he cannot remember it. Spend the day with H. M., depart and return minutes later, and he will not recall having met you. He forgets that he has recently eaten and reads magazines over and over as if he has never seen them before. A favorite uncle has died, but H. M. cannot remember. Thus every time H. M. asks how his uncle is, he experiences shock and grief as though it were the first time he learned of his uncle's death.

H. M.'s surgery actually took place in 1953, and researchers have followed his case for over 40 years (Postle & Corkin, 1998; Scoville & Milner, 1957). No matter how many years pass, H. M.'s memory for events contains little after 1953. He cannot consciously remember new facts, nor retain the meaning of words that have entered the English language since his operation. He once guessed, for example, that "biodegradable" meant "two grades." Even his sense of identity is frozen in time. H. M. recalls himself looking like a young man, and cannot remember the aging image of himself that he sees in the mirror. Here, H. M. describes what his existence is like:

> Every day is alone in itself. . . . You see, at this moment, everything looks clear to me, but what happened just before? It's like waking from a dream. I just don't remember. (Milner, 1970, p. 37)

Memory refers to the processes that allow us to record and later retrieve experiences and information. As H. M.'s case illustrates, memory is precious and complex. What prevents H. M. from recalling new experiences, while leaving most of his pre-1953 memories intact? Why is it, as Figure 7.1 shows, that H. M. can learn and remember how to perform new tasks, yet swear each time he encounters these tasks that he has never seen them before? In this chapter, we explore these and other fascinating questions about memory.

❯ MEMORY AS INFORMATION PROCESSING

➤ 1. How is memory likened to an information-processing system?

Psychological research on memory has a rich tradition, dating back to late 19th-century Europe where Hermann Ebbinghaus (1885) studied the rate at which new information is forgotten and Sir Francis Galton (1883) investigated people's memories for personal events. Decades later, the cognitive revolution within North American psychology and the advent of computers ushered in a metaphor that has influenced memory research since the 1960s: the mind as a processing system that encodes, stores, and retrieves information (Bower, 2000).

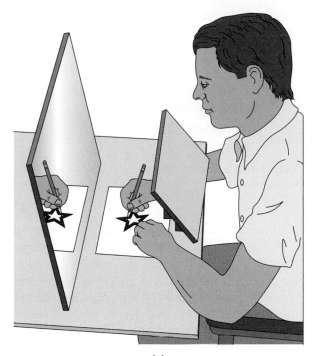

(a)

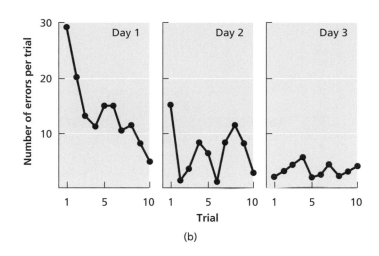

(b)

FIGURE 7.1 (a) On this complex task, participants trace a pattern while looking at its mirror image, which shows their hand moving in the direction opposite to its actual movement. (b) H. M.'s performance rapidly improved over time, indicating that he had retained a memory of *how* to perform the task. Yet each time he performed it, he stated that he had never seen the task before, and had to have the instructions reexplained.
Adapted from Milner, 1965.

Encoding refers to getting information into the system by translating it into a neural code that your brain processes. This is a little like what happens when you type on a computer keyboard, as your keystrokes are translated into an electrical code that the computer can understand and process. **Storage** involves retaining information over time. Once in the system, information must be filed away and saved, as happens when a computer stores information on a hard drive. Finally, there must be a way to pull information out of storage when we want to use it, a process called **retrieval.** On a computer, retrieval occurs when you give a software command (e.g., "Open File") that transfers information from the hard drive back to the screen where you can view it. Keep in mind, however, that this analogy between human and computer is crude. For one thing, we routinely forget and distort information, and may "remember" events that never occurred (Loftus, 1979; Schacter & Curran, 2000). Human memory is highly dynamic and its complexity cannot be fully captured by any existing information-processing model.

Encoding, storage, and retrieval represent what our memory system does with information, and they could not take place without memory having some type of organization, or structure. Thus before exploring these processes in more detail, let us examine some basic components of memory.

A Three-Component Model

Our encounter with H. M. suggests an interesting possibility regarding how memory might be organized. If you told H. M. your name or read him a series of numbers, he could recall it for a short time. Yet he could not form a lasting memory; once his train of thought changed, that information was lost forever. Could it be, as William James (1890) suggested long ago, that memory has distinct yet interacting components, one temporary and the other more permanent?

FIGURE 7.2 In this model, memory has three major components: (1) sensory registers, which detect and briefly hold incoming sensory information; (2) working memory, which processes certain information received from the sensory registers and information retrieved from long-term memory; and (3) long-term memory, which stores information for longer periods of time.

Adapted from Atkinson & Shiffrin, 1968.

➤ 2. What is sensory memory? How did Sperling assess the duration of iconic memory?

FIXATION

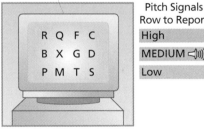

DISPLAY (1/20 sec) plus Tone

REPORT

FIGURE 7.3 After a participant fixates on a screen, a matrix of letters is flashed for 1/20 of a second. In one condition, participants do not hear any tone and must immediately report as many letters as they can. In another condition, a high-, medium-, or low-pitched tone signals the participant to report either the top, middle, or bottom row. If the tone occurs immediately, participants typically can report three or all four letters, no matter which row is signaled.

The model shown in Figure 7.2 incorporates this assumption. Originally developed by Richard Atkinson and Richard Shiffrin (1968), and subsequently modified, it proposes that memory has three major components: sensory memory, short-term or "working" memory, and long-term memory. The model does not assume that each component corresponds to a specific structure within the brain. Rather, the components may involve interrelated neural sites and memory researchers use these terms in a more abstract sense.

Sensory Memory

Sensory memory holds incoming sensory information just long enough for it to be recognized. It is comprised of different subsystems, called *sensory registers*, which are the initial information processors. Our visual sensory register is called the *iconic store*, and in 1960 George Sperling conducted a classic experiment to assess how long it stores information. Twelve letters, arranged in three rows and four columns like those in Figure 7.3, were flashed on a screen for 1/20 of a second, after which participants immediately recalled as many letters as they could. Typically, they were able to recall only three to five letters.

Sperling wondered whether the participants had actually processed the whole array, only to have their iconic memory fade in the few seconds it took to report the letters. To test this possibility, Sperling modified his experiment. This time, just as the letters were flashed off, participants heard either a high-, medium-, or low-pitched tone, which signaled them to report either the top, middle, or bottom row of letters (Figure 7.3).

If the tone occurred immediately, participants often could report all four letters in whichever row was signaled. Because they did not know which row would be signaled ahead of time, this implies that their iconic memory had stored an image of the whole array, and they now had time to "read" their iconic image of any one line before it rapidly disappeared. If this logic is correct, then even participants who have to report only one row should do poorly if the signaling tone is delayed. Indeed, recall dropped rapidly with a 1/3 second delay and after 1 second had elapsed, performance was no better than without the tone. As Figure 7.4 illustrates, it is difficult, perhaps impossible, to retain complete information in purely visual form for more than a fraction of a second (Barsalou, 1992).

The auditory sensory register, called the *echoic store*, is studied by asking participants to recall different sets of numbers or letters that are simultaneously presented to their left and right ears via headphones. Echoic memory lasts longer than iconic memory. A nearly complete echoic trace may last about 2 seconds and a partial trace may linger for several more (Darwin et al., 1972).

Short-Term/Working Memory

Because our attentional capabilities are limited, most information in sensory memory simply fades away. But through selective attention, a small portion enters **short-term memory,** which holds the information that we are conscious of at any given time. Short-term memory also is referred to as **working memory,** because it consciously processes, codes, and "works on" information (Atkinson & Shiffrin, 1968; Baddeley, 1986).

Mental representations. Once information leaves sensory memory, it must be represented by some type of code if it is to be retained in short-term and eventually long-term memory. For example, the words that someone just spoke to you ("please buy some gum") or the phone number that you just looked up must somehow become represented in your mind. Such *mental representations,* or memory codes, can take various forms (Jackendoff, 1996). We may try to form a mental image (visual encoding), code something by sound (phonological encoding), or focus on the meaning of a stimulus (semantic encoding). For physical actions, such as learning sports or playing musical instruments, we code patterns of movement (motor encoding).

Realize that the form of a memory code often does not correspond to the form of the original stimulus. For example, as you read these words (visual stimuli) you probably are not storing images of the way the letters look. Rather, you are likely forming phonological codes (saying the words silently to yourself) and, as you think about the material, semantic codes that represent their meaning. When people are presented with lists of words or letters and asked to recall them immediately, the errors that they make often are phonetic. They might recall a V instead of a B because of the similarity in how the letters sound (Conrad, 1964). Likewise, given word lists such as (1) *man, mad, cap, can, map;* (2) *old, late, thin, wet, hot;* and (3) *big, huge, broad, long, tall,* people become most confused recalling the first list, in which the words sound similar (Baddeley, 1966). Such findings suggest that phonological codes play an important role in short-term memory.

Capacity and duration. Short-term memory can hold only a limited amount of information at a time. Depending upon the stimulus, such as numbers, letters, or words, most people can hold no more than five to nine meaningful items in short-term memory, leading George Miller (1956) to set the capacity limit at "the magical number 7, plus or minus 2." To demonstrate this, try administering the *digit-span task* in Table 7.1 to some people you know.

If our short-term memory capacity is so limited, how can we remember and understand sentences as we read? To answer this, read the line of letters below (about one per second), then cover it up and write down as many letters as you can remember, *in the order presented.*

B I R C Y K A E U Q S A S A W T I

Did you have trouble remembering even half of these 17 letters in order? Now we rearrange (reverse) the letters and again ask you to write them down in order. Here are the 17 letters: "It was a squeaky crib." No doubt, you find this task much easier. The limit on short-term memory capacity concerns the number of meaningful *units* that can be recalled, and the original 17 letters have been combined into five meaningful units (words). Combining individual items into larger units of meaning is called **chunking,** and it can greatly aid recall.

Short-term memory is limited in duration as well as capacity. Have you ever experienced rapid forgetting, such as being introduced to someone, starting a conversation, and then suddenly realizing that you don't have the foggiest idea what her or his name was? Without rehearsal, the "shelf-life" of information in short-term memory is indeed short, perhaps lasting about 20 seconds. Lloyd and Margaret Peterson (1959) demonstrated this by presenting participants with

FIGURE 7.4 The arc of light that you see traced by a twirling "sparkler," or the lingering flash that you see after observing a lightning bolt, results from the brief duration of information in iconic memory. Because iconic memory stores complete information for a fraction of a second, the image quickly vanishes.

➤ 3. Describe the limitations of short-term memory, and how they can be overcome.

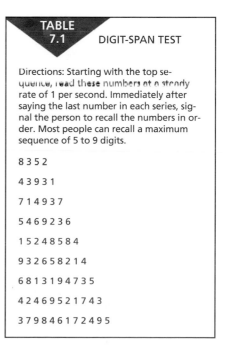

TABLE 7.1	DIGIT-SPAN TEST

Directions: Starting with the top sequence, read these numbers at a steady rate of 1 per second. Immediately after saying the last number in each series, signal the person to recall the numbers in order. Most people can recall a maximum sequence of 5 to 9 digits.

8 3 5 2

4 3 9 3 1

7 1 4 9 3 7

5 4 6 9 2 3 6

1 5 2 4 8 5 8 4

9 3 2 6 5 8 2 1 4

6 8 1 3 1 9 4 7 3 5

4 2 4 6 9 5 2 1 7 4 3

3 7 9 8 4 6 1 7 2 4 9 5

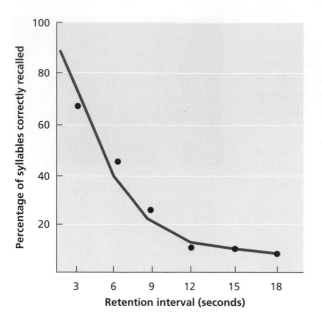

FIGURE 7.5 Participants who were prevented from rehearsing three-letter syllables in working memory showed almost no recall of the letters within 18 seconds, illustrating the rapid forgetting of information in short-term memory.
Based on Peterson & Peterson, 1959.

➤ 4. Why do researchers refer to short-term memory as "working memory"?

➤ 5. Identify three components of working memory.

three-letter syllables (all consonants), such as BSX, followed by a three-digit number, such as 140. Upon seeing the number, participants counted backward by threes, which prevented them from rehearsing the letters. As Figure 7.5 indicates, after counting backward for as little as 18 seconds, few syllables were recalled.

By rehearsing information we can extend its duration in short-term memory indefinitely. This occurs when you look up a telephone number and keep saying it to yourself, either out loud or silently, while waiting to use a phone. This simple repetition of information is called **maintenance rehearsal.** In contrast, **elaborative rehearsal** involves focusing on the meaning of information or relating it to other things we already know. Thus you could rehearse the term "iconic memory" by thinking about examples of iconic memory in your own life. Both types of rehearsal keep information active in short-term memory, but elaborative rehearsal is more effective in transferring information into long-term memory, which is our more permanent memory store (Gardiner et al., 1994; Mäntylä, 1986).

Putting short-term memory "to work."   Picture the seemingly endless stacks of a library (representing long-term memory), and a tiny "loading platform"(representing short-term memory) outside the building. New books (pieces of information) rapidly arrive and, because there isn't enough space, knock other ones off the platform. According to the original three-stage model, items that remain on the short-term loading dock long enough—such as through maintenance rehearsal—eventually get transferred into the long-term library.

The original three-stage model of memory focused on short-term memory primarily as a loading platform or holding station for information along the route from sensory to long-term memory. Many cognitive scientists now reject this view of short-term memory as too passive and too sequential. Instead, they view short-term memory as a *working memory*—a "mental workspace" that actively and simultaneously processes different types of information and supports other cognitive functions, such as problem solving and planning. Metaphorically, rather than a loading platform, working memory "is instead more like the office of a busy librarian, who is energetically categorizing, cataloging, and cross-referencing new material" (Reisberg, 1997, p. 139).

To illustrate how working memory stores information, processes it, and supports problem solving, add the numbers 27 and 46 "in your head." Your working memory stores the numbers, calls up information from long-term memory on "how to add," keeps track of the interim steps (7 + 6 = 13, carry the 1), and coordinates these mental processes.

One model, proposed by Alan Baddeley (1986, 1998), divides working memory into three components. First, we maintain some information in an *auditory working memory* (the "phonological loop"), such as when you repeat a phone number, name, or new vocabulary terms to yourself mentally. A second component, *visual-spatial working memory* (the "visuo-spatial sketchpad"), allows us to temporarily store and manipulate images and spatial information, as when forming mental "maps" of the route to some destination. Finally, a control process, called the *central executive,* directs the action. It decides how much attention to allocate to mental imagery and auditory rehearsal, calls up information from long-term memory, and integrates the input. Research suggests that the prefrontal cortex, the seat of "executive functions" described in Chapter 3, is heavily involved in directing the processing of information in working memory (Nelson et al., 2000).

Long-Term Memory

As already noted, **long-term memory** is our vast library of more durable stored memories. Perhaps there have been times in your life, such as periods of intensive study during finals, when you have felt as if "the library is full," with no room for storing so much as one more new fact inside your brain. In reality, barring brain damage, we remain capable of forming new long-term memories until we die. And, as far as we know, long-term storage capacity essentially is unlimited. Once formed, a long-term memory can endure for up to a lifetime (Bahrick et al., 1994).

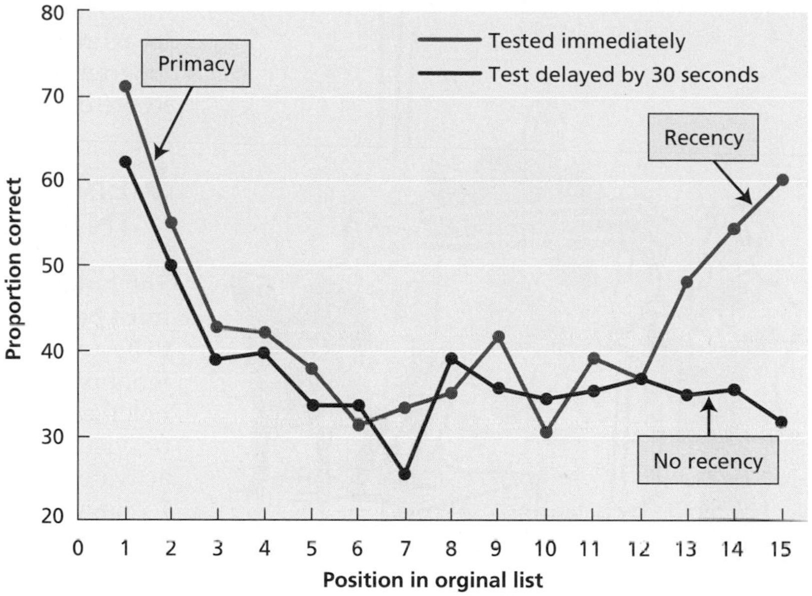

Are short-term and long-term memory really distinct? Case studies of amnesia victims like H. M. support this distinction, but another source of evidence comes from laboratory experiments in which participants with normal memory learn lists of words. Suppose that we present you with a series of unrelated words, one word at a time. The list might contain 10, 15, 20, or even 30 items. Immediately after the last word is presented, you will recall as many words as you can, in any order you wish. As Figure 7.6 illustrates, most experiments find that words at the end and beginning of the list are the easiest to recall. This U-shaped pattern is called the **serial position effect,** meaning that recall is influenced by a word's position in a series of items. The serial position effect has two components, a *primacy effect* reflecting the superior recall of early words and a *recency effect* representing the superior recall of the most recent words.

What causes the primacy effect? According to the three-stage model, as the first few words enter short-term memory, we can quickly rehearse them and transfer them into long-term memory. However, as the list gets longer, short-term memory rapidly fills up and there are too many words to keep repeating before the next word arrives. Therefore, beyond the first few words, we cannot rehearse the items and they are less likely to get transferred into long-term memory. If this hypothesis is correct, then the primacy effect should disappear if we can prevent people from rehearsing the early words, say by presenting the list at a faster rate. Indeed, this is what happens (Glanzer, 1972).

As for the recency effect, the last few words have the benefit of not being "bumped out" of short-term memory by any new information. Thus if we try to recall the list immediately, all we have to do is "read out" the last words while they linger in short-term memory. In sum, according to the three-stage model, the primacy effect is due to the transfer of early words into long-term memory, whereas the recency effect is due to short-term memory.

If this explanation is correct, then we should be able to wipe out the recency effect—but not the primacy effect—by eliminating the last words from short-term memory. This happens when the recall test is delayed, even for as little as 15 or 30 seconds, *and* you are prevented from rehearsing the last words. To prevent rehearsal, we might briefly ask you to count a series of numbers immediately after presenting the last word (Glanzer & Cunitz, 1966; Postman & Phillips, 1965). Now by the time you try to recall the last words, they will have faded from short-term memory and been "bumped out" by the arithmetic task (6 . . . 7 . . . 8 . . .9 . . .). Figure 7.6 shows that, indeed, under these delayed conditions, the last words are recalled no better than the middle ones, while a primacy effect remains.

FIGURE 7.6 Immediate recall of word lists produces a serial position curve, where primacy and recency effects are both evident. However, even a short delay of 30 seconds in recall (during which rehearsal is prevented) eliminates the recency effect, indicating that the later items in the word list have disappeared from short-term memory. Adapted from Glanzer & Cunitz, 1966.

➤ 6. What is the serial position effect? Under what conditions do primacy and recency effects occur?

➤ 7. According to the three-component model, why do primacy and recency occur?

"The matters about which I'm being questioned, Your Honor, are all things I should have included in my long-term memory but which I mistakenly inserted in my short-term memory."

FIGURE 7.7 Ineffective encoding can have practical as well as theoretical significance.

➤ 8. Provide some examples of effortful and automatic processing in your own life.

➤ 9. Explain the concept of "depth of processing."

Having examined some of the basic components of memory, let us now explore more fully how information is encoded into long-term memory, how it is stored, and factors that affect our ability to retrieve it.

❯ ENCODING: ENTERING INFORMATION

The holdings of your long-term memory, like those of a library, must be organized in terms of specific codes if the information is to be available when you wish to retrieve it. In a library, new material is assigned a call number before it is placed in storage. As noted earlier, our "call numbers" come in various forms—semantic, visual, phonological, and motor codes—that later enable us to activate information in long-term memory and access it. As Figure 7.7 suggests, the more effectively we encode material into long-term memory, the greater the likelihood of retrieving it (Hunt & Ellis, 1999).

Effortful and Automatic Processing

Think of the parade of information that you have to remember: names, phone numbers, computer passwords, and mountains of schoolwork on which you expect to be tested. Learning such information involves *effortful processing*, encoding that is initiated intentionally and requires conscious attention (Hasher & Zacks, 1979). Rehearsing, making lists, and taking class notes illustrate effortful processing.

In contrast, have you ever been unable to answer an exam question, and said to yourself "Why can't I answer this? I can even picture the diagram; it was on the upper portion of the left page!" Here incidental information about the diagram's location on the page (that you were not trying to learn) appears to have been transferred into long-term memory through *automatic processing*, encoding that occurs without intention and requires minimal attention.

Information about the frequency, spatial location, sequence, and timing of events often is encoded automatically (Hasher & Zacks, 1984; Mangels, 1997). For example, if I ask you what you did yesterday, you probably will have little trouble remembering your sequence of activities, despite the fact that you never had to sit down and intentionally memorize this information.

Levels of Processing: When Deeper Is Better

Imagine that you are participating in a laboratory experiment, and are about to be shown a list of words, one at a time. Each word will be followed by a question, and all you have to do is answer "yes" or "no." Here are three examples:

1. POTATO   "Is the word in capital letters?"
2. horse   "Does the word rhyme with course?"
3. TABLE   "Does the word fit in the sentence, 'The man peeled the _____'?"

Each question requires effort, but differs from the others in an important way. The first question requires superficial *structural encoding*, as you only have to notice how the word looks. Question 2 requires a little more effort. You must engage in *phonological* (also called *phonemic*) *encoding* by sounding out the word to yourself and then judging whether it matches the sound of another word. The last question requires *semantic encoding* because you must pay attention to what the word means.

In this experiment, every word shown to you will be followed by a question similar to one of these. Unexpectedly, you will then be given a memory test. Which group of words will be recognized most easily: those processed structurally, phonologically, or semantically?

According to the **levels of processing** concept developed by Fergus Craik and Robert Lockhart (1972), the more deeply we process information, the better it will be remembered. In the study above, semantic encoding involves the deepest processing because it requires us to focus on the *meaning* of information. Merely perceiving the structural properties of the words (e.g., capitalized vs. lowercase) involves shallow processing, and phonemically encoding words is intermediate. You can see in Figure 7.8 that the results of a study conducted by Craik and Endel Tulving (1975) support the value of deeper, semantic encoding.

Although many experiments have replicated this finding (Gabrielli et al., 1996), at times the concept of "depth of processing" can be difficult to measure. Suppose that some randomly assigned students study a chapter by creating hierarchical outlines and notes. A second group creates flash cards, jumbles them up, and rehearses them. Which study method represents deeper processing? If the first group performs better on a test, should we assume that they must have processed the information more deeply? To do so, warns Alan Baddeley (1990), is to fall into a trap of circular reasoning. Then again, there are situations where few would argue with at least a broad distinction between shallow and deep processing. Here is one of them.

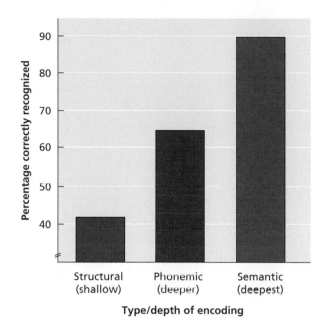

FIGURE 7.8 Depth of processing facilitates memory. Participants were shown words and asked questions that required superficial structural processing of a word, somewhat deeper phonemic processing, or deeper semantic processing. Depth of processing increased later recognition of the words in a larger list. Data from Craik & Tulving, 1975.

Exposure and Rehearsal

Years ago a student came to my office after failing the first exam in my introductory psychology course. He told me he had been to all the lectures, completed the chapters ahead of time, and reread each chapter twice more just before the exam. Yet when I looked through his textbook, not a word or sentence had been underlined or highlighted. I asked if he took notes as he read or paused to reflect on the information, and he said "No." Instead, he read each chapter quickly, much like a novel, and assumed that merely by looking at everything three times the information would somehow "sink in."

Unfortunately, this student's approach stood little chance of success. To learn factual and conceptual information presented in most academic or job settings, we need to employ effortful, deep processing. Yet simple repeated exposure to a stimulus without stopping to think about it represents shallow processing. To demonstrate this, try drawing from memory a picture of the smallest-denomination coin in your country (e.g., a penny in Canada or the United States), accurately locating all the markings. Few of our students can do this. Thus even thousands of shallow exposures to a stimulus do not guarantee long-term retention (Jones, 1990; Nickerson & Adams, 1979).

Rehearsal goes beyond mere exposure because we are thinking about the information. Of course, not all thinking is created equal, and neither is all rehearsal. As noted earlier, *maintenance rehearsal* involves simple repetition, as when silently repeating an unfamiliar phone number while waiting to use the phone. Maintenance rehearsal is most useful for keeping information active in short-term, working memory, and it may help transfer some information into long-term memory (Naveh & Jonides, 1984; Wixted, 1991). However, it is an inefficient method for bringing about long-term transfer.

➤ 10. How effectively do maintenance and elaborative rehearsal process information into long-term memory?

In contrast, *elaborative rehearsal* focuses on the meaning of information—we *elaborate* on the material in some way. Organizing information, thinking about how it applies to our own lives, and relating it to concepts or examples we already know illustrate such elaboration. According to Craik and Lockhart (1972), elaborative rehearsal involves deeper processing than maintenance rehearsal and should be more effective in transferring information into long-term memory. In contexts as varied as college students learning word-lists to sixth-graders learning CPR (cardiopulmonary resuscitation), experiments support the greater effectiveness of elaborative rehearsal (Gardiner et al, 1994; Mäntylä, 1986; Rivera-Tovar & Jones, 1990). Even thinking about examples of concepts that other people provide for us facilitates later recall (Palmere et al., 1983).

Organization and Imagery

Dining at the Colorado restaurant where J.C. is a waiter can be an awe-inspiring experience. Perhaps you would like a filet mignon, medium-rare, with a baked potato, and Thousand Island dressing on your salad? Whatever you choose, it represents only one of over 500 possible options that can be ordered (7 entrees × 5 serving temperatures × 3 side dishes × 5 choices of salad dressing). Yet you and 20 or so of your best friends can place your selections with J.C., and he will remember them perfectly without writing them down. How does he do it?

Psychologists K. Anders Ericsson and Peter Polson (1988), who studied J.C., found that he invented an overall organizational scheme to aid his memory. He divided his customers' orders into four categories (entrees, temperatures, side dish, dressing) and then used a different system to encode the orders in each category. For example, he represented dressings by their initial letter, so orders of Thousand Island, oil and vinegar, blue cheese, and oil and vinegar would become TOBO.

Imposing organization on a set of stimuli is an excellent way to enhance memory. An organizational scheme can enhance the meaningfulness of information and also serve as a cue that helps trigger our memory for the information it represents, just as the word *TOBO* jogs J. C.'s memory of the four orders of salad.

Hierarchies and Chunking

Organizing material in a *hierarchy* takes advantage of the principle that memory is enhanced by associations between concepts. Gordon Bower and his coworkers (1969) demonstrated this experimentally by presenting some participants with a logically organized list of words, based on a hierarchical tree like the one in Figure 7.9*a*. Other participants received the same words placed randomly within the tree. As Figure 7.9*b* shows, participants presented with a meaningful hierarchy remembered more than three times as many words.

Notice that the hierarchy in Figure 7.9*a* does not reduce the amount of information to be remembered. With or without it, there are 26 words to learn. Rather, a logical hierarchy enhances our *understanding* of how these diverse elements are related, and as we proceed from top to bottom, each category can serve as a cue that triggers our memory for the associated items below it. Because the hierarchy has a visual organization, there also is a greater possibility of using imagery as a supplemental memory code.

Chunking refers to combining individual items into a larger unit of meaning, and it widens the information-processing bottleneck caused by the limited capacity of short-term memory (Gobet & Simon, 1998; Miller, 1956). To refresh your memory, read the line of letters below to yourself (about one per second) and try to recall as many as you can, in the same sequence.

I R S Y M C A I B M K G B F B I

If you remembered four to eight of the letters in order, you did quite well. Now we can reorganize these sixteen individual bits of information into five larger,

> 11. Why do hierarchies, chunking, mnemonic devices, and imagery enhance memory?

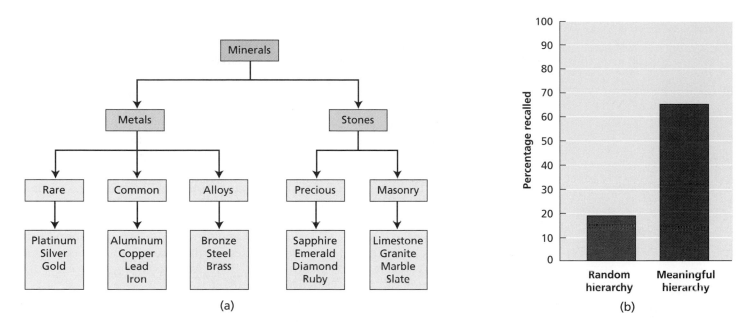

(a)

(b)

FIGURE 7.9 Words presented in a logically organized hierarchical structure (a) are remembered better (b) than the same words placed randomly in a similar-looking structure.

Bower et al., 1969.

more meaningful chunks: IRS, YMCA, IBM, KGB, and FBI. This rearrangement is easier to keep active in short-term memory and, should you be so motivated, to rehearse and transfer into long-term memory. A common example of chunking in everyday life is the way we encode and later retrieve phone numbers from long-term memory. Thus if you periodically call someone who lives far away, you probably encode the number as a set of three chunks (e.g., 206-543-2640) rather than as ten individual numbers.

Mnemonic Devices

The search for memory aids dates back thousands of years. In fact, the term "mnemonics" (nee-mon'-iks), which refers to "the art of improving memory," derives from the name Mnemosyne, the Greek goddess of memory. A *mnemonic device* is any type of memory aid. Hierarchies and chunking represent two types of mnemonic devices. So are acronyms, which combine one or more letters (usually the first letter) from each piece of information you wish to remember. For example, many students learn the acronyms HOMES and ROY G. BIV to help remember the names of the five Great Lakes of North America (Huron, Ontario, Michigan, Erie, Superior) and the hues in the visible spectrum—the "colors of the rainbow" (red, orange, yellow, green, blue, indigo, violet). Acronyms are one of the most popular mnemonic techniques among college students (Soler & Ruiz, 1996).

Keep in mind that when you are learning new material, mnemonic devices do not reduce the amount of *raw* information you have to encode into memory. Rather, they reorganize information into more meaningful units and provide extra cues to help retrieve information from long-term memory. When chunking seven digits into 543-2640, you still have to encode seven digits. And the acronym HOMES is useful only when you have also encoded the names of the Great Lakes into long-term memory. Thus some researchers argue that acronyms—DAM—*d*on't *a*id *m*emory, or at least do so only when you are already familiar with the material (Carney et al., 1981, 1994).

Visual Imagery

How many windows are there in your home? Can you tell me, in as much detail as possible, what your bedroom looked like during your high school years? To answer these questions, you might try to construct and scan a series of mental images in your working memory, based on information that you draw out of long-term memory.

Allan Paivio (1969, 1995) proposes that information is stored in long-term memory in two forms: verbal codes and visual codes. According to his **dual coding theory,** if we encode information using both verbal and visual codes, the chances improve that at least one of the two codes will be available later to support recall. In short, two codes are better than one, though dual coding is harder to use with some types of stimuli than others. Try to construct a mental image for each of the following two words: (1) fire truck, (2) lightbulb. Now construct an image for these words: (1) jealousy, (2) knowledge. You probably found the second task more difficult, because the latter words represent abstract concepts rather than concrete objects (Sadoski et al., 1997). Abstract concepts are easier to encode semantically than visually.

Memory improvement books often recommend using imagery to dual-code information, and research supports this approach (Tye, 1991). The ancient Greeks developed an effective and well-known imagery technique called the *method of loci* (loci is Latin for "places"). To use this technique, imagine a physical environment with a sequence of distinct landmarks, such as the rooms in a house or places on your campus. In one psychology class, students rapidly learned to use the 40 locations on the Monopoly game board as their visual reference (Schoen, 1996).

To remember a list of items or concepts, take an imaginary stroll through this environment and form an image linking each place with an item or concept. To remember the three components of working memory, you might imagine walking into the president's office at your college (executive control system), then watching a band rehearsal in your gym (phonological loop), and finally visiting an art class (visuo-spatial sketchpad). Many studies support the method of loci's effectiveness (Crovitz, 1971; Roediger, 1980).

How Prior Knowledge Shapes Encoding

Long-term memory is densely populated with semantic codes that represent the meaning of information. Typically, when we read, listen to someone speak, or experience some other event, we do not precisely record every word, sentence, or moment. Rather, we form a mental representation that captures the essential meaning or gist of that event. For example, in the two preceding paragraphs we described the method of loci. Can you recall those paragraphs word for word? More likely, what you have encoded is the gist—the general theme—that the method of loci involves forming images that link items to places.

Schemas: Our Mental Organizers

> ➤ 12. What is a schema? Explain how schemas influence encoding.

The themes that we extract from events and store in memory are often organized around schemas. A **schema** (plural: *schemas,* or *schemata*) is a "mental framework"—an organized pattern of thought about some aspect of the world, such as a class of people, events, situations, or objects (Bartlett, 1932; Koriat et al., 2000). We form schemas through experience, and they can strongly influence the way we encode material in memory. To demonstrate this, read the following paragraph:

> The procedure is actually quite simple. First you arrange things into different groups. Of course, one pile may be sufficient depending on how much there is to do. If you have to go somewhere else due to lack of facilities, that

is the next step; otherwise you are pretty well set. It is important not to overdo things. That is, it is better to do too few things at once than too many. In the short run this might not seem important, but complications can easily arise. A mistake can be expensive as well. . . . After the procedure is completed, one arranges the materials into different groups again. Then they can be put into their appropriate places. Eventually they will be used once more, and the whole cycle will have to be repeated. However, that is part of life. (Bransford & Johnson, 1972, p. 722)

Asked to recall as much as you can of the preceding paragraph, you would probably have difficulty remembering much of it. Certainly, participants in the original experiment did. However, suppose we tell you that the paragraph is about a common activity: washing clothes. Now if you read the material again, you will find that the abstract and seemingly unrelated ideas suddenly make sense. Your schema—your mental framework for "washing clothes"—helps you organize these ideas and recall a great deal more.

This example illustrates that how we perceive a stimulus shapes the way we mentally represent it in memory. Essentially, schemas create a perceptual set, which is a readiness to perceive—*to organize and interpret*—information in a certain way.

Schemas and Expert Knowledge

When people who have never learned to "read notes" look at a musical score, they see an uninterpretable mass of information. In contrast, musicians see organized patterns that they can easily encode, eventually learning to play a piece "from memory." In music as in other fields, acquiring *expert knowledge* can be viewed as a process of developing schemas—mental frameworks—that help encode information into meaningful patterns.

> 13. In what sense are schemas and expert knowledge related?

William Chase and Herbert Simon (1973) demonstrated the relation between expertise, schemas, and encoding in an intriguing study. Three chess players—an expert ("master"), an intermediate player, and a beginner—were allowed to look at a chess board containing about 25 pieces for only 5 seconds. Then they looked away and, on an empty board, attempted to reconstruct the placement of the pieces from memory. This was repeated over several trials, each with a different arrangement of pieces. On some trials, the chess pieces were arranged in *meaningful positions* that actually might occur in game situations. With only a 5-second glance, the expert typically recalled 16 pieces, the intermediate player 8, and the novice only 4. What may surprise you is that, when the pieces were in *random positions*, there was no difference in recall between the three players. They each did poorly, accurately recalling only 2 or 3 pieces.

How would you explain these results? We have to reject the conclusion that the expert had better overall memory than the other players, because he performed no better than they did with the random arrangements. But the concepts of schemas and chunking do explain the findings (Chase & Simon, 1973; Gobet & Simon, 1998). When the chess pieces were arranged in meaningful positions, the expert could apply well-developed schemas to recognize patterns and group together pieces. For example, he would treat as a unit all pieces that were positioned to attack the king. The intermediate player and especially the novice, who did not have well-developed chess schemas, could not construct the chunks and had to try to memorize the position of each piece. However, if the pieces were not in positions that would occur in a real game, they were no more meaningful to the expert than to the other players. In this case, the expert lost the advantage of schemas and had to approach the task on a piece-by-piece basis just as the other players did. Similarly, football coaches show much better recall than novices do after looking at diagrams of football plays (patterns of X's and O's), but only when the plays are logical (Figure 7.10).

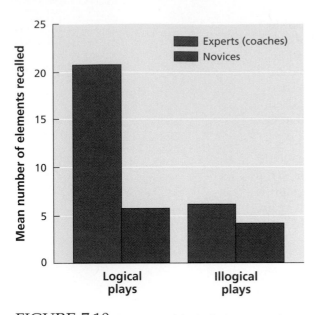

FIGURE 7.10 Diagrams of football plays were shown to football coaches (experts) and people who had played football, but were not coaches (novices). Allowed to see each play for just 5 seconds, coaches displayed excellent memory—but only when the plays were logical. Their well-developed football schemas were of little use when the patterns of X's and O's were illogical. The findings are very similar to those obtained when expert and novice chess players tried to reproduce meaningful and random arrangements of chess pieces.

Data from Garland & Barry, 1991.

➤ 14. Explain the concepts of associative networks and priming.

You may not be an advanced chess player, but there are many areas in which you possess expert knowledge. You have used language for most of your life and have years of experience about how the world works. As the washing machine example illustrates, your own "expert schemas" strongly influence what you encode and remember.

❯ STORAGE: RETAINING INFORMATION

After information is encoded, how is it organized and stored in long-term memory? Consider the following statements, indicating as quickly as possible whether each is true or false:

1. A raccoon has wings.
2. Moscow is in Russia.
3. A bat is a fish.
4. Coca-Cola is green.
5. An apple is a fruit.
6. Some fire engines are red.

Chances are, you were able to respond to each statement almost instantaneously. Considering their diversity, it is remarkable that you could access the information so quickly. The fact that we are able to perform such tasks routinely—that we can recall an incredible wealth of information at a moment's notice—has influenced many cognitive models of how knowledge is stored and organized in memory.

Memory as a Network

We noted earlier that memory is enhanced by elaborative rehearsal, which involves forming associations between new information and other items already in memory. The general principle that memory involves associations goes to the heart of the network approach.

Associative Networks

One group of theories proposes that memory can be represented as an **associative network,** a massive network of associated ideas and concepts (Collins & Loftus, 1975). Figure 7.11 shows what a small portion of such a network might be like. In this network, each concept or unit of information—fire engine, red, and so on—is represented by a *node* somewhat akin to each knot in a huge fishing net. The lines in this network represent associations between concepts, with shorter lines indicating stronger associations. For simplicity, Figure 7.11 shows only a few connections extending from each node, but there could be hundreds or more. Notice that items within the same category—types of flowers, types of fruits, colors, and so on—generally have the strongest associations and therefore tend to be clustered closer together.

Alan Collins and Elizabeth Loftus (1975) theorize that when people think about a concept, such as "fire engine," there is a *spreading activation* of related concepts throughout the network. For example, when you think about a "fire engine" related concepts like "truck," "fire," and "red" should be partially activated as well. The term **priming** refers to the activation of one concept (or one unit of information) by another. Thus "fire engine" primes the node for "red," making it more likely that our memory for this color will be accessed.

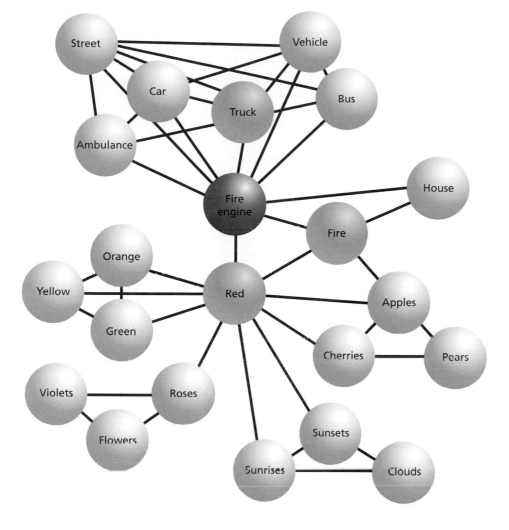

FIGURE 7.11 A network of concepts in semantic memory. The lines in the semantic network represent associations between concepts, with shorter lines indicating stronger associations.
Adapted from A. M. Collins and E. F. Loftus, 1975.

The notion that memory stores information in an associative network provides one possible explanation for why "hints" and mnemonic devices help stimulate our recall (Reisberg, 1997). For example, when I ask "Name the colors of the rainbow," the nodes for "color" and "rainbow" jointly activate the node for ROY G. BIV, which in turn primes our recall for "red," "orange," and so forth.

Neural Networks

The neural network approach provides a different and increasingly popular model of memory and cognition (Chappell & Humphreys, 1994; McLelland & Rumelhart, 1985). A neural network has nodes that are linked to each other, but these nodes are physical in nature and do not contain individual units of information. There is no single node for "red," for "fire engine," and so on. Instead, each node is more like a small information-processing unit. As an analogy, some proponents would say: Think of each neuron in your brain as a node. A neuron processes inputs and sends outputs to other neurons, but as far as we know, the concepts of "red" or "fire engine" or your mental image of an elephant are not stored within any single neuron.

Where, then, is the concept "red" stored? In a **neural network,** each concept is represented by a particular *pattern* or *set of nodes* that becomes activated simultaneously. When node 4 is activated simultaneously (i.e., in parallel) with nodes 9 and 42, the concept "red" might come to mind. But when node 4 is simultaneously activated with nodes 75 and 690, another concept enters our thoughts.

> 15. How do neural network models differ from associative network models?

Looking across the entire network, as a multitude of nodes *distributed* throughout the brain fire in *parallel* at each instant and spread their activation to other nodes, concepts and information are retrieved and thoughts arise. For this reason, neural network models are often called *parallel distributed processing models*.

Neural network models have numerous supporters and are generating interest in many fields, including psychology, neuroscience, engineering, computer science, philosophy, mathematics, and physics (Levine, 2000; Nyberg et al., 2000). They are likely to remain an area of intensive research for years to come.

Types of Long-Term Memory

> ➤ 16. Use the concepts of declarative versus procedural memory, and explicit versus implicit memory, to explain the pattern of H. M.'s amnesia.

Think back to the nature of H. M.'s amnesia. Since his brain operation, H. M. has been unable to consciously recall new facts or personal experiences once they leave his short-term memory. Each time he meets you he will believe it is the first time. Yet with practice, H. M. learned new tasks even though he would never remember having seen them before (Milner, 1965).

Based on research with amnesia patients, brain-imaging studies, and animal experiments, many cognitive scientists believe that we possess several long-term memory systems that interact with one another (Squire & Zola-Morgan, 1991; Tulving, 2000). This view is consistent with the concept, described in Chapter 5, that the mind involves distinct yet interrelated modules.

Declarative and Procedural Memory

Declarative memory involves factual knowledge, and includes two subcategories (Figure 7.12). **Episodic memory** is our store of factual knowledge concerning personal experiences: when, where, and what happened in the *episodes* of our lives. My recollection that I ate pizza last night is an episodic memory. **Semantic memory** represents general factual knowledge about the world and language, including memory for words and concepts. You know that Mt. Everest is the world's tallest peak, and that $e = mc^2$. Episodic and semantic memories are called *declarative* because, to demonstrate our knowledge, we typically have to "declare it"—we tell other people what we know.

H. M.'s brain damage severely impaired both components of his declarative memory, but this is not always the case. Some brain-injured children with amnesia cannot remember their daily personal experiences but can retain general factual knowledge, enabling them to learn language and attend mainstream schools (Vargha-Khadem et al., 1997).

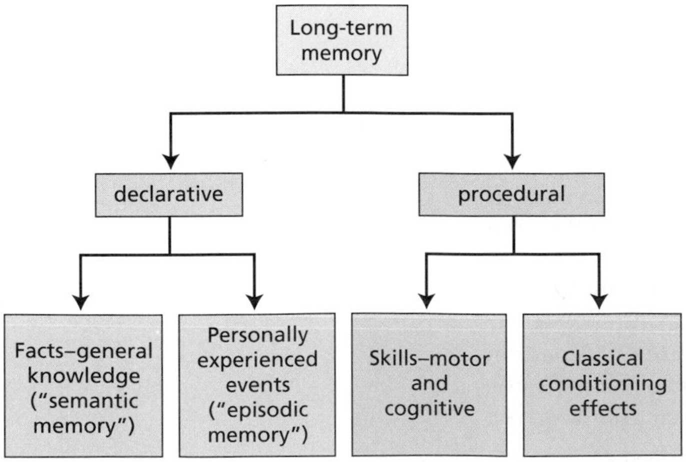

In contrast to declarative memory, whose contents are verbalized, **procedural memory** (nondeclarative memory) is reflected in skills and actions. One component of procedural memory consists of *skills* that are expressed by "doing things" in particular situations, such as typing, riding a bicycle, playing a musical instrument. *Classically conditioned responses* also reflect procedural memory (Gabrieli, 1998). After a tone was repeatedly paired with a puff of air blown toward H. M.'s eye, he began to blink involuntarily to the tone alone (Woodruff-Pak, 1993). Although H. M. could not recall undergoing this procedure, his brain stored a memory for the association between the tone and the air puff, affecting his actions (he blinked) when subsequently exposed to the tone alone.

FIGURE 7.12 Some theorists propose that we have separate but interacting declarative and procedural memory systems. Episodic and semantic memories are declarative; their contents can be verbalized. Procedural memory is nondeclarative; its contents cannot readily be verbalized.

Explicit and Implicit Memory

Many researchers distinguish between explicit and implicit memory. **Explicit memory** involves conscious or intentional memory retrieval, as when you consciously recognize or recall something (Graf & Schacter, 1985). *Recognition* requires us to decide whether a stimulus is familiar, as when an eyewitness is asked to pick out a suspect from a police lineup, or students take multiple-choice tests. In recognition tasks, the "target" stimuli (possible suspects or answers) are provided to you. *Recall* involves spontaneous memory retrieval, in the sense that you must retrieve the target stimuli or information on your own. This occurs when you are briefly shown a list of words and then asked to recall them. With *cued recall*, hints are given to stimulate memory. If you cannot recall the word "hat" from the list, we might say, "It rhymes with 'bat.' " In academics, essay, short-answer, and fill-in-the-blank questions involve recall or cued recall.

➤ 17. Describe some ways to measure explicit and implicit memory.

Implicit memory occurs when memory influences our behavior without conscious awareness. H. M. was able to remember how to perform the mirror-tracing task, although he had no conscious awareness of having learned it. His memory for the task (in this case, procedural memory) was implicit. In Chapter 5 we encountered another amnesia patient, whose hand Edouard Claparède (1911) intentionally pricked with a pin during a handshake. Shortly thereafter she could not consciously recall this incident, but despite her amnesia, she showed implicit memory of their encounter by withdrawing her hand when Claparède offered to shake it again.

In less dramatic ways, all of us demonstrate memory without conscious awareness. Riding a bicycle, driving, or performing any well-learned skill provides a common example. You may be consciously thinking about an upcoming school test or last night's party, while your implicit, procedural memory enables you to keep executing the skill.

Priming tasks provide another example. You might read a list of words (one word per second) that includes "kitchen," "moon," and "defend." Later—even a year later—you are rapidly shown many word stems, some of which might be KIT——, MO——, and DE——, and are asked to complete each stem to form a word. You are not aware that this is a memory test. Compared with people not given the original list of words, you will be more likely to complete the stems with words on the original list (e.g., MOon, rather than MOther). The word stems have activated or "primed" your stored mental representations of these words—the information is still in your memory—even though you may be unable to consciously recall the original words (Schacter, 1992; Sloman et al., 1988).

❯ RETRIEVAL: ACCESSING INFORMATION

Storing information is useless without the ability to retrieve it. Imagine looking for a specific title in a library, searching book by book because items are placed onto shelves without call numbers. In contrast, if we have a call number and the book is shelved correctly, we can easily gain access to it.

A **retrieval cue** is any stimulus, whether internal or external, that stimulates the activation of information stored in long-term memory. If I ask you, "Have you seen Sally today?" the word *Sally* is intended to serve as retrieval cue. Likewise, seeing a yearbook picture of a high school classmate can act as a retrieval cue that triggers memories of that person. *Priming* is a good example of how a retrieval cue ("fire engine," "MO——") can trigger associated elements ("red," "MOon") in memory, presumably via a process of spreading activation.

The Value of Multiple and Self-Generated Cues

Timo Mäntylä (1986) conducted a series of experiments that vividly show the value of having not just one, but multiple retrieval cues. In one experiment, Swedish college students were presented with a list of 504 words. Some students were asked to think of and write down an association for each word, while

➤ 18. Why does having multiple, self-generated retrieval cues enhance recall?

others were asked to think of and write down three associations. To illustrate, what three words come to your mind when I say "banana"? Perhaps you might think of "monkey," "peel," and "fruit."

The students had no idea that their memory for these words would be tested, and once the association task was completed, they were given an unexpected immediate recall test for 252 of the words. For some words, students were first shown the one or three associations that they had previously generated. As a control, for other words they were first shown one or three associations that *another* participant had generated. Then they were asked to recall the original word.

The results were astounding. When the associations (i.e., retrieval cues) were self-generated, students shown one cue correctly recalled 61 percent of the words, and those shown three cues correctly recalled 91 percent. In contrast, when students were shown cues that someone else had generated, recall with one cue dropped to 11 percent and with three cues to 55 percent. Finally, when given another surprise recall test one week later on the remaining words, students still remembered 65 percent of the words when they were first provided with three self-generated retrieval cues, far better than any other condition.

In seven experiments, Mäntylä consistently found that having multiple, self-generated retrieval cues was the most effective approach to maximizing recall (Mäntylä, 1986; Mäntylä & Nilsson, 1988). Why might this be? On the encoding side of the equation, generating our own associations involves deeper, more elaborative rehearsal than does being presented with associations generated by someone else. Similarly, generating three associations involves deeper processing than thinking of only one. On the retrieval side, these self-generated associations become cues that have personal meaning. And with multiple cues, if one fails, another may activate the memory. The implication for studying academic material is clear. Think about the material, and draw one or preferably more links to items you already have in memory.

The Value of Distinctiveness

There is a quick exercise that you can perform to demonstrate a simple point. A list of words appears below. Say each word silently to yourself (about one per second), then when you see the word *WRITE,* look away and jot down as many words as you can recall, in any order. Here are the words: *robin, eagle, nest, crow, feather, goose, owl, tomato, rooster, fly, sparrow, nightingale, chirp, hawk, pigeon, WRITE.*

Recall that in the serial position effect, words in the middle of a list usually are recalled less well. Yet, if you are like 95 percent of my students, you will have recalled the word *tomato,*" which occurred in the middle. In this list, tomato is distinctive. It stands out from the crowd (or at least, from the flock) and catches our attention. Upon retrieval, it is less likely to become "blended in" with all the other words. In general, distinctive stimuli are better remembered than nondistinctive ones (Eysenck & Eysenck, 1980; Hirsham & Jackson, 1997). This principle also applies to the events of our lives. In one study, college students were asked to list their three clearest memories (Rubin & Kozin, 1984). Distinctive events such as weddings, romantic encounters, births and deaths, vacations, and accidents, were among the most frequently recalled.

Can we enhance the memorability of nondistinctive stimuli by associating them with other stimuli that help make them distinctive? According to Mäntylä (1986), this is a key reason why students who generated their own three-word associations were able to remember almost all of the 500 words on their list. Associating each word with three others helped form a distinctive, personally meaningful set of cues. Thus when studying, one way to increase your recall when all the material "starts looking alike" is to make it distinctive by associating it with other information that is personally meaningful to you.

Flashbulb Memory: Fogging Up the Picture?

Do you remember the moment when you heard that Princess Diana had been killed in a car crash? Particularly if you are over age 20, do you recall what you were doing when you learned that the space shuttle *Challenger* exploded after take-off? Like others of our generation, we can vividly recall the moment about 40 years ago when we heard that President John F. Kennedy had been assassinated.

Flashbulb memories are recollections that seem so vivid, so clear, that we can picture them as if they were a "snapshot" of a moment in time. They are most likely to occur for distinctive, positive or negative events that evoke strong emotional reactions and which are repeatedly recalled in conversations with other people (Brown & Kulik, 1977).

Because flashbulb memories are vivid and easily recalled, we are confident of their accuracy. But are they accurate? The day after the *Challenger* disaster, Ulric Neisser and Nicole Harsch (1993) asked college students to describe how they learned of the accident, where they were, and so on. Reinterviewed three years later, about half of them remembered some details correctly, but recalled other details inaccurately. A fourth of the students completely misremembered all the major details, and were astonished over how inaccurate their memories were after reading their original descriptions.

For a captivated public that followed the 1995 O. J. Simpson murder trial, the jury's verdict seemed to be an unforgettable moment. Was it? Three days after Simpson's acquittal, college undergraduates were asked how, when, with whom, and where they had learned of the verdict (Schmolck et al., 2000). Students also reported whether they agreed with the verdict and how emotional they felt about it. When some students' memory was retested 15 months later, only 10 percent made major mistakes in recalling the event. Over time, however, the flashbulb seemed to fade. Among other students retested 32 months after the verdict, 43 percent misremembered major details. Memory accuracy was not related to whether students originally had agreed or disagreed with the verdict, but those who reported a stronger emotional reaction in 1995 displayed better memory 32 months later. Perhaps most striking, among those students with grossly inaccurate recall, 61 percent were highly confident of their memories.

Although the accuracy of flashbulb memories declines over time for many people, how does it compare to our memory for more mundane events? Days after the United States bombed Iraq in the 1991 Gulf War, Charles Weaver (1993) recorded college students' accounts of how they learned of the event. He had just collected other data from these students concerning a routine interaction with a roommate or friend. Both 3 months and 1 year later, students recalled the bombing no more accurately than the routine event, but had become more confident in their memory of the bombing. In short, flashbulb memories "feel" especially accurate, even when—in truth—they may be a bit foggy.

Context, State, and Mood Effects on Memory

Years ago, two Swedish researchers reported the case of a young woman who was raped while out for a jog (Christianson & Nilsson, 1989). When found by a passerby she was in shock and could not remember the assault. Over the next three months the police took her back to the crime scene several times. Although she could not recall the rape she became emotionally aroused, suggesting implicit memory of the event. While jogging one day shortly thereafter, she consciously recalled the rape.

Because this is a case study we cannot be sure what caused her memory to return. One possibility, the **encoding specificity principle,** states that memory is enhanced when conditions present during retrieval match those that were present during encoding (Tulving & Thompson, 1973). This occurs because stimuli associated with an event may become encoded as part of the memory and later serve as retrieval cues.

➤ 19. Do flashbulb memories always provide an accurate picture? Describe some evidence.

➤ 20. Explain how context-dependent and state-dependent memory illustrate the encoding specificity principle.

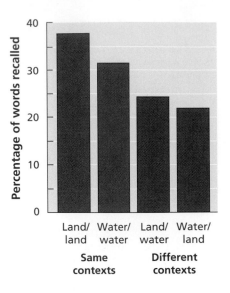

FIGURE 7.13 Context-dependent memory. Scuba divers who learned lists of words while underwater later recalled them best while underwater, whereas words learned on land were best recalled on land. Recall was poorer when the learning and testing environments were mismatched.

Data from Godden & Baddely, 1975.

FIGURE 7.14 State-dependent memory. In the film *City Lights*, a drunken millionaire befriends and spends the evening partying with Charlie Chaplin after Chaplin saves his life. The next day, in a sober state, the millionaire doesn't remember Chaplin and considers him an unwanted pest. After getting drunk again, he remembers Chaplin and treats him like a good buddy.

➤ 21. Identify practical principles of encoding and retrieval that can be used to enhance memory.

Context-Dependent Memory: Returning to the Scene

Applying the encoding specificity principle to *external* cues leads us to **context-dependent memory:** It typically is easier to remember something in the same environment in which it was acquired. Thus upon returning to your elementary school or old neighborhood, sights and sounds may trigger memories of teachers, classmates, and friends. As with the Swedish jogger, police detectives may take an eyewitness or crime victim back to the crime scene, hoping to stimulate the person's memory.

In a classic experiment, Duncan Godden and Alan Baddeley (1975) asked scuba divers to learn some lists of words underwater and some on dry land. As Figure 7.13 shows, when the divers were later retested in the two environments, lists learned underwater were recalled better underwater and those learned on land were better recalled while on land. Similarly, when randomly assigned college students studied material in either a quiet or noisy room, they later displayed better memory on short-answer and multiple-choice questions when tested in a corresponding (quiet or noisy) environment (Grant et al., 1998). Thus if you take exams in quiet environments, try to study in a quiet environment.

State-Dependent Memory: Arousal, Drugs, and Mood

Moving from external to internal cues, the concept of **state-dependent memory** proposes that our ability to retrieve information is greater when our *internal* state at the time of retrieval matches our original state during learning. The Swedish jogger who was raped consciously remembered her assault for the first time while jogging. In her case, both context-dependent cues (similar environment) and state-dependent cues (arousal while jogging) may have stimulated her memory.

Diverse experiments support this effect. Many students at the campus gym read course materials while exercising on a bicycle, treadmill, or stairclimber machine. Christopher Miles and Elinor Hardman (1998) found that material learned while we are aroused during aerobic exercise is later recalled more effectively if we are once again aerobically aroused, rather than at rest. Conversely, material learned at rest is better recalled at rest.

Many drugs produce physiological effects that directly impair memory, but state-dependency is another reason why events experienced in a drug state may be difficult to recall later while in a drug-free state (Figure 7.14). Experiments examining alcohol, marijuana, amphetamines, barbiturates, nicotine, caffeine, antihistamines, and other drugs have often found that information recall is poorer when there is a mismatch between the person's state during learning and testing (Carter & Cassady, 1998; Eich et al., 1975; Peters & McGee, 1982). This *does not* mean, by the way, that drugs improve memory relative to not taking drugs during initial learning.

Does state-dependent memory extend to mood states? Is material learned while in a happy mood or a sad mood better recalled when we are in that mood again? Inconsistent findings suggest that such *mood-dependent memory* is not a reliable phenomenon, although researchers continue to study whether it might occur under certain conditions (Ryan & Eich, 2000). Instead, there is more consistent evidence of **mood-congruent recall:** We tend to recall information or events that are congruent with our current mood (Teasdale & Fogarty, 1979; Fiedler, 2000). When happy we are more likely to remember positive events, and when sad we tend to remember negative events. This helps perpetuate our mood and may be one factor that maintains depression once people have entered a depressed state (Pyszczynski et al., 1991).

Clearly, many factors affect how we encode, store, and retrieve information. Our *Applications of Psychological Science* feature highlights some principles that are particularly relevant to helping you improve your memory.

APPLICATIONS OF PSYCHOLOGICAL SCIENCE

Improving Memory and Academic Learning

Memory enhancement strategies fall into three broad categories (Park et al., 1990; Soler & Ruiz, 1996):

- *external aids,* such as shopping lists, notes, appointment calendars, and placing objects (such as keys) in the same location;
- *general memory strategies,* such as organizing and rehearsing information; and
- *formal mnemonic techniques,* such as acronyms and other systems that take training to be used effectively.

Overall, memory researchers most strongly recommend using external aids and general strategies to enhance memory (Park et al., 1990). Of course, in situations such as "closed-book" college exams, using external aids may land you in the Dean's office! Here, following sound psychological principles can best enhance memory.

▶ Use Elaborative Rehearsal to Process Information Deeply

Elaborative rehearsal—focusing on the meaning of information—enhances deep processing and memory (Gabrieli et al., 1996). Put simply, *if you are trying to commit information to memory, make sure that you understand what it means.* You may feel that we're daffy for stating such an obvious point, but let us ask you this: Do you always seek assistance when you encounter material that you have trouble understanding? Unfortunately, some students who find material confusing simply try to rote memorize it, an approach that usually fails. The "directed questions" that appear in this book's margins can help you process the course material more deeply, and also serve as good retrieval cues.

▶ Link New Information to Examples and Items Already in Memory

Once you understand the material, process it more deeply by associating it with information you already know. This creates memory "hooks" onto which you can hang new information. Because you already have many memorable life experiences, *make new information personally meaningful* by relating it to your life.

Pay attention to examples, even if they are unrelated to your own experiences. In one study, participants read a 32-paragraph essay about a fictitious African nation. Each paragraph presented a topic sentence stating a main theme along with zero, one, two, or three examples illustrating that theme. The greater the number of examples, the better the participants recalled the themes (Palmere et al., 1983).

▶ Organize Information

Organizing information keeps you actively thinking about the material and makes it more meaningful. Before reading a chapter, look at the outline to determine how the material is logically developed. When studying, take notes from a chapter and use outlining to organize the information. This hierarchical structure forces you to arrange main ideas above subordinate ones and becomes an additional retrieval cue that facilitates recall (Bower et al., 1969).

▶ Overlearn the Material

Overlearning refers to continued rehearsal past the point of initial learning, and it significantly improves performance on memory tasks (Driskell et al., 1992). In general, the greater the amount of overlearning, the greater the benefit. Moreover, much of this memory boost persists for weeks after overlearning ends. In short, just as elite athletes keep practicing their skills, continue to rehearse material after you have first learned it.

▶ Distribute Learning Over Time

You have finished the readings and organized your notes for an upcoming test. Now it's time to study and review. Are you better off with *massed practice,* a marathon session of highly concentrated learning, or with *distributed practice,* several shorter sessions spread out over a few days? Research suggests that you will retain more information with distributed practice (Smith & Rothkopf, 1984; Underwood, 1970). It can reduce fatigue and anxiety, both of which impair learning.

▶ Minimize Interference

Interference, as we soon discuss more fully, occurs when one piece of information encoded in memory impairs our ability to remember some other piece of information. Distributed practice is effective because the rest periods between study sessions reduce interference from competing material. However, when studying for several exams on the same or consecutive days, there really are few rest periods. There is no simple solution to this problem. Suppose you have a psychology exam on Thursday and a sociology exam on Friday. Try to arrange several sessions of distributed practice for each exam over the preceding week. On Wednesday, limit your studying to psychology if possible. Once your psychology exam is over, turn your attention to your second test. This way, the final study period for each course will occur as close as possible to test time and minimize interference from other cognitive activities.

—Continued

Studying before you go to sleep may enhance retention by temporarily minimizing interference, but most of all, a typical college course load illustrates why overlearning is so important. Realistically, interference cannot be avoided, so study the material beyond the point where you feel you have learned it.

▶ Use Imagery

Among formal mnemonic techniques, memory researchers view imagery as the most valuable (Park et al., 1990). As dual-coding theory predicts, images provide a splendid second "cognitive hook" on which to hang and retrieve in-formation (Paivio, 1969, 1995). Instead of writing down customers' orders, some restaurant waiters and waitresses form images, such as visualizing a man who has ordered a margarita turning light green. As one waitress remarked, "After a while, customers start looking like drinks" (Bennett, 1983, p. 165). Perhaps an image of a camera flashbulb with a big red X through it will help you remember that flashbulb memories often are less accurate than people think they are. In sum, although there may not be any "magic" or effortless way to enhance memory, psychological research has established numerous principles that you can put to your advantage.

〉 FORGETTING

Some very bright people are legendary for their memory failures, or "absent-mindedness." The eminent French writer Voltaire began a passionate letter "My Dear Hortense" and ended it "Farewell, my dear Adele." The splendid absent-mindedness of Canon Sawyer, an English nobleman, once led him, while welcoming a visitor at the railroad station, to board the departing train and disappear (Bryan, 1986). Indeed, how we forget is nearly as interesting a scientific question as how we remember.

The Course of Forgetting

German psychologist Hermann Ebbinghaus (1885/1964) pioneered the study of forgetting by testing only one person—himself (Figure 7.15). He created over 2,000 *nonsense syllables*, meaningless letter combinations (e.g., *biv, zaj, xew*), to study memory with minimal influence from prior learning, as would happen if he used actual words. A dedicated scientist, in one study Ebbinghaus spent over 14,000 practice repetitions trying to memorize 420 lists of nonsense syllables.

Ebbinghaus typically measured memory by using a method called *relearning* and computing a savings percentage. For example, if it initially took him 20 trials to learn a list, but only half as many trials to relearn it a week later, then the savings percentage was 50 percent. In one series of studies, he retested his memory at various time intervals after mastering several lists of nonsense syllables. As Figure 7.16*a* shows, forgetting occurred rapidly at first and slowed noticeably thereafter.

Perhaps you are dismayed by this finding, which suggests that we quickly forget most of what we learn. Ebbinghaus, however, studied so many lists that his ability to distinguish among them undoubtedly suffered. If you learned just one or a few lists of syllables, the general shape of your forgetting curve might resemble Ebbinghaus's over the first 24 hours, but the amount you forget would likely be much less. Moreover, when material is meaningful (unlike nonsense syllables), we are likely to retain more of it for a longer time.

Consider the forgetting curve shown in Figure 7.16*b*, based on a study examining the vocabulary retention of people who had studied Spanish in school anywhere from 3 to 50 years earlier and then rarely used it (Bahrick, 1984). Once again, forgetting occurred more rapidly at first, then more slowly as time passed. Notice, however, that we are now employing a time frame of years rather than hours and days as Ebbinghaus did. Similarly, in another study college freshmen and sophomores accurately recalled 73 percent of their grades from senior year in high school, and their recall for grades from earlier years was almost as good (Bahrick et al., 1996). Of course, although participants in these studies retained considerable information over time, their memory was far from perfect.

▶ 22. Describe Ebbinghaus's "forgetting curve" and factors that contributed to his rapid, substantial forgetting.

FIGURE 7.15 Hermann Ebbinghaus was a pioneering memory researcher.

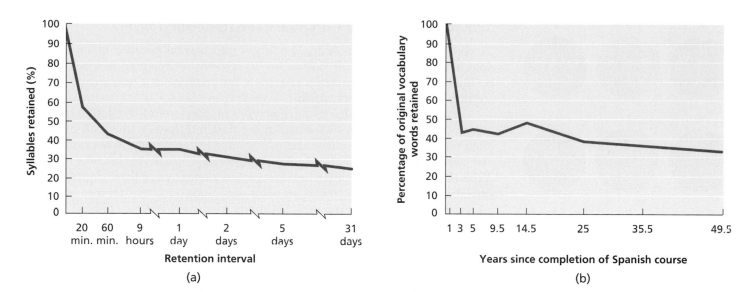

FIGURE 7.16 (a) Hermann Ebbinghaus's forgetting curve shows a rapid loss of memory for nonsense syllables at first, then a more gradual decline. The rapid decline is probably due to the meaningless nature of the nonsense syllables. (b) The forgetting of vocabulary from high school Spanish language classes follows a similar curve, except that the time frame is in years, not days.
Data from (a) Ebbinghaus (1964) and (b) Bahrick (1984).

Why Do We Forget?

Given that some memories last a lifetime, why do we forget so much? Researchers have proposed several explanations for normal memory loss, emphasizing difficulties in encoding, storage, and retrieval.

➤ 23. Identify encoding, storage, retrieval, and motivational processes that have been hypothesized to contribute to forgetting.

Encoding Failure

If memory is in some respects like a giant library, then one reason we do not remember information is that the book was never put on the shelf. Many memory failures result not from "forgetting" information that we once knew well, but from failing to encode the information into long-term memory in the first place. Much of what we sense is not processed deeply enough to commit to memory, which is understandable given the flood of stimuli that enter the sensory registers every day.

We noted earlier that few people can draw a penny (or other coin) from memory, with accurate detail. Even when the task is made easier by requiring only recognition, as in Figure 7.17, most people cannot identify the correct coin (Jones, 1990; Nickerson & Adams, 1979). The details of a coin's appearance are not meaningful to most of us, so we do not encode them no matter how often we see coins in our daily lives.

Decay of the Memory Trace

Turning from encoding to storage, one early explanation for forgetting was **decay theory,** which proposed that with time and disuse the physical memory trace in the nervous system fades away. Decay theory soon fell into disfavor because scientists could not identify what physical memory traces were, where they were located, or how physical decay could be measured.

Decay theory's prediction that the longer the interval of disuse between learning and recall, the less should be recalled, was also problematic. When participants learn a list of words or a set of visual patterns and are retested at two different times, they sometimes recall *more* material during the second testing than during the first. This phenomenon, called *reminiscence,* seems inconsistent with the concept that a memory trace decays over time (Greene, 1992; Klimesch, 1979).

FIGURE 7.17 Which of the coins pictured here corresponds to a real penny? Most people have difficulty choosing the correct one because they have never bothered to encode all of the features of a real penny. The answer is in the margin on page 298.

Nickerson & Adams, 1979.

Interference, Retrieval Failure, and the Tip-of-the-Tongue

According to *interference theory,* we forget information because other items in long-term memory impair our ability to retrieve it (Postman & Underwood, 1973). Many cognitive psychologists view interference as a major cause of forgetting (Anderson & Neely, 1996).

Figure 7.18 illustrates two major types of interference. **Proactive interference** occurs when material learned in the past interferes with recall of newer material. Suppose that Charles changes residences, acquires a new phone number, and memorizes it. That night he sees a friend who asks for his new number. When Charles tries to recall it, he can remember only two or three digits, and instead keeps remembering the digits of his old phone number. Memory of his old phone number is interfering with his ability to retrieve the new one.

Retroactive interference occurs in the opposite direction. Here newly acquired information interferes with the ability to recall information learned at an earlier time (Tulving & Psotka, 1971). Suppose Charles has now had his new phone number for several months, and recalls it perfectly each time. If we ask him, "What was your old phone number?" Charles may have trouble remembering it, perhaps mixing up the digits with his new number. In general, the more similar two sets of information are, the more likely it is that interference will occur. You would probably experience little interference in recalling highly dissimilar material, such as French vocabulary and mathematical formulas.

Some researchers believe that interference is caused by competition among retrieval cues (Anderson & Neely, 1996; Runquist, 1975). When different memories become associated with similar or identical retrieval cues, confusion can result and accessing a cue may "call up" the wrong memory. Retrieval failure also can occur because we have too few retrieval cues or the cues may be too weak (Tulving & Psotka, 1971).

Almost all of us have experienced the so-called *tip-of-the-tongue (TOT) phenomenon,* in which we cannot recall a fact or name (a target word), but feel that we are on the verge of recalling it. Often we keep recalling an incorrect word that sounds similar to or resembles the target word. TOT states are common, perhaps occurring on average about once a week (Brown, 1991). Eventually, we retrieve the correct answer about half the time, and when we cannot, we often recall related information that makes us feel "I really do know the answer" (Brown, 1991; Riefer et al., 1995).

Do TOT states always reflect a retrieval problem? In one experiment, Bennett Schwartz (1998) asked college students a series of general factual questions, some of which actually had no correct answer. Yet when asked these impossible questions, all students claimed at least once that the answer was on the tip of their tongue. In short, some TOT experiences seem to be illusory. Rather than retrieval failure, perhaps we never knew the answer to begin with (Schwartz, 2000).

Motivated Forgetting

Psychodynamic theorists and other psychologists suggest yet another reason for some forgetting. They maintain that motivational processes, such as **repression,** may protect us by blocking the recall of anxiety-arousing memories (Singer, 1990, 1999).

During therapy sessions Sigmund Freud often observed that his patients remembered traumatic or anxiety-arousing events that had long seemed "forgotten." For example, one of his patients suddenly remembered with great shame that while standing beside her sister's coffin, she had thought, "Now my brother-in-law is free to marry me." Freud concluded that the thought had been so shocking and anxiety arousing that the woman had *repressed* it—pushed

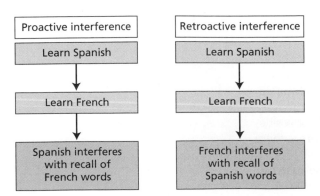

FIGURE 7.18 Interference is a major cause of forgetting. With proactive interference, older memories interfere with the retrieval of newer ones. With retroactive interference, newer memories interfere with the retrieval of older ones.

it down into her unconscious mind—there to remain until it was uncovered years later during psychoanalysis.

The concept of motivated forgetting is controversial. Some evidence supports it, and other evidence does not (Bonanno & Kaltman, 2000; Weinberger, 1990). People certainly do forget unpleasant events (and pleasant ones as well), but it has been difficult to demonstrate experimentally that a process akin to "repression" is the cause of such memory loss (Holmes, 1990; Schooler & Eich, 2000). We will return to this topic shortly.

Amnesia

The most dramatic instances of forgetting occur in amnesia, which takes several forms. **Retrograde amnesia** represents memory loss for events that occurred *prior to* the onset of amnesia. For example, H. M. suffered mild memory loss for events in his life that had occurred during the year or two *before* his operation. A football player who is "knocked out" in a concussion, regains consciousness, and cannot remember the events just before being hit, is experiencing retrograde amnesia.

Anterograde amnesia refers to memory loss for events that occur *after* the initial onset of amnesia. H. M.'s brain operation, and particularly the removal of much of his hippocampus, produced severe anterograde amnesia and robbed him of the ability to consciously remember new experiences and facts. The woman whose hand was pinpricked by Claparède during a handshake also experienced anterograde amnesia; moments later she could not consciously remember the episode. Unlike H. M., her anterograde amnesia was caused by *Korsakoff's syndrome,* which can result from chronic alcoholism and may also cause severe retrograde amnesia (Kopelman et al., 1999).

Alzheimer's disease, which affects millions and mostly elderly adults, produces severe retrograde and anterograde amnesia. This memory loss may be due to a decline in the operation of several neurotransmitter systems, especially the *acetylcholine* system (Kimble, 1992). Acetylcholine plays a key role in synaptic transmission in several brain areas involved in memory.

Finally, there is one type of amnesia that all of us experience: an inability to remember personal experiences from the first few years of our lives. This memory loss for early experiences is called **infantile amnesia** (also known as *childhood amnesia*). Our memories of childhood typically do not include events that occurred before the age of 3 or 4, although some adults can partially recall major events that happened when they were as young as 2 years of age (Eacott & Crawley, 1998; Usher & Neisser, 1993). Major events might be the birth of sibling, hospitalization, or a death in the family.

This does not mean that infants and preschool children don't form long-term memories. They clearly do. Newborns retain memories for sensory information (e.g., they can distinguish between the sound of their mother's vs. another woman's voice) and can remember behaviors that produce rewards (DeCasper & Fifer, 1980). But we are not able to consciously recall the events of our infancy and earliest childhood. Indeed, even 9- and 10-year-old children have difficulty remembering the faces of their preschool classmates (Newcombe & Fox, 1994).

What causes infantile amnesia? One possibility is that brain regions responsible for encoding long-term memories are still immature in the first years after birth. Another hypothesis is that we do not encode our early experiences deeply, and fail to form rich retrieval cues for them. For example, older children are more likely than younger children to spontaneously discuss, and thus rehearse, their recent experiences (Fivush, 1994). Additionally, because infants and very young children lack a clear self-concept, they do not have a personal frame of reference around which to organize rich memories (Howe & Courage, 1993; Harley & Reese, 1999).

➤ 24. Describe the nature and some possible causes of retrograde, anterograde, and infantile amnesia.

The Lincoln penny
In Figure 7.17, penny "A" is the correct answer.

Forgetting to Do Things: Prospective Memory

Have you ever forgotten to mail a letter, turn off the oven, keep an appointment, or purchase something at the market? In contrast to *retrospective memory*, which refers to memory for past events, **prospective memory** concerns remembering to perform an activity in the future (Meacham & Singer, 1977). That people forget to do things as often as they do is interesting, because prospective memories typically involve little content (Baddeley, 1990). Often we need only recall that we must perform some event-based task ("Remember, on your way out, mail the letter") or time-based task ("Remember, take your medication at 4 P.M."). Successful prospective memory, however, draws upon other cognitive abilities, such as planning and allocating attention while performing other tasks (Marsh et al., 1998). The frontal lobes, which direct these executive processes, appear to be centrally involved in prospective memory (McDaniel et al., 1999).

Are people with better retrospective memory less likely to be forgetful on prospective memory tasks? Some findings suggest not, at least when retrospective memory is measured explicitly by recall and recognition tasks (McDaniel & Einstein, 1993). In one experiment, researchers assessed participants' retrospective memory ability by having them recall lists of words (Wilkins & Baddeley, 1978). Next participants performed a prospective, simulated pill-taking task by carrying around a small box with a button. Four times a day at a specified time they had to remember to press the button, which time-stamped their response. Overall, participants who performed better on the word-recall task did not display better memory on the simulated pill-taking task.

During adulthood, do we become increasingly absentminded about remembering to do things, as a common stereotype suggests? Numerous laboratory experiments support this view (Einstein et al., 1998; Mäntylä & Nilsson, 1997). Typically, participants perform a task that requires their ongoing attention while trying to remember to signal the experimenter at certain time intervals or whenever specific events take place. Older adults generally display poorer prospective memory, especially when signaling is time-based. However, when prospective memory is tested outside the laboratory using tasks such as simulated pill-taking, healthy adults in their sixties to eighties often perform as well as or better than adults in their twenties (Rendell & Thomson, 1993, 1999). Perhaps older adults are more motivated to remember in such situations or rely more on a standard routine (Anderson & Craik, 2000). In sum, prospective memory—like other areas of memory—is far from simple.

❭ MEMORY AS A CONSTRUCTIVE PROCESS

Retrieving information from long-term memory is not like viewing a taped replay on a video cassette recorder. Usually, our memories of things past are incomplete and sketchy. In such situations we may literally *construct* (or as some researchers prefer to say, *reconstruct*) a memory by piecing together bits of stored information in a way that intuitively "makes sense," and which therefore seems real and accurate (Schacter & Curran, 2000). Memory construction can be amusing at times, but it also can have serious personal and societal consequences.

Memory Distortion and Schemas: On Ghosts, "Gargoils," and Scenes Beyond the Edge

➤ 25. How do Bartlett's research and studies of boundary extension illustrate memory construction?

A classic experiment by Sir Frederick Bartlett (1932) provides an excellent illustration of memory construction. Bartlett asked residents of Cambridge, England, to read and then retell stories months, or in some cases years, later. Table 7.2 presents one story, "The War of the Ghosts," which is a Pacific North-

TABLE 7.2	ONE OF BARTLETT'S STORIES, AND ONE SUBJECT'S RECONSTRUCTION AFTER 20 HOURS

Original	Reconstruction
The War of the Ghosts	Bartlett asked his English participants to try to retell the story. About 20 hours later, one person recalled the story this way.
One night two young men from Egulac went down to the river to hunt seals, and while they were there it became foggy and calm. Then they heard war-cries, and they thought: "Maybe this is a war-party." They escaped to the shore and hid behind a log. Now canoes came up, and they heard the noise of paddles and saw one canoe coming up to them. There were five men in the canoe, and they said:	**The War of the Ghosts**
"What do you think? We wish to take you along. We are going up the river to make war on the people."	Two men from Edulac went fishing. While thus occupied by the river they heard a noise in the distance.
One of the young men said: "I have no arrows."	"It sounds like a cry," said one, and presently there appeared some men in canoes who invited them to join the party on their adventure. One of the young men refused to go, on the ground of family ties, but the other offered to go.
"Arrows are in the canoe," they said.	"But there are no arrows," he said.
"I will not go along. I might be killed. My relatives do not know where I have gone. But you," he said, turning to the other, "may go with them."	"The arrows are in the boat," was the reply.
So one of the young men went, but the other returned home.	He thereupon took his place, while his friend returned home. The party paddled up the river to Kaloma, and began to land on the banks of the river. The enemy came rushing upon them, and some sharp fighting ensued. Presently some one was injured, and the cry was raised that the enemy were ghosts.
And the warriors went up the river to a town on the other side of Kalama. The people came down to the water, and they began to fight, and many were killed. But presently the young man heard one of the warriors say: "Quick, let us go home: that Indian has been hit." Now he thought: "Oh, they are ghosts." He did not feel sick, but they said he had been shot.	The party returned down the stream, and the young man arrived home feeling none the worse for his experience. The next morning at dawn he endeavoured to recount his adventures. While he was talking something black issued from his mouth. Suddenly he uttered a cry and fell down. His friends gathered round him.
So the canoes went back to Egulac, and the young man went ashore to his house, and made a fire. And he told everybody and said: "Behold I accompanied the ghosts, and we went to fight. Many of our fellows were killed and many of those who attacked us were killed. They said I was hit, and I did not feel sick."	But he was dead.
He told it all, and then he became quiet. When the sun rose he fell down. Something black came out of his mouth. His face became contorted. The people jumped up and cried.	
He was dead.	

Source: Bartlett, 1932.

west Indian tale about a man who meets a group of warriors and goes on a raid with them. During the raid, he discovers that his companions are ghosts; subsequently, he dies a supernatural death.

Bartlett's participants, however, were 20th-century residents of England, not 18th-century Native Americans. When these English participants retold the story, they reconstructed it in a way that made sense to them. Table 7.2 shows an example, retold after only 20 hours. The story is shorter and the plot has changed significantly. Now the hero was fishing rather than hunting seals, the word "boat" is introduced, and most importantly the enemy—not the war party—is described as ghosts. Bartlett found that the longer the time interval between the reading and retelling of the story, the more the story changed to fit English culture.

Earlier we described how schemas (such as the concept "washing clothes") shape encoding. Bartlett, who coined the term *schema,* believed that people have generalized ideas (schemas) about how events happen and that they use these ideas to organize and reconstruct their memories. In reading "The War of the Ghosts," our preexisting schemas no doubt affect how we encode the story, but they also influence how we "fill in the gaps" and reconstruct the story when we later recall it.

In general, the use of appropriate schemas improves memory by helping us organize information as we encode and retrieve it. Remember that whether we are a chess player, coach, musician, or simply an experienced user of language, schemas are a key component of "expert knowledge." But schemas can exact a cognitive price. Fitting information into our schemas is sometimes like trying to squeeze a square peg into a round hole, requiring us to reshape and distort information so that it "makes sense" and fits in with preexisting assumptions about the world.

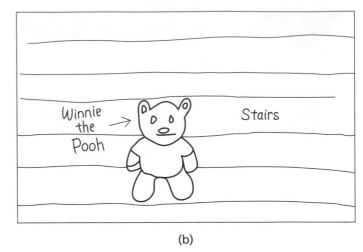

(a)   (b)

FIGURE 7.19   Boundary extension. (a) What you see. (b) What you remember. Helene Intraub and her colleagues (1996) have found that when people briefly look at close-up pictures, such as this one of a teddy bear, and then draw the pictures from memory, they unknowingly convert the image into a "wider-angle scene" in which the size of the main object (e.g., the teddy bear) shrinks. This effect is less likely to occur if the original picture already is a wide-angle scene.

Images courtesy of Helene Intraub.

Advertisers often exploit people's tendency to elaborate and change their memories, thereby skirting laws against false advertising. Consider the following commercial for the mouthwash Listerine.

"Wouldn't it be great," asks the mother, "if you could make him coldproof? Well, you can't. Nothing can do that. [Boy sneezes.] But there is something you can do that may help. Have him gargle with Listerine antiseptic. Listerine can't promise to keep him cold-free, but it may help him fight off colds. During the cold-catching season, have him gargle twice a day with full-strength Listerine. Watch his diet, see he gets plenty of sleep, and there's a good chance he'll have fewer colds, milder colds, this year." (Anderson, 1980, p. 203)

This commercial, with the name of the product changed to *Gargoil,* (alas, not Gargoyle) was used in a memory experiment (Harris, 1977). When participants were asked to recall the commercial, they agreed with the statement "Gargoil antiseptic helps prevent colds," even though the commercial *did not* say that. (The advertisement said it *may* help.) Participants elaborated on what the ad said when they reconstructed it in their memories. Undoubtedly, this is what the advertisers hoped would happen.

Memory construction extends, quite literally, to how we visualize the world. As Figure 7.19 illustrates, when college students look at photographs that have a main object within a scene, and then draw the pictures from memory, they consistently display *boundary extension,* remembering a scene as more expansive—as being "wider-angle"—than it really was (Intraub et al., 1996, 1998). In real life, objects occur against an expansive background, creating a schema for how we expect scenes to look. Thus when remembering close-up images, our schemas lead us to "see beyond the edge" and retrieve a broader scene, not the one we saw.

The Misinformation Effect and Eyewitness Testimony

If memories are constructed, then information that occurs *after* an event may shape that construction process. This **misinformation effect,** the distortion of a memory by misleading postevent information, has been investigated most thoroughly in relation to mistaken eyewitness testimony. In one celebrated case, Father Bernard Pagano, a Roman Catholic priest, was positively identified by seven eyewitnesses as the perpetrator of a series of armed robberies in the Wilmington, Delaware, area. He was saved from almost certain conviction when the true robber, dubbed the "gentleman bandit" because of his politeness and concern for his victims, confessed to the crimes. You can see in Figure 7.20 that there was little physical resemblance between the two men.

Two pieces of information may have affected the witnesses' memory. First, the gentlemanly and concerned manner of the robber is consistent with the schema many people have of priests. Second, before presenting pictures of suspects to the eyewitnesses, the police let it be known that the suspect might be a priest. Father Pagano was the only suspect wearing a clerical collar, and the witnesses' memories may have been strongly affected by this information (Rodgers, 1982; Tversky & Tuchin, 1989).

The misinformation effect can be subtle, produced by changing a single word while questioning an eyewitness. Imagine that after you witness a two-car crash, a police officer takes your statement and simply asks you, "About how fast were the cars going when they smashed into each other?" In one experiment, college students viewed a brief film of a car accident and then judged how fast the cars were going. Their judgments varied by almost 25 percent, depending upon how the question was asked (Loftus & Palmer, 1974). The recalled speed became progressively slower when the words *smashed into* (40.8 mph) were changed to *collided* (39.3 mph), *bumped* (38.1 mph), *hit* (34.0), and *contacted* (31.8 mph).

Confusing the Source

Misinformation effects also occur because of **source confusion,** our tendency to recall something or recognize it as familiar, but to forget where we encountered it. Suppose an eyewitness to a crime looks through a series of mugshots and reports that none of the individuals is the perpetrator. Several days later, the eyewitness is brought back to view a lineup and is asked to identify the person who committed the crime. In reality, none of the people in the lineup did, but one suspect was pictured in a mugshot that the eyewitness had seen days ago. "That's the person," says the eyewitness. Source confusion (also called *source amnesia* or *source misattribution*) occurred because the eyewitness recognized that individual's face was familiar, but failed to remember that this familiarity stemmed from the mugshot. Instead, the witness mistakenly assumed that he or she saw the familiar-looking suspect committing the crime.

In an experimental analog to this situation, 29 percent of participants who witnessed a staged event and later viewed mugshots misidentified *innocent* suspects as having been involved in the event because of source confusion (Brown et al., 1977). Source confusion also occurs when participants are exposed to several misleading statements about an event that they have witnessed (Zaragoza & Mitchell, 1996). They eventually forget that the source of the misinformation (e.g., that a barehanded thief wore gloves) was a statement made by someone else, and come to believe it was part of what they saw while witnessing the event.

Does postevent information permanently alter a witness's original memory, so that the original memory can never again be retrieved? Researchers debate the answer, but all agree that eyewitness reports can be influenced by postevent information. Results like these have raised concerns about the reliability of eyewitness testimony not only from adults, but also from children in cases of alleged physical and sexual abuse. We now explore this issue in our *Psychological Frontiers* feature.

(a)

(b)

FIGURE 7.20 Seven eyewitnesses to armed robberies committed by Ronald Clouser (a) mistakenly identified Father Bernard Pagano (b) as the robber, probably as a result of information from police that influenced their memory reconstructions.
United Press International.

➤ 26. Explain how source confusion contributes to misinformation effects.

➤ 27. Are younger and older children equally susceptible to misinformation effects, and equally accurate in recalling traumatic events? Describe some evidence.

PSYCHOLOGICAL FRONTIERS

How Accurate Are Young Children's Memories?

Research on the accuracy of children's memory has grown dramatically in the past 15 years. This interest stems from at least three factors. First, basic researchers seek to understand how memory capabilities develop with age. Second, misinformation experiments with adults raise the question of whether children's memory is as malleable. Third, society's increasing sensitivity to the tragedy of child abuse raises legal and scientific debates about the possible overreporting (false reporting) and underreporting of abuse (Ceci et al., 2000).

In cases of alleged sexual abuse there often is no conclusive corroborating medical evidence (sexual abuse often does not involve intercourse) and the child usually is the only witness (Bruck et al., 1998). If the charges are true, the thought of failing to convict the abuser and returning the child to an environment where the abuse might continue is frightening. Conversely, if the charges are false, the consequences of convicting an innocent person are equally distressing. Thus the accuracy and believability of children's recall is of paramount concern.

▶ Children's Susceptibility to Suggestive Questioning

As with adults, misinformation experiments indicate that a single instance of suggestive questioning can distort children's memory. Moreover, among children and adults, suggestive questioning most often leads to false memories when it is repeated (Ceci et al., 1994; Zaragoza & Mitchell, 1996). In both situations, young children typically are more susceptible to misleading suggestions than older children (Ceci et al., 2000; Templeton, & Wicox, 2000).

In one experiment by Michelle Leichtman and Stephen Ceci (1995), 3- to 6-year-old children were told about a man named Sam Stone. During interviews over several weeks, some children were repeatedly told stories that portrayed Sam as clumsy. Later "Sam" visited the children's classroom, was introduced to them, and behaved innocuously. In class the next day, the children were shown a ripped book and soiled teddy bear, things that Sam clearly had not done. Over the next 10 weeks children were interviewed several times and some were asked suggestive questions about Sam (e.g., "When Sam Stone tore the book, did he do it on purpose or was he being silly?"). Two weeks later a new interviewer asked all the children to describe Sam's visit to the classroom.

Children who only heard suggestive stories about Sam *before* his classroom appearance, and those who only were asked suggestive questions *after* his appearance, made more false reports about Sam's behavior than a control group receiving neither type of suggestive treatment. Moreover, children who received both types of misinformation made the highest number of false reports, and younger children were much more likely to do so. One child stated that after soaking the teddy bear in the bath, Sam smeared it with a crayon.

Many researchers believe that these findings have troubling implications. In many cases where abuse allegations are investigated, the child initially offers no statements about being abused, or denies it if questioned. Over time and with repeated suggestive questioning during therapy or police investigation, the child acknowledges having been abused, may later deny it again, and then admits it once more (Bruck et al., 1998; Sorensen & Snow, 1991).

▶ Accurate Versus False Reports: Can We Tell Them Apart?

Can adults, even trained professionals, distinguish between children's accurate and false reports of personal events? The answer appears to be "no," at least when false reports arise after repeated, suggestive questioning. When judges, mental-health professionals, social workers, and prosecutors were shown videotapes of the children's reports in the Leichtman and Ceci (1995) experiment, they could not reliably tell which were true and which were false. The false reports were often judged as highly credible, perhaps because many children who make such false reports are not intentionally lying. Rather, like adults in misinformation experiments, they believe that what they are remembering is accurate (Bruck et al., 1998).

▶ Children's Memory for Traumatic Events

Some researchers have moved outside the laboratory to study children's memory for naturally occurring events that involve traumatic physical touch, such as medical exams. Gail Goodman and her colleagues (1994) obtained permission to study 46 children who, because of health problems, underwent a painful medical procedure involving forced genital contact (a catheter had to be inserted through the urethra, and liquid was infused into each child's bladder). About two weeks later, the children's memory of the procedure was tested.

The children's free recall was assessed first using general questions (e.g., "Tell me everything you can remember about what happened."). Then they were asked nonleading questions that did not present any inaccurate informa-

–Continued

tion (e.g., "Was the doctor a man or a woman?"), and misleading questions that contained false information (e.g., "Didn't the doctor look in your ears when he gave you that test?"). The results showed that misleading questions did not influence children's memories for this particular traumatic event. However, although the oldest children correctly answered 82 percent of both nonleading and misleading questions, the youngest children answered only 48 percent accurately. Overall, children who underwent multiple operations did not have more accurate memories than did children who had only one operation. Still, although the youngest children misremembered many details of the situation, all of them remembered something. There was no evidence for memory repression, at least of this experience.

▶ Conclusions

From the standpoint of basic science, it appears that young children remember a great deal, but like adults, they also misremember and seem more susceptible to misinformation effects. On the applied side, mental-health and legal professionals are now paying greater attention to how children's admissions of abuse are elicited, and training programs are helping practitioners minimize suggestive interviewing techniques (Bruck et al., 1998; Ceci et al., 2000). For researchers, the applied goal is not to discredit children's allegations of abuse. To the contrary, the hope is that by minimizing the risk of false allegations, nonsuggestive interviewing will elicit allegations judged as even more compelling, thereby helping to ensure that justice is done.

The "Recovered Memory" Controversy: Repression or Reconstruction?

In 1997 a woman from Illinois settled a lawsuit against two psychiatrists and their hospital for $10.6 million. She alleged that her psychiatrists used hypnosis, drugs, and other treatments that led her to develop false memories of having been a high priestess in an abusive satanic cult. That same year, criminal charges were brought against a group of Houston mental-health professionals, alleging that they "used techniques commonly associated with mind control and brainwashing" with seven patients, creating false memories of having been abused in a satanic cult (APA Montior, December 1997, p. 9). Yet only years earlier, there had been a wave of cases in which adults—usually in the course of psychotherapy—began to remember long-forgotten childhood abuse and sued their parents, other family members, and former teachers for the alleged trauma (Figure 7.21).

The debate over the validity of "recovered memories" of childhood trauma has escalated the long-running scientific controversy over Freud's concept of repression (Brown, 2000; Loftus et al., 2000). This controversy can be broken down into two issues, though unfortunately they are often intertwined. First, when a recovered memory of sexual abuse occurs, is it accurate? Second, if the abuse really happened, what caused the memory to be forgotten for so long—repression, or some other psychological process? For the person having the memory, the alleged abuser, and the legal system, accuracy is what matters most. For researchers and therapists, both issues are important.

Let's briefly examine the second issue. Many scientists and therapists question Freud's concept of repression. Repression implies a special psychological mechanism that actively pushes traumatic memories into the unconscious mind, and we have already noted that researchers have had difficulty demonstrating it experimentally. Elizabeth Loftus (1998) and other researchers propose that recovered memories of childhood abuse should not be taken as automatic evidence of repression. Alternative explanations include the possibility that the memory loss occurred because of ordinary (nonmotivated) sources of forgetting, or that the event itself never happened. In contrast, primarily based on numerous case studies, other researchers and many therapists believe that repression is a valid concept (Singer, 1999). This controversy will not be resolved soon.

What about the more basic question? Is it possible that someone could forget their childhood sexual abuse, by whatever psychological mechanism, and then recover that memory as an adult? We know that memory loss can occur following a psychological trauma. Trauma victims may report not remembering the event at all or may report partial memory loss and confusion.

▶ 28. Do people ever forget traumatic personal events? Why are recovered memories and repression controversial topics?

Shahn Kermuni, Gamma Liason.

FIGURE 7.21 In a famous 1990 repressed memory case, George Franklin was convicted of murdering Susan Nason, an 8-year-old girl killed in 1969. Franklin's 28-year-old daughter Eileen (shown above), who had been Susan's childhood friend, provided the key evidence. During therapy Eileen recovered memories of her father sexually assaulting and killing Susan. A judge overturned the conviction after learning that Eileen's memories had been recovered under hypnosis. All of the details about the case that Eileen recalled had been published in the newspapers, creating the possibility of source confusion in her memory. Eileen also had other recovered memories that were proven to be untrue, such as those of her father killing two other girls.

Amnesia without obvious signs of brain damage has been reported among survivors of natural disasters, children who witnessed the violent death of a parent, victims of rape, and combat veterans (Arrigo & Pezdek, 1997). In cases of child sexual abuse, some victims do not recall their trauma when they are adults (Williams, 1994; Kluft, 1999). Moreover, laboratory experiments indicate that a mentally shocking event (e.g., viewing a sudden, violent film scene) can produce retrograde amnesia for information presented just before the shocking event occurred (Loftus & Burns, 1982).

In some cases it appears that accurate memories can indeed return after decades of posttrauma forgetting (Arrigo & Pezdek, 1997; Kluft, 1999). Yet memory loss after psychological trauma usually is far shorter, with memory returning over weeks, months, or perhaps a few years. In many cases of trauma the victim's primary problem is not memory loss, but rather an *inability* to forget, which may involve recurrent nightmares and flashbacks (Ross et al., 1989). Experiments with adults and children also indicate that false memories of personal events can be created ("implanted") by suggestive questioning or comments, or merely by having someone imagine that the event took place (Bruck et al., 1998; Loftus & Pickrell, 1995). Many memory researchers are concerned that in "recovered memory therapy," therapists repeatedly suggest the possibility of abuse to people who already are emotionally vulnerable. Given everything science has taught us about forgetting, constructive memory, and the "fogging up" of even flashbulb memories, they argue that it is naive to take the accuracy of recovered memories of long-past events at face value.

While this debate rages, therapists and the courts in Canada, the United States, and abroad are being urged to recognize the possibility of false memory implantation during therapy (Gothard & Ivker, 2000; Prout & Dobson, 1998). Several members of the Royal College of Psychiatrists in Great Britain wrote:

> . . . when memories are "recovered" after long periods of amnesia, particularly when extraordinary means were used to secure the recovery of memory, there is a high probability that the memories are false. (Brandon et al., 1998, p. 296)

"High probability," of course, is not certainty. As is the case in research on the accuracy of children's testimony about sexual abuse, the message from science is not that anyone who claims a recovered memory of trauma should be dismissed out of hand. Rather, it is to urge caution in unconditionally accepting those memories, particularly in cases where suggestive techniques are used to recover the memories.

〉 THE BIOLOGY OF MEMORY

Since the early 1900s, the scientific quest to determine the biological basis of memory has taken some remarkable twists and turns. Karl Lashley, a pioneering physiological psychologist, spent decades searching for the *engram*—the physical "memory trace" that presumably was stored somewhere in the brain when a memory was formed. Lashley (1950) trained animals to perform various tasks, such as running mazes, and later removed or damaged (lesioned) specific regions of their cortex to see if they would forget how to perform the task. No matter what small area was lesioned, the animals' memory remained intact. Large lesions affected memory, but even then, it didn't seem to matter where the lesion was made. Lashley never found the engram and concluded that a memory is stored throughout the brain.

Other research initially suggested that, indeed, engrams exist. While performing neurosurgery, Wilder Penfield and his colleagues (1963) electrically stimulated specific sites on the cerebral cortex of patients who were under local anesthesia and fully conscious. Penfield reported that the stimulation sometimes triggered patients' memories. One patient reported seeing the office in which she had worked a long time ago, with a man leaning on her desk, pencil in hand.

Unfortunately, when other researchers reviewed Penfield's data, they concluded that such instances were rare and probably involved inaccurate, "reconstructed" images (Loftus & Loftus, 1980). For example, people sometimes reported memories of being in places where, in fact, they had never been.

Perhaps most striking was James McConnell's (1962) discovery of "memory transfer." He classically conditioned flatworms to a light that was paired with an electric shock, eventually causing the worms to contract to the light alone. Next he chopped them up and fed a chemical from their cells, RNA (ribonucleic acid), to a sample of untrained worms. Amazingly, the new worms showed some conditioning to the light. This suggested that RNA might be a chemical engram, a "memory molecule" that stored experiences. Some scientists found memory transfer effects with rats, mice, and goldfish, but others were unable to replicate these findings. Controversy ensued, and McConnell gave up on the idea (Rilling, 1996). Yet despite the inevitable "dead ends," neuroscientists have made considerable progress in understanding the biological bases of memory.

Where in the Brain Are Memories Formed?

Scientists rely on three approaches to map the "geography" of memory (Gabrieli, 1998). In *human lesion studies*, they examine memory loss following naturally occurring damage (e.g., from disease, accidents) to different parts of the brain. In *nonhuman animal lesion experiments*, researchers damage a specific part of the brain and observe how memory is affected. Finally, *brain-imaging studies* examine the healthy brain as participants perform various memory tasks. Together, these lines of research reveal that memory involves many interacting brain regions, several of which are shown in Figure 7.22.

➤ 29. What three approaches do scientists use to study the brain regions involved in memory?

The Hippocampus and Cerebral Cortex

The hippocampus and its adjacent tissue help to encode and retrieve long-term declarative memories (Rolls, 2000). Like H. M., most patients with hippocampal damage retain short-term memory, but cannot form new, explicit long-term memories of personal experiences and facts (Squire & Zola-Morgan, 1991). For example, one

➤ 30. What major roles do the hippocampus, cerebral cortex, thalamus, amygdala, and cerebellum play in memory?

FIGURE 7.22 Many areas of the brain, such as the regions shown here, play key roles in memory.

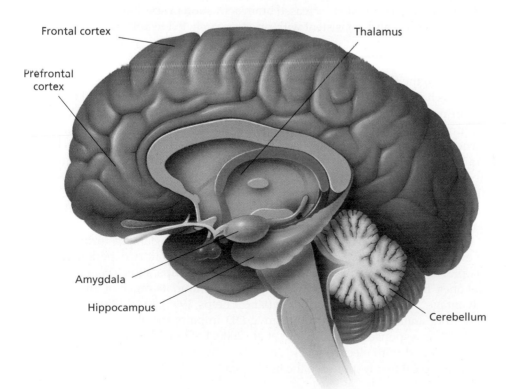

Frontal cortex

Prefrontal cortex

Thalamus

Amygdala

Hippocampus

Cerebellum

patient could recall the names of presidents elected before his brain injury occurred, but not the names of presidents elected after his injury (Squire, 1987).

The hippocampus does not seem to be the site where long-term memories are permanently stored, which is why H. M. retained his long-term memories acquired earlier in life. Rather, it seems to be an "encoding station" that helps to convert short-term memories into more permanent ones. Brain-imaging studies show that specific hippocampal regions become highly active during encoding and retrieval (Lepage et al., 1998; Tulving et al., 1994).

The cerebral cortex plays a vital role in encoding by processing information from the sensory registers. The diverse components of an experience—where something happened, what the scene or people looked like, sounds we heard, the meaning of events or information, and so on—may be processed in different regions of the cortex and then gradually "bound" together in the hippocampus (Squire & Stuart Zola-Morgan 1991). This hypothetical and gradual "binding" process is called **memory consolidation,** and it may involve the creation of codes that allow information to be transferred from short-term memory into long-term memory.

The cerebral cortex also appears to store semantic memories across wide-ranging sites. As John Gabrieli (1998, p. 94) notes, "knowledge in any domain [e.g., for pictures or words] . . . is distributed over a specific, but extensive, neural network that often extends over several lobes." Similarly, the various components of an episodic memory are stored across wide areas of the cortex (Schacter et al., 1998; Squire, 1992). Yet we retrieve and reintegrate these components as a "unified memory," thanks to their previous consolidation in the hippocampus.

Finally, brain-imaging studies suggest that the frontal lobes—especially the prefrontal cortex—play a central role in carrying out the functions of working memory (Nelson et al., 2000; Cabeza & Nyberg, 2000). In one experiment, John Gabrieli and his colleagues (1996) used functional MRI imaging to study brain activity during shallow and deep processing. In the shallow (structural) processing task, young adults identified whether each word was capitalized or lowercase. The deep (semantic) processing task required them to pay attention to the meaning of the words by identifying whether a word referred to an abstract concept (e.g., trust, love) or a concrete object (e.g., chair, book). As Figure 7.23 shows, the researchers found that deep processing increased brain activation in specific regions of the left prefrontal cortex and, consistent with prior research, led to better recall.

The Thalamus and Amygdala

Damage to the thalamus can produce severe amnesia, although we are not sure why this happens (Gabrieli, 1998). In a famous case, a young U.S. Air Force technician named N. A. was injured in a freak accident (Squire, 1987). While his roommate was practicing thrusts with a miniature fencing foil, N. A. suddenly turned around in his seat and was stabbed through the right nostril, piercing his brain and damaging a portion of his thalamus. The damage permanently limited his ability to form new declarative memories (Cohen & Squire, 1981). He also could not recall events from the two-year period prior to the accident, but over time this retrograde amnesia improved. In many cases, however, thalamic damage results in permanent, extensive anterograde and retrograde amnesia.

The amygdala seems to encode emotionally arousing and disturbing aspects of events (Gabrieli, 1998; LaBar & Phelps, 1998). In laboratory experiments, most people remember emotionally arousing stimuli (film clips, slides) better than neutral ones. But damage to your amygdala would eliminate much of this "memory advantage" from arousing stimuli (LaBar & Phelps, 1998). In addition, for humans and other animals, damage to the amygdala impairs the ability to form conditioned fear responses (Amorapanth et al., 2000; LeDoux, 1992). For example, if a light is paired with electric shock, animals with amygdala damage will not develop a typical fear response to the light alone.

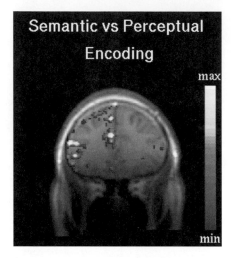

FIGURE 7.23 Four of the participants in this experiment performed shallow (i.e., perceptual/structural) encoding and deep (semantic) encoding tasks while undergoing functional magnetic resonance imaging (fMRI). Activity in a section of their prefrontal cortex was imaged every 1.5 seconds, yielding a total of 224 images per participant. The results, shown here for 1 participant, revealed that semantic encoding was accompanied by greater neural activity in specific regions of the left prefrontal cortex.

Photo courtesy of John Gabrieli.

The Cerebellum

Along with several other parts of the brain, the cerebellum plays an important role in the formation of procedural memories (Gabrieli, 1998; Sanes et al., 1990). This helps explain why H. M., whose cerebellum was not damaged by the operation, showed improved performance at various hand-eye coordination tasks (such as mirror-tracing) even though he was unable to consciously remember having performed the tasks.

Focusing on another type of procedural memory, Richard Thompson and his coworkers established a classically conditioned eyeblink response in rabbits by pairing a tone (CS) with a puff of air to the eye (UCS). As the rabbits learned the conditioned response, electrical recordings revealed increased electrical activity in the cerebellum (Thompson, 1985; Thompson & Steinmetz, 1992). Later Thompson found that removing a tiny portion of the cerebellum completely abolished the memory for the *conditioned* eyeblink, but did not affect a general (unconditioned) eyeblink response. Similarly, eyeblink conditioning fails to work with human patients who have damaged cerebellums (Green & Woodruff, 2000).

How Are Memories Formed?

One of the enduring mysteries of memory research is perhaps the most basic one: How are memories formed within the nervous system? To many researchers, the answer lies in physical and chemical changes in the brain's neural circuitry (Hebb, 1949; Martin et al., 2000).

➤ 31. How has research with *Aplysia* aided our understanding of memory formation?

Eric Kandel and his colleagues have studied a marine snail, *Aplysia californica,* for over 25 years (Abel & Kandel, 1998; Carew & Kandel, 1973). *Aplysia* is no mental giant, but it can learn, form memories, and has only about 20,000 neurons (compared with our 100 billion) that are larger and easier to study than ours. For example, *Aplysia* retracts its gill slightly when the gill is gently squirted with water. But if a squirt is paired with electric shock to its tail, *Aplysia* covers up its gill with a protective flap of skin. After repeated pairings, *Aplysia* acquires a conditioned response and will cover its gills when the water is squirted alone. In other words, *Aplysia* forms a simple procedural memory.

When water is squirted before conditioning begins, sensory neurons in the gill fire and release neurotransmitters that stimulate motor neurons, causing the gill to move. During conditioning, electric shock causes sensory neurons in the tail to release a flood of neurotransmitters that reach the sensory neurons from the gill and activate an enzyme called *protein kinase.* In turn, protein kinase activation causes the gill sensory neurons to release more of their own neurotransmitters.

Crucially, the length of time that protein kinase is active seems to determine whether short-term memories become long-term ones. If only a few shocks are paired with the squirt of water, the protein kinase "shuts off" after a brief period and no permanent memory is formed. But with repeated pairings, the protein kinase remains in a long-term state of activation and a longer-term memory is formed. Days later, sensory neurons in the gill will still react more strongly to a squirt of water than they did before conditioning.

During this process the axon terminals of the sensory neurons from the gill become densely packed with neurotransmitter release points, and postsynaptic neurons develop more receptor sites (Bailey & Chen, 1992; Baudry & Davis, 1991). These structural changes result in greater ease of synaptic transmission and the development of a neural circuit that may be the basis for memory consolidation (Abel & Kandel, 1998; Martin et al., 2000).

A radically different line of research, involving rats and other species with more complex nervous systems, supports this hypothesis. In numerous experiments, researchers have sought to mimic (albeit very crudely) a process of long-term memory formation by stimulating specific neural pathways with low-intensity, rapid bursts of electricity (say, 100 impulses per second for several

➤ 32. What is long-term potentiation, and what role does it appear to play in memory?

TABLE 7.3

"S." memorized this 50-digit matrix in 3 minutes and recalled it in 40 seconds. He recalled it in any pattern that Luria requested, such as the second column from bottom to top (30 seconds) and a zig-zag pattern (35 seconds) shown here by the italicized numbers.

```
6 6 8 0
5 4 3 2
1 6 8 4
7 9 3 5
4 2 3 7
3 8 9 1
1 0 0 2
3 4 5 1
2 7 6 8
1 9 2 6
2 9 6 7
5 5 2 0
0 1
```

Adapted from Ericsson & Chase, 1982.

➤ 33. According to some researchers, what basic memory principles account for exceptional memory? Do you agree with this position?

seconds). They find that once this rapid stimulation ends, the neural pathway becomes stronger—synaptic connections are activated more easily—for days or even weeks (Bliss & Dolphin, 1982; Martinez et al., 1998). This enduring increase in synaptic strength, called **long-term potentiation,** has been studied extensively in the hippocampus, which plays a key role in memory consolidation.

How does long-term potentiation occur? Some findings suggest that presynatpic neurons increase their release of certain neurotransmitters and postsynaptic neurons become more receptive by developing additional tiny branches (spines) on their dendrites (Trommald et al., 1996). Protein kinase also appears to play a key role. Long-term potentiation does not occur when protein kinase activity is inhibited by drugs, and mice with a genetically bred protein kinase deficiency not only have impaired long-term potentiation, but also display memory deficits on a variety of learning tasks (Nayak et al., 1998; Silva et al., 1992).

In sum, research points to increased synaptic efficiency as one neural basis of long-term memory, and to the important role of protein kinase. However, protein kinase is not a "memory molecule." Rather, it appears to facilitate other chemical actions inside neurons that allow long-term memories to form.

❯ EXCEPTIONAL MEMORY

H. M., the amnesia patient whose story began this chapter, became famous for his extraordinary forgetting. In contrast, some people (called *mnemonists*) display extraordinary remembering. The distinguished Italian conductor Arturo Toscanini reputedly could recall from memory each note for every instrument in 250 symphonies, as well as the music and lyrics for 100 operas (Marek, 1982). Russian newspaper reporter S.V. Shereshevski had a remarkable capacity to remember numbers, mathematical formulas, nonsense syllables, sounds, and poems in foreign languages. At one point psychologist Aleksandr Luria (1968), who studied "S." for decades, presented him with the 50-digit matrix shown in Table 7.3. S. took only 3 minutes to learn it, could rapidly recall the digits in any direction—up, down, left, right, and zigzag—and could recite them years later. In 1981, former psychology major Rajan Mahevedan set a world record by reciting from memory the first 31,811 digits of pi (π).

To what should we attribute these remarkable memory feats? Is exceptional memory a "natural" trait or an acquired skill? This question brings us to our featured study in the *Research Close-Up.*

RESEARCH CLOSE-UP

Is Exceptional Memory Really Exceptional?

▶ **Background**

In this classic case study, K. Anders Ericsson and his colleagues hypothesized that the remarkable feats of mnemonists do not require unique memory abilities and can be explained by basic memory principles. They tested their hypothesis by examining whether a person with average memory skills could, with practice, develop exceptional memory.

▶ **Method**

S. F., a college student, practiced a digit-span task for 1 hour a day, 3 to 5 days a week, for 20 months. If he correctly recalled a string of digits (1 digit was presented per second), the next string was increased by a digit. If he made an error, the next sequence was decreased by a digit. In total, he spent about 230 hours at the task. At 6 months

—Continued

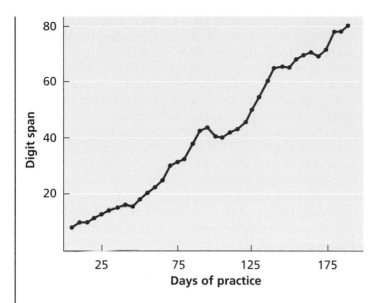

FIGURE 7.24 S. F.'s performance on digit span tests improved dramatically with practice. This graph shows 190 practice sessions.
Source: Ericsson, et al., 1980.

and again a year later, the researchers also measured how long it took S. F. to learn the 50-digit matrix shown in Table 7.3. Four students who had not undergone digit-span practice also were tested on the 50-digit matrix.

▌ Results

As Figure 7.24 shows, S. F.'s digit-span recall improved dramatically. He also learned the 50-digit matrix far more quickly than the control participants (187 vs. 860 seconds), performing at a level comparable to that previously displayed by the famous mnemonist S. (180 seconds). S. F. also could recall the 50-digit matrix in various patterns that, overall, matched S.'s performance.

Interviews revealed that S. F., on his own, learned to use chunking, associations, and hierarchical organization. S. F. was an experienced runner, so on the digit-span task he grouped sequences into 4-digit chunks that he remembered as "running times." Thus 3492 would become "3 minutes and 49.2 seconds, near world-record time for running a mile." He also used ages and dates as schemas for chunking (893 became "89.3 years old, a very old person," and 1944 became "near the end of World War II"). As the strings of digits became longer, S. F. used hierarchical organization to

arrange the individual chunks into 3-chunk "supergroups," and then into additional hierarchical groupings. S. F.'s system was taught to another student (also a runner), whose digit-span recall increased to 60 digits over 300 practice days.

▌ Critical Discussion

Did S. F.'s practice increase the general capacity of his short-term memory? The authors argued that it did not. After 3 months of S. F.'s digit-span practice, they tested him on a letter-span task, and his recall immediately dropped to six items (letters). Instead, it appeared that S. F. had found a way to use *chunking*, *associations*, and *hierarchical organization* to rapidly transfer digits into long-term memory. The authors concluded that with the proper mnemonic strategies and practice, there is no limit to how much memory can improve. The keys to exceptional memory, they argue, are (1) prior knowledge and extensive practice, (2) meaningful associations, and (3) efficient storage and retrieval structures (Ericsson & Chase, 1982).

Should we accept the authors' conclusion? Even with thousands of hours of practice, can an average person really remember over 30,000 digits of pi? Likewise, with further practice, would S. F. have been able to duplicate S's extraordinary ability to recall numerous types of stimuli *decades* later? These are testable questions and the answer might be "yes," but at present we simply do not know. According to the researchers who studied Rajan and S., although they used certain mnemonic techniques, Rajan and S. also possessed special abilities that allowed them to employ these techniques to an extraordinary extent (Luria, 1968; Thompson et al., 1991).

The present study also does not address the cases of *savants*, individuals with mental disabilities who display exceptional memory for particular tasks. Some savants can reproduce complex musical pieces or highly detailed drawings after being exposed to them only once. Others, such as the man portrayed by actor Dustin Hoffman in the movie *The Rain Man*, are "human calendars." Give them a date from the past or future and they will tell you what day of the week it was—or will be (Hurts & Mulhall, 1988). Researchers continue to debate whether savants' skills reflect special "natural abilities" or extensive rote memorization and basic memory processes (Miller, 1999; Winner, 2000).

Despite these issues, the present study makes an intriguing point. Exceptional memory truly may be exceptional in its accomplishments, but not in its underlying mechanisms. Instead, it is possible that exceptional memory involves only the highly motivated and skilled application of basic memory principles.

K. Anders Ericsson, William G. Chase, and Steve Faloon (1980). Acquisition of a memory skill. *Science, 208,* 1181–1182. (Data also reported in K. Ericsson and William Chase (1982). Exceptional memory, *American Scientist, 70,* 615.)

❯ A FINAL THOUGHT: THE "CURSE" OF EXCEPTIONAL MEMORY

There is one obvious sense in which normal forgetting is a blessing, for it can dull the unpleasant experiences of the past. All of us forget most of the details of daily life, both positive and negative ones, although the scales are not necessarily

➤ 34. In what ways is "forgetting" adaptive? How might perfect memory be a burden?

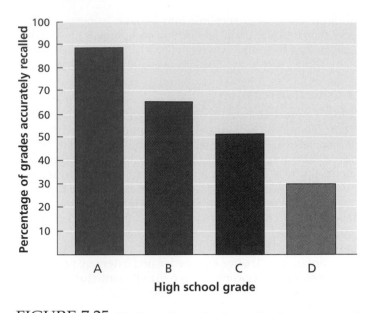

FIGURE 7.25   The lower the grade, the smaller the percentage of students who accurately recalled it. Note also that almost all recall "errors" for grades of B, C, and D overestimated how well the student did.
Bahrick et al., 1996.

balanced. As Figure 7.25 shows, when college students in one study recalled their high school grades, the worse the grade the less often students remembered it accurately (Bahrick et al., 1996). In addition, errors were positively biased; B's were misremembered as A's, C's as B's, and D's as C's. Thus students tended to reconstruct their academic past through slightly rosy glasses.

There is another, more important way in which it pays to forget. Most of us would at times (especially around final exam periods) like to have a photographic long-term memory from which we could retrieve everything we ever saw, heard, or learned. We seldom stop to think what a curse this could be. Luria (1968) describes how S. was tyrannized by his seeming inability to forget meaningless information. Almost any retrieval cue might unleash a flood of trivial memories that dominated S.'s consciousness and made it difficult for him to concentrate or think abstractly. If you had a photographic memory, you would be paralyzed trying to answer a question as simple as "What does a dog look like." Instead of easily generating a dog's abstract qualities (four legs; wagging tail; tendency to seek out foul, smelly objects), you would be mired in images of every dog your ever saw and of how different they actually looked (Reisberg, 1997). In short, we should appreciate just how wonderfully our memory system is balanced between the adaptiveness of remembering and the benefits of forgetting. Figure 7.26 highlights some of the biological, psychological, and environmental factors that cause us to forget.

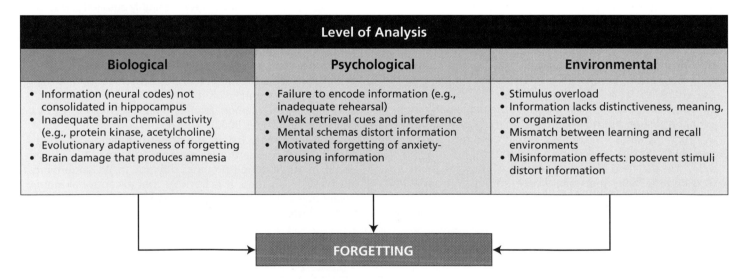

FIGURE 7.26   Understanding the Causes of Behavior: Factors that cause forgetting.

CHAPTER SUMMARY

Memory as Information Processing

- Memory involves three main processes: encoding (placing information into the system), storage, and retrieval. According to one model, these processes are organized around three components: sensory memory, short-term (working) memory, and long-term memory.

- Incoming sensory information is briefly held in sensory registers. Only a small portion of this information reaches short- and long-term memory, where it is mentally represented by phonological, visual, semantic, or motor codes.

- Short-term memory holds about five to nine units of information for about 20 seconds, but rehearsal can extend this duration. Short-term memory is called working memory because it actively processes information and supports other cognitive functions. Working memory has auditory, visuospatial, and executive (coordinating) components.

- Long-term memory can store enormous amounts of information for up to a lifetime. Studies of amnesia patients and research on the serial position effect support the distinction between short- and long-term memory.

Encoding: Entering Information

- Effortful processing involves intentional encoding and conscious attention, as when we study material in school. Automatic processing occurs without intention and requires minimal effort. Information about the frequency, spatial location, sequence, and timing of events often is encoded automatically.

- The more deeply we process information, the better we will remember it. Maintenance rehearsal (repetition) provides somewhat deeper processing than simple exposure, but elaborative rehearsal provides the deepest processing.

- Memory aids (mnemonics) that organize information and generate additional retrieval cues, such as forming hierarchies, chunking material, and forming visual images to supplement other memory codes, enhance encoding and facilitate deep processing.

- Schemas are mental frameworks that shape how we encode information. As we become experts in any given field, we develop schemas that allow us to encode information into memory more efficiently.

Storage: Retaining Information

- Associative network models view long-term memory as a network of associated nodes, with each node representing an idea or concept. Activating any one node within this network creates spreading activation that primes related nodes, thereby increasing the likelihood that associated concepts will be accessed.

- Neural network models propose that each piece of information in memory is represented not by a single node, but by multiple nodes distributed throughout the brain. Each memory is represented by a unique pattern of simultaneously activated nodes.

- Declarative long-term memories involve factual knowledge and include episodic memories (facts concerning personal experiences) and semantic memories (facts about the world and language). In contrast, procedural memory is reflected in skills and actions.

- Explicit memory involves conscious or intentional memory retrieval, whereas implicit memory occurs when memory influences our behavior without conscious awareness.

Retrieval: Accessing Information

- Retrieval cues are internal and external stimuli that activate information stored in long-term memory. Memory retrieval is more likely when we have multiple cues, self-generated cues, and distinctive cues.

- The encoding specificity principle states that memory is enhanced when cues present during retrieval match those that were present during encoding. Context-dependent memory and state-dependent memory illustrate encoding specificity.

- To learn academic information more effectively, process it deeply by using elaborative rehearsal, organization, and overlearning. Distribute study sessions over time and use imagery to create multiple retrieval cues.

Forgetting

- Forgetting often is more rapid relatively soon after initial learning, but the time frame and degree of forgetting can vary widely depending on numerous factors.

- We often cannot recall information because of encoding failure: We never entered it into long-term memory in the first place.

- Decay theory proposes that we forget because physical memory traces deteriorate with disuse over time, but today interference theories are more influential. Proactive interference occurs when material learned in the past interferes with recall of newer material. Retroactive interference occurs when newly acquired information interferes with the ability to recall information learned at an earlier time.

- Psychodynamic theorists propose that we may forget anxiety-arousing material through an unconscious process of motivated forgetting called repression.

- Retrograde amnesia represents memory loss for events that occurred *prior to* the onset of amnesia. Anterograde amnesia refers to memory loss for events that occur *after* the initial onset of amnesia. Our inability to remember personal experiences from the first few years of our lives is called infantile amnesia.

- Whereas retrospective memory refers to memory for past events, prospective memory refers to our ability to remember to perform some activity in the future.

Memory as a Constructive Process

- Our schemas often cause us to remember events not as they actually occurred, but in a way that "makes sense" and fits in with our preexisting assumptions about the world.

- Misinformation effects occur when our memory is distorted by misleading postevent information, and often occur because of source confusion—our tendency to recall something or recognize it as familiar, but to forget where we encountered it.

- Children experience misinformation effects. Vulnerability is greatest among younger children and when misleading questions are asked repeatedly. Experts cannot reliably tell when children are reporting accurate versus sincerely believed false memories.

- Psychologists hotly debate whether recovered memories of child abuse are accurate, and whether they are caused by repression. Increasing concern about misinformation effects caused by therapist influence have led many researchers and legal experts to urge caution in accepting the validity of recovered memories without corroborating evidence.

The Biology of Memory

- Memory involves numerous brain regions. The hippocampus helps consolidate long-term declarative memories. The cerebral cortex processes sensory information, stores declarative memories across distributed sites, and is the seat of working memory.

- The amygdala encodes emotionally arousing aspects of events, the cerebellum helps form procedural memories, and damage to the thalamus can produce severe amnesia.

- Classical conditioning research with sea snails and studies of long-term potentiation in other species indicate that, as memories form, complex chemical and structural changes occur in neurons that enhance synaptic efficiency. Protein kinase, an enzyme, appears to facilitate chemical actions inside neurons that allow long-term memories to form.

Exceptional Memory

- People who display exceptional memory are called mnemonists. Researchers debate whether mnemonists have unique memory abilities, or instead employ basic memory skills to an extraordinary degree.

- Although people sometimes wish for a perfect memory, our memory system strikes a highly adaptive balance between the benefits of remembering and benefits of forgetting.

KEY TERMS AND CONCEPTS*

anterograde amnesia (297)
associative network (286)
chunking (277)
context-dependent memory (291)
decay theory (295)
declarative memory (288)
dual coding theory (284)
elaborative rehearsal (278)
encoding (275)
encoding specificity principle (291)
episodic memory (288)
explicit memory (288)
flashbulb memories (291)
implicit memory (289)
infantile amnesia (297)

levels of processing (281)
long-term memory (279)
long-term potentiation (308)
maintenance rehearsal (278)
memory (274)
memory consolidation (306)
misinformation effect (300)
mood-congruent recall (292)
neural network (286)
overlearning (293)
priming (286)
proactive interference (295)
procedural memory (288)
prospective memory (298)

repression (296)
retrieval (275)
retrieval cue (289)
retroactive interference (295)
retrograde amnesia (297)
schema (284)
semantic memory (288)
sensory memory (276)
serial position effect (279)
short-term memory (277)
source confusion (301)
state-dependent memory (292)
storage (275)
working memory (277)

* Each term has been boldfaced in the text on the page indicated in parentheses.

APPLYING YOUR KNOWLEDGE

These questions allow you to apply your understanding of the material in this chapter.

1. As you look at a blank computer screen, a matrix of twelve letters (three rows by four columns) is rapidly flashed on the screen for 1/20 of a second. Immediately, you try to recall as many of the twelve letters as you can. (There is no tone signaling you to report only one row.) You probably will be able to recall _____ of the letters because _____ .
   a) almost all; your iconic memory will store the letters for about 5 seconds
   b) almost all; you can rapidly transfer all the letters into short-term memory
   c) less than half; the letters were flashed too rapidly for you to see all of them
   d) less than half; your complete iconic memory will fade in a fraction of a second

2. An experimenter reads you a list of twenty words at a rate of one word per second, and then immediately asks you to recall as many of the words on the list as you can. Your pattern of recall most likely will demonstrate
   a) a primacy effect.
   b) a recency effect.
   c) a primacy effect and a recency effect.
   d) neither a primacy effect nor a recency effect.

3. To draw a rough analogy, your working memory can best be likened to
   a) the reference desk at a library, where attention is allocated to diverse tasks and information is processed and retrieved.
   b) a temporary transfer station in which, if information simply remains present long enough, it will be moved into more permanent storage.
   c) a video camera that faithfully records all the information it receives on a fleeting, moment-to-moment basis.
   d) the hard drive of a computer, where information can be permanently stored.

4. Because chess experts use _____ more effectively than novice chess players, they can more accurately recall _____ arrangements of pieces after viewing these arrangements for just a few seconds.
   a) maintenance rehearsal; meaningful
   b) maintenance rehearsal; both meaningful and random
   c) schemas and chunking; meaningful
   d) schemas and chunking; both meaningful and random

5. Your ability to _____ best illustrates episodic memory.
   a) ride a bicycle or swim
   b) tell me about what you did last summer
   c) solve a set of arithmetic problems
   d) name the capital city and leader of your country

6. Just before Gail leaves college at the end of her senior year, she returns to visit the dormitory where she lived as a first-year student. Upon walking down her old hallway, Gail suddenly remembers many dorm-life events that she thought she had forgotten. Her enhanced memory best illustrates
   a) state-dependent memory.
   b) context-dependent memory.
   c) mood-congruent recall.
   d) the serial position effect.

7. Lori has about 10 hours in her schedule over the next three days to spend studying for her introductory psychology test. You should advise Lori to
   a) use elaborative rehearsal more extensively than maintenance rehearsal.
   b) study in two or three distributed sessions rather than a single, massed session of 8 hours.
   c) overlearn the material.
   d) do all of the above.

8. Last semester Sal took a sociology course, and this semester he is taking psychology. Unfortunately, Sal is having difficulty remembering some of the psychology terms because they were defined differently in his sociology course, and he gets them mixed up. Sal's difficulty in learning the psychology terms is most likely due to
   a) encoding failure.
   b) motivated forgetting.
   c) retroactive interference.
   d) proactive interference.

9. One night as Edith was walking home a man quickly snatched her purse. The police showed Edith a series of mug shots, but she could not identify the robber. Later in a police lineup, Edith identified one of the suspects as being the robber. Actually, this person was not the robber, but Edith had previously seen his face in a mug shot. This example best illustrates how misinformation effects can be caused by
   a) source confusion.
   b) overlearning.
   c) repression.
   d) implicit memory.

10. Paul, a college sophomore, recently experienced a brain trauma that damaged extensive portions of his hippocampus. As a result, he now has a severe memory deficit. Most likely, Paul is unable to
    a) learn new physical skills.
    b) remember the meaning of words that he used to know.
    c) consciously remember new facts or personal experiences.
    d) retrieve memories of his childhood and teenage years.

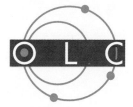

For additional quizzing and a variety of interactive resources, visit the book's Online Learning Center at www.mhhe.com/passer.

INTELLIGENT THOUGHT
AND BEHAVIOR

"A moment's insight is sometimes worth a life's experience."
—*Oliver Wendell Holmes*

8

CHAPTER 8 OUTLINE

FIGURE 8.1 The successful landing of Flight 118 was a tribute to the power of human reasoning, language, and problem-solving abilities.

➤ 1. What are mental representations? How are they involved in thinking and communicating?

▼▼▼▼▼▼▼▼▼▼▼▼▼▼▼▼▼▼▼▼▼▼▼▼▼▼▼▼▼▼▼▼▼▼▼▼▼▼

For the crew and passengers of United Airlines Fight 118, the skies over Maui were about to become the scene of a terrifying test of human resourcefulness, with survival at stake. On a routine flight 20,000 feet above the Pacific Ocean, the unthinkable happened. With an explosive popping of rivets and a shriek of tearing metal, part of the surface at the front of the plane suddenly ripped away from the rest of the aircraft, leaving the flight deck and forward passenger compartments exposed to the air. Inside, terrified passengers and flight attendants quite literally hung on for dear life as gale-force winds swirled through the cabin and the plane threatened to spin out of control.

The sudden change in the aerodynamics of the plane meant that it could not be flown normally. The captain, an experienced pilot, needed to develop a mental model of the plane in its altered form to keep it from plunging into the ocean. Thanks to his flight experience and his knowledge of the principles under which the aircraft normally responded to its controls, the captain quickly recognized what needed to be done, formulated a plan for doing it, and then executed the appropriate actions. The captain and the first officer could not communicate with one another verbally because of the noise from the engines and the roar of the wind, so they used hand signals to coordinate their activities. Through perfect teamwork, they landed the aircraft safely at an auxiliary airfield, a feat that was labeled by one aeronautical engineer as "astonishing" (Figure 8.1).

Incidents like this one illustrate the power of human reasoning, communication, and problem-solving abilities—cognitive skills that underlie adaptive behavior. Yet as we shall see, the basic mental operations and communication procedures the aviators used to deal with this life-and-death challenge were really no different from many of the mundane reasoning, problem-solving, and linguistic activities that we engage in each day.

Though human beings are physically puny and relatively defenseless in comparison with some other species, we dominate our world because we think better and communicate more effectively than other animals do. Humans have remarkable abilities to create "mental representations" of the world and to manipulate them in the forms of language, thinking, reasoning, and problem solving (Simon, 1990). Mental representations take a variety of forms, including images, ideas, concepts, and principles. You are engaged in some of these mental activities at this very moment. To the extent that we are communicating effectively via the written word, mental representations are being transferred from our minds to yours through the medium of language. Indeed, the process of education is all about transferring ideas and skills from mind to mind.

〉 LANGUAGE

According to anthropologists who have studied the skulls of prehistoric humans, the brain probably achieved its present form some 50,000 years ago (Pearson, 1998; Pilbeam, 1984). Why then did it take another 35,000 years before lifelike paintings began to appear on cave walls, and another 12,000 years for humans to develop a way to store knowledge outside the brain in the form of writing (Kottak, 2000; Rose, 1973)? These time lags tell us that human thought and behavior depend on more than the physical structure of the brain. Although the structure of the brain may not have changed much in the last 50,000 years, human cognitive skills clearly have.

Language, which various scientists have labeled "the jewel in the crown of cognition" (Pinker, 2000) and "the human essence" (Chomsky, 1972), may well be the most important of these cognitive skills. Evolutionary theorists believe that language evolved as humans gathered to form larger social units. The ability to form cooperative social systems, develop social customs, communicate thoughts to others, create divisions of labor, and pass on knowledge and wisdom were made easier by the development of language (Goody, 1997; Kottak, 2000; Figure 8.2). Given the enormous adaptive value of language for the emerging human way of life, it is not surprising that there developed in the human brain an inborn capacity to acquire any of the thousands of languages that are spoken in the world.

The Nature and Structure of Language

Language consists of a system of symbols and rules for combining these symbols in ways that can produce an infinite number of possible messages or meanings. This definition implies three critical properties that are essential to any language.

First, language is *symbolic*. It uses sounds, written signs, or gestures to refer to objects, events, ideas, and feelings. Language allows communicators to form and then transfer mental representations to the mind of another person. Thus you can tell another person about your house, what you did last week, your plans after graduation, how you feel about your current life situation, and the meaning of the word *cognition*. The linguistic feature of **displacement** refers to the fact that past, future, and imaginary events and objects that are not physically present can be symbolically represented and communicated through the medium of language. Language thus helps free us from being restricted to the present.

Second, language has a *structure*, with rules that govern how symbols can be combined to create meaningful communication units. Thus if I ask you if *zpflrovc* is an English word, you will almost certainly say that it is not. Why? Because it violates rules of the English language that *z* is not to be followed by *pf* and that five consonants are not to be combined. Likewise, you would not consider the string of words "Bananas have sale for I no" an appropriate English sentence. You may not be able to verbalize the formal rules of English that are violated in these examples, but you know them implicitly because they are part of the language you speak.

Third, language is *generative*. This means that its symbols can be combined to generate an infinite number of messages that can have novel meaning. Thus you can create and understand a sentence like "Who put the nightingale under my strudel?" even though you are unlikely to have heard anything like it before. Indeed, in reading that sentence, you may already have formed a mental representation (most likely, an image) of that unlikely scene, illustrating the concept of displacement.

Surface and Deep Structure

Psycholinguists, who study the psychological properties of language and the underlying mechanisms that produce it, describe language as having both a surface structure and a deep structure. The **surface structure** consists of the way symbols are combined within a given language. The rules for such combination are called the **syntax** (rules of grammar) of a language. Thus the word *zpflrovc* and the "banana" sentence described above violate English syntax.

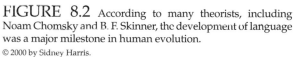
"GOT IDEA. TALK BETTER. COMBINE WORDS. MAKE SENTENCES."

FIGURE 8.2 According to many theorists, including Noam Chomsky and B. F. Skinner, the development of language was a major milestone in human evolution.
© 2000 by Sidney Harris.

➤ 2. Define three properties common to any human language.

➤ 3. Differentiate between surface structure and deep structure.

Deep structure refers to the underlying meaning of the combined symbols. The rules for connecting the symbols to what they represent are known as **semantics.** To distinguish surface structure from deep structure, consider the following sentences:

1. Eloise ran over the attacking pit bull with her Big Wheel.
2. The Big Wheel driven by Eloise ran over the attacking pit bull.
3. The police must stop drinking after midnight.

The first two sentences have different surface structures but they share the same deep structure. In other words, they have different syntax but similar semantic meaning. Either way, the pit bull got it. The third sentence is an ambiguous one that can have two different deep structures, one relating to police duties, the other to their personal conduct. The rules for surface structure and deep structure are both stored in long-term memory. However, when we recall something, we are likely to retrieve deep structure (meaning) rather than the specific words. That's why, as you may have experienced to your sorrow on essay examinations, you can sometimes "understand" a concept without being able to reproduce the precise definition. Or you can recall what someone said without being able to reconstruct the exact sentences.

In considering the formal structure of language, we can retreat to an even more elemental level and consider the basic building blocks that are combined into the symbols that convey meaning.

Language From the Bottom Up

> 4. What are phonemes and morphemes? Where do they fit in the hierarchy of language?

Human languages have a hierarchical structure. The lowest rung on the ladder is the phoneme. **Phonemes** are the smallest units of sound that are recognized as separate in a given language. English uses about 40 phonemes, consisting of the various vowel and consonant sounds, as well as certain letter combinations such as *th* and *sh.* Thus the sounds *h, a,* and *t* can be combined to form the three-phoneme word *hat.*

Humans are capable of producing about 100 phonemes, including clicking sounds used in some African languages, but no language uses all of these sounds. The world's languages vary considerably in phonemes, some employing as few as 15 and others more than 80.

At the next level of the hierarchy, phonemes are combined into **morphemes,** the smallest units of meaning in a language. Morphemes consist of a single syllable. Thus *hat, sick,* and *tel* are all morphemes, as are prefixes and suffixes such as *-ed, un-, -ous,* and *pre-.* The suffix *-ous* is formed from two phonemes, *uh* and *s.* In every language, syntax rules determine how phonemes can be combined into morphemes. English's 40 phonemes can be combined into more than 100,000 morphemes.

Morphemes, in turn, are the stuff of which words are formed. English morphemes can be combined into nearly half a million words, words into countless phrases, and phrases into an almost infinite number of sentences. Thus from the humble phoneme to the elegant sentence, we have a five-step language hierarchy (Figure 8.3).

Acquiring a Language

Language acquisition is one of the most striking events in human cognitive development. Many language experts believe that humans are born linguists, inheriting a biological readiness to recognize and eventually produce the sounds and structure of whatever language they are exposed to (Chomsky, 1965; Lieberman, 1984).

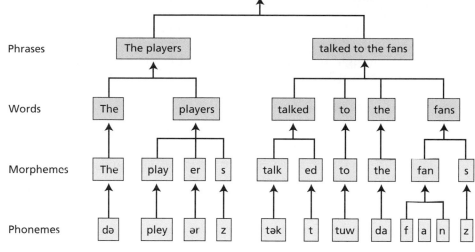

FIGURE 8.3 Human language is structured hierarchically with phonemes being the most basic unit. The line of phonemes contains symbols used by linguists to denote particular sounds.

Biological Foundations

Several facts suggest a biological basis for language acquisition. First, human children, despite their limited thinking skills, begin to master language early in life without any formal instruction. Moreover, despite their differences at the phoneme level, all adult languages throughout the world—including sign languages for the deaf that have developed independently in different parts of the world—seem to have a common underlying deep structure (Anderson & Lightfoot, 1999). Language acquisition thus represents the unfolding of a biologically primed process within a learning environment as part of the more general growth of cognitive capacities in the developing human (Aitchison, 1996; Chomsky, 1987).

> 5. What scientific evidence supports the notion that human language has a biological basis?

Whether born in Toledo, Taiwan, or Tanzania, infants vocalize the entire range of phonemes found in the world's languages. At about 6 months of age, however, they begin to make the sounds of their native tongue and discard those of other languages. For example, Japanese children lose the ability to distinguish between the *r* and *l* sounds because their language does not make this phonetic distinction, but children exposed to English can discriminate these sounds at an early age. Likewise, Japanese-speaking children learn to put the object before the verb ("Sadahara the ball threw"), whereas English-speaking children learn the syntactic rule that the verb comes before the object ("John threw the ball"). The noted linguist Noam Chomsky (1987) likens our innate language acquisition capacity to a huge electrical panel with banks of linguistic switches that are thrown as children hear the words and syntax of their native language.

> 6. What findings indicate that learning interacts with biology to affect language development? What evidence exists for a sensitive period?

Some linguists are convinced that there is a *sensitive period* during which language is most easily learned. This period typically extends from infancy to puberty (Lenneberg, 1967). Support for a sensitive period comes from studies of children who lived by themselves in the wild or who were isolated from human contact by disturbed parents. One such child was found when she was 6 years old. She immediately received language training and seemed to develop normal language abilities (Brown, 1958). In contrast, language-deprived children who were found when they were past puberty seemed unable to acquire normal language skills despite extensive training (Clarke & Clarke, 2000; Curtiss, 1977).

The importance of early language exposure applies to any language, not just spoken language. Because sign languages share the deep structure characteristics of spoken languages, deaf children who learn sign language before puberty develop normal linguistic and cognitive abilities even though they never hear a spoken word (Marschark & Mayer, 1998). In contrast, deaf people who are not exposed to sign language before the age of 12 show a distinct language-learning deficit even at 30 years of age (Meier, 1991).

Social Learning Processes

Social learning plays a central role in acquiring a language. Early on, mothers and fathers maintain their children's interest and attract their attention by conversing with them in what has been termed *motherese*, a high-pitched intonation that seems to be used all over the world (Fernald et al., 1989). Parents also teach their children words by pointing out objects and naming them, by reading aloud to them, and by responding to the never-ending question, "What dat?"

The behaviorist B. F. Skinner (1957, 1985) developed an operant conditioning explanation for language acquisition. His basic premise was that children's language development is strongly governed by adults' reinforcing appropriate language and nonreinforcement of inappropriate verbalizations. However, most modern psycholinguists doubt that operant learning principles alone can account for language development. For one thing, children learn too much too fast. By 30 months of age they already have learned several hundred words. By age 6, children are learning an average of more than 15 words per day, and their vocabularies have grown to between 8,000 and 14,000 words (Carey, 1977; Smith, 1926). Moreover, observational studies have shown that parents do *not* typically correct their children's grammar as language skills are developing. Rather, parents' corrections focus primarily on the "truth value" (or deep structure) of what the child is trying to communicate. Thus they are less likely to correct a young child's statement that "I have two foots" than they are to correct one who says, "I have three feet," even though the latter statement is grammatically correct. As this point also shows, much of children's language is very different from that of their parents, and thus it can't be explained simply as an imitative process. Certainly, social learning is crucial, but it seems unlikely that it is the sole factor in acquiring a language.

As biological (including the maturation of speech production mechanisms) and experiential factors combine their influences, language acquisition proceeds according to a developmental timetable that is common to all cultures. As shown in Table 8.1, children progress from reflexive crying at birth through stages of cooing, babbling, and one-word utterances. By the second year of life, children are uttering two-word sentences called **telegraphic speech** that consist of a noun and a verb ("Want cookie"). In the short span of five years, an initially nonverbal creature has come to understand and produce a complex language.

Bilingualism: Learning a Second Language

For those of us laboring to learn a second language (or to fully master our native language), there are models to inspire us. M. D. Berlitz, inventor of the system for teaching languages that bears his name, spoke 58 of them. Sir John Bowring, once the British governor of Hong Kong, could speak 100 languages and read 100 more. And some sort of record must be held by Benjamin Schulze (1699–1760), who could recite the Lord's Prayer in 215 languages (Bryan, 1986).

➤ 7. What factors affect the learning of a second language and its effects on thinking?

A second language is learned best and spoken most fluently when it is learned during the sensitive period of childhood. A study of Korean and Chinese immigrants to the United States showed that if they learned English early in life, they could master that grammar about as well as the grammar of their first language. After about age 7, however, mastery of English grammar became progressively more difficult (Johnson & Newport, 1989).

TABLE 8.1	COURSE OF NORMAL LANGUAGE DEVELOPMENT IN CHILDREN
Age	Speech Characteristics
1–3 months	Infants can distinguish speech from nonspeech sounds, and they prefer speech sounds (phonemes); undifferentiated crying gives way to cooing when happy.
4–6 months	Babbling sounds begin to occur. These contain sounds from virtually every language. Child vocalizes in response to verbalizations of others.
7–11 months	Babbling sounds narrow to include only the phonemes heard in the languages spoken by others in the environment. Child moves tongue with vocalizations ("lalling"). Child discriminates between some words without understanding their meaning and begins to imitate word sounds heard from others.
12 months	First recognizable words typically spoken as one-word utterances to name familiar people and objects (e.g., *da-da* or *block*).
12–18 months	Child increases knowledge of word meanings and begins to use single words to express whole phrases or requests (e.g., *out* to express a desire to get out of the crib); primarily uses nouns.
18–24 months	Vocabulary expands to 50–100 words. First rudimentary sentences appear, usually consisting of two words (e.g., *more milk*) with little or no use of articles (*the, a*), conjunctions (*and*), or auxiliary verbs (*can, will*). This condensed, or telegraphic speech, is characteristic of first sentences throughout the world.
2–4 years	Vocabulary expands rapidly at the rate of several hundred words every 6 months. Two-word sentences give way to longer sentences that, though often grammatically incorrect, exhibit basic language syntax. Child begins to express concepts with words and to use language to describe imaginary objects and ideas. Sentences become more correct syntactically.
4–5 years	Most children have learned the basic grammatical rules for combining nouns, adjectives, articles, conjunctions, and verbs into meaningful sentences.

Positive correlates of bilingualism, such as greater thinking flexibility and higher performance on intelligence tests, have been shown in a number of countries, including Switzerland, South Africa, Israel, and Canada. However, such effects are not likely to appear until both languages are well learned (Lambert et al., 1993). In fact, learning a second language when a child's native language is not well developed can actually have negative effects on cognitive performance at that time because the child may be unable to use either language effectively. Research shows that non-English-speaking immigrant children perform best in bilingual educational settings in which they are taught in both their native language and in English. Compared with similar children who are placed in English-only classrooms and left to struggle, those in bilingual classes drop out of school less frequently, develop higher self-esteem, and exhibit better academic performance and English fluency (Thomas & Collier, 1997).

When a second language is learned, is it represented in the same part of the brain as the first language? Again, the answer may depend on how early in life the new language is acquired and how well it is learned. At the University of Milan, Daniela Perani and her coworkers (1998) used PET scans to measure cortical activation patterns in the brains of bilingual Italians as they listened to stories read aloud in Italian and in English. People who were highly proficient in English and who had learned the second language before the age of 10 showed representation of the two languages in the same cortical areas. The two languages had, in a sense, become one, as was suggested by the fluent participants' ability to use the languages interchangeably. In contrast, Italians who had learned English later in life and were less fluent than in their native language showed brain activity in different areas than those activated by native language stories when they read stories in English, indicating different patterns of language processing. Such people were also less able to switch rapidly back and forth from one language to the other.

Linguistic Influences on Thinking

➤ 8. Define the linguistic relativity hypothesis and evaluate its validity. How does language influence thought?

Despite the fact that many politicians prove on a daily basis that a well-developed larynx bears little relation to the capacity for sound thinking, a relation between language and thinking has long been assumed. The linguist Benjamin Lee Whorf (1956) took an extreme position on this matter, contending in his **linguistic relativity hypothesis** that language not only influences, but also *determines* what we are capable of thinking. For example, he suggested that people reared in a culture whose language lacks a past tense, such as the Hopi Indians of the United States, would have difficulty remembering past events.

In the hindsight provided by nearly a half century of research, Whorf's position clearly was overstated. For example, if the linguistic relativity hypothesis were correct, then people whose cultures have only a few words for colors should have greater difficulty in perceiving the spectrum of colors than do people whose languages have many different color words. To test this proposition, Eleanor Rosch (1973) studied the Dani of New Guinea, who have only two color words in their language, one for bright warm colors, the other for cool dark ones. She found that, contrary to what strict linguistic determinism would suggest, the Dani could discriminate among and remember a wide assortment of hues in much the same manner as can speakers of the English language, which contains many color names.

Today most linguists do not agree with Whorf that language *determines* how we think. They would say instead that language can *influence* how we think, how efficiently we can categorize our experiences, and perhaps how much detail we attend to in our daily experience (Hunt & Agnoli, 1991). Language can also color our perceptions and the conclusions we draw. Consider, for example, the ability of sexist language to evoke gender stereotypes. Thirty years ago, it was convention to use the male pronoun *he* to refer to people in general: "As *man* masters *his* thoughts and feelings, *he* will attain new heights." Does such language make any difference? Indeed it does, at least to people who have now become accustomed to gender-neutral language. In one study, college students read one of the following two statements about psychology:

a. "The psychologist believes in the dignity and worth of the individual human being. He is committed to increasing man's understanding of himself and others."

b. "Psychologists believe in the dignity and worth of the individual human being. They are committed to increasing people's understanding of themselves and others."

The students then were asked to rate the attractiveness of a career in psychology for men and women. Those who had read the first statement rated psychology as a less attractive profession for women than did the students who read the second statement, written in gender-neutral language (Briere & Lanktree, 1983). Apparently, statement *a* implied that psychology is a male profession. In such ways, language can help create and maintain stereotypes.

The fact that language influences what and how we think is of no minor importance, for, as we have seen, how we encode information affects perception and memory in important ways. As their vocabularies expand, children become capable of thinking in more sophisticated ways. The power of language to influence thinking makes vocabulary development a critical part of the educational process in any field. For example, the vocabulary you are learning in this course provides new concepts that will influence how you think about your own and others' behavior in the future.

Language not only influences how we think, but also may influence how well we think in certain domains. For example, English-speaking children consistently score lower than children from Asian countries in mathematical skills such as counting, addition, and subtraction (Geary, 1995). One reason may be the words and symbols the languages use to represent numbers. Asian languages make it far easier to learn the base 10 number system, particularly the numbers between 10 and 100. For example, in Chinese, the number 11 is "ten one," 13 is "ten three," and 46 is "four ten six." In contrast, English speakers struggle with such words as "eleven," "twelve," and "thirteen," which bear little conceptual relation to a 10-base mode of thinking. Regardless of their counting proficiency, American and British children fail to grasp the base 10 system by age 5, whereas many Chinese children do, enabling them to do addition and subtraction with greater ease (Miller & Stigler, 1987). In this manner, the English language hampers the development of skills in using numbers, whereas Asian languages facilitate the development of mathematical skills.

Thinking may be considered the internal "language of the mind," but it actually includes a wide range of mental activities. One mode of thought takes the form of verbal sentences that we seem to "hear" in our minds. This is called **propositional thought** because it expresses a proposition, or statement. Another thought mode, **imaginal thought,** consists of images that we can "see," "hear," or "feel" in our mind. There also is a third mode, **motoric thought,** which relates to mental representations of motor movements, like throwing an object. All three of these modes of thinking enter into our abilities to reason, solve problems, and engage in many forms of "intelligent" behavior.

➤ 9. Describe three major modes of thought.

Concepts and Propositions

Much of our thinking occurs in the form of **propositions,** statements that express facts. "College students are intelligent people" is a proposition. All propositions consist of concepts combined in a particular way. Typically, one concept is a *subject* and another is a *predicate* (Figure 8.4). **Concepts** are basic units of semantic memory—mental categories into which we place objects, activities, abstractions (such as "liberal" and "conservative," for example), and events that have essential features in common (Medin et al., 2000). Every psychological term you are learning in this course is a concept. Concepts can be acquired through explicit instruction or by our own observations of similarities and differences among various objects and events.

➤ 10. What are propositions, and how are they formed?

Many concepts are difficult to define explicitly. For example, you are quite familiar with the concept "vegetable," yet you might be hard-pressed to come up with an explicit definition of what a vegetable is. However, you can quickly think of a good example of a vegetable. According to Eleanor Rosch (1977), many concepts are defined by **prototypes**—the most typical and familiar members of the class. Rosch suggests that we often decide which category something belongs to by its degree of resemblance to the prototype (Figure 8.5).

➤ 11. What are concepts, and what is the role of prototypes in concept formation?

Consider the following questions:

1. Is a sparrow a bird?
2. Is a penguin a bird?
3. Is a bat a bird?

According to the prototype view, you should have come to a quicker decision on the first question than on the last two. Why? Because a sparrow fits most people's "bird" prototype better than does a penguin (which is a bird, though it lacks some essential prototypic

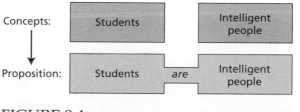
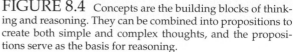

FIGURE 8.4 Concepts are the building blocks of thinking and reasoning. They can be combined into propositions to create both simple and complex thoughts, and the propositions serve as the basis for reasoning.

FIGURE 8.5 Which of the following are birds? The speed with which you make the decision is based on the extent to which the creature conforms to your prototype of the concept "bird."

➤ 12. What evidence supports the position that animals can exhibit true language? What evidence is used to dispute that position?

features, like the ability to fly) or a bat (which is not a bird, even though it flies). Experiments measuring speed of "yes" and "no" responses to the questions found on page 323 have found that it does indeed take most people longer to decide whether penguins or bats are birds (Rips, 1997).

The use of prototypes is perhaps the most elementary method of forming concepts. It requires *only* that we note similarities among objects. Thus children's early concepts are based on prototypes of the objects and people they encounter personally. They then decide if new objects they encounter are similar enough to the prototype to be a "Mommy," a "cookie," a "doggie," and so on (Smith & Zarate, 1992). Because prototypes may differ as a result of personal experience, there is considerable room for arbitrariness and individual differences in prototypic concepts. Thus one person's concept of a "political radical" may differ sharply from another's.

How we state propositions about a problem or decision can influence how we try to solve the problem, reason through to a decision, or make a judgment (Anderson, 1991). For example, assume that a loved one has received a cancer diagnosis. You are told about a new experimental treatment that removes cancerous cells in successful cases. Would it make a difference to you if you were told that the treatment has a "50 percent success rate" as opposed to a "50 percent failure rate"?

Research suggests that these two propositions for representing the potential outcomes of the treatment, though logically equivalent, are not at all psychologically equivalent. Participants in an experiment who were told that the treatment has a 50 percent success rate judged the treatment to be significantly more effective and expressed a greater willingness to have it administered to a family member than did participants who were told that it has a 50 percent failure rate (Kahneman & Tversky, 1979). Representing outcomes in terms of positives or negatives has this effect because people tend to assign greater costs to negative outcomes (such as losing $100) than they assign value to an equivalent positive outcome (earning $100). Therefore the proposition that "there is a 50 percent chance of failure" causes the "50-50" treatment to appear more risky (Tversky & Kahneman, 1981). Thus differences in how we verbally represent choices and goals can make a difference in our perceptions and decisions.

PSYCHOLOGICAL FRONTIERS

Can Animals Acquire Human Language?

Noam Chomsky referred to language as the "human essence." Yet nonhuman species communicate in diverse ways. Many have special "calls" that warn of predators and attract mates (Alcock, 1998). When a honeybee discovers nectar, it returns to the hive and performs a "waggle dance" (von Frisch, 1953). The dance pattern and duration convey information about the nectar's location, which other bees receive by sensing vibrations as they stay in contact, behind the dancer. Using this information and odor cues, they can zero in on the food source (Kirchner & Grasser, 1998).

In some species communication shows interesting parallels to human language (Figure 8.6). Just as humans have different languages, each songbird species has its own songs. Remarkably, some songbirds also have "local dialects" (Catchpole & Rowell, 1993). Thus experts can tell whether a male white-crowned sparrow lives in certain areas north, south, or east of San Francisco by how it sings (Marler & Tamura, 1964). And just as humans have a sensitive period in childhood for language acquisition, songbirds are unlikely to sing "normally" in adulthood unless they hear the songs of their species while growing up (Marler, 1970).

Research with apes provides the most controversial challenge to the assumption that only humans are capable of language. At first, investigators tried to teach chimpanzees to speak, but chimps lack a vocal system that would permit humanlike speech.

❯ Washoe: Early "Signs" of Success

A breakthrough came in 1966 when Allen and Beatrice Gardner (1969) of the University of Nevada took advantage of chimps' hand and finger dexterity, and began teaching American Sign Language to a 10-month-old chimp named Washoe. They "cross-fostered" Washoe (i.e., raised her in a home and treated her like a human child), and by age 5 Washoe had learned 160 signs. More importantly, at times she combined signs (e.g., "more fruit," "you tickle Washoe"), sometimes in novel ways. For example, when a researcher showed Washoe a baby doll inside a cup and signed "What that?", Washoe signed back: "Baby in my drink." The Gardners cross-fostered four other chimpanzees from birth and replicated their findings; the chimps' signing skills steadily advanced and at times they signed with each other (Gardner et al., 1989; Gardner & Gardner, 1998). Other researchers also had success. A gorilla named Koko learned over 600 signs (Bonvillian & Patterson, 1997), and a chimp named Lana was taught to communicate with lexigrams—visual symbols on a keyboard (Rumbaugh, 1977).

"Although humans make sounds with their mouths and occasionally look at each other, there is no solid evidence that they actually communicate with each other."

FIGURE 8.6 Human scientists debate whether dolphins possess language. Could the opposite also be occurring? © 2000 by Sidney Harris.

❯ Project Nim: Dissent From Within

At Columbia University, Herbert Terrace taught sign language to a chimp he named Nim Chimpsky—a play on the name of linguist Noam Chomsky (Terrace, 1979). Terrace was optimistic, envisioning that one day Nim might serve as a chimp "interpreter" for communication between humans and wild chimpanzees. But after years of work and videotape analysis of Nim's "conversations," Terrace concluded that Nim was not displaying language and was not even capable of creating a sentence. He found that when Nim combined symbols into longer sequences, he was either imitating his trainer's previous signs or "running on" with his hands until he got what he wanted. And unlike human language, as Nim's "sentences" got longer, they didn't convey additional information (e.g., "eat Nim eat," or "play me Nim play"). Moreover, Nim spontaneously signed only when he wanted something, which is not how humans use language.

❯ The Controversy Heats Up

Ape-language researchers criticized Terrace's conclusions and the way that Nim was trained. They argued that apes do combine symbols in informative ways. How could Washoe's signing "Baby in my drink" be imitation when a researcher had just signed "What that?" Lana, the chimp who used keyboard symbols, saw an orange and wanted it. Having a symbol for the color, but not for the fruit itself, she punched in "Lana want eat ball which is orange" (Rumbaugh, 1977). And although apes mainly signed to request things, other types of communications

—Continued

were reported. For example, Chantek, an orangutan who had been taught a symbol for "dirty" in regard to feces and urine, spontaneously began applying the symbol to spilled food, soiled objects, and toilets (Miles et al., 1996).

Roger and Deborah Fouts of Central Washington University continued working with Washoe and other cross-fostered chimps. They intentionally refrained from signing in front of Loulis, Washoe's adopted son, and found that Loulis acquired over 50 signs by observing other cross-fostered chimps communicate (Fouts et al., 1989). By using remote video cameras, Fouts (1994) also discovered that the chimps signed with each other even when humans were not present. Moreover, chimp-to-chimp signing occurred across various contexts, such as play, feeding, and fighting (Cianelli and Fouts, 1998).

▶ Kanzi: Chimp versus Child

Sue Savage-Rumbaugh (1986, 1998) of Georgia State University has worked extensively with a primate species of chimp called the *bonobo*. At age 1 1/2, a bonobo named Kanzi spontaneously showed an interest in using plastic geometric symbols that were associated with words (Figure 8.7a). By age 4, with only informal training during social interactions, Kanzi had learned more than 80 symbols (Figure 8.7b) and produced a number of two- and three-"word" communications. Kanzi typically combined gestures and symbols that he pointed to on a laminated board or typed on a specially designed keyboard. For example, Kanzi created the combinations "Person chase Kanzi" and "Kanzi chase person," and "Person chase person" to designate who should chase whom during play. Kanzi also responded readily to spoken English commands.

Savage-Rumbaugh also tested Kanzi's ability to understand unfamiliar spoken sentences under controlled conditions (Savage-Rumbaugh et al., 1993). For example, when told "Give the doggie a shot," Kanzie picked up a toy dog, grabbed a hypodermic needle, and gave the dog a shot. Kanzi also appeared to understand syntax. Given slightly different requests, such as "Make the [toy] snake bite the [toy] doggie," and "Make the doggie bite the snake," Kanzi responded appropriately. For comparison, one of the researcher's daughters, Alia, was tested under the same conditions between the ages of 2 to 2 1/2. Kanzi correctly responded to 74 percent of the novel requests, Alia to 65 percent. In short, Kanzi was comprehending speech at the level of a human toddler.

▶ Conclusion: Is it Language?

At present, neither side in the debate has convinced the other. Proponents believe the data strongly show that great apes can acquire rudimentary language skills (Savage-Rumbaugh et al., 1998). If it were anatomically possible, argues Sue Savage-Rumbaugh, Kanzi would be speaking. But critics—even those impressed by Kanzi's feats—are not persuaded (Kako, 1999). Some argue that operant conditioning and imitation account for most of the apes' accomplishments. Others disagree with how the researchers define "language," and some believe that am-

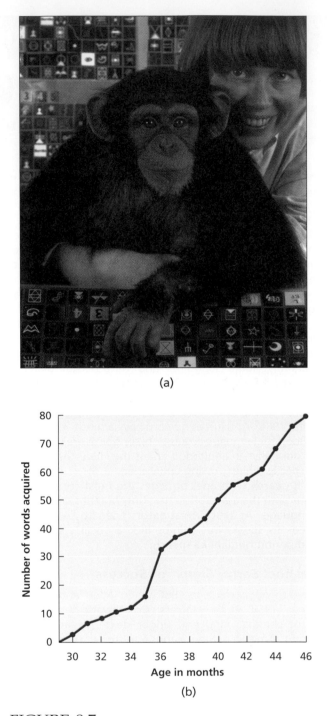

(a)

(b)

FIGURE 8.7 (a) Kanzi, a bonobo chimpanzee, communicates using complex symbols with his trainer, psychologist Sue Savage-Rumbaugh. Kanzi uses the symbols to signify objects and qualities. (b) This figure shows the rate of Kanzi's symbol acquisition over 17 months of informal training.

Adapted from Savage-Rumbaugh et al., 1986.

biguous ape communications are interpreted as language because the researchers erroneously assume what must be going on "inside the apes' minds."

What then should we conclude about apes' language abilities? The answer depends in large part on how we define "language." Recall that language is (1) symbolic, (2) struc-

–Continued

tured, and (3) generative. Evidence is strongest for the first criterion. Apes clearly are capable of communicating with symbols and hand signs, and they can learn a small "vocabulary" of several hundred words. Whether the apes perceive the symbols and signs as "words" in the sense that humans do is still debated. As for structure and generativity, the evidence remains mixed and highly controversial. Both sides, for example, can point to examples of how apes are sensitive to—or disregard—syntax. Whatever linguistic abilities do exist, however, are quite modest, similar at best to those of a very young child. In any case, the scientific exploration of animals' language capabilities reminds us to appreciate something that we tend to take for granted, namely, the seemingly "natural" ease with which humans acquire language.

❯ REASONING AND PROBLEM SOLVING

What is "intelligent " thinking? Certainly, it involves the ability to reason and think logically. Such thinking helps us to acquire knowledge, make sound decisions, and solve problems. Cognitive scientists believe that our capacity for logical thinking has been honed by evolutionary forces because of its adaptive value (Eisenstadt & Simon, 1997; Rips, 1997).

The most primitive ways of solving problems is through trial and error, in which we try one solution after another in the real world until the problem is solved. Reasoning helps us avoid the hazards and time-consuming efforts of trial and error. Most of the time, people solve problems by developing solutions in their minds before applying them in the external world. For example, if you decide to build a bookcase, you are unlikely to nail or screw boards together at random in the hope that the finished product will serve your purposes. Instead, you will develop mental representations to guide your efforts. These will likely include a visual image of the finished product as well as general principles for successful construction, which are likely to be expressed in linguistic terms (e.g., "Build from the bottom up").

Reasoning

Two types of reasoning underlie many of our attempts to make decisions and solve problems (Figure 8.8). In **deductive reasoning,** we reason from the "top down,'" that is, from general principles to a conclusion about a specific case. People reason deductively when they begin with a set of premises (propositions assumed to be true) and determine what they imply about a specific situation. Deductive reasoning is the basis of formal mathematics and logic. Logicians regard it as the strongest and most valid form of reasoning because the conclusion *cannot be false* if the premises (factual statements) are true. More formally, the underlying deductive principle may be stated: Given a proposition, *if X then Y*, if X occurs, then you can infer *Y*. Thus to use the classic deductive argument, called a syllogism,

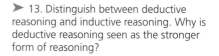 13. Distinguish between deductive reasoning and inductive reasoning. Why is deductive reasoning seen as the stronger form of reasoning?

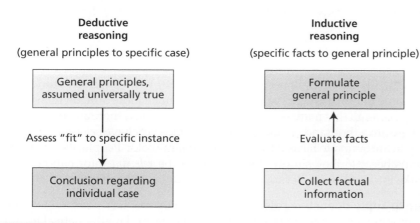

FIGURE 8.8 Comparing deductive and inductive reasoning.

if all humans are mortal (first premise), and

if Socrates is a human (second premise),

then Socrates must be mortal (conclusion).

In **inductive reasoning,** we reason in a "bottom-up" fashion, starting with specific facts and trying to develop a general principle (Figure 8.8). For example, scientists use induction when they discover general principles, or laws, as a result of observing a number of specific instances of a phenomenon. If enough apples fall on our heads, we may conclude that there exists a general force that pulls objects toward the earth. Likewise, after Ivan Pavlov observed a number of instances in which the dogs began to salivate when approached by the experimenter who fed them, he began to think in terms of a general principle that later was formalized as classical conditioning.

An important difference between deductive and inductive reasoning lies in the certainty of the results. Deductive conclusions are certain to be correct, *if* the premises are true, but inductive reasoning leads to likelihood rather than certainty. Even if we reason inductively in a flawless manner, the possibility of error always remains because some new observation may disprove our conclusion.

In both daily life and in science, inductive and deductive reasoning may be used at different points in problem solving and decision making. For example, psychologists often make informal observations that cause them to construct an initial explanation for a particular behavioral phenomenon (such as the failure of many bystanders to help in emergencies). But they know that the explanation they have derived through inductive reasoning from specific observations could be wrong, even if it is consistent with all the known facts. Therefore they move to a deductive process in which they design experiments to formally test specific *if–then* hypotheses. If the results of these experimental tests do *not* support their hypotheses, they conclude that their explanation or theory cannot be correct and needs to be revised or discarded. This latter process is formally known as the *hypothetico-deductive* approach to scientific theory building.

Stumbling Blocks in Reasoning

The ability to reason effectively is a key factor in critical thinking, in making sound decisions, and in solving problems. Unfortunately, several factors may prevent us from selecting the information needed to draw sound conclusions.

Distraction by irrelevant information.   Distinguishing relevant from irrelevant information can at times be challenging. Consider, for example, the following problem. As you solve it, analyze the mental steps you take, and do not read on until you have decided on an answer.

> Your drawer contains 19 black socks and 13 blue socks. Without turning on the light, how many socks do you have to pull out of the drawer to be sure you have a complete set?

As you solved the problem, what information entered into your reasoning? Did you take into account the fact that there were 19 black socks and 13 blue ones? If so, you're like many of Robert Sternberg's (1988) Yale University students who did the same thing, thereby making the problem much more difficult than it should be. In this case, all that matters is how many *colors* of socks there are. It doesn't matter if there are a thousand socks of each color; once you have selected any three of them, you are bound to have at least two of the same color. People often fail to solve problems because they simply don't focus on the *relevant* information. Instead, they take into account irrelevant information that leads them astray.

Failure to apply deductive rules.   Even when people have learned to use general problem-solving methods, such as formal logic and mathematical formulas, they tend to think of them as methods to be used only in certain situations and

➤ 14. How is a combination of inductive and deductive reasoning involved in scientific activity?

➤ 15. Summarize three factors that can interfere with the correct application of deductive reasoning. What is meant by belief bias?

may fail to apply them to new problems. For example, all of us have encountered arithmetic-progression problems, in which a variable is set at an initial value and then is increased by a constant amount per interval for a number of intervals. An example is "If your car was going 30 mph and you increased your speed by 5 mph every minute for 7 consecutive minutes, how fast would you be going at the end?" The appropriate formula is $Y = B + (a)D$, where Y is the correct answer, B is the original value, D is the amount added, and (a) is the number of times it is added, providing a Y of 65 mph in this case.

Both mathematics and physics students learn this formula for solving such problems. However, students in physics classes learn to solve arithmetic-progression problems only as they apply to physics, whereas students in mathematics classes solve arithmetic-progression problems drawn from a variety of areas. What happens if physics students are presented with arithmetic-progression problems from a mathematics class and mathematic students are given similar problems used in the physics class? Will math and physics students be equally adept at "plugging in" the correct problem-solving method?

Figure 8.9 shows the results of one experiment (Bassok & Holyoak, 1989). The mathematics students, who had practiced recognizing when to use the $Y = B + (a)D$ problem-solving method in different situations, quickly applied it to the physics problems. In contrast, the physics students failed to apply their knowledge in the novel math situations. Sometimes, knowledge is not enough; one must have the wisdom to know when and how to apply the knowledge.

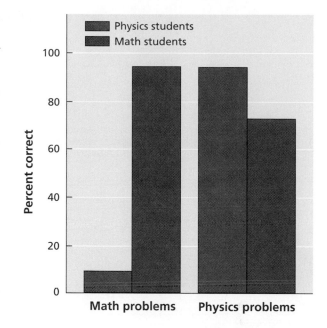

FIGURE 8.9 Percentage of arithmetic-progression problems solved by students who were trained to use the same equations, either as a type of mathematics or as a tool in solving physics problems. The specificity of the physics students' previous use apparently interfered with their ability to generalize what they knew to the mathematics problems.
Data from Bassok & Holyoak, 1989.

Belief bias. **Belief bias** is the tendency to abandon logical rules in favor of our own personal beliefs. To illustrate, let us consider an experiment in which college students were asked to judge whether conclusions followed logically from syllogisms like the following:

> All things that are smoked are good for one's health.
>
> Cigarettes are smoked.
>
> Therefore cigarettes are good for one's health.

What do you think? Is the logic correct?

Actually, it is. If we accept (for the moment) that the premises are true, then the conclusion *does* follow logically from the premises. Yet students frequently claimed that the conclusion was not *logically correct* because they disagreed with the first premise that all things smoked are good for the health. In this case, their beliefs about the harmful effects of smoking got in the way of their logic. When the same syllogisms were presented with nonsense words like *ramadians* substituted for cigarettes, the errors in logic were markedly reduced (Markowitz & Nantel, 1989). Incidentally, we agree that the conclusion that cigarettes are good for one's health is factually false. However, it is false because the major premise is false, not because the logic is faulty. Unfortunately, many people confuse factual correctness with logical correctness. The two are not at all the same.

Problem Solving

Humans have an unmatched ability to solve problems and adapt to the challenges of their world. People can systematically use inductive and deductive reasoning to solve problems. Such problem solving proceeds through four stages (Figure 8.10). How well we carry out each of these stages determines our success in solving the problem.

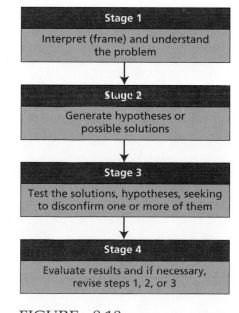

FIGURE 8.10 Stages of problem solving.

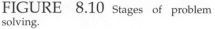

> 16. Describe the four stages of problem solving.

Understanding, or Framing, the Problem

Most of us have had the experience of feeling totally frustrated in our attempts to solve a problem. We may even think that the problem is unsolvable. Then someone suggests a new way of looking at the problem and the solution suddenly becomes obvious. How we mentally represent, or *frame,* a problem can make a huge difference. Consider the problem illustrated in Figure 8.11.

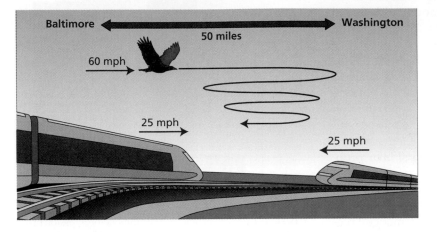

FIGURE 8.11 The Crow and the Trains problem described in the text. (The answer appears on p. 359.)

➤ 17. How does the Crow and Trains problem demonstrate the role of framing?

Train A leaves Baltimore for its 50-mile trip to Washington, D.C., at a constant speed of 25 mph. At the same time, Train B leaves Washington, bound for Baltimore at the same speed of 25 mph. An energetic crow leaves Baltimore at the same time as Train A, flying above the tracks toward Washington at a speed of 60 mph. When the crow encounters Train B, it turns and flies back to Train A, then instantly reverses its direction and flies back to Train B. The supercharged bird continues this sequence until Trains A and B meet midway between Baltimore and Washington. Try to solve this problem before reading on: *What is the total distance the bird will have traveled in its excursions between Trains A and B?*

Many people approach the problem as a distance problem, which is quite natural because the question was stated in terms of distance. They try to compute how far the bird will fly during each segment of its flight between Trains A and B, sometimes filling up several pages with computations in the process. But suppose you approach the problem by asking *how long* it will take the trains to meet? The crow will have flown the same period of time at 60 mph. Now that you have reframed it as a time problem, the problem becomes much easier to solve. (You can check your solution against the answer given on page 359.)

As you can see, our initial understanding of a problem is a key step toward a successful solution. If we frame a problem poorly, we can easily be led into a maze of blind alleys and ineffective solutions. If we frame it optimally, we at least have a chance to generate an effective solution.

Generating Potential Solutions

Once we have interpreted the problem, we can begin to formulate potential solutions or explanations. Ideally, we might proceed in the following fashion:

1. Determine which procedures and explanations will be considered.
2. Determine which of these solutions are consistent with the evidence that has so far been observed. Rule out any solutions that do not fit the evidence.

Testing the Solutions

Consider the possible solutions that remain. If the solution requires you to choose between specific explanations, ask if there is any test that should give one result if one explanation is true and another result if a different explanation is true. If so, make that test and evaluate the explanations again in light of the evidence from that test. This is essentially what scientists do when they design experiments.

Let us consider a common problem that can arise in the process of discovering and applying solutions to problems. Figure 8.12 shows a series of seven problems that we invite you to solve. Here is the first of those problems:

Suppose you have a 21-cup jug, a 127-cup jug, and a 3-cup jug. Drawing and discarding as much water as you like, how will you measure out exactly 100 cups of water?

This problem is followed by the remaining six problems in Figure 8.12. Try to solve all of them in order and write your calculations before reading on. Does a common solution emerge? If so, see if you can specify what it is.

As you worked the problems, you probably discovered that they are all solvable by the same formula, namely $B - A - (2 \times C)$ = desired amount—for example, in Problem 1, $127 - 21 - (2 \times 3) = 100$. If you discovered this, it gave you a logical formula that you could apply to the rest of the problems. And it worked, didn't it? However, by applying the successful formula used on Problems 1 through 5 to Problems 6 and 7, you may have missed even easier solutions for these last two problems, namely $A - C$ for Problem 6 and $A + C$ for Problem 7.

Abraham Luchins (1942) developed the water jars problems to demonstrate the manner in which a **mental set**—the tendency to stick to solutions that have worked in the past—can result in less effective problem solving. Luchins found that most people who worked on Problems 6 and 7 were blinded by the mental set they had developed by working the first five problems. In contrast, people who had not worked on Problems 1 through 5 almost always applied the simple solutions to Problems 6 and 7. Studies of mental set show how easy it is to become rigidly fixated on one particular approach if we enjoy some degree of success with that approach.

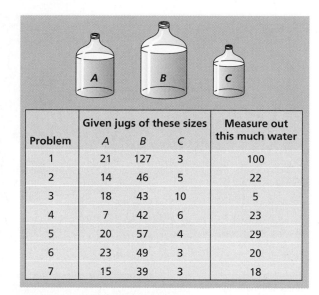

Problem	Given jugs of these sizes			Measure out this much water
	A	B	C	
1	21	127	3	100
2	14	46	5	22
3	18	43	10	5
4	7	42	6	23
5	20	57	4	29
6	23	49	3	20
7	15	39	3	18

FIGURE 8.12 Luchins's water jars problems. Using containers A, B, and C with the capacities shown in the table, how would you measure out the volumes indicated in the right-hand column? You may discover a general problem-solving formula that fits all seven problems.

Evaluating Results

The final stage of problem solving is to evaluate the solutions. As we saw in the water jars problems, even solutions that prove successful may not be the easiest or the best. Thus after solving a problem, we should ask ourselves, "Would there have been an easier or more effective way to accomplish the same objective?" This can lead to the development of additional problem-solving principles that may be applicable to future problems.

➤ 18. Which problem-solving pitfall is revealed by Luchin's water jars problems?

Problem-Solving Schemas

In solving problems, people often learn to employ shortcut problem-solving methods that apply to specific situations (Johnson-Laird, 1997; Rips, 1994). **Problem-solving schemas** can be likened to mental blueprints, or step-by-step scripts for selecting information and solving specialized classes of problems. We have all learned a great many of them, from schemas for cooking dinner or getting acquainted with a person we've just met to schemas for studying and mastering academic course content. Once they are mastered, we seem to "know what to do" without having to engage in step-by-step formal problem-solving procedures.

➤ 19. What are problem-solving schemas? How do they relate to expertise, and to the strengths and weaknesses of human memory?

Schemas help explain what it means to be an expert. For example, masters and grand masters in chess far exceed the playing ability of even the brightest novices. They can glance at a chess board and quickly plan strategies and make adjustments in the heat of competition. The world's best players can store in memory as many as 50,000 board configurations, together with the locations of each of the individual pieces (Chase & Simon, 1973). For years, world chess champion Gary Kasparov's sophisticated schemas enabled him to regularly defeat chess-playing computers that used logical rules, even those capable of logically analyzing up to 100,000 moves per second. It took Deep Blue, a 1.4-ton behemoth capable of "thinking" at a rate of 200 million positions and 200,000 moves per second, to finally defeat the schemas within Kasparov's 3 pound brain (Figure 8.13).

Expert athletic coaches, surgeons, military leaders, and political consultants all rely on the schemas they have developed with experience. Planning military strategy, chess playing, running a political campaign, and piloting aircraft are very different activities. Nevertheless, researchers have found that there is a common factor underlying expertise: Experts have developed a great many schemas

(a)

(b)

FIGURE 8.13 Chess master Gary Kasparov (a) has developed chess schemas that make him a worthy opponent for even the most sophisticated computers, including IBM's Deep Blue, whose operating system is shown in (b).

➤ 20. Differentiate between an algorithm and a heuristic.

➤ 21. Describe two commonly used problem-solving heuristics.

to guide problem solving in their field, and they are much better than novices at recognizing when each schema should be applied (Bedard & Chi, 1992). Applying the correct mental blueprint provides a proven route to solving problems quickly and effectively.

Consider what this difference in schema application means in terms of what we know about human memory. As we learned in Chapter 7, human long-term memory is quite good, and that is where schemas reside. Because they rely on learned schemas, experts depend on their spacious long-term memory. They can quickly analyze a problem, select the retrieval cues needed to pull the appropriate schema from memory, and apply it to solve the problem at hand. In contrast, novices who haven't yet learned specialized schemas must use general problem-solving methods that force them to solve problems in working memory, on the space-limited "blackboard of the mind" (Newell & Simon, 1972). In so doing, they tax their working memories—the weakest link in the human mind.

Algorithms and Heuristics

Algorithms and heuristics are two important strategies for problem solving. **Algorithms** are formulas or procedures that automatically generate correct solutions. Mathematical and chemical formulas are algorithms; if you use them correctly, you will always get the correct answer. Another algorithm is that if the letters of a word are scrambled in random order to produce an anagram like *teralbay,* then the word can be discovered by a process in which the letters are recombined in all possible combinations.

As this last example illustrates, using algorithms can at times be very time-consuming. In this case, the eight letters can be rearranged in no fewer than 40,320 different ways, and applying the algorithm might significantly delay your finishing this chapter. We may therefore decide to use some more general rule-of-thumb strategy, such as trying out only consonants in the first and last positions because we know that more words begin and end in consonants than begin and end in vowels. When we adopt rule-of-thumb approaches like this, we are using heuristics.

Heuristics are general problem-solving strategies that we apply to certain classes of situations. They are mental shortcuts that may or may not provide correct solutions. In using heuristics, we typically compare the present facts with some concept or schema that seems applicable to the present situation.

Means-ends analysis is one example of a heuristic (Newell & Simon, 1972). In using this strategy, we identify differences between the present situation and one's desired state, or goal, and then make changes that will reduce these differences. Assume, for example, that you have a 30-page paper due at the end of the term and have not begun working on it yet. The present situation is zero pages written; the desired end state is a 30-page paper. What, specifically, needs to be done to reduce that discrepancy, and how are you going to do it?

Means-ends analysis often involves the use of another heuristic known as **subgoal analysis.** People can attack a large problem by formulating subgoals, or intermediate steps toward a solution. For example, it is unlikely that you can write a 30-page paper at one sitting. Instead, your expertise as a student will likely lead you to break this big task down into subgoals, such as (a) choosing a topic; (b) doing library and Internet research on the topic to get the facts you need; (c) organizing the facts within a general outline of the paper; (d) writing a first draft, or specific sections of the paper; (e) reorganizing and refining the first draft, and so on. In so doing, a huge task becomes a series of smaller and more manageable tasks, each with a subgoal that leads you toward the ultimate goal of a quality 30-page paper.

The value of setting subgoals can be seen in the Tower of Hanoi problem, depicted in Figure 8.14. The ultimate goal for this problem is to move all three rings on peg 1 to peg 3 using no more than seven moves. There are, however, two restrictions. First, only the top ring on a peg can be moved. Second, a ring must never be placed above a smaller ring. Can you solve this challenging problem? It can be done in seven steps.

Breaking this task into subgoals helps us solve the problem. The first subgoal is to get ring C to the bottom of peg 3. The second subgoal is to get ring B over to peg 3. With these two subgoals accomplished, the final subgoal of getting ring A to peg 3 is quite easy. The solution requires planning (hypothesis formation), checking, and revising hypotheses—all processes discussed previously. The correct seven-step sequence of moves is presented on page 359.

Heuristics enter not only into problem-solving strategies but also into judgments and decisions. As we shall see, they can also contribute to errors in judgment.

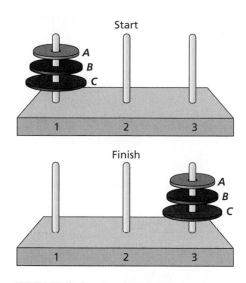

FIGURE 8.14 The Tower of Hanoi problem. The object is to move the rings one at a time from peg 1 to peg 3 in the smallest number of moves possible. (It can be done in seven moves.) Only the top ring on a peg can be moved, and a large ring can never be placed on top of a smaller one. (The answer appears on p. 359.)

Uncertainty, Heuristics, and Decision Making

Few decisions in everyday life can be made with the absolute certainty that comes from applying some mathematical formula. Typically, the best we can hope for is a decision that has a high probability of a positive outcome. Because we seldom know what the exact probabilities are (e.g., how likely it is that the stock market will be up or down when you need your money at a specific time in the future, or how probable it is that a new dating relationship will become permanent), we tend to apply certain heuristics to form judgments of likelihood.

In daily life, we routinely make decisions about what other people are like. Suppose, for example, you are given the following description of a young woman:

> Linda is 31 years old, single, outspoken, and very bright. She majored in philosophy. As a student, she was deeply concerned with issues of discrimination and social justice, and she also participated in antinuclear demonstrations.

Now rate the likelihood that each of the following hypotheses is true. Use 1 to indicate the most likely statement, 8 to indicate the least likely statement, and any number between 2 and 7 to indicate the likelihood of the second most likely statement.

_____ A Linda is active in the feminist movement.

_____ B Linda is a bank teller.

_____ C Linda is active in the feminist movement and is a bank teller.

This problem was used in a series of experiments conducted by cognitive psychologists Amos Tversky and Daniel Kahneman to study the role of heuristics in judgment and decision making. Kahneman and Tversky (1980, 1982) showed that certain heuristics underly much of our inductive decision making (drawing conclusions from facts), and that their misuse results in many of our thinking errors. Let us examine how that occurs.

The representativeness heuristic.   "What does it look [or seem] like?" This is probably the first task faced by our perceptual system when it processes incoming stimuli. Earlier, we discussed the importance of prototypes in concept formation. We use the **representativeness heuristic** to infer how closely something or someone fits our prototype for a particular concept, or class, and therefore how likely it is to be a member of that class. In essence, we are asking, "How likely is it that this [person, object, event] *represents* that class?" Sometimes, our use of representativeness can cause us to make decisions that fly in the face of logic.

For example, what was your order of likelihood judgments concerning Linda? Figure 8.15 shows the mean likelihood estimates that college students attached to each statement (a low number indicating greater likelihood). First of all, there is a clear tendency to favor Hypothesis A (Linda is a feminist). This is not surprising; the description of her does sound like a feminist. However, the significant finding is that Hypothesis C (Linda is a feminist bank teller) was favored over Hypothesis B (Linda is a bank teller). But this cannot possibly be correct. Why not? Because everyone who is both a feminist and a bank teller is also "just" a bank teller. Furthermore, there are many bank tellers who are not feminists, and Linda could be one of them. Stated differently, any person is more likely to be just a bank teller than to be a bank teller *and* a feminist—or for that matter, a bank teller and anything else. People who say that Hypothesis C is more likely than Hypothesis B (and about 85 percent of participants given this problem do so) violate the logical principle that the combination of two events cannot be more likely than either event alone.

Tversky and Kahneman believe that the reason people make this sort of error is that they confuse representativeness with probability. Linda represents our prototype for a feminist bank teller better than she fits our prototype for a bank teller. Therefore the former is (we erroneously think) more likely than the latter. Notice how this argument fits with the ideas about memory discussed in Chapter 7. The description of Linda as "outspoken" and "concerned with issues of discrimination and social justice" serves a priming function, activating the elements in memory that are associated with the concept of *feminist,* so it is hard to think of Linda without thinking of a feminist. On the other hand, there is nothing in Linda's description that would activate the concept of bank teller. Thus if Linda is to be a bank teller at all, we think she must be a feminist bank teller.

The availability heuristic. Another heuristic that can sometimes lead us astray is the **availability heuristic,** which causes us to base judgments and decisions on the availability of information in memory. We tend to remember events that are most important and significant to us. Usually that principle serves us well, keeping important information at the forefront in our memories, ready to be applied. But if something easily comes to mind, we may exaggerate the likelihood that it could occur. For example, a recent memorable event, such as the terrorist bombing of an airliner, is readily accessible to memory and can increase people's belief that they could suffer a similar fate (Fiske & Taylor, 1991). After several such terrorist acts in the mid-1980s, U.S. and Canadian tourism declined sharply in Europe for nearly a year. Instead of going to Europe, what did people do? They chose to drive their automobiles to vacation spots in North America, a decision that, on statistical grounds, made it far more likely that they would be killed than if they had gone to Europe, terrorists or not. Similarly, the year after Steven Spielberg's movie *Jaws* provided graphic images of a great white shark devouring swimmers at New England beaches, tourism in that area fell off so drastically that many beachfront resorts nearly went bankrupt. The vivid images available in memory increased people's perceived likelihood that they, too, could become shark bait.

➤ 22. Describe the representativeness heuristic and indicate how it applies to people's response to the Linda problem.

➤ 23. How does the availability heuristic influence judgments of likelihood or probability?

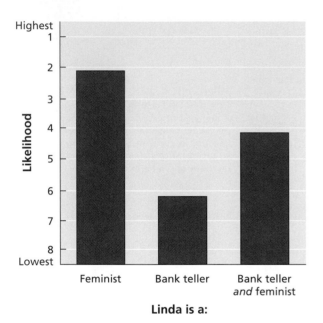

Linda is a:

FIGURE 8.15 Mean likelihood judgments made by students on the basis of the description of Linda cited in the text. Data from Tversky & Kahneman, 1982.

Confirmation Bias

Sometimes, one of the most challenging problem-solving tasks is obtaining new evidence to test our hypothesis or solution. Here is another mind-teaser that tests your ability to choose the evidence you need to test a hypothesis.

Imagine that the four cards shown in Figure 8.16 are placed in front of you. Each card has a single letter written on one side and a number on the other side. The following rule may apply to the cards: "If the card has a vowel on one side, then it has an even number on the other side." Your task is to choose two cards that you could turn over to determine whether the rule is valid. Which cards should you choose? (Please make your choices now by putting check marks above the chosen cards.)

Now here is a principle that may seem puzzling to you: Rationally, the best thing we can do to test our ideas is to seek evidence that will *disconfirm* them, rather than trying to solidify our ideas by looking for evidence that supports them. Why? Because the most informative piece of evidence we can obtain is one that rules out a hypothesis or causes us to change our ideas. Disconfirming evidence proves conclusively that our idea *cannot* be true in its current form. In contrast, confirming evidence only supports our idea. It doesn't prove it with certainty, for it is possible that some future observation will disconfirm it, or that another explanation fits the facts even better.

Following this disconfirmation principle is easier said than done, because people are often unwilling to challenge their cherished beliefs. Instead, they are prone to fall into a trap called **confirmation bias:** They tend to look for evidence that will confirm what they currently believe rather than looking for evidence that could disconfirm their beliefs.

Confirmation bias can occur even when the hypothesis we're testing doesn't relate to a cherished belief. To illustrate, let's return to the four-cards problem in Figure 8.16. The hypothesis to be tested was "If there is a vowel on one side of the card, then there is an even number on the other side." Most people realize immediately that the card with the A needs to be turned over to ensure that it has an even number on the other side. The illustration of confirmation bias comes in the choice of the second card to be turned over. Which other card did you choose? The correct choice is the card with the 7. Why? Because the only way to truly *test* the proposition is by examining the card with the odd number (the 7) on one side. If you turn over the card with the 7 and it has a vowel on it, the proposition is disconfirmed and cannot be true.

Most people do not choose the 7 card, however. Instead, over 95 percent of them try to *confirm* the proposition by examining as their second choice the 4 card to see if it has a vowel on the other side (Wason & Johnson-Laird, 1972). But this is a totally uninformative choice, for whether it has a vowel or not is irrelevant to the proposition being tested. After all, the rule does *not* state that a card with a consonant *cannot* have an even number on the other side. Thus , if you turn over the 4 and it doesn't have a vowel, you could mistakenly conclude that the proposition is not true when in fact it is.

The confirmation bias shown in the laboratory study of the four-cards problem applies to real-life situations as well. Given the choice of what kinds of information they would like to have about themselves, people have a strong tendency to seek, elicit, and recall feedback from others that confirms their beliefs about themselves. They tend to avoid and "forget" evidence that disconfirms these self-beliefs (Swann et al., 1992). In their personal lives, people find it difficult to test and challenge their ideas. They want to see them confirmed.

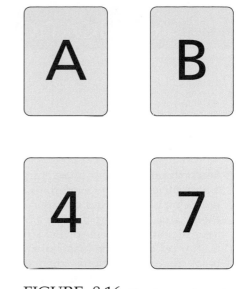

FIGURE 8.16 The four-cards problem. Each card has a letter on one side and a number on the other. Which two cards could you turn over to test the rule "If the card has a vowel on one side, it has an odd number on the other side?"

➤ 24. What is confirmation bias? Why does it occur, and how can it interfere with problem solving?

➤ 25. Differentiate between convergent and divergent thinking. What is meant by incubation?

APPLICATIONS OF PSYCHOLOGICAL SCIENCE

Guidelines for Creative Problem Solving

Research on reasoning offers insights into how effective and creative problem solvers think and how they approach problems. In some ways, as experts so often demonstrate, there is no substitute for experience, for it teaches us heuristics and problem-solving schemas that can be very useful. Yet one of the marks of creativity is the ability to break out of conventional schemas when the occasion demands it and engage in **divergent thinking,** the generation of novel ideas that depart from the norm (Guilford, 1959). In part, this means being able to apply concepts or propositions from one domain to another unrelated domain in a manner that produces a new insight (Chi, 1997). It also means refusing to be constrained by traditional approaches to the problem. Creative people are, in this respect, intellectual rebels.

Such constraints can be difficult to overcome. Consider, for example, the nine-dot problem in Figure 8.17. The task is this: Without lifting your pencil from the paper, draw no more than four straight lines that will pass through all nine dots.

Many people have difficulty solving this problem. Did you? If so, it is probably because you imposed a "traditional" but unnecessary constraint on yourself and tried to stay within the boundary formed by the dots. But nothing in the statement of the problem forced you to do so. To solve the problem, you have to "think outside the box." Two different solutions to the problem are shown on page 359.

Creative problem solvers are often able to ask themselves questions like the following to stimulate divergent thinking (Simonton, 1999):

1. What would work instead?
2. Are there new ways to use this? How else could it be used if I modified it in some way? By adding, subtracting, or rearranging parts, or by modifying the sequence in which things are done, could I make it more useful?
3. Do the elements remind me of anything else? What else is like this?

Try using some of these questions in the following problem. Look at the objects in Figure 8.18. How could you use these objects to mount a candle on the wall and light it so that you could study for your next exam if the power went out. One solution is on page 359.

Solving the candle problem requires using some of the objects in the figure in unconventional ways. People are often prevented from doing so by **functional fixed-**

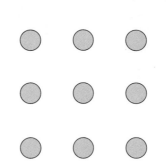

FIGURE 8.17   Without lifting your pencil from the paper, draw no more than four straight lines that will pass through all nine dots. (The answer appears on p. 359.)

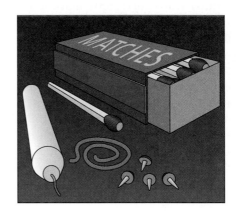

FIGURE 8.18   Using these objects, find a way to mount the candle on the wall so it functions like a lamp. (The answer appears on p. 359.)

ness, the tendency to be so fixed in their perception of the proper function of an object or procedure that they are blinded to new ways of using it.

Sometimes, creative solutions to problems seemingly appear out of the blue, suddenly popping into the problem solver's mind in a flash of insight after the problem solver has temporarily given up and put the problem aside. **Incubation** is the name given to this phenomenon; it is as if the problem is "incubating" and being worked on at a subconscious level (Cattell, 1971). Sometimes the best approach when we are stymied by a problem is to put it aside for a while and gain a bit of psychological distance from it. Perhaps this causes mental sets and other biases to dissipate somewhat, allowing a new idea to emerge (Ander-

—Continued

son, 1985). Additionally, as time passes, new internal or external stimuli may activate a different perspective on the problem, aiding its solution (Bastik, 1982).

As you can see, creative problem solving involves many of the principles discussed earlier. We see the operation of means-ends reasoning, the testing of hypotheses, and the need to overcome biases that may cause us to overestimate or underestimate the likelihood of certain outcomes. Here are some other general problem-solving guidelines suggested by the previous discussion:

1. When you encounter a new problem you haven't solved before, ask yourself if it has any similarities to others you've solved. Maybe the schema for solving a problem with common features can be modified to solve this one. (The principle involved is that our long-term memories are better than our working memories.)
2. If you are testing your ideas, really test them! Try to find evidence that would disconfirm your ideas, not evidence that confirms what you already believe. In particular, if you are asked if statement X is true, see if you can imagine situations in which X would be false. (The principle is that you should be aware of your bias toward confirming your cherished hypotheses.)
3. Beware of confusing representativeness with probability. The odds are overwhelming that the bird that is "a little big" for a sparrow but looks to be exactly the right size for the rare Patagonian warbler is probably . . . a big sparrow, because there are so many more sparrows (even oversized ones) than Patagonian warblers.
4. Make use of the means-ends problem-solving heuristic. Ask yourself what you are trying to accomplish, what the present state of affairs is, and what means you have for reducing the discrepancy.
5. Don't be afraid to use pencil and paper. Orderly notes and schematics can substitute for our rather limited working memories and allow us to have more information at hand to work with.

❯ INTELLIGENCE

So far, we have considered general principles of human thinking, reasoning, and problem solving. Yet it is readily apparent that there are important individual differences in how effectively people think and behave. Is it true that some people are generally more "intelligent" than others? If so, can we measure these differences and use the measures to predict success and failure in real-life settings? What is the nature of intelligence, and what factors account for the differences we observe in people's cognitive, emotional, and behavioral skills? These and related questions have inspired more than a century of scientific research (and more than 20,000 published scientific studies since 1967 alone). Attempts to answer them have had an enormous influence on our culture. Yet today, there is still no universally accepted definition of intelligence, nor is there agreement on whether there is one general form or multiple, specific forms of intelligence. In our discussion, we use the following definition, which accommodates most viewpoints: **Intelligence** is a concept, or construct, that refers to the ability to acquire knowledge, to think and reason effectively, and to deal adaptively with the environment.

❯ 26. How is intelligence defined?

Intelligence in Historical Perspective

Historically, two scientists with different agendas played seminal roles in the study and measurement of mental skills. In England, Sir Francis Galton's work grew out of a purely scientific desire to extend Darwin's theory of evolution to the inheritance of mental abilities. In France, Alfred Binet's concern was the practical one of finding a means to identify "mentally defective" children who would be unable to profit from normal educational experiences.

Sir Francis Galton: Quantifying Mental Ability

Galton, who was highly influenced by the theory of evolution developed by his cousin, Charles Darwin, conducted the first scientific studies of mental skills in England in the late 19th century. In his book *Hereditary Genius* (1869), Galton showed through the study of family trees that eminence and genius seemed to occur across generations within certain families. These studies convinced him that such people had "inherited mental constitutions" that made them more fit for thinking than their less successful counterparts. Exhibiting his own belief bias, Galton, an avowed hereditarian, dismissed the fact that the successful people he studied almost invariably came from privileged environments.

Galton then attempted to demonstrate a biological basis for eminence by showing that people who were more socially and occupationally successful would also perform better on a variety of laboratory tasks thought to measure the efficiency of the nervous system. He developed measures of reaction speed, hand strength, and sensory acuity, and even measured the size of people's skulls on the grounds that skull size reflects brain size and hence intelligence. However, Galton's approach to mental skills measurement fell into disfavor because his measures of "nervous system efficiency" proved unrelated to socially relevant measures of mental ability, such as academic and occupational success. Nonetheless, Galton's work created an interest in the measurement of mental abilities, setting the stage for the pioneering work of Alfred Binet.

Alfred Binet's Mental Tests

The modern intelligence testing movement began at the turn of the 20th century, when the French psychologist Alfred Binet was commissioned by France's Ministry of Public Education to develop the test that was to become the forerunner of all modern "intelligence tests." Unlike Galton (with whom he had trained), Binet was interested in solving a practical problem rather than supporting a theory. Certain children seemed unable to benefit from normal public schooling. Educators wanted an objective way to identify these children as early as possible so that some form of special education could be arranged for them.

➤ 27. What two assumptions did Alfred Binet make in developing his measure of intelligence?

In developing his tests, Binet made two assumptions about intelligence. The first was that mental abilities develop with age. The second was that the rate at which people gain mental competence is a characteristic of the person and is fairly constant over time. If this is true, then a child who is less competent than expected at age 5 should also be lagging at age 10.

To develop a measure of mental skills, Binet asked experienced teachers what sorts of problems children could solve at ages 3, 4, 5, and so on, up through the school years. He then used their answers to develop a "standardized interview" in which an adult examiner posed a series of questions to a child to determine whether the child was performing at the correct mental level for his or her age (Table 8.2). The result of the testing was a score called the **mental age.** For instance, if a child of 8 could solve problems at the level of the average 10-year-old, the child would be said to have a mental age of 10. For the French school system, the practical implication was that educational attainment could be enhanced if placement in school were based at least in part on the child's mental age. An 8-year-old child with a mental age of 6 could hardly be expected to cope with the academic demands of a normal classroom for 8-year-olds.

➤ 28. What was Stern's original IQ ratio? Why was it abandoned, and what replaced it?

The concept of mental age was subsequently expanded by the German psychologist William Stern to provide a relative score—a common yardstick of intellectual attainment—for people of different chronological ages. Stern's **intelligence quotient,** or **IQ** was originally based on the ratio of mental age to chronological age, according to the formula:

$$IQ = (\text{Mental age/chronological age}) \times 100.$$

Thus a child who was performing at exactly his or her age level would have an IQ of 100. In our previous example, the child with a mental age of 10 and a chronological age of 8 would have an IQ of $(10/8) \times 100 = 125$. A 12-year-old with a mental age of 16 would also have an IQ of 125, so the two children would be comparable in intelligence even though their ages differed.

Today's tests no longer use the concept of mental age. One problem is that increases in mental age begin to slow down dramatically at about age 16. Because

TABLE 8.2	SAMPLE PROBLEMS FROM THE STANFORD-BINET INTELLIGENCE TEST THAT SHOULD BE ANSWERED CORRECTLY AT PARTICULAR AGES
Age 3—Child should be able to:	Point to objects that serve various functions such as "goes on your feet." Name pictures of objects such as *chair, flag*. Repeat a list of 2 words or digits—e.g., *car, dog*.
Age 4—Child should be able to:	Discriminate visual forms such as squares, circles, and triangles. Define words such as *ball* and *bat*. Repeat 10-word sentences. Count up to 4 objects. Solve problems such as "In daytime it is light; at night it is . . ."
Age 6—Child should be able to:	State the differences between similar items such as a *bird* and a *dog*. Count up to 9 blocks. Solve analogies such as "An inch is short; a mile is . . ."
Age 9—Child should be able to:	Solve verbal problems such as "Tell me a number that rhymes with tree." Solve simple arithmetic problems such as "If I buy 4 cents worth of candy and give the storekeeper 10 cents, how much money will I get back? Repeat 4 digits in reverse order.
Age 12—Child should be able to:	Define words such as *skill* and *muzzle*. Repeat 5 digits in reverse order. Solve verbal absurdities such as "One day we saw several icebergs that had been entirely melted by the warmth of the Gulf Stream. What is foolish about that?"

Source: Terman & Merrill, 1972.

many of the skills measured by intelligence tests are learned by that age through normal life experiences and schooling, mental age works pretty well for children, but not for adults. A 40-year-old cannot be expected to have twice the level of mental skill of a 20-year-old. (Indeed, some 20-year-olds seem convinced that the opposite is the case.) A second problem is that some intellectual skills show an actual decline at advanced ages rather than the growth assumed by the concept of mental age. Finally, a notable discovery by New Zealand researcher James Flynn (1987, 1998) suggests that much of the world's population is scoring progressively higher on intelligence tests. This "rising curve" phenomenon has produced IQ increases of 28 points in the United States since 1910 and a similar increase in Britain since 1942. Whether this increase is due to better nutrition, richer learning environments, or some unknown factor is unclear at this time (Neisser et al., 1998). What is clear, however, is that the intelligence score distribution has to be recalibrated upward if the average IQ is to remain at 100, the traditional midpoint of the intelligence range. To deal with these problems, today's intelligence tests provide an "IQ" score that is not a quotient at all, but rather is based on a person's performance relative to the scores of a large sample of other people his or her age.

The Stanford-Binet and Wechsler Scales

Lewis Terman, a professor at Stanford University, revised Binet's test for use in the United States, translating it into English and rewriting some of its items so they were relevant to American culture. Terman's revision became known as the Stanford-Binet test. By the mid-1920s, it had been widely accepted in North America. The Stanford-Binet contained mostly verbal items, and it yielded a single IQ score.

Somewhat later, a major competitor to the Stanford-Binet emerged in the form of the Wechsler scales. Psychologist David Wechsler believed that intelligence should be measured as a group of distinct but related verbal and nonverbal abilities. He therefore developed intelligence tests for adults and for children that measured a range of intellectual skills. In 1939, the Wechsler Adult Intelligence Scale

Wechsler Adult Intelligence Scale (WAIS)		
Subtest	**Description**	**Example**
Verbal scale		
Information	Taps general range of knowledge	On what continent is Italy?
Comprehension	Tests understanding of social conventions and ability to evaluate past experience	Why are children required to go to school?
Arithmetic	Tests arithmetic reasoning through verbal problems	How many hours will it take to drive 120 miles at 40 miles per hour?
Similarities	Asks in what way certain objects or concepts are similar; measures abstract thinking	How are a computer and a typewriter alike?
Digit span	Tests attention and rote memory by orally presenting series of digits to be repeated forward or backward	Repeat the following numbers backward: 7 3 5 1 6 8
Vocabulary	Tests ability to define increasingly difficult words	What does "formidable" mean?
Performance scale		
Digit symbol	Tests speed of learning through timed coding tasks in which numbers must be associated with drawings of various shapes	Shown: 1 2 3 4 ○□△◇ Fill in appropriate symbol: 1 4 3 2 _ _ _ _
Picture completion	Tests visual alertness and visual memory through presentation of an incompletely drawn figure; the missing part must be discovered and named	What is missing in this picture? 
Block design	Tests ability to perceive and analyze patterns by presenting designs that must be copied with blocks	Assemble blocks to match this design: 
Picture arrangement	Tests understanding of social situations through a series of comic-strip-type pictures that must be arranged in the right sequence to tell a story	Put the pictures in the correct order: 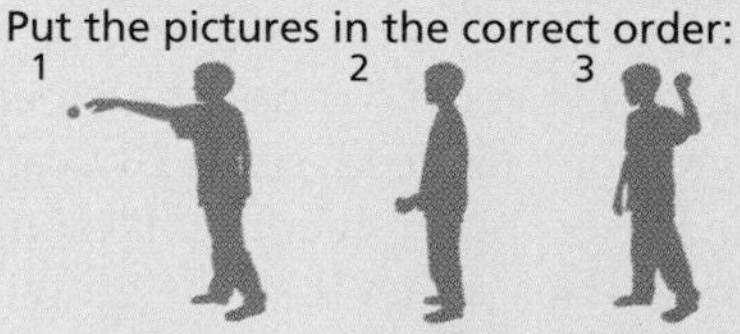 1 2 3
Object assembly	Tests ability to deal with part/whole relationships by presenting puzzle pieces that must be assembled to form a complete object	Assemble the pieces into a complete object: 

FIGURE 8.19 Sample items resembling those found on the subscales of the Wechsler Adult Intelligence Scale.

(WAIS) appeared, followed by the Wechsler Intelligence Scale for Children (WISC) in 1955 and the Wechsler Preschool and Primary Scale of Intelligence (WPPSI) in 1967. Like the Stanford-Binet, the Wechsler scales are regularly revised. Today the Wechsler tests (WAIS-III and WISC-III) are the most widely used individually administered intelligence tests in the United States (Groth-Marnat, 1999).

The Wechsler scales consist of a series of subtests that fall into two classes: Verbal Tests and Performance Tests (Figure 8.19). A psychologist can therefore plot a profile of the scores on each of the subtests to assess a person's pattern of intellectual strengths and weaknesses. The test yields three different summary scores: a Verbal IQ based on the sum of the Verbal subscales; a Performance IQ based on the Performance subscales; and a Full-Scale IQ based on all of the scales. For some purposes, it is useful to examine differences between the Verbal IQ and the Performance IQ. For example, a person from an impoverished environment with little formal schooling might score higher on the Performance scales than on the Verbal scales, suggesting that the overall IQ might be an underestimate of intellectual potential. Sometimes, too, various types of brain damage are reflected in large discrepancies between certain subtest scores (Goldstein, 2000).

A newer version of the Stanford-Binet published in 1986 is also designed to measure more specific mental functions. It consists of 15 subtests designed to measure four areas of intellectual functioning: verbal reasoning, abstract/visual reasoning, quantitative reasoning, and short-term memory (Thorndike et al., 1986). A score similar to an IQ can be computed for each of the four intellectual domains, for any combination of them, or for the test as a whole.

Group Tests of Aptitude and Achievement

Intelligence tests like the Stanford-Binet and the Wechsler scales are administered to an individual by a trained tester. They typically take as long as 2 hours to administer and are therefore impractical for large-scale screening purposes. Group tests of intelligence can be used to obtain IQ scores from groups of people at the same time, using written questions rather than the verbal ones asked by an examiner using a test like the Wechsler. Group tests such as the Lorge-Thorndike Intelligence Test and the Otis-Lennon School Ability Test are routinely used by many school districts, and you may very well have taken one of these tests during your school years.

Other group tests do not provide IQ scores, but measure specific mental skills. These include the Scholastic Aptitude Test (SAT), widely used to select college applicants in the United States, the Graduate Record Examination (GRE), used to select applicants for postgraduate study, the Medical College Admission Test (MCAT), the Law School Aptitude Test (LSAT), and the Armed Services Vocational Aptitude Battery (ASVAB), presently used to screen recruits for the U.S. Armed Services.

Using written tests for selection purposes highlights an issue that Binet faced and that continues to plague test developers today. Should we test a person's abstract "aptitude for learning," or should we test what a person already knows? Consider an example. In selecting applicants for college, we could either give students an **achievement test** designed to find out how much they have learned in high school, or we could present them with an **aptitude test** containing novel puzzlelike problems that presumably go beyond prior learning and are thought to measure the applicant's potential for future learning and performance.

The argument for achievement testing is that it is usually a good predictor of future performance in a similar situation. The argument against achievement testing is that it assumes that everyone has had the same opportunity to learn the material being tested. In the college selection example, if there are marked differences in the quality of the high schools the applicants have attended, a person's test score could depend on whether that person went to a good school rather than on his or her ability to learn in college.

The argument for aptitude testing is that it is "fairer," since aptitude tests are supposed to depend less on prior knowledge than on a person's ability to react to the problems presented on the test. The argument against aptitude testing is that it is difficult to construct a test that is independent of prior learning. When such a test is constructed, it may require an "ability to deal with puzzles" that is not relevant to success in situations other than the test itself.

In fact, most intelligence tests measure a combination of aptitude and achievement, reflecting both native ability and previous learning. This fact has raised major scientific and social issues concerning the meaning of test scores and the usefulness of the measures for describing mental competence and predicting performance in nontest situations.

➤ 29. What is the distinction between achievement and aptitude tests? What controversy exists concerning their respective values for measuring mental skills?

Scientific Standards for Psychological Tests

A **psychological test** is a method for measuring individual differences related to some psychological concept, or construct, based on a sample of relevant behavior in a scientifically designed and controlled situation. In the case of intelligence testing, intelligence is the construct in question. To design a test, we need to decide which specific behaviors serve as indicators or reflections of intellectual abilities. Then we need to devise test items that allow us to assess individual differences in those behaviors. We will, of course, need evidence that our sample of items (a sample, because we can't ask every conceivable question) actually measures the abilities we are assessing. As in designing an experiment (see Chapter 2), we will want to collect that "sample of relevant behavior" under standard conditions, attempting to control for other factors that could influence responses to the items. To understand how psychologists meet these requirements, we must examine three key measurement concepts: reliability, validity, and standardization.

Reliability

> 30. Define reliability and describe three different kinds of reliability that apply to psychological tests.

Reliability refers to consistency of measurement, and consistency can take several forms (Table 8.3). One is consistency over time. If you step on your bathroom scale five times in a row, you should expect it to register the same weight each time unless you have a very unusual metabolism. Likewise, if we assume that intelligence is a relatively stable trait (which virtually all psychologists do), then scores on our measure should be stable, or consistent, over time. Where psychological tests are concerned, this type of measurement consistency is defined as **test-retest reliability,** and it is assessed by administering the measure to the same group of participants on two separate occasions and correlating the two sets of scores.

After about age 7, scores on intelligence tests show considerable stability, even over many years (Gregory, 1998). Over a short interval (2 to 12 weeks) the test-retest correlation of adult IQs on the WAIS is .96, or nearly perfect (Wechsler, 1997). Correlations between IQs at age 9 and age 40 are in the .70 to .80 range (McCall, 1977), indicating a high degree of stability. Thus *relative to her age group,* a person who achieves an above-average IQ at age 9 is very likely to also be above the average for 40-year-olds when she reaches that age. Even during childhood, when children's cognitive skills are developing rapidly, IQs are quite stable. In one large-scale study, test-retest correlations of .87, .87, and .91 were

TABLE 8.3	TYPES OF RELIABILITY AND VALIDITY IN PSYCHOLOGICAL TESTING
Types of Reliability	**Meaning and Critical Questions**
Test-retest reliability	Are scores on the measure stable over time?
Internal consistency	Do all of the items on the measure seem to be measuring the same thing, as indicated by high correlations among them?
Interjudge reliability	Do different raters or scorers agree on their scoring or observations?
Types of Validity	
Construct validity	To what extent is the test actually measuring the construct of interest (e.g., intelligence)?
Content validity	Do the questions or test items relate to all aspects of the construct being measured?
Predictive validity	Do scores on the test predict some present or future behavior or outcome assumed to be affected by the construct being measured?

found for Wechsler Verbal, Performance, and Full-Scale IQs, respectively, over an interval of nearly 3 years (Canivez & Watkins, 1998).

Another form of reliability, **internal consistency,** has to do with consistency of measurement *within* the test itself. If a test is internally consistent, all of the items within a test are measuring the same thing. For example, the items on the Vocabulary subtest of the Wechsler test all correlate highly with one another (Gregory, 1998).

Finally, **interjudge reliability** refers to consistency of measurement when different people score the same test. Ideally, two different psychologists who independently score the same test would assign exactly the same scores. To attain high interjudge reliability, the scoring instructions must be so explicit that trained professionals will use the scoring system in the same way.

Validity

Validity refers to how well a test actually measures what it is designed to measure. As in the case of reliability, there are several types of validity (Table 8.3).

➤ 31. Define validity and distinguish between construct, content, and predictive (criterion-related) validity.

Is this test actually measuring intelligence, or is it measuring something else? Such a question addresses the issue of **construct validity.** If an intelligence test had perfect construct validity, individual differences in IQs would be due to differences in intelligence and nothing else. This ideal is never attained, for other factors such as motivation and educational background also influence test scores.

Two other kinds of validity contribute to construct validity. **Content validity** refers to whether the items on a test measure all the knowledge or skills that are assumed to comprise the construct of interest. For example, if we want the Arithmetic subtest of the WAIS-III to measure general mathematical reasoning skills, we would not want that subtest to have only addition problems; we would want the items to sample other relevant mathematical abilities as well.

If an intelligence test is valid, the IQ it yields should allow us to predict other behaviors that are assumed to be influenced by intelligence, such as school grades or job performance. These outcome measures are called *criterion* measures. **Predictive validity** is defined by how highly test scores correlate with, or can predict, criterion measures. Thus we could determine how well your IQ predicts your current or future college grades.

Intelligence tests were originally developed to predict academic and other forms of achievement. How well do they do so? Correlations of IQ with school grades are in the +.60 range for high school students and in the +.30 to +.50 range for college students (Aiken, 1996). In general, then, people who score well on the tests tend to do well academically. Likewise, the college entrance examination you took while in high school is designed to predict the criterion of grades in college. In fact, SAT scores do predict college grades, with correlations slightly below +.50 (Willingham et al., 1990). This correlation, which is about the same magnitude as the correlation between people's height and weight, is high enough to justify using the tests for screening purposes, but low enough to suggest the use of other predictors (such as high school grades) in combination with SAT scores. After all, would you let a tailor design a $600 suit of clothes on the basis of your height alone?

➤ 32. How well do intelligence tests predict academic and job performance?

Intelligence test scores also predict military and job performance, yielding correlations of +.20 to +.50 with various measures of job performance across different occupations (Hartigan & Wigdor, 1989; Hunter & Hunter, 1984). Generally, intelligence tests are better at predicting academic success (which requires the kinds of cognitive skills they measure) than job success, which may require other skills as well. However, they are far from perfect predictors in any achievement domain. In many performance settings, including college, a certain level of intellectual ability is needed to survive, but for people who have that requisite level, other factors, such as motivation and work habits, may assume greater importance.

FIGURE 8.20 A psychologist administers the Wechsler Intelligence Scale for Children (WISC-III) using explicit instructions and procedures to create a standard testing environment.

➤ 33. What are the two meanings of the term *standardization?*

Standardization and Norms

The third measurement requirement, **standardization,** has two facets. The first has to do with creating a well-controlled, or *standardized,* environment for administering the intelligence test so that other uncontrolled factors will not influence scores. Tests like the Stanford-Binet and Wechsler scales have very detailed instructions that must be closely adhered to, even to the point of reading the instructions and items to the person being tested (Figure 8.20).

The second aspect of standardization is especially important in providing a meaningful IQ score. It involves the collection of **norms,** or test results derived from a large sample that represents particular age segments of the population. These normative scores provide a basis for interpreting a given individual's score, just as the distribution of scores in a course exam allows you to determine how well you did relative to your classmates.

When norms are collected for mental skills (and for many other human characteristics), the scores usually form a bell-shaped curve known as a **normal distribution,** with most scores clustering around the center of the curve. On intelligence tests, the center of the distribution for each age group from childhood to late adulthood is assigned an IQ score of 100. Because the normal distribution has known statistical properties, we can specify what percentage of the population will score higher than a given score. Thus as Figure 8.21 shows, an IQ score of 100 cuts the distribution in half, with an equal percentage of the population scoring above and below this midpoint. The farther we move from this average score of 100 in either direction, the fewer people attain the higher or lower scores. The figure also shows the percentage of people who score above certain IQ levels. On modern intelligence tests, this method of assigning an IQ score has replaced the original formula of mental age divided by chronological age.

The relative nature of the IQ has important implications for interpreting the meaning of intelligence test scores. Consider two people, one with an IQ of 150 and another with an IQ of 75. Because the scores are computed relative to a population norm, it makes no sense whatsoever to say that the first person is "twice as intelligent" as the second. What can be said is that in a random sample of 100 people we would expect only 1 person to have a score higher than 150, while 95 people would have a score higher than 75.

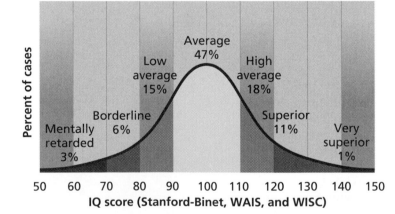

FIGURE 8.21 When administered to large groups of people, intelligence tests yield a normal, or bell-shaped, distribution of IQ scores that has known statistical properties. The mean of the distribution is set at 100. It is possible to specify for any given score which percentage of the standardization group achieved higher or lower scores. Common descriptive labels are shown relative the bell-shaped distribution. The range of scores from 90 to 110 is labeled average and includes nearly half of the population.

The Nature of Intelligence

Two major approaches have been taken to studying intelligence. The *psychometric approach* attempts to map the structure of intellect and to specify the kinds of mental ability that underlie test performance. Is intelligence a single dimension of general mental competence, or is it a loose collection of very specific abilities? A second approach, the *cognitive processes approach,* studies the specific thought processes that underlie mental competencies.

The Psychometric Approach: The Structure of Intellect

➤ 34. Differentiate between the psychometric and cognitive psychology approaches to intelligence.

Psychometrics is the statistical study of psychological tests. Thus standardization, reliability, and validity are all psychometric concepts. The psychometric approach to intelligence tries to identify and measure the abilities that underlie individual differences in performance on intelligence tests. In essence, the psychometric approach tries to produce a measurement-based map of the mind.

One of the major tools used by psychometric researchers is **factor analysis,** which analyzes patterns of correlations between test scores to discover clusters of measures that correlate highly with one another but not with measures in other clusters. When such clusters, or factors, are found, the investigator tries to decide what common underlying ability accounts for the high correlations. For example, if we were to find that four different tests were highly correlated with one another and that the tests all required subjects to solve mathematical problems, we might conclude that the underlying factor is "mathematical reasoning ability." If another cluster of correlated tests all required the ability to define and use words, we might conclude that the underlying intellectual factor is "verbal ability." (A more extensive discussion of factor analysis can be found in Appendix A.)

Psychometric theorists disagree on the nature of intelligence. Some believe that intelligence is a single global mental capability that cuts across all of what we would call "thinking." At the other extreme are those who regard intelligence not as a unitary trait, but as a set of specific abilities to do different types of thinking.

The *g* factor: intelligence as general mental capacity. The psychometric argument for intelligence as a general ability was first advanced by the British psychologist Charles Spearman (1923), who pioneered the use of factor analysis. He observed that school grades in very different subjects, such as English and mathematics, were almost always positively correlated but that the correlations were not perfect. Spearman found the same to be true for different types of Binet intelligence test items, such as vocabulary questions, arithmetic reasoning problems, and the ability to construct puzzles.

Faced with this pattern of results, Spearman concluded that intellectual performance is determined partly by "general intelligence" (usually indicated by the symbol *g*), and partly by whatever special abilities might be required to perform that particular task. Spearman contended that since the general factor—the *g* factor—was so important on virtually all tasks, it constituted the most important aspect of intelligence. For instance, Spearman would argue that your performance in a mathematics course would depend mainly on your general intelligence, but also on your specific ability to learn mathematics. Today many theorists continue to believe that the *g* factor is the core of what we call intelligence (Jensen, 1998).

Intelligence as specific mental abilities. Spearman's conclusion concerning the *g* factor was soon challenged by L. L. Thurstone of the University of Chicago. Where Spearman had been impressed by the fact that scores on different mental tasks are correlated, Thurstone was impressed by the fact that the correlations are far from perfect. Thurstone concluded that human mental performance depends not on a general factor, but rather on seven distinct abilities, which he called **primary mental abilities** (Table 8.4). Contesting Spearman's position,

> 35. What kinds of evidence gave rise to the *g* factor and specific mental abilities conceptions of intelligence?

TABLE 8.4 THURSTONE'S PRIMARY MENTAL ABILITIES	
Ability Name	Description
S—Space	Reasoning about visual scenes
V—Verbal comprehension	Understanding verbal statements
W—Word fluency	Producing verbal statements
N—Number facility	Dealing with numbers
P—Perceptual speed	Recognizing visual patterns
M—Rote memory	Memorization
R—Reasoning	Dealing with novel problems

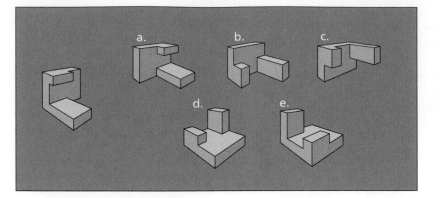

FIGURE 8.22 Spatial-visual skills are assessed with problems like this one. Which of the five objects on the right is the same as the object on the left? (The answer appears on p. 359.)

➤ 36. Differentiate between crystallized and fluid intelligence. How is their utilization related to age?

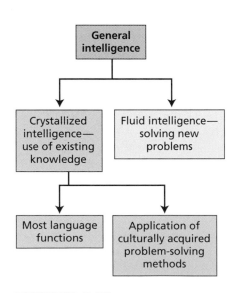

FIGURE 8.23 The structure of general intelligence, according to Cattell and Horn, includes an important distinction between crystallized and fluid intelligence.

➤ 37. What types of competencies are represented in Gardner's theory of multiple intelligences?

Thurstone maintained that performance on any mental task is more influenced by the specific abilities relevant to that task than by any underlying *g* factor. Following Thurstone's lead, other investigators claimed to have found even more factors. One prominent theorist maintained that there are over a hundred distinct and measurable mental abilities (Guilford, 1967, 1998).

Despite the lack of agreement as to whether intelligence is best conceived as a single ability that is applicable in many settings, or as a set of specialized abilities, there are some trends that are found in almost every population. The clearest of these is a distinction between the ability to deal with verbal information and the ability to solve spatial-visual problems, such as the one shown in Figure 8.22. These appear to be two relatively distinct abilities. Mathematical reasoning is more strongly related to spatial-visual reasoning than it is to verbal reasoning (Hunt, 1997).

Crystallized and fluid intelligence. Current knowledge about the nature of mental abilities suggests a position intermediate between Spearman's general intelligence and Thurstone's separate factors of the mind (Hunt, 1997). This position, originally developed by Raymond Cattell (1971) and subsequently extended by John Horn (1985), accounts for the facts quite well. Horn and Cattell break down Spearman's general intelligence into two correlated (around .50) but distinct abilities (Figure 8.23). **Crystallized intelligence** is the ability to apply previously acquired knowledge to current problems. Vocabulary and information tests are good measures of crystallized intelligence. Crystallized intelligence depends in large part on the ability to retrieve information and previously learned problem-solving schemas from long-term memory (Hunt, 1997).

Cattell and Horn's second general factor is **fluid intelligence,** defined as the ability to deal with novel problem-solving situations for which personal experience does not provide a solution. It involves inductive reasoning and creative problem-solving skills like those discussed earlier in the chapter. The four-card, Tower of Hanoi, and nine-dot problems you worked on earlier in the chapter are fluid intelligence tasks. Fluid intelligence requires the abilities to reason abstractly, think logically, and manage information in working (short-term) memory so that new problems can be solved on the "blackboard of the mind" (Hunt, 1997). Thus long-term memory contributes strongly to crystallized intelligence and working memory to fluid intelligence.

Cattell and Horn argue that over our life span we progress from using fluid intelligence to depending more on crystallized intelligence. This makes sense in terms of problem-solving schemas, discussed earlier. Early in life, we encounter many problems for the first time, so fluid intelligence is needed to figure out solutions. As experience makes us more "expert," we have less need to approach each situation as a new problem. We simply call the appropriate information and schemas up from long-term memory and use them. Now we are being served by our crystallized intelligence.

Reflecting the "wisdom" of experience, performance on tests of crystallized intelligence improves or remains stable well into late adulthood. In contrast, performance on tests of fluid intelligence begins to decline as people enter late adulthood (Schaie, 1994, 1998). Thus the issue of whether intelligence declines in old age depends on whether you are talking about crystallized or fluid intelligence (Cattell, 1998).

FIGURE 8.24 According to Howard Gardner, these people are exhibiting specific forms of intelligence—musical, body-kinesthetic, and personal, respectively—that are not measured on traditional intelligence tests.

Multiple intelligences: beyond mental competencies.   All the conceptions of intelligence discussed so far view intelligence in terms of *mental* competence. Yet if we regard intelligence as the ability to adapt to environmental demands, a broader conception beckons. Some psychologists suggest that intelligence may be more broadly conceived as relatively independent *intelligences* that relate to different adaptive demands. Harvard psychologist Howard Gardner (1983) is one of the strongest proponents of this view. Gardner has advanced a theory of multiple intelligences that defines six distinct varieties of intelligence: (1) linguistic; (2) mathematical; (3) visual-spatial; (4) musical (the ability to perceive pitch and rhythm); (5) bodily-kinesthetic (the ability to control body movements and skill-fully manipulate objects, as might be personified in a great ballerina, athlete, or skilled surgeon); and (6) personal (understanding of ourselves and others).

The first three abilities are measured by existing intelligence tests, but the other three are not. Indeed, some of Gardner's critics insist that these abilities are not really part of intelligence. However, Gardner replies that the form of intelligence that is most highly valued within a given culture depends on the adaptive requirements of that culture. In Gardner's view, the abilities exhibited by Albert Einstein, Tiger Woods, and a "street-smart" gang leader exemplify different forms of intelligence that are highly adaptive within their respective environments (Figure 8.24). Gardner further believes that these six classes of abilities require the functioning of separate but interacting modules in the brain. He bases his argument on studies of brain damage, which often leaves some abilities devastated while sparing others, and on the characteristics of **savants.** These people are intellectually disabled in a general sense, yet they exhibit striking skills in specific areas, such as the ability to memorize hundreds of television commercials word-for-word after hearing them only once or the ability to mentally compute mathematical problems such as the square root of 2,349,867 $\times$ 43,978. A g factor alone would not allow for these specific areas of extraordinary ability. Gardner's approach is provocative but remains controversial because it goes far beyond traditional conceptions of intelligence as mental skills.

Emotional intelligence.   Another form of adaptive ability that is attracting the attention of psychologists relates to the emotional realm. **Emotional intelligence** involves the abilities to read others' emotions accurately, to respond to them appropriately, to motivate oneself, to be aware of one's own emotions, and to regulate and control one's own emotional responses (Epstein, 1998; Mayer & Salovey, 1997). Proponents of emotional intelligence point to the important adaptive

➤ 38. Describe the five abilities that comprise emotional intelligence.

TABLE 8.5	SAMPLE ITEMS FROM A TEST OF EMOTIONAL INTELLIGENCE

I am aware of the nonverbal messages I send to others.

I help other people feel better when they're down.

I have control over my emotions.

I easily recognize my emotions as I experience them.

I motivate myself by imagining a good outcome to tasks I take on.

I know why my emotions change.

Note: Items are answered on a 5-point scale ranging from 1, *strongly disagree*, to 5, *strongly agree*.
Source: Schutte et al., 1998.

advantages of skills in managing the emotional challenges of daily life. Emotionally intelligent people, they suggest, form stronger emotional bonds with others, enjoy greater success in careers, marriage, and childrearing, modulate their own emotions so as to avoid strong depression, anger, or anxiety, and work more effectively toward long-term goals by being able to control impulses for immediate gratification. In the end, those high in emotional intelligence may enjoy more success in life than do others who surpass them in mental intelligence (Salovey et al., 1997).

Table 8.5 shows sample items from one recently developed measure of emotional intelligence. Scores on this measure were unrelated to cognitive measures, but did predict higher college grades. In accord with predictions, psychotherapists achieved higher emotional intelligence scores, on average, than did nonprofessionals, and women scored higher on the measure than did men (Schutte et al., 1998).

Critics of noncognitive forms of intelligence are concerned that the concept of intelligence is being stretched too far from its original focus on mental ability (e.g., Cooper, 1998). Proponents respond that if we regard intelligence as adaptive abilities, we ought not limit ourselves to the purely cognitive realms of human ability. This debate promises to continue into the future.

Cognitive Process Approaches: Processes Underlying Intelligent Thinking

Psychometric theories of intelligence are statistically sophisticated ways of describing *how* people differ from one another. What psychometric theories don't explain is *why* people vary in these ways. **Cognitive process theories** try to do so by relating the types of individual variation described in the psychometric approach to the cognitive skills presented in the first part of the chapter. Recall that this was the logic behind Galton's early attempts to relate thinking ability to speed of reaction and sensory acuity.

Sternberg's triarchic theory.   Robert Sternberg (1998) is a leading proponent of the cognitive processes approach to intelligence. His **triarchic theory of intelligence** addresses both the psychological processes involved in intelligent behavior and the diverse forms that intelligence can take. Sternberg's theory divides the cognitive processes that contribute to intelligent behavior into three specific classes: metacomponents, performance components, and knowledge acquisition components (Figure 8.25).

Metacomponents are the higher-order processes used to plan and regulate task performance. They include the problem-solving skills discussed earlier in the chapter: identifying problems, formulating hypotheses and strategies, testing them logically, and evaluating performance feedback. Sternberg believes that metacomponents are the fundamental sources of individual differences in fluid intelligence. He finds that intelligent people spend more time framing problems and developing strategies than do less intelligent people, who have a tendency to plunge right in without sufficient forethought.

The second-level components, **performance components,** are the actual mental processes used to perform the task. They include perceptual processing, retrieving appropriate memories and schemas from long-term memory, and making responses. The third-level components are **knowledge-acquisition components,** which allow us to learn from our experiences, store information in memory, and combine new insights with previously acquired information. These abilities underlie individual differences in crystallized intelligence. Thus Sternberg's theory addresses the processes that underlie the important distinction made by Cattell and Horn between fluid and crystallized intelligence.

Sternberg's theory also addresses intelligent behavior as it relates to the individual's culture and environment. Sternberg (1986, 1998) suggests that environmental demands may call for three different manifestations of intelligence, and that people differ in their intellectual strengths in these areas:

1. *Analytical* intelligence involves the kinds of academically oriented problem-solving skills assessed by traditional intelligence tests.

2. *Practical* intelligence refers to the skills needed to cope with everyday demands and to manage oneself and other people effectively. Emotional intelligence would fall within this category.

3. *Creative* intelligence is the mental skills needed to deal adaptively with novel problems.

Sternberg believes that educational programs should teach all three classes of skills, not just the analytical/academic skills. In studies with elementary school children, he and his colleagues have shown that a curriculum that also teaches practical and creative skills results in greater mastery of course material than does a traditional analytic memory-based approach to learning course content (Sternberg et al., 1998). As Sternberg's work illustrates, cognitive science is leading us in a new direction in which the focus is on understanding and enhancing the mental processes that underlie intelligent behavior.

Galton resurrected: intelligence and neural efficiency. The scientific study of intelligence began in part with Sir Francis Galton's attempts to develop measures of nervous system efficiency that might underlie mental skills. As noted earlier, these attempts fell into disfavor because scores on his measures were unrelated to one another and to external criteria of success. As tools for directly measuring brain functions become more sophisticated, however, Galton's legacy lives on in current attempts to relate neural measures to IQ.

Two types of evidence suggest that this line of research may bear fruit. The first comes from electrophysiological studies of brain responses to visual and auditory stimuli. Modest relations have been shown between traditionally measured IQ and both the nature and speed of the brain's electrical response to stimuli. These electrical responses may reflect the speed and efficiency of information processing in the brain (Barrett & Eysenck, 1992; Caryl, 1994).

The second line of evidence comes from studies of brain metabolism. PET scans of people's brains taken while they engage in problem-solving tasks have shown lower levels of glucose consumption in people of high intelligence, suggesting that their brains are working more efficiently and expending less energy (Haier et al., 1993). Whether these findings herald a new way of measuring intelligence is an unanswered question. The proof of this pudding will be in the ability of such measures to predict external achievement criteria, as traditional intelligence tests do.

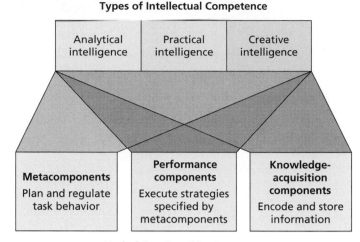

Types of Intellectual Competence

Analytical intelligence	Practical intelligence	Creative intelligence

Metacomponents Plan and regulate task behavior	**Performance components** Execute strategies specified by metacomponents	**Knowledge-acquisition components** Encode and store information

Underlying Cognitive Processes

FIGURE 8.25 Sternberg's theory of intelligence deals with the specific cognitive processes assumed to underlie intelligent behavior, and it illustrates the current interest of cognitive psychology in underlying processes.

➤ 39. What are the three levels of psychological processes that underlie intelligence in Sternberg's triarchic theory? What are the three different kinds of "intelligence"?

➤ 40. What evidence is there that intelligence might involve neural efficiency?

Heredity, Environment, and Intelligence

"To what extent is intelligence determined by people's genetic inheritance in comparison with the environment in which they are raised?" This seemingly simple question has long served as a lightning rod for controversy and, at times, bitter debate.

➤ 41. What is the relation between genetic similarity and similarity in IQ? How much group variation in IQ is accounted for by genetic variation?

Suppose that intelligence was totally determined by genes. (No one thinks that it is, but examining the extreme view can be instructive.) In that case, any two individuals with exactly the same genes would have identical test scores, so that the correlation between the test scores of identical (monozygotic) twins would be +1.00. Nonidentical brothers and sisters (including fraternal twins, who result from two fertilized eggs) share only half their genes. Therefore the correlation between the test scores of fraternal twins and other siblings should be substantially lower. Extending the argument, the correlation between a parent's test scores and his or her children's scores should be about the same as that between siblings, because a child inherits only half of his or her genes from each parent.

What do the actual data look like? Table 8.6 summarizes the results from many studies. As you can see, the correlations between the test scores of identical twins are substantially higher than any other correlations. In fact, the correlation for identical twins reared together is nearly as high as when the same people are tested twice. Identical twins separated early in life and reared apart are of special interest because they have identical genes but different environments. The correlation for identical twins raised apart is higher than the figure for nonidentical twins raised together and nearly as high as that for identical twins reared together (Bouchard et al., 1990). This is very strong evidence that genes play an important role in intelligence.

Notice, however, that the figure for twins raised together is higher than the figure for twins raised apart. The same thing is true for other types of siblings raised together and raised apart. This rules out an entirely genetic explanation. Although genetic constitution seems to be an important factor in determining intelligence test scores, it probably accounts for only 50 to 70 percent of the IQ variation between people in the U.S. population today (Bouchard et al., 1990; Plomin, 1997). Thus environment counts, too. Obviously, then, the question

TABLE 8.6 CORRELATIONS IN INTELLIGENCE AMONG PEOPLE WHO DIFFER IN GENETIC SIMILARITY AND WHO LIVE TOGETHER OR APART

Relationship	Correlation of IQ Scores
Identical twins reared together	.86
Identical twins reared apart	.75
Nonidentical twins reared together	.57
Siblings reared together	.45
Siblings reared apart	.21
Parent–offspring reared by parent	.36
Parent–offspring not reared by parent	.20
Adopting parent–offspring	.19
Adopted children reared together	.02

Source: Data from Bouchard & McGue, 1981; Bouchard et al., 1990; Scarr, 1992.

with which this section began is too simplistic. The real question should be: "How do heredity and environment *interact* to affect intelligence?"

Biological Reaction Range, Environment, and Intelligence

The concept of reaction range contributes to our understanding of genetic-environmental interactions. The **reaction range** for a genetically influenced trait is the range of possibilities—the upper and lower limits—that the genetic code allows. Thus to say that intelligence is genetically influenced does not mean that intelligence is fixed at birth. Instead, it means that an individual inherits a range for potential intelligence that has upper and lower limits. Environmental effects will then determine where the person falls within these genetically determined boundaries. In other words, each of us has a range of intellectual potential that is jointly influenced by our genetic inheritance and the opportunities our environment provides for acquiring intellectual skills.

At present, genetic reaction ranges cannot be measured directly, and we do not know if their sizes differ from one person to another. But studies of IQ gains associated with environmental enrichment and adoption programs suggest that the ranges could be as large as 15 to 20 points on the IQ scale (Dunn & Plomin, 1990). If this is indeed the case, then the influence of environmental factors on intelligence could be highly significant.

Some practical implications of the reaction range concept are illustrated in Figure 8.26. First, consider Persons B and H. They have identical reaction ranges, but B develops in a very deprived environment and H in an enriched environment with many cultural and educational advantages. H is able to realize her innate potential and has an IQ that is 20 points higher than B's. Now compare Persons C and I. C actually has greater intellectual potential than I, but ends up with a lower IQ as a result of living in an environment that does not allow that potential to develop. Finally, note Person G, who was born with high genetic endowment and reared in an enriched environment. His IQ of 110 is lower than we would expect, suggesting that he did not take advantage of either his biological capacity or his environmental advantages. This serves to remind us that intellectual growth depends not only on genetic endowment and environmental advantage, but also on other personal characteristics, such as interests and motivation, that affect how much we take advantage of our genetic and environmental endowments.

Cultural and Group Differences in Intelligence

We know that you highly esteem the kind of learning taught in those colleges. . . . But you, who are wise, must know that different nations have different conceptions of things: and you will not therefore take it amiss, if our ideas of this kind of education happen not to be the same with yours. We have had some experience of it; several of our young people were formerly brought up at the colleges of the Northern provinces; they were instructed in all your sciences; but, when they came back to us, they were bad runners, ignorant of every means of living in the woods, unable to bear either cold or hunger, knew neither how to build a cabin, take a deer, nor kill an enemy, spoke our language imperfectly, were therefore neither fit for hunters, warriors, nor counselors; they were totally good for nothing. . . . We are, however not the less obligated by your kind offer, though we decline accepting it; and to show our grateful sense of it, if the gentlemen of Virginia will send us a dozen of their sons, we will take care of their education, instruct them in all we know,

➤ 42. How does the concept of reaction range help account for the interaction between heredity and environment?

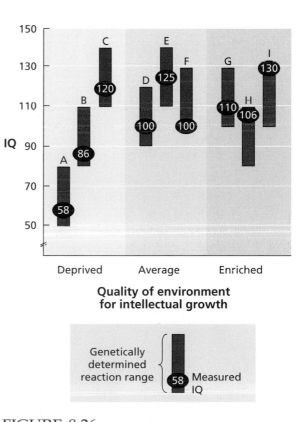

FIGURE 8.26 Reaction ranges, environment, and intelligence. Genetic endowment is believed to create a reaction range within which environment exerts its effects. Enriched environments are expected to allow a person's intelligence to develop to the upper region of his or her reaction range, whereas deprived environments may limit intelligence to the lower portion of the range. Where intelligence is concerned, the reaction range may cover as much as 15 to 20 points on the IQ scale.

and make men of them. (A Native American leader quoted in Benjamin Franklin's *Remarks Concerning the Savage of North America* [1784]).

This response to a well-intentioned offer by colonists to provide Native American children with access to White educational opportunities reminds us that if we view intelligence as adaptive behavior, people in other cultures may have an entirely different conception concerning which behaviors are "intelligent" ones. Thus intelligence is in some respects a cultural construction, based on the adaptive demands that confront a culture and the behaviors that are required to cope with those demands. Consider, for example, what the items on an intelligence test constructed within that Native American culture might be like. Undoubtedly, they would bear little resemblance to Wechsler intelligence test items.

Ethnic group differences.   Some of the most controversial debates in psychology have concerned the existence and meaning of ethnic and racial group differences in intelligence. Discussions of intellectual differences between ethnic groups and between men and women touch on deeply held notions of social equality. To make matters worse, the evidence does not warrant any simple conclusion.

> 43. What differences are found in the average IQ between ethnic groups in the United States?

Where ethnic groups are concerned, everyone agrees on certain facts. Today there are consistent differences in the average intelligence test scores of members of different racial and national groups. National comparisons indicate that Japanese children have the highest mean IQ in the world (Hunt, 1995). Their mean score of 111 places 77 percent of Japanese children above the mean scores of U.S. and European children. Within the United States, significant ethnic differences also exist. Asian-Americans test somewhat above the White norms, especially on tests related to visual-spatial and mathematical reasoning. Hispanics who have become U.S.-acculturated score at about the same level as White Americans. African-Americans score, on average, about 12 to 15 IQ points below the White American average (Jencks et al., 1998). This, of course, does not mean that all Whites and Hispanics test lower than Asian-Americans, or that all African-Americans test lower than the other ethnic groups; in all groups, some individuals score at the highest levels. Nonetheless, the average group differences are large enough to have practical consequences. The unanswered question is where these differences come from.

Keep in mind that these findings apply to test scores, which are the standard operational definition of the construct we call intelligence. Concerns have been expressed that these tests underestimate the mental competence of minority group members because the tests are culturally biased, based on Euro-American White culture. But defenders of the tests point out that racial differences appear throughout intelligence tests, not just on those items that would, on their face, appear to be culturally biased (Jensen, 1980, 1998). Second, they point out that intelligence test scores predict the performance of minority group members as well as they predict White performance (Barrett & Depinet, 1991; Hartigan & Wigdor, 1989). For example, even though African-Americans as a group score lower than Whites, the tests predict academic and occupational performance equally well for both racial groups, indicating that they are measuring relevant mental skills (Hunt, 1995).

> 44. How well do intelligence tests predict the performance of different ethnic groups?

> 45. Are IQ differences between Blacks and White increasing or decreasing? What does this imply?

The next dispute about racial differences is a rather different one. The nature-nurture argument tentatively accepts the differences in measures of mental abilities as being real and then asks why they exist. Consider the differences between White Americans and African-Americans. On the nurture side, there is no question that a higher proportion of African-American than White children in the United States are raised and schooled in environments that do not optimize the development of cognitive skills. However, social changes over the past 25 years have provided African-Americans with greater access to educational and vocational opportunities and have coincided with a reduction in the IQ difference between African-Americans and White Americans (Jencks et al., 1998). These shrinking ethnic differences also extend to reading and mathematics achievement tests in grades 1 through 12, as well as to scores on the SAT

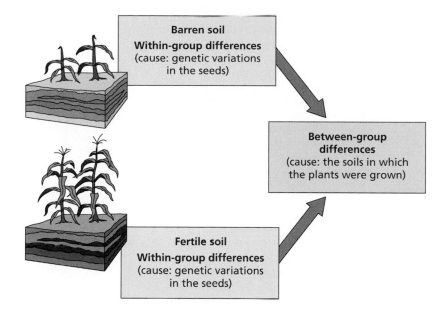

FIGURE 8.27 The interaction of heredity and environment is shown in this agricultural analogy. Seeds planted in a fertile field will be, on the average, larger than those planted in poor soil. This between-groups variability is attributable to environment. Within each field, however, plants will also differ in size as a result of genetic factors. Applied to intelligence, this analogy indicates how between-group differences could result from environmental factors despite the fact that intelligence has a strong genetic component.

(Linn, 1989). People who are impressed by this decreasing test gap tend to attribute racial differences to environmental differences that could be changed (Nisbett, 1998). Meredith Phillips and her coworkers (1998) analyzed a wide range of family environment factors in relation to intellectual differences between 5- and 6-year-old African-American and White children. They concluded that family environment factors alone could account for about two thirds of the test score gap. Figure 8.27 provides an agricultural analogue of how an environment could produce group differences even for a genetically affected variable.

The key role played by the cultural environment also may be illustrated by a historical example involving a different minority group. Early in the 20th century, the average Italian-American child had an IQ of 87, about the same as the average score of African-Americans today. Henry Goddard (1917), a leading hereditarian researcher of the time,, concluded that 79 percent of Italian-American immigrants were "feeble minded" and posed a danger to the gene pool of the United States. Today the average Italian-American student obtains an above-average IQ (Ceci, 1996). Obviously, genetic changes could not produce a result of this size in such a short time. Cultural assimilation and educational and economic opportunity seem much more reasonable explanations for this pronounced increase in test scores.

Another factor worth noting is a tendency, even among some scientists, to overemphasize genetic differences between groups. Indeed, where measured directly, gene differences tend to be greater *within* any given racial group than they are between racial groups (Rowe, 1999). For example, both African-Americans and Whites exhibit greater genetic variation among themselves than exists between the average Black and the average White.

Sex differences in cognitive abilities.   Men and women differ in physical attributes and reproductive function. They also differ in their abilities to perform certain types of intellectual tasks. The gender differences lie not in levels of general intelligence but rather in the patterns of cognitive skills that men and women exhibit. These ability differences have been reported quite consistently by researchers (Halpern, 2000; Hampson & Kimura, 1992).

Figure 8.28 summarizes the most consistent differences, though most of them are relatively small. Men, on average, tend to outperform women slightly on certain spatial tasks; they are more accurate in target-directed skills, such as throwing and catching objects; and they tend to perform slightly better on tests of mathematical reasoning. Women, on average, perform better on tests of perceptual speed, verbal fluency, mathematical calculation, and precise manual tasks requiring fine motor

➤ 46. What are the major differences between men and women in cognitive skills? What biological and environmental factors might be responsible for them?

Problem-solving tasks favoring women

Women tend to perform better than men on tests of perceptual speed, in which people must rapidly identify matching items—for example, pairing the house on the far left with its twin:

In addition, women remember whether an object, or a series of objects, has been displaced:

On some tests of ideational fluency, for example, those in which people must list objects that are the same color, and on tests of verbal fluency, in which participants must list words that begin with the same letter, women also outperform men:

L _ _ _	Limp, Livery, Love, Laser, Liquid, Low, Like, Lag, Live, Lug, Light, Lift, Liver, Lime, Leg, Load, Lap, Lucid ...

Women do better on precision manual tasks—that is, those involving fine-motor coordination—such as placing the pegs in holes on a board:

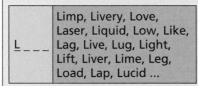

And women do better than men on mathematical calculation tests:

77	14 x 3 – 17 + 52
43	2 (15 + 3) + 12 – 15/3

Problem-solving tasks favoring men

Men tend to perform better than women on certain spatial tasks. They do well on tests that involve mentally rotating an object or manipulating it in some fashion, such as imagining turning this three-dimensional object:

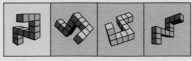

or determining where the hole punched in a folded piece of paper will fall when the paper is unfolded:

Men also are more accurate than women in target-directed motor skills, such as guiding or intercepting projectiles:

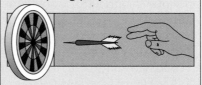

They do better on disembedding tests, in which they have to find a simple shape, such as the one on the left, once it is hidden within a more complex figure:

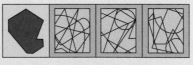

And men tend to do better than women on tests of mathematical reasoning:

1,100	If only 60 percent of seedlings will survive, how many must be planted to obtain 660 trees?

FIGURE 8.28 Gender differences in cognitive abilities reported in the scientific literature.

Source: Kimura, 1992; reprinted by permision.

coordination (Collins & Kimura, 1997). Keep in mind, however, that men and women also vary considerably among themselves in all of these skills, and the performance distributions of males and females overlap considerably.

Explanations for these gender differences have emphasized both biological and environmental factors. The environmental explanations typically focus on the socialization experiences that males and females have as they grow up, especially the kinds of sex-typed activities that boys and girls are steered into (Crawford & Chaffin, 1997). Until relatively recently, for example, boys were far more likely to play sports that involve throwing and catching balls, which might help account for their general superiority in this ability.

Biological explanations have increasingly focused on the effects of hormones on the developing brain. These influences begin shortly after conception when, during a critical period, the sex hormones establish sexual differentiation. The hormonal effects go far beyond reproductive characteristics, however. They also alter brain organization and appear to extend to a variety of behavioral differences between men and women, including aggression and problem-solving approaches (Becker et al., 1992). One intriguing finding is that fluctuations in women's hormonal levels during the menstrual cycle are related to fluctuations in task performance. When women are high in the female hormone estrogen, they perform better on some of the "feminine" abilities in Figure 8.28, while showing declines in performance on some of the "male" ones (Kimura, 1992; Moody, 1997).

Beliefs, Expectations, and Cognitive Performance

Cognitive abilities are not the only mental determinants of how well people perform on intellectual and academic measures. Beliefs are also very important. Our beliefs about others' capabilities can affect how we respond to them. For example, teachers' beliefs that a particular child has hidden potential (or, alternatively, has intellectual limitations) may affect the amount of attention and effort expended with that child, affecting the development of cognitive skills (Rosenthal, 1985).

Even more important at times than what others believe are our own self-beliefs. These beliefs are like unquestioned commands, telling us who we are and what we can and cannot do. Can self-beliefs and widely held social beliefs about groups we identify with affect performance on cognitive tasks? A new line of research, described in the *Research Close-Up*, suggests that stereotypes about the capabilities of minorities and women may indeed affect their performance.

> 47. How do beliefs about self and others influence cognitive performance?

> 48. What is stereotype threat, and how does it operate? How has it been shown to affect academic performance?

RESEARCH CLOSE-UP

Gender and Racial Stereotypes, Self-Concept, and Cognitive Performance

▶ Background

Our self-concept is based on numerous experiences that convey to us who we are, how valued we are, and what we are capable of achieving in our lives. Some of this information comes from observing the consequences of our own behavior. But our self-concept can also be influenced by our membership in racial and gender groups. If certain stereotypes are widely associated with these groups, we may incorporate them into our self-concept. Once accepted, these self-beliefs may push us to behave in a way that is consistent with our self-concept. But even if not incorporated into the self, group members could believe that certain behaviors on their part would confirm the negative stereotype in the minds of others. Such beliefs could produce what social psychologist Claude Steele terms **stereotype threat** and evoke anxiety that undermines performance. To test this hypothesis, Steele

—Continued

and his coworkers assessed the academic performance effects of evoking two widely held stereotypes—that Blacks are less academically able than Whites and that women have less mathematical ability than men do.

▶ Method

Two studies were conducted with students at Stanford University (Spencer et al., 1999; Steele & Aronson, 1995). In the first, men and women who were good in math were given a difficult mathematics exam whose items were taken from the advanced Graduate Record Examination. Participants were randomly assigned to one of two experimental conditions designed to either activate the stereotype or not. Participants in the *stereotype-relevant* condition were told that the test generally showed sex differences (expected to activate the stereotype of women being inferior to men in math). In the other condition, the students were told that scores on the test showed no sex differences. The dependent variable was the students' scores on the math problems.

In the second study, African American and Caucasian American students were tested on the most difficult items from the Graduate Record Examination Verbal test. Again, there were two experimental conditions, this time varying the racial relevance of the test. In one condition, the students were told that the test was a measure of intelligence (expected to activate the stereotype of African Americans as being less intelligent). In the other condition, the students were told that the items were part of a laboratory task that was unrelated to general intellectual ability.

▶ Results

The results of the two experiments, shown in Figure 8.29, were strikingly similar. In the first (Figure 8.29a), women and men performed at an equivalent level on the math problems when they were told there were no sex differences on the test. However, the picture changed dramatically when the task was made relevant to the gender stereotype. Women's performance dropped and men's performance increased, producing a marked performance difference between the two sexes. In Figure 8.29b, we see a similar pattern of results when the racial stereotype was made relevant to the task. African American students performed more poorly than Caucasians when it was implied that test performance was influenced by intellectual level, but there were no racial differences in performance when students were told that the task was not affected by level of mental ability.

▶ Critical Analysis

This research dramatically illustrates how stereotype-based aspects of the self-concept can affect behavior, in this case, cognitive performance. Steele (1997) believes that in the stereotype-relevant conditions, the threat of doing poorly on the test and being "branded" as a math-deficient woman or an academically inferior African American aroused anxiety that lowered their performance.

The results have broad societal implications and might help explain the fact that over the course of their academic

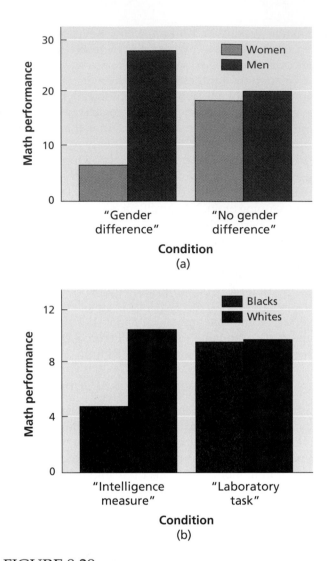

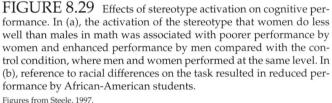

FIGURE 8.29 Effects of stereotype activation on cognitive performance. In (a), the activation of the stereotype that women do less well than males in math was associated with poorer performance by women and enhanced performance by men compared with the control condition, where men and women performed at the same level. In (b), reference to racial differences on the task resulted in reduced performance by African-American students.

Figures from Steele, 1997.

careers, women exhibit less inclination to pursue mathematics, even though, on average, they are slightly superior to men in mathematical calculation skills (Collins & Kimura, 1997; Lee, 1998). Perhaps stereotype threat also helps account for the fact that African American children become progressively less identified with and invested in academics as they progress through school, and many drop out altogether (Major et al., 1998). In both cases, the sex and racial ability differences are slight to nonexistent when the children first enter school. What happens thereafter as females and minorities confront (and perhaps come to believe) the stereotypes about their mental abilities may be an important environmental determinant of their performance.

Source: Claude M. Steele, 1997. A threat in the air: How stereotypes shape intellectual identity and performance. *American Psychologist, 52,* 613–629.

Extremes of Intelligence

Because of the many genetic and environmental influences on intelligence, there are individuals at both ends of the intelligence distribution who have exceptional mental abilities. At the low end are those labeled mentally retarded or cognitively disabled; at the upper end are the intellectually gifted.

The Cognitively Disabled

Approximately 3 to 5 percent of the U.S. population, or about 10 million people, are classified as mentally retarded, or cognitively disabled. The American Psychiatric Association has devised a four-level classification system that characterizes cognitive disability as mild, moderate, severe, and profound on the basis of IQ scores. Table 8.7 describes these classifications. As you can see, the vast majority are mildly disabled, obtaining IQs between about 50 and 70. Most of the mildly disabled are capable of living in the mainstream of society, given appropriate support. They are capable of marrying and holding jobs. Progressively greater environmental support is needed as we move toward the profoundly disabled range, where institutional care is usually required.

Mildly disabled children can attend school, but they have difficulties with tasks requiring reading, writing, memory, and mathematical computation. Many of their difficulties result from poorly developed problem-solving strategies. They often have difficulties in reasoning, planning, and evaluating feedback from their efforts.

Cognitive disability has a variety of causes, some genetic, some due to other biological factors, and some environmental. About 25 percent of cases have known biological causes. More than a hundred different genetic

> 49. What are the behavioral capabilities of mildly disabled people?

TABLE 8.7	ADAPTIVE CAPABILITIES OF COGNITIVELY CHALLENGED PEOPLE OVER THE LIFE SPAN		
		Characteristics From Birth to Adulthood	
Category	Percent of Retarded Population	Birth through Five	Six through Twenty	Twenty-one and Over
Mild 50–70 IQ	85%	Often not noticed as delayed by casual observer but is slower to walk, feed him- or herself, and talk than most children.	Can acquire practical skills and master reading and arithmetic to a third- to sixth-grade level with special education. Can be guided toward social conformity.	Can usually achieve adequate social, vocational, and self-maintenance skills; may need occasional guidance and support when under unusual social or economic stress.
Moderate 35–50 IQ	10%	Noticeable delays in motor development, especially in speech; responds to training in various self-help activities.	Can learn simple communication, elementary health and safety habits, and simple manual skills; does not progress in functional reading or arithmetic.	Can perform simple tasks under sheltered conditions; participate in simple recreation; can travel alone in familiar places; usually incapable of self-maintenance.
Severe 20–35 IQ	4%	Marked delay in motor development; little or no communication skill; may respond to training in elementary self-help, such as self-feeding.	Usually walks, barring specific disability; has some understanding of speech and some response; can profit from systematic habit training.	Can conform to daily routines and repetitive activities; needs continuing direction and supervision in protective environment.
Profound below 20 IQ	1%	Gross disability; minimal capacity for functioning in sensorimotor areas; needs nursing care.	Obvious delays in all areas of development; shows basic emotional responses; may respond to skillful training in use of legs, hands, and jaws; needs close supervision.	May walk, need nursing care, have primitive speech; usually benefits from regular physical activity; incapable of self-maintenance.

Source: American Pyschiatric Associaton, 1994.

causes of retardation have been identified (Shaffer, 1989). For example, Down syndrome (formerly called mongolism), which is characterized by mild to severe mental retardation, is caused by an abnormal division of the 21st chromosome pair. Retardation can also be caused by accidents at birth, such as severe deprivation of oxygen (anoxia), and by diseases contracted from the mother during pregnancy, such as syphilis and fetal alcohol syndrome. Despite this range of potential biological causes, however, 75 to 80 percent of cases lack a clear biological cause. These cases may be due to undetectable brain damage, extreme environmental deprivation, or a combination of the two.

In the United States, federal law requires that cognitively disabled children, who were formerly segregated into special education classes, be given individualized instruction in the "least restrictive environment." This has resulted in a practice called *mainstreaming,* or inclusion programs, which allows many cognitively challenged children to attend school in regular classrooms and experience a more normal peer environment (Gaylord-Ross, 1990).

The Intellectually Gifted

Like children at the other end of the competence continuum, gifted children often need special educational opportunities. They may become bored in regular classrooms and even drop out of school if they are not sufficiently challenged (Fetterman, 1988).

Like the cognitively disabled, the gifted are often the victims of stereotypes that depict them as eccentric and socially maladjusted. One of the first studies to challenge this stereotype was conducted by Lewis Terman, who helped develop the Stanford-Binet test. He identified some 1,500 California children who had an average IQ of 150 and began an extensive study of them that has continued for over 70 years. Terman and other researchers found these children to be above average not only in intelligence but also in height, weight, strength, physical health, emotional adjustment, and social maturity. They continued to exhibit high levels of adjustment throughout their adolescent and adult years. By midlife, they had authored 92 books, 2,200 scientific articles, and 235 patents. Their marriages tended to be happy and successful, and they seemed well adjusted psychologically. In essence, the gifted children became gifted and happy adults (Sears, 1977).

It would be a mistake to assume that high intelligence alone will result in the kind of eminence that we term "genius." To make enduring contributions to one's field, people are likely to need, in addition to high intelligence, exceptionally good creative problem-solving skills and high motivation to develop their gifts and to perform at an extraordinary level (Renzulli, 1986).

As we have seen, intelligent thinking and behavior has many causal factors. Some of these factors are summarized in Figure 8.30.

➤ 50. What did Terman's longitudinal study of gifted children reveal about their success as adults?

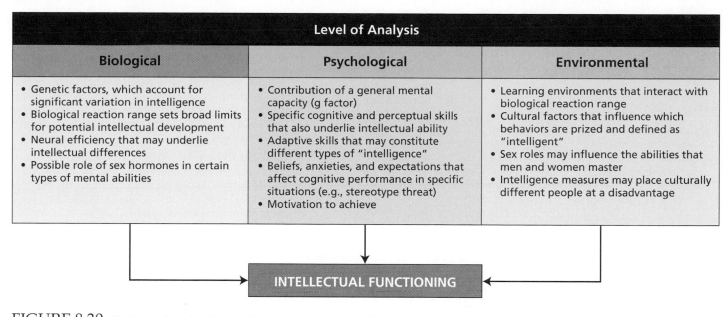

Level of Analysis		
Biological	**Psychological**	**Environmental**
• Genetic factors, which account for significant variation in intelligence • Biological reaction range sets broad limits for potential intellectual development • Neural efficiency that may underlie intellectual differences • Possible role of sex hormones in certain types of mental abilities	• Contribution of a general mental capacity (g factor) • Specific cognitive and perceptual skills that also underlie intellectual ability • Adaptive skills that may constitute different types of "intelligence" • Beliefs, anxieties, and expectations that affect cognitive performance in specific situations (e.g., stereotype threat) • Motivation to achieve	• Learning environments that interact with biological reaction range • Cultural factors that influence which behaviors are prized and defined as "intelligent" • Sex roles may influence the abilities that men and women master • Intelligence measures may place culturally different people at a disadvantage

INTELLECTUAL FUNCTIONING

FIGURE 8.30 Understanding the Causes of Behavior: Factors that influence intellectual functioning.

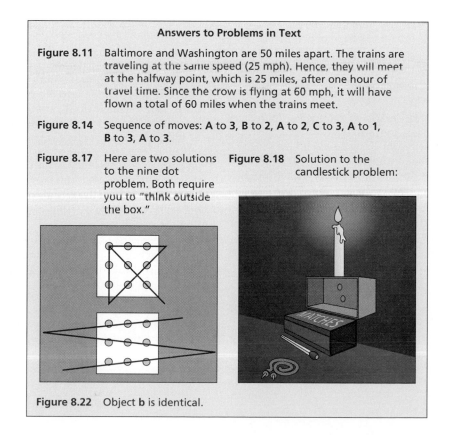

Answers to Problems in Text

Figure 8.11 Baltimore and Washington are 50 miles apart. The trains are traveling at the same speed (25 mph). Hence, they will meet at the halfway point, which is 25 miles, after one hour of travel time. Since the crow is flying at 60 mph, it will have flown a total of 60 miles when the trains meet.

Figure 8.14 Sequence of moves: **A to 3, B to 2, A to 2, C to 3, A to 1, B to 3, A to 3**.

Figure 8.17 Here are two solutions to the nine dot problem. Both require you to "think outside the box."

Figure 8.18 Solution to the candlestick problem:

Figure 8.22 Object **b** is identical.

▼▼

CHAPTER SUMMARY

Language

- Human language is symbolic, structured, and generative. The surface structure of a language refers to how symbols are combined; the deep structure refers to the underlying meaning of the symbols. Language elements are hierarchically arranged from the phoneme to morphemes, and on to words, phrases, and sentences.

- In infancy, babies emit all the phonemes that exist in the languages of the world. At about 6 months of age, babbling sounds narrow to include only the languages spoken by others in the environment. By ages 4 to 5, most children have learned the basic grammatical rules for combining words into meaningful sentences.

- Language development seems to depend heavily on innate mechanisms that permit the learning and production of language, provided that the child is exposed to an appropriate linguistic environment. There may be a sensitive period for exposure to language that extends from early childhood to puberty. Thereafter normal linguistic development does not occur.

- When both languages are well learned, bilingualism has been shown to have positive influences on cognitive performance. A second language is most easily mastered and fluently spoken if it is learned during the sensitive period of childhood.

- Language does not appear to determine thought, but it does influence what and how effectively people think. Expansion of vocabulary allows people to encode and process information in more sophisticated ways.

- Concepts are classes that share certain characteristics. Many concepts are based on prototypes, the most typical and familiar members of a class. How much something resembles the prototype determines whether the concept is applied to it. Propositional thought involves the use of concepts in the form of statements having subjects and predicates.

- The issue of whether animals can acquire human language is controversial. Animals clearly can communicate. There is little doubt that apes are capable of learning, combining, and communicating symbols at a level similar to that of a young child, but skeptics question whether they can learn syntax and generate novel ideas.

Reasoning

- In deductive reasoning, we reason from general principles to a conclusion about a specific case. Inductive reasoning in-volves reasoning from a set of specific facts or observations to a general principle. Deduction is regarded as the strongest and most valid form of reasoning, because the conclusion cannot be false if the premises are true. Inductive reasoning can produce conclusions that have a high likelihood of being valid, but cannot yield certainty.

- Unsuccessful deductive reasoning can result from (1) failure to select the appropriate information; (2) failure to apply the appropriate deductive reasoning rules, particularly in novel situations; and (3) belief bias, the tendency to abandon logical rules in favor of personal beliefs.

Problem Solving

- Reason-based problem solving proceeds through a number of steps: (1) understanding the nature of the problem, (2) establishing initial hypotheses or potential solutions, (3) testing the solutions against existing evidence to rule out hypotheses that do not apply, and (4) evaluating results.

- Problem-solving schemas are shortcut methods for solving specialized classes of problems. They are stored in long-term memory and can help overcome the limitations of working memory. Expertise in a given area consists largely in having acquired a range of successful problem-solving schemas through training and practical experience, as well as knowing when to apply each schema.

- Algorithms are formulas or procedures that guarantee correct solutions. Heuristics are general strategies that may or may not provide correct solutions. Means-ends analysis is one commonly used heuristic. Several biases that can produce faulty conclusions involve the misapplication of heuristics. The representativeness heuristic is the tendency to judge evidence according to whether it is consistent with an existing concept or schema. The availability heuristic is the tendency to base conclusions and probability judgments on what is readily available in memory. Humans have a marked confirmation bias, a tendency to look for facts to support hypotheses rather than to disprove them.

- Problem solving is often facilitated by the application of learned schemas. In some situations, however, divergent thinking is needed for generating novel ideas or variations on ideas. Functional fixedness, which can blind us to new ways of using an object or procedure, can interfere with creative problem solving. In some cases, a period of incubation permits problem solving to go on at a subconscious level while giving the problem solver psychological distance from the problem.

Intelligence and Its Measurement

- Intelligence is a construct that refers to the ability to acquire knowledge, to think and reason effectively, and to deal adaptively with the environment.

- The IQ is a relative measure that indicates where the person falls within the normal distribution of IQ scores derived in the process of standardization. The concept of mental age introduced by Binet is no longer used.

- The Wechsler scales, separately developed for adults, children, and preschoolers, are the most widely used individual intelligence tests. They consist of a series of verbal and performance subscales that yield separate Verbal and Performance IQs, as well as a Full-Scale IQ.

- An aptitude test is designed to measure potential for future learning and performance, whereas achievement tests are designed to measure what one has already learned. In practice, most intelligence tests measure both aptitude and achievement.

- Among the standards that are required for a psychological test are reliability, or consistency of measurement. Such consistency can refer to consistency over time (test-retest reliability), consistency of measurement by items within a scale (internal consistency), and agreement between scorers (interjudge reliability). Standardization involves both standard items and procedures for obtaining scores and the development of norms. Validity refers to whether the test is measuring what it is intended to measure, such as a theoretical construct (construct validity). Predictive validity refers to how well test scores predict other outcomes, or criteria. IQ is a better predictor of academic success than of job success, which often requires abilities that are not measured by the tests.

The Nature of Intelligence

- The psychometric approach attempts to map the structure of intellect and establish how many different classes of mental ability underlie test performance. A newer approach, the cognitive processes approach, focuses on the specific thought processes that underlie mental competencies.

- Spearman believed intelligence is determined both by specific cognitive abilities and a general intelligence (g) factor that constituted the core of intelligence. Thurstone disagreed, viewing intelligence as a set of specific abilities. Thurstone's position is best supported by observed distinctions between verbal and visual-spatial abilities.

- Cattell and Horn have differentiated between crystallized intelligence, based on the ability to apply previously learned knowledge to current problems, and fluid intelligence, the ability to deal with novel problem-solving situations for which experience does not provide a solution. Cattell and Horn argue that over the life span, we show a progressive shift from using fluid to using crystallized intelligence as we attain wisdom.

- Gardner has suggested that there are separate and distinct forms of intelligence, including linguistic, mathematical, spatial, musical, bodily-kinesthetic, and personal intelligence. Emotional intelligence refers to people's ability to read and respond appropriately to others' emotions, to motivate themselves, and to be aware of and in control of their emotions.

- Cognitive process theories of intelligence have focused on the elementary information-processing abilities that contribute to intelligence. Sternberg's theory of intelligence includes a componential subtheory that addresses the specific cognitive processes that underlie intelligent behavior. Recent physiological evidence suggests that the brains of intelligent people may function more efficiently.

Heredity, Environment, and Intelligence

- Intelligence is determined by interacting hereditary and environmental factors. Heredity establishes a reaction range with upper and lower limits for intellectual potential. Environment affects what point within that range will be reached.

- Cultural and racial differences in intelligence exist (though they may be narrowing), but the relative contributions of genetic and environmental factors are still in question. Evidence exists for both genetic and environmental determinants.

- Although the differences are not large, men tend as a group to score higher than women on certain spatial and mathematical reasoning tasks. Women perform slightly better than men on tests of perceptual speed, verbal fluency, mathematical calculation, and fine motor coordination. Both environmental and biological bases of such differences have been suggested. Stereotype threat is one potential environmental factor for both sex-based and racial performance differences.

Extremes of Intelligence

- Cognitive disability can be caused by a number of factors. Biological causes are identified in only about 25 percent of cases. Cognitive disability can range from mild to profound. The vast majority of disabled individuals are able to function in the mainstream of society, given appropriate support.

- Lewis Terman's study of gifted children indicated that these individuals tended to be well adjusted and to have happy and productive adulthoods.

▼▼

KEY TERMS AND CONCEPTS*

achievement test (341)

algorithm (332)

aptitude test (341)

availability heuristic (334)

belief bias (329)

cognitive process theories (348)

concept (323)

confirmation bias (335)

construct validity (343)

content validity (343)

crystallized intelligence (346)

deductive reasoning (327)

deep structure (318)

displacement (317)

divergent thinking (336)

emotional intelligence (347)

factor analysis (345)

fluid intelligence (346)

functional fixedness (336)

heuristics (332)

imaginal thought (323)

incubation (336)

inductive reasoning (328)

intelligence (337)

intelligence quotient (IQ) (338)

interjudge reliability (343)

internal consistency (343)

knowledge-acquisition
    components (349)

language (317)

linguistic relativity hypothesis (322)

means-ends analysis (332)

mental representations (316)

mental age (338)

mental set (331)

metacomponents (348)

morpheme (318)

motoric thought (323)

normal distribution (344)

norms (344)

performance components (349)

phoneme (318)

predictive validity (343)

primary mental abilities (345)

problem-solving schemas (331)

proposition (323)

propositional thought (323)

prototype (323)

psychological test (342)

psychometrics (344)

reaction range (351)

reliability (342)

representativeness heuristic (333)

savant (347)

semantics (318)

standardization (344)

stereotype threat (355)

subgoal analysis (332)

surface structure (317)

syntax (317)

telegraphic speech (320)

test-retest reliability (342)

triarchic theory of intelligence (348)

validity (343)

* Each term has been boldfaced in the text on the page indicated in parentheses.

▼▼

APPLYING YOUR KNOWLEDGE

1. "Tom eats hamburgers. Pizza eats Tom." Which statement about these two sentences is correct?
   a) Both sentences are semantically correct.
   b) Only one sentence has correct syntax.
   c) Neither sentence is semantically correct.
   d) Both sentences have correct syntax.

2. A mother instructs her son to tell her neighbor, "I'll be home at four, but I'll be out until then." He tells the neighbor, "Mother will be gone most of the day, but she'll be back by four." The son clearly remembered the
   a) surface structure, but not the deep structure
   b) syntax of the message, but not the semantics
   c) deep structure, but not the surface structure
   d) phonemes, but not the morphemes

3. Shelley is trying to develop a theoretical principle. She considers the facts she knows to be true of the phenomenon she is studying. She then tries to reason from these facts to a conclusion about causal factors. Shelley is engaging in
   a) inductive reasoning
   b) propositional reasoning
   c) syllogistic inference
   d) deductive reasoning

4. You ask twenty of your acquaintances to rate the likelihood of the following statements: (a) There will be a flood in southern California; (b) There will be an earthquake in California that causes a flood. Sixteen of your participants

choose statement b as more likely. Their decision is _____ and shows the use of _____.
a) correct; inductive reasoning
b) incorrect; the representativeness heuristic
c) correct; the availability heuristic
d) correct; confirmation bias

5. A middle-aged woman tells you, "The chances are very good that I will die of breast cancer. Three of my friends have been diagnosed with it in the past two years." Her prediction has probably been influenced by
a) availability.
b) incubation.
c) representativeness.
d) confirmation bias.

6. After hearing a lecture on abnormal psychology, John became sure that he had a particular personality disorder. Thereafter he focused on every nuance of his behavior and thinking that was consistent with that disorder and ignored his "normal" behaviors. John was exhibiting
a) means-ends analysis
b) heuristic reasoning
c) confirmation bias
d) functional fixedness

7. Jason takes a Wechsler intelligence scale and receives a verbal IQ of 115 on the basis of the scores obtained by hundreds of people his age. This ability to derive Jason's IQ is due to which characteristic of the Wechsler test?
a) reliability
b) construct validity
c) internal consistency
d) standardization

8. Melanie has to do a major science project for school. She starts out by planning the steps of her project and devises a highly creative method for solving a problem. Melanie is using which component of Sternberg's triarchic model?
a) performance components
b) metacomponents
c) knowledge-acquisition components
d) semantic memory components

9. Consider a set of identical twins that is separated at birth and raised in different homes. Jack is raised in a stimulating and nurturing home, whereas Mack is reared in a cold, dull family environment. By adolescence, Jack has an IQ of 120 and Mack an IQ of 105. This difference best illustrates
a) reaction range
b) heritability
c) the role of genetic factors
d) lack of a genetic component to IQ

10. A psychologist wants to develop an intelligence test that is not affected by cultural factors. His test has a series of novel spatial puzzle problems that are unlike anything people in any culture have encountered. His test would best be described as measuring
a) analytical intelligence
b) practical intelligence
c) performance components
d) fluid intelligence

For additional quizzing and a variety of interactive resources, visit the book's Online Learning Center at www.mhhe.com/passer.

MOTIVATION

One can never consent to creep when one feels an impulse to soar.
— *Helen Keller*

9

CHAPTER OUTLINE

9

▼▼▼▼▼▼▼▼▼▼▼▼▼▼▼▼▼▼▼▼▼▼▼▼▼▼▼▼▼▼▼▼▼

Born in Scotland, Evelyn Glennie is one of the world's foremost percussionists (Figure 9.1). She began studying percussion at age twelve, attended London's Royal Academy of Music, received its most prestigious award, and won a Grammy Award a few years later. Symphony orchestras around the globe invite her to perform as a guest artist.

Becoming a consummate musician takes tremendous motivation and skill under any circumstance, but Glennie also is profoundly deaf. She hears sounds at a reduced volume and their quality is poor. To her, a phone ring sounds like crackling and she must lip-read to understand speech. As a young student, Glennie stood with her hands against the classroom wall, listening and sensing vibrations while her music teacher played. Her husband explains:

> Eventually, Evelyn managed to distinguish the rough pitch of notes by associating where on her body she felt the sound with the sense of perfect pitch she had before losing her hearing. The low sounds she feels mainly in her legs and feet and high sounds might be particular places on her face, neck, and chest. (Malcangi, 1997)

FIGURE 9.1 Evelyn Glennie is a world-renowned percussionist. Her perseverance and years of training exemplify the human striving to achieve.

To others, Evelyn Glennie's deafness makes her extraordinary achievements seem all the more so. But to her, hearing loss is just a fact of life. Once, when a reporter kept dwelling on her deafness, Glennie replied: "If you want to know about deafness, you should interview an audiologist. My specialty is music" (Malcangi, 1997).

▼▼

Sara gained 15 pounds during her first year of college, thanks to late night pizza-and-beer parties. She dieted and returned to her normal weight of 115 pounds. Proud of her success, 5'1" Sara continued dieting and lost 25 more pounds. Her menstrual period stopped, but she was so afraid of gaining weight that she could not bring herself to eat normally. Finally, weighing 80 pounds, she was hospitalized and began psychotherapy.

Lisa also gained weight during her freshman year and felt like a "big fat failure." Then she began to eat lightly during the day, but binge at night on pizza and cookies. After bingeing she waited for the laxatives to kick in—the fifty laxatives she usually ate along with ten diet pills during the prior breakfast. Lisa sought help after a laxative-consuming friend suffered a heart attack at age twenty (Hubbard et al., 1999).

The term "motivation" often triggers images of people who, like Evelyn Glennie, persevere to attain their dreams and stretch the boundaries of human achievement. But to psychologists, motivational issues are broader. What motivates eating, sexual behavior, thrill seeking, and affiliation? What motivated Sarah's self-starvation? **Motivation** is a process that influences the direction, persistence, and vigor of goal-directed behavior. The word *motivation* derives from the Latin term meaning "to move," and psychologists who study motivation identify factors that move us toward our goals, whether they be obtaining food, a mate, success, or even peace and quiet.

❯ PERSPECTIVES ON MOTIVATION

Psychology's diverse theoretical perspectives view motivation through different lenses. Let's examine some of their basic motivational concepts.

Instinct Theory and Modern Evolutionary Psychology

Darwin's theory of evolution inspired early psychological views that instincts motivate much of our behavior. An **instinct** (also called a *fixed action pattern*) is an inherited characteristic, common to all members of a species, that automatically produces a particular response when the organism is exposed to a particular stimulus. William James (1890) proposed about three dozen human instincts, and by the 1920s researchers had proposed thousands (Atkinson, 1964).

Human instinct theories faded because there was little evidence to support them and they often relied on circular reasoning. Why are people greedy? Because greed is an instinct. How do we know that greed is an instinct? Because people are greedy. This explains nothing. Today scientists examine hereditary contributions to human motivation more productively. By conducting twin and adoption studies, behavior geneticists seek to establish how strongly heredity

➤ 1. According to evolutionary psychologists, how does the concept of adaptive significance help us understand human motivation?

accounts for differences among people in many aspects of motivated behavior, such as tendencies to be outgoing or antisocial (Neiderhiser et al., 1999).

Modern evolutionary psychologists propose that many "psychological" motives have evolutionary underpinnings expressed through the actions of genes (Buss, 2000; Cosmides & Tooby, 1987). From this perspective, the *adaptive significance* of behavior is a key to understanding motivation. For example, why are we such social creatures? Presumably, affiliation produced survival advantages—such as sharing resources and better protection against predators—that afforded our ancestors a greater opportunity to pass their genes on to successive generations. Over the ages the genes of "affiliative people" made up an increasing part of the human gene pool, and we became biologically predisposed to be social rather than reclusive.

Homeostasis and Drive Theory

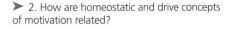

> 2. How are homeostatic and drive concepts of motivation related?

Your body's biological systems are delicately balanced to ensure survival. For example, when you are hot your body automatically tries to cool itself by perspiring. When you are cold, your body generates warmth by shivering. In 1932, Walter Cannon proposed the concept of **homeostasis,** a state of internal physiological equilibrium that the body strives to maintain.

Maintaining homeostasis requires a sensory mechanism for detecting changes in the internal environment, a response system that can restore equilibrium, and a control center that receives information from the sensors and activates the response system (Figure 9.2). The control center functions somewhat like the thermostat in a furnace or air-conditioning unit. Once the thermostat is set at a fixed temperature, or *set point*, the sensors detect significant temperature changes in either direction. The control unit responds by turning on the furnace or air conditioner until the sensor indicates that the set point temperature has been restored, and then turns it off. Homeostatic regulation also can involve learned behaviors. When we're hot we not only perspire, but also may seek a shady place or deliciously cool drink.

According to Clark Hull's (1943, 1951) influential **drive theory** of motivation, physiological disruptions to homeostasis produce *drives*, states of internal tension that motivate an organism to behave in ways that reduce this tension. Drives such as hunger and thirst arise from tissue deficits (e.g., lack of food and water) and provide a source of energy that pushes an organism into action. Hull, a prominent learning theorist, proposed that reducing drives is the ultimate goal of motivated behavior.

Homeostatic models currently are applied to many aspects of motivation, such as the regulation of hunger, thirst, body temperature, weight, and sleep (Woods et al., 2000). But drive concepts are less influential than in the past. For one thing, people often behave in ways that seem to increase rather than reduce states of arousal, as when people skip meals in order to diet or flock to tension-generating horror movies.

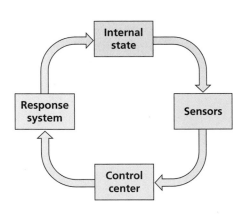

FIGURE 9.2 Your body's internal environment is regulated by homeostatic mechanisms. Sensors detect bodily changes and send this information to a control center, which in turn regulates a response system that restores bodily equilibrium.

Incentive and Expectancy Theories

> 3. According to expectancy × value theory, why might people respond differently to the same incentive?

Whereas drives are viewed as internal factors that "push" organisms into action, **incentives** represent environmental stimuli that "pull" an organism toward a goal. To a student, receiving a good grade can be an incentive for studying.

Incentive theories focus attention on external stimuli that motivate behavior, though historically the concepts of incentives and drives were often linked. Clark Hull (1943, 1951) argued that all reinforcement involves some kind of biological drive reduction (e.g., food is an incentive because it reduces the drive of hunger), but this view is no longer held.

Some learning theorists urged that we do away with the concept of motivation entirely. B. F. Skinner believed that psychologists need not muddy their thinking with unobservable concepts like "drives" and "motives" when they could study measurable variables like "hours of food deprivation." In Skinner's view, rather than attribute a student's poor performance to a "lack of motivation," teachers should modify the environment to provide the student with more effective reinforcers.

Why is it, however, that people often respond differently to the same incentive? Consider James, Lenora, and Harrison, students in a calculus class who have similar math aptitude. Yet James studies hard in hopes of getting an A, whereas Lenora and Harrison put in just enough effort to pass with a C.

According to the cognitive perspective, the answer lies in their thoughts about this situation. One cognitive approach, called **expectancy × value theory,** proposes that goal-directed behavior is jointly determined by two factors: the strength of the person's expectation that particular behaviors will lead to a goal, and the value the individual places on that goal—often called *incentive value* (Brehm & Self, 1989). These two factors are multiplied, producing the following equation: Motivation = *expectancy × incentive value*. James works hard because he believes that the more you study the greater the probability of getting an A, and he values an A highly. Lenora also believes that studying hard will lead to an A, but getting an A holds little value for her in this course. In contrast, Harrison values an A, but believes that because the tests are tricky, studying hard is unlikely to produce a high grade.

Can external incentives ever decrease motivation? Many cognitive theorists distinguish between **extrinsic motivation,** performing an activity to obtain an external reward or avoid punishment, and **intrinsic motivation,** performing an activity for its own sake—because you find it enjoyable or stimulating. According to *the overjustification hypothesis,* giving people extrinsic rewards to perform activities that they intrinsically enjoy may "overjustify" that behavior and reduce intrinsic motivation (Lepper et al., 1974). In essence, say supporters, if we begin to perceive that we are performing for the extrinsic rewards rather than for enjoyment, the rewards will turn "play" into "work" and it may be difficult to return to "play" if those rewards cease.

Overall, research indicates that extrinsic rewards reduce intrinsic motivation most strongly when they are tangible (e.g., prizes or money, rather than praise), given merely for performing a task (regardless of how well), and the performer expects rewards to be offered (Deci et al., 1999). But when extrinsic rewards such as praise are perceived as *informative*—as a means of positive feedback rather than as an attempt to control behavior—they can increase feelings of competence and intrinsic motivation.

Psychodynamic and Humanistic Theories

The psychodynamic and humanistic perspectives view motivation within a broader context of personality development and functioning, but take radically different approaches. Freud's (1923) psychoanalytic theory highlighted the motivational underworld. To Freud, much of our behavior results from a never-ending battle between unconscious impulses struggling for release and psychological defenses used to keep them under control. Energy from these unconscious motives—especially from instinctive sexual and aggressive drives—is often disguised and expressed through socially acceptable behaviors. Thus hidden aggressive impulses may fuel one's career as a trial attorney, businessperson, or athlete.

Although research offers little support for Freud's "dual-instinct" model, his work stimulated other psychodynamic theories that highlighted different needs, such as needs for self-esteem and relatedness to other people (Adler, 1927;

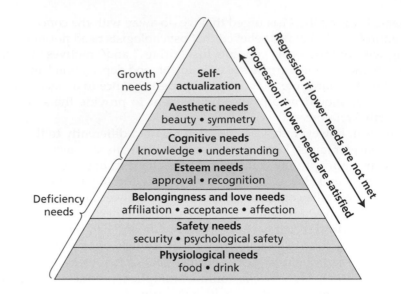

FIGURE 9.3 Maslow proposed that needs are arranged in a hierarchy. After meeting our more basic needs, we experience *need progression* and focus on needs at the next level. If a need at a lower level is no longer satisfied, we experience *need regression* and focus once again on meeting that lower-level need. Critics wonder, might people focus on belonging, love, esteem, and higher-level needs even when their physiological and safety needs are not met? What do you think?

Kohut, 1977). Today's diverse psychodynamic theories continue to emphasize that along with conscious mental processes, unconscious motives, and tensions guide how we act and feel (Westen, 1998). Experiments in cognitive psychology and neuroscience increasingly support this view, although as discussed in Chapter 5, cognitive models of the unconscious differ from psychodynamic ones (Bargh & Chartrand, 1999; Wenzlaff & Wegner, 2000).

➤ 4. Explain Maslow's concept of a need hierarchy. Do you agree with this model?

    Humanist Abraham Maslow believed that psychology's other perspectives ignored a key motive: our striving for personal growth. Maslow (1954) distinguished between *deficiency needs,* which are concerned with physical and social survival, and *growth needs,* which are uniquely human and motivate us to develop our potential. He proposed the concept of a **need hierarchy,** a progression of needs containing deficiency needs at the bottom and growth needs at the top (Figure 9.3). Once our basic physiological needs are satisfied, we focus on our needs for safety and security. After these needs are met, we turn our attention to needs at the next highest level, and so on. **Self-actualization** represents the need to fulfill our potential, and it is the ultimate human motive. To echo a U.S. Army recruiting slogan, self-actualization is striving to "be all that you can be."

    Critics question the validity of Maslow's need hierarchy and believe that the concept of "self-actualization" is vague (Heylighen, 1992). How does the hierarchy explain why prisoners of war endure torture rather than betray their comrades, or why millions of women live in constant hunger to be thin? Still, the model draws valuable attention to the human desire for growth, incorporates a wide range of psychological and biological motives, and has influenced thinking in diverse fields such as philosophy, education, and business (Muchinsky, 2000).

    In sum, each of these theoretical approaches raises provocative questions about human motivation and has strong proponents and critics, just as some perspectives no doubt resonate more closely than others with your own views about motivation. Taken together, they underscore the complexity of behavior and the value of studying it from multiple levels of analysis. We begin that analysis with one of our most basic motives: hunger.

〉 HUNGER AND WEIGHT REGULATION

If you could give up all food forever and satisfy your hunger and nutritional needs with a daily pill, would you? Eating is a necessity, but for many people it also is one of life's delicious pleasures. Thus while biology provides a "push" to eat, the anticipated and actual good taste of food offers a powerful "pull" (Bolles, 1980). Indeed, numerous biological, psychological, and environmental factors regulate our food intake.

The Physiology of Hunger

Eating and digestion supply the body with the fuel it needs to function and survive. **Metabolism** is the body's rate of energy (or caloric) utilization, and about two thirds of the energy we normally use goes to support *basal metabolism,* the resting, continuous metabolic work of body cells. Several mechanisms attempt to keep the body in energy homeostasis by regulating food intake (Kennedy, 1953; Woods et al., 2000). There are "short-term" signals that start meals by producing hunger and stop food intake by producing *satiety* (the state where we no longer feel hungry due to eating). Your body also monitors "long-term" signals based on how much body fat you have. These signals adjust appetite and metabolism to compensate for when you overeat or eat too little in the short term.

Before we describe some of these signals, consider three points. First, many students believe that hunger occurs when we begin to "run low on energy," and that we feel "full" when immediate energy supplies are restored (Assanand et al., 1998). Your body does monitor its immediate energy supplies, but this information interacts with other signals to regulate food intake. Thus hunger is not necessarily linked to immediate energy needs (Pinel, 1997; Woods et al., 1998). Second, homeostatic mechanisms are designed to *prevent* you from "running low" on energy in the first place. In evolutionary terms, an organism that does not eat until its energy supply starts to become low (in any absolute sense) would be at a serious survival disadvantage.

Finally, many researchers believe that there is a *set point*—an internal physiological standard—around which body weight (or more accurately, our fat mass) is regulated (Powley & Keesey, 1970). This view holds that if we overeat or eat too little, homeostatic mechanisms return us close to our original weight. The set point concept is well ingrained in popular culture, but some researchers believe it is flawed (Pinel, 1997). They propose that, as we gain or lose weight, homeostatic mechanisms kick in and make it harder to keep gaining or losing weight, but do not necessarily return us to our original weight. Over time, we may "settle in" at a new weight.

Signals That Start and Terminate a Meal

Is hunger produced by those familiar muscular contractions ("hunger pangs") of an empty stomach? In an early experiment, A. L. Washburn showcased a unique scientific talent: He swallowed a balloon. When it reached his stomach the balloon was inflated and hooked up to an amplifying device to record his stomach contractions. Washburn then pressed a key every time he felt hungry (Figure 9.4). The findings revealed that Washburn's stomach contractions did indeed *correspond* with subjective feelings of hunger (Cannon & Washburn, 1912). But did they *cause* the "experience" of hunger?

Surprisingly, other research indicates that "hunger pangs" do not depend on an empty stomach, or any stomach at all! Animals display hunger and satiety even if all nerves from their stomach to their brain are cut, and people who have had their stomach surgically removed for medical reasons continue to feel

〉 5. Describe some physiological signals that initiate hunger.

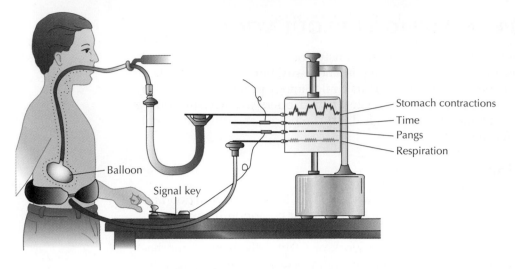

FIGURE 9.4 A. L. Washburn swallowed a balloon and inflated it in his stomach. A machine recorded stomach contractions by amplifying changes in the pressure on the balloon, and Washburn pressed a telegraph key every time he felt a hunger pang. Hunger pangs occurred when the stomach contracted. Based on Cannon and Washburn, 1912.

➤ 6. What physiological signals cause us to stop eating?

hungry and "full" (Brown & Wallace, 1980). Thus other signals must help trigger hunger.

When you eat, digestive enzymes break food down into various nutrients. One key nutrient is **glucose,** a simple sugar that is the body's (and especially the brain's) major source of immediately usable fuel. After a meal some glucose is transported into cells to provide energy, but a large portion is transferred into your liver and fat cells, where it is converted into other nutrients and stored for later use. Sensors in the hypothalamus and liver monitor blood glucose concentrations. When blood glucose levels decrease, the liver responds by converting stored nutrients back into glucose. This produces a drop-rise glucose pattern.

L. Arthur Campfield and his colleagues have found that humans and rats display a temporary drop-rise glucose pattern prior to experiencing hunger (Campfield & Smith, 1990; Campfield et al., 1996). This occurs not only when glucose levels fall and rise naturally (by about 10 percent), but also when they are manipulated experimentally. The meaning of this drop-rise pattern is not certain, but it may contain information that helps the brain regulate hunger (Campfield, 1997).

As we eat, several bodily signals combine and ultimately cause us to end our meal. *Stomach and intestinal distention* are "satiety signals" (Stricker & Verbalis, 1987). The walls of these organs stretch as food fills them up, sending nerve signals to the brain. This does not mean that the stomach literally has to be "full" for us to feel satiated. Nutritionally rich food seems to produce satiety more quickly than an equal volume of less nutritious food, suggesting that some satiety signals respond to food content.

Patients who have had their stomachs removed continue to experience satiety not only due to intestinal distention, but also due to chemical signals. The intestines respond to food by releasing several hormones—called *peptides*—that help terminate a meal. For example, **CCK (cholecystokinin)** is released into your bloodstream by the small intestine as food arrives from the stomach. It travels to the brain and stimulates receptors in several regions that decrease eating. Hungry animals injected with CCK will stop feeding or reduce the size of their meals, and humans who receive small doses of peptides report feeling full after eating less food (Gibbs et al., 1973; Konkle et al., 2000).

Signals That Regulate General Appetite and Weight

Fat cells are not passive storage sites for fat. Rather, they actively regulate food intake and weight by secreting **leptin,** a hormone that decreases appetite (Halaas et al., 1995). As we gain fat, more leptin is secreted into the blood and reaches the brain, where receptor sites on certain neurons detect it. These leptin signals influence neural pathways to decrease appetite and increase energy expenditure (Woods et al., 1998, 2000).

Leptin is a "background" signal. It does not make us feel "full" like CCK and other satiety signals that respond directly to food intake during a meal. Instead, leptin may regulate appetite by increasing the potency of these other signals (Woods et al., 1998). Thus as we gain fat and secrete more leptin, we tend to eat less because these mealtime satiety factors make us feel full sooner. As we lose fat and secrete less leptin, it takes more food and a greater accumulation of satiety signals to make us feel full. In essence, high leptin levels may tell the brain "There is plenty of fat tissue, so it's time to eat less."

Evidence for leptin's important role grew out of research with genetically obese mice (Coleman, 1978; Zhang et al., 1994). A gene called the *ob* gene (*ob* = obesity) normally directs fat cells to produce leptin, but mice with an *ob* gene mutation lack leptin. As they gain weight the brain does not receive this "curb your appetite" signal, and the mice overeat and become obese. Daily leptin injections reduce their appetite and increase their energy expenditure, and the mice become thinner. Another strain of obese mice produces ample leptin, but because of a mutation in a different gene (the *db* gene), their brain receptors are insensitive to leptin (Chen et al., 1996; Halaas et al., 1995). The "curb your appetite" signal is there, but they can't detect it and become obese. Injecting these mice with leptin does not reduce their food intake and weight.

Are these specific *ob* and *db* gene mutations a major source of human obesity? Probably not, for both genetic conditions seem to be rare among humans (Clement, 1999). However, when they do occur, these conditions are associated with extreme obesity, suggesting the importance of normal leptin functioning in human weight regulation. Might leptin injections be the "magic bullet" that helps most obese people lose weight? Unfortunately, there is reason for doubt, because obese people already have ample leptin in their blood due to their fat mass (Jequier & Tappy, 1999; Ravussin & Gautier, 1999). For presently unknown reasons, their brain appears to be "resistant" to that information.

Brain Mechanisms

Many parts of the brain—ranging from the primitive brain stem to the lofty cerebral cortex—play a role in regulating hunger and eating (Logue, 1991). But is there a "master control center"? Early experiments pointed to two regions in the hypothalamus (Stellar, 1954). Areas near the side, called the *lateral hypothalamus (LH)*, seemed to be a "hunger on" center (Figure 9.5a). Electrically stimulating a rat's LH would cause it to start eating, and lesioning (damaging or destroying) the LH would cause it to refuse to eat, even to the point of starvation (Anand & Brobeck, 1951).

In contrast, structures in the lower-middle area, called the *ventromedial hypothalamus* (VMH), seemed to be a "hunger off" center. Electrically stimulating the VMH caused even a hungry rat to stop eating, and lesioning the VMH produced gluttons—like the rat in Figure 9.5b—who ate frequently and doubled or tripled their body weight (Hetherington & Ranson, 1942). Medical case studies of people with damage to these hypothalamic areas also found that normal weight regulation was disrupted (Gazzaniga et al., 1979).

As scientists explored further, they learned that although the LH and VMH played a role in hunger regulation, they were not really "hunger on" and

➤ 7. Explain how leptin regulates appetite. How did scientists learn about leptin's role?

➤ 8. What evidence suggested that the LH and VMH were hunger "on" and "off" centers? What evidence suggests otherwise?

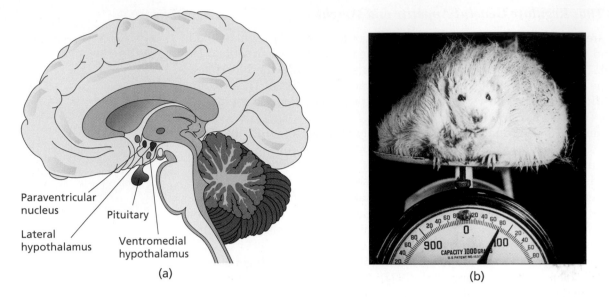

Paraventricular
nucleus   Pituitary

Lateral
hypothalamus   Ventromedial
hypothalamus

(a)   (b)

FIGURE 9.5   (a) Various structures within the hypothalamus play a role in regulating hunger, thirst, sexual arousal, and body temperature. The lateral hypothalumus (LH), ventromedial hypothalamus (VMH), and paraventricular nucleus (PVN) are involved in hunger regulation. (b) After this rat's VMH was lesioned, it overate and became obese. Its weight of 1,080 grams is about triple that of a normal rat.

"hunger off" centers (Pinel, 1997; Schwartz, 1984). For example, rats with LH damage stop eating and lose weight in part because they develop trouble swallowing and digesting, and they become generally unresponsive to external stimuli, not just to food. Moreover, axons from many brain areas funnel into the hypothalamus and then fan out again upon leaving it. Cutting these nerve tracts anywhere along their path—not just within the hypothalamus—duplicates some of the effects of the LH and VMH lesions (Schwartz, 1984).

Researchers are now examining how various neural circuits within the hypothalamus regulate food intake. Many pathways involve the **paraventricular nucleus (PVN),** a cluster of neurons packed with receptor sites for various transmitters that stimulate or reduce appetite (Figure 9.5a). One transmitter, *neuropeptide Y,* is a powerful appetite stimulant (Leibowitz, 1992). Rats in one experiment quickly became obese when they received three daily injections of neuropeptide Y into their PVN for 10 days. Their food intake doubled, their fat mass tripled, and their total body weight increased sixfold (Stanley et al., 1986).

A fascinating finding about leptin and the PVN in rats may help explain why we become so hungry when trying to lose weight. When leptin reaches the hypothalamus, it seems to *inhibit* the activity of neurons that release neuropeptide Y into the PVN, and therefore appetite is reduced. But when rats lose fat, less leptin is secreted and therefore neuropeptide Y neurons become more active, increasing appetite (Woods et al., 1998, 2000).

Psychological Aspects of Hunger

From a behavioral perspective, eating is positively reinforced by the good taste of food and negatively reinforced by hunger reduction. Cognitively, we develop an expectation that eating will be pleasurable, and this becomes an important motivator to seek and consume food. Even the mere thought of food can trigger hunger, as you may find by closing your eyes and concentrating on the aroma, sight, and taste of your favorite dish.

(a)   (b)   (c)

FIGURE 9.6 Throughout much of Western history, a full-bodied woman's figure was esteemed. In recent decades, the norm of "sexy = thin" has evolved. (a) Peter Paul Rubens's 17th-century painting, "The Three Graces." (b) Actress Lillian Russell, who represented the American ideal of feminine beauty a century ago. (c) Contemporary supermodel, Naomi Campbell.

Our beliefs about the caloric content of food, and our memory of when and how much we last ate, also affect food consumption. Consider amnesia patients who cannot form new long-term memories, and who therefore forget that they have eaten within a minute or two after finishing a meal. Paul Rozin and his colleagues (1998) presented two amnesia patients with multiple lunches on various days. The patients fully or partially ate the second meal (presented 10 to 30 minutes after the initial lunch), and partially ate a third meal shortly thereafter. In contrast, patients without amnesia rejected all of the additional lunches.

Attitudes, habits, and psychological needs also regulate food intake. Have you ever felt "stuffed" after gobbling up part of a meal, yet finished it and even had dessert? Beliefs such as "don't leave food on your plate" and conditioned habits ("autopilot" snacking while watching TV) may lead us to eat even when we do not feel hungry. Conversely, countless dieters intentionally restrict their food intake even though they *are* hungry.

> 9. Describe some factors that contribute to the pressure women feel to be thin.

Especially for women, such food restriction often stems from social pressures to conform to cultural standards of beauty (Figure 9.6). Studies of *Playboy* magazine centerfolds, Miss America contestants, and fashion models indicate a clear trend toward a thinner, leaner, and increasingly unrealistic "ideal" female body shape between the 1950s and 1980s (Garner et al., 1980; Wiseman et al., 1992). Correspondingly, relative to men, women have become increasingly dissatisfied with their body image over the past 50 years (Feingold & Mazzella, 1998).

A classic study by April Fallon and Paul Rozin (1985) suggests an additional reason why this is so. College women overestimated how thin they needed to be to conform to men's preferences, whereas men overestimated how

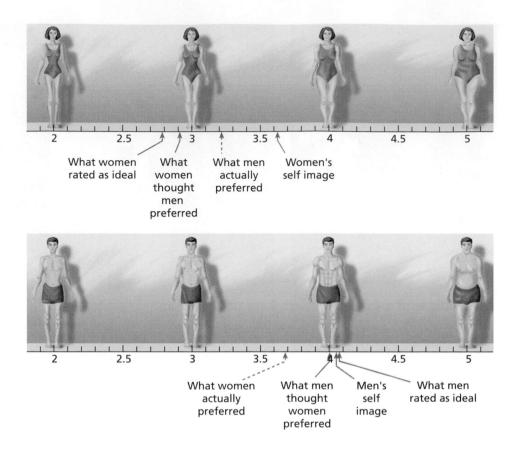

FIGURE 9.7 College women overestimated how thin they needed to be to conform to men's preferences and viewed their own body shape as heavier than ideal. In contrast, men overestimated how bulky they should be to conform to women's preferences and viewed their body shape as close to ideal. Data from Fallon & Rozin, 1985.

bulky they should be to conform to women's preferences (Figure 9.7). Women also perceived their body shape as heavier than ideal, whereas men viewed their body shape as close to ideal. As Fallon and Rozin noted, "Overall, men's perceptions serve to keep them satisfied with their figures, whereas women's perceptions place pressure on them to lose weight" (1985, p. 102).

People who perceive themselves as heavy tend to have lower self-esteem, but this relation is stronger among women than men (Miller & Downey, 1999). According to Barbara Fredrickson and Tomi Ann Roberts's (1997) *objectification theory*, American culture teaches women to view their bodies as objects, much as external observers would. This increases body shame and anxiety, which in turn leads to eating restriction and even eating disorders (Fredrickson et al., 1998). Laboratory experiments suggest that women do indeed restrict eating to restore self-esteem. In one experiment, college women ate less food in the presence of a desirable versus undesirable male, particularly when their feelings of femininity had been publicly threatened beforehand (Mori et al., 1987).

The norm that "thin = attractive" is ingrained by adolescence. In one study, about half of eighth- and ninth-grade girls felt that "a girl has to be thin to be popular with boys" (Nichter & Vuckovic, 1994, p. 121). To a degree, they are right. A two-year study of adolescent girls found that weight was significantly related to dating frequency. "The 5 ft. 3 in. girl who weighed 110 pounds was twice as likely to date as a girl of the same height and level of pubertal maturity who weighed 126 pounds" (Halpern et al., 1999, p. 732).

Environmental and Cultural Factors

Food availability is the most obvious environmental regulator of eating. For millions of people who live in poverty or famine-ravaged regions, food scarcity limits consumption. In contrast, abundant low-cost food (including high-fat foods) in many countries contributes to a high rate of obesity among children and adults (Hill & Peters, 1998).

Food taste and variety powerfully regulate eating. Good-tasting food positively reinforces eating and increases food consumption, but during a meal and from meal to meal, we can become "tired of eating the same thing" and terminate a meal more quickly (Rolls et al., 1981). In contrast, food variety increases consumption, which you know all too well if you attend buffet meals. Rats also seem to enjoy a buffet, or what technically is called a *cafeteria diet.* At each meal they may focus mostly on one type of food, but overall they eat more when their menu has variety (Rogers & Blundell, 1984).

Through classical conditioning we learn to associate the smell and sight of food with its taste, and these food cues can trigger hunger. Eating may be the last thing on your mind until your nose detects the sensuous aroma wafting from a bakery, pizzeria, or popcorn machine. Rats who have recently eaten and do not appear to be hungry (e.g., they have food available but ignore it) will eat again when presented with classically conditioned buzzers and lights that they have learned to associate with food (Weingarten, 1983). Similarly, does the musical jingle of the neighborhood ice cream truck tweak your hunger?

Many other environmental stimuli affect food intake. We typically eat more when dining with other people rather than alone, in part because meals take longer (Feunekes et al., 1995). Cultural norms influence when, how, and what we eat. In countries such as Spain and Greece, people often begin dinner in the late evening (say, around 9 P.M.), by which time most North Americans have finished their supper. And although we like variety, we usually feel most comfortable selecting from among familiar foods and often have difficulty "getting past" our squeamish thoughts about unfamiliar dishes (Figure 9.8). Figure 9.9 summarizes several factors that help to regulate hunger and eating.

> ➤ 10. Identify several environmental and cultural factors that influence eating.

FIGURE   9.8 Cultural upbringing strongly affects food preferences. Grubs, traditionally eaten by Australian Aboriginal peoples, are now served in fine restaurants. Not interested? Perhaps you would prefer some other insects, reptiles, camel eyes, or dog—all delicacies in other cultures.

Level of Analysis		
Biological	**Psychological**	**Environmental**
• Genetic factors that influence energy metabolism • Bodily sensations, such as stomach distention • Chemical signals (e.g., glucose utilization, CCK, leptin) • Neural circuits within and passing through the hypothalamus	• Thinking about food; anticipation of tasty food • Learned food preferences and eating habits • Memory of when and how much we have recently eaten • Beliefs and feelings concerning body image	• The abundance or scarcity of food • Food appearance, aroma, taste, and variety • Other stimuli (e.g., time of day, people) associated with eating • Norms that affect what, when, how, and how much we eat

EATING

FIGURE 9.9   Understanding the Causes of Behavior: Factors that regulate hunger and eating.

Obesity

The heaviest known man and woman in recorded history, both Americans, weighed 1,400 and 1,200 pounds at their respective peaks in 1978 and 1987 (*Guinness Book,* 2000). (After hospitalization and dieting, the man lost 920 pounds over 16 months, and the woman lost 917 pounds over 7 years.) Although few people even approach such extreme weight, a staggering 54 percent of American adults and 25 percent of children are either overweight or obese (Flegal et al., 1998; Troiano & Flegal, 1999). In Canada, about one in three men and one in four women are obese (Trakas et al., 1999). In general, a body weight of more than 20 percent over the average for a given height is considered obese.

Obesity is often blamed on a lack of willpower, a weak character, or emotional disturbances, but research does not consistently find such psychological differences between obese and nonobese people. Some scientists hypothesize that obese people eat to cope with stress, or that they react more strongly than nonobese people to food cues, such as the aroma and appearance of food (Schachter, 1968). But again, evidence that these factors cause obesity is mixed (Greeno & Wing, 1994).

Genes and Environment

➤ 11. What evidence suggests a genetic role in obesity? How does obesity among the Pima Indians illustrate a gene-environment interaction?

Do you know people who seem to gain weight easily, and other envied souls who eat even more food without adding pounds? Data from over 25,000 pairs of twins and 50,000 other biological and adoptive family members point to heredity as one source of such differences. Heredity influences our basal metabolic rate and tendency to store energy as either fat or lean tissue (Bouchard et al., 1990). Overall, genetic factors appear to account for about 40 to 70 percent of the variation in body mass among women and among men (Maes et al., 1997; Comuzzie & Allison, 1998). Identical twins reared apart are about as similar in body mass as identical twins reared together, and adopted children resemble their biological parents more closely than their adoptive parents (Stunkard et al., 1990). And yes, obese people are more likely than nonobese people to have parents and grandparents who are obese (Noble, 1997).

Over 200 genes have been identified as possible contributors to human obesity, and in most cases it is the combined effect of a subset of genes—rather than "single-gene" variations—that produce an increased risk (Comuzzie & Allison, 1998). However, although heredity affects our susceptibility to obesity, so does the environment. Genes have not changed much in recent decades, but obesity rates in Canada and the United States have increased significantly. According to experts such as James Hill and John Peters (1998), the culprits are:

- an abundance of inexpensive, tasty, high-fat foods available almost anywhere;
- a cultural emphasis on "getting the best value," which contributes to the "supersizing" of menu items; and
- technological advances that decrease the need for daily physical activity and encourage a sedentary lifestyle.

The Pima Indians of Arizona provide a striking example of how genes and environment interact to produce obesity. Despite the fact that the Pimas are genetically predisposed to obesity and diabetes, both conditions were rare among tribe members before the 20th century (Savage & Bennett, 1992). Their native diet and way of life prevented their genetic predisposition from expressing itself. But particularly among Pimas born after World War II, obesity rates increased dramatically as they adopted a westernized diet and sedentary lifestyle (Price et al., 1993; Esparza et al., 2000). Today they have one of the highest rates of obesity (and diabetes) in the world. In contrast, Pimas living in northwest Mexico still eat a more traditional diet and perform more physical labor, and among these men and women the obesity rate is much less than that of their Arizonan counterparts (Ravussin et al., 1994).

Dieting and Weight Loss

Unfortunately, being fat primes people to stay fat, in part by altering body chemistry and energy expenditure (Logue, 1991). For example, obese people generally have higher levels of insulin (a hormone secreted by the pancreas) than people of normal weight, which increases the conversion of glucose into fat. Substantial weight gain also makes it harder to exercise vigorously, and dieting slows basal metabolism because the body responds to food deprivation with decreased energy expenditure. Along with a genetic predisposition to obesity, these factors enable many obese people to maintain excess weight with fewer calories than people who are gaining the same weight for the first time. In contrast to earlier reports, however, there is not consistent evidence that the body's energy-saving metabolic slowdown becomes more pronounced with each weight loss attempt (Brownell & Rodin, 1994, National Task Force, 1994). Thus, whether repeated *"yo-yo dieting"* makes it more difficult to lose weight is debatable.

> 12. Why is it especially hard for obese people to lose weight? Are diets doomed to fail?

Are diets doomed to fail? The common adage that "95 percent of people who lose weight regain it within a few years" evolved from just one study decades ago. According to Albert Strunkard, one of the researchers, 100 obesity patients were "just given a diet and sent on their way. That was state of the art in 1959" (Fritsch, 1999). Certainly, achieving weight loss is not easy, and combining healthy eating (reduced energy input) with exercise (increased energy output) has a greater chance of success than dieting alone. But in truth, we do not have good estimates of weight-loss success rates, partly because people who succeed (or fail) on their own without going to clinics or treatment programs are rarely heard from (Schachter, 1982). For example, the National Weight Control Registry (2000) has a database of over 2,000 successful, long-term dieters who, on average, have lost about 60 pounds and kept it off for about 5 years. About half of these participants did so on their own, without any type of formal program.

We do know that about one third of Americans report that they are trying to lose weight, although there are significant ethnic differences (Figure 9.10). For example, compared to their White peers, African-American women are more satisfied with their weight and body shape, are less concerned about dieting, and feel that a woman's ideal weight should be heavier (Desmond et al., 1989; Halpern et al., 1999).

Health concerns motivate some dieters, but psychological and social concerns are the primary motivators for many others. Many *nonobese* adolescent girls and women diet, including those of average and below-average weight (Halpern et al., 1999; Miller et al., 2000). Unfortunately, as Figure 9.11 illustrates and as we now explore, what begins as a diet may evolve into a health-threatening eating disorder.

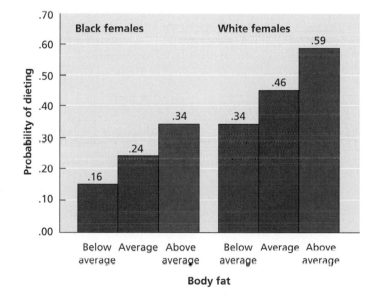

FIGURE 9.10 Among 200 adolescent girls (average age = 13.8 years), Carolyn Halpern and her colleagues (1999) found that Whites were more likely to diet than Blacks. These data are for *nonobese girls* who were divided into three body fat groups. The likelihood of dieting increased with greater body fat, but for each body fat group, Whites were more likely to diet than Blacks. Notice that a significant percentage of girls with below-average body fat dieted.

Based on Halpern, et al., 1999.

FIGURE 9.11 Anorexia nervosa is a potentially life threatening disorder in which people virtually starve themselves to be thin. This anorexic woman returned to normal weight after therapy.

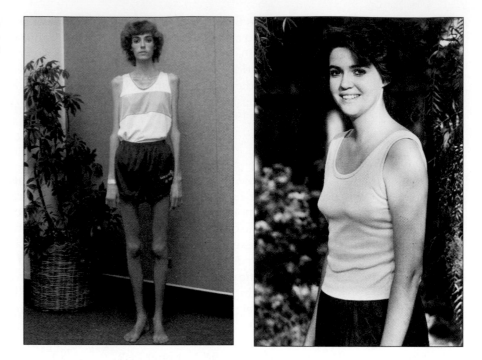

➤ 13. Describe some of the symptoms and causes of anorexia and bulimia.

PSYCHOLOGICAL FRONTIERS

Eating Disorders: Anorexia and Bulimia

Sara and Lisa, the college freshmen described at the beginning of the chapter, both suffered from eating disorders. Victims of **anorexia nervosa,** like Sara, have an intense fear of being fat and severely restrict their food intake to the point of self-starvation. Despite looking emaciated and weighing less than 85 percent of what would be expected for their age, anorexics continue to view themselves as fat. They often crave food, but have what amounts to an eating phobia that can be life threatening. About 90 percent of anorexics are female, mostly adolescents and young adults (Becker et al., 1999). Anorexia causes menstruation to stop, strains the heart, produces bone loss, and increases the risk of death (Neumäker, 2000). In 1982 the death of a famous singer, Karen Carpenter, was attributed to heart strain caused by her anorexia.

People who suffer from **bulimia nervosa,** like Lisa, are overconcerned about becoming fat, but instead of self-starvation they binge eat and then purge the food, usually by inducing vomiting or using laxatives. Bulimics often consume 2,000 to 4,000 calories during binges, and in some cases may consume 20,000 calories per day (Crandall, 1989; Geracioti et al., 1995). About 90 percent of bulimics are female.

Although most bulimics are of normal body weight, repeated purging can produce severe physical consequences, including gastric problems and badly eroded teeth. Some surveys indicate that up to 10 percent of college women exhibit symptoms of bulimia, although its general prevalence among North American women is 1 to 3 percent—compared with 0.5 percent for anorexia (Becker et al., 1999; Walsh & Devlin, 1998).

▶ Causes of Anorexia and Bulimia

What motivates people to develop such abnormal eating patterns? The answer—as with general eating regulation—seems to lie in a combination of environmental, psychological, and biological factors. Anorexia and bulimia are more common in industrialized cultures where beauty is equated with "thinness." Variations in beauty norms

–Continued

among different ethnic groups also may help explain why, in North America, eating disorders are more common among Whites than Blacks (Zhang & Snowden, 1999). Consistent with objectification theory, a study of 16- to 21-year-old female college students suggests that a cultural emphasis on viewing one's body as an object contributes to eating disorders (Noll & Fredrickson, 1998).

Cultural norms alone cannot account for eating disorders, because only a small percentage of women within a particular culture are anorexic or bulimic. Some researchers believe that personality factors are another piece of the puzzle. Anorexics often are perfectionists—high achievers like Sara (a high school valedictorian) who often strive to live up to lofty self-standards, including distorted standards concerning an acceptably thin body (Garfinkel & Garner, 1982). In one study, Monique Smeets (1999) showed anorexic and normal women a "morphing movie" in which a woman's thin body transforms into an obese one. When asked to judge the transition points at which the body changes from "thin" to "normal," "fat," and "obese," anorexics set harsher standards (e.g., lower weight levels to meet the transition point) for their own *and* other women's bodies.

For anorexics, losing weight becomes a battle for success and control: "Me versus food, and I'm going to win." Their perfectionism and need for control may partly stem from their upbringing. Anorexics describe their parents as disapproving and as setting abnormally high achievement standards, and they report more stressful events related to their parents than do nonanorexics (Waller & Hartley, 1994).

A different pattern emerges for bulimics, who tend to be depressed and anxious, exhibit low impulse control, and seem to lack a stable sense of personal identity and self-sufficiency (Strober & Humphrey, 1987). Bingeing is often triggered by life stress, and guilt and self-contempt follow it—recall Lisa's feeling that she was a "big fat failure."

The purging may be a means of reducing depression and anxiety triggered by the bingeing (Rosen & Leitenberg, 1982).

On the biological side, genetic factors may create a predisposition toward eating disorders. Concordance rates for eating disorders are higher among identical twins than fraternal twins, and higher among first-degree relatives than second- or third-degree relatives (Fichter & Noegel, 1990; Woodside et al., 1998). Anorexics and bulimics exhibit abnormal activity of serotonin and other body chemicals that help regulate eating (Bruch, 1973; Walsh & Devlin, 1998). However, because the findings are correlational, it is not clear whether these chemical abnormalities help cause eating disorders, or are a reaction to self-starvation and binge-purge eating.

Many researchers believe that these physiological changes initially are a *response* to abnormal eating patterns, but once started, they *perpetuate* eating and digestive irregularities (Walsh & Devlin, 1998). For example, because leptin is secreted by fat cells and anorexics have low fat mass, the amount of leptin circulating in their bloodstream is abnormally low (Mantzoros et al., 1997). But when anorexics begin to eat more, their leptin levels rebound more quickly than their weight gain. Because leptin is a signal that reduces appetite, this leptin rebound may make it more difficult for anorexics to keep gaining weight (Walsh & Devlin, 1998). Similarly, stomach acids expelled into the mouth during vomiting cause bulimics to lose taste sensitivity, making the normally unpleasant taste of vomit more tolerable (Rodin et al., 1990). This helps to perpetuate bulimics' willingness to keep purging in this manner.

Treating eating disorders is difficult and may take years, but with professional help about half of anorexics and bulimics fully recover (Becker et al., 1999; Walsh & Devlin, 1998). Others are able to eat more normally, but maintain their preoccupation with weight.

❭ SENSATION-SEEKING

In contrast to the drive-reduction goal assumed by some theories, humans and other animals often seek out stimulation, preferring novel, complex, or arousing stimuli to familiar and simple ones (Figure 9.12). Monkeys will repeatedly push open a spring door just to see what is happening on the other side, and will spend hours working on mechanical puzzles without any tangible reward for doing so. Anyone who has taken small children to a gift store and seen a sign that says, "If they break it, you've bought it," knows how common exploratory behaviors are in humans from infancy on.

Sensation-seeking refers to the motivation to seek out stimulation and novelty, and its strength varies across people. Psychologist Marvin Zuckerman (1979, 1991) developed the Sensation-Seeking Scale to measure this motive (Table 9.1). People who score high on sensation-seeking scales tend to enjoy higher-risk sports and other physically risky activities, such as skydiving, hang-gliding, motorcycle riding, and fire fighting (Jack & Ronan, 1998).

❭ 14. What evidence suggests that sensation-seeking has a biological basis.

FIGURE 9.12 Humans and other animals often seek out novelty and stimulation. These young monkeys will spend hours on mechanical puzzles without external reinforcers. From extreme sports to riding roller coasters and attending scary movies, many people seek thrills and excitement in diverse ways.

TABLE 9.1	SENSATION-SEEKING SCALE

Sample Items

Choose A or B for each item:

1a.   I prefer people who are calm and even tempered.
1b.   I prefer people who are emotionally expressive, even if they are a bit unstable.

2a.   A good painting should shock or jolt the senses.
2b.   A good painting should give one the feeling of peace and security.

3a.   I enter cold water gradually, giving myself time to get used to it.
3b.   I like to dive or jump right into the ocean or a cold pool.

Scoring: Choices 1b, 2a, and 3b reflect higher sensation-seeking. Based on Zuckerman, 1979, 1991.

Perhaps because they prefer unpredictable environments, high sensation seekers are less likely to become psychologically distressed in the face of negative life changes (Smith et al., 1978). However, there is a downside to high sensation-seeking, particularly among adolescent girls and boys. They are more likely than low sensation seekers to perform illegal actions (such as stealing and destroying property) and to use drugs—a finding replicated across many ethnic groups (Howard et al., 1999; Newcomb & McGee, 1991; Pilgrim et al., 1999). Zuckerman suggests that it is important to steer high sensation seekers into socially acceptable activities such as sports, where their needs for excitement and stimulation can be satisfied in a more desirable manner.

Among college students, high sensation seekers drink more alcohol, participate in more drinking games (even compared with other students who are equally intoxicated), and engage in a wider range of sexual activities with more partners (Johnson & Cropsey, 2000). Moving from the bedroom to the living room, sensation-seeking is even related to television-watching habits. High sensation seekers do not watch more television, but they have a greater preference for action-adventure and music-video programs, and they change channels more often out of boredom (Perse, 1996).

Sensation seeking may have a biological basis. One theory is that high sensation seekers are less reactive to external stimulation than are low sensation seekers (Goldman et al., 1983; Larsen & Zarate, 1991). EEG recordings indicate that when high and low sensation seekers are exposed to a constant stimulus, brain activity in the cerebral cortex of high sensation seekers decreases more quickly. For them, the stimulation loses its effect more quickly. Thus to maintain a particular level of cortical activity, high sensation seekers may need stronger levels of stimulation than low sensation seekers. In contrast, low sensation seekers have stronger cortical responses to weak stimuli, suggesting their greater reactivity to stimulation (Zuckerman, 1991).

A less sensitive nervous system may be one reason why high sensation seekers experience boredom more easily and therefore seek high-risk activities, whereas low sensation seekers are prone to overstimulation and therefore seek less-arousing activities. In addition, impulsive sensation-seeking related to criminality, drug use, and sex is related to under- and overactivity of different neurotransmitter systems (Zuckerman, 1996).

〉 SEXUAL MOTIVATION

Why do people have sex? If you are thinking, "Isn't it obvious?" let's take a look. Sex often is described as a biological "reproductive motive," yet people usually do not have sex to conceive children. Moreover, a drive to reproduce does not explain why people masturbate, have oral sex, use birth control, and have sex into their seventies and eighties. Pleasure, then, must be the key. Evolution has shaped our physiology so that sex feels good; periodically this leads to childbirth, and our genes are passed on. But consider the following:

- In a study asking adolescents why they have sex, both genders cited peer pressure far more often than "sexual gratification" (Stark, 1989).
- In the 1920s, British sex researcher Helena Wright found that most women she surveyed viewed sex as an unenjoyable marital duty (Kelly, 2001).
- Many women find their first sexual intercourse disappointing (Sprecher et al., 1995). Some sex researchers call this reaction "Peggy Lee syndrome," named for a singer who had a hit song entitled, "Is That All There Is?" (Hyde & DeLamater, 2000).
- About 10 percent of American men and 20 percent of women report that sex is not pleasurable (Laumann et al., 1994).

In reality, people engage in sex for a host of noble and not so noble reasons: to reproduce, obtain and give pleasure, express love, foster intimacy, build one's ego, fulfill one's "duty," conform to peer pressure, get over a broken relationship, and for millions of people worldwide, to earn money (Byer et al., 1999).

Sexual Behavior: Patterns and Changes

Because most people are reluctant to let researchers into their bedrooms, scientists typically learn about people's sexual activities by conducting surveys. Alfred Kinsey and his colleagues (1948, 1953) at Indiana University conducted the first large-scale American sex surveys in the late 1930s. One of the best and more recent U.S. surveys, based on a nationally representative sample of 18- to 59-year-olds, found that about 70 percent of this age group has sex with a partner at least a few times per month (Table 9.2; Laumann et al., 1994; Michael et al., 1994). Overall, single adults who cohabit (are not married but live with a sexual partner) are the most sexually active, followed by married adults. Single adults who do not cohabit are the least active.

The survey also found that, although men and women have sex with a partner about equally often, men masturbate and fantasize about sex more often than women do. About 25 percent of men and 10 percent of women masturbate one or more times per week, and 60 percent of men and 40 percent of women report masturbating at least once a year. The common belief that adults masturbate

TABLE 9.2 FREQUENCY OF SEX IN THE PAST 12 MONTHS BY GENDER AND MARITAL STATUS

Social characteristics	Not at all	A few time per year	A few times per month	2 or 3 times a week	4 or more times a week
Men					
Noncohabitating	23	25	26	19	7
Cohabiting	0	8	36	40	16
Married	1	13	43	36	7
Women					
Noncohabiting	32	23	24	15	5
Cohabiting	1	8	35	42	14
Married	3	12	47	32	7

Source: From Sex in America. Copyright © 1994 by C.S.G. Enterprises, Inc., Edward O. Laumann, Robert T. Michael, and Gina Kolata. By permission of Little, Brown and Company.

simply because they do not have a sex partner *is false:* 85 percent of men and 45 percent of women with regular sex partners masturbate at least once a year.

Overall, males tend to have first intercourse about one to two years earlier than females, but data from the U.S. Centers for Disease Control and Prevention (CDC, 1996) reveal that by their senior year of high school, similar percentages of females and males have had sexual intercourse at least once (females, 66 percent; males, 67 percent) and are currently sexually active (females, 52 percent; males, 48 percent).

Surveys also reveal that premarital intercourse has become more common in a number of countries over the past half century. Among unmarried American females in the early 1960s, about 4 percent of 15-year-olds and 27 percent of 19-year-olds had engaged in sexual intercourse. In 1995, the corresponding figures were 21 and 72 percent (CDC, 1997). Changing social norms, a trend toward having first intercourse at a younger age, and a tendency to delay marriage have contributed to this rise in premarital sex. Among adolescent and young women, about two-thirds are "going steady" when they first have sexual intercourse (CDC, 1997).

Some findings suggest, however, that these premarital trends may be leveling off and possibly reversing (CDC, 1997). This may be a response to an increased cultural emphasis on the depth of relationships (Wade & Cirese, 1992) and to the crisis concerning AIDs and other sexually transmitted diseases (STDs). According to the World Health Organization, about 360,000 people worldwide contract an STD each day, yielding 125 million new cases each year (Alexander, 1996.) In America, the overall incidence of STDs is higher among 15- to 19-year-olds than any other age group (Byer et al., 1999).

The Physiology of Sex

In 1953, William Masters and Virginia Johnson (Figure 9.13) began a landmark study in which they examined the sexual responses of 694 men and women under laboratory conditions. In total, they physiologically monitored about 10,000 sexual episodes in which volunteers masturbated, had intercourse, and performed other sexual activities. By putting a camera into a transparent penis-shaped case, Masters and Johnson were able to film vaginal reactions during simulated intercourse.

The Sexual Response Cycle

Masters and Johnson (1966) concluded that most people go through a four-stage **sexual response cycle** when sexually aroused (Figure 9.14). During the *excitement phase* arousal builds rapidly. Blood flow increases to arteries in and around the genital organs, nipples, and women's breasts, pooling and causing these body areas to swell (this process is called *vasocongestion*). The penis and clitoris begin to become erect, the vagina becomes lubricated, and muscle tension increases throughout the body. In the *plateau phase,* respiration, heart rate, vasocongestion, and muscle tension continue to build until there is enough muscle tension to trigger orgasm.

During the *orgasm phase* in males, rhythmic contractions of internal organs and muscle tissue surrounding the urethra project semen out of the penis. In females, orgasm involves rhythmic contractions of the outer third of the vagina, surrounding muscles, and the uterus. In males, orgasm is ordinarily followed by the *resolution phase,* during which physiological arousal decreases rapidly and the genital organs and tissues return to their normal condition. During the resolution phase, males enter a *refractory period* during which they are temporarily incapable of another orgasm. Females may have two or more successive orgasms before the onset of the resolution phase, but Masters and Johnson reported that most women experienced only one. Moreover, sexual response varies across people and time, and this four-stage model only represents an "average." People may experience orgasm on some occasions but not others, and orgasm is neither the only goal nor necessarily the ultimate goal of all sexual activity.

FIGURE 9.13 William Masters and Virginia Johnson conducted groundbreaking research on the physiology of human sexual response.

➤ 15. Explain the stages of the sexual response cycle.

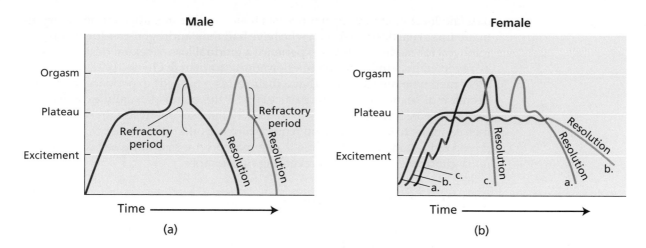

FIGURE 9.14 Masters and Johnson discovered a four-stage pattern of sexual response. (a) In males, there is a refractory period after orgasm during which no further response is possible. (b) In females, pattern "a" represents one or more orgasms followed by resolution, pattern "b" shows a plateau stage with no orgasm, and pattern "c" shows an orgasm with no preceding plateau stage
Based on Masters & Johnson, 1966.

Hormonal Influences

As with hunger, the hypothalamus plays a key role in sexual motivation. It controls the pituitary gland, which regulates the secretion of hormones called *gonadotropins* into the bloodstream. In turn, these hormones affect the rate at which the *gonads* (testes in the male and ovaries in the female) secrete *androgens,* the so-called "masculine" sex hormones such as testosterone, and *estrogens,* the so-called "feminine" sex hormones such as estradiol. Realize that, despite these labels, both men and women produce androgens and estrogens.

Sex hormones have *organizational effects* that direct the development of male and female sex characteristics (Breedlove, 1992; Byer et al., 1999). In the womb, male and female embryos form a primitive gonad that has the potential to develop into either testes or ovaries. If genetically male, the embryo forms testes about 8 weeks after conception. Then as the testes release sex hormones during a key period of prenatal development, there typically is sufficient androgen activity to produce a male pattern of genital, reproductive, brain, and other organ development. Years later, as part of this pattern, the hypothalamus stimulates an increased release of sex hormones from the testes when the male reaches puberty. In contrast, a genetically female embryo does not form testes and, in the absence of sufficient androgen activity during this prenatal period, a female pattern of development ensues. As part of this pattern, at puberty the hypothalamus stimulates the release of sex hormones from the ovaries on a cyclical basis that regulates the female menstrual cycle.

Sex hormones also have *activational effects* that stimulate sexual desire and behavior. In nonhuman animals, mature males have a relatively constant secretion of sex hormones and their readiness for sex is largely governed by the presence of environmental stimuli (e.g., a receptive female). In contrast, hormone secretions in female animals follow an "estrus" cycle, and they are sexually receptive only during periods of high estrogen secretion (i.e., when they are "in heat"). Sex hormones also influence human sexual desire, as when the hormonal surge of puberty results in increased sexual motivation for most people. But in humans, normal short-term hormonal fluctuations have relatively little effect on sexual arousability (Morrell et al., 1984). Women may experience high sexual desire at any time during their menstrual cycle.

In men and women, androgens—rather than estrogens—appear to have the primary influence on sexual desire (Kelly, 2001). However, desire does not go up and down like a yo-yo as blood levels of sex hormones change. Rather, a

> 16. Describe the organizational and activational effects of sex hormones. How do the activational effects differ in humans versus nonhumans?

baseline level of certain hormones, such as testosterone, appears necessary to maintain sexual desire. Women who have had their androgen-producing organs removed for medical reasons experience a gradual loss of sexual desire that can be reversed by administering sex hormones (Kaplan & Owett, 1993). Similarly, most men who are castrated (have their testes removed) experience a gradual decrease of sexual desire. But particularly if the man is sexually experienced, sexual responsiveness declines more slowly than sexual desire. In some cases, men continue to have sexual intercourse for years after they have been castrated (Hyde & DeLamater, 2000). This is one reason why castrating sex offenders is not a guaranteed method of preventing future rapes.

The Psychology of Sex

➤ 17. What psychological factors stimulate and inhibit sexual functioning?

Sexual arousal involves more than physiological responses. It typically begins with desire and a sexual stimulus that is *perceived* positively (Walen & Roth, 1987). Such stimuli can even be imaginary.

Sexual Fantasy

Sexual fantasy is an important component of many people's lives. Among 18- to 59-year-old American adults, about half of men and a fifth of women fantasize about sex at least once a day (Laumann et al., 1994). Fantasy illustrates how mental processes can affect physiological functioning. Indeed, sexual fantasies alone may trigger genital erection and orgasm in some people, and are often used to enhance arousal during masturbation (Byrne & Osland, 2000).

Most men and women also fantasize at least occasionally during sexual intercourse (Leitenberg & Henning, 1995), as comedian Rodney Dangerfield acknowledged with his quip, "Last time I tried to make love to my wife nothing was happening, so I said to her, 'What's the matter, you can't think of anybody either?'" However, in contrast to what Dangerfield's joke implies, sexual fantasy typically is not a response to dissatisfaction with one's partner. Rather, people who are more sexually active also tend to fantasize more (Kelly, 2001).

Desire, Arousal, and Sexual Dysfunction

Psychological factors can not only trigger sexual arousal, but also inhibit it. A person may be anticipating an evening of lovemaking, or be engaged in sexual activity, and then become "turned off" by something a partner does. Many people who are physiologically capable of becoming sexually aroused simply do not have the desire. About one in three women and one in six men report that they lack an interest in sex (Laumann et al., 1994).

Other people desire sex, but have difficulty becoming or staying aroused. Stress, fatigue, and anger at one's partner can lead to temporary arousal problems. *Sexual dysfunction* refers to chronic, impaired sexual functioning that distresses a person. It may result from injuries, diseases, and drug effects, but some causes are psychological. About 10 percent of men report difficulty maintaining an erection, and about 20 percent of women have difficulty lubricating and becoming aroused (Laumann et al., 1994). Performance anxiety can cause both types of problems, and arousal difficulties also may be a psychological consequence of sexual assault or childhood sexual abuse (Byers et al., 1999).

Cultural and Environmental Influences

➤ 18. How do cultural norms and environmental stimuli influence sexual behavior?

The psychological meaning of sex depends strongly upon cultural contexts and learning. For example, some religions discourage or prohibit premarital sex, extramarital sex, and public behavior that arouses sexual desire. In turn, most people who view themselves as very religious believe it is important to bring their sexual practices into harmony with their religious beliefs (Janus & Janus, 1993).

Cultural Norms

Anyone who doubts culture's power to shape the expression of human sexuality need only examine sexual customs around the globe. Consider that childhood sexuality is suppressed in our culture, but is permitted and even encouraged in others. In the Marquesas Islands of French Polynesia, families sleep together in one room and children have ample opportunity to observe sexual activity. When a baby boy is distressed, Marquesan parents may masturbate the child. Boys and girls begin to masturbate at age two or three, and most engage in casual homosexual contacts during their youth. When they reach adolescence, an adult of the opposite sex instructs them in sexual techniques and has intercourse with them (Suggs, 1962).

Although North Americans are less sexually permissive than the Marquesans, they are not as repressive as the inhabitants of Inis Beag, an island off the coast of Ireland. Sex is a taboo topic among these people and nudity is abhorred. Only infants are allowed to be completely naked. The genders are separated from early childhood until marriage, and during marital sex both partners keep their underwear on. Sexual revulsion is so intense that dogs and other animals are often beaten if they are caught licking their genitals. In contrast to Marquesan women, who customarily experience orgasm in sexual interactions, orgasm among the women of Inis Beag is rare and viewed as abnormal (Messenger, 1971). Clearly, what is considered proper, moral, and desirable varies enormously across cultures.

Arousing Environmental Stimuli

The environment affects sexuality not only through cultural experiences, but also by providing sexually arousing stimuli. A lover's caress can trigger sexual desire in an instant. So too can watching a partner undress, which ranks second only to vaginal intercourse as the sexual activity that most men and women find appealing (Laumann et al., 1994).

Erotic portrayals of sex can trigger arousal and sexual behavior as long as people perceive those stimuli positively (Davis & Bauserman, 1993). In one study, Julia Heiman (1975) measured the genital arousal and self-reported arousal of sexually experienced college students as they listened to tape recordings of erotic and nonerotic stories from popular novels. Women and men experienced sexual arousal to descriptions of explicit sex, but not to descriptions devoid of sexual content (romantic or general conversations). Both genders showed the strongest arousal when erotic stories focused on the female character, and when she was the one who initiated sex.

Pornography, Sexual Violence, and Sexual Attitudes

By today's standards, depictions of sex in popular novels are a tame form of erotica. Sexually explicit magazines and movies, telephone sex lines, nude dance clubs, and Internet "cyberporn" comprise a multi-billion-dollar pornography industry. Most pornography consumers are men, though about one third of people who have purchased or rented X-rated video tapes are women (Laumann et al., 1994).

Given the appalling incidence of sexual assault in some countries, the public and scientists alike have asked whether exposure to pornography fosters sexual violence against women. Twenty percent of 15- to 44-year-old American women report that they have experienced forced sexual intercourse at least once during their lives, and about 25 to 30 percent of female college students have experienced some type of sexual assault (CDC, 1997; Koss, 1988). Contrary to a common belief, as Figure 9.15 shows, most rapes are *not* committed by strangers (Laumann et al., 1994).

Two psychological viewpoints are especially relevant to predicting pornography's effects. According to *social learning theory*, people learn through observation. Many pornographic materials model "rape myths," themes that sex is

Who Commits Rape?

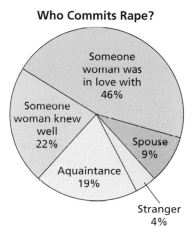

FIGURE 9.15 In a national sample of 18- to 59-year-old Americans, women who had been victims of forced sex indicated that the offender typically was someone they knew (Laumann et al., 1994). A national study of college women (Koss et al., 1988) found similar results, based on the following categories of rape offenders: boyfriend or other steady date (31%), nonromantic acquaintance (26%), casual date (22%), stranger (11%), and family members, including spouses (9%).

Data from Edward O. Laumann, Robert T. Michael, and Gina Kolata.

➤ 19. According to social learning and catharsis principles, how should viewing pornography affect sexual aggression? What does research find?

impersonal, that men are entitled to sex when they want it, and that women enjoy being dominated and coerced into sex (Burton, 1980; Malamuth, 1998). Men who view such materials should become more likely to treat women as objects and sexually aggress toward them. In contrast, Freud and other psychoanalysts advocated a *catharsis principle,* which states that as inborn aggressive and sexual impulses build up, actions that release this tension provide a "catharsis" that temporarily returns us to a more balanced physiological state. Thus viewing pornography—especially materials that contain aggressive or violent content— should provide people with a safe "outlet" for releasing sexual and aggressive tensions, and should decrease sexually aggressive behavior toward women.

Correlational studies of real-world sexual violence do not clearly support either viewpoint. For example, although some sex offenders use pornography to arouse themselves in preparation for a crime, overall, they do not report having been exposed to pornography at a younger age or to a substantially larger degree than males in general (Bauserman, 1996). More broadly, some countries with high rape rates have little pornography, whereas others have a great deal. In some countries, pornography is widely available but rape rates are low (Bauserman, 1996).

To isolate pornography's possible effects on behavior, controlled experiments are needed. In one such experiment, Edward Donnerstein and Leonard Berkowitz (1981) randomly divided male college students into four groups. Group 1 saw a nonsexual film of a talk show. Group 2 watched a sexually explicit film in which a young couple made consensual love. Groups 3 and 4 watched explicit depictions of a woman being sexually assaulted by two men. In one film (Group 3)—a "rape myth" version—the woman resisted at first but then became a willing sexual participant. In the other film (Group 4), she was shown resisting and then suffering during the entire experience.

Next, in a supposedly unrelated second experiment, these male participants interacted with a woman (actually, an accomplice of the experimenter). During this interaction, she intentionally angered half of the participants. Later the men were given the opportunity to aggress against her by giving her electric shocks as punishment for errors made on a learning task she was performing. As Figure 9.16 shows, watching the "rape myth" film (Group 3) increased the

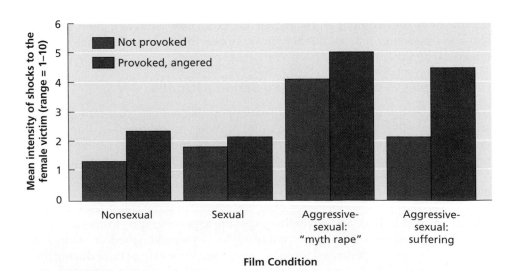

FIGURE 9.16 Viewing an aggressive-sexual "rape myth" film in which the victim did not appear to suffer increased the aggression of both angered and nonangered male participants toward a woman. After seeing an aggressive-sexual film in which the female victim did appear to suffer, only angered men showed substantially higher aggression toward a woman. A sexually explicit film without violent content did not increase later aggression.

Data from Donnerstein & Berkowitz, 1981.

aggression of both angered and nonangered men. Further, *for angered men,* aggression increased even when they saw the rape depiction showing the woman suffering (Group 4). This heightened aggression was specifically directed toward women; in a related experiment, viewing these rape depictions increased men's aggression toward a female confederate, but *not* toward a male confederate.

Based on over two dozen experiments, researchers still debate whether nonviolent sexually explicit materials increase men's aggression toward women, but the clearest and strongest effects emerge for violent pornography (Allen et al., 1995; Byrne & Osland 2000; Donnerstein & Malamuth, 1997). At least temporarily, such films seem to increase men's aggressive behavior toward women. Pornography also promotes a view that sex is impersonal and decreases viewers' satisfaction with their own sexual partners (Donnerstein & Malamuth, 1997; Zillmann, 1994). In combination with a hostile attitude toward women, the belief that sex is impersonal contributes to rape (Malamuth, 1998). Incarcerated rapists and students who have admitted committing date rape both display an impersonal orientation to sex.

Should violent pornography, or all pornography, be banned? This is a moral and political question that goes beyond what the data can answer. Like everyone else, researchers have personal values and some take a strong stand on this issue. In an encouraging vein, research also shows that providing men with realistic information about sexual assault can lead them to reject rape myths (Linz & Donnerstein, 1989). Strong messages against coercive sexual practices may promote attitudes that help reduce sexual crimes against women.

> ➤ 20. Do you believe that research findings should influence societal decisions about pornography? Why or why not?

Sexual Orientation

Sexual orientation refers to one's emotional and erotic preference for partners of a particular sex (Byer et al., 1999). On one level, defining sexual orientation seems simple: Heterosexuals prefer opposite-sex partners, homosexuals prefer same-sex partners, and bisexuals are sexually attracted to members of both sexes. So how would you classify the sexual orientation of the following 25-year-olds?

> ➤ 21. Why is the issue of defining sexual orientation complicated?

- Earl is attracted to and has sex only with men, and views himself as homosexual.
- Susan feels sexually attracted to men and women, but has had sex only with men and thinks of herself as heterosexual.
- Larry has had sex with other men twice since puberty, yet isn't attracted to men and views himself as heterosexual.

Prevalence of Different Sexual Orientations

For decades, researchers viewed sexual orientation as a single dimension ranging from "exclusively heterosexual" to "exclusively homosexual," with "equally heterosexual and homosexual" at the midpoint (Kinsey 1948). But this concept is too simplistic and modern researchers propose that sexual orientation has three dimensions: *self-identity, sexual attraction,* and *actual sexual behavior* (Kelly, 2001).

Figure 9.17 shows that about 3 percent of American men and 1 percent of women identify themselves as homosexual or bisexual, but higher percentages report same-gender attraction and at least one same-gender sexual experience (Laumann et al., 1994). National surveys in England and France report slightly lower rates of same-gender sexual activity (Johnson et al., 1992).

Overall, 10 percent of American men and 9 percent of women answered affirmatively to at least one of the items in Figure 9.17. Of this group, roughly half report same-gender attraction but have never had same-gender sex and do not think of themselves as homosexual. In contrast, almost all individuals who have

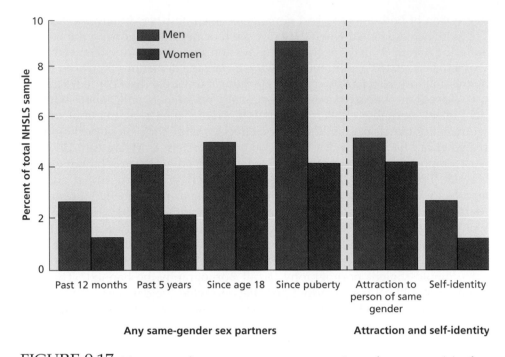

FIGURE 9.17 More men and women report same-sex attraction and same-sex activity than view themselves as homosexual or bisexual.

Data from Laumann et al., 1994.

a homosexual or bisexual self-identity also report same-gender attraction and same-gender sexual activity.

Determinants of Sexual Orientation

During the 20th century theory after theory about the origins of sexual orientation fell by the scientific wayside. An early and unsupported biological theory was that homosexual and heterosexual males differ in their adult levels of sex hormones. One psychodynamic view proposed that male homosexuality develops when boys grow up with a weak ineffectual father and identify with a domineering or seductive mother. Another hypothesized that being sexually seduced by an adult homosexual caused children to divert their sex drive toward members of their own sex. Behaviorists suggested that homosexuality was a conditioned response, developed by associating adolescent sexual urges with the presence of same-sex peers.

These early theories took a scientific beating. In an extensive study of nearly 1,000 homosexual and over 500 heterosexual men and women in the San Francisco area, Alan Bell and his colleagues (1981) asked participants more than 200 questions about their childhood, adolescence, and adulthood. They searched in vain for a common pattern of early experiences that might suggest clues about the determinants of sexual orientation, and concluded:

> No particular phenomenon of family life can be singled out, on the basis of our findings, as especially consequential for either homosexual or heterosexual development. . . . What we seem to have identified . . . is a pattern of feelings and reactions within the child that cannot be traced back to a single social or psychological root. (pp. 191–192)

Overall, there was one notable pattern: Even in childhood, homosexual men and women felt that they were somehow different from their same-sex peers and were more likely to engage in gender-nonconforming behaviors. Similarly, a cross-cultural study found that compared with heterosexual women, homosex-

➤ 22. What do you believe determines sexual orientation? Does your belief correspond to theories that have been rejected?

ual women in Brazil, Peru, the Phillipines, and the United States were about twice as likely during childhood to be considered tomboys, engage in pretend play with men's clothes or other items, and be interested in boys' toys (Whitam & Mathy, 1991).

Still, why do such patterns arise? At present, many researchers believe that human sexual orientation has genetic roots. J. Michael Bailey and Richard Pillard (1991) found that among gay men who had a brother, the concordance rates for sexual orientation (i.e., the brother was gay also) were 52 percent among identical twins, 22 percent among fraternal twins, and 11 percent among adoptive brothers. Similarly, among lesbian women with sisters, the concordance rates were 48, 16, and 6 percent among identical twins, fraternal twins, and adopted sisters (Bailey et al., 1993). In sum, the closer the genetic relatedness, the higher the concordance rates for sexual orientation.

On another biological front, altering animals' prenatal exposure to sex hormones can influence their sexual orientation (Collaer & Hines, 1995; Money, 1987). According to one view, the brain develops a neural pattern that predisposes organisms to prefer either female or male sex partners, depending upon whether prenatal sex hormone activity follows a masculine or feminine path (Ellis & Ames, 1987). Scientists do not conduct similar experiments with humans, but some women have used medications during pregnancy that altered fetal exposure to sex hormones. Additionally, in rare cases some genetically male fetuses are insensitive to their own androgen secretions and some female fetuses experience an atypical buildup of androgens. Several studies of these individuals suggest a relation between their prenatal sex hormone exposure and adulthood sexual orientation (Dessens et al., 1999; Williams et al., 2000).

These findings are intriguing, but the human research is correlational and many investigators believe that there is no clear evidence that prenatal sex hormones directly affect human sexual orientation (Byne, 1997; Doell, 1995). For example, male fetuses who have androgen insensitivity develop the external anatomy of females, typically are raised as girls, and socialization could account for their sexual orientation.

What about environmental influences? Despite identical genes, in about half the cases when one identical twin is homosexual, the other is heterosexual. Thus several biological factors, or a biological predisposition and socialization experiences, may combine to determine our sexual orientation (Money, 1987). At present, we do not know what those factors are. It is also possible, argues Daryl Bem (1996), that heredity affects sexual orientation only indirectly by influencing children's basic personality style. He proposes that different personality styles steer children toward different socialization experiences, which then play the key role in determining sexual orientation. Finally, there may be multiple paths toward developing a sexual orientation, and the paths for men and women may differ (Byne, 1997; Peplau et al., 1998). Although much more research is needed to examine these models, one point is clear. No matter our sexual orientation, close relationships provide us with much more than the mere opportunity for sexual expression.

> 23. What evidence suggests that sexual orientation has biological roots? Describe the limitations of this evidence.

〉 THE DESIRE FOR AFFILIATION AND INTIMACY

What makes your life most meaningful? To many people, close relationships are one key. Abraham Maslow (1954) viewed belongingness and love as basic psychological needs, and considerable research indicates that ". . . the need to belong is a powerful, fundamental, and extremely pervasive motivation" (Baumeister & Leary, 1995, p. 497).

➤ 24. From evolutionary and social comparison viewpoints, why are humans such social creatures.

FIGURE 9.18 Affiliation brings us companionship, intimacy, love, and also basic social contact. To satisfy these desires we form friendships, interact with family members, join groups, converse with strangers, and flock together in crowds.

➤ 25. How does fear influence affiliation?

➤ 26. How and why does proximity influence affiliation and attraction?

Why Do We Affiliate?

Humans are social beings, and we affiliate in many ways (Figure 9.18). Some theorists argue that, over the course of evolution, individuals whose biological makeup predisposed them to affiliate were more likely to survive and reproduce than those ancestors who were reclusive. By affording greater access to sexual mates, more protection from predators, an efficient division of labor, and the passing of knowledge across generations, a socially oriented lifestyle had considerable adaptive value (Flinn, 1997; Kottak, 2000).

Psychologically, Craig Hill (1987) suggests that we affiliate for four basic reasons: to obtain positive stimulation, to receive emotional support, to gain attention, and to permit social comparison. **Social comparison** involves comparing our beliefs, feelings, and behaviors with those of other people. This helps us determine whether our responses are "normal" and enables us to judge the level of our cognitive and physical abilities (Festinger, 1954).

People differ in how strongly they desire to affiliate. In one study, college students who scored high on a personality test of *need for affiliation* made more friends during the semester than students who scored low (Byrne & Greendlinger, 1989). In another study, high school students wore beepers over a one-week period. They were signaled approximately every two hours, and recorded their thoughts and activities. Participants with a high need for affiliation were more likely than their peers to report that they were thinking about friends and wishing that they could be with people (Wong & Csikszentmihalyi, 1991).

People with a high need for affiliation also show a stronger *psychological sense of community*—the feeling of being part of a larger collective, of being engaged with others in pursuing common goals (Burroughs & Eby, 1998). People with a strong sense of community are more likely to engage in extracurricular school activities and keep abreast of local and national news (Davidson & Cotter, 1997). Clearly, our desire to feel connected can express itself in many ways.

Many situational factors affect our tendency to affiliate. For example, fear-inducing situations increase our desire to be with others (Schachter, 1959). During emergencies, as in the aftermath of earthquakes, floods, and hurricanes, many people find themselves bonding to strangers (Humphriss, 1989). When afraid, we most prefer to be with people who have been through the feared situation we are facing. This way, we can gauge the normalcy of our reactions and learn information about what to expect. In one study, hospital patients awaiting open-heart surgery expressed a stronger desire to have a roommate who already had been through the surgery than a preoperative roommate like themselves (Kulik & Mahler, 1989). And when such patients were assigned to postoperative rather than preoperative roommates, they became less anxious and later recovered from surgery more quickly (Kulik et al., 1996).

Initial Attraction

Attraction is the first phase of most friendships and romantic relationships. What causes us to "connect" with some people, but not others?

Proximity and Mere Exposure: "Haven't I Seen You Somewhere?"

People cannot develop a relationship unless they first meet, and proximity (nearness) is the best predictor of who will cross paths with whom. Movies like *Sleepless in Seattle* and *You've Got Mail* spotlight "long-distance" encounters, but in reality we interact most with people who are physically closer (Latané et al., 1995). Residents in married-student apartments are most likely to form friendships with other residents who live close by; students placed in assigned classroom seats are most likely to become friends with students seated nearby; and many adults meet their spouse or current dating partner at school, work, or a place of worship (Festinger et al., 1950; Michael et al., 1994).

Proximity increases the chance of frequent encounters, and over 200 experiments provide evidence of a **mere exposure effect:** Repeated exposure to a stimulus typically increases our liking for it. No matter the stimuli—college classmates, photographs of faces, random geometric shapes, foreign words, and so on—as long as they are not unpleasant and we are not oversaturated, exposure generally enhances liking (Zajonc, 1968; Winograd et al., 1999).

Similarity: Birds of a Feather

When it comes to attraction, folk wisdom covers all the bases. On the one hand, "opposites attract." On the other, "birds of a feather flock together." So which is it? The evidence is overwhelming: People most often are attracted to others who are similar to themselves (Byrne, 1997). For psychological attributes, similarity of attitudes, beliefs, and values seems to matter the most (Buss, 1985).

In the laboratory, college students' degree of liking for a stranger can be predicted very accurately simply by knowing the proportion of similar attitudes that they share (Byrne, 1997; Byrne & Nelson, 1965). This similarity-attraction relationship has been found across many groups, including people in Mexico, India, and Japan who ranged from fourth-graders to retirees. Outside the laboratory, Donn Byrne and his colleagues (1970) matched college students on a brief 30-minute date, pairing people with partners who had either highly similar or dissimilar attitudes. Students were more attracted to similar partners, talked with them more during the rest of the semester, and had a stronger desire to date them. One reason we like people with similar attitudes is that they validate our view of the world.

So like mismatched roommates Felix Unger (an uptight neatnik) and Oscar Madison (a carefree slob) in the classic movie *The Odd Couple,* do opposites ever attract? At times, of course. But much more often, opposites repel (Krueger & Caspi, 1993; Rosenbaum, 1986). When choosing potential friends or mates, we typically screen out people who are dissimilar to us. And when dissimilar people do form relationships, they tend not to last as long (Byrne, 1997). As Diane Felmlee (1998) found, dissimilarity increases the risk of "fatal attractions": we initially find some characteristic of another person appealing, but over time we come to dislike it. In short, what is intriguing and different today may repel us tomorrow!

Physical Attractiveness: Spellbound by Beauty

It may be shallow and in many ways unfair, but most people seem drawn to beauty like moths to a flame (Figure 9.19). In many studies, when men and women rate the desirability of hypothetical short-term dating partners, their judgments are influenced most strongly by how good-looking the person is (Wiederman & Dubois, 1998). When faced with a potential dating partner who is attractive rather than unattractive, women and men are more likely to misrepresent their personal qualities in a way that makes themselves appear more similar to the potential date (Rowatt et al., 1999). And when Donn Byrne (1970) matched college students on an *actual* brief date, students rated physically attractive partners as more desirable and were more interested in dating them.

In a classic study, Elaine Walster and her colleagues (1966) randomly paired over 700 first-year University of Minnesota students on blind dates for a "Welcome Week" dance. Earlier, the researchers had given all the participants a battery of personality, intelligence, and social skills tests, and had other students rate each participant's physical attractiveness. During an intermission at the dance, students rated how desirable they found their partner. Did any of psychological characteristics predict who would like whom? No. Only one factor did. Women

➤ 27. Do birds of a feather flock together, or do opposites attract? Describe the evidence.

FIGURE 9.19 Hey, good lookin! The way that both sexes initially judge someone is influenced by that person's attractiveness and other physical features. We are not alone. Many species, such as these Frigate birds (male on the right), have evolved distinct features and ritualized mating displays to attract a potential mate's attention.

and men who dated physically attractive partners liked them more and had a stronger desire to date them again. Similarly, among 100 homosexual men who researchers paired together for a date, men's liking for their partner and desire to date him again were most strongly influenced by the partner's physical attractiveness (Sergios & Cody, 1986).

> 28. Identify two factors that may underlie the desire to affiliate more with attractive people.

What motivates our desire to affiliate with attractive people? One factor may be the widespread stereotype that "what is beautiful is good"; we often assume that attractive people have more positive personality characteristics than unattractive people (Dion et al., 1972; Feingold, 1992). The popular media reinforces this stereotype. Analyzing five decades of top-grossing U.S. movies, Stephen Smith and his colleagues (1999) found that good-looking male and female characters were portrayed as more intelligent, moral, and sociable than less attractive characters. Because we are often judged by the company we keep, we also may prefer to associate with attractive people to buttress our self-esteem. Self-conscious people who are highly concerned about how they come across to others are especially likely to gravitate toward attractive people (Richardson, 1991; Snyder et al., 1985).

Lest you conclude that beauty is the key to happiness, we should note that physical attractiveness during the college years is unrelated to life satisfaction in middle age (Kaner, 1995). And physically attractive people do not necessarily have the highest levels of self-esteem (Major et al., 1984). Beauty is sometimes linked with self-doubt, because highly attractive individuals may attribute the positive responses of others solely to their "surface" beauty rather than to their inner personal qualities.

Although we are attracted to "beautiful people," we are most likely to have a dating partner or spouse whose level of physical attractiveness is similar to our own—a **matching effect** (Feingold, 1988). In this case, "birds of equally attractive feathers flock together." One reason for this is that the most attractive people may match up first and are "taken," then the next most attractive, and so on (Kalick & Hamilton, 1988). Another factor is that, to lessen the risk of rejection, some people may refrain from approaching potential dating partners who are more attractive than they are (Huston, 1973). Among dating couples, those who are best matched on attractiveness are most likely to fall deeply in love, and couples who eventually marry are more similar in attractiveness than dating couples in general (White, 1980).

Close Relationships: As Attraction Deepens

People may share an initial attraction, but have different goals regarding what form they want a relationship to take. Compared with women, men show more interest in short-term mating (e.g., dating without developing a committed relationship) and perceive short-term mates as more desirable (Wiederman & Dubois, 1998). Men typically have more permissive attitudes than women about both casual and premarital sex, and have more sexual partners over their lifetime (Clark & Hatfield, 1989; Hyde and Oliver, 2000). Women—even those who have permissive attitudes about premarital sex—are more likely than men to want partners who make an emotional investment in the relationship.

What Do Men and Women Seek in a Mate?

> 29. Describe some gender differences in mate preferences.

Whether initial attraction leads to a close relationship also depends on the degree to which each partner perceives the other to have desired characteristics. But what do women and men want in a mate? Men typically prefer younger women, whereas women prefer older men. In terms of personal qualities, Table 9.3 shows the overall results of a worldwide study of mate preferences in 37 cultures (Buss et al., 1990). Men and women show considerable overall agreement, but some gender

> ### TABLE 9.3 WHAT DO YOU LOOK FOR IN A MATE?

Women and men from 37 cultures rated each characteristic on a 4-point scale. From top to bottom, the numbers represent the order (rank) and most to least highly rated, for Buss's worldwide sample. How would you rate their importance?

| | Preferred by | |
Characteristic	Women	Men
Mutual attraction/love	1	1
Dependable character	2	2
Emotional stability/maturity	3	3
Pleasing disposition	4	4
Education/intelligence	5	6
Sociability	6	7
Good health	7	5
Desire for home/children	8	8
Ambitious	9	11
Refinement	10	9
Similar education	11	14
Good financial prospect	12	13
Good looks	13	10
Social status	14	15
Good cook/housekeeper	15	12
Similar religion	16	17
Similar politics	17	18
Chastity	18	16

Data from Buss et al., 1990.

differences also emerge. Men place greater value on a potential mate being physically attractive and possessing good domestic skills, whereas women place greater value on a potential mate's earning potential, status, and ambitiousness.

The evolution of desire. To some evolutionary psychologists, our mating strategies and preferences reflect inherited tendencies, shaped over the ages in response to different types of adaptive problems that men and women faced (Buss et al., 1998; Trivers, 1972). In evolutionary terms, our most successful ancestors were those who survived and passed down the greatest numbers of their genes to future generations. Men who had sex with more partners increased the likelihood of fathering more children. Men also may have used a woman's youth and attractive, healthy physical appearance as signs that she was fertile and had many years left to bear children (Buss, 1989).

In contrast, ancestral women had little to gain and much to lose by mating with many men. According to **parental investment theory** (Trivers, 1972), the gender with a greater investment (costs) in producing offspring will be more selective in choosing a mate. In humans and other mammals, females typically make a greater investment than males: They carry the fetus, incur health risks, and nourish the newborn. Engaging in short-term sexual relationships with multiple men can create uncertainty about which one is the father, thereby decreasing a

> 30. How do evolutionary and social structure models explain gender differences in mate preferences?

male's willingness to commit resources to raising the child. Thus women maximized their reproductive success by being selective and choosing mates who were willing and able to commit time, energy, and other resources (e.g., food, shelter, protection) to the family (Buss, 1989). Through natural selection, according to evolutionary psychologists, the differing qualities that maximized men and women's reproductive success eventually became part of their biological nature.

Social-cultural perspectives.   Many scientists challenge evolutionary psychologists' explanations for human mating patterns and other social behaviors (Scher, 1999; Lynn, 1989). Adaptive behavior patterns may have been passed from parents to children not through genes, but through learning. In addition, **social structure theory** proposes that men and women display different mating preferences because society directs them into different social roles (Eagly & Wood, 1999). Even in this day and age, women generally have less power, lower wages, and less access to resources than men do. In two-income marriages, women are more likely to be the partner who switches to part-time work or a full-time homemaker role after childbirth. Thus society's division of labor still tends to socialize men into the "breadwinner" role and women into the "homemaker" role.

It makes sense, then, for women to seek men who will be successful wage earners, and for men to seek mates who can fulfill the domestic worker role. An older male–younger female age gap is favorable because older men are likely to be further along in earning power, younger women are more economically dependent, and this conforms to cultural expectations of marital roles. This division-of-labor hypothesis does not directly address why men emphasize a mate's physical attractiveness more than women, but Alice Eagly and Wendy Wood (1999) speculate that attractiveness is viewed as part of what women "exchange" in return for a male's earning capacity.

We now have two competing explanations for gender differences in mating behavior: the evolutionary approach and the social structure view. Which view is more valid? Our *Research Close-Up* looks at one attempt to answer this question.

> 31. How consistent are gender differences in mate preferences across cultures? How might this support both evolutionary and social structure views?

RESEARCH ⬧ CLOSE-UP

Gender Differences in the Ideal Mate: Evolution or Social Roles?

▶ Background

How can we possibly test the hypothesis that over the ages, evolution has shaped the psyche of men and women to be inherently different? Evolutionary psychologist David Buss proposes that, as a start, we can examine whether gender differences in mating preferences are consistent across cultures. If they are, this would be consistent with the view that men and women follow universal, biologically based mating strategies that transcend culture. Based on principles of evolutionary psychology, Buss hypothesized that *across cultures:*

- Men will prefer to marry younger women, because such women have greater reproductive capacity.

- Men will value a potential mate's attractiveness more than women will, because men use attractiveness as a sign of health and fertility.
- Women will place greater value than men on a potential mate's earning potential, because this provides survival advantages for the women and her offspring.

Method

A team of 50 scientists administered questionnaires to women and men from 37 cultures around the globe. Although random sampling could not be used, the sample of 10,047 participants was ethnically, religiously, and socioeconomically diverse. Participants reported the ideal ages at

–Continued

which they and a spouse would marry, rank-ordered (from "most to least desirable") a list of 13 qualities that a potential mate might have, and rated the importance of 18 mate qualities on a second list (Table 9.3).

▶ Results and Evolutionary Interpretation

In every culture, men desired to marry younger women. Overall, they believed that the ideal ages for men and women to marry were 27.5 and 24.8 years, respectively. (In every culture, women preferred older men, reporting on average an ideal marriage age of 28.8 for husbands and 25.4 for wives.) In every culture, men valued having a physically attractive mate more than women did, and in 36 of 37 cultures, women attached more importance than men did to a mate's earning potential. Buss concluded that the findings strongly supported the predictions of evolutionary theory.

▶ Reanalysis and Social Roles Interpretation

David Buss made his data available to social structure theorists Alice Eagly and Wendy Wood, who tested several predictions from their theory.

- Men place greater value than women on a mate's having good domestic skills, because this is consistent with culturally defined gender roles.
- If economic and power inequalities cause men and women to attach different values to a mate's age, earning potential, and domestic skills, then these gender differences should be smaller in cultures where there is less inequality between men and women.

The item "good cook and housekeeper" produced large overall gender differences, with men valuing it more highly. Eagly and Wood then used the United Nations Gender Empowerment Measure to assess the degree of gender equality in each culture. This measure reflects women's percentage share of administrative, managerial, professional, and technical jobs, seats in parliament, and earned income relative to men.

As predicted by the social structure model, in cultures with greater gender equality men showed less of a preference for younger women, women displayed less of a preference for older men, and the gender gap decreased in mate preferences for a good housekeeper and good financial prospect. Recall that this division-of-labor model does not directly address why men value physical attractiveness more than women, and this gender difference was *not* smaller in cultures with greater gender equality.

▶ Critical Discussion

Buss's research provides evidence of remarkably consistent gender differences in worldwide mate preferences. Buss interprets this cross-cultural consistency as evidence that men and women follow universal, biologically based mating strategies. Yet the fact that behavior is consistent across cultures does not, by itself, demonstrate *why* those patterns occur (Wood & Eagly, 2000). Eagly and Wood's analysis suggests that a common social condition found across cultures—gender inequality—accounts for some of the gender differences in mating preferences.

In science, such controversy stimulates opposing camps to find more sophisticated ways to test their hypotheses. Ultimately, everyone's goal is to arrive at the most plausible explanation for behavior. This is why scientists make their data available to one another, knowing that their peers may use the data to bolster an opposing point of view.

Although men and women consistently differ in some of their mating preferences and strategies, it is important not to stereotype men and women as "coming from different planets." The similar overall order of mate preferences shown in Table 9.3 indicates that we are talking about shades of the same color, not different colors. In fact, Buss and his colleagues (1990) found that cross-cultural differences in mating preferences were *stronger* overall than gender differences, noting that "there may be more similarity between men and women from the same culture than between men and men or women and women from different cultures" (p. 17).

Sources: David M. Buss, 1989. Sex differences in human mate preferences: Evolutionary hypotheses tested in 37 cultures. *Behavioral and Brain Sciences, 12,* 1–49.

Alice H. Eagly & Wendy Wood, 1999. The origins of sex differences in human behavior: Evolved dispositions versus social roles. *American Psychologist, 54,* 408–423.

Social penetration and social exchange.   How do close relationships grow? According to **social penetration theory,** relationships progress as interactions between people become *broader,* involving more areas of their lives, and *deeper,* involving more intimate and personally meaningful areas (Altman & Taylor, 1973). Partners may share activities, other experiences, or physical intimacy, but *self-disclosure*—the sharing of innermost thoughts and feelings—plays a key role in fostering close relationships (Harvey & Omarzu, 1997). In friendships, dating relationships, and marriages, more extensive and intimate self-disclosure is associated with greater emotional involvement and relationship satisfaction (Hendrick, 1989; Miller, 1990). This relation is reciprocal. Self-disclosure fosters intimacy and trust, and intimacy and trust encourage self-disclosure.

> 32. According to social penetration and social exchange theories, what factors influence whether a relationship will deepen, be satisfying, and continue?

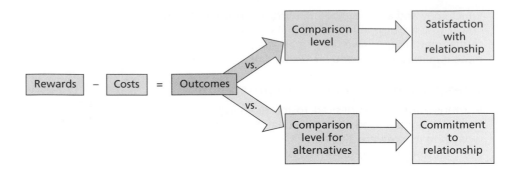

FIGURE 9.20 According to Thibaut and Kelley's social exchange theory, rewards minus costs equal the outcome of a relationship. Comparing our outcomes with two standards, the comparison level and the comparison level for alternatives, determines our satisfaction and commitment in the relationship, respectively.

According to John Thibaut and Harold Kelley's (1959) **social exchange theory,** the course of a relationship also is governed by rewards and costs that the partners experience. Rewards include companionship, emotional support, and the satisfaction of other needs. Costs may include effort spent to maintain the relationship, arguments and conflicts, and so forth. The overall *outcome* (rewards minus costs) in a relationship can be positive or negative.

Outcomes are evaluated against two standards (Figure 9.20). The first, called the *comparison level,* is the outcome that a person has grown to expect in relationships, and it influences the person's *satisfaction* with the present relationship. Outcomes that meet or exceed the comparison level are satisfying; those that fall below this standard are dissatisfying. The second standard, called the *comparison level for alternatives,* focuses on potential alternatives to the relationship, and it influences the person's degree of *commitment* (Floyd & Wasner, 1994; Honeycutt, 1995). Thus a person may leave a satisfying relationship if something even better is available, or may remain committed to a relationship that is unsatisfying because the alternatives seem even worse.

Love

Love must be a powerful motive if it indeed "can make the world go round," but which type of love does this? In his book *The Art of Loving,* psychoanalyst Erich Fromm (1956) identified five fundamental types of love: parental love, erotic (sexual) love, self-love, love for humanity, and love of God. Even restricting ourselves to friendships and romantic relationships, poet Elizabeth Barrett Browning 's insight, "How do I love thee? Let me count the ways" is most applicable.

Types of Love

Passionate love involves intense emotion, arousal, and yearning for the partner (Hatfield, 1988). We may ride an emotional roller coaster that ranges from ecstasy when the partner is present to heartsickness when the person is absent. **Companionate love** involves affection, deep caring about the partner's well-being, and a commitment to "being there" for the other (Caspi & Herbener, 1990; Hatfield, 1988). Both types of love contribute to satisfaction in the long-term romantic relationships (Sprecher & Regan, 1998). In general, passionate love is less stable and declines more quickly over time than companionate love, but this does not mean that the flames of passionate love inevitably extinguish (Tucker & Aron, 1993).

The distinction between passionate and companionate love is one of psychology's most basic. However, Robert Sternberg (1988, 1997) proposes a

➤ 33. How does Sternberg's model expand upon the passionate-companionate love distinction?

three-component **triangular theory of love** that focuses on *intimacy* (closeness, sharing, and valuing one's partner), *commitment* (the decision to remain in the relationship), and *passion* (feelings of romance, physical attraction, and sexual desire). Research suggests that these three qualities do a good job of capturing the way people commonly think about love (Aron & Westbay, 1996).

Figure 9.21 shows that different combinations of these components characterize seven types of love (plus "nonlove," which is the absence of all three). Sternberg proposes that the ultimate form of love between people—*consummate love*—occurs when intimacy, passion, and commitment are all present.

The Cognitive-Arousal Model: Why Does My Heart Pound?

Our culture believes in the concept of love and we are exposed to love themes from childhood. Woman meets Prince Charming; they fall in love, get married, and live happily ever after. By adolescence, we are eagerly awaiting the glories of love.

According to the **cognitive-arousal model of love,** the passionate component of love has interacting cognitive and physiological components (Berscheid, 1984; Hatfield & Rapson, 1987). Primed with our beliefs and expectations about love, if we experience high arousal in the presence of someone whom we perceive as attractive and desirable, we may conclude that we must be "falling in love." This model suggests that emotional arousal actually caused by some other factor may sometimes be misinterpreted as love. This phenomenon is known as **transfer of excitation:** arousal due to one source is perceived ("misattributed") as due to another source (Zillmann, 1984).

Consider an experiment by Donald Dutton and Arthur Aron (1974). An experimenter—either a male or attractive young female—approached male participants as they crossed over one of two bridges just north of Vancouver, Canada. The "arousing" bridge was the Capilano Suspension Bridge, a narrow 450-foot-long structure that wobbles and sways on cables 230 feet above a deep ravine and river (Figure 9.22). The "nonarousing" bridge was broader, sturdy, and much lower over the same river. Participants were asked to write stories in response to a series of pictures, after which the experimenter offered his or her name and phone number to the participant and told him to call if he wanted more information about the study. When the researchers analyzed the stories, they found sexual themes only in the stories of participants who had encountered the female experimenter on the suspension bridge. This group also made the most follow-up calls to the experimenter.

Dutton and Aron (1974) concluded that men's sexual attraction toward the woman was increased by the arousal produced by being on the suspension bridge, and a meta-analysis of over 30 experiments supports this model (Foster et al., 1998). When we are in the presence of someone we find attractive, other sources of arousal—whether a wobbly bridge, physical exercise, or a frightening movie—increase our sexual attraction even if we recognize those outside sources. If we are not aware of these sources, our attraction increases even more.

Of course, for close relationships to develop and endure, they need more than passion alone. Intimacy, self-disclosure, and commitment provide a basis for the trust and friendship that sustains and increases love. As our *Applications of Psychological Science* feature highlights, other behaviors also help to make close relationships successful.

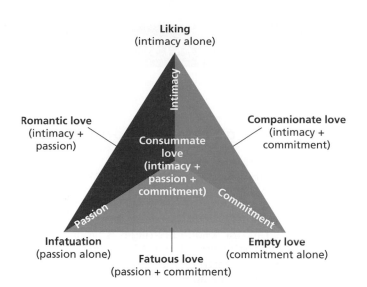

FIGURE 9.21 According to Sternberg, different types of love involve varying combinations of intimacy, commitment, and passion. Consummate love involves the presence of all three factors, whereas nonlove represents the absence of all three.

➤ 34. Explain how transfer of excitation can influence our feelings of love.

FIGURE 9.22 The Capilano Suspension Bridge provided a novel setting for a study testing the cognitive-arousal model of love.

➤ 35. Based on marital research, give some advice to a newlywed couple about behaviors that will help keep their relationship strong.

APPLICATIONS OF PSYCHOLOGICAL SCIENCE

Making Close Relationships Work: Lessons From Psychological Research

Close relationships go through good times and bad, persisting or dissolving over time. Consider marriage. Though highly intimate, this union often is fragile. In the United States, about half of first marriages end in divorce, and the failure rate for second marriages is higher. How can people make their close relationships more satisfying and stable? Recent research on marriage suggests several answers that also can be applied to dating relationships and friendships.

For decades, most marital research simply asked people about their marriages. But as Figure 9.23 shows, researchers are now bringing couples into laboratories to videotape their interactions and to chart their facial and physiological responses as they discuss emotionally charged issues (Gottman et al., 1999; Kiecolt-Glaser et al., 1998). Rather than focusing only on unhappy couples to find out what is going wrong in their relationships, researchers are also studying happy couples to discover the secrets of their success.

Using these methods and new marital interview techniques, psychologists have predicted whether marriages will last or dissolve with impressive accuracy (Carrière et al., 2000). In one laboratory study, John Gottman and his coworkers (1998) collected behavioral and physiological data from 130 newlywed couples as they discussed areas of marital conflict (e.g., in-laws, finances, sex) during the first six months of their marriage. Six years later, participants reported being happily married, unhappily married, or divorced. Using data collected while the couples were newlyweds, the researchers predicted which marriages would end in divorce with 83 percent accuracy, and the degree of marital satisfaction in still-married couples with 80 percent accuracy.

Surprisingly, the amount of anger expressed by husbands and wives in their laboratory interactions predicted neither stability nor happiness six years later. Instead, the crucial factor was the manner in which couples dealt with their anger. Particularly important were four behaviors that Gottman (1994) calls "The Four Horsemen of the Apocalypse": *criticism, contempt, defensiveness,* and *stonewalling* (listener withdrawal and nonresponsiveness).

Couples headed for unhappiness or divorce often exhibit these behaviors while discussing conflict, thereby escalating their conflict and negative emotions. When the wife criticizes the husband, he often stonewalls and withdraws from her attempts to reach some resolution. Her resulting frustration leads to stronger emotional displays and criticism, and the interaction degenerates into exchanges of contempt in which the partners tear down

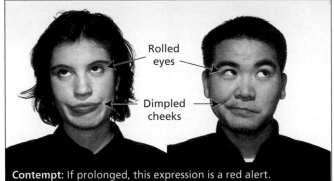

Contempt: If prolonged, this expression is a red alert. Especially when accompanied by sarcasm and insults, it suggests a marriage in serious trouble.

FIGURE 9.23 In John Gottman's "love lab," married couples (husband visible in rear) are filmed while interacting. Facial expressions, actions, heart rate, breathing rate, perspiration, fidgeting, and other responses are measured.

each other. Once this negative cycle develops, even positive overtures by one spouse are likely to evoke a negative response from the other (Margolin & Wampold, 1981).

Happily married couples experience conflict and anger too, but do not allow the spiral of negativity to get out of control. Instead, they make frequent "repair attempts" to resolve their differences in a spirit of mutual respect and support. Gottman and his coworkers (1998) found that in happy marriages, the wife often introduced the conflict topic in a softened or low-intensity manner, rather than

–Continued

with sarcasm, criticism, and strong emotion. Next a key factor occurred: The husband responded to the issues she raised in a concerned and respectful manner that de-escalated negative emotion. A husband who turns off the television and listens to his wife, or who says, "I can see you're upset, so let's work this out," demonstrates that her concerns are important to him. In happy marriages, after the husbands' responsiveness de-escalated the conflict, couples tended to "soothe" one another (and themselves) with positive comments and humor, resulting in more emotionally positive interchanges and lowered physiological arousal.

Happily married partners also make the effort to get to know each other's psychological world—their fears and dreams, philosophy of life, attitudes, and values—and they continually update their knowledge. This "love map," as Gottman (1998) calls it, allows each partner be more responsive to the other's needs and to navigate around relationship roadblocks. Such behavior contributes to an essential aspect of happy marriages: a deep and intimate friendship between the partners. Gottman (1994) notes that the lessons of happy

TABLE 9.4	HOW STRONG IS YOUR RELATIONSHIP?		
Answer each question True (T) or False (F):			
I can tell you about some of my partner's dreams.		T	F
We just love talking to each other.		T	F
My partner is one of my best friends.		T	F
My partner listens respectfully, even when we disagree.		T	F
We generally mesh well on basic values and goals in life.		T	F
I feel that my partner knows me pretty well.		T	F

The greater the number of "True" answers, the stronger your relationship. (Courtesy of John Gottman.)

marriages can be applied to other types of close relationships. Affirmative answers to the questions in Table 9.4 suggest that such relationships are on solid psychological ground.

❯ ACHIEVEMENT MOTIVATION

Extraordinary accomplishments like those of percussionist Evelyn Glennie vividly demonstrate the desire to achieve. As a college student, you are keenly aware of society's emphasis on achievement, and you know that some people seek out and thrive on challenges, whereas others do not. In the 1950s, David McClelland, John Atkinson, and their associates (1953) began to explore these individual differences in **need for achievement,** which represents the desire to accomplish tasks and attain standards of excellence. They viewed the need for achievement as a relatively stable personality characteristic that energizes and guides our achievement behavior.

❯ 36. What types of achievement goals are associated with a high motive for success, and with a high fear of failure?

Motivation for Success: The Thrill of Victory

People can strive to succeed for two radically different reasons. The first is a positively oriented *motive for success* and the second is a negatively oriented motivation to avoid failure, more commonly called *fear of failure*. McClelland and his colleagues (1953) measured the motive for success by showing participants a series of pictures like the one in Figure 9.24 and asking them to make up a story about each one. Other researchers use psychological tests that ask participants about their own achievement behavior (Elliot & Church, 1997).

People who have a strong motive for success are attracted to the "thrill of victory" that comes about from mastering skills or outperforming other people. Andrew Elliot and Marcy Church (1997) report that college students with a high motivation for success focus on *mastery goals* and *performance-approach goals*. Mastery goals reflect intrinsic motivation and include "I want to learn as much as possible from this class" and "I prefer course material that arouses my curiosity, even if it is difficult to learn." Students who view mastery as important study hard, think about the material deeply, and display better long-term retention than their peers. In contrast, performance-approach goals involve social comparison, such as "I am motivated by the thought of outperforming my peers in this class." Striving to outperform classmates also leads to high effort and predicts somewhat higher course grades (Elliot & Church, 1997; Elliot et al., 1999).

FIGURE 9.24 Pictures like this are used to elicit stories that are scored for the motive to succeed. Which of the following two stories, written by different people, reflects a stronger motive to succeed? (1) This young man is sitting in school, but he is dreaming about the day when he will become a doctor. He . . . will study and work harder than anyone else. He goes on to become one of the top medical researchers in the world. (2) The boy is daydreaming about how much he hates being in school. . . . He would like to run away from home and just take it easy on a tropical island. However, he is doomed to be in the rat race the rest of his life.

Fear of Failure: The Agony of Defeat

Fear of failure usually is measured by psychological tests that ask people to report how much anxiety they experience in achievement situations. People with a high fear of failure show an interesting pattern of achievement goals (Elliot & Church, 1997; Elliot & McGregor, 1999). They tend to adopt *performance-approach goals* in which it is important to outperform peers, but they also have strong *performance-avoidance goals* (e.g., "My fear of performing poorly in this class is often what motivates me").

Common sense might suggest that a strong motive for success combined with a strong fear of failure might lead a person to perform better on challenging tasks than someone who is motivated only by a desire for success. But this is not the case. The worry associated with fear of failure and performance-avoidance goals impairs task performance. Anxiety makes it difficult to process information effectively and attend to the task requirements, and performance deteriorates (Sarason & Sarason, 1990). In sports, this is the athlete who "chokes" under pressure (Smith et al., 1996).

Achievement Needs and Situational Factors

People with a strong need for achievement—particularly those who score high on motivation for success and low on fear of failure—are ambitious and persist longer after encountering difficulty than do people with a low need for achievement. College students with high achievement motivation (which researchers call *need achievement*) tend to seek out and enter more prestigious occupations (Heckhausen, 1991). But this striving for success does not apply equally to all situations.

In the laboratory and the workplace, high-need achievers generally do not outperform individuals with low achievement motivation when conditions are relaxed and tasks are easy. But when tasks are challenging or the importance of doing well is stressed, high-need achievers outshine low-need achievers (McClelland, 1989). Competitive situations decrease low-need achievers' task enjoyment, but are music to the ears of high-need achievers (Epstein & Harackiewicz, 1992). In general, high-need achievers are most likely to strive hard for success when:

- they perceive themselves as personally responsible for the outcome;
- they perceive some risk of not succeeding; and
- there is an opportunity to receive performance feedback (Koester & McClelland, 1990).

> 37. How do people with high versus low achievement needs differ in the difficulty of tasks they select? Explain why this occurs.

What would you predict? When given a choice of performing a task that is very easy (a high probability of success), moderately difficult (a 40 to 60 percent probability of success), or very difficult (a low probability of success), which task will high-need achievers choose? Contrary to what you might expect, they prefer intermediate rather than extremely high or low risks (Atkinson & Birch, 1978). On a ring-toss task, they tend at first to select an intermediate distance to toss the ring at the peg. This distance is the most challenging because the outcome—success versus failure—*is most uncertain*. People with a high fear of failure are more likely to choose tasks that are easy (where success is almost assured) or very difficult (where success is not expected).

The key to understanding this behavior is to recognize that it is the individual's *perception* of task uncertainty that counts. For most of us, the probability of successfully climbing Mt. Everest is virtually zero. But to highly trained mountaineers, the task is neither impossible nor easy. Decades ago, sociologist and mountain climber Dick Emerson (1966) joined a Mt. Everest expedition. He predicted that the climbers' communications with one another would strike a balance between optimistic and pessimistic comments about reaching their goal to keep their perceived chance of success–failure at 50-50, thereby maintaining maximum motivation. Not only did Emerson find such a pattern when he monitored the climbers' spontaneous communications, but he also tested this hypothesis by randomly making optimistic or pessimistic statements to individual members of the climbing team. Most of the time, the climbers' replies were opposite to Emerson's, thereby "balancing out" their interaction and maintaining a perception that the climb had an intermediate chance of success.

Family and Cultural Influences

➤ 38. How do cultural factors influence the expression of achievement needs?

High need for achievement develops when parents encourage and reward achievement, but do not punish failure (Koestner & McClelland, 1990). Conversely, fear of failure seems to develop when successful achievement is taken for granted by parents, but failure is punished. Therefore the child learns to dread the possibility of failing (Weiner, 1992). Providing children with a cognitively stimulating home environment that has many opportunities for learning fosters their intrinsic motivation to perform academic tasks (Gottfried et al., 1998).

Individualistic cultures, like those in North America and much of Europe, tend to stress personal achievement. In cultures that nurture collectivism, such as those in China and Japan, achievement motivation more strongly reflects a desire to fit into the family and social group, meet its expectations, and work for its goals (Markus & Kitayama, 1991). Chinese high school students, for example, typically care more about meeting their parents' expectations for academic success than do American students (Chen & Lan, 1998).

These cultural differences, however, do not portray a black-and-white picture. As Sushila Niles (1998) found in comparing the achievement goals of Sri Lankans (collectivistic) and Anglo-Australians (individualistic), both groups supported the concept of individual responsibility and a strong work ethic. As expected, Sri Lankans' achievement goals were more group and family oriented than those of the Australians, but they also reported important individual goals. Conversely, the Australians held some group-oriented goals, particularly as concerns the family.

The relation between cultural values and achievement motivation also is suggested by the correspondence between the amount of achievement imagery in children's storybooks and measures of national accomplishment. Presumably, the level of concern for achievement in children's books reflects the motivational level of the adults in the country at that time, as well as the values that are being transmitted to children. In one study, achievement motivation scores based on the content of second- and fourth-grade schoolbooks corresponded

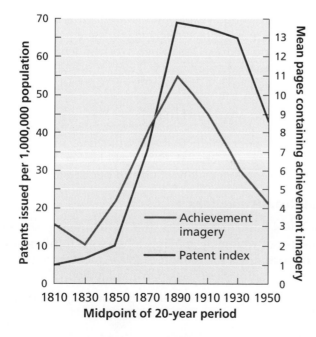

FIGURE 9.25 Relation between achievement imagery found in children's stories and number of patents per million population issued in the United States between 1810 and 1950.

From deCharms & Moeller, 1962.

closely to the number of patents issued per million population in the United States between 1810 and 1950 (Figure 9.25; de Charms & Moeller, 1962).

〉 MOTIVATION IN THE WORKPLACE

The workplace is one of life's most important achievement arenas. You may devote forty to fifty years of your life to a career, and you probably desire that work to be motivating and satisfying. Motivation also is vital to organizations. To succeed, an organization needs workers who are motivated to join it and perform their jobs well (Steers & Porter, 1991).

Why Do People Work?

➤ 39. In the workplace, are most people motivated primarily by money? Explain.

The earliest theory of work motivation, advanced by Frederick Taylor (1911), held that workers are motivated almost entirely by money. This view may characterize some workers, but research indicates that many more view personal accomplishment as the most important job attribute. Opportunities for mastery, growth, and satisfying interpersonal relationships are key motivators for many employees (Buckingham & Coffman, 1999; McGregor, 1960).

Cultural factors influence work motivation (Figure 9.26). In collectivistic Japan, traditional business organizations adopt a concept of *Kaizen* (continuous improvement), encouraging workers to develop skills and increase productivity (Berry, 1998). Companies assume responsibility for their employees' welfare, promote them slowly, and are willing to retain them for life (Ouichi, 1981). The company becomes integral to the workers' identity and they are strongly motivated by loyalty to their managers and the organization (Misumi, 1985).

FIGURE 9.26 In Japan, achievement motivation generally manifests itself as a desire to conform to the expectations of the social group and to contribute to the attainment of group goals. Demanding but caring managers and leaders are highly effective because they foster a sense of obligation that causes employees to work hard.

Job Satisfaction and Performance

If we tell you that satisfied employees perform much better than unsatisfied employees, this conclusion seems so obvious that you may wonder why researchers bother to study it. There is just one problem: It is not true. Major research reviews have found that *job productivity* (making more sales, building better products, and so on) and job satisfaction are only weakly related (Brayfield & Crockett, 1955; Iaffaldano & Muchinsky, 1985). At present, there is no agreed-upon explanation for why this relation is so weak. *Absenteeism* and *turnover* (leaving the organization) are other important aspects of job performance. Dissatisfied workers tend to be absent slightly more often than satisfied workers and, especially when the job market is good, they are somewhat more likely to quit their current job (Gerhart, 1990).

➤ 40. How strongly is job satisfaction related to job productivity? Do you have any ideas why this might be?

Enhancing Work Motivation

Given the high cost of poor productivity, absenteeism, and turnover to organizations, industrial/organizational (I/O) psychologists have designed many programs to enhance employee motivation and performance.

Enriching and Redesigning Jobs

➤ 41. Describe three types of programs that psychologists have designed to enhance work motivation. What major perspectives do these programs rest upon?

Reflecting Maslow's humanistic theory, **job enrichment** programs attempt to increase intrinsic motivation by making jobs more fulfilling and providing workers with opportunities for growth. A job is most intrinsically motivating and satisfying when it provides (Hackman and Lawler, 1971):

- *skill variety.* A variety of tasks must be performed, requiring many talents and skills.

- *task identity.* A "whole" product is completed from beginning to end.
- *task significance.* Tasks have an impact on the lives or work of other people.
- *autonomy.* The worker has some freedom to determine work procedures and schedules.
- *job feedback.* The job provides clear feedback about performance effectiveness.

Job enrichment has promoted better work outcomes in manufacturing plants, white-collar and police organizations, and other work settings (van der Vegt et al., 1998). At a truck assembly plant owned by Volvo in Sweden, job enrichment improved performance, lowered absenteeism, and reduced turnover (Wexley & Yukl, 1977). Production teams of five to twelve workers replaced assembly lines (which were low on all five core job dimensions). Team members elected their own coordinator, decided task distribution, managed their own quality control, and could vary their work as long as they met production standards.

Modifying External Incentives

Learning theory predicts that performance will increase when reinforcers are made contingent on productivity. Union National Bank instituted a program in which it paid workers for the number of customers served and new accounts opened. As a result, employees' take-home pay increased by 25 percent and the bank's profits doubled (Aamodt, 1991). Another program reduced tardiness and absenteeism among industrial workers in an unusual way. Every day, each worker who arrived on time was dealt a card from a poker deck. At the end of the week, the worker with the best five-card poker hand (and who therefore had to be on time every day) won a $20 prize (Pedalino & Gamboa, 1974)!

Money is not the only external incentive than modifies performance. The Emory Air Freight Corporation used praise and recognition to reinforce desired employee behaviors, and a large department store improved the performance of its salespeople by reinforcing them with "time off" for desired behaviors (Luthans et al., 1981).

Goal-Setting and Management by Objectives

Goal setting is a powerful motivational technique that has increased employee productivity in almost every study conducted, and **management by objectives (MBO)** combines goal setting with employee participation and feedback (Locke & Latham, 1990). These approaches reflect the cognitive assumption that motivation is maximized when people pursue valued goals that they perceive as attainable. Effective goal setting involves developing specific goals (rather than general goals or "do your best goals") that are challenging yet attainable (rather than easy) *and* planning a clear strategy for achieving them (Locke, 1996).

Employee participation is the second component of MBO. Employees meet at least once a year with their managers to develop employee goals and plan how to attain them. Goals may focus on individual or group performance. Participation is designed to increase employees' acceptance of the goals and enhance the likelihood that goals will be attained. The third MBO component, *objective feedback,* is essential to effective goal setting (Locke & Latham, 1990; Wilk & Resmon, 1998). It provides opportunities to recognize success and, when goals are not met, it encourages a search for new methods to reach them.

Robert Rodgers and John Hunter (1991) meta-analyzed 70 studies that tested MBO in different organizations. Productivity increased in 97 percent of the studies, but the amount of improvement depended strongly upon whether top management actively supported the program. Even well-planned motivation programs will be less effective when an organization is not highly committed to it.

➤ 42. Explain three main types of motivational conflict. Can you think of examples from your own life?

"C'mon, c'mon—it's either one or the other."

FIGURE 9.27   An unfortunate avoidance-avoidance conflict.

〉 MOTIVATIONAL CONFLICT

Motivational goals sometimes conflict with one another. Achievement and affiliation motives may clash, for example, when we have to choose between studying for an exam and attending a party. This conflict places us in a motivational bind that can affect our well-being. Kurt Lewin (1935) described such conflicts in terms of two opposing tendencies: approach and avoidance. When something attracts us, we tend to approach it; when something repels us, we tend to avoid it. Different combinations of approach and avoidance tendencies can produce three basic types of conflict.

Approach-approach conflict involves opposition between two attractive alternatives. Selecting one means losing the other. Conflict is at its greatest when both alternatives, such as a choice between two desirable career paths, are equally attractive and important. The reverse dilemma is **avoidance-avoidance conflict,** in which a person faces two undesirable alternatives (Figure 9.27). Do I spend all week studying boring material for my test, or do I skip studying and fail the exam?

Approach-avoidance conflict involves being attracted to and repelled by *the same goal.* These are sometimes the most difficult conflicts to resolve. A college senior, thinking of changing majors, is attracted to job opportunities in this new major but is repelled by the possibility of a fifth year of classes. Seeing a person on a bench hold out some food, a squirrel is motivated by hunger to approach and by fear to keep its distance.

In approach-avoidance relationships the tendency to approach a desired goal and the desire to avoid it both grow stronger as we get nearer to the goal (Miller, 1944). A critical factor, however, is that the avoidance tendency usually increases in strength faster than the approach tendency does (Figure 9.28). Thus at first we may be attracted to a goal and only slightly repelled by its drawbacks. As we get closer to it, the negative aspects become more dominant. We may stop and then retreat, approach again, and continue to vacillate in a state of conflict.

Some methods of coping with motivational conflict can be maladaptive. Of these, *defensive avoidance* may be the most common (Janis and Mann, 1977). Here, the decision-maker procrastinates and generally avoids coming to grips with the decision. We see in Chapter 13 that psychodynamic models often focus on unconscious ways in which people resolve such conflicts.

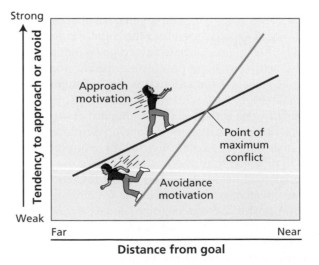

FIGURE 9.28   According to Neal Miller (1944), the tendency to approach and the tendency to avoid grow stronger as one moves closer to the goal. However, the tendency to avoid increases faster than the tendency to approach. Maximum conflict is experienced where the two gradients cross, because at this point the opposing motives are equal in strength.

▼▼

CHAPTER SUMMARY

Perspectives on Motivation

- Motivation is a process that influences the direction, vigor, and persistence of behavior. Evolutionary psychologists propose that in our ancestral past, motivational tendencies that had adaptive significance were more likely to be passed from one generation to the next, eventually evolving into genetically based predispositions to act in certain ways.

- Homeostatic models view motivation as an attempt to maintain equilibrium in bodily systems. Drive theories propose that tissue deficits create drives, such as hunger, that motivate or "push" an organism from within to reduce that deficit and restore homeostasis.

- Incentive theories emphasize the role of environmental factors that "pull" people toward a goal. The cognitive expectancy × value theory explains why the same incentive may motivate some people, but not others.

- Psychodynamic theories emphasize that unconscious motives and mental processes guide much of our behavior. Humanist Abraham Maslow proposed that needs exist in a hierarchy, from basic biological needs to the ultimate need for self-actualization.

Hunger and Weight Regulation

- The body monitors several chemicals involved in energy utilization. Changing patterns of glucose usage provide one signal that helps initiate hunger. Upon eating, hormones such as CCK are released into the bloodstream and help signal the brain to stop eating. Fat cells release leptin, which acts as a long-term signal that helps to regulate appetite. The hypothalamus and other brain regions play a role in hunger regulation.

- The expected good taste of food motivates eating and the thought of food can trigger hunger. Our memory, attitudes, habits, and psychological needs affect our food intake.

- The availability, taste, and variety of food powerfully regulate eating. Through classical conditioning, neutral stimuli can acquire the capacity to trigger hunger. Cultural norms affect our food preferences and eating habits.

- Heredity and the environment affect our susceptibility to becoming obese. Homeostatic mechanisms make it difficult to lose substantial weight.

- Anorexia and bulimia are eating disorders that have serious physical consequences, occur more often in cultures that value thinness, and are associated with different psychological profiles and childhood patterns of family interaction.

Sensation-Seeking

- Humans and other animals tend to seek out novelty and stimulation. High sensation seekers are more likely to engage in risky activities than are low sensation seekers.

- Sensation seeking may have a biological basis. High sensation seekers may be less reactive to external stimulation than are low sensation seekers.

Sexual Motivation

- The last half century has witnessed changing patterns of sexual activity, such as an increase in premarital sex.

- During sexual intercourse people often experience a four-stage physiological response pattern consisting of excitement, plateau, orgasm, and resolution.

- Sex hormones have organizational effects that guide the prenatal development of internal and external organs along either a male or female pattern. Sex hormones also have activational effects that influence sexual desire.

- Sexual fantasy can trigger arousal, whereas stress and psychological difficulties can interfere with sexual arousal. Cultural norms determine the sexual practices and beliefs that are considered moral, proper, and desirable.

- Environmental stimuli affect sexual desire. Viewing sexual violence reinforces men's belief in rape myths and increases men's aggression toward women, at least temporarily.

- Sexual orientation involves dimensions of self-identity, sexual attraction, and actual sexual behavior. No single biological, social, or psychological factor—and no specific combination of causes—has been clearly identified as the cause of sexual orientation.

The Desire for Affiliation and Intimacy

- Affiliation has adaptive advantages and allows people to engage in social comparison.

- Proximity, mere exposure, similarity of attitudes, and physical attractiveness typically enhance our liking for someone else.

- Evolutionary theorists propose that cross-cultural gender differences in mate preferences reflect inherited biological tendencies, whereas social structure theory argues that they result from sex-role socialization and societal gender inequities in economic opportunities.

- Relationships deepen as partners self-disclose and exchanges between them become more intimate and broader. According to social exchange theory, people will be satisfied when their relationship outcomes exceed their comparison level, and they will remain in the relationship if the outcomes exceed their comparison level for alternatives.

- Different combinations of intimacy, commitment, and passion lead to different types of love. Due to transfer of excitation, arousal caused by some other factor may be misattributed as increased feelings of passion toward someone we find attractive.

- Partners are more likely to remain happily married when they understand each other and deal with conflicts by de-escalating their emotions and providing mutual support.

Achievement Motivation

- People who have a high motivation for success are attracted to the thrill of victory. They value mastery and social comparison. People who have a high fear of failure experience anxiety in achievement settings. They are motivated by social comparison and a fear of performing poorly.

- High-need achievers seek moderately difficult tasks that are challenging but attainable. Low-need achievers are more likely to choose easy tasks where success is assured or very difficult tasks where success is not expected. Child-rearing and cultural factors influence our level and expression of achievement motivation.

Motivation in the Workplace

- For most workers, opportunities for accomplishment and growth are stronger motivators than money. Dissatisfied workers are higher in absenteeism and job turnover than satisfied employees, but job satisfaction is correlated weakly with job productivity.

- Job enrichment programs attempt to increase employees' motivation by making work tasks more intrinsically motivating. Incentive programs make external reinforcers contingent on certain types of performance. Goal-setting programs set challenging goals and plan a strategy to reach them. Management by objectives includes goal setting, employee participation, and objective performance feedback.

Motivational Conflict

- Motivational goals may conflict with one another. Approach-approach conflicts occur when a person has to select between two attractive alternatives. Avoidance-avoidance goals involve choosing between two undesirable alternatives.

- Approach-avoidance conflicts occur when we are attracted to, and repelled by, the same goal. As we approach the goal, the avoidance tendency usually increases in strength more rapidly than the approach tendency.

▼▼

KEY TERMS AND CONCEPTS*

anorexia nervosa (380)

approach-approach conflict (406)

approach-avoidance conflict (406)

avoidance-avoidance conflict (406)

bulimia nervosa (380)

CCK (cholecystokinin) (372)

cognitive-arousal model of love (399)

companionate love (398)

drive theory (368)

expectancy × value theory (369)

extrinsic motivation (369)

glucose (372)

homeostasis (368)

incentive (368)

instinct (367)

intrinsic motivation (369)

job enrichment (404)

leptin (373)

management by objectives (MBO) (405)

matching effect (394)

mere exposure effect (393)

metabolism (371)

motivation (367)

need for achievement (401)

need hierarchy (370)

paraventricular nucleus (PVN) (374)

parental investment theory (395)

passionate love (398)

self-actualization (370)

sensation-seeking (381)

sexual orientation (389)

sexual response cycle (384)

social comparison (392)

social exchange theory (398)

social penetration theory (397)

social structure theory (396)

transfer of excitation (399)

triangular theory of love (399)

* Each term has been boldfaced in the text on the page indicated in parentheses.

▼▼

APPLYING YOUR KNOWLEDGE

These questions allow you to apply your understanding of the material in this chapter.

1. Brianna is 35 years old. According to Abraham Maslow's need hierarchy, if Brianna is able to satisfy all of her other needs, she will finally be in a position to satisfy her need for _____ , which Maslow regarded as the ultimate human need.
   a) self-actualization
   b) self-esteem
   c) intimacy and love
   d) helping others

2. Aaron is 25 pounds overweight and is going on a diet. As he loses weight, his reduced fat mass will secrete _____ , increasing his overall appetite.
   a) more leptin
   b) less leptin
   c) more CCK
   d) less CCK

3. Joni, a college junior, is anorexic. If we were to study her personality, it is most likely that we find Joni to be
   a) an antisocial person who dislikes being with other people.
   b) someone who normally maintains a calm, quiet exterior, but who is easily angered by the slightest provocation.
   c) a depressed, anxious, impulsive person who lacks a stable sense of identity.
   d) a perfectionistic achiever who sets high standards for herself and needs to feel in control.

4. After celebrating the first anniversary of their marriage with a romantic dinner and movie, Sophie and Antonio are enjoying an evening of lovemaking. After their arousal increases during the excitement phase, it is most likely that they will proceed through the _____ stages of the sexual response cycle.
   a) plateau, orgasm, and resolution
   b) resolution, orgasm, and plateau
   c) orgasm, resolution, and plateau
   d) orgasm, plateau, and resolution

5. Nathan produces pornographic films that often depict men sexually subduing women who at first resist, but who then "give in and enjoy it." In a news interview, Nathan states that his films give male viewers a safe outlet for releasing their sexual and aggressive tensions, and therefore reduce the chances that men would actually display sexual aggression toward women. Nathan's view reflects _____, and overall, scientific research _____ this view.
   a) social learning theory; does
   b) social learning theory; does not
   c) the catharsis principle; does
   d) the catharsis principle; does not

6. To predict Kirsten's commitment to remaining in her dating relationship with Tom, social exchange theory proposes that we should look most closely at whether
   a) Kirsten and Tom have similar personalities.
   b) Kirsten's relationship outcomes are positive or negative.
   c) Kirsten's relationship outcomes exceed her comparison level.
   d) Kirsten's relationship outcomes exceed her comparison level for alternatives.

7. Evelyn and Nigel are happy newlyweds. Which of the following styles of dealing with anger-producing conflicts will most likely predict that they will still be happily married five or six years from now?
   a) They allow themselves to get very hostile with one another, so that their negative emotions don't stay bottled up.
   b) They try to avoid discussing conflicts and keep their negative thoughts to themselves, to avoid hurting each other.
   c) They express anger but try to solve their conflict in a way that de-escalates their negative emotions.
   d) None of these patterns can predict marital success that far into the future.

8. Alethia has high achievement motivation. When she selects achievement tasks to work on, she will
   a) most likely choose easy tasks that have a high probability of success.
   b) most likely choose moderately difficult tasks that have an intermediate probability of success.
   c) most likely choose very difficult tasks that have a low probability of success.
   d) be equally likely to choose any of the above tasks.

9. Dr. Chavez is an industrial/organizational psychologist who is designing a motivation program at a large factory. Her program will give workers more freedom to determine their work procedures, each worker will perform a greater variety of tasks, and each worker will be part of team that assembles an entire product, rather than just one component of it. Of these three options, Dr. Chavez's approach best illustrates
   a) a job enrichment program.
   b) management by objectives.
   c) an incentive program.

10. Derrick, a college sophomore, has been offered a part-time job. The thought of making extra money sounds good to him, but the job sounds boring. Derrick is experiencing a(n)
    a) avoidance-avoidance conflict.
    b) approach-avoidance conflict.
    c) approach-approach conflict.
    d) transfer of excitation.

Answers

1. a) (page 370); 2. b) (page 373); 3. d) (page 381); 4. a) (page 384); 5. d) (page 385); 6. d) (page 398); 7. c) (page 400); 8. b) (page 402); 9. a) (page 404); 10. b) (page 406)

For additional quizzing and a variety of interactive resources, visit the book's Online Learning Center at www.mhhe.com/passer.

EMOTION, STRESS,
AND HEALTH

Some guy hit my fender the other day, and I said unto him,
Be fruitful and multiply, But not in those words.
— *Woody Allen*

10

CHAPTER OUTLINE

▼▼

A damp fog hugged the ground as the downed fighter pilot slipped silently through the moonlit forest. The pilot knew that enemy patrols would be out searching for him. He had radioed his position shortly after parachuting from his damaged aircraft and now, navigating by compass, was making his way to a designated point to the south where a rescue helicopter was to pick him up. A clammy sweat born of fear had long since drenched the underarms of his uniform, and his heart pounded in his chest. His eyes and ears strained to pick up telltale signs of human presence, and he was now nearly oblivious to the dull ache from the gash in his thigh.

Ahead was a small clearing strewn with boulders whose tops projected like ghostly islands above the ground fog. The pilot carefully scanned the area. "I'd be too exposed," he thought. "I'd better keep to the woods and skirt the clearing." He quickly planned a route around the left side of the clearing and began to pick his way cautiously through the trees.

Almost before the faint click and the reflection of light on metal registered in his awareness, the pilot's legs propelled him into a headlong dive for cover behind a tree stump. A stream of bullets from the enemy soldier's assault rifle ripped through the air inches above his diving form. As he hit the ground, the pilot realized that he was now hidden under the protective mantle of ground fog. He slid silently down a leaf-covered slope into the protective cover of the forest and continued his journey toward the rescue site. Behind him the sounds of the enemy patrol faded in the distance. Ahead, he could hear the faint throbbing sound of the rescue helicopter's approach. Thoughts of safety and images of being reunited with his wife and children replaced fear with emotions of gratitude and joy.

In this struggle for survival, emotions played a central role. The dangers to well-being created by this stressful situation evoked a pattern of responses in the pilot. Some of the responses were mental ones, including the pilot's subjective feelings of fear (eventually replaced by joy), his perceptions of danger (which turned to anticipations of rescue and safety), and his mental problem-solving attempts. Others were physiological, involving a state of bodily arousal reflected in his fear-produced sweating and his pounding heart. There were also behavioral responses, such as the seemingly "instinctive" dive out of harm's way. In the end, the fear-produced responses helped him survive. In many ways, this episode illustrates important principles about emotion, stress, and coping that you will learn in this chapter.

❭ THE NATURE AND FUNCTIONS OF EMOTIONS

Life without emotion would be bland and empty. Our subjective experiences of love, anger, joy, fear, and other emotions energize and add color to our lives. Emotions can foster happiness and well-being, or they can contribute to psychological and physical dysfunction. Modern psychology's focus on the study of emotion echoes a timeless fascination—expressed in songs, paintings, stories, poems, and scholarly treatises—with human emotions.

Emotions are positive or negative feeling (affect) states consisting of a pattern of cognitive, physiological, and behavioral reactions to events that have relevance to important goals or motives. The events in question may be external situations, such as that faced by the pilot, or they may be internal thoughts, memories, or images, such as his thoughts about being killed or his later images of rescue and family.

➤ 1. What is an emotion?

The concepts of motivation and emotion have always been closely linked, and the dividing line between them is not always clear (Carlson & Hatfield, 1992; Edwards, 1998). One reason is that motivation and emotion both involve states of arousal, and they both can trigger patterns of action (e.g., flight in the case of fear and attack in the case of anger). Indeed, the terms *motivation* and *emotion* are both derived from the Latin word *movere,* "to move." The link between motivation and emotion involves more than a common linguistic root, however. Emotion theorist Richard Lazarus (1991a) believes that there is *always* a link between motives and emotions, because we react emotionally only when our motives and goals are gratified, threatened, or frustrated. Emotional reactions are especially strong when an experience is pertinent to goals that are very important to us (Figure 10.1). Clearly, perceived threat to his very survival were the basis for the fear the pilot experienced, and his later relief and joy were triggered by desires for safety and reunion with family.

➤ 2. How are emotions related to motivation?

How then shall we distinguish between motivation and emotion? One way is to place them within a stimulus-response framework. Some theorists suggest that motives operate as internal *stimuli* that energize and direct behavior toward some goal or incentive, whereas emotions are basically reactions, or *responses,* to events that relate to important goals (Mandler, 1984; Scherer, 1988).

The Adaptive Value of Emotions

Like other psychological processes, emotions have important adaptive functions. First, they signal that something important is happening, and they direct our attention to that event. In an evolutionary sense, some emotions are part of an emergency arousal system that increases the chances of survival by energizing, directing, and sustaining adaptive behaviors. Probably the most basic of these behavioral tendencies, seen in virtually all species, is fighting or fleeing when confronted by threat or danger. The physiological arousal that is so central to the emotions of anger and fear energizes and intensifies such behaviors.

Barbara Fredrickson (1998) suggests that positive and negative emotions have different adaptive functions. Negative emotions have been sculpted by evolutionary survival pressures to *narrow* attention and action tendencies so that the organism can respond to a threatening situation with a focused set of responses. An animal threatened with attack should selectively attend to attack-relevant stimuli and respond by either fighting or fleeing. We saw this tendency in the pilot described earlier. He was so focused and vigilant to cues of danger in the external environment that he was largely oblivious to his leg wound. Thus even before the presence of the enemy soldier registered fully in his awareness, the pilot reacted in a way that saved his life.

FIGURE 10.1 The intimate relations between motivation and emotion are seen in the strong emotional responses that can occur when important goals are either attained or lost.

What good, then, are positive emotions? Fredrickson suggests that unlike negative emotions, positive emotions usually arise under conditions of safety and goal attainment, in which high physiological arousal is not needed. Rather than narrowing attention and behavior tendencies, positive emotions like interest, joy, contentment, and love actually *broaden* our thinking and behavior so that we explore, consider new ideas, try out new ways to achieve goals, play, and savor what we have. These activities help individuals to build new resources, some of which are intellectual (gaining new knowledge and insights), some physical (finding new ways to complete tasks, or new physical skills), and some social (building and strengthening relationships). Fredrickson believes that in these ways, positive emotions also are highly adaptive for humans.

➤ 3. What are the adaptive functions of positive and negative emotions?

Emotions are also a form of social communication. By providing observable information about our internal states and intentions, emotions influence how other people behave toward us (Isaacs, 1998). Consider, for example, the effects of a baby's crying and smiling on adults. Parents and other adults report

➤ 4. In what ways are emotions modes of communication?

FIGURE 10.2 Emotional responses communicate our internal states, and they can influence the responses of others, thereby providing the aid, comfort, or assistance we need.

feeling irritated, annoyed, disturbed, distressed, sympathetic, or unhappy when babies cry, and they become more physiologically aroused themselves (Frodi et al., 1978). Parents and other adults generally respond to crying infants with caretaking responses that have obvious survival value for the infant. Positive emotions also pay off for babies. A smiling infant is likely to increase parents' feelings of love and caring, thereby increasing the likelihood that the child's biological and emotional needs will be satisfied.

Emotional messages begin to have an impact early in life (Figure 10.2). Within 1 to 3 days after birth, human infants respond to another infant's crying with crying of their own. Children who are less than a year old respond with negative affect to vocal expressions of fear by their mother (Mumme et al., 1996), and by two years of age they react to their mother's real or simulated signs of distress with efforts to help or comfort her (Sagi & Hoffman, 1976; Zahn-Waxler et al., 1979, 1992). Adults' expressions of sadness and distress also evoke concern, empathy, and helping behavior from others (Izard, 1989).

The Nature of Emotions

Psychologist James Averill (1980) found more than 550 words in the English language that refer to various positive and negative emotional states. We surely do not have 550 different emotions, but the emotions we do have share four common features.

➤ 5. Name the four major components of emotions, including the two classes of behavioral responses.

- First, emotions are responses to external or internal *eliciting stimuli.*

- Second, emotional responses result from our interpretation or **cognitive appraisal** of these stimuli, which gives the situation its perceived meaning and significance.

- Third, our *bodies respond physiologically* to our appraisal. We may become physically "stirred up," as in fear, joy, or anger, or we may experience decreased arousal, as in contentment or depression.

- Fourth, emotions include *behavior tendencies.* Some are *expressive behaviors* (e.g., exhibiting surprise, smiling with joy, or crying). Others are *instrumental behaviors,* ways of doing something about the stimulus that aroused the emotion (e.g., studying for an anxiety-arousing test, fighting back in self-defense, or running away).

Figure 10.3 illustrates the general relations among these four emotional components. For example, an insulting remark from another person (eliciting stimulus) may evoke a cognitive appraisal that one has been unfairly demeaned, an increase in physiological arousal, a clenching of jaw and fists (expressive behavior), and a verbal attack on the other person (instrumental behavior). As the two-way arrows indicate, these emotional components can influence one another. Cognition can trigger physiological changes and expressive behavior which can, in turn, affect what we think about the situation and about ourselves (Forgas, 2000).

Emotion is a dynamic ongoing *process.* Thus any of its four elements can change rapidly as the situation and our responses to it influence one another. For example, as anger begins to escalate during a disagreement, you might choose to make a conciliatory response that evokes a positive reaction or apology from the other person, helps defuse the situation, and reduces your negative appraisal of the other person and your level of

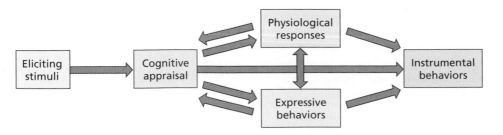

FIGURE 10.3 Components of emotion, showing the relations between eliciting stimuli, cognitive appraisal processes, physiological arousal, expressive behaviors, and instrumental behaviors. Note the reciprocal (two-way) causal relations that are thought to exist among the appraisal, physiological arousal, and expressive behavior components.

emotional arousal. This dynamic, ever-changing property of emotional reactions makes them a challenging "moving target" for scientific study.

Eliciting Stimuli

Emotions do not occur in a vacuum. They are responses to situations, people, objects, or events. We become angry *at* something or someone; fearful or proud *of* something; in love *with* someone. Moreover, the stimuli that trigger cognitive appraisals and emotional responses are not always external; they can be internal stimuli, such as mental images and memories. Most of us can work up a state of anger simply by recalling or imagining a painful injustice or insult from the past, or evoke warm feelings by recalling significant positive experiences.

Innate biological factors help determine which stimuli have the greatest potential to arouse emotions. Newborn infants come equipped with the capacity to respond emotionally with either interest or distress to events in their environment (Davidson & Fox, 1988; Galati & Lavelli, 1997). Adults, too, may be biologically primed to experience emotions in response to certain stimuli that have evolutionary significance. This may help explain why the majority of human phobias involve "primal" stimuli such as heights, water, sharks, snakes, or spiders, rather than modern threats like guns, electrical transformers, and automobiles (Öhman, 1993). As discussed in Chapter 6, fear responses can be classically conditioned more easily to pictures of snakes and spiders than to more innocuous stimuli, such as flowers, when these stimuli are paired with mild electric shocks (Hygge & Öhman, 1978).

Learning also influences the ability of particular objects or people to arouse emotions. Previous experiences can make certain people or situations eliciting stimuli for emotions. The mere sight of one's lover can evoke feelings of passion, and the sight of a disliked person an instantaneous feeling of revulsion that seems almost reflexive in nature. On the broadest level, cultures have different standards for defining the good, the bad, and the ugly, and these standards affect how eliciting stimuli will be appraised and responded to emotionally. Physical features that provoke sexual arousal and feelings of infatuation in one culture, such as ornamental facial scars or a bone through the nose, may elicit feelings of disgust in another. In Western societies, recent increases in the popularity and acceptability of body piercing and tattoos illustrates how quickly cultural standards can change.

The Cognitive Component

You are walking across campus with a group of people from one of your classes when you encounter a person you met at a party the previous night and to whom you are attracted. The person looks at you as you warmly say "Hello!", responds with a blank stare, and then turns away without responding. Which emotions would the following thoughts trigger in you?

- "Oh no! What a total put-down. What do my classmates think of me now?"
- "What a jerk, ignoring me like that."
- "Just like always. I'll never find anyone who likes me."
- "What a relief! Now I won't be distracted from my usual 50-hour study week and my thimble collection."

Embarrassed? Angry? Depressed? Relieved? As you think, so shall you feel.

Cognitions are involved in virtually every aspect of emotion. They can evoke emotional responses, they are part of our subjective experience of the emotion, and they influence how we express our emotions and act on them. A situation may evoke pleasure or distress, depending on how we appraise it. For example, sexual stimulation may elicit anger, fear, or disgust instead of pleasure if it is deemed inappropriate or unwanted.

Appraisal processes.   Emotions are always responses to our perceptions of the eliciting stimuli. While all perceptions involve attaching meaning to sensory

> ➤ 6. In what sense can eliciting stimuli be external or internal? What is the role of biological and learning factors?

> ➤ 7. How do cognitive appraisals enter into emotion? Do they need to involve conscious thought?

FIGURE 10.4 Differences in appraisal can trigger entirely different emotional reactions, as in this instance. What kinds of appraisals are likely occurring in these school children?

➤ 8. What evidence exists for (a) universal and (b) culturally determined appraisals? Provide examples of each.

➤ 9. How strongly are wealth, health, relationships, intelligence, and religiosity related to happiness?

➤ 10. Describe the role of comparison processes in happiness.

➤ 11. What evidence is there that genetics and culture can influence happiness?

stimuli, the appraisals involved in emotion are especially evaluative and personal; they relate to what we think is desirable or undesirable for us or for the people we care about (Lazarus, 1998).

Often we are not consciously aware of the appraisals that underlie emotional responses (Bargh & Chartrand, 1999; Cacioppo & Gardner, 1999). Some appraisals involve little more than an almost automatic interpretation of sensory input (Lazarus, 1998; Zajonc, 1984). Your emotional reaction to the sight of a milk truck bearing down upon you would probably not require an extended contemplation of the impending outcomes. More likely, you'd reflexively jump out of the way and experience an instantaneous fear response.

Infants who have no formal language obviously experience emotions, providing further evidence for the role of primitive appraisals. As our cognitive abilities develop, however, appraisals are more likely to become tied to language, whether or not we are consciously aware of the actual appraisals (Izard & Malatesta, 1987). Indeed, many language-based appraisals become so habitual that they run off in a subconscious shorthand with little or no awareness on our part (Bargh, 1997; Beck, 1976). We often fail to appreciate how arbitrary can be our interpretations of "the way things are." To us, they're simply "reality," but someone else can appraise the same situation in a manner that creates an entirely different "reality" and triggers a different emotional response.

The idea that emotional reactions are triggered by cognitive appraisals rather than external situations helps to account for the fact that different people (or even the same person at different times) can have very different emotional reactions to the same object, situation, or person (Figure 10.4). Statements like "I have a new attitude toward her now" or "I've decided what's really important in life" reflect changes in appraisals of certain situations or people.

Culture and appraisal.   Like theorists who study the situations that elicit emotion in various cultures, those who study cognitive appraisal have looked for cross-cultural similarities and differences in the thoughts and perceptions that precede emotions (Scherer, 1984; Smith & Ellsworth, 1985). Respondents in a variety of cultures have been asked to recall events that evoked certain emotions, then to answer questions about how they appraised or interpreted the situations. In one study conducted in 27 different countries, the researchers found strong cross-cultural similarities in the types of appraisals that evoked joy, fear, anger, sadness, disgust, shame, and guilt (Wallbott & Scherer, 1988). In another cross-cultural study comparing American and Asian people in Japan and Hong Kong, Robert Mauro and his coworkers (1992) found that Americans reported feeling happiness, pride, and hope more frequently than did the Japanese. The Japanese, in turn, reported more frequent feelings of shame and regret than did people from Hong Kong. Nonetheless, whenever any of these emotions did occur, similar appraisals were involved, regardless of the culture.

Despite these cross-cultural commonalities in appraisal, the same type of situation can also evoke different appraisals and resulting emotional reactions, depending on one's culture. Consider, for example, the circumstance of "being alone." For Tahitians, being alone is appraised as an opportunity for bad spirits to bother a person, and fear is the most common emotional response. In the close-knit Utku Inuit, an Eskimo culture, being alone signifies social rejection and isolation, triggering sadness and loneliness. In Western cultures, being alone may at times represent a welcome respite from the frantic pace of daily life, evoking contentment and happiness (Mesquita et al., 1997). Thus where appraisals are concerned, there seem to be certain universals, but also some degree of cultural diversity in some of the more subtle aspects of interpreting situations (Mesquita et al., 1997; Scherer, 1998).

Perhaps the most universally desired of all human conditions is happiness. How do external conditions and inner psychological processes determine how content and happy we are?

PSYCHOLOGICAL FRONTIERS

What Makes People Happy?

Among psychological researchers, there recently has been a surge of interest in the topic of happiness, or its more technical term, subjective well-being (Myers & Diener, 1995). **Subjective well-being (SWB)** includes people's emotional responses and their degree of satisfaction with various aspects of their life (Diener, 1999). SWB is typically assessed by means of self-report ratings of contentment, happiness, and satisfaction.

How happy are people in general? Ed and Carol Diener (1996) reviewed findings derived from nearly 1,000 representative samples in 43 westernized and developing nations. The mean rating of personal happiness on a scale ranging from 0 (most unhappy) to 10 (most happy) was 6.33, indicating mild happiness. Only in two economically poor nations, India and the Dominican Republic, did SWB fall into the unhappy range of the scale. In the United States, all ethnic groups scored well above the neutral point on the happiness scale (Andrews, 1991).

▶ The Causes of Happiness

Under what circumstances do people experience happiness? Some researchers have examined the *resources* that might contribute to happiness, such as youth, attractiveness, intelligence, wealth, and health. Others have studied the internal *psychological processes* that underlie our experiences of happiness or unhappiness.

Personal Resources and Happiness

If you're "healthy, wealthy, and wise," will you be happier? Not necessarily. Although people who are happy *believe* they are healthier, they are not according to external measures of physical well-being, such as physicians' evaluations and doctor visits (Brief et al., 1993; Watten et al., 1997). On average, individuals with severe and disabling medical conditions like paralyses do report lower levels of life satisfaction than do nondisabled people, yet about two thirds of the disabled rate their lives as somewhat or very satisfying (Mehnert et al., 1990).

If only you had more money, you'd be happier, correct? Well, perhaps not. Although people in affluent countries are happier on average than people who live in abject poverty, such countries differ in many ways besides wealth (e.g., in terms of social and political turmoil) that could affect SWB. When wealth and SWB are correlated within the same country, whether the country be poor or affluent, wealth is only weakly related to happiness, with correlations typically less than +.20 (Diener, 1999). Moreover, extreme changes in wealth have only a temporary positive impact on SWB (Brickman et al., 1978; Smith & Razzell,

1975; Thoits & Hannan, 1979). Thus where health and wealth are concerned, not having the resource may create unhappiness because important basic needs can't be met, but once an adequate level is attained, further increases seem to do little to promote happiness.

How about being wise? Overall, intelligence bears little relation to happiness (Diener, 1999). Educational level does have a weak positive relation to SWB, probably because it helps people avoid poverty and compete for satisfying jobs (Witter et al., 1994). Unemployment is one of the strongest predictors of life dissatisfaction, and an adequate educational level can help people avoid this fate (Clark, 1998).

If being healthy, wealthy, and wise won't guarantee happiness, perhaps intimate relationships and a sense of meaning in life will. Researchers do find a consistent positive relation between life satisfaction and marriage for both men and women, but the meaning of this correlational result is not clear. Does marriage promote greater life satisfaction, or are happier, better-adjusted people more likely to be able to establish and sustain good marital relationships?

Many people report that their religious beliefs contribute to a sense of meaning, both in daily life and during life crises (McIntosh et al., 1993; Pollner, 1989). But, again, causality is difficult to infer. It is possible that happier people are more likely to gravitate toward religion, or that some third factor, such as being raised in a loving religious home, causes both religiosity and SWB (Diener, 1999).

Overall, age is unrelated to happiness, probably because there are rewards and challenges at all stages of living. Likewise, men and women are about equal in global happiness, but there is an important qualifier: Women on average experience *both* positive and negative emotions more intensely than men do (Wood et al., 1989). The more extreme emotional responses of women balance out, resulting in a level of happiness similar to that produced by men's less extreme highs and lows.

Psychological Processes Underlying Happiness

Overall, external circumstances are now thought to account for only about 15 to 20 percent of the variability between people in happiness ratings (Argyle, 1999). Perhaps psychological *processes*, rather than resources, are the keys to happiness. For example, research has shown that feelings of life satisfaction are based on how we compare ourselves and our circumstances with other people, their circumstances, and with past conditions we have experienced (Bruunk & Gibbons, 1997). When we engage in **downward comparison**, seeing ourselves as better off than the standard for comparison, we experience increased satisfaction. A discrepancy

–Continued

that involves an **upward comparison,** where we view ourselves as worse off than the standard of comparison, produces dissatisfaction. In one study, researchers asked college students to keep a written record of every time they compared their appearance, grades, abilities, possessions, or personality with someone else's over a 2-week period. At the same time, the students recorded their current mood. Downward comparisons with less fortunate or talented people were consistently associated with positive moods, and upward comparisons with negative emotional reactions (Wheeler & Miyake, 1992). Thus depending on what or whom you compare yourself with, you can be an eagle among starlings or a fly among butterflies.

Just as our senses adapt to stimuli over time, we also adapt to positive or negative life events. This helps account for the ability of ill and disabled people to "bounce back" from their misfortunes and become less dissatisfied over time. It also helps explain why an increase in income or in grades may produce a temporary surge of happiness that wears off after a while. In one study, participants were followed over a 2-year period during which they regularly reported on life events and level of happiness. At any given point in time, only events that had occurred within the past 3 months were related to current happiness or unhappiness (Suh et al., 1996).

Biological and Cultural Factors

Is it possible that people come into the world with a biologically based predisposition to be happy or unhappy? David Lykken and Auke Tellegen (1996) measured happiness in a sample of 2,310 identical and fraternal twins. Identical twins were far more similar in SWB than were fraternal twins regardless of their life circumstances. The possibility that one's genes, perhaps by influencing brain hormones and neurotransmitter activity, can predispose us to experience positive or negative affect is certain to be an important focus of future research (Hamer & Copeland, 1998).

Culture may also influence which factors are related to happiness. Indeed, the basic assumption that subjective well-being is synonymous with positive emotions may not hold in other cultures. Eunkook Suh and coworkers (1998) found that the frequency and intensity of positive emotional experiences are positively correlated with SWB in the individualistic "me" societies of North America and Europe. In contrast, little relation was found between emotions and ratings of life satisfaction in collectivistic cultures of Southeast Asia. There the well-being of the group may be a more important factor in personal happiness than one's own emotional life.

The Physiological Component

One of the first things we notice is the bodily changes that occur when our feelings are "stirred up." Many parts of the body are involved in emotional arousal, but certain brain regions, the autonomic nervous system, and the endocrine system play especially significant roles.

➤ 12. Which subcortical and cortical structures are involved in emotion? How does LeDoux's theory explain unconscious emotional phenomena?

Brain structures and neurotransmitters. The brain's involvement in emotion is complex, and many aspects are not well understood. It is clear, however, that emotions involve important interactions between cortical and subcortical areas (Borod, 2000; Edwards, 1998).

Subcortical structures, such as the hypothalamus, the amygdala, the hippocampus, and other limbic system structures play major roles in emotion (Figure 10.5). If animals are electrically stimulated in specific areas of the limbic system, they will growl at and attack anything that approaches them. Destroying the same sites produces an absence of aggression, even if the animal is provoked or attacked (LeDoux, 1996). Other areas of the hypothalamus and limbic system show the opposite pattern: lack of emotion when they are stimulated and unrestrained emotion when they are removed (Thompson, 1988).

The cerebral cortex has many connections with the hypothalamus and limbic system, allowing constant communication between cortical and subcortical regions. Cognitive appraisal processes surely involve activities in the cortex, where the mechanisms for language and complex thought reside. Moreover, the ability to regulate emotion depends heavily on the executive functions of the *prefrontal cortex,* which lies immediately behind the forehead (Gross, 1998).

Groundbreaking research and theorizing by psychologist Joseph LeDoux (1986) has revealed important links between the cortex and the limbic system. As shown in Figure 10.6, the key brain structures in this model are the thalamus, which routes sensory input to various parts of the brain, the amygdala, which helps coordinate and trigger physiological and behavioral responses to emotion-arousing situations, and the cortex, where sensory input is organized as per-

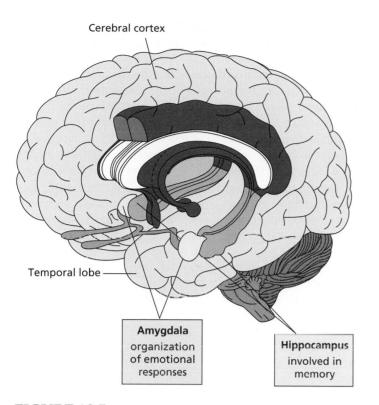

FIGURE 10.5 The limbic system plays a key role in emotion. The amygdala is involved in the organization of emotional responses.

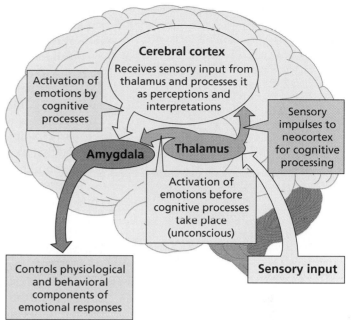

FIGURE 10.6 Parallel neural processes may produce conscious and unconscious emotional responses at about the same time. LeDoux's research suggests that sensory input to the thalamus can be routed directly to the amygdala in the limbic system, producing an "unconscious" emotional response before cognitive responses evoked by the other pathway to the cortex can occur.

ceptions and evaluated by the "thinking" or linguistic part of the brain. LeDoux's key discovery was that the thalamus sends messages along two independent neural pathways, one traveling to the cortex and the other directly to the amygdala. This means that the amygdala can receive direct input from the senses and generate emotional reactions before the cerebral cortex has had time to fully interpret what is causing the reaction. LeDoux suggests that this primitive mechanism (which is the only emotional mechanism in species like birds and reptiles) has survival value because it enables the organism to react with great speed. Shortly afterward, the cerebral cortex responds with a more carefully processed cognitive interpretation of the situation. This may be what occurs when a hiker sees an object that looks like a snake and jumps out of the way, only to realize an instant later that the object is a rope.

The existence of a dual system for emotional processing may help explain some puzzling aspects of our emotional lives. For example, most of us have had the experience of suddenly feeling emotional without understanding why. LeDoux (2000) also suggests that people are capable of having two simultaneous emotional reactions to the same event, a conscious one occurring as a result of cortical activity and an unconscious one triggered by the amygdala. This might help explain instances in which people are puzzled by behavioral reactions that seem to be at odds with the emotion they are consciously experiencing: "I don't know why I came across as being angry. I felt very warm and friendly."

Many of our emotional responses are based on previous learning experiences. As psychodynamic and cognitive researchers have shown, some memories are not consciously experienced but may affect our behavior nonetheless (Bargh & Chartrand, 1999; Westen, 1998). LeDoux (1989) has shown that the amygdala can indeed learn on its own, providing a possible mechanism for "unconscious" emotional memories. First, he surgically removed the visual cortex of rats so that visual stimuli could not be processed in the cortex. Then using a classical conditioning

➤ 13. What experimental and clinical evidence supports the role of the amygdala in emotional learning?

procedure, he paired a light with electric shock. Although the rat's visual cortex couldn't "see" the light, the rats developed a conditioned fear response to this CS, indicating that the amygdala learned to fear it.

Studies with humans suggest emotional processing by the amygdala without conscious awareness. British scientists measured neural activity in the amygdala while participants viewed pictures of faces. Some of the faces had been previously paired with an aversive noise to establish a conditioned negative emotional response to them. Even when the faces were presented in such a manner that the participants could not consciously report their presence, brain recordings showed that the amygdala in the right (nonverbal) hemisphere reacted to the aversively conditioned faces, but not to the nonconditioned faces (Morris et al., 1998).

Research with brain-damaged patients suggests different neural bases for conscious awareness and emotional responses. Two limbic system structures that have been studied are the hippocampus, which is involved in forming memories, and the amygdala. Patients with damage to their hippocampus suffer memory impairment. They can develop a classically conditioned emotional response even though they cannot consciously learn the connection between the CS and the UCS. In contrast, people with no hippocampal damage but a damaged amygdala can describe the CS-UCS contingency ("that picture was paired with the shock"), but fail to develop a conditioned fear response (Bechara et al., 1995). Some psychodynamic theorists are hailing these discoveries as support for the existence of unconscious emotional processes (Bucci, 1997; Westen, 1998). Indeed, there is now little doubt that important aspects of emotional life can occur out of conscious awareness (Bargh & Chartrand, 1999; Cacioppo & Gardner, 1999).

Neuroscientist Candace Pert (1997) argues that because all of the neural structures involved in emotion operate biochemically, it is the ebbs and flows of various neurotransmitter substances that activate the emotional programs residing in the brain. For example, dopamine activity appears to underlie some pleasurable emotions, and endorphins may also play a role (Panksepp, 1998; Robinson, 1997). Serotonin and norepinephrine play a role in anger. Despite these linkages, however, it seems unlikely that specific brain substances will be found to produce specific emotions on their own. When the final story of the brain and emotion can at last be told, it will undoubtedly describe complex interactions between brain chemicals and neural structures.

Hemispheric activation and emotion. Years ago in Italy, psychiatrists treated clinically depressed patients with electroshock treatments to either the right or the left hemisphere. The electric current temporarily disrupted activity in the hemisphere to which it was applied. With the left hemisphere knocked out (forcing the right hemisphere to take charge), patients had what physicians termed a "catastrophic" reaction, wailing and crying until the shock effects wore off. When shock was applied to the right hemisphere, allowing the left hemisphere to dominate, the patients reacted quite differently, They seemed unconcerned, happy, and sometimes even euphoric. A similar pattern of emotions was noted in patients in whom one hemisphere had been damaged by lesions or strokes. Left hemisphere damage, particularly in the frontal lobe, accentuated negative emotions like depression; right frontal damage was linked to indifference or euphoria (Gainotti, 1972).

These findings suggested that left-hemisphere activation might underlie certain positive emotions, and right-hemisphere functioning negative ones. To test this proposition, Richard Davidson and Nathan Fox obtained EEG measures of frontal lobe activity as people experienced various emotions (Davidson & Fox, 1988; Fox & Davidson, 1991). They found that when people felt positive emotions by recalling pleasurable experiences or watching a happy film, the left hemisphere was relatively more active than the right. But when sadness or other negative emotions were evoked, the right hemisphere became relatively more active. This pattern seems to be innate. Infants only three to four days old

➤ 14. Which neurotransmitters are involved in specific emotional responses?

➤ 15. What clinical and research evidence is there to support an "L+, R−" theory of hemispheric activation differences for positive and negative emotions?

showed a similar pattern of hemispheric activation when given sucrose solutions, which evoke positive reactions, or a citric acid solution, which apparently disgusts them (Davidson & Fox, 1988).

As we saw in the previous discussion of subjective well-being, people differ in their tendency to experience positive or negative emotions. Individual differences in typical or *resting* hemispheric activation, measured under emotionally neutral conditions, seems related to this tendency. Davidson and Fox (1989) found that human infants with resting right-hemisphere dominance were more likely to become upset and cry if their mothers left the room than were those with left-hemisphere dominance (Figure 10.7). In adults, a higher resting level of right-hemisphere EEG activity appears to be a risk factor for the later development of adult depressive disorders (Marshall & Fox, 2000; Tomarken & Keener, 1998).

Autonomic and hormonal processes. You are afraid. Your heart starts to beat faster. Blood is drawn from your stomach to your muscles, and digestion slows to a crawl. You breathe harder and faster to get more energy-sustaining oxygen. Blood sugar level increases, producing more nutrients for your muscles. The pupils of your eyes dilate to let in more light so you can see the danger better. Your skin perspires to keep you cool and to flush out waste products created by extra exertion. Your muscles tense, ready for action.

Some theorists call this state of arousal the *fight-or-flight response*. It is produced by the sympathetic branch of the autonomic nervous system and by hormones from the endocrine system. The sympathetic nervous system produces arousal within a few seconds by directly stimulating the organs and muscles of the body. Meanwhile, the endocrine system pumps epinephrine, cortisol, and other stress hormones into the bloodstream. These hormones produce physiological effects like those triggered by the sympathetic nervous system, but their effects are longer lasting and can keep the body aroused for a considerable length of time.

Do different emotions produce different patterns of arousal? Many investigators conclude that complex and subtle emotions like jealousy and tenderness do not involve distinct patterns of arousal (Panksepp, 1998). On the other hand, autonomic patterns do show subtle differences in certain basic emotions, like anger and fear (Levenson, 1992). For example, heart rate speeds up in both fear and anger, but there are differences in where the blood gets pumped (Ekman et al., 1983). Anger causes more blood to flow to the hands and feet, whereas fear reduces blood flow to these areas (providing a scientific basis for the colloquial expression "cold feet"). But whether people can detect such subtle physiological differences in a manner that would allow them to identify and label their emotions is an unanswered question.

"I cannot tell a lie": the lie detector controversy. Given what you have learned so far about the physiology of emotion, do you think emotional arousal could tell us whether someone is telling the truth or lying? A scientific instrument known as a **polygraph** (Figure 10.8a) can measure physiological responses, such as respiration, heart rate, skin conductance (which increases in the presence of emotion due to sweat gland activity). Because people have less control over physiological responses than over many other behaviors, the polygraph is regarded by some as a nearly infallible means of establishing whether or not someone is telling the truth. However, this approach to detecting "lying" by increases in emotional arousal is highly controversial.

Figure 10.8b shows a portion of a polygraph record. Polygraph examiners compare physiological responses to critical questions (e.g., "Were you present at the National Bank when it was robbed the night of August 4, 2001?") with responses to control questions ("Have you ever lived in Arizona?"). In this case, note the changes that occurred on the autonomic measures after an emotionally loaded question was asked (point A to point B).

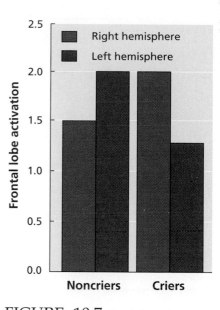

FIGURE 10.7 Resting activation in the left and front frontal hemispheres differed in infants who later reacted with distress or no distress when their mothers left. The criers showed relatively greater right hemisphere activation, the noncriers greater left-hemisphere activation.

Data from Davidson & Fox, 1989.

➤ 16. How are the sympathetic and endocrine systems involved in emotion? Do different emotions have different patterns of autonomic arousal?

(a)

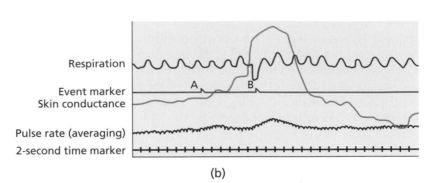

Respiration

Event marker
Skin conductance

Pulse rate (averaging)
2-second time marker

(b)

FIGURE 10.8   The polygraph (a) records physiological changes (b) that are part of emotional responses. Between points A and B, an emotionally loaded question was asked. Within 2 seconds, the effects of the question were visible in the subject's respiration, skin conductance, and pulse rate. Does this mean he was lying?

➤ 17. What considerations and research evidence challenges the validity of the "lie detector"? What kinds or errors are most likely?

But does this emotional response mean that the subject was lying? Herein lies one major problem with polygraph tests. Innocent people may appear guilty when doubt, fear, or lack of confidence increases their autonomic activity. Even a thought like "What if my answer makes me look guilty, even though I'm not?" in response to a critical question could send the polygraph pens into spasms that might suggest a lie. As David Lykken, a leading critic of the lie detector, has noted, "polygraph pens do no special dance when we are lying" (1981, p. 10).

Not only can innocent people appear guilty, but guilty people can also learn to "beat" the polygraph. For example, by biting their tongue, curling their toes, or contracting their anal sphincter when control questions are asked, they can produce an arousal response to those questions that look similar to the arousal that occurs when they actually lie on critical questions. William Casey, former director of the CIA, used to delight in his ability to fool the lie detector (Carlson & Hatfield, 1992). Fred Fay, a prison convict who had been falsely convicted of murder partly on the basis of a polygraph test, later became an expert at defeating polygraph tests. (He obviously could have saved himself considerable grief by learning these skills earlier.) On one occasion, Fay coached 27 fellow inmates who were scheduled for polygraph tests. All of the inmates told Fay they were guilty of the relevant crimes. Yet after only 20 minutes of instruction, 23 of the 27 inmates managed to beat the polygraph (Lykken, 1981). Such results sharply contradict the notion of an infallible lie detector.

This conclusion is supported by research in which experienced polygraph examiners were given the polygraph records of suspects known to be either innocent or guilty on the basis of other evidence. The experts were asked to judge the guilt or innocence of the suspects. The examiners often did quite well in identifying the guilty, attaining accuracy rates of 80 to 98 percent (Honts & Perry, 1992). However, they did less well in identifying the innocent, judging as many as 55 percent of the truly innocent suspects guilty in some studies (Honts & Perry, 1992; Kleinmuntz & Szucko, 1984; Lykken, 1984). These error rates call into question the adage that an innocent person has nothing to fear from a polygraph test.

Largely because of an unacceptably high likelihood that an innocent person might be judged guilty, the American Psychological Association has supported legal challenges to polygraph testing. Congressional testimony by psychologists strongly influenced passage of the Employee Polygraph Protection Act of 1988, which prohibits most nongovernmental polygraph testing. Moreover, polygraph results alone cannot be used to convict people of crimes in most states. Nonetheless, the federal government continues to use polygraph tests in internal criminal investigations and in national security screening, despite the fact that their use for hiring and security clearance decisions has been shown to lack validity (Honts, 1991).

The Behavioral Component

So far, we have examined the situational, cognitive, and physiological components of emotion. We now turn to the directly observable behaviors that are part of emotional responses.

Expressive behaviors.   Although we can never directly experience another person's feelings, we can often infer that someone is angry, sad, fearful, or happy on the basis of his or her emotional displays, or **expressive behaviors.** When exposed to slides showing angry or happy faces, college students responded with subtle facial muscle responses that denote displeasure or pleasure within 1/3 of a second (Dinberg & Thunberg, 1998). Sometimes, too, others' emotional displays can evoke similar emotional responses in us, a process known as **empathy.** Perhaps you have found yourself experiencing the same emotion as the central character while reading a novel or viewing a movie. Professional actors sometimes find that they become so immersed in the expressive behaviors of a character they are playing that the boundaries between self and role begin to fade. Kirk Douglas reported one such experience when he played Vincent Van Gogh in *Lust for Life* (Figure 10.9):

> I was close to getting lost in the character of Van Gogh . . . I felt myself going over the line, into the skin of Van Gogh. . . . Sometimes I had to stop myself from reaching my hand up and touching my ear to find out if it was actually there. It was a frightening experience. That way lies madness . . . I could never play him again. (Lehman-Haupt, 1988, p. 10)

Evolution and emotional expression.   Where do emotional expressions come from? In his classic work, *The Expression of Emotions in Man and Animals* (1872/1965), Charles Darwin argued that emotional displays are products of evolution and that they developed because they contributed to species survival. Darwin emphasized the basic similarity of emotional expression from other animals to humans. For example, both wolves and humans bare their teeth when they are angry. As Darwin explained it, this behavior makes the animal look more ferocious and thus decreases its chances of being attacked and perhaps killed in a fight. Darwin did not maintain that all forms of emotional expression are innate, but he believed that many of them are.

Like Darwin, modern evolutionary theorists stress the adaptive value of emotional expression (Izard, 1984; Plutchik, 1994; Tomkins, 1991). Two key findings suggest that humans have innate, or **fundamental emotional patterns.** First, the expressions of certain emotions (e.g., rage and terror) are similar across a variety of cultures, suggesting that certain expressive behavior patterns are wired into the nervous system. Second, children who are blind from birth seem to express these basic emotions in the same ways that sighted children do, ruling out the possibility that they are learned solely through observation (Eibl-Eibesfeldt, 1973). The fundamental emotional patterns proposed by three leading evolutionary theorists are shown in Table 10.1. Other emotions are seen as resulting from some combination of these innate emotions. The evolutionary view does *not* assume that all emotional expressions are innate, nor does it deny that innate emotional expressions can be modified or inhibited as a result of social learning.

Emotions can be organized in terms of a hierarchy ranging from the most universal expressions to the more subtle subordinate categories (Fischer et al., 1990). Positive and negative affect, expressed as interest and distress, are the most basic categories, the most universal, and the first to manifest themselves after birth.

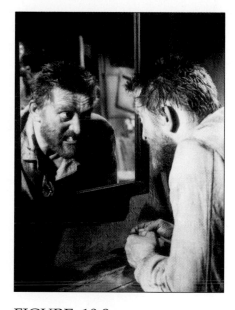

FIGURE 10.9 Kirk Douglas, shown playing Vincent Van Gogh in the movie *Lust for Life,* reported that by virtue of behaving like Van Gogh, he at times lost the ability to separate himself from the character. It appears that voluntary expressions, postures, and actions can affect emotions.

➤ 18. What evidence exists for fundamental emotional patterns of expression? How do they fit into an emotional hierarchy?

TABLE 10.1	FUNDAMENTAL OR PRIMARY INNATE EMOTIONS PROPOSED BY THREE LEADING EVOLUTIONARY THEORISTS	
Carroll Izard	Silvan Tomkins	Robert Plutchik
Anger	Anger	Anger
Fear	Fear	Fear
Joy	Joy	Enjoyment
Disgust	Disgust	Disgust
Interest	Interest	Anticipation
Surprise	Surprise	Surprise
Contempt	Contempt	
Shame	Shame	
	Sadness	Sadness
	Distress	
Guilt		
		Acceptance

Source: Based on Izard, 1984; Tomkins, 1991; and Plutchik, 1991.

The basic emotions described by evolutionary theorists appear at the second level of the hierarchy. These basic emotions are assumed to apply across all cultures, but they appear later in a child's development than do the positive and negative affect observed in infants. The third level consists of more subtle emotions derived from the basic emotions. These emotions and the ways they are expressed are more heavily influenced by cultural learning. For example, distinctions are made in Western cultures between many different varieties of love, including passionate love, friendship love, parental love, possessive love, and infatuation (Lee, 1988; Sternberg, 1988). In contrast, only two forms of love are distinguished in India: mother love and erotic love (Lynch, 1990). Children learn these cultural distinctions much later in their development.

Facial expression of emotion. Most of us are fairly confident in our ability to "read" the emotions of others. Although many parts of the body can communicate feelings, we tend to concentrate on what the face tells us. Most lower animals have relatively few facial muscles, so their facial expressions are limited. Only monkeys, apes, and humans have enough well-developed facial muscles to produce a large number of expressions.

Interest in studying facial expressions was spurred by the development of sophisticated measuring procedures, such as the Facial Action Coding System (FACS). Developed by Paul Ekman and Wallace Friesen (1978), the FACS requires a trained observer to dissect an observed expression in terms of all the muscular actions that produced it. The system is so complex that it takes about 100 minutes to score each minute of observed facial expression (Ekman et al., 1988).

Common lore has it that the eyes are particularly good sources of information about what is being felt: "if looks could kill"; "the look of love"; "her eyes twinkled with amusement." Research tells us, however, that other parts of the face are at least as important, if not more so. In fact, it appears that different emotions are expressed through different parts of the face.

In one experiment, judges first agreed on the emotions being expressed in a set of 32 posed facial photographs. Each photograph was then cut into three parts, a brow-forehead part, an eyes part, and a mouth part. People were then asked to rate these partial photos in terms of six basic emotions: anger, fear, happiness, surprise, sadness, and disgust. The results showed that different parts of

➤ 19. What results concerning emotional perception, sex differences, and universal expressions of emotion have been found using the FACS?

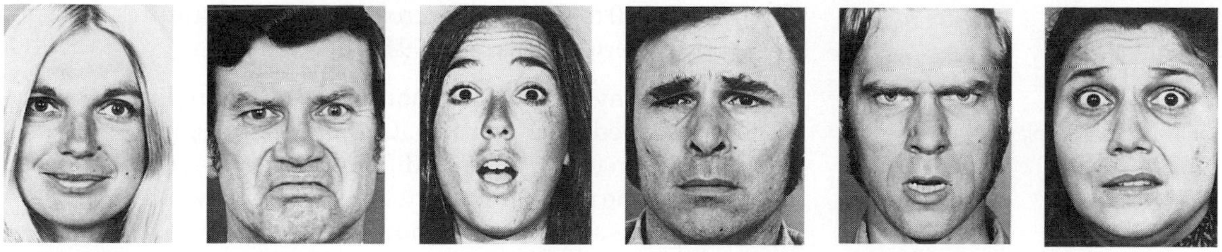

	Happiness	Disgust	Surprise	Sadness	Anger	Fear
United States						
(N = 99)	97%	92%	95%	84%	67%	85%
Brazil						
(N = 40)	95%	97%	87%	59%	90%	67%
Chile						
(N = 119)	95%	92%	93%	88%	94%	68%
Argentina						
(N = 168)	98%	92%	95%	78%	90%	54%
Japan						
(N = 29)	100%	90%	100%	62%	90%	66%

FIGURE 10.10 Percentage of agreement in judgments of facial expressions of emotion by people in five different cultures.
Source: Ekman, 1973.

the face provided the best cues for recognizing the various emotions. The eyes provided the most important cues for fear and sadness, but the mouth was the major cue for happiness and disgust, and the forehead was the best indicator of surprise. Anger appeared to be a more complex emotion, requiring information from all facial areas to be recognized accurately (Boucher & Ekman, 1975).

Although facial expressions can be valuable cues for judging emotion, even people within the same culture may learn to express the same emotions differently. Thus some people have learned to appear very calm when they are angry. Fortunately, we usually know something about the situation to which the person is reacting, and this often is an important basis for judging emotions. For example, if a woman is crying, is she crying because of sadness or because of happiness? A background showing her being declared the winner of a lottery will result in a different emotional judgment than one showing her at a graveside. Many experiments have shown that people's accuracy and agreement in labeling emotions from pictures is considerably higher when the pictures show a background situation (Ekman & Davidson, 1994).

Across many cultures, women have generally proven to be more accurate judges of emotional expressions than men (Ekman, 1982; Zuckerman, 1976). Perhaps the ability to accurately read emotions has greater adaptive significance for women, whose traditional role within many cultures has been to care for others and attend to their needs (Buss, 1991). This ability may also result from cultural encouragement for women to be sensitive to others' emotions and to express their feelings openly. Men who work in professions that emphasize these skills, such as psychotherapy, drama, and art, are as accurate as women are in judging emotions, suggesting that these skills can be learned (Rosenthal et al., 1974).

What of Darwin's claim that certain facial expressions are universal indicators of specific emotions? Modern researchers have approached this question by determining the extent to which people in different cultures agree on the emotions being expressed in facial photographs (Ekman, 1973; Russell et al., 1997). The results of one such study are shown in Figure 10.10. You can see that there is generally high agreement on these photos of basic emotions, but also some cultural variations. Other researchers have found levels of agreement ranging from 40 to 70 percent across a variety of cultures, well above chance but still far from perfect (Russell, 1994).

Cultural display rules.   The norms for emotional expression within a given culture are called **display rules.** Certain gestures, body postures, and physical movements can convey vastly different meanings in different cultures. For example, using the familiar upright thumb gesture while hitchhiking in certain regions of Greece and Sardinia could result in decidedly negative consequences, such as tire tracks on one's body. In those regions, an upright thumb is the equivalent of a raised middle finger in the United States (Morris et al., 1979). Likewise, spitting on someone is a sign of contempt in most cultures. Yet the Masai tribe of Africa traditionally considered being spat on a great compliment, particularly if the person doing the spitting was a member of the opposite sex (Thomson, 1887). One can only imagine what a Masai singles bar would be like.

Do emotional expressions differ across cultures in the same way that gestures do? To some extent they do, for the display rules of a particular culture dictate *when* and *how* particular emotions are to be expressed. In the Orissa culture of India, sticking out one's tongue is the display rule for expressing feelings of shame (Menon & Schweder, 1994). Some Asian cultures, such as the Japanese, are more subdued in their expression of emotion in public settings than Europeans and Americans are (Mesquita et al., 1997). Within the Utku Inuit Eskimo culture, the expression of anger is nearly absent. The only exceptions occur toward individuals who have been ostracized from the community and toward dogs, who are the frequent targets of vented aggression (Briggs, 1970). A number of emotion theorists, including Silvan Tomkins (1991), Paul Ekman (1994), and Carroll Izard (1989), conclude that innate biological factors and cultural display rules combine to shape emotional expression.

Instrumental behaviors.   Emotional responses are often "calls to action," requiring some sort of response to the situation that aroused the emotion. A highly anxious student must find some way to cope with an impending test. A mother angered by her child's behavior must find a nondestructive way to get her point across. These are **instrumental behaviors,** directed at achieving some goal.

Batja Mesquita, Nico Frijda, and Klaus Scherer (1997) analyzed cross-cultural studies and concluded that instrumental actions fall into five broad categories: moving toward others (e.g., love), moving away from others (fear, revulsion), moving against others (anger), helplessness, and submission. Within each of these broad categories, many different goal-directed behaviors can occur. Whether an instrumental behavior will be successful depends on the appropriateness of the response to the situation, the skill with which it is carried out, and the level of emotional arousal that accompanies the behaviors.

People often assume that high emotional arousal enhances task performance, as when athletes try to "psych themselves up" for competition. Yet as students who have experienced extreme anxiety during tests could testify, high emotional arousal can also interfere with performance. In many situations, the relation between emotional arousal and performance seems to take the shape of an upside-down, or inverted, U. As physiological arousal increases up to some optimal level, performance improves. But beyond that optimal level, further increases in arousal impair performance. It is thus possible to be either too "flat" or too "high" to perform well.

The relation between arousal and performance depends not only on arousal level, but also on task complexity (Yerkes & Dodson, 1908). Task complexity involves how complicated the task is, how much precision is required to do the task, and how well the task has been learned. Generally speaking, as task complexity *increases,* the optimal level of arousal for maximum performance *decreases.* Thus even a moderate level of arousal can disrupt performance on a highly complex task.

Figure 10.11 illustrates these two principles. Note that the inverted U relation applies for all three tasks and that the more complex the task, the lower is

➤ 20. What are cultural display rules? How do they affect emotional behavior?

➤ 21. How do level of arousal and task complexity combine to affect task performance?

the optimal arousal level. One other feature of Figure 10.11 is worth noting: Performance drops off less at high levels of arousal for the simple task than for the others. In fact, even the highest levels of arousal can enhance performance of very simple tasks, such as running or lifting something. This fact may account for seemingly "superhuman" feats we hear about occasionally, such as one incident in which a highly distraught 102-pound mother lifted up the front end of a truck to free her child, who was trapped under one of its wheels (*Honolulu Star-Bulletin*, January 6, 1980).

For complex tasks, the relation between arousal and performance is different. High emotionality can interfere with the ability to attend to and process information effectively. Thus people may underachieve on intelligence test items that require complicated mental processing if they are too anxious, and the performance of air traffic control officers can suffer in highly stressful circumstances (Joslyn & Hunt, 1998; Pierce et al., 1998). On physical tasks, muscle tension can interfere with the skillful execution of complex movements. For example, in the sport of golf, which requires precise and complex movements, the optimal level of arousal should be quite low. Robert Weinberg and Marvin Genuchi (1980) studied the effects of anxiety on performance during an intercollegiate golf tournament. Before the tournament began, they administered a questionnaire to identify players who were low, moderate, or high in performance anxiety. Although the three groups of golfers were similar in ability and performed equally well during practice rounds, their golf scores differed sharply during the anxiety-arousing tournament rounds. On the first day of competition, the average performance of golfers in the low-anxiety group was five strokes better than the performance of those in the high-anxiety group. On the pressure-packed last day of the tournament, this difference rose to nearly seven strokes. The moderate-anxiety group had intermediate scores.

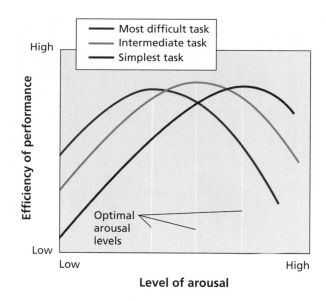

FIGURE 10.11 The relation between arousal and performance often takes the form of an inverted U, with performance declining above and below an optimal arousal level. However, the more difficult or complex a task is, the lower is the optimal level of arousal for performing it.

❯ INTERACTIONS AMONG THE COMPONENTS OF EMOTION

Emotions involve complex interactions among eliciting stimuli, thoughts, physiological responses, and behaviors. For more than 100 years, theorists and researchers have explored the nature of these interactions.

➤ 22. Compare the James-Lange (somatic) and Cannon-Bard explanations for emotional perception and labeling.

The James-Lange Somatic Theory

In 1890, the eminent psychologist William James ignited considerable controversy with this counterintuitive statement:

> Common sense says . . . we meet a bear, are frightened, and run; we are insulted by a rival, are angry, and strike. The hypothesis here to be defended says that this order of sequence is incorrect . . . and that the more rational statement is that we feel sorry *because* we cry, angry *because* we strike, afraid *because* we tremble. (James, 1890/1950, p. 451, italics ours)

At about the same time that James advanced his theory, a Danish psychologist named Carl Lange reached a similar conclusion, so the theory was attributed to both men. Today, the *James-Lange theory* lives on as the **somatic theory of emotion** (Papanicolaou, 1989). To proponents of this theory, body informs mind. We know we are afraid or in love only because our bodily reactions tell us so.

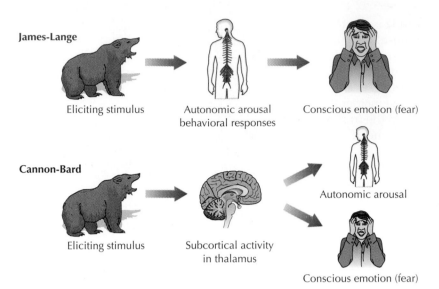

James-Lange

Eliciting stimulus → Autonomic arousal behavioral responses → Conscious emotion (fear)

Cannon-Bard

Eliciting stimulus → Subcortical activity in thalamus → Autonomic arousal / Conscious emotion (fear)

FIGURE 10.12 Two early theories of emotion continue to influence current-day theorizing. The James-Lange theory holds that the experience of emotion is caused by somatic feedback and physiological arousal. According to the Cannon-Bard theory, the thalamus receives sensory input and simultaneously stimulates physiological responses and cognitive awareness.

➤ 23. How does research on animals and people deprived of sensory feedback bear on the validity of the James-Lange and Cannon-Bard theories?

The Cannon-Bard Theory

It wasn't long before the James-Lange theory was challenged. In 1927, the physiologist Walter Cannon fired back. He pointed out that people's bodies do *not* respond instantaneously to an emotional stimulus; several seconds may pass before signs of physiological arousal appear. Yet people typically experience the emotion immediately. This would be impossible according to the James-Lange theory. Cannon and his colleague L. L. Bard concluded that cognition must be involved as well.

The *Cannon-Bard theory* proposed when we encounter an emotion-arousing situation, the thalamus simultaneously sends sensory messages to the cerebral cortex *and* to the body's internal organs. The message to the cortex produces the experience of emotion, and the one to the internal organs produces the physiological arousal. Thus neither cognition nor arousal causes the other; they are independent responses to stimulation from the thalamus. The James-Lange and Cannon-Bard theories are compared in Figure 10.12.

The Role of Autonomic Feedback

The James-Lange and Cannon-Bard theories differ on one critical point. According to the James-Lange theory, feedback from the body's reactions to eliciting stimuli tells the brain that we are experiencing an emotion. Without such feedback, there would be no emotional response. In contrast, the Cannon-Bard theory maintains that experiencing emotion results from signals sent from the thalamus to the cortex, not from bodily feedback. Is there any situation that would provide a test of whether bodily feedback is necessary?

In fact, there is. What if organisms were deprived of sensory feedback from their internal organs, so they never knew when these organs were aroused? Would they be devoid of emotional reactions? To answer this question, Cannon (1929) carried out experiments with animals in which he severed the nerves that provide feedback from the internal organs to the brain. He found that even after surgery, the animals still exhibited emotional responses, supporting his theory over that of James and Lange.

But perhaps people are different from other species. Obviously, Cannon's animal experiments could never be replicated with people, but nature provides a tragic parallel. Like Cannon's animals, people whose spinal cords have been severed in accidents receive no sensory feedback from body areas below the injury. Given this fact, what are their emotional lives like? To find out, Kathleen Chwalisz, Ed Diener, and Dennis Gallagher (1988) administered self-report measures of emotional experience to people who had sustained spinal injuries. For comparative purposes, the same measures were administered to individuals having physical handicaps that did not affect sensory feedback, and to a group of nonhandicapped people.

As shown in Figure 10.13, the people with spinal cord injuries did not differ from the other two groups in the reported intensity of either their positive or negative emotions. Indeed, some reported that they frequently experienced very intense emotions—sometimes more intense than those they had experienced before their injury. Moreover, people with upper and lower spinal cord injuries—who differed in the amount of bodily feedback they could receive—did not differ in the intensity of their emotions. These results, like those of Cannon's animal studies, appear to cast doubt on the claim that arousal feedback from the body is absolutely necessary for people to experience intense emotions. But let us take this issue one step further.

The Facial Feedback Hypothesis

Arousal feedback is not the only kind of bodily feedback the somatic theory considers important. Facial muscles involved in emotional displays also feed messages to the brain, and these muscles are active even in patients with spinal injuries who may receive no sensory input from below the neck. According to the **facial feedback hypothesis**, this feedback to the brain might play a key role in determining the nature and intensity of emotion that we experience, as the James-Lange theory would suggest (Adelmann & Zajonc, 1989; McIntosh et al., 1997).

Research shows that positive or negative emotional responses can indeed be triggered by contraction of specific facial muscles. Especially noteworthy are studies in which participants do not know that they are activating muscles used in specific emotional expressions. In one such study, Fritz Strack and his coworkers (1988) found that when participants held pens in their teeth, activating muscles used in smiling (Figure 10.14a), they rated themselves as feeling more pleasant than when they held the pens with their lips (Figure 10.14b), which activates muscles involved in frowning. Participants also rated cartoons as funnier while holding pens in their teeth and activating the "happy muscles" than while holding pens with their lips (Figure 10.14c). In another study, Robert Zajonc and his colleagues compared the subjective experiences of subjects who pronounced different sounds, such as *eee* and *ooh*. Saying the *eee* sound, which activates muscles used in smiling, was associated with more pleasant feelings than saying the *ooh* sound, which activates muscles involved in negative facial expressions (Zajonc et al., 1989). Perhaps photographers should force us to say "cheese" not only when they take our picture, but also later when they show us proofs that not even our mothers could love.

How might facial feedback trigger emotional experience? According to the **vascular theory of emotional feedback** (McIntosh et al., 1997; Zajonc, 1985), tensing facial muscles alters the temperature of blood entering the brain by controlling the volume of air inhaled through the nose. Cooling the blood increases positive affect, whereas warming it produces negative affect, perhaps by influencing the release of different neurotransmitters in the brain. Proponents of this theory have shown that activating the muscles involved in smiling not only cools the blood supply to the forehead as more air is inhaled through the nostrils, but also increases pleasant feelings. Conversely, activating the muscles involved in negative facial expressions reduces air flow, raises forehead temperature as the blood supply warms, and evokes negative affect (McIntosh et al., 1997). Perhaps the vascular theory can help explain how body influences mind in the experiencing of emotions.

Cognitive-Affective Theories

Nowhere are mind-body interactions more obvious than in the emotions, where thinking and feeling are intimately connected. Cognitive-affective theories focus on the ways in which cognitions and physiological responses interact. Historically, Richard Lazarus and Stanley Schachter have been major figures in this approach.

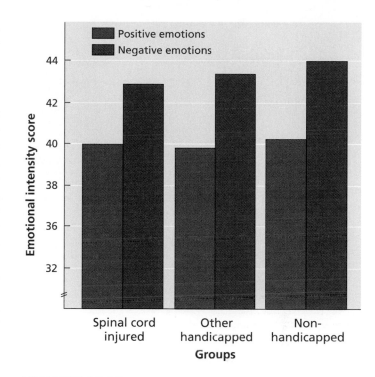

FIGURE 10.13 Intensity of positive and negative emotions reported by people with spinal cord injuries, by handicapped people with no spinal damage, and by nonhandicapped people. The lack of differences casts doubt on the assertion that feedback from physiological arousal is essential for the experiencing of normal emotional responses. Data from Chwalisz et al., 1988.

➤ 24. What is the facial feedback hypothesis? What research evidence supports it? What might be the role of vascular feedback?

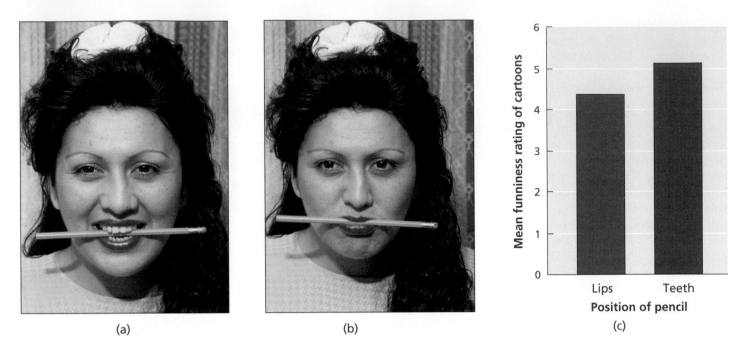

FIGURE 10.14 Holding a pen in the teeth (a) so as to activate the muscles used in smiling evokes more pleasant feelings than holding the pen in one's lips (b), which activates muscles used in frowning. This finding (c) provides support for the facial feedback hypothesis. Data from Strack et al., 1988.

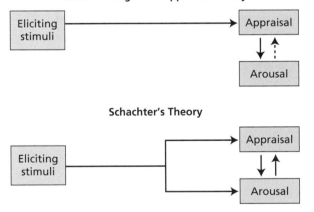

FIGURE 10.15 Two theories of cognitive-arousal interactions. The cognitive appraisal theory of Richard Lazarus holds that cognitive appraisal processes stimulate emotional arousal, which may then affect subsequent appraisals. Stanley Schachter's two-factor theory also focuses on the interactive role of cognition and arousal. Schachter emphasized the role of appraisals of the environment in our labeling of the emotions we experience.

➤ 25. According to Schachter, what influences perceptions of emotional intensity? What tells us which emotion we are experiencing?

➤ 26. How did Lazarus and coworkers show that appraisals influence level of arousal? How did Schachter and Wheeler show that arousal level can affect appraisals?

Lazarus strongly emphasizes the link between cognitive appraisal and arousal, insisting that all emotional responses require some sort of appraisal, whether we are aware of that appraisal or not.

> The fundamental premise is that in order to survive, animals (humans particularly) are constructed biologically to be constantly evaluating (appraising) their relationship with the environment with respect to significance for well-being. . . . If a person (or animal) appraises his or her relationship with the environment in a particular way, then a specific emotion, which is tied to the appraisal, always results; and if two persons make the same appraisal, then they will experience the same emotion regardless of the actual circumstances. (Lazarus, 1991, p. 825)

As noted earlier, the appraisal itself need not be a conscious thought; it may be some instantaneous perception that does not enter conscious awareness. Once the appraisal has triggered the arousal response, arousal cues may feed back into the ongoing appraisal process (Figure 10.15). Thus if you feel yourself becoming aroused in the presence of another person, you may begin to appraise the person as more desirable and attractive than before.

Like Lazarus, Stanley Schachter emphasized links between cognition and arousal. He was intrigued with the question of how we know both *what* we are feeling and *how strongly* we are feeling it. Schachter's **two-factor theory of emotion** states that arousal and cognitive labeling based on situational cues are the critical ingredients in emotional experience. The intensity of physiological arousal tells us *how strongly* we are feeling something, but situational cues give us the information we need in order to tell us *what* we are feeling—fear, anger, love, or some other emotion (Schachter, 1966). Lazarus would agree, viewing these cues as an important determinant of the appraisal process (Figure 10.15). Thus both theories view situation, cognition, and arousal as highly interrelated. Two classic experiments conducted in the Lazarus and Schachter labs explored the links between cognition and arousal.

RESEARCH   CLOSE-UP

Cognition-Arousal Relations: Two Classic Experiments

Manipulating Appraisal to Influence Arousal

❱ Introduction

Richard Lazarus and his University of California colleagues examined how differences in cognitive appraisal can influence physiological arousal. To do so, they needed to measure physiological arousal in response to visual stimuli that were held constant for all participants while influencing the manner in which these eliciting stimuli were appraised. If people in different appraisal conditions showed different arousal responses to the same eliciting stimuli, it would support the notion that arousal is influenced by appraisal.

Method

The researchers monitored college students' physiological responses while they watched an anthropology film, *Subincision in the Arunta,* which depicts in graphic detail an aboriginal puberty rite during which the penises of adolescent boys are cut with a jagged flint knife. The film typically elicits a high level of physiological arousal in viewers (and, according to the researchers, many leg-crossing responses in males). The dependent variable, measured by recording electrodes attached to the participants' palms, was changes in electrical skin conductance caused by sweat gland activity.

To study the effects of participants' appraisal of the filmed visual stimuli on arousal, the researchers experimentally varied the film's sound track. Four different sound track conditions were used to manipulate the independent variable:

- A *trauma* sound track emphasized the pain suffered by the boys, the danger of infection, the jaggedness of the flint knife, and other unpleasant aspects of the operation.
- A *denial* sound track was just the opposite; it denied that the operation was excessively painful or traumatic and emphasized that the boys looked forward to entering adulthood by undergoing the rite and demonstrating their bravery.
- The *intellectualization* sound track, also designed to produce a more benign appraisal, ignored the emotional elements of the scenes altogether and focused on the traditions and history of the tribe.
- In a *silent* control condition, the film was shown without any sound track at all, leaving viewers to make their own appraisals.

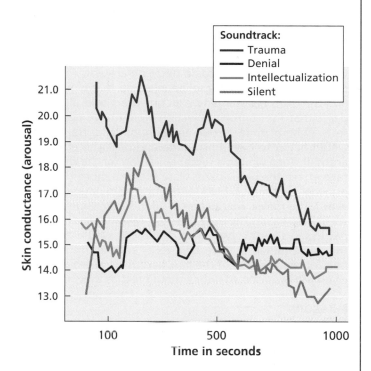

FIGURE 10.16 Appraisal influences arousal. Participants who viewed a film showing a tribal subincision rite in vivid detail exhibited different levels of physiological arousal, depending on the sound track that accompanied the film.

Data from Speisman, et al., 1964.

❱ Results

As shown in Figure 10.16, the sound tracks produced markedly different levels of arousal. As predicted, the trauma sound track resulted in the highest arousal, followed by the silent film condition, which likely evoked dire appraisals as well. The denial and intellectualization sound-tracks, designed to create more benign appraisals, resulted in much lower levels of arousal. This classic study supported Lazarus's contention that appraisal can influence arousal.

Manipulating Arousal to Influence Appraisal

❱ Introduction

Is the reverse also true? Can level of arousal influence people's appraisal of an eliciting stimulus? To test this hypothesis, one must cause people to experience different levels

—Continued

of arousal without knowing the true reason. The level of arousal should then be attributed to whatever eliciting stimuli are present in the situation.

▶ Method

In Stanley Schachter's laboratory at Columbia University, participants were told they were in a study involving the effects of a new vitamin called suproxin on visual perception. The researchers directly manipulated level of physiological arousal by injecting participants with one of three difference "suproxin" substances. In one condition, participants received epinephrine, a drug that increases arousal. In a second experimental condition, participants received a tranquilizer drug that would decrease arousal. A placebo control group received a saline injection that would have no effects on arousal. The experimenters told all participants that the suproxin injection would have no side effects (when, in fact, the epinephrine and tranquilizer would begin to have immediate and opposite effects on arousal). Then while presumably waiting for the vitamin to take effect, the participants were shown a short movie "to provide continuous black-and-white stimulation to the eyes." The movie was a comedy film that included a slapstick chase scene. The experimenters hypothesized that the participants in the two drug conditions would attribute their heightened or lowered level of arousal to the funniness (or lack thereof) of the film, because they would know of no other reason why they should feel as they did.

▶ Results

Participants were observed from behind a one-way mirror while they watched the movie. The observers, who were unaware of which participants had received which injections, recorded how frequently the participants smiled, grinned, laughed, threw up their hands, slapped their legs, or doubled over with laughter. These behaviors were combined into an "amusement score" that served as the dependent variable measure of how funny the participants found the film to be.

It appears that arousal cues can indeed influence one's appraisal of the situation. As Figure 10.17 shows, the results supported the experimenters' hypothesis that level of arousal would influence participants' appraisal of the film. The aroused participants in the epinephrine group found the film funnier than the tranquilized participants did, and the placebo control group fell in the middle. Thus a person injected with epinephrine might think, "Here I am watching this film and getting all excited. This film's really funny!"

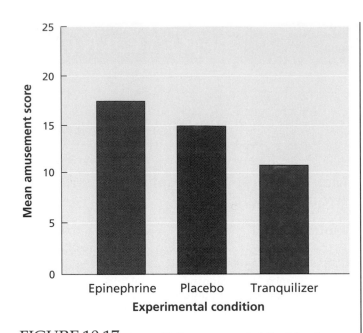

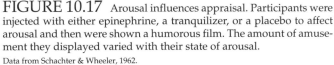

FIGURE 10.17 Arousal influences appraisal. Participants were injected with either epinephrine, a tranquilizer, or a placebo to affect arousal and then were shown a humorous film. The amount of amusement they displayed varied with their state of arousal.
Data from Schachter & Wheeler, 1962.

▶ Critical Discussion

These two studies were among the first to experimentally manipulate appraisal and arousal so as to study their effects upon one another. In the first study, even though it was not possible to completely control for participants' own tendencies to appraise situations in certain ways, the four sound track conditions did have effects on the arousal responses of participants as they watched the subincision film. When Schachter and Wheeler turned Lazarus's procedure around and manipulated arousal levels with the stimulant and tranquilizing drugs, they found the expected differences in appraisal of the films. Moreover, they were able to measure these differences in terms of observable behavior.

Taken together, these two studies show that appraisal influences arousal and that arousal can influence appraisals, demonstrating the two-way causal relation between cognition and arousal shown in the model of emotion originally presented in Figure 10.3 (p. 414).

Sources: Joseph Speisman, Richard Lazarus, Arnold Mordkoff, and Les Davison, 1964. Experimental reduction of stress based on ego-defense theory. *Journal of Abnormal and Social Psychology, 68,* 367–380.

Stanley Schachter and Ladd Wheeler, 1962. Epinephrine, chlorpromazine, and amusement. *Journal of Abnormal and Social Psychology, 65,* 121–128.

The concepts of emotion and stress are closely related, for negative emotions such as anxiety, anger, frustration, shame, or depression are prominent features of our stress responses. Many of the insights achieved in the study of emotion apply directly to understanding and managing stress. Conversely, research and theorizing about stress has contributed greatly to an understanding of emotions.

❭ STRESS, COPING, AND HEALTH

Priscilla, now 15, had anything but an idyllic childhood. She grew up in an impoverished inner city home with an alcoholic father who sexually abused her and her younger sister. Her mother was hospitalized twice with "nervous breakdowns." When Priscilla was 7 years of age, her father called his family together in the living room and told them, "You drove me to this." He then put a gun to his head and committed suicide as his wife and children watched in horror. From that time on, Priscilla had to work after school to help support the family. Her mother became increasingly disturbed and sometimes beat her.

Considering her background, we might expect Priscilla to be an unhappy, maladjusted child, her emotional life dominated by anxiety, anger, and depression. Instead, she grew into a delightful and popular young woman who was emotionally well adjusted, president of her high school class, a talented singer, and an honor student. Children like Priscilla have been termed "invulnerable" or "resilient" youngsters (Garmezy, 1983; Masten & Coatsworth, 1998; Werner & Smith, 1982).

What allows resilient people to rise above extraordinarily stressful environments, while other individuals blessed with more benign life histories collapse under the weight of less severe stresses? The answer will show us that our psychological and physical well-being depends on complex interactions among environmental demands, the personal and environmental resources that we have to deal with them, and the individual vulnerabilities that make us susceptible to certain kinds of demands.

The Nature of Stress

Psychologists have viewed stress in three different ways: as a stimulus, as a response, and as an organism-environment interaction. Some define stress in terms of eliciting stimuli, or events that place strong demands on us. These situations are termed **stressors.** We use the term stress in this "stimulus" fashion when we make statements such as, "There's all kinds of stress in my life right now. I have three exams next week, I lost my backpack, and my car just broke down."

Stress has also been viewed as a *response* having cognitive, physiological, and behavioral components (Keyse, 2000). Thus a person might say, "I'm feeling all stressed out. I'm tensed up, I can't concentrate because I'm really worried, and I've been flying off the handle all week." The presence of negative emotions is an important feature of the stress response and links the study of stress with the field of emotion (Borod, 2000; Fink, 2000).

A third way of thinking about stress combines the stimulus and response definitions into a more inclusive model. Here stress is viewed as a *person-situation interaction*, or, more formally, as a *transaction* between the organism and the environment (Lazarus, 1991, 1998). The transactional conception of stress forms the basis for the model shown in Figure 10.18 and will guide our discussion of stress. From this perspective, **stress** is a pattern of cognitive appraisals, physiological responses, and behavioral tendencies that occurs in response to a perceived imbalance between situational demands and the resources needed to cope with them. You will recognize this as an adaptation of the general model of emotion presented earlier (Figure 10.3).

27. Describe three ways that theorists have defined the term, "stress."

Stressors

Stressors are specific kinds of eliciting stimuli. Whether physical or psychological, they place demands on us that endanger well-being, requiring us to adapt in some manner. The greater the imbalance between demands and resources, the

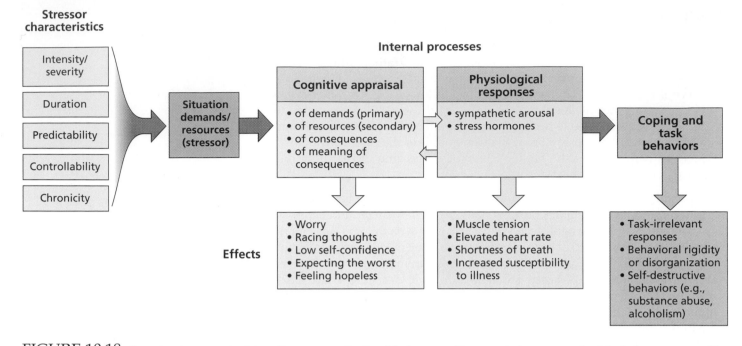

Stressor characteristics

Intensity/ severity

Duration

Predictability

Controllability

Chronicity

Situation demands/ resources (stressor)

Internal processes

Cognitive appraisal
- of demands (primary)
- of resources (secondary)
- of consequences
- of meaning of consequences

Physiological responses
- sympathetic arousal
- stress hormones

Coping and task behaviors

Effects

- Worry
- Racing thoughts
- Low self-confidence
- Expecting the worst
- Feeling hopeless

- Muscle tension
- Elevated heart rate
- Shortness of breath
- Increased susceptibility to illness

- Task-irrelevant responses
- Behavioral rigidity or disorganization
- Self-destructive behaviors (e.g., substance abuse, alcoholism)

FIGURE 10.18 Stress involves complex interactions among situational factors, cognitive appraisal processes, physiological responses, and behavioral attempts to cope with the situational demands. Stressor characteristics that increase stress responses are shown. The lower panels show potential cognitive, physiological, and behavioral stress responses that can interfere with well-being.

more stressful a situation is likely to be. Stressors can range in severity from *microstressors*—the daily hassles and everyday annoyances we encounter at school, on the job, and in our family relations—to very severe stressors. *Catastrophic events* often occur unexpectedly and typically affect large numbers of people. They include such events as natural disasters, acts of war, and concentration camp confinement (Figure 10.19). *Major negative events* such as being the victim of a major crime or sexual abuse, the death or loss of a loved one, an academic or career failure, or a major illness, also require major adaptation. As we shall see, all three classes of stressors can have significant negative impacts on psychological and physical well-being (Baum et al., 2000).

In addition to intensity or severity, several other characteristics of stressors have been identified as important and are listed in Figure 10.18. In general, events over which the person has little or no control, which occur suddenly and unpredictably, and which impact a person over a long period of time seem to take the greatest toll on physical and psychological well-being (Lazarus & Folkman, 1984; Taylor, 1999).

Measuring stressful life events. Sometimes it is possible to verify the life events a person has experienced. We may know that a person has lived through a natural disaster or lost a loved one to death. In other cases, researchers must rely on people's self-reports. To study linkages between life events and well-being, researchers have devised **life event scales** to quantify the amount of life stress that a person has experienced over a given period of time (e.g., the last six months or the past

FIGURE 10.19 Stressful life events can vary from catastrophic ones to microstressors, or "daily hassles." Both classes of stressor take their toll on physical and psychological well-being.

TABLE 10.2	SAMPLE ITEMS FROM A SELF-REPORT MEASURE OF POSITIVE AND NEGATIVE LIFE EVENTS					
Experience	Happened in Last 6 Months?		Good or Bad?		"Day-to-day" or "Major"	
Parents discover something you didn't want them to know	No	Yes	Good	Bad	Day-to-Day	Major
Pressures or expectation by parents	No	Yes	Good	Bad	Day-to-Day	Major
Receiving a gift	No	Yes	Good	Bad	Day-to-Day	Major
Having plans fall through (not going on a trip, etc.)	No	Yes	Good	Bad	Day-to-Day	Major
Losing job (quitting, getting fired, laid off, etc.)	No	Yes	Good	Bad	Day-to-Day	Major
Making honor roll or other school achievement	No	Yes	Good	Bad	Day-to-Day	Major
Making love or sexual intercourse	No	Yes	Good	Bad	Day-to-Day	Major
Something good happens to a friend	No	Yes	Good	Bad	Day-to-Day	Major
Work hassles (rude customers, unpleasant jobs, etc.)	No	Yes	Good	Bad	Day-to-Day	Major
Death of a friend or family member	No	Yes	Good	Bad	Day-to-Day	Major

Source: Scale used in Smith et al., 1990.

two years). The life event scale shown in Table 10.2 asks people to indicate not only whether a particular event occurred, but also their appraisal of whether the event was a positive or a negative one, and whether it was a major event (defined as having a significant and long-term impact on the person's life) or a "day-to-day" event (Smith et al., 1990). Moreover, additional information can be obtained. For example, respondents could be asked to rate the predictability, controllability, and duration of each event they experienced, permitting an analysis of these factors as well. Life event scales have been widely used in life stress research. Like other self-report measures, however, they are subject to possible distortion and failures of recall.

Some early theorists believed that any life event that requires adaptation, whether negative or positive in nature, is a stressor (Holmes & Rahe, 1967; Selye, 1956). Because later research showed that only negative life changes consistently predicted adverse health and behavioral outcomes, most modern researchers now define stress in terms of negative life changes only (Cohen et al., 1995; Lazarus, 1998). Indeed, positive life events sometimes counter or even cancel out the negative impact of negative events (Thoits, 1983).

The Stress Response

We respond to situations as we perceive them. The starting point for the stress response is therefore our appraisal of the situation and of its implications for us. As Figure 10.19 indicates, four aspects of the appraisal process are of particular significance:

➤ 28. What four types of appraisal occur in response to a potential stressor? How do these correspond to primary and secondary appraisal?

1. appraisal of the *demands* of the situation (primary appraisal);
2. appraisal of the *resources* available to cope with it (secondary appraisal);
3. judgments of what the *consequences* of the situation could be; and
4. appraisal of the *personal meaning,* that is, what the outcome might imply about us.

Let us apply these appraisal steps to a real-life situation. You are about to have an important job interview. According to Richard Lazarus (1991), you will first engage in a **primary appraisal** of this situation as either benign, neutral/irrelevant, or threatening in terms of its demands (how difficult an interview it will be) and its significance for your well-being (how badly you want or need the job). At the same time, you will be appraising your perceived ability to cope with the situation, that is, the resources available to deal with it. Lazarus calls this resource-appraisal step **secondary appraisal.** Coping resources include your knowledge and abilities, your verbal skills, and your social resources, such as people who will give you emotional support and encouragement. If you believe that the demands of the interview greatly exceed your resources, you will likely experience stress. Primary and secondary appraisal correspond with aspects 1 and 2 above, respectively.

You will also take into account the *potential consequences* of failing to cope successfully with the situation, including both the seriousness of the consequences and the likelihood that they will occur. Will you be able to pay your tuition if you perform poorly and don't get the job? How likely is it that you will fail? Appraising the consequences of failing as very costly and very likely to occur increases the perceived stressfulness of the situation.

Finally, the *psychological meaning of the consequences* may be related to your basic beliefs about yourself or the world. Certain beliefs or personal standards can make people vulnerable to particular types of situational demands. For example, if your feelings of self-worth depend on how successful you are in situations like this one, you may regard doing poorly during the interview as evidence that you are a worthless failure.

Distortions and mistaken appraisals can occur at any of the four points in the appraisal process, causing inappropriate stress responses. People may overestimate the seriousness of the situation, they may underestimate their own resources, they may exaggerate the seriousness of the consequences and the likelihood that they will occur, or they may have irrational self-beliefs that confer inappropriate meaning on the consequences (e.g., "If I don't succeed at this, it means I am and always will be a total loser"). The fact that appraisal patterns can differ from person to person in so many ways helps us understand why there can be so much individual variation in how people respond to the same event or situation, and it also helps us understand why some people are particularly vulnerable to certain types of demands.

As soon as we make appraisals, the body responds to them (Borod, 2000; Tomaka et al., 1997). Although appraisals begin the process, appraisals and physiological responses mutually affect one another, since autonomic and somatic feedback can affect our reappraisals of how stressful a situation is and whether our resources are sufficient to cope with it. Thus if you find yourself trembling as you enter the interview room, you may appraise the situation as even more threatening than you did initially.

Endocrinologist Hans Selye (1976) was a pioneer in studying the body's response to stress. He described a physiological response pattern to strong and prolonged stressors that he termed the **general adaptation syndrome (GAS).** The GAS consists of three phases: alarm, resistance, and exhaustion (Figure 10.20).

In response to a physical or psychological stressor, organisms exhibit an immediate increase in physiological arousal as the body mobilizes itself to respond to the threat. This *alarm* reaction occurs because of the sudden activation of the sympathetic nervous system and the release of stress hormones by the endocrine system. The alarm stage cannot last indefinitely, however, and the body's natural tendency to maintain the stable internal state of homeostasis results in parasympathetic nervous system activity, which reduces arousal. The body continues to remain on red alert, however, responding with the second stage, resistance.

During *resistance*, the body's resources are mobilized by the continued outpouring of adrenaline and other stress hormones released by the endocrine system, particularly the adrenal glands. Resistance can last for a relatively long time, but the body's resources are being depleted, and immune system functioning is being

➤ 29. Describe the three stages of Selye's GAS.

partially suppressed by the stress hormones (Chiapelli, 2000). If the stressor is intense and persists too long, the body may reach a stage of *exhaustion,* in which there is increased vulnerability to disease and, in some extreme cases, collapse and death (Hancock & Desmond, 2000). Selye believed that whichever body system of the body is weakest will be the first to be affected. A mild form of this process is familiar to students who deal successfully with the rigors of the end of the academic term and final exams (resistance), only to become ill as soon as the stressors end and vacation begins.

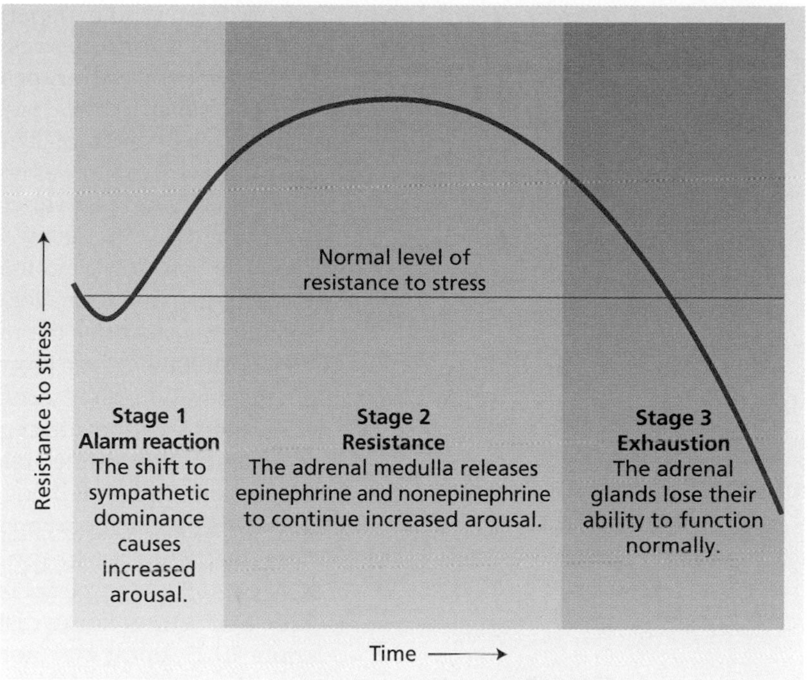

Stress and Health

Selye's work inspired a generation of medical and psychological researchers to explore the effects of stress on both physical and psychological well-being. As we shall now see, stress can result in physical and psychological deterioration. One conclusion is that a physical mobilization system sculpted by evolution to help organisms deal with life-threatening *physical* stressors may not be as adaptive for dealing with the *psychological* stressors we face in modern life. As noted by one medical authority, "Stone Age physiological and biochemical responses to emotion have become inappropriate in a Space Age setting, and can pave the way to psychosomatic diseases" (Carruthers, 1981, p. 239).

FIGURE 10.20 Hans Selye described the general adaptation syndrome. When a person is exposed to a stressor, the alarm reaction mobilizes the body's resources. During the stage of resistance, stress hormones maintain the body's defensive changes, and the body signs characteristic of the alarm reaction virtually disappear. But if the stress persists over a long time, the body's resources become depleted and exhaustion occurs; the organism can no longer cope and is highly vulnerable to breakdown. (Selye, 1976.)

Stress and Psychological Well-Being

Effects of stress on psychological well-being are clearest and most dramatic among people who have experienced catastrophic life events. Anthony Rubonis and Leonard Bickman (1991) surveyed the results of 52 studies of catastrophic floods, hurricanes, and fires. In the wake of natural disasters, they found an average increase of 17 percent in rates of psychological disorders such as anxiety and depression.

Some stressors are so traumatic that they can have a strong and long-lasting psychological impact. More than 50 years after the horror of the Holocaust, psychological scars remain for Jewish survivors of the Nazi concentration camps (Nadler & Ben-Shushan, 1989; Valent, 2000; Zahava & Ginzburg, 1998). Many survivors are still troubled by high levels of anxiety and recurrent nightmares about their traumatic experiences. Children who lost their parents and siblings continue to experience sudden fears that something terrible will happen to their spouses or children whenever they are out of sight. Depression and crying spells are also common, as are feelings of insecurity and difficulties in forming close relationships. As one researcher reported, "child survivors (now in their 50s and 60s) . . . despite their outward normalcy, remain entrapped in this survival mode" (Valent, 1998, p. 751).

Long-lasting psychological symptoms have also been found among American soldiers who experienced trauma during the Vietnam War. Paula Schnurr and her coworkers (1998) found a significantly greater number of stress symptoms in traumatized servicemen compared with veterans from the same era who did not experience combat or noncombat trauma.

➤ 30. What are the characteristics of the rape trauma syndrome?

➤ 31. Describe three possible causal paths between self-reported stress and distress.

Women who experience the trauma of rape sometimes find that its aftermath can be nearly as stressful as the incident itself. Many victims experience a reaction known as the **rape trauma syndrome** (Burgess & Holmstrom, 1974). For months or even years after the rape, victims may feel nervous and may fear another attack by the rapist. Many victims change their place of residence but continue to have nightmares and to be frightened when they are alone, outdoors, or in crowds. Victims frequently report decreased enjoyment of sexual activity long after the rape, even when their ability to have orgasms is not affected (Feeny & Foa, 2000; Holmes & St. Lawrence, 1983). In one long-term study of rape victims, one fourth of the women felt that they had not recovered psychologically 6 years after the rape (Meyer & Taylor, 1986).

Fortunately, the majority of stressors that people experience are not as severe as concentration camp confinement, combat, or rape. How do more typical but less serious stressors affect psychological well-being? To answer this question, researchers have examined relations between self-reported life events and measures of psychological well-being. Findings consistently show that the more negative life events people report on measures like the one shown in Table 10.2 (p. 435), the more likely they are to also report symptoms of psychological distress (Holahan & Moos, 1990; Monroe & Peterman, 1988). We might therefore be tempted to conclude that "stress causes distress." This causal interpretation is shown in path 1 in Figure 10.21, but it may not be accurate because the data are correlational in nature and other causal interpretations are possible. For example, path 2 reverses the first causal interpretation, suggesting that people's levels of distress may influence their reporting of negative life events. That is, distressed people may be more likely to remember negative things that have happened to them. Or they may tend to view more events as negative, resulting in higher negative life change scores. Psychological distress also might cause more negative events to occur in people's lives because of their own behavior. For example, distressed people tend to evoke negative reactions from others (Coyne et al., 1991; Joiner et al., 1992).

A third causal possibility, shown in path 3, is that a third variable causes both negative life events and psychological distress. The personality trait of **neuroticism** might be one such factor. People who are high in neuroticism have a heightened tendency to experience negative emotions and to get themselves into stressful situations through their maladaptive behaviors (Eysenck, 1989; Suls et al., 1998). In one longitudinal study of Dutch adults, Johan Ormel and Tamar Wohlfarth (1991) found that initial scores on a neuroticism scale were positively related to both the number of stressful events and the amount of psychological distress reported over the next 6 years. Thus we are again reminded that stressful life events are part of a network of causal relations that involve ongoing transactions between people and situations. It appears that stressful life events can function as both cause and effect (Cohen & Edwards, 1989; Suls et al., 1998).

Stress and Illness

Stress can combine with other physical and psychological factors to influence the entire spectrum of physical illnesses, from the common cold to cancer, heart disease, diabetes, and sudden death (Cohen et al., 1998; Dougall & Baum, 2000). Sometimes, the effects are immediate. On the day of the 1994 Los Angeles earthquake, the number of sudden deaths due to heart attacks in that city increased from an average of 35.7 per day during the 7 previous days to 101 fatalities (Leor et al., 1996). Other effects of major stressors on physical well-being are less immediate but no less severe. Within a month following the death of a spouse, bereaved widowers and widows begin to show a higher mortality rate than married people of the same age who have not lost a spouse (Kaprio et al., 1987).

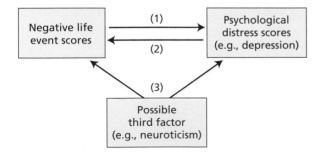

FIGURE 10.21 Statistical relations between stressful life events and psychological distress may reflect a number of different casual relations: (1) stressful life events may cause distress; (2) distress may cause higher stressful life event scores; or (3) a third factor, such as neuroticism, may cause both distress and high negative life change scores.

Stressful life events have also been linked to an increased likelihood of developing cancer later on (Skylar & Anisman, 1981).

A traumatic life event can worsen an already existing medical condition, as in the case of a 7-year-old African-American girl with sickle-cell anemia.

> This little girl was bused to a new elementary school in a white neighborhood. . . . She and other black children were met with cries by angry whites to "go back to where you belong!" The little girl was quite upset by the incident. After some time at the school she went to the principal's office crying and complaining of chest pains. She died later that day in the hospital, apparently from a sickle-cell crisis brought on by stress. As she died, she kept repeating "go back where you belong." (Friedman & DiMatteo, 1989, p. 169)

Linkages between long-term stress and illness are not surprising, for physiological responses to stressors can directly harm other body systems. For example, the secretion of stress hormones by the adrenal gland is an important part of the stress response. These hormones affect the activity of the heart, and excessive secretions can damage the lining of the arteries. By reducing fat metabolism, the stress hormones can also contribute to the fatty blockages in arteries that cause heart attacks and strokes (Kimble, 1992; Willenberg et al., 2000).

Stress can also trigger illness by causing breakdowns in immune system functioning (Ader, 1995; Maier & Watkins, 1999; Marsland et al., 2000). Janice Kiecolt-Glaser and her coworkers (1998) brought 90 newly married couples into a laboratory and asked them to discuss areas of conflict in their relationship. They coded the couples' behavior during the discussions and measured their physiological and immune responses. Among those couples whose interactions became hostile during the conflict discussions, measurable decreases in immune function occurred within 24 hours (Figure 10.22). Similar results were observed in an older sample of 31 couples who had been married an average of 42 years. In this older sample, one of the immune functions that decreased after hostile interchanges helps protect against influenza and pneumonia, leading causes of death in elderly people.

Stress can also contribute to health breakdowns by causing people to behave in ways that increase the risk of illness. For example, people with adult-onset diabetes can frequently control their disease by means of medication and diet. When under stress, however, diabetics are less likely to regulate their diets and take their medication, resulting in an increased risk of serious medical consequences (Brantley & Garrett, 1993). People are more likely to quit exercising when under stress, even if the primary reason they began exercising in the first place was to reduce stress (Stetson et al., 1997). Stress may also lead to smoking, alcohol and drug use, sleep loss, undereating and overeating, and other health-compromising behaviors.

Vulnerability and Protective Factors

Some individuals seem able to tolerate extremely demanding stressors over a long period of time; others appear to quickly fall prey to even relatively minor stressors. **Vulnerability factors** increase people's susceptibility to stressful events. They include lack of a support network, poor coping skills, tendencies to become anxious or pessimistic, and other factors that reduce stress resistance. In contrast, **protective factors** are environmental or personal resources that help people cope more effectively with stressful events. They include social support, coping skills, and personality factors such as optimism.

Social Support

Social support is one of the most important environmental resources that people can have (Wills & Filer, 2000). The knowledge that we can rely on others for help and support in a time of crisis helps blunt the impact of stress

> 32. By what physiological and behavioral mechanisms can stress contribute to illness?

FIGURE 10.22 Research has shown that the stress produced by marital conflict can produce decreases in immune function.

> 33. Differentiate between vulnerability and protective factors, and give examples of each.

> 34. What evidence exists that social support is a protective factor? In what ways can it protect against stressful events?

FIGURE 10.23 Social support is one of the strongest protective factors against stress.

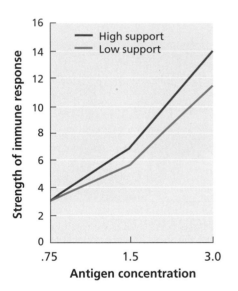

FIGURE 10.24 Relation of social support to immune function in spouses of cancer patients. Immune cell activity in response to antigens was greater in spouses high in social support, particularly at high antigen levels that place people at increased risk.

Data from Baron et al., 1990.

➤ 35. Can disclosing upsetting experiences to others enhance well-being? Cite relevant data.

(Figure 10.23). In contrast, social isolation is an important vulnerability factor. Studies carried out in the United States, Finland, and Sweden carefully tracked the well-being of some 37,000 people for up to 12 years. Even after taking into account medical risk factors such as age, smoking, high blood pressure, high cholesterol levels, obesity, and lack of physical exercise, the researchers found that people with weak social ties were twice as likely to die during the period of the study as those with strong ties (House et al., 1988). The relation between social isolation and poor health was stronger for men than for women.

One way that social support protects against stress is by enhancing immune system functioning. Robert Baron and his coworkers (1990) studied distressed people whose spouses were being treated for cancer. The participants agreed to be injected with an antigen so that their immune responses could be measured. As Figure 10.24 shows, the immune systems of the spouses who rated themselves high in social support produced more immune cells, particularly at high levels of the antigens, than did the immune systems of those who indicated lower social support in their lives. These results may help explain why people who have high levels of social support are more disease-resistant when they are under stress (House et al., 1988). Many other studies show that social support decreases psychological distress in people who are dealing with stressful life events of all kinds (Holahan & Moos, 1986, 1990; Rodin & Salovey, 1989; Schwarzer, 1998).

Why is social support such a strong protective factor? One possibility is that people who feel that they are part of a social system experience a greater sense of identity and meaning in their lives, which in turn results in greater psychological well-being (S. Cohen, 1988; Rodin & Salovey, 1989). Social networks also reduce exposure to other risk factors, such as loneliness, and having the backing of others can increase their feelings of control over stressors. Finally, true friends can apply social pressure to prevent people from coping with stressors in maladaptive ways (e.g., through alcohol or drug use). Any of these buffering effects can help to counteract the impact of stressful life events.

A series of studies conducted by James Pennebaker (1995, 1997) suggests the importance of having someone to talk to about upsetting experiences. College students talked about traumas they had experienced to an experimenter in an adjoining room, or they tape recorded or wrote about them. Many tearfully recounted incidents of personal failure, family tragedies, shattered relationships, sexual or physical abuse, or traumatic accidents. Participants in a control group were asked to talk or write about trivial everyday matters. At the end of the session, blood samples taken from the students indicated enhanced immune functioning in those who had purged themselves of negative emotions, but not in those who had not. Moreover, the students who had disclosed the traumatic incidents had 50 percent fewer visits to the campus health center over the next 6 months compared with the control group. In another study, Pennebaker invited 33 Holocaust survivors to talk about their horrible ordeal. Many discussed their traumatic experiences in greater detail than ever before and even showed friends and families videotapes of the Holocaust. Those who were the most disclosing had the most improved health 14 months later. Pennebaker's results are intriguing but controversial, and more research is needed to determine when emotional "purging" is helpful and whether there are circumstances when it is not. Likewise, because participants in these studies could choose to purge their emotions or not, it is possible that some other factor, such as a personality trait, contributes to both the emotional disclosure and the health consequences.

Returning to the case of Priscilla described earlier, how was she able to overcome her traumatic childhood—the abuse, the suicide of her father, the absence of a mother? Studies of resilient children like Priscilla have repeatedly highlighted the role of social support in helping blunt the impact of the terrible stressors they experienced in their daily lives (Garbarino, 1995; Garmezy, 1983; Masten & Coatsworth, 1998; Werner & Smith, 1982). Summarizing the findings of her 30-year longitudinal study of resilient children, psychologist Emmy Werner noted, "Without exception, all of the children who thrived had at least one person that provided them with consistent emotional support—a grandmother, an older sister, a teacher or a neighbor" (*New York Times*, October 13, 1987, p. C11). For Priscilla, that person was a schoolteacher who cared enough to befriend and encourage her during her childhood years.

Cognitive Protective Factors: The Importance of Beliefs

Considering the important role that appraisal processes play in emotions and stress, we should not be surprised that the ways we think about situations and ourselves are important protective and vulnerability factors.

Hardiness. In the 1970s, Suzanne Kobasa of the University of Chicago began an intensive study of 200 executives who worked in highly stressful jobs. She found that some of them responded to their circumstances with psychological distress and physical illness, whereas others continued to function well both physically and psychologically. How did the two groups differ? The answer came in the form of three beliefs that comprised a stress-protective factor that she termed **hardiness.** The "three Cs" of hardiness are *commitment, control,* and *challenge.*

> ➤ 36. What three "C" beliefs underlie the protective factor called hardiness?

Hardy people are committed to their work, their families, and their other involvements, and they believe that what they are doing is important. Second, they view themselves as having control over their outcomes, as opposed to feeling powerless to influence events. Finally, they appraise the demands of the situations as challenges, or opportunities, rather than as threats. As a result, demanding situations not only become less stressful, but they can actually stimulate higher levels of performance (Kobasa et al., 1985).

Of these three hardiness components, control apparently is the strongest active ingredient in buffering stress (Funk, 1992; Steptoe, 2000). A 5-year longitudinal study showed that women who felt in control of their lives did not show increases in future illness when stress increased, whereas those low in perceived control did (Lawler & Schmeid, 1992).

Coping self-efficacy. When confronted by a stressor, one of the most significant appraisals we make is whether or not we have sufficient resources to cope with the demands (Bandura, 1997). Small wonder, then, that **coping self-efficacy**—the conviction that we can perform the behaviors necessary to cope successfully—is an important protective factor (Bandura, 1989). Even events that are appraised as extremely demanding may generate little stress if we believe that we have the skills needed to deal with them.

Self-efficacy is always specific to the particular situation: Can I handle *these* demands? Previous successes in similar situations increase efficacy; failures undermine it (Bandura, 1997). People can also increase efficacy expectancies by observing others cope successfully and through social persuasion and encouragement from others. The teacher who befriended Priscilla constantly gave her the message, "I believe in you. You can do it!" Finally, experiencing a low level of physiological arousal in the face of a stressor can convey a sense of strength and ability to cope, demonstrating another way in which arousal can affect appraisal.

> ➤ 37. What four types of information increase coping self-efficacy?

Feelings of self-efficacy may fortify our body as well our mind against stressful events. An intriguing finding is that when people experience an increase in self-efficacy while confronting a stressful situation, their immune system actually begins to function more effectively (Wiedenfeld et al., 1992).

Optimism. Our beliefs about how things are likely to turn out also play an important role in stress. Optimists have a rosy view of the future, expecting that in the long run, things will work out well. Pessimists tend to focus on the black cloud surrounding any silver lining.

> ➤ 38. What evidence is there that optimism-pessimism affect response to stress?

Recent research indicates that optimistic people are at lowered risk for anxiety and depression when they confront stressful events. Edward Chang

(1998) found that optimists appraised themselves as being less helpless in the face of stress and adjusted better to negative life events than did pessimists. Optimism is also a health protective factor. In a year-long study, optimists had about half as many infectious illnesses and visits to doctors as did pessimists (Peterson & Seligman, 1987). In another study, women who came to the National Cancer Institute for breast cancer treatment were followed for 5 years. On average, optimists lived longer than pessimists even where the physical severity of the disease was the same at the beginning of the 5-year period (Levy et al., 1989).

➤ 39. In what ways do spiritual and religious beliefs affect response to stressful events?

Finding meaning in stressful life events.   Humanistic theorists emphasize the human need to find meaning in one's life, and the psychological benefits of doing so (May, 1961; Watson & Greenberg, 1998; Yalom, 1980). Some people find personal meaning through spiritual beliefs, which can be a great source of comfort in the face of crises. Daniel McIntosh and coworkers (1993) studied 124 parents who had lost their babies to sudden infant death syndrome. They found that religious beliefs that helped the grieving parents find some higher meaning in their loss were related to greater well-being and less distress 18 months later. In another study, researchers studied people who had recently lost a family member to death. In following up the survivors over a period of 18 months, the researchers discovered that people who were able to find meaning in the loss experienced less distress during the first year. Finding a sense of meaning from their own process of coping with the loss (e.g., by growing spiritually) had even longer-term positive effects (Davis et al., 1998).

Religious beliefs can be a two-edged sword, however. They can either decrease or increase stress, depending on their nature and the type of stressor to which they are applied. In one study of medically ill elderly adults, poorer physical and psychological adjustment occurred in patients who viewed God as punishing them, saw themselves as the victims of demonic forces, expressed anger toward God, clergy, or church members, or questioned their faith (Koenig et al., 1998). Religious beliefs may have positive effects in dealing with some types of stressors, but not with others. Such beliefs seem to help people cope more effectively with losses, illnesses, and personal setbacks. In contrast, they can increase the negative impact of other stressors such as marital problems and abuse, perhaps by inducing guilt or placing internal pressures on individuals to remain in the stressful relationship (Strawbridge et al., 1998).

As we have now seen, a variety of biological, cognitive, and environmental factors influence stress and its effects on us. Figure 10.25 summarizes these important influences.

Coping With Stress

> My courage sank, and with each succeeding minute it became less possible to resist this horror. My cue came, and on I went to that stage where I knew with grim certainty I would not be capable of remaining more than a few minutes. . . . I took one pace forward and stopped abruptly. My voice had started to fade, my throat closed up and the audience was beginning to go giddily round." (Aaron, 1986, p. 24)

This account of "stage fright" was given not by a novice actor in his first play, but by Sir Laurence Olivier, considered by many to be the greatest actor of his generation (Figure 10.26). Few people were aware that for most of his career, Olivier experienced a private hell before every performance. His audiences saw only what happened once he stepped onto the stage: another flawless performance. Olivier had a remarkable ability to purge the terror from his mind, relax his body, and concentrate fully on his role once showtime arrived (Aaron, 1986).

➤ 40. Define and give an example of the three major classes of coping strategies.

Although there are countless ways people might respond to a stressor, coping strategies can be divided into the three broad classes shown in Figure 10.27. (Carver et al., 1989; Folkman & Lazarus, 1988; Smith et al., 1999). **Problem-focused coping** strategies attempt to confront and directly deal with the demands of the situation,

Level of Analysis		
Biological	**Psychological**	**Environmental**
• Physiological responses of autonomic and endocrine systems to situational stressors • Stress effects on immune system • Individual differences in emotional reactivity to stressors	• Cognitive appraisal of environmental demands, resources, potential consequences, and personal meaning of consequences • Personality factors, such as optimism and hardiness, that affect responses to stressors • Coping strategies and skill with which they are applied • Self-efficacy and expectations of available social support	• Number and nature of the stressful events • Availability of social support • Cultural factors that teach one how to respond to stressors

STRESS

FIGURE 10.25 Understanding the Causes of Behavior: Stress and its effects.

FIGURE 10.26 The renowned actor Sir Laurence Olivier suffered from extreme stress responses before every performance, yet was able to apply coping skills that resulted in award-winning performances once he was onstage.

Coping Strategies

Problem-focused coping	Emotion-focused coping	Seeking social support
• Planning • Active coping and problem-solving • Suppressing competing activities • Exercising restraint • Assertive confrontation	• Positive reinterpretation • Acceptance • Denial • Repression • Escape–avoidance • Wishful thinking • Controlling feelings	• Help and guidance • Emotional support • Affirmation of worth • Tangible aid (e.g., money)

FIGURE 10.27 Coping strategies fall into three general categories: (1) problem-focused coping, consisting of active attempts to respond to situational demands; (2) emotion-focused coping, directed at minimizing emotional distress; and (3) seeking or accepting social support.

or to change the situation so that it is no longer stressful. Examples include studying for a test, going directly to another person to work out a misunderstanding, and signing up for a course in time management in order to deal with time pressures.

Rather than dealing directly with the stressful situation, **emotion-focused coping** strategies attempt to manage the emotional responses that result from it. As Figure 10.27 shows, some forms of emotion-focused coping involve appraising the situation in a manner that minimizes its emotional impact. A person might deal with the stress from an interpersonal conflict by denying that any problem exists. Other forms involve avoidance or acceptance of the stressful situation. Thus a student might decide to deal with anxiety about an upcoming test by going to a party and forgetting about it. Informed that he has a terminal illness, a man might simply accept grim reality, realizing that there is nothing that can be done to change the situation.

A third class of coping strategies involves **seeking social support,** that is, turning to others for assistance and emotional support in times of stress. Thus the man with the terminal illness might choose to join a support group for the terminally ill, and the student might seek help in preparing for the test.

Effectiveness of Coping Strategies

Which of the three general classes of coping strategies would you expect to be most generally effective? Whenever we ask this question in our classes, the majority of students vote for problem-focused coping. This response is understandable, for many people approach problems with the attitude that if something needs fixing, we should fix it.

What does the research literature say? Charles Holahan and Rudolf Moos (1990) studied coping patterns and psychological outcomes in more than 400 California adults over a one-year period. They found that problem-focused coping methods and seeking social support were associated with favorable adjustment to stressors. In contrast, emotion-focused strategies that involved avoiding feelings or taking things out on other people predicted depression and poorer adjustment. Other studies have yielded similar results. In both children and adults, and across many different types of stressors, emotion-focused strategies that involve avoidance, denial, and wishful thinking seem to be related to less effective adaptation (Aldwin, 1994). On the other hand, there are adaptive emotion-focused strategies, such as identifying and changing irrational negative thinking and learning relaxation skills to control arousal. These emotion-focused methods can reduce stress responses without avoiding or distorting reality, and can be effective ways of dealing with stress (DeLongis, 2000; Meichenbaum, 1985).

Controllability and Coping Efficacy

➤ 41. How does controllability influence the effectiveness of coping strategies?

Despite the evidence generally favoring problem-solving coping, attempts to change the situation are not always the most adaptive way to cope with a stressor. When we cannot influence or modify a situation, problem-focused coping may do us little good, and could even make things worse. In such cases emotion-focused coping may be the most adaptive approach we can take, for even if we cannot master the situation, we may be able to prevent or control maladaptive emotional responses to it (Auerbach, 1989; Taylor, 1991). Of course, reliance on emotion-focused coping is likely to be maladaptive if it prevents us from acting to change situations in which we actually *do* have control.

Thomas Strantz and Stephen Auerbach (1988) demonstrated the effectiveness of emotion-focused coping in adapting to a stressful situation with limited personal control. As part of a training program conducted by the Federal Bureau of Investigation, airline employees who might be future victims of hijackings volunteered to participate in an exercise in which they were abducted by FBI agents posing as terrorists and held hostage for 4 days under very realistic and stressful conditions.

Before their abduction, the employees were randomly assigned to two experimental conditions and a control condition. In one condition, employees were trained in problem-focused techniques that hostages can use to actively deal with and modify the situation. They were shown how to interact with captors and maintain a facade of dignity and composure through appearance and behavior. They also learned ways of supporting one another nonverbally and communicating with one another through use of the prisoner-of-war tap code.

Training for the second experimental group focused on the emotional reactions the hostages would likely experience and techniques they could use to minimize their stress responses. These emotion-focused techniques included deep breathing, muscular relaxation, stopping unwanted thoughts, and generating pleasant fantasies. Hostages in the control condition were given no coping skills training.

At various points during their captivity, all of the hostages completed self-report measures of emotional distress and psychiatric symptoms. In addition, the adaptiveness of their behavior was coded by trained observers. The hostage groups trained in either problem-focused or emotion-focused strategies fared better than the untrained employees on both the self-report and the behavioral measures. However, employees who had received emotion-focused training adapted better to the largely uncontrollable conditions of captivity than did those who had received problem-focused coping instruction (Figure 10.28).

The important principle is that no coping strategy or technique is equally effective in all situations. Instead, effectiveness depends on the characteristics of the situation, the appropriateness of the technique, and the skill with which it is carried out. People are likely to adapt most effectively to the stresses of life if they have mastered a variety of coping techniques and know how and when to apply them most effectively. The importance of controllability in the choice of techniques recalls the wisdom in the theologian Reinhold Niebuhr's famous prayer that asks for the courage to change those things that can be changed, the forbearance to accept those that cannot be changed, and the wisdom to discern the difference.

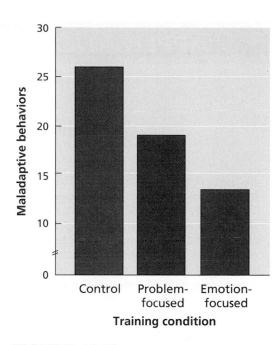

FIGURE 10.28 Behavioral ratings of adjustment to the stress of captivity by airline personnel given instruction in problem- or emotion-focused coping techniques prior to the abduction by FBI agents posing as terrorists. The control group received no coping skills instruction. Higher scores indicated more disturbed behaviors.

Data from Strantz & Auerbach, 1988.

Gender, Culture, and Coping

Many factors, including gender roles and culture, influence our tendency to favor one coping strategy over another. Although men and women both use problem-focused coping, men are more likely to favor it as the first strategy they use when they confront a stressor (Ptacek et al., 1992). On the other hand, women, who tend to have larger support networks and higher needs for affiliation than men, are more likely than men to seek social support (Billings & Moos, 1984; Schwarzer, 1998). Women also are somewhat more likely than men to report using emotion-focused coping (Carver et al., 1989; Pearlin & Schooler, 1978). This general pattern of coping preferences is consistent with the socialization that boys and girls traditionally experience. In most cultures, boys are pushed to be more independent, assertive, and self-sufficient, whereas girls are expected to be more emotionally expressive, supportive, and dependent (Eccles, 1991; Lytton & Romney, 1991).

Cultural differences in coping have also been found. North Americans and Europeans show a tendency to use problem-focused coping more than do Asian and Hispanic peoples (Essau & Trommsdorff, 1996; Jung, 1995). The latter two groups tend to favor greater use of emotion-focused coping and social support. Asians also show a greater tendency to avoid the stressful situation, particularly interpersonal stressors, reflecting their culture's emphasis on interpersonal harmony (Chang, 1996). In a study of how American married couples deal with marital stress, African-Americans reported a greater tendency than Caucasians to seek social support (Sistler & Moore, 1996).

➤ 42. How do gender and cultural factors affect the tendency to use particular coping strategies?

➤ 43. What coping skills can be used to control (a) cognitive appraisal and (b) physiological arousal components of the stress response? Describe the integrated coping response.

APPLICATIONS OF PSYCHOLOGICAL SCIENCE

Cognitive-Affective Stress Management Skills

Because of the toll that stress takes on people's physical and psychological well-being, much effort has gone into developing methods for reducing stress. In many coping skills programs, people are taught to modify habits of thought that trigger inappropriate emotional responses and are also taught to control physiological arousal responses through relaxation skills (Barlow & Rapee, 1991; Meichenbaum, 1985; Smith & Rohsenow, 1989).

▶ Cognitive Coping Skills

Because cognitive appraisal processes play a central role in generating stress, Richard Lazarus, Albert Ellis, and other cognitive theorists maintain that the most powerful means of regulating feelings is by controlling how we think about stressful situations and about ourselves. Ellis (1962) suggests that a relatively small number of "irrational" core beliefs lie at the root of most maladaptive negative feelings. For example, he says, we tell ourselves that we *must* achieve and be approved of in virtually every respect if we are to consider ourselves worthwhile people; that it is terrible, awful, and *catastrophic* when life or other people are not the way we *demand* that they be; that people who do not behave as we wish are bad and therefore deserving of punishment. These and other ideas generate anxiety, despair, and anger. When people use the technique of *cognitive restructuring* to systematically detect, challenge, and replace these irrational ideas, their feelings can change dramatically, as in the following case:

> Whenever I find myself getting guilty or upset, I immediately tell myself that there must be some silly sentence that I am saying to myself to cause this upset; and almost immediately . . . I find this sentence . . . [It] invariably takes the form of "Isn't it terrible that . . ." or "Wouldn't it be awful if . . ." And when I look at and question these sentences and ask myself, "How is it really terrible that . . . ? or "Why would it actually be awful if . . . ?" I always find that it isn't terrible or wouldn't be awful, and I get over being upset very quickly. . . . I can hardly believe it, but I seem to be getting to the point, after so many years of worrying over practically everything and thinking I was a slob no matter what I did, of now finding that nothing is so terrible or awful, and I now seem to be recognizing this in advance rather than after I have seriously upset myself. (Ellis, 1962, pp. 31–32)

A somewhat different approach to changing cognitions is *self-instructional training* (Meichenbaum, 1985).

Rather than attacking irrational ideas that cause disturbance, people learn to "talk to themselves" and guide their behavior in ways that help them cope more effectively at four critical stages of the stressful episode: preparing for the stressor; confronting the stressor; dealing with the feeling of being overwhelmed; and appraising coping efforts after the stressful situation. Table 10.3 provides examples of self-instructions that can be used at these stages of the coping process.

▶ Controlling Arousal Through Relaxation Training

Coping skills training can also help people control their physiological responses in stressful situations. Because one cannot be relaxed and tense at the same time, *relaxation training* provides a means of voluntarily reducing or preventing high levels of arousal. People can generally learn this skill within about a week of practice. Here is a procedure you can use to learn muscle relaxation:

1. While sitting comfortably, bend your arms at the elbow. Now make a hard fist with both hands, and bend your wrists downward while simultaneously tensing the muscles of your upper arms. This will produce a state of tension in your hands, forearms, and upper arms. Hold this tension for 5 seconds and study it carefully. Then slowly let out the tension halfway while concentrating on the sensations in your arms and fingers as the tension decreases. Hold the tension at the halfway point for 5 seconds, and then slowly let the tension out the rest of the way and let your arms rest comfortably in your lap. As you breathe normally, concentrate on those muscles, and give yourself a mental command to "relax" each time you exhale. Do this for 7 to 10 breaths.

    Use the same procedure of tensing the muscles, letting the tension out halfway, letting it out completely, and using breathing in conjunction with the word *relax*. This will help condition this word to the state of relaxation so that it serves as an eliciting cue to relax you.
2. Tense the calf and thigh muscles in your legs. You can do this by straightening your legs while pointing your toes downward.
3. Cross the palms of your hands in front of your chest, and press them together so as to tense the chest and shoulder muscles. At the same time, tense your stomach muscles.

—Continued

TABLE 10.3	SELF-INSTRUCTIONAL TRAINING: EXAMPLES OF ADAPTIVE SELF-STATEMENTS THAT CAN BE APPLIED AT VARIOUS STAGES OF THE COPING PROCESS

Phase of Coping Process	Self-Statements
Preparing for the stressor	• What do I have to do? • I can work out a plan to deal with it. • Remember, stick to the issues and don't take it personally. • Stop worrying. Worrying won't help anything.
Confronting and handling the stressor	• As long as I keep my cool, I'm in control of the situation. • I can meet this challenge. This tenseness is just a cue to use my coping techniques. • Don't think about stress, just about what I have to do. • Take a deep breath and relax. Ah, good.
Coping with the feeling of being overwhelmed	• Keep my focus on the present. What is it I have to do? • Relax and slow things down. • Don't try to eliminate stress totally; just keep it manageable. • Let's take the issue point by point.
Evaluation and self-reinforcement	• OK, what worked and what didn't? • I handled it pretty well. • It didn't work, but that's OK. I'll do better next time. • Way to go! You did it!

Source: Meichenbaum, 1985.

4. Arch your back, and push your shoulders back as far as possible so as to tense your upper and lower back muscles. (Be careful not to tense these muscles too hard.)

5. Tense your neck and jaw muscles by thrusting your jaw outward and drawing the corners of your mouth back, or by bending your neck forward, backward, or to one side. Experiment to find the way that's best for you.

6. Wrinkle your forehead and scalp upward to tense those muscles.

7. While sitting in a totally relaxed position, take a series of short inhalations, about one per second, until your chest is filled and tense. Hold this for about 5 seconds, then exhale slowly while repeating silently the word *relax.* Most people can produce a deeply relaxed state by doing this. Repeat this exercise three times.

8. Finish your relaxation practice by concentrating on breathing comfortably into your abdomen (rather than into your chest area). Abdominal breathing is far more relaxing than breathing into the chest.

9. Once you have been through the individual muscle groups (steps 1 through 6) at least five times, you can concentrate on quickly relaxing yourself. Tense all the muscle groups at once, hold for 5 seconds, release the tension while exhaling and giving the mental command to relax. You will soon find that you can relax yourself almost instantaneously by simply exhaling as you say the word *relax.* This is a valuable arousal control skill that can be used to control either anxiety or anger. (Barlow & Rapee, 1991)

▶ Mind-Body Control: The Integrated Coping Response

Once you have learned the cognitive and relaxation coping responses, you can combine them into an *integrated coping response* that can be used anywhere, at any time, without disrupting what you are doing. The key is to tie the elements into the breathing cycle. You'll recall that during relaxation training, relaxation is paired with exhalation and the trigger word *relax.* To integrate the cognitive skills with the relaxation response, you simply add in a stress-reducing self-statement derived from either cognitive restructuring or self-instructional training during the inhalation phase of the breathing cycle. Thus as you inhale, say to yourself the appropriate self-statement, followed by a connecting word like *so* or *and.* Then as you exhale, say the word *relax* and relax your body. The sequence, with some examples included, is shown in Figure 10.29. You can repeat the sequence as often as you wish, changing self-statements as needed. Use of this coping response has been shown to reduce stress responses and enhance feelings of self-efficacy, and to improve performance in both athletic and academic settings (Crocker, 1989; Smith & Nye, 1989).

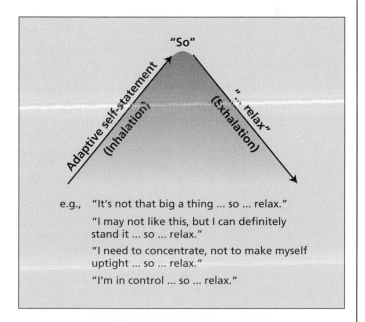

e.g., "It's not that big a thing ... so ... relax."

"I may not like this, but I can definitely stand it ... so ... relax."

"I need to concentrate, not to make myself uptight ... so ... relax."

"I'm in control ... so ... relax."

FIGURE 10.29 The integrated coping response acquired through cognitive restructuring, self-instructional training, and relaxation training provides a means of controlling appraisals and physiological arousal when incorporated into the breathing cycle. (Smith, 1993).

▼▼

CHAPTER SUMMARY

The Functions of Emotions

- An emotion is a positive or negative feeling (or affective) state consisting of a pattern of cognitive, physiological, and behavioral reactions to events that have relevance to important goals or motives. Negative emotional responses are a central feature of the stress response.

- Emotions further our well-being in several ways: by rousing us to action, by helping us communicate with others, and by eliciting empathy and help. Negative emotions narrow attention and behavior, whereas positive thoughts tend to broaden our thinking and behavior.

The Nature of Emotions

- The primary components of emotion are the eliciting stimuli, cognitive appraisals, physiological arousal, and expressive and instrumental behaviors. Individual differences in personality and motivation affect the experience and expression of emotion, as do cultural factors.

- Although innate factors can affect the eliciting properties of certain stimuli, learning can also play an important role in determining the arousal properties of stimuli.

- The cognitive component of emotional experience involves the evaluative and personal appraisal of the eliciting stimuli. The ability of thoughts to elicit emotional arousal has been demonstrated clinically and in experimental research. Cross-cultural research indicates considerable agreement across cultures in the appraisals that evoke basic emotions, but also some degree of variation in more complex appraisals.

- Our physiological responses in emotion are produced by the hypothalamus, the limbic system, and the cortex, and by the autonomic and endocrine systems. There appear to be two systems for emotional behavior, one involving conscious processing by the cortex, the other unconscious processing by the amygdala.

- Recent studies suggest that negative emotions reflect greater relative activation of the right hemisphere, whereas positive emotions are related to relatively greater activation in the left hemisphere.

- The validity of the polygraph as a "lie detector" has been questioned largely because of the difficulty of establishing which emotion is being expressed.

- The behavioral component of emotion includes expressive and instrumental behaviors. Different parts of the face are important in the expression of various emotions. The accuracy of people's interpretation of these expressions increases when situational cues are also available. Based in part on similarities in facial expression of emotions across widely separate cultures, evolutionary theorists propose that certain fundamental emotional patterns are innate. They agree, however, that cultural learning can influence emotional expression in important ways.

- Research on the relation between arousal and performance suggests that there is an optimal level of arousal for the performance of any task. This optimal level varies with the complexity or difficulty of the task; complex tasks have lower optimal levels.

Interactions Among the Components of Emotion

- Several past and present theories posit causal relations among emotional components. The James-Lange/somatic theory maintains that we first become aroused and then judge what we are feeling. The Cannon-Bard theory proposes that arousal and cognition are simultaneously triggered by the thalamus. Cognitive appraisal theory states that appraisals trigger emotional arousal. According to Schachter's two-factor theory, arousal tells us how strongly we feel, while cognitions derived from situational cues help us to label the specific emotion.

- The facial feedback hypothesis, derived from the James-Lange/somatic theory, states that feedback from the facial muscles associated with innate emotional displays affects cognitive and physiological processes. Recent evidence provides support for the theory.

- Because of the two-way relations between the cognitive and physiological components of emotion, it is possible to manipulate appraisals and thereby influence level of arousal. Arousal changes can also affect appraisal of the eliciting stimuli.

The Nature of Stress

- Stress has been viewed by various theorists as a stimulus; as a response having cognitive, physiological, and behavioral components; and as a person-situation interaction, i.e., a transaction between the person and the environment.

- A transactional model of stress specifies interactions among situational factors, cognitive appraisal processes, physiological responses, and behavioral attempts to cope. This model by its nature predicts individual differences in response to stressors.

- Stressors are events that place physical or psychological demands on organisms. The stressfulness of a situation is defined by the balance between demands and resources. Life events can vary in terms of how positive or negative they are, as well as in predictability, controllability, chronicity, and other dimensions that affect their impact.

- Cognitive appraisal processes play an essential role in people's responses to stressors. People appraise the nature of the demands, the resources available to deal with them, their possible consequences, and the personal meaning of these consequences. Distortions at any of these levels can result in inappropriate stress responses.

- The physiological response to stressors is mediated by the autonomic and endocrine systems and involves a pattern of arousal that mobilizes the body to deal with the stressor. Selye described a general adaptation syndrome, which includes the stages of alarm, resistance, and exhaustion.

Stress and Health

- Measures of both major negative life events and microstressors are associated with negative psychological outcomes. Causal linkages may be difficult to identify in the relation between negative life events and psychological distress.

- Life stress can decrease immune function, worsen preexisting medical conditions, and increase the risk of illness and death.

Vulnerability and Protective Factors

- Social support is an important protective factor for people who are confronting stressors. Such support has both direct and buffering effects that help people cope with stress.

- Hardiness is a protective factor against stress. Hardy individuals are characterized by commitment, feelings of personal control, and a tendency to perceive stressful situations as a challenge. Other cognitive protective factors are self-efficacy and optimism. Spiritual beliefs often help people cope more effectively with stressful life events, but certain religious beliefs are negatively related to adjustment.

Coping with Stress

- Three major ways of coping with stressors are problem-focused coping, emotion-focused coping, and seeking social support.

- Problem-focused coping and seeking social support generally relate better to adjustment than emotion-focused coping. However, the outcome of a coping strategy depends on its appropriateness to the situation and the skill with which it is carried out. In situations involving low personal control, emotion-focused coping may be the most appropriate and effective strategy.

- Stress management can also be accomplished through coping skills training. Cognitive restructuring and self-instructional training can be used to develop cognitive coping responses; and relaxation training can be used to develop greater control of physiological arousal.

KEY TERMS AND CONCEPTS*

cognitive appraisal (414)

coping self-efficacy (441)

display rules (426)

downward comparison (417)

emotion (412)

emotion-focused coping (444)

empathy (423)

expressive behaviors (423)

facial feedback hypothesis (429)

fundamental emotional patterns (423)

general adaptation syndrome (436)

hardiness (441)

instrumental behaviors (426)

life event scales (434)

neuroticism (438)

polygraph (421)

primary appraisal (436)

problem-focused coping (442)

protective factors (439)

rape trauma syndrome (438)

secondary appraisal (436)

seeking social support (444)

somatic theory of emotions (427)

stress (433)

stressors (433)

subjective well-being (SWB) (417)

two-factor theory of emotion (430)

upward comparison (418)

vascular theory of emotional feedback (429)

vulnerability factors (439)

* Each term has been boldfaced in the text on the page indicated in parentheses.

APPLYING YOUR KNOWLEDGE

1. As you enter class, your instructor announces that there will be a surprise quiz. Your palms become sweaty, your heart starts pounding, and your mouth feels like cotton. This physiological response is caused by activity of your
   a) hippocampus.
   b) somatic nervous system.
   c) sympathetic nervous system.
   d) frontal cortex.

2. Julie is a very upbeat, cheerful, and happy person. Were you to obtain a resting EEG measure of her brain activity, you would expect to find
   a) greater relative activity in the left hemisphere.
   b) strong activity in the amygdala.
   c) strong relative activity in the right hemisphere.
   d) consistently strong sympathetic activation.

3. Clem has very low academic self-confidence and experiences high test anxiety. "I'm just not very smart," he says. Which aspect of cognitive appraisal would you focus on if you were trying to help him become more confident?
   a) appraisal of demands
   b) appraisal of consequences
   c) appraisal of resources
   d) primary appraisal

4. While watching a movie at night, you suddenly realize that tears are streaming down your face and conclude that you are sad. This is most consistent with which theory of emotion?
   a) Cannon-Bard
   b) James-Lange
   c) cognitive appraisal
   d) LeDoux's theory

5. I don't understand it. When I first saw that person, I had an instantaneous queasy feeling." Joseph LeDoux's theory would suggest that this reaction was probably triggered in
   a) the left cerebral cortex.
   b) the thalamus.
   c) the hippocampus.
   d) the amygdala.

6. An acquaintance tells you that all people accused of sexually abusing a child should be required to take a polygraph test. You disagree, saying that the greatest danger is that
   a) many innocent people might appear guilty.
   b) guilty people will not be identified.
   c) sex abusers do not react emotionally.
   d) polygraph tests are totally inaccurate.

7. You are a sport psychologist who teaches athletes relaxation skills to help them keep their physiological arousal at a low level during competition. Which of the following athletes would be most likely to profit from such training?
   a) a sprinter
   b) a weight lifter
   c) a golfer
   d) a football lineman

8. Which of the following skills is not needed to use the integrated coping response described in this chapter?
   a) control of facial expressions
   b) abdominal breathing skills
   c) stress-reducing self-statements
   d) muscle relaxation skills

9. During the Watergate crisis, President Richard Nixon showed no visible ill effects of the stressful circumstances. Immediately upon resigning and returning to his California home, however, he developed a painful case of phlebitis. Selye would likely say that he had moved from the _____ phase of the GAS to the _____ phase.
   a) alarm; resistance
   b) exhaustion; alarm
   c) resistance; exhaustion
   d) exhaustion; alarm

10. The chief executive officer of a medical supply company is dealing with internal conflict between two of her middle managers that is affecting productivity and creating stress for her. Given the circumstances, which coping strategy is most likely to be effective for her?
   a) seeking social support
   b) problem-focused coping
   c) cognitive restructuring
   d) emotion-focused coping

Answers

1. c) (page 421); 2. a) (page 420); 3. c) (page 435); 4. b) (page 427); 5. d) (page 419); 6. a) (page 422); 7. c) (page 427); 8. a) (page 447); 9. c) (page 437); 10. b) (page 444).

For additional quizzing and a variety of interactive resources, visit the book's Online Learning Center at www.mhhe.com/passer.

DEVELOPMENT OVER THE LIFE SPAN

There are only two lasting bequests we can hope to give our children. One of these is roots; the other, wings.

— *Hodding Carter*

11

CHAPTER OUTLINE

FIGURE 11.1   Victor, the "Wild Boy of Aveyron."

▼▼▼▼▼▼▼▼▼▼▼▼▼▼▼▼▼▼▼▼▼▼▼▼▼▼▼▼▼▼▼▼▼▼▼▼▼

In 1799 three hunters discovered a remarkable child living in the forests of Aveyron, France. Most likely abandoned at a young age, he grew up isolated from human contact, foraging for food and surviving naked in the wild. About 12 years old, he easily climbed trees, ate nuts and roots, scratched and bit people who interfered with him, and made few sounds. He could walk upright, yet ran quickly on all fours. Some regarded him as half-human, half-beast, and they called him the "Wild Boy of Aveyron" (Itard, 1894/1962).

Several medical experts concluded that the boy was incurably "mentally deficient," but others disagreed, noting that it took intelligence to survive in the wild. They argued that special education and care would enable the child to flower into a normal, civilized adult. In Paris, the boy was placed under the care of a prominent young physician, Jean-Marc Itard, who named him Victor and diligently supervised his training (Figure 11.1).

Victor initially was unresponsive to stimuli that most people find aversive. Unfazed, he would stick his hand into boiling kitchen water to grab food or eagerly roll around half-naked on the cold winter ground. Eventually, he learned to sense temperature differences, dress himself, and perform other self-care behaviors. Victor's emotional responses, which at first fluctuated without reason, began to fit the situation. He laughed in playful situations, shed tears over someone's death, and displayed some signs of affection toward Itard. Victor learned to read and write some words, communicate basic needs, and perform simple tasks.

Although Victor changed in important ways, his progress slowed considerably. He never learned to speak and after five years of education his cognitive, emotional, and social development remained limited. Pessimism over further progress grew and the "project" ended. Victor was moved nearby and cared for by a woman for the rest of his life.

At the time, people expected Victor's case study to help answer an intense debate about the role of "nature versus nurture" in shaping who we are. But it raised more questions than it answered. Was Victor a normal, inherently noble infant who became irreparably harmed by his childhood isolation, or was he born "mentally deficient"?

Modern research tells us that, although unfavorable environments can significantly impair development, some children exposed to extreme adversity are highly resilient and thrive later in life (Masten & Coatsworth, 1998). Although we cannot pinpoint the causes of Victor's stunted development and failure to recover, this famous case highlights a broader issue: Just how does the miracle of human development unfold, and what conditions are required for normal growth?

❭ MAJOR ISSUES AND METHODS

Developmental psychology examines biological, physical, psychological, and behavioral changes that occur as we age. Four broad issues guide much developmental research.

➤ 1. Describe four broad issues that guide developmental research.

- *Nature and nurture.* To what extent is our development the product of heredity (nature) and the product of environment (nurture)? How do nature and nurture interact?

- *Critical and sensitive periods.* Are some experiences especially important at particular ages? A **critical period** is an age range during which certain experiences *must occur* for development to proceed normally or along a certain path. A **sensitive period** is an *optimal* age range for certain experiences, but if those experiences occur at another time, normal development will still be possible.

- *Continuity versus discontinuity.* Is development continuous and gradual, as when a sapling slowly grows into a tree? Or is it discontinuous, progressing through qualitatively distinct *stages,* as when a creeping caterpillar emerges from its cocoon as a soaring butterfly?

- *Stability versus change.* Do our characteristics remain consistent as we age?

Developmental psychologists often use special research designs to investigate these and other questions (Figure 11.2). Suppose we wish to study how intellectual abilities change from age 10 to age 60. Using a **cross-sectional design** we would compare people of different ages at the same point in time. Thus in the next month we could administer intellectual tasks to 10-, 20-, 30-, 40-, 50-, and 60-year-olds. We would test each person only once and compare how well the different age groups perform. The cross-sectional design is widely used because data from many age groups can be collected relatively quickly, but a key drawback is that the different age groups, called *cohorts,* grew up in different historical periods. Thus if 60-year-olds have poorer intellectual abilities than 20-year-olds, is this due to aging or possibly to broad environmental differences (e.g., perhaps poorer nutrition or medical care) between growing up in the 1940s versus 1980s?

To avoid this problem a **longitudinal design** repeatedly tests the same cohort as it grows older. We could test a sample of 10-year-olds this month and then retest them every 10 years, up to age 60. Now everyone is exposed to the same historical time frame. Unfortunately this design can be time consuming and, as years pass, our sample may shrink substantially as people move, drop out of the study, or die. Further, suppose we find that intelligence declines at age 60. Is this really due to aging or to developmental experiences unique to our particular cohort? Researchers can answer this question by using a *sequential design* that combines the cross-sectional and longitudinal approaches. That is, we can repeatedly test *several* age cohorts as they grow older and determine whether they follow a similar developmental pattern. This design is the most comprehensive but also the most time consuming and costly.

These research approaches provide much of our knowledge about human development, which we now explore from conception through death. We begin with the *prenatal period,* approximately 266 days during which we develop from a single-cell organism barely larger than a pinhead into a wondrously complex newborn human.

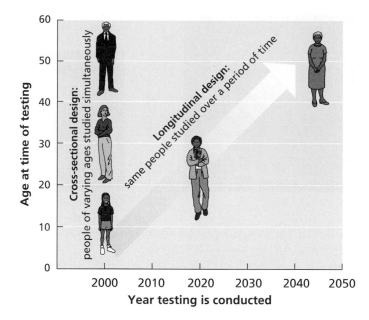

FIGURE 11.2 Using a cross-sectional design we would test different age groups in the year 2000 and compare their performance. Using a longitudinal design, we would test one age group and then retest them every 10 years until age 60. Using a sequential design (there are many types), we might test 10- through 60-year-olds in the year 2000 and then retest them every 10 years until age 60. Suppose that in the year 2000 the 60-year-olds perform worse than younger adults. Also suppose that, as the 10- through 50-year-olds age, their performance worsens at age 60. We are now more confident that this decline, replicated over different age cohorts, represents a true effect of aging.

➤ 2. Explain how cross-sectional, longitudinal, and sequential designs differ.

〉 PRENATAL DEVELOPMENT

Prenatal development consists of three stages (Figure 11.3). The *germinal stage* comprises approximately the first two weeks of development, beginning when one sperm fertilizes a female egg (ovum). This fertilized egg is called a **zygote,** and through repeated cell division it becomes a mass of cells that attaches to the mother's uterus about 10 to 14 days after conception.

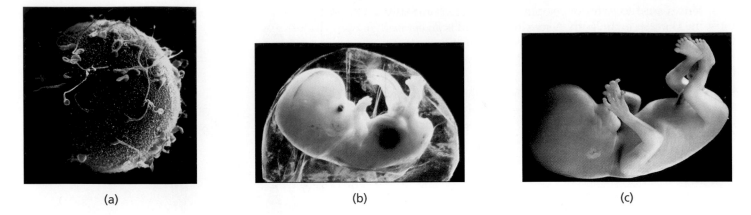

FIGURE 11.3 These remarkable photos show (a) the moment of conception, as one of many sperm cells fertilizes the ovum, (b) the embryo at 6 to 7 weeks, and (c) the fetus at 3 months of age.

The *embryonic stage* extends from the end of the second week through the eighth week after conception, and the cell mass is now is called an **embryo.** Two life-support structures, the placenta and umbilical cord, develop at the start of this stage. Located on the uterine wall, the *placenta* contains membranes that allow nutrients to pass from the mother's blood to the umbilical cord. In turn, the *umbilical cord* contains blood vessels that carry these nutrients and oxygen to the embryo, and waste products back from the embryo to the mother. Supplied with nutrients, embryonic cells rapidly divide and become specialized. Bodily organs and systems begin to form, and by week 8 the heart of the inch-long embryo is beating, the brain is forming, and facial features such as eyes can be recognized.

At the ninth week after conception, the embryo is now called a **fetus.** During this *fetal stage,* which lasts until birth, muscles become stronger and other bodily systems continue to develop. At about 24 weeks the eyes open and by 28 weeks the fetus attains the *age of viability,* meaning that it is likely to survive outside the womb in case of premature birth (Hetherington & Parke, 1999).

Genetics and Sex Determination

➤ 3. What determines the sex of a child?

Throughout history many women have been blamed and belittled for failing to give birth to a male heir. Ironically, any father who feels a need to "lay blame" should look in the mirror, for his genetic contribution determines the sex of a baby. Recall from Chapter 3 that a female's egg cells and a male's sperm cells each have only 23 chromosomes. At conception an egg and sperm unite to form the zygote, which now contains the full set of 23 *pairs* found in other human cells. The 23rd pair of chromosomes determines the baby's sex. A genetic female's 23rd pair contains two X chromosomes (XX), so called because of their shape (Figure 11.4). Because women carry only X chromosomes, the 23rd chromosome in the egg is always an X. A genetic male's 23rd pair contains an X and a Y chromosome (XY). Thus the 23rd chromosome in the sperm is an X in about half of the cases and a Y in the other half. The Y chromosome contains a specific gene, known as the *TDF gene,* that triggers male sexual development. The union of an egg with a sperm cell having a Y chromosome results in an XY combination and therefore a boy. A sperm containing an X chromosome produces an XX combination and so a baby girl.

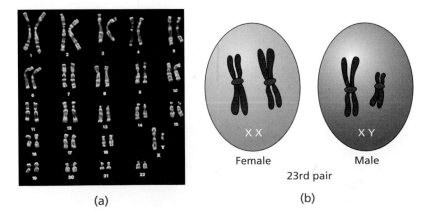

Female   Male
23rd pair

FIGURE 11.4 (a) Most human cells contains 23 pairs of chromosomes. Each pair consists of one chromosome from each parent. The 23rd pair determines a person's sex. (b) In males the 23rd pair consists of an X chromosome and a Y chromosome. In females, the 23rd pair contains two X chromosomes.

How does the Y chromosome determine our sex characteristics? If a Y chromosome is present, its *TDF* gene initiates the development of testes at roughly 6 to 8 weeks after conception. In fact, the term *TDF* stands for "testis-determining factor." Once formed, the testes secrete sex hormones called androgens that continue to direct a male pattern of organ development. If the *TDF* gene is not present, as happens with an XX pair on the 23rd chromosome, testes do not form and—in the absence of sufficient androgen activity during this prenatal *critical period*—an inherent female pattern of organ development ensues (Hyde & De-Lamater, 2000).

Environmental Influences

Our genetic blueprint sets forth a path of prenatal development, but nature and nurture become intertwined even before we are born. Because the embryo and fetus receive their nutrients from the mother, severe *maternal malnutrition* is associated with a greater risk of miscarriage, premature birth, stillbirth, smaller birth size, and impaired prenatal brain development (Read, 1982).

Teratogens are environmental agents that cause abnormal prenatal development. The placenta prevents many dangerous substances from reaching the embryo and fetus, but some harmful chemical molecules and diseases can pass through. Stress hormones can cross the placenta and prolonged *maternal stress* is associated with increased risk of premature birth, infant irritability, and attentional deficits (Weinstock, 1997). If the mother contracts *rubella (German measles)*—especially when the embryo's eyes, ears, heart, and central nervous system are beginning to form early in pregnancy—it can cause blindness, deafness, mental retardation, and heart defects in the infant (Murdoch, 1984).

➤ 4. How do STDs, alcohol, and other drugs affect prenatal development? Identify other broad classes of teratogens.

Sexually transmitted diseases can be passed from mother to fetus and produce serious harm that may include brain damage, blindness, and deafness depending upon the disease. Among pregnant women with untreated syphilis, about 25 percent of fetuses are born dead. Similarly, without medical treatment during pregnancy, about 25 percent of fetuses born to mothers with the HIV virus that causes AIDS also are infected (Vander Zanden, 1997).

Mercury, lead, radiation, and many other *environmental toxins* produce birth defects, as do many *drugs*. **Fetal alcohol syndrome (FAS)** is a severe group of abnormalities that results from prenatal exposure to alcohol (Streissguth et al., 1982, 1998). FAS children have facial abnormalities and small, malformed brains (Figure 11.5). Psychological symptoms include mental retardation, attentional and perceptual deficits, irritability, and impulsivity (Aronson & Hagberg, 1998). Other children exposed to alcohol in the womb display only some or milder forms of these deficits, a pattern most commonly called *fetal alcohol effects* (FAE) (Streissguth et al., 1998).

FAS is a major cause of mental retardation in Western countries, and the threshold level of alcohol exposure needed to produce FAS is unknown. About one third to a half of infants born to alcoholic mothers have FAS, but even "social drinking" or an episode of binge-drinking can increase the risk of prenatal damage and long-term cognitive impairment (Hunt et al., 1995; Larroque & Kaminski, 1998). Clearly, because no amount of prenatal alcohol exposure has been confirmed to be "absolutely safe," pregnant women and those trying to become pregnant are best advised to completely avoid drinking alcohol.

Nicotine is a teratogen and maternal smoking increases the risk of miscarriage, premature birth, and low birth weight. Due to secondhand smoke, regular tobacco use by fathers also has been linked to low infant birth weight and increased risk of respiratory infections (Wakefield et al., 1998). Babies of pregnant mothers who regularly use *heroin* or *cocaine* are often born addicted and experience withdrawal symptoms after birth. Their cognitive functioning and ability to regulate their arousal and attention may also be impaired (Mayes et al., 1998).

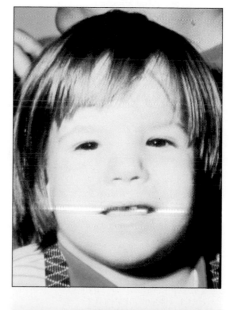

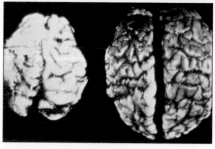

FIGURE 11.5 Children who suffer from fetal alcohol syndrome (FAS) not only look different, but have brains (left) that are underdeveloped compared with those of normal children (right).

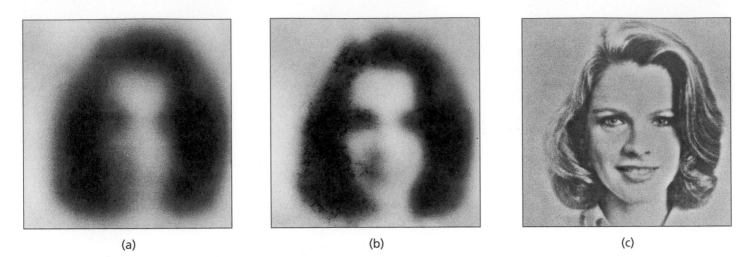

(a)   (b)   (c)

FIGURE 11.6 Seeing through an infant's eyes. These three images approximate the visual acuity of an infant at (a) age 1 month, (b) 3 months, and (c) 12 months.

➤ 5. How can scientists measure newborn's sensory capabilities and perceptual preferences? What are some of those preferences?

〉 INFANCY AND CHILDHOOD

Studying infancy poses interesting challenges. During research infants may start to fuss, cry, drool, spit up, soil their diapers, or simply fall asleep! Further, because infants cannot describe their experiences, researchers must find clever ways to take advantage of those responses that infants can make, such as sucking and moving their eyes, to draw inferences about their capabilities and preferences.

The Amazing Newborn

After a newborn emerges from the comfort of its mother's womb, does its world become a "buzzing, blooming confusion" as pioneering psychologist William James (1890) proposed? Contrary to a long-held view of newborns as helpless and passive, research reveals that they are surprisingly sophisticated information processors who respond to many features of their environment.

Sensory Capabilities and Perceptual Preferences

Newborns' visual systems are immature. Their eye movements are not as well coordinated as ours and they are very nearsighted (Dobson & Teller, 1978). Still, infants scan their environment and although objects look blurry, they can perceive some forms only a few days after birth. Newborns can reasonably see objects about a foot away, the typical distance between their eyes and their mothers' eyes while nursing. As Figure 11.6 shows, visual acuity improves with age.

Infants also display visual preferences, which Robert Fantz (1961) studied using the *preferential looking procedure.* He placed infants on their backs, showed them two or more stimuli at the same time, and filmed their eyes to record how long they looked at each stimulus. Infants preferred patterns to solid colors, and complex patterns—such as realistic or scrambled drawings of a human face—to simpler patterns (Figure 11.7). Indeed, newborns prefer to look at faces, especially ones that move (Morton & Johnson, 1991; Simion et al., 1998).

Just as you would make different facial expressions after tasting sweet, sour, or bitter substances, newborns' facial responses tell us that they have a reasonably well-developed sense of taste. Newborns also respond to touch, sense changes in temperature and body position, and distinguish different odors. If exposed to pads taken from inside the bras of several nursing mothers, week-old infants will orient toward the odor of their own mother's pad (MacFarlane, 1975;

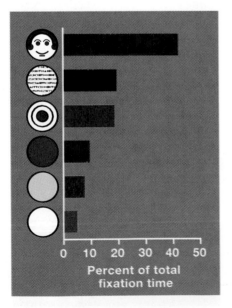

FIGURE 11.7 Whether 2 days old or 2 to 3 months old, infants prefered to look at complex patterns more than simple patterns or solid colors.

Based on R. L. Frantz, 1961.

Porter & Winberg, 1999). Their hearing capabilities do not approach adult levels until late childhood, but newborns can hear reasonably well. They turn toward the source of sounds, prefer human voices to other sounds, and prefer high-pitched tones—more typical of a mother's voice—to low-pitched sounds (Aslin, 1987). As Figure 11.8 describes, newborns also seem to prefer sounds that become familiar to them during their last months of fetal development, during which time they can hear sounds transmitted through the womb (DeCasper & Spence, 1986). These findings provide important evidence of a capacity for *prenatal learning*.

Reflexes and Learning

Neonates are equipped with many **reflexes**—automatic, inborn behaviors that occur in response to specific stimuli. Some, including breathing, have obvious adaptive significance. Touch a baby's cheek and it will turn its head toward the direction it was touched and open its mouth—the *rooting reflex*. When something is placed in the infant's mouth, it will suck on it—the *sucking reflex*. Together, these reflexes increase the infant's ability to feed. In general, healthy reflexes indicate normal neurological maturity at birth.

Infants display many of the learning mechanisms described in Chapter 6. They habituate to routine, repetitive nonthreatening stimuli and can acquire classically conditioned responses. For example, after a tone (CS) is repeatedly paired with a gentle puff of air to the eye (UCS), infants as young as 10 days old will develop a conditioned eyeblink response to the tone alone (Lipsitt, 1990). Through operant conditioning, newborns learn that they can "make things happen." Thus 3-day-old infants can learn to suck a plastic nipple with a certain pattern of bursts to activate a tape recorder playing their mother's voice (Moon & Fifer, 1990). Newborns also can learn to kick their legs or turn their head in a particular direction to receive various reinforcers.

What about observational learning? As Figure 11.9 shows, researchers have found that within weeks or even days after birth, newborns can reproduce a simple facial expression made by an adult model (Meltzoff & Moore, 1977). Some developmentalists argue that this merely is a reflexive response, but psychologist Andrew Meltzoff views it as evidence of a more flexible, biologically based capacity for imitation (Meltzoff & Moore, 1999). Meltzoff (1988) also has found that 9-month-olds can view a model's behavior and then, a day later, reproduce that behavior from memory.

In sum, a consistent pattern emerges from research on infants' sensory capacities, perceptual preferences, reflexes, and learning abilities: Infants appear to be born "prewired" with an array of mechanisms that help them respond to caretakers, begin to recognize their primary caretakers, and learn other important information.

Physical, Motor, and Brain Development

Our bodies and movement (motor) skills develop rapidly during infancy and childhood. On average, by our first birthday body weight triples, height increases by 50 percent, and we are standing easily and learning to walk. **Maturation** is the

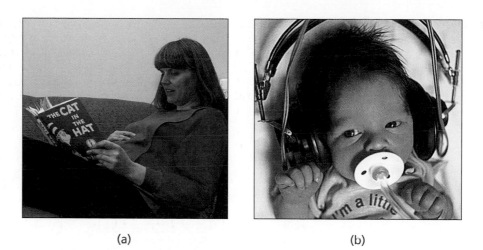

(a)   (b)

FIGURE 11.8 Can the fetus learn? (a) Twice a day during their last 6 weeks of pregnancy mothers read out loud the same passage of nursery rhyme from Dr. Seuss's story, *The Cat in the Hat*. (b) Two or 3 days after birth, newborns were able to turn on a recording of their mother reading either the *Cat in the Hat* rhyme or an unfamiliar rhyme by sucking on a sensor-equipped nipple at different rates. Compared with infants in a control condition, these newborns more often altered their sucking rate on a sensor-equipped nipple in whichever direction (faster or slower) selected the familiar rhyme (DeCasper & Spence, 1986).

➤ 6. Can newborns learn through classical and operant conditioning, and modeling?

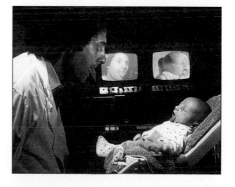

FIGURE 11.9 Young infants have been found to reproduce tongue protrusion after watching an adult model. Here researcher Andrew Meltzoff models the behavior and records an infant's response.

➤ 7. Explain how nature and nurture jointly influence physical growth and motor development during infancy.

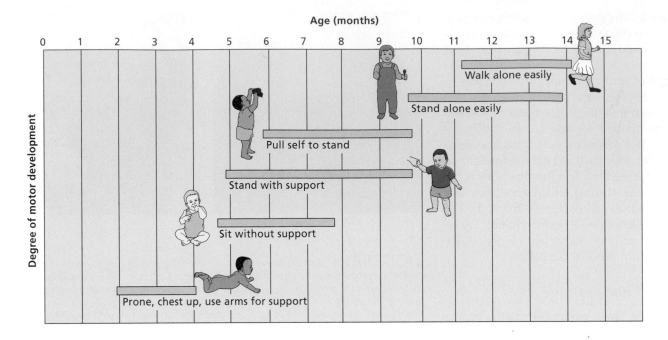

FIGURE 11.10 Infant motor development occurs in an orderly sequence, but the age at which abilities emerge varies across children. The left end of each bar represents the age by which 25 percent of children exhibit the skill; the right end represents the age by which 90 percent have mastered it.

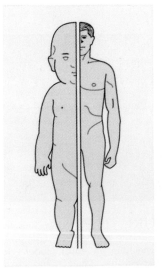

FIGURE 11.11 The cephalocaudal principle. Compared with adults, a newborn's head is disproportionately large relative to rest of the body, reflecting the tendency for development to proceed in a head-to-foot direction. In a fetus, the head represents an even greater proportion of the body (look carefully at Figure 11.3c).

genetically programmed biological process that governs our growth. As Figure 11.10 shows, infants vary in the age at which they acquire a particular skill, but the sequence in which skills appear normally is the same across children.

Physical and motor development follow several biological principles. The **cephalocaudal principle** reflects the tendency for development to proceed in a head-to-foot direction. Thus the head of a fetus or infant is disproportionately large because physical growth concentrates on the head and proceeds toward the lower part of the body (Figure 11.11). The **proximodistal principle** states that development begins along the innermost parts of the body and continues toward the outermost parts. Thus a fetus's arms develop before hands and fingers, and at birth infants can control their shoulders but not their arm or hand muscles.

No organ in the human body develops more rapidly and dramatically than the brain (Kolb, 1989). Still, at birth the newborn's brain it is far from mature and is only about 25 percent of its eventual adult weight. By age 6 months, however, the brain already is 50 percent of its adult weight. What makes the brain heavier? Cells become larger, many axons develop an insulating myelin sheath, and as Figure 11.12 shows, neural networks that form the basis for cognitive and motor skills develop rapidly.

From the embryonic stage through childhood, brain growth occurs in an orderly fashion. The first areas to develop and mature, such as the brain stem, lie deep within the brain and regulate basic survival functions like heartbeat and breathing. The last areas to mature include the association areas of the frontal cortex, which are vital to our highest-level cognitive functions such as thinking and language.

The rapid rate of growth during infancy and early childhood slows in later childhood. Five-year-olds' brains have reached almost 90 percent of adult size and they are closer to adult weight than any other part of the body (Tanner, 1978). Although brain size increases little between the ages of 5 and 10 years, its maturation continues. New synapses form, the association areas of the cerebral cortex mature, and the cerebral hemispheres become more highly specialized.

Environmental and Cultural Influences

Though guided by genetics, physical and motor development are also influenced by experience. Diet is an obvious example. Chronic, severe malnutrition not only stunts general growth and brain development, but also is a major source of infant death worldwide (Sigman, 1995).

Physical touch and environmental enrichment also affect growth in infancy. Properly nourished newborn rats show stunted development if they are deprived of normal physical contact with their mothers, but vigorously stroking the rats with a brush helps maintain normal physical growth (Kuhn & Schanberg, 1998). Similarly, premature and full-term human infants who are regularly massaged gain weight more rapidly and show faster neurological development (Field, 2000). In addition, rats raised in an enriched environment develop heavier brains, larger neurons, more synaptic connections, and greater amounts of acetylcholine, a brain neurotransmitter that enhances learning (Rosenzweig & Bennett, 1996).

Finally, experience also can affect the development of basic movement skills. The Ache people roam the dense rain forests of eastern Paraguay, foraging for food and making temporary camp in different sites. For safety, mothers keep their children in direct physical contact almost constantly until the age of 3, providing them little opportunity to move about. Ache infants typically do not begin to walk until they are almost age 2, about a year later than the average North American infant (Kaplan & Dove, 1987). In contrast, Kipsigis infants of Kenya receive training to sit up and walk at a early age, and acquire these skills about a month sooner than North American infants (Super, 1976). Experience also affects the types of complex movement skills that toddlers and children acquire (Figure 11.13).

Our discussion of physical growth and motor development reinforces three points that apply across the realm of human development:

- *Biology sets limits on environmental influences.* The best nutrition will not enable most people to grow 7 feet tall, and no infant can be toilet-trained before the nerve fibers that help regulate bladder control have biologically matured.

- *Environmental influences can be powerful.* Nurturing environments foster physical and psychological growth, and impoverished environments can stunt growth. Especially in combination, severe and prolonged environmental stressors may produce a lasting physical and psychological failure to thrive (Buergin, 1999).

- *Biological and environmental factors interact.* Enriched environments enhance brain development. In turn, brain development facilitates our ability to learn and benefit from environmental experiences (Rosenzweig, 1984).

Cognitive Development

What are the thought processes of a child like, and how do they change with age? Swiss psychologist Jean Piaget (1926, 1977) spent over 50 years exploring these questions, and his ideas have influenced generations of developmental researchers (De Vries et al., 2000).

Piaget's Stage Model

Early in his career Piaget worked for French psychologist Alfred Binet, the pioneer of intelligence testing. Piaget became intrigued by the patterns of errors children made on test questions, with children of the same age often making similar mistakes. He came to believe that the key issue in understanding how children think was not whether they got the right answers, but *how* they arrived at their answers.

Piaget relied on observational research, carefully watching children and listening to them reason as they tried to solve problems. He proposed that children's

At birth

1 month

3 months

15 months

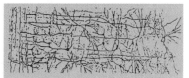

24 months

FIGURE 11.12 Increases in the density of neural networks during early development are apparent in these drawings of tissue from the human cerebral cortex.

➤ 8. Describe assimilation and accommodation. How are they related to cognitive development?

FIGURE 11.13 At the Parker Ranch in Hawaii, this 2-year-old is learning to ride a horse and use a lasso.

thinking changes *qualitatively* with age, and that it differs from the way adults think. Piaget believed that cognitive development results from an interplay of maturation and experience, and he viewed children as natural-born "scientists" who actively explore and seek to understand their world.

To achieve this understanding the brain builds **schemas,** which are organized patterns of thought and action. Think of a schema as an "internal framework" that guides our interaction with the world. For example, infants are born with a sucking reflex that provides a primitive framework—a schema—for interacting with physical objects. To the infant, the world is meant to be sucked. In a sense, sucking is a basic way in which the infant "knows" the world. Similarly, when a child says "doggie" to describe the family pet, this word reflects an underlying schema—a concept or framework—that the child is using to understand this particular experience.

Cognitive development occurs as we acquire new schemas, and as our existing schemas become more complex. According to Piaget, two key processes are involved. **Assimilation** is the process by which new experiences are incorporated into existing schemas. For example, when a young infant encounters a new object—a small plastic toy, a blanket, a doll—she will try to suck it. She tries to "fit" this new experience into a schema that she already has: Objects are suckable. Similarly, a child who sees a horse for the first time may exclaim "big doggie." After all, the horse has four legs and a tail, so the child tries to make sense of this new experience by applying his familiar schema: "doggie."

Accommodation is the process by which new experiences cause existing schemas to change. As the infant tries to suck different objects, she will eventually encounter ones that are too big to go into her mouth or that taste bad. Similarly, the child who calls a horse a "big doggie" eventually will realize that this "big doggie" doesn't bark, sit, fetch, or otherwise behave like a dog. This imbalance or *disequilibrium* between existing schemas and new experiences ultimately forces those schemas to change. Thus the infant's "suckability" schema will become more complex; some objects are suckable, some are not. The child's "doggie" schema also will change, and he will begin to develop new schemas for "horsey," "kitty," and so on. This may not seem earth-shaking to us, but to them, their understanding of the world has changed fundamentally. Every time a schema is modified it helps create a better balance, an *equilibrium*, between the environment and the child's understanding of it.

Cognitive growth thus involves a give-and-take between trying to understand new experiences in terms of what we already know (assimilation), and having to modify our thinking when new experiences don't fit into our current schemas (accommodation). As Table 11.1 shows, Piaget charted four major stages of cognitive growth.

➤ 9. How do infants develop cognitively during the sensorimotor stage?

Sensorimotor stage.   In the **sensorimotor stage,** which lasts from birth to about age 2, infants understand their world primarily through sensory experiences and physical (motor) interactions with objects. Their reflexes are the earliest schemas that guide thought and action, but as sensory and motor capabilities increase, babies begin to explore their surroundings. Eventually, they realize that they can "make things happen": They bang spoons, take objects apart, and find amazing ways to get themselves into trouble. One 18-month-old peeled sheets of latex paint from a nursery wall, proudly proclaiming the guiding schema to his shocked parents: "Band-Aid!"

For young infants, said Piaget, "out of sight" literally means "out of mind." If you hide 3-month-old Cindy's favorite toy from view she will not search for it, as if the toy no longer exists (Figure 11.14). But when Cindy is older, about age 8 months according to Piaget, she will pull back the blanket and retrieve the hidden toy. The infant now understands that an object continues to exist even when it no longer can be seen, a concept Piaget called **object permanence.** This major

TABLE 11.1	PIAGET'S MODEL OF COGNITIVE DEVELOPMENT	
Stage	Age (years)	Major Characteristics
Sensorimotor	Birth to 2	• Infant understands world through sensory and motor experiences • Achieves object permanence • Emergence of symbolic thought
Preoperational	2–7	• Symbolic thinking; child uses words and images to represent objects and experiences; pretend play • Thinking displays egocentrism, irreversibility, and centration
Concrete operational	7–12	• Child can think logically about concrete events • Grasps concepts of conservation and serial ordering
Formal operational	12 on	• Adolescent can think more logically, abstractly, and flexibly • Can form hypotheses and systematically test them

developmental milestone frees the child from immediate sensory experience and keeps things that are unseen a part of the child's conscious experience.

Infants begin to acquire language after age 1 and toward the end of the sensorimotor period they increasingly use words to represent objects, needs, and actions. Thus in the space of 2 years, infants have grown into planful thinkers who can form simple concepts, solve some problems mentally, and communicate their thoughts to others.

Preoperational stage. Children enter the **preoperational stage** around age 2: They represent the world symbolically through words and mental images, but do not yet understand basic mental operations or rules. Rapid language development helps children label objects and represent simple concepts, such as that two objects can be "the same" or "different." Children become capable of thinking about the past ("yesterday") and future ("tomorrow," "soon"), they become better at anticipating the consequences of their actions, and symbolic thinking enables them to engage in "make-believe," otherwise known as *pretend play.*

Despite these advances, their cognitive abilities still have important limitations. According to Piaget, the preoperational child does not understand the concept of **conservation,** the principle that basic properties of objects, such as

 10. Identify some achievements and limitations of children's thinking in the preoperational stage.

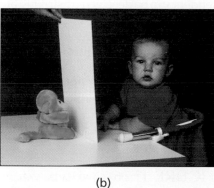

(a)   (b)

FIGURE 11.14 During the early sensorimotor period a baby will reach for a visible toy (a), but not for one that has been hidden from view while the infant watches (b). According to Piaget, the child lacks the concept of object permanence; when something is out of sight, it ceases to exist.

(a)   (b)   (c)

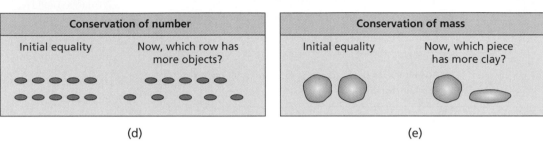

(d)   (e)

FIGURE 11.15 (a,b,c) *Conservation of volume.* At the end of this sequence (from left to right), when the preoperational child is asked which beaker contains more liquid, he points to the taller one. (d) *Conservation of number.* Two rows with an equal number of objects are aligned. After one row is spread out, preoperational children will say that it has more objects than the other row. (e) *Conservation of mass.* Preoperational children watch as one of two identically sized clay balls is rolled into a new shape. They typically will say that it now has more clay.

(a)

(b)

their volume, mass, or quantity stay the same (are "conserved") even though their outward appearance may change (Figure 11.15). For example, suppose we have two short, wide beakers containing equal amounts of liquid. To many people's surprise, when the liquid from one is poured into a tall, narrow beaker, a 4-year-old often will say that the taller glass now has more liquid.

Whereas you understand that the water can be poured back into the short beaker to return to the original state of affairs, the child's thinking displays *irreversibility:* It is difficult for them to mentally reverse an action. You also pay attention to height and width, recognizing that the water is "taller" because the beaker is narrower. But the child exhibits *centration,* focusing (centering) on only one aspect of the situation. Usually, this is the most striking feature, such as the height of the water. Centration also contributes to young preoperational children's more general tendency to be deceived by striking but false appearances, as Figure 11.16 illustrates.

Preoperational children often display *animism,* attributing lifelike qualities to physical objects and natural events. When it rains "the sky is crying" and stars twinkle at night "because they're winking at you." Their thinking also reflects **egocentrism,** difficulty in viewing the world from someone else's perspective. By "egocentrism" Piaget did not mean "selfishness." Rather, children at this stage believe that other people perceive things in the same way they do (Figure 11.17).

FIGURE 11.16 (a) Rheta De Vries (1969) individually showed 3- to 6-year-old children a black cat named Maynard. They correctly identified Maynard as a "cat" and played with him briefly. (b) While each child watched, De Vries hid the front half of Maynard's body behind a screen and placed a realistic mask of a growling dog on his head. When De Vries showed Maynard to the children and asked them questions ("Can it bark? Is it really a dog?"), 3-year-olds often stated that Maynard was now a dog, whereas 6-year-olds knew that Maynard was still a cat.

Concrete operational stage.   In the **concrete operational stage,** which Piaget believed lasts from about ages 7 to 12, children can perform basic mental operations concerning problems that involve tangible (i.e., "concrete") objects and situations. Because they now grasp the concept of reversibility and display less centration, these children easily solve the water-beaker task and other conservation problems that baffled them as preschoolers.

Unlike younger children, concrete operational children grasp the concept of serial ordering and can easily arrange a set of objects along various dimensions, such as from "shortest" to "tallest." These children also can form mental representations of a series of actions. For example, a concrete operational child could draw a map showing the route to get to school. A preoperational child might be able to lead you to school, but would have difficulty representing the route symbolically.

When concrete operational children confront problems that are hypothetical or require abstract reasoning, however, they often have difficulty or show rigid types of thinking. To demonstrate this, ask a few 9-year-olds: "If you could have a third eye, where on your body would you put it? Draw a picture." Then ask them to explain their reason. David Shaffer (1989) reports that 9-year-olds typically draw a row of three eyes across their face. Their thinking is concrete, bound by the reality that eyes appear on the face, and their justifications often are unsophisticated (e.g., ". . . so I could see you better"). Many find the task silly because "Nobody has three eyes" (Shaffer, 1989, p. 324).

Formal operational stage.   Piaget's model ends with the **formal operational stage,** in which individuals are able to think logically and systematically about both concrete and abstract problems, form hypotheses, and test them in a thoughtful way. Formal thinking begins around ages 11 to 12 and increases through adolescence (Ward & Overton, 1990).

Children entering this stage begin to think more flexibly when tackling hypothetical problems, such as "brain-teasers," and typically enjoy the challenge. Shaffer (1989) reports that 11½- to 12-year-olds provide more creative answers and better justifications to the "third-eye problem" than do 9-year-old concrete thinkers. One child placed the eye on the palm of his hands so that he could use it to ". . . see around corners. . . . " Another placed it on top of his head, so that he could "revolve the eye to look in all directions." Formal operational children loved this hypothetical task and begged their teacher for more. We will return to this stage when discussing adolescence.

Stages, Ages, and Culture

Piaget's theory has been tested in diverse cultures around the world. First, it appears that *the general cognitive abilities associated with Piaget's four stages occur in the same order across cultures* (Berry et al., 1992). For example, children understand object permanence (stage 1) before symbolic thinking blooms (stage 2). Formal operational thinking (stage 4) may not be as common as Piaget believed, but when it occurs, it is mastered after concrete reasoning (stage 3) develops.

Second, *children acquire many cognitive skills at an earlier age than Piaget believed.* As Figure 11.18 shows, even 3½- to 4½-month-olds display a basic grasp of objective permanence when they are tested on special tasks that do not require them to physically search for a hidden object (Baillargeon, 1987). Similarly, young children make fewer conservation errors and show less egocentric thinking when tested on tasks that are more familiar or depend less on language than the tasks Piaget used (Borke, 1975).

Third, *cognitive development within each stage seems to proceed inconsistently.* A child may perform at the preoperational level on some tasks, yet solve other tasks at a concrete operational level (Dasen, 1975; Siegler, 1981). This problem goes to

FIGURE 11.17 Piaget used the three-mountain problem to illustrate the egocentrism of young children. Suppose that a preoperational child named Ted is looking at the mountains just as you are. Another child, Susan, is standing at the opposite (far) side of the table. Ted is asked what Susan sees. Because Ted is able to see the road he will mistakenly say that Susan also can see it, indicating that he has failed to recognize Susan's perspective as different from his own.

➤ 11. How does thinking change during the concrete and formal operational stages?

➤ 12. In what major ways does research support and contradict Piaget's basic ideas?

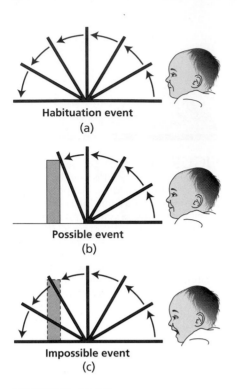

Habituation event
(a)

Possible event
(b)

Impossible event
(c)

FIGURE 11.18 (a) *Habituation.* Renée Baillargeon (1987) repeatedly exposes young infants to a screen that slowly rotates 180°. Eventually, they habituate and become bored. Then the infants watch as a box is placed in the screen's path. (b) *Possible event.* The screen rotates, conceals the infant's view of the box, and then stops as the box blocks it. (c) *Impossible event.* The screen rotates, conceals the view of the box, and continues a full 180° because the box is secretly removed. Infants stare longer at the "impossible" than at the "possible" event, as if they are surprised that the box did not stop the screen. This can only happen, reasons Baillargeon, if the infants understand that the box continues to exist even when concealed from view (i.e., object permanence).

Adapted from Baillargeon, 1987.

➤ 13. What is the "zone of proximal development" and why is it important?"

the heart of the continuity-discontinuity debate. If development proceeds in qualitatively distinct stages, then a child at a given stage should *not* show large inconsistencies in solving conceptually similar tasks.

Fourth, *culture influences cognitive development.* Piaget's Western perspective equated "cognitive development" with scientific-logical thinking, but many cultures do not share this view. As David Matsumoto and Philip Hull note:

> Different societies value and reward different skills and behaviors. . . . Many cultures . . . consider cognitive development to be more relational, involving the thinking skills and processes to engage in successful interpersonal contexts. (Matsumoto & Hull, 1994, p. 105)

Compared with Westerners, people from underdeveloped countries or tribal societies often appear to show a large "age-delay" or achieve less success in solving Piaget's concrete and formal operational tasks. But these differences shrink or disappear when culturally appropriate tasks are chosen, when researchers speak the native language, or when children receive special training or formal schooling (Jahoda, 1983).

So what are we to conclude? Newer research challenges some of Piaget's ideas, but he revolutionized thinking about children's cognitive development. His work continues to guide many researchers, called *neo-Piagetians,* who have modified his theory to account for some of the issues discussed above (Flavell et al., 1985).

Vygotsky: The Social Context of Cognitive Development

Whereas Piaget focused mainly on children's independent exploration of the physical world, Russian psychologist Lev Vygotsky (1935/1978) emphasized that children also live in *social* world, and that cognitive development occurs in a sociocultural context. In all types of daily interactions, including fantasy play, adults and older peers stimulate children's cognitive growth and provide them with knowledge about the world.

To illustrate a key aspect of Vygotsky's approach, suppose that 5-year-olds Ray and Juanita have similar scores on cognitive tests, and that neither child can solve Piaget's conservation problems. However, with guidance from a parent, teacher, or older sibling, Juanita "gets it" and can now solve these problems. Ray, even with assistance, just doesn't understand. Were these two children really at the same cognitive level to begin with? Vygotsky says no, introducing a concept called the **zone of proximal development:** the difference between what a child can do independently, and what the child can do with assistance from adults or more advanced peers.

Why is the zone of proximal development important? For one thing, it helps us recognize "those functions that have not yet matured but are in the process of maturation . . ." (Vygotsky, 1935/1978, p. 86). In other words, it gives us an idea of what children may soon be able to do on their own. Second, this concept emphasizes that people can provide experiences and feedback that "move" a child's cognitive development forward within limits (the "zone") dictated by the child's level of biological maturation (Plumert & Nichols-Whitehead, 1996).

Even having older siblings around the house may stimulate a younger child's cognitive development, as long as the child is biologically ready for the input. In one study of 2- to 6-year-old English and Japanese children, those over age 3 who grew up with older brothers and sisters performed better on a cognitive task than children who grew up alone or with younger brothers and sisters (Ruffman et al., 1998). However, 2- to 3-year-olds performed poorly on the task regardless of how many older or younger siblings they had. The task was simply beyond their current cognitive capacity.

Information-Processing Approaches

Many researchers believe that cognitive development is best examined within an information-processing framework. For example, young children may be unable to solve conservation problems because they pay insufficient attention to the task, don't search for key information, or are unable to simultaneously hold enough pieces of information in memory (Siegler, 1986, 1996).

Consider children's *information-search strategies.* Look at the two houses in Figure 11.19. Are they identical or different? This visual scanning task is easy for you or me, but not for young children. Elaine Vurpillot (1968) recorded the eye movements of 3- to 10-year-olds while they examined these and other sets of houses. Older children methodically scanned the houses, but preschoolers often looked at only a few windows and failed to compare each window in the house on the left to the corresponding window in the house on the right. In short, preschoolers were less able to systematically search for relevant details.

Information-processing speed also improves during childhood, as Robert Kail's (1991) review of 72 studies shows in Figure 11.20. Notice that processing speed improves continuously and that the relatively rapid rate of change between ages 8 to about 12 slows during adolescence.

Memory capabilities expand significantly during childhood. When it comes to organizing information and using strategies to improve memory, preschoolers fall far short of school-aged children. John Flavell (1970) gave children lists of words or numbers to remember. Preschoolers rarely used rehearsal spontaneously, whereas 8- to 10-year-olds often could be heard rehearsing words or numbers under their breath. Similarly, young children do not make effective use of "chunking," an organizational strategy for grouping related objects or words together (Brown et al., 1983).

Metacognition refers to an awareness of one's own cognitive processes. Older children display greater awareness of their own mental processes than do younger children (Flavell, 1985). For example, older children are better at judging how well they understand material for a test or directions to someone's house. In turn, this can help them decide whether they need to study more or ask for a map.

> ➤ 14. Describe how information-processing capabilities improve during childhood. How is this relevant to the continuity-discontinuity debate?

FIGURE 11.19 Stimuli used by Vurpillot to assess visual inspection through filmed eye movements. Preschoolers fail to scan the pictures systematically, which often leads them to claim that the two houses are identical.

Based on Vurpillot, 1968.

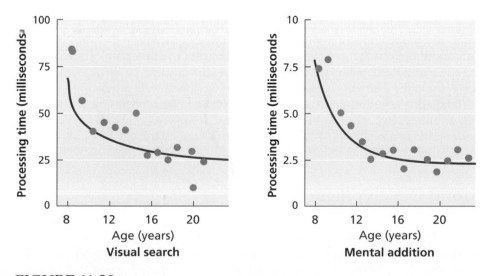

FIGURE 11.20 These two graphs show how information processing speed for visual search and mental addition tasks becomes faster with age. The relatively rapid rate of change between ages 8 to about 12 slows during adolescence. A similar nonlinear pattern also occurs on name retrieval, mental rotation, and other cognitive tasks.

Data from Kail (1988, 1991).

Many researchers who adopt an information-processing approach believe that cognitive development is a continuous, gradual process in which the same set of processing abilities become more efficient over time. But neo-Piagetian theorists believe that children also acquire new modes of processing information as they age (Flavell, 1985). This debate is far from resolved, and some argue that development involves both discontinuity (stages) *and* continuity. For example, Susan Gathercole (1998) suggests that memory capabilities change qualitatively (i.e., new abilities emerge) between infancy and age 7, but then undergo only gradual quantitative improvements through adolescence. Robbie Case (1987, 1996) offers another integrative view, proposing that gradual increases in information-processing capabilities within stages enable children to move qualitatively from one stage of cognitive development to the next. More research is needed to determine which of these approaches proves most useful.

Theory of Mind: Children's Understanding of Mental States

> ➤ 15. At what age do children begin to understand other people's thinking? How have researchers established this?

The term **theory of mind** refers to a person's beliefs about the "mind" and ability to understand other people's mental states. Piaget believed that children younger than 6 or 7 poorly understand how mental processes work and therefore have trouble recognizing what other people are thinking. Indeed, this is what Piaget's concept of egocentrism is all about: not being able to understand how someone else is perceiving a situation. But consider the following story:

> Susie puts a candy bar inside a green box on the table, and then she goes away. Then her mother takes the candy bar out of the box and puts it inside a red bag on the bed. Susie doesn't see her mother do this. Later, Susie comes back and wants to get her candy because she is hungry. Where will Susie look for her candy bar?

On problems like this, most 2- and 3-year-olds indicate that Susie will look in the red bag, as if she had the same knowledge that they have. Piaget would not be surprised. But most 4-year-olds say she will choose the green box, recognizing that Susie does not have the information they do. Thus at some level, they comprehend that Susie's mental state—her "mind"—is different from theirs. Using culturally equivalent examples, studies with young children from African tribal societies, Canada, China, Japan, the United Kingdom, and the United States obtain similar findings (Avis & Harris, 1991; Ruffman et al., 1998).

Lying and deception also provide evidence of theory of mind. They imply an ability to recognize that one person can have information that another does not, and therefore that we can influence what other people think by withholding the truth. Researchers find that most 3-year-olds are capable of trying to deceive someone else and recognize the difference between providing someone with false information due to a lie, and providing false information due to an innocent mistake (Carlson et al., 1998). Overall, it appears that children begin to understand some aspects of other people's thinking by the age of 3 to 4, well before Piaget proposed (Ritblatt, 2000).

Moral Development

All societies have norms of moral conduct, and a major goal of socialization is to help children recognize "right" from "wrong" and become moral adults. Sigmund Freud (1935) believed that children develop a moral conscience (i.e., they *internalize* society's moral norms) by identifying with their parents. B. F. Skinner (1971) proposed that we learn which behaviors and values are "good" and "bad" through their association with reinforcement and punishment. And Piaget (1932) viewed moral development as a cognitive process in which children pass from a simple stage of believing that actions are good or bad because adults say so, to a more complex stage of believing that morality involves subjective judgments about fairness.

Kohlberg's Stage Model

Drawing upon Piaget's model of cognitive development, Lawrence Kohlberg (1963, 1984) developed a highly influential theory of moral reasoning. He presented children, adolescents, and adults with hypothetical moral dilemmas like the following:

> Heinz's wife was dying from cancer. A rare drug might save her, but the druggist who made the drug for $200 would not sell it for less than $2,000. Heinz tried hard, but he could only raise $1,000. The druggist refused to give Heinz the drug for that price even though Heinz promised to pay the rest later. So Heinz broke into the store to steal the drug. What do you think? Should Heinz have stolen the drug? Why or why not?

Kohlberg was interested not in whether people agreed or disagreed with Heinz's behavior, but in the *reasons for their judgment.* He analyzed responses to various moral dilemmas and concluded that there are three main levels of moral reasoning, with two substages within each level (Table 11.2).

Preconventional moral reasoning is based on anticipated punishments or rewards. Consider reasons given for stealing the drug. In stage 1, children focus on punishment: "Heinz should steal the drug because, if he lets his wife die he'll get into trouble." In stage, 2 morality is judged by anticipated rewards and doing what is in the person's own interest: "Heinz should steal the drug because that way he'll still have his wife with him."

Conventional moral reasoning is based on conformity to social expectations, laws, and duties. In stage 3, conformity stems from the desire to gain people's approval: "People will think that Heinz is bad if he doesn't steal the drug

➤ 16. How do preconventional, conventional, and postconventional moral reasoning differ?

TABLE 11.2 KOHLBERG'S STAGES OF MORAL REASONING	
Level of Moral Reasoning	**Basis for Judging What Is Moral**
Level 1: Preconventional	Actual or anticipated punishment and rewards, rather than internalized values
Stage 1: Punishment/obedience orientation	Obeying rules and avoiding punishment
Stage 2: Instrumental/hedonistic orientation	Self-interest and gaining rewards
Level 2: Conventional	Conformity to the expectations of social groups; person adopts other people's values
Stage 3: Good child orientation	Gaining approval and maintaining good relations with others
Stage 4: Law and order orientation	Doing one's duty, showing respect for authority, and maintaining social order
Level 3: Postconventional	Moral principles that are well thought out and part of one's belief and value system
Stage 5: Social contract orientation	General principles agreed upon by society that foster community welfare and individual rights; recognition that society can decide to modify laws that lose their social utility
Stage 6: Universal ethical principles	Abstract ethical principles based on justice and equality; following one's conscience

Source: Based on Kohlberg, 1963, 1984.

to save his wife." In stage 4, children believe that laws and duties must be obeyed simply because rules are meant to be followed. Thus: "Heinz should steal the drug because it's his duty to take care of his wife."

Postconventional moral reasoning is based on well thought out, general moral principles. Stage 5 involves recognizing the importance of societal laws, but also taking individual rights into account. Thus "Stealing breaks the law, but what Heinz did was reasonable because he saved a life." In stage 6, morality is based on abstract, ethical principles of justice that are viewed as universal. For example, "Saving life comes before financial gain, even if the person is a stranger. The law in this case is unjust, and stealing the drug is the morally right thing to do."

Kohlberg believed that progress in moral reasoning depends upon general cognitive maturation and the opportunity to confront moral issues, particularly when such issues can be discussed with someone who is at a higher stage of development. Moral education programs based on Kohlberg's theory have been applied in schools, prisons, and with at-risk youth (Higgins, 1991).

Culture, Gender, and Moral Reasoning

▶ 17. What aspects of Kohlberg's model have been supported? What are its limitations?

Researchers have studied moral reasoning throughout North, Central, and South America, Africa, Asia, Europe, and India (Colby et al., 1983; Eckensberger & Zimba, 1997). Overall, findings indicate that

- As we age from childhood through adolescence, moral reasoning changes from preconventional to conventional levels (Figure 11.21).
- Even in adulthood, postconventional reasoning is relatively uncommon, though its frequency varies across cultures.
- Levels are not skipped. Preconventional reasoning occurs before conventional reasoning, and when it occurs, postconventional reasoning is last to emerge.
- A person's moral judgments do not always reflect the same level or stage within levels.

Research using Kohlberg's tasks also finds that postconventional reasoning occurs more often among people from Westernized, formally educated, and middle- or upper-class backgrounds than among people in developing countries. Critics, however, claim that the theory has a Western cultural bias. Fairness and justice are Kohlberg's postconventional ideals, but in many cultures the highest moral values focus on principles that do not fit easily into Kohlberg's model: benevolence, nonviolence, respect for all animal life, protecting the souls of dead ancestors from harm, respect for the elderly, and collective harmony (Eckensberger & Zimba, 1997). Critics charge that when people respond to Kohlberg's moral dilemmas, answers that involve such concepts are often "scored" as reflecting a lower level of reasoning than they should be.

Another criticism concerns gender bias. Carol Gilligan (1982) argued that Kohlberg's emphasis on "justice" primarily reflects a male perspective. She claimed that highly moral women place greater value than men do on caring and responsibility for others' welfare. Overall, however, evidence of such gender bias is mixed, and most cross-cultural studies find that females and males display similar levels of moral reasoning (Eckensberger & Zimba, 1997). Females use justice reason-

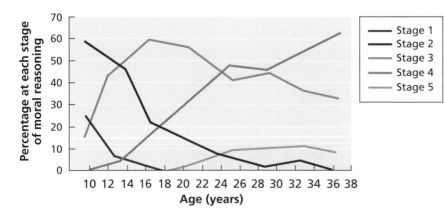

FIGURE 11.21 In this study based on Kohlberg's model, 58 American boys responded to moral dilemmas over more than 20 years. As they aged, preconventional morality (stages 1 and 2) decreased and conventional morality (stages 3 and 4) took precedence during adolescence. Postconventional moral reasoning was not common at any age.
Based on Colby et al., 1983.

ing when the situation calls for it, and males use reasoning based on caring and relationships when appropriate (Friedman et al., 1987; Walker, 1987). Nevertheless, Gilligan's analysis reinforces the key point that high-level moral reasoning can be based on values other than "justice" (Gump et al., 2000).

Critics also charge that the model focuses too heavily on moral thinking and not enough on moral behavior. We cannot assume, for example, that people at more advanced stages in Kohlberg's model always behave more morally (Richards et al., 1992). Remember, what determines someone's stage of reasoning is not whether they feel that stealing or other actions are right or wrong, but the types of justification given for their belief. Further, moral behavior may vary across situations: Cheating, honesty, or altruism in academic situations may not necessarily predict similar behaviors elsewhere. In general, moral behavior is more consistent across situations and is tied more strongly to moral beliefs in adulthood than in childhood (Blasi, 1980).

In sum, research relating culture and gender to moral behavior reminds us of an important point. Moral development is not just a cognitive process: It has a behavioral component, it overlaps with other aspects of personality development, and it occurs within a social context (Killen et al., 2000).

Personality and Social Development

Children grow not only physically and mentally, but also socially and emotionally. They form attachments and relationships, and each child displays a unique *personality*—a distinctive yet somewhat consistent pattern of thinking, feeling, and behaving. Sigmund Freud (1933/1964) believed that adult personality is largely established during the first five years of our life. Research does not support this view, but it supports Freud's general point that childhood is a special period of personality and social development.

Erikson's Psychosocial Theory

Psychoanalytic psychologist Erik Erikson (1963, 1968) believed that personality develops through confronting a series of eight major **psychosocial stages,** each of which involves a different "crisis" (i.e., conflict) over how we view ourselves in relation to other people and the world. Each crisis is present throughout life, but takes on special importance during a particular age period. As Table 11.3 shows, four crises occur in infancy and childhood:

➤ 18. What does Erikson's model imply regarding the stability of personality?

- *Basic trust versus basic mistrust.* During the first year of life we depend totally on our parents or other caretakers. How adequately our needs are met, and how much love and attention we receive, determine whether we develop a basic trust or basic mistrust of the world.

- *Autonomy versus shame and doubt.* During the next two years, children become ready to separate themselves from their parents and exercise their individuality. If parents unduly restrict children or make harsh demands during toilet training, children develop shame and doubt about their abilities and later lack the courage to be independent.

- *Initiative versus guilt.* From age three through age five, children display great curiosity about the world. If they are allowed freedom to explore and receive answers to their questions, they develop a sense of initiative. If they are held back or punished, they develop guilt about their desires and suppress their curiosity.

- *Industry versus inferiority.* From age six until puberty, the child's life expands into school and peer activities. Children who experience pride and encouragement in mastering tasks develop "industry"—a striving to achieve. Repeated failure and lack of praise for trying leads to a sense of inferiority.

TABLE 11.3 ERIKSON'S PSYCHOSOCIAL STAGES

Age (years)	Major Psychosocial Crisis
First year	Basic trust vs. mistrust
1–2	Autonomy vs. shame and doubt
3–5	Initiative vs. guilt
6–12	Industry vs. inferiority
12–20	Identity vs role confusion
20–40	Intimacy vs. isolation
40–65	Generativity vs. stagnation
65+	Integrity vs. despair

Although critics argue that Erikson's model lacks detail and question its "stage" approach, the model successfully captures several major issues that developing children confront. Because each stage of life creates new opportunities, personality is not fixed in childhood. Yet, as Erikson proposed and as some research supports, successfully resolving each crisis helps prepare us to meet the next (Hazen & Durrett, 1982; Kahn et al., 1985). Like the early chapters of a novel, themes that emerge in childhood help set the stage for the unfolding story of our lives.

➤ 19. Does infants' temperament predict their childhood behavior? Does children's temperament predict their adult functioning?

Do the roots of adult personality truly reside in childhood? Our *Psychological Frontiers* feature examines another approach to this issue.

PSYCHOLOGICAL FRONTIERS

You Were Such a Fussy Baby: Does Early Temperament Predict Adult Functioning?

From their moment of birth, infants differ from one another in **temperament**—a biologically based general style of reacting emotionally and behaviorally to the environment. Some infants are calm and happy, others are irritable and fussy. Some are outgoing and active, others shy and inactive. Indeed, within any age group—children, adolescents, or adults—people differ in temperament (McCrae & Costa, 1990; Shiner, 1998). The question is, does our early temperament predict how we will function as adults?

In a pioneering study, Alexander Thomas and Stella Chess (1977, 1986) had parents describe their babies' behavior and found that most infants could be classified into three groups. *Easy infants* (40 percent of the sample) had regular sleeping and feeding patterns, reacted positively to new situations, were playful, and accepted frustration with little fuss. *Difficult infants* (about 10 percent) were irritable, had irregular eating and sleeping patterns, reacted negatively to new situations, and threw tantrums when frustrated. *Slow to warm-up infants* (about 15 percent) were the least active, had mildly negative responses to new situations, but slowly adapted over time. Over the next 10 years children's temperamental styles were moderately consistent, and those who had been "difficult infants" were most likely to have subsequent emotional and behavior problems.

This study attracted much admiration, but many researchers criticized its classification system and exclusive reliance on parental reports. Alternative categories were developed, and researchers now try to measure temperament by directly observing infants and children, and by getting ratings from parents *and* other adults.

▶ Temperament in Infancy and Childhood

Based on these newer approaches, it appears that temperament is only weakly to moderately stable during infancy (Plomin et al., 1993; Carnicero et al., 2000). Some infants maintain a consistent temperament between their first and second years of life, while others change. Consider shyness, which forms part of a more general temperament style called *behavioral inhibition* (Reznick et al., 1992). Inhibited infants are quiet and timid, but cry and withdraw when exposed to unfamiliar people, places, objects, and sounds. Uninhibited infants are more sociable, verbal, and spontaneous.

Jerome Kagan and his Harvard coworkers (Kagan et al., 1988; Kagan & Snidman, 1991) found that about 20 to 25 percent of infants displayed this inhibited pattern, which remained moderately stable during infancy. Compared with their uninhibited peers, inhibited infants became more physiologically aroused when exposed to novel stimuli, which Kagan attributes to fear and anxiety that causes them to withdraw.

The infants were studied into childhood, up to age 7 1/2 years. For the vast majority—those who were only mildly to moderately inhibited or uninhibited between the ages of 1 and 2 years—their temperament did not predict how shy or outgoing they would be as children. But for infants who were *extremely* uninhibited or inhibited (the "top" 15 percent of each group) the findings were different. Highly uninhibited infants became sociable and talkative 7-year-olds. Extremely inhibited infants developed into quiet, cautious, and socially avoidant 7-year-olds who, when exposed to novel stimuli, had faster heart rates and higher stress hor-

–Continued

mone levels than their peers. Thus for older infants who are highly inhibited or uninhibited, temperament may predict childhood shyness and sociability (Kagan, 1989).

Is there just one type of shyness? At Arizona State University, Nancy Eisenberg and her colleagues (1998) observed 6- to 8-year-olds during natural play. They also had parents and teachers fill out questionnaires about the children at this age, and two and four years later. They found that one type of shyness reflected caution and timidity when interacting with unfamiliar people, and a second type involved concern about evaluation when interacting with classmates. Both types of shyness were moderately stable over four years and occurred to a similar degree in boys and girls. Individually, some children were in both ways, others in just one.

▶ Does Childhood Temperament Predict Adult Outcomes?

Demonstrating that temperament has some stability during childhood is one thing. Showing that it can predict how we function as adults is another. Avshalom Caspi of the University of Wisconsin and his coworkers (1988) followed shy, behaviorally inhibited boys and girls from the time they were 10 to 12 years of age into their forties. Men who had been shy boys tended to delay marriage, fatherhood, and establishing a career for several years, possibly reflecting their reluctance to enter new and unfamiliar social situations. Women who had been shy girls were more likely to quit work after marriage and become homemakers. In a Swedish study, men who had been shy boys displayed this same tendency to delay marriage and fatherhood, whereas shy girls delayed marriage and attained less education (Kerr et al., 1996).

Does temperament in *early* childhood also predict adult functioning? Denise Newman, Caspi, and their colleagues (1997) measured the temperament of 961 New Zealanders at age 3, based on a 90-minute observation of each child. At age 21, participants completed questionnaires about their life, and either a spouse, close friend, or relative described each participant's strengths and problems. Compared with 3-years-olds with a *well-adjusted* temperament, those who were *undercontrolled* (e.g., irritable, impulsive, inattentive, physically overactive) or *inhibited* (socially shy and fearful, low self-confidence) functioned differently as adults. The undercontrolled group reported more antisocial behavior, greater conflict in family and romantic relationships, and was more likely to have been fired from a job. Other people rated them as unreliable.

In contrast, the inhibited group showed normal adjustment in their romantic relationships and at the workplace, but reported having less overall companionship, less emotional nurturance, and less guidance in their lives. In general, they had a smaller social support network, and other people rated them as less affiliative and less socially attractive.

In sum, most infants and young children fall within a middle range on temperamental traits. They are either well adjusted, or mildly to moderately inhibited or undercontrolled. *Within* this group, differences in early temperament do not substantially predict who will function best as adults. But for those who have strong temperamental traits, early temperament can give us a peek into later childhood and early adulthood functioning.

Newman, Caspi, and their colleagues emphasize that we should not expect early temperament to do a good job of predicting any single adult behavior. Rather, temperament better predicts different overall *patterns* of functioning. As they note, it is remarkable that a mere 90-minute observation of children at age 3 can modestly predict different patterns of adjustment 18 years later.

Attachment

Imagine a single-file procession of ducklings following you around campus and everywhere you go, as if you were their mother. For this to happen, we need only isolate the ducklings after they hatch and then expose them to you at a certain time. If they later encounter their real parents the ducklings will ignore them and continue to follow you. If the only moving object the ducklings see for their first 24 hours is a model duck or ball, they will faithfully follow that object as they grow up (Hess, 1959).

German ethologist Konrad Lorenz (1937) called this sudden, biologically primed form of attachment **imprinting** (Figure 11.22*a*). It occurs in some species of birds, including ducks, chickens, and geese, and in a few mammals, such as shrews. Imprinting illustrates the concept of *critical periods*. In mallard ducklings, for example, the strongest imprinting takes place within a day after hatching, and by 2½ days the capacity to imprint is lost (Hess, 1959). Thus depending on the species, offspring *must* be exposed to parents within hours or days after entering the world to attach to them.

Attachment refers to the strong emotional bond that develops between children and their primary caregivers (Figure 11.22*b*). Human infants do not automatically imprint on a caregiver the way that ducklings do, and there is not an immediate postbirth critical period where contact is required for infant-caregiver bonding. Instead, the first few years of life seem to be a *sensitive period* when we

➤ 20. How does imprinting illustrate the concept of critical periods?

(a)   (b)

FIGURE 11.22 (a) During a short critical period after birth the offspring in some species permanently "imprint" on their parents—or in this case—on ethologist Konrad Lorenz. (b) In humans, infant-caretaker attachment is more complex and forms over a much longer period.

➤ 21. How did Harlow demonstrate the importance of contact comfort?

FIGURE 11.23 Infant monkeys reared with a cloth-covered surrogate from birth clung to it as they would a real mother, and they preferred to remain in contact with the terry cloth mother even though the wire mother satisfied nutritional needs.

From Harlow, 1958.

➤ 22. According to Bowlby, what are the phases of attachment in infancy?

➤ 23. Does separation anxiety follow a similar pattern across cultures? What is the adaptive value of separation anxiety?

most easily form a first attachment to caregivers, a bond that enhances our social and personality adjustment later in life (Masten & Coatsworth, 1998; Schore, 1996). But although it may be more difficult, strong first attachments to caregivers can still be formed later in childhood.

The attachment process. For decades, people assumed that infant-caregiver bonding resulted primarily from the mother's role in satisfying the infant's need for nourishment. Harry Harlow (1958) tested this notion by separating infant rhesus monkeys from their biological mothers shortly after birth. Each infant was raised in a cage with two artificial, "surrogate" mothers. One was a bare wire cylinder with a feeding bottle attached to its "chest." The other was a wire cylinder covered with soft terry cloth, without a feeding bottle (Figure 11.23).

Faced with this choice, the infant monkeys became attached to the cloth mother. When they were exposed to frightening situations or removed from their cages and later returned, the infants ran to the terry cloth figure and clung tightly to it. They even maintained contact with the cloth mother while feeding from the wire mother's bottle. Thus Harlow showed that *contact comfort*—body contact with a comforting object—is more important in fostering attachment than the provision of nourishment.

Coinciding with Harlow's monkey research, pioneering studies of human attachment were conducted in several societies, ranging from rural Africa to urban Europe and North America (Ainsworth, 1967; Bowlby, 1958). Based on this work, British psychoanalyst John Bowlby (1969) proposed that attachment during infancy develops in three phases:

- *Indiscriminate attachment behavior.* Newborns cry, vocalize, and smile, and they emit these behaviors toward everyone. In turn, these behaviors evoke caregiving from adults.

- *Discriminate attachment behavior.* Around 3 months of age, infants direct their attachment behaviors more toward familiar, regular caregivers, than toward strangers.

- *Specific attachment behavior.* By 7 or 8 months of age, infants develop their first meaningful attachment to specific caregivers. Infants smile more at these caregivers, hold out their arms to be picked up by them, and want to be in their presence. The caregiver becomes a "secure base" from which the infant can crawl about and explore the environment.

Interestingly, as an infant's attachment becomes more focused, two types of anxiety occur. Typically, **stranger anxiety** occurs first, often emerging around age 6 or 7 months, and ending before the infant is 18 months old. If a stranger approaches and touches the infant, or if the infant is handed over by a caregiver to a stranger, the infant will become afraid, cry, and reach for the caregiver. **Separation anxiety** typically begins a little later, peaks around age 12 to 16 months, and disappears between 2 and 3 years of age (Kagan et al., 1978). Here the infant becomes anxious and cries when the caregiver is out of sight. Both forms of anxiety show a similar pattern across many cultures (Figure 11.24).

Some theorists propose that these responses may stem from infants' increasing cognitive abilities (Kagan, 1972). For example, newborns don't have well-formed schemas that enable them to distinguish strangers from nonstrangers. However, as these schemas develop, stranger anxiety emerges. Others suggest that stranger and separation anxiety are adaptive reactions shaped over the course of evolution (Bowlby, 1973). At an age when infants master crawling and then learn to walk, fear of strangers and of separation help prevent infants from wandering beyond the sight of their caretakers, especially in unfamiliar situations.

Around age 3 to 4, as children's cognitive and verbal skills grow, they develop a better understanding of their attachment relationships. According to Bowlby (1969), a stage of *goal-corrected partnership* emerges in which children and caregivers can describe their wishes and feelings to each other, and their relationship can be maintained whether they are together or apart.

Variations in attachment.   Infants progress through similar attachment stages, but they develop different types of attachments with their caretakers. Psychologist Mary Ainsworth and her colleagues (1978) developed a standard procedure called the **strange situation** for examining infant attachment. The infant, typically a 12- to 18-month-old, first plays with toys in the mother's presence. Then a stranger enters the room and interacts with the child. Soon the mother leaves the child with the stranger. Later the stranger leaves and the child is alone. Finally, the mother returns. The infant's behavior is observed throughout this procedure.

In the mother's presence *securely attached* infants explore the playroom and react positively to strangers (Ainsworth et al., 1978). They are distressed when she leaves and happily greet her when she returns. In contrast, there are two types of *insecurely attached* infants. *Anxious-resistant* infants are fearful when the mother is present, demand her attention, and are highly distressed when she leaves. They are not soothed when she returns and may angrily resist her attempts at contact. *Anxious-avoidant* infants show few signs of attachment and seldom cry when the mother leaves. They don't seek contact when she returns, but won't resist contact if the mother initiates it.

Across most cultures studied, about half to three quarters of infants are securely attached. Correlational studies find that mothers who are sensitive to their babies' needs at home tend to have infants who are securely attached in the "strange situation" (Ainsworth et al., 1978). In contrast, mothers who respond to their babies more slowly and inconsistently tend to have insecure infants.

Attachment and later behavior.   Most researchers believe that early attachment has a long-term influence on children's adjustment (Ainsworth & Bowlby, 1991; Masten & Coatsworth, 1998). Elementary school children who are securely attached as infants seem better adjusted socially, have higher self-esteem, and are better behaved in school. In contrast, those who are insecurely attached as infants are more likely to have behavioral problems in school, be overly aggressive, and show attention-seeking behavior in the classroom (Ainsworth, 1989). This research lends credence to Erikson's view that establishing a stable, trusting relationship with a caregiver is an important component of early social development.

Attachment Deprivation

If infants and young children are deprived of a stable attachment with a caregiver, how do they fare in the long run?

Isolate monkeys and children.   Harry Harlow studied this issue under controlled conditions. After rearing "isolate" monkeys either alone or with artificial surrogate mothers, Harlow returned them to the monkey colony at 6 months of age. Exposed to other monkeys, the isolates were indifferent, terrified, or aggressive. When they became adults, these monkeys could not copulate normally. Some female isolates were artificially inseminated, and as parents they were

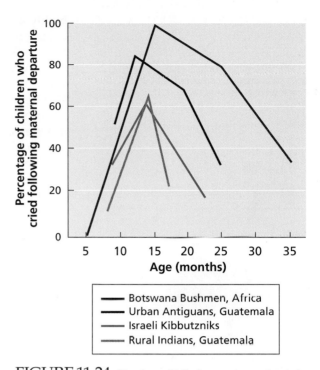

FIGURE 11.24   The rise and fall of separation anxiety in infancy shows a similar pattern across cultures.
Based on Kagan et al., 1978.

➤ 24. What is the "strange situation"? Describe the styles of attachment identified by this procedure.

➤ 25. How do studies of monkey and human child isolates, and of children in orphanages, help us resolve whether attachment involves critical or sensitive periods?

➤ 26. Why might Victor's recovery have been so limited, as compared with that of the Czech twins?

FIGURE 11.25 Stephan Suomi and Harry Harlow (1972) raised four male monkeys in social isolation for 6 months after birth. They were then exposed several months to normal female monkeys who were three months younger. In this photo, the younger monkey is comforting the older isolate monkey. In the presence of an energetic but nonthreatening young companion, the isolates gradually became interactive, playful, and well adjusted.

➤ 27. Does day care impair infants' attachment? Does it seem to have long-term effects on children?

highly abusive toward their firstborns (Harlow & Suomi, 1970). Clearly, having being raised without attachment to a real, interactive caregiver produced long-term social impairment.

What of isolate human children? Victor, the Wild Boy of Aveyron, was severely impaired after his isolation and showed only limited recovery after intensive remedial training. But was it a lack of human contact that severely stunted Victor's development, or was it brain damage, possibly present from birth? And if severe isolation was the cause, are its negative effects impossible to reverse?

In the 1960s, in Czechoslovakia, twin boys were forced by their father and stepmother to live in extreme isolation beginning at age 1½. The twins were discovered at age 7, emotionally and socially retarded, with the cognitive development of a 3-year-old and speech skills of a 2-year-old. Jarmila Koluchova (1972, 1991) studied the boys for over 20 years and found that they became happy, sociable, and firmly attached to their foster family. Their IQ increased to normal levels and they became well-adjusted adolescents and young adults.

Why the difference? In case studies such as these, we can only speculate. Unlike Victor, the twins had each other's company, though this cannot explain why "single" isolate children have recovered. The twins' isolation ended—and their rehabilitation began—at a younger age when the brain's neural plasticity is greater (Victor was about 12). Moreover, in their first year of recovery, the twins were well cared for in a home that allowed them to interact with younger, nonthreatening preschool children. Harlow's monkey research had already demonstrated the value of this "younger companion" approach (Figure 11.25).

Children raised in orphanages. Even when orphaned children are raised with little attention in substandard institutions, those adopted during their first year or two typically become attached to their new caregivers and show normal intellectual functioning within a few years (Dennis, 1973). But what about children adopted at an older age? Barbara Tizard and Jill Hodges (1978) studied children raised in stimulating, high-quality orphanages. The nurses were attentive, but the turnover was so high that the children had no opportunity to form a stable bond with any caregiver. Yet the vast majority adopted between ages 2 to 8 years formed healthy attachments with their adopted parents, though in adolescence many had difficulty forming peer relationships because they came across as needing "too much attention" (Hodges & Tizard, 1989).

In sum, it appears that infancy is a sensitive (not critical) period where an initial attachment to caregivers forms most easily and facilitates subsequent development. Prolonged attachment deprivation creates developmental risks, but when deprived children are placed into a nurturing environment at a young enough age, most become attached to their caretakers and grow into well-adjusted adults.

The Day-Care Controversy

As a child, were you in day care? Over half of American preschoolers are cared for during the day by someone other than a parent, and most who enter day care do so before age 1 (Scarr, 1998). High-quality day care provides a stimulating environment with well-trained caretakers, few children per caretaker, and low staff turnover, whereas poor day care does the opposite. But in either case, many parents worry about how day care will affect their child's development. Thirty years of research—mostly in North America, Sweden, and other European countries—suggests some surprising conclusions.

- *Attachment.* Overall, as measured by the *strange situation procedure*, day care *does not* seem to disrupt infants' attachment to their parents, even when day care begins in early infancy and occurs for many hours a week (National Institute of Child Health and Human Development/NICHD, 1997; Scarr, 1998). However, if several negative factors combine—day care is poor, the child spends many hours there, parents are not sensitive to the child at home, and the child has multiple day-care arrangements—the risk of insecure attachment increases.

- *Other parent-child interactions.* Compared with families not using day care, infants and toddlers in day care are slightly less engaged and sociable toward their mothers when tested during a play situation, and their mothers are slightly less sensitive (e.g., less supportive, more intrusive) toward them (NICHD, 1999). But there is no relation between these patterns and children's attachment to their mother.

- *Long-term effects.* Infants and preschoolers from low-income families who receive high-quality day care tend to be better adjusted socially and perform better in elementary school than their peers who either receive poor-quality day care or do not attend day care (Scarr, 1998). For infants and preschoolers from middle- and upper-income homes, their day-care experience—regardless of quality—seems to have little carry-over effect to their elementary school years. Rather, the quality of their family experiences is more important in predicting social adjustment and academic performance in school.

This last point is underscored in a study of *after-school care* (Vandell & Ramanan, 1991). Among 390 third- through fifth-graders who either attended adult-supervised after-school programs, cared for themselves, or were cared for by their mothers, the type of after-school care was a less important predictor of children's psychological adjustment than was the quality of their relationships with their families.

Concerns about disrupted parent-child relations also surface when parents divorce. Our *Applications of Psychological Science* feature examines this societally important issue.

➤ 28. In the short and long term, how do children generally respond to parental divorce? What factors enhance their adjustment to divorce and remarriage?

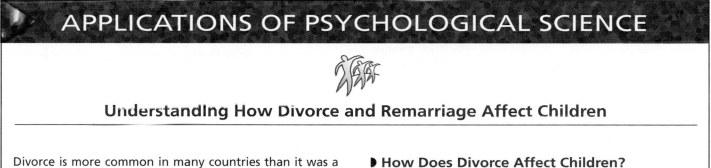

APPLICATIONS OF PSYCHOLOGICAL SCIENCE

Understanding How Divorce and Remarriage Affect Children

Divorce is more common in many countries than it was a half-century ago, and it creates a stressful life transition for parents and their children. Because most divorced parents remarry, they and their children also experience a second major transition: becoming part of a stepfamily. In the United States, about half of children from divorced families have to make this adjustment within only four years after their parents' divorce (Hetherington et al., 1998).

Decades ago there was little scientific information on children of divorce and remarriage, but research now provides us with a better understanding of how these major events affect children. With this knowledge, local governments in over 35 American states now require soon-to-be-divorced parents to take special classes that focus on helping children cope with divorce.

▶ How Does Divorce Affect Children?

Many children report that parental divorce is one of the most painful experiences of their lives. In the short term, they may experience anxiety, fear, anger, confusion, and depression, regress to immature forms of behavior, and develop behavior problems at school (Hetherington et al., 1998; Wallerstein & Kelly, 1980).

In the long term, children of divorce remain at greater risk for a variety of difficulties, including academic problems, troubled relationships with family members and peers, low self-esteem, and depression (Morrison & Coiro, 1999). When they become adolescents, children of divorce are more likely to disengage themselves from their family (or stepfamily), spending as little time at home as possible. They also are more likely to drop out of school, become unemployed, use

—Continued

drugs, have sex at an earlier age, and become unmarried teen parents (Simons & Chao, 1996). In adulthood, they display poorer problem-solving skills during marital interactions, experience more marital conflict, and have a higher divorce rate (O'Connor et al., 1999).

Most of these problems, however, are interrelated; they tend to cluster together into an overall pattern of "maladjustment." Leading divorce researcher E. Mavis Hetherington and her colleagues (1998) estimate that about 20 to 25 percent of children in divorced families, versus 10 percent of children in nondivorced families, experience this cluster of problems. This is a significantly elevated risk for maladjustment, but most children of divorce do not experience these long-term effects and grow up to be normally adjusted adults.

Some early studies suggested that boys were more likely to respond to divorce by becoming aggressive and "acting out," whereas girls were more likely to internalize their negative emotions and become depressed (Emery, 1982). But such gender differences are weaker and less consistent than they first appeared to be. Similarly, children's age at the time of divorce is weakly related to how well they ultimately cope (Hetherington et al., 1998).

▶ Should We Stay Together "For the Sake of the Child?"

Many couples considering divorce wonder whether they should stay together for the child's sake. The answer depends on the amount of conflict present in the marriage (Hetherington et al., 1998). Reviewing 92 studies, Paul Amato and Bruce Keith (1991) found that children living with married but contentious parents had poorer school achievement, lower self-esteem, and more behavior problems than children from divorced families and children from intact families with low parental conflict. When divorce ends a highly conflicted marriage, children's psychological adjustment typically benefits in the long run (Morrison & Coiro, 1999). But many unhappy marriages do not involve extensive conflict, and in such cases divorce usually puts children at greater risk for maladjustment (Amato et al., 1995).

▶ How Can Divorced Parents Help Their Children?

The major factor affecting a child's adjustment to divorce is the quality of life within the postdivorce family, and it of-

ten takes about two to three years for divorced parents and children to redevelop stable family relations (Cherlin & Furstenberg, 1994). The period during and after divorce can intensify parents' anger and conflicts. Fighting over the children and immersing them in "loyalty" battles that cause children to become "caught in the middle" are particularly damaging to their well-being. In contrast, the negative effects of divorce can be cushioned by cooperative and amicable parental behaviors during this rocky transition (Hetherington et al., 1998). For children, the lasting problems of divorce often lie in a disruption of parenting that follows marital breakdown, in conflicts between divorced parents, and in the failure of many parents to stabilize their own lives.

▶ How Do Children Respond to Remarriage and Stepfamilies?

Loving stepfamilies in which children develop close relationships with their new stepparent and stepsiblings are to be admired, because it is more difficult to make a stepfamily function well than a nondivorced family. When one or both spouses bring children from a previous marriage with them, the odds of remarriage ending in divorce may increase by as much as 50 percent (Tzeng & Mare, 1995).

Forming a stepfamily requires new adaptations, temporarily disrupts children's relations with the remarried custodial parent, and typically increases children's short-term problem behaviors. It some cases it takes up to seven years for parents and children to adjust to their new roles within the stepfamily (Hetherington et al., 1998). The transition from divorce to remarriage benefits some children but not others, and such benefits appear to be greater for preadolescent boys than for girls. In general, young adolescents seem to have the most difficulty coping with the transition into a stepfamily.

In remarriages, children may be hostile and reject the stepparent, especially when the stepparent attempts to be a strong disciplinarian. Research suggests that children usually adjust better to living in a stepfamily when discipline is handled in the following way. First, the custodial parent is warm but firm, and has primary responsibility for discipline. Second, the stepparent is warm toward the child but supports the custodial parent's authority (Bray & Berger, 1993; Hetherington, 1989).

Styles of Parenting

➤ 29. What parenting styles are associated with the most and least positive child outcomes?

Beyond the issues of divorce and remarriage, how do different child-rearing practices affect children's development in general? After studying how parents interacted with their preschool children, Diana Baumrind (1967, 1980) identified two key dimensions of parental behavior. The first is *warmth versus hostility*. Warm parents communicate love and caring for the child, and respond with greater sensitivity and empathy to the child's feelings. Hostile parents express rejection and behave as if they do not care about the child. The second dimension is *restrictiveness versus permissiveness*. Parents differ in the extent to which they make and enforce rules, place demands on children, and discipline children. As Figure 11.26

shows, combining these dimensions yields four parenting styles that are associated with different patterns of child development (Maccoby & Martin, 1983).

Authoritative parents are controlling but warm. They establish clear rules, consistently enforce them, and reward children's compliance with warmth and affection. They communicate high expectations, caring, and support. This style is associated with the most positive childhood outcomes (Baumrind, 1983, 1991). Children with authoritative parents tend to have higher self-esteem, are higher achievers in school, have fewer conduct problems, and are more considerate of others.

Authoritarian parents also exert control over their children, but do so within a cold, unresponsive, or rejecting relationship. Their children tend to have lower self-esteem, be less popular with peers, and perform more poorly in school than children with authoritative parents (Dornbusch et al., 1987).

Indulgent parents have warm and caring relationships with their children, but do not provide the guidance and discipline that helps children learn responsibility and concern for others. Their children tend to be more immature and self-centered (Patterson, 1982).

Neglectful parents provide neither warmth nor rules and guidance. Their children are most likely to be insecurely attached, have low achievement motivation and disturbed relationships with peers and adults at school, and to be impulsive and aggressive. Neglectful parenting is associated with the most negative developmental outcomes (Ainsworth, 1989).

Do these findings extend to adolescence? Laurence Steinberg and his colleagues (1994) studied several thousand high school students in California and Wisconsin. Consistent with earlier research, they found that authoritative parenting generally was associated with the most positive developmental outcomes among adolescents, and neglectful parenting was associated with the poorest outcomes. Many of the findings held true across African-, Asian-, Caucasian-, and Hispanic-American students (Lamborn et al., 1991).

Keep in mind, however, that parent-child influences are bidirectional. Children who have an irritable, hostile, and difficult temperament tend to elicit harsher and less warm parenting behaviors. Moreover, parents do not mold their children's personality and behavior like lumps of clay. Parenting makes a difference, but the way children "turn out" depends on interactions among their inherited characteristics, parental behaviors, and other environmental experiences (Collins et al., 2000). For example, schizophrenia is a serious mental disorder that has a strong genetic component. In one study, biologically "at-risk" children (i.e., they had schizophrenic biological parents) placed into good adoptive homes were no more likely to develop various mental disorders in adulthood than adopted children who were not at biological risk (Tienari et al., 1994). But when the adoptive family environment was dysfunctional, the "at-risk" children later developed significantly more disorders than the children who were not at risk.

Gender Identity and Socialization

Parents also play a role in helping children develop a **gender identity,** a sense of "femaleness" or "maleness" that becomes a central aspect of our personal identity. Most children develop a basic gender identity between the ages of 2 and 3 and can label themselves (and others) as being either a boy or girl, but their understanding of gender is still fragile. Just as young children often report that a cat wearing a dog mask has suddenly become a dog, they may believe that a boy wearing a dress is a "girl" and that a girl can grow up and become a man. **Gender constancy,** which is the understanding that being male or female is a permanent part of a person, develops around age 6 to 7 (Gouze & Nadelman, 1980; Szkrybalo & Ruble, 1999).

As gender identity develops children also acquire **sex-role stereotypes,** which are beliefs about the types of characteristics and behaviors that are appropriate for

	Warmth/ acceptance	Hostility/ rejection
Restrictive	**Authoritative**	**Authoritarian**
	Demanding, but caring; good child-parent communication	Assertion of parental power without warmth
Permissive	**Indulgent**	**Neglecting**
	Warm toward child, but lax in setting limits	Indifferent and uninvolved with child

FIGURE 11.26 The combination of two basic dimensions of parental behavior (warmth-hostility and restrictiveness-permissiveness) yields four different styles of child rearing.
Based on Maccoby & Martin, 1983.

➤ 30. How does socialization shape children's beliefs about gender?

FIGURE 11.27 If you were told that an infant is a boy, would you behave in the same way as if you were told the infant was a girl? People expect male and female infants to have different qualities and treat them differently. Mothers and fathers are more likely, for example, to use adjectives like "cute" and "pretty" when describing baby daughters. Cathy © 1986 Cathy Guisewite. Reprinted with permission of Universal Press Syndicate. All rights reserved.

FIGURE 11.28 In subtle and not so subtle ways, cultures socialize most female and male children in gender-stereotypic ways.

boys and girls to possess. **Socialization,** which refers to the process by which we acquire the beliefs, values, and behaviors of a group, plays a key role in shaping our gender identity and sex-role stereotypes. Every group, including our family and cultural groups, has norms that set standards for expected and accepted behavior. Through socialization, we ultimately internalize these expectations and standards, and they become part of our identity (Valsiner & Lawrence, 1997). Sex-role stereotypes are no exception.

Sex-typing, which involves treating others differently based on whether they are female or male, is one socialization process that accounts for gender differences in children's attitudes and behaviors (Eccles, 1991; Maccoby, 1988). From infancy onward, girls and boys are viewed and treated differently (Figure 11.27). Fathers use more physical and verbal prohibition with their 12-month-old sons than with their daughters and they steer their sons away from activities that are considered stereotypically feminine (Snow et al., 1983). Mothers talk more and use more supportive speech with daughters than with sons (Leaper et al., 1998).

Sex-role stereotypes are also transmitted through observational learning and operant conditioning (Figure 11.28). Children observe parents, other adults, peers, and television and movie characters, and often attempt to emulate what they see (Bandura, 1965). In ways both obvious and subtle, others approve of us and reinforce our behavior when we meet their expectations, and disapprove of us when we don't. In turn, this influences the way children think about gender. Some children as young as 2 to 3 years of age display sex-role stereotypes in their ability to identify objects, such as hammers and brooms, as "belonging with" one gender or the other (Fagot et al., 1992). By age 7 or 8, stereotyped thinking is firmly in place; children believe that boys and girls possess different personality traits and should hold different occupations as adults (Best et al., 1977; Miller & Budd, 1999).

As children make the transition to adolescence and enter junior high school they generally display more flexible thinking about gender. Some come to believe that traditionally masculine and feminine traits can be blended within a single person—what is called an *androgynous* gender identity—as when a person is both assertive and compassionate. During the remaining junior high and high school years some adolescents maintain this view. Overall, however, stereotypes about men's and women's psychological traits seem to become a little more rigid, and most people continue to adhere to relatively traditional beliefs (Alfieri et al., 1996; Lamke, 1982).

❭ ADOLESCENCE

We call it Sunrise Dance. It's the biggest ceremony of the White Mountain Apache—when a girl passes from childhood to womanhood. . . . On Friday evening Godmother dressed me . . . Saturday is like an endurance test. Men begin prayer chants at dawn. Godmother tells me to dance. . . . When the time comes for running, I go fast around a sacred cane. . . . Next, my father pours candies and corn kernels over me to protect me from famine. My Godfather directs my dancing on Sunday. . . . Godfather paints me. . . . On Monday there is more visiting and blessing. (Quintero, 1980, pp. 262–271)

In some cultures, ceremonies like the Sunrise Dance represent *rites of passage* that mark a transition from childhood into adulthood status (Figure 11.29). But what of *adolescence*, the well-known period between childhood and adulthood? Alice Schlegel and Herbert Barry (1991) found that among almost 200 nonindustrial societies worldwide, nearly all recognize some type of transition period between childhood and adulthood. Yet in many societies this period is brief and is not marked by a special term analogous to "adolescence."

As we know it, the lengthy period called "adolescence" is largely an invention of 18th- to 20th-century Western culture (Valisner & Lawrence, 1997). In preindustrial times, biological maturity was a major criterion for adult status. In many cultures, for example, girls were expected to marry once they became capable of bearing children. But as the Industrial Revolution brought new technology and a need for more schooling, recognition of adult status was delayed and the long transition period we call adolescence evolved.

FIGURE 11.29 A White Mountain Apache girl participates in the Sunrise Dance, a four-day ceremony that initiates her into womanhood.

Physical Development and its Psychological Consequences

Adolescence begins at **puberty**, a period of rapid maturation in which the person becomes capable of sexual reproduction. The brain's hypothalamus signals the pituitary gland to increase its hormonal secretions. This stimulates other glands and physical growth throughout the body, speeding up maturation of the *primary sex characteristics* (the sex organs involved in reproduction). Hormonal changes also produce *secondary sex characteristics* (nonreproductive physical features, such as breasts in girls, and facial hair in boys).

The pubertal landmark in girls is *menarche*, the first menstrual flow. For boys, it is the production of sperm and the first ejaculation. In North America and Europe, these events occur most often around age 12 or 13 for girls and 14 for boys, but variations occur across people, cultures, and lifestyles. In parts of New Guinea, 50 percent of girls have their first menstrual period after they turn 17 (Roche, 1979). Girls who participate in high-level figure skating, gymnastics, and ballet often experience delayed menarche, possibly from restricting their diet and exercising vigorously (Warren, 1992). Puberty is a biological process, but it can be affected by environmental factors (Graber et al., 1995).

The physical changes of puberty have psychological consequences. For one thing, hormones that steer puberty also can affect mood and behavior (Buchanan et al., 1992). But there is a social component too. Did your parents and peers react to you differently as you matured? Did your self-image change? In one study, African- and Caucasian-American girls whose mothers were supportive and helped them prepare for menarche ended up feeling most positive about it (Scott et al., 1989).

Psychological reactions to puberty are influenced by whether it occurs early or late. Overall, early maturation tends to be associated with more positive outcomes for boys than for girls. Early maturing boys acquire physical strength and

❭ 31. Describe some factors that influence adolescents' psychological reactions to experiencing puberty.

➤ 32. Discuss how adolescents' reasoning abilities change, and the ways in which their thinking is egocentric.

FIGURE 11.30 When adolescents attain formal operational thought, they can use deductive reasoning to solve scientific problems systematically.

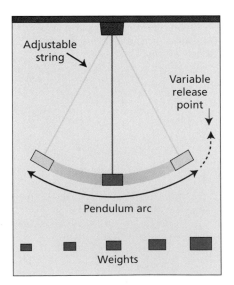

FIGURE 11.31 The materials for the pendulum problem used by Inhelder and Piaget include an adjustable string and a set of weights. The problem is to determine what factors influence how long it takes the pendulum to move through its arc. String length is the only relevant factor: the shorter the string, the less time it takes the pendulum to swing back and forth.

Adapted from B. Inhelder & J. Piaget, 1958.

size, facilitating their success in athletics and other physical activities that contribute to a male's popularity and positive body image (Sigelman & Shaffer, 1991).

In contrast, early maturing girls are more likely to develop eating disorders, smoke, drink, have problems in school, and experience psychological distress than girls who mature later (Ge et al., 1996). Some early maturing girls welcome their mature appearance, but others develop a negative body image and feel they are too fat (Peterson, 1987). However, it is not just the absolute timing of puberty that matters, but also the individual's *perception* of whether maturation is occurring too early or too late (Lerner, 1987).

Cognitive Development

Cognitive changes during adolescence can be as dramatic as physical ones. Many teenagers acquire a new maturity that enables them to reason abstractly and reflect more deeply on their own and others' thoughts.

Abstract Reasoning Abilities

Piaget (1926, 1970) proposed that the final stage of cognitive development, *formal operational thinking*, is attained during adolescence. Adolescents can more easily contemplate abstract and hypothetical issues, ranging from scientific problems to questions about social justice and the meaning of life (Figure 11.30). They reason more flexibly and creatively than concrete thinkers, and use both the deductive and inductive problem-solving methods described in Chapter 8.

Consider the "pendulum problem" in Figure 11.31. Which variable(s)—length of string, weight of object, how hard it is pushed, and release point (height in the arc)—influence(s) how quickly the pendulum oscillates? This problem is best solved by forming and testing an organized set of deductive hypotheses (e.g., "*If* string length is a factor, *then* the swing time with a short versus long string should differ"). Concrete operational children find this task difficult (Inhelder & Piaget, 1958). For example, when they adjust the string length they often adjust the weight as well, making it impossible to draw a conclusion about either variable. In contrast, adolescents think more systematically and manipulate each variable while holding the others constant.

Clearly the capacity for abstract reasoning increases substantially during adolescence (Chapell & Overton, 1998). Still, task performance partly depends on formal schooling and exposure to scientific-abstract tasks. Even with schooling, however, many teens and adults struggle at formal operational tasks. Some people frequently use abstract reasoning, but others rarely do.

Social Thinking

Adolescent thinking can be highly self-focused, particularly in the earlier teenage years. David Elkind (1967) proposes that such **adolescent egocentrism** has two main parts. First, adolescents overestimate the uniqueness of their feelings and experiences, which is called the *personal fable*. Examples would be "My parents can't possibly understand how I really feel," and "Nobody's ever felt love as deeply as ours." Second, many adolescents feel that they are always "on stage" and that "Everybody's going to notice" how they look and what they do. Elkind calls this oversensitivity to social evaluation the *imaginary audience.*

Adolescents who think more egocentrically tend to be more depressed and are more likely to underestimate the negative consequences of risky behaviors, such as sex without contraception, drunk driving, or using psychoactive drugs

(Baron & Hanna, 1990). In short, "They don't know me . . . I can handle it." Yet some researchers believe that adolescent egocentrism is an outgrowth of the search for individuality and independence (Vartanian, 1997). Thus, it may be as much a social phenomenon as a cognitive one.

Social and Personality Development

G. Stanley Hall (1904), the first psychologist to study adolescence, viewed it as a time of "storm and stress." As they cross the bridge between childhood and adulthood, adolescents may grapple with issues concerning parental and peer relations, career goals, gender roles and ethnicity, sexuality, drug use, politics, and religion. Indeed, some adults recall adolescence as a period of conflict and alienation, but other people find it to be a positive, relatively carefree period of life (Rosenberg, 1985).

The Search for Identity

"Who am I?" "What do I believe in?" "How do I want to live my life?" Erik Erikson (1968) proposed that questions such as these reflect the pivotal crisis of adolescent personality development, which he termed *identity versus role confusion* (see Table 11.3, p. 471). Erikson believed that an adolescent's "identity crisis" (a term he coined) can be resolved positively, leading to a stable sense of identity, or can end negatively, leading to confusion over one's identity and values.

> ➤ 33. Identify some of the different ways that adolescents' approach the challenge of establishing an identity.

James Marcia (1966, 1994) built upon Erikson's work. He interviewed adolescents and young adults, and found many adolescents in a condition or "status" that Marica called *identity diffusion:* They have not yet gone through an identity crisis and remain uncommitted to a coherent set of values or roles. Some may be unconcerned or cynical about identity issues. Other adolescents are in *foreclosure,* adopting an identity without first going through a crisis. For example, an adolescent may automatically adopt peer group or parental values without giving them much thought.

In contrast, two other groups have experienced an identity crisis. Adolescents in a status of *moratorium* are currently experiencing a crisis but have not resolved it. They want to establish a clear identity, but are unsure which way to go. Those in *identity achievement* have gone through a crisis and successfully resolved it. They have adopted a coherent set of values and are pursuing goals to which they are committed.

Figure 11.32 shows that most young adolescents are in identity diffusion or foreclosure; they have not experienced an identity crisis. But with age many identity-diffused teens think more deeply about who they are and most teens in foreclosure reconsider their prematurely adopted values. They experience an identity crisis and over half successfully resolve it by young adulthood.

Although we have discussed "identity" as a single concept, our sense of identity actually has multiple components (Camilleri & Malewska-Peyre, 1997). These include:

- our gender, ethnicity, and other attributes by which we define ourselves as members of social groups ("daughter," "student," "athlete");

- how we view our personality and other characteristics ("shy," "friendly"); and

- our goals and values pertaining to areas we view as important, such as family and peer relations, career, religion, and so forth.

Typically, we achieve a stable identity regarding some of these components before others (Skorikov & Vondracek, 1998). And even after an identity

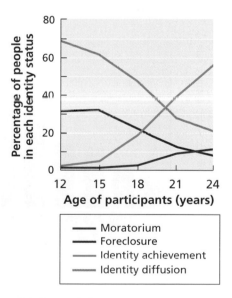

FIGURE 11.32 Based on interviews in one study, this graph shows the percentage of participants in each of Marcia's four identity statuses at various ages. These data suggest that most young people attain identity a few years later than Erikson suggested.

Adapted from P. W. Meilman, 1979.

crisis has been resolved, changing situations may trigger new ones and cause us to reevaluate prior goals and values.

Finally, culture plays an important role in identity formation, one that goes beyond the simple idea that we view ourselves as belonging to certain cultural groups. Our cultural upbringing influences the very way we view concepts such as "self" and "identity." Having grown up in an individualistic culture, my sense of identity assumes that "I" am an autonomous individual with clear boundaries separating me from other people. But in collectivistic cultures, the concept of "self" traditionally is based more strongly on the interdependence and connectedness between people (Kagitçibasi, 1997). Thus the question "Who am I" is more likely to be answered in ways that reflects a person's relationships with family members, friends, and others.

Relationships With Parents

➤ 34. To what extent are parent-teen relationships characterized by "storm and stress?"

Research around the world has examined teenagers' relationships with their parents, and it appears that "storm and stress" is the exception rather than the rule. In a national survey conducted during the socially turbulent 1970s, 56 percent of American teenagers reported getting along "very well" with their parents, and 41 percent reported getting along "fairly well" (Gallup, 1988). More recently, a study of over 600 Dutch teenagers found little evidence of conflicting tastes and negative relationships with parents (Van Wel, 1994). Judith Smetana and Cheryl Gaines (1999) reported that, among 51 African-American middle-class families, conflicts between parents and young teens centered around routine issues such as chores, neatness, and bedtime. Though moderately frequent conflicts usually were mild in intensity.

In a larger project, Andrew Fuligni (1998) studied 1,341 female and male American students in sixth, eighth, and tenth grades. They came from immigrant and native-born families of Mexican, Chinese, Filipino, and European ancestry. Fuligni found that, among all four ethnic groups:

- Adolescents agreed with their parents' right to "make the rules," but more for some issues than others (Figure 11.33).

- Older adolescents felt it was less appropriate for parents to make the rules.

- Girls believed their parents would "grant them autonomy" at a later age than boys did.

So what about actual conflicts with parents?

- Overall, there was somewhat more conflict with mothers than fathers, *but:*

- Regardless of adolescents' gender, ethnic group, or age, conflict was low with *both* mothers and fathers.

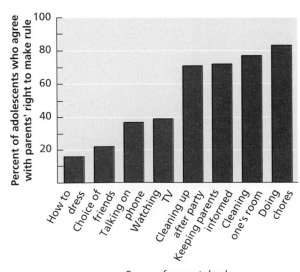

Focus of parental rule

FIGURE 11.33 Using a questionnaire developed by Judy Smetana (1988), Andrew Fuligni (1998) found that the percentage of teenagers who agree that their parents have the right to "make the rules" depends on the particular issue.

Data courtesy of Andrew Fuligni.

Of course, some parents and teenagers do struggle a lot, and parent-teen conflict is correlated with other signs of distress. Chuansheng Chen and colleagues (1998) studied 600 seventh- and eighth-graders from America (European- and Chinese-Americans), Taiwan, and Beijing, China. Parent-teen conflict generally was low in each cultural group, but young teens who reported more conflict had higher levels of school misconduct (e.g., cheating, skipping school) and more antisocial behavior (e.g., getting into fistfights, damaging property). Teens who report more conflict with parents also report greater hopelessness, lower self-esteem, and less life satisfaction (Shek, 1998). Although parent-teen conflict may contribute to teens' psychological problems, we should remember that it also is likely to be caused by such problems.

Peer and Friendship Relationships

Peer relationships increase in importance during the adolescent years. From Alabama to the Arctic, teens like to spend time "hanging out" with their friends. According to some studies, adolescents spend more time with peers than doing almost any other activity, and they tend to identify more with peers than with adults (Csikszentmihalyi & Larson, 1984). But this pattern may be stronger in Canada and the United States than in Europe or Asia, where teens generally place a relatively stronger emphasis on family relationships (Chen et al., 1998).

Adolescent friendships typically are more intimate than those at previous ages, involving a greater sharing of problems and better mutual understanding (Hunter & Youniss, 1982). Perhaps one reason intimacy with peers increases is that, in choosing best friends, adolescents (like older adults) tend to select peers who are similar to themselves (Tolson & Urberg, 1993). This increase in peer intimacy seems to fit with another shift in peer interactions that occurs over the high school years: The amount of time spent in groups decreases and time spent with individual friends increases.

Peer relationships also play a part in the process of separating from parents and establishing one's own identity. Because they help satisfy the adolescent's needs for intimacy, approval, and belonging, peers can strongly influence a teenager's values and behaviors. For some adolescents, peer pressure increases the risk of misconduct, such as cheating, skipping school, damaging property, or disobeying parental rules about smoking and drinking. Fortunately, peer pressure *against* committing misdeeds typically has an even stronger effect in inhibiting misconduct, and closeness to parents is an added buffer that helps many teenagers resist peer pressure to do misdeeds (Brown et al., 1986; Chen et al., 1998). Despite increased peer influence on dress, hairstyles, and attitudes toward other people, parental influence remains high on issues of politics and religion, morality, and career decisions (Bachman et al., 1987). In these and other important areas, the so-called "generation gap" is far narrower than we might expect.

❯ ADULTHOOD

It was a grand birthday party. Jeanne Calment was born in France 10 years after the American Civil War. By age 60, she had lived through a world war and the invention of the radio, telephone, motion picture, automobile, and airplane. Still to come was another world war, television, space flight, computers, the Internet, and riding a bicycle until age 100. Yes, her 120th birthday was grand indeed. When a reporter asked how her future looked, Jeanne replied with a wry sense of humor, "Very brief" (Figure 11.34).

Older adults are the fastest-growing segment of the population in many countries. By 2025, almost one in five Americans will be over 65 years of age (Bureau of the Census, 2000). Here, we examine some of the physical, cognitive, and social changes that occur during young (roughly 20 to 40 years), middle (40 to 60 years), and late adulthood (60 years and over).

Physical Development

Young adults are at the peak of their physical, sexual, and perceptual functioning. Maximum muscle strength in the legs, arms, and other parts of the body is reached at age 25 to 30. Vision, hearing, reaction time, and coordination are at peak levels in the early to mid-twenties (Hayslip & Panek, 1989). Although

➤ 35. How do peer relationships change during adolescence?

FIGURE 11.34 Jeanne Calment of Arles, France, was born in 1875 and died in 1997 at the age of 122. Although other individuals have claimed to live this long or beyond, Calment's life is the longest that has been verified.

➤ 36. What are some of the major bodily changes that occur from early through late adulthood?

(a)

(b)

FIGURE 11.35 Many older adults maintain a physically active lifestyle. (a) Astronaut John Glenn made a space flight at age 77. (b) These 70- to 76-year-old Jacksonville Super Moms are Senior Games medalists.

➤ 37. Discuss how information-processing abilities and memory change throughout adulthood.

many physical capacities decline in the mid-thirties, the changes aren't noticeable until years later.

Physical status typically declines at midlife (Troll, 1985). Visual acuity often worsens and muscles become weaker and stiffer, especially among sedentary people. After age 40 the *basal metabolic rate,* the rate at which the resting body converts food into energy, slows and produces a tendency to gain weight. The efficiency of oxygen consumption decreases and it is harder for middle-aged adults to maintain the physical endurance needed for sustained exercise. Around age 50 women's ovaries stop producing estrogen, they lose their fertility, and experience *menopause,* the end of menstruation. Men remain capable of fathering children, but their fertility gradually declines in middle age.

Despite these declines, many middle-aged adults are in excellent health and vigorously active. Growing experience in job and recreational skills can offset much of the age-related declines. From climbing mountains to running marathons, they may achieve physical goals well beyond those attained by many younger adults.

The physical changes of middle adulthood become more pronounced in late adulthood. About 80 percent of a young adult's body consists of so-called lean body mass (muscles, organs, and bone), and the remaining 20 percent consists of fatty tissue. By age 70, the balance between lean and fat body mass may be 50-50. Bones lose calcium, becoming more brittle and slower to heal, and hardened ligaments make movements stiffer and slower (Weg, 1983). At age 90 the brain of a healthy adult has lost 5 to 10 percent of its early adult weight, due to a normal loss of neurons that occurs as we grow older (Whitbourne, 1985). But with regular exercise, good nutrition, the right attitude, and barring major disease, many adults maintain physical vigor and an active lifestyle well into old age (Figure 11.35).

Cognitive Development

Piaget believed that formal operational thinking was the fourth and final stage of cognitive development. He argued that adults do not develop new modes of thinking; rather, they simply use formal operations in new and more complex ways.

Several theorists disagree, proposing a fifth stage of cognitive development called **postformal thought,** in which people can reason logically about opposing points of view and accept contradictions and irreconcilable differences (Riegel, 1973; Rakfeldt et al., 1996). Postformal thinkers also realize that, from social behavior to ethics and politics, life involves many interacting factors (Kramer, 1983). When reasoning about social problems, postformal thinkers are more likely to acknowledge opposing points of view and see both sides of a disagreement as having legitimate arguments.

Information Processing and Memory

Many people assume that cognitive functioning declines throughout middle and late adulthood. Research shows that this is true in some ways, but not others (Craik and Salthouse, 2000). For example:

- *Perceptual speed* (reaction time) declines steadily after the mid-thirties. Thus it takes older adults longer to visually identify and evaluate stimuli (Scialfa & Joffe, 1997).
- *Memory for new factual information* declines during adulthood. Compared with younger adults, older adults find it harder to remember new series of

numbers, names and faces of unfamiliar people, map directions, and directions for using new prescription drugs (Morrell et al., 1989).

- *Recall* declines more strongly than recognition, because recall requires more processing resources (Craik & McDowd, 1998).

On the other hand, certain types of verbal memory show less of a decline with aging. Thus the ability to repeat just-heard sentences decreases more slowly than the ability to repeat single, unrelated words. Healthy elderly adults also do well in recalling personal events and recognizing *familiar* stimuli from long ago, such as the faces of high school classmates (Bahrick et al., 1975).

Intellectual Changes

How do our intellectual abilities change in adulthood? The conclusion from early research seemed clear: After 30 we were "over the hill." When the IQ scores of different age groups were compared in cross-sectional studies, they began to decline noticeably beginning between ages 30 and 40 (Doppelt & Wallace, 1955).

Researchers made a breakthrough when they examined separate intellectual abilities rather than overall IQ. They studied *fluid intelligence,* which reflects the ability to perform mental operations (such as abstract reasoning, solving logic problems, and mentally rotating objects), and *crystallized intelligence,* which reflects the accumulation of verbal skills and factual knowledge (Horn & Cattell, 1966). *Cross-sectional* research comparing different age groups typically found that fluid intelligence began to decline steadily in young adulthood, whereas crystallized intelligence peaked during middle adulthood and then began to decline in late adulthood (Figure 11.36*a*).

➤ 38. How do intellectual abilities change with age? To what extent does the answer depend on the research design used?

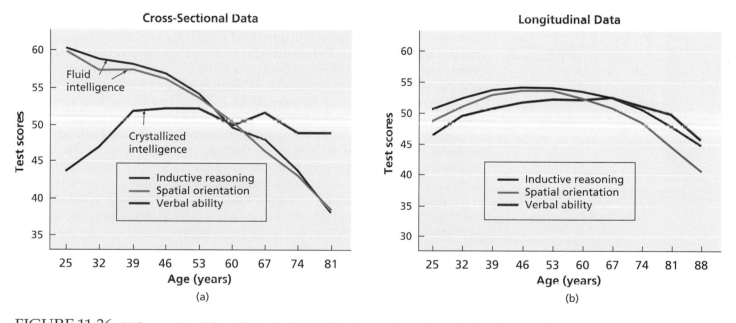

FIGURE 11.36   (a) Cross-sectional data indicate that fluid abilities (reasoning and spatial task performance) begin to decline in young adulthood, whereas crystallized intelligence (verbal ability) begins to decline in late adulthood. However, (b) longitudinal data from the same study indicate that *both* fluid and crystallized intelligence remain fairly stable through young and middle adulthood and do not decline significantly until late adulthood. The longitudinal and cross-sectional data are consistent in showing that crystallized abilities decline at a later age than fluid abilities.

Adapted from Schaie, 1994.

Some researchers wondered whether this early decline in fluid abilities was really a function of aging or the result of different experiences encountered by the various age generations. The older groups may have had less exposure to scientific problem solving in school, or may have had jobs requiring less use of abstract intellectual skills. Such factors could have artificially depressed the scores of older adults.

To answer this question, K. Warner Schaie of Pennsylvania State University and his coworkers (Schaie, 1994, 1998) began a study in 1956 that has now involved about 5,000 adults. This study uses a sequential design that includes both longitudinal and cross-sectional components. The *longitudinal data* do not support an early decline in either fluid or crystallized intelligence. Rather, most abilities are relatively stable (or even increase slightly) throughout young and middle adulthood, and do not begin to reliably decline until late adulthood (Figure 11.36*b*). But both the cross-sectional and longitudinal data add further support to the previously established finding that certain fluid intellectual abilities (such as reasoning and spatial ability) begin to decline at a somewhat earlier age than crystallized intelligence (such as verbal abilities). On average, verbal abilities at ages 25 and 88 were similar.

Age-related intellectual declines are partly due to poorer perceptual speed, memory, vision, and hearing (Fristoe et al., 1997). Thus we find a bigger intellectual decline during old age when test questions call for quick responses (i.e., *"timed tests"*) than when they involve unlimited or ample time (*"untimed tests"*). This decrease in intellectual speed shows up in various real-world tasks, such as learning to use a computer. But although 75- to 89-year-olds may take longer to acquire computer skills and need more assistance than their 60- to 74-year-old counterparts, the key is that many retain the intellectual capacity to learn (Echt et al., 1998).

Use It or Lose It? Maintaining Cognitive Functioning

➤ 39. Identify some factors associated with greater retention of cognitive abilities during late adulthood.

The average intellectual decline in old age shown in Figure 11.36*b* is a bit deceiving, disproportionately influenced by a minority of Schaie's older participants who declined a lot. For each intellectual ability, Schaie found that about 70 percent of his participants *maintained* their level of functioning between ages 67 and 74, and 65 percent maintained it between ages 74 and 81.

Can we predict who will maintain their level of intellectual functioning the longest? According to (Schaie, 1994), it appears to be people who have above-average education and cognitively stimulating jobs, are involved in cognitively stimulating personal activities, (e.g., reading, travel, continuing education), marry a spouse with greater intellectual abilities than their own, and maintain a higher level of perceptual processing speed.

As in the case of maintaining physical fitness, the moral for intellectual fitness appears to be "use it or lose it." In fact, regular physical exercise and perceptual-motor activities may help preserve cognitive abilities in late adulthood (Clarkson-Smith & Hartley, 1990). In one study, Dutch researchers randomly assigned some elderly adults (ages 69 to 90 years) to play the video game "Super Tetris" for 5 hours a week, for 5 weeks (Goldstein et al., 1997). This challenging game requires progressively faster perceptual-motor responses at each new level. Compared with a non-playing control group, the Tetris players improved their reaction time on a standard psychological test.

➤ 40. Does theory of mind research support the notion that elderly adults are "older but wiser"?

In sum, remaining intellectually and physically active may help slow the age decline of some cognitive functions. With age we also accumulate knowledge that can lead to "wisdom" (Erikson et al., 1986). Our *Research Close-Up* examines one component of being "older but wiser."

RESEARCH CLOSE-UP

Older but Wiser? Mind-Reading in Elderly and Young Adults

▶ Background

During childhood each of us develops a *theory of mind,* a set of beliefs about the mind and an ability to understand what other people "are thinking." Of course, the ability to read other people's minds remains important throughout life. We judge whether people are being sincere or deceitful, predict how others will behave based on what is "going on in their head," and infer what people "must have been thinking" to have acted as they did. Because previous theory of mind research largely ignored adulthood, Francesca Happé and her colleagues compared the ability of young and elderly adults to make judgments about other people's thought processes.

▶ Method

The experiment involved 19 healthy, elderly adults (average age = 73 years) and 15 young adults (average age = 22.5 years) living in the Boston area, and 52 young adults (average age − 21 years) living in London. The groups had a balance of men and women.

Each participant silently read 24 short paragraphs. After finishing each one, they turned the page and were asked a question about it. The 24 paragraphs were divided into three categories, representing the independent variable: theory of mind stories, control stories, and jumbled passages. Theory of mind stories examined participants' ability to make a judgment about another person's mental state. For example:

A burglar who has just robbed a shop is making his getaway. As he is running home, a policeman on his beat sees him drop his glove. He doesn't know the man is a burglar, he just wants to tell him he dropped his glove. But when the policeman shouts out to the burglar, "Hey, you! Stop!" the burglar turns round, sees the policeman, and gives himself up.

Question: Why did the burglar do that?

Control stories also involved making a judgment, but not about a mental state. For example, a burglar breaks into a jewelry store and avoids setting off the electronic detector beam, which would trigger an alarm if it were broken. He sees the gems, and

As he reaches out . . . he steps on something soft. He hears a screech and something small and furry runs out past him, towards the shop door. Immediately the alarm sounds.

Question: Why did the alarm go off?

The jumbled passages involved meaningful but disconnected sentences that didn't form a story; they simply tested participants' memory ability. Here is part of a jumbled passage:

Today, at college, it is Jim's worst class—mathematics. She has only one dollar left, which she must keep for her bus fare. He buys a bright tie to go with his new shirt.

Question: Does she have two dollars left?

Two dependent variables were measured: the time it took to read the paragraphs and the quality of the answers. Answers received full, partial, or no credit depending on how explicit and accurate they were.

▶ Results

The responses of young adults from Boston and London were similar, and were combined into one "young adult" group. Overall, the older adults took slightly longer to read the paragraphs and performed less well than younger adults on the jumbled passages, which tested simple memory. But the two groups performed equally well on the nonsocial control stories, and on the theory of mind tasks the elderly adults achieved 93 percent of the possible points, compared with 80 percent for the younger adults.

▶ Critical Discussion

The results suggest evidence of superior social reasoning abilities in healthy, elderly adults. Both groups did well, but if this were an academic test on social insight, we might give the older adults an A and the younger adults a B. The findings clearly contradict a stereotype of the elderly as "feebleminded," supporting instead a notion that there indeed is "wisdom in the aged."

By cleverly including two types of control conditions (control stories and jumbled passages) the authors reduced the plausibility of several alternative explanations for the findings. For example, is it possible that the older adults simply had better memory skills? Not likely: The younger adults scored higher on the simple recall task. Might the older adults have been more intelligent or better educated than the younger ones? If so, why didn't they perform better on the "control" reasoning tasks? The authors also ensured that

—Continued

participants' answers were scored in an unbiased manner. The scorer used a standardized system and was blind to the purpose of the study and to each participant's age group.

Like all research, this study has limitations. Strictly speaking, because the design is cross-sectional, we cannot conclude that social reasoning ability increases *as a function of aging.* The elderly participants might have per-formed even better when they were younger. Further, per-formance differences between the age groups might be due to different socialization experiences they had while growing up. Nevertheless, the authors called attention to an important question: How do social reasoning abilities change in adulthood? Now it is up to further research to explore this question more fully.

Source: Francesca Happé, Ellen Winner, and Hiram Brownell, 1998. The getting of wisdom: Theory of mind in old age. *Developmental Psychology, 34,* 358–362.

Social and Personality Development

Adults follow a great diversity of life paths. As Bernice Neugarten notes, "If you look at people's lives, they're like the spreading of a fan. The longer they live, the greater the differences between them" (Neugarten & Hall, 1980, p. 78). Yet all adults confront the biological realities of aging. Most are also influenced by a tick-ing **social clock,** a set of cultural norms concerning the optimal age range for work, marriage, parenthood, and other major life experiences to occur (Neugarten, 1979).

Stages and Critical Events

➤ 41. According to Erikson, what are the three major developmental challenges of adulthood?

Many researchers view adult social development as a progression through age-re-lated stages (Levinson, 1990; Vaillant, 1977). According to Erik Erikson (1959/1980), whose model we introduced earlier, *intimacy versus isolation* is the major develop-mental challenge of young adulthood (ages 20 to 40). Intimacy is the ability to open oneself to another person and to form close relationships. This is the period of adult-hood when many people form close adult friendships, fall in love, and marry.

Middle adulthood (ages 40 to 60) brings with it the issue of *generativity versus stagnation.* Through their careers, volunteer work, raising children, or involvement in religious and political activities, people achieve generativity by doing things for others, exercising leadership, and making the world a better place. Certainly, many young adults make such contributions to society, but generativity typically be-comes a more central issue later in adulthood (Strough et al., 1996).

Late adulthood (over 60) accentuates the final crisis, *integrity versus despair.* Older adults review their life and evaluate its meaning. If the major crises of ear-lier stages have been successfully resolved, the person experiences integrity: a sense of completeness and fulfillment. Older adults who have not achieved pos-itive outcomes at earlier stages may experience despair, regretting that they can-not relive their lives in a more fulfilling way.

Consistent with Erikson's model, many of our goals vary in importance as we age and successfully resolving certain life tasks may contribute to mastering others (Cross & Markus, 1991; McAdams & de St. Aubin, 1998). But critics cau-tion that we should avoid viewing early, middle, and late adulthood as strict "stages" or dividing lines where one life task takes over while others fade away. For example, "intimacy" goals may be as important in middle adulthood as in early adulthood (Strough et al., 1996).

Another way to view adult social development is through the major life events that people experience. Sigmund Freud once defined psychological adjust-ment as "the ability to love and work" (1935, p. 112), and research confirms that many key life events revolve around these two themes (Holmes & Rahe, 1967).

Marriage and Family

The vast majority of adults marry at some point in their lives. Most expect a great deal from marriage, including satisfaction of social, emotional, and sexual needs. Although many couples realize these goals, a high divorce rate in many countries indicates that happiness is by no means an automatic outcome. Successful marriages are characterized by emotional closeness and physical intimacy, positive communication and problem-solving, agreement on basic values and expectations, and a willingness to accept and support changes in the partner (Gottman & Levenson, 1992).

Cohabitation.   Some people in committed relationships *cohabit*—that is, live together without being married. In 1960, the ratio of married to cohabiting households in the United States was about 95:1. By 1998, that ratio had shrunk to 14:1, representing over 4 million cohabiting households (Bureau of the Census, 1999). Although some couples cohabit as a permanent alternative to marriage, many more do so as a "trial marriage" to determine if they are compatible before tying the knot. In Sweden, premarital cohabitation appears to be the norm among newlyweds (Duvander, 1999).

Does premarital cohabitation decrease the chances that a marriage will end in divorce? To the contrary, national surveys in several countries find that premarital cohabitation is associated with a higher risk of subsequent divorce (Bennett et al., 1988; Bumpass & Sweet, 1988; Hall & Zhao, 1995). This relation, however, does not seem to be causal. Rather, couples who cohabit before marriage differ psychologically from couples who don't cohabit first. For example, they tend to be less religious and report less commitment to marriage as an institution, and some are ambivalent about whether to marry. Taken together, these preexisting factors would increase the risk of divorce even if these couples had not cohabited. When researchers limit their analysis to cohabiting couples who start out with a strong orientation toward marriage, the risk of divorce is no higher and the quality of marital relations is no poorer than among couples who did not cohabit prior to marriage (Brown & Booth, 1996; Bruederl, 1997).

What's love got to do with it? Culture and marriage.   Suppose someone had all the qualities you desired in a mate, but you didn't love the person. Would you still marry him or her? Robert Levine and his colleagues (1995) posed this question to 1,163 college students from 11 countries. Table 11.4 shows that in five Western countries, 80 percent or more of women and men said they would not marry such a person. But in the least economically developed Eastern countries of India, Pakistan, and Thailand, only 24 to 39 percent said "No." In fact, half of the Indian and Pakistani students said they would marry someone they didn't love, versus only 4 percent of American students. There were few gender differences, but on the individualism-collectivism dimension, students from collectivistic countries were less likely to believe that love is prerequisite to marriage.

Do these results surprise you? In many cultures, marriages are "arranged" by family members. To some extent, the notion that romantic love is a prerequisite to marriage is a well-ingrained but culture-bound norm.

Marital satisfaction, parenthood, and the empty nest.   On average, marital satisfaction declines in the first few years after the knot is tied (Kurdek, 1991, 1999; Glenn, 1998). This does not mean, however, that most couples are unhappy. They are still satisfied, just less than they were. In a sense, the honeymoon is over.

The birth of a first baby represents a major change in the way couples spend their time. For many couples, marital satisfaction decreases in the year or two after their first child is born (Cowan & Cowan, 1988, 2000; Shapiro et al., 2000). Compared with husbands, wives are more likely to leave their outside job, spend more time parenting, and feel that their spouse is not helping enough. Disagreements over the division of labor and parenting are a major contributor to the drop in marital satisfaction (Belsky & Hsieh, 1998).

Over a broader age period, many cross-sectional studies suggest a U-shaped relation between marital satisfaction and progression through various major life events. The percentage of couples reporting that they are "very satisfied"

| TABLE 11.4 | LOVE AND MARRIAGE |

If someone had all the other qualities you desired, would you marry this person if you were not in love with him/her?

Country	Percentage* No	Yes
India	24	49
Thailand	34	19
Pakistan	39	50
Philippines	64	11
Japan	64	2
Hong Kong	78	6
Australia	80	5
Mexico	83	10
England	84	7
Brazil	86	4
United States	86	4

*The remaining students selected "Undecided" as their response.
Source: Adapted from Levine et al., 1995.

➤ 42. How does marital satisfaction typically change over time? What major events are associated with these changes?

in their marriage typically is highest before or just as the first child is born, drops during the child-rearing years, and increases in the years after all the children have left home (Orbuch et al., 1996; Rollins & Feldman, 1970). Although a longitudinal study did not find this late adulthood rebound in marital satisfaction (Glenn, 1998), this research still challenges a myth about the so-called "empty nest" years after the last grown child leaves home. Contrary to popular stereotypes, most middle-aged couples do not become significantly depressed or suffer a crisis when their children leave (Chiriboga, 1989). Spouses maintain meaningful relationships with their children, but have more time to spend with each other and pursue leisure activities.

Despite the stresses that accompany marriage and parenthood, married people are happier; have lower rates of chronic illness, depression, and stress; and live longer than unmarried adults (Shumaker & Hill, 1991; Verbrugge, 1979). Moreover, although raising children is demanding, parents often report that "having children" is one of best things that has ever happened in their lives. The knowledge that many married couples experience a drop in marital satisfaction over time can help newlyweds establish more realistic expectations, and perhaps encourage couples to take a more active role in maintaining a satisfying relationship.

Establishing a Career

➤ 43. Describe some major differences between women and men's typical career paths.

One of the first questions a new acquaintance typically asks is, "What do you do?" A career not only helps us earn a living, but also defines part of our identity and allows us to express "who we are" (Super, 1981). Work provides an outlet for achievement and feelings of success, gives us structure, counteracts boredom, and is a significant source of social interactions (Berry, 1998). A 14-country study suggests that having satisfying interpersonal relationships at work is particularly important in collectivistic countries (Hui et al., 1995).

According to Donald Super (1957), a pioneer in the field of vocational psychology, in childhood through our mid-twenties we first enter a *growth stage* of career interests in which we form initial impressions about the types of jobs we like or dislike, followed by a more earnest *exploration stage* in which we form tentative ideas about a preferred career and pursue the necessary education or training. During their first two years in college, however, most students cannot accurately predict their future occupations and many change their majors during college. Both of your authors did; neither of us entered college intending to become psychologists.

From their mid-twenties to mid-forties, people often enter an *establishment phase* during which they begin to make their mark. Initially, they may experience some job instability. After college, for example, many people are likely to change careers at least once (Holland, 1985). Careers tend to become more stable by the end of this period and people enter a *maintenance stage* that continues through the rest of middle adulthood and into late adulthood. In general, older workers tend to be more satisfied with their jobs than younger workers, but there are also developmental changes in what workers view as most important (Berry, 1998). Younger workers are more interested in salary and advancement, but in middle adulthood, job security becomes more important (Krausz, 1982). Finally, during the *decline stage,* one's investment in work tends to decrease, and we eventually retire.

Though useful as a general model, people's career paths may vary quite a bit, and this is especially true for women. Nora Keating and Barbara Jeffrey (1983) traced the work histories of women who had retired from lengthy, nonprofessional careers. Most who never married had a continuous, nondelayed career, but all of the married women experienced career gaps or postponed a career until their thirties for family reasons. Similarly, Joy Schneer and Frieda Reitman (1995, 1997) found that among students who obtained an M.B.A. (Master of Business Administration) degree and then pursued managerial careers, women were more likely than men to experience work gaps by mid career. Such work gaps tend to retard professional advancement and salary level.

Childbirth is one of the major causes of work gaps for women. About 75 percent of women who hold outside jobs become pregnant during their working years, and over half return to work within a year (Muchinsky, 1997). Career gaps also occur when adults must temporarily leave the workforce to care for their elderly parents. As in raising children, women disproportionately fill this eldercare role. Not surprisingly, married women in the workforce experience greater *interrole conflict* than married men, as they try to juggle the demands of career and family (Berry, 1998; Gustafson & Magnuson, 1991). But as children grow up and leave home, this conflict decreases. During middle adulthood women who work outside the home report higher self-esteem, better physical health, and less psychological distress than homemakers do (Frankenheuser et al., 1991). Indeed, after raising a family, many women enter the workforce for the first time, reinvigorate an earlier career, or return to college in preparation for a new one.

Midlife Crisis: Fact or Fiction?

Popular wisdom holds that along the developmental path of career and family, people hit a massive pothole called "midlife crisis." Is it true? Daniel Levinson and his coworkers (1978, 1986) longitudinally studied 85 men and women and found that many experienced a turbulent midlife transition between the ages of 40 and 45. They began to focus on their mortality and realize that some of their life's dreams pertaining to career, family, and relationships would not come true.

Critics note that Levinson's sample was small and nonrepresentative. In fact, there is considerable evidence that the notion of a full-blown, turmoil-filled midlife crisis is largely a myth. Research conducted around the world shows that happiness and life satisfaction generally are unrelated to age (Diener et al., 1999). In one study of adolescents and people in young, middle, and late adulthood from eight Western European countries, about 80 percent of each age group reported they were "satisfied" or "very satisfied" with their lives (Ingelhart & Rabier, 1986). Moreover, people in their forties *do not* have higher rates of divorce, suicide, depression, feelings of meaninglessness, or emotional instability than younger or older adults (Figure 11.37; McCrae & Costa, 1990).

In sum, adults surely experience conflicts, disappointments, frustrations, and worries as they enter midlife, but so do people of all ages. As Erikson emphasized, there are major goals to achieve, crises to resolve, and rewards to experience in every phase of life.

Retirement and the Golden Years

Retirement is an important milestone in life. Some adults view it as a reminder that they are growing older, but many look forward to leisure time, volunteer work, and other opportunities they were unable to pursue during their careers. Most retired people do not become more anxious, depressed, or lonely due to retirement, although those who have strong work values are most apt to miss their jobs (George, 1980; Hardy & Quadagno, 1995).

The decision to retire or keep working typically involves many factors, such as feelings about the job, leisure interests, one's physical health, and family relationships (Shultz et al., 1998). In one study, workers were more likely to choose retirement if their marriage was satisfying and their spouse was not working (Reitzes et al., 1998). In this case, retirement meant an opportunity to spend more time with a loved one.

Some people, of course, do not have the luxury to choose their work status. They may be forced into retirement or feel compelled to keep working for economic reasons, and this has an important impact on well being. Whether in their fifties or seventies, adults who are working or retired because this is what

➤ 44. Is midlife crisis a myth? Discuss the evidence.

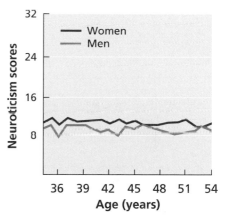

FIGURE 11.37 In a national health survey of over 10,000 men and women, the percentage of individuals measured to have "emotional instability" remained steady between the ages of 33 and 54.
From McCrae & Costa, 1990.

➤ 45. Does retirement cause psychological problems for most retirees? Under what situation are such problems most likely?

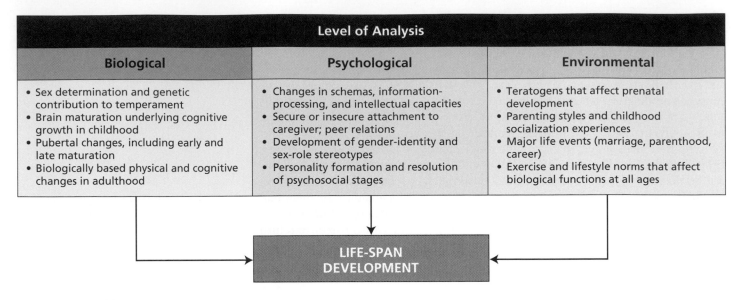

Level of Analysis		
Biological	**Psychological**	**Environmental**
• Sex determination and genetic contribution to temperament • Brain maturation underlying cognitive growth in childhood • Pubertal changes, including early and late maturation • Biologically based physical and cognitive changes in adulthood	• Changes in schemas, information-processing, and intellectual capacities • Secure or insecure attachment to caregiver; peer relations • Development of gender-identity and sex-role stereotypes • Personality formation and resolution of psychosocial stages	• Teratogens that affect prenatal development • Parenting styles and childhood socialization experiences • Major life events (marriage, parenthood, career) • Exercise and lifestyle norms that affect biological functions at all ages

LIFE-SPAN DEVELOPMENT

FIGURE 11.38 Understanding the Causes of Behavior: Factors that influence life-span development.

they prefer report higher life satisfaction and better physical and mental health than adults who are involuntarily working or retired (Shultz et al., 1998; Swan et al., 1991).

Death and Dying

All of us eventually face the specter of death. Like other aspects of life-span development summarized in Figure 11.38, death can be viewed at several levels; it is an inevitable biological process but one with important psychological and environmental components.

➤ 46. Why is it incorrect to say that there is a "normal" or "proper" way to confront death?

In her pioneering work on dying, Elisabeth Kübler-Ross (1969) found that terminally ill patients often experienced five stages as they coped with impending death. *Denial* typically came first, as the person refused to accept that the illness was terminal. Next denial often gave way to *anger* and then to *bargaining,* such as "Lord, please let me live long enough to see my grandchild." *Depression* ushered in the fourth stage, as patients began to grieve. Finally, many experienced *acceptance* and a resigned sense of peacefulness.

It is essential to keep in mind that these stages do not represent a "normal" or "correct" way to face death, and that terminally ill patients' reactions may not typify those of people facing death under other circumstances (Doka, 1995). Even among terminally ill patients, some move back and forth between stages, do not experience all the stages, or look forward to death (Schulz & Aderman, 1980). Nevertheless, Kübler-Ross's work spurred interest in understanding and helping people cope with death, and this may be her most enduring legacy.

As Figure 11.39 illustrates, beliefs and customs concerning death vary across cultures and individuals (Seale, 1998). To some, death means the complete end of one's existence. Others believe in reincarnation or that the soul enters an afterlife. Death also means different things to people of different ages (Cicirelli, 1998). Older adults typically have lost more friends and loved ones, and have thought more about their own deaths than have younger people. Understandably, the elderly are more accepting of their own deaths than any other age group (Kalish & Reynolds, 1977). In the midst of a fatal heart attack, one 81-year-old man reassuringly told his family, "It's my time. It's been a good life." We should all wish for this blessing of a fulfilled life's journey.

FIGURE 11.39 Many cultures honor a person's death with a ceremony that involves family, friends, and the wider community. In some cultures this traditionally is a somber occasion; in others it is more joyous celebration. In Seoul, Korea, this family has gathered at the national cemetery on Family Memorial Day.

▼▼

CHAPTER SUMMARY

Major Issues and Methods

- Developmental psychology studies the process of aging. Cross-sectional designs compare people of different age groups at a single point in time. A longitudinal design repeatedly tests the same age group as it grows older. A sequential design tests several groups as they grow older.

Prenatal Development

- Prenatal development involves the zygote, embryonic, and fetal stages.

- The 23rd chromosome in a mother's egg cell always is an X chromosome. If the 23rd chromosome in the father's sperm cell is an X, the child will be genetically female (XX); if a Y, the child will be born genetically male (XY). Maternal malnutrition, stress, illness, drug use, and environmental toxins can cause abnormal prenatal development.

Infancy and Childhood

- Newborns are nearsighted, but can distinguish between different visual patterns, sounds, odors, and tastes. They display perceptual preferences, can learn through classical and operant conditioning, and may have a primitive capacity for imitation.

- The cephalocaudal principle reflects the tendency for development to proceed in a head-to-foot direction. The proximodistal principle states that development begins along the innermost parts of the body and continues toward the outermost parts.

- According to Piaget, cognitive development depends on processes of assimilation and accommodation, and occurs in four stages: sensorimotor, preoperational, concrete operational, and formal operational.

- Although the general cognitive abilities associated with Piaget's four stages occur in the same order across cultures, children acquire many cognitive skills at an earlier age than Piaget believed. Vygotsky emphasized that cognitive development occurs in a sociocultural context. Each child has a zone of proximal development, reflecting the difference between what a child can do independently and what the child can do with assistance from others.

- Information-processing capacities improve with age. Older children search for information more systematically, process it more quickly, and display better memory.

- Kohlberg proposed that moral reasoning proceeds through three levels. Preconventional moral judgments are based on anticipated rewards and punishments. Conventional morality is based on conformity to social expectations, laws, and duties. Postconventional moral judgments are based on well thought out moral principles. Critics argue that the model contains cultural and gender biases.

- Erikson proposed that personality development proceeds through eight major psychosocial stages. Each stage involves a major crisis and the way we resolve it influences our ability to meet the challenges of the next stage.

- Temperament reflects a biologically based pattern of reacting emotionally and behaviorally to the environment. Extreme temperamental styles in infancy and childhood can predict some aspects functioning years later.

- Infant-caretaker attachment develops in three phases, and infants experience periods of stranger and separation anxiety. Secure attachment is associated with better developmental outcomes in childhood and adolescence than is insecure attachment. For most children, day care does not disrupt attachment. Divorce, however, disrupts children's psychological adjustment in the short term and, for some children, is associated with a long-term pattern of maladjustment.

- Parenting styles vary along dimensions of warmth-hostility and restrictiveness-permissiveness. The children of authoritative parents generally display the best developmental outcomes. Gender identity begins to form early in childhood and socialization influences children's acquisition of sex-role stereotypes.

Adolescence

- In Western cultures puberty marks the onset of adolescence. Generally, early maturation is a more positive experience for boys than it is for girls.

- Abstract thinking capabilities increase during adolescence, but young adolescents often show egocentrism in their social thinking. The search for identity is a key task of adolescence. With age, teens who have not yet experienced an identity crisis become more likely to do, and most resolve it successfully.

- During adolescence peer relationships become more important and intimate. Most teens maintain good relations with their parents.

Adulthood

- Young adults are at the peak of their physical capabilities. Information-processing speed declines steadily after reaching one's thirties. Longitudinal data show that many intellectual abilities do not begin to decline reliably until late adulthood.

- Erikson proposed that intimacy versus isolation, generativity versus stagnation, and integrity versus despair are the main crises of early, middle, and late adulthood.

- Premarital cohabitation is associated with a higher risk of marital divorce, though this does not appear to be a causal relation. For many couples marital satisfaction tends to decline in the years following the birth of children, but increases later in adulthood.

- Work serves important psychological and social functions. Overall, women experience more career gaps and their career paths are more variable than men's. Most adults do not experience a full-blown "midlife crisis." Similarly, most retired people do not become more anxious, depressed, or lonely due to retirement.

- Many terminally ill patients experience similar psychological reactions as they cope with their impending death, but beliefs and feelings about death vary with culture and age, and there is no "normal" way to approach death.

KEY TERMS AND CONCEPTS*

accommodation (462)

adolescent egocentrism (482)

assimilation (462)

attachment (473)

authoritarian parents (479)

authoritative parents (479)

cephalocaudal principle (460)

concrete operational stage (465)

conservation (463)

conventional moral reasoning (469)

critical period (454)

cross-sectional design (455)

egocentrism (464)

embryo (456)

fetal alcohol syndrome (FAS) (457)

fetus (456)

formal operational stage (465)

gender constancy (479)

gender identity (479)

imprinting (473)

indulgent parents (479)

longitudinal design (455)

maturation (459)

neglectful parents (479)

object permanence (462)

postconventional moral reasoning (470)

postformal thought (486)

preconventional moral reasoning (469)

preoperational stage (463)

proximodistal principle (460)

psychosocial stages (471)

puberty (481)

reflexes (459)

schema (462)

sensitive period (455)

sensorimotor stage (462)

separation anxiety (474)

sex-role stereotypes (479)

social clock (490)

socialization (480)

strange situation (475)

stranger anxiety (474)

temperament (472)

teratogens (457)

theory of mind (468)

zone of proximal development (466)

zygote (455)

*Each term has been boldfaced in the text on the page indicated in parentheses.

APPLYING YOUR KNOWLEDGE

These questions allow you to apply your understanding of the material in this chapter.

1. Dr. Yee wishes to study how children's memory changes with age. She obtains a sample of 100 4-year-olds, 100 6-year-olds, 100 8-year-olds, and 100 10-year-olds. Over the next few weeks, each child is tested once on the same memory task (a digit span task in which they are presented with series of numbers of different lengths). Dr. Yee finds that older children recall more numbers than younger children. In this study, Dr. Yee has used
   a) a sequential design.
   b) a cross-sectional design.
   c) a longitudinal design.
   d) a case study approach.

2. Roberta and Paul are the proud parents of a newborn baby girl. This means that when they conceived their child, the 23rd chromosome in Roberta's egg cell was a(n) _____ , and the 23rd chromosome in Paul's sperm cell was a(n) _____ .
   a) X; X
   b) X; Y
   c) Y; X
   d) Y; Y

3. William was born with facial and heart abnormalities, and a small, malformed brain. He has difficulties in visual perception and is mentally retarded. It is most likely that William's mother _____ during pregnancy.
   a) smoked a pack or more of cigarettes a day
   b) contracted German measles
   c) regularly consumed large amounts of alcohol
   d) used cocaine at least once a week

4. Susan is a young child, and she knows that fish swim. One day, at the zoo, a penguin is swimming in the water. Susan points to the penguin and says to her parents, "Look, the black and white fish is swimming." The fact that Susan calls the penguin a fish because it is swimming best illustrates
   a) the process of assimilation.
   b) the process of accommodation.
   c) egocentric thinking.
   d) a failure to understand the principle of object permanence.

5. Geraldine is a middle-aged adult. As she enters late adulthood, we would expect her fluid intellectual abilities to begin to decline _____ her crystallized intellectual abilities
   a) at an earlier age than
   b) at a later age than
   c) at the same age as

6. You show Shawnda two identical short and wide glasses filled with an equal amount of water. You then take the water from one glass and pour it into a tall, narrow glass. When you ask Shawnda whether the remaining short glass and the tall glass have the same amount of water, or whether one has more water, Shawnda says, "The tall glass has more water." Based on her response, it is most likely that Shawnda is in the _____ stage of cognitive development.
   a) formal operational
   b) sensorimotor
   c) concrete operational
   d) preoperational

7. Ms. and Mr. Rodriguez are concerned about the psychological effects of placing their 1-year-old daughter into day care, and are seeking advice. We should inform them that, according to research, placing their daughter into day care will most likely
   a) cause her to become less securely attached to her parents.
   b) increase the risk, when she grows up, of behavior and adjustment problems during elementary school.
   c) cause her to become less securely attached and also increase the risk of long-term adjustment problems.
   d) not cause insecure attachment, nor increase the risk of long-term adjustment problems.

8. Cheryl is the first girl in her class, and Billy is the first boy in his, to enter puberty. On the basis of this early maturation, we would expect Cheryl to experience more _____ outcomes, and Billy to experience more _____ outcomes than their classmates who mature later.
   a) positive; positive
   b) positive; negative
   c) negative; positive
   d) negative; negative

9. Keith and Tracy have just turned 40 years old. If they are like most people their age, then we should expect that _____ will experience a severe midlife crisis within the next five or so years, becoming depressed and emotionally unstable.
   a) Keith
   b) Tracy
   c) both Keith and Tracy
   d) neither Keith nor Tracy

10. Leon is a healthy 65-year-old office manager who has voluntarily decided to retire. Studies indicate that once he retires, Leon most likely will
   a) show a much greater decline in physical health than if he had stayed on the job.
   b) become more dissatisfied in his marriage and social life.
   c) experience feelings of anxiety and depression that may last up to a year.
   d) maintain positive feelings about being retired.

Answers

1. b) (page 455); 2. a) (page 456); 3. c) (page 457); 4. a) (page 462); 5. a) (page 487); 6. d) (page 463); 7. d) (page 476); 8. c) (page 481); 9. d) (page 493); 10. d) (page 493).

For additional quizzing and a variety of interactive resources, visit the book's Online Learning Center at www.mhhe.com/passer.

BEHAVIOR IN A SOCIAL CONTEXT

Without the human community, one
single human being cannot survive.
— *The Dalai Lama*

12

CHAPTER OUTLINE

The prison had become a living hell. Hidden behind their mirrored sunglasses, the guards asserted their total authority over the prisoners. The guards' permission was required to do virtually anything, including going to the toilet. After they quickly put down a prisoners' rebellion, cruelty became the order of the day. The guards conducted roll calls in the middle of the night to assert their power and disrupt the prisoners' sleep. Prisoners were forced to do push-ups, sometimes with a guard's foot pushing down on the prisoner's back. For their part, the prisoners became increasingly passive and depressed. They hated the guards, but were powerless against them. After a few days, one prisoner cracked emotionally. Soon another broke down. Before long, the demoralized prisoners became what the guards expected them to be—objects of scorn and abuse.

This prison was not in some brutal dictatorship, the prisoners were not hardened criminals, nor were the guards sadistic psychopaths. Instead, this prison was in the basement of the Psychology Building at Stanford University and the guards and prisoners were intelligent, well-adjusted college students. Social psychologist Philip Zimbardo watched in disbelief as scenes of callous inhumanity unfolded before him.

What began as a two-week simulation of prison life had to be stopped after only six days. Zimbardo and his associates held several sessions with the participants to help them work through their powerful emotional reactions, and they maintained contact over the following year to ensure that participants did not experience lasting negative effects.

What transformed normal college students into people they would not have recognized a week earlier? As one guard recalled, "I was surprised at myself. I made them . . . clean out the toilets with their bare hands. I practically considered the prisoners cattle. . . ." (Zimbardo et al., 1973, p. 42). Decades later, the "Stanford Prison Study" remains a landmark for dramatically illustrating a basic concept: Behavior is determined not only by our biological endowment and past learning experiences, but also by the power of the immediate social situation (Haney & Zimbardo, 1998).

As social beings, we belong. We spend our lives in a stream of social environments that profoundly shape how we behave, think, and feel. In this chapter we explore the field of social psychology, which studies how other people influence our behavior (*social influence*), how we think about and perceive our social world (*social thinking and social perception*), and how we behave toward other people (*social relations*).

〉 SOCIAL INFLUENCE

Patricia, a novice piano player, makes more mistakes after her parents enter the room to listen to her practice. Shawn donates money to a charity after seeing his coworkers contribute. A "guard" in the Stanford Prison Study mistreats a fellow student "prisoner." These diverse situations share one basic ingredient: They all involve social influence.

The Mere Presence of Others

➤ 1. When does the mere presence of other people enhance or impair performance? Why?

Norman Triplett (1898) helped launch the field of social psychology by testing a deceptively simple hypothesis: The presence of others energizes performance. Triplett, who loved bicycle racing, analyzed the records from numerous competitions. In some races, cyclists performed individually against the clock; in other races of similar distance, they performed together in a "pack." As Triplett predicted, cyclists' average speed per mile was much faster in group races than in individual races. Next, in a laboratory experiment, Triplett had children perform a simple physical task as rapidly as they could, either alone or in the presence of another child (called a *coactor*) who independently performed the same task. Again, performance improved when people were in each other's presence (Triplett, 1898).

Many early studies replicated this finding; the *mere presence* of coactors or a passive, silent audience enhanced performance. Even ants carried more dirt when in the presence of other ants (Chen, 1937). Yet other experiments found that performance on learning tasks worsened when coactors or an audience were present.

In 1965, Robert Zajonc proposed a theory to explain this seeming paradox. First, the mere physical presence of another person (or member of the same species) increases our arousal. Second, as arousal increases, we become more likely to perform whatever behavior happens to be our *dominant response* (i.e., our most typical response) to that specific situation. When a task is difficult and complex, and we are first trying to learn it, our dominant response is to make errors. Therefore performing in front of an audience or with coactors should impair performance. But when a task either is simple or is complex but well learned, our dominant response usually is to perform the task correctly. In these situations, performing in the presence of others will enhance performance (Figure 12.1). This phenomenon is called **social facilitation,** an increased tendency to perform one's dominant response in the mere presence of others (Blascovich et al., 1999).

Social facilitation occurs in species ranging from cockroaches and fruit flies to rats and hens (Duncan et al., 1998; Zajonc, 1980). Meta-analyzing the results of 241 studies involving almost 24,000 participants, Charles Bond and Linda Titus (1983) found that social facilitation produced small but reliable effects on human performance. In one study, James Michaels and his colleagues (1982) identified pairs of pool players who had either above average or below average skill. Then four observers (researchers) sauntered over to the pool tables at the college student union building to watch the players. As predicted, the presence of an audience increased the performance of the accomplished players (whose dominant responses were assumed to be correct), but decreased the performance of the less skilled players (whose dominant responses were assumed to be incorrect). Social facilitation may be the most basic of all social influence processes, and it has an important practical implication: When learning complex tasks, minimize the presence of other people.

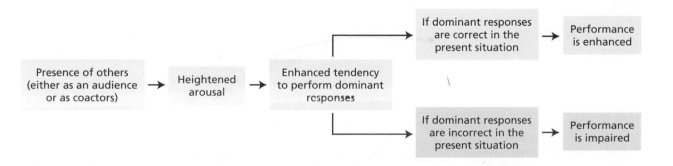

FIGURE 12.1   Will this young musician's performance improve or worsen if other people stop by to listen? Zajonc's (1965) theory of social facilitation proposes that the presence of other people increases our arousal, which then makes us more likely to perform our dominant response. If the dominant response (e.g., a particular finger movement) happens to be correct—as typically occurs on simple tasks or complex tasks that have been mastered—then performance will be enhanced. But if the dominant response is incorrect—as often occurs when a novice is trying to learn a complex task—then the presence of other people most likely will impair performance.

➤ 2. How do norms and roles guide our behavior?

Social Norms: The Rules of the Game

Years ago a professor on our campus gave his class an unusual assignment: Without doing anything illegal, they were to violate some "unspoken rule" of social behavior and observe people's reactions. One student licked her plate clean at a formal dinner, receiving cold stares from other guests. Another boarded a city bus, sat down next to the only other passenger, and said "Hi." The passenger sat up stiffly and stared out the window. The assignment ended when a third student entered class—attired only in a thin coat of oil.

Social norms are shared expectations about how people should think, feel, and behave, and they are the cement that binds social systems together (Cialdini & Trost, 1998). Some norms are formal laws and regulations, but many are implicit and unspoken. As the "break-a-norm" examples illustrate, such norms powerfully regulate daily behavior without our conscious awareness; we take them for granted—until they are violated.

A **social role** consists of a *set* of norms that characterizes how people in a given social position ought to behave. The roles of "college student," "professor," "police officer," and "spouse" carry different sets of behavior expectations. Because we may wear many hats in our daily life, *role conflict* can occur when the norms accompanying different roles clash. College students who hold jobs or who have children often experience role conflict as they try to juggle the competing demands of school, work, and parenthood.

Norms and roles can influence behavior so strongly that they compel a person to act uncharacteristically. The guards in the Stanford Prison Study were well-adjusted students, yet norms related to the role of "guard" and to concepts of "crime and punishment" seemed to override their values, leading to dehumanizing treatment of the prisoners.

Culture and Norm Formation

Social norms lose invisibility not only when they are violated, but also when we examine behavior across cultures and historical periods. In doing so, we see that social customs we take for granted as *"normal"*—from gender roles to sexual practices and views of love and marriage—are merely arbitrary (Figure 12.2). Norms even regulate such subtle aspects of social behavior as the amount of *personal space* that we prefer when interacting with people. For example, Japanese sit farther apart when conversing than Venezuelans do, and Americans prefer an intermediate distance (Sussman & Rosenfeld, 1982). Italians and Greeks are more likely to touch while interacting than are Europeans from more northern regions (Remland et al., 1995).

Indeed, it is difficult to imagine any society, organization, or social group functioning well without norms. In a classic experiment, Muzafer Sherif (1935) found that even randomly created groups develop norms. The task involved an optical illusion called the *autokinetic effect:* When people stare at a dot of light projected on a screen in a dark room, they begin to perceive the dot as moving, even though it really is stationary. When Sherif tested college students individually over several trials, each student perceived the light to move a different amount, from an inch or two to almost a foot.

Later the students were randomly placed into groups of three and made further judgments. As the members within each group heard one another's judgments over several sessions, their judgments converged and a group norm evolved. The participants did not explicitly communicate or "decide" to develop a group norm. It just happened. Moreover, just as norms vary across cultures, the norm that evolved for how far the dot of light moved varied from group to group, and it was not the simple average of the original judgments (Figure 12.3). When participants were retested *individually* a year later, their judgments continued to reflect their group's norm (Rohrer et al., 1954).

(a)

(b)

FIGURE 12.2 Norms may vary over time and across cultures (a) A century ago it was not "normal" for many Western women to have the right to vote, or to become doctors, business managers, and police officers. (b) Women in many countries wear skirts, shorts, sleeveless blouses, and bikinis in public. Yet some cultures consider it inappropriate and sexually suggestive for women to display any part of their body in public.

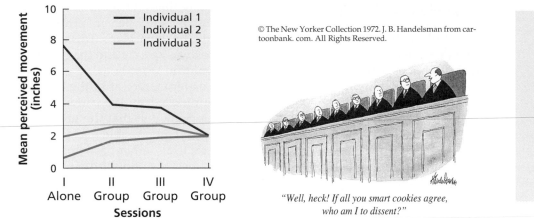

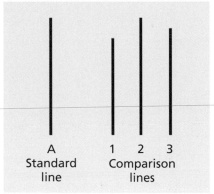

© The New Yorker Collection 1972. J. B. Handelsman from cartoonbank. com. All Rights Reserved.

"Well, heck! If all you smart cookies agree, who am I to dissent?"

FIGURE 12.3 In Sherif's experiments, individuals' autokinetic judgments made alone (Session I) began to converge when they were made in the presence of two other participants (Sessions II, III, IV). Each mean is based on 100 judgments per session. These data are from one of the three-person groups. Based on Sherif, 1935.

FIGURE 12.4 Often we conform to a majority because we believe that their opinion "must be right."

FIGURE 12.5 In Asch's (1955) conformity experiments, students were asked to judge which of three lines was the same length as another line. They performed this task for multiple trials, using a different set of standard and comparison lines each time.

Sherif's finding has been replicated in other countries and with different types of tasks (Khoury, 1985). Whether at a cultural level or in small random groups, humans placed together seem to develop common standards for behavior and judgment.

Conformity and Obedience

Norms can influence behavior only if people conform to them. Without *conformity*—the adjustment of individual behaviors, attitudes, and beliefs to a group standard—we would have social chaos. It is no accident therefore that all social systems exert overt and subtle pressures on their members to conform.

Why Do People Conform?

Psychologically, our desire to understand the world and respond to it effectively provides one basic motive for conforming (Biener & Boudreau, 1991). As Figure 12.4 illustrates, at times we follow the opinions or behavior of other people because we believe they have accurate knowledge and what they are doing is "right." This is called **informational social influence.** We also may conform to obtain rewards that come from being accepted by other people, while at the same time avoiding their rejection. This is called **normative social influence** (Deutsch & Gerard, 1955).

Solomon Asch's (1951, 1956) landmark conformity experiments illustrated both types of influence. In the experimental condition, groups of college students performed several trials of a simple visual task, shown in Figure 12.5. Only one member of the group, however, actually was a participant. The rest were accomplices (called "confederates") of the experimenter. Group members sat around a table and were called on in order. The real participant sat next to last. According to plan, every confederate intentionally gave the same wrong answer on some trials. Imagine, for example, that the first member says "Line 1." (You think to yourself, "Huh?"). Then the next four members also say "Line 1." (You're wondering, "Can this really be?"). Now it is your turn.

Would anybody conform to the group's incorrect judgments? Asch found that a quarter of the participants never conformed, a quarter conformed

> 3. Explain the difference between informational and normative social influence.

frequently, and the rest conformed once or a few times. Overall, participants conformed 37 percent of the time compared with a mere 1 percent error rate in a control condition where people judged the lines by themselves. This conformity rate stunned many scientists because the task was so easy and the confederates did not overtly pressure participants to conform.

During debriefing discussions with the experimenter after the task was over, many participants said that they were puzzled by the difference between their own and the group's perceptions. Some felt that the group was wrong, but went along to avoid "making waves" and possible rejection. This reflects normative social influence. After several trials, other participants succumbed to informational social influence and began to doubt their eyesight and judgment.

Factors That Affect Conformity

➤ 4. Identify some situational factors that influence people's degree of conformity.

Asch demonstrated that complex social behavior could be studied scientifically under controlled conditions. In subsequent experiments he manipulated different independent variables and measured their effects on conformity. Consider two examples.

- *Group size.* Conformity increased from about 5 to 35 percent as group size increased from one to about four or five confederates, but contrary to common sense, further increases in group size did not increase conformity. Participants were just as likely to conform when there were four or five confederates giving incorrect answers as when there were ten or fifteen.

- *Presence of a dissenter.* When one confederate (according to plan) disagreed with the others, this greatly reduced real participants' conformity. Even when the dissenter gave an incorrect answer (e.g., the majority said "Line 3" and the dissenter said "Line 1"), participants made many fewer errors. The key is that, when someone else dissents, this person serves as a model for remaining independent from the group.

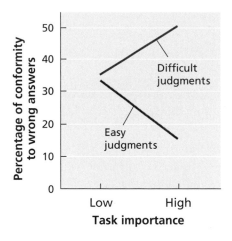

FIGURE 12.6 In this experiment, college students made a series of eyewitness memory judgments. For each judgment, one participant and two accomplices were shown a slide of a person. Next they had to pick out that person from a second slide showing four people. The second slide was presented for 5 seconds (easy task) or 0.5 seconds (hard task), and the accomplices intentionally gave wrong answers on some trials. Participants were told that the task was important (including a possible $20 prize for high accuracy) or unimportant. The high incentive decreased conformity on the easy task, but increased conformity when the task was difficult.

Based on Baron et al., 1996.

Would Asch's participants have conformed less if the task had been made more important to them, say, by offering a financial incentive for giving correct answers? As Figure 12.6 shows, when the correct answer is obvious (the task is easy, as was Asch's), conformity decreases when the consequences of going along with the group's erroneous judgment are made more costly (Baron et al., 1996). But when we are less sure of the right way to behave (the task is hard), conformity increases as the stakes become higher.

Reviewing 97 conformity experiments conducted in the United States from 1951 to 1990, Rod Bond and Peter Smith (1996) found that the overall level of conformity has decreased slightly over recent decades. Around the globe, conformity tends to be greater among research participants from collectivist cultures, where group harmony is valued more highly than in individualistic cultures. Overall, gender differences in conformity have been weak or nonexistent (Bond & Smith, 1996; Eagly & Carli, 1981).

Minority Influence

➤ 5. When is the minority most likely to influence the majority?

Although majority influence is powerful, in some cases the group minority may influence the majority's behavior. Serge Moscovici (1985) proposes that, to maximize its influence, the minority must be highly committed to its point of view, remain independent in the face of majority pressure, be consistent over time, yet appear to keep an open mind. Dissenting information presented by the minority may cause majority members to change their view, at least on a private level (Maass & Clark, 1984). In reviewing almost a hundred studies, Wendy Wood and her colleagues (1994) found that minority influence is strongest when it maintains a highly consistent position over time. However, if the minority appears too unreasonable, deviant, or negative, it may cause the majority to become entrenched or lead some people to shift their attitudes even further away from the minority's positon.

Obedience to Authority

Like conformity to a group, obedience to an authority figure is inherently neither good nor bad. As an airplane passenger, you would not be amused if the copilot disregarded the pilot's commands simply because he or she "didn't feel like obeying," putting the flight and your life at risk. Without obedience, society would face chaos.

But obedience can also produce tragic results. After World War II, the famous Nuremberg trials were held to judge Nazi war criminals who had slaughtered millions of innocent people in concentration camps. In many instances, the defense offered by the defendants was that they had "only followed orders." In the massacre of men, women, and children at My Lai during the Vietnam War, American soldiers accused of atrocities gave the same explanation. No doubt we will hear the cry of "I was just following orders" again as accountability is judged for more recent mass atrocities in Kosovo, Rwanda, and elsewhere around the globe.

Just as the Nuremberg court did, many of us reject justifications based on obedience to authority as mere rationalizations, secure in our conviction that we would behave more humanely in such situations. But would we? Our *Research Close-Up*—part of the most famous series of studies ever conducted in social psychology—suggests some provocative answers.

➤ 6. Describe Milgram's obedience experiment. Do you believe the results would be similar today? Why or why not?

RESEARCH ◢ CLOSE-UP

The Dilemma of Obedience: When Conscience Confronts Malevolent Authority

❭ Background

Stanley Milgram wanted to examine conformity in a more powerful situation than Asch had. Rather than have participants judge lines, Milgram thought about testing whether people would conform to group pressure and give electric shocks to a protesting victim. But he realized that a control condition was needed to measure how much shock people would give without group pressure. Here the experimenter would instruct each participant to give the shocks. As he thought about it, Milgram wondered: Would ordinary citizens obey such malevolent orders? How far would they go? At that moment, Milgram shifted his focus from conformity to obedience. Fueled by his desire to better understand the horrors and lessons of the Holocaust, Milgram conducted 18 obedience experiments between 1960 and 1963 (Milgram, 1974).

❭ Method

The following experiment was conducted twice, first with 40 men and then with 40 women. Participants ranged in age from 20 to 50 years and represented a cross section of occupations and educational backgrounds.

At the laboratory each participant met a middle-aged man who was introduced as another participant, but who actually was a confederate. They were told that the experiment examined the effects of punishment on memory. Then, through a supposedly random draw (it was rigged), the real participant became the *teacher* and the confederate became the *learner*. The teacher presented a series of memory problems to the learner through a two-way intercom system. Each time the learner made an error the teacher was instructed to administer an electric shock using a machine that had thirty switches, beginning with 15 volts and increasing step-by-step to 450 volts (Figure 12.7a). As the teacher watched, the learner was strapped into a chair in an adjoining room and hooked up to wires from the shock generator (Figure 12.7b). The learner expressed concern about the shock and mentioned that he had a slight heart problem.

Returning to the main room, the experimenter gave the teacher a sample shock (45 volts) and then ordered the experiment to begin. Unbeknownst to the teacher, the learner actually did *not* receive any shock and intentionally committed many errors. The learner made verbal protests

—Continued

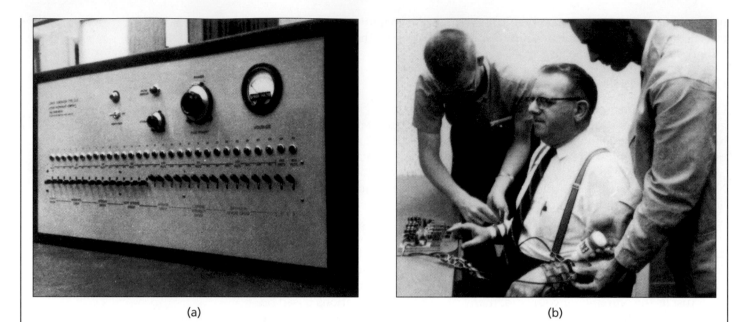

(a)   (b)

FIGURE 12.7   (a) Switches on the shock generator ranged form 15 volts ("slight shock") to 450 volts ("XXX"). (b) The participant (teacher) saw the learner being strapped into the chair.

that were standardized on a tape recorder, so that they were the same for all participants.

As the learner's errors mounted the teacher increased the shock. If the teacher balked at continuing, the experimenter issued one or more escalating commands, such as "Please continue," "You must continue," and "You have no other choice." At 75 volts the learner moaned when the teacher threw the switch. At 150 volts the learner's reaction was "Ugh!!! Experimenter! That's all. Get me out of here. I told you I had heart trouble. My heart's starting to bother me now. Get me out of here, please . . . I refuse to go on. Let me out." Beyond 200 volts he emitted agonized screams every time a shock was delivered, yelling "Let me out! Let me out!" At 300 volts the learner refused to answer and continued screaming to be let out. At 345 volts and beyond, there was only silence. Full obedience was operationally defined as continuing to the maximum shock level of 450 volts.

▶ **Results**

Participants wrestled with a dilemma. Should they continue to hurt this innocent person, as the experimenter commanded, or should they stop the learner's pain by openly disobeying? Most participants became stressed. Some trembled, sweated, laughed nervously, or in a few cases, experienced convulsions. But would they obey? Make a prediction: What percent of people obeyed to 450 volts, and were there any gender differences?

When Milgram asked psychiatrists, professors, university students, and middle-class adults to predict the outcome, they estimated a 1 percent obedience rate. Indeed, most participants balked or protested at one time or another and said they would not continue. But ultimately, 26 of the 40 men and an identical 26 of 40 women (65 percent) obeyed to the end (Figure 12.8).

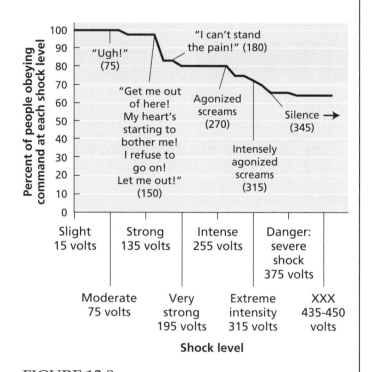

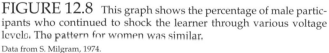

FIGURE 12.8   This graph shows the percentage of male participants who continued to shock the learner through various voltage levels. The pattern for women was similar.

Data from S. Milgram, 1974.

▶ **Critical Discussion**

Milgram's research has generated controversy for decades (Blass, 2000). On one level, its ethics were harshly criticized (Baumrind, 1964): Participants were deceived, exposed to substantial stress, and risked long-lasting

—*Continued*

negative effects to their self-image. Milgram countered that the research was so socially significant as to warrant the deception, that participants were carefully debriefed afterward, and that psychiatric follow-ups of a sample of obedient participants suggested no long-term ill effects. Weighing the costs and benefits, do you believe that this research was justified?

Researchers also debate why obedience was high, but many agree with Milgram's view that participants psychologically transferred much of the "responsibility" for the teacher's fate to the experimenter (Blass, 1996; Darley, 1995). While administering the shock, some participants stated that they "were not responsible" for what happened. Others asked, "Who is responsible if something happens to the learner?" When the experimenter replied, "I am responsible," participants felt greater freedom to continue. Yet they were the ones flipping the switch.

Would similar results occur today? We suspect so. For 25 years after Milgram's research, experiments in different coun-tries, in "real-world" settings, and with children, adolescents, and adults, yielded depressingly consistent results (Miller, 1986). In the 1980s, Dutch researchers Wim Meeus and Quinten Raaijmakers (1986, 1995) conducted 19 obedience studies. In one, 92 percent of male and female participants completely obeyed an experimenter's orders to repeatedly disrupt the performance of a job applicant (actually a confederate) taking a very important job screening test. To no avail, the applicant pleaded with participants to stop.

How would you have responded? Almost all of our own students say they would have disobeyed. So suppose we conduct the experiment today, but with real electric shock and with you as the learner. The teacher will be a randomly selected student from your class. Are you confident that this student will disobey? Few of our students express such confidence. In short, virtually all of us are confident that *we* would not obey, but we are not so sure about other people—and in turn they are not so sure about *us*.

Source: Stanley Milgram, 1974. *Obedience to Authority.* New York: Harper & Row.

Factors That Influence Destructive Obedience

By changing various aspects of the experimental situation, Milgram and other researchers obtained obedience rates ranging from zero to over 90 percent.

➤ 7. What situational factors increase obedience?

- *Remoteness of the victim.* Obedience was greater when the learner was out of sight. When the teacher and learner were placed in the same room, obedience dropped to 40 percent. Further, when the teacher had to make physical contact and force the learner's hand onto a "shock plate," obedience dropped to 30 percent (Figure 12.9).

- *Closeness and legitimacy of the authority figure.* Obedience was highest when the authority figure was close and perceived as legitimate. When the experimenter left the scene and gave orders by phone, or when an "ordinary person" (a confederate) took over and gave the orders, obedience dropped to about 20 percent.

- *Cog in a wheel.* When another "participant" (actually a confederate) flipped the shock switch and real participants only had to perform another aspect of the task, 93 percent obeyed. In short, *obedience increases when someone else does the "dirty work."* In contrast, when Harvey Tilker (1970) made participants feel fully responsible for the learner's welfare, not a single person obeyed to the end.

- *Personal characteristics.* Milgram compared the political orientation, religious affiliation, occupations, education, length of military service, and psychological characteristics of obedient versus disobedient participants. Differences were weak or nonexistent. Likewise, gender is not consistently related to obedience rates (Milgram, 1974; Shanab & Yahya, 1977).

Lessons Learned: From the Holocaust to Airline Safety

What lessons shall we draw from this research? Certainly, it is *not* that people are apathetic or evil. Participants became stressed precisely because they did care about the teacher's welfare. Neither is the lesson that we are sheep. If we

FIGURE 12.9 In one of Milgram's studies (Touch Proximity), the teacher was ordered to physically force the learner's hand onto a shock plate after the learner refused to continue. Here, 30 percent of participants obeyed fully to 450 volts. Although touch proximity strongly reduced obedience, that a significant minority still obeyed raises considerable concern.

were, obedience would be high across all situations, which is not the case. Rather, Milgram sums up a key lesson as follows:

> "... it would be a mistake ... to make the simple-minded statement that kindly and good persons disobey while those who are cruel do not ... often, it is not so much the kind of person a man is as the kind of situation in which he finds himself that determines how he will act." (Milgram, 1974, p. 205)

In other words, by arranging the situation appropriately, most people—ordinary, decent citizens—can be induced to follow orders from an authority figure they perceive as legitimate, even when doing so contributes to harming innocent people. The applicability of this principle to the Holocaust and other atrocities seems clear. During the Holocaust, obedience was made easier because most of the personnel working at the concentration camps were cogs in a horrendous wheel: They didn't pull the switch to flood the chambers with gas, but instead performed other tasks. Their victims also were "remote" at the moment of their murder. Further, to lessen concentration camp worker's feeling of responsibility, Hitler's subordinate Heinrich Himmler told them in manipulative speeches that only he and Hitler were personally responsible for what took place (Davidowicz, 1975).

Does obedience research suggest that we are not responsible for following orders? This is a moral and legal question, not a scientific one. But if anything, this research should heighten our responsibility for being aware of the pitfalls of blind obedience and prevent us from being so smug or naive as to feel that such events "could never happen here."

Increased sensitivity to the power of obedience pressures also has had concrete applications. As an airline passenger, there are times when you would want the copilot to challenge a pilot's commands, such as when the pilot's actions pose a clear threat to flight safety. But traditionally, copilots have been reluctant to do this (National Transportation Safety Board, 1979). Actual cockpit recordings and flight simulator experiments suggest that several jetliner crashes might have been prevented had copilots been more assertive in taking over control or questioning pilots' decisions (Foushee, 1984; Helmreich, 1997). Responding to concerns raised by aviation psychologists and others, several commercial airlines currently use a program called Crew Resource Management to enhance crew communication and increase copilots' assertiveness (Helmreich et al., 1999).

➤ 8. Describe deindividuation and how conditions in the Stanford Prison Study may have fostered it.

Crowd Behavior and Deindividuation

Years ago in New York City, a handyman sat perched on a ledge for an hour while a crowd of nearly 500 people on the street below shouted at him to jump. Fortunately, police managed to rescue the man. New York is hardly alone, as Australian psychologist Leon Mann (1981) found when he analyzed newspaper reports of 21 cases in which crowds were present when a person threatened to jump off a building. In 10 cases, the crowd had encouraged the person to jump.

What could prompt people to encourage distraught human beings to end their lives? In the 19th century, French physician Gustave LeBon (1895) suggested that the anonymity that exists in mobs leads to a loss of personal identity and a weakening of restraints that prompts people to engage in behaviors they would not perform as individuals (Figure 12.10). This condition is called

FIGURE 12.10 Deindividuation can lead to a loss of restraint that causes people to engage in uncharacteristic behaviors. In 1997, students at the University of Colorado, Boulder, rioted to protest a new campus policy designed to curb their partying.

deindividuation, a loss of individuality that leads to disinhibited behavior (Festinger et al., 1952). The concept of deindividuation has been applied to diverse types of antisocial behavior, from cheating and stealing to riots by sports fans and acts of genocide (Staub et al., 1996).

But what is the primary aspect of deindividuation that disinhibits behavior? Tom Postmes and Russell Spears (1998) meta-analyzed 60 deindividuation studies and determined that *anonymity to outsiders* was the key. Conditions that make an individual less identifiable to people *outside* the group reduce feelings of accountability and, slightly but consistently, increase the risk of antisocial actions. Postmes and Spears suggest that being anonymous to outsiders enhances the individual's tendency to focus on his or her identity with the group and makes the person more responsive to emerging group norms.

Reinforcing the importance of anonymity to outsiders, Mann (1981) found that people were most likely to encourage a potential suicide victim to jump when the crowd was large and it was dark outside. During the Stanford Prison Study, no names were used and guards had to be called "Mr. Correctional Officer." All guards wore identical uniforms and reflecting sunglasses that prevented the prisoners from making direct eye contact. The guards were unaware that their behavior was being monitored by the experimenters, and antisocial norms evolved from the role of "tough prison guard" adopted by those participants who spontaneously took over leadership roles (Zimbardo et al., 1973). These factors led Zimbardo to conclude that deindividuation was a key factor in the cruelty exhibited by the guards. Reducing anonymity—and thereby increasing public accountability—may be the most basic approach to counteracting deindividuation.

Group Influences on Performance and Decision Making

Much of our behavior occurs in groups, from family and friendship groups to social clubs, work groups, and athletic teams. People often form groups to make decisions or perform tasks that are too complex or physically demanding to be accomplished by one person. We now consider some factors that enhance or interfere with group productivity.

Social Loafing: Failing to Pull Your Own Weight

In 1913, Max Ringelmann, a French agricultural engineer, measured the force that men exerted while pulling on a rope as hard as they could. Individually, the men averaged 63 kilograms (kg) of pull. In groups of 3, you might expect a combined pull of about 3×63 kg = 189 kg, and 504 kg for groups of 8. But this isn't what happened. The total pull in 3- and 8-man groups was 16 percent and 51 percent below expectations, respectively.

Why did this happen? Perhaps the men didn't coordinate the timing of their pull precisely, and there was a loss of mechanical efficiency. Or perhaps each person exerted less effort when in a group. To resolve this issue, Alan Ingham and his colleagues (1974) led blindfolded participants to believe that they were pulling a rope (connected to a force meter) either alone or in groups of various sizes. In reality, participants were always alone, and therefore any performance drop had to be due to diminished effort. Overall, participants exerted 18 percent less force when they thought they were in a group.

The tendency for people to expend less individual effort when working in a group than when working alone is called **social loafing.** In contrast to social facilitation experiments, where a person performs a task individually (in front of an audience or with a coactor) and *does not pool* her or his effort with anyone, social loafing involves collective performance. Thus contrary to what common sense may tell you, when college students and high school cheerleaders are asked to be as loud as possible, they individually clap, shout, and

➤ 9. What is social loafing and when is it most likely to occur?

cheer *less* loudly when performing as a group than when they are alone (Hardy & Latané, 1986).

Social loafing also occurs on cognitive tasks, such as when people have to evaluate written materials, make decisions in simulated juries, and monitor the concentration of gases in the air (Hoeksema et al., 1998). Why does social loafing occur? Steven Karau and Kipling Williams (1993) propose a *collective effort model:* On a collective task, people will put forth effort only to the extent that they expect their effort to contribute to obtaining a valued goal. In support of this model, their meta-analysis of 78 social loafing studies revealed that social loafing is *more* likely to occur when

- people believe that individual performance within the group is not being monitored;
- the task (goal) has less value or meaning to the person;
- the group is less important to the person; and
- the task is simple and the person's input is redundant with that of other group members.

Fatigue also seems to increase social loafing. By having participants work on various cognitive tasks for 20 hours without sleep, Dutch researchers demonstrated that we are more likely to "skate by" on other group members' shoulders when we are tired (Hoeksema et al., 1998). Social loafing also depends on gender and culture (Karau & Williams, 1993). It occurs more strongly in all-male groups than in all-female or mixed-sex groups, possibly because women may be more concerned about group outcomes than are men. Participants from individualistic cultures (Canada and the United States) exhibit more social loafing than people from collectivistic cultures (China, Japan, Taiwan), where group goals are especially valued.

When are groups more productive than individuals?   Social loafing suggests that, in terms of group performance, "the whole is less than the sum of its parts." But this is not always the case. Social loafing may disappear when individual performance is monitored or when members highly value their group or the task goal (Karau & Hart, 1998). In fact, to achieve a highly desired goal, some members may engage in *social compensation:* They will work harder in a group than alone if they expect that their colleagues either don't have enough ability or will slack off.

Even when social loafing occurs, groups still accomplish physical feats that individuals cannot—from pulling a car out of a ditch to building a commercial jetliner. On problem-solving tasks, groups frequently develop better solutions than individuals do (Hellriegel et al., 1989). Groups provide a greater diversity of resources and more opportunities for errors to be corrected. Groups are especially likely to be more effective than individuals on tasks that can be subdivided easily.

Group Polarization: Going to Extremes

Groups are often called upon to make key decisions. Governments, educational institutions, and corporations frequently develop policies through committees. The fate of defendants often rests in the hands of juries. Such decisions are often entrusted to groups because they are assumed to be more conservative than individuals and less likely to "go off the deep end." Is this assumption correct? It is, as long as the group is generally conservative to begin with. In such cases, the group's final opinion or attitude will likely be even *more conservative.* But if the group members lean toward a more liberal or risky viewpoint to begin with, the group's decision will tend to become *more liberal or riskier.* This principle is called **group polarization:** When a group of like-minded people discusses an issue, whether face to face or over e-mail, the "average" opinion of group members tends to become more extreme (Liu & Latané, 1998; Moscovici & Zavalloni, 1969).

Why does group polarization occur? One reason, reflecting *normative social influence,* is that individuals who are attracted to a group may be motivated to

➤ 10. Identify two causes of group polarization.

adopt a more extreme position to gain the group's approval. A second reason, reflecting *informational social influence,* is that during group discussions people hear arguments supporting their positions that they had not previously considered. These new arguments tend to make the initial positions seem even more valid (Burnstein, 1983).

Groupthink: Suspending Critical Thinking

After the U.S. military ignored warning signs of imminent attack by Japan in 1941, the fleet at Pearl Harbor was destroyed in a "surprise" attack. In 1961, President Kennedy and his advisors launched the hopelessly doomed Bay of Pigs invasion of Cuba. In 1972, five men broke into Democratic Party offices at the Watergate hotel, and the following cover-up forced President Nixon to resign. According to Yale social psychologist Irving Janis (1983), the decision-makers involved in each of these historical blunders fell victim to a process called **groupthink,** the tendency of group members to suspend critical thinking because they are striving to seek agreement.

Janis developed the concept of groupthink, shown in Figure 12.11, after analyzing historical accounts of group deliberations that resulted in disastrous decisions. He proposed that groupthink is most likely to occur when a group

- is under *high stress* to reach a decision;
- is *insulated* from outside input;
- has a *directive leader* who promotes her or his personal agenda; and
- has *high cohesion,* reflecting a spirit of closeness and ability to work well together.

Under these conditions, the group is so committed to reaching a consensus while remaining loyal and agreeable, that members suspend their critical judgment.

Various symptoms signal that groupthink is at work. For example, group members who express doubt are faced with *direct pressure* to stop "rocking the boat." Some members serve as *mind guards* by preventing negative information from reaching the group. Ultimately, members display *self-censorship* and withhold their doubts, creating a potentially disastrous *illusion of unanimity* in which each member comes to believe that "everyone else seems to agree with the decision" (Figure 12.12).

Many aspects of groupthink were present during the decision process leading up to the fatal launch of the space shuttle *Challenger* in 1986 (Esser & Lindoerfer, 1995; Moorhead et al., 1991). A Presidential Commission found that the engineers who designed the rocket boosters had strongly opposed the launch, fearing that subfreezing weather would make rubber seals too brittle to contain hot gasses from the rocket. NASA, however, was under high stress and leadership was directive. This shuttle mission was to be historic, carrying America's first civilian into space. There had been several delays and NASA did not want another one. To foster an illusion of unanimity, a key NASA executive polled only management officials, excluding the engineers from the final decision-making process (Magnuson, 1986). Thanks to mind guarding, the NASA official who gave the final go-ahead was never informed of the concerns expressed by the engineers.

In general, research supports Janis's belief that directive leaders impair effective group decision making (Esser, 1998). A meta-analysis of 17 experiments found that high cohesion does indeed impair good decision making, but *only when the other antecedent conditions of groupthink are also present* (Mullen et al., 1994). When a group has procedures in place to stimulate critical thinking, high cohesion enhances good decision making.

Can groupthink be prevented? Janis suggested that the leader should remain impartial during discussions, regularly encourage critical thinking, bring in outsiders to offer their opinions, and divide the larger group into subgroups—to see if each subgroup independently reaches the same decision. Of course, even groups that display poor decision-making procedures may still end up making a

➤ 11. What are some causes, symptoms, and consequences of groupthink?

Antecedent conditions
1. High stress to reach a decision
2. Insulation of the group
3. Directive leadership
4. High cohesiveness

↓

Some symptoms of groupthink
1. Illusion of invulnerability (group overestimates itself)
2. Direct pressure on dissenters
3. Self-censorship
4. Illusion of unanimity
5. Self-appointed mind guards

↓

Groupthink increases risk of defective decision making
1. Incomplete survey of alternatives
2. Incomplete survey of objectives
3. Failure to examine risks of preferred choice
4. Poor information search
5. Failure to reappraise alternatives

FIGURE 12.11 Antecedents, symptoms, and negative effects of groupthink on decision making.
Adapted from I. L. Janis, 1983.

"*All those in favor say 'aye'.*"
  "*Aye.*"   "*Aye.*"   "*Aye.*"
          "*Aye.*"   "*Aye.*"   "*Aye.*"

(a)

(b)

FIGURE 12.12 (a) The illusion of unanimity occurs when group members collectively fail to speak their true minds. (b) This illusion contributed to the ill-fated decision to launch the space shuttle *Challenger* on January 28, 1986. The *Challenger* exploded shortly after takeoff, killing all astronauts on board.

➤ 12. Why did LaPiere's study raise doubts about attitude-behavior consistency?

➤ 13. Discuss three broad conditions under which attitudes best predict behavior.

correct decision, or at least may "get away" with a bad one (Raven, 1998). Conversely, critical debate will not guarantee a positive outcome, but it will enhance the odds.

❭ SOCIAL THINKING AND PERCEPTION

Beyond decision making, we spend a great deal of time thinking about our social world. We hold countless attitudes and beliefs, wonder about why people act as they do, and develop impressions of people. Social psychologists have devoted considerable attention to these three aspects of social thinking and perception.

Attitudes and Attitude Change

In 1935, Gordon Allport called attitude "social psychology's most indispensable concept" (p. 798). Our attitudes help define our identity, guide our actions, and influence how we judge people (Maio & Olson, 2000). Indeed, attitudes help steer the course of world events, from political elections to war to the latest fashion craze.

An **attitude** is a positive or negative evaluative reaction toward a stimulus, such as a person, action, object, or concept (Tesser & Shaffer, 1990). Whether disagreeing with a governmental policy or agreeing with a movie review, you are expressing evaluative reactions. Sometimes, as shown in Figure 12.13, our attitudes are supported by an extensive personal belief and value system.

Do Our Attitudes Influence Our Behavior?

If we tell you that, according to research, people's attitudes strongly guide their behavior, you might reply "So what? That's just common sense." But consider a classic study by Richard LaPiere (1934). In the 1930s he toured the United States with a young Chinese couple, stopping at 251 restaurants, hotels, and other establishments. At the time, prejudice against Asians was widespread, yet the couple—who often entered the establishment before LaPiere did—was refused service only once. Later LaPiere wrote to all of the places they had visited, asking if they would provide service to Chinese patrons. More than 90 percent of those who responded stated that they would not.

In LaPiere's study we cannot be sure that the people who expressed negative attitudes in the survey were the same individuals who, months earlier, had actually served the Chinese couple. Yet the discrepancy between stated prejudicial attitudes and nondiscriminatory behavior seemed so overwhelming that it called the "commonsense" assumption of attitude-behavior consistency into question. Better-controlled studies found similar results, and in a 1969 research review, Allen Wicker concluded that there was little evidence that attitudes predict behavior.

After this wake-up call psychologists explored the attitude-behavior link in greater detail, leading Stephan Kraus (1995) to conclude in a more recent review that, overall, attitudes predict behavior to a modest degree. Most importantly, we now understand three factors that help explain why the attitude-behavior relationship is strong in some cases, but weak in others.

First, *attitudes influence behavior more strongly when counteracting situational factors are weak*. Financial incentives, conformity and obedience pressures, deindividuation, groupthink, and other conditions may lead people to behave in ways that are at odds with their inner convictions. According to the **theory of planned behavior** and similar models (Ajzen, 1991; Fishbein, 1980), our intention to engage in a behavior is strongest when we have a positive attitude toward that behavior, when *subjective norms* (our perceptions of what other people think we should do) support our attitudes, and when we believe that the behavior is under our control. Based on this approach researchers have successfully predicted numerous behaviors, including whether people will undergo breast cancer screenings, become smokers, use condoms, attend church, donate blood, and seek out therapy (Courneya et al., 1999; Rutter, 2000).

Second, *attitudes have a greater influence on behavior when we are aware of them and when they are strongly held.* Sometimes we seem to act "without thinking," out of impulse or habit. Attitude-behavior consistency increases when people consciously think about their attitudes before acting (Powell & Fazio, 1984; Snyder & Swann, 1976). In addition, attitudes are stronger and more predictive of behavior when they are formed through direct personal experience, rather than through secondhand, indirect information (Millar & Millar, 1996).

Third, *general attitudes do best at predicting general classes of behavior, and specific attitudes do best at predicting specific behaviors.* For example, Martin Fishbein and Icek Ajzen (1974) found almost no relation between people's general attitudes toward religion and 70 specific religious behaviors (such as the frequency of praying before meals or attending services). However, when they combined the 70 specific behaviors into a single "global index" of religious behavior, the relation between general religious attitudes and overall religious behavior was substantial.

Does Our Behavior Influence Our Attitudes?

As we have just seen, under the proper conditions people's attitudes guide their behavior. But attitude-behavior consistency is not a one-way street: We also come to develop attitudes that are consistent with how we behave. In the Stanford Prison Study, as the guards slipped into their roles and began mistreating the prisoners, they began to view the prisoners as little more than animals. Why should this be?

Self-justification.   Imagine that you volunteer for an experiment, arrive at the laboratory, and perform two extremely boring tasks emptying and filling a tray with spools over and over, and repeatedly turning 48 pegs stuck into holes. After 60 minutes of the laboratory equivalent of being bit to death by ducks, the experimenter enters, thanks you for participating, and asks for your help. It is important for the next student to begin the study with a "positive attitude" about the tasks, and all you have to do is tell the student that the boring tasks are interesting. Depending upon the condition to which you have been randomly assigned, the experimenter offers to pay you either $1 or $20 for, essentially, lying to the next participant. To help out, you agree to do so. Afterward, you go to the psychology department's main office to collect your money and fill out a "routine form" that asks how much you enjoyed the tasks in the experiment.

Make a prediction: Comparing participants who received $1 and who received $20 with a control group that simply rated the boring tasks without telling any lie beforehand, which of the three groups rated the task most positively? Why?

Common sense might suggest that participants paid $20 would feel happiest about the experiment and rate the task most highly. However, as Figure 12.14 shows, and as Leon Festinger and J. Merrill Carlsmith (1959) predicted, participants who were paid $1 gave the most positive ratings. Indeed, they actually rated the boring tasks as slightly enjoyable!

According to Festinger's (1957) **theory of cognitive dissonance,** people strive for consistency in their cognitions. When two or more cognitions contradict one another (such as "I am a truthful

FIGURE 12.13 The components of a person's attitude toward smoking. Around the attitude object (smoking) are beliefs related to smoking. The plus and minus signs show the positive or negative value the person associates with each belief. The minus sign in the center indicates the resulting overall negative attitude toward smoking cigarettes.

Adapted from Sears et al., 1985.

➤ 14. What causes cognitive dissonance, and how can it produce attitude change?

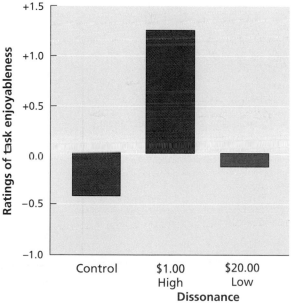

FIGURE 12.14 Participants lied to a fellow student by saying that a boring task was interesting. Those offered $1 to lie later rated the task most positively. Presumably, they reduced their cognitive dissonance about lying by convincing themselves that the task was interesting after all. Participants offered $20 had an external justification to lie, experienced little dissonance, and therefore did not need to convince themselves that the task was enjoyable. They and control participants who had no lied rated the task less favorably than the $1 group.

Based on Festinger & Carlsmith, 1959.

person" and "I just told another student that those boring tasks were interesting"), the person experiences an uncomfortable state of tension that Festinger calls *cognitive dissonance,* and becomes motivated to reduce this dissonance.

The theory predicts that to reduce dissonance and restore a state of cognitive consistency, people will change one of their cognitions or add new cognitions. Participants who received $20 could justify their behavior by adding a new cognition—"Who wouldn't tell a little lie for $20?"—and there was little reason for them to change their attitude toward the boring tasks. Those who had lied for only $1 could not use this trivial monetary gain to justify their behavior. But if they could convince themselves that the tasks were actually enjoyable, then they wouldn't have been lying after all! In short, they changed their attitude about the task to bring it more in line with how they had behaved.

Behavior that is inconsistent with one's attitude is called *counterattitudinal* behavior, and it produces dissonance only if we perceive that our actions were freely chosen, rather than coerced. Dissonance is maximized when the behavior threatens our sense of self-worth or produces negative consequences that were foreseeable (Cooper & Fazio, 1984; Petty & Wegener, 1998; Steele, 1988).

Dissonance, however, does not always lead to attitude change. People can reduce dissonance by rationalizing that their attitude or their behavior wasn't important, by finding external justification, or by making other excuses (Simon et al., 1995; Stalder & Baron, 1998). In surveys of over 3,300 Scandinavian adolescents and adults, people who drank alcohol despite having negative attitudes toward drinking often emphasized that "Other people drink more than I do." As researcher Klaus Mäkelä (1997) noted, the general rationalization seemed to be "I may not be perfect, but other people are still worse."

Despite the many ways to reduce dissonance, the theory has successfully inspired researchers to change people's attitudes by inducing them to engage in counterattitudinal behaviors. For example, college students who agree to write essays advocating positions opposite to their own (such as supporting a tuition increase) often shift their attitudes in the direction of the essay they have produced (Croyle & Cooper, 1983; Stalder & Baron, 1998). Mediators in labor disputes occasionally use this principle by asking company executives and labor leaders to switch roles for a time and present each other's arguments.

➤ 15. According to self-perception theory, why does counterattitudinal behavior produce attitude change?

Self-perception.   If we observe someone campaigning for a political candidate, we will likely assume that this person has a positive attitude toward the candidate. If we see someone exerting great effort to achieve a goal, we will logically judge that the goal was important to that person. In short, we infer what other people's attitudes "must be" by watching how they behave. According to Daryl Bem's (1972) **self-perception theory,** we make inferences about our own attitudes in much the same way: by observing how *we* behave. Knowing that for very little external justification ($1), you have told a fellow student that the boring experimental tasks are enjoyable, you logically conclude that "deep down" you *must* feel that the tasks were at least somewhat enjoyable. In Bem's view, your attitude is not produced by a mysterious concept called "cognitive dissonance." Rather, you simply observe how you act, and infer how you *must* have felt to have behaved in this fashion.

➤ 16. What evidence supports dissonance theory? What evidence favors self-perception theory?

Self-perception theory and cognitive dissonance theory both predict that counterattitudinal behavior produces attitude change. How then can we determine which theory more accurately explains the reason behind such attitude change? One key difference is that only dissonance theory assumes that we experience heightened physiological arousal (tension produced by dissonance) when we engage in counterattitudinal behavior. Do we? At least in some instances, it appears so (Elliot & Devine, 1994). In one study, college students consumed an unpleasant-tasting drink and were then asked to write a sentence stating that they liked the taste. Students who were given a high degree of choice to write this counterattitudinal statement showed higher arousal and greater attitude change than participants who were simply told to generate such arguments (Harmon-Jones et al., 1996).

Moreover, if unpleasant arousal motivates attitude change, then factors that reduce arousal should reduce attitude change. When research participants experience arousal from dissonance-producing behaviors but are led to believe that their arousal is a side effect caused by a pill (which in reality, is a placebo), they do not change their attitudes to be more in line with their behavior (Cooper, 1998; Zanna & Cooper, 1974) The pill gives participants an external justification (albeit a false one) for why they are feeling aroused.

These and other findings indicate that dissonance theory best explains why people change their views after behaving in ways that openly contradict their clearly defined attitudes, particularly when such behaviors threaten one's self-image. However, in situations where counterattitudinal behavior does not threaten one's self-worth, and we have weak attitudes to begin with, such behavior is less likely to create significant arousal—yet people may still alter their attitudes to be more consistent with how they have behaved. In this case, self-perception theory may provide the better explanation. Thus, both dissonance theory and self-perception theory appear to be correct, but under different circumstances (Fazio et al., 1977; Tesser & Shaffer, 1990). Both theories, however, agree that *our behaviors can influence our attitudes.*

Persuasion

Whether through political speeches, advertisements, or discussions with family and friends, persuasion is a fact of everyday life (Maio & Olson, 2000). Persuasion involves a *communicator* who delivers a *message* through a *channel* (e.g., in writing, verbally, visually) to an *audience* within a surrounding *context* (e.g., a cultural setting) (Petty & Cacioppo, 1986). Here, we briefly examine three components that have been studied most extensively.

The communicator. **Communicator credibility**—how believable the communicator is—often is a key to effective persuasion. In fact, audience members who do not enjoy thinking deeply about issues may pay little attention to the content of a message and simply go along with the opinions of a highly credible source (Chaiken & Maheswaran, 1994). Credibility has two major components: *expertise* and *trustworthiness*. The most effective persuader is one who appears to be an expert and to be presenting the truth in an unbiased manner (Hovland et al., 1953). Perceived expertise may be particularly important when the issue is complex (Cooper et al., 1996).

> ➤ 17. Identify communicator and message characteristics that increase persuasiveness.

Communicators who are physically attractive, likable, and similar to us (such as in interests or goals) also may persuade us more, which is why advertisers spend millions of dollars hiring likable, attractive stars to promote their products. But the positive impact of communicator characteristics—including credibility—tends to dissipate with time *if* we remember the message, but forget the messenger (Chaiken, 1987).

The message. In trying to persuade someone, is it more effective to present only your side of the issue, or to also present the opposition's arguments and then refute them? A meta-analysis indicates that, overall, the *two-sided refutational approach* is most effective (Allen, 1991). Especially if an audience initially disagrees with a message or is aware that there are two sides to the issue, a two-sided message will be perceived as less biased.

In stating your position to an audience that disagrees with you, should you "go for broke" and present extreme arguments, hoping that the audience will compromise toward your position? Or should you present a position that is only moderately discrepant with their viewpoint? A highly credible communicator

FIGURE 12.15 Fear appeals are a common approach to persuasion. They are most effective when people believe that a feared event could occur ("Driving after drinking can increase my risk of an accident"), that the consequences would be highly aversive ("I could lose my license, or be killed), that there is an effective way to reduce the risk ("If I drink, I won't drive"), and that they can carry out this behavior without great cost (have a designated driver; call a friend).

➤ 18. Describe the central and peripheral routes to persuasion. For whom is the central route more likely to be effective?

➤ 19. How are the norm of reciprocity, door-in-the-face and foot-in-the-door techniques, and lowballing used to manipulate behavior?

can afford to present a more discrepant viewpoint than a low-credibility communicator (Aronson et al., 1963), but in general, a *moderate degree of discrepancy* is most effective (Bochner & Insko, 1966).

Messages that attempt to persuade by arousing fear, such as those in Figure 12.15, can be effective under certain conditions (Wood, 2000). Overall, fear arousal works best when the message evokes *moderate fear* (Johnson, 1991). If the message is too frightening, people may reduce their anxiety simply by denying the message or the communicator's credibility.

The audience. A message loaded with logical arguments and facts may prove highly persuasive to some people, yet fall flat on its face with others. One reason is that people differ in their *need for cognition*. Some enjoy analyzing issues; others prefer not to spend much mental effort (Cacioppo et al., 1983, 1996).

According to Richard Petty and John Cacioppo (1986), there are two basic routes to persuasion. The **central route to persuasion** occurs when people think carefully about the message and are influenced because they find the arguments compelling. The **peripheral route to persuasion** occurs when people do not scrutinize the message, but are influenced mostly by other factors such as a speaker's attractiveness or a message's emotional appeal. Attitude change that results from the central route tends to have a deeper foundation, lasts longer, and predicts future behavior more successfully.

People who have a high need for cognition tend to follow the central route to persuasion. In forming attitudes about consumer products, for example, they are influenced by information about product characteristics. In contrast, people with a low need for cognition are more strongly influenced by peripheral cues, such as the attractiveness of the person who endorses the product (Haugtvedt et al., 1992).

APPLICATIONS OF PSYCHOLOGICAL SCIENCE

Detecting and Resisting Persuasion Tactics

From telemarketers and salespeople to TV and Internet advertisements, we live in an era of unprecedented persuasive attempts. Would-be persuaders often come armed with techniques that may get us to say "Yes" when we want to say "No." By learning to identify these techniques, you will be in a better position to resist them (Cialdini, 1988).

◗ The Norm of Reciprocity

The powerful **norm of reciprocity**—"Do unto others as they do unto you"—includes the expectation that when others treat us well, we should respond in kind. Thus to get you to comply with a request, I can do something nice for you now—such as an unsolicited favor—in the hopes that you will feel pressure to reciprocate later (Cialdini, 1988). Free food samples offered at the supermarket are another example. People may buy a product they don't want because the salesperson did something "nice" for them.

Our self-imposed pressure to "repay our debt" can dissipate over time (Burger et al., 1997). Thus persuaders often perform an unsolicited favor and then quickly ask us to reciprocate. As Figure 12.16 describes, the Hare Krishna Society (a religious sect) cleverly used "flower power" to manipulate the norm of reciprocity and raise millions of dollars in donations.

◗ Door-in-the-Face Technique

As you walk across campus, a representative of a "County Youth Program" asks if you would donate two hours a week, for at least two years, to serve as a counselor to juvenile delinquents. You politely refuse. Then he presents a smaller request: Would you help chaperone a group of delinquents on one trip to the zoo? In an actual experiment with college students, 51 percent agreed to the second, smaller request (Cialdini et al., 1975). In contrast,

—Continued

FIGURE 12.16   In the 1970s, members of the Hare Krishna Society approached passersby and gave them a small flower. If a passerby refused, the member said "Please. It is a gift for you." Reluctantly, people often accepted. Then the member asked for a donation. People felt pressure to reciprocate, donated money, and often threw the flower away.

among control group students presented only with the smaller (zoo) request, merely 17 percent agreed. Similarly, people are more likely to donate $2 to a charity after they have first declined a $25 request, than if they are directly asked for $2 (Wang et al., 1989).

These examples illustrate the **door-in-the-face technique**: A persuader makes a large request, expecting you to reject it (you "slam the door" in the persuader's face), and then presents a smaller request. To be effective, the same persuader must make both requests, suggesting that the *norm of reciprocity* is involved. Because the persuader "compromised" by making a smaller request, this pressures us to reciprocate and accept it (Cialdini, 1988). Refusing the first request also may produce guilt, so to reduce it and to feel socially responsible we comply with the second request (O'Keefe & Figge, 1997; Tusing & Dillard, 2000).

◗ Foot-in-the-Door Technique

The door-in-the-face-technique involves shifting from a larger to a smaller request. In contrast, the **foot-in-the-door technique** does the opposite: The persuader gets you to comply with a small request first (getting the "foot-in-the-door"), and later presents a larger request (Freedman & Fraser, 1966). When residents of suburban Toronto were directly asked to donate money to the Cancer Society, 46 percent did so (Pliner et al., 1974). But when other residents were merely asked to wear a "Cancer Drive" pin (small request) and then a day later were asked for money (larger request), the donation rate almost doubled.

This technique typically works regardless of whether the two requests are made by the same person or by different people (Chartrand et al., 1999). However, although hypotheses abound, we are not sure why it is effective.

◗ Lowballing

With **lowballing,** a persuader gets you to commit to some action and then—*before you actually perform the behavior*—he or she increases the "cost" of that *same behavior*. For example, when college students were asked to participate in an experiment at 7:00 A.M., only 24 percent consented. Other students were asked to participate, but the 7:00 A.M. time was not mentioned. Now 56 percent agreed. Then after they consented, the researcher informed them of the 7:00 A.M. time and allowed them to change their mind. Not a single student backed out over the phone, and 95 percent showed up at 7:00 A.M. for the experiment (Cialdini et al., 1978)!

Similarly, imagine negotiating to buy a used car for $7,000, a "great price." The salesperson says, "I need to confirm this with manager," comes back shortly, and states, "I'm afraid my manager says the price is too low. But you can have the car for only $300 more. It's still a great price." At this point, you are more likely to go through with the deal than you would have been had the "real" $7,300 price been set at the outset.

Like the foot-in-the-door technique, lowballing involves moving from a smaller request to a larger (more costly) one. But with the foot-in-the-door, the smaller request (e.g., wearing a pin) and the larger request (e.g., donating money) typically are different acts, and the larger request is not made until after the smaller request actually is performed. In lowballing, the stakes for the *same* behavior are raised after the person commits to it, but *before* the behavior is consummated. Having made a commitment, people may find it easier to rationalize the added costs, and may feel a sense of obligation to the person to whom the commitment was made (Burger & Petty, 1981).

◗ Resisting Social Influence

By recognizing when influence techniques are being used to manipulate our behavior, we are in a better position to resist them. Consider the norm of reciprocity. Robert Cialdini (1988), an expert on influence techniques, suggests that the key is not to resist the initial gift or favor. Instead, accept the unsolicited "favor," but if the person then asks you for a favor in return, recognize this as a manipulative technique. As Cialdini notes, "The rule says that favors are to be met with favors; it does not require that tricks be met with favors."

If you agree to a small request, and later the person asks for a larger favor, recognize that the foot-in-the-door technique is a "trick" being used to manipulate you. Similarly, if a telemarketer or door-to-door solicitor first asks you to agree to a very large request, and then after you decline immediately asks for a smaller commitment, respond by thinking or even saying, "I see; the door-in-the-face technique." Of course, you can still choose to comply if you believe it is the right thing to do. The goal is not to automatically reject every social influence attempt, but to avoid feeling coerced into behaving in ways that you do not wish to.

Attribution: Perceiving the Causes of Behavior

In everyday life we often make **attributions,** judgments about the causes of our own and other people's behavior and outcomes. Was my A on the midterm due to hard work and ability, or was it just an easy test? Did Bill criticize Carl because he is a rude person, or was he provoked? Attributions influence our subsequent behavior and emotions. If I attribute my A to hard work and ability, I will feel greater pride and continue to exert more effort than if I attribute it to an easy test (Weiner, 1985). In the courtroom, jurors' attributions about a defendant's behavior influence their decisions about guilt versus innocence.

Personal Versus Situational Attributions

➤ 20. What types of information lead us to form a situational, rather than personal attribution?

Fritz Heider (1958), a pioneer of attribution theory, maintained that our attempts to understand why people behave as they do typically involve either personal attributions or situational attributions. *Personal (internal) attributions* infer that people's behavior is caused by their characteristics: Bill insulted Carl because he (Bill) is a rude person; my A on an exam reflects my high ability. *Situational (external) attributions* infer that aspects of the situation cause a behavior: Bill was provoked into insulting Carl; I received an A because the test was easy.

How do we decide whether a behavior is caused by personal or situational factors? Suppose you ask Kim for advice on whether to take a particular course (say, Art 391) and she tells you that the course is terrible. Is Art 391 really poor (a situational attribution), or is it something about Kim (a personal attribution) that led to this response? According to Harold Kelley (1973), three types of information determine the attribution we make: *Consistency, distinctiveness,* and *consensus.* First, is Kim's response consistent over time? If you ask Kim again two weeks later and she still says that Art 391 is terrible, then consistency is high. Second, is her response distinctive? If Kim dislikes only Art 391, then distinctiveness is high. If she thinks that most of her courses are terrible, then distinctiveness is low. Finally, how do other people respond? If other students agree with Kim that Art 391 is poor, then consensus is high. But if they disagree with her, then consensus is low.

As Figure 12.17 illustrates, when consistency, distinctiveness, and consensus are all high, we are likely to make a situational attribution: The course is bad.

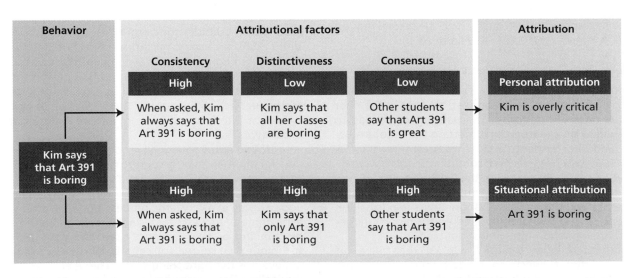

Behavior	Attributional factors			Attribution
	Consistency	**Distinctiveness**	**Consensus**	
	High	Low	Low	**Personal attribution**
	When asked, Kim always says that Art 391 is boring	Kim says that all her classes are boring	Other students say that Art 391 is great	Kim is overly critical
Kim says that Art 391 is boring	High	High	High	**Situational attribution**
	When asked, Kim always says that Art 391 is boring	Kim says that only Art 391 is boring	Other students say that Art 391 is boring	Art 391 is boring

FIGURE 12.17 According to Harold Kelley, consistency, distinctiveness, and consensus information help us determine whether to make personal or situational attributions for someone else's behavior. Note that in both examples, above, consistency is high. If a person's behavior has low consistency (suppose that above sometimes Kim says Art 391 is boring, and other times she says it's interesting), we typically attribute the behavior to transient conditions (e.g., changes in Kim's mood) rather than to stable personal or situational factors.

But when consistency is high and the other two factors are low, we make a personal attribution: Perhaps Kim is overly critical, or just doesn't like college.

At times, people do respond thoughtfully and take consistency, distinctiveness, and consensus information into account when making attributions. But at other times people take mental shortcuts and make snap judgments that bias their attributions (Ross & Nisbett, 1991).

Attributional Biases

Think back to the guards' brutal behavior in the Stanford Prison Study, or to the people who obediently shocked a protesting victim in Milgram's experiments. Were the college students who served as guards evil? Were Milgram's participants weak and callous? Social psychology teaches us that the immediate social environment profoundly influences behavior. Yet we often form negative opinions about the participants in these studies because we tend to make a **fundamental attribution error:** We underestimate the impact of the situation and overestimate the role of personal factors when explaining other people's behavior (Ross, 1977).

In a classic experiment, college students read either a favorable or unfavorable speech about Cuban President Fidel Castro, presumably written by a member of a college debating team (Jones & Harris, 1967). They then estimated the writer's attitude toward Castro. Half the students were told that the debate team member freely chose the favorable or unfavorable position. The others were told that the favorable or unfavorable viewpoint had been assigned by the debate coach—it was not the debater's choice. Figure 12.18 shows that when the speech was freely chosen, students logically assumed that the debater had a correspondingly positive or negative attitude about Castro. Yet when told that the role was assigned, students paid insufficient attention to this situational factor and still perceived the pro-Castro and anti-Castro debaters to have different personal beliefs. Figure 12.19 provides another example.

The fundamental attribution error applies to how we perceive other people's behavior, rather than our own. As comedian George Carlin once noted, the slow driver ahead of us is a "moron," and the fast driver trying to pass us is a "maniac." Yet we do not think of ourselves as a "moron" or "maniac" when *we* are driving slowly or trying to pass another driver. One reason is that we have more information about the present situation when making judgments about ourselves, as when we are driving slowly to follow unfamiliar directions. Second, the perceptual principle of figure-ground relations comes into play. When you watch someone else behave, they are the "figure" that stands out against the background. But when we behave, we are not "watching" ourselves. We are part of the background, and the situation that we are in stands out. If you watch yourself on a videotape, you now become the figure, and are more likely to make personal attributions for your own behavior—just as if you were observing someone else (Storms, 1973).

Is the fundamental attribution error inevitable? Certainly not. On April 20, 1999, Eric Harris and Dylan Klebold went on a shooting rampage in Littleton, Colorado, killing 12 of their Columbine High School schoolmates and a teacher, and then committing suicide. In the following days, Gallup polls found that most Americans rated situational factors such as parenting, gun availability, TV and movie violence, and media coverage of past shootings as bearing considerable blame. On one set of questions, only 11 percent made a personal attribution for the shooters' behavior, such as "mental problems," "bad kids," "anger," or "wanting attention" (Gillespie, 1999; Saad, 1999).

When people have time to reflect on their judgments or are highly motivated to be careful, the fundamental attribution error is reduced (Burger, 1991; Gilbert & Malone, 1995). The Littleton shooting was preceded by a tragic string of similar and highly publicized incidents across the United States. The

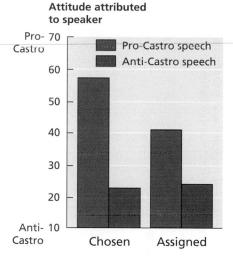

> 21. Describe the fundamental attribution error and the self-serving bias. How do cultural norms affect these attributional tendencies?

FIGURE 12.18 These data illustrate a fundamental attribution error. When told that a debate coach had *assigned* a team member to write a pro- or anti-Castro speech, college students still attributed a more anti-Castro attitude to the writter of the anti-Castro speech. Data from Jones & Harris, 1967.

FIGURE 12.19 Unlike Mr. Spock, the logical and emotionless Vulcan from the series *Star Trek*, actor Leonard Nimoy has feelings just like the rest of us. TV and movie fans make the fundamental attribution error when they expect media stars to have the same traits as the characters they play. The title of Nimoy's autobiography, *I Am Not Spock,* emphasizes this point.

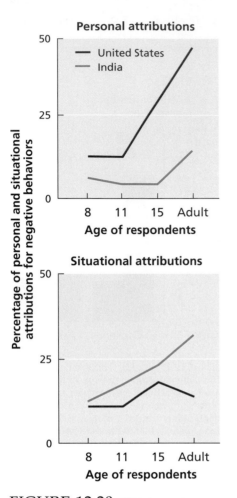

Personal attributions

Percentage of personal and situational attributions for negative behaviors

— United States
— India

Age of respondents: 8 11 15 Adult

Situational attributions

Age of respondents: 8 11 15 Adult

FIGURE 12.20 With increasing age from childhood to adulthood, Americans show a greater tendency to make personal attributions for other people's behaviors. In contrast, participants from India show an increased tendency to make situational attributions.

Data from J. G. Miller, 1984.

➤ 22. Why do primacy effects occur in impression formation? How can they be reduced?

American public was already highly engaged in this issue and had considerable time to think about the causes of school violence.

When it comes to explaining our own behavior, we tend to protect our self-esteem by displaying a **self-serving bias:** making relatively more personal attributions for success and situational attributions for failures (Ross & Nisbett, 1991). In one study of athletes' postgame statements, successes tended to be attributed to personal factors, such as "We played great defense and hung in there," whereas losses were more frequently attributed to external causes, such as poor officiating or "Everything they shot was going in" (Lau & Russell, 1980). The strength of the self-serving bias depends on various factors, ranging from one's psychological state to cultural norms. Depressed people, for example, often display the opposite attributional pattern—taking too little credit for successes and too much credit for failures—a pattern that helps keep them depressed.

Culture and Attribution

Just as culture influences how we perceive the physical world (see Chapter 4), it affects how we perceive the social world. Consider the fundamental attribution error. Does the tendency to attribute other people's behavior to personal factors reflect a westernized emphasis on individualism? In a study by J. G. Miller (1984), participants of varying ages from India and the United States attributed causality for several behaviors. As Figure 12.20 shows, with increasing age participants from India made more situational attributions and those from America made more personal attributions. Similarly, American college students and British schoolchildren make more personal attributions for other people's criminal behavior than do Korean college students and Nigerian schoolchildren, who come from less individualistic cultures (Na-Eun-Yeong & Loftus, 1998; Pfeffer et al., 1998).

Culture also influences attributions for our own behavior (Singh et al., 1979). Modesty is highly valued in China's collectivistic culture, and Chinese college students take less credit for successful social interactions than do American students, while accepting more responsibility for their failures (Anderson, 1999).

Forming and Maintaining Impressions

As social beings we constantly form impressions of other people, just as they form impressions of us. Attributions play a key role in impression formation: Does a person's behavior say something about her or him, or is it caused by the situation? Other factors, however, also affect how we form and maintain impressions.

Primacy Versus Recency: Are First Impressions More Important?

Try this simple exercise. Tell some people that you know a person who is "intelligent, industrious, impulsive, critical, stubborn, and envious." Tell others that this person is "envious, stubborn, critical, impulsive, industrious, and intelligent." Then ask for their impression of this person. Both groups receive the same information, but in reverse order. In a classic experiment, Solomon Asch (1946) found that the person in the first description was perceived more positively—as being more sociable and happier—than the person in the second description. In another experiment, participants read a two-paragraph story about a boy named Jim. One paragraph described Jim as outgoing, the other as introverted. Participants' impression of Jim was influenced more strongly by whichever paragraph they read first (Luchins, 1957a).

When forming impressions, the **primacy effect** refers to our tendency to attach more importance to the initial information that we learn about a person. New information can change our opinion, but it has to "work harder" to overcome that initial impression for two reasons. First, we tend to be most alert to information we receive first. Second, initial information may shape how we perceive subsequent information. Imagine a student and an athlete who, respectively, get off to a great start in class or in training camp. The teacher and the coach attribute high ability to these people, but as time goes on, suppose that performance declines. To maintain their positive initial impression, the teacher and coach need only attribute the performance decline to fatigue, a drop in motivation, or a string of bad breaks.

Primacy is the general rule of thumb in impression formation, especially for people who dislike ambiguity and uncertainty (Kruglanski & Webster, 1996). We seem to have a remarkable capacity for forming snap judgments based on small amounts of initial information, and some evolutionary psychologists propose that evaluating stimuli quickly (such as rapidly distinguishing friend from foe) was adaptive for our survival (Krebs & Denton, 1997). But we are not slaves to primacy. Primacy effects decrease—and *recency effects* (giving greater weight to the most recent information) may occur—when we are asked to avoid making snap judgments, are reminded to carefully consider the evidence, and are made to feel accountable for our judgments (Luchins, 1957b; Webster et al., 1996).

Mental Sets and Schemas: Seeing What We Expect to See

Imagine that we are going to a party and I tell you that the host, George, is a distant, aloof, cold person. You meet him and try to make pleasant conservation. George doesn't say much in response to your questions, avoids eye contact, and doesn't ask you about your life. A bit later, you say to me, "You were right, he's really a cold fish." Now let's roll back this scene. Suppose that I had described George as nice, but extremely shy. Later when you try to make conservation, he doesn't say much, avoids eye contact, and doesn't ask you about your life. You say to me, "You were right, he's really shy." Same behavior, different impression. This example reminds us of a key perceptual principle highlighted in Chapter 4. Whether perceiving objects or people, the same stimulus can be "seen" in different ways. Our mental *set*, which is a readiness to perceive the world in a particular way, powerfully shapes how we interpret a stimulus (see Figure 4.2, p. 133).

What creates our mental sets? One important factor that we have encountered throughout the book is *schemas*, mental frameworks that help us organize and interpret information. By telling you that our host is "cold," "shy" or "distracted," I activate a set of concepts and expectations (your schema) for how such a person is likely to behave. Although the host's behavior can be interpreted in multiple ways, you "fit" his behavior into the particular schema that is already activated.

A **stereotype,** which is a generalized belief about a group or category of people, represents a powerful type of schema. In one experiment, participants watched a videotape of a 9-year-old girl named Hannah and were asked to judge her academic potential. Half of the participants were told that Hannah came from an upper-middle-class environment and that her parents had white-collar careers. Other participants were told that Hannah came from a poor neighborhood and that her parents were blue-collar workers. On the videotape, Hannah performed at an average level, answering some difficult questions and missing some others. Although all participants saw the same performance, those who thought Hannah came from an affluent setting rated her higher in ability than did those who thought she came from a disadvantaged background (Darley & Gross, 1983). In a real sense, participants' stereotypes about blue-collar and white-collar workers created a mental set that biased their perception of Hannah's subsequent behavior.

Self-Fulfilling Prophecies: Creating What We Expect to See

Seeing what we expect to see is only one way we confirm our initial expectations and impressions. Usually without conscious awareness, a **self-fulfilling prophecy** occurs when people's erroneous expectations lead them to act toward

➤ 23. How do mental sets shape the way we perceive people? How do stereotypes create mental sets?

➤ 24. Explain how our incorrect expectations can become self-fulfilling.

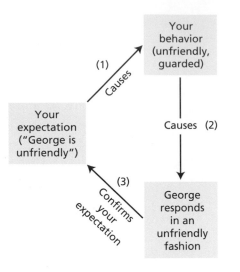

FIGURE 12.21 The self-fulfilling prophecy begins when a false expectation that we have about someone else influences how we treat that person. Next, influenced by our behavior, the person responds in a particular way. Finally, we interpret the person's behavior as evidence that our expectation was correct all along—unaware of the role that we played in shaping the person's behavior.

others in a way that brings about the expected behaviors, thereby confirming the original impression. Returning to our "party" example, if you expect the host to be cold and aloof, your behavior toward him may change in subtle ways. You make conversation, but perhaps you smile less, stand further away, and give up a little earlier than you would have, had I simply told you that he was a great guy. His reserved response, in part, could be a reaction to *your* behavior (Figure 12.21).

Robert Rosenthal and Lenore Jacobson (1968) demonstrated this effect by telling elementary school teachers that, according to a new psychological test, certain children would be "intellectual bloomers" and would likely experience a large intellectual growth spurt during the coming year. In reality, these children had been chosen *at random* by the experimenters. Eight months later, the researchers readministered intelligence tests and found that in some of the school grades, the so-called "late bloomers" had actually bloomed, showing greater IQ gains than the other children. The teachers felt that they had treated their students equally, but somehow, their expectations must have influenced the students' behavior. For example, teachers may have provided more encouragement and attention to the expected "bloomers."

Some researchers questioned the strength of these findings, but self-fulfilling prophecies have since been demonstrated in hundreds of studies across different countries and settings, including schools, business organizations, the military, sports, and dating and marital relationships (Downey et al., 1998; McNatt, 2000; Rosenthal, 1991). In interacting with other people, our initially unfounded expectations can influence how we behave toward them, thereby shaping other people's behavior in a way that ultimately confirms our expectations.

❯ SOCIAL RELATIONS

Our relations with other people take many forms. In Chapter 9 we examined the human desire to affiliate and form close personal relationships. Here we explore three other types of social interactions that help define who we are, both individually and collectively: prejudice, altruism, and aggression.

Prejudice and Discrimination

Walk into a party, classroom, job interview—any social situation—and just by looking at your body build people will start to form an impression of you (Gacsaly & Borges, 1979). If they perceive you as "fat," for example, you may be judged as less likable, as having poorer will power and social skills, and as being more unhappy with yourself than your nonfat peers (Crandall & Martinez, 1996).

Attractiveness matters too. Both children and adults tend to form less favorable impressions of people who are less attractive. They expect them to have less desirable personality traits and to achieve less success and happiness in life, even though correlational studies typically find that such variables are unrelated or only weakly related to attractiveness and other facial features (Dion et al., 1972; Zebrowitz et al., 1996).

Perhaps above all, ethnicity and gender matter. They are likely to be the first characteristics someone notices about you, and like so many other personal qualities, can be the basis for prejudice and discrimination (Fiske, 1998). **Prejudice** refers to a negative attitude toward people based on their membership in a group. Thus we *prejudge* people—dislike them or hold negative beliefs about them—simply because they are female or male, belong to one ethnic group or religion rather than to another, are "gay" or "straight," and so on. **Discrimination** refers to overt behavior: It involves treating people unfairly based on the group to which they belong.

Overt and Covert Prejudice: Have Times Changed?

Even in this day and age, overt prejudice and discrimination are in abundant supply. Armed conflicts based on ethnic or religious divisions continue across the globe; supremacist groups and hate crimes persist; and people's race, gender, religion, and sexual orientation spark unfair treatment (Herek, 2000). In some ways, however, the most blatant forms of prejudice and discrimination have decreased in many countries. Racial segregation is no longer sanctioned by government policy in the United States and South Africa, and opinion polls indicate that fewer people express prejudiced attitudes toward other ethnic groups than was the case decades ago (Newport, 1999, March 1, March 29).

Although prejudiced attitudes truly seem to have faded a bit, in many ways modern racism, sexism, and other forms of prejudice have gone underground and are more difficult to detect (Dovidio et al., 1997; Sigall & Page, 1971). Many people consciously hide their prejudices, expressing them only when they feel it is safe or socially appropriate. In other cases people may honestly believe that they are not prejudiced, but still show biases when tested in sophisticated ways (Fazio et al., 1995).

➤ 25. How do psychologists use reaction time tasks to detect people's covert prejudice?

To measure covert prejudice, Anthony Greenwald and his coworkers (1998) developed an *implicit association test* in which a series of word-pairs, such as "black—pleasant" and "white—pleasant" are flashed on a computer screen. As soon as you see each pair, your task is to press a computer key as quickly as you can, and this represents your reaction time. The principle underlying this test is that people react more quickly when they perceive that the two words in each pair are associated with one another (i.e., the words "fit" together) than when they don't fit together. Thus without conscious control, a person prejudiced against Blacks will react more slowly to the "black—pleasant" pair than to the "white—pleasant" pair. The larger the discrepancy in reaction times, the stronger are the person's underlying negative attitudes. Greenwald and his associates found large reaction time differences of this kind even among White males who claimed—in response to standard questions—to have no prejudice toward Blacks. Likewise, Japanese and Koreans, whose nations have a history of conflict, react differently toward pairs such as "Japanese—pleasant" and "Korean—pleasant."

Cognitive Roots of Prejudice

Whether overt or subtle, prejudice and discrimination are caused by a constellation of factors, including historical and cultural norms that legitimize differential treatment of various groups. Here, we examine several cognitive and motivational causes of prejudice.

➤ 26. Identify cognitive processes that foster prejudice

Categorization and us-them thinking. To organize and simplify our world, we have a normal perceptual tendency to categorize objects and people. At times, this helps us react to the environment quickly and predict others' behavior (Smith & Zarate, 1992). But our automatic tendency to categorize people also helps to lay a foundation for prejudice (Dovidio et al., 1997; Glick & Fiske, 1999).

Categorization leads to the perception of "in-groups" and "out-groups," groups to which we do and do not belong, respectively. In turn, in-group versus out-group distinctions spawn two common biases. First, we display *in-group favoritism*, a tendency to favor in-group members and attribute more positive qualities to "us" than to "them." In-group favoritism emerges in laboratory experiments across the globe, even when participants are assigned to temporary groups based on the flip of a coin or some trivial characteristic (Reichl, 1997; Tajfel, 1971).

Second, people display an *out-group homogeneity bias*. They generally view members of out-groups as being more similar to one another than are members of in-groups. In other words, we perceive that "they are all alike," but recognize that "we are diverse" (Linville & Jones, 1980). The mere fact that we identify people as

"Asian," "Hispanic," "Black," and "White" reflects such a bias, because each of these ethnic categories contains many subgroups. In one study, Anglo-American college students were less likely to distinguish among "Hispanic" subgroups than were Cuban-American, Mexican-American, and Puerto Rican-American college students (Huddy & Virtanen, 1995). But just like Anglo students, the Cuban-, Mexican-, and Puerto Rican-American students also engaged in us-them thinking: They saw their own subgroup as distinct from the others, but did not differentiate between the other two Hispanic subgroups.

Stereotypes and attributional distortions.   Categorization and in-group biases lead us to respond quickly to out-group members based on perceived group characteristics—stereotypes—rather than based on their individual characteristics. Recall that merely labeling Hannah's parents as "blue-collar" or "white-collar" created a mental set that shaped how people perceived her behavior (Darley & Gross, 1983). Similarly, 73 percent of White college students who observed a videotape of a Black man shoving a White man perceived the behavior as "violent," but when the tape showed a White man shoving a Black man, only 13 percent of students saw it as violent (Duncan, 1976). Figure 12.22 also illustrates how racial and gender stereotypes affect our perceptions.

> 27. How can people maintain their stereotypes in the face of contradictory information?

What happens when we encounter individual members of out-groups whose behavior clearly contradicts our stereotypes? One possibility is that we may change our stereotype, but someone who is motivated to hold on to their prejudiced belief can "explain away" discrepant behavior in several ways. For example, the out-group member may be seen as an "exceptional case" or as having succeeded at a task not because of high ability, but due to tremendous effort, good luck, or special advantage (Pettigrew, 1979). People who stereotype women as passive and dependent may respond to a strong and assertive woman by placing her in a special subcategory, such as "feminist," thereby leaving the general stereotype intact.

(a)   (b)

FIGURE 12.22   (a) Who is holding the razor knife? Allport and Postman (1947) showed this picture to one person, who then told another, who then told another, and so forth. Typically, by the sixth telling, the Black man was erroneously described as holding the razor. (b) Which person contributes most strongly to this research team? When the drawing shows an all-male group, all-female group, or mixed-sex group with a male at the head of the table (seat 3), participants say that the person in seat 3 is the strongest member. But in this mixed-gender drawing, most male and female participants do not pick the woman in seat 3. Instead, they pick one of the two men (Porter & Geis, 1981).

Motivational Roots of Prejudice

People's well-ingrained ways of perceiving the world—categorizing, forming in-groups and out-groups, and so forth—appear to set the wheels of prejudice in motion, but motivational factors affect how fast those wheels spin.

Competition and conflict.   According to **realistic conflict theory,** competition for limited resources fosters prejudice. In the United States and Europe, hostility toward minority groups increases when economic conditions worsen (Hovland & Sears, 1940; Pettigrew & Meertens, 1995). Originally, it was believed that a threat to one's personal welfare was the prime motivator of prejudice, but research suggests that prejudice is triggered more strongly by a *perceived threat to one's in-group* (Tajfel & Turner, 1986). As the Robbers Cave summer camp experiment illustrated in Chapter 1, competition between groups often breeds hostility and derogation of the out-group (Sherif et al., 1961). Likewise, among Whites, prejudice toward Blacks is not related to personal resource gains and losses, but to the belief that White people as a group are in danger of being overtaken (Bobo, 1988).

Enhancing self-esteem.   According to **social identity theory,** prejudice stems from a need to enhance our self-esteem. Some experiments find that people express more prejudice after their self-esteem is threatened (such as by receiving negative feedback about their abilities) and that the opportunity to derogate others helps to restore self-esteem (Fein & Spencer, 1997). Self-esteem, however, is based on two components: a personal identity and a "group" identity that reflects membership in various groups (Tajfel & Turner, 1986). We can raise self-esteem by associating ourselves with our in-group's accomplishments, and conversely, threats to the in-group threaten our self-esteem. Our group identity thus creates a tendency to take pride in one's in-group while also derogating out-groups (Perdue et al., 1990). Compared with relatively unprejudiced people, prejudiced individuals show greater concern with accurately determining who is an in-group versus out-group member (Blascovich et al., 1997).

> 28. According to realistic conflict theory and social identity theory, what are the motivational roots of prejudice?

How Prejudice Confirms Itself

Self-fulfilling prophecies are one of the most invisible yet damaging ways of maintaining prejudiced beliefs. A classic experiment by Carl Word and his colleagues (1974) illustrates this point. The researchers began with the premise—supported by research at the time—that Whites held several negative stereotypes of Blacks. In the experiment, White male college students interviewed White and Black high school students who were seeking admission into a special group. The participants used a fixed set of interview questions provided by the experimenter and, unknown to them, each applicant was an "accomplice" who had been trained to respond in a standard way to the questions. The findings indicated that these White participants sat farther away, conducted shorter interviews, and made more speech errors when the applicants were Black. In short, their behavior was discriminatory.

> 29. Discuss how self-fulfilling prophecies and stereotype threat perpetuate prejudice.

But this is only half the picture. In a second experiment—a job interview simulation—White male undergraduates served as *job applicants.* Through random assignment they were treated either as the White applicants had been treated in the first experiment, or as the Black applicants had been treated. In other words, for half the participants, the interviewer sat farther away, held a shorter interview, and made more speech errors. The findings revealed that White participants who were treated more negatively performed worse during the job interview, were less composed, made more speech errors, and rated the interviewer as less friendly. In short, these experiments suggest that an interviewer's negative stereotypes can lead to discriminatory treatment during a job interview, and this discriminatory behavior can cause the applicant to perform more poorly—ultimately confirming the interviewer's initial stereotype.

FIGURE 12.23 Like this rescue worker, many people seek out careers or join volunteer organizations that allow them to help other people.

➤ 30. According to sociobiologists, what is the evolutionary basis of helping behavior?

FIGURE 12.24 Spotting a hawk or other predator, this female ground squirrel may sound an "alarm call" that warns other squirrels. Is the call truly a prosocial act, much like a human yells "Look out"? Perhaps it simply indicates the squirrel's own sense of alarm, much as we might scream out of fear for our own safety. But if this is the case, why is she more likely to sound this call when her own kin—rather than other squirrels—are nearby?

Stanford psychologist Claude Steele (1997) has demonstrated another debilitating way that prejudice ends up "confirming itself." As described in Chapter 8, his concept of **stereotype threat** proposes that stereotypes create a fear and self-consciousness among stereotyped group members that they will "live up" to other people's stereotypes. This can occur even if the group members do not accept the stereotype themselves. Given the stereotype that "Blacks are not as intelligent as Whites," Black college students who take a difficult test composed of SAT (Scholastic Aptitude Test) items perform more poorly than White students when the test is described as "an intelligence test." But Blacks perform as well as Whites when the items are described merely as being a "laboratory task." Stereotypes that Whites are inferior to Asians in math, and that women are inferior to men at math, produce analogous results. When a difficult standardized math test is given in situations that activate these stereotypes, Whites and women perform more poorly than when the test is presented in a more neutral way (Aronson et al., 1999; Spencer et al., 1999).

Psychologists are concerned not only about the causes of prejudice, but also in identifying conditions and designing programs that reduce it (Allport, 1954; Gaertner et al., 2000). One famous principle, *equal status contact*, states that prejudice between two people or groups is most likely to be reduced when they engage in close contact, have equal status within this interaction, and work together to achieve a common goal that would be difficult to attain without such cooperation (Allport, 1954). In the Robbers Cave experiment, conflict did *not* end when the two hostile groups of boys merely were brought together to share enjoyable social activities, such as watching a movie. Rather, conflict was resolved by providing equal status to the two groups and then having them cooperate to solve a series of "crises" that were staged by the researchers (Sherif, 1961). In Chapter 16 we examine prejudice reduction programs more closely.

Prosocial Behavior: Helping Others

Helping behavior comes in many forms, from heroic acts of bravery and charitable donations to tutoring a classmate or returning a lost wallet. It characterizes the entire being of people like Mother Teresa, who devoted her life to the world's poor. Acts of violence often grab the news headlines, but we should not lose sight of the mountains of good deeds performed around the world each day (Figure 12.23).

Why Do People Help?

What motivates prosocial behavior? The debate over this question has practical consequences and profound implications for our conception of human nature.

Helping, evolution, and genetics. Prosocial behavior occurs throughout the animal kingdom. In some bird species, adults feign injury to lead predators away from their young. One investigator observed a male baboon watching two juveniles playing on a ledge below. Suddenly, a rock began to fall toward the juveniles. The male grabbed the rock and held it in place, releasing it only after the juveniles were out of harm's way (Rushton, 1989). Interpreting the meaning of such behavior, however, can be difficult (Figure 12.24).

Sociobiologists propose that helping has a genetic basis, shaped by evolution (Hamilton, 1964). According to the principle of **kin selection,** organisms are most likely to help others with whom they share the most genes, namely, their offspring and genetic relatives. By protecting their kin, prosocial individuals increase the odds that their genes will survive across successive generations, and the gene pool of the species increasingly represents the genes of its prosocial members (Buck & Ginsburg, 1991). In this manner, over the course of evolution, helping became a biologically predisposed response to certain situations. To support their view that genetics influence helping behavior, sociobiologists note that identical twins are more similar in the behavioral trait of helpfulness than siblings or fraternal twins (Davis et al., 1994; Rushton, 1989).

But what accounts for the abundant helping and care that humans display toward friends and strangers, and that some other species also display toward nonrelatives (Schaeff et al., 1999)? Sociobiologists propose the concept of *reciprocal altruism:* helping others increases the likelihood that they will help us or our kin in return, thereby enhancing the survival of our genes (Trivers, 1971).

Critics question sociobiologists' generalizations from nonhumans to humans, and in some cases kin selection and reciprocal altruism do not adequately explain why people cooperate (Palmer, 1991; Wonderly, 1996). Sociobiologists reply that genetic factors only predispose us to act in certain ways, and that experience also plays a role in shaping helping behavior.

Social learning and cultural influences.   Socialization, modeling, and reinforcement play a key role in fostering prosocial behavior and attitudes (Eisenberg & Mussen, 1989; Janoski et al., 1998). Beginning in childhood, we are exposed to helpful models and taught prosocial norms. Recall from Chapter 6 that children were more likely to place several dogs' welfare above their own if they had first seen adults rescue a puppy on a TV program (Sprafkin et al., 1975). A survey of nearly 200 studies suggests that television programs that model acts of kindness and helping have a strong positive effect on viewers' prosocial behavior (Hearold, 1986).

Two social norms are especially relevant to helping behavior (Berkowitz, 1972; Miller et al., 1990). First, the *norm of reciprocity* states that we should reciprocate when others treat us kindly. Second, the *norm of social responsibility* states that people should help others and contribute to the welfare of society. We are reinforced with approval when we adhere to these norms, receive disapproval when we do not, and observe other people receive praise for conforming to these norms. Eventually, we internalize prosocial norms and values as our own, enabling powerful *self-reinforcers* such as pride, self-praise, and feelings of satisfaction to maintain prosocial behaviors even when external reinforcement is absent.

Studies in Europe, Asia, and North America confirm that socialization matters. Children are more likely to act prosocially when they have been raised by parents who have high moral standards, who are warm and supportive, and who encourage their children to develop empathy and "put themselves in other people's shoes" (Janssens & Dekovic, 1997; Krevans & Gibbs, 1996). However, there also are cross-cultural differences in beliefs about when and why we should help (Eckensberger & Zimba, 1997). Joan Miller and her colleagues (1990) found that Hindu children and adults in India believe that one has a moral obligation to help friends and strangers, whether their need is serious or mild. In contrast, when a person's need for assistance is mild, American children and adults feel less obligated to help and view helping as more of a choice.

Empathy and altruism.   Are all prosocial acts, regardless of how noble they appear, ultimately motivated by self-reinforcement, or do we have a capacity for *altruism,* the desire to aid another without concern for oneself? According to C. Daniel Batson's **empathy-altruism hypothesis,** altruism does exist, and it is produced by *empathy,* the ability to put oneself in the place of another and to share what that person is experiencing (Batson, 1991; Batson et al., 1997)

In one study, female students' empathy for another female participant (actually, an accomplice) was increased or decreased by leading them to believe that her values were either similar or dissimilar to their own (Batson et al., 1981). Then by a rigged coin flip, the accomplice was selected to receive supposedly painful electric shocks while performing a task, while the real participant acted as an observer. When the experiment began, the accomplice expressed great fear of the shocks. At this point, the participant was told that she could leave after watching only two shock trials or, if she wished, could change places with the woman, thereby saving her from the trauma of being shocked. Consistent with the empathy—altruism hypothesis, Figure 12.25 shows that high empathy participants were much more likely to voluntarily change places.

➤ 31. How do social norms, self-reinforcers, and empathy influence helping behavior?

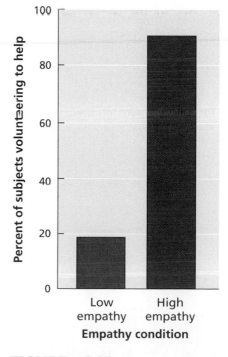

FIGURE 12.25 Compared with women in a low empathy condition, women who were led to feel high empathy for a fellow research participant were more likely to volunteer to receive electric shocks in her place.

Data from Batson et al., 1981.

FIGURE 12.26 Catherine ("Kitty") Genovese, a 28-year-old bar manager, was raped and murdered outside her New York City apartment building in 1964 when she came home from work at about 3 A.M. The attack lasted half an hour, and as discussed in Chapter 2 (p. 42), about 40 of her neighbors heard her screams. Yet no one intervened or called the police until it was too late.

➤ 32. Identify two key ways (two stages of intervention) in which the presence of other bystanders often inhibits people from responding to an emergency.

As critical thinkers, we need to ask whether participants exchanged places not by virtue of empathy, but because they would have felt guilty for not doing so. Or perhaps, as the **negative state relief model** proposes, high empathy causes us to feel distress when we learn of others' suffering, so by helping them we reduce *our own* personal distress—a self-focused goal, not an altruistic one (Cialdini et al., 1987). Indeed, there are many reasons for acts of helping, but Batson's research suggests that at least some prosocial behavior is motivated by unselfish goals and not by the reduction of guilt, sadness, or one's own distress (Batson et al., 1997). Other researchers are not convinced, however, and the larger philosophical debate of whether people are ever truly altruistic rages on (Cialdini et al., 1997).

When Do People Help?

Ordinary citizens often go to great lengths to help strangers, but as the infamous Kitty Genovese murder illustrates, at times bystanders fail to assist victims who are clearly in distress (Figure 12.26). What influences whether a bystander will intervene?

Bibb Latané and John Darley (1970) view bystander intervention as a five-step process (Figure 12.27). First, a bystander will not help unless she or he notices the situation. Imagine that as you walk along a street, you hear two people yelling and then hear a single scream coming from inside a house. You've noticed the situation, but now what? In everyday life, many social situations are ambiguous, and step 2 involves deciding whether this is an emergency. Is someone really in danger? To answer this question, we often engage in *social comparison:* We look around to see how other people are responding. You might say to yourself, "No one else seems concerned, so it mustn't be anything too serious." In Kitty Genovese's murder, some bystanders mistakenly thought that because nobody else intervened they were merely witnessing a "lover's quarrel" that didn't warrant their "butting in" (Darley & Latané, 1968).

Laboratory experiments confirm the importance of social comparison. In one classic study, participants were filling out a questionnaire when smoke started to pour into the room from underneath a locked side-door (Latané & Darley, 1968). Among those who were alone, three-quarters left the room to report the smoke. But when three participants were in the room together, only 38 percent of the groups reported the smoke. Astonishingly, most groups kept working while the room filled with smoke. Each person looked around, saw that nobody else was doing anything, and became convinced that the smoke didn't represent an emergency!

If you conclude that a situation is an emergency, then you move to the next step: assuming responsibility to intervene. If you are the only person to hear someone screaming, then responsibility for helping falls squarely on you. But if others are present, there may be a *diffusion of responsibility*— "If I don't help, someone else will"—and if each bystander has this thought, the victim won't receive help. In the Kitty Genovese murder, many bystanders who *did* interpret the incident as an emergency failed to intervene because they were certain that someone must already have called the police (Darley & Latané, 1968). Similarly, in a experiment where college students were isolated in individual cubicles and listened to another student who indicated he was having a seizure, participants were less likely to assist the seizure victim if they believed that other bystanders were present (Darley & Latané, 1968).

If you take responsibility, whether you actually intervene still depends on a fourth factor, your *self-efficacy* (confidence) in dealing with the situation. Sometimes, we fail to help because we don't know how or believe that our help won't be effective. In one survey, 269 college students and faculty indicated they had witnessed a public episode of child abuse, yet only a quarter reported that they had intervened (Christy & Voigt, 1994). Of those who intervened, 71 percent said that they had been certain about what to do. Among those who did not intervene, 80 percent said they were *not* certain about what action to take.

Finally, a bystander might decide not to intervene because of the perceived costs (Dovidio et al., 1991). Potential costs include not only possible physical danger but also negative social consequences, such as "appearing foolish" by trying to help inappropriately.

As this model indicates, the commonsense adage "there is safety in numbers" is not always true when it comes to receiving help. Many experiments find a **bystander effect:** The presence of multiple bystanders inhibits each person's tendency to help, largely due to social comparison or diffusion of responsibility. This inhibition is more likely to occur when the bystanders are strangers rather than friends (Latané & Rodin, 1969).

Beyond the bystander effect, other factors also help to explain why people may be helpful on some occasions but not on others. First, we are more likely to help when we are in a *good mood* (Salovey et al., 1991). Ironically, *preexisting guilt*—feeling guilty about something we have recently done—also increases helping (Regan et al., 1972). Apparently, assisting others eases our guilt, even when the two actions are unrelated. Observing a *helpful role model,* such as someone assisting a stranded motorist or donating blood, increases prosocial behavior (Sarason et al., 1991). Finally, we help more when there is a lack of time pressure and we are *not in a hurry.*

Whom Do We Help?

Some people are more likely to receive help than others. Three prominent factors are

- *Similarity.* Perceiving that a person is similar to us increases our willingness to provide help. The similarity may be in dress, attitudes, nationality, or other characteristics (Dovidio, 1984), and it may make it easier for us to identify with the victim's plight.

- *Gender.* Women are more likely to receive help than men *if* the bystander is male (Eagly & Crowley, 1986). Women and men are equally likely to be helped by female bystanders.

- *Perceived responsibility.* People are more likely to receive help when their need for aid is viewed as being caused by factors beyond their control (Weiner, 1996). Thus people who are homeless because of a natural disaster are more likely to receive help than those who are perceived as being homeless because they are unwilling to work.

Because our attributions regarding why a person needs help can be inaccurate, this last factor—perceived responsibility—can take an odd twist. Ironically, one factor that can lead attributions astray is a belief that the world is a just place. The **just world hypothesis** (Lerner, 1980) holds that because people want to view the world as fair, they perceive that people get what they deserve and deserve what they get. This belief may lead some people to conclude that victims of rape, AIDS, and other misfortunes somehow *deserve* their fate (Ford et al., 1998; Wyer et al., 1985). This irrational blaming of victims may reduce people's feelings of responsibility to help.

Increasing Prosocial Behavior

Can prosocial behavior be increased? "Mandatory volunteerism" is one approach used in some high schools, colleges, and businesses. Obviously, the students and workers who are required to donate their time to charitable organizations provide a valuable service, but do these programs increase participants' intrinsic volunteerism later in life? Unfortunately, research results are mixed (Janoski et al., 1998;

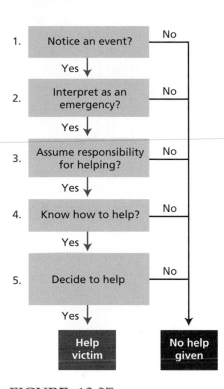

FIGURE 12.27 Bystander intervention in an emergency situation can be viewed as a five-step process. If the answer at each step is "yes," help is given.
Based on Latané & Darley, 1970.

➤ 33. Who are we most likely to help? How might the belief in a just world inhibit us from helping?

Stukas, 1999). The outcome probably depends on the personal rewards that volunteers experience and their increased awareness of human needs.

Another approach, consistent with social learning theory, is to expose people to prosocial models. Psychologists used prosocial modeling as part of a nationwide program to increase blood donations (Sarason et al., 1991). Students in 66 high schools watched an audiovisual program showing high-school donors giving blood. Compared with a control condition presented with a standard appeal from the local blood bank, the prosocial video increased blood donations by 17 percent.

Research suggests that developing feelings of empathy and connectedness with others also may make people more likely to help (Eisenberg, 2000). Margaret Clark and her coworkers (1987) found that people who felt a greater sense of connectedness to their communities were more likely to experience a need to be socially responsible and to help others.

Finally, simply learning about factors that hinder bystander intervention may increase the tendency to help someone in distress. Arthur Beaman and his coworkers (1978) exposed some college students to information about the *bystander effect*. Control participants did not receive this information. Two weeks later, more than half of the students who had learned about the bystander effect provided aid to the victim of an accident (staged by the researchers), compared with only about one fourth of the control group participants.

Aggression: Harming Others

We love. We nurture. We help. But as current events and the history of humankind attest, we also harm. In humans, *aggression* represents any form of behavior that is intended to harm another person, and it can be analyzed at biological, environmental, and psychological levels.

Biological Factors in Aggression

➤ 34. What evidence supports a genetic role in aggression?

Is aggression rooted in heredity? From bulls, roosters, and dogs to laboratory mice and rats, animals can be selectively bred over generations to be more or less aggressive (Lagerspetz et al., 1968). In some species, like the stickleback fish shown in Figure 12.28, certain aggressive behaviors represent a fixed-action pattern that is reflexively triggered by specific environmental stimuli. Humans do not display such rigid, reflexive aggressive responses, but behavior geneticists argue that heredity partly determines why some people are more aggressive than others. Identical twins are more similar in their aggressive behavior patterns than are fraternal twins, even when the identical twins are raised in different homes with presumably different social environments (Bouchard et al., 1990; Coccaro et al., 1997; Plomin & Rende, 1991). Sociobiologists propose that a genetic predisposition toward aggression can be traced to evolutionary adaptation. As in nonhumans, aggression at the proper time helped our ancestors compete successfully for mates, food, and shelter, defend territory, and survive against attack. This increased the odds that such individuals would pass their genes on to the next generation (Rushton, 1989).

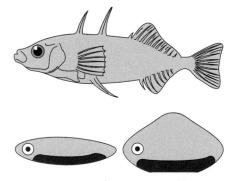

FIGURE 12.28 During the mating season the male stickleback fish develops a red belly. The sight of another red-bellied male—a potential rival for a mate—reflexively triggers an attack by the first male. The key releaser stimulus for this fixed action pattern is the red marking. A male stickelback will not attack a realistic-looking male model that has no red belly, but will attack unrealistic fish models that have this red marking.

Based on Tinbergen, 1951.

The search for biological causes of aggression also has led researchers deep within the brain, to the *hypothalamus, amygdala,* and other subcortical structures (Flynn, 1975; Siegel et al., 1999). Electrically stimulate certain neural pathways in a cat's hypothalamus, and it will arch its back and attack. Surgically destroy areas of the amygdala—an approach that has sometimes been used with violent human criminals—and in many species defensive aggression will decrease (Aggleton, 1993). There is, however, no single brain structure that "turns on" and "turns off" aggression. Different types of aggression—defending oneself, defending one's offspring, predatory aggression, establishing dominance, and so forth—may involve different neural circuits (Siegel et al., 1999).

➤ 35. Describe some brain regions and body chemicals that play a role in aggression.

Especially in humans, aggression also involves activity in the *frontal lobes*—the seat of reasoning, forethought, and impulse control (Hawkins & Trobst, 2000). Adrian Raine and his colleagues (1998) examined the brain functioning of 24 adults who had murdered someone either out of emotional, momentary impulse or as a planned predatory act. PET scans revealed that both groups of murderers showed more subcortical activity than a control group of nonmurderers, but the impulsive murderers also had lower frontal lobe activity. Deficient frontal lobe activity may make it more difficult to regulate aggressive impulses generated by subcortical brain regions.

Just as there is no single brain center for aggression, there is no one "aggression chemical." In humans and other animals, however, atypically low levels of *serotonin* activity may play a role in impulsive aggression, as when people lash out from emotional rage (Siegel et al., 1999; Siever et al., 1999). When a drug designed to boost serotonin activity is administered to men who physically abuse their partners and also to psychiatric patients who have difficulty controlling aggressive impulses, both groups show a relatively weak response to the drug (Rosenbaum et al., 1997).

And what about the sex hormone *testosterone,* which is found in males and also in females (though in smaller amounts)? In many species of mammals, higher testosterone levels contribute to greater *social aggression:* unprovoked aggressive acts that are designed to establish a dominance hierarchy among members of the same species. Injecting adult males with testosterone increases social aggression, whereas castration decreases it. But in humans and other primates, the association between testosterone and aggression is weaker and less consistent (Pinel, 1997; Tremblay et al., 1997).

Aversive Environmental Stimuli: Beyond Frustration

Aggression is influenced not only by biology, but also by our present environment and past learning experiences (Eron, 2000; Rotton & Cohn, 2000). Frustration, which occurs when some stimulus or event interferes with our progress toward a goal, often contributes to aggression. In 1939, several leading psychologists proposed the **frustration-aggression hypothesis,** stating that (1) frustration inevitably leads to aggression, and (2) all aggression is the result of frustration (Dollard et al., 1939).

Both of these sweeping assertions have since been disproved. From human infants to adults, frustration does increase the risk of verbal or physical aggression (Calkins & Johnson, 1998). At the workplace, it contributes to acts of employee hostility, theft, and sabotage (Spector, 1997). But people do not always respond to frustration by aggressing. Instead, they may exhibit despair, resignation, or nonaggressive ways of dealing with conflict (Björkqvist, 1997).

The second postulate is false as well. Aggression can be increased not only by frustration, but also by exposure to a wide range of aversive stimuli (Berkowitz, 1990). For example, *painful stimuli* can trigger irritability and aggression in humans and other animals. *Provocation* is another stimulus to aggress. Experiments with college students confirm that we often retaliate against someone who insults us or causes us physical harm (Ohbuchi & Kambara, 1985). In other species, even animals that are normally passive and prefer to flee when attacked will fight if they become cornered (Enquist & Leimar, 1990).

Crowding can trigger aggression in many species, as the remarkable study by John Calhoun (1962) shown in Figure 12.29a illustrates. In humans, when people feel crowded and believe they have little control over the situation, they report greater stress, have higher levels of stress hormones, and tolerate frustration more poorly (Fleming et al., 1987). For some motorists, increasingly congested roads and being trapped in inescapable traffic jams set the stage for high stress and aggressive acts of "road rage" (Figure 12.29b).

> 36. Identify some major types of environmental stimuli that increase the risk of aggression.

(a)

(b)

FIGURE 12.29 (a) John Calhoun (1962) built a utopian environment with abundant food, water, and nesting materials for rats, and observed them for 27 months. The rats flourished, and at the rate they were multiplying Calhoun could have expected a final colony of over 5,000. But as the population exploded, the rats' behavior became pathological: Aggression increased and infant mortality rose, in some cases when mothers ate their litter. Eventually, the colony stabilized at about 150 rats. (b) Increasingly crowded roads and stressed drivers have made road rage a national problem in the United States.

Heat also increases the risk of aggression (Anderson & Anderson, 1998). Assaults, rapes, family disturbances, and riots increase in summer months. These correlational findings are supported by several controlled experiments. In one, Dutch police officers were exposed to two temperature conditions (27° and 21° C/80.6° and 69.8° F) and shown firearm-training videotapes portraying interactions with crime suspects (Vrij et al., 1994). When the temperature was hotter, police perceived suspects as more threatening and responded with greater aggression.

Learning to Aggress: Reinforcement and Modeling

> ➤ 37. Discuss how reinforcement and modeling contribute to aggression.

Nonaggressive animals can be trained to become vicious aggressors if conditions are arranged so that they are consistently victorious in fights with weaker animals. Conversely, if conditions are arranged so that an animal is defeated in its early battles, it becomes submissive. The younger an animal is when it first suffers repeated defeats, the more submissively it will react to attacks by other animals (Zillmann, 1979).

Reward affects human aggression in much the same way. In one study of 4-year-old nursery-school children, the investigators recorded a total of 2,583 aggressive acts and their consequences. Children became increasingly aggressive when their aggressive behavior produced positive outcomes for them (as when an aggressive act resulted in another child's giving up a desired toy). Children whose aggressive behavior was unsuccessful or who experienced unpleasant consequences were less likely to be aggressive in the future (Patterson et al., 1967). Unfortunately, about 80 percent of the aggressive behaviors were rewarding for the aggressor.

Aggression also can be learned by observing others (Huesmann 1997). As Albert Bandura's (1965) famous "Bobo doll" experiments clearly demonstrated, children learn "how to aggress" even when they witness an aggressive model being punished (p. 264). Later, if the punishing agent is not present, or if rewards are available for aggressing, children can reproduce the model's actions. Correlational studies, while not establishing cause and effect, find that aggressive and delinquent children tend to have parents who frequently model aggressive behavior (Bandura, 1973; Stormshak et al., 2000).

Psychological Factors in Aggression

> ➤ 38. How do cognitive factors determine whether we respond to a stimulus aggressively?

Numerous cognitive factors influence whether we behave aggressively in a particular situation. From gang violence to "road rage" and war, people may employ several types of *self-justification* to make it psychologically easier to aggress toward others (Schlenker & Weigold, 1992; White, 1968). Aggressors may blame the victim for imagined wrongs, thereby convincing themselves that the victim "deserves it." They may minimize the seriousness of their own aggression by believing that other people's acts are even more repulsive, or by displacing responsibility. They may also "dehumanize" their victims by stripping them of human qualities and regarding them as objects or animals, as the guard in the Stanford Prison Study did when he began to view the prisoners as "cattle."

Perceived intent, empathy, and emotional regulation. Other cognitive factors, such as the *attribution of intentionality*, affect how we respond to provocation. When we perceive that someone's negative behavior toward us was intended or controllable, we are more likely to become angry and retaliate (Betancourt & Blair, 1992; Graham et al., 1992). Unfortunately, people who are generally angry and aggressive tend to perceive others as having greater hostile intent, which may contribute to a vicious cycle of aggression (Epps & Kendall, 1995).

Our degree of *empathy* for someone also influences how we react to provocation. When someone offends us and then apologizes, the likelihood that we will forgive them depends, in part, on how well we can understand their viewpoint (McCullough et al., 1997). And even when we don't forgive, whether we respond to provocation calmly or lash out depends on our *ability to regulate our emotions.* Some children and adults seem to be more physiologically reactive to provocation than others, and reduced frontal lobe activity may impair the ability to control aggressive impulses (Raine et al., 1998). But cultural norms and cognitive factors also influence how we regulate our emotions and manage conflict (Bjoerkqvist, 1997). Thus when nonviolent married men listen to audiotaped interactions designed to induce anger, they respond with more anger-controlling thoughts than do men with a history of domestic abuse (Eckhardt & Kassinove, 1998).

Psychodynamic processes.   Sigmund Freud believed that human aggression is instinctive, a view shared by the famous ethologist Konrad Lorenz (1966) and some modern psychodynamic thinkers (Raphling, 1998). Freud proposed that in a never-ending cycle, aggressive impulses build up over time, eventually have to be released, and then build up again. His principle of **catharsis** stated that performing an act of aggression discharges aggressive energy and *temporarily* reduces our impulse to aggress. But how does one do this in a world where violence is discouraged and punished? One method of releasing aggressive impulses is to channel them into socially acceptable "aggressive" behaviors, such as participating in verbal debates, vigorous exercise, competitive sports, hunting, and so forth. Another approach is to discharge aggressive impulses *vicariously* by watching and identifying with other people who behave aggressively.

If people cannot express their aggressive impulses in direct or disguised forms, will the unreleased pressures build up to an explosion point? In some cases, seemingly meek or unassertive people commit shocking and brutal crimes. These individuals, who psychologist Edwin Megargee (1966) describes as having *overcontrolled hostility,* show little immediate reaction to provocations. Instead, they bottle up their anger and over time the pressure to aggress builds up. At a critical point, they erupt into violence. Often, the provocation that triggers their destructive outburst is trivial. For example, one 10-year-old boy with no previous history of aggression stabbed his sister more than 80 times with an ice pick after she changed the channel during his favorite television show. After the aggressive outburst, such people revert to their former passive, unassertive state (Quinsey et al., 1983).

Cases of overcontrolled hostility are consistent with the concept of catharsis, but other research is not. For example, when people are aroused from just-completed vigorous physical exercise, it is easier—not harder—to provoke them into aggression (Zillmann, 1979). Psychodynamic theory also predicts that viewing violent pornography should help people discharge aggressive impulses, but as noted in Chapter 9, this is not what happens. After watching scenes of rape and sexual coercion, men act *more* aggressively toward women (Donnerstein & Berkowitz, 1981). And what about watching violent movies and television programs? Do these activities help people "blow off steam," as some stars in the entertainment industry claim?

Media Violence: Catharsis Versus Social Learning

Many movies, as well as fiction and nonfiction television programs, are saturated with violence. Analyzing 6,000 hours of American TV programming from 1994 to 1997, researchers found that 60 percent of shows contained acts of violence (National Television Violence Study, 1998). On premium cable channels, the figure was 92 percent.

According to psychodynamic theory, movie and TV violence should be a cathartic pot of gold. But social learning theorists argue that, by providing

➤ 39. According to the catharsis and social learning viewpoints, what role does media violence play in regulating human aggression?

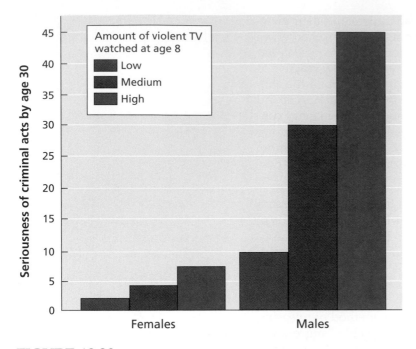

FIGURE 12.30 Children who watched more violent television at age 8 committed more serious criminal behavior by age 30. Although criminal behavior is higher overall for males than females, their general pattern of results is the same. These findings are correlational (Can you think of alternative explanations for this TV-crime relation?), but in conjunction with controlled experiments the weight of evidence convinces most experts that viewing media violence has psychological consequences. Data from Eron, 1987.

➤ 40. Based on research, how does media violence affect people's behavior and attitudes?

➤ 41. According to learning principles, how might violent video games teach people to behave aggressively? Does evidence support this view?

FIGURE 12.31 Do children who play graphically violent video games become desensitized to violence and more likely to behave aggressively toward other people?

numerous aggressive models—including many who are reinforced—media violence is more likely to increase viewers' aggressive behavior than to reduce it. From a social learning perspective, it is particularly disturbing that (National Television Violence Study, 1998):

- Forty percent of violent incidents on television were initiated by "good guys" who viewers were likely to perceive as attractive role models and identify with.

- About 75 percent of violent scenes contained no remorse or penalty for violence, and the "bad guys" went unpunished in 40 percent of the programs.

- Only 15 percent of TV programs portrayed long-term negative consequences of violence.

Headline-making "copycat" acts of violence clearly illustrate social learning effects. Still, hundreds of millions of people view media violence, and such horrendous acts thankfully are rare. What, then, are the more general effects of media violence on aggression? Over the past 30 years, hundreds of experiments and correlational studies have shed light on the "catharsis versus social learning" debate.

To most experts, the verdict is clear: The preponderance of evidence favors the social learning view (Eron, 2000; Huesmann, 1997; Smith & Donnerstein, 1998). Exposure to television and movie violence is related to the tendency of both children and adults to behave aggressively.

For example, using data collected over 22 years, Leonard Eron (1987) found that American children who watched greater amounts of violent television violence at age 8 were more likely to have committed serious criminal activity by age 30 (Figure 12.30). In Finland, Vappu Viemeroe (1996) found that boys and girls who watched more violent TV when they were 7 to 9 years old were more likely to have been arrested by their mid-twenties. In Belgium, Jacque Leyens and his colleagues (1975) went into a facility for high-school-age juvenile delinquents and held a special "movie week" in which they showed different groups of boys either violent or nonviolent movies each night. The result: Among boys who watched the violent films, physical and verbal aggression increased.

Media violence appears to exert its effects through multiple avenues (Huesman, 1997; National Television Violence Study, 1998).

- Viewers learn new aggressive behaviors through modeling.
- Viewers come to believe that aggression usually is rewarded, or at least, rarely punished.
- Viewers become desensitized to the sight and thought of violence, and to the suffering of victims.
- Viewers' fear of becoming a target of crime or violence increases.

Beyond movies and TV, violent video games have become more graphic and realistic in the past decade. Does playing violent video games also promote aggressive behavior? (Figure 12.31).

PSYCHOLOGICAL FRONTIERS

Do Violent Video Games Promote Aggression?

Sociologist Tracy Dietz (1998) recently examined 33 popular video games marketed by Nintendo and Sega (two major manufacturers). Almost half involved direct aggression toward other characters and one fifth included violence toward women. Especially in some arcade games, players use realistic "guns" to kill human or humanlike characters, whose deaths are graphically portrayed. Successful aggression is rewarded. The more targets you kill, the more points you score and the longer the game plays on.

Do violent video games stimulate aggression, or even prime some children and adolescents to kill? Few Americans believe that such games are the primary cause of shootings like the highly publicized 1999 Columbine High School murders in Littleton, Colorado, but 58 percent feel that the federal government should do more to regulate video game violence (Newport, 1999, May 10). Clearly, both the public and scientists are concerned.

▶ Video Games as Target Practice: Conditioning and Desensitization?

To psychologist David Grossman of Arkansas State University, the issue of media and video game violence has special meaning. He lives in Jonesboro, where in March 1998 an 11- and 13-year-old boy staged a false fire alarm, lured classmates out of school, then fatally shot four girls and a teacher and wounded 10 other people. Three years earlier, before a shocking string of similar schoolground killings across the United States, Grossman (1995) published *On Killing: The Psychological Cost of Learning to Kill in War and Society.* His major point: In order to kill, we must learn to overcome a natural inhibition *against* killing members of our own species. And, he argues, violent video games can be a powerful disinhibitor and teacher.

Grossman, a retired U.S. Army officer, points to a history of warfare in which soldiers have been reluctant to kill the enemy face-to-face. In World War II, the U.S. Army found that for every 100 soldiers who had a clear shot at the enemy, only 15 percent fired at their target: a 15 percent "kill rate." To counteract this situation, the army trained soldiers by using operant and classical conditioning principles. A "shooting" response was gradually shaped via increasingly realistic target practice, progressing from bull's-eye targets to human silhouettes and "pop-up" human figures, and finally to video combat simulations. Over time, soldiers became desensitized to shooting at human forms and by the Korean and Vietnam Wars, the kill rates increased to 55 and 90 percent, respectively. For over 20 years, police and other law en-

forcement agencies also have conditioned their personnel to shoot—and to discern when not to shoot—using video simulations (Cummins, 1999, March 2).

▶ Experiments on Video Game Violence

Does evidence support Grossman's view that video games can be training grounds for violence? Unfortunately, there are relatively few experiments, they focus on short-term effects, and some (particularly in the 1980s) involve "violent" video games that are tame by today's standards.

In one of the best studies to date, Roland Irwin and Alan Gross (1995) of the University of Mississippi randomly assigned 60 7- and 8-year old boys to play either a violent or nonviolent Nintendo video game for 20 minutes. In the violent game, *Double Dragon,* the player assumes the role of a martial arts hero who kicks, punches, and uses a rope or chain to whip and defeat ruthless street gang members. In the nonviolent game, *Excitebike,* the player races a motorcycle against the clock.

After playing one of the games, each child engaged in a 10-minute "free-play" period with another boy (an accomplice). Next as each participant competed against this boy on a task for a prize, the boy (according to plan) cheated. Observers who were blind to each child's video game condition coded the participants' behavior during both the free-play period and the frustrating event. Compared with participants who had played *Excitebike,* those who played *Double Dragon* displayed more physical and verbal aggression toward inanimate objects (e.g., toys), more verbal aggression toward the other boy during the free-play period, and more physical aggression toward the other boy during the frustrating competition.

Let us think critically about this result. Did *Double Dragon's* violent *content* increase participants' aggression, or was it simply a more exciting game? If so, perhaps it was only *greater arousal* that led to more aggression? To help decide between these two alternatives, Irwin and Gross measured participants' heart rate both before and during the video game play. The result: no heart rate differences between the two video game conditions, strengthening the conclusion that the aggressive content of the violent game was the key factor.

This experiment, like others, measured short-term effects. Still, aggression increased after only a single 20-minute exposure to the violent game. We can only speculate as to what effect hundreds of hours of playtime has on people. Other studies also suggest that playing—and even observing—violent video games temporarily increases

—Continued

some children's aggressive behavior, though some have failed to obtain such findings. But overall, research tentatively provides stronger support for the social learning view that violent video games promote aggression than for the belief that such games provide a catharsis by helping children or adults "blow off steam" (Anderson & Dill, 2000; Griffiths, 1997). Violent video games also may affect how children perceive other people's actions. In one experiment with third- and fourth-graders, playing a violent game for just a few minutes increased children's tendency to perceive that a peer who caused a negative event did so intentionally (Kirsh, 1998).

Clearly, the overwhelming majority of children and adults who play violent video games do not go out and commit crimes or kill people. But aggression comes in many forms, physical and verbal, obvious and subtle, and more research is needed to pinpoint how children are affected by a video world full of *Mortal Kombat* and *Doom*.

In closing, Figure 12.32 highlights some of the biological, psychological, and environmental factors that contribute to human aggression.

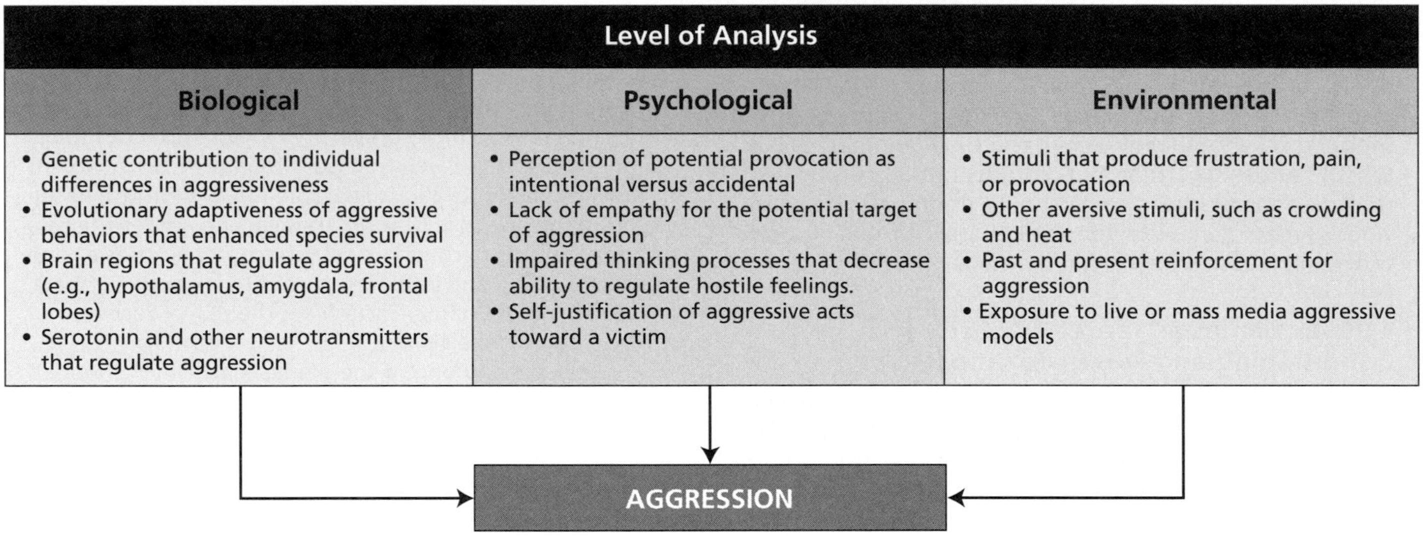

Level of Analysis		
Biological	**Psychological**	**Environmental**
• Genetic contribution to individual differences in aggressiveness • Evolutionary adaptiveness of aggressive behaviors that enhanced species survival • Brain regions that regulate aggression (e.g., hypothalamus, amygdala, frontal lobes) • Serotonin and other neurotransmitters that regulate aggression	• Perception of potential provocation as intentional versus accidental • Lack of empathy for the potential target of aggression • Impaired thinking processes that decrease ability to regulate hostile feelings. • Self-justification of aggressive acts toward a victim	• Stimuli that produce frustration, pain, or provocation • Other aversive stimuli, such as crowding and heat • Past and present reinforcement for aggression • Exposure to live or mass media aggressive models

AGGRESSION

FIGURE 12.32   Understanding the Causes of Behavior: Why do people aggress?

CHAPTER SUMMARY

Social Influence

- Social psychologists study how the social environment affects the way we behave, think, and feel.

- Zajonc's theory of social facilitation states that the mere presence of others increases our arousal and tendency to perform our dominant response. If our dominant response to a task is incorrect, as when learning complex tasks, performance usually is impaired. If our dominant response is correct, as when performing simple or well-learned tasks, the presence of others usually enhances performance.

- A social norm is a rule or expectation shared by the members of a group about how they should think, feel, and behave. A social role is a set of norms that defines a particular position in a social system. Norms vary across cultures and times.

- People conform to be accepted by others and because they believe that what other people are doing or saying is "right." The size of the majority, the presence or absence of dissenters, and the importance of the situation influence the degree of conformity to a group. Minority influence is strongest when the minority maintains a consistent position over time but does not appear too deviant.

- Milgram's obedience research raised strong ethical concerns and found unexpectedly high percentages of people willing to obey destructive orders. Such obedience is stronger when the victim is remote and when the authority figure is close by, legitimate, and assumes responsibility for what happens.

- Deindividuation is a temporary lowering of restraints that can occur when a person is immersed in a group. Anonymity to outsiders appears to be the key factor in producing deindividuation.

- Social loafing occurs when people exert less individual effort when working as a group than when working alone. Social loafing decreases when the goal or group membership is valued highly, and when people's performance within the group can be individually monitored. Culture and gender influence the tendency to socially loaf.

- When the members of a decision-making group initially share the same conservative or liberal viewpoint, the group's final decision often reflects a polarization effect, and becomes more extreme than the average opinion of the individual members. Cohesive decision-making groups also may display groupthink, a tendency to suspend critical thinking and agree on a decision to maintain cohesion and loyalty to the leader's viewpoint.

Social Thinking and Perception

- Attitudes predict behavior best when (1) the role of situational influences is minimized, (2) the attitude is strong and we consciously think about it, and (3) general attitudes are used to predict general classes of behavior, or specific attitudes are used to predict specific behaviors.

- Our behavior also influences our attitudes. Counterattitudinal behavior is most likely to create cognitive dissonance—an unpleasant state of tension—when the behavior is freely chosen and has negative implications for our sense of self-worth. To reduce dissonance, we may change our attitude to become more consistent with how we have behaved. In situations where our attitudes are weaker or don't threaten our self-worth, counterattitudinal behavior may produce attitude change through a process of self-perception.

- Communicator, message, and audience characteristics influence the effectiveness of persuasion. Communicator credibility is highest when the communicator is perceived as expert and trustworthy. Fear-arousing communications may be highly effective if they arouse moderate fear and provide behavioral guidelines for avoiding the feared consequence. Audience members' need for cognition influences the effectiveness of messages that take a central versus peripheral route to persuasion.

- Persuaders often use special influence tactics such as manipulating the norm of reciprocity, the door-in-the-face technique, the foot-in-the-door technique, and lowballing.

- An attribution is a judgment about the causes of our own or someone else's behavior. Consistency, distinctiveness, and consensus information jointly influence whether we make a personal or situational attribution for a particular act.

- The fundamental attribution error is the tendency to attribute other people's behavior to personal factors while underestimating the role of situational factors. The self-serving bias is the tendency to attribute one's successes to personal factors and one's failures to situational factors. Cultural norms influence the degree to which people display these tendencies.

- Though our impressions of people may change over time, the initial information we learn about someone generally carries extra weight. Stereotypes and schemas create mental sets that powerfully shape our impressions of people. Through self-fulfilling prophecies, our initially false expectations about someone shape the way we act toward her or him. In turn, this person responds to our behavior in a way that confirms our initially false belief.

Social Relations

- Overt prejudice and discrimination have decreased in some ways, but often have been replaced by covert prejudice. Sophisticated tasks, such as the implicit association test, help to reveal nonconscious forms of prejudice.

- The cognitive roots of prejudice stem from our tendency to categorize objects and people, which leads us to perceive in-groups and out-groups. People typically display in-group favoritism and an outgroup homogeneity bias. Stereotypes affect how we perceive out-group members' behavior and shape our impressions of them. Inconsistent information may be ignored or rationalized away.

- Motivationally, prejudice stems from perceived threats to one's in-group and a need to enhance one's self-esteem. In part, our self-esteem derives from identifying with certain in-groups.

- Self-fulfilling prophecies and stereotype threat maintain prejudice. In stereotype threat, out-group members' self-conciousness about confirming a stereotype affects their behavior in a way that, indeed, ends up confirming the stereotype.

- One of the most effective ways to reduce prejudice is to have in-group and out-group members work closely together, with equal status, on tasks in which common goals can be achieved only through cooperation.

- Sociobiologists propose that through kin selection and reciprocal altruism, evolution has helped shape a genetic predisposition toward prosocial behavior among humans. The social learning view emphasizes the role of social norms, modeling, reinforcement, and self-reinforcement, in socializing prosocial attitudes and behavior. The empathy-altruism hypothesis proposes that feelings of empathy for a victim lead us to engage in truly altruistic behavior without any concern for personal benefit, whereas the negative state relief model argues that empathic people, by helping others, benefit by reducing their own distress.

- The presence of multiple bystanders may actually decrease bystander intervention through social comparison processes and a diffusion of responsibility for helping. We are most likely to help others when we perceive they are similar to us and are not responsible for their plight.

- Prosocial behavior can be increased by enhancing people's feelings of empathy for victims and providing prosocial models.

- Aggression has biological, environmental, and psychological causes. Animals can be bred to be more or less aggressive, illustrating the role of genetics. No single brain region or body chemical controls human aggression, though it appears that the hypothalamus, amygdala, frontal lobes, and neurotransmitter serotonin play especially important roles in certain types of aggression.

- Stimuli that cause frustration, pain, and provocation increase the risk of aggression, as do high levels of heat and crowding under some circumstances. Learning experiences, including modeling and reinforcement, help shape a tendency to behave more or less aggressively.

- People are more likely to aggress when they find ways to justify and rationalize their aggressive behavior, when they perceive provocation as intentional, have little empathy for others, and have difficulty regulating their emotions.

- According to the classic psychodynamic concept of catharsis, performing direct or vicarious acts of aggression helps people to release their aggressive urges and temporarily reduces the tendency toward further aggression. Although research on people with overcontrolled hostility is consistent with this view, research on media violence and violent pornography is not. Viewing such stimuli tends to increase aggressive behavior as social learning theory predicts, and desensitizes viewers to violence. Tentatively, a small body of research suggests that violent video games also may stimulate aggressive behavior in some children.

KEY TERMS AND CONCEPTS*

attitude (512)
attribution (518)
bystander effect (529)
catharsis (533)
central route to persuasion (516)
communicator credibility (515)
deindividuation (509)
discrimination (522)
door-in-the-face technique (517)
empathy-altruism hypothesis (527)
foot-in-the-door technique (517)
frustration-aggression hypothesis (531)
fundamental attribution error (519)

group polarization (510)
groupthink (511)
informational social influence (503)
just world hypothesis (529)
kin selection (526)
lowballing (517)
negative state relief model (528)
norm of reciprocity (516)
normative social influence (503)
peripheral route to persuasion (516)
prejudice (522)
primacy effect (520)
realistic conflict theory (525)

self-fulfilling prophecy (521)
self-perception theory (514)
self-serving bias (520)
social facilitation (501)
social identity theory (525)
social loafing (509)
social norm (502)
social role (502)
stereotype (521)
stereotype threat (526)
theory of cognitive dissonance (513)
theory of planned behavior (512)

* Each term has been boldfaced in the text on the page indicated in parentheses.

APPLYING YOUR KNOWLEDGE

These questions allow you to apply your understanding of the material in this chapter.

1. Dianna, a college drama major, is trying to learn some complicated dance movements for her role in an upcoming play. Dianna finds dancing difficult in general, and this dance sequence is complex. She rehearses at night in the living room of her dormitory suite, making many errors. If her roommates watch her practice, this probably will _____ the frequency of Dianna's dominant response and _____ the quality of her performance.
   a) increase; impair
   b) increase; enhance
   c) decrease; impair
   d) decrease; enhance

2. Elliot and three friends have been drinking alcohol at a party. When they are ready to leave and drive home, Elliot knows it is dangerous and that they should call a taxi, but he doesn't say anything because he's afraid that his friends will disapprove or make fun of him. In this case, Elliot's conformity to his friends' decision to drive home primarily reflects
   a) informational social influence.
   b) normative social influence.
   c) deindividuation.
   d) social loafing.

3. Helena is behaving in a way that is inconsistent with her attitudes. She will most likely experience cognitive dissonance if
   a) she freely chose to engage in this behavior.
   b) her attitudes are weak to begin with.
   c) she has a strong external justification for behaving the way she did.
   d) her behavior does not threaten her sense of self-worth.

4. Claude, a new worker, is 30 minutes late and nowhere in sight. His boss assumes that Claude is "unreliable," but doesn't realize that Claude actually arrived at the building early and has been stuck in a broken elevator (without a cell phone) for the last 50 minutes. The boss's immediate tendency to judge Claude as "unreliable" best reflects
   a) the self-serving bias.
   b) the central route to persuasion.
   c) the fundamental attribution error.
   d) social facilitation.

5. The Faculty Curriculum Committee at your college is debating whether to increase the number of foreign language courses that students will have to take for a general breadth requirement. In which of the following cases would the committee's decision most likely reflect the presence of "groupthink"?
   a) The committee makes a fast, high-quality decision because they first divide into subcommittees that independently discuss the issue.
   b) After a two-hour debate, committee members are still unable to agree on a decision.
   c) To maintain positive feelings of group cohesiveness, the committee accepts the chairperson's solution without thinking carefully about the issue.
   d) The committee seeks assistance from outside advisors because group members realize they do not have the expertise to make a proper decision.

6. A classmate who you do not know asks to borrow your class notes from the entire quarter. You say "No," which is exactly what he expected. Then he asks, "OK, well, can I borrow your notes just from the last week." In fact, the second request was the one he really was interested in all along. What manipulative technique is this person using?
   a) the norm of reciprocity
   b) lowballing
   c) the foot-in-the-door technique
   d) the door-in-the face technique

7. Two groups of children, each representing a different ethnic group, are expressing prejudice and hatred toward one another. According to the "contact hypothesis," what should you do to most effectively reduce their prejudice?
   a) Have the two groups engage in a series of enjoyable, noncompetitive activities, such as field trips to museums, the zoo, or movies.
   b) Have the two groups compete against one another in enjoyable activities, such as spelling contests or sports.
   c) Separate the groups, have them avoid all contact for a while, and then gradually allow them to spend more time in each other's presence.
   d) Have the two groups work together on common assignments that require them to cooperate to succeed.

8. Herbert expresses a lot of prejudice toward members of other ethnic groups. According to social identity theory, the fundamental cause of Herbert's prejudice is his
   a) need to enhance his self-esteem.
   b) belief that he is competing against members of other ethnic groups for limited resources (e.g., job, spaces for admission to college).
   c) lack of exposure to members of other ethnic groups during childhood.
   d) perception that members of other ethnic groups are "all alike."

9. Teresa is a volunteer for several charitable organizations. She likes to help people because it gives her great pride and personal satisfaction, and makes her feel like she is a "good person." Teresa's motives best reflect the _____ viewpoint of why people help others.
   a) sociobiological
   b) empathy-altruism
   c) negative state relief model
   d) social learning

10. Brad believes that violent movies and TV programs serve a valuable function by letting people "blow off steam" and get rid of their aggressive urges. In short, he believes in the principle of _____, which the majority of scientific research _____ when it comes to the issue of media violence.
    a) catharsis; supports
    b) catharsis; does not support
    c) deindividuation; supports
    d) deindividuation; does not support

Answers

1. a) (page 501); 2. b) (page 503); 3. a) (page 513);
4. c) (page 519); 5. c) (page 511); 6. d) (page 516);
7. d) (page 526); 8. a) (page 525); 9. d) (page 527);
10. b) (page 533).

For additional quizzing and a variety of interactive resources, visit the book's Online Learning Center at www.mhhe.com/passer.

PERSONALITY

Much of our lives is spent in trying to understand others and
in wishing others understood us better than they do.
— *Gordon Allport*

13

CHAPTER OUTLINE

Bathed in the early spring sunlight, three college women sat on their front porch. Donna spoke first. " I'm not sure how much longer I can take Julia's moodiness. She jumped down my throat again the other day when I asked her to turn down her stereo. She seems to have all this anger inside that gets directed at us for no real reason. At first she seemed really nice, but now I regret the day she moved in with us."

"I talked to someone who knew her in middle school and high school," replied Kim. "He told me Julia was always tough to get close to. Her sister's the same way. Maybe it's the family genes, or maybe she was just raised as a spoiled brat. The strange thing is that she can be totally different in other situations. She's friendly and nice when we go to parties or when she's in a large group of people where things are pretty superficial. It's when you try to get close to her that she goes into attack mode. That's what Brad said, too, when he broke up with her."

Ellen had been listening closely. "You know, I think that deep down, Julia has a pretty negative self-image that she covers over by being arrogant. I wonder if she really understands what she's doing. I wouldn't be surprised if she's been hurt in the past and is really scared of letting her guard down. Maybe if we can just hang in with her a little longer, she can relax her defenses. I think I've seen that start to happen a bit."

Why does Julia act as she does? Do the roots of her behavior lie in "the family genes"? Did overindulgent parents turn her into "a spoiled brat"? Or has she been "deeply hurt" in the past, leaving lots of unresolved anger that bubbles over and gets directed at others inappropriately? Does Julia indeed have a negative self-concept, and are her behaviors really an unconscious defense to keep people from getting close enough to hurt her? How is she able to be such a different person in different situations? Can she change in meaningful ways? As we shall see in this chapter, Donna's, Kim's, and Ellen's hypotheses are similar to those that might be advanced by various personality theorists who try to understand human individuality and the reasons people behave as they do.

❯ WHAT IS PERSONALITY?

➤ 1. What two common observations give rise to the concept of personality?

The concept of personality arises from the fascinating spectrum of human individuality. We observe that people differ meaningfully in the ways they customarily think, feel, and act. Thus Julia differs from Donna, Kim, and Ellen, and this distinctive behavior pattern helps define her identity as a person. As one group of theorists noted, each of us is in certain respects like *all other* people, like *some other* people, and like *no other* person who has lived in the past or will exist in the future (Kluckhohn & Murray, 1953).

The concept of personality also rests on the observation that people seem to behave somewhat consistently over time and across different situations. At least from middle school on, we are told, Julia has been "hard to get close to." From this perceived consistency comes the notion of "personality traits" that characterize individuals' customary ways of responding to their world. Although only modest stability is found from childhood personality to adult personality, consistency becomes greater as we enter adulthood (Caspi & Roberts, 1999). Nonetheless, even in adulthood, there remains a capacity for meaningful personality change (Lewis, 1999). Combining these notions of individuality and consistency, we can define **personality** as the distinctive and relatively enduring ways of thinking, feeling, and acting that characterize a person's responses to life situations.

The thoughts, feelings, and actions that are seen as reflecting an individual's personality typically have three characteristics. First, they are seen as components of identity that distinguish that person from other people. Second, the behaviors are viewed as being caused primarily by internal rather than environmental factors. Third, the person's behaviors seem to "fit together" in a meaningful fashion, suggesting an inner personality that guides and directs behavior (Figure 13.1).

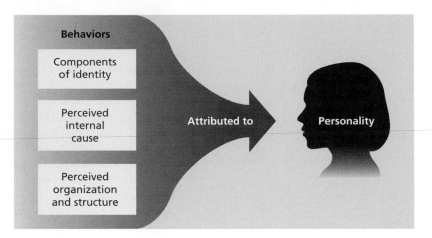

FIGURE 13.1 Perceived characteristics of behaviors that are seen as reflecting an individual's personality.

Perhaps more than any other topic, the study of personality has been guided by the psychodynamic, humanistic, biological, behavioral, cognitive, and sociocultural perspectives. These perspectives provide different conceptions of what personality is and how it functions. As one pair of observers noted, "It seems hard to believe that all the theorists are talking about the same creature, who is now angelic and now depraved, now a black-box robot shaped by reinforcers and now a shaper of its own destiny, now devious . . . and now hardheadedly oriented to solid reality" (Stone & Church, 1968). Yet this very diversity arises from the fact that the theorists have their own personalities that influence how they perceive and understand themselves and their world. No doubt, you will find some of the theories more in accord with your own life views than others. But for personality psychologists, their subjective "truth" is less important than their *usefulness* as scientific theories. As discussed in Chapter 2, a theory is scientifically useful to the extent that it (1) provides a comprehensive framework within which known facts can be incorporated, (2) allows us to predict future events with some precision, and (3) stimulates the discovery of new knowledge. We will evaluate each of the theories we describe in terms of these scientific standards.

➤ 2. What three standards are used to evaluate the usefulness of a personality theory?

❭ THE PSYCHODYNAMIC PERSPECTIVE

Psychodynamic theorists look for the causes of behavior in a dynamic interplay of inner forces that often conflict with one another. They also focus on unconscious determinants of behavior. Sigmund Freud's psychoanalytic theory was the first and most influential of these theories, and his ideas continue to influence Western thought today.

Freud's Psychoanalytic Theory

Freud (1856–1939) spent most of his life in Vienna, where he attended medical school with the intention of becoming a medical researcher (Figure 13.2). He was particularly interested in brain functioning. A pivotal event in his life occurred when he was awarded a fellowship to study in Paris with the famous French neurologist Jean Charcot. Charcot was treating patients who suffered from a disorder called *conversion hysteria* in which physical symptoms such as paralysis and blindness appeared suddenly and with no apparent physical cause. Freud's experiences in treating these patients convinced him that their symptoms were related to painful memories and feelings that seemed to have been repressed, or pushed out of awareness. When his patients were able to reexperience these traumatic

FIGURE 13.2 Sigmund Freud is shown here with his daughter Anna, who also became an influential psychoanalytic theorist.

➤ 3. Which clinical phenomena convinced Freud of the power of the unconscious mind?

memories and unacceptable feelings, which were often sexual or aggressive in nature, their physical symptoms often disappeared or improved markedly.

These observations convinced Freud that an unconscious part of the mind exerts great influence on behavior. He began to experiment with various techniques to unearth the buried contents of the unconscious mind, including hypnosis, free association (saying whatever comes to mind, no matter how trivial or embarrassing), and dream analysis. In an attempt to relieve painful bouts of depression that he was experiencing, Freud also conducted an extensive self-analysis based on his own dreams.

In 1900 Freud published, *The Interpretation of Dreams.* The book sold only 600 copies in its first six years, but his revolutionary ideas began to attract followers. His theory also evoked scathing criticism from a Victorian society that was not ready to regard the human being as a seething cauldron of sexual and aggressive impulses. In the words of one commentator, "It is a shattering experience for anyone seriously committed to the Western tradition of morality and rationality to take a steadfast, unflinching look at what Freud has to say. It is humiliating to be compelled to admit the grossly seamy side of so many grand ideals. . . . To experience Freud is to partake a second time of the forbidden fruit" (Brown, 1959, p. xi).

Freud based his theory on careful clinical observation and constantly sought to expand it. Over time, psychoanalysis became a theory of personality, an approach to studying the mind, and a method for treating psychological disorders.

Psychic Energy and Mental Events

➤ 4. How did hydraulic systems of his time contribute to Freud's psychodynamic concepts?

Inspired by the hydraulic models of 19th-century physics, which emphasized exchanges and releases of physical energy, Freud considered personality to be an energy system, somewhat like the steam engines of his day. According to Freud, instinctual drives generate **psychic energy,** which powers the mind and constantly presses for either direct or indirect release. For example, a buildup of energy from sexual drives might be discharged directly in the form of sexual activity, or indirectly through such diverse behaviors as sexual fantasies, farming, or painting.

Mental events may be *conscious, preconscious,* or *unconscious.* The conscious mind consists of mental events that we are presently aware of. The preconscious contains memories, thoughts, feelings, and images that we are unaware of at the moment but that can be recalled. A friend's telephone number or memories of your sixteenth birthday are likely to reside in the preconscious mind.

Because we are aware of their contents, we are likely to see the conscious and preconscious areas of the mind as the most prominent ones. But Freud believed that these areas are dwarfed in both size and importence by the unconscious mind, a dynamic realm of wishes, feelings, and impulses that lies beyond our awareness. Only when impulses from the unconscious are discharged in one way or another, such as in dreams, slips of the tongue, or some disguised behavior does the unconscious reveal itself. Thus in the throes of passion, a young man proclaimed his love for his fiancé by whispering, "I love you, Marcia." The only problem was that his fiancé's name was Amy. Freud would probably have concluded (as did Amy!) that the slip of the tongue was a sign that erotic feelings for Marcia (which the man vehemently denied) were still there, buried in his subconscious mind. Psychoanalysts believe that such verbal slips are holes in our armor of conscious control and expressions of our true feelings.

The Structure of Personality

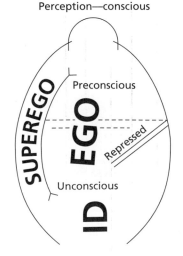

FIGURE 13.3 Freud's own drawing of his three-part conception of personality shows the relation of the id, ego, and superego to the conscious, preconscious, and unconscious areas of the mind.

Freud divided personality into three separate but interacting structures: id, ego, and superego. The **id** exists totally within the unconscious mind (Figure 13.3). It is the innermost core of the personality, the only structure present at birth, and the source of all psychic energy. Freud described the id as "a chaos, a cauldron of seething excitations" (Freud, 1900/1964, p. 73). The id has no direct contact with reality and functions in a totally irrational manner. Operating according to the **pleasure principle,** it seeks immediate gratification or release, regardless of rational considerations and environmental realities. Its dictum: "Want . . . take!"

➤ 5. Discuss the roles of the pleasure principle, the reality principle, and identification in relation to Freud's three personality structures.

The id cannot directly satisfy itself by obtaining what it needs from the environment because it has no contact with the outer world. Therefore in the course of development, a new structure develops out of the id that has direct contact with reality. The **ego** functions primarily at a conscious level, and it operates according to the **reality principle.** It tests reality to decide when and under what conditions the id can safely discharge its impulses and satisfy its needs. For example, the ego would seek sexual gratification within a consenting relationship rather than allowing the pleasure principle to dictate an impulsive sexual assault on the first person who happened by.

The last personality structure to develop is the **superego,** the moral arm of the personality. Developing by the age of 4 or 5, the superego contains the traditional values and ideals of society. These ideals are internalized by the child through identification with his or her parents, who also use reinforcement and punishment to teach the child what is "right," what is "wrong," and how the child "should" be. With the development of the superego, self-control is substituted for external control.

Like the ego, the superego strives to control the instincts of the id, particularly the sexual and aggressive impulses that are condemned by society. In a sense, the id says, "I want!" and the superego replies, "Don't you dare! That would be evil!" Whereas the ego simply tries to postpone instinctual gratification until conditions are safe and appropriate, the superego, in its blind quest for perfection, tries to block gratification permanently. For the superego, moralistic goals take precedence over realistic ones, regardless of the potential cost to the individual. Thus the superego might cause a person to experience intense guilt over sexual activity even within marriage because it has internalized the idea that sex is "dirty."

With the development of the superego, the ego is squarely in the eye of a psychic storm. It must achieve compromises between the demands of the id, the constraints of the superego, and the demands of reality. This balancing act has earned the ego the title, "executive of the personality."

➤ 6. Why is the ego sometimes referred to as the "executive of the personality"?

Conflict, Anxiety, and Defense

The dynamics of personality involve a never-ending struggle between instincts and drives in the id striving for release and counterforces generated by the ego and superego to contain them. Observable behavior often represents compromises between motives, needs, impulses, and defenses. When the ego confronts impulses that threaten to get out of control or is faced with dangers from the environment, anxiety results. Like physical pain, anxiety serves as a danger signal and motivates the ego to deal with the problem at hand. In many instances, the anxiety can be reduced through realistic coping behaviors, as when a person who is extremely angry at someone works out the problem through rational discussion instead of a murderous assault. However, when realistic strategies are ineffective in reducing anxiety, the ego may resort to **defense mechanisms** that deny or distort reality. Some of the defense mechanisms permit the release of impulses from the id in disguised forms that will not conflict with forces in the external world or with the prohibitions of the superego. The major defense mechanisms are described in Table 13.1.

➤ 7. How and why do defense mechanisms develop? What specific forms do they take?

Psychoanalysts believe that repression is the primary means by which the ego "keeps the lid on the id." In **repression,** the ego uses some of its energy to prevent anxiety-arousing memories, feelings, and impulses from entering consciousness. Repressed thoughts and wishes remain in the unconscious, striving for release, but they may be expressed indirectly, as in slips of the tongue or in

TABLE 13.1	PSYCHOANALYTIC EGO DEFENSE MECHANISMS	
Defense Mechanism	**Description**	**Example**
Repression	An active defensive process through which anxiety-arousing impulses or memories are pushed into the unconscious mind.	A person who was sexually abused in childhood develops amnesia for the event.
Denial	A person refuses to acknowledge anxiety-arousing aspects of the environment. The denial may involve either the emotions connected with the event or the event itself.	A man who is told he has terminal cancer refuses to consider the possibility that he will not recover.
Displacment	An unacceptable or dangerous impulse is repressed, then directed at a safer substitute target.	A man who is harassed by his boss experiences no anger at work, then goes home and abuses his wife and children.
Intellectualization	The emotion connected with an upsetting event is repressed, and the situation is dealt with as an intellectually interesting event.	A person who has been rejected in an important relationship talks in a highly rational manner about the "interesting unpredictability of love relationships."
Projection	An unacceptable impulse is repressed, then attributed to (projected onto) other people.	A woman with strong repressed desires to have an affair continually accuses her husband of being unfaithful to her.
Rationalization	A person constructs a false but plausible explanation or excuse for an anxiety-arousing behavior or event that has already occurred.	A student caught cheating on an exam justifies the act by pointing out that the professor's tests are unfair and, besides, everybody else was cheating, too.
Reaction formation	An anxiety-arousing impulse is repressed, and its psychic energy finds release in an exaggerated expression of the opposite behavior.	A mother who harbors feelings of hatred for her child represses them and becomes overprotective of the child.
Sublimation	A repressed impulse is released in the form of a socially acceptable or even admired behavior.	A man with strong hostile impulses becomes an investigative reporter who ruins political careers with his stories.

dreams. They may even be channeled into socially desirable and admirable behaviors through the defense mechanism of **sublimation,** completely masking the sinister underlying impulses. For example, hostile impulses may find expression in tracking down criminals or being a successful trial lawyer. Although Freud described several defense mechanisms, his primary interest was in repression. His daughter Anna Freud, also a psychoanalyst, extended his ideas and described many of the defense mechanisms shown in Table 13.1.

Defense mechanisms operate unconsciously, so people are usually unaware that they are using self-deception to ward off anxiety. Almost everyone uses them at times, but maladjusted people use them excessively in place of more realistic approaches to dealing with problems. For example, Freud might suggest that Julia, the college woman described earlier, is filled with repressed rage stemming from perceived parental favoritism toward her younger sister. That rage, too threatening for her to confront consciously, is now being directed at other people through the defense mechanism of displacement.

Psychosexual Development

> 8. How does each of Freud's psychosexual stages contribute to adult personality?

Freud's clinical experiences convinced him that personality is powerfully molded by experiences in the first years of life. He proposed that children pass through a series of **psychosexual stages** during which the id's pleasure-seeking tendencies are focused on specific pleasure-sensitive areas of the body called *erogenous zones.* Potential deprivations or overindulgences can arise during any of these stages, resulting in *fixation,* a state of arrested psychosexual development in which instincts are focused on a particular psychic theme.

The first of these stages is the *oral stage,* which occurs during infancy. Infants gain primary satisfaction from taking in food and from sucking on a breast, a thumb, or some other object. Freud proposed that either excessive gratification or frustration of oral needs can result in fixation on oral themes of self-indulgence or dependency as an adult.

In the second and third years of life, children enter the *anal stage*, and pleasure becomes focused on the process of elimination. During toilet training, the child is faced with society's first attempt to control a biological urge. According to Freud, harsh toilet training can produce compulsions, overemphasis on cleanliness, obsessive concerns with orderliness, and insistence on rigid rules and rituals. In contrast, Freud speculated that extremely lax toilet training results in a messy, negative, and dominant adult.

The most controversial of Freud's stages is the *phallic stage*, which begins at 4 or 5 years of age. This is the time when children begin to derive pleasure from their sexual organs. Freud believed that during this stage of early sexual awakenings, the male child experiences erotic feelings toward his mother, desires to possess her sexually, and views his father as a rival. At the same time, however, these feelings arouse strong guilt and a fear that the father might castrate him, hence the term *castration anxiety*. This conflictual situation is the **Oedipus complex,** named for the Greek character Oedipus, who unknowingly killed his father and married his mother. Girls, meanwhile, discover that they lack a penis, blame the mother for their lack of what Freud considered the more desirable sex organ, and wish to bear their father's child as a substitute for the penis they lack. The female version of the Oedipus complex was termed the **Electra complex.** Freud believed that the phallic stage is a major milestone in the development of gender identity, for children normally resolve these conflicts by repressing their sexual impulses and moving from a sexual attachment to the opposite-sex parent to *identification* with the same-sex parent, boys taking on the traits of fathers and girls those of their mothers. Identification allows the child to possess the opposite-sex parent indirectly, or vicariously, and also helps form the superego as children internalize the parent's values and moral beliefs.

As the phallic stage draws to a close at about 6 years of age, children enter the *latency stage,* during which sexuality becomes dormant for about 6 years. Sexuality normally reemerges in adolescence as the beginning of a lifelong *genital stage* in which erotic impulses find direct expression in sexual relationships.

Research on Psychoanalytic Theory

Freud was committed to testing his ideas through case studies and clinical observations. He believed that careful observations of everyday behavior and clinical phenomena were the best source of evidence. He opposed experimental research, believing that the complex phenomena he had identified could not be studied under controlled conditions (Rosenzweig, 1992). Most modern psychologists do not believe that clinical observations are sufficient proof, but they do acknowledge the difficulty of studying psychoanalytic concepts under controlled laboratory conditions (Carver & Scheier, 2000; Mischel, 1999). Indeed, a major shortcoming of psychoanalytic theory is that many of its concepts are ambiguous and difficult to operationally define and measure (Westen & Gabbard, 1999). How, for example, can we measure the strength of an individual's id impulses and unconscious ego defenses, or study processes that are by definition unconscious and inaccessible to the person?

Fortunately, cognitive psychologists have developed new methods to identify and measure unconscious processing of information, and a growing body of research has shown that much of our moment-to-moment mental and emotional life occurs outside of awareness (Bargh & Chartrand, 1999; Kirsch & Lynn, 1999). On the biological front, cognitive neuroscience has provided methods for tapping into mental processes as they occur by measuring brain activity (Posner, 1999). Increasingly, researchers are using these tools to test hypotheses derived from psychoanalytic theory with greater scientific precision. The following *Research Close-Up* provides one example.

➤ 9. Describe how Shevrin and his colleagues tried to establish the existence of unconscious psychodynamics. What were their findings?

RESEARCH CLOSE-UP

Using Neuropsychology to Study Unconscious Psychodynamics

▶ Background

Freud's original medical specialty was neurology, and this background influenced many of his concepts. In his first comprehensive account of psychoanalysis, *Project for a Scientific Psychology* (1895/1950), Freud tried to link psychoanalytic concepts to the neurophysiology of his time. He soon abandoned this approach in favor of clinical observation, largely because there were no scientific tools available to test his ideas about brain processes. Today, however, the tools Freud lacked are available and are being used in pioneering efforts to test psychodynamic concepts. One such project, carried out by Howard Shevrin and coworkers at the University of Michigan Medical Center, was designed to investigate unconscious mental processes using recordings of brain activity. If the brain reacts differently to psychodynamically meaningful stimuli than it does to other stimuli, the researchers believe that the concept of unconscious psychodynamics receives a level of support that goes beyond clinical observations.

▶ Method

The researchers selected 11 patients who had applied for psychological treatment for either anxiety disorders or depression. Each patient underwent a detailed psychiatric workup, including three audiotaped clinical interviews and a battery of personality tests designed to identify unconscious psychodynamic conflicts. The interview tapes and the test materials were carefully reviewed by a panel of four experienced psychoanalytic therapists who arrived at agreement on the patient's psychiatric diagnosis, consciously expressed symptoms, and the specific unconscious conflicts believed to underlie the symptoms.

For example, Patient A suffered from severe social anxiety that threatened to ruin his career. He feared disapproval and rejection by others, and he avoided social situations in which he might be negatively evaluated. Upon careful consideration of all the data available to them, the panel of psychoanalysts concluded that the underlying unconscious conflict involved hidden rage toward others who might stand in the way of his grandiose ambitions and desire to control others. The anxiety not only provided a "safe" outlet for the physiological arousal produced by the unconscious rage, keeping him unaware of its existence, but it also kept him away from people toward whom the rage might be unleashed. The rage was also projected onto others so that he could view them, and not himself, as dangerous.

Based on their evaluation of each patient, the clinical panel then selected four sets of eight words that the patient had actually spoken or written during the clinical interviews and testing. One set of words was related to the patient's conscious symptoms. For Patient A, they included words such as *tense, dancing,* and *groups.* The second set of words related to the patient's hypothesized unconscious conflicts. For A, these included *penetrate, take control,* and *violence.* In addition, the clinicians selected two other sets of words, one positive (e.g., *happy*) and the other negative (e.g., *stench*) that were unrelated to the patient's symptoms or hypothesized dynamics. Different sets of words were selected for each patient.

Using a subliminal stimulation method, these customized words were then flashed on a screen for 1/1,000 of a second, so briefly that they cannot be consciously recognized but can nevertheless be processed by the brain. As the stimuli were being presented, the researchers recorded brain-wave patterns (evoked potentials) through EEG electrodes attached to the patient's scalp.

▶ Results

Each patient's brain responses to the four classes of words were compared through sophisticated analyses of the evoked potentials. The researchers found that distinctly different brain-wave patterns occurred in response to the unconscious conflict words than to the patients' symptom words or the ordinary unpleasant words. The authors therefore concluded that the hidden and emotionally "loaded" meaning of the conflict words caused the brain to process them differently. Finally, in support of their conclusion that the brain processing of the conflict words reflected defensive processes, the researchers found that the most distinctive brain responses to the conflict words occurred among patients who had high scores on a psychological test that measures the tendency to avoid and repress unpleasant stimuli. Presumably, such people would be most highly motivated to keep the stimuli at an unconscious level.

▶ Critical Evaluation

A strength of this research was the careful study of the individual patients. This represented quite well the psychoanalytic approach to understanding the unique features of the individual. The stimuli presented subliminally were carefully tailored to each person's psychological symptoms and hypothesized conflict and were different for each patient. In this case, the patients served as their own control group, since they each received all four classes of words.

The Michigan group's research suggests that it might be possible to realize Freud's dream of relating internal psychodynamics to brain processes. The fact that the patients'

—Continued

brains reacted differently to the conflict words than to the other classes of words suggests the possibility that such stimuli are indeed being processed differently. However, as the authors themselves point out, their measure of brain activity reflects the electrical activity of large groups of neurons at different levels of the brain, so that their data provide little information on the precise nature of the brain's activities. Greater understanding of the brain struc-

tures and processes that are involved awaits more precise measurement of brain functioning.

Despite these limitations, the study is an intriguing illustration of how new scientific approaches may permit experimental tests of psychoanalytic hypotheses. Perhaps this is the kind of research Freud foresaw when he wrote, "Let the biologists go as far as they can, and let us go as far as we can. One day the two will meet" (Freud, 1900, p. 276).

Source: Howard Shevrin, James A. Bond, Linda A. W. Brakel, Richard K. Hertel, & William J. Williams, 1996. *Conscious and unconscious processes: Psychodynamic, cognitive, and neurophysiological convergences.* New York: Guilford Press.

Evaluating Psychoanalytic Theory

Although it has profoundly influenced psychology, psychiatry, and other fields, psychoanalytic theory has often been criticized on scientific grounds. One reason is that many of its specific propositions have not held up under the scrutiny of research (Fisher & Greenberg, 1996). To some critics, psychoanalytic theory seems to be more science fiction than science. A great drawback of the theory is that it is hard to test, not because it doesn't explain enough, but because it often explains too much to allow clear-cut behavioral predictions (Meehl, 1995). For example, suppose we predict on the basis of psychoanalytic theory that participants in an experimental condition will behave aggressively, and they behave instead in a loving manner. Is the theory wrong, or is the aggression being masked by the operation of a defense mechanism such as reaction formation (which produces exaggerated behaviors that are the opposite of the impulse)? The difficulties in making clear-cut behavioral predictions mean that some psychoanalytic hypotheses are untestable, and this detracts greatly from the theory's scientific usefulness.

Freud's emphasis on the unconscious was scorned by a Victorian society that emphasized rationality and condemned as unscientific by generations of personality psychologists with a behaviorist orientation. However, research over the past 20 years has vindicated Freud's belief in unconscious psychic events by showing that nonconscious mental and emotional phenomena do indeed occur and can affect our behavior (Bargh & Chartrand, 1999; Erdelyi, 1995). On the other hand, the nonconscious processes that have been experimentally demonstrated are by no means as exotic as those described by Freud (Kihlstrom, 1999). Rather than a seething cauldron of forbidden wishes and desires, current research is unearthing what one theorist describes as "a kinder, gentler unconscious" (Greenwald, 1992).

Freud's ideas about psychosexual development are the most controversial feature of his theory. Although many theorists reject Freud's assertions about childhood sexuality as well as the notion of specific psychosexual stages, there is strong evidence that childhood experiences do indeed influence the development of personality (Lewis, 1999).

➤ 10. Why is it difficult to test psychoanalytic theory? What is the current status of unconscious processes and psychosexual development?

Freud's Legacy: Neoanalytic and Object Relations Approaches

Freud's ideas were so revolutionary that they generated disagreement even within his circle of disciples. *Neoanalysts* were psychoanalysts who disagreed with certain aspects of Freud's thinking and developed their own theories. Among them were Alfred Adler, Karen Horney, Erik Erickson, and Carl Jung. The neoanalysts believed that Freud did not give social and cultural factors a sufficiently important role in the development and dynamics of personality. In particular, they believed that he stressed infantile sexuality too much (Kurzweil, 1989). The second major criticism was that Freud laid too much emphasis on the events of childhood as determinants of adult personality. Neoanalytic theorists agreed that

➤ 11. Explain how neoanalytic theorists Adler and Jung departed from Freudian theory. What is the focus of the object relations approach?

FIGURE 13.4 In Alfred Adler's theory, people have an inborn *social interest* that can cause them to put society's welfare above their interests. Here, volunteer relief workers provide assistance to sick and starving children.

childhood experiences are important, but some of them, such as Erik Erikson, believed that personality development continues throughout the life span as individuals confront challenges that are specific to particular phases in their lives.

In contrast to Freud's assertion that behavior is motivated by inborn sexual and aggressive instincts and drives, Alfred Adler (1870–1937) insisted that humans are inherently social beings who are motivated by *social interest,* the desire to advance the welfare of others. They care about others, cooperate with them, and place general social welfare above selfish personal interests (Figure 13.4). In contrast, Freud, seemed to view people as savage animals caged by the bars of civilization. Perhaps influenced by his own struggles to overcome childhood illnesses and accidents, Adler also postulated a general motive of *striving for superiority,* which drives people to compensate for real or imagined defects in themselves (the *inferiority complex*) and to strive to be ever more competent in life.

Like Adler, Carl Jung (1875–1961) was Freud's friend and associate before he broke away and developed his own theory of **analytic psychology.** Jung expanded Freud's notion of the unconscious in unique directions. For example, he believed that humans possess not only a *personal unconscious* based on their life experiences, but also a *collective unconscious* that consists of memories accumulated throughout the entire history of the human race. These memories are represented by **archetypes,** inherited tendencies to interpret experiences in certain ways. Archetypes find expression in symbols, myths, and beliefs that appear across many cultures, such as the image of a God, an evil force, the hero, the good mother, and the quest for self-unity and completeness (Figure 13.5).

Following Freud's death in 1939, a new psychodynamic emphasis known as object relations became highly influential. **Object relations** theorists, including Melanie Klein (1991), Otto Kernberg (1976), Margaret Mahler (1968), and Heinz Kohut (1975), focus on the images or mental representations that people form of themselves and other people as a result of early experiences with caregivers. Whether realistic or distorted, these internal representations of important adults—for example, of the mother as kind or malevolent, the father as protective or abusive—become lenses, or "working models" through which later social interactions are viewed, and these relational themes exert an unconscious influence on a person's relationships throughout life (Westen, 1998). People who have difficulties forming and maintaining intimate relationships tend to mentally represent themselves and others in negative ways, expecting painful interactions and attributing malevolence or rejection to others (Kernberg, 1984; Nigg et al., 1992). These working models often create self-fulfilling prophesies, influencing the recurring relationships people form with others.

John Bowlby's (1969, 2000a) attachment theory, discussed in Chapter 11, is an outgrowth of the object relations approach. Correlational research relating early attachment experiences to later adult relationships is yielding provocative results (Lewis, 1999). For example, college students with a history of positive early attachments tend to have longer and more satisfying romances (Shaver & Clark, 1996). In contrast, child-abusing parents often have mental representations of their own parents as punitive, rejecting, and abusive (van Ijzendoorn, 1995). Table 13.2 shows descriptive statements that characterize people who manifest secure, avoidant, and anxious-ambivalent adult attachment styles. Today a large

FIGURE 13.5 One of Carl Jung's archetypes, the notion of a holistic self, is expressed in this Tibetan *mandala* (Sanskrit for circle), which symbolizes wholeness and completion. The mandala symbol occurs within numerous cultures and religions of the world, suggesting to Jung that it is a reflection of the collective unconscious.

proportion of psychodynamic theorists and clinicians claim to rely more heavily on object relations concepts than on classical psychoanalytic theory (Aron, 1996; Westen, 1998). The concepts in object relations theories are also easier to define and measure, making them more amenable to research.

❯ THE HUMANISTIC PERSPECTIVE

Humanistic theories were in part a reaction to Freud's conception of the human as being driven by "those half-tamed demons that inhabit the human beast" (Freud, 1900, p. 202). Instead, humanists embrace a positive view that affirms the inherent dignity and goodness of the human spirit. They emphasize the central role of conscious experience, as well as the individual's creative potential and inborn striving for **self-actualization,** the total realization of one's human potential (Figure 13.6). As described in Chapter 9, humanist Abraham Maslow considered self-actualization to be the ultimate human need and the highest expression of human nature.

Carl Rogers's Self Theory

Carl Rogers (1902–1987) was one of the most influential humanistic theorists. In contrast to Freud, Rogers believed that our behavior is not a reaction to unconscious conflicts, but a response to our immediate conscious experience of self and environment (Rogers, 1951). He believed that the forces that direct behavior are within us and that, when they are not distorted or blocked by our environment, they can be trusted to direct us toward self-actualization.

The Self

The central concept in Rogers's theory is the **self,** an organized, consistent set of perceptions of and beliefs about oneself (Rogers, 1959). Once formed, the self plays a powerful role in guiding our perceptions and directing our behavior.

Rogers theorized that at the beginning of their lives, children cannot distinguish between themselves and their environment. As they interact with their world, children begin to distinguish between the "me" and the "not-me." The self-concept continues to develop in response to our life experiences, though many aspects of it remain quite stable over time.

Once the self-concept is established, there is a tendency to maintain it, for it helps us to understand ourselves in relation to the world. We therefore have needs for **self-consistency** (an absence of conflict among self-perceptions) and **congruence** (consistency between self-perceptions and experience). Any experience we have that is inconsistent with our self-concept, including our perceptions of our own behavior, evokes **threat** and anxiety. Well-adjusted individuals can respond to threat adaptively by modifying the self-concept so that the experiences are congruent with the self. But other people choose to deny or distort their experiences to remove the incongruence, a strategy that can lead to what Rogers termed "problems in living."

Suppose that an important aspect of a young man's self-concept is the belief that he is so charming and handsome that every woman finds him irresistible. He meets a young woman whom he finds very attractive but who shows a total lack of interest in him. This incongruence between his self-concept and his experience produces threat and anxiety because his basic view of himself is challenged. He could react adaptively by modifying his self-concept to acknowledge that he is not, after all, irresistible to *all* women. On the other hand, he might resolve the incongruence by distorting reality. He might deny the woman's lack of interest ("She's just playing hard to get"), or he might distort his perception of the woman ("She would have to be crazy not to appreciate how special I am—thank heaven I found out in time").

| TABLE 13.2 | ATTACHMENT STYLES IN ADULT RELATIONSHIPS |

Question: Which of the following best describes your feelings?*

A. I find it relatively easy to get close to others and am comfortable depending on them and having them depend on me. I don't often worry abut being abandoned or about someone getting too close to me.

B. I am somewhat uncomfortable being close to others; I find it difficult to trust them completely, difficult to allow myself to depend on them. I am nervous when anyone gets too close, and often, love partners want me to be more intimate than I feel comfortable being.

C. I find that others are reluctant to get as close as I would like. I often worry that my partner doesn't really love me or won't want to stay with me. I want to merge completely with another person, and this desire sometimes scares people away.

*The first type of attachment style is described as "secure," the second as "avoidant," and the third as "anxious/ambivalent."
Source: Shaver et al., 1988

➤ 12. What is self-actualization? How does this concept conflict with Freud's conception of human nature?

FIGURE 13.6 The motivations underlying behavior are much different for humanistic theorists than they are for Freudians. In the view of humanistic theorists like Maslow and Rogers, creative and artistic accomplishments like this one are a product not of intrapsychic conflict and sublimation, but an expression of an innate tendency toward self-actualization.

➤ 13. Describe the roles of self-consistency and congruence in Rogers's self theory. How do these concepts relate to adjustment?

"I can't say I like the looks of that bunch."

FIGURE 13.7 Tendencies to behave in accordance with one's self-concept can at times have ominous implications.

The self-consistency knife can cut in both directions, however. At the other extreme, consider a young man who believes that he is totally unattractive to women. If a desirable woman expresses interest, he might appropriately revise his self-concept in a positive direction. But it is often as difficult for people with negative self-concepts to accept success as it is for those with unrealistically positive self-concepts to accept failure (Rogers, 1959). Thus he might find it necessary to give a congruent explanation. ("She's just trying to be nice. She doesn't really like me.") Such interpretations will allow the young man maintain his negative image of himself.

To preserve their self image, people not only interpret situations in self-congruent ways, but they also behave in ways that will lead others to respond to them in a self-confirming fashion (Brown, 1997). Recall Ellen's speculation that Julia's obnoxious behavior stems from an image of herself as unloveable and certain to be rejected if she lets people get close enough to hurt her. Julia's self-protective hostility is, however, almost certain to alienate others and prompt rejection, confirming in her mind that she is indeed unloveable. As Rogers frequently noted, people are pushed by self-consistency needs to behave in accord with their self-concept (Figure 13.7).

According to Rogers, the degree of congruence between self-concept and experience helps define one's level of adjustment. The more rigid and inflexible people's self-concepts are, the less open they will be to their experiences and the more maladjusted they will become (Figure 13.8a). If there is a significant degree of incongruence between self and experience, and the experiences are forceful enough, the defenses used to deny and distort reality may collapse, resulting in extreme anxiety and a temporary disorganization of the self-concept.

The Need for Positive Regard

Rogers believed that we are born with an innate **need for positive regard**—that is, for acceptance, sympathy, and love from others. Rogers viewed positive regard as essential for healthy development. Ideally, positive regard received from the parents is unconditional—that is, independent of how the child behaves. **Unconditional positive regard** communicates that the child is inherently worthy of love. *Conditional positive regard,* on the other hand, is dependent on how the child behaves. In the extreme case, love and acceptance are given to the child *only* when the child behaves as the parents want.

➤ 14. How do conditions of worth develop and how can they hinder adjustment?

People need positive regard not only from others, but also from themselves. We all want to feel good about ourselves. Thus a **need for positive self-regard** also develops. Lack of unconditional positive regard from parents and other significant people in the past teaches people that they are worthy of approval and love only when they meet certain standards. This fosters the development of **conditions of worth** that dictate when we approve or disapprove of ourselves. A child who has experienced parental approval when behaving in a friendly fashion but disapproval whenever she became angry or aggressive may come to disapprove of her own "angry" feelings, even when they are justified. She therefore may come to deny in herself all feelings of anger and struggle to preserve a self-image of being totally loving. Rogers believed that conditions of worth can tyrannize people and cause major incongruence between self and experience, together with a need to deny or distort important aspects of experience. Conditions of worth are similar to the "shoulds" that populate Freud's superego.

Fully Functioning Persons

Toward the end of his career, Rogers became particularly interested in people who had achieved self-actualization. As Rogers viewed them, **fully functioning persons** do not hide behind masks or adopt artificial roles. They feel a sense of inner freedom, self-determination, and choice in the direction of their growth. They have no fear of behaving spontaneously, freely, and creatively. Because they are fairly free of conditions of worth, they can accept inner and outer experiences as they are, without modifying them defensively to suit a rigid self-concept or the expectations of others. Thus a fully functioning unmarried woman would be able to state quite frankly that her career is more important to her than a role as wife and mother *if* she truly felt that way, and to act comfortably on those feelings. In a sense, she could be true to herself (Figure 13.8*b*).

Research on the Self

By giving the self a central place in his theory, Rogers helped stimulate a great deal of research on the self-concept (Brown, 1997; Robins et al., 1999). Two topics at the forefront are (1) the development of self-esteem and its effects on behavior, and (2) the roles played by self-enhancement and self-consistency motives.

Self-Esteem

Self-esteem (how positively or negatively we feel about ourselves) is a very important aspect of personal well-being, happiness, and adjustment (Brown, 1998; Diener, 2000). Self-esteem is related to many positive behaviors and life outcomes. People with high self-esteem are less susceptible to social pressure, have fewer interpersonal problems, are happier with their lives, achieve at a higher and more persistent level, and are more capable of forming satisfying love relationships (Baumeister, 1999). In contrast, people with a poor self-image are more prone to psychological problems like anxiety and depression, to physical illness, and to poor social relationships and underachievement (Brown, 1998). Men and women do not differ in overall level of self-esteem (Feingold, 1994; Maccoby & Jacklin, 1974).

What conditions foster the development of high self-esteem? Children develop higher self-esteem when their parents communicate unconditional acceptance and love, establish clear guidelines for behavior, and reinforce compliance while giving the child freedom to make decisions and express opinions within those guidelines (Coopersmith, 1957; Harrington et al., 1987). One study showed that when low self-esteem children were exposed to highly supportive youth sport coaches who gave them much positive reinforcement and encouragement, the children's self-esteem increased significantly over the course of the sport season (Smoll et al., 1993). Apparently, the positive feedback caused the children to revise their self-concepts in a positive direction.

Self-Verification and Self-Enhancement Motives

Rogers proposed that people are motivated to preserve their self-concept by maintaining self-consistency and congruence. Modern researchers call this need **self-verification,** and it has received considerable research support. In one

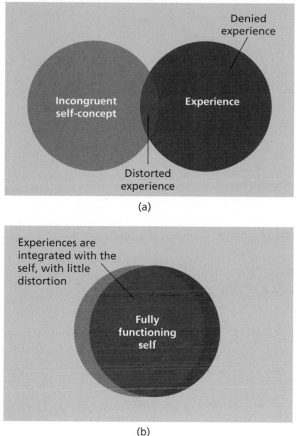

(a)

(b)

FIGURE 13.8 Rogers defined psychological adjustment in terms of the degree of congruence between self-concept and experience. Maladjustment (a) occurs when a person faced with incongruities between self and experience distorts or denies reality to make it consistent with the self-concept. In contrast, extremely well-adjusted, or fully functioning, people integrate experiences into the self with minimal distortion (b), so that they are able to profit fully from their experiences.

Source: After Rogers, 1951.

➤ 15. How do differences in self-esteem affect behavior? What conditions affect self-esteem development?

➤ 16. Define self-verification and self-enhancement. What research evidence is there to support these processes?

study, researchers measured college students' self-concepts. In a later experiment, the students interacted with other participants and received fake feedback from them in the form of adjectives that were either consistent or inconsistent with their self-concept. Later when the students were asked to recall and identify the adjectives that had been attributed to them, they showed greater recall for the consistent adjectives, suggesting that people selectively attend to and recall self-consistent information (Suinn et al., 1962).

Self-verification needs are also expressed in people's tendency to seek out self-confirming relationships. One study found that if people with firmly held negative self-views marry spouses who appraise them favorably, they tend to eventually withdraw from the marriage. Such people are more likely to remain with spouses who agree with the negative image they have of themselves. In contrast, people with positive self-concepts prefer spouses who share their positive view of themselves (Swann et al., 1992).

Rogers also suggested that people have a need to regard themselves positively, and research confirms a strong and pervasive tendency to gain and preserve a positive self-image. These processes are known as **self-enhancement** (Brown, 1998; Swann, 1996). Several self-enhancement strategies have been identified. For example, people show a marked tendency to attribute their successes to their own abilities and effort but to attribute their failures to environmental factors. Furthermore, most people rate themselves as better than average on virtually any socially desirable characteristic that is subjective in nature (Steele, 1988). The vast majority of businesspeople and politicians rate themselves as more ethical than the average. In defiance of mathematical possibility, about 80 percent of high-school students rate themselves in the top 10 percent in their ability to get along with others. Even people who have been hospitalized after causing auto accidents rate themselves as more skillful than the average driver (Pyszczynski & Greenberg, 1987). Indeed, as evidence on self-serving biases in self-perception continues to accumulate, researchers are concluding that positive illusions of this sort are the rule rather than the exception in well-adjusted people and that these self-enhancement tendencies, or "positive illusions," contribute to their psychological well-being (Taylor & Brown, 1988; Taylor et al., 2000).

Culture, Gender, and the Self

Culture provides a learning context in which the self develops. Individualistic cultures like those in North America and northern Europe place an emphasis on independence and personal attainment, whereas collectivistic cultures like those found in many parts of Asia, Africa, and South America emphasize connectedness between people and the achievement of group goals (Cross & Markus, 1999; Triandis, 1989). What kinds of self-concept differences would you predict in people from these two types of cultures?

In one study, American and Japanese college students were given a self-concept questionnaire on which they listed their five most important attributes. The researchers then classified each statement according to whether it referred to a personal attribute (e.g., I am honest, I am smart), a social identity (e.g., I am an oldest son; I am a student), or something else, such as a physical trait. As Figure 13.9 shows, the Americans were far more likely than the Japanese to list personal traits, abilities, or dispositions, whereas the Japanese more frequently described themselves in social identity terms. Thus the social embeddedness of the collectivist Japanese culture was reflected in their self-perceptions, as was cultural individualism in the Americans' self-concepts (Cousins, 1989).

Gender-role socialization provides us with **gender schemas,** organized mental structures that contain our understanding of the attributes and behaviors that are appropriate and expected for males and females (Bem, 1981). Within a given culture, gender schemas tell us what the typical man or woman "should"

➤ 17. What cultural and gender differences have been found in self-concept research?

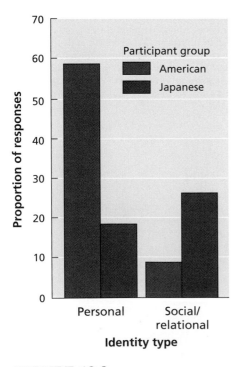

FIGURE 13.9 Cultural differences in the self-concept. Percentages of personal identity and social/relational self-attributes given by Japanese and American college students as key aspects of their self-concept. Data from Cousins, 1989.

be like. In Western cultures, men tend to prize attributes related to achievement, emotional strength, athleticism, and self-sufficiency, whereas women especially prize interpersonal competencies, kindness, and helpfulnes to others (Beyer, 1990; Brown, 1998; Marsh, 1990). In a sense, men in Western cultures tend to develop more of an individualistic self-concept, emphasing achievement and separateness from others, whereas women's self-concepts tend to be more collectivistic, emphasizing their social connectedness with others (Kashima et al., 1995; Markus & Oyserman, 1989). Nonetheless, we should keep in mind that significant individual differences exist within each gender group, with many women being highly individualistic and many men collectivistic (Brown, 1998).

Evaluating Humanistic Theories

Humanistic theorists focus on the individual's subjective experiences. What matters most is how people view themselves and the world (Nye, 1992). Some critics believe that the humanistic view relies too much on individuals' reports of their personal experiences. For example, psychoanalytic theorists maintain that accepting what a person says at face value may easily lead to erroneous conclusions because of the always-present influence of unconscious factors. Some critics also believe that it is impossible to define an individual's actualizing tendency except in terms of the behavior that it supposedly produces. This would be an example of circular reasoning: "Why did the person achieve such success? Because of self-actualization." "How do we know self-actualzation was at work? Because the person achieved great success."

Though humanism may indeed seem nonscientific to some, Carl Rogers (1959) dedicated himself to developing a theory whose concepts could be measured and its laws tested. One of his most notable contributions was a series of groundbreaking studies on the process of self-growth that can occur in psychotherapy. To assess the effectiveness of psychotherapy, Rogers and his coworkers measured the discrepancy between clients' *ideal selves* (how they would like to be) and their *perceived selves* (their perceptions of what they are actually like). The studies revealed that when clients first enter therapy, the discrepancy is typically large, but it gets smaller as therapy proceeds, suggesting that therapy may help the client to become more self-accepting and perhaps also more realistic. Rogers and his coworkers also discovered important therapist characteristics that either aid or impede the process of self-actualization in therapy. This research will be described in Chapter 15.

❯ TRAIT AND BIOLOGICAL PERSPECTIVES

How do people differ in personality? The goals of trait theorists are to describe the basic classes of behavior that define personality, to devise ways of measuring individual differences in personality traits, and to use these measures to understand and predict a person's behavior.

The starting point for the trait researcher is identifying the behaviors that define a particular trait. But here we have an embarrassment of riches. Years ago, the trait theorist Gordon Allport went through the English dictionary and painstakingly recorded all of the words that could be used to describe personal traits. The result: a gigantic list of 17,953 words (Allport & Odbert, 1936). Obviously, it would be impractical if not impossible to describe people in terms of where they fall on some 18,000 dimensions. The trait theorist's goal is to condense all of these behavioral descriptors into a manageable number of basic traits that can capture personal individuality.

Two major approaches have been taken to define what Allport (1937) called "the building blocks of personality." One approach is to propose traits (e.g.,

➤ 18. How is factor analysis based on correlation, and how is it used to identify personality traits?

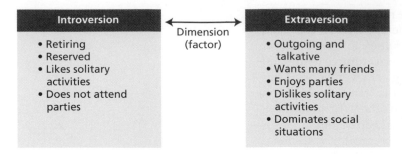

FIGURE 13.10 Factor analysis allows researchers to reduce many behaviors to a smaller number of basic dimensions, or factors. A factor comprises behaviors that are highly correlated with one another and are therefore assumed to have common psychological meaning. Here, we see the kinds of behaviors that might fall on the two ends of the introversion-extraversion dimension. The two groups of behaviors are negatively correlated with one another.

"dominance," "friendliness," or "self-esteem") on the basis of intuition or a personality theory. A more systematic approach uses the statistical tool of **factor analysis** to identify clusters of specific behaviors that are correlated with one another so highly that they can be viewed as reflecting a basic dimension, or trait, on which people vary. For example, you might find that most people who are socially reserved also avoid parties, like quiet activities, and enjoy being alone. At the other end of the spectrum are people who are very talkative and sociable, like parties and excitement, dislike solitary activities like reading, and constantly seek out new acquaintances. These behavioral patterns define a general factor or dimension that we might label *introversion-extraversion* (or simply *extraversion*). At one end of the dimension are highly introverted behaviors, and at the other end are highly extraverted behaviors (Figure 13.10). Presumably, each of us could be placed at some point along this dimension in terms of our customary behavior patterns. In fact, as we shall see, factor analytic studies have found introversion-extraversion to be a major dimension of personality.

Cattell's Sixteen Personality Factors

If you were asked to describe and compare every person you know, how many different traits would it take to do the job? This is where trait theorists begin to part company. Because factor analysis can be used and interpreted in different ways, trait theorists have cut up the personality pie into smaller or larger pieces. For example, the pioneering trait theorist Raymond B. Cattell (1965, 1990) asked thousands of people to rate themselves on numerous behavioral characteristics and also obtained ratings from people who knew the participants well. When he subjected this mass of data to factor analysis, he identified 16 basic behavior clusters, or factors. These personality dimensions are shown in Figure 13.11. Using this information, Cattell developed a widely used personality test called the 16 Personality Factor Questionnaire (16PF) to measure individual differences on each of the dimensions and provide a comprehensive personality description. He was able to develop personality profiles not only for individuals, but also for groups of people. For example, Figure 13.11 compares average scores obtained by creative artists and Olympic athletes.

The Five Factor Model

Other trait researchers believe that Cattell's 16 dimensions may be more than we need. Their factor analytic studies suggest to them that five "higher-order" factors, each including several of Cattell's more specific factors, are all that is needed to capture the basic structure of personality (Digman, 1990; McCrae & Costa, 1999). These theorists also believe that these "Big Five" factors may be universal to the human species, for the same five factors have been found consistently in trait ratings within diverse North American, Asian, Hispanic, and European cultures (John & Srivastava, 1999; Trull & Geary, 1997).

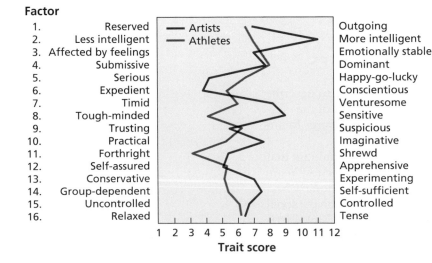

FIGURE 13.11 Cattell identified 16 basic personality traits through factor analysis. Here we see personality profiles (mean scores) for Olympic athletes and creative artists on the 16PF, the test developed by Cattell to measure the traits.
Based on data from Cattell, 1965.

TABLE 13.3	THE BIG FIVE PERSONALITY FACTORS AND THEIR LOWER-ORDER TRAITS

Big Five Factors	Lower-Order Traits
Openness	Artistically sensitive vs. artistically insensitive
	Intellectual vs. unreflective, narrow
	Polished, refined vs. crude, boorish
	Imaginative vs. simple, direct
Conscientiousness	Fussy, tidy vs. careless
	Responsible vs. undependable
	Scrupulous vs. unscrupulous
	Persevering vs quitting, fickle
Extraversion	Talkative vs. silent
	Frank, open vs. secretive
	Adventurous vs. cautious
	Sociable vs. reclusive
Agreeableness	Good-natured vs. irritable
	Not jealous vs. jealous
	Mild, gentle vs. headstrong
	Cooperative vs. negativistic
Neuroticism	Poised vs. nervous, tense
	Calm vs. anxious
	Composed vs. excitable
	Emotionally stable vs. moody, unstable

The Big Five factors are shown in Table 13.3. (The acronym OCEAN—for Openness, Conscientiousness, Extraversion, Agreeableness, and Neuroticism—may help you remember them.) Proponents of the Five Factor Model believe that when a person is placed at a specific point on each of these five dimensions by means of a psychological test, behavior ratings, or direct observations of behavior, the essence of his or her personality has been captured (McCrae & Costa, 1999).

> 19. What does *OCEAN* stand for in the Five Factor model?

What do you think about that conclusion? Your reaction may be one of skepticism, since it seems that there *must* be more to individuality than can be captured by only five dimensions. However, we should remember that, as discussed in Chapter 4, the incredible number of colors that humans can discriminate is based on the activity patterns of only *three* types of cones. Thus the many variations that can occur from the blending of five personality dimensions could account for enormous variations in the pattern of people's behavioral tendencies.

Eysenck's Extraversion-Stability Model

We've now seen that among trait theorists there are "splitters" like Cattell who posit a large number of basic traits and "lumpers" like the Big Five theorists who favor a smaller number. Hans J. Eysenck (1916–1997), one of Britain's leading psychologists, was the ultimate lumper, for he maintained that normal personality can be understood in terms of only *two* basic dimensions. These dimensions of Introversion-Extraversion and Stability-Instability (sometimes called Neuroticism) blend together to form all of the more specific traits. Eysenck's two "supertraits" are comparable to the Big Five traits of Extraversion and Neuroticism.

The Extraversion dimension reflects the tendency to be sociable, active, and willing to take risks versus a tendency toward social inhibition, passivity, and caution. The Stability dimension represents a continuum from high emotional stability to an unstable and emotionally reactive behavior pattern that involves

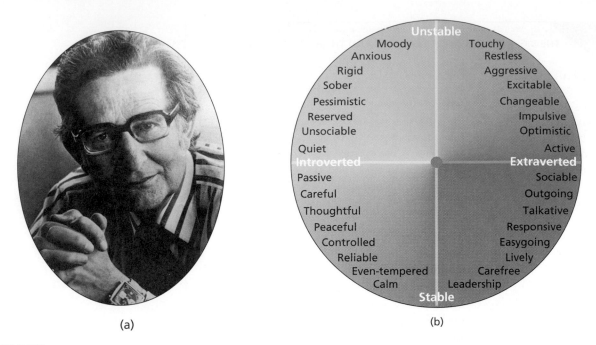

(a)   (b)

FIGURE 13.12   According to Hans Eysenck (a), various combinations of two major dimensions of personality, introversion-extraversion and stability-instability, combine to form the more specific traits shown in (b).

From H. J. Eysenck, The Biological Basis of Personality, Figure 13, 1967. Courtesy of Charles C Thomas, Publisher, Ltd., Springfield, Illinois.

moodiness, anxiety, and depression. Eysenck (Figure 13.12*a*) believed that normal personality is captured quite well within this two-dimensional model.

Eysenck's Extraversion-Stability model is shown in Figure 13.12*b*. Note that the two basic dimensions intersect at right angles (meaning that they are statistically independent, or uncorrelated). Thus knowing how extraverted a person is tells us nothing about her level of emotional stability; she could fall anywhere along the stability dimension. The secondary traits shown in the circle reflect varying combinations or "mixtures" of these two primary dimensions. Thus we can see that the emotionally stable extravert is a carefree, lively person who tends to be well adjusted and to seek out leadership roles. In contrast, unstable (neurotic) extraverts tend to be touchy, aggressive, and restless. The stable introvert is calm, reliable, and even-tempered, but the unstable introvert tends to be rigid, anxious, and moody. Different combinations of the two basic personality dimensions can thus produce very diverse personality patterns.

Traits and Behavior Prediction

➤ 20. What are the predictive advantages of (a) broad general traits and (b) narrow, specific ones? What's the research evidence?

Trait theorists not only try to describe the basic structure of personality, but also attempt to predict real-life behavior on the basis of a person's traits. Even if a limited number of general traits like the Big Five seem adequate to describe important features of personality, it is entirely possible that a larger number of specific traits like Cattell's would be more likely to capture nuances of behavior within particular situations and would therefore be better for predictive purposes.

To address this issue, Bryan Mershon and Richard Gorsuch (1988) used scores derived from the 16PF test to predict real-life outcomes such as choice of occupation, job performance and promotions, marijuana smoking, and the development of psychological disorders. They scored the 187 items of the 16PF in two different ways. First, they calculated scores for each of Cattell's 16 factors. Then they scored the test for broader factors that corresponded to the Big Five. Finally, they determined which set of scores did a better job of predicting the various behaviors.

Mershon and Gorsuch found that although the Big Five factors were able to predict the behaviors to a moderate degree, the 16 factors were far superior in their ability to predict specific behaviors. In fact, they did, on average, about twice as well, though different combinations of the 16 scores were most strongly correlated with each of the various behaviors. It thus appears that broad traits like the Big Five and Eysenck's "big two" may do an adequate job of predicting behavior across a whole range of situations, as a wide-beamed floodlight illuminates a large area. However, like a narrowly focused and intense spotlight, specific traits like Cattell's may do better in specific situations that call for the behaviors measured by the narrower traits.

Biological Foundations of Personality Traits

Both nature and nurture influence the development of personality traits, but their contributions differ depending on the trait in question (Plomin & Caspi, 1999). Biological explanations for personality differences focus on three levels. Some researchers search for differences in the functioning of the nervous system (Pickering & Gray, 1999). Others seek the genetic bases for trait inheritance (Plomin, 1997). Some psychologists have used evolutionary principles to explain why these traits exist in the human species (e.g., Buss, 1999).

Personality and the Nervous System

Hans Eysenck (1967) was one of the first modern theorists to suggest a biological basis for major personality traits. He linked Introversion-Extraversion and Stability-Instability to differences in individuals' normal patterns of arousal within the brain. He started with the notion that there is an optimal, or preferred, level of biological arousal in the brain. Eysenck believed that extreme introverts are chronically *overaroused*; their brains are too electrically active, so they try to minimize stimulation and reduce arousal to get down to their optimal arousal level, or "comfort zone." In contrast, the brains of extreme extraverts are chronically *underaroused*, so they need powerful or frequent stimulation to achieve an optimal level of cortical arousal and excitation. The extravert thus seeks social contact and physical arousal, likes parties, takes chances, is assertive, and suffers boredom easily.

Whereas Introversion-Extraversion reflects a person's customary level of arousal, Stability-Instability represents the suddenness with which shifts in arousal occur. Unstable people have hair-trigger nervous systems that show large and sudden shifts in arousal, whereas stable people show smaller and more gradual shifts (Pickering & Gray, 1999). Eysenck also called this stability dimension Neuroticism because he found that people with extremely unstable nervous systems are more likely to experience emotional problems that require clinical attention.

Eysenck believed that the arousal patterns that underlie Introversion-Extraversion and Stability-Instability have genetic bases. A growing body of evidence from twin studies supports his view. Identical twins are much more alike on these traits than are fraternal twins, and about half of the variance among people can be attributed to hereditary factors (Loehlin et al., 1988; Pederson et al., 1988; Plomin, 1997). Eysenck believed that although personality is strongly influenced by life experiences, the ways people respond to those experiences may be at least partly programmed by biological factors.

Behavior Genetics and Personality

Twin studies are particularly informative for studying the role of genetic factors because they compare the degree of personality resemblance between monozygotic twins, who have identical genetic makeup, and dizygotic twins, who do not (Rowe, 1999). On a great many psychological characteristics, identical twins

➤ 21. In Eysenck's theory, what are the biological bases for individual differences in Extraversion and Stability?

are more similar to one another, suggesting a role for genetics. However, the issue is clouded by the possibility that identical twins may also have more similar environments than fraternal twins. Because they are more similar in appearance, size, and other physical characteristics than are fraternal twins, others may be inclined to treat them more similarly.

The ideal solution to this problem would be to compare personality traits in identical and fraternal twins who were either raised together or reared apart. If the identical twins who were reared in different families were as similar as those reared together, a more powerful argument could be made for the role of genetic factors. Moreover, this research design would allow us to divide the total variation among individuals on each personality trait into three components: (1) variation attributable to genetic factors; (2) variation due to a shared family environment in those raised together; and (3) variation attributable to other factors, including unique individual life experiences. The relative influence of these sources of variation can be estimated by comparing personality test correlations in the four groups of twins (Plomin & Caspi, 1999; Scarr, 1992).

Several studies using this research design with different personality measures have now appeared (Bouchard et al., 1990; Pederson et al., 1988; Tellegen et al., 1988). These studies have shown that identical twins are far more similar in personality than are fraternal twins, and it makes little difference whether they were reared together or in different families (Figure 13.13). Indeed, contrary to what many personality psychologists would expect, differences in family environment had little influence on personality differences in these studies.

The results of one of the studies, conducted by Auke Tellegen and his colleagues at the University of Minnesota, is shown in Table 13.4. The four groups of twin pairs completed measures of 14 different personality traits. As you can see, genetic factors accounted for 39 to 58 percent of the variation among people in trait scores. In contrast, the degree of resemblance did not differ much whether the twin pairs were reared together or apart, showing that general features of the family environment, such as its emotional climate and degree of affluence, accounted for little variance in any of the traits. However, this does not mean that experience is not important. Rather than the family environment, it was individuals' unique environmental experiences, such as their school experiences and interactions with peers, that accounted for considerable personality variance. Even within the same family, individual children can have quite different experiences while growing up, and it is these unique experiences that help shape personality development.

Evolutionary Approaches

Behavior genetics researchers attempt to understand how biological factors contribute to differences between individuals on personality traits. An approach called **evolutionary personality theory** (Buss, 1999) asks an even more basic question: Where did the traits come from in the first place?

Consider the Big Five personality factors. Why should we find these traits so consistently in cultures around the world? According to David Buss, an evolutionary personality theorist, they exist in humans because they have helped us achieve two overriding goals: physical survival and reproduction of the species (Buss, 1999). Traits such as extraversion and emotional stability were helpful in attaining positions of dominance and mate selection. Conscientiousness and agreeableness might be particularly important in group survival, as well as in reproduction and the care of children. Finally, because openness to experience may be the basis for problem solving and creative activities that could affect the ultimate survival of the species, there has always been a need for intelligent and creative people. Thus evolutionary theorists regard the Big Five as having been sculpted by natural selection pressures until they have become part of human nature. They may also reflect the ways in which we are biologically

➤ 22. What do twin studies suggest about the respective roles of (a) genetic factors, (b) family environment, and (c) individual environment in personality traits?

FIGURE 13.13 Jim Springer and Jim Lewis are identical twins who were separated when 4 weeks old and raised in very different environments. When reunited in adulthood as part of a behavior genetics study of personality, they showed striking similarities in personality and interests. Both men had even built benches around trees in their yards.

➤ 23. According to evolutionary theorists, what is the origin of the Big Five factors?

TABLE 13.4	ESTIMATES OF THE PERCENTAGES OF GROUP VARIANCE IN 14 PERSONALITY TRAITS ATTRIBUTABLE TO GENETIC AND ENVIRONMENTAL FACTORS		
Trait	Genetic	Familial Environment	Unique Environment
Well-being	.48	.13	.39
Social-potency	.54	.10	.36
Achievement	.39	.11	.50
Social closeness	.40	.19	.41
Stress reaction	.53	.00	.47
Alienation	.45	.11	.54
Aggression	.44	.00	.56
Control	.44	.00	.56
Harm avoidance	.55	.00	.45
Traditionalism	.45	.12	.43
Absorption	.50	.03	.47
Positive emotionality	.40	.22	.38
Negative emotionality	.55	.02	.43
Constraint	.58	.00	.42

*Note: The variance estimates are based on a comparison of the degree of personality similarity in identical and fraternal twins who were reared together or apart.

Source: Data from Tellegen et al., 1988.

prepared to think about and discriminate among people. Lewis Goldberg (1981) suggests that over the course of evolution, people have had to ask five basic questions when they interact with another person. In order of importance, these questions have survival and reproductive implications:

1. Is Person X active and dominant or passive and submissive? Can I dominate X or will I have to submit to X?
2. Is Person X agreeable and friendly, or hostile and uncooperative?
3. Can I count on X? Is X conscientious and dependable?
4. Is X sane (stable, rational, predictable) or crazy (unstable, unpredictable, possibly dangerous)?
5. How smart is X, and how quickly can X learn and adapt?

Not surprisingly, according to Goldberg, these questions map onto the Big Five trait factors. He believes that this is why factor analyses of trait ratings reveal Big Five consistency across very diverse cultures.

The Stability of Personality Traits

Because traits are defined as enduring behavioral predispositions, they should show some degree of stability over time and across situations. Where stability over time is concerned, the research literature shows evidence for both stability and change (Caspi & Roberts, 1999). Some personality dimensions tend to be more stable than others. For example, introversion-extraversion, as well as temperamental traits such as emotionality and activity level, tend to be quite stable from childhood into adulthood and across the adult years (Eysenck, 1990; Mc-Crae & Costa, 1990; Zuckerman, 1991).

Certain habits of thought may also be fairly stable. One is our tendency to think optimistically or pessimistically. Melanie Burns and Martin Seligman

➤ 24. How does research evidence bear on the assumption of stability across time and across situations?

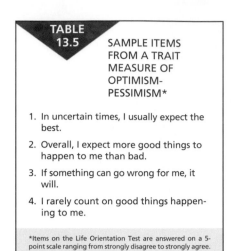

TABLE 13.5 SAMPLE ITEMS FROM A TRAIT MEASURE OF OPTIMISM-PESSIMISM*

1. In uncertain times, I usually expect the best.

2. Overall, I expect more good things to happen to me than bad.

3. If something can go wrong for me, it will.

4. I rarely count on good things happening to me.

*Items on the Life Orientation Test are answered on a 5-point scale ranging from strongly disagree to strongly agree.
Source: Scheier & Carver, 1985.

➤ 25. What three factors make it difficult to predict behavior from individual personality traits?

TABLE 13.6 SAMPLE ITEMS FROM THE SELF-MONITORING SCALE*

1. In different situations and with different people, I often act like very different persons.

2. I am not always the person I appear to be.

3. I have trouble changing my behavior to suit different people and different situations.

4. I would not change my opinion (or the way I do things) in order to please someone or win their favor.

*Items 1 and 2 are keyed *true*, and items 3 and 4 *false* for self-monitoring.
Source: Snyder, 1974.

(1989) coded diaries and letters that elderly people had written approximately 50 years earlier for the tendency to respond either optimistically or pessimistically to life events. The elderly people also completed a questionnaire that measured their current optimistic-pessimistic tendencies. Although little consistency over time was shown for dealing optimistically or pessimistically with positive events, Burns and Seligman found a stable tendency to respond with optimism or pessimism to negative life events. The authors suggested that this tendency to be pessimistic might constitute an enduring risk factor for depression, low achievement, and physical illness, and they are presently studying such linkages. Table 13.5 contains items from the Life Orientation Test (Scheier & Carver, 1985), used by personality researchers to measure the disposition to be optimistic or pessimistic.

When it comes to stability of behavior across situations, personality again shows both a degree of stability and some capacity for change (Mischel & Shoda, 1999). Because behavior always results from a person interacting with a situation, we would be foolish to expect people to behave in the same manner from situation to situation. Even on a trait so central as honesty, people can show considerable behavioral variability across situations. In a classic study, Hugh Hartshorne and Mark May (1928) tested the honesty of thousands of children. The children were given opportunities to lie, steal, and cheat in a number of different settings—at home, in school, at a party, and in an athletic contest. The rather surprising finding was that "lying, cheating and stealing as measured by the test situations in this study are only very loosely related. . . . Most children will deceive in certain situations but not in others" (p. 411). More than a half-century later, Walter Mischel (1984) reported similar findings for college students on the trait of "conscientiousness." A student might be highly conscientious in one situation (e.g., coming to work on time) without being conscientious in another (turning in class assignments on time).

Three factors make it difficult to predict on the basis of personality traits how people will behave in particular situations. First, personality traits interact with other traits as well as with characteristics of different situations. This melding accounts for the incredible richness we see in personality, but it also poses a challenge to psychologists who want to predict behavior. When two or more traits, such as honesty, dominance, and agreeableness influence a behavior in a particular situation, our ability to predict on the basis of only one of the traits is bound to be quite limited (Ahadi & Diener, 1989).

Second, the degree of consistency across situations is influenced by how important a given trait is for the person. A person for whom honesty is a central component of the self-concept may show considerable stability in honest behaviors across situations because feelings of self-worth may be linked to living up to moral standards regardless of the circumstances (Kenrick & Funder, 1991).

Third people differ in their tendency to tailor their behavior to what is called for by the situation. This personality trait is called called **self-monitoring** (Table 13.6). People who are high in self-monitoring are very attentive to situational cues and adapt their behavior to what they think would be most appropriate. Extreme self-monitors resemble behavioral chameleons who act very differently in different situations. Low self-monitors, on the other hand, tend to act primarily in terms of their internal beliefs and attitudes rather than the demands of the situation. The saying "What you see is what you get" applies well to low self-monitors, and such people show greater consistency across situations than do high self-monitors (Snyder, 1987).

According to some trait theorists, the stability and distinctiveness that we see in personality does not come from the fact that we behave the same way in every situation. Rather, it results from our exhibiting an *average* amount of extraversion, emotional stability, agreeableness, honesty, and other traits across many different situations (Epstein, 1983; Kenrick & Funder, 1988). Nonetheless, if they wish to understand more about these interactions between personality traits, situations, and behavior, personality researchers need to define the relevant characteristics of both the person and the situation (Shoda & Mischel, 2000).

Evaluating the Trait Approach

Despite differences of opinion concerning the nature and number of basic personality dimensions, trait theorists have made an important contribution by focusing attention on the value of identifying, classifying, and measuring stable, enduring personality dispositions. Several challenges confront trait theorists, however. More attention must be paid to how traits interact with one another to affect various behaviors if we are to capture the true complexities of personality (Ahadi & Diener, 1989; Choca et al., 1992; Smith et al., 1990). All too often, researchers try to make specific predictions on the basis of a single measured personality trait without taking into account other personality factors that might also influence the behavior in question. This approach sells short the complexity of personality.

In evaluating the trait perspective, we must remember the distinction between description and explanation. To say that someone is outgoing and fun-loving *because* she is high in extraversion is merely to describe the behavior with a trait name, not to explain the inner disposition and how it operates. Traditionally, the trait perspective has been more concerned with describing the structure of personality, measuring individual differences in personality traits, and predicting behavior than with understanding the psychological processes that produce the traits (McAdams, 1992). Eysenck's theory of brain arousal is a notable exception, for it attempts to explain the biological bases for behavioral differences produced by extraversion and stability.

The next crucial task for trait theorists is to understand how biological, psychodynamic, cognitive, and environmental factors combine to determine personality, and how these personality dispositions affect behavior and well-being. An example of this emphasis is found in research on personality and health, described in the following *Psychological Frontiers*.

➤ 26. Describe Type A, Type B, and Type C personalities, as well as the risk factors inherent in the Type A and Type C patterns.

➤ 27. How do differences in optimism-pessimism and conscientiousness relate to health and longevity?

PSYCHOLOGICAL FRONTIERS

Personality and Health

Are personality differences related to one's physical health? Can your personality make you more or less vulnerable to illnesses such as coronary heart disease and cancer? There is increasing evidence that the answer is yes.

Consider, for example, a personality style known as the Type A personality. The Type A pattern is said to have been discovered by an upholsterer who came to repair the chairs in the office of a physician who specialized in treating heart attack victims. The upholsterer noticed an unusual wear pattern: The chairs were worn at the front of the seat, not the back, indicating that the patients were constantly sitting on the edges of their seats and moving about during their appointments.

The upholsterer's observation typifies many of the behaviors seen in **Type A personalities.** Type A people tend to live under great pressure and are demanding of themselves and others (Shaw, 2000). Their behaviors include rapid talking, moving, walking, and eating. They have an exaggerated sense of time urgency and become very irritated at delays or failures to meet their deadlines. Many of them are workaholics who tend to schedule more and more activities in less and less time and try to do several things at once. Figure 13.14 shows a page from the

–Continued

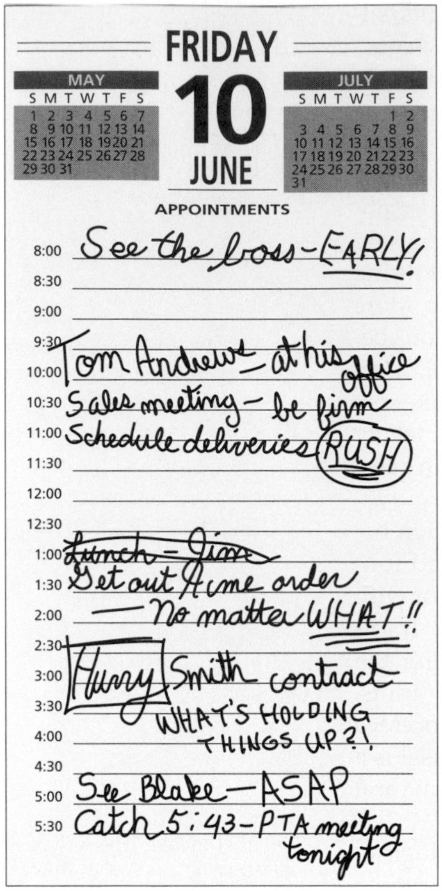

FIGURE 13.14 The Type A personality experiences a constant sense of time urgency as well as irritable impatience and hostility. The owner of this appointment book died of a heart attack shortly after the date on this schedule.

From Carver, C. S. & Scheier, M. F., *Perspectives on Personality*. Copyright © 1988 by Allyn & Bacon. Reprinted by permission.

appointment book of a Type A person who later died of a heart attack (Carver & Scheier, 1988). Type A people are also characterized by high levels of competitiveness and ambition, as well as aggressiveness and hostility when things get in their way. They stand in sharp contrast to *Type B* persons, who are more relaxed, more agreeable, and have far less sense of time urgency (Strube, 1989). Several large-scale studies suggest that even when other physical risk factors, such as obesity and smoking, are taken into account, Type A men and women have about double the risk for coronary heart disease (CHD) (Haynes et al., 1980; Rosenman et al., 1975).

Not all components of the Type A pattern increase vulnerability to CHD. The fast-paced, time-conscious lifestyle and high ambition apparently are not the culprits. Rather, the crucial component seems to be negative emotions. The Type A behavior pattern virtually guarantees that these people will encounter many stressful situations, such as time pressures of their own making and barriers that anger them (Booth-Kewley & Friedman, 1987; Friedman, 1991). A cynical hostility marked by suspiciousness, resentment, frequent anger, distrust, and antagonism seems particularly important (Barefoot et al., 1989; Miller, 2000). This aspect of the Type A pattern is likely to alienate others, produce conflict, and reduce the amount of social support they receive. Adding to the risk equation is the tendency of Type A people to overreact physiologically to events that arouse anger, a biological factor that may contribute to their tendency to develop heart disease (Fichera & Andreassi, 1998; Taylor, 1999). John Hunter, an 18th-century pioneer in cardiovascular medicine, recognized his own vulnerability when he said, "My life is in the hands of any rascal who chooses to put me in a passion." Hunter's statement was all too prophetic; he died of a heart attack during an angry debate at a hospital board meeting.

Quite a different personality style, known as the **Type C** pattern, may be a risk factor for cancer (Eysenck, 1994; Sanderman & Ranchor-Adelita, 1997). Type Cs are almost the mirror image of the Type A pattern. They are highly sociable and "nice" people who are very inhibited in expressing negative emotions. Their tendency to bottle up such emotions, particularly anger and anxiety, seems to get in the way of active coping, and they tend to feel helpless and hopeless in the face of severe stress. The emotional inhibitions may take a toll on their bodies as well. In one large-scale European study that extended over 10 years, people with the Type C pattern were far more likely than others to develop cancer (Eysenck & Grossarth-Maricek, 1991). Once diagnosed with cancer, patients who continue to suppress their negative emotions are less likely to survive the disease (Salovey et al., 2000; Sanderman & Ranchor-Adelita, 1997). In contrast, those who learn to release negative emotions are more likely to survive. In Eysenck's (1994) longitudinal study, those Type C people who became more emotionally expressive had only a 4 percent death rate from cancer over the next 13 years, compared with a 43 percent cancer mortality rate in the most extreme Type C group. Other research also shows that bottling up negative feelings can be hazardous to one's health (Traue & Deighton, 2000).

Recent research indicates that optimism is good for your health as well as your happiness (Scheier & Carver, 2000). Pessimistic people are at greater risk for helplessness and depression when they confront stressful events, and are at greater risk for illness and death (Peterson & Park, 1998). In one study, infectious illnesses and number of doctor visits were counted over a one-year period for optimistic and pessimistic college students. Pessimists had about twice as many illnesses and visits to doctors as did optimists (Peterson & Seligman, 1987). In another study, women who came to the National Cancer Institute for treatment of breast cancer were followed for 5 years. On average, pessimists died sooner than optimists even when the physical severity of the disease was the same at the beginning of the 5-year period (Levy et al., 1989). The increased vulnerability to disease and death may lie in a link between pessimism and reduced immune functioning in the face of stress. A study of law students during the stressful first year of law school revealed that optimists not only maintained a more positive mood over the course of the year, but also had higher levels of immune system functioning (Segerstrom et al., 1998).

—Continued

Longitudinal studies suggest that pessimists may suffer more illnesses over their lifetimes and may die at a younger age from both natural and accidental causes. At age 25, members of the Harvard classes of 1939–1944 completed questionnaires from which a measure of optimism-pessimism was later derived. Since that time, they have been studied and have had periodic physical checkups. The researchers found that pessimism at age 25 predicted poorer health beginning at about age 45, perhaps because pessimists (who tend to expect the worst) were less likely to engage in self-protective patterns of healthy behavior, such as regular exercise and good dietary habits (Peterson et al., 1998).

Among the Big Five personality factors, conscientiousness seems to have the strongest links to physical health and longevity. In one study, a large group of children have been followed for over 70 years. Those children who were judged by their parents and teachers to be highly conscientious at age 11 have lived significantly longer and are about 30 percent less likely to die in any given year (Friedman et al., 1995). Conscientious people were less likely to engage in risky behaviors, and therefore less likely to die from violent deaths in accidents or fights. They were also less likely to smoke and drink to excess and more likely to exercise regularly, eat a balanced diet, have regular physicals, and follow medical prescriptions when ill. Thus the effects of being carefree and careless add up during one's life and can be quite harmful in the end.

Considerable evidence exists that personality plays a role in health and longevity (Contrada et al., 1999). Researchers continue to explore links between personality and health, and their findings may shed important light on psychological processes that can affect physical well-being.

〉 SOCIAL COGNITIVE THEORIES

The psychology of learning has great relevance for understanding personality. Many behaviors ascribed to personality are acquired through classical conditioning, operant conditioning, and modeling (Bandura, 1999). However, the learner is not simply a passive reactor to environmental forces. Instead, as the cognitive perspective tells us, the human is a perceiver, a thinker, and a planner who mentally interprets events, thinks about the past, anticipates the future, and decides how to behave. Whatever effects the environment has are filtered through these cognitive processes and are influenced—even changed—by them. **Social cognitive** theorists such as Julian Rotter (1954, 1966), Albert Bandura (1986, 1999), and Walter Mischel (1973, 1999) have combined the behavioral and cognitive perspectives into an approach to personality that stresses the interaction of a thinking human with a social environment that provides learning experiences.

To understand behavior, psychodynamic, humanistic, and trait theorists emphasize internal personal causes of behavior, such as unconscious conflicts, self-actualization tendencies, and personality traits. In a sense, they account for behavior from "the inside out." In contrast, radical behaviorists emphasize environmental causes and view humans as reactors to external events (Parker et al., 1998). To them, behavior is to be explained from "the outside in." Social-cognitive theorists take an intermediate position, focusing on both internal and external factors. They believe that the debate on whether behavior is more strongly influenced by personal factors or by the person's environment is basically a meaningless one. Instead, according to the social cognitive principle of **reciprocal determinism** (Bandura, 1978), the person, the person's behavior, and the environment all influence one another in a pattern of two-way causal links (Figure 13.15). As an example, let us consider how these interactions or linkages might operate in the case of Julia, the difficult housemate described at the beginning of the chapter.

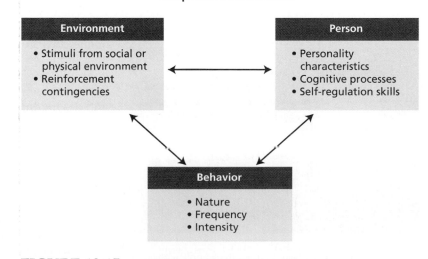

FIGURE 13.15 The social cognitive concept of reciprocal determinism states that the characteristics of the person, the person's behavior, and the environment all affect one another in reciprocal, or two-way causal relations.

➤ 28. How does reciprocal determinism apply to Julia's personality pattern? Specify the two-way causal links.

There seems little doubt that Julia is low on the Big Five personality trait of Agreeableness. Her disagreeableness trait manifests itself as the irritable, cynical, and uncooperative behavior pattern described by her roommates (i.e., Julia's personality influences her behavior). Julia's disagreeable behaviors tend to evoke negative responses from others (her behavior causes her social environment to respond to her in kind). These negative social consequences reinforce and strengthen still further Julia's personality trait (including her expectations that others will eventually reject her), and they also strengthen her disagreeable behavior tendencies (her environment influences both her personality trait and her social behavior). Thus Julia's personality, her behavior, and her environment all influence one another.

Julian Rotter: Expectancy, Reinforcement Value, and Locus of Control

➤ 29. Define Rotter's concepts of expectancy and reinforcement value and explain how they jointly influence behavior.

In 1954, Julian Rotter (whose name is pronounced like "motor") laid the foundation for today's social cognitive approaches. According to Rotter, the likelihood that we will engage in a particular behavior in a given situation is influenced by two factors: expectancy and reinforcement value. *Expectancy* is our perception of how likely it is that certain consequences will occur if we engage in a particular behavior within a specific situation. *Reinforcement value* is basically how much we desire or dread the outcome that we expect the behavior to produce. Thus a student who strongly values academic success and expects that studying will result in high grades is quite likely to study. Note that this approach makes use of reinforcement, a central behaviorist concept, but views its effects within a cognitive framework that emphasizes how we think about our behavior and its expected outcomes.

Locus of Control

➤ 30. Describe Rotter's concept of locus of control and how it affects behavior.

One of Rotter's most influential concepts is **internal-external locus of control,** an expectancy concerning the degree of personal control we have in our lives. People with an *internal* locus of control believe that life outcomes are largely under personal control and depend on their own behavior (Figure 13.16). In contrast, people with an *external* locus of control believe that their fate has less to do with their own efforts than with the influence of external factors, such as luck, chance, and powerful others. Table 13.7 contains items from Rotter's (1966) Internal-External (I-E) Scale, used to measure individual differences in locus of control.

Locus of control is a highly researched personality variable. Quite consistently, people with an internal locus of control behave in a more self-determined fashion (Burger, 2000). In the 1960s, for example, African-Americans who actively participated in the civil rights movement were more internal on the I-E Scale than were those who did not (Rotter, 1966). Internal college students achieve better grades than do external students of equal academic ability, probably because they link their studying to degree of success and work harder. Internals are more likely to actively seek out the information needed to succeed in a given situation (Ingold, 1989). Interpersonally, internals tend to be independent but cooperative in their dealings with others and are more resistant to social influence, whereas externals tend to give in to high-status people who they see as powerful others. Internals are more likely than externals to engage in health-promoting behaviors, such as exercising regularly, maintaining a healthy diet, using seat belts, and abstaining from smoking (Marshall, 1991; Wallston, 1993).

FIGURE 13.16 Research shows that people with an internal locus of control are more likely to take an active role in social change movements.

TABLE 13.7	SAMPLE ITEMS FROM ROTTER'S INTERNAL-EXTERNAL SCALE

Choose statement a or b

1a. Many times I feel that I have little influence over the things that happen to me.

1b. It is impossible for me to believe that chance or luck plays an important part in my life.

2a. The average citizen can have an influence in government decisions.

2b. The world is run by the few people in power and there isn't much the little guy can do about it.

3a. In the long run, people get the respect they deserve in this world.

3b. Unfortunately, an individual's worth often passes unrecognized no matter how hard one tries.

Note: 1b, 2a, and 3a are the internal alternatives.
Source: Rotter, 1966.

Internal locus of control is positively related to self-esteem and feelings of personal effectiveness, and internals tend to cope with stress in a more active and problem-focused manner than do externals (Jennings, 1990). They are also less likely to experience psychological maladjustment in the form of depression or anxiety (Hoffart & Martinson, 1991). Locus of control is called a *generalized expectancy* because it is thought to apply across many life domains as a general worldview.

Albert Bandura: Social Learning and Self-Efficacy

Albert Bandura has made major contributions to the development of the social cognitive approach. His early studies of modeling, described in Chapter 6, helped meld the psychology of learning with the cognitive perspective. Bandura's social learning analyses of aggression, moral behavior, and behavioral self-control demonstrated the wide applicability of the social cognitive approach (Bandura, 1973, 1988, 1991). Perhaps his most influential contribution, however, is his theory development and research on self-efficacy.

> 31. Define self-efficacy. What four sources of information influence efficacy beliefs?

Self-Efficacy

According to Bandura (1997), a key factor in how people regulate their lives is their sense of **self-efficacy,** their beliefs concerning their ability to perform the behaviors needed to achieve desired outcomes. People whose self-efficacy is high have confidence in their ability to do what it takes to overcome obstacles and achieve their goals.

A good deal of research has been done on the factors that create differences in self-efficacy (Figure 13.17). Four important determinants have been identified (Bandura, 1997; Maddux, 1999). The most important is our previous *performance attainments* in similar situations. Such experiences shape our beliefs about our capabilities. For example, as shown in Figure 13.18, college women who felt that they had mastered the martial arts and emotional control skills taught in a physical self-defense training program showed dramatic

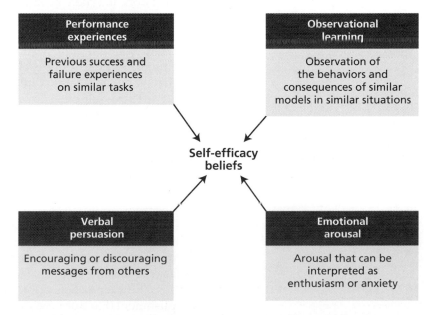

FIGURE 13.17 Four classes of information that affect self-efficacy beliefs.
After Bandura, 1997.

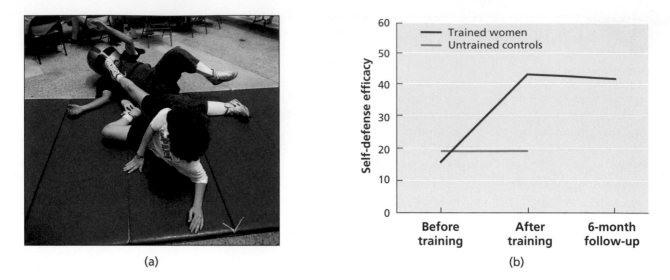

(a)   (b)

FIGURE 13.18 Physical self-defense training (a) has dramatic effects on women's self-efficacy to perform the behaviors needed to defend themselves (b). The physical defense self-efficacy scores in this study could extend from 6 to 60.
Based on Data from Weitlauf et al., 2000.

increases in their belief that they could escape from or disable a potential assailant or rapist (Weitlauf et al., 2000). Bandura stresses that self-efficacy beliefs are always specific to particular situations. Thus we may have high self-efficacy in some situations and low self-efficacy in others. For example, the women who mastered the physical self-defense skills did not feel more generally capable in all areas of their lives, despite their enhanced self-defense efficacy.

A second source of information comes from *observational learning,*—that is, observing others' behaviors and their outcomes. If you observe a person similar to yourself accomplish a particular goal, then you are likely to believe that if you perform those same behaviors, you will also succeed. A striking example of how powerful such expectations can be comes from the world of sports. At one time, physiologists insisted that it was physically impossible for a human being to run a mile in less than four minutes, and no one in the history of track and field had ever done it. When the Englishman Roger Bannister broke the four-minute barrier in 1954, that limiting belief was shattered. The impact on other runners' performance was immediate and dramatic. In the year following Bannister's accomplishment, 37 other runners broke the barrier, and the year after that, nearly 300 runners did the "impossible." Apparently, a great many people came to believe that "if he can do it, so can I."

Third, self-efficacy can be increased or decreased by *verbal persuasion.* The messages we get from other people who affirm our abilities or downgrade them affect our efficacy beliefs. Thus inspirational teachers who convey high standards and a "you can do it" conviction can inspire their students to great accomplishments.

Finally, high *emotional arousal* that is interpreted as anxiety or fatigue tends to decrease self-efficacy. On the other hand, if we find ourselves able to control negative arousal, it may enhance efficacy beliefs and subsequent performance. For example, test-anxious college students who mastered the relaxation skills taught in Chapter 10 (p. 446) showed increases in their belief that they could remain relaxed and focused during tests, and their performance on tests increased as well (Smith, 1989).

Efficacy beliefs are strong predictors of future performance and accomplishment (Bandura, 1997). They become a kind of self-fulfilling prophesy. In the words of Henry Ford, "Whether you believe you can do something or you believe you can't, you're probably right."

➤ 32. Summarize six principles of effective goal setting.

APPLICATIONS OF PSYCHOLOGICAL SCIENCE

Increasing Self-Efficacy Through Systematic Goal Setting

Because positive self-efficacy beliefs are consistently related to success in behaving effectively and achieving goals, Bandura and other social cognitive theorists have been strongly interested in practical measures for enhancing self-efficacy. When people are successful and when they attribute their success to their own competencies (internal locus of control), their self-efficacy increases and assists them in subsequent goal-directed efforts (Maddux, 1999). Moreover, successful people have usually mastered the skills involved in setting challenging and realistic goals, figuring out what they need to do on a day-by-day basis to achieve them, and making the commitment to do what is required. As they achieve each goal they have set, they become more skillful and increase their sense of personal efficacy (Bandura, 1997).

Not all goal setting procedures are created equal, and it is important to apply the principles that make goal-setting programs most effective (Locke & Latham, 1990). Here are some research-derived guidelines for effective goal setting.

1. **Set specific, behavioral, and measurable goals.** The first step in changing some aspect of your life is to set a goal. The kind of goal you set is very important, because certain kinds of goals encourage us to work harder, enjoy success, and increase self-efficacy.

   Specific and fairly narrow goals have been shown to be far more effective than general "do your best" goals (Locke & Latham, 1990). A goal such as "improving my tennis game" is less likely to be helpful than "increasing the percentage of serves I put in play by 20 percent." The latter goal refers to a specific behavior that you can focus on and measure.

   One of the most important aspects of goal setting is systematically measuring progress toward the goal. This was shown in a study by Bandura and Daniel Cervone (1983) in which participants worked on a strenuous bicycle-pedaling task over a number of trials. Two independent variables were manipulated: (a) whether the participants were given specific improvement goals, and (b) whether the participants were given feedback about their performance on the previous trial. A control condition got neither goals nor feedback and provided a basis for evaluating the effects of goals and feedback, alone or in combination. The dependent variable was the speed and power with which the participants pedaled.

   As shown in Figure 13.19, simply having goals was not enough, nor was feedback effective by itself. The participants who had both goals and feedback

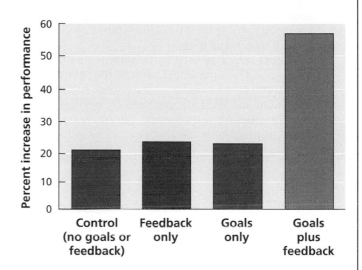

FIGURE 13.19 The effects of improvement goals and performance feedback on performance improvement on a grueling bicycling task. Clearly, the combination of explicit goals and performance feedback resulted in the greatest improvement in performance. Data from Bandura & Cervone, 1983.

showed by far the greatest improvement. This shows how important it is to find a way to measure your progress toward the goal so that you get performance feedback and can see your improvement. Visible movement toward realistic goals builds self-efficacy.

2. **Set performance, not outcome, goals.** Many of our goals relate to outcomes in the future, such as "getting an A in this course." You are more likely to achieve such goals if you use the means-ends heuristic discussed in Chapter 8 and think about the specific things you must do to achieve that outcome goal. Performance goals (what one has to do) work better than outcome goals because they keep the focus on the necessary behaviors. A performance goal might be "read the book and outline the lecture notes for one hour each day." Achieving this performance goal can also be measured quickly and repeatedly, giving you constant feedback. Many people focus on outcome goals and forget what has to be done on a day-to-day basis to achieve them. It has been said that there are three kinds of people in this world: those who make things happen, those who wait for things to happen, and those who wonder what happened. Make sure you're someone who makes things happen.

—Continued

3. **Set difficult but realistic goals.** Moderately difficult goals challenge and motivate us and give us a sense of hope. When reached, they increase self-efficacy. Easy goals do not provide a sense of accomplishment, and extremely difficult goals do not provide the success experiences you need to increase self-efficacy.

4. **Set positive, not negative, goals.** Chapter 6 discussed the advantages of positive reinforcement over punishment. Working toward positive goals, such as "getting a B," is better than avoiding a negative consequence, as in "not flunking." Again, positive goals keep you focused on the positive steps that you need to take to achieve them.

5. **Set short-range as well as long-term goals.** Short-range goals are important because they provide the opportunity for immediate mastery experiences, and they keep you working positively. A long-term goal like "graduating with honors" can easily be broken into a series of subgoals that you can be working to-

ward right now. Short-term goals are like the steps on a staircase leading to the long-term goal. As they are accomplished, they not only provide mastery experiences but also lead you toward your ultimate goal. In reaching any goal, "divide and conquer" is a cliche that works.

6. **Set definite time spans for achievement.** It is said that the road to hell is paved with good intentions. To keep a goal-setting program on track, it is important to specify the dates by which specific performance goals or subgoals will be met, together with the behaviors needed to attain them in that time span.

Goal setting is a motivational technique that has resulted in remarkable improvements in productivity in many work, social, and academic settings (Locke & Latham, 1990). Moreover, for purposes of increasing self-efficacy, it has the added advantage of providing the repeated mastery experiences that are the most powerful sources of efficacy information.

Walter Mischel and Yuichi Shoda: The Cognitive-Affective Personality System

Walter Mischel, who studied under Julian Rotter at Ohio State and was a colleague of Albert Bandura's at Stanford, is a third key figure in social cognitive theory. Mischel's major contribution is drawing together social cognitive concepts, some from Rotter's and Bundura's theories, that help account for individual differences in personality.

> 33. Describe the five psychological variables that comprise the CAPS.

In the most recent formulation of social cognitive theory, Mischel and Yuichi Shoda describe five variables that account for how a given person might respond to a particular situation. These factors, summarized in Table 13.8, are organized into a **cognitive-affective personality system (CAPS)** (Mischel, 1999; Shoda & Mischel, 2000). The dynamic interplay among these five factors, together with the characteristics of the situation, account for individual differences between people as well as differences in people's behavior across different situations (Figure 13.20). As a result of interactions between situations and the personality system, people exhibit distinctive **behavioral signatures,** consistent ways of responding in particular classes of situations. These behavioral signatures are the outward manifestation of personality that establish a person's unique identity.

> 34. What are behavioral signatures? How do they explain situational consistency and inconsistency in behavior?

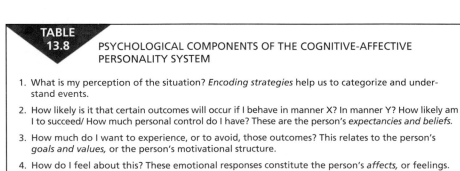

TABLE 13.8	PSYCHOLOGICAL COMPONENTS OF THE COGNITIVE-AFFECTIVE PERSONALITY SYSTEM

1. What is my perception of the situation? *Encoding strategies* help us to categorize and understand events.

2. How likely is it that certain outcomes will occur if I behave in manner X? In manner Y? How likely am I to succeed/ How much personal control do I have? These are the person's *expectancies and beliefs.*

3. How much do I want to experience, or to avoid, those outcomes? This relates to the person's *goals and values,* or the person's motivational structure.

4. How do I feel about this? These emotional responses constitute the person's *affects,* or feelings.

5. Do I have the behavioral skills needed to deal with this situation? What should I do? *Personal competencies and self-regulatory processes* affect behavior as well.

Source: After Mischel, 1999.

Research shows that people can have very distinctive behavioral signatures. For example, Figure 13.21 shows the behavioral patterns of two verbally aggressive children in a residential summer camp (Shoda et al., 1994). The children's behaviors were systematically observed and coded for more than 150 hours per child. Overall, these two children were quite similar in the overall number of verbally aggressive responses they made. However, inspection of the *situational patterns* of aggression reveals that Child A reacted very aggressively toward adults, whether they were behaving toward the child in a warm or a punitive fashion. In contrast, this child showed relatively little aggression toward peers. Child B showed quite a different pattern, consistently reacting with low levels of aggression toward adults or when being teased by peers. On the other hand, a consistently high level of aggression occurred when peers approached this child in a friendly manner. An important lesson here is that if we simply averaged the aggressive behavior counts across the five situations, the two children would look equally "aggressive." But in so doing, we would mask the distinctive and consistent behavior signatures that define the children's individuality. Let us now describe the internal "person factors" that produce behavioral signatures

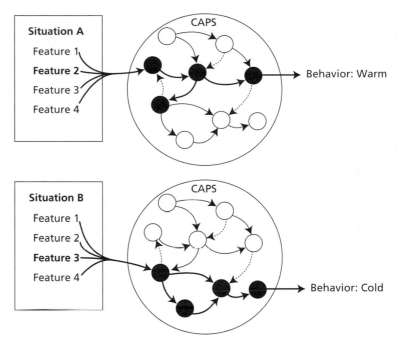

FIGURE 13.20 The cognitive-affective personality system (CAPS), consisting of the components shown in Table 13.8, processes and responds to relevant characteristics of the situation and is responsible for generating the behavior that occurs. Feature 2 of situation A activates the network of CAPS elements that produce warm behavior. The person's focus on Feature 3 in situation B results in cold behavior.

Encoding Strategies

People differ greatly in how they customarily encode (represent, interpret, construe) situations. A talkative man who steps onto an elevator holding a snake in his arms might be labeled as "wierd" by one person and "an intriguing person I'd like to get to know" by another. Our encodings determine how we respond emotionally and behaviorally to situations. For example, studies of highly aggressive youth reveal that they have a strong tendency to perceive others as having disrespect for them and hostile intent toward them (Berkowitz, 1998). Thus they are primed to react to an innocuous event, such as being unintentionally brushed against on a stairway at school, with a violent response (Dodge, 1986) Other individuals tend to encode ambiguous interpersonal events, such as not being greeted by a fellow student, as instances of personal rejection and to

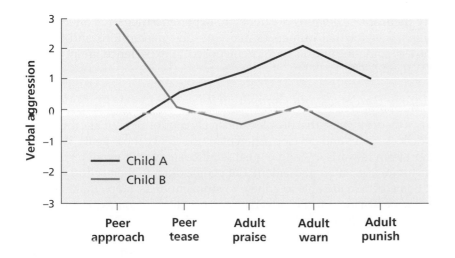

FIGURE 13.21 Aggressive responses of two children, A and B, in five different summer camp situations, showing the manner in which they have distinctive "behavioral signatures" for aggressive responding even though their aggression scores averaged across the five settings are quite similar. The vertical line in the graph at the "0" point represents the average amount of verbal aggression shown in each situation by all the children in the study. Data from Shoda et al., 1994.

become depressed as a result (Downey & Feldman, 1996). As object relations theorists have suggested, the internal representations or working models we have of relationships influence how we perceive (encode) and respond to others in our later relationships. This is an example of how the social cognitive approach can incorporate concepts and insights from other theories.

Expectancies and Beliefs

As Rotter emphasized, what we expect will happen if we behave in a particular way is a strong determinant of our behavioral choices. *Behavior-outcome expectancies* represent the *if . . . then* links between alternative behaviors and possible outcomes. What will happen to my grade point *if* I take that course in organic chemistry? How likely is it that I'll be forgiven *if* I apologize? Will I make enough money to support myself *if* I become a teacher? People may have very different answers to such questions and therefore respond quite differently to the same situation (Bugenthal, 2000). For example, some people believe that assertively approaching someone with whom they desire a romantic relationship is most likely to pay off, so they do so. Others may believe that to do so is to court disaster and possible rejection, so they do not take the initiative.

In addition to behavior-outcome expectancies, beliefs about our competencies and about the degree of personal control we have over our lives strongly influence our actions. Thus Mischel also includes Bandura's self-efficacy and Rotter's locus of control as important expectancy variables.

Goals and Values

Motivation plays a central role in attempts to understand behavior, and is represented in the CAPS system as goals and values that guide our behavior, cause us to persist in the face of barriers, and determine the outcomes and situations we seek and our reactions to them (Higgins, 1996). People differ in important ways in the goals that are important to them and the values that guide their lives. These differences can cause people to behave very differently in situations that are relevant to these important personality factors (Little, 1999).

Affects (Emotions)

Anything that implies important consequences for us, whether beneficial or harmful, can trigger an emotional response (Ferguson, 2000; Smith & Lazarus, 1990). Once aroused, emotions color our perceptions and influence our behavior. For example, if one is already feeling bad and then gets negative feedback about performance on a test, it is easy to become demoralized and suspend academic effort for a time. Research shows that people exhibit stable individual differences in emotionality. For example, people who are high on Eysenck's trait of instability (neuroticism) have a tendency to experience negative affect in an intense fashion, a factor that influences many of their perceptions and behaviors. In contrast, some individuals are predisposed to experience mainly positive affect (Watson & Clark, 1992).

Self-Regulatory Processes and Competencies

Social cognitive theorists stress that people extensively control, or regulate, their own behavior. We choose goals and develop action plans to achieve those goals. We often put aside short-term rewards or endure great sacrifices to work toward a goal that lies far in the future (e.g., after graduation). But people differ in their self-regulation capabilities. Some people are able to adhere to stringent diets, stop smoking after many years, and persist in the face of adversity and negative outcomes, whereas others are not able to do so. By the end of January, about 45 percent of New Year's resolutions have been abandoned, but 55 percent of people are still persisting (Norcross et al., 1989). People's ability to control their own behavior is a distinguishing aspect of personality, as are the competencies they develop that allow them to successfully adapt to life and pursue important goals (Metcalfe & Mischel, 1998). Some of these competencies are cognitive problem-solving methods that allow them to plan successful strategies, whereas others involve the ability to exert personal control over thoughts, emotions, and behaviors (DeLongis, 2000; Gross, 1999).

One important way people regulate their own behavior is through self-administered consequences. **Self-reinforcement processes** refer to internal, self-administered rewards and punishments (Bandura, 1999; Mischel, 1999). In response to our own behaviors, we generate positive evaluations and emotions like pride, self-approval, and the conviction that we did "the right thing." In contrast, we may respond with negative responses like self-reproach, shame, and guilt when we violate our personal standards. Self-reinforcement processes often override external consequences, making us more autonomous and self-directed.

Resolving the Consistency Paradox

As noted in our earlier discussion of the trait perspective, people's behavior often shows a notable lack of consistency across situations, a fact that has caused some to call the traditional concept of personality trait into question (Mischel, 1968). In CAPS theory, however, personality is defined in terms of the five person variables and the interactions among them that produce the person's behavioral signatures. How a person behaves depends on the features of the situation, how these features are encoded, the expectancies and beliefs that are activated, the goals that are relevant, the emotions that might occur, and the plans and self-regulatory processes that help determine the behavior. Thus it is entirely possible for people to behave inconsistently from situation to situation. They will behave similarly in situations that have important characteristics in common, but inconsistently in situations that differ in ways that evoke different responses by the CAPS (Shoda & Mischel, 2000).

Let us return once more to Julia, the hostile roommate, whose behavior differs greatly in different situations. We are told that she is charming, agreeable, and friendly in social situations like parties, where interactions are relatively superficial. In close relationships, however, she becomes hostile and self-protective. In trying to understand Julia's behavioral inconsistency, Mischel and Shoda might suggest that because of hurtful experiences in the past, she perceives threat (encodings) and becomes anxious (affect) in intimate relationships because she expects that others will reject or hurt her if she gets too close (expectancy). She strongly fears this outcome (value) and doesn't have the competencies to deal with her insecurity and control her anxiety (self-regulatory skills and competencies). Therefore as relationships become more intimate over time, she pushes others away with her hostility. By understanding Julia's CAPS factors and how they relate to critical features of a given situation, we are able to understand her behavioral inconsistency in casual versus close relationships. In the *if . . . then* language of behavioral signatures, we might summarize this aspect of her personality as: *If* in a superficial relationship, *then* friendly and charming, but *if* a close or potentially intimate relationship, *then* guarded and hostile.

Evaluating Social Cognitive Theories

A strength of the cognitive-behavioral approach is its strong scientific base. It brings together two perspectives, the behavioral and the cognitive, that have strong research traditions. The constructs of social cognitive theory can be defined, measured, and researched with considerable precision. As a result, the social cognitive approach has advanced our understanding of how processes within the person and characteristics of the situation interact with one another to influence behavior. Another strength is its ability to translate insights derived from other perspectives into cognitive-behavioral concepts (Carver & Scheier, 2000).

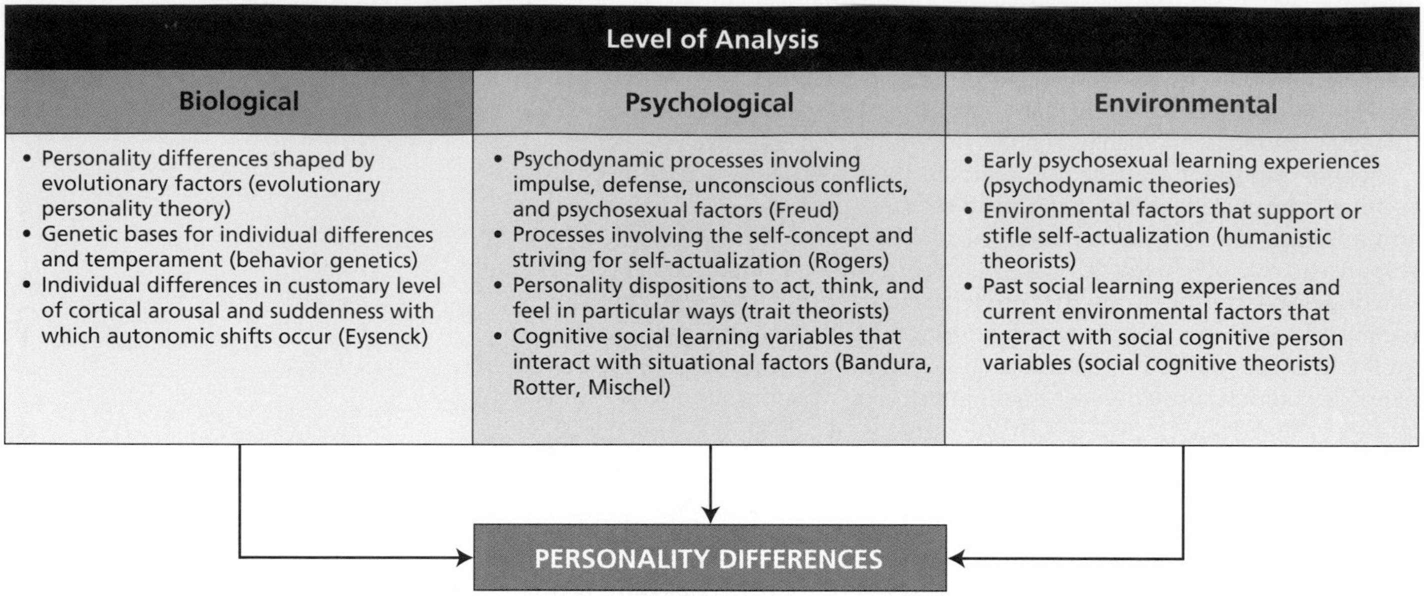

Level of Analysis		
Biological	**Psychological**	**Environmental**
• Personality differences shaped by evolutionary factors (evolutionary personality theory) • Genetic bases for individual differences and temperament (behavior genetics) • Individual differences in customary level of cortical arousal and suddenness with which autonomic shifts occur (Eysenck)	• Psychodynamic processes involving impulse, defense, unconscious conflicts, and psychosexual factors (Freud) • Processes involving the self-concept and striving for self-actualization (Rogers) • Personality dispositions to act, think, and feel in particular ways (trait theorists) • Cognitive social learning variables that interact with situational factors (Bandura, Rotter, Mischel)	• Early psychosexual learning experiences (psychodynamic theories) • Environmental factors that support or stifle self-actualization (humanistic theorists) • Past social learning experiences and current environmental factors that interact with social cognitive person variables (social cognitive theorists)

PERSONALITY DIFFERENCES

FIGURE 13.22 Understanding the Causes of Behavior: Personality differences.

Social cognitive theory also helps resolve an apparent contradiction between the central assumption that personality produces stability in behavior and research findings that people's behavior is not very consistent across different situations. The CAPS theory of Mischel and Shoda suggests that the inconsistency of a person's behavior across situations is actually a manifestation of a stable underlying cognitive-affective personality structure that reacts to certain features of situations. However, the ability of CAPS to predict behavior needs further examination.

We have seen that the various perspectives focus on different determinants of personality. Figure 13.22 summarizes the determinants stressed by the various theories at the biological, psychological, and environmental levels of analysis.

〉 PERSONALITY ASSESSMENT

If we were to introduce you to a woman you have never met and give you one week to provide a complete personality description of her, what would you do?

Chances are, you would seek information in a variety of ways. You might start by interviewing the woman and finding out as much as you could about her. Based on your knowledge of the theories we have discussed, what questions would you ask? Would you ask about early childhood experiences and dreams? About how she sees herself and others? Would you be interested in the kinds of traits embodied in the Big Five or in Eysenck's dimension of Introversion-Extraversion? Would you want to know how the woman customarily feels and responds in various situations? Your answers to these questions and your other assessment decisions would in some sense reflect your own theory of what is important in describing personality.

You probably would not be content simply to interview the woman. You might also decide to interview other people who know her well and get their views of what she is like. You might even ask them to rate her on a variety of traits, such as those found in Cattell's model of personality or in the Five Factor model, and you could ask the person you are studying to rate herself on the same measures to see if her self-concept agrees with how others see her.

Finally, you might decide that it would be useful to actually observe how the woman behaves in a variety of situations. You would want to observe her in such a way that you got as "natural" and characteristic a sample of her behavior as possible. This information, together with that obtained from the person and from those who know her best, might provide a reasonable basis for a personality description.

Figure 13.23 shows the major methods that psychologists use to assess personality characteristics. As you can see, they use some of the same methods you might have chosen: the interview; trait ratings and behavior reports; and behavioral assessment, or direct observation and measurement of the person's behavior. In addition, they have developed several types of psychological tests, including objective self-report measures and "projective" tests that ask respondents to interpret ambiguous stimuli, such as inkblots or pictures. Finally, physiological measures can be used to measure various aspects of personality, such as emotional reactivity or levels of cortical arousal.

The task of devising valid and useful personality measures is anything but simple, and it has taxed the ingenuity of psychologists for nearly a century. To be useful from either a scientific or a practical perspective, personality tests must conform to the standards of reliability and validity discussed in Chapter 8 (p. 342). *Reliability*, or consistency of measurement, takes several forms. A test that measures a stable personality trait should yield similar scores when administered to the same individuals at different times (test-retest reliability). Another aspect of reliability is that different professionals should score and interpret the test in the same way (interjudge reliability). *Validity* refers to the most important question of all: Is the test actually measuring the personality variable that it is intended to measure? A valid test allows us to predict behavior that is influenced by the personality variable being measured. Research on test reliability and validity is an important activity of personality psychologists, and good measures of personality are an absolute must for scientific research on personality and for ethical clinical application (Domino, 2000).

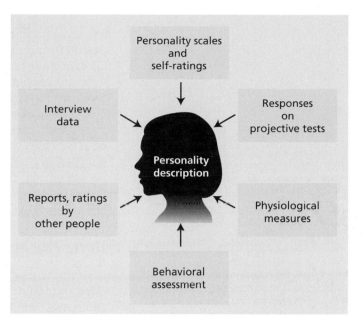

FIGURE 13.23 Measurement approaches used to assess personality.

➤ 35. Cite six methods that can be used to measure personality variables.

Interviews

Interviews are one of the oldest methods of assessment. Long before the invention of writing, people undoubtedly made judgments about others by observing them and talking with them. Interviewers can obtain information about a person's thoughts, feelings, and other internal states, as well as information about current and past relationships, experiences, and behavior.

Structured interviews, frequently used to collect research data or to make a psychiatric diagnosis, contain a set of specific questions that are administered to every participant. An attempt is made to create a standardized situation so that interviewees' responses to more-or-less identical stimuli can be interpreted and compared.

Good interviewers do not limit their attention to what an interviewee says; they also look at how she or he says it. They note interviewees' general appearance and grooming, their voice and speech patterns, the content of their statements, and their facial expressions and posture. Sometimes, attitudes that are not expressed verbally can be inferred from behavior, as in this instance:

➤ 36. What is a structured interview? What are its advantages over informal approaches?

> During the interview she held her small son on her lap. The child began to play with his genitals. The mother, without looking directly at the child, moved his hand away and held it securely for a while. . . . Later in the interview the mother was asked what she ordinarily did when the child masturbated. She replied that he never did this—he was a very "good" boy. She was evidently entirely unconscious of what had transpired in the very presence of the interviewer. (Maccoby & Maccoby, 1954, p. 484)

The interview is valuable for the direct personal contact it provides, but it has some limitations. First, characteristics of the interviewer may affect how the person responds in ways that can affect the validity of the information. The validity of information obtained in an interview also depends on the interviewee's desire to cooperate, to respond honestly, and to report accurately what the interviewer is trying to assess. Some interview data may be valid, others invalid.

Despite its limitations, the face-to-face interview is essential for certain purposes. A clinical psychologist needs to observe and converse with someone who is being considered for admission to a mental hospital. Interviews are often used in research. For example, in this chapter's *Research Close-Up* study, experienced psychoanalytic therapists interviewed each patient on several occasions to assess symptoms and to make inferences about their underlying conflicts so that appropriate subliminal word stimuli could be selected.

Behavioral Assessment

➤ 37. How are behavioral assessments designed, and what three questions are they designed to answer?

Personality psychologists can sometimes observe the behaviors they are interested in rather than asking people about them. In **behavioral assessment,** psychologists devise an explicit coding system that contains the behavioral categories of interest. Then they train observers until they show high levels of agreement (interjudge reliability) in using the categories to record behavior (Figure 13.24). Behavioral assessment can provide valuable information about how frequently and under what conditions certain classes of behavior occur (Haynes, 2000). This method was used by the social cognitive researchers to measure the "behavioral signatures" of the verbally aggressive children in the summer camp environment (Shoda et al., 1994).

Behavioral assessment requires precision in defining the behaviors of interest and the conditions under which they occur. For example, observers studying a young child who is having problems in school do not simply say "Jerry is disruptive." Instead, they try to answer the question, "What, specifically, does Jerry *do* that causes disruption?" Once they have identified Jerry's specific behaviors, the next questions are, "How often and under what conditions does the disruptive behavior occur?" and "What kinds of outcomes do the behaviors produce?" Answers to these questions can be particularly important not only in measuring differences in people's personality characteristics but also in identifying potential situational causes of their behavior (Greene & Ollendick, 2000).

FIGURE 13.24 In behavioral assessment, carefully trained observers code specific classes of behavior and the conditions under which they occur.

Remote Behavior Sampling

➤ 38. Describe remote behavior sampling procedures and the types of reports that can be collected.

It is not practical or possible for behavioral assessors to follow people around from situation to situation on a daily basis. In addition, assessors are frequently interested in unobservable events, such as emotional reactions and thinking patterns, that may shed considerable light on personality functioning. Through **remote behavior sampling,** researchers and clinicians can collect samples of behavior from respondents as they live their daily lives. A tiny computerized device carried by respondents pages them at randomly determined times of the day. When the "beeper" sounds, respondents record their current thoughts, feelings, or behaviors, depending on what the researcher or therapist is assessing (Csikszentmihalyi, 1990; Singer, 1988; Stone et al., 2000). Respondents may also report on the kind of situation they are in so that situation-behavior interactions can be examined. The data can either be stored in the computer or transmitted directly to the assessor.

Remote sampling procedures can be used over weeks or even months to collect a large behavior sample across many situations. This approach to personality assessment holds great promise, for it enables researchers and clinicians to detect patterns of personal functioning that might not be revealed by other methods.

Personality Scales

Personality scales, or inventories, are widely used for assessing personality in both research and clinical work. Personality scales are termed *objective* measures because they include standard sets of questions, usually in a true-false or rating scale format, that are scored using an agreed-upon scoring key (Nezami & Butcher, 2000). Their advantages include the ability to collect data from many people at the same time, the fact that all people respond to the same items, and ease of scoring. Their major disadvantage is the possibility that some people will choose not to answer the items truthfully, in which case their scores will not be valid reflections of the trait being measured. To combat this threat to validity, some widely used tests have special *validity scales* that detect tendencies to respond in a socially desirable manner or to present an overly negative image of oneself.

The items on personality scales are developed in two major ways. In the **rational approach,** items are based on the theorist's conception of the personality trait to be measured. For example, to develop a measure of introversion-extraversion, we would ask ourselves what introverts and extraverts would be likely to say about themselves, then write items that capture those kinds of self-descriptions (e.g., "I love to be at large social gatherings" or "I'm very content to spend time by myself"). One frequently used measure developed using the rational approach is the NEO-PI, which measures the Big Five personality traits of Openness, Conscientiousness, Extraversion, Agreeableness, and Neuroticism (Costa & McCrae, 1992).

In a second approach to personality test development known as the **empirical approach,** items are chosen not because their content seems relevant to the trait on rational grounds, but because previous research has shown that the items were answered differently by groups of people known to differ in the personality characteristic of interest. The empirical approach was used to develop the **Minnesota Multiphasic Personality Inventory** (MMPI; Hathaway & McKinley, 1983), the most widely used personality inventory. Developed in the 1940s, the MMPI was originally designed to provide an objective basis for psychiatric diagnosis. Its 567 true-false items consist of statements that were answered differently by groups of patients who were diagnosed as having specific psychiatric disorders (e.g., hysteria, paranoia, and schizophrenia) than they were by a nonpsychiatric comparison sample of "normal" people. The items vary widely in content; some are concerned with attitudes and emotions, others relate to overt behavior and symptoms, and still others refer to the person's life history.

The revised MMPI-2, like the original, has ten clinical scales and three validity scales (Table 13.9). The validity scales are used to detect tendencies to present either an overly positive picture or to exaggerate degree of psychological disturbance. The clinical scales were originally intended to measure severe personality deviations such as schizophrenia, depression, and psychopathic personality, and they do. In addition, however, the pattern or *configuration* of scores obtained on the various scales also reveals important aspects of personality functioning in people who do not display such disorders. The MMPI-2 is used not only for personality description and as an aid to psychiatric diagnosis, but also as a screening device in industrial and military settings.

Responses on the MMPI-2 are scored and then plotted on a graph, or profile sheet, that reflects the degree to which the individual's responses resemble those of the psychiatric groups. Figure 13.25 shows the MMPI profile of mass murderer Jeffrey Dahmer, who mutilated and dismembered his victims, sometimes eating their body parts. According to MMPI expert Alex B. Caldwell (1994), several aspects of this profile are consistent with his bizarre and destructive behavior. The extraordinarily high score on the Psychopathic Deviate scale reflects an extreme antisocial impulsiveness coupled with a total lack of capacity for compassion and empathy. His victims were in all likelihood regarded as little more than objects to

➤ 39. Contrast the rational and empirical approaches to personality test development. Give an example of a test developed by each approach.

TABLE 13.9	THE VALIDITY AND CLINICAL SCALES OF THE MINNESOTA MULTIPHASIC PERSONALITY INVENTORY-2 (MMPI-2) AND THE BEHAVIORAL CHARACTERISTICS ASSOCIATED WITH HIGH SCORES ON THE SCALES.	

Scale	Abbreviation	Behavioral Correlates
Validity scales		
Lie	L	Lies or is highly conventional
Frequency	F	Exaggerates complaints, answers haphazardly
Correction	K	Denies problems
Clinical scales		
Hypochondriasis	Hs	Expresses bodily concerns and complaints
Depression	D	Is depressed, pessimistic, guilty
Hysteria	Hy	Reacts to stress with physical symptoms, lacks insight into negative feelings
Psychopathic Deviate	Pd	Is impulsive, in conflict with the law, involved in stormy relationships
Masculinity, Femininity	Mf	Has interests characteristic of the opposite sex
Paranoia	Pa	Is suspicious, resentful
Psychasthenia	Pt	Is anxious, worried, high-strung
Schizophrenia	Sc	Is confused, disorganized, disoriented, and withdrawing from others
Hypomania	Ma	Is energetic, active, restless
Social Introversion	Si	Is introverted, with little social contact

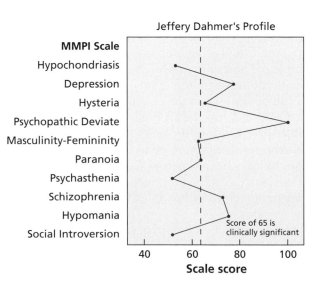

FIGURE 13.25 The MMPI profile of convicted mass murderer Jeffrey Dahmer reflects his severe psychological disturbance and is consistent with his pattern of unrestrained and vicious victimization of others. Scores greater than the dotted line are considered clinically significant.

Caldwell Report, 1994.

satisfy his perverse needs. Caldwell viewed the profile as reflecting Dahmer's sense of being fated or doomed to repeat his acts until he would be caught (the high Depression score), together with an absence of fear that, in normal people, might inhibit murderous behavior (the low Psychasthenia [anxiety] score). Although the profile clearly indicates his high level of psychological disturbance (a normal score on each scale is 50), it also reflects an ability to mask his pathology and put up the normal facade that for years fooled law enforcement officials.

Projective Tests

Freud and other psychodynamic theorists emphasized the importance of unconscious factors in understanding behavior. By definition, however, people are unaware of unconscious dynamics, so they cannot report them to interviewers or on questionnaires like the NEO-PI or the MMPI. Other methods were therefore needed to assess them. The assumption underlying **projective tests** is that when a person is presented with an ambiguous stimulus whose meaning is not clear, the interpretation attached to the stimulus will have to come partly from within. The person's interpretation may thus reflect the "projection" of inner needs, feelings, and ways of viewing the world onto the stimulus.

> ➤ 40. What is the assumption underlying projective tests? Describe two widely used projective tests.

Perhaps the following fictional story will help illustrate the rationale for projective techniques. During the administration of a set of Rorschach inkblots, the man being tested saw every one of the inkblots as either sex organs or people engaging in sexual acts. After the last inkblot, the psychologist exclaimed, "I've never in my entire career seen anyone so obsessed with sex as you seem to be." The man responded indignantly, "What do you mean, *I'm* obsessed with sex? *You're* the one with all the dirty pictures!"

Rorschach Inkblots

The Rorschach test consists of 10 inkblots. The person being tested is shown each one in succession and asked, "What does this look like? What might it be?" (Figure 13.26). After responding, the person is asked what specific feature of the inkblot (e.g., its shape or its color) caused it to be seen in that manner. Examiners write down the responses word for word. They also carefully note subjects' behavior during testing, including gestures, mannerisms, and expressed attitudes. They categorize and score responses in terms of the kinds of objects reported, the features attended to (e.g., the whole blot, colored portions, tiny details), and the emotional tone associated with particular types of responses (Erdberg, 2000).

Interpretations made by Rorschach examiners are often based on what the responses seem to symbolize. For example, people who see peering eyes and threatening figures in the inkblots are likely to be viewed as projecting their own paranoid fears and suspicions onto the stimuli. A problem is that different examiners may interpret the same response very differently, producing unreliability among examiners. In an attempt to minimize clinician subjectivity in interpreting Rorschach responses, John Exner (1991) developed a Comprehensive System with specific coding categories and scoring criteria. Although this system created greater uniformity in scoring, many of the personality interpretations derived from the Rorschach lack research support, and the usefulness of the test for predicting behavior is still hotly debated (e.g., Dawes, 1994; Wood et al., 1996). Nonetheless, many psychodynamic clinicians maintain their faith in the usefulness of the Rorschach, insisting that they find it useful for gaining insight into unconscious processes.

FIGURE 13.26 During a Rorschach administration, the person is presented with 10 inkblots and asked to indicate what each resembles and what feature of the stimulus (e.g., its shape or its color) makes it appear that way.

Thematic Apperception Test

The Thematic Apperception Test (TAT) consists of a series of pictures derived from paintings, drawings, and magazine illustrations. Although the pictures are more ambiguous than most photographs, they are less ambiguous than the Rorschach inkblots. Respondents are asked to describe what is going on in each scene, what has led up to the current situation, what the characters are thinking and feeling, and what the outcome of the situation will be. The stories are analyzed for recurrent themes that are assumed to reflect important aspects of the respondent's personality. These might include the kinds of relationships depicted in the stories, the types of motives and feelings that are attributed to the characters, whether positive or negative outcomes occur, and factors that produce such outcomes, such as personal weaknesses or forces in the environment.

The TAT, like the Rorschach, has the problem of nonstandardized or subjective interpretation of responses, which can result in different interpretations of the same stories. Since not everyone can be right, the possibility of erroneous interpretations is obvious. Where specific systems have been developed to score stories, the TAT has proven to be a useful and valid test (Atkinson, 1958). As discussed in Chapter 9 (p. 401), this method is used by researchers to measure motivational variables such as the needs for achievement, affiliation, and power. The TAT appears to provide a more valid measure of these needs than do objective self-report measures of the same motives, showing stronger relations with motivated behavior (Ferguson, 2000; McClelland, 1988). Despite such exceptions, however, objective measures of personality have generally been found to have better reliability and validity than projective measures (Nezami & Butcher, 2000; Groth-Marnat, 1999).

Personality Theory and Personality Assessment

> 41. What kinds of personality measures are favored within the various perspectives?

Personality assessment is intimately related to theory. Theories provide us with a framework that specifies how thoughts, feelings, and bodily processes relate to one another and to behavior. Assessment provides tools for measuring personality variables and testing the theory. A clinician's or researcher's theoretical perspective therefore influences which assessment approach he or she is likely to use.

Projective techniques are favored by psychodynamic theorists who believe that people's responses to tests like the Rorschach and TAT reveal unconscious processes. Humanistic theorists favor self-report measures of the self-concept and personal aspirations (Wylie, 1989). Social cognitive researchers use behavioral assessments and ask people to rate their expectations about what will happen in the future and how well they will do in particular situations. Remote behavior sampling is also useful in studying interactions between the person and the situation. Paper-and-pencil inventories like the MMPI and the NEO-PI are favored by trait theorists who want to measure specific personality traits and by behavior geneticists who want to estimate genetic contributions to traits through twin or adoption studies. Researchers interested in biological processes that underlie personality functioning, such as emotional reactivity or brain processes, use physiological measures. For example, our *Research Close-Up* described the measurement of electrical activity as the brain processed psychodynamically meaningful stimuli. All of these assessment methods have their place in studying personality and can help illuminate important aspects of individuality.

▼▼

CHAPTER SUMMARY

What Is Personality?

- The concept of personality arises from observations of individual differences and consistencies in behavior. Personality is the distinctive and relatively enduring ways of thinking, feeling, and acting that characterize a person's responses to life situations. Behaviors attributed to personality are viewed as establishing an individual's personal identity, having an internal cause, and having a meaningful organization and structure.

- Personality theories differ considerably in their conceptions of what personality is and how it functions. Scientifically useful theories organize existing knowledge, allow prediction of future events, and stimulate the discovery of new knowledge.

The Psychodynamic Perspective

- Freud's psychoanalytic theory views personality as an energy system. Personality dynamics involve modifications and exchanges of energy within this system. Mental events may be conscious, preconscious, or unconscious.

- Freud divided the personality into three structures: id, ego, and superego. The id is irrational and seeks immediate instinctual gratification on the basis of the pleasure principle. The ego operates on the reality principle, which requires it to test reality and to mediate between the demands of the id, the superego, and reality. The superego is the moral arm of the personality.

- The dynamics of personality involve a continuous conflict between impulses of the id and counterforces of the ego and superego. When dangerous id impulses threaten to get out of control or when danger from the environment threatens, the result is anxiety. To deal with threat, the ego may develop defense mechanisms, which are used to ward off anxiety and permit instinctual gratification in disguised forms.

- Freud's psychosexual theory of personality development held that adult personality is basically molded by how children deal with instinctual urges and social reality during the oral, anal, and phallic stages.

- Neoanalytic theorists modified and extended Freud's ideas in important ways, stressing social and cultural factors in personality development. Modern object relations theorists focus on the mental representations that people form of themselves, others, and relationships.

The Humanistic Perspective

- Humanistic theories emphasize the subjective experiences of the individual and thus deal with perceptual and cognitive processes. Self-actualization is viewed as an innate positive force that leads people to realize their positive potential if not thwarted by the environment.

- Carl Rogers's theory attaches central importance to the role of the self. Experiences that are incongruous with the established self-concept produce threat and may result in a denial or distortion of reality. Conditional positive regard may re-sult in realistic conditions of worth that can conflict with self-actualization. Rogers described a number of characteristics of the fully functioning person.

- Rogers's theory helped stimulate a great deal of research on the self-concept, including studies on the origins and effects of differences in self-esteem, self-enhancement and self-verification motives, and cultural and gender contributions to the self-concept.

Trait and Biological Perspectives

- Trait theorists try to identify and measure the basic dimensions of personality. They disagree concerning the number of traits needed to adequately describe personality. Cattell suggested 16 basic traits; other theorists insist that as few as 5 may be adequate. Eysenck posits two major dimensions, extraversion and stability. Prediction studies indicate that the larger number of more specific traits may be superior for prediction of behavior in specific situations.

- Traits have not proved to be highly consistent across situations, and they also vary in stability over time. Individuals differ in their self-monitoring tendencies, and this variable influences the amount of cross-situational consistency they exhibit in social situations. Traits interact not only with situations but also with one another, thereby producing inconsistency.

- Biological perspectives on traits focus on differences in the nervous system, the contribution of genetic factors, and the possible role of evolution in the development of universal human traits and ways of perceiving behavior. Studies comparing identical and fraternal twins reared together or apart indicate that genetic factors may account for as much as half of the variance in personality test scores, with individual experiences accounting for the rest. Evolutionary theories of personality attribute some personality dispositions to genetically controlled mechanisms based on natural selection.

- Researchers are exploring relations between personality factors and health. Evidence exists for a Type A personality that is a risk factor in coronary heart disease, a Type C cancer-prone pattern, and for the roles of optimism and conscientiousness in promoting health and longevity.

Social Cognitive Theories

- Social cognitive theories are concerned with how social relationships, learning mechanisms, and cognitive processes jointly contribute to behavior. A key concept is reciprocal determinism, relating to two-way causal relations between personal characteristics, behavior, and the environment.

- Rotter's theory viewed behavior as influenced by expectancies and the reinforcement value of potential outcomes. His concept of locus of control is a generalized belief in the extent to which we can control the outcomes in our life.

- Bandura's concept of self-efficacy relates to our self-perceived ability to carry out the behaviors necessary to achieve goals in a particular situation.

- According to Mischel and Shoda, situational features activate the person's cognitive-affective personality system (CAPS).

The CAPS involves individual differences in encoding strategies, expectancies and beliefs, goals and values, affects, and competencies and self-regulatory processes. Both self-efficacy and self-regulation skills can be enhanced through the application of systematic goal setting procedures.

Personality Assessment

- Methods used by psychologists to assess personality include the interview, behavioral assessment, remote behavior sampling, physiological measures, objective personality scales, and projective tests.

- The major approaches to constructing personality scales are the rational approach, in which items are written on an intuitive basis, and the empirical approach, in which items that discriminate between groups known to differ on the trait of interest are chosen. The MMPI-2 is the best-known test developed with the empirical approach. The NEO-PI, developed via the rational approach, measures individual differences in the Big Five factors.

- Projective tests present ambiguous stimuli to subjects. It is assumed that interpretations of such stimuli give clues to important internal processes. The Rorschach inkblot test and the Thematic Apperception Test are the most commonly used projective tests.

KEY TERMS AND CONCEPTS*

analytic psychology (550)

archetypes (550)

behavioral assessment (576)

behavioral signatures (570)

cognitive-affective personality system (CAPS) (570)

conditions of worth (552)

congruence (551)

defense mechanisms (545)

ego (545)

Electra complex (547)

empirical approach (577)

evolutionary personality theory (560)

factor analysis (556)

fully functioning persons (553)

gender schema (554)

id (544)

internal-external locus of control (566)

Minnesota Multiphasic Personality Inventory (MMPI) (577)

need for positive regard (552)

need for positive self-regard (552)

object relations theories (550)

Oedipus complex (547)

personality (542)

pleasure principle (545)

projective tests (579)

psychic energy (544)

psychosexual stages (546)

rational approach (577)

reality principle (545)

reciprocal determinism (565)

remote behavior sampling (576)

repression (545)

self (551)

self-actualization (551)

self-consistency (551)

self-efficacy (567)

self-enhancement (554)

self-esteem (553)

self-monitoring (562)

self-reinforcement processes (573)

self-verification (553)

social cognitive theory (565)

sublimation (546)

superego (545)

threat (551)

Type A personality (563)

Type C personality (564)

unconditional positive regard (552)

* Each term has been boldfaced in the text on the page indicated in parentheses.

APPLYING YOUR KNOWLEDGE

1. Ted stands before a jewelry store window late at night admiring an expensive watch. His _____ says, "Break the window and snatch it." His _____ replies, "Don't! That would be an evil thing to do, you loser." Finally, his _____ says, "Get a job and you can not only afford to buy the watch, but also stay out of jail."
   a) superego; id; ego
   b) superego; ego; id
   c) id; superego; ego
   d) id; ego; superego

2. Emily's little brother Jack gets into all her things and messes them up, or even destroys them. He also gets more attention from their parents than she does. Emily insists repeatedly that she adores Jack. In fact, she loves him so much that she often carries him about. Emily's behavior likely reflects the defense mechanism of
   a) reaction formation.
   b) displacement.
   c) projection.
   d) sublimation.

3. Sally is a very introverted person. She prefers a quiet, predictable life and is very introspective. According to Eysenck's theory, brain recordings would show that she tends to have
   a) low cortical arousal.
   b) very rapid shifts in electrical activity.
   c) chronically high levels of cortical arousal.
   d) low cortical arousal, but high subcortical arousal.

4. Clint believes that he is a gifted and exceptional student. When he gets to college, he finds that he can earn only average grades. According to Rogers, if Clint is well adjusted, he will _____. If he is maladjusted, he will _____.
   a) adjust his self-concept; blame his professors for giving unfair tests.
   b) alter his self-concept; change his behavior.
   c) seek self-verification; change his self-concept.
   d) develop a negative working model of college; develop self-efficacy.

5. Which research finding would be most damaging to the proposition that personality is inherited?
   a) if newborns showed differences in sociability
   b) if adopted children were more similar to their biological parents than to their adoptive parents
   c) if identical twins were more similar in personality than fraternal twins
   d) if identical twins raised apart were much less similar than identical twins raised together

6. The first time you saw Brent, he was arguing with the professor about a test question. The next time you see him, he is playing intramural basketball. When the referee makes a call against his team, you expect him to begin arguing. Your expectation is most consistent with which personality perspective?
   a) trait
   b) biological
   c) evolutionary
   d) social cognitive

7. A woman tends to be outgoing and assertive at home, but shy and passive in social situations outside the home. Mischel and Shoda's social cognitive theory would attribute this difference to
   a) her self-concept
   b) working models of social relationships
   c) the cognitive-affective personality system
   d) an external locus of control

8. According to the I–E scale, Heathcliffe has an external locus of control. Which of the following statements would he be most likely to make?
   a) "If my luck changed, I could recoup my losses."
   b) "Hard work and perseverence always pays off."
   c) "There's no such thing as luck or chance."
   d) "If everybody dedicates themselves, we can eliminate crime."

9. A psychologist at a mental health center wants test data to help make a diagnostic decision about a client. Which objective test would he most likely choose?
   a) NEO-PI
   b) 16PF
   c) MMPI-2
   d) Thematic Apperception Test

10. During a visit to a psychologist, a child is asked to draw a picture of his family and tell a story about the picture. The psychologist concludes that the child is suffering from feelings of rejection. This assessment approach would best be described as a
    a) personality inventory
    b) projective technique.
    c) behavioral assessment.
    d) remote behavior sampling.

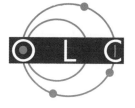

For additional quizzing and a variety of interactive resources, visit the book's Online Learning Center at www.mhhe.com/passer.

PSYCHOLOGICAL DISORDERS

*How come when we talk to God we're praying,
but when God talks to us we're schizophrenic?*
— *Lili Tomlin*

14

14

▼▼▼▼▼▼▼▼▼▼▼▼▼▼▼▼▼▼▼▼▼▼▼▼▼▼▼▼▼▼▼▼▼▼▼▼▼▼▼

Mark has been depressed for several years, but things are even worse now. He feels totally inadequate and inferior. The future looks hopeless, and he cannot sleep at night. During the day, he can barely function, and his moods alternate between deadening depression and intense anxiety. A friend has suggested that he seek professional counseling, but Mark is convinced that he has slipped too deeply into the black hole of despair to ever feel good again. He wonders how long he wants to go on living in his private hell.

▼▼▼▼▼▼▼▼▼▼▼▼▼▼▼▼▼▼▼▼▼▼▼▼▼▼▼▼▼▼▼▼▼▼▼▼▼▼▼

Sarah was walking across campus the first time it happened. Suddenly, her heart began pounding and skipping beats. She grew weak and shaky, began sweating profusely, and felt an indescribable sense of impending doom. She was sure she was either going to die or become insane on the spot. Gathering all her strength, she made it to her dormitory room and began to feel better. Now, after several such incidents while on campus, she is afraid to leave her dorm.

▼▼▼▼▼▼▼▼▼▼▼▼▼▼▼▼▼▼▼▼▼▼▼▼▼▼▼▼▼▼▼▼▼▼▼▼▼▼▼

Unwashed, unshaven, and wearing tattered clothes, Eddie lives in the downtown area of the city. He is frequently seen sitting in a park mumbling to himself. Some nights he eats and sleeps at a shelter, but more often he rolls himself in a filthy blanket and sleeps in an alley. Eddie has been committed to a state mental hospital on more than 10 occasions. In the hospital, he responds quickly to antipsychotic drugs and begins to behave more normally. But soon after being released back into the community, he stops taking his medication and begins his slide back into a deteriorated mental state. Today he is noticed by a social service caseworker, who asks him how he's doing. Staring vacantly into space, he replies, "Life is trouble."

These three people could very well live in your city, on your campus, or in your neighborhood. In December 1999, the Surgeon General of the United States issued a comprehensive report that summarized the results of hundreds of mental health studies (Satcher, 1999). Among the conclusions:

- At any given point in time, 22 percent of the U.S. population suffers from a diagnosable mental disorder.
- Nearly half of all Americans between the ages of 15 and 54 will experience a psychological disorder at some time in their lives.
- Psychological disorders are the second leading cause of disability, after heart disease.
- Medications used to treat anxiety and depression are among the most frequently prescribed drugs in the United States.
- One adolescent commits suicide every 90 seconds.
- Each year, more than a million students withdraw from college because of emotional problems.
- One in four Americans will have a substance abuse disorder during his or her lifetime. Alcohol abuse alone costs the U.S. economy about $117 billion a year.

These cold statistics, startling though they may be, cannot possibly capture the intense suffering that they reflect. They cannot communicate the confusion and terror felt by the schizophrenic patient whose psychological world is disintegrating, the intense personal misery of a depressed person who is sinking into a quagmire of hopelessness, or the suffering endured by the families and friends of those who have psychological disorders.

This chapter is therefore not just about the problems of "someone else." Even if you do not at some point in your life experience a psychological disorder, statistics suggest that a family member, friend, or acquaintance almost surely will.

〉 HISTORICAL PERSPECTIVES ON PSYCHOLOGICAL DISORDERS

The pages of history are filled with accounts of prominent people who suffered from psychological disorders. Tamerlane, the 14th-century Mongol conquerer of much of central Asia and Europe, was particularly fond of building pyramids out of human skulls. One of his creations reportedly contained 40,000 of them. The 18th-century French philosopher Jean-Jacques Rousseau developed marked paranoid symptoms in the latter part of his life and was obsessed with fears of secret enemies. During the time he was composing his requiem, Mozart was convinced he was being poisoned. Abraham Lincoln suffered recurrent bouts of depression and on one occasion was so depressed that he failed to show up for his own wedding (Figure 14.1).

These dysfunctional behaviors did not go unnoticed. Human society has explained and responded to abnormal behavior in different ways at different times, based on its values and assumptions about human life and behavior. At various times, psychological disorders have been viewed as the work of demons, as physical diseases, as the result of psychological conflicts, as learned maladaptive behaviors, and as a product of the ways in which we perceive our world.

FIGURE 14.1 Abraham Lincoln, a victim of severe depression, is among the many famous historical figures who suffered from psychological disorders.

The Demonological View

The belief that abnormal behavior is caused by supernatural forces goes back to the ancient Chinese, Egyptians, and Hebrews, all of whom attributed deviance to the work of the devil. One ancient "treatment" was based on the notion that bizarre behavior reflected an evil spirit's attempt to escape from a person's body. In order to "release" the spirit, a procedure called *trephination* was carried out. A sharp tool was used to chisel a hole in the skull about 2 centimeters in diameter (Figure 14.2). It seems likely that in many cases, this procedure did indeed result in the elimination of abnormal behaviors, as well as all others.

In the Middle Ages, the demonological model of abnormality reigned supreme. Religious dogma held that disturbed people either were possessed involuntarily by the devil or had voluntarily made a pact with the forces of darkness (Figure 14.3). The killing of witches was justified on theological grounds, and various "diagnostic" tests were devised. One test was to bind a woman's hands and feet and throw her into a lake or pond. Based on the notion that impurities float to the surface, a woman who sank and drowned was declared pure (which undoubtedly was of great consolation to the victim). Of course, a woman who floated was in *real* trouble. During the 16th and 17th centuries, it is estimated that more than 100,000 people with psychological disorders were identified as witches, hunted down, and executed.

➤ 1. Describe the demonological perspective on abnormal behavior and its implications for dealing with deviant behavior.

Early Biological Views

About the 5th century B.C., the Greek physician Hippocrates suggested that mental illnesses are diseases just like physical disorders. He insisted that people with disordered behavior were sick, not possessed by evil spirits. Hippocrates believed that the site of illness was the brain, which he saw as the organ of the

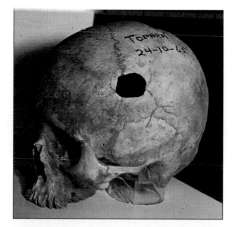

FIGURE 14.2 An early treatment for disordered behavior was trephination, in which a hole was chiseled through the skull to release the evil spirit thought to be causing the abnormal behavior. Some people survived the operation; in this case, healing of the skull is evident around the hole.

FIGURE 14.3 This painting by Francisco Jose Goya reflects the widespread belief that disordered people were possessed by the devil. *Sabbath* portrays the weekly gathering of Satan and the witches he possessed.

➤ 2. What was the historical importance of discovering the cause of general paresis?

➤ 3. What concepts are used by the psychodynamic, behavioral, cognitive, humanistic, and sociocultural perspectives to explain abnormal behavior?

mind. Hippocrates was the first to suggest that a mental or behavioral disorder could be caused by a physical dysfunction, a belief that is now reflected in the biological perspective on psychological disorders.

By the 1800s, attempts were being made to extend medical diagnoses to mental disorders, which were increasingly being viewed as biological disorders. The biological emphasis was given impetus by the discovery that *general paresis*, a disorder characterized in its advanced stages by mental deterioration and bizarre behavior, resulted from massive brain deterioration caused by syphilis. This was a breakthrough, the first demonstration that a psychological disorder was linked to an underlying physical malady.

Psychological Perspectives

In the early 1900s, Sigmund Freud's theory of psychoanalysis emerged as a new way of viewing deviant behavior. Freud was convinced that psychological disorders are caused by unresolved conflicts from childhood that make the person vulnerable to certain kinds of life events. These situations arouse anxiety, and the person tries to cope with the anxiety by using defense mechanisms such as repression, projection, reaction formation, and displacement. Inappropriate or extreme use of the defense mechanisms results in maladaptive patterns of behavior. Some disorders, such as obsessions, phobias, and depression that do not involve a loss of contact with reality were called *neuroses*. Freud thought that in some instances, however, the anxiety caused by these unresolved conflicts may become so great that the person can no longer deal with reality and withdraws from it. These more severe disorders, such as schizophrenia, were called *psychoses*.

The behavioral perspective views disordered behaviors not as a reflection of internal psychodynamics and unconscious conflicts, but rather as learned responses that, like normal behaviors, are learned through classical conditioning, operant conditioning, and modeling. The behavioral perspective has profoundly influenced our understanding of how environmental factors help shape abnormal behavior.

Cognitive theorists emphasize the important role played by people's thoughts and perceptions about themselves and the environment. Aaron Beck and other cognitive researchers have identified maladaptive and self-defeating thought patterns that are linked to a number of different disorders, such as depression and anxiety. From this perspective, the key to understanding many maladaptive behaviors is to isolate the specific thought patterns, beliefs, and attitudes that underlie them.

The humanistic perspective views abnormality as the result of environmental forces that frustrate or pervert people's inherent self-actualization tendencies and search for meaning in life. Conditions of worth imposed by parents and others can result in the development of a negative self-concept and the need to deny or distort important aspects of experience. If experience, including one's inner feelings, become so incongruous with the self-concept that they arouse severe threat, a breakdown or disorganization of the self may occur.

In recent years, the sociocultural perspective has had a major impact on the study of psychological disorders (Lopez & Guarnaccia, 2000; Tanaka-Matsumi & Draguns, 1997). Increasingly, it is apparent that psychological disorders cannot be totally understood without taking into account the cultural context in which they occur and the cultural factors that influence the forms they take.

Today's Vulnerability-Stress Model

Biological, psychological, and environmental/sociocultural factors play important roles in the psychological disorders. How these complex factors interact in a given disorder, or even in a particular individual who exhibits that disorder, can vary. One useful way to think about the causal factors is in terms of the relation between vulnerabilities and stress (Figure 14.4). According to the **vulnerability-stress model,** each and every one of us has some degree of vulnerability (ranging from very low to very high) for developing a given psychological disorder. The **vulnerability,** or predisposition, can have a biological basis, such as our genotype, a brain malfunction, or a hormonal factor. It could also arise from a personality factor, such as low self-esteem or extreme pessimism, or from previous environmental factors, such as poverty or a severe trauma or loss earlier in life. Likewise, cultural factors can create vulnerability to certain kinds of disorders.

But vulnerability is only part of the equation. In most instances, a predisposition creates a disorder only when a **stressor**—some recent or current event that requires a person to cope—combines with a vulnerability to trigger the appearance of the disorder. Thus a person who has a genetic predisposition to depression or who suffered a traumatic loss of parents early in life may be primed to develop a depressive disorder *if* faced with the stress of another loss later in life. The biological, psychological, and environmental levels of analysis have all contributed to the vulnerability-stress model and to our understanding of behavior disorders and how they develop.

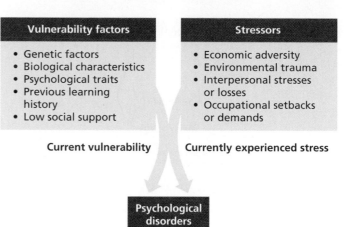

FIGURE 14.4 The vulnerability-stress model views behavior disorders as resulting from an interaction between personal vulnerability factors and life stressors.

➤ 4. How does the vulnerability-stress model illustrate person-situation interactions?

❯ DEFINING AND CLASSIFYING PSYCHOLOGICAL DISORDERS

So far, we have discussed historical and contemporary accounts of abnormal behavior without actually defining what is meant by the term. Defining what is normal and what is abnormal is not as easy as it might at first appear.

What Is "Abnormal"?

Judgments about where the line between normal and abnormal should be drawn differ depending on the time and the culture. In the 1940s, a woman who decided to forsake marriage and children in favor of a career in engineering would have been seen by many segments of society, including some psychologists and psychiatrists, as deviant and possibly in need of psychotherapy. Today most people would regard the woman's choice as a valid one. In certain Hispanic cultures, a woman who loses a loved one exhibits a range of symptoms that would merit a diagnosis of major depression in the United States. However, in Ecuador, she would be viewed not as psychologically disturbed, but as suffering from *susto,* or "soul loss," a normal bereavement pattern that quickly subsides after a mourning ritual designed to help the person deal with the loss (Goleman, 1995).

Abnormality is, in the final analysis, a social construction (Neimeyer & Raskin, 2000). As such, it can be affected by value judgments and political agendas. In the 1840s, for example, a census commissioned by Senator John Calhoun of South Carolina concluded that 1 in every 14 former slaves in the state of Maine "is either an idiot, or lunatic" (Gamwell & Tomes, 1995). In contrast, the census identified almost no insane slaves in the South. Calhoun concluded in an 1845 letter to the Speaker of the House that "the data on insanity . . . is (sic) unimpeachable. From it, our nation must conclude that the abolition of slavery would be to the African a curse rather than a blessing." Medical experts soon defined a new mental disorder called *"drapetomania"* (from the Latin word *drapeta,* fugitive), an obsessive desire for freedom that drove some slaves to flee from captivity. The criteria specified that this diagnosis be applied to any slave who tried more than twice to escape.

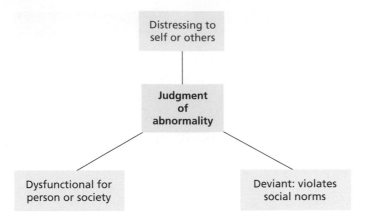

FIGURE 14.5 Whether a behavior is or is not considered abnormal involves a social judgment made on the basis of the "three Ds."

➤ 5. Cite the "three Ds" that typically underlie judgments that behavior is abnormal.

More recently, a spirited political battle was fought over the proposed inclusion of *self-defeating/masochistic personality disorder* in the psychiatric diagnostic system. The diagnosis was to be applied to people who repeatedly involve themselves in hurtful circumstances and relationships. Critics vigorously protested that this label would be applied to many women who remained in abusive relationships, thereby shifting the responsibility from the abuser to the woman's "personality disorder." Following years of debate, the critics prevailed and this category was not included in the diagnostic system despite many clinicians' reports that they frequently encounter such individuals in their practices (Widiger, 1995).

Despite the arbitrariness introduced by time, place, and value judgments, there are certain criteria that seem to govern decisions about abnormality. These are sometimes referred to as the "three Ds," and one or more of them seem to apply to virtually any behavior regarded as abnormal (Figure 14.5).

First, we are likely to label behaviors as abnormal if they are intensely *distressing* to the individual. People may be viewed as having a psychological disorder when they are inordinately anxious, depressed, dissatisfied, or otherwise seriously upset about themselves or about life circumstances, particularly if they seem to have little control over these reactions. On the other hand, personal distress is neither necessary nor sufficient to define abnormality. For example, some seriously disturbed mental patients are so out of contact with reality that they seem to experience little distress, and yet their bizarre behaviors are considered very abnormal. Conversely, almost all of us experience suffering as a part of our lives. Nonetheless, when such suffering is disproportionate to the situation, or too long-lasting, it may be viewed as abnormal.

Most behaviors that are labeled as abnormal are *dysfunctional* either for the individual or for society. Behaviors that interfere with a person's ability to work and to experience satisfying relationships with other people are likely to be seen as maladaptive and self-defeating, especially if an individual seems unable to control such behaviors. Sometimes, behaviors are labeled as abnormal because they interfere with the well-being of society. But even here, the standards are not cut and dried. For example, is a political terrorist who plants a bomb in a public market psychologically disturbed, a criminal, or a patriot?

The third criterion for abnormality is based on society's judgments of the *deviance* of a given behavior. As we have seen, conduct within every society is regulated by norms, behavioral rules that specify how people are expected to behave. Some norms are explicitly codified as laws, and violation of these norms defines criminal behavior. Other norms, however, are far less explicit. For example, it is generally expected in our culture that one should not carry on animated conversations with people who are not present and should not face the rear of the elevator staring intently into the eyes of one's fellow passengers. (You might try engaging in the latter behavior if you want to see an elevator empty out quickly.) People are likely to be viewed as psychologically disturbed if they violate these unstated norms, especially if the violations cannot be attributed to environmental causes and if they make others uncomfortable.

To summarize, both personal and social judgments of behavior enter into judgments of what is abnormal. Nonetheless, as a working definition, we might define **abnormal behavior** as *behavior that is personally distressful, personally dysfunctional, and/or so culturally deviant that other people judge it to be inappropriate or maladaptive.*

Diagnosing Psychological Disorders

Classification is a necessary first step toward introducing order into discussions of the nature, causes, and treatment of psychological disorders. To be scientifically and practically useful, however, a classification system has to meet standards of reliability and validity. **Reliability** means that clinicians using the system should show high levels of agreement in their diagnostic decisions. Because professionals with different types and amounts of training—including psychologists, psychiatrists, social workers, and general physicians—make diagnostic decisions, the system should be couched in terms of observable behaviors that can be reliably detected and should minimize subjective judgments (American Psychiatric Association, 1994). **Validity** means that the diagnostic categories should accurately capture the essential features of the various disorders. Thus if research and clinical observations show that a given disorder has four behavioral characteristics, the diagnostic category for that disorder should also have those four features. Moreover, the diagnostic categories should allow us to differentiate one psychological disorder from another.

The *Diagnostic and Statistical Manual of Mental Disorders, Fourth Edition* (DSM-IV), is the most widely used diagnostic classification system in the United States. For each of its more than 350 diagnostic categories, DSM-IV contains detailed lists of observable behaviors that must be present in order for a diagnosis to be made. Table 14.1 samples the range of major DSM-IV categories.

The DSM-IV allows diagnostic information to be represented along five dimensions, or axes, that take both the person and his or her life situation into account. Axis I, the primary diagnosis, represents the person's primary clinical symptoms. Axis II reflects long-standing personality or developmental disorders, such as ingrained, inflexible aspects of personality, that could influence the

➤ 6. What is meant by reliability and validity of diagnostic classification systems?

➤ 7. How do the five axes of DSM-IV describe an individual's abnormal behavior and factors that may contribute to it or predict its future course?

| TABLE 14.1 | A SAMPLE OF MAJOR DIAGNOSTIC CATEGORIES IN DSM-IV |

1. Anxiety disorders
   Intense, frequent, or inappropriate anxiety, but no loss of reality contact; includes phobias, generalized anxiety reactions, panic disorders, obsessive-compulsive disorders and posttraumatic stress disorders

2. Mood (affective) disorders
   Marked disturbances of mood, including depression and mania (extreme elation and excitement)

3. Somatoform disorders
   Physical symptoms, such as blindness, paralysis, or pain, that have no physical basis and are assumed to be caused by psychological factors; also, excessive preoccupations and worry about health (hypochondriasis)

4. Dissociative disorders
   Psychologically caused problems of consciousness and self-identification, including amnesia and multiple personalities (dissociative identity disorder)

5. Schizophrenic and other psychotic disorders
   Severe disorders of thinking, perception, and emotion that involve loss of contact with reality and disordered behavior

6. Substance abuse disorders
   Personal and social problems associated with the use of psychoactive substances, such as alcohol, heroin, or other drugs

7. Sexual and gender identity disorders
   Inability to function sexually or enjoy sexuality (sexual dysfunctions); deviant sexual behaviors, such as child molestation and arousal by inappropriate objects (fetishes); strong discomfort with one's gender accompanied by the desire to be a member of the other sex

8. Eating disorders
   Includes anorexia nervosa (self-starvation) and bulimia nervosa (patterns of bingeing and purging)

9. Personality disorders
   Rigid, stable, and maladaptive personality patterns, such as antisocial, dependent, paranoid, and narcissistic disorders

Source: Derived from American Psychiatric Association, 1994.

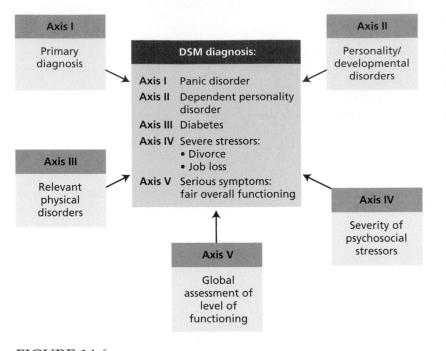

FIGURE 14.6 The DSM-IV uses a five-axis system to arrive at a comprehensive diagnosis that takes into account not only deviant behaviors, but also other relevant personal and environmental factors.

person's behavior and response to treatment. Axis III notes any physical conditions that might be relevant, such as high blood pressure. Reflecting the vulnerability-stress model discussed earlier, the clinician also rates the intensity of environmental stressors in the person's recent life on Axis IV, and the person's coping resources as reflected in recent adaptive functioning on Axis V. Figure 14.6 shows how the axes are represented in a DSM-IV diagnosis.

Although the reliability and validity of DSM-IV have not yet been thoroughly evaluated, it appears that the highly specific behavioral criteria in the DSM-IV categories have improved Axis I reliability over earlier versions (Widiger, 1995). On the other hand, the criteria are sometimes so strict that many people don't fit into the categories. Moreover, debate continues over the validity of some of the categories. Especially problematic are the Axis II personality disorders, which overlap extensively with one another and with Axis I disorders (Widiger et al., 2000). As many as half of all people who receive a specific personality disorder diagnosis could easily be classified differently (Morey, 1988). Such overlap reduces both reliability and validity. Although this state of affairs has led some to call for a complete revision of the personality disorder categories and, perhaps, their abandonment (Trull & McCrae, 1994), many other categories of DSM-IV appear to be diagnostically useful and reliable. Nonetheless, we may expect to see another revision in coming years.

Critical Issues in Diagnostic Labeling

Beyond their clinical and scientific utility, diagnostic labels can have important personal, social, and legal consequences for people who receive them.

Social and Personal Implications

➤ 8. What effects do psychiatric labeling have on social- and self-perceptions?

Once a diagnostic label is attached to a person, it becomes all too easy to accept the label as an accurate description of the *individual* rather than of the *behavior*. It then becomes difficult to look at the person's behavior objectively, without preconceptions about how he or she will act. It is also likely to affect how we will interact with that person. Consider for a moment what your reaction might be if you were informed that your new next-door neighbor had been diagnosed as a "sexual psychopath." It would be surprising indeed if this label did not influence your perceptions and interactions with that person, whether or not the label was accurate.

In one famous study, eight normal individuals, including psychologist David Rosenhan (1973), got themselves admitted to mental hospitals in five different states by stating that they had been hearing voices. Understandably, they received diagnoses of schizophrenia. Once in the hospitals, however, they acted completely normal. Although the false patients never exhibited any abnormal behavior, when they were discharged after intervals ranging from 7 to 52 days, they typically received the diagnosis, "schizophrenia, in remission." This label means that the disorder was still presumed to be present, though not currently active. Once attached, diagnostic labels are not easily shed.

Diagnostic labels may also play a role in creating or worsening psychological disorders (Wright, 1991). When people become aware that a psychiatric label has been applied to them, they may accept the new identity implied by the label and develop the expected role and outlook. Because psychiatric labels often carry degrading and stigmatizing implications, the effects on morale and self-esteem can be devastating. Moreover, a person may despair of ever changing, and therefore give up attempts to deal with life circumstances that may be responsible for the problems. In this way, the expectations that accompany a label may result in a self-fulfilling prophecy, in which expectation becomes reality.

Legal Consequences

Psychiatric diagnoses also have important legal consequences. Individuals judged to be dangerous to themselves or others may be involuntarily committed to mental institutions under certain circumstances. When so committed, they lose some of their civil rights and may be detained indefinitely if their behavior does not improve.

The law tries to take into account the mental status of individuals accused of crimes. Two particularly important legal concepts are competency and insanity. **Competency** refers to a defendant's state of mind at the time of a judicial hearing (not at the time the crime was committed). A defendant judged to be too disturbed to understand the nature of the legal proceedings may be labeled as *not competent to stand trial* and institutionalized until judged competent.

Insanity, a far more controversial issue, relates to the presumed state of mind of the defendant at the time the crime was committed. Defendants may be declared *not guilty by reason of insanity* if they are judged to have been so severely impaired during the commission of a crime that they lacked the capacity either to appreciate the wrongfulness of their acts or to control their conduct. It is important to understand that insanity is a legal term, not a psychological one.

Despite the fact that the insanity plea is entered only once in every 500 felony cases and that in 85 percent of those cases the prosecution agrees that the person was indeed insane, the insanity defense has long been hotly debated. The acquittal of John Hinckley, who attempted to assassinate President Ronald Reagan in 1981, created an uproar (Figure 14.7). Twelve years later, Jeffrey Dahmer, accused of the grisly murders and mutilations of 15 men, also entered a plea of not guilty by reason of insanity. The defense contended that no sane person could have committed the shocking acts that Dahmer freely admitted, which included storing and eating victims' body parts. As you saw in Chapter 13 (p. 578), psychological test results also indicated severe psychological disturbance. Yet the insanity plea was rejected, and Dahmer was found guilty.

Both defendants clearly had serious mental disorders. Why the different verdicts? An important change had occurred in the legal requirement for proving sanity or insanity. At the time Hinckley was tried, the law required the prosecution to prove that Hinckley was *sane*. They could not do so beyond a reasonable doubt, and Hinckley was acquitted. Partly in response to Hinckley's acquittal, the law was changed, and the burden of proof was shifted to the defense. Dahmer's attorneys were not able to prove that their client was *insane* at the time he committed his crimes, so Dahmer was convicted of murder.

To balance punishment for crimes with concern about a defendant's mental status and possible need for treatment, Canada and an increasing number of U.S. jurisdictions have adopted a verdict of *guilty but mentally ill*. This verdict imposes a normal sentence for a crime but sends the defendant to a mental hospital for treatment. If the defendant is considered recovered before the end of the sentence, he or she is sent to prison to serve the remainder of the sentence.

➤ 9. Differentiate between the legal concepts of competency and insanity. What is the current burden of proof in insanity hearings?

FIGURE 14.7 Both John Hinckley (top), who shot Ronald Reagan and his press secretary, and the mass murderer Jeffrey Dahmer (bottom) pleaded not guilty by reason of insanity. Hinckley won his plea, whereas Dahmer's was rejected. These cases focused considerable attention on the insanity defense.

"Do I Have That Disorder?"

Having considered issues of diagnosis, we now move to a description of the disorders themselves. First, however, you should be aware of a common phenomenon that in medical education is termed "medical students' disease." When people read descriptions of disorders, whether physical or psychological, they often see some of those symptoms or characteristics in themselves. In the case of psychological disorders, this is quite understandable. We all experience problems in living at various times, and we may react to them in ways that bear similarities to the behaviors you will be reading about. Seeing such a similarity does not necessarily mean that you have the disorder. On the other hand, if you find that maladaptive behaviors like those described in this chapter are interfering with your happiness or personal effectiveness, then you should not hesitate to seek help in changing these behaviors. Some guidelines for doing so are presented in Chapter 15 (p. 662).

〉 ANXIETY DISORDERS

All of us have experienced anxiety, the state of tension and apprehension that is a natural response to perceived threat. But in **anxiety disorders,** the frequency and intensity of anxiety responses are out of proportion to the situations that trigger them, and the anxiety interferes with daily life.

 10. Describe the three components of anxiety.

Anxiety responses have three components: (1) a *cognitive* component, including subjective feelings of apprehension, a sense of impending danger, and a feeling of inability to cope; (2) *physiological* responses, including increased heart rate and blood pressure, muscle tension, rapid breathing, nausea, dry mouth, diarrhea, and frequent urination; and (3) *behavioral* responses, such as avoidance of certain situations and impaired task performance (Noyes & Hoehn-Saric, 1999).

Anxiety disorders take a number of different forms, including phobic disorders, generalized anxiety disorders, panic disorders, posttraumatic stress disorders, and obsessive-compulsive disorders. Large-scale population studies indicate that anxiety disorders are the most prevalent of all psychological disorders in the United States, affecting 17.6 percent of Americans during their lifetimes. (Kessler et al., 1994; Robins & Regier, 1991; Satcher, 1999). Figure 14.8 shows lifetime prevalence rates for the various anxiety disorders. All of the anxiety disorders tend to occur more frequently in females than in males.

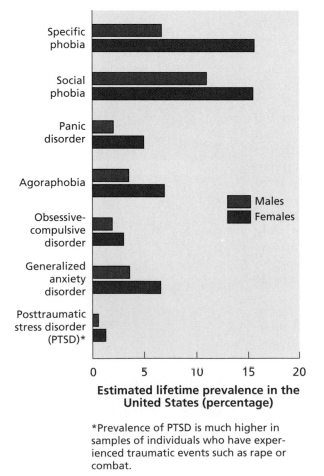

Males
Females

0   5   10   15   20

Estimated lifetime prevalence in the United States (percentage)

*Prevalence of PTSD is much higher in samples of individuals who have experienced traumatic events such as rape or combat.

FIGURE 14.8 Lifetime prevalence rates for the anxiety disorders in men and women. All occur more frequently in women.
Based on data from Kessler et al., 1994; Robins & Regier, 1991.

Phobic Disorder

Laura's fear of the water dates back to her childhood. She recalled her mother, who had a similar fear, vividly describing an incident in which one of her own childhood friends had drowned at a school picnic. Laura's fear of water intensified after she breathed in some water and panicked when she was "dunked" by a playmate at a swimming pool. She floundered and was sure she was going to drown until a lifeguard pulled her to safety. For the past 15 years, Laura has avoided outings that would take her into deep water. Although she knows how to swim, she dreads the thought of going swimming. She makes excuses to avoid boating trips and once turned down a free trip to Hawaii because of the anxiety she knew she would experience flying over the ocean.

Phobias are strong and irrational fears of certain objects or situations. The word was originally derived from *Phobos*, the Greek god of fear, whose likeness was painted on masks and shields to frighten enemies in battle. Today's phobic fights a different kind of battle, with fears of a less realistic but no less intense nature.

People with phobias realize that their fears are out of all proportion to the danger involved, but they feel helpless to deal with these fears. Instead, they make strenuous efforts to avoid the phobic situation or object. Among the most common phobias in Western society are **agoraphobia,** a fear of open and public places, **social phobias** (excessive fear of situations in which the person might be evaluated and possibly embarrassed), and **specific phobias;** such as fears of dogs, snakes, spiders, airplanes, elevators, enclosed spaces, water, injections, illness, or death. Phobias can develop at any point in life, but many of them develop during childhood, adolescence, and early adulthood. Once phobias develop, they seldom go away on their own, and they may broaden and intensify over time.

The degree of impairment produced by a phobia depends in part on how often the phobic stimulus is encountered in the individual's normal round of activities. For example, fear of flying is a common phobia that occurs in some 25 million Americans (Bruce & Sanderson, 1998). An airplane phobia may be a relatively minor inconvenience for a person who never needs to travel by air, but it may be a debilitating condition for an executive who has to travel frequently. Some people simply refuse to fly even at great personal inconvenience (Figure 14.9).

Generalized Anxiety Disorder

> On initial assessment, Dr. J, who is manifestly tense, complains of never being entirely free of a sense of impending disaster, although he cannot further specify the nature of this anticipated catastrophe. He notes a number of signs of autonomic hyperarousal that he experiences on virtually a daily basis, emphasizing in particular excessive sweating, which has become a source of embarrassment. He is medicating himself for persistent attacks of diarrhea. He complains of an inability to attain a refreshing level of sleep even on those rare occasions when he can count on a few uninterrupted off-duty hours, and his very few waking "leisure" hours are filled with restless irritability. (Carson et al., 1988, p. 195)

Dr. J is suffering from a **generalized anxiety disorder,** a chronic state of diffuse, or "free-floating," anxiety that is not attached to specific situations or objects. In such cases, the anxiety may last for months on end with the signs almost continuously present. Emotionally, Dr. J feels jittery, tense, and constantly on edge. Cognitively, he expects something awful to happen but doesn't know what. Physically, he experiences a mild chronic emergency reaction. Dr. J sweats, his stomach is usually upset, he has diarrhea, and so forth.

As we might expect, this disorder can markedly interfere with daily functioning. The person may find it hard to concentrate, to make decisions, and to remember commitments. One large-scale study found that 5 percent of people between the ages of 15 and 45 reported having experienced the symptoms of generalized anxiety disorder. Onset tends to occur in childhood and adolescence (Wittchen et al., 1994).

Panic Disorder

In contrast to generalized anxiety disorder, which involves chronic tension and anxiety, **panic disorders** occur suddenly and unpredictably, and they are much more intense. The symptoms of panic attacks can be terrifying. As in the case of Sarah, the college student described at the beginning of the chapter, it is not unusual for victims to feel that they are dying (Ballenger, 2000).

> ➤ 11. What is a phobia, and what are the three major types of phobias?

FIGURE 14.9 Many people suffer from a fear of flying. One famous figure is John Madden, formerly a professional football coach and currently a television analyst, who travels to his weekly assignments (sometimes separated by thousands of miles) in this specially equipped motor home.

> ➤ 12. How does a generalized anxiety disorder differ from a phobic disorder? From a panic disorder?

> ➤ 13. What occurs in a panic disorder, and how do these experiences frequently result in development of agoraphobia?

In most cases, panic attacks occur out of the blue and in the absence of any identifiable stimulus. It is this unpredictable quality that makes panic attacks so mysterious and terrifying to their victims. Many people with panic attacks develop *agoraphobia*, a fear of public places, because of their fear that they will have an attack in public. In extreme cases, they may fear leaving the familiar setting of the home, and agoraphobics have been known to be housebound for years at a time because of their "fear of fear" (Milrod et al., 1997). This case shows the development of an agoraphobic pattern:

> As the attacks continued, Ms. Watson began to dread going out of the house alone. She feared that while out she would have an attack and would be stranded and helpless. She stopped riding the subway to work out of fear she might be trapped in a car between stops when an attack struck, preferring instead to walk the 20 blocks between her home and work. Social and recreational activities, previously frequent and enjoyed, were severely curtailed because an attack might occur. (Adapted from Spitzer et al., 1983)

Panic disorders with or without agoraphobia tend to appear in late adolescence or early adulthood and affect about 3.5 percent of the population (Kessler et al., 1994). Even more common are occasional panic attacks. In one survey of Canadian students, 34 percent reported having had at least one unexpected panic attack within the previous year, usually during periods of extreme stress (Norton et al., 1985). Under DSM-IV criteria, these students would *not* be diagnosed as having a panic disorder unless they developed an inordinate fear of having future attacks.

Obsessive-Compulsive Disorder

A thirty-eight-year-old mother of one child had been obsessed by fears of contamination during her entire adult life. Literally hundreds of times a day, thoughts of being infected by germs would occur to her. Once she began to think that either she or her child might become infected, she could not dismiss the thought. The constant concern about infection resulted in a series of washing and cleaning rituals that took up most of her day. Her child was confined to one room only, which the woman tried to keep entirely free of germs by scrubbing it—floor to ceiling—several times a day. Moreover, she opened and closed all doors with her feet, in order to avoid contaminating her own hands. (Rachman & Hodgson, 1980)

➤ 14. Differentiate between obsessions and compulsions. How are they typically related to one another?

This woman was diagnosed as having an **obsessive-compulsive disorder.** Such disorders usually consist of two components, one cognitive, the other behavioral, although either can occur alone. **Obsessions** are repetitive and unwelcome thoughts, images, or impulses that invade consciousness, are often abhorrent to the person, and are very difficult to dismiss or control. This mother was tyrannized by thoughts and images of contamination. **Compulsions** are repetitive behavioral responses—like the woman's cleaning rituals—that can be resisted only with great difficulty. Compulsions are often responses to obsessive thoughts and function to reduce the anxiety associated with the thoughts (De Silva & Rachman, 1998). Once the mother had performed her compulsive cleanliness acts, she was relatively free from anxiety, at least until the thoughts of contamination intruded once more.

Behavioral compulsions are extremely difficult to control. They often involve checking things repeatedly, cleaning, and repeating tasks endlessly. If the person does not perform the compulsive act, he or she may experience tremendous anxiety, perhaps even a panic attack. Like phobic avoidance responses, compulsions appear to reduce anxiety and to be strengthened through a process of negative reinforcement because they allow a person to avoid anxiety (Jenicke, 1998).

Recent studies have found the lifetime prevalence of obsessive-compulsive disorder in the United States and Canada to be about 2.5 per 100 people. Onset typically occurs in the twenties (Robins & Regier, 1991; Weissman et al., 1994).

Posttraumatic Stress Disorder

People who have been exposed to traumatic life events may experience a **posttraumatic stress disorder (PTSD).** Four major symptoms commonly occur in this anxiety disorder:

➤ 15. Describe the four common features of PTSD.

- The person experiences severe symptoms of anxiety, arousal, and distress that were not present before the trauma;

- The person relives the trauma recurrently in "flashbacks," in dreams, and in fantasy (Pitman et al., 2000);

- The person becomes numb to the world and avoids stimuli that remind him or her of the trauma; and

- In instances where others are killed, the person may experience extreme guilt about surviving the catastrophe when others did not (Valent, 2000).

The PTSD category arose in part from studies of soldiers who had been subjected to the horrors of war. One study found the incidence of PTSD to be seven times more likely for Vietnam veterans who spent significant time in combat and were wounded than in other veterans (Centers for Disease Control, 1988). Yet the catastrophe that brings about a posttraumatic stress reaction need not be experienced by a mass of people, as occurs in wars and natural disasters; it can be an individual experience.

The trauma of being raped is experienced by many women, and its aftermath can be nearly as traumatic as the incident itself. For months or even years after the rape, victims may feel nervous and may fear retaliation by the rapist. They may experience sudden flashbacks or nightmares that force them to relive the traumatic experience. Many victims change their place of residence but continue to have nightmares and to be frightened when they are alone, outdoors, or in crowds. Victims frequently report decreased enjoyment of sexual activity long after the rape, even when they are still capable of having orgasms (Burgess & Holmstrom, 1974; Holmes & St. Lawrence, 1983; Masters et al., 1988). Figure 14.10 shows the incidence of PTSD symptoms reported by victims during the three months following the rape (Foa et al., 1995). In another long-term followup of rape victims, one quarter of the women felt that they had not recovered psychologically at the end of a six-year period following the rape (Meyer & Taylor, 1986). Moreover, women who had been subjected to earlier physical abuse exhibited a post-rape prevalence of PTSD symptoms three times higher than in a nonabused comparison group (Watson et al., 1997). In general, traumas caused by human actions, such as war, rape, and torture, tend to precipitate more severe PTSD reactions than do natural disasters, such as hurricanes or earthquakes (O'Donohue & Elliot, 1992).

The psychological wreckage caused by PTSD may increase vulnerability to the later development of other disorders. One study found that women who experienced PSTD had double the risk of developing a depressive disorder and three times the risk of developing alcohol-related problems in the future (Bresalau et al., 1997). Such findings highlight the importance of prompt posttrauma intervention to prevent the development of PTSD (Yule, 2000).

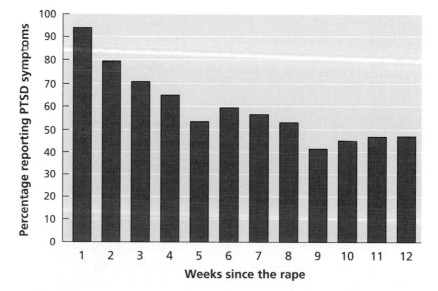

FIGURE 14.10 Symptoms of PTSD reported over three months following being raped. Nearly half of the women continue to be diagnosed with PTSD three months after the traumatic event.

Data from Foa et al., 1995.

Causal Factors in the Anxiety Disorders

Anxiety is a complex phenomenon having biological, psychological, and environmental causes. Within the vulnerability-stress model presented earlier, any of these factors can create predispositions to respond to stressors with an anxiety disorder.

Biological Factors

➤ 16. What evidence is there for a genetic predisposition to anxiety disorders? What form might the vulnerability factor take?

Genetic factors may create a vulnerability to anxiety disorders (Blackwood, 2000). David Barlow (1988) suggests that such vulnerability may take the form of an autonomic nervous system that overreacts to perceived threat, creating high levels of physiological arousal. Hereditary factors may cause overreactivity of neurotransmitter systems involved in emotional responses (Mineka et al., 1998).

Studies of identical and fraternal twins raised together and apart provide important clues to the importance of genetic causes. Identical twins are far more similar to one another in scores on psychological tests that measure anxiety than are fraternal twins, even when the identical twins were separated early in life and raised in different families. Heritability estimates indicate that about 50 to 60 percent of the variation in anxiety scores can be attributed to genetic factors, with the remaining 40 to 50 percent attributable to individuals' life experiences (Blackwood, 2000; Tellegen et al., 1988). Where clinical levels of anxiety are concerned, identical twins have a concordance rate (if one twin has it, so does the other) of about 40 percent for anxiety disorders, compared with a 4 percent concordance rate in fraternal twins (Carey & Gottesman, 1981). Although such findings indicate a genetic predisposition, the concordance rate even in identical twins is far from 100 percent, indicating the importance of psychological and environmental factors.

➤ 17. How might GABA be related to anxiety disorders?

The search for biological processes associated with the anxiety disorders has focused on several neurotransmitters in the brain. One such transmitter is *GABA (gama-aminobutyric acid)*. GABA is an inhibitory transmitter that reduces neural activity in the amygdala and other brain structures that stimulate physiological arousal. Some researchers believe that abnormally low levels of inhibitory GABA activity in these arousal areas may cause some people to have highly reactive nervous systems that quickly produce anxiety responses in response to stressors (Bremner, 2000). Such people could also be more susceptible to classically conditioned phobias because they already have a strong unconditioned arousal response in place, ready to be conditioned to new stimuli. The fact that certain drugs reduce anxiety by increasing GABA activity offers support for this theory, but other transmitter systems are probably also involved (Davidson, 1999).

➤ 18. What factors might produce the sex difference seen in the prevalence of the anxiety disorders?

As noted earlier, women exhibit anxiety disorders more often than men do (Leibenluft, 1999). In a large epidemiological study of adolescents, Peter Lewinsohn and coworkers (1998) found that this sex difference emerges as early as 7 years of age. The contributing role of biological factors is suggested by Lewinsohn's finding that even when 11 psychosocial factors (including negative life events, self-esteem, and social support) that differentiated males from females were controlled for statistically, the large sex difference remained.

Such findings suggest a sex-linked biological predisposition for anxiety disorders, but social conditions that give women less power and personal control may also contribute (Kessler et al., 1994). As in other instances of sex differences, it seems likely that biological, psychological, and environmental factors combine in complex ways.

Finally, we should recall the possible role of evolutionary factors in predisposing people to fear certain types of stimuli that might have had survival significance in the past, such as snakes, spiders, storms, and heights. As discussed in Chapter 6, evolutionary theorists believe that **biological preparedness** makes it easier for us to learn to fear certain stimuli and may explain why phobias seem to center on certain classes of "primal" stimuli and not on more dangerous modern ones, such as guns and electrical power stations (Oehman, 1993).

Psychological Factors

Psychodynamic theories. Anxiety is a central feature of psychoanalytic conceptions of abnormal behavior. According to Freud, **neurotic anxiety** occurs when unacceptable impulses threaten to overwhelm the ego's defenses and explode into action. How the ego's defense mechanisms deal with neurotic anxiety determines the form of the anxiety disorder. Freud believed that in phobic disorders, neurotic anxiety is displaced onto some external stimulus that has symbolic significance in relation to the underlying conflict. For example, in one of Freud's most celebrated cases, a little boy named Hans suddenly developed a fear of horses and the possibility of being bitten. To Freud, the phobia resulted from the boy's unresolved Oedipus complex. The powerful horse represented Hans's father, and the fear of being bitten symbolized Hans's unconscious fear of being castrated by his father if he acted on his sexual desire for his mother.

Obsessions and compulsions are also ways of handling anxiety. According to Freud, the obsession is symbolically related to, but less terrifying than, the underlying impulse. A compulsion is a way of "taking back," or undoing, one's unacceptable urges, as when obsessive thoughts about dirt and compulsive handwashing are used to deal with one's "dirty" sexual impulses. Finally, generalized anxiety and panic attacks are thought to occur when one's defenses are not strong enough to control or contain anxiety but are strong enough to hide the underlying conflict.

Although psychoanalytic theory has stimulated considerable thinking about the causes and treatment of the anxiety disorders, the notion of anxiety disorder symptoms as symbolic expressions of underlying conflicts has not received much research support (Fisher & Greenberg, 1996). Cognitive and behavioral approaches are far more influential today in guiding research on anxiety disorders and their treatment.

> ➤ 19. How does psychoanalytic theory explain the development of anxiety disorders?

Cognitive factors.   Cognitive theorists stress the role of maladaptive thought patterns and beliefs in anxiety disorders. Anxiety-disordered people "catastrophize" about demands and magnify them into threats. They anticipate that the worst will happen and feel powerless to cope effectively (Clark, 1988; Mineka et al., 1998). Edna Foa and coworkers (1996) asked social phobics (1) how likely it was that they would embarrass themselves in a social situation and (2) how serious and costly the consequences of performing poorly would be for them. Compared with nonphobics, the social phobics judged both the likelihood and the costs to be much higher. Interestingly, these judgments were restricted to social situations. The social phobics did not differ in their likelihood and cost judgments in nonsocial situations.

Cognitive processes also play an important role in panic disorders. According to David Barlow (1991, 1997), panic attacks are triggered by exaggerated misinterpretations of normal anxiety symptoms, such as heart palpitations, dizziness, and breathlessness. The panic-disordered person appraises these as signs that a heart attack or a psychological loss of control is about to occur, and these catastrophic appraisals create even more anxiety until the process spirals out of control, producing a full-blown state of panic (Figure 14.11). Helping panic patients to replace such "mortal danger" appraisals with more benign interpretations of their bodily symptoms (e.g., "It's only a bit of anxiety, not a heart attack") results in a marked reduction in panic attacks (Barlow, 1997; Craske, 1999).

> ➤ 20. How do cognitive factors enter into the anxiety disorders, particularly panic disorder? What research supports these explanations?

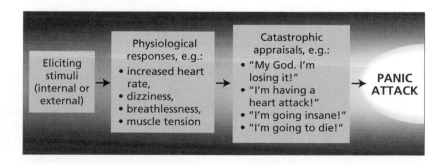

FIGURE 14.11   Current cognitive explanations of panic attacks depict a process in which normal manifestations of anxiety are appraised catastrophically, ultimately resulting in a full-blown panic attack.

➤ 21. Explain anxiety disorders in terms of classical conditioning, negative reinforcement, and observational learning.

Anxiety as a learned response.   From the behavioral perspective, anxiety disorders result from emotional conditioning (Öhman, 2000; Rachman, 1998). Some fears are acquired as a result of traumatic experiences that produce a classically conditioned fear response. For example, a person who has a traumatic fall from a high place may develop a fear of heights (a CR) because the high place (CS) was associated with the pain and trauma of the fall (UCS).

Classical conditioning cannot be the whole story, however, because many phobics have never had a traumatic experience with the phobic object or situation that they now fear (Bruce & Sanderson, 1998; Menzies & Clarke, 1995). Most people who are afraid to fly have never been in an air crash themselves. So how did they learn their fear? Clearly, phobias can also be acquired through observational learning. For example, televised images of air crashes can evoke high levels of fear in some people. Yet most people do not develop phobias under these conditions, so there must be still more going on. It may be that biological dispositions and cognitive factors help determine whether a person develops a phobia from observing a traumatic event. Thus if a person has a biological disposition toward intense fear and if the person comes to believe that "sooner or later, the same thing will happen to me," the likelihood of developing a phobia on the basis of observational learning may increase.

Once anxiety is learned, it may be triggered either by cues from the environment or by internal cues, such as thoughts and images (Pitman et al., 2000). In the case of phobic reactions, the cues tend to be external ones relating to the feared object or situation. In panic disorders, on the other hand, the anxiety-arousing cues tend to be internal ones, such as bodily sensations (e.g., one's heart rate) or mental images (such as the image of collapsing and having a seizure in a public place) (Craske, 1999).

People are highly motivated to avoid or escape anxiety because it is such an unpleasant emotional state. Here is where operant conditioning enters the picture. Behaviors that are successful in reducing anxiety, such as compulsions or phobic avoidance responses, are strengthened through a process of negative reinforcement. Thus the obsessive-compulsive mother's scrubbing ritual reduces anxiety about contamination, and the water phobic's avoidance of swimming prevents her from experiencing anxiety. Unfortunately, successful avoidance prolongs the problem because it prevents extinction of the learned anxiety response, which would occur eventually if these people could expose themselves to the feared stimuli enough times.

Sociocultural Factors

➤ 22. Describe four culture-bound disorders that involve anxiety.

Social and cultural factors also play a role in the development of anxiety disorders (Lopez & Guarnaccia, 2000). The role of culture is most dramatically shown in **culture-bound disorders** that occur only in certain places. *Koro* is a Southeast Asian anxiety disorder in which a man fears that his penis is going to retract into his abdomen and kill him. Another culture-specific disorder, found in Japan, is a social phobia called *Taijin Kyofushu* (Tanaka-Matsumi, 1979). People with this disorder are pathologically fearful of offending others by emitting offensive odors, blushing, staring inappropriately, or having a blemish or improper facial expression. Taijin Kyofushu has been attributed to the Japanese cultural value of extreme interpersonal sensitivity and to cultural prohibitions against expressing negative emotions (Kleinknecht et al., 1997; Russell, 1989).

Several culture-bound anxiety-based disorders occur in the United States. *Windigo* is an anxiety disorder found among certain North American Indians. Persons with Windigo are fearful of being possessed by monsters who will turn them into homicidal cannibals. A more familiar culturally based anxiety occurs in *anorexia nervosa*. Though formally classified as an eating disorder, anorexia nervosa has a strong phobic component, namely the fear of getting fat. This eating disorder is found almost exclusively in developed countries, where the emphasis on being thin has become a cultural obsession (Becker et al., 1999).

❯ MOOD (AFFECTIVE) DISORDERS

Another set of emotion-based disorders are the **mood disorders,** which involve depression and mania (excessive excitement). Together with the anxiety disorders, mood disorders are the most frequently experienced psychological disorders (Kessler et al., 1994; Robins & Regier, 1991).

Depression

Almost everyone has experienced depression, at least in its milder and more temporary forms. Loss and pain are inevitable parts of life, and when they occur, most of us feel blue, sad, discouraged, apathetic, and passive. The future looks bleak, and some of the zest goes out of living. Such reactions are normal; at any given point in time, 25 to 30 percent of college undergraduates are experiencing mild depression (Seligman, 1991). These feelings usually fade away after the event has passed or as the person becomes accustomed to the new situation. In clinical depression, however, the frequency, intensity, and duration of depressive symptoms are out of proportion to the person's life situation (Oatley & Jenkins, 1992). Thus some people may respond to a minor setback or loss with an intense **major depression** that leaves them unable to function effectively in their lives. Mark, the young man described at the beginning of the chapter, typifies a major depression. Other people exhibit a less intense form of depression called **dysthymia** that has less dramatic effects on personal and occupational functioning. Dysthymia is, however, a more chronic and long-lasting form of misery, occurring for years on end with intervals of normal mood that never last more than a few weeks or months.

Although depression is primarily a disorder of mood, there are three other types of symptoms: cognitive symptoms, motivational symptoms, and somatic (physical) symptoms (Figure 14.12).

The *negative mood state* is the core feature of depression. When depressed people are asked how they feel, they most commonly report sadness, misery, and loneliness (Figure 14.13). Whereas people with anxiety disorders retain their capacity to experience pleasure, depressed people lose it (Mineka et al., 1998). Activities that used to bring satisfaction and happiness feel dull and flat. Even biological pleasures, such as eating and sex, lose their appeal.

Cognitive symptoms are also a central part of depression. Depressed people have difficulty concentrating and making decisions. They usually have low self-esteem, believing that they are inferior, inadequate, and incompetent. When setbacks occur in their lives, depressed people tend to blame themselves; when failure has not yet occurred, they expect that it will and that it will be caused by their own inadequacies. Depressed people almost always view the future with great pessimism and hopelessness (Clark et al., 1999).

Motivational symptoms in depression involve an inability to get started and to perform behaviors that might produce pleasure or accomplishment. A depressed student may be unable to get out of bed in the morning, let alone go to class or study. Everything seems too much of an effort. In extreme depressive reactions, the person may have to be prodded out of bed, clothed, and fed. In some cases of severe depression, movements slow down and the person walks or talks slowly and with excruciating effort.

Somatic (bodily) symptoms often include loss of appetite and weight loss in moderate and severe depression. Sleep disturbances, particularly insomnia, commonly occur. Sleep disturbance and weight loss lead to fatigue and weakness,

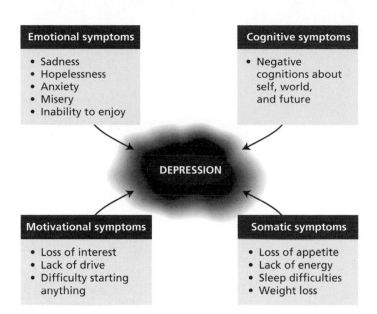

FIGURE 14.12 Depression includes emotional, cognitive, motivational, and somatic features.

➤ 23. Differentiate between major depression and dysthymia.

➤ 24. Describe the four classes of symptoms that characterize (a) depression and (b) mania.

FIGURE 14.13 The most notable emotional feature of depression is profound sadness.

which tend to add to the depressed feelings. Depressed people also may lose sexual desire and responsiveness. In mild depression, weight gain sometimes occurs as a person eats compulsively.

Bipolar Disorder

When a person experiences only depression, the disorder is called *unipolar* depression. In a **bipolar disorder,** depression (which is usually the dominant state) alternates with periods of **mania,** a state of highly excited mood and behavior that is quite the opposite of depression. In a manic state, mood is euphoric and cognitions are grandiose. The person does not believe there are limits to what can be accomplished and does not recognize the negative consequences that may ensue if grandiose plans are acted upon. At a motivational level, manic behavior is hyperactive. The manic person engages in frenetic activity, be it in work, in sexual relationships, or elsewhere. The 19th-century composer Robert Schumann produced 27 works during one manic year, but his productivity ground to a halt when he sank back into the depressive phase of his bipolar disorder (Jamison, 1995).

In a manic state, speech is often rapid or pressured, as if the person must say as many words as possible in the time allotted. With all this flurry of activity comes a greatly lessened need for sleep. Manic people may go for several days without sleeping, until exhaustion inevitably sets in and the mania slows down. The following case illustrates a manic episode:

> Robert B, a 56-year-old dentist awoke one morning with the idea that he was the most gifted dental surgeon in his tri-state area; his mission then was to provide service for as many persons as possible so that they could benefit from his talents. Consequently, he decided to enlarge his 2-chair practice to a 20-chair one, and his plan was to reconstruct his two dental offices into 20 booths so that he could simultaneously attend to as many patients. That very day he drew up the plans for this arrangement and telephoned a number of remodelers and invited them to submit bids for the work.
>
> Toward the end of that day he became irritated with the "interminable delays" and, after he attended to his last patient, rolled up his sleeves and began to knock down the walls of his dental offices. When he discovered that he couldn't manage this chore with the sledge hammer he had purchased for this purpose earlier, he became frustrated and proceeded to smash his more destructible tools, washbasins, and X-ray equipment. He justified this behavior in his own mind by saying, "This junk is not suitable for the likes of me; it'll have to be replaced anyway."
>
> He was in perpetual motion and his speech was "overexcited." When Robert was later admitted to a hospital, he could not sit in his chair; instead he paced the office floor like a caged animal. (Kleinmuntz, 1980, pp. 309–310)

Prevalence and Course of Mood Disorders

Epidemiological studies in the United States suggest that at this moment, about 1 in 20 Americans is severely depressed (Satcher, 1999). Statistically, the chances are nearly 1 in 5 that an American will have a depressive episode of clinical proportions at least once in his or her lifetime (Hamilton, 1989). No age group is exempt from depression. It appears in infants as young as 6 months who have been separated from their mothers for prolonged periods. The rate of depressive symptoms in children and adolescents is as high as the adult rate (Essau & Petermann, 1999).

Data from numerous studies indicate that depression is on the rise in young groups, with the onset of depression increasing dramatically in 15- to 19-year-olds (Burke et al., 1991). People born after 1960 are 10 times more likely to experience depression than are their grandparents, even though their grandparents have lived much longer (Seligman, 1989). The reasons for this striking increase are not totally clear, but we will consider one possible explanation later.

Prevalence of depressive disorders is similar across socioeconomic and ethnic groups, but there is a major sex difference in our culture. Though men and women do not differ in prevalence of bipolar disorder, women appear to be about twice as likely as men to suffer unipolar depression (Figure 14.14). Biological theories suggest that genetic factors, biochemical differences in the nervous system, or the monthly premenstrual depression that many women experience could increase vulnerability to depressive disorders (Donaldson, 1998). In contrast, environmental theories focus on possible cultural causes. One suggestion is that the traditional sex role expectation for females in Western cultures is to be passive and dependent in the face of stress or loss and to focus on their feelings, whereas men are more likely to distract themselves through activities such as physical activity and drinking (Nolen-Hoeksema et al., 1994).

Most people who suffer depressive episodes never seek treatment. What is likely to happen to such people? Perhaps the one positive thing that can be said about depression is that it usually dissipates with time. After the initial episode, which typically comes on suddenly after a stressful experience, depression typically lasts an average of 5 to 10 months when untreated (Tollefson, 1993).

Once a depressive episode has occurred, one of three patterns may follow. In perhaps half of all cases, depression will never recur. Many other cases show a second pattern: recovery with recurrence. On the average, these people will remain symptom-free for perhaps three years before experiencing another depressive episode of about the same severity and duration. The time interval between subsequent episodes of depression tends to become shorter over the years (Rubin, 2000). Finally, about 10 percent of people who have a major depressive episode will not recover and will remain chronically depressed (Figure 14.15).

Manic episodes, though less common than depressive reactions, are far more likely to recur. Fewer than 1 percent of the population experience mania, but more than 90 percent of those who do have a recurrence (American Psychiatric Association, 1994; Kessler et al., 1994).

Causal Factors in Mood Disorders

Biological Factors

Both genetic and neurochemical factors have been linked to depression (Donaldson, 1998). Genetic factors surface in both twin and adoption studies. Identical twins have a concordance rate of about 67 percent for experiencing clinical depression, compared with a rate of only 15 percent for fraternal twins (Gershon et al., 1989). Among adopted people who developed depression, biological relatives were found to be eight times more likely than adoptive relatives to also suffer from depression (Wender et al., 1986). What is likely inherited is a predisposition to develop a depressive disorder, given certain kinds of environmental factors such as significant losses and low social support (Barondes, 1999).

Research has also focused on the possible role of brain chemistry in depression. One influential theory holds that depression is a disorder of motivation caused by underactivity in a family of neurotransmitters that include norepinephrine, dopamine, and serotonin (Davidson, 1998). These transmitters play important roles in several brain regions known to be important sites for experiencing reward and pleasure. When neural transmission decreases in these brain regions, the result is the lack of pleasure and loss of motivation that characterizes depression (Donaldson, 1998; White & Milner, 1992). In support of this theory, several highly effective antidepressant drugs operate by increasing the activity of these neurotransmitters, thereby increasing stimulation of the neural systems that underlie positive mood and goal-directed behavior (Sen et al., 1999).

> 25. How prevalent is depression in men and women? Why the difference? What is its course if left untreated, and its likelihood of recurrence?

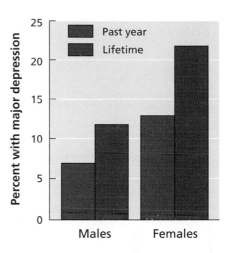

FIGURE 14.14 Prevalence rates for major depression in men and women. Data from Kessler et al., 1994.

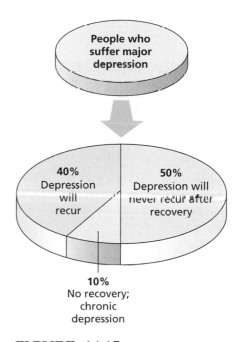

FIGURE 14.15 Course of outcome following a major depressive episode. About half never have a recurrence, a sizable proportion do have a recurrence, and about 10 percent suffer chronic depression.

> 26. What evidence exists for a genetic factor in depression?

> 27. What biochemical processes might underlie depression? Mania?

Bipolar disorder, in which depression alternates with less frequent periods of mania, has been studied primarily at the biological level because it appears to have a stronger genetic basis than does unipolar depression (Young & Joffe, 1997). Among both men and women, the lifetime risk of developing a bipolar disorder is just below 1 percent. Yet about 50 percent of patients with bipolar disorder have a parent, grandparent, or child with the disorder (Barondes, 1999; Rubin, 2000). The concordance rate for bipolar disorder is five times higher in identical twins than in fraternal twins, suggesting a genetic link.

Manic disorders may stem from an *overproduction* of the same neurotransmitters that are underactive in depression. This might explain the symptom picture that is quite the opposite of that seen in depression. Significantly, lithium chloride, the drug most frequently used to calm manic disorders, works by decreasing the activity of these transmitters in the brain's motivational/pleasure activation system (LeMoal, 1999; Robinson, 1997).

Psychological Factors

Biological factors seem to increase vulnerability to certain types of psychological and environmental events that can then trigger the disorders. Other perspectives specify what those events might be.

Personality-based vulnerability.   Psychoanalysts Karl Abraham (1911) and Sigmund Freud (1917) believed that early traumatic losses or rejections create vulnerability for later depression by triggering a grieving and rage process that becomes part of the individual's personality (Figure 14.16). Subsequent losses and rejection reactivate the original loss and cause a reaction not only to the current event, but also to the unresolved loss from the past.

Were he alive today, Freud would surely point to research by the British sociologists George Brown and Terrill Harris (1978) to support his theory of early loss. Brown and Harris interviewed women in London and found that the rate of depression among women who had lost their mothers before age 11 and who had also experienced a severe recent loss was almost three times higher than the rate of depression among women who had experienced a similar recent loss but had not lost their mothers before age 11. Other research has shown that death of the father while a child is young is also associated with a greatly increased risk of later depression (Barnes & Prosen, 1985; Bowlby, 2000a).

The humanistic perspective also addresses causes of depression. In attempting to explain the dramatic increase in depression among people born after 1960, Martin Seligman (1989) has suggested that the "me" generation, with its overemphasis on individuality and personal control, has sown the seeds for its own depression. Because people define their self-worth in terms of individual attainment and have fewer commitments to traditional values of family, religion, and the common good, they are likely to react much more strongly to failures, to view negative events as reflecting their own inadequacies, and to experience a sense of meaninglessness in their lives.

Cognitive processes.   According to Aaron Beck (1976), depressed people victimize themselves through their own beliefs that they are defective, worthless, and inadequate. They also believe that whatever happens to them is bad, and that negative things will continue happening because of their personal defects (Clark et al., 1989). This **depressive cognitive triad** of negative thoughts concerning (1) the world, (2) oneself, and (3) the future seems to pop into consciousness automatically, and many depressed people report that they cannot control or suppress the negative thoughts (Wenzlaff et al., 1988). Depressed people also tend to recall most of their failures and few of their successes, and they tend to focus much of their attention on their perceived inadequacies (Haaga et al., 1991; Clark et al., 1999). Such thoughts trigger depressed affect.

➤ 28. What evidence is there to support the notion that early losses create a risk factor for later depression?

FIGURE 14.16 Early catastrophic losses are thought by psychoanalysts to increase vulnerability to later depressive disorders.

➤ 29. How does Seligman explain the dramatic increase in depression among people born after 1960?

➤ 30. Describe (a) the cognitive triad and (b) the depressive attributional pattern described by Beck.

Depressive attributional pattern

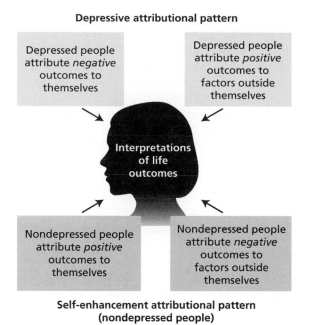

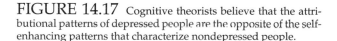

FIGURE 14.17 Cognitive theorists believe that the attributional patterns of depressed people are the opposite of the self-enhancing patterns that characterize nondepressed people.

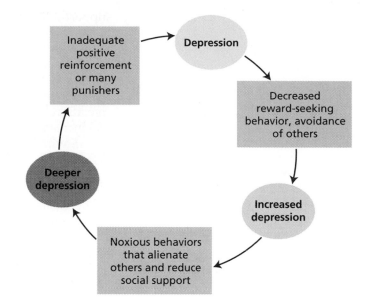

FIGURE 14.18 Lewinsohn's behavioral model of depression focuses on the environmental causes and effects of depression. Depression results from loss of positive reinforcement and produces further declines in reinforcement and social support in a vicious-cycle fashion.

As noted in the discussion of self-enhancement tendencies in Chapter 13, most people tend to take personal credit for the good outcomes in their lives and to blame their misfortunes on factors outside of themselves, thereby maintaining and enhancing their self-esteem. According to Beck, depressed people do exactly the opposite: They interpret successes or other positive events as being due to factors outside the self while attributing negative outcomes to personal factors (Figure 14.17). Beck believes that this **depressive attributional pattern** of taking no credit for successes but blaming themselves for failures maintains depressed people's low self-esteem and their belief that they are worthless failures. Quite literally, they can't win!

Another prominent cognitive account of depression, **learned helplessness theory,** holds that depression occurs when people expect that bad events will occur and that there is nothing they can do to prevent or cope with them (Abramson et al., 1978; Seligman & Isaacowitz, 2000). The depressive attributional pattern described above plays a central role in the learned helplessness model, but learned helplessness theorists take it a step further by specifying what the negative attributions for failures are like. They suggest that chronic and intense depression occurs as the result of negative attributions for failures that are *personal* ("It's all *my* fault"), *stable* ("I'll *always* be this way"), and *global* ("I'm a *total* loser"). Thus people who attribute negative events in their lives to factors such as low intelligence, physical repulsiveness, or an unlovable personality tend to believe that their personal defects will render them helpless to avoid negative events in the future, and they are therefore at significantly greater risk for depression.

Learning and environmental factors. Peter Lewinsohn and his colleagues (1985) believe that depression is usually triggered by a loss, some other punishing event, or by a drastic decrease in the amount of positive reinforcement that the person receives from her or his environment (Figure 14.18). As the depression begins to take hold, people stop performing behaviors that previously provided reinforcement, such as hobbies and socializing. Moreover, depressed people tend to make those who come in contact with them feel anxious, depressed, and hostile (Joiner & Coyne, 1999). Eventually, these other people begin to lose patience, failing to understand why the person doesn't "snap out of it." This diminishes social

➤ 31. According to learned helplessness theory, what kinds of attributions trigger depression?

➤ 32. How does Lewinsohn's learning theory explain the spiraling downward course that occurs in severe depression?

support still further and may eventually cause depressed people to be abandoned by those who are most important to them (Nezlek et al., 2000).

Behavioral theorists believe that to begin feeling better, depressed people must break this vicious cycle by initially forcing themselves to engage in behaviors that are likely to produce some degree of pleasure. Eventually, positive reinforcement produced by these behaviors will begin to counteract the depressive affect, undermine the sense of helplessness that characterizes depression, and increase feelings of personal control over the environment.

Environmental factors may also help explain why depression tends to run in families. Constance Hammen (1991) studied the family histories of depressed people and concluded that children of depressed parents often experience poor parenting and many stressful experiences as they grow up. As a result, they may fail to develop good coping skills and a positive self-concept. They are therefore vulnerable later in life to stressful events that can trigger depressive reactions.

Sociocultural Factors

➤ 33. How are cultural factors related to the prevalence, manifestations, and sex differences in depression?

Although depression is found in virtually all cultures, its prevalence, symptom pattern, and its causes reflect cultural variation (Lopez & Guarnaccia, 2000). For example, compared with Western nations, the prevalence of depressive disorders is far lower in Hong Kong and Taiwan, where strong connections to family and other groups helps reduce the negative impact of loss and disappointments and provides strong social support when they occur (Tseng et al., 1990).

Cultural factors also can affect the ways in which depression is manifested. Feelings of guilt and personal inadequacy seem to predominate in North American and western European countries, whereas somatic symptoms of fatigue, loss of appetite, and sleep difficulties are more often reported in Latin, Chinese, and African cultures (Manson, 1994).

Finally, cultural factors may influence who develops depression. As noted earlier, women are about twice as likely as men to report feeling depressed in technologically advanced countries like Canada, the United States, and other Western nations. Yet this sex difference is not found in developing countries (Culbertson, 1997; Nolen-Hoeksema, 1990). At present, we do not know why this pattern occurs, but attempts are under way to learn more about how the cultural environment influences the development of depression.

➤ 34. What is the relation between depression and suicide? What are the major motives and risk factors for suicide? Describe four practical guidelines for helping a suicidal person.

At one time or another, many depressed people consider suicide as a way to escape from the unhappiness of their lives. We now examine suicide, its causes, and what can be done to prevent this tragic event.

APPLICATIONS OF PSYCHOLOGICAL SCIENCE

Understanding and Preventing Suicide

Suicide is defined as the willful taking of one's own life. The World Health Organization estimates that nearly 500,000 people worldwide commit suicide annually, about 1.4 every minute. Ten times that number attempt suicide. In the United States, suicide is now the second most frequent cause of death (after accidents) among high school and college students, and suicide rates among 15- to 24-year-olds have tripled since 1960 (National Center for Health Statistics, 1995; Figure 14.19).

Women make about three times as many suicide attempts as men, but men are three times more likely to actually kill themselves. These differences may be due to (a) a higher incidence of depression in women and (b) men's choice of more lethal methods, such as shooting themselves

—Continued

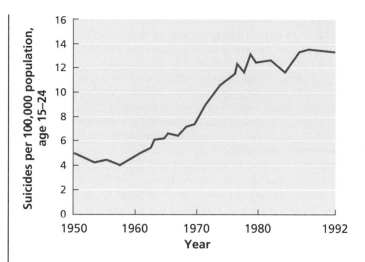

FIGURE 14.19 Suicide rate per 100,000 persons aged 15 to 24, from 1950 to 1992.

Data from National Center for Health Statistics, 1998.

or jumping off buildings. The suicide rate for both men and women is higher among those who have been divorced or widowed. Women who commit suicide have a relatively greater tendency to be motivated by failures in love relationships, whereas men have a greater tendency to be motivated by failure in their occupations (Shneidman, 1976). A history of sexual or physical abuse significantly increases the likelihood of later suicide attempts (Fergusson & Lynskey, 1997; Garnefski & Arends, 1998).

Depression is one of the strongest predictors of suicide. About 15 percent of clinically depressed individuals will eventually kill themselves, a rate that is 22 to 36 times higher than the suicide rate for the general population. An estimated 80 percent of suicidal people are significantly depressed. It is noteworthy, however, that suicides do not usually occur when depression is deepest. Instead, suicide often occurs unexpectedly as a depressed person seems to be emerging from depression and feeling better. The lifting of depression may provide the energy needed to complete the suicidal act without affecting the person's underlying sense of hopelessness and despair.

◗ Motives for Suicide

There appear to be two fundamental motivations for suicide: the desire to end one's life and the desire to manipulate and coerce other people into doing what the suicidal person wants (Beck et al., 1979). Those who wish to end their lives have basically given up. They see no other way to deal with intolerable emotional distress, and in death they see an end to their problems. In one study, 56 percent of suicide attempts were classified as having been motivated by the desire to die (Beck, 1976). These attempts were accompanied by high levels of depression and hopelessness, and they tended to be more lethal than other suicide attempts (Figure 14.20).

The second primary motivation for suicide is manipulation of others. Many *parasuicides* (suicide attempts that

FIGURE 14.20 From 1988 to 1994, Ray Combs charmed television audiences as the playful host of *Family Feud*. Fans were shocked when he hung himself in 1996 after a series of personal and professional setbacks that left him depressed and hopeless.

do not end in death) are cries for help or attempts to coerce people to meet one's needs. Trying to prevent a lover from ending a relationship and trying to dramatize one's suffering are manipulative motives. Manipulative suicide attempters tend to use less lethal means (such as drug overdoses or wrist-slashing) and to make sure help is available. In the study cited earlier (Beck, 1976), 13 percent of the suicide attempts were classified as manipulative. The remaining 31 percent combined the two types of motivation. A small minority of suicides result from altruistic decisions to sacrifice one's life for the survival of others. Examples are the soldier who dives on a hand grenade to save comrades or a mother who elects to give birth rather than aborting her baby, knowing that she will die in the process.

◗ Warning Signs for Suicide

The best predictor of suicide attempts in both men and women is a verbal or behavioral threat to commit suicide, and such threats should always be taken seriously. One of the most destructive myths about suicide is that people

—Continued

who talk openly about suicide don't actually carry out the act. Yet research shows that a high proportion of suicide attempts—perhaps 80 percent—are preceded by some kind of warning (Bagley & Ramsay, 1997; Chiles & Strossahl, 1995). Sometimes the warning is an explicit statement of intent, such as "I don't want to go on living" or "I won't be a burden much longer." Other times, the warnings are more subtle, as when a person expresses hopelessness about the future, withdraws from others or from favorite activities, gives away treasured possessions, or takes unusual risks. Other important risk factors are a history of previous suicide attempts and a detailed plan that involves a lethal method (Chiles & Strossahl, 1995; Shneidman, 1998).

▶ Suicide Prevention

Much has been learned about the dynamics and prevention of suicide as a result of scientific research. These findings provide guidelines for preventing this tragic answer to life's problems. For example, another myth about suicide is that broaching the topic with a potentially suicidal person may prompt the person to carry out the act. In truth, the best first step if you suspect that someone may be suicidal is to ask the person directly whether he or she is considering suicide: "Have you thought about hurting yourself, or ending your life?" If the person responds affirmatively, try to find out if he or she has a plan or a timetable in mind. Do not be hesitant to approach the person. *Diffusion of responsibility* (discussed in Chapters 2 and 12) could result in your assuming that someone else is helping a potentially suicidal person, when in fact no one is (Kalafat et al., 1993). Your ul-timate goal should be to help the person to receive assistance from a qualified professional as soon as possible, not to treat the person yourself. Nonetheless, you can take some immediate steps that may be helpful.

Many suicidal people feel alone in their misery. It is important to provide social support and empathy at this critical juncture. An expression of genuine concern can pave the way for other potentially helpful interventions (Barnett & Porter, 1998). For example, a frank discussion of the problem that is foremost in the person's life can be helpful. Suicidal people often feel totally overwhelmed by life, and focusing on a specific problem may help the person realize that it is not un-solvable and need not cloud his or her total perception of life.

When people are distressed and hopeless, their time orientation tends to narrow, and they have difficulty seeing beyond their current distress. Try to help the person see his or her present situation within a wider time perspective and to consider positive possibilities that might exist in the future. In particular, discuss reasons for continuing to live and focus on any doubts the person might have about electing suicide. For example, if the person indicates that his or her family will suffer greatly from the suicide, adopt this as one of your arguments for a different solution to the problem. Many suicidal people would like to feel that they do not have to commit suicide. Capitalize on such feelings.

If a person is suicidal, stay with him or her and seek professional assistance. Most cities have suicide prevention centers that offer 24-hour services, including telephone and direct counseling. These centers are usually listed under *suicide* or *crisis* in the phone book.

❭ SOMATOFORM DISORDERS

▶ 35. Describe three varieties of somatoform disorders. What causal factors might be involved in somatoform disorders?

Somatoform disorders involve physical complaints or disabilities that suggest a medical problem, but which have no known biological cause and are not produced voluntarily by the person (Finell, 1997). In **hypochondriasis,** people become unduly alarmed about any physical symptom they detect, and are convinced that they have or are about to have a serious illness. People with **pain disorder** experience intense pain that either is out of proportion to whatever medical condition they might have or for which no physical basis can be found. Somatoform disorders differ from *psychophysiological disorders,* in which psychological factors cause or contribute to a real medical condition, such as an ulcer, asthma, hypertension (chronic high blood pressure), or a cardiac problem.

Perhaps the most fascinating of the somatoform disorders is **conversion disorder,** in which serious neurological symptoms, such as paralysis, loss of sensation, or blindness suddenly occur. People with conversion disorders often exhibit *la belle indifference,* a strange lack of concern about their symptom and its implications (Pajer, 2000). In some cases, the complaint itself is physiologically impossible. An example is the so-called *glove anesthesia,* in which a person loses all sensation below the wrist. As Figure 14.21 shows, the hand is served by nerves that also provide sensory input above the hand, making glove anesthesia anatomically impossible.

Conversion disorders are relatively rare, occurring in about 3 in 1,000 Americans during peacetime (American Psychiatric Association, 1994), but such disorders occur more frequently under wartime conditions (Slavney, 1990).

Thus a soldier about to return to the trauma of combat may suddenly develop blindness or paralysis for which no physical cause can be found.

Although "psychogenic blindness" is quite rare in the general population, researchers have discovered the largest known civilian group of people in the world having trauma-induced blindness. They are Cambodian refugees who escaped from their country and settled in Long Beach, California. These survivors of the "killing fields" of Cambodia were subjected to unspeakable horror at the hands of the Khmer Rouge in the years following the Vietnam War (Cooke, 1991). More than 150 of them are functionally blind, even though their eyes appear intact and electrophysiological monitoring shows that visual stimuli "register" in their visual cortex (Figure 14.22). The doctors who studied this remarkable group are convinced that they are not faking blindness. Many of the victims reported that their blindness occurred suddenly after witnessing traumatic scenes of murder. Were the sights from the outer world so painful that in these people, the visual system involuntarily shut down? An intriguing but as yet unanswered question is how cultural factors might have affected the development of this response to trauma.

To Freud, such symptoms were a symbolic expression of an underlying conflict that aroused so much anxiety that the ego kept the conflict in the unconscious by converting the anxiety into a physical symptom that in some way symbolized the conflict. Contemporary psychodynamic theorists continue to accept this explanation (Fisher & Greenberg, 1995). In one of Freud's cases, a young woman who was forced to take care of her hostile, verbally abusive and unappreciative father suddenly developed paralysis in her arm. According to Freud, this occurred when her repressed hostile impulses threatened to break through and cause her to strike him using that arm (Freud, 1935).

A predisposition to somatoform disorders may involve a combination of biological and psychological vulnerabilities. Somatoform disorders tend to run in families, though it is not clear whether this reflects the role of genetic factors, environmental learning and social reinforcement for bodily symptoms, or both (Guze, 1993). Other theorists have suggested that some people may experience internal sensations more vividly than others, or may focus more attention on them (Barsky, 1992). If this results in a person being self-absorbed in his or her own body sensations, it could set the stage for increased apprehension about the body. The incidence of somatoform disorders tends to be much higher in cultures that discourage open discussion of emotions or that stigmatize psychological disorders (Tanaka-Matsumi & Draguns, 1997). In such settings, somatic symptoms may be the only acceptable outlet for emotional distress. The same may occur in people who are so emotionally constricted that they cannot acknowledge their emotions or communicate them to others verbally (Trae & Deighton, 2000).

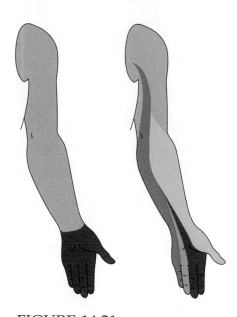

FIGURE 14.21 Glove anesthesia is a conversion disorder in which all feeling is lost below the wrist. The skin areas served by nerves in the arm make this symptom physiologically impossible.

FIGURE 14.22 A physician examines one of the Cambodian refugees who appear to be suffering from psychologically-induced blindness. There is nothing wrong with their eyes, but they cannot see.

❯ DISSOCIATIVE DISORDERS

Ordinarily, personality has unity and coherence, and the many facets of the self are integrated so that people act, think, and feel with some degree of consistency. Memory plays a critical role in this integration, for it connects past with present and provides a sense of personal identity that extends over time. **Dissociative disorders** involve a breakdown of this normal integration, resulting in significant alterations in memory or identity. Three forms that such disorders can take are psychogenic amnesia, psychogenic fugue, and dissociative personality disorder.

In **psychogenic amnesia,** a person responds to a stressful event with extensive but selective memory loss. Some people can remember nothing about their past. Others can no longer recall specific events, people, places, or objects, although other contents of memory, such as language and cognitive or motor skills remain intact.

❯ 36. What is the central feature of dissociative disorders? Describe the three major types of dissociative disorders.

FIGURE 14.23 Chris Sizemore, the actual person depicted in the book and movie, *The Three Faces of Eve.*

Psychogenic fugue is a more profound dissociative disorder in which a person loses all sense of personal identity, gives up his or her customary life, wanders to a new faraway location, and establishes a new identity. Usually, the fugue is triggered by a highly stressful event or trauma, and it may last from a few hours or days to several years. Some adolescent runaways have been found to be in a fugue state, and married fugue victims may wed someone else and start a new career (Loewenstein, 1991). Typically, the fugue ends when the person suddenly recovers his or her original identity and "wakes up," mystified and distressed at being in a strange place under strange circumstances.

Dissociative identity disorder (DID), formerly called *multiple personality disorder,* is the most striking and widely publicized of the dissociative disorders. Several celebrated cases of DID have been dramatized in books and movies, such as *Sybil* and *The Three Faces of Eve* (Figure 14.23). In this disorder, two or more separate personalities coexist in the same person. A primary, or *host personality* appears more often than the others (called *alters*), but each personality has its own integrated set of memories and behaviors. The personalities may or may not know about the existence of the others. They can also differ in their age and gender, with one being male, another female. The personalities can differ not only mentally and behaviorally but also physiologically, as in the following case.

A 38-year-old woman named Margaret was admitted to a hospital with paralysis of her legs following a minor car accident. During the course of her interview the woman, a member of an ultrareligious sect, reported that she sometimes heard a strange voice inside her threatening to "take over completely." The physician suggested that she let the voice "take over." Here is his report of what happened:

> The woman closed her eyes, clenched her fists, and grimaced for a few moments during which she was out of contact with those in the room. Suddenly she opened her eyes and one was in the presence of another person. Her name, she said, was "Harriet." Whereas Margaret had been paralyzed, and complained of fatigue, headache, and backache, Harriet felt well and she at once proceeded to walk around the room unaided. She spoke scornfully of Margaret's religiousness, her invalidism, and her puritanical life, professing that she herself liked to drink and "go partying" but that Margaret was always going to church and reading the Bible.... At length, at the interviewer's suggestion, Harriet reluctantly agreed to "bring Margaret back" and after more grimacing and fist clenching, Margaret reappeared paralyzed, complaining of her headache and backache, and completely amnesic for the brief period of Harriet's release from her prison. (Nemiah, 1978, pp. 179–180)

➤ 37. How does the trauma-dissociation theory account for the development of DID?

According to **trauma-dissociation theory,** the development of new personalities occurs in response to severe stress. For a vast majority of patients, this begins to occur in early childhood, frequently in response to physical or sexual abuse. Frank Putnam (1989) studied the life histories of 100 diagnosed DID cases and found that 97 of them reported severe abuse and trauma in early and middle childhood, a time when children's identities are not well established and it is quite easy for them to dissociate. Putnam believes that in response to the trauma and their helplessness to resist it, children may engage in something akin to self-hypnosis and dissociate from reality. They create a new alternate identity to detach themselves from the trauma, to transfer what is happening to someone else who can handle it, and to blunt the pain. Over time, it is theorized, the protective functions served by the new personality remain separate in the form of an alternate personality, rather than being integrated into the host personality (Meyer & Osborne, 1987; Putnam, 1989).

Dissociative identity disorder has become a controversial topic, and some question its very existence. We now consider some of the reasons why.

➤ 38. On what grounds have critics questioned the validity of DID, and what explanations do they offer instead?

PSYCHOLOGICAL FRONTIERS

Dissociative Identity Disorder: A Clinical and Scientific Puzzle

Scientists at the National Institute of Mental Health (NIMH) in Washington, D.C., have studied more than 150 cases of DID (Putnam, 1989, 1998). In many cases, they were able to study the physiological responses of the patients when different personalities were active. The results of these studies suggest that the alternate selves may be different in both mind and body. If Eve had three faces, she may also have had three voices, three memory systems, and, in a limited sense, three biological response systems.

Prior to the NIMH studies, physicians and mental-health workers had frequently reported dramatic physical differences among the alternate personalities of DID patients. The differences include physical health differences, voice changes, and even changes in right- and left-handedness. Some patients had severe allergies when one personality was present but no allergies when the others were active. One patient nearly died of a violent allergic reaction to a bee sting. A week later, when an alternate personality was active, another sting produced no reaction. Female patients frequently have different menstrual cycles for each female personality; one patient had three periods per month. Other patients need eyeglasses with different prescriptions for different personalities; one may be farsighted, another nearsighted (Miller et al., 1991). Epileptic patients with DID often have their seizures in one personality but not another (Drake et al., 1988).

Physiological studies of DID patients under controlled laboratory conditions have also shown differences between the various personalities (Atchison & McFarlane, 1994). Indeed, the responses of the various personalities frequently appear as different as if they had come from different people (Figure 14.24). For example, Christine Ludlow did computerized spectral analyses ("voice prints") of audio recordings made by alternate personalities, and found that the voices were very distinct from one another (Putnam, 1984). Using electrical recording and brain-scanning techniques to study brain differences associated with alternate personalities, Frank Putnam (1984) found that cerebral blood-flow patterns differed among the personalities. Moreover, Putnam found shifts in EEG measures of hemispheric dominance when the individual had right-handed and left-handed personalities. When a left-handed personality appeared, the right hemisphere became more active. In another study, ophthalmologists found shifts in visual acuity and eye-muscle balance as DID patients shifted from one personality to another. Such changes did not occur among control subjects who were asked to simulate another personality (Miller et al., 1991).

As dramatic as these physiological differences between DID alters might appear, they are not universally accepted by critics who correctly point out that many of

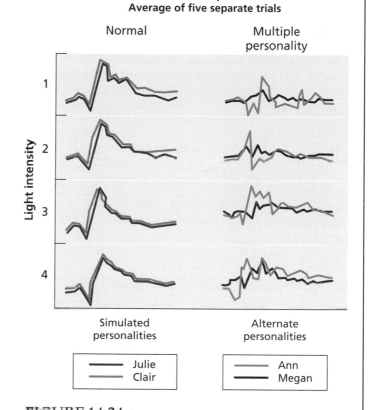

Visual evoked potentials
Average of five separate trials

FIGURE 14.24 Comparisons of evoked potentials of a DID patient (Ann and her alternate personality, Megan) and a control participant (Julie) simulating a second personality (Clair) to four levels of visual stimulation. The DID patient's EEG records differed more from one another.

Adapted from Putnam, 1984.

the observations are based on uncontrolled case studies. Could the average person asked to role play separate personalities exhibit such differences as well? There is indeed some evidence that EEG differences can be produced by such role playing in normal individuals (Coons et al., 1982), but so far none of the other more exotic physiological phenomena described above have been shown in role-playing controls (Gleaves, 1996). In some studies, such as the visual acuity and eye muscle study described above, role-players have been unable to produce the responses shown by DID patients. Nonetheless, it is clear that additional controlled studies of physiological alterations are needed.

—Continued

Some critics consider the notion of multiple personalities to be nothing more than science fiction, and they dispute the existence of DID as a valid clinical disorder (Beahrs, 1994; Spanos, 1994). Troubling to many psychologists and legal experts is a tendency for some people who have committed serious crimes to disclaim personal responsibility on the grounds that they are DID victims and that one of the alternative personalities committed the crime (Beahrs, 1994). Other critics wonder if DID is, in reality, a therapist-produced phenomenon. They point out that prior to 1970, only about 100 cases of what was then called multiple personality disorder had been reported worldwide. Even today, it is virtually unknown in many cultures, including Japan (Takahashi, 1990). But after the disorder was highly publicized in the book and movie *Sybil,* many additional cases began to be reported by therapists until they numbered in the tens of thousands by the mid-1990s. The number of alternate personalities also increased from two or three to an average of about fifteen (Spanos, 1994). Could this dramatic increase in prevalence and number of alters be the result of publicity and therapist expectations? Some critics of DID believe that many features of the cases, including the memories of previous abuse, could be false memories and suggestions of multiple identities that are unintentionally implanted by overzealous therapists. The widespread use of hypnosis in the treatment of suspected DID only adds to the danger of a therapist-induced clinical picture that is based on susceptibility to suggestion. As we saw in our discussion of hypnosis in Chapter 5, people can become so immersed in an imagined role that it becomes quite real to them, and they act accordingly (Spanos, 1996).

In some instances, clients have filed lawsuits against therapists, charging them with creating the disorder in them. In one bizarre case, a Wisconsin woman and her insurance company successfully sued a psychiatrist who used hypnosis to allegedly unearth 120 different personalities in her, including Satan and a duck, then billed the insurance company at the higher group therapy rate on the grounds that he was treating multiple people! The woman charged the therapist with implanting false memories of sexual abuse, rape, being pushed into an open grave, and aborting a baby. She maintained that she had never had any of the memories before beginning therapy and that the false memories caused nightmares, flashbacks, suicidal impulses, and, eventually, the need for hospitalization (*Associated Press,* December 12, 1997). Such extreme instances, which by no means typify the efforts of ethical therapists to help their clients, serve to fuel the concerns of critics.

Is DID real? Suppose it were to be convincingly demonstrated in experimental studies that role-playing by average people can produce all of the DID phenomena described at the beginning of this feature. Would this prove that true dissociation does not occur in *any* of the cases seen by mental-health workers? Not at all, supporters maintain, any more than a compelling depiction of a schizophrenic person by a skilled actor like Jack Nicholson would prove that all cases of schizophrenia involve nothing more than acting. The controversy that swirls around DID can help fuel continued investigation of the cognitive and physiological phenomena that are seen in DID. Such research may advance our understanding of factors that can produce dramatic alterations in memory, physiological responses, and behavior.

❭ SCHIZOPHRENIA

Of all the psychological disorders, schizophrenia is the most serious and, in many ways, the most puzzling. Despite many theories of schizophrenia and thousands of research studies, a complete understanding of this disorder continues to elude us.

Schizophrenia is a psychotic disorder that involves severe disturbances in thinking, speech, perception, emotion, and behavior. The term *schizophrenia* was introduced by the Swiss psychiatrist Eugen Bleuler in 1911. Literally, the term means "split mind," which has often led people to confuse schizophrenia with dissociative identity disorder or with a Dr. Jekyll–Mr. Hyde phenomenon. But multiple personalities is not what Bleuler had in mind when he coined the term. Instead, Bleuler intended to suggest that certain psychological functions, such as thought, language, and emotion, which are joined together in normal people, are somehow split apart or disconnected in schizophrenia.

Characteristics of Schizophrenia

A diagnosis of schizophrenia requires evidence that a person misinterprets reality and exhibits disordered attention, thought, or perception. In addition, withdrawal from social interactions is common, communication is strange or inappropriate, personal grooming may be neglected, and behavior may become disorganized (American Psychiatric Association, 1994).

The schizophrenic thought disorder sometimes includes delusions (Nadelson & Reinburg, 1999). **Delusions** are false beliefs that are sustained in the face

➤ 39. What is meant by the term schizophrenia? What are the major cognitive, behavioral, emotional, and perceptual features of these disorders?

FIGURE 14.25 The bizarre and terrifying perceptual world of schizophrenia is shown in this series of cat paintings made by the English artist Louis Wain as he deteriorated from a normal state into a progressively more severe schizophrenic state.

of evidence that normally would be sufficient to destroy them. A schizophrenic person may believe that his brain is being turned to glass by ray guns operated by his enemies from outer space, or that Jesus Christ is a special agent of his. The first is a *delusion of persecution,* the second a *delusion of grandeur.*

Several aspects of the thought disorder were described by a schizophrenic during a period of recovery:

> The most wearing aspect of schizophrenia is the fierce battle that goes on inside my head in which conflicts become unresolvable. I am so ambivalent that my mind can divide on a subject, and those two parts subdivide over and over until my mind feels like it is in pieces, and I am totally disorganized. At other times, I feel like I am trapped inside my head, banging against its walls, trying desperately to escape while my lips can utter only nonsense. (*New York Times,* March 18, 1986, p. C12)

Perceptual disorganization and disordered thought become more pronounced as people progress into a schizophrenic condition. What the world might come to look like from "inside" is shown in the pictures of cats drawn by artist Louis Wain as he became progressively more disturbed (Figure 14.25). Some experience **hallucinations,** false perceptions that have a compelling sense of reality. Auditory hallucinations (typically voices speaking to the patient) are most common, although visual and tactile hallucinations may also occur. This patient describes his hallucinations:

> Recently, my mind has played tricks on me, creating The People inside my head who sometimes come out to haunt me and torment me. They surround me in rooms, hide behind trees and under the snow outside. They taunt me and scream at me and devise plans to break my spirit. The voices come and go, but The People are always there, always real. (*New York Times,* March 18, 1986, p. C12)

The language of schizophrenic patients is often disorganized, and can contain strange words.

> I am here from a foreign university . . . and you have to have a "plausity" of all acts of amendment to go through for the children's code . . . and it is no mental disturbance or "putenance" . . . it is an "amorition" law . . . it is like their "privatilinia." (Vetter, 1969, p. 189)

Patients' language sometimes contains word associations that are based on rhymes or other associations rather than meaning. Consider the following conversation between a psychologist and a hospitalized schizophrenic:

> After two weeks, the psychologist said to him: "As you say, you are wired precisely wrong. But why won't you let me see the diagram?" Carl answered: "Never, ever will you find the lever, the eternalever that will sever me forever with my real, seal, deal, heel. It is not on my shoe, not even on the sole. It walks away." (Rosenhan & Seligman, 1989, p. 369)

Emotions can be affected in a number of ways. Many people with schizophrenia have *blunted affect,* manifesting less sadness, joy, and anger than most people. Others have *flat affect,* showing almost no emotions at all. Their voices are monotonous, their faces impassive. *Inappropriate affect* can also occur, as in the following case:

> The psychologist noted that Carl "smiles when he is uncomfortable, and smiles more when in pain. He cries during television comedies. He seems angry when justice is done, frightened when someone compliments him, and roars with laughter on reading that a young child was burned in a tragic fire." (Rosenhan & Seligman, 1989, p. 369)

Subtypes of Schizophrenia

➤ 40. Describe the four major types of schizophrenic disorders.

Schizophrenia has cognitive, emotional, and behavioral facets that can vary widely from case to case. DSM-IV differentiates among four major subtypes of schizophrenia:

- **Paranoid type.** The most prominent features in paranoid schizophrenics are delusions of persecution, in which people believe that others mean to harm them, and delusions of grandeur, in which they believe they are enormously important. Suspicion, anxiety, or anger may accompany the delusions, and hallucinations may also occur in this subtype.
- **Disorganized type.** The central features are confusion and incoherence, together with severe deterioration of adaptive behavior. Thought disorganization is often so extreme that it is difficult to communicate with them. Their behavior often appears silly and childlike, and their emotional responses are highly inappropriate. These people are usually unable to function on their own.
- **Catatonic type.** The catatonic subtype shows striking motor disturbances ranging from muscular rigidity to random or repetitive movements. Catatonics sometimes alternate between stuporous states in which they seem oblivious to reality and agitated excitement during which they can be dangerous to others. While in a stuporous state, they may exhibit a *waxy flexibility* in which their limbs can be molded by another person into grotesque positions that they will then maintain for hours (Figure 14.26).
- **Undifferentiated type.** This category is for people who exhibit some of the symptoms and thought disorders of the above categories but do not have enough of the specific criteria to be diagnosed in those categories.

FIGURE 14.26 The woman pictured here exhibits catatonic rigidity. She might hold this position for several hours.

➤ 41. Distinguish between Type I and Type II schizophrenia. How are positive and negative symptoms related to past history and future prognosis?

In addition to these formal DSM-IV categories, many mental-health workers and researchers categorize schizophrenic reactions into two main categories on the basis of two classes of symptoms. **Type I schizophrenia** is characterized by a predominance of **positive symptoms,** such as delusions, hallucinations, and disordered speech and thinking. These symptoms are called *positive* because they represent pathological extremes of normal processes. **Type II schizophrenia** features **negative symptoms**—an absence of normal reactions,—such as lack of emotional expression, loss of motivation, and an absence of normal speech (Johnstone et al., 1999).

The distinction between positive and negative symptom subtypes seems to be an important one. Researchers have found differences in brain function between schizophrenics having positive symptoms and those with primarily negative symptoms (Gur et al., 1998; Zakzanis, 1998). The subtypes also show differences in life history and prognosis. Negative symptoms are likely to be associated with a long history of poor functioning prior to hospitalization and with a poor outcome following treatment (McGlashan & Fenton, 1992). In contrast, positive symptoms, especially those associated with a diagnosis of paranoid schizophrenia, are associated with good functioning prior to breakdown and a better prognosis for eventual recovery, particularly if the symptoms came on suddenly and were preceded by a history of relatively good adjustment (Fenton & McGlashan, 1991a, 1991b).

Schizophrenia afflicts only 1 to 2 percent of the population, yet schizophrenic patients occupy about half of all psychiatric hospital beds in the United States (Satcher, 1999). Many others like Eddie, the man described at the beginning of the chapter, barely function as homeless "street people" in large cities (Herman et al., 1998). About 10 percent of people with schizophrenia remain permanently impaired, and 65 percent show intermittent periods of normal functioning. The other 25 percent recover from the disorder (American Psychiatric Association, 1994). Schizophrenia affects equal numbers of males and females, but it appears earlier in males, frequently between the ages of 15 and 30 (Jeste & Heaton, 1994).

Causal Factors in Schizophrenia

Because of the seriousness of the disorder and the many years of anguish and incapacitation that its victims are likely to experience, schizophrenia is perhaps the most widely researched of the psychological disorders. There is a growing consensus that schizophrenia results from a biologically based vulnerability factor that is set into motion by psychological and environmental events (Fowles, 1992; Gottesman, 1991; Green, 1997).

> 42. Describe the evidence for genetic and neurological factors in schizophrenia.

Biological Factors

Strong evidence exists for a genetic predisposition to schizophrenia, though the specific genes involved and their roles in creating the disposition are still unknown (Franzek & Beckmann, 1999). As Figure 14.27 shows, the closer the biological relationship to a person diagnosed with schizophrenia, the greater the risk for developing the disorder during one's lifetime (Gottesman, 1991). Twin studies show that identical twins have higher concordance rates than fraternal twins, and adoption studies show much higher concordance with biological parents than with adoptive parents (Kety, 1988; Wahlberg et al., 1997). Figure 14.28 shows a remarkable set of identical quadruplets, all of whom developed schizophrenia. But, again, genetics do not by themselves account for the development of schizophrenia. If they did, the concordance rate in identical twins would be 100 percent, not 48 percent.

Brain scans have indicated a number of structural abnormalities in the brains of

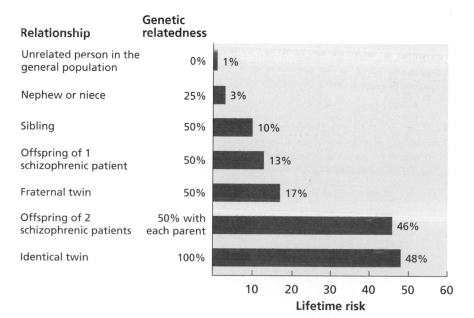

FIGURE 14.27 The degree of risk for developing schizophrenia in one's lifetime correlates highly with the degree of genetic relationship with someone who has that disorder. These data summarize the results of 40 concordance studies conducted in many countries. Based on data from Gottesman, 1991.

FIGURE 14.28 The Genain quadruplets, whose family tree contained several disordered people, all developed schizophrenia during their adolescent and young adult years. They have been studied for most of their adult lives at the National Institute of Mental Health. The quadruplets show remarkable similarities in abnormal brain functioning and in their patterns of behavior.
Source: National Institute of Mental Health.

➤ 43. What is the dopamine hypothesis? What evidence supports it?

➤ 44. What concepts do (a) psychoanalytic and (b) cognitive theorists use to explain the symptoms of schizophrenia?

schizophrenic patients. First, 20 to 35 percent show mild to moderate *brain atrophy,* a general loss or deterioration of neurons in the cerebral cortex and limbic system (Jernigan et al., 1991). The atrophy is centered in brain regions that influence cognitive processes and emotion, which may help explain the thought disorders and inappropriate emotion that are seen in such patients. Likewise, the thalamus, which collects and routes sensory input to various parts of the brain, shows MRI abnormalities. This may help account for the disordered attention and perception reported by schizophrenic patients whose cerebral cortex may be getting garbled or unfiltered information from the thalamus (Andreason et al., 1994). All of these structural differences are more common in patients who exhibit the Type II negative symptom pattern (Green, 1997). As we have seen, these patients have a poorer chance of recovery than those with the Type I positive symptom pattern.

Dopamine, a major excitatory transmitter substance, may play a key role in schizophrenia. The **dopamine hypothesis** states that the symptoms of schizophrenia—particularly positive symptoms—are produced by overactivity of the dopamine system in areas of the brain that regulate emotional expression, motivated behavior, and cognitive functioning (White & Milner, 1992). People diagnosed with schizophrenia have more dopamine receptors on neuron membranes than do nonschizophrenics and these receptors seem to be overreactive to dopamine stimulation (Black et al., 1988; Wong et al., 1986). Additional support comes from the finding that the effectiveness of antipsychotic drugs used to treat schizophrenia is directly related to their effectiveness in reducing dopamine-produced synaptic activity (Creese et al., 1976; Green, 1997). Other neurotransmitter systems are probably involved in this complex disorder as well.

The biological findings concerning schizophrenia are intriguing. What is not clear is whether they cause the disorder or are caused by it. Future research is almost certain to reveal other biological bases for the complex disorders of schizophrenia.

Psychological Factors

Freud and other psychoanalytic thinkers viewed schizophrenia as a retreat from unbearable stress and conflict. For Freud, schizophrenia represented an extreme example of the defense mechanism of **regression,** in which a person retreats to an earlier and more secure (even infantile) stage of psychosocial development in the face of overwhelming anxiety. Other psychodynamic thinkers, focusing on the interpersonal withdrawal that is an important feature of schizophrenia, view the disorder as a retreat from an interpersonal world that has become too stressful to deal with. Although Freud's regression explanation has not received much direct research support (Fisher & Greenberg, 1996), the belief that life stress is a causal factor is generally accepted today (Crook & Copolov, 2000).

Cognitive theorists believe that schizophrenics have a defect in the attentional mechanism that filters out irrelevant stimuli, so that they are overwhelmed by both internal and external stimuli. Thus sensory input becomes a chaotic flood, and irrelevant thoughts and images flash into consciousness. The stimulus overload produces distractability, thought disorganization, and the sense of being overwhelmed by disconnected thoughts and ideas. As one schizophrenic noted, "Everything seems to come pouring in at once . . . I can't seem to keep anything out" (Carson et al., 1988, p. 329). The recent MRI findings of thalamic abnormalities described above may help explain how this stimulus overload could occur through malfunction of the brain's "switchboard."

Environmental Factors

Stressful life events seem to play an important role in the emergence of schizophrenic behavior. These events tend to cluster in the two or three weeks preceding the "break" when the acute signs of the disorder appear (Day et al., 1987). Stressful life events seem to interact with biological or personality vulnerability factors. A highly vulnerable person may require little in the way of life stress to reach the breaking point (Fowles, 1992).

Family dynamics have long been a prime suspect in the origins of schizophrenia, but the search for parent or family characteristics that might cause the disorder has been largely unsuccessful. Significantly, children of biologically normal parents who are raised by schizophrenic adoptive parents do not show an increased risk of developing schizophrenia (Kety, 1988). Although persons with schizophrenia often come from families with problems, the nature and seriousness of those problems are not different from those of families in which nonschizophrenics are raised.

This does not mean that family dynamics are not important; rather, it may mean that a biological vulnerability factor must be present if stressful familial events are to cause their damage. Indeed, there is evidence that this vulnerability factor may appear early in life. In one study, researchers analyzed home movies showing children who were later to develop schizophrenic behaviors, as well as movies of their nonschizophrenic brothers and sisters. Even at these early ages—sometimes as young as 2 years of age—preschizophrenic children tended to show more odd and uncoordinated movements and less emotional expressiveness, especially for positive emotions (Grimes & Walker, 1994). These behavioral oddities may not only reflect a vulnerability factor, but they may also help to create environmental stress by evoking negative reactions from others.

Although researchers have had difficulty pinpointing family factors that contribute to the *initial* appearance of schizophrenia, one consistent finding is that previously hospitalized schizophrenics are more likely to relapse if they return to a home environment that is high in a factor called **expressed emotion** (Vaughn & Leff, 1976). Expressed emotion involves high levels of *criticism* ("All you do is sit in front of that TV"), *hostility* ("We're getting sick and tired of your craziness") and *overinvolvement* ("You're not going out unless I go with you"). One review of 26 studies showed that within 9 to 12 months of their return home, an average relapse rate of 48 percent occurred in patients whose families were high in expressed emotion, compared with a relapse rate of 21 percent when families were low in this factor (Kavanaugh, 1992). Before we conclude that high expressed emotion causes patients to relapse, however, we should note a finding from another study in which researchers videotaped actual interactions involving patients and their families (Rosenfarb et al., 1995). Analyses of the videotapes revealed that families high in expressed emotion did indeed make more negative comments to patients when they engaged in strange behaviors, but they also showed that the patients in these families engaged in about four times as many strange and disruptive behaviors, clouding the issue of what causes what. Thus high expressed emotion may be either a cause of or a response to patients' disordered behaviors.

Sociocultural Factors

Sociocultural factors are undoubtedly linked to schizophrenia (Freeman, 1994). Many studies have found that the prevalence of schizophrenia is highest in lower socioeconomic populations (Figure 14.29). Why is this? Is poverty a cause of schizophrenia, or is it an effect of the disorder? Two theories give opposite answers. The *social causation hypothesis* attributes the higher prevalence of schizophrenia to the higher levels of stress that low-income people experience, particularly within urban environments. In contrast, the *social drift hypothesis* proposes that as people develop schizophrenia, their personal and occupational functioning deteriorates, so that they drift down the socioeconomic ladder into poverty and migrate to low-cost urban environments. Perhaps social causation and social drift are both at work, for the factors that link poverty, social and environmental stressors, and schizophrenia are undoubtedly complex.

In contrast to most of the disorders we have described so far, schizophrenia may be a "culture-free" disorder. A worldwide epidemiological study sponsored by

➤ 45. How successful have researchers been in identifying family factors that cause schizophrenia? What role does expressed emotion play as a family variable?

➤ 46. Contrast the social causation and social drift hypotheses concerning social class and prevalence of schizophrenia.

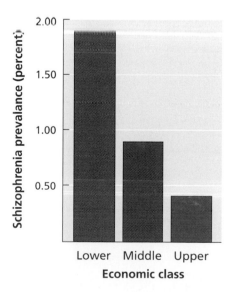

FIGURE 14.29 Relation between economic status and prevalence of schizophrenia. Is economic status a cause or an effect of schizophrenia?
Based on data from Keith et al., 1991.

the World Health Organization indicated that the prevalence of schizophrenia is not dramatically different throughout the world (Jablensky et al., 1992). On the other hand, researchers have found that the likelihood of *recovery* is greater in developing countries than in developed nations like the United States and Canada. This may reflect a stronger community orientation and greater social support extended to disturbed people in developing countries (Tanaka-Matsumi & Draguns, 1997).

〉 PERSONALITY DISORDERS

People diagnosed with **personality disorders** exhibit stable, ingrained, inflexible, and maladaptive ways of thinking, feeling, and behaving. When they encounter situations in which their typical behavior patterns do not work, unresolved conflicts tend to reemerge, they are likely to intensify their inappropriate ways of coping, and their emotional controls may break down (Millon et al., 1998).

Table 14.2 briefly describes the 10 personality disorders in Axis II of DSM-IV. The disorders are divided into three clusters that capture important commonalities: dramatic and impulsive behaviors; anxiety and fearfulness; or odd and eccentric behaviors. We focus here on the personality disorder that has received the greatest attention from clinicians and researchers over the years, namely, antisocial personality disorder.

TABLE 14.2	DSM-IV AXIS II PERSONALITY DISORDERS AND THEIR MAJOR FEATURES

Dramatic/impulsive Cluster

Antisocial personality disorder
Severe irresponsible and antisocial behavior beginning in childhood and continuing past age 18; impulsive need gratification and lack of empathy for others; often highly manipulative and seem to lack conscience

Histrionic personality disorder
Excessive, dramatic emotional reactions and attention seeking; often sexually provocative; highly impressionable and suggestible; out of touch with negative feelings

Narcissistic personality disorder
Grandiose fantasies or behavior, lack of empathy, and oversensitivity to evaluation; constant need for admiration from others; proud self-display

Borderline personality disorder
Pattern of severe instability of self-image, interpersonal relationships, and emotions, often expressing alternating extremes of love and hatred toward the same person; high frequency of manipulative suicidal behavior

Anxious/fearful Cluster

Avoidant personality disorder
Extreme social discomfort and timidity; feelings of inadequacy and fearfulness of being negatively evaluated

Dependent personality disorder
Extreme submissive and dependent behavior; fears of separation from those who satisfy dependency needs

Obsessive-compulsive personality disorder
Extreme perfectionism, orderliness, and inflexibility; preoccupied with mental and interpersonal control

Odd/eccentric cluster

Schizoid personality disorder
Indifference to social relationships and a restricted range of experiencing and expressing emotions

Schizotypal personality disorder
Odd thoughts, appearance, and behavior, and extreme discomfort in social situations

Paranoid personality disorder
An unwarranted tendency to interpret the behavior of other people as threatening, exploiting, or harmful

Source: Abstracted from DSM-IV Axis II, American Psychiatric Association, 1994.

Antisocial Personality Disorder

In the past, individuals with antisocial personality disorder have been referred to as *psychopaths* or *sociopaths*. They are among the most interpersonally destructive and emotionally harmful individuals. Males outnumber females three to one in this diagnostic group (American Psychiatric Association, 1994).

People with antisocial personality disorder seem to lack a conscience. In the 19th century, they were sometimes referred to as "moral imbeciles." They exhibit little anxiety or guilt and tend to be impulsive and unable to delay gratification of their needs. They also exhibit a lack of emotional attachment to other people, as suggested in this report by a man diagnosed as having an antisocial personality:

> When I was in high school my best friend got leukemia and died and I went to his funeral. Everybody else was crying . . . (but) . . . I suddenly realized I wasn't feeling anything at all. . . . That night I thought about it some more and found I wouldn't miss my mother and father if they died and that I wasn't too nuts about my brothers and sisters for that matter. I figured there wasn't anybody I really cared for but, then, I didn't need any of them anyway so I rolled over and went to sleep. (McNeil, 1967, p. 87)

Lack of the capacity to care about others can make antisocial individuals a danger to society (Black, 1999). For example, mass murderers Charles Manson, Ted Bundy, and Jeffrey Dahmer failed to show any remorse for their serial murders or sympathy for their victims (Figure 14.30). Although antisocial individuals often verbalize feelings and commitments with great sincerity, their behaviors indicate otherwise. They often appear very intelligent and charming, and they have the ability to rationalize their inappropriate behavior so that it appears reasonable and justifiable. Consequently, they are often virtuosos at manipulating others and talking their way out of trouble. One researcher who wanted to study nonincarcerated antisocial personalities quickly attracted 25 of them from the Boston area with the following classified ad:

> Wanted: Charming, aggressive, carefree people who are impulsively irresponsible but are good at handling people and at looking after Number One. Send name, address, phone, and short biography proving how interesting you are to . . . (Widom, 1983, p. 72)

People with antisocial personalities also display a perplexing failure to respond to punishment. Because of their lack of anxiety, punishment does not deter them from engaging in self-defeating or illegal acts again and again. As a result some of them develop imposing prison records.

To be diagnosed as having an antisocial personality disorder, a person must be at least 18 years of age. However, the diagnostic criteria also require substantial evidence of antisocial behavior before the age of 15, including such acts as habitual lying, early and aggressive sexual behavior, excessive drinking, theft, vandalism, and chronic rule violations at home and school. Thus antisocial personality disorder is the culmination of a behavior pattern that typically begins in childhood (Kernberg, 2000).

➤ 47. Describe the major characteristics of the antisocial personality disorder.

FIGURE 14.30 The serial killer Theodore Bundy exhibited many features of the antisocial personality, including a charismatic personality and an ability to injure others without remorse or guilt.

Causal Factors

Biological Factors

Biological research on the antisocial personality disorder has focused on both genetic and physiological factors. A genetic factor is indicated by consistently higher rates of concordance for antisocial behavior among identical twins than among fraternal twins (Rutter, 1997). Adoption studies suggest a similar conclusion. In one study, researchers compared the criminal records of men who had been adopted early in life with those of their biological fathers and their adoptive fathers. Men whose biological fathers had no criminal record showed a low incidence of criminal behavior themselves, even if their adoptive fathers were criminal offenders. In contrast, the criminality rate was nearly twice as high if the biological father had a criminal record and the adoptive father did not, clearly suggesting the operation of genetic factors. However, the rate of criminality in the sons was still greater when both the biological *and* the adoptive fathers were criminals. These sons probably inherited a tendency toward criminality from their biological fathers and learned criminal behaviors from their adoptive fathers, showing the additive influences of genetic and environmental factors (Cloninger & Gottesman, 1987).

➤ 48. How are biological factors implicated in the antisocial personality disorder?

How might genetic factors predispose individuals to engage in antisocial behavior? One clue might lie in the relative absence of anxiety and guilt that seems to underlie many of the behaviors in the antisocial disorder. Many researchers have suggested that the physiological basis for the disorder might lie in some dysfunction in brain structures that govern emotional arousal and behavioral inhibition, resulting in a chronically underaroused state that impairs avoidance learning, causes boredom and a search for excitement, and fosters behavioral impulsiveness (Arnett et al., 1997; Patrick et al., 1994). Support comes from MRI findings that individuals diagnosed with the disorder have subtle neurological deficits in the prefrontal lobes, the seat of executive functions such as planning, reasoning, and behavioral inhibition, and that these neurological deficits are associated with reduced autonomic activity (Raine et al., 2000). It thus appears, as long suspected, that antisocial individuals may indeed be "wired" differently at a neurological level.

Psychological and Environmental Factors

Psychodynamic theorists regard antisocial personalities as people without a conscience. Psychoanalytic theorists suggest that such people lack anxiety and guilt because they did not develop an adequate superego (Gabbard, 1990). In the absence of a well-developed superego, the restraints on the id are reduced, resulting in impulsive and hedonistic behavior. The failure to develop a strong superego is thought to result from inadequate identification with appropriate adult figures because these figures were either physically or psychologically unavailable to the child (Kernberg, 2000).

➤ 49. How are classical conditioning and modeling concepts used to account for the development of antisocial personality disorder?

Like some biological theories, learning explanations suggest that persons with the disorder lack impulse control because of impaired ability to develop conditioned fear responses when punished. This results in a deficit in avoidance learning. Hans Eysenck (1964) maintained that developing a conscience depends on the ability to learn fear and avoidance responses through classical conditioning, and people who fail to do so will be less able to inhibit their behavior. In accord with this hypothesis, Adrian Raine and coworkers (1996) did a 14-year follow-up of males who had been subjected at age 15 to a classical conditioning procedure in which a soft tone was used as the CS and a loud, aversive tone as the UCS. The conditioned fear response was the participant's skin conductance response when the CS occurred after a number of pairings with the loud UCS. The researchers found that men who had accumulated a criminal record by age 29 had shown much poorer emotional conditioning at age 15 than had those with no criminal record.

Learning through modeling may also play an important role. Many antisocial individuals come from homes where parents exhibit a good deal of aggression and are inattentive to their children's needs (Rutter, 1997). Such parents provide role models for both aggressive behavior and disregard for the needs of others. Another important environmental factor is exposure to deviant peers. Children who become antisocial often learn some of their deviant behaviors from peer groups who both model antisocial behavior and reinforce it with so-

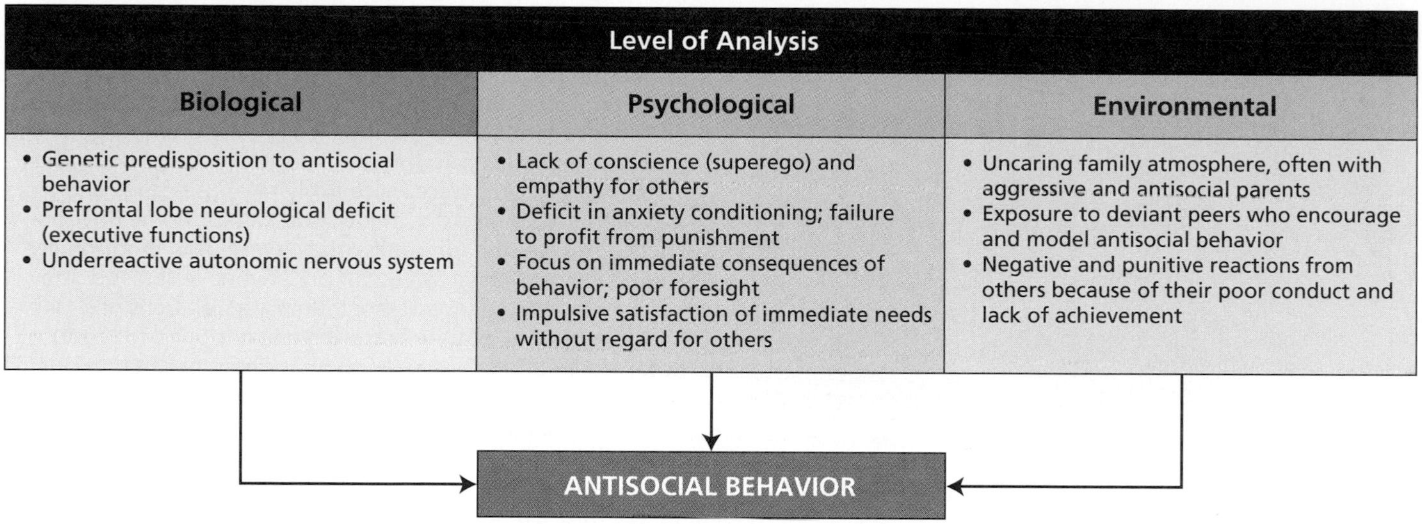

Level of Analysis		
Biological	**Psychological**	**Environmental**
• Genetic predisposition to antisocial behavior • Prefrontal lobe neurological deficit (executive functions) • Underreactive autonomic nervous system	• Lack of conscience (superego) and empathy for others • Deficit in anxiety conditioning; failure to profit from punishment • Focus on immediate consequences of behavior; poor foresight • Impulsive satisfaction of immediate needs without regard for others	• Uncaring family atmosphere, often with aggressive and antisocial parents • Exposure to deviant peers who encourage and model antisocial behavior • Negative and punitive reactions from others because of their poor conduct and lack of achievement

ANTISOCIAL BEHAVIOR

FIGURE 14.31 Understanding the Causes of Behavior: Antisocial personality disorder.

cial approval (Bandura, 1997). Combined with a possible genetic predisposition for antisocial behavior, such environmental factors would surely encourage the development of deviant behavior patterns (Figure 14.31).

Cognitive theorists believe that another deficit in antisocial personalities is their consistent failure to think about or anticipate the long-term negative consequences of their acts. As a result, they behave impulsively, thinking only of what they want at that moment (Bandura, 1997).

Though people with antisocial personality disorders often lack the capacity to form intimate and caring relationships, they frequently do marry. Our *Research Close-up* suggests that such individuals may be among a troubling population, namely men who abuse their wives physically and emotionally.

➤ 50. Describe the psychological and physiological characteristics of the two types of battering men discovered by Jacobson and Gottman.

RESEARCH CLOSE-UP

Personality Disorders in Men Who Batter Women

❱ **Background**

An estimated 2 to 4 million women in the United States are beaten periodically by the men who have taken a vow to love and honor them, namely, their husbands (Figure 14.32). Whereas only 6 percent of murdered men are killed by women with whom they've had intimate relationships, half of all murdered women are killed by their husbands, ex-husbands, boyfriends, and ex-boyfriends (Bergen, 1998; Koss & Ingram, 2000). What kinds of men commit such acts? How many have antisocial and other personality disorders? Within abusive relationships, does the violence ever end? Can women escape such relationships, or is their fear and the risk of reprisal too great? These questions and others were the focus of an eight-year research project carried out

by psychologists Neil Jacobson and John Gottman. Most previous studies of spousal abuse were based on after-the-fact reports by batterers and their victims, which may not be reliable. In this research project, the investigators decided to actually observe and measure what happens during arguments involving couples in abusive relationships.

❱ **Method**

Couples who were experiencing distress in their marriages were invited through newspaper ads and public service announcements to participate in a study of marital interactions. More than 200 Seattle-area couples responded. Within this larger sample, the researchers found 63 couples with marriages in which severe physical battering occurred,

—Continued

FIGURE 14.32 Spousal abuse is a serious, and sometimes fatal, social problem. What are the personality characteristics of men who batter their wives?

as well as a comparison group of nonviolent couples who were equally dissatisfied with their marriages. The couples completed extensive interviews about their interactions, including incidents of physical abuse, and they were given a series of personality tests. In the laboratory, they engaged in nonviolent arguments about conflictual areas in their relationship. During the arguments, the researchers videotaped them and obtained physiological measures of emotional arousal, including heart rate, blood pressure, and skin conductance. Two years and five years after this initial assessment, the couples were again interviewed about their marriages and the nature of their interactions.

▶ Results

On the basis of the personality, behavioral, and physiological data that they collected, Jacobson and Gottman concluded that the majority of men who battered their wives tended to fall into two distinct groups having different patterns of motivation, behavior, and physiology. The larger group of batterers confined their violence to family members and did not tend to have criminal records. They were basically contemptuous of women but extremely dependent on their wives and so fearful of being abandoned by them that they used violence to gain total domination over them. In a sense, they "sunk their teeth into their partners and wouldn't let go," so the researchers called them "pit bulls." Their violence was marked by a gradual increase in emotional arousal that culminated in an emotional outburst and physical assault on the spouse. During the controlled nonviolent arguments in the laboratory, their physiological arousal increased gradually in a "slow burn" pattern as they grew more angry with their wives. About a third of the "pit bulls" qualified for a diagnosis of antisocial personality disorder.

The second group of men, comprising about 20 percent of the batterers, were much different. When they grew increasingly angry during the laboratory arguments, their physiological measures actually showed a *decrease* in emotional arousal—a cold fury. These men calmed themselves internally while reacting with almost instantaneous verbal aggression in the controlled environment. This remarkably

cold-blooded emotional pattern combined with their quick-strike aggression prompted the researchers to refer to them as "cobras." Almost all of these men qualified for a diagnosis of antisocial personality disorder, and many of them had histories of criminal violence outside of their marriages. They also were more likely to threaten to kill their wives with guns and knives. Cobras were more likely to abuse drugs and alcohol and to come from chaotic and violent home environments. Unlike the pit bulls, they were not emotionally dependent on their wives or on anyone else, and they seemed to lack the capacity for intimacy in relationships. Like that of the pit bulls, their battering was designed to produce total domination, but only so that their partners would never hesitate to cater to their every desire.

The results of the two- and five-year follow-ups were also revealing. In no instance did the abuse within a relationship ever stop, whether the batterer was a pit bull or a cobra. Sometimes, after the wife was totally dominated, the physical abuse was replaced by vicious emotional abuse and explicit threats of physical assault. Nonetheless, by the end of five years, 75 percent of the women married to pit bulls and 25 percent of those married to cobras had left or divorced their battering husbands. The reactions of the husbands varied. Pit bulls seemed more likely to stalk or retaliate violently against their former spouses because of their psychological issues relating to abandonment and betrayal. Although the cobras were more severely violent than the pit bulls, these men, being less psychologically invested in the relationship, were more likely to simply move on to another victim who would gratify their needs.

▶ Critical Analysis

This study is the first to identify subgroups of abusers based on both behavioral and physiological patterns. The cobras showed a remarkable dissociation of physiology from other aspects of anger. They also exhibited many of the "cold-blooded" qualities of the antisocial personality, including the capacity to use others for need gratification. The research also dispelled some myths about spousal abuse, including the belief that over time, abusive relationships will improve. Once begun, the abuse never ended.

Although about half of the women physically aggressed against their husbands at times, their aggression was usually to defend themselves and was unlikely to injure their spouse. Yet some of the pit bulls seized upon these incidents to describe themselves as victims. Some even describe themselves as "battered husbands." Finally, this study demonstrates that it is possible to study important aspects of behavior under controlled conditions and that doing so may yield important findings, such as the two patterns of physiological arousal in the abusive husbands. As unexpected and interesting as the lowered emotional arousal exhibited by the cobras was, however, a question as yet unanswered is whether the same pattern occurs when they are actually being physically violent, or whether it might have occurred only in the controlled laboratory setting as they tried to inhibit their physically aggressive behavior.

Source: Neil S. Jacobson and John M. Gottman, 1998. *When men batter women.* New York: Simon & Schuster.

▼▼

CHAPTER SUMMARY

Defining and Classifying Psychological Disorders

- Abnormality is largely a social judgment. Behavior that is judged to reflect a psychological disorder typically is (1) distressing to the person or to other people; (2) dysfunctional, maladaptive, or self-defeating; and (3) socially deviant in a way that arouses discomfort in others and cannot be attributed to environmental causes. The major psychiatric classification system in the United States is the DSM-IV, which describes the current status of the individual using five different dimensions, or axes.

- Among the important issues in psychiatric diagnosis are the reliability and validity of the diagnostic categories and the potential negative effects of labeling on social perceptions and self-perceptions. Legal implications of competency and insanity judgments are also receiving attention.

Anxiety Disorders

- Anxiety involves three components: (1) cognitive processes involving perceptions of threat and lack of control; (2) physiological arousal; and (3) behaviors that reflect the anxious state and often are designed to escape or avoid the feared object or situation.

- The anxiety disorders include phobic disorders (irrational fears of specific objects or situations), generalized anxiety disorder (recurrent anxiety reactions that are difficult to link to specific environmental stimuli), panic disorder, obsessive-compulsive disorder (which involves uncontrollable and unwelcome thoughts and repetitive behaviors), and posttraumatic stress disorders.

- Biological factors in anxiety disorders include both genetic and biochemical processes, possibly involving the action of neurotransmitters, such as GABA, within parts of the brain that control emotional arousal.

- Psychoanalytic theorists believe that neurotic anxiety results from the inability of the ego's defenses to deal with conflicts involving the id and the superego. The cognitive perspective stresses the role of cognitive distortions, including the tendencies to magnify the degree of threat and danger and, in the case of panic disorder, to misinterpret normal anxiety symptoms in ways that can evoke panic. The behavioral perspective views anxiety as a learned response established through classical conditioning or vicarious learning. The avoidance responses in phobias and compulsive disorders are seen as operant responses that are negatively reinforced through anxiety reduction.

- Sociocultural factors are also involved in anxiety disorders, as illustrated by certain culture-bound anxiety disorders. The greater prevalence of anxiety disorders in women has been explained in both biological and sociocultural terms.

Mood (Affective) Disorders

- Mood disorders include several depressive disorders and bipolar disorder, in which intermittent periods of mania (intense mood and behavior activation) occur. Depression has four sets of symptoms: emotional, motivational, cognitive, and somatic. The negative emotions, thoughts, loss of motivation, and behavioral slowness symptoms are reversed in mania.

- Both genetic and neurochemical factors have been linked to depression. One prominent biochemical theory links depression to underactivity of neurotransmitters (norepinephrine, dopamine, and serotonin) that activate brain areas involved in pleasure and positive motivation. Drugs that relieve depression increase the activity of these transmitters. Bipolar disorder seems to have an even stronger genetic component than unipolar depression does.

- Psychoanalytic theorists view depression as a long-term consequence of traumatic losses and rejections early in life that create a personality vulnerability pattern.

- Cognitive theorists emphasize the role of negative feelings about the self, the world, and the future (depressive triad) and describe a depressive attributional pattern in which negative outcomes are attributed to personal causes and successes are attributed to situational causes. Seligman's theory of learned helplessness suggests that attributing negative outcomes to personal, stable, and global causes fosters depression.

- The behavioral approach focuses on the vicious cycle in which depression-induced inactivity and aversive behaviors reduce reinforcement from the environment and thereby increase depression still further.

- Desire to escape distress and manipulation are the two major motives for suicide. Suicide potential increases if the person has a lethal plan and a past history of parasuicide.

Somatoform Disorders

- Somatoform disorders involve physical complaints that do not have a physical basis sufficient to explain them. They include hypochondriasis, pain disorder, and conversion disorders, in which a physical symptom or disability occurs in the absence of physical pathology.

- Familial similarities in somatoform disorders may have a biological basis or they may be the result of environmental shaping through attention and sympathy. Somatoform patients may be highly vigilant and reactive to somatic symptoms. Such disorders tend to occur with greater frequency in cultures that discourage open expression of negative emotions.

Dissociative Disorders

- Dissociative disorders involve losses of memory and personal identity. The major dissociative disorders are psychogenic amnesia, psychogenic fugue, and dissociative identity disorder (DID).

- The trauma-dissociation theory holds that DID emerges when children dissociate to defend themselves from severe physical or sexual abuse. This model has been challenged by other theorists who believe that the "multiple personalities" result from role immersion and therapist suggestion.

Schizophrenia

- Schizophrenia is a psychotic disorder featuring disordered thinking and language; poor contact with reality; flat, blunted, or inappropriate emotion; and disordered behavior. The cognitive aspect of the disorder can involve delusions (false beliefs) or hallucinations (false perceptions).

- Schizophrenias have been categorized in a number of ways. The DSM-IV lists five subcategories: paranoid, disorganized, catatonic, undifferentiated, and residual. Another categorization is based on the nature of the symptoms (positive vs. negative). Positive symptoms involving delusions or persecutions predict a better outcome.

- There is strong evidence for a genetic predisposition to schizophrenia that makes some people particularly vulnerable to stressful life events. The dopamine hypothesis states that schizophrenia involves overactivity of the dopamine system, resulting in too much stimulation.

- Psychoanalytic theorists regard schizophrenia as a profound regression to a primitive stage of psychosocial development in response to unbearable stress, particularly within the family. Negative expressed emotion is a family variable related to relapse among formerly hospitalized schizophrenics.

- Cognitive theorists focus on the thought disorder that is central to schizophrenia. One idea is that schizophrenics have a defect in their attentional filters, so that they are overwhelmed by internal and external stimuli and become disorganized.

Personality Disorders

- Personality disorders are rigid, maladaptive patterns of behavior that characterize an individual's behavior over a long period of time. They fall on Axis II of DSM-IV.

- Research on the antisocial disorder suggests that genetic and physiological factors that result in underarousal may contribute to the disorder's causes. Psychoanalysts view the disorder as a failure to develop a superego, that could restrain their impulsive self-gratification. Learning explanations focus on the failure of punishment to inhibit maladaptive behaviors and exposure to aggressive, uncaring models. It seems likely that there is a genetic predisposition that increases the risk of antisocial behavior, especially if the person is exposed to deviant models.

- Research on men who batter their wives has identified two subtypes who exhibit different motivational and physiological patterns.

▼▼

KEY TERMS AND CONCEPTS*

abnormal behavior (590)

agoraphobia (595)

anxiety disorders (594)

biological preparedness (598)

bipolar disorder (602)

catatonic schizophrenia (614)

competency (legal) (593)

compulsion (596)

conversion disorder (608)

culture-bound disorders (600)

delusions (612)

depressive attributional pattern (605)

depressive cognitive triad (604)

disorganized schizophrenia (614)

dissociative disorders (609)

dissociative identity disorder (DID) (610)

dopamine hypothesis (616)

dysthymia (601)

expressed emotion (617)

generalized anxiety disorder (595)

hallucinations (613)

hypochondriasis (605)

insanity (legal) (593)

learned helplessness theory (605)

major depression (601)

mania (602)

mood disorders (601)

negative symptoms (612)

neurotic anxiety (599)

obsession (596)

obsessive-compulsive disorder (596)

pain disorder (608)

panic disorder (595)

paranoid schizophrenia (614)

personality disorder (618)

phobias (594)

positive symptoms (612)

posttraumatic stress disorder (PTSD) (597)

psychogenic amnesia (609)

psychogenic fugue (610)

regression (616)

reliability (diagnosis) (591)

schizophrenia (612)

social phobia (595)

somatoform disorder (608)

specific phobia (595)

stressor (589)

suicide (606)

trauma-dissociation theory (610)

Type I schizophrenia (614)

Type II schizophrenia (614)

undifferentiated schizophrenia (614)

validity (diagnosis) (591)

vulnerability (589)

vulnerability-stress model (589)

* Each term has been boldfaced in the text on the page indicated in parentheses.

APPLYING YOUR KNOWLEDGE

1. Trephination as a method for treating abnormal behavior was inspired by
   a) the biological perspective.
   b) the humanistic perspective.
   c) the demonological perspective.
   d) the psychodynamic perspective.

2. There is a history of depression in Brent's family. Brent has never shown any sign of depression, but his sister Julie became severely depressed when her best friend moved to another city. Which model best explains the different outcomes for Brent and Julie?
   a) biological perspective
   b) behavioral perspective
   c) humanistic perspective
   d) vulnerability-stress model

3. Stuart is going to stand trial on a felony assault charge. He increasingly seems to be out of touch with reality. On the day of his trial, his lawyer is unable to get him to focus on what is happening. Instead, Stuart carries on a conversation with a nonexistent friend. His lawyer might move to get him declared, for purposes of the trial,
   a) incompetent.
   b) insane.
   c) guilty but mentally ill.
   d) possessed by a demon.

4. A woman becomes very anxious whenever she leaves her home. Soon she will not go out alone because she fears that she will "fall apart" in public. The woman would most likely be diagnosed with
   a) agoraphobia.
   b) obsessive-compulsive disorder.
   c) mood disorder.
   d) psychogenic fugue.

5. Whenever Thomas studies, he has trouble concentrating because unwanted thoughts about failure intrude into consciousness. The thoughts upset him greatly. Thomas is experiencing
   a) compulsions.
   b) a panic disorder.
   c) obsessions.
   d) a preschizophrenic reaction.

6. Jenny confides to you that she has had a terrible fear of bees that prevents her from enjoying the outdoors. With the wisdom gained in your psychology course, you explain to her that the major reason phobias are maintained is that
   a) they are learned early in life before the ego matures.
   b) they are reinforced by classical conditioning.

   c) avoidance responses prevent extinction of the anxiety response.
   d) the fear response becomes stronger over time.

7. On Saturday, Claire was on top of the world, optimistic, and very energetic. The next day, she awoke feeling sad, worthless, and convinced that life had nothing to offer her. She may be exhibiting the signs of
   a) a dissociative identity disorder.
   b) antisocial personality disorder.
   c) unipolar depression.
   d) a bipolar disorder.

8. An acquaintance has seemed very depressed for the past month. One day she gives you a prized possession and you become concerned about the possibility of suicide. You should
   a) not bring up the topic of suicide, because it might put the idea into her mind.
   b) not broach the topic because people who are contemplating suicide never talk about it anyway.
   c) allay your concern because women are far less likely than men to attempt suicide.
   d) talk frankly about your concern and find out if she has a suicide plan, then assist her in getting professional help.

9. Gregory experiences hallucinations of monsters stalking him, delusions that people are spying him, and bizarre speech. Clement exhibits no emotion, has lost most speech, and does not relate to others at all. Which person has the better chance of recovery?
   a) Gregory
   b) Clement
   c) They have an equal chance of recovery, but Clement will recover first
   d) Neither person has any chance of recovering

10. A stockbroker has been arrested for convincing 20 people to invest their life savings in a nonexistent company. The man expresses no guilt for cheating the people and declares, "The greedy suckers got what they deserved." A check of his history reveals a long history of conduct problems in adolescence. He is most likely to be diagnosed with
    a) paranoid schizophrenia.
    b) antisocial personality disorder.
    c) adult conduct disorder.
    d) being misunderstood, but honest.

Answers

1. c) (page 587); 2. d) (page 589); 3. a) (page 593); 4. a) (page 595); 5. c) (page 596); 6. c) (page 600); 7. d) (page 602); 8. d) (page 608); 9. a) (page 615); 10. b) (page 619).

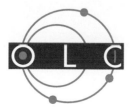

For additional quizzing and a variety of interactive resources, visit the book's Online Learning Center at www.mhhe.com/passer.

TREATMENT OF PSYCHOLOGICAL DISORDERS

It is a process, a thing-in-itself, an experience,
a relationship, a dynamic.

–Carl Rogers

15

15

CHAPTER OUTLINE

▼▼▼▼▼▼▼▼▼▼▼▼▼▼▼▼▼▼▼▼▼▼▼▼▼▼▼▼▼▼▼▼▼

I fought my way through Harvard in the midst of psychosis and "spaciness." . . . There is no doubt in my mind that therapy helped me get through school. . . . For so long I wondered why my therapist insisted on talking about my relationship with him. He was not my problem; the problem was my life—my past, my fears, what I was going to do tomorrow, how I would handle things, sometimes just how to survive. . . . I took a long time, but finally I saw why it was important to explore my relationship with my therapist—it was the first real relationship I had ever had: that is, the first I felt safe enough to invest myself in. I rationalized that it was all right because I would learn from this relationship how to relate to other people and maybe even one day leave behind the isolation of my own world. . . . I often felt at odds with my therapist until I could see that he was a real person and he related to me and I to him, not only as patient and therapist, but as human beings. Eventually I began to feel that I too was a person, not just an outsider looking in on the world.

Medication or superficial support is not a substitute for the feeling that one is understood by another human being. For me, the greatest gift came the day I realized that my therapist really had stood by me for years and that he would continue to stand by me and help me achieve what I wanted to achieve. With that realization, my viability as a person began to grow. ("A Recovering Patient," 1986, pp. 68–70)

➤ 1. What two therapeutic elements combine in the treatment of behavior disorders?

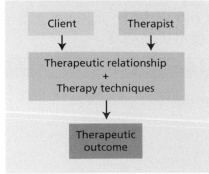

FIGURE 15.1 The process of therapy involves a relationship between a client and a therapist who applies the techniques dictated by his or her approach to treatment.

In this poignant account, written by a person who had suffered from schizophrenia for much of her life, we see that even in this most serious of behavior disorders, humans can reach out and help one another. This chapter explores the many approaches that are being taken to treat psychological disorders, as well as the critical issue of their effectiveness. Although first-person reports like that offered by the "recovering patient" suggest that many people derive considerable benefit from psychotherapy, psychologists demand much more in the way of evidence. Nearly 40 years of research on psychological treatments has taught us that the question of efficacy, or treatment outcome, is a tremendously complex one that has no simple answers. Yet as we shall see, much has been learned about the effectiveness of these various therapeutic approaches and about the factors that influence treatment outcome.

❭ THE HELPING RELATIONSHIP

The basic goal of all treatment approaches is to help people change maladaptive, self-defeating thoughts, feelings, and behavior patterns so that they can live happier and more productive lives. As the remarks of the "recovering patient" suggest, the relationship between the client and the person providing help is a prime ingredient of therapeutic success (Beutler et al., 1994; Binder & Strupp, 1997; Rogers, 1980). Within that helping relationship, therapists use a variety of treatment techniques to promote positive changes in the client. These techniques vary widely, depending on the therapists' own theories of cause and change, and they may range from biomedical approaches (such as administering psychoactive drugs) to a wide range of psychological treatments. Both of these elements, relationship and techniques, are important to the success of the treatment enterprise (see Figure 15.1).

A majority of people with mental health problems first seek help not from mental health professionals, but from family members, physicians, members of the clergy, acquaintances, or self-help groups (Seligman, 1995). Often, however, these sources of psychological support are not enough, and distressed people are increasingly seeking help from professional counselors and therapists. Surveys indicate that nearly 30 percent of Americans have sought psychological counseling from professionals at some point in their lives, a dramatic rise from the 13 percent who had done so in the mid-1950s (Gaylin, 2000; Meredith, 1986). These people receive treatment from mental health professionals who fall into several categories.

Counseling and clinical psychologists make up one group. These psychologists, who typically hold the Ph.D. (Doctor of Philosophy) or the Psy.D. (Doctor of Psychology) degree, have received five or more years of intensive training and supervision in a variety of psychotherapeutic techniques as well as training in research and psychological assessment techniques. A second group, *psychiatrists*, are medical doctors who specialize in psychotherapy and in biomedical treatments, such as drug therapy.

In addition to psychologists and psychiatrists, a number of other professionals provide treatment. These professionals typically receive master's degrees based on two years of highly focused and practical training. They include *psychiatric social workers*, who often work in community agencies; *marriage and family counselors*, who specialize in problems arising from family relations; *pastoral counselors*, who tend to focus on spiritual issues; and *abuse counselors*, who work with substance and sexual abusers and their victims.

Having previewed the nature of therapy and those who provide it, we now consider the therapeutic approaches that have developed within the major perspectives on human behavior. Figure 15.2 provides an overview of the therapies we will consider.

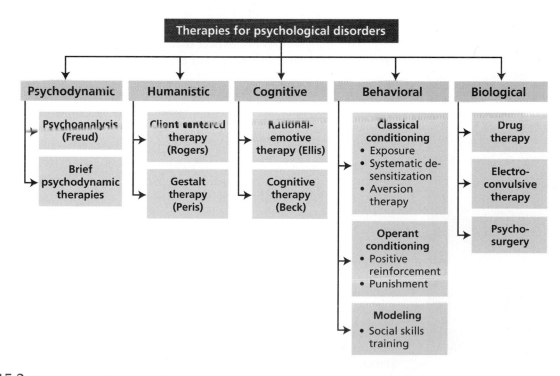

FIGURE 15.2 An overview of the major treatment approaches to the behavior disorders, organized according to five major perspectives on behavior.

❯ PSYCHODYNAMIC THERAPIES

The psychodynamic approach to psychotherapy focuses on internal conflicts and unconscious factors that underlie maladaptive behavior. The historical roots of psychodynamic approaches are to be found in Sigmund Freud's development of psychoanalysis. The term *psychoanalysis* refers not only to Freud's theory of personality, but also to the specific approach to treatment that he developed. Although both the theory and the techniques of therapy were later modified by his followers and by those who defected to pursue rival approaches, the psychodynamic principles underlying Freud's approach continue to exert a major influence today.

Psychoanalysis

➤ 2. What is the major therapeutic goal in psychoanalysis?

The goal of psychoanalysis is to help clients achieve **insight,** the conscious awareness of the psychodynamics that underlie their problems. Such awareness permits clients to adjust their behavior to their current life situations, rather than continuing to repeat the old maladaptive routines learned in childhood. Analysts believe that as the client repeatedly encounters and deals with buried emotions, motives, and conflicts both within and outside of therapy, the psychic energy that was previously devoted to keeping the unconscious conflicts under control can be released and redirected to more adaptive ways of living.

Free Association

➤ 3. How are free association and dream analysis used in psychoanalysis?

Freud believed that mental events are meaningfully associated with one another, so that clues to the contents of the unconscious are to be found in the constant stream of thoughts, memories, images, and feelings we experience. In his technique of **free association,** Freud asked his clients to recline on a couch and to verbally report without censorship any thoughts, feelings, or images that entered awareness. Freud sat out of sight behind the client so that the client's thought processes would be determined primarily by internal factors (Figure 15.3).

The analyst does not expect that free association will necessarily lead directly to unconscious material but rather that it will provide clues concerning important themes or issues. For example, a client's stream of thoughts may suddenly stop after she has mentioned her father, suggesting the possibility that she was approaching a "loaded" topic that activated repressive defenses.

Dream Interpretation

Psychoanalysts believe that dreams express impulses, fantasies, and wishes that the client's defenses keep in the unconscious during waking hours. Even in dreams, which Freud termed "the royal road to the unconscious," defensive processes usually disguise the threatening material to protect the dreamer from the anxiety that the material might evoke. In dream interpretation, the analyst tries to help the client search for the unconscious material contained in the dreams. One means of doing so is to ask the client to free associate to each element of the dream and try to help the client arrive at an understanding of what the symbols in the dream really represent.

Resistance

Although clients come to therapists for help, they also have a strong unconscious investment in maintaining the status quo. After all, their problems result from the fact that certain unconscious conflicts are so painful that the ego has resorted to maladaptive defensive patterns to deal with them. These avoidance patterns emerge in the course of therapy as **resistance,** defensive maneuvers that hinder the process of therapy. Resistance can be manifested in many differ-

FIGURE 15.3 In classical Freudian psychoanalysis the client reclines on a couch, with the analyst sitting out of the client's view. This photo shows the office where Freud saw his clients.

ent ways. A client may experience difficulty in free-associating, may come late or "forget about" a therapy appointment, or may avoid talking about certain topics. Resistance is a sign that anxiety-arousing sensitive material is being approached. An important task of analysis is to explore the reasons for resistance, both to promote insight and to guard against the ultimate resistance: the client's decision to drop out of therapy prematurely.

Transference

As noted earlier, the analyst sits out of view of the client and reveals nothing to the client about himself or herself. Nonetheless, clients will eventually begin to project onto the "blank screen" of the therapist important perceptions and feelings related to their underlying conflicts. **Transference** occurs when the client responds irrationally to the analyst as if he or she were an important figure from the client's past. Transference is considered a most important process in psychoanalysis, for it brings out into the open repressed feelings and maladaptive behavior patterns that the therapist can point out to the client.

➤ 4. How do resistance and transference reflect underlying conflicts?

Transference takes two basic forms. *Positive transference* occurs when a client transfers feelings of intense affection, dependency, or love to the analyst, whereas *negative transference* involves irrational expressions of anger, hatred, or disappointment. Analysts believe that until transference reactions are analyzed and resolved, there can be no full resolution of the client's problems. In the following excerpt from a psychoanalytic session, a client traces her transference reaction to its source and then recognizes the operation of similar reactions in other relationships.

Client: I don't want to like you. I'd rather not like you.

Therapist: I wonder why?

Client: I feel I'll be hurt. Liking you will expose me to being hurt.

Therapist: But how do you feel about me?

Client: I don't know. I have conflicting emotions about you. Sometimes I like you too much and sometimes I get mad at you for no reason. I often can't think of you, even picture you. . . . Yes, I don't want to like you. If I do, I won't be able to help myself. I'll get hurt. But why do I feel or insist that I'm in love with you?

Therapist: Are you?

Client: Yes. And I feel so guilty and upset about it. At night I think of you and get sexual feelings and it frightens me.

Therapist: Do I remind you of anyone?

Client: Yes. (Pause) There are things about you that remind me of my brother. (Laughs) I realize this is silly.

Therapist: Mmhmm.

Client: My brother Harry, the one I had the sex experiences with when I was little. He made me do things I didn't want to. I let him fool with me because he made me feel sorry for him.

Therapist: Do you have any of the same feelings toward me?

Client: It's not that I expect that anything will really happen, but I just don't want to have feelings for you. . . . I know it's the same thing. I'm afraid of you taking advantage of me. If I tell you I like you, that means you'll make me do what you want.

Therapist: Just like Harry made you do what he wanted.

Client: Yes. I didn't want to let him do what he did, but I couldn't help myself. I hated myself. That's why I know it now because there is no reason why I should feel you are the same way. That's why I act that way with other people too. . . . I don't like to have people get too close to me. The whole thing is the same as happens with you. It's all so silly and wrong. You aren't my brother and the other people aren't my brother. I never saw the connection until now. (Wolberg, 1967, pp. 660–661)

In this interchange, we see both positive and negative transference reactions based on an important past relationship. The client's feelings about her brother continue be played out in her fear of getting close to others and becoming vulnerable to being exploited once again.

Interpretation

> ➤ 5. What are interpretations, and how are they used by analysts?

How can analysts help clients detect and understand resistances, the meaning of dream symbols, and transference reactions? The analyst's chief therapeutic technique for these purposes is interpretation of the material the client presents. An **interpretation** is any statement by the therapist intended to provide the client with insight into his or her behavior or dynamics. An interpretative statement confronts clients with something that they have not previously admitted into consciousness: "It's almost as if you're angry with me without realizing it."

A general rule in psychoanalytic treatment is to interpret what is already near the surface and just beyond the client's current awareness. Offering "deep" interpretations of strongly defended unconscious dynamics is considered poor technique because even if they are correct, such interpretations are so far removed from the client's current awareness that they cannot be informative or helpful. This is one reason that even after the analyst fully understands the causes of the client's problems, psychoanalysis may require several more years of treatment. It is the client who must eventually arrive at the insights.

Brief Psychodynamic Therapies

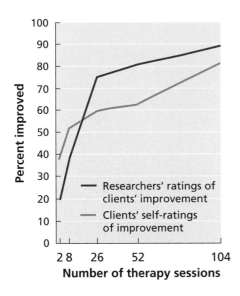

FIGURE 15.4 Clients' improvement (based on researchers' and clients' ratings) in relation to the number of sessions of psychotherapy the clients received. These data suggest that many improve by the eighth session and that most researcher-rated improvement occurs within the first 26 sessions.
Data from Howard et al., 1986.

> ➤ 6. What two research results favor the use of brief therapies over classical psychoanalysis? How do brief psychodynamic therapies differ from it?

Classical psychoanalysis, as practiced by Freud and by a declining number of contemporary analysts, is an expensive and time-consuming process. In classical psychoanalysis, it is not uncommon for a client to be seen five times a week for five years or more. Many therapists consider this level of client and therapist commitment both impractical and unnecessary. Their conclusion is supported by studies in which researchers and clients rated the degree of improvement that had occurred by the end of therapy. Figure 15.4 plots amount of improvement in relation to the length of therapy. As you can see, about half of the clients improved within 8 sessions, and most of the therapeutic effects occurred within 26 sessions. Moreover, there is no evidence that long-term classical analysis yields better therapeutic outcomes than briefer forms of psychodynamic therapy (Fisher & Greenberg, 1996).

Like psychoanalysis, brief psychodynamic psychotherapies emphasize understanding the maladaptive influences of the past and relating them to current patterns of self-defeating behavior. Many of these brief therapies utilize basic concepts from psychoanalysis, such as the importance of insight and the use of interpretation, but they employ them in a more focused and active fashion. The therapist and client are likely to sit facing one another, and conversation typically replaces free association. Clients are seen once or twice a week rather than daily, and the goal is typically limited to helping the client deal with specific life problems rather than attempting a complete rebuilding of the client's personality. Therapy is therefore more likely to focus on the client's current life situations than on past childhood experiences.

One brief psychodynamic therapy is called **interpersonal therapy** (Weissman & Markowitz, 1994). This therapy, which is highly structured and seldom takes longer than 15 to 20 sessions, focuses on the client's current interpersonal problems. These include dealing with role disputes such as marital conflict, adjusting to the loss of a relationship or to a changed relationship, and identifying and correcting deficits in social skills that make it difficult for the client to initiate or maintain satisfying relationships. The therapist collaborates very actively with the client in finding solutions to these problems. In controlled outcome studies, interpersonal therapy has proven to be one of the more effective current therapies for depression (Chambless & Hollon, 1998; DeRubeis & Crits-Christoph, 1998).

〉 HUMANISTIC PSYCHOTHERAPIES

In contrast to psychodynamic theorists, who view behavior as a product of unconscious processes, humanistic theorists view humans as capable of consciously controlling their actions and taking responsibility for their choices and behavior. These theorists also believe that everyone possesses inner resources for self-healing and personal growth and that disordered behavior reflects a blocking of the natural growth process. This blocking is brought about by distorted perceptions, lack of awareness about feelings, or a negative self-image.

When these assumptions about human nature are applied to psychotherapy, they inspire treatments that are radically different from psychoanalysis. Humanistic psychotherapy is seen as a human encounter between equals. The therapist's goal is to create an environment in which clients can engage in self-exploration and remove the barriers that block their natural tendencies toward personal growth (Greenberg & Rice, 1997). These barriers often result from childhood experiences that fostered unrealistic or maladaptive standards for self-worth. When people try to live their lives according to the expectations of others rather than in terms of their own desires and feelings, they often feel unfulfilled and empty, and unsure about who they really are as people.

In contrast to psychoanalytic therapy, humanistic approaches focus primarily on the present and future instead of the past. Therapy is directed at helping clients to become aware of feelings as they occur rather than to achieve insights into the childhood origins of the feelings.

> ➤ 7. What is the goal of humanistic therapies, and how do the therapies try to achieve this goal?

Client-Centered Therapy

The best-known and most widely used form of humanistic therapy is the client-centered (now sometimes called person-centered) approach developed by Carl Rogers (1959, 1980; Figure 15.5) In the 1940s, Rogers began to depart from psychoanalytic methods. He became convinced that the important "active ingredient" in therapy is the relationship that develops between client and therapist, and he began to focus his attention on the kind of therapeutic environment that seemed most effective in fostering self-exploration and personal growth (Lakin, 1998). Rogers's research and experiences as a therapist identified three important and interrelated therapist attributes:

FIGURE 15.5 "Psychotherapy is the releasing of an already existing capacity in a potentially competent individual, not the expert manipulation of a more or less passive personality."—Carl Rogers

1. **Unconditional positive regard** is communicated when therapists show clients that they genuinely care about and accept them, without judgment or evaluation. The therapist also communicates a sense of trust in clients' ability to work through their problems. In part, this sense of trust is communicated in the therapist's refusal to offer advice or guidance.

2. **Empathy,** the willingness and ability to view the world through the client's eyes, is a second vital factor. In a good therapeutic relationship, the therapist comes to sense the feelings and meanings experienced by the client and communicates this understanding to the client. The therapist does this by *reflecting* back to the client what he or she is communicating—perhaps by rephrasing something the client has just said in a way that captures the meaning and emotion involved.

➤ 8. Define the three important therapist attributes described by Rogers.

3. **Genuineness** is the third important therapist attribute. There must be consistency between the way the therapist feels and the way he or she behaves. A therapist must be open enough to honestly express feelings, whether positive or negative. In the case of negative feelings, this may seem to be contradictory to the attribute of unconditional positive regard, but that is not necessarily the case. Indeed, the most striking demonstrations of both attributes occur when a therapist can express displeasure with a client's behavior and at the same time communicate acceptance of the client as a person. For example, a therapist might say, "I feel frustrated with the way you handled that situation because I want things to work out better than that for you."

Rogers believed that when therapists can express these three critical therapeutic attributes, they create a situation in which the client feels accepted, understood, and free to explore basic attitudes and feelings without fear of being judged or rejected. Within such a relationship, clients experience the courage and freedom to grow.

These therapeutic attitudes are exhibited in the following excerpt from one of Rogers's therapy sessions:

Client: I cannot be the kind of person I want to be. I guess maybe I haven't the guts or the strength to kill myself, and if someone else would relieve me of the responsibility or I would be in an accident, I—just don't want to live.

Rogers: At the present time things look so black that you can't see much point in living. (Note the use of empathic reflection and the absence of any criticism.)

Client: Yes, I wish I'd never started this therapy. I was happy when I was living in my dream world. There I could be the kind of person I wanted to be. But now there is such a wide, wide gap between my ideal and what I am. . . . (Notice how the client responds to reflection with more information.)

Rogers: It's really tough digging into this like you are and at times the shelter of your dream world looks more attractive and comfortable. (Reflection.)

Client: My dream world or suicide. . . . So I don't see why I should waste your time coming in twice a week—I'm not worth it—what do you think?

Rogers: It's up to you. . . . It isn't wasting my time. I'd be glad to see you whenever you come, but it's how you feel about it. . . . (Note the genuineness in stating an honest desire to see the client and the unconditional positive regard in trusting her capacity and responsibility for choice.)

Client: You're not going to suggest that I come in oftener? You're not alarmed and think I ought to come in every day until I get out of this?

Rogers: I believe you're able to make your own decision. I'll see you whenever you want to come. (Trust and positive regard.)

Client: (Note of awe in her voice.) I don't believe you are alarmed about— I see—I may be afraid of myself but you aren't afraid for me. (She experiences the therapist's confidence in her.)

Rogers: You say you may be afraid of yourself and are wondering why I don't seem to be afraid for you. (Reflection.)

Client: You have more confidence in me than I have. I'll see you next week, maybe. (Based on Rogers, 1951, p. 49)

[The client did not attempt suicide.]

Rogers believed that as clients experience a constructive therapeutic relationship, they exhibit increased self-acceptance, greater self-awareness, enhanced self-reliance, increased comfort with other relationships, and improved life functioning (Rogers, 1959). Research does indicate that therapists' characteristics have a strong effect on the outcome of psychotherapy. Therapy is most likely to be successful when the therapist is perceived as genuine, warm, and empathic (Beutler et al., 1994; Bohart & Greenberg, 1997).

Gestalt Therapy

Frederick S. (Fritz) Perls, a European psychoanalyst who was trained in Gestalt psychology, developed another humanistic approach to treatment (Figure 15.6). As noted in Chapter 4, the term *gestalt* ("organized whole") refers to perceptual principles through which people actively organize stimulus elements into meaningful "whole" patterns. Ordinarily, in whatever we perceive, whether external stimuli, ideas, or emotions, we concentrate on only part of our whole experience—the figure—while largely ignoring the background against which the figure appears. For people who have psychological difficulties, that background includes important feelings, wishes, and thoughts that are blocked from ordinary awareness because they would evoke anxiety. Like Rogers, Perls believed that people have an inherent tendency toward self-actualization but that they can be blocked from achieving their potential when they cut off important aspects of their experience.

Gestalt therapy is often carried out in groups, and gestalt therapists have developed a variety of imaginative techniques to help clients get in touch with their inner selves. These methods are much more active and dramatic than client-centered approaches, and sometimes even confrontational in nature. Therapists often ask clients to role-play different aspects of themselves so that they may directly experience their inner dynamics. In this example, John discloses that he has difficulty talking to Mary, another member of the therapy group, because he experiences a wall between them. The gestalt therapist asks him to play the "wall."

> *John:* (as the wall) I am here to protect you against predatory women who will eat you alive if you open yourself to them.

The therapist asks John to talk with his wall so that he can experience the conflict that keeps him from close relationships with others.

> *John:* (to the wall) Aren't you exaggerating? She looks pretty safe to me. In fact, she looks more scared than anything.
>
> *John:* (as the wall) Of course she's scared. I'm responsible for that. I'm a very severe wall and I make lots of people scared. . . . You're scared of me even though I'm really on your side.
>
> *John:* (to the wall) I *am* scared of you and I even feel you inside me, like I have become like you. I feel my chest as if it was iron, and I really feel mad about that.
>
> *John:* (as the wall) Mad—at what? I'm your strength and you don't even know it. Feel how strong you are inside.
>
> *John:* (to the wall) Sure, I feel the strength, but I also feel rigid when my chest feels like iron. I'd like to beat on you, knock you over and go over to Mary.
>
> *Therapist:* Go ahead. Beat on your iron.
>
> *John:* (beats his chest and shouts) Get out of my way—get *out* of my *way*! (silence of a few moments) My chest feels strong—but not like it's made of iron. (after another silence, John begins to cry and talks to Mary) I don't feel any wall between us anymore and I really want to talk with you. (Polster & Polster, 1973, pp. 53–54)

FIGURE 15.6 *"If the patient can become truly aware at every instant of himself and his actions on whatever level—fantasy, verbal, or physical—he can see how he is producing his difficulties and he can solve them in the present, in the here and now."*—Fritz Perls

➤ 9. How is gestalt therapy derived from gestalt psychology principles?

In this exercise, the gestalt therapist created a situation that allowed John to directly experience the intimidating shell that he used to keep others from getting close enough to hurt him, as well as the many emotions resulting from his conflict.

Despite their common commitment to humanistic principles, Rogers and Perls differed sharply in their attitudes toward doing research on humanistic therapies. Rogers was committed to research that would help identify the factors that contribute to therapeutic success. He was a pioneer in tape-recording therapy sessions and analyzing them to study what went on in therapy (Rogers & Dymond, 1954). In contrast, Perls had a strongly antiscientific attitude that kept him and his followers from doing systematic research on the effectiveness of gestalt therapy. As a result, the influence of the gestalt movement began to wane following Perls's death in 1970, although some of its techniques have been integrated into other therapies (Lazarus, 1995).

❯ COGNITIVE THERAPIES

As we have seen, many behavior disorders involve maladaptive ways of thinking about oneself and the world. Cognitive approaches to psychotherapy focus on the role of irrational and self-defeating thought patterns, and therapists who employ this approach try to help clients discover and change the cognitions that underlie their problems.

In contrast to psychoanalysts, cognitive therapists do not emphasize the importance of unconscious psychodynamic processes. They do, however, point out that because our habitual thought patterns are so well practiced and ingrained, they tend to "run off" almost automatically, so that we may be only minimally aware of them and may simply accept them as reflecting "reality" (Clark et al., 1999). Thus clients often need help in identifying the beliefs, ideas, and self-statements that trigger maladaptive emotions and behaviors. Once identified, these cognitions can be challenged and, with practice and effort, changed. Albert Ellis and Aaron Beck are the most influential figures in the cognitive approach to therapy.

Ellis's Rational-Emotive Therapy

Ellis's theory of emotional disturbance and his rational-emotive therapy are embodied in his ABCD model (Figure 15.7).

- *A* stands for the *activating event* that seems to trigger the emotion.
- *B* stands for the *belief system* that underlies the way in which a person appraises the event.
- *C* stands for the emotional and behavioral *consequences* of that appraisal.
- *D* is the key to changing maladaptive emotions and behaviors: *disputing*, or challenging, an erroneous belief system.

Ellis (Figure 15.8) points out that people are accustomed to viewing their emotions (*C*s) as being caused directly by events (*A*s). Thus a young man who is turned down for a date may feel rejected and depressed. However, Ellis would insist that the woman's refusal is *not* the true reason for the emotional reaction. Rather, that reaction is caused by the young man's irrational belief that "to be a worthwhile person, I must be loved and accepted by virtually everyone, especially those I consider important." If the young man does not want to feel depressed and rejected, this belief must be countered and replaced by a more rational interpretation (e.g., "It would have been nice if she had accepted my invitation, but I don't need to turn it into a catastrophe and believe that no one will ever care about me").

➤ 10. What do ABCD stand for in rational-emotive therapy, and how is this model used in therapy?

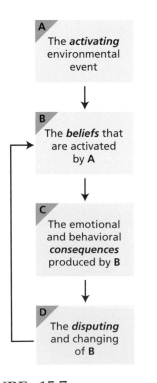

FIGURE 15.7 Albert Ellis's ABCD model describes his theory of the cause—and cure—of maladaptive emotional responses and behaviors. In therapy, the goal is to discover, dispute, and change the client's maladaptive beliefs.

Rational-emotive therapists introduce clients to common irrational ideas (Table 15.1) and then train them to ferret out the particular ideas that underlie their maladaptive emotional responses. Clients are given homework assignments to help them analyze and change self-statements. They may also be asked to place themselves in challenging situations and practice control over their emotions by using the new self-statements. For example, a shy person might be required to go to a party and practice rational thoughts that counteract social anxiety. By learning and practicing cognitive coping responses, clients can eventually modify underlying belief systems in ways that enhance well-being.

Beck's Cognitive Therapy

Like Ellis, Aaron Beck's goal is to point out errors of thinking and logic that underlie emotional disturbance and to help clients identify and reprogram their overlearned "automatic" thought patterns (Figure 15.9). In treating depressed clients, a first step is to help clients realize that their thoughts, not the situation, causes their maladaptive emotional reactions. This sets the stage for identifying and changing the maladaptive thoughts.

Client: I get depressed when things go wrong. Like when I fail a test.

Beck: How can failing a test make you depressed?

Client: Well, if I fail, I'll never get into law school.

Beck: So failing a test means a lot to you. But if failing a test could drive people into clinical depression, wouldn't you expect everyone who failed a test to have a depression? Did everyone who failed get depressed enough to require treatment?

Client: No, but it depends on how important the test was to the person.

Beck: Right, and who decides the importance?

Client: I do.

Beck: Now what did failing mean?

Client: (Tearful) That I couldn't get into law school.

Beck: And what does that mean to you?

FIGURE 15.8 "The essence of effective therapy according to rational-emotive therapy is full tolerance of people as individuals combined with a ruthless campaign against their self-defeating ideas.... These can be easily elicited and demolished by any scientist worth his or her salt; and the rational-emotive therapist is exactly that: an exposing and nonsense-annihilating scientist." —Albert Ellis

TABLE 15.1 IRRATIONAL IDEAS THAT CAUSE DISTURBANCE, AND ALTERNATIVES THAT MIGHT BE OFFERED BY A RATIONAL-EMOTIVE THERAPIST	
Irrational Belief	**Rational Alternative**
It is a dire necessity that I be loved and approved of by virtually everyone for everything I do.	Although we might prefer approval to disapproval, our self-worth need not depend on the love and approval of others. Self-respect is more important than giving up one's individuality to buy the approval of others.
I must be thoroughly competent and achieving to be worthwhile. To fail is to be a *failure*.	As imperfect and fallible human beings, we are bound to fail from time to time. We can control only effort; we have incomplete control over outcome. We are better off focusing on the process of doing rather than on demands that we do well
It is terrible, awful, and catastrophic when things are not the way I demand that they be.	Stop catastrophizing and turning an annoyance or irritation into a major crisis. Who are we to demand that things be different from what they are? When we turn our preferences into dire necessities, we set ourselves up for needless distress. We had best learn to change those things we can control and accept those that we can't control (and be wise enough to know the difference).
Human misery is externally caused and forced on one by other people and events.	Human misery is produced not by external factors but rather by what we tell ourselves about those events. We feel as we think, and most of our misery is needlessly self-inflicted by irrational habits of thinking.
Because something deeply affected me in the past, it must continue to do so.	We hold ourselves prisoner to the past because we continue to believe philosophies and ideas learned in the past. If they are still troubling us today, it is because we are still propagandizing ourselves with irrational nonsense. We *can* control how we think in the here and now and thereby liberate ourselves from the "scars" of the past.

FIGURE 15.9 "The formula for treatment may be stated in simple terms: The therapist helps the patient to identify his warped thinking and to learn more realistic ways to formulate his experience." —Aaron Beck

➤ 11. Which disorders have responded most favorably to Beck's cognitive therapy? What is the focus of the therapy in these disorders?

Client: That I'm just not smart enough.

Beck: Anything else?

Client: That I can never be happy.

Beck: And how do those thoughts make you feel?

Client: Very unhappy.

Beck: So it is the *meaning* (italics ours) of failing a test that makes you very unhappy. In fact, believing that you can never be happy is a powerful factor in producing unhappiness. So you get yourself into a trap—by definition, failure to get into law school equals "I can never be happy." (Based on Beck et al., 1979, pp. 145–146)

Beck's contributions to the understanding and treatment of depression have made his cognitive therapy a psychological treatment of choice for that disorder. More recently, cognitive therapy has been extended to the treatment of anger and anxiety disorders, with equally encouraging results (Craske, 1999; Rush, 1998). As we shall see, cognitive therapy is also being combined with other therapeutic techniques to form highly effective treatment "packages" for certain disorders (Hollon et al., 1991).

〉 BEHAVIOR THERAPIES

In the 1960s, behavioral approaches emerged as a dramatic departure from the assumptions and methods that characterized psychoanalytic and humanistic therapies. The new practitioners of behavior therapy denied the importance of inner dynamics. Instead, they insisted that (1) behavior disorders are learned in the same ways normal behaviors are, and (2) these maladaptive behaviors can be unlearned by application of principles derived from research on classical conditioning and operant conditioning. Behaviorists demonstrated that these learning procedures could be applied to change the behaviors of schizophrenics, to effectively treat anxiety disorders, and to modify many child and adult behavior problems that seemed resistant to traditional therapy approaches (Bandura, 1969).

In Chapter 6, we described three important learning mechanisms: classical conditioning, operant conditioning, and modeling. We now consider therapy techniques based on each of these forms of learning.

Classical Conditioning Treatments

Classical conditioning procedures have been used in two major ways. First, they have been used to reduce, or decondition, anxiety responses. Second, they have been used in attempts to condition new anxiety responses to a particular class of stimuli, such as alcoholic beverages or inappropriate sexual objects. The most commonly used classical conditioning procedures are exposure therapies, systematic desensitization, and aversion therapy.

Exposure: An Extinction Approach

➤ 12. What are the classical and operant conditioning procedures used in exposure therapy? How was this procedure used to treat agoraphobics?

From a behavioral point of view, phobias and other fears result from classically conditioned emotional responses. The conditioning experience is assumed to involve a pairing of the phobic object (the neutral stimulus) with an aversive unconditioned stimulus (UCS). As a result, the phobic stimulus becomes a conditioned stimulus (CS) that elicits the conditioned response (CR) of anxiety. According to the two-factor learning theory discussed in Chapter 6, avoidance responses to the phobic situation are then reinforced by anxiety reduction (operant conditioning based on negative reinforcement). Thus a person who is injured in an automobile accident may find herself afraid to ride in a car. Moreover, each time she avoids exposure to cars, her avoidance response is strengthened through anxiety reduction.

According to this formulation, the most direct way to reduce the fear is through a process of classical extinction of the anxiety response. This requires **exposure** to the feared CS in the absence of the UCS while using **response prevention** to keep the operant avoidance response from occurring. This is the theoretical basis for the exposure approach (Marks, 1991; Zinbarg et al., 1992). The client may be exposed to real-life stimuli or may be asked to imagine scenes involving the stimuli (Figure 15.10). These stimuli will, of course, evoke considerable anxiety, but the anxiety will extinguish in time if the person remains in the presence of the CS and the UCS does not occur.

Exposure has proved to be a highly effective technique for extinguishing anxiety responses in both animals and humans (Bruce & Sanderson, 1998; DeRubeis & Crits-Christoph, 1998). In one study, agoraphobics who feared leaving the safety of their homes and going into public places were treated. The researchers used an exposure therapy that required these clients to confront feared situations such as driving alone and going into crowded shopping centers. Both before and after the exposure therapy, each client was assessed on a series of real-life performance tasks. For example, an agoraphobic who feared being in public might be asked to go and stand in a long checkout line in a crowded supermarket. Before exposure treatment began, the phobics were able to pass only 27 percent of these performance tasks. At the end of treatment, they were able to perform 71 percent of the tasks. Moreover, this degree of improvement was maintained or even increased at follow-ups ranging from three months to two years (Williams et al., 1989). These are extremely encouraging results, since agoraphobics are difficult to treat with nonbehavioral methods. An additional advantage is that clients can administer exposure treatment to themselves under a therapist's direction, with high success rates (Marks, 1991).

FIGURE 15.10 Exposure to feared stimuli can extinguish phobic behavior. In this photo, a therapist is accompanying a client with a severe height phobia (acrophobia) during an exposure session as a co-therapist records her accomplishments and her ratings of anxiety.

Systematic Desensitization: A Counterconditioning Approach

In 1958, Joseph Wolpe introduced **systematic desensitization**, a new learning-based treatment for anxiety disorders. Wolpe also presented impressive outcome data for 100 phobics he had treated with the technique. Systematic desensitization remains a widely used treatment today. In many controlled studies, its success rate in treating a wide range of phobic disorders has been 80 percent or better (Rachman, 2000; Spiegler & Guevremont, 1998).

Wolpe viewed anxiety as a classically conditioned emotional response. His goal was to eliminate the anxiety by using a procedure called **counterconditioning,** in which a new response that is incompatible with anxiety is conditioned to the anxiety-arousing CS.

➤ 13. How does systematic desensitization differ from exposure in terms of its (a) underlying principle and (b) specific techniques?

The first step in systematic desensitization is to train the client in the skill of voluntary muscle relaxation, using an approach similar to that described in Chapter 10 (p. 446). Next the client is helped to construct a **stimulus hierarchy** of 10 to 15 scenes relating to the fear. The hierarchy is carefully arranged in roughly equal steps from low-anxiety scenes to high-anxiety ones. Table 15.2 shows a stimulus hierarchy that was used in treating a college student with high test anxiety.

In the desensitization sessions, the therapist deeply relaxes the client and then asks the client to vividly imagine the first scene in the hierarchy (the least anxiety-arousing one) for several seconds. The client can't be both relaxed and anxious at the same time, so if the relaxation is strong enough, it replaces anxiety as the CR to that stimulus—the counterconditioning process. When the client can imagine that scene for increasingly longer periods without experiencing anxiety, the therapist proceeds to the next scene. When low-arousal scenes have been deconditioned, some of the total anxiety has been reduced and the

TABLE 15.2	A STIMULUS HIERARCHY USED IN THE SYSTEMATIC DESENSITIZATION TREATMENT OF A TEST-ANXIOUS COLLEGE STUDENT
Scene 1.	Hearing about someone else who has a test
Scene 2.	Instructor announcing that a test will be given in 3 weeks
Scene 3.	Instructor reminding class that there will be a test in 2 weeks
Scene 4.	Overhearing classmates talk about studying for the test, which will occur in 1 week
Scene 5.	Instructor reminding class of what it will be tested on in 2 days
Scene 6.	Leaving class the day before the exam
Scene 7.	Studying the night before the exam
Scene 8.	Getting up the morning of the exam
Scene 9.	Walking toward the building where the exam will be given
Scene 10.	Walking into the testing room
Scene 11.	Instructor walking into room with tests
Scene 12.	Tests being passed out
Scene 13.	Reading the test questions
Scene 14.	Watching others finish the test
Scene 15.	Seeing a question I can't answer
Scene 16.	Instructor waiting for me to finish the test

➤ 14. How does classical conditioning underlie aversion therapy? What additional training can enhance its effectiveness?

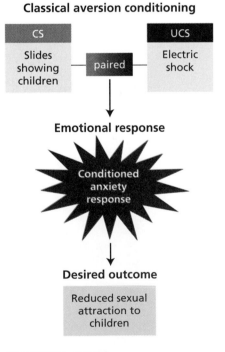

FIGURE 15.11 The classical conditioning that occurs in aversion therapy is illustrated in the treatment of a pedophile who receives electric shocks when pictures of children are presented. The goal of the treatment is the development of a conditioned anxiety response that reduces the sexual attractiveness of children.

person is now able to imagine more anxiety-arousing ones without becoming anxious. Desensitization can also be accomplished through carefully controlled exposure to a hierarchy of real-life situations (e.g., having a height phobic actually stand on a step stool and, eventually, to walk across a suspension bridge while voluntarily relaxed), rather than to imagined scenes. Both desensitization approaches are highly effective in reducing anxiety (Barlow, 1988).

Although both exposure therapy based on extinction and systematic desensitization are very effective in reducing fear responses, systematic desensitization is sometimes preferred because the client will experience far less anxiety during the treatment. On the other hand, exposure often reduces anxiety more quickly than does systematic desensitization (Bruce & Sanderson, 1998).

Aversion Therapy

For some clients, the therapeutic goal is not to reduce anxiety, but to actually condition it to a particular stimulus so as to reduce deviant approach behaviors. In **aversion therapy,** the therapist pairs a stimulus that is attractive to a person and stimulates deviant or self-defeating behavior (the CS) with a noxious UCS in an attempt to condition an aversion to the CS. For example, aversion treatment for alcoholics may involve injecting the client with a nausea-producing drug, then having him or her drink alcohol (the CS) as nausea (the UCS) develops. Similarly, pedophiles (child molesters) have undergone treatment in which strong electric shock is paired with slides showing children similar to those the offenders sexually abused (Figure 15.11). To measure the effects of the treatment for males, readings from a physiological recording device that measures penile blood volume responses to the slides can be compared before and after treatment (Sandler, 1986).

Aversion therapies have been applied with variable results to a range of disorders. In one study of 278 alcoholics who underwent aversion therapy, 190 (63 percent) were still abstinent a year after treatment had ended. Three years later, a third of the patients were still abstinent, an impressive result given the traditionally high relapse rate in chronic alcoholics (Wiens & Menustik, 1983). Unfortunately, however, treatment effects from aversion therapies often fail to generalize from the treatment setting to the real world. Some experts believe that aversion therapy is most likely to succeed if it is part of a more comprehensive treatment program in which the client also learns specific coping skills for avoiding relapses (Marlatt & Gordon, 1985).

Operant Conditioning Treatments

The term **behavior modification** refers to treatment techniques that involve the application of operant conditioning procedures in an attempt to increase or decrease a specific behavior. These techniques may use any of the operant procedures for manipulating the environment that were discussed in Chapter 6: positive reinforcement, extinction, negative reinforcement, or punishment. The focus in behavior modification is on externally observable behaviors, and measurement of the behaviors targeted for change occurs throughout the treatment program. This measurement allows the therapist to track the progress of the treatment program and to make modifications if behavior change begins to lag.

Behavior modification techniques have been successfully applied to many different behavior disorders. They have yielded particularly impressive results when applied to populations that are difficult to treat with more traditional therapies, such as chronic hospitalized schizophrenics, profoundly disturbed children, and mentally retarded individuals (Azrin & Ayllon, 1968; DeRubeis & Crits-Christoph, 1998; Lovaas, 1977). We now consider the use of positive reinforcement and punishment in two of these populations.

> ➤ 15. How do token economies work, and what evidence exists for their effectiveness?

Positive Reinforcement

One of the dangers of long-term psychiatric hospitalization is the gradual loss of social, personal-care, and occupational skills needed to survive outside the hospital. Such deterioration is common among chronic schizophrenic patients who have been hospitalized for an extended period. Verbal psychotherapies have very limited success in rebuilding such skills.

In the 1960s, Teodoro Ayllon and Nathan Azrin (1968) introduced a revolutionary approach to the behavioral treatment of hospitalized schizophrenics. The **token economy** is a system for strengthening desired behaviors—such as personal grooming, appropriate social responses, housekeeping behaviors, working on assigned jobs, and participation in vocational training programs—through the systematic application of positive reinforcement. Rather than giving tangible reinforcers, such as food or grounds privileges, a kind of "menu" is derived in which a specified number of plastic tokens is given for performance of each desired behavior. The tokens can be redeemed by the patients for a wide range of tangible reinforcers, such as a private room, exclusive rental of a radio or television set, selection of personal furniture, freedom to leave the ward and walk around the grounds, recreational activities, and items from the hospital commissary. The long-term goal of token economy programs is to get the desired behaviors started with tangible reinforcers until they eventually come under the control of social reinforcers and self-reinforcement processes (such as self-pride), which will be needed to maintain them in the world outside the hospital. When this begins to occur, the tokens can be phased out and the desired behaviors continue to occur (Kazdin, 1982).

Token economy programs have proven highly effective with some of the most challenging populations. Figure 15.12 shows how quickly the introduction of a token economy

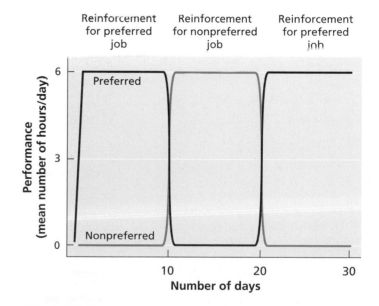

FIGURE 15.12 Average number of hours hospitalized schizophrenic patients worked per day on a job they preferred and a job they did not prefer when tokens were used as reinforcement. Note how quickly and how strongly their behavior is influenced by the reinforcement contingency.

Data from Ayllon & Azrin, 1965.

increased the work behavior of chronic schizophrenic patients who were supposedly too disturbed to engage in a work-retraining program (Ayllon & Azrin, 1965). In another study, a token economy program was carried out over a 4-year period with severely disturbed schizophrenic patients who had been hospitalized an average of more than 17 years. During the course of the program, 98 percent of the patients from the behavioral treatment program were able to be released from the hospital (most to shelter-care facilities in the community), compared with only 45 percent of a control group that received the normal hospital treatments (Paul & Lentz, 1977). Token economies have also been applied successfully within business, school, prison, and home environments to increase desirable behaviors (Sullivan & O'Leary, 1990).

Therapeutic Use of Punishment

In the view of most psychologists, punishment is the least preferred way to control behavior because of its aversive qualities and the potential negative side effects described in Chapter 6 (p. 245). Therefore before deciding to use punishment as a therapy technique, therapists ask themselves two important questions: (1) Are there alternative, less painful approaches that might be effective? (2) Is the behavior to be eliminated sufficiently injurious to the individual or to society to justify the severity of the punishment?

> ➤ 16. Under what conditions is punishment used as a behavior modification technique? What evidence is there for its effectiveness?

Sometimes, the answers to these questions lead to a decision to use punishment. For example, some of the most startling self-destructive behaviors imaginable occur in certain severely disturbed autistic children. Such children may strike themselves repeatedly, bang their heads on sharp objects, bite or tear pieces of flesh from their bodies, or engage in other self-mutilating behaviors. O. Ivar Lovaas (1977), a UCLA psychologist who pioneered the use of operant conditioning techniques in the treatment of such children, successfully eliminated such behaviors with a limited number of contingent electric shocks. One 7-year-old boy had been self-injurious for 5 years and had to be kept in physical restraints. During one 90-minute period when his restraints were removed, he struck himself more than 3,000 times. With the consent of his parents, shock electrodes were attached to the boy and he was given a painful electric shock each time he struck himself. Only 12 shocks were needed to virtually eliminate the self-destructive behavior. In another case, 15 shocks eliminated self-destructive behavior in a severely disturbed girl with a history of banging her head against objects. Punishment is never employed without consent of the client or the client's legal guardian in the event that the client is mentally incompetent to give consent.

Modeling and Social Skills Training

Modeling is one of the most important and effective learning processes in humans, and modeling procedures have been used to treat a variety of behavioral problems. One of the most widely used applications is designed to teach clients social skills that they lack.

> ➤ 17. How is modeling used in social skills training? How is self-efficacy involved in its effectiveness?

In **social skills training,** clients learn new skills by observing and then imitating a model who performs a socially skillful behavior. In the following example, a therapist served as a model for his client, a socially anxious college student who had great difficulty asking women for dates. The client began by pretending to ask for a date over the telephone:

> *Client:* By the way (pause), I don't suppose you want to go out Saturday night?
>
> *Therapist:* Up to actually asking for the date you were very good. However, if I were the girl, I might have been offended when you said, "By the way." It's like asking her out is pretty casual. Also, the way you

posed the question, you are kind of suggesting to her that she doesn't want to go out with you. Pretend for the moment I'm you. Now, how does this sound: *'There's a movie at the Varsity Theater that I want to see. If you don't have other plans, I'd very much like to take you.'*

Client: That sounded good. Like you were sure of yourself and like the girl, too.

Therapist: Why don't you try it? (Masters et al., 1987, p. 100).

Social skills training has been used with many populations, including individuals who have minor deficits in social skills, delinquents who need to learn how to resist negative peer pressures, and even hospitalized schizophrenic patients who need to learn social skills in order to function adaptively outside the hospital. It is often used in conjunction with other psychological or biological treatments to "jump start" new adaptive behaviors that can then be strengthened by natural reinforcers in the client's everyday environment.

Research demonstrates that a key factor underlying the effectiveness of social skills training is increased self-efficacy. When clients come to believe that they are capable of performing the desired behaviors, they succeed in doing so (Bandura, 1997; Maddux, 1999). Observing successful models also increases self-efficacy by encouraging the view, "If she can do that, so can I."

❯ GROUP, FAMILY, AND MARITAL THERAPIES

Most of the therapeutic approaches we have discussed can be carried out with groups of clients as well as with individuals (Beck & Lewis, 2000). Therapy groups typically include six to eight clients and a single therapist. Within a group, clients can experience acceptance, support, and a sense of belonging. They soon see that other people also struggle with problems, a realization that helps to counter feelings of isolation and deviance. Clients can also observe how others approach problems, and the interpersonal relations that develop within the group can be a training ground for learning new interpersonal skills. Furthermore, clients can gain insight into how they are perceived by others (Jongsma, 2000).

Family Therapy

Sometimes, the group being treated is a family. Family therapy had its roots in the clinical observation that many clients who had shown marked improvement in individual therapy—often in institutional settings—suffered relapses when they returned home and began interacting with their families. This observation led to an important concept in the field of psychotherapy, namely, that the disorder shown by the "identified patient" may reflect disordered relationships within the family system, and that permanent change in the client may require that the entire family system be the focus of therapy (Minuchin, 1974; Nichols et al., 2000). Family therapists therefore try to help the family understand how it functions and how its unique patterns of interactions contribute to conflicts and to the problems of one or more members (Figure 15.13).

> In one family, an anorexic 14-year-old girl was the identified patient. However, as the therapist worked with the family, he saw a competitive struggle for the father's attention and observed that the girl, Laura, was able to compete and get "cuddly" affection from her father only when she presented herself to him as a "sick" person. To bring the hidden dynamics out into the open, the therapist worked at getting the family members to express their desires more directly—in words instead of through hidden behavioral messages. In time, Laura became capable of expressing her need for affection directly to her father, and her anorexia disappeared. (Aponte & Hoffman, 1974)

> ➤ 18. What clinical observation stimulated the development of family therapy, and what are its key assumptions?

FIGURE 15.13 Family therapists focus on the total pattern of family interactions, and they include the entire family in treatment.

Marital Therapy

Today's soaring divorce rate is a stark reflection of the difficulties that exist in many marriages. Nearly half of all first marriages end in divorce, and the divorce rate is even higher among people who remarry (Hetherington et al., 1998). Couples frequently seek marital therapy because they are troubled by their relationship or because they are contemplating separation or divorce. Typically, the therapist works with both partners together, and therapy focuses on clarifying and improving the interactions between them. Research has shown that happily married couples differ from distressed couples in that they talk more to one another, keep channels of communication open, show more sensitivity to each other's feelings and needs, and are more skilled at solving problems (Gottman & Levinson, 1992). Marital therapy targets improvement in these areas.

Distressed couples frequently have faulty communication patterns, as demonstrated in the following case:

> *Husband:* She never comes up to me and kisses me. I am always the one to make the overtures.
>
> *Therapist:* Is this the way you see yourself behaving with your husband?
>
> *Wife:* Yes, I would say he is the demonstrative one. I didn't know he wanted me to make the overtures.
>
> *Therapist:* Have you told your wife you would like this from her—more demonstration of affection?
>
> *Husband:* Well, no. You'd think she'd know.
>
> *Wife:* No, how would I know? You always said you didn't like aggressive women.
>
> *Husband:* I don't, I don't like dominating women.
>
> *Wife:* Well, I thought you meant women who make the overtures. How am I to know what you want?
>
> *Therapist:* You'd have a better idea if he had been able to tell you. (Satir, 1967, pp. 72–73)

➤ 19. How has acceptance been integrated into marital therapy?

An important recent addition to marital therapy is a focus on *acceptance* (Jacobson & Christensen, 1996). This addition was based on findings that in well-functioning couples, as well as those who profit from treatment, partners make a decision to accept those aspects of the partner's behavior that probably are too ingrained to change. For example, it makes little sense to demand that a person with a highly introverted personality style suddenly become a social gadfly and life of the party. The therapeutic emphasis is on helping couples work toward change in those areas where change is possible and to learn to accept aspects of the partner and the relationship that seem unlikely to change. Doing so reduces frustration, lessens demands on the other spouse, and allows the couple to focus on and enjoy the positive aspects of their relationship. The addition of acceptance training to the other elements of marital therapy has improved treatment outcomes (Jacobson et al., 2000).

〉 INTEGRATING AND COMBINING THERAPIES

➤ 20. What is eclecticism? Give an example of an integration of therapies.

We have now surveyed a variety of therapeutic orientations. To an increasing extent, clinicians are becoming **eclectic,** combining treatments and making use of whatever orientations and therapeutic techniques seem appropriate for the particular client they are treating (Lazarus, 1995; Snyder & Ingram, 2000). In part, this tendency reflects a responsiveness to research findings that certain approaches to therapy are well suited for some problems and ill suited for others. For example, Gestalt techniques are highly effective for helping people to discover underlying feelings, but a behavioral approach would be the treatment of choice for treating a phobia and cognitive therapy is highly effective for depression. A therapist could choose to use any combination of techniques in a case having multiple problems. Also prompting the move toward eclecticism is the fact that modern therapists are being trained in a variety of perspectives and therapy approaches, so that they emerge as professionals with a wider range of therapeutic competencies (Norcross, 1991). One national survey of eclectic therapists revealed that 72 percent included psychodynamic principles within their version of treatment, 54 percent included cognitive approaches, 45 percent used behavioral techniques, and a smaller percentage used various humanistic techniques (Jensen et al., 1990).

The move toward eclecticism has resulted in some integrations that would have been unthinkable 30 years ago. For example, **psychodynamic behavior therapy,** developed by Paul Wachtel (1997), involves an integration of psychoanalysis and behavior therapy. These would appear to be strange bedfellows indeed, but Wachtel, originally trained as a psychoanalyst, has skillfully blended them into an approach that seems capable of being applied to a wide range of problems. For example, consider a highly submissive man who is unaware of unresolved anger that has contributed to the development of an ulcer. Wachtel might treat this client with psychodynamic techniques to help him achieve insight into his unconscious anger and its origins in his early life. Having achieved such insight, the irrational aspects of his anger may disappear, but he may still find himself unable to be assertive even when it would be appropriate. At this point, psychoanalysis has reached its limits of therapeutic effectiveness and the therapist might switch to a behavioral social skills training program to allow the person to develop and practice the needed assertiveness skills.

The search for more effective therapy techniques has resulted not only in a tendency to combine various therapy approaches, but also in a search for new technologies. Our *Psychological Frontiers* feature focuses on attempts to use the high-tech capabilities of virtual reality as a therapy tool.

➤ 21. Which specific attributes of VR make it potentially useful in therapy? What evidence is there that VR can work therapeutically?

PSYCHOLOGICAL FRONTIERS

Virtual Reality as a Therapeutic Technique

Virtually all therapeutic perspectives are based on the assumption that therapy outcomes are likely to be most favorable if clients are able to vividly experience or reexperience important environmental, emotional, and relationship elements that underlie their problems. **Virtual reality (VR)** involves the use of computer technology to create highly realistic "virtual environments" that simulate actual experience so vividly that they evoke many of the same reactions that a comparable real-world environment would create. Observers typically wear helmets containing two small video monitors (one for each eye) attached to a high-speed computer. The image to each eye is slightly different to produce binocular depth perception cues that result in a 3-D image. With the aid of position-tracking devices, the computer monitors the person's physical movements and adjust the images and sounds accordingly. Observers thus have a vivid experience of *presence* in a "different place" when navigating through the virtual world. This power to immerse the user in a simulated environment derives not so much from the realism of the displays as from the fact that perception and action are integrated as they are in real life (Glantz et al., 1996).

Several other aspects of VR heighten its potential usefulness as a therapy tool. VR is highly flexible and programmable, allowing a therapist to present a variety of controlled situations and monitor their effects on a client. Scenes can be easily changed, depending on the actions of the client. Moreover, the therapist can don his or her

–Continued

own helmet and accompany the client into the virtual world, experiencing exactly what the client does and providing input to the client at appropriate moments. These shared experiences in the virtual world could enable clients to overcome old problems, experiment with new social roles, and learn new skills with the guidance of the therapist.

VR's use in psychotherapy is in its infancy, but it has already been applied to a variety of problems (Hoffman et al., 2000; Rothbaum et al., 2000). Most of these applications have been in the treatment of phobias and PTSD, where VR allows clients to interact with feared stimuli or situations while undergoing exposure or systematic desensitization therapy. For example, researchers have produced simulations of heights (e.g., a virtual elevator that could produce the sensations of being at various heights under different conditions, such as with or without walls, inside or on the outside of a building). Compared with a no-treatment control group of height phobics, those who received a seven-session VR graded exposure treatment showed significant reductions in anxiety and less avoidance of heights. Over a third of the VR participants spontaneously exposed themselves to heights after the treatment, including one who rode up 72 stories in a glass-walled elevator (Rothbaum et al., 1995). VR therapy has also been applied successfully to fear of flying by taking the client on trips, accompanied by the therapist, in a virtual Apache helicopter that takes off and flies over the airport and city (Klein, 1999; North et al., 1997).

A case study by Albert Carlin, Hunter Hoffman, and Suzanne Weghorst (1997) provides an example of how several sensory modalities can be combined to immerse people in a virtual environment. The client was a 37-year-old woman with a debilitating spider phobia that had interfered with her life for 20 years. At the time she entered treatment, any encounter with a spider or a spider web evoked panic, weeping, and shame about her "out of control" fear. She took elaborate precautions to avoid spiders, including fumigating and vacuuming her car before entering it, sealing her bedroom door and windows with duct tape each night, placing each piece of her clothing in a separate plastic bag immediately after washing or ironing it, and avoiding the outdoors where she might encounter a spider. Even viewing photographs or drawings of spiders evoked anxiety.

Over a period of 12 weekly sessions, VR was used to create a "virtual kitchen" where the client had encounters with either a small black spider in a web or a large brown virtual spider with a furry texture. Using a computer mouse to move about the 3-D virtual kitchen and a glove that operated her "virtual hand" inside the scene, the client exposed herself to spider experiences that gradually increased in intensity (Figure 15.14). When she opened a cupboard in the kitchen, she might encounter a spider that would crawl toward her. The spiders were preprogrammed to jump into the air when touched, swing toward her in their webs, and engage in other frightening behaviors. Later in treatment, when she began touching

FIGURE 15.14 Virtual reality (VR) was used to treat this spider phobic. The client views a virtual "spiderworld" inside the helmet. Psychologist Hunter Hoffman brings a virtual spider (shown on monitor) closer by slowly moving the VR position sensor in his right hand closer to the client's face. The sensor can also be attached to a furry toy spider to increase stimulus exposure.

Courtesy of Hunter Hoffman; photo by Mary Levin, University of Washington.

the large hairy brown spider with her virtual hand, another sensory modality was brought into the virtual world in the form of a palm-sized replica of a fur-covered Guyana bird-eating tarantula. When the client reached out with her virtual hand to touch the brown spider, her real hand encountered the furry tarantula, and any movement of the toy spider caused a similar movement of the virtual spider. These experiences, which evoked considerable anxiety at first, resulted in a dramatic reduction in spider anxiety both within the virtual world and in her real-life environment. Her ritualistic avoidance behaviors disappeared and she was able to stand over a spider that she encountered in her home for 20 minutes, to crush another one, and to go camping for the first time since adolescence. A controlled experimental study has since confirmed the effectiveness of the VR treatment for spider phobics (Hoffman et al., 2000).

The promising results achieved so far point to the need for systematic studies of VR therapy to explore several questions. Is it more effective than exposure through imagination or in real life? Is it cost effective in terms of computer and programming costs and number of therapy sessions needed? Up to now, most VR applications have depicted physical aspects of the environment. Can it be extended to social situations where a client might be able to have realistic interactions with significant virtual others from the client's past or present life? Could it be used in aversion therapies to classically condition negative emotional responses to depictions of children in the case of pedophiliacs, or to alcohol in the case of alcoholics? These are just a few of the questions that researchers might explore on the frontier of VR-assisted therapy.

〉 CULTURAL AND GENDER ISSUES IN PSYCHOTHERAPY

Psychological treatments reflect the cultural context in which they develop. Within the dominant cultures of western Europe and North America, personal problems are seen as originating within people in the form of dysfunctional thinking, conflict, and stress responses. People are assumed capable of expressing their feelings and taking personal responsibility for improving themselves. We can easily see these values and assumptions reflected in the therapies we have discussed. Psychodynamic, humanistic, and cognitive treatments all focus on changing these internal factors.

These values are not shared by all cultures and ethnic groups, however. For example, people from some Asian cultures might view the "therapeutic" expression of hostility toward one's parents as unthinkable (Sue et al., 1994). Likewise, the suggestion that assertiveness training would be helpful in competing more successfully with others and standing up for one's rights could be appalling to a person from a highly collectivistic culture (Cooper & Denner, 1998). Given diverse cultural norms and values, we should not be surprised that some individuals from non-Western cultures view psychotherapy as a totally inappropriate, and even shameful, option for the solution of their problems in living (Foulks et al., 1995).

Cultural Factors in Treatment Utilization

Although overall rates of psychopathology do not differ greatly among ethnic groups in the United States, utilization of mental health services is far less for minority groups than it is for the majority White population. Even when minorities do seek out mental-health services, they often fail to stay in treatment. As a result, many problems that could benefit from psychological treatment go untreated (Burnam et al., 1987; Sue, 1998). The growing cultural diversity in North America has important implications for the practice of psychotherapy, and researchers are trying to identify the barriers to psychological treatment and what can be done to lower them.

Psychologists Derald Sue and David Sue (1990) have identified several of these barriers. One of them is cultural norms against turning to professionals outside one's own culture for help. Instead, the family, clergy, acupuncturists, herbalists and folk healers are looked to for assistance. Moreover, many minority members have a history of frustrating experiences with White bureaucracies that make them unwilling to approach a hospital or mental-health center. There may also be language barriers.

> ➤ 22. What factors serve as barriers to therapy for ethnic minorities?

Sometimes, access to treatment is a major problem. Because many minority groups suffer high rates of unemployment and poverty, they may not have health insurance and cannot afford therapy. Likewise, many community mental-health agencies and professional therapists are located outside the areas where the underserved populations live.

But according to Stanley Sue and Nolan Zane (1987), the biggest problem of all is that there are too few skilled counselors who could provide culturally responsive forms of treatment. Therapists often have little familiarity with the cultural backgrounds and personal characteristics of ethnic groups other than their own. Sometimes they operate on the basis of inaccurate stereotypes. This can result in unrealistic and possibly inappropriate goals and expectations on the part of a therapist, as well as great difficulty in establishing the positive relationship that has been shown to be a powerful factor in therapeutic success.

What can be done to increase access of culturally diverse groups to psychological treatment? One answer is to take therapy to the people. Studies have shown that establishing mental health service agencies in minority population

FIGURE 15.15 Before starting relaxation training, this culturally competent White therapist has determined that systematic desensitization is compatible with the cultural background of his Southeast Asian client.

➤ 23. What skills are found in culturally competent therapists?

areas increases utilization of mental health services, particularly if agencies are staffed by culturally skilled counselors (S. Sue, 1998). Another solution might be to train more therapists from these ethnic groups. Stanley Sue and his coworkers (1991) found that dropout rates were reduced and number of therapy sessions increased when clients saw ethnically similar therapists. However, for clients who elect to remain in therapy, it has *not* been demonstrated that treatment outcomes are better for clients who are seen by therapists from their own ethnic group. What seems more important than ethnic match is for the therapist and client to form a good relationship and to share similar viewpoints regarding goals for treatment and preferred means for resolving problems (Figure 15.15).

Stanley Sue (1998) suggests that **culturally competent therapists** are able to use knowledge about the client's culture to achieve a broad understanding of the client. At the same time they are attentive to how the client may differ from the cultural stereotype, thereby balancing cultural understanding with the individual characteristics and needs of the client. They also are able to introduce *culture-specific elements* into the therapy. Thus a therapist might draw upon some of the techniques used by folk healers within that culture (e.g., prayer or a specific ritual) to effect changes in the client. Obviously, this would require a good working knowledge of the culture from which the client comes, plus a willingness to take advantage of what "works" in that culture.

Can therapists be trained to be more culturally sensitive? Indeed they can. In one study, experienced African-American and White therapists were assigned to either a four-hour cultural sensitivity training program or to a control condition that received no training. The therapists then treated African-American clients from the community and the outcome of therapy was carefully assessed. The results showed that exposure to the ethnic training was more important to therapeutic outcome than whether the therapist was African-American or White. Clients rated the therapists who had received training (whether African-American or White) as having greater empathy and expertise, and these clients also attended more therapy sessions (Wade & Bernstein, 1991). It thus appears that cultural sensitivity can be acquired and used to enhance the process of therapy for members of minority cultures.

Gender Issues in Therapy

Even within the same culture, the lives of men and women can differ in many ways, as can the life demands they are called upon to cope with. As we saw in Chapter 14, psychological disorders, particularly those involving anxiety and depression, occur more frequently among women in Western cultures. This may reflect the impact of specific stressors that women face, such as poverty (women are overrepresented at the poverty level), lack of opportunity fostered by sexism, strains created by the demanding multiple roles of mother, worker, and spouse among married women, and the violence and histories of abuse that many have been subjected to. In many instances, psychological problems arise not so much from the internal problems and conflicts, but from oppressive elements in the family, social, and political worlds. As women strive for more egalitarian relationships with men and for equal opportunity to develop their potential, they often meet external barriers that are deeply embedded in their culture's traditional sex roles.

In the eyes of many therapists, it may be more important to focus on what can be done to change women's life circumstances than to help them adapt to sex-role expectations that constrain them (Brown, 1994). It is important for both men and women therapists to support people in making choices that meet their needs, whether it be a man who wishes to stay at home and care for children or a woman who wants a career in the military. Consistent with the research on cultural similarity between therapist and client, research on therapy with women clients indicates that it is not necessary that women be treated by female therapists. Rather, what seems important is the therapist's sensitivity to gender issues (Worell & Remer, 1992).

〉 EVALUATING PSYCHOTHERAPIES

Given the human suffering created by psychological disorders, the effects of psychotherapy have both personal and societal implications. Practicing clinicians and clinical researchers want to know which approaches are most effective, what kinds of problems are best treated with each approach, and what "active ingredients" of each treatment produce its effects.

Today the basic question "Does psychotherapy work?" is viewed as a gross oversimplification of a much more involved question known as the **specificity question:** "Which types of therapy, administered by which kinds of therapists to which kinds of clients having which kinds of problems, produce which kinds of effects?" After nearly a half century of psychotherapy research involving many hundreds of studies this complex question is still not fully answered (Snyder & Ingram, 2000). Nonetheless, for many reasons, this question demands answers. Selecting and administering the most appropriate kind of intervention is vital in human terms. It is also important for economic reasons. Billions of dollars are spent each year on psychological treatments, and an increasing share of these costs is being paid by so-called third parties, such as insurance companies, health maintenance organizations, and government agencies. As the costs rise, those who bear the financial burden increase their demands for accountability and for demonstrations that the treatments are useful.

Designing good psychotherapy research is one of the most challenging tasks in all of psychology because there are so many variables that cannot be completely controlled. In contrast to laboratory studies, in which the experimental conditions can be highly standardized, therapist-client interactions are by their nature infinitely varied. Another difficulty involves measuring the effects of psychotherapy. Figure 15.16 shows some of the typical ways of measuring change. These measures differ in the outcome variable assessed (emotions, thoughts, or behaviors) and in the source of the data (the client, the therapist, or other informants). Which measures of change are most important or valid? A behaviorist will insist that direct observations of behavior are the best measures, whereas a psychodynamic therapist may be most interested in how clients feel and how much insight they have achieved into the childhood roots of their problems. A humanistic therapist may place the greatest stock in self-concept changes. What if one set of measures indicates improvement, another indicates no change, and a third suggests that the client is worse off than before treatment? How should we evaluate the effects of the therapy? These are just a few of the vexing issues that can arise in psychotherapy research.

Psychotherapy Research Methods

In the 1930s and 1940s, individual case studies provided most of the psychotherapy outcome data. Indeed, Freud and other psychoanalysts opposed the use of experimental methods to evaluate psychoanalysis, insisting that case studies left no doubt regarding its effectiveness (Fisher & Greenberg, 1996; Rosenzweig, 1992). They assumed that without therapy, patients would not improve, and they saw plenty of people who did improve in analysis.

In 1952, British psychologist Hans Eysenck mounted a frontal assault on this assumption. Using recovery data from insurance companies on people who

➤ 24. What is the "specificity question" in psychotherapy research?

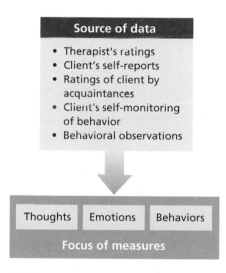

FIGURE 15.16 The measures used to assess the outcome of psychotherapy may come from a variety of data sources, and they may measure different aspects of the client's functioning.

➤ 25. What types of measures are used to assess the outcome of therapy?

➤ 26. Describe Eysenck's challenge to therapy effectiveness and the data on which it was based.

applied for disability because of psychological problems, Eysenck (1952) concluded that the rate of **spontaneous remission**—symptom reduction in the absence of any treatment—was as high as the success rates reported by psychotherapists. He therefore concluded that troubled people who receive psychotherapy are no more likely to improve than are those who go untreated. He also pointed out, quite correctly, that virtually all of the existing outcome data were based on therapists' evaluations of their clients' improvement, and he suggested that these evaluations could be biased by therapists' needs to see themselves as competent and successful.

Eysenck's conclusions sparked intense debate—even outrage—among clinicians, and it now appears that his conclusions were overly pessimistic. More importantly, Eysenck's challenge stimulated a vigorous increase in research on psychotherapy and the development of more sophisticated methods for evaluating treatment outcomes. Fifty years and many hundreds of studies later, we have reached the point where the American Psychological Association's Division of Clinical Psychology has taken the lead in reviewing all of this research to identify *empirically validated therapies* that research shows to be effective for specific disorders (APA Task Force on Psychological Intervention Guidelines, 1995; DeRubeis & Crits-Christoph, 1998).

What Is a Good Psychotherapy Research Design?

> ➤ 27. Summarize desirable standards for designing psychotherapy research studies with regard to design, treatment standardization, and follow-up.

For many of the reasons discussed in Chapter 2, where we discussed experimental methods and their value in drawing conclusions about causality, most psychotherapy researchers favor **randomized clinical trials** involving participants having well-defined psychological disorders and being similar on other variables that might affect response to treatment (age and ethnic status, for example). These individuals are *randomly assigned to either an experimental condition that gets the treatment or to a control condition.* The control group may be either a no-treatment condition or (even better) a **placebo control group** that gets an intervention that is not expected to work but that controls for client expectations of improvement because clients are being seen by a therapist and think they're getting an effective treatment. (Clients in the control group, whether it be a no-treatment or placebo condition, are often given the real treatment later for ethical reasons.)

Another control condition, which avoids the ethical dilemma of withholding or delaying treatment for some people, involves randomly assigning participants to either the treatment being studied or to another kind of treatment that has proven effective for that disorder. If the treatment being tested in the experimental condition is equally or more effective than the established treatment, the new therapy is deemed effective. Sometimes, the design of a study involves a group in which the treatment is combined with another intervention such as a drug treatment. It is then possible to see if the group that received the drug *plus* therapy does better than the groups that got only the drug or only the therapy (Hollon, 1996).

To *standardize* the treatment much as one would do in a laboratory experiment, the APA treatment evaluation group recommends that there be a manual containing procedures that the therapists have to follow exactly, and that therapists' compliance with these procedures be evaluated by observing them or taping their sessions. Some therapists, particularly those who do psychodynamic or humanistic therapies, object to this requirement on the grounds that every therapy case they see is different in its course, client characteristics, and procedures used. As a result, most of the current empirically validated therapies are cognitive-behavioral in nature, because these therapies are more often "manualized" into a step-by-step procedure that therapists can apply in a uniform manner. However, there is a movement toward standardizing even psychodynamically oriented therapies so that they can be evaluated more effectively (Crits-Christoph, 1992; Weissman & Markowitz, 1994).

In evaluating the treatment, at least some of the measures of improvement should be behavioral in nature. Interviewers or observers should not know what condition the clients were in so as to minimize experimenter bias in evaluating change during interviews or behavioral observations following treatment.

Finally, researchers should *collect follow-up data*. This is extremely important, for we want to know not only how the treatment conditions differ at the end of the clinical trial, but also how lasting the effects are. For example, in some studies comparing psychotherapy for depression with the effects of antidepressant drugs, the drug treatment effects occurred more quickly and were stronger at the end of the treatment period, suggesting a superiority for drug therapy. But follow-up data showed psychotherapy to be ultimately more effective, with fewer relapses into depression because clients had learned specific psychological skills that they could apply after therapy ended (Hollon & Beck, 1994; Weissman & Markowitz, 1994). Such information is important in today's managed health care environment, where there is an emphasis on choosing and paying for whichever treatment not only works most quickly and inexpensively, but also has the most lasting effects (Beitman, 1998).

Meta-Analysis: A Look at the Big Picture

As discussed in Chapter 2, the technique of **meta-analysis** allows researchers to combine the results of many studies to arrive at an overall conclusion. In the psychotherapy research literature they can compute an **effect size statistic** that represents a common measure of treatment effectiveness. The effect size tells researchers what percentage of clients who have received therapy had a more favorable outcome than that of the average control client who did not receive the treatment.

In 1977, Mary Ann Smith and Gene Glass used meta-analysis to combine the effects of 375 studies of psychotherapy involving 25,000 clients and 25,000 control participants. These studies differed in many ways, but they all compared a treatment condition with a control condition. The results indicated that the average therapy client had a more favorable outcome than 75 percent of the untreated cases. Smith and Glass therefore disputed Eysenck's earlier conclusion, maintaining that therapy does indeed have positive effects beyond spontaneous remission. More recent meta-analyses support this conclusion. Robert Grissom (1997) found that across a large number of studies, clients who received therapy were likely to have a more favorable outcome than 70 percent of those in no-treatment control conditions and 66 percent of those in placebo conditions.

What about differences among therapies? Smith and Glass broke down their meta-analysis in terms of many of the therapies described in this chapter. As shown in Figure 15.17, psychodynamic, client-centered, and behavioral approaches were quite similar in their effectiveness, and all of them seemed to yield somewhat more positive effects than gestalt therapy. A more recent meta-analysis of brief psychodynamic therapy outcome studies supports a similar conclusion: That form of therapy yielded significantly better outcomes than did no-treatment or placebo control conditions, but did not differ in effectiveness from other forms of therapy with which it was compared (Anderson & Lambert, 1997).

In evaluating the results of meta-analyses, we should remember that the studies lumped together in a meta-analysis can differ in many ways, including the nature and severity of the problems that were treated, the outcome measures that were used, and the quality of the methodology. Psychotherapy researchers point out that combining good studies with less adequate ones can produce misleading results (Kazdin, 1998; Matt & Navarro, 1997). When studies that meet

> ➤ 28. How is meta-analysis used to assess therapy effects? What have meta-analyses shown about overall effectiveness and the effects of different forms of therapy?

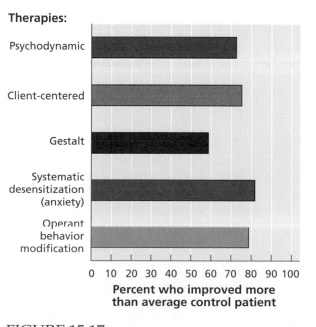

FIGURE 15.17 This meta-analysis of 375 studies of psychotherapy outcome yielded effectiveness data on various types of psychotherapy. The bars indicate the percentage of treated clients who improved more than the average control client. Data from Smith & Glass, 1977.

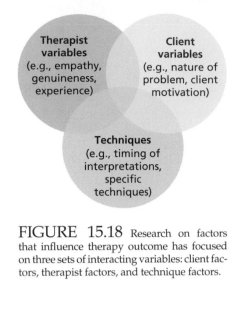

FIGURE 15.18 Research on factors that influence therapy outcome has focused on three sets of interacting variables: client factors, therapist factors, and technique factors.

➤ 29. What client variables are important to treatment outcome?

➤ 30. Which therapist factors affect treatment outcome?

➤ 31. Define and give examples of common factors in psychotherapy.

rigorous research standards are compared in meta-analyses with less rigorous studies, the rigorous studies tend to yield more favorable outcomes for therapy conditions (Matt & Navarro, 1997). Apparently, the rigorous methods used in such studies allow effective therapies to show their true effects.

Factors Affecting the Outcome of Therapy

Clearly, not everyone who enters therapy profits from it. There is even evidence that some clients—perhaps 10 percent—may get worse as a result of treatment (Binder & Strupp, 1997; Lambert et al., 1986). What then are the factors that influence treatment outcome? Three sets of factors have been the focus of research designed to answer this question, namely, client variables, therapist variables, and technique variables (Figure 15.18).

Where client variables are concerned, three important factors are an openness to therapy, self-relatedness, and the nature of the problem. **Openness** involves clients' general willingness to invest themselves in therapy and take the risks required to change themselves. **Self-relatedness** refers to their ability to experience and understand internal states such as thoughts and emotions, to be attuned to the processes that go on in their relationship with their therapist, and to be able to apply what they learn in therapy to their lives outside of treatment (Howard et al., 1993). The third important client factor is the nature of the problem and its degree of "fit" with the therapy being used. For example, specific problems like phobias may respond best to a behavioral anxiety-reduction treatment like systematic desensitization or exposure, whereas a more global problem, such as a search for self-discovery and greater meaning in life, may respond better to a psychodynamic, cognitive, or humanistic approach.

A second important determinant of therapy outcome is the quality of the relationship that the therapist is able to establish with the client (Lafferty et al., 1989; Strupp, 1989). Carl Rogers's emphasis on the importance of therapist qualities such as empathy, unconditional acceptance of the client as a person, and genuineness has been borne out in a great many studies (Beutler et al., 1994; Bohart & Greenberg, 1997). The establishment of an empathic, trusting, and caring relationship forms the foundation upon which the specific techniques employed by the therapist can have their most beneficial effects. When therapists do not manifest these behaviors, the effects of therapy are not simply null; clients can actually get worse. For example, hostile interchanges between therapist and client can contribute to a *deterioration effect* in therapy (Binder & Strupp, 1997).

We do not mean to imply that as long as a therapist has a good relationship with a client, it does not matter what therapy techniques are used or how they are used. It does matter. Therapists must be skilled in what they do. For example, a large-scale study at the University of Pennsylvania revealed that the correctness of the interpretations made by psychoanalytic therapists, as measured by expert ratings, was related to more positive treatment outcome (Crits-Christoph et al., 1988). Likewise, in a detailed analysis of the audiotaped therapy sessions of 21 psychotherapists, Enrico Jones and coworkers (1988) found that the most effective therapists adjusted their techniques to the specific needs of their clients. They concluded that "general relationship factors, such as therapeutic alliance, are closely bound with the skillful selection and application of psychotherapeutic techniques" (p. 55).

Despite dramatic differences in the techniques they employ, various therapies tend to enjoy similar success rates, probably because people who differ on the client variables are lumped together. This finding has led many experts to search for **common factors** shared by these diverse forms of therapy that might contribute to their success. These common factors include the following:

- faith in the therapist and a belief on the part of clients that they are receiving help;

- a plausible explanation for their problems, and an alternative way of looking at themselves and their problems;

- a protective setting where clients can experience and express their deepest feelings within a supportive relationship;

- an opportunity to practice new behaviors; and

- increased optimism and self-efficacy.

The complexities of psychotherapy pose a formidable challenge for clinical researchers. Our *Research Close-up* describes one notable attempt to assess client perceptions of treatment outcome.

➤ 32. What were the major findings of the *CR* survey? On what bases were its conclusions criticized?

RESEARCH CLOSE-UP

The Effectiveness of Psychotherapy: Feedback From the Consumer

▶ Background

Martin Seligman (1995) drew a distinction between two important questions about psychotherapy and its effects. The first is **efficacy,** a scientific term referring to whether a therapy can produce positive outcomes exceeding those in appropriate control conditions. Efficacy is best demonstrated in experimental clinical trials, where the form of therapy and the nature of the clinical problems are controlled. The second is **effectiveness,** meaning the outcomes that psychotherapy has in the real-life settings of clinical practice, where clients are free to pursue any kind of treatment they wish and the nature of the treatment is left uncontrolled. Seligman (1995) argued that highly controlled efficacy studies may not provide a true indication of psychotherapy's effectiveness in "real-life" clinical practice. He therefore assisted the periodical *Consumer Reports (CR)* in a large-scale survey of its readership to assess consumers' evaluations of their treatment experiences and the professionals they worked with.

▶ Method

Each year, *CR* sends questionnaires to over 4 million of its subscribers on which they rate various products and services. One form of the 1994 annual survey, mailed to 184,000 randomly selected subscribers, contained a section on stress and mental health. Readers were asked to complete the mental health section if they had sought help for emotional problems in the past three years. A total of 22,000 readers responded to the questionnaire—a 13 percent response rate that is typical of *CR* surveys. Of these, 35 percent reported that they had a mental-health problem, and 40 percent of this latter group (approximately 2,900 respondents) reported that they had sought professional help from a psychologist, psychiatrist, social worker, or marriage counselor. The respondents were asked to indicate the nature of the problem(s) for which they sought therapy, how much they improved as a result of treatment, and how satisfied they were with the treatment they received.

▶ Results

Clients most frequently sought treatment for depression, followed by marital and sexual problems, anxiety, and family or social problems. Forty-three percent said they were feeling either "very poorly" or "poorly" when they began therapy, and 44 percent reported feeling "so-so." As shown in Figure 15.19, the majority of clients said they had improved as a result of treatment and were satisfied with their therapist. Those who were in treatment longer than six months said that they improved more than did those who were treated less than six months, even when the nature and severity of their problem was held constant. No overall outcome differences were found among mental health professionals, but clients were less satisfied with marriage counselors than with psychologists, psychiatrists, or social workers. As in the meta-analyses described earlier, the *CR* survey found no effectiveness differences between the various types of psychotherapy the clients said they had received.

▶ Critical Discussion

Seligman concluded that "*CR* has provided empirical validation of the effectiveness of therapy" (1995, p. 974). Further, he concluded that the survey method used in this study might actually have provided data that are more representative of "real-life" outcomes than data yielded by highly controlled clinical trials.

Given what you've learned about psychotherapy research, do you agree with Seligman's conclusions? Can you think of any aspects of the *CR* methods that might limit your ability to conclude that psychotherapy is effective?

—Continued

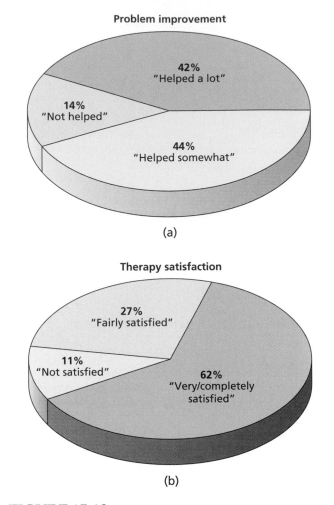

Problem improvement

42%
"Helped a lot"

14%
"Not helped"

44%
"Helped somewhat"

(a)

Therapy satisfaction

27%
"Fairly satisfied"

11%
"Not satisfied"

62%
"Very/completely satisfied"

(b)

FIGURE 15.19 Ratings of (a) self-perceived improvement and (b) satisfaction with therapy outcome made by about 2,900 subscribers of *Consumer Reports* who had been in psychotherapy for the treatment of psychological disorders.

Data from Consumer Reports, 1995.

Seligman's conclusions were strongly contested on scientific grounds, and the American Psychological Association devoted an entire issue of its flagship publication (*American Psychologist,* November, 1996) to reactions from leading psychotherapy researchers. Here are some of the issues they raised:

1. Consider the nature of the sample. Only 1.6 percent of the original 184,000 people contacted described their therapy experience. Is it possible that among the other 98.4 percent are a significant percentage of people who had been in therapy with unfavorable results and chose not to share their experiences? If so, the effectiveness of therapy could be exaggerated in this self-selected sample.

2. What about the nature and quality of the data? We have only global after-the-fact reports from clients. There is no way to corroborate respondents' reports with other sources of data. How do we know that they are not biased by memory distortions or affected by cognitive dissonance ("If I spent that much time and money, I must have gotten better"). A dissonance effect could also account for the apparent superiority of long-term therapy, where more time and money were expended, as well as the tendency to return the questionnaire and share the success story.

3. What has this study told us about the more important specificity question? We don't know if some matches of clinical problems with specific forms of therapy yielded better outcomes than others. In fact, we can't even be sure what kinds of therapy were administered because respondents didn't describe their treatments in detail.

4. How about the absence of a control group? Can we rule out spontaneous remission of symptoms? As we saw in Chapter 14, many mental-health problems (e.g., depression and anxiety) fluctuate or improve with time. People who are assessed at their low points, when they are most likely to seek therapy, are almost certain to improve, with or without therapy (Mintz et al., 1996). Could this factor alone explain the respondents' perceptions that they had improved? As Seligman himself conceded:

> Because there are no control groups, the *CR* . . . study cannot tell us directly whether talking to sympathetic friends or merely letting time pass would have produced just as much improvement as treatment by a mental-health professional. (1995, p. 972)

We chose to feature this study because it illustrates how difficult it can be to draw causal conclusions from studies that lack the precision of randomized clinical trials that are designed to control for all of the above factors. It may be that Seligman's conclusions are indeed correct, but we simply can't be sure when there are so many alternative explanations for the results.

Sources: *Consumer Reports* (1995, November). Mental health: Does therapy help? 734–739. Martin E. P. Seligman (1995). The effectiveness of psychotherapy: The Consumer Reports study. *American Psychologist, 50,* 965–974.

❯ BIOLOGICAL APPROACHES TO TREATMENT

In the previous chapter, we found that biological factors play an important role in many psychological disorders. Thus a direct biological approach designed to alter the brain's functioning is an alternative (or an addition) to psychological treatment.

Drug Therapies

Drug therapies are the most commonly used biological interventions. Discoveries in the field of psychopharmacology (the study of how drugs affect cognitions, emotions, and behavior) have revolutionized the treatment of the entire range of behavior disorders. Each year in the United States alone, more than 200 million prescriptions are filled for drugs that affect mood, thought, and behavior (Lieberman, 1998). The most commonly prescribed drugs fall into three major categories: antianxiety drugs, antidepressant drugs, and antipsychotic drugs.

Antianxiety Drugs

Surveys have shown that more than 15 percent of Americans between the ages of 18 and 74 use antianxiety or tranquilizing drugs such as Valium, Xanax, and BuSpar. These drugs are designed to reduce anxiety as much as possible without affecting alertness or concentration. Sometimes antianxiety drugs are used in combination with other therapies to help clients cope successfully with problematic situations (Stahl, 1998). A temporary reduction in anxiety from the use of a drug may allow a client to enter anxiety-arousing situations and learn to cope more effectively with them.

➤ 33. How do antianxiety drugs achieve their effects? Do they have any drawbacks?

One drawback of antianxiety drugs is psychological and physical dependence that can result from their long-term use. As with any other addictive drug, people who have developed physiological dependence on tranquilizers can experience characteristic withdrawal symptoms, such as intense anxiety, nausea, and restlessness when they stop taking them (Lieberman, 1998). Another problem is that anxiety symptoms often return when people stop taking the drugs.

A newer antianxiety drug, *buspirone* (BuSpar), is slow acting, has fewer fatiguing side effects, and seems to have less potential for abuse. It has proven effective in the treatment of generalized anxiety and posttraumatic stress disorder (Lieberman, 1998; Stahl, 1998). Like the other antianxiety drugs, BuSpar works by slowing down excitatory synaptic activity in the nervous system. One mechanism for doing so is by enhancing the postsynaptic activity of GABA, an inhibitory transmitter that reduces neural activity in areas of the brain associated with emotional arousal (Pies, 1998).

Antidepressant Drugs

Antidepressant drugs fall into three major categories: *tricyclics* (trade names Elavil, Tofranil); *monoamine oxidase (MAO) inhibitors* (Nardil, Parnate); and *selective serotonin reuptake inhibitors, or SSRIs* (Prozac, Zoloft, Paxil). The first two classes increase the activity of the excitatory neurotransmitters norepinephrine and serotonin, whose lowered level of activity in brain regions involved in positive emotion and motivation is related to depression. The tricyclics work by preventing reuptake of the excitatory transmitters into the presynaptic neurons, allowing them to continue stimulating postsynaptic neurons. The MAO inhibitors reduce the activity of monoamine oxidase, an enzyme that breaks down the neurotransmitters in the synapse.

➤ 34. How do the three classes of antidepressant drugs achieve their effects biologically? How effective are they compared/combined with therapy?

Copyright 1996 Nick Hobart

"How about that! I take Prozac too."

MAO inhibitors have more severe side effects than the tricyclics. They can cause dangerous elevations in blood pressure when taken with certain foods, such as cheeses and some types of wine. Many patients have abandoned their antidepressant medications because of severe side effects. The SSRIs were designed to decrease side effects by increasing the activity of just one transmitter, serotonin (Pies, 1998). Like the other antidepressants, however, SSRIs do have side effects. For example, about 30 percent of patients on Prozac report nervousness, insomnia, sweating, joint pain, or sexual dysfunction (Hellerstein et al., 1993). Nonetheless, the SSRIs are gradually replacing the tricyclics because, in addition to milder side effects, they reduce depressive symptoms more rapidly and also reduce anxiety

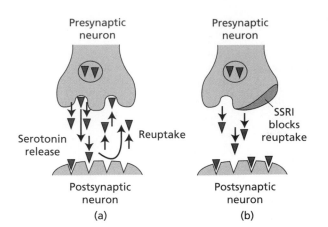

Presynaptic neuron   Presynaptic neuron

Serotonin release   Reuptake

SSRI blocks reuptake

Postsynaptic neuron   Postsynaptic neuron

(a)   (b)

FIGURE 15.20 Serotonin activity is low in many depressed clients. When a presynaptic neuron releases serotonin into the synaptic space, a pumplike reuptake mechanism begins to pull neurotransmitter molecules back into the "sending" neuron, limiting the stimulation of the postsynaptic neuron (a). By blocking the reuptake of serotonin into the presynaptic neuron, (b), the selective serotonin reuptake inhibitors (SSRIs) allow serotonin to continue its stimulation of postsynaptic neurons.

symptoms, including panic disorder, obsessive-compulsive behaviors, and social phobia (Lickey & Gordon, 1991; Lieberman, 1998). Figure 15.20 shows how the SSRIs produce their effects.

Increasingly, depression researchers are studying the effects of combining drugs and psychotherapy. A meta-analysis of such studies revealed that recovery rates for psychotherapy and the combined treatments did not differ for less severely depressed people. However, the combination of psychotherapy and drug treatment yielded the best recovery rates in more severe cases of depression (Thase et al., 1997).

Antipsychotic Drugs

Perhaps the most dramatic effects of drug therapy have occurred in the treatment of severely disordered people, permitting many of them to function outside of the hospital setting (Shorter, 1998). As shown in Figure 15.21, a sharp decline in the number of inpatients in public mental hospitals has occurred since 1955, when antipsychotic drugs were first introduced on a wide scale.

The revolution in drug therapy for severe psychological disorders began when it was accidentally discovered that reserpine, a drug derived from the root of the snakeroot plant, calmed psychotic patients. This discovery resulted in the development of synthetic antipsychotic drugs (also called *major tranquilizers*) used today to treat schizophrenic disorders. The primary effect of the major tranquilizers is to decrease the action of dopamine, the neurotransmitter whose overactivity is thought to be involved in schizophrenia (Pies, 1998). These drugs have dramatic effects in reducing positive symptoms, such as hallucinations and delusions. However, they have little effect on negative symptoms, such as apathy and withdrawal. Antipsychotic drugs are now so widely used that nearly all schizophrenic patients living in the United States, Canada, and western Europe have received them at one time or another. Because patients often relapse very quickly if they stop taking the drugs, it is common practice to recommend that the medication be continued indefinitely once the individual has returned to the community (Carpenter & Heinrichs, 1983).

Although antipsychotic drugs have allowed many patients to be released from hospitals and reduced the need for padded cells, straitjackets, and other re-

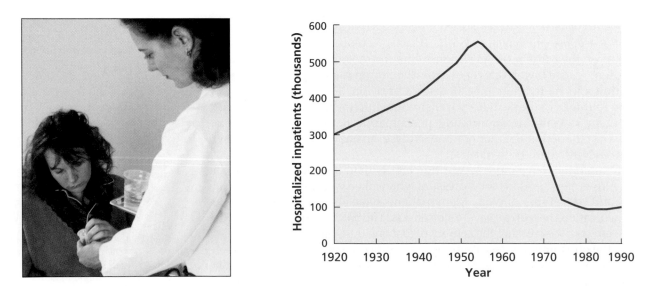

FIGURE 15.21 Antipsychotic drugs have revolutionized the treatment of severely disturbed individuals, allowing many of them to leave mental hospitals. Note the decline in hospitalized inpatients that occurred following the introduction of antipsychotic drugs in the mid-1950s.

straints that were used to control the behavior of hospitalized patients, these drugs can produce is a severe movement disorder known as **tardive dyskinesia** (Kane, 1992). Uncontrollable and grotesque movements of the face and tongue are especially prominent in this disorder, and sometimes the patient's arms and legs flail uncontrollably. Tardive dyskinesia can be more debilitating than the psychotic symptoms that prompted the drug treatment, and it appears to be irreversible once it develops (Barnes, 1994). One study found that within four years of beginning antipsychotic medications, 18.5 percent of young adults and 31 percent of those over 55 developed tardive dyskenesia symptoms (Saltz et al., 1991).

➤ 35. What is tardive dyskinesia, and how is it caused?

Researchers are working to develop new drugs that can control schizophrenic symptoms without producing side effects, such as the devastating symptoms of tardive dyskinesia. A new drug called *clozapine* (Clozaril) reduces not only positive symptoms, but also negative ones, and it appears not to produce tardive dyskenesia (Lieberman, 1998). Unfortunately, it produces a fatal blood disease in 1 to 2 percent of people who take it, requiring expensive weekly blood tests for patients who use the medication.

Antipsychotic drugs can often be used effectively in conjunction with psychotherapy. For example, drugs may be used to bring psychotic symptoms under control so that other approaches such as social skills training, family therapy, and group therapy can be applied to maintain the initial improvement.

Electroconvulsive Therapy

Another biologically based treatment, **electroconvulsive therapy (ECT),** was based on the observation by a Hungarian physician that schizophrenia and epilepsy rarely occur in the same person. (Apparently, he didn't stop to consider the fact that the probability of epilepsy and *any* other disorder occurring together is very low.) The physician therefore suggested that seizure induction might be useful in the treatment of schizophrenia. Two Italian physicians, Ugo Cerletti and Lucio Bini, began to treat schizophrenic patients by attaching electrodes to their skulls and inducing a seizure by means of an electric current administered to the brain.

When ECT was first introduced in the 1930s, it was applied to a wide range of disorders, but later research revealed that it cannot relieve anxiety disorders and it is of questionable value for schizophrenic patients (Herrington & Lader, 1996; Weiner & Coffey, 1988). However, ECT can be useful in treating severe depression, particularly if there is a high risk of suicide. In such cases, the use of antidepressant drugs may be impractical because they will likely take several weeks to begin reducing the depression. In contrast, the effects of ECT can be immediate, and controlled studies indicate that 60 to 70 percent of severely depressed people given ECT improve (Rey & Walter, 1997).

➤ 36. Which disorders do and do not respond favorably to ECT?

Dramatizations of ECT in the mass media sometimes portray a procedure that appears barbaric. In early applications of ECT, a wide-awake patient was strapped to a table, electrodes were attached to the patient's scalp, and roughly 100 volts of electricity was applied to the brain, producing violent convulsions and momentary unconsciousness. Sometimes, the seizures were so violent that patients fractured their arms or legs.

Today, however, the procedure is quite different (Figure 15.22). A patient is first given a sedative and a muscle relaxant to prevent injuries from convulsions. The patient is then placed on a well-padded mattress, and electrodes are attached to his or her scalp. A modified procedure in which electrodes are placed on only one side of the head is often used (Martin, 1986). The duration of the shock is less than a second, causing a seizure of the central nervous system. There is little observable movement in the patient, other than a twitching of the toes and a slight facial grimace. The patient wakes up 10 to 20 minutes after ECT, possibly with a headache, sore muscles, and some confusion. Recently, scientists have been able to calibrate the amount of electric current a patient needs so that treatments can

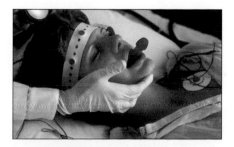

FIGURE 15.22 A severely depressed and possibly suicidal patient is prepared for electroconvulsive therapy. The patient has been sedated and given a muscle relaxant to minimize limb movements during the brief electrical stimulation of the brain. The rubber object in her mouth prevents her from biting her tongue or damaging teeth during the convulsion.

be individualized, and research is being carried out to determine whether certain drugs can further reduce seizure-induced confusion and amnesia.

ECT has many critics, despite its effectiveness in alleviating major depression. Critics note that even where the effects are dramatically positive, the possibility of a depressive relapse is high. Concerns have been raised about the safety of ECT because in some instances permanent memory loss has been reported, and there are also concerns about possibly permanent brain damage when ECT is used repeatedly. Today the number of ECT treatments is limited to less than 10, but in the past, many patients received numerous treatments. One person who suffered a tragic outcome was the author Ernest Hemingway.

> In December 1960, Hemingway underwent 11 shock treatments at the Mayo Clinic in Rochester, Minnesota. Three months later he was back for another series. His friend and biographer, A. E. Hotchner, described him at that time: "Ernest was even more infuriated with these treatments than the previous ones, registering bitter complaints about how his memory was wrecked and how he was ruined as a writer." Hemingway told Hotchner, "What these shock doctors don't know is about writers and such things as remorse and contrition and what they do to them. What is the sense of ruining my head and erasing my memory, which is my capital, and putting me out of business? It was a brilliant cure but we lost the patient." Shortly afterwards, Hemingway committed suicide. (Friedberg, 1975, pp. 25–26)

Steps have been taken to increase the safety of ECT, and available scientific evidence suggests that today's ECT is a safer treatment than previous forms were. MRI studies of the brains of patients who received brief pulse treatment to both sides of the brain revealed no evidence of brain damage (Coffey et al., 1991). After reviewing both sides of the issue, the American Psychiatric Association (1990) concluded that this therapy should be regarded as a useful procedure for major depression in patients who cannot take or do not respond to medication and has published guidelines for its use.

Psychosurgery

Psychosurgery refers to surgical procedures that remove or destroy brain tissue to change disordered behavior. It is the least used of the biomedical procedures, but such was not always the case. In the 1930s, before the advent of antipsychotic drugs, Portuguese surgeon Egas Moniz reported that cutting the nerve tracts that connect the frontal lobes with subcortical areas of the brain involved in emotion resulted in a calming of psychotic and uncontrollably violent patients. The operation eliminated emotional input from the limbic system into the areas of the brain connected with executive functions of planning and reasoning. Walter Freeman developed a 10-minute *lobotomy* operation performed by inserting an icepick-like instrument with sharp edges through the eye socket into the brain, then wiggling it back and forth to sever the targeted nerve tracts. During the 1930s and 1940s, tens of thousands of patients—50,000 in the United States alone—underwent the operation. Moniz received a Nobel prize for his contribution (Shorter, 1998).

Initial enthusiasm for lobotomy was soon replaced by a sober recognition that the massive neural damage it caused had severe side effects on mental and emotional functioning, including seizures, stupor, memory and reasoning impairments, and listlessness. With the development of antipsychotic drugs in the 1950s, lobotomies decreased and are hardly ever used today. However, more precise and limited psychosurgery procedures are still used at times in the most extreme cases and when every other avenue has been tried (Pressman, 1998). One procedure called *cingulotomy* involves cutting a small fiber bundle near the corpus callosum that connects the frontal lobes with the limbic system. Cingulotomy has been used successfully in treating severe depressive and obsessive-compulsive disorders that

> 37. What was the rationale and the effects of prefrontal lobotomy?

have failed to improve with drug treatment or psychotherapy. However, this more limited procedure can also produce side effects, including seizures (Herrington & Lader, 1966; Pressman, 1998). Appropriately, cingulotomy and other forms of psychosurgery are considered to be last-resort procedures.

Mind, Body, and Therapeutic Interventions

The impact of drug and electroconvulsive therapies on psychological disorders illustrates once again the important interactions between biological and psychological phenomena. In the final analysis, both psychological and biological treatments affect brain functioning in ways that can change disordered thoughts, emotions, and behavior. For example, Lewis Baxter and coworkers (1992) used PET scans to study cortical brain metabolism changes in patients who were being treated for obsessive-compulsive disorders with either behavior therapy or drug therapy. Those patients who showed improvement in their obsessive-compulsive behaviors exhibited a specific pattern of changes in brain activity that was the same whether they had undergone drug therapy or psychotherapy. Clients who did not improve did not show the "signature" changes in brain activity. Thus different forms of therapy, whether "psychological" or "biological" in nature, may result in similar changes at a neurological level and, ultimately, at a behavioral level.

An important factor to keep in mind is that drug treatments, however effective they may be in modifying some disordered behaviors in the short term, do not "cure" the disorder. They suppress symptoms, but do not teach the client coping and problem solving skills that might be used to deal with stressful life situations (DeLongis et al., 2000; Nezu et al., 2000). Many therapists believe that one of the major benefits of psychological treatments is their potential not only for helping clients to deal with current problems but also for increasing their personal resources so that they might enjoy a higher level of adjustment and life satisfaction in the future (Hollon, 1996).

We have now considered a wide spectrum of approaches to treating abnormal behavior. Figure 15.23 summarizes the mechanisms for therapeutic change that are emphasized by the various psychological and biological approaches.

Level of Analysis		
Biological	**Psychological**	**Environmental**
• Changes in neurotransmitter, autonomic, or hormonal activity brought about by drug treatment, psychotherapy, or surgical procedures	• Cognitive and emotional changes brought about by cognitive therapies • Modification of conditioned emotional responses by deconditioning procedures such as exposure, desensitization, and aversion therapy • Behavioral changes produced by operant procedures • Self-concept changes brought about by psychotherapy (e.g., client-centered, Gestalt therapy) • Insight into unconscious dynamics and development of more mature defenses brought about by short- and long-term psychodynamic therapies	• Life situation changes brought about by constructive behavior changes learned in therapy or produced by biological means • Exposure to specific therapeutic techniques administered by a mental-health expert • A positive therapeutic relationship that helps promote change and allows therapy techniques to be effective • Cultural factors that affect access to therapy, type of therapy, and exposure to a culturally competent therapist

THERAPEUTIC BEHAVIOR CHANGE

FIGURE 15.23   Understanding the Causes of Behavior: Mechanisms of therapeutic behavior change.

❭ PSYCHOLOGICAL DISORDERS AND SOCIETY

Since the days of insane asylums, first established in the 16th century to segregate the insane from society, severe behavior disorders have been treated in institutional settings. In the United States, a national network of nearly 300 state-funded mental hospitals was built between 1845 and 1945. Many private facilities were also built. The number of patients being treated in public mental hospitals increased steadily from about 250,000 in 1920 to more than 500,000 in 1950. By 1955, half of all hospital beds in the United States were occupied by psychiatric patients. However, it was readily apparent to mental-health experts that although there were some high-quality institutions, many public mental hospitals were not fulfilling their intended role as treatment facilities. They were overcrowded, understaffed, and underfinanced. Many of them could provide little more than minimal custodial care and a haven from the stresses and demands of the outer world. Moreover, people who were admitted to such hospitals often sank into a chronic "sick" role in which passive dependence and "crazy" behavior were not only tolerated, but expected (Goffman, 1961; Scheff, 1964). They lost the self-confidence, motivation, and skills needed to reenter and adapt to the outside world and had little chance of surviving outside the hospital.

Deinstitutionalization

By the 1960s, the stage was set for a new approach to the treatment of behavior disorders. Concerns about the inadequacies of mental hospitals, together with the ability of antipsychotic drugs to "normalize" patients' behavior, resulted in a **deinstitutionalization** movement to transfer the primary focus of treatment from the hospital to the community.

In 1963, Congress passed the Community Mental Health Centers Act, which provided for the establishment of one mental health center for every 50,000 people. Community mental health centers are designed to provide comprehensive services for their local communities. Their major function is to provide outpatient psychotherapy and drug treatment so that clients can remain in their normal social and work environments. They can also arrange for short-term inpatient care, usually at a local general hospital, when clients are acutely disturbed. Many have crisis centers and telephone "hot lines" to respond to emergency situations encountered by people in the community. Finally, community mental health centers provide education and consultation for their communities. For example, staff members may provide drug education programs to local schools or educate police officers on how to deal with seriously disturbed people they might encounter in the line of duty.

Combined with the development of effective drug treatments, the impact of deinstitutionalization on the treatment of behavior disorders has been dramatic. According to the National Institute of Mental Health, 77.4 percent of all patients were being treated as inpatients in public and private hospitals in 1955. By 1990, the inpatient figure had shrunk to 27.1 percent. As Figure 15.24 indicates, the average length of hospitalization for patients having severe (typically schizophrenic) disorders has also decreased markedly.

The concept of community treatment is a good one, for it allows people to remain in their social and work environments and to be treated with minimal disruption of their lives. However, it requires the availability of high-quality mental health care in community clinics, halfway houses, sheltered workshops, and other community facilities. When these facilities are available, deinstitutionalization can work. Unfortunately, however, many communities never were able to fund the needed facilities, and the 1980s saw sharp cutbacks in federal fund-

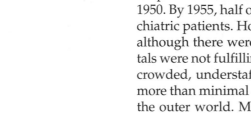

➤ 38. What is the rationale for deinstitutionalization? What prevents it from achieving its goals?

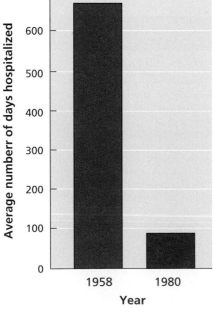

FIGURE 15.24 Average length of psychiatric hospitalization at Veterans Administration Hospitals in 1958 and 1980.
Data from National Institute of Mental Health, 1992.

ing of community mental-health centers. As a result, many patients are being released into communities that are ill-prepared to care for their needs. The result is a *revolving door phenomenon* involving repeated rehospitalizations. Nearly three fourths of all hospital admissions involve formerly hospitalized patients. While in the hospital, they respond well to antipsychotic medications and are soon released back into a community that cannot offer them the care they require. Soon they stop taking their medication. In the absence of treatment, their condition deteriorates to the point where they must be hospitalized, and so the cycle begins again. One result is a growing population of disturbed and homeless people who have nowhere to go for help (Figure 15.25). In some states with large urban populations, the largest mental wards exist not in hospitals but on city streets. There are as many as 1 million homeless people in the United States, and approximately one-third have a severe mental disorder, typically schizophrenia (Torrey, 1997).

Deinstitutionalization can work only if society has the will to make it work. Time will tell if funding will be provided for the community programs needed to slow the revolving door and provide the help so desperately needed by the many people who are being left without treatment and without hope.

Preventive Mental Health

Up to now, we have focused entirely on what can be done to help people once they have developed a behavior disorder. Successful treatment is one way to reduce the toll of human suffering produced by failures to adapt. Another way is to try to *prevent* the development of disorders through psychological intervention. In terms of economic, personal, and societal costs, it may indeed be the case that "an ounce of prevention is worth a pound of cure." If current efforts to enhance personal well-being and to slow the rise of health care costs are to be successful, a focus on prevention of behavior disorders must be a focal point in social policy (Munoz et al., 1996).

People may become vulnerable to psychological disorders as the result of situational factors, personal factors, or both. Thus prevention can be approached from two perspectives (Figure 15.26). **Situation-focused prevention** is directed at reducing or eliminating the environmental causes of behavior disorders or in enhancing situational factors that help prevent the development of disorders. Psychologist George Albee (1996), who champions this approach, insists that prevention must focus on efforts to reduce the stresses of unemployment, economic exploitation, discrimination, and poverty. Programs designed to enhance the functioning of families, reduce stress within organizations, provide better educational opportunities for children, and develop a sense of "connection" to other people and the community at large all have the potential to help prevent the development of behavior disorders (Albee, 1997; Taylor & Wang, 2000).

The personal side of the equation is addressed by **competency-focused prevention,** which is designed to increase personal resources and coping skills. Such programs may focus on strengthening resistance to stress, improving social and vocational competencies, enhancing self-esteem, and helping people to gain the skills needed to build stronger social support systems. One illustrative program, developed by Edna Foa and her coworkers (1995), focused on preventing the development of posttraumatic stress disorder in women who had recently been raped or assaulted.

The victims were randomly assigned to either a treatment condition or to a nontreatment control condition. Over a four-week period, the women in the treatment group underwent an educational program designed to increase their stress management coping skills. They learned about the common psychological reactions to being raped, showing them that their responses were normal, and they emotionally relived their trauma through imagery to defuse their lingering fears through exposure. They also learned stress coping skills such as relaxation, and they went through a cognitive therapy procedure so they could replace their

FIGURE 15.25 The "revolving door" phenomenon created by inadequate funding of community-based treatment facilities has produced a large population of severely disturbed homeless people who live on our nation's streets.

➤ 39. Define the two major approaches to prevention.

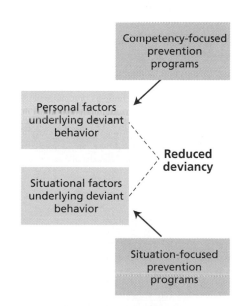

FIGURE 15.26 Two approaches to prevention of psychological disorders, based on the principle that deviant behavior represents the interaction of personal and situational factors. Situation-focused approaches increase situational protective factors or reduce vulnerability factors in the environment. Competency-focused approaches reduce personal vulnerability factors or strengthen personal competencies and coping skills.

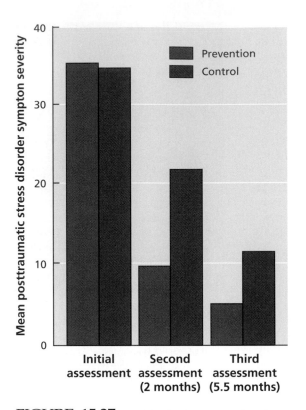

FIGURE 15.27 Results of a competency-based prevention project designed to prevent PTSD in women who were victims of rape and assault. The program, which combined a number of behavioral and cognitive therapy techniques to increase stress management coping skills, sharply reduced the likelihood of developing PTSD.

Based on Foa et al., 1995.

negative beliefs about themselves and their stress-producing cognitions with more realistic appraisals.

The results of the prevention program are shown in Figure 15.27. The women exposed to the prevention treatment had less severe symptoms at both the 2-month and 5.5-month assessments. Moreover, 2 months after their trauma, diagnostic interviews with the women in the two groups revealed that 70 percent of the women in the control condition met the DSM-IV criteria for PTSD compared with only 10 percent of the women who had received the prevention program. Thus for many of the women, an efficient four-hour program prevented what might have been a PTSD disorder that would have created tremendous personal misery and required a far more expensive and time-consuming course of therapy (Rasmussen & Charney, 2000).

Many mental-health experts believe that more resources need to be focused on prevention so that the occurrence of maladaptive behavior can be reduced. However, prevention presents its own challenges. For one, we cannot develop an intervention program until we understand the causes of the disorder we want to reduce. Even where causal factors are known, we also need to understand what kinds of interventions will be successful in modifying them. This requires careful research into which types of programs are most effective in preventing which types of problems in which types of people—our old specificity question. Another practical problem is that the effects of prevention are usually not immediately obvious. It may take years for their effects to become evident. Moreover, their effects (which usually involve the *absence* of a disorder) can be hard to measure. For these reasons, prevention programs can be difficult to justify when funding priorities are being set, even though the programs may, in the long run, have greater positive impact than programs that focus on treating disorders that have already developed.

Having described the nature and benefits of treatments, we end this chapter with guidelines for seeking and profiting from therapy.

APPLICATIONS OF PSYCHOLOGICAL SCIENCE

When and Where to Seek Therapy

No one is immune to problems in living. Every day, each of us does the best we can to balance our personal and social resources against the demands created by our life circumstances. We all have certain vulnerabilities, and if environmental demands and our vulnerabilities combine to exceed our resources, we may experience psychological problems for which professional assistance would be helpful. Here are some general guidelines for seeking such help and profiting from it.

First is the issue of when to seek help. In general terms, you should consider seeking professional assistance if any of the following apply:

- You are experiencing serious emotional discomfort, such as feelings of depression or anxiety, that are adversely affecting your personal, work, or family life.
- You are encountering a serious problem or life transition that you feel unable to handle on your own.

—Continued

- A problem that has interfered with your life or personal happiness in the past is worsening or has suddenly resurfaced.
- You have experienced some traumatic event, either in the past or recently, that you find yourself thinking about, dreaming about, or responding to with negative emotions.
- You are preoccupied with your weight or body image and are taking extreme steps such as bingeing, then purging by vomiting or taking laxatives.
- You hear voices telling you what to do or feel that others are controlling your thoughts.

How does one go about getting help in dealing with psychological problems? Help may be sought at a school counseling center, at a community agency, a health maintenance organization (HMO), or from a professional in private practice. The counseling center is often a good place for a student to start, for it can provide either help or an appropriate referral to a reputable mental health professional. If you are at a larger university that has a graduate program in clinical psychology, there may also be a psychology clinic administered by that program.

How expensive is treatment? It is often offered free or at a nominal fee at a campus facility or HMO. Community agencies typically have a sliding fee scale based on the client's income. Thus financial considerations need not be a barrier to seeking professional assistance. A private practitioner may charge a fee similar to that charged by doctors, dentists, and attorneys, perhaps exceeding $100 per 50-minute session. A prospective client should always ask beforehand about the fee. You should also check into the mental health benefits provided by your health insurance policy. You should realize, however, that in this era of managed care and health cost containment, a person totally untrained in mental health delivery may decide on the number of sessions and the kind of therapy an insurance company will pay for. Unfortunately, to the enormous frustration of many mental health professionals, bottom-line profit motives too often take precedence over the needs of the client as determined by a clinical assessment (Beitman, 1998; Tuckfelt et al., 1997).

In choosing a therapist, what should you look for? It is important that your therapist be fully trained and licensed. Ask the therapist about his or her degree, license, training, therapeutic orientation, and the problems in which she or he specializes. This chapter has provided an overview of the major theoretical orientations, and one or more of them may be especially attractive to you.

As we've seen, the relationship between client and therapist is of the utmost importance. You will want a therapist who can create a good working relationship with you. Degree of value similarity between you and the therapist can be important. Timothy Kelly and Hans Strupp (1992) found that the most positive therapeutic outcomes were achieved when the client and therapist were neither very similar nor very dissimilar in values. High similarity may result in a failure to explore value-related issues that should be explored, whereas too much dissimilarity may interfere with building a good therapeutic relationship. One exception to this general rule may occur in the area of religious values. Clients who have strong and committed religious values may profit most from a therapy that supports those values and uses them to help change problem behaviors (Probst et al., 1992).

Some clients prefer to work with either a male or female therapist, depending in part on the nature of the personal issues that have caused them to seek counseling. As we have seen, research has shown that personal warmth, sincere concern, and empathy are important therapist characteristics. You should like and feel comfortable with your therapist, and you should feel at ease with the methods the therapist uses. Under no circumstances should your therapeutic relationship involve physical intimacy of any kind, and if a therapist should ever make inappropriate advances, a client should immediately terminate treatment with that therapist and notify the appropriate professional organization, such as the state psychological or medical association. Such conduct is a serious breach of professional ethics and cannot be condoned under any circumstances.

You and your therapist should have explicit, agreed-on goals for the treatment program. If therapy proceeds well, you will experience beneficial changes that indicate movement toward these goals. It may take some time for these changes to occur, however, since long-standing personal vulnerabilities are not easily changed, and significant change seldom occurs overnight. If you do not see any progress after several months, or if you seem to be functioning less well than before, you should discuss your progress with the therapist. It is possible that the therapist is more satisfied with your progress than you are. However, if you continue to be dissatisfied with your progress or with the therapeutic relationship, you may at some point decide to terminate it. This should not prevent you from seeking help from another therapist.

Entering a helping relationship is a courageous step, and resolving problems in living may involve taking risks and experiencing pain. However, many clients look back on the pain and risks and feel that the process has been a valuable one that has enabled them to live happier lives than they could otherwise have. Here is a reflection by Dr. Sandra L. Harris, a prominent clinical psychologist, on the course of therapy she undertook as a college student:

When I think about the girl I was in my freshman year at the University of Maryland and the young woman I was when I graduated four years later, it is clear that it was not only the issues Jim and I discussed, but how we talked that made the difference. The intangibles of trust, respect, and caring were at least as important as the active problem solving that transpired in our weekly meetings. It was not a dramatic transformation, rather it was a slight shifting of a path by a few degrees on the compass. Over the years that shift has had a cumulative effect and I walk a very different road than I would have without him. (Harris, 1981, p. 3)

▼▼▼

CHAPTER SUMMARY

Psychodynamic Therapies

- The goal of Freudian psychoanalysis is to help clients achieve insight into the unconscious dynamics that underlie their behavior disorders so that they can deal adaptively with their current environment.

- The chief means for promoting insight in psychoanalysis are the therapist's interpretations of free associations, dream content, resistance, and transference reactions.

- Brief psychodynamic psychotherapies have become increasingly popular alternatives to lengthy psychoanalysis. Their goal is also to promote insight, but they tend to focus more on current life events. Interpersonal therapy is a structured therapy that focuses on current interpersonal problems and the development of needed interpersonal skills.

Humanistic Psychotherapies

- Humanistic psychotherapies attempt to liberate the client's natural tendency toward self-actualization by establishing a growth-inducing therapeutic relationship.

- Rogers's client-centered therapy emphasizes the importance of three therapist characteristics: unconditional positive regard, empathy, and genuineness.

- The goal of gestalt therapy is to remove blockages to clients' awareness of the wholeness of immediate experience by making them more aware of their feelings and the ways in which they interact with others.

Cognitive Therapies

- Ellis's rational-emotive therapy and Beck's cognitive therapy focus on discovering and changing maladaptive beliefs and logical errors of thinking that underlie maladaptive emotional responses and behaviors.

Behavior Therapies

- Behavioral treatments based on classical conditioning are directed at modifying emotional responses. Exposure to the CS and prevention of avoidance responses promote extinction. Systematic desensitization is designed to countercondition a response that is incompatible with anxiety, such as relaxation, to anxiety-arousing stimuli. Aversion therapy is used to establish a conditioned aversion response to an inappropriate stimulus that attracts the client.

- Operant procedures have been applied successfully in many behavior modification programs. The token economy is a positive reinforcement program designed to strengthen adaptive behaviors. Punishment has been used to reduce self-destructive behaviors in disturbed children.

- Modeling is an important component of social skills training programs, which help clients to learn and rehearse more effective social behaviors.

Group, Family, and Marital Therapies

- Group approaches offer clients a number of advantages, including opportunities to form close relationships with others, to gain insights into how they interact with others and are perceived by them, and to observe how others approach problems.

- Family therapy is based on the notion that individuals' problems are often reflections of dysfunctional family systems. Such systems should be treated as a unit.

- Marital therapies help couples to improve their communication patterns and resolve difficulties in their relationships. The recent addition of acceptance training has improved outcomes.

Integrating and Combining Therapies

- An important trend toward eclecticism—the willingness to combine perspectives and techniques from several different therapies, is now seen in the field. There is also a movement to develop more effective therapies by combining different forms of therapy into new therapeutic techniques.

Cultural and Gender Issues in Psychotherapy

- Research has shown that members of minority groups underutilize mental health services. Barriers include lack of access to therapists who can provide culturally responsive forms of treatment. More important to outcome than a cultural match is a therapist who can understand the client's cultural background and share similar viewpoints on therapy goals and the means used to achieve them. Culturally competent therapists take into account both cultural and individual factors in understanding the client.

- Awareness of oppressive environmental conditions that adversely affect women and a willingness to support life goals that do not necessarily conform to gender expectations can increase therapeutic outcomes. Whether the therapist is a man or a woman seems less important to outcome than gender sensitivity.

Evaluating Psychotherapies

- Eysenck challenged the effectiveness of psychotherapy and stimulated research using increasingly more sophisticated methods to evaluate outcomes of various therapies. The randomized clinical trial is the most powerful approach to researching the effects of therapy, and a number of standards have been established for conducting psychotherapy research.

- Three sets of interacting factors affect the outcome of treatment: client characteristics (including the nature of the problem), therapist characteristics, and therapy techniques.

- Meta-analysis is a method for combining the results of many studies into an effect size statistic. Large-scale meta-analyses of treatment outcome studies indicate that therapy clients improve more than 70 to 75 percent of control clients, and that various therapies seemed to differ little in effectiveness.

- Many therapy researchers have concluded that the most important common factor in the success of various therapies is the quality of the relationship that the therapist establishes with the client. The three characteristics suggested by Rogers—empathy, unconditional positive regard, and genuineness—seem to be particularly important.

Biological Approaches to Treatment

- Drugs have revolutionized the treatment of many behavior disorders and have permitted many hospitalized patients to function outside of institutions.

- Effective drug treatments exist for anxiety, schizophrenia, and depression. Some of these drugs have undesirable side effects and can be addictive. All have their effects by affecting neurotransmission within the brain, and they work on specific classes of neurotransmitters.

- Electroconvulsive therapy is used less frequently than in the past, and its safety has been increased. It is used primarily to treat severe depression, particularly when a threat of suicide exists.

- Drugs and psychotherapy may be combined to hasten relief of symptoms while establishing more effective coping responses to deal with the sources of the disorder.

- Psychosurgery techniques have become more precise, but they are still generally used only after all other treatment options have failed.

Psychological Disorders and Society

- The introduction of drug therapies that normalize disturbed behavior, as well as concerns about deterioration of life skills during hospitalization, have helped to stimulate a move toward deinstitutionalization—the treatment of people in their communities.

- Research has shown that deinstitutionalization can work when adequate community treatment is provided. Unfortunately, the needed facilities have not been funded, resulting in a "revolving door" of release and rehospitalization, as well as a new generation of homeless people who live in the streets and do not receive needed treatment.

- Prevention programs may be classified as either situation-focused or competency-focused, depending on whether they are directed at changing environmental conditions or personal factors.

KEY TERMS AND CONCEPTS*

aversion therapy (640)

behavior modification (641)

common factors (652)

competency-focused prevention (661)

counterconditioning (639)

culturally competent therapist (648)

deinstitutionalization (660)

eclectic (644)

effect size statistic (651)

effectiveness (653)

efficacy (653)

electroconvulsive therapy (ECT) (657)

empathy (633)

exposure (639)

free association (630)

genuineness (634)

insight (630)

interpersonal therapy (632)

interpretation (632)

meta-analysis (651)

openness (652)

placebo control group (650)

psychodynamic behavior therapy (645)

psychosurgery (658)

randomized clinical trial (650)

resistance (630)

response prevention (639)

▼▼

KEY TERMS AND CONCEPTS (CONTINUED)

self-relatedness (652)

situation-focused prevention (661)

social skills training (642)

specificity question (649)

spontaneous remission (650)

stimulus hierarchy (639)

systematic desensitization (639)

tardive dyskinesia (657)

token economy (641)

transference (631)

unconditional positive regard (633)

virtual reality (VR) (645)

* Each term has been boldfaced in the text on the page indicated in parentheses.

▼▼

APPLYING YOUR KNOWLEDGE

1. In a recent session with her analyst, Paula mentioned a "strange" camping trip she took with her father when she was eight years old. But every time the analyst asks her to tell her more about it, Paula claims she can't remember anything about it and switches the subject to something else. The analyst may well suspect that Paula's behavior is a sign of
   a) negative transference.
   b) resistance.
   c) working through.
   d) positive transference.

2. Dennis, diagnosed with schizophrenia, has been taking antipsychotic medication for several years. Although these drugs have reduced his disordered thoughts and behavior, he has gradually begun to develop grotesque, uncontrollable, facial and tongue movements. Dennis has developed
   a) Parkinson's disease.
   b) Alzheimer's disease.
   c) positive symptoms.
   d) tardive dyskinesia.

3. Someone tells you that he wants a psychodynamic therapy, but doesn't want to expend the time and money needed for traditional psychoanalysis. Which of the following approaches would you recommend to him as an alternative?
   a) interpersonal therapy
   b) aversion therapy
   c) gestalt therapy
   d) rational-emotive psychotherapy

4. Sandy seeks therapeutic help because she feels that her life has little meaning. Her therapist guides her to explore who she is as a person and what she really wants, frequently reflecting back what she has said. Sandy comes to realize that she has been living her life in terms of her parents' expectations rather than her own needs and values. Her therapist is most likely
   a) Sigmund Freud.
   b) Carl Rogers.
   c) Fritz Perls.
   d) Aaron Beck.

5. Vincent has a phobia about heights. During his second therapy session, his therapist takes him into a glass-sided elevator and they ride up and down the 48-story building. Which therapy technique is the therapist using?
   a) modeling therapy
   b) gestalt therapy
   c) exposure
   d) aversion therapy

6. In the course of therapy, it becomes apparent that one of Margaret's problems is that she is unable to express her real feelings to people. This is particularly a problem in her relationship with her husband. The therapist has Margaret talk to an empty chair, pretending that her husband is sitting in it. Margaret's therapist is most likely a practitioner of
   a) behavior therapy.
   b) gestalt therapy.
   c) client-centered therapy.
   d) psychoanalysis.

7. Donna has a panic disorder. Her therapist has shown her that her panic arises when she interprets normal anxiety symptoms as a sign that she is going to die or "fall apart" in public) He helps her replace these thoughts with reminders that her symptoms are "just normal anxiety." Her therapist is most likely
   a) Carl Rogers.
   b) Joseph Wolpe.
   c) Aaron Beck.
   d) Paul Wachtel.

8. Martha is depressed and is also experiencing a social phobia. Her physician prescribes a drug that affects only one neurotransmitter system and relieves both depression and anxiety. The drug is most likely to be
    a) an SSRI.
    b) a major tranquilizer.
    c) a tricyclic.
    d) an MAO inhibitor.

9. You have decided that you want to work out some issues in your life, and you know that the outcome of treatment depends on certain therapist variables. Which of the following would be the most important factor to look for?
    a) a therapist who is a member of your ethnic group
    b. someone whose values are identical to yours
    c) a therapist who is empathic and accepting of you
    d) a person of the same sex as you

10. Many cities have established recreational and athletic programs for disadvantaged youth to counteract gang influences and drug use by providing a supportive environment and good role models. Such programs are an example of
    a) tertiary prevention.
    b) situation-focused prevention.
    c) competency-focused prevention.
    d) social skills training.

Answers

1. b) (page 630); 2. d) (page 657); 3. a) (page 632); 4. b) (page 633); 5. c) (page 639); 6. b) (page 635); 7. c) (page 637); 8. a) (page 655); 9. c) (page 634); 10. b) (page 661)

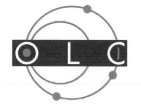

For additional quizzing and a variety of interactive resources, visit the book's Online Learning Center at www.mhhe.com/passer.

PSYCHOLOGY AND SOCIETY: FROM BASIC RESEARCH TO SOCIAL APPLICATION

The difference between what we do and what we are capable
of doing would suffice to solve most of the world's problems.
–Gandhi

16

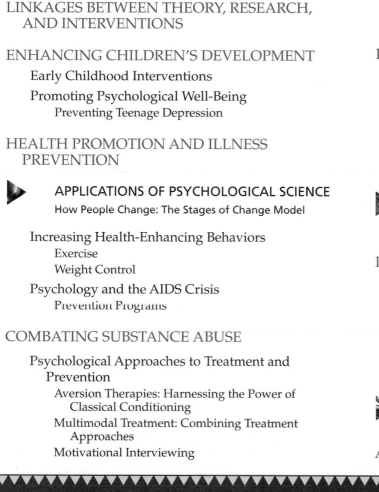

As we entered the 21st century, the National Defense Foundation Council reported that 65 of the world's 193 nations were embroiled in civil or cross-border wars. Within this context of violent confrontation, an increasing number of unstable countries are acquiring weapons of mass destruction.

Domestic crime and violence occur in epidemic proportions, with their perpetrators becoming increasingly younger and their crimes, including fatal shooting sprees at school, more horrifying.

Despite medical advances that have extended the human life span, many people engage in health-endangering behaviors that threaten their physical and psychological well-being. Millions more suffer the scourges of deadly communicable diseases such as AIDS.

Many children are raised in destructive and impoverished environments that leave lifelong psychological scars and cognitive deficits. In the United States, half of all marriages end in divorce, and many others are marked by instability and domestic violence.

Widely perceived failures of our educational, legal, and social welfare systems have eroded citizens' confidence in their political and social institutions, and cries for reforms are tempered with a pervasive sense that little can be done to improve them.

The problems that confront modern society are formidable and demand solutions. Some of them threaten our very existence as a species. As the science of behavior, psychology can and should play a major role in the solution of humanity's major problems. As we have seen in the preceding chapters, basic research has provided major insights into the causes of many varieties of behavior, including virtually all of the problem behaviors cited above. Likewise, we have seen many examples of applied science, which carries this knowledge of causal factors into the natural world to effect desired changes in people and environments.

To review just a few examples, perceptual principles discovered in controlled research were applied to reveal an illusion that caused mysterious airline crashes at night, leading to remedies that should prevent similar tragedies in the future (see Chapter 4). Principles of learning find application in many areas, including improved teaching techniques, clinical interventions, and the expansion of individual freedom through self-regulation strategies (see Chapters 6 and 14). People are being helped to improve memory and problem-solving skills, thanks to advances in cognitive psychology (see Chapters 7 and 8). Research findings from social psychology and personality are being used to help people establish more satisfying relationships with others and to find greater self-acceptance and meaning in their own lives (see Chapters 9 and 13).

Advances in the biological areas of psychology are being applied in countless ways, including the diagnosis and treatment of deviant behavior and disorders of the nervous system (see Chapters 3 and 15). In this chapter, we review large-scale social interventions that illustrate the positive role that psychological science can play in human betterment.

❯ LINKAGES BETWEEN THEORY, RESEARCH, AND INTERVENTIONS

Psychological theories, research, and **interventions** (systematically applied programs designed to solve a practical problem) are intimately related to one another, giving a unity to psychology that links basic research and applied work. As shown in Figure 16.1, theories, research, and interventions all influence one another, hence the two-way arrows between them. Theories provide a framework for understanding a behavioral phenomenon by specifying causal factors and how they operate. Research evidence usually gives birth to a theory, and subsequent research is used to test the theory. Ideally, an intervention should be based on a body of scientific evidence or on a theory that specifies how the application should be designed (Stricker, 1992). Once implemented, the results of the intervention should be scientifically evaluated, ideally against a randomly assigned control group of similar participants who did not receive the intervention. Evaluation provides new scientific data from an applied setting and also tests the adequacy of the theory (Dishion & Patterson, 2000). Unexpected or disconfirming results may indicate that the theory needs revision.

In a sense, programs designed to deal with society's problems can be viewed as social experiments having independent and dependent variables (Campbell, 1969; Figure 16.2). The interventions are like independent variables; they involve application of previously identified causal factors that are designed to have an effect on people, situations, or problems. For example, in a child abuse prevention program for high-risk families, we might choose to teach the parents positive parenting skills that are known to reduce abusive interactions. The medical, behavioral, or social indicators used to evaluate the impact of the interventions (in this case, measures of physical or psychological abuse or of positive parent-child interactions) are like dependent, or outcome, variables. But while the similarities between interventions and scientific experiments are evident, it is equally obvious that the complexity of the settings and the number of uncontrollable factors that exist in "social" experiments far exceed anything that the laboratory experimenter has to contend with.

How do we know whether an intervention works? Can we measure its effects, both intended and unintended, and isolate the reasons for its success or lack of success? Do the benefits of the program outweigh its costs? Is the program the most efficient way to use limited resources? These are the kinds of questions that are the focus of **program evaluation** research (Lipsey & Cordray, 2000). To be deemed effective, an intervention has to pass these scientific tests of its value.

In this final chapter, we explore how psychology's avowed goal of promoting human welfare is being pursued

❯ 1. How do theory, research, and interventions influence one another? Provide an example of each of the six possible influences.

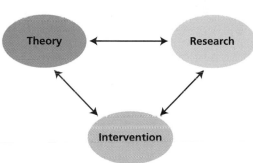

FIGURE 16.1 Theory, research, and interventions all influence one another. Theories inspire research and interventions, and research and interventions are ways of testing a theory. Previous research results, as well as theories, suggest what causal factors should be targeted in an intervention, and research is needed to test the effects of an intervention. The best interventions are based on solid research evidence and theories that explain how and why they work.

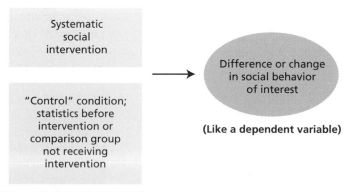

(Like an independent variable)

FIGURE 16.2 Systematic social interventions can be viewed as experiments, with the intervention being the manipulated independent variable that affects a causal factor identified in previous research. This causal factor, in turn, is expected to affect the outcome measures, which can be viewed as dependent variables. Program evaluation research examines the outcomes of the intervention and tries to identify the factors within the intervention that produced the outcome.

➤ 2. What important scientific and policy questions can be answered through good program evaluation research?

in relation to some of society's most urgent and intractable problems. In so doing, we will draw upon many of the concepts, principles, and research results you have encountered in previous chapters.

〉 ENHANCING CHILDREN'S DEVELOPMENT

Perhaps the greatest investment any society can make is in the well-being and development of its children, for they represent that society's future. Children's development is the product of interactions with parents and family, schools, the social structure of neighborhoods, media influences, physical environments, culture, and the period in which they are growing up (Lerner, 1995; Sampson, 1997). Even under the best of conditions, today's world is a challenging place for rearing children. Many parents feel as if they are swimming against a tide created by a culture that promotes destructive behaviors and contradicts deeply held values, such as the sanctity of the family and traditional standards of morality. Moreover, an increasing proportion of children are growing up in what James Garbarino (1995) has labeled **socially toxic environments** marked by poverty, crime and violence, child abuse, family disintegration, low levels of social support, lack of helpful and friendly interactions among neighbors, and physical danger (Figure 16.3). The percentage of American children living in such conditions rose from 3 percent in 1970 to 17 percent in 1990 (Annie E. Casey Foundation, 1997). Such children have high levels of delinquency and aggressive behavior, substance abuse, psychological and behavior problems, and poor educational and occupational outcomes (Black & Krishnakumar, 1998; Marqolin & Gordis, 2000).

As we saw in Chapter 11, developmental research provides guidelines for what might be done to enhance the well-being of developing children. We know that an authoritative parenting style marked by a warm, accepting relationship with the child combined with clear limits on behavior is associated with the most positive outcomes for children (Baumrind, 1983, 1991). We also know that quality day care with well-trained staff and an educationally stimulating environment produces positive long-term psychological and social outcomes for disadvantaged children (Scarr, 1998). Educational programs that promote the development of thinking, problem-solving skills, insights into one's own thought processes, and learning strategies yield good educational outcomes (Brown, 1998). Can knowledge of positive causal factors like these be systematically applied to counteract the adverse conditions that place so many children at risk?

FIGURE 16.3   Being raised in an impoverished environment with little intellectual stimulation retards intellectual growth in a manner that is often irreversible.

Early Childhood Interventions

The belief that early childhood education can positively influence the lives of poor children is found in the 18th-century writings of the French social philosopher Jean Jacques Rousseau. In the United States today, that belief translates into the annual expenditure of more than $10 billion dollars on early intervention programs designed to reverse the downward course of cognitive and social development, school dropout, and joblessness that is so often seen in children from low-income minority families (Ramey et al., 1998). The early environment of the poor or socially disadvantaged child may not support the level of cognitive development needed for later school success. Progressively lower intelligence test scores are found in such children as they grow older and their barren environment retards brain development (Garber, 1988; Ramey & Ramey, 1998).

In the 1960s, researchers and educators began to design early childhood intervention programs like Head Start in an attempt to compensate for the limited learning environments of disadvantaged children. Head Start began as a summer program and gradually increased in scope. But even when it was extended to a

➤ 3. What two factors might have limited the outcomes from Project Head Start? How did such speculation influence later childhood interventions?

full school year, Head Start was only a half-day program that did not begin until age 4. The results were disappointing. Within two years, Head Start children were performing no better in school than comparison children (McKey et al., 1985).

What had gone wrong? Was the Head Start program too little too late? How much might a more intensive program begun earlier in life help disadvantaged children? These questions inspired several notable intervention programs, namely, the Abecedarian Program and the High/Scope Perry Preschool Program.

Participants in the Abecedarian Program were biologically healthy infants born to impoverished families in a southern U.S. community. Most were African-American. The children were randomly assigned to an experimental preschool program or to a control group whose families received normal social services. The preschool group was given an intensive early childhood educational program beginning when they were 6 months old and continuing until they began kindergarten at 5 years of age. Within an educational child-care setting, highly trained preschool personnel exposed the children to many stimulating learning experiences designed to foster the growth of cognitive skills (Figure 16.4). At age 5, the preschool program ended, but half of the preschool children and half of the control children were enrolled in a special home-and-school educational program during the first three years of school. This experimental design allowed the researchers to test the effects of early versus later intervention.

The long-term effects of the program have now been evaluated. At age 15, the children in the preschool condition had higher IQs and higher scores on standardized tests of reading and mathematics than did the control group children. As Figure 16.5 shows, fewer of the children in the preschool group were placed in special education or retained in grade. A particularly notable effect was found for children in the preschool condition whose mothers were mentally retarded, having IQs below 70. In this subgroup, every one of the children who had the early intervention attained an IQ at least 20 points higher than the control children. They also averaged 32 IQ points higher than their mothers (Landesman & Ramey, 1989). A difference of this magnitude is truly remarkable for children of a mentally retarded parent, one reason being that such parents are unable to provide much in the way of intellectual stimulation for their children. Apparently, the preschool program provided the environmental stimulation needed for normal intellectual development to occur.

What of the control children who did not have the preschool program but were exposed to the special program from 5 to 8 years of age? This later training had little effect on any of the outcome measures. It also had minimal added effects on the children who had been in the preschool program. Thus early intervention has a much stronger effect than does later training. By the time disadvantaged children are in school, it may be too late to accelerate their future cognitive development to any great degree (Ramey & Ramey, 1998).

The Abecedarian Program showed positive intervention effects that were still apparent in adolescence. What effect does early intervention have on later adult functioning? Here we turn to another program, the High/Scope Perry Preschool Program, carried out with African-American children who lived in an impoverished area of Ypsilanti, Michigan. The children were considered at high risk for educational and social problems. They were 2 or 3 years old when they were matched on IQ and family variables and randomly assigned to either an intensive preschool program or to a control group that did not receive the program. During the next three years, trained teachers spent five mornings a week with groups of children in the preschool group and made weekly 90-minute home visits to see each child and mother. The teachers provided learning experiences involving logic and mathematics, language and literacy, music and

FIGURE 16.4 The Abecedarian project provided preschool learning experiences for low-income high-risk children. Here a trainer in an early intervention program teaches number concepts to preschool children.

➤ 4. What were the major outcomes of the Abecedarian early intervention project? What evidence suggests that such interventions must occur before school age?

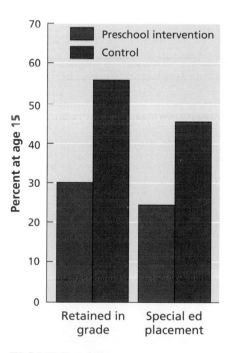

FIGURE 16.5 Educational outcomes of the Abecedarian project at age 15. Children who received the preschool intervention were less likely to be retained in grade or placed in special education classes during their school careers.

Data from Ramey et al., 1998.

movement, creative activities, and initiative. Many of the logic and mathematics experiences were based on Piaget's theory of cognitive growth.

The two groups of children have been followed up through age 27, and the results are remarkable. Figure 16.6 compares the two groups at that point on several key outcome measures. In the 22 years since the program ended, the preschool group had lower crime rates, required less welfare assistance, exhibited better academic performance and progress, and had higher income and home ownership. A cost-benefit analysis showed that the early intervention program provided taxpayers with a return of $7.16 for every dollar invested in the program (Schweinhart & Weikart, 1998).

Does early intervention work? The Abecedarian and High/Scope Perry programs prove it can provide social, intellectual, educational, and psychological dividends if the program is intensive enough and administered very early in life (Masten & Coatsworth, 1998; Reppucci et al., 1999). Perhaps the most meaningful conclusion is provided by the directors of the High/Scope Perry Preschool Program:

> High quality preschool programs for children living in poverty are no panacea; but then, nothing is. These programs can lead to an extraordinary variety of important effects later in life. They are worth doing well for all young children living in poverty. To do less is not just to shortchange our children, but ourselves. (Schweinhart & Weikart, 1998, p. 161)

Administered to disadvantaged children, early intervention can have dramatic positive effects. Do such programs also benefit children from middle- and upper-income families? Here the long-term picture is far less clear. Whatever positive effects do occur tend to be small and temporary (Hetherington, 1998). For poor children, quality intervention programs offer learning opportunities, social stimulation, and emotional supports that the children would not experience at home. In contrast, children from higher income and socioeconomic backgrounds are more likely to already experience these benefits in their own homes, so that early intervention can add little to what they already have.

➤ 5. What social and educational outcomes were found in the 22-year follow-up of the High/Scope Perry Preschool Program?

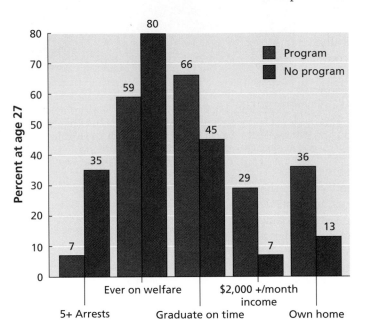

FIGURE 16.6 Differences between children who received the High/Scope Perry Preschool Program and matched controls at age 27. Source: Schweinhart & Weikart, 1998.

Promoting Psychological Well-Being

The "happy years of childhood" are anything but that for many children. Between 15 and 22 percent of children and adolescents have diagnosable psychological disorders, and between 25 and 50 percent of them engage in behaviors, such as drug use, delinquency, and school dropout, that endanger their future welfare as adults (Lewinsohn et al., 1993; McDermott & Weiss, 1995). Psychologists have developed a number of effective training programs designed to teach children coping skills that help them deal constructively with important challenges in their lives (Reppucci et al., 1999).

One such program was designed to teach middle school children skills in self-control of emotions and behavior, communication, problem-solving, conflict resolution, and resisting the social influence of conduct-disordered classmates. The young people were taught the skills in school, and therapists also worked with their parents to enlist their support for the skill-building. Children who were taught these skills over a two-year period showed the ability to think of more productive solutions to teen problems, were more popular with their peers, and were less likely to engage in troublesome behaviors in school (Weissberg & Bell, 1997).

Preventing Teenage Depression

As noted in Chapter 14, depressive disorders are on the rise in adolescents and children. A recent longitudinal study of people from birth to age 21 showed that nearly 25 percent of the girls and 10 percent of the boys experienced a clinically significant episode of depression by age 21 (Hankin et al., 1998). The incidence of depression increased with age, with the greatest increase in cases occurring during the period from age 15 to 19 (Figure 16.7). Can anything be done in childhood to reduce the likelihood of later depression?

The Penn Optimism Project, conducted by clinical psychologists from the University of Pennsylvania, is attempting to teach cognitive and behavioral coping skills that will reduce the likelihood of later depression (Gillham et al., 1995). The project is based on the finding that people who think in an optimistic fashion seldom develop depression, whereas pessimism is a major risk factor (Scheier & Carver, 2000).

The researchers focused on preadolescents who appeared at risk for later depression. Children in the fifth and sixth grades who scored high on a screening test for pessimistic thinking were placed into either an intervention or a no-treatment control condition. In the intervention condition, the children met in small groups with a professional leader who used procedures derived from cognitive therapy and problem-solving training to teach them coping skills. In the cognitive therapy component, the children learned to identify and reconsider negative beliefs about themselves and to replace these thoughts with more constructive and realistic ones. They were also taught to replace pessimistic attributions for their successes ("I wasn't really responsible") and failures ("It happened because of my inadequacies") with more optimistic ones that acknowledged their role in their successes. The behavioral problem-solving component used modeling and role playing to teach the children constructive ways to solve problems with parents, teachers, and peers. The goal here was to help children reduce stressful life events that might trigger depression, and to increase their sense of self-efficacy concerning their own coping abilities.

Children in the intervention and control groups have been followed for two years since the program ended. The results, shown in Figure 16.8 for the one- and two-year follow-up measures of depression, indicate that the control group is showing the developmentally predicted increase in depression, whereas the intervention group is considerably lower. A definitive conclusion awaits assessments of the two groups during the critical ages of 15 to 19 years, but so far, the results of the program appear promising. Because depression deprives so many people of joy in living, preventing or reducing its occurrence or intensity is a worthy objective for psychological interventions, and childhood is an optimal time to learn the needed skills. Helping ensure that children have the developmental experiences needed to become healthy, happy, and productive adults is a high-priority enterprise in contemporary psychology.

〉 HEALTH PROMOTION AND ILLNESS PREVENTION

In 1979, the Surgeon General of the United States issued a report entitled *Healthy People* (U.S. Public Health Service, 1979). The report concluded that improvements in the health of Americans are more likely to result from efforts to prevent disease and promote health than from new drugs and medical technologies.

That conclusion is borne out by comparing the leading modern causes of death in the United States with those in 1900.

FIGURE 16.7 Longitudinal studies of mental health have revealed a major increase in the prevalence of clinical depression between the ages of 15 and 19. Current prevention programs for children are seeking to reduce the later likelihood of developing depressive disorders.

➤ 6. What is the goal of the Penn Optimism Project? What techniques does it use, and what effects have been found?

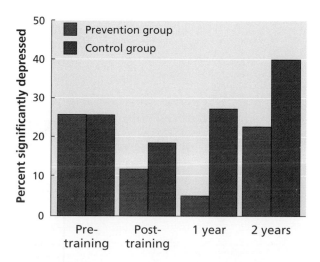

FIGURE 16.8 Results of the Penn Optimism Project at one- and two-year follow-ups. The children given the intervention showed less depression and did not exhibit the age-related increase shown by the controls.
Data from Gillham et al., 1995.

Death rates per 100,000

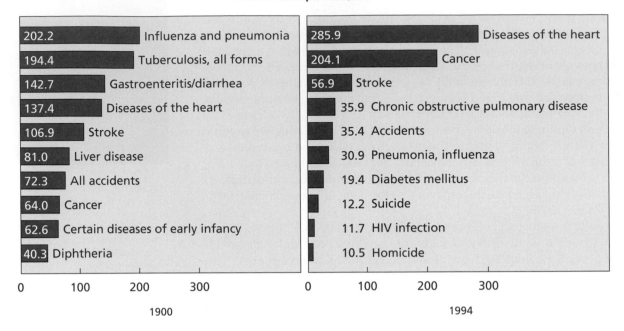

FIGURE 16.9 Causes of death, 1900 versus 1994. Modern causes of death are far more attributable to health-endangering behaviors.
Based on data from Sexton, 1979 and U.S. Department of Commerce, 1997.

➤ 7. What changes have occurred in the major causes of death during the 20th century? How do these changes suggest the potential contributions of health psychology?

As Figure 16.9 indicates, the leading culprits have changed from influenza, pneumonia, tuberculosis, and gastroenteritis to heart disease, cancer, and stroke. The major killers of the early 1900s have been largely controlled by medical advances. In contrast, the death rate has doubled for heart disease and tripled for cancer since 1900. As shown in Table 16.1, these diseases and today's other killers are strongly influenced by behavioral factors. Health authorities estimate that half the early mortality (deaths occurring prior to the life expectancy age within a culture) from the 10 leading causes of death can be traced to cigarette smoking, excessive alcohol consumption, insufficient exercise, poor dietary habits, use of illicit drugs, failure to adhere to doctors' instructions, and other self-defeating behaviors, such as risky sex practices and failure to wear auto seat belts (Centers for Disease Control; 1994; Taylor, 1999).

Recognition of the crucial role that behavior plays in health maintenance has added impetus to the field of **health psychology,** which studies psychological and behavioral factors in the prevention and treatment of illness and in the

TABLE 16.1	BEHAVIORAL RISK FACTORS FOR THE LEADING CAUSES OF DEATH IN THE UNITED STATES
Disease	Risk Factors
Heart disease	Tobacco, obesity, elevated blood pressure, cholesterol, sedentary lifestyle
Cancer	Tobacco, improper diet, alcohol, environmental exposure
Cerebrovascular disease (stroke)	Tobacco, elevated blood pressure, cholesterol, sedentary lifestyle
Accidental injuries	Safety belt nonuse, alcohol, home hazards
Chronic lung disease	Tobacco, environmental exposure

Source: Based on McGinnis, 1994.

TABLE 16.2	AVERAGE COSTS OF TREATING VARIOUS PREVENTABLE MEDICAL CONDITIONS ONCE THEY OCCUR	
Condition	Avoidable Intervention	Cost per Patient
Heart disease	Coronary bypass surgery	$30,000
Cancer	Lung cancer treatment	$29,000
Injuries	Quadriplegia treatment and rehabilitation	$570,000 (lifetime)
	Hip fracture treatment and rehabilitation	$40,000
Low-birth weight baby	Respiratory distress syndrome treatment	$26,500

Source: Intellimed International Corp., 2000

maintenance of health. Research by psychologists has helped identify many of the psychological and social causes for risky health behaviors, and the clear need for lifestyle interventions has spurred attempts around the world to promote positive changes in such behaviors (Stokols, 1995; Taylor, 1999). This effort is also driven by attempts to contain rising medical costs. Table 16.2 shows average costs for treating certain diseases once they occur. Prevention of illness by modifying people's health behaviors before they ever become ill has the potential for both financial savings and the avoidance of illness-produced human distress.

Health-related behaviors fall into two main categories. **Health-enhancing behaviors** serve to maintain or increase health. Such behaviors include exercise, healthy dietary habits, safe sexual practices, regular medical checkups, and breast and testicular self-examination. **Health-compromising behaviors** are those that promote the development of illness. They include smoking, fatty diets, a sedentary lifestyle, and unprotected sexual activity. Psychologists have developed programs that are focused on both classes of behavior. Designing effective programs depends on understanding the factors that control the health behaviors of interest. Such information comes from basic research.

If we wish to change behavior, we need to understand the processes that underlie behavior change in general. The following *Applications of Psychological Science* feature describes one influential model of how people change, and its implications for designing effective interventions.

➤ 8. What are the two major categories of health-related behaviors? Given an example of each type.

➤ 9. Describe the stages of change that lead to successful modification of behavior.

➤ 10. What are stage-matched interventions? How do they move people from precontemplation to action?

APPLICATIONS OF PSYCHOLOGICAL SCIENCE

How People Change: The Stages of Change Model

In the 1980s, psychologists James Prochaska and Carlo DiClemente became convinced that a common pattern of change occurs in people as they modify their thoughts, feelings, and behaviors in positive ways, either on their own or with professional help. The Stages of Change model that emerged from their research focuses on six major stages, shown in Figure 16.10 (Prochaska & DiClemente, 1984; Prochaska et al., 1998). The model does not assume that people go through the stages in a smooth sequence.

Longitudinal studies have shown that many people move forward and backward through the stages as they try to change their behavior over time, and many people make repeated efforts to change before they finally succeed (Evers et al., 1998). It is assumed, however, that failure at a particular stage is likely to occur if the previous stages have not been mastered.

The first stage is *precontemplation*. People in this stage have no desire to change their behavior. Often

—Continued

Stages of Change

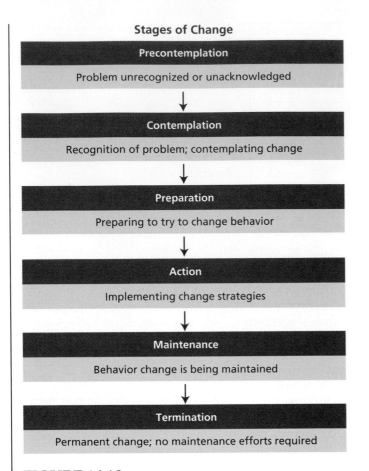

FIGURE 16.10 The Stages of Change model identifies a series of phases through which people pass as they modify their behavior. People may pass up and down through the stages several times before they reach the final stage of termination.
Prochaska et al., 1998.

they don't perceive themselves as having a problem, or they deny that their behavior has negative consequences. For example, public opinion polls suggest that there may be as many as 10 million smokers in the United States who still refuse to believe that smoking leads to premature death (Prochaska et al., 1994). Some precontemplators who do perceive a problem feel powerless to change their behavior, so they have no interest in trying.

Some precontemplators move on to the stage of *contemplation.* Here, the person perceives a problem or the desirability of a behavior change, but has not yet decided to take action. Thus some smokers are well aware of the problems that could be created by their habit, yet are not ready to quit. Until the perceived benefits of changing outweigh the costs or effort involved, contemplators will not take action.

In the *preparation* stage, people have decided that they want to change their behavior, but have not actively begun to do so. Typically, they plan to take action within the next month and are making the final adjustments to do so. People in this stage have often begun making small changes, such as reducing the number of cigarettes they are smoking, signing up for a health club membership, or identifying conditions that affect the target behavior.

In the *action* stage, people actively begin to modify their behavior and their environment. They stop smoking altogether, remove fattening foods from the house, pour the last bottle of liquor down the drain, or begin their planned exercise program. Success at this stage requires the behavior control skills needed to carry out the plan of action. The action stage requires the greatest commitment of effort and energy.

If the person has been successful in avoiding relapse and has controlled the target behavior for six months, he or she is in the stage of *maintenance.* This does not mean that the struggle is over, for many people do lapse back into their former behavior pattern. A *relapse* (a complete return to the former pattern) should not be confused with a *lapse* (an occasional slip). Most people do have lapses, and lapses are to be expected when one is trying to change deeply ingrained habits. The big challenge is not to give up when a lapse occurs and abandon the change program. It typically takes smokers three to five cycles through action before they finally quit, and New Year's resolutions are typically made for five or more consecutive years before they are finally carried out successfully (Prochaska et al., 1994; Schachter, 1982). The message is clear: If at first you don't succeed, don't give up. Instead, acquire the behavioral skills you need to succeed.

The final stage, *termination,* occurs when the change in behavior is so ingrained and under personal control that the original problem behavior will never return. It is the ultimate goal for all people who seek change.

The Stages of Change model is noteworthy not only because it helps us understand how people change, but also because it has important applied implications. One is that different intervention procedures are needed for people at various stages. Precontemplators need consciousness-raising information that finally convinces them that there is a problem, as well as social support to change (De Vries et al., 1998). Contemplators often need to have an emotional experience that increases their motivation to change or causes them to begin to reevaluate themselves in relation to the behavior. For example, a problem drinker may not confront the fact that his abusive behavior when drunk is incompatible with his desire to be a loving spouse and father until he hurts a loved one or his spouse threatens to leave him. In the preparation stage, the person needs to develop a specific plan (ideally, based on the goal-setting procedures described in Chapter 13 (p. 569) and the skills to carry it out before action is likely to be successful. Figure 16.11 shows the effects of an action-stage smoking-cessation program on people who were in the precontemplation, contemplation, and preparation stages when treatment began. Clearly, the smokers who were in the preparation stage profited most from the action techniques in the program. Those in earlier stages were not ready for them (Prochaska et al., 1992).

These insights have led psychologists to develop ways of determining what stage people are in so that they can apply *stage-matched interventions* designed to move

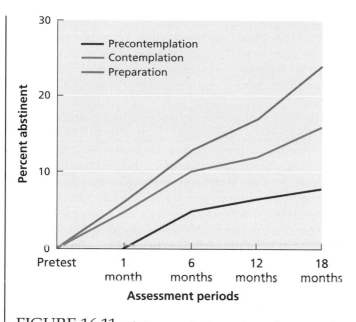

FIGURE 16.11 Abstinence rates for smokers who were at the stages of precontemplation, contemplation, and preparation at the time they began a smoking cessation program. The closer to the action stage the smokers were at the beginning, the more likely they were to be abstinent 18 months later. Very few could jump from precontemplation to action.

Source: Prochaska et al., 1994.

the person toward the action and maintenance stages. For example, in a large-scale AIDS prevention project for women being carried out by the U.S. Centers for Disease Control and Prevention, the goal is to promote condom use during sexual activity, thereby helping to protect high-risk women from HIV infection as well as reducing unplanned pregnancies that might produce HIV-infected babies (Galavotti et al., 1997). Preliminary research showed that most of the women, who were engaged in prostitution and drug use, were in the precontemplation stage. Because they had little awareness of the danger they were in, they saw no reason to change their high-risk sexual and drug behaviors. For these women, it would have been futile to try to increase safe-sex practices without first making them aware of the dangers of their actions and motivating them to change. Once they moved into the contemplation or preparation stages, training in specific skills, including how to acquire condoms and require their use by sexual partners, was necessary before they could move to the action and maintenance stages. When they proceed to action and maintenance, the women need continued social support from a counselor to help them maintain their safer sexual behaviors. Stage-matched interventions have enhanced the effectiveness of many behavior change programs (DiClemente et al., 1998; Rosen 2000). We will see the Stages of Change model applied in several other interventions to be described in this chapter.

Increasing Health-Enhancing Behaviors

Exercise

The couch potato lives! (But apparently, not as long.) A sedentary lifestyle is a significant risk factor for a variety of health problems, including coronary heart disease and obesity (Rodin & Salovey, 1989; Taylor, 1999). Despite this widely publicized fact, about 70 percent of Americans are inactive (Baum et al., 1997; Dishman, 1988). Inactivity has helped double the rate of obesity since 1900 despite a 10 percent decrease in daily caloric intake over the same period (Friedman & DiMatteo, 1989).

Aerobic exercise is sustained activity, such as jogging, swimming, and bicycling, that elevates the heart rate and increases the body's need for oxygen. This kind of exercise has many physiological benefits. In a well-conditioned person, the heart beats more slowly and efficiently, oxygen is better utilized, cholesterol levels may be reduced, faster adaptation to stressors occurs, and more calories are burned (Baum & Posluszny, 1999; deGeus, 2000).

Exercise is associated with both physical health and longevity (Figure 16.12). A study that followed 17,000 Harvard undergraduates into middle age revealed that death rates were one-quarter to one-third lower among moderate exercisers than among those in a less active group. Surprisingly, perhaps, very high levels of exercise were not associated with enhanced health; instead, moderate exercise (burning 2,000 to 3,500 calories per week) on a regular basis produced the best health benefits (Paffenbarger et al., 1986). Performing at 70 to 85 percent of maximal heart rate nonstop for 15 minutes three times a week is related to reduced risk for coronary heart disease (Dishman, 1982).

Findings like these have inspired behavioral interventions designed to promote regular exercise. Typically, these programs have an educational component

➤ 11. What is aerobic exercise? What evidence is there that it promotes health and longevity?

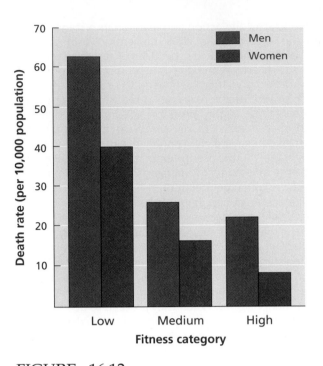

FIGURE 16.12 Aerobic exercise is an important health-enhancing behavior, contributing to physical well-being. Significantly higher death rates occur for both men and women who are low in physical fitness.

Based on Blair et al., 1989.

➤ 12. How large are exercise dropout rates? What factors predict dropout and compliance?

FIGURE 16.13 An alarmingly large percentage of adults and children are overweight, increasing health risks. Family-based interventions are directed at modifying bad dietary habits, such as high-fat diets.

that provides information on the benefits of regular exercise and the best ways to exercise. They may also include other components of behavior change, such as goal setting, writing explicit contracts that specify an exercise regimen, monitoring one's exercise behavior on a daily basis, and increasing social support by choosing an exercise partner or group.

Despite the demonstrated benefits of regular exercise, people have a strong tendency to either avoid doing it or to discontinue it after a short period. When employers offer exercise programs to their employees, it is uncommon for more than 30 percent to participate. Dropout rates of 50 percent within six months are quite typical in virtually all exercise programs that have been studied (Dishman, 1988; Wing, 1995). On the other hand, people who are able to persist for three to six months are likely to continue as exercise becomes a healthy habit (McAuley, 1992).

What factors predict dropout? This is an important research question, for once the risk factors are identified, measures can be taken to counteract them. As we might anticipate from our discussion of attitude-behavior discrepancies in Chapter 12, general attitudes toward physical fitness do *not* predict adherence or dropout; the attitudes of dropouts and people who adhere to their exercise programs are equally favorable. However, low self-efficacy for success in exercising regularly ("I can't do this"), Type A personality ("Sorry, too busy to exercise"), inflated estimates of current physical fitness ("I'm already in great shape from walking from my couch to the refrigerator"), and inactive leisure-time pursuits (such as watching television and walking to the refrigerator) all predict dropout (Martin & Dubbert, 1985; Wilcox & Storandt, 1996). The strongest social-environmental factor related to dropout is lack of social support from friends, family, or other exercisers (Feist & Brannon, 1989).

Psychologists have been able to increase compliance by helping exercisers identify these impediments and prepare specific strategies to deal with them before they occur (Rosen, 2000; Simkin & Gross, 1994). For example, a person who anticipates feeling "too tired" to work out at the end of the day might prepare a set of self-statements about how much better she will feel after exercising. If she is not receiving social support and encouragement from others, she could also arrange for a pleasurable activity after exercise so as to positively reinforce her exercising (Courneya, 1995).

Weight Control

About one third of the adult American population is obese, defined as being more than 20 percent overweight (Figure 16.13). Since 1980, the average American adult's body weight has increased by about 8 pounds, with the upward trend continuing (Brody, 1995; Taylor, 1999). A significant proportion of children (13.7 percent) and adolescents (11.5 percent) are also obese (Buet & Harris, 1994).

Obesity is a risk factor for a variety of chronic diseases, such as cardiovascular disease, kidney disease, and diabetes (Baum & Posluszny, 1999). Women who are 30 percent overweight are more than three times more likely to develop heart disease than normal weight women (Manson et al., 1990). For reasons yet unknown, fat that is localized in the abdomen is a far greater risk factor for cardiovascular disease, diabetes, and cancer than is excessive fat in the hips, thighs, or buttocks (Taylor, 1999). The accumulation of abdominal fat is increased by **yo-yo dieting** that results in big up-and-down weight fluctuations. Such dieting markedly increases the risk of dying from cardiovascular disease, an excellent reason to avoid this practice (Hafen & Hoeger, 1998; Rodin et al., 1990).

TABLE 16.3	A SAMPLE OF EFFECTIVE BEHAVIORAL WEIGHT CONTROL TECHNIQUES	
Keep an eating diary	Keep problem foods out of sight	
Examine your eating patterns	Serve and eat one portion at a time	
Prevent automatic eating	Use gradual shaping for behavior change	
Examine triggers for eating	Distinguish hunger from cravings	
Do nothing else while eating	Focus on behavior, not weight loss	
Eat in one place	Cope positively with slips, lapses	
Put fork down between bites	Keep an exercise diary	
Pause during the meal	Understand benefits of exercise	
Shop on a full stomach	Know calorie values of various exercise activities	
Buy foods that require preparation	Program exercise activity	

Source: After Brownell, 1994.

Behavioral interventions for weight loss usually begin with a period of self-monitoring in which clients keep careful records of what they eat, how much they eat, and under what circumstances. This is designed to make them more aware of their eating habits and to identify situational factors (antecedents) that affect their eating. They then are taught to take control over those antecedents. For example, they make low-calorie foods such as raw vegetables freely available, while limiting high-calorie foods in the house. Stimulus control techniques are then used, such as confining eating to one location in the house and eating only at certain times of the day. Because overeaters tend to wolf down their food and overload their stomachs, clients also learn to slow down their eating by putting down eating utensils until the food is chewed and swallowed, and they pause between mouthfuls. These behaviors reduce food intake and allow clients to pay attention to how full they are. They are told to savor each mouthful of food. The goal is to eat less, but enjoy it more. Finally, they chart the amount of food they eat to provide constant feedback, and they arrange to reinforce themselves for successful performance. These behavioral practices are combined with nutritional and attitudinal guidelines. Table 16.3 shows specific guidelines from a highly successful weight-reduction program developed by Yale psychologist Kelly Brownell (1994).

Research shows that the addition of an exercise program increases the positive effects of the behavioral eating control program (Jeffery & Wing, 1995; Wadden et al., 1997). High levels of physical activity are associated with initial weight loss and maintenance of the weight loss, and it adds to the effectiveness of other weight loss methods, such as dietary change. Many people are able to attain gradual weight loss of about 2 pounds per week for up to 20 weeks, and to keep the weight off over two years, whereas others are less successful.

Nearly one in four American children is overweight (National Center for Health Statistics, 1996). Recent interventions have focused on obese children under age 11, whose numbers have increased dramatically in the past 25 years. Many of these programs are targeting parents, training them to adopt dietary guidelines and sound eating habits that they can convey to their children. Obesity is much more effectively treated in children than in adults (Taylor, 1999), so that this approach may help prevent overweight children from becoming overweight adults.

Psychology and the AIDS Crisis

On June 5, 1981, the Centers for Disease Control reported the first case of acquired immune deficiency syndrome (AIDS). In the two decades that followed, AIDS grew from an unknown disease into a devastating worldwide epidemic

➤ 13. Why is yo-yo dieting an undesirable practice?

➤ 14. What are the major behavior-change techniques used in behavioral weight control programs?

➤ 15. What is the scope of the worldwide AIDS crisis?

for which there is currently no medical cure. According to the World Health Organization, about 16,000 new infections occur each day. Worldwide, 1 in every 100 adults ages 15 to 49 is infected with the AIDS virus, and the disease has claimed the lives of nearly 17 million people. Of the 2.3 million people who died from AIDS in 1997, 46 percent were women and 20 percent were children. Worldwide, only 5 to 10 percent of the cases presently occur in homosexual men, the population that is most often identified with the affliction (Centers for Disease Control and Prevention, 1996). The AIDS epidemic threatens to overwhelm our health care financing and delivery systems.

AIDS is caused by the *human immunodeficiency virus (HIV)*, which cripples the immune system by killing cells that coordinate the body's attack against invading viruses, bacteria, and tumors, which become the actual killers. Because the AIDS virus changes rapidly, vaccines are at present ineffective in preventing its spread. Moreover, the incubation period between initial infection and the appearance of the disease may be as long as 10 years, meaning that an infected person may unknowingly pass the virus on to many other people. The major modes of transmission are direct exposure to infected semen, vaginal fluids, and blood through either homosexual or heterosexual contact, the sharing of infected needles in intravenous drug use, and exposure to infected blood through transfusion or in the womb.

Prevention Programs

In the absence of a vaccine, the only existing means of controlling the AIDS epidemic is by changing the high-risk behaviors that transmit the virus. In this respect, AIDS is as much a psychological problem as a medical one. In recent years, principles derived from educational psychology, social psychology, and the psychology of learning have been applied in designing and carrying out prevention programs. Such programs typically are designed to (1) educate people concerning the risks that attend certain behaviors, such as having sex without using a condom; (2) motivate people to change their behavior and convince them that they can do so; (3) provide specific guidelines for changing the risky behaviors and teach the skills needed for change; and (4) give support and encouragement for the desired changes.

➤ 16. Summarize the four features of most AIDS prevention projects, and the outcomes of a program directed at homosexual men. How do cultural factors influence outcomes?

Early AIDS interventions were directed at homosexual men, who were originally the major at-risk group. In this population, a major mechanism of HIV transmission is anal intercourse without use of a condom. In one early prevention study (Kelly & St. Lawrence, 1989), 42 homosexual men went through a program that provided them with information on the risks accompanying unprotected intercourse, helped them develop and rehearse strategies for avoiding high-risk situations (such as sexual relations with strangers), and taught them how to be more assertive in refusing to engage in high-risk behaviors such as sexual relations without a condom. Another group of 43 homosexual men also completed the program after serving as an initial control group.

Both groups were assessed before and after the first group went through the program and then were followed for eight months after completion of the program to assess long-term behavior changes. As shown in Figure 16.14, the intervention program resulted in substantial and lasting changes in the use of condoms during sexual activity. Similar programs are now being conducted with adolescent populations, where unprotected heterosexual intercourse is resulting in a surge of new infections (Jemmott et al., 1998). Another target for interventions is heterosexual women, who not only are the fastest-rising segment of the HIV population, but who also have the potential to infect their babies (Stevens & Bogart, 1999).

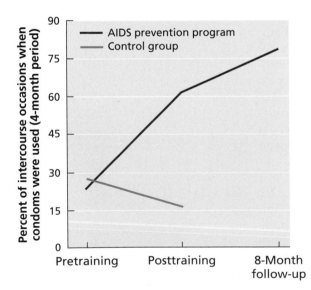

FIGURE 16.14 Effects of an AIDS prevention program for homosexual men on their use of condoms during sexual activity. The program educated the men on the risks involved in sexual behaviors (especially unprotected sex), promoted use of condoms, and taught them coping skills to deal with high-risk situations.

Data from Kelly and St. Lawrence, 1989.

Even where something as urgent as AIDS prevention is involved, research has shown that the success of prevention programs depends on the extent to which the individual's social system supports the desired changes. Where the use of condoms runs contrary to the values of an individual or cultural group, people may continue to engage in high-risk behaviors even though they have been informed of the dangers involved (Herdt & Lindenbaum, 1992; Huff et al., 1999). Likewise, within both homosexual and heterosexual populations, and particularly among adolescents and young adults, many individuals continue to have an irrational sense of invulnerability to infection, and this belief contributes to a failure to engage in safe sexual practices (Kelly et al., 1991). Counteracting these barriers to safe sexual behavior is a major challenge for health psychologists.

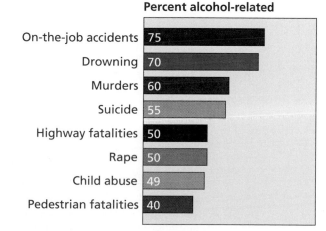

➤ 17. What cultural and belief factors promote unsafe sexual behavior?

Behavior-based AIDS prevention programs are now being applied in Africa, where two thirds of the world's HIV infections occur. One intervention was directed at native healers in the Central African Republic (Somse et al., 1998). Like their patients, the healers were quite ignorant of AIDS and its transmission. They were trained in the diagnosis, treatment, and prevention of sexually transmitted diseases. Healers were also taught how to promote condom use, how to conduct AIDS education at the community level, and how to provide psychosocial support for people with AIDS. Follow-ups indicated that the intervention had its intended educational effect on the healers, which is a step in the right direction. However, future studies will be needed to determine whether the healers can influence the sexual behavior of their patients and help slow down the rate of HIV infections.

To control the spread of AIDS, effective community-based interventions directed at specific at-risk groups are badly needed. Psychologists are in perhaps the best position of any profession to design, carry out, and evaluate such interventions because of their knowledge about health behaviors, understanding of cultural factors, expertise in behavior change techniques, and research skills. Intervention programs do not have to change every at-risk person's behavior in order to be valuable. Given the fatal consequences of AIDS infection, even modest changes in risk behaviors can have high social significance.

❱ COMBATING SUBSTANCE ABUSE

Substance abuse exacts a fearsome toll on society. In the United States alone, alcohol abuse alone costs over $100 billion a year in decreased work productivity and treatment costs, and $13.8 billion in alcohol-related automobile accidents (Pedersen-Pietersen, 1997). Alcohol is implicated in half of all fatal automobile accidents, and it is a leading factor in industrial and farm accidents as well (Figure 16.15). Alcohol abuse is also highly damaging to health. Compared with people who do not abuse alcohol, death rates among those who do are two to four times higher for men and three to seven times higher for women, depending on the disease in question. Life expectancy is 10 to 12 years less (U.S. Bureau of the Census, 1996). Alcohol affects the welfare of others as well, resulting in children born with fetal alcohol syndrome and disrupted family relationships, including domestic violence. For every person who has a problem with alcohol, an average of four other people's lives are adversely affected on a daily basis (Levinthal, 1996)

Other varieties of substance abuse also have adverse effects. Tobacco use damages both smokers and those who breathe their secondhand smoke. Smoking ranks as the single largest cause of preventable death, killing more than half a million Americans each year (American Cancer Society, 2000). Many crimes are committed by users of illicit drugs to support their habit (Kendall, 1998). Moreover,

Percent alcohol-related

On-the-job accidents 75
Drowning 70
Murders 60
Suicide 55
Highway fatalities 50
Rape 50
Child abuse 49
Pedestrian fatalities 40

FIGURE 16.15 Societal costs of alcohol abuse, showing the percentage of common negative events that are alcohol-related. Data from Carroll et al., 1993.

substance abuse is highly associated with psychological disorders, often being part of a larger pattern of maladjustment in both adolescents and adults (Miller, 1997).

Psychological Approaches to Treatment and Prevention

A variety of psychological principles discussed in earlier chapters have been applied to the treatment of substance abuse (Larimer et al., 1998; Marlatt, 1996; Prochaska et al., 1998). Disappointing results from traditional psychotherapy, such as long-term psychodynamic approaches, and limited effectiveness of biological treatments, pointed the way to cognitive-behavioral approaches, which have proven to be more cost-effective and successful in reducing abuse (Institute of Medicine, 1990; Marlatt et al., 1998; Miller et al., 1995).

Aversion Therapies: Harnessing the Power of Classical Conditioning

> ➤ 18. How are classical conditioning principles applied in aversion therapies for smoking and drinking? What are the outcomes for alcoholics?

One of the earliest behavioral approaches was aversion therapy, which is based on principles of classical conditioning. As discussed in Chapter 15, aversion therapy is designed to condition a negative response, or aversion, to a positive stimulus, such as the sight and taste of alcohol, tobacco, or some other drug. In treating substance abuse, the procedure involves pairing a negative stimulus, such as electric shock or drug-produced nausea, with the substance in question. A widely used form of chemical aversion treatment for alcohol abuse involves Antabuse, a drug that is taken in pill form each day. Within two days, Antabuse produces nausea and other unpleasant physiological effects if a person drinks alcohol. This should, over time, create a classically conditioned alcohol aversion that reduces the urge to drink. The intended aversion does appear to occur within the treatment setting where the procedure is applied, and many alcoholics lose their craving for alcohol (Marlatt, 1996). Unfortunately, aversion therapy effects often fail to generalize to the outside environment, where many people relapse or, in the case of Antabuse, stop taking the medication.

Multimodal Treatment: Combining Treatment Approaches

> ➤ 19. What kinds of behavior change procedures are employed in multimodal treatments for substance abuse?

Today, aversion therapy is sometimes part of a **multimodal treatment approach** that involves multiple treatment elements such as

- teaching relaxation and stress management techniques as a more adaptive means of dealing with stressful situations;
- applying self-monitoring procedures to help the person identify the antecedents and consequences of the abuse behaviors;
- coping and social skills training for dealing with high-risk situations that trigger abuse;
- marital and family counseling to reduce conflicts and increase social support for change; and
- use of positive reinforcement procedures to strengthen change.

This broad-based multiple-technique approach appears to produce favorable outcomes for many people who have substance addictions (Miller, 1997; Nathan, 1997; Rohsenow & Smith, 1985). For example, in one multimodal therapy outcome study, 427 alcoholic patients were followed for 12 to 20 months after completion of an inpatient program that included drug-based aversion therapy and counseling. The follow-ups revealed that 65.1 percent were totally abstinent for one year after treatment. The best outcome occurred in cases where urges to drink had been eliminated (presumably by aversion therapy) and alternate coping skills increased through the use of cognitive-behavioral techniques like those described above (Smith & Frawley, 1993).

Motivational Interviewing

Motivation powerfully influences the ability to change problem behaviors. The Stages of Change model discussed earlier shows us that even the most effective program will not work if the person is in precontemplation or contemplation and does not have the motivation to take and sustain action to change the behavior. In recent years, a technique called **motivational interviewing** has been developed by psychologist William Miller to help abusers increase their awareness of problems, desire to take action, and self-efficacy for doing so (Miller & Rollnick, 1991; Miller, 1996). Instead of confronting the person with his or her problem (which often drives people who need help away), the interviewer leads the person to that very conclusion by asking questions that focus on discrepancies between what is presently occurring and the individual's ideal self-image, desired behaviors, and desired outcomes. Focusing on these discrepancies may produce a state of *cognitive dissonance* (see Chapter 12) that helps motivate change (Draycott & Dabbs, 1998). Consider the following exchange:

> *Client:* I really don't believe I have a drinking problem.
>
> *Counselor:* You're the best judge of that. How many drinks do you have a day?
>
> *Client:* Oh, it varies. Probably 5 or 6.
>
> *Counselor:* Is that about what you'd like to be drinking?
>
> *Client:* Well, I'd probably be better off if I cut down a little—maybe to 3 or 4.
>
> *Counselor:* What would that do for you?
>
> *Client:* Well, I could study better, and reduce the arguments with my roommate. I can get pretty nasty when I'm buzzed. I hate being nasty; I'm not that kind of person. Our relationship is going downhill and I'd hate to lose a friend.
>
> *Counselor:* Well, you know, you don't have to have a big problem in order to want to make a change. I'm sure you could do so if you really want to.
>
> *Client:* I can see that I'd be more the person I want to be if I worked on this.
>
> *Counselor:* And I'd be happy to help you make your change.

Following a client's decision to pursue behavior change, the counselor helps the client set specific goals and select from a menu of behavior change strategies the ones he or she would like to employ. Thereafter the counselor provides feedback and support for the client's efforts.

Motivational interviewing has proven to be a highly effective and low-cost treatment approach for substance abusers (Miller, 1997). In one large-scale study of alcohol abuse patients, a 4-session motivational interviewing intervention proved to be as effective as a 12-session program modeled on Alcoholics Anonymous (Project MATCH Research Group, 1997). Increasingly, like the Stages of Change model, motivational interviewing is finding its way into substance abuse programs.

Relapse Prevention

High dropout rates are a major problem in treating substance abuse. For example, the Alcoholics Anonymous (AA) program seems to be moderately effective in reducing drinking if people remain in the program and adhere to its procedures (Morgenstern et al., 1997). Yet only 10 percent of those who begin the AA program remain in it, become abstinent, and remain abstinent for a year (Tonigan et al., 1996). As we've already noted, aversion therapy programs such as Antabuse treatment suffer from the same dropout problem. Overall, fewer than

➤ 20. What are the major goals and techniques in motivational interviewing? How effective is this approach?

➤ 21. How severe is the problem of relapse in substance abuse treatment?

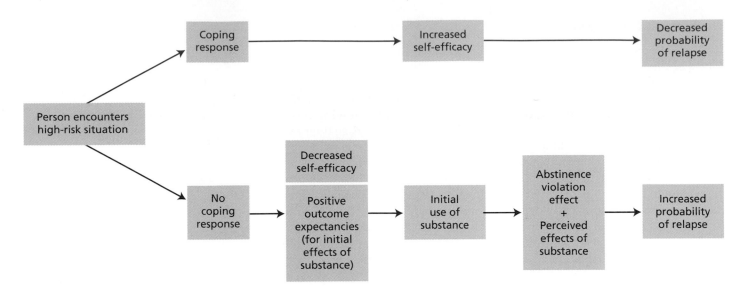

FIGURE 16.16 A model of relapse prevention. Relapse is most likely to occur as a result of inadequate coping skills for dealing with high-risk situations, a focus on anticipated positive effects of substance use, and a resulting abstinence violation effect that causes the person to feel incapable of successful change and to abandon attempts at behavior control.

Source: Marlatt & Gordon, 1985.

30 percent of treated alcoholics remain improved one year after treatment, and 80 percent of people who quit smoking relapse within a year (Baker et al., 1987; Baum et al., 1997). Virtually every behavior change program has the same problem, even New Year's resolutions. These self-initiated change attempts are maintained for more than four months by only 40 to 45 percent of people (Marlatt & Kaplan, 1972; Norcross et al., 1989).

Why do people relapse into their problem behaviors, and what can be done to prevent it? Research on these questions led G. Alan Marlatt and Judith Gordon (1985) to develop the model of relapse shown in Figure 16.16, together with an intervention known as *relapse prevention*. Research with substance abusers showed that most **relapses** (a return to the undesirable behavior pattern) tended to occur after the person had suffered a **lapse** (a one-time "slip") when confronted with a high-risk situation. High-risk situations included stressful events, interpersonal conflicts, social pressure to perform the undesirable behavior, being in the company of other individuals using the substance, and experiencing negative emotions (Marlatt, 1996).

Increased likelihood of relapse occurred when people had not developed strong enough coping skills to deal successfully with the high-risk situation. Consequently, they felt a lack of self-efficacy for resisting the temptation, or they allowed expected positive benefits (such as enjoyment of the substance or anticipated stress reduction) to prompt their decision to perform the undesirable behavior. A lapse would then occur, followed by a critically important reaction called the **abstinence violation effect:** The person became upset and self-blaming over the failure to remain abstinent and viewed the lapse as proof that he or she would never be strong enough to resist temptation. This self-blaming sense of hopelessness placed people at great risk to abandon all attempts to change, and in many cases a total relapse would occur. In contrast, people with sufficient coping skills who confront high-risk situations feel confident in their ability to handle them and are far less likely to relapse, even if they slip once in a while.

Relapse prevention strategies involve teaching people that a lapse means nothing more than the fact that they have encountered a situation that exceeded their current coping skills. Moreover, the episode has given them valuable information about the specific situational, cognitive, and emotional antecedents

➤ 22. What is the difference between a lapse and a relapse? How does the abstinence violation effect contribute to relapse?

that they must learn to handle more effectively. When they master the needed skills, they will be better able to resist high-risk situations. Attention is then directed at learning and practicing the required skills so that self-efficacy improves. The continuing focus is on "progress, not perfection."

Relapse prevention, which was developed from a research-based theory of why people relapse, is increasingly being incorporated into many behavior change programs (Marlatt, 1996). It is an important addition to the Stages of Change model, as being prepared for occasional lapses helps people to move more smoothly from the preparation stage to the action and maintenance stages (Prochaska et al., 1998). Building in relapse prevention training appears to increase the effectiveness of many behavior change programs (Taylor, 1999). As a stand-alone approach to alcohol abuse, studies have shown relapse prevention to have an overall effectiveness equal to AA programs, even though it is usually a much briefer intervention (Ouimette et al., 1997).

➤ 23. How does relapse prevention treatment try to keep lapses from becoming a relapse? How effective is this approach?

Harm Reduction Approaches to Prevention

Substance abuse not only has negative effects on physical well-being, but often results in other severe consequences, such as self-defeating sexual and aggressive behaviors. **Harm reduction** is a prevention strategy that is designed not to eliminate a behavior, but rather to reduce the harmful effects of a behavior when it occurs (MacCoun, 1998; Weingardt & Marlatt, 1998). In the area of drug abuse, harm reduction approaches include needle and syringe exchange programs to reduce the spread of HIV infections. Another example is methadone maintenance programs for heroin addicts that are targeted at reducing their need to engage in criminal activity to feed their heroin habit. The reasoning is that even if an addictive behavior cannot be eliminated, it is possible to modify how often and under what conditions it occurs and to thereby minimize its harmful effects on the person and society.

➤ 24. What is a harm reduction approach, and how does it differ from an abstinence based one?

Many college students fail to realize the extent to which they place themselves in harm's way through their use of alcohol. In one national study carried out by the Harvard School of Public Health, binge drinking was defined as having more than four (for women) or five (for men) drinks at a time on at least three occasions during the previous two weeks (Wechsler et al., 1994). Data from 18,000 students at 140 U.S. colleges revealed that 50 percent of the males and 40 percent of the women met this bingeing criterion, yet fewer than 1 percent saw themselves as having an alcohol problem. However, the dangerous consequences of their drinking became clear when binge drinkers were asked about alcohol-related problems (Table 16.4). Frequent binge drinkers were 7 to 10 times more likely than moderate drinkers to engage in unplanned and unprotected intercourse, to suffer injuries, to drive under the influence of alcohol, to damage property, and to get into trouble with the police. At schools with the highest alcohol consumption

➤ 25. How serious are the consequences of heavy drinking among college students?

TABLE 16.4 PERCENTAGE OF BINGE-DRINKING COLLEGE STUDENTS WHO REPORTED DRINKING-RELATED PROBLEMS	
Missed a class	61%
Forgot where they were or what they did	54%
Engaged in unplanned sex	41%
Got hurt	23%
Had unprotected sex	22%
Damaged property	22%
Got into trouble with campus or local police	11%
Had 5 or more alcohol-related problems in school year	47%

Source: Data from Wechsler et al., 1994.

rates, nondrinkers and moderate drinkers were two to three times more likely to report physical assault, sexual harassment, destruction of their property, and interruption of their sleep and studying by heavy drinkers. Some college women (obviously, sound sleepers) complained that they woke up Sunday after Sunday to find a strange man in bed with their roommate (and all too frequently, the heavy-drinking roommate didn't know him either).

Previous attempts to convince heavy-drinking college students to abstain from alcohol have met with limited success (Marlatt, 1998). Typically, it seems, problem drinkers laugh all the way to the liquor store after being told to simply stop drinking. As a result, a new generation of intervention programs is focused on helping drinkers control how much and under what conditions they drink so as to reduce harmful consequences to themselves and others. In one harm reduction project carried out at a large U.S. university, incoming freshmen were screened for alcohol problems before they arrived on campus (Marlatt et al., 1998). Once on campus, those identified as problem drinkers were randomly assigned to either an intervention condition or to a no-treatment control condition. Over the next two years, the students in both conditions regularly reported on their alcohol consumption and alcohol-related problems. People who knew them well also furnished reports, and high agreement between the two sources of data indicated that the students were being truthful and accurate. Students' degree of alcohol dependence (craving for alcohol and withdrawal symptoms when not drinking) was assessed through psychological tests and interviews.

The brief intervention, occurring in the winter of the freshman year, was based on the motivational interviewing approach described earlier. The goal was to prevent or reduce harmful consequences of drinking by increasing motivation to make constructive changes, rather than to stop students' drinking. Clinical psychologists met with each student individually for one session. The interviewer reviewed the drinking data submitted by the student over the previous academic term and gave individualized feedback in graphic form. The graph compared the student's drinking rates with college student averages, which were invariably much lower. This feedback actually surprised many students. Because most of their friends drank as much as they did, they thought the same was true for college students in general. Potential risks for heavy drinkers (such as those shown in Table 16.4) were pointed out. The psychologists also told the students about the physiological effects of alcohol, including the biphasic effect described in Chapter 5 (an initial stimulating effect followed by a depressive one) to show that the expectation that "drinking more will make me feel better" is incorrect. Environmental risk factors, such as being in a fraternity or sorority or having heavy-drinking friends, were also discussed if relevant.

The interviewers were never confrontational, but instead helped students to evaluate their situation ("What do you make of this? Are you surprised?"), to think about present and possible future problems ("Would you be worried about something like this happening to you? What impact would it have on your life?"), and to consider the possibility of change. Specific goals of behavior change were left to the student and not imposed by the interviewer. Later, during the winter of their second year in college, students in the intervention condition were mailed individualized feedback on their self-reported drinking data and alcohol-related problems over the previous year so that they could evaluate possible changes in their situations.

Did this very brief program have positive effects on the at-risk students? At the end of two years, the students in the intervention group were drinking less than were the students in the control condition, but still nearly 80 percent more than the average college student. However, only 11 percent of the intervention students were judged to be alcohol-dependent, compared with 27 percent in the control group. Although they continued to have more alcohol-related problems than did a comparison group of average college students, the inter-

> 26. What methods and outcomes occurred in Marlatt et al.'s alcohol harm reduction study with high-risk college students?

vention group had far fewer alcohol-related problems than did the untreated high-risk group (Figure 16.17). Thus despite the lack of an explicit focus on reducing drinking, the brief one-session intervention had significant positive effects. In particular, students learned to moderate their drinking when in potentially hazardous situations, thereby reducing harmful consequences.

Changing health-related and substance abuse behaviors is challenging. This is why advances from theory development and research are such important foundations for interventions, and why program evaluations provide important information on how to make them better. Moreover, given the widespread nature of health-endangering behaviors, even modest increases in success are socially significant. For example, an estimated 18 million Americans try to quit smoking each year (Wetter et al., 1998). Even if an improved intervention results in an increase of only 10 percent in the success rate, this translates into 1.8 million additional people (plus those affected by their secondhand smoke) whose health and life expectancy are positively affected.

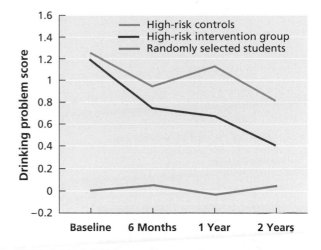

FIGURE 16.17 Effects of a brief harm reduction intervention based on motivational interviewing. One year and two years after the intervention, high-risk drinkers who underwent the program still reported more alcohol-related problems than the average college student, but fewer than the high-risk drinkers in the control group. Data from Marlatt et al., 1998.

❯ REDUCING VIOLENCE

Few of us will live our lives without being personally or indirectly victimized by violence. According to the National Crime Victimization Survey carried out by the U.S. Department of Justice (1999), 37 of every 1,000 American citizens were victims of a violent crime in 1998. One murder occurred every 29 minutes, one forcible rape every 5 minutes, and one aggravated assault every 34 seconds. One child under age 5 was murdered every 15 hours (FBI Supplementary Homicide Reports, 1999). From the 1980s to the 1990s, homicides and aggravated assaults committed by juveniles both increased more than 50 percent (Snyder & Sickmund, 1995). If U.S. statistics are not chilling enough, United Nations statistics indicate that in other countries, such as Iraq, Jamaica, the Russian Federation, and Colombia, murder rates are three to nine times higher than in the United States. Behind each of these statistics lies a story of human tragedy and suffering that extends beyond the victims themselves, as you yourself know if you or a loved one has been a victim.

There are few safe havens from violence or from aggressors, who come in all shapes and sizes. Debra Pepler and Wendy Craig (1995) set up hidden cameras and microphones on Canadian schoolgrounds and captured an average of one act of bullying every seven minutes. In an investigation carried out in Great Britain, one third of the secondary school students who were studied reported having experienced bullying incidents that created fear and concentration difficulties in school, as well as psychological distress and recurring memories of the incidents (Sharp, 1995). A Minnesota study by Nicki Crick and Maureen Bigbee (1998) revealed that girls are less likely than boys to use physical aggression, but nearly three times more likely to inflict "wounds of the heart" through **relational aggression,** which involves spreading of vicious rumors, exclusion from peer groups, and withdrawal from friendships. They speculated that relational aggression may be even more psychologically damaging than physical bullying.

Approaches to Violence Reduction

As with other problematic behaviors, to reduce violence we must understand its causes and find ways to alter them. Current approaches to reducing violent behavior focus on these biological, psychological, and environmental causes and their implications for intervention (Reppucci et al., 1999).

❯ 27. What evidence indicates that violence and bullying, especially by young people, is a major social problem? What sex difference is found in bullying behavior?

Antecedents and Consequences of Violence

Violent acts are carried out for many different reasons. One useful way of categorizing violent behavior is in terms of the antecedents (internal and external stimuli) that precede the violent act and the consequences, or outcomes, that the act produces (Mattaini et al., 1996). This type of analysis, which is based in part on the principles of learning discussed in Chapter 6, also helps to identify environmental and cognitive factors that might be the focus of intervention efforts.

Many violent behaviors are strengthened and maintained by *negative reinforcement* resulting from the removal of some unpleasant or aversive antecedent. For example, perceived insult or disrespect is a powerfully unpleasant experience that motivates many violent acts in young people (Anderson, 1994). A violent act that removes the disrespect is negatively reinforced. In other cases, the aversive stimulation produced by a crying or misbehaving child can trigger violent acts designed to quiet the child down (Emery & Laumann-Billings, 1998).

Some habitually violent individuals use aggression because they feel that others will hurt them if they do not strike first. In this case, aggression reduces anxiety about personal safety, thereby strengthening violent behaviors through negative reinforcement (Toch, 1992). The intervention implications are clear: If people who behave violently in order to terminate unpleasant states can be taught more constructive ways to prevent aversive situations or react to them, the violent solution they now favor might be altered (Malott, 1994).

Other violent acts are carried out for *positive reinforcement*. Violent acts may result in tangible rewards such as acquiring a victim's money or personal belongings. Commission of a violent act (sometimes, a murder) is required for admission to some youth gangs (Figure 16.18). Perpetrators of violent acts also gain increased status within such subcultures. As one youth involved in a gang fight later said,

> If I would of got the knife, I would have stabbed him. That would have gave me more of a build up. People would have respected me for what I've done and things like that. They would say, "There goes a cold killer." (Yablonsky, 1962, p. 8)

The positive reinforcer for some men who batter their wives is increased dominance and control over one's spouse so that the spouse will not hesitate to meet whatever needs the batterer has (Jacobson & Gottman, 1998). In his classic study of violent men, Hans Toch (1992) identified a subset that he called *bullies and sadists* who derived great pleasure from simply hurting other people. In cases where the positive reinforcers are adaptive ones, such as status and respect from others, violent individuals could be taught constructive ways of obtaining these prized outcomes. Preventing school dropout and fostering educational and vocational success can liberate many young people from social environments that promote violent and criminal behavior (Reiss & Roth, 1993).

Rage and Violence

Many acts of a violent nature are responses to emotional antecedents, such as frustration, anger, or rage (Figure 16.19). These acts often occur impulsively and with little forethought. For example, incidents of "road rage" are becoming all too common on our highways, and many instances of child abuse are triggered by anger (Emery & Laumann-Billings, 1998). Interventions for people whose violent behavior is driven by emotion typically focus on (a) teaching them to anticipate high-risk situations, (b) training in methods for reducing physiological arousal, such as relaxation (Feindler & Scalley, 1998). Such people need to develop well-rehearsed tactics for delaying impulsive acts and for dealing with the source of the emotion in more adaptive ways (Gottlieb, 2000; Novaco, 1975). Abusing parents need to learn more constructive child management techniques

➤ 28. What are the roles of negative and positive reinforcement in violent behavior? Cite examples of each.

FIGURE 16.18 An alarming increase in gang-related violence has occurred over the past decade. Murders often occur as a result of feeling disrespected or to gain entry or status within a gang.

FIGURE 16.19 "Road rage" is becoming a major source of violence. One approach to reducing such behavior is emotional control training.

➤ 29. What can be done to reduce violent behavior in people for whom emotions like anger are a strong antecedent?

that can help eliminate the child's aversive behaviors that trigger the emotional responses (Howe, 1999).

Using the Mass Media to Teach Nonviolence

As noted earlier, exposure to violent models, either directly or through the mass media, increases the likelihood that observers will behave aggressively (Bandura, 1983; Eron, 2000). Fortunately, the opposite is also true; exposure to models who demonstrate nonviolent ways of responding to provocations decreases aggressive behavior in observers (Donnerstein & Donnerstein, 1976). Building on this principle, the American Psychological Association (APA) has begun a joint project with Music Television (MTV) to reduce violence among youthful viewers (Zabriskie, 1999). As part of MTV's *True Life* series, leading psychologists who study violence are creating media materials to teach teens how to deal with situations that lead to violence. A "Warning Signs" guide developed by APA is available free through a toll-free number shown during the MTV presentations. Psychologists around the country have volunteered to be present in schools when young people watch the MTV productions and then to lead discussions on how to cope with anger and frustration. This partnership between the world's largest psychological organization and a cable channel that attracts many young viewers promises to transmit important information about violence prevention to many millions of youngsters, and to provide high-status peer models for nonviolent solutions to problems. Program evaluation research can then assess the impact of this intervention.

Changing Cultural Beliefs That Encourage Violence Against Women

In recent years, projects conducted under the auspices of the United Nations and the World Health Organization have investigated violence on a worldwide basis (United Nations, 1996). The widespread differences in violent crime rates among nations has served to focus attention on cultural factors that affect violent behavior. Some of these factors have deep historical roots. In the Russian Republic, where, according to government reports, an average of 14,000 women die annually as the result of domestic violence, some long-standing beliefs and traditions may help create an environment that legitimizes their abuse:

> ➤ 30. How do cultural beliefs contribute to violence against women?

> Throughout Russian folklore and religious literature, women were believed to possess evil and magical powers, which called for rules and punishments to control them. . . . These beliefs gave rise to the "Domostroi," a household manual that dictated that women were to devote themselves solely to domestic duties and men were responsible for physically disciplining wives who disregarded their duties. The Domostroi described appropriate dimensions for whips and instructed that a wife should be lashed with her blouse removed so that it was done privately. . . . As late as the end of the 19th century, the Russian wedding custom of passing a whip from the bride's father to her husband was observed. (Horne, 1999, p. 56)

Studies of abused Russian women have revealed that, like the men who beat them, they have accepted the long-standing cultural norms (Pisklakova, 1995). In one study, 26 percent of the women interviewed related having been beaten by their husbands, but half of these women maintained that they "deserved it." (Russian Association of Crisis Centers for Women, 1995). The Russian government, which is developing educational and legal programs in an attempt to reduce violence against women, is well aware that reducing domestic violence will require changing long-standing cultural supports for such behavior. Russia is by no means the only country where such beliefs exist, but it is one nation taking active and constructive steps to reduce violence against women.

TABLE 16.5 BEHAVIORAL INDICATORS OF STAGES OF CHANGE IN A MEXICAN WIFE-ABUSE REDUCTION PROGRAM

Precontemplation

Denial or self-blame

Nonrecognition of behaviors as abusive

Culturally reinforced tolerance (That's just the way it is)

Contemplation

Recognition of violence as abuse

Knowing where to go for help

Willingness to disclose abuse to friends or family

Preparation

Asking for help from family or friends

Emergency planning

Seeking assistance from formal institutions

Participation in a support group

Threatening to leave

Leaving the abuser for short periods of time

Action

Adopting active strategies to "manage" the abuse (fighting back)

Leaving for good

Seeking a protection order

Taking legal action

Source: Fawcett et al., 1999.

➤ 31. How do the results from the Oak Ridge study demonstrate the important role of personality in offenders' responses to treatment?

In Mexico, domestic violence is also a major problem, with as many as 57 percent of low-income women reporting that they live in a violent household (Ramirez & Uribe, 1993). Yet the majority of these women never disclose their abuse to anyone else and suffer in silence because they accept it as part of their gender role. The goal of one project in a low-income suburb of Mexico City is a modest one: to bring the abuse out into the open and to help women get support and assistance in ending the abuse (Fawcett et al., 1999). The project is designed around the Stages of Change model described earlier (Table 16.5). It involves a 12-session consciousness-raising and skills-development workshop for women and a large-scale community education campaign. The goals of the campaign are to shift the problem of abuse from a private "family matter" to a community issue that deserves everyone's attention, to reduce victim-blaming, and to promote supportive responses from the friends and family of women living in abusive relationships. The effects of this new program are currently being evaluated.

Biological Approaches to Violence Reduction

Like all other forms of behavior, violence results from processes occurring within the brain. As these neurochemical processes are understood through basic research, it may be possible to intervene at a biological level to reduce aggression in violence-prone individuals. For example, basic research shows that in both animals and in humans, aggressive behavior is associated with low levels of serotonin (Cleare & Bond, 1997; Manuck et al., 1998). Serotonin seems to act as a braking mechanism on acts of impulsive aggression. Moreover, animal studies and clinical reports indicate that decreases in aggressive behavior occur when the activity of serotonin in the brain is increased by certain antidepressant drugs. Similar effects can be produced by drugs that mimic the effects of serotonin (Deckel & Fuqua, 1998; Karper & Krystal, 1997; Lopez-Mendoza et al., 1998). These findings could herald the development of new pharmacological approaches to the problem of violence.

Again, however, it well to remember that violent behavior occurs as biological and environmental events interact with one another, so that attention to both sets of factors will be important if we wish to reduce violent behavior. As the following study shows, it is also important to take individual differences into account when planning interventions. And sometimes research designed to assess the efficacy of a treatment yields surprises that have major social policy implications.

RESEARCH   CLOSE-UP

A Therapeutic Community Treatment Approach for Violent Offenders— And Its Surprising Outcomes

▌Background

For ages, society has wrestled with the question of how to deal with people who commit acts of violence. In many countries the current answer has swung in the direction of building more and larger prisons (Kendall, 1999). Critics of this approach view prison as a "school for criminals" that

serves only to harden them further and insist that the primary goal should be rehabilitation rather than punishment or removal from society (Haney & Zimbardo, 1998).

Which approach—rehabilitation or imprisonment—works better, and for whom? This study compared long-term outcomes for two approaches to the treatment of violent male offenders. The first was conventional imprisonment.

—Continued

The second was a highly progressive and intensive "therapeutic community" approach that exposed participants to a comprehensive intervention designed to alter personality factors that predisposed them to violence.

▶ Method

In the 1960s and 1970s, the maximum-security Oak Ridge Division of the Mental Health Centre in Ontario, Canada, was the site of an ambitious therapeutic community treatment program for violent offenders. The program extended over two years and had 80 hours per week of therapeutic group and individual treatment that was administered by carefully chosen and highly trained prisoners. The program was designed "to produce insight and promote the development of cooperation, responsibility, caring, and empathy" (Rice, 1997, p. 414). Acquiring these characteristics was expected to reduce the likelihood of violent behavior once the men were released. The program was deemed especially appropriate for men with antisocial personality disorder (also known as psychopaths), who lack the above qualities. Indeed, blue-ribbon panels of experts who reviewed the program gave it glowing evaluations, such as "Here the impossible is apparently happening—psychopaths are being treated with success." The techniques were hailed as "the most fruitful of any in the universe at the present time" (Rice, 1997, p. 415). At that time, however, the long-term effects of the program on future violence had not been evaluated.

To assess the impact of the program, the investigators did a 10-year followup of two groups of men: 146 men who had been sent to prison, and 146 men who had been through the Oak Ridge program. To compare groups that were as similar as possible, each untreated offender was matched with a treated participant who was the same age, had committed the same offense, and had an equally serious criminal history. Psychopathic characteristics were measured using a psychological test. The two groups were equivalent overall on mean psychopathy scores, although within each group some men had high scores and some had low scores. The dependent variable was *violent recidivism,* defined as being arrested for one or more violent acts (assaults, homicides, or rapes) in the 10-year period following treatment or release from prison.

▶ Results

Despite experts' glowing evaluations of the program while it was being implemented, the results 10 years later were disappointing. The violent recidivism rate was 40 percent for those treated in the therapeutic community, with little difference between the Oak Ridge and prison groups. These overall results masked an even more important result, however. When the investigators broke down the prison and Oak Ridge groups into psychopaths and nonpsychopaths using scores on the psychological test, the pattern shown in Figure 16.20 emerged.

Overall, the psychopaths had a significantly higher rate of repeat violence, whether treated at Oak Ridge or sent to prison. That in itself is no real surprise, for people

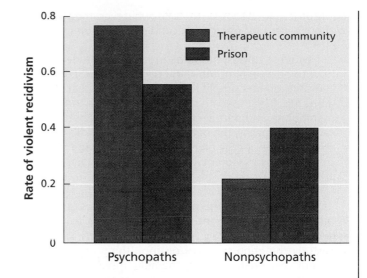

FIGURE 16.20 Repeat violence over a 10-year period following release from either prison or a therapeutic community program designed to change personality factors related to aggressive behavior. Data from Rice, 1997.

with antisocial personality disorders generally have a higher rate of repeat violence (Rice, 1997). The real surprise was the different responses of the psychopaths and nonpsychopaths to the two programs. The rate of repeat violence among nonpsychopaths treated in the therapeutic community was about half that of the nonpsychopaths who went to prison. Apparently the Oak Ridge program had its desired effects on the nonpsychopaths. In contrast, the therapeutic community was associated with a significantly *higher* rate of repeat violence for the psychopaths than was being sent to prison. Indeed, this group had a rate of repeat violence double that of the psychopaths who went to prison and four times higher than the nonpsychopaths who were treated in the therapeutic community. We can thus conclude that the therapeutic program was a success—but only for nonpsychopaths.

▶ Critical Analysis

This study shows why it is so important to systematically evaluate intervention programs, and particularly their long-term effects. In this case, a program described by experts as "the most fruitful in the universe" for treating violent offenders with antisocial personality disorder was associated with the highest rate of repeat violence after the psychopaths returned to the community. As discussed in Chapter 14, no group is in greater need of developing responsibility, caring, and empathy than people with antisocial personality disorders, and the program was specifically designed to enhance these qualities. Moreover, the treatment approach was based on our best theories of psychopathy. What went wrong?

The investigators suggested two possibilities. One was that the treatment program raised psychopath's self-esteem, with the unintended effect of making them even more

—*Continued*

egocentric and disposed to take whatever they wanted without regard for others. A second possibility was that

> . . . whereas nonpsychopaths in the program learned how to be more empathic and concerned with others, the psychopaths simply learned how to appear more empathic. They used this information so as to better manipulate and deceive others. . . . In the absence of any true empathy, the better manipulation skills of the treated psychopaths allowed them to use and abuse others (in both violent and nonviolent ways). (Rice, 1997, p. 415)

One lesson from this project is clear: In designing and evaluating social interventions, it is important to discover *when* and *for whom* they work or do not work. We see in this study the importance of distinguishing between two different personality types, namely, psychopathic and nonpsychopathic defenders. The positive side, of course, is the low rate of repeat violence on the part of the nonpsychopaths who were exposed to the therapeutic community. This was a very intensive and expensive treatment program, and one could reasonably conclude from these re-

sults that it is best administered to offenders who are not psychopathic. For psychopaths, prison may be a better—and less expensive—alternative.

Recent studies of treatments for juvenile delinquents (who are frequently tomorrow's antisocial personality disorders) show a surprising result that parallels this one in some important respects. Across a number of studies in which delinquents were treated in groups or went to "therapeutic" summer camps, the treated groups had significantly worse long-term outcomes of criminal behavior, violence, and substance abuse than did nontreated delinquents (Dishion et al., 1999). Apparently, when such youngsters are put together, even in what should be a highly effective treatment program, they reinforce each others' deviant attitudes and behaviors with attention and approval, thereby strengthening antisocial tendencies. Thus after many years of application, longterm program evaluations are challenging what is historically the most popular approach to treating delinquents, namely, peer group rehabilitation programs. A more effective approach may be to isolate them from other delinquents so that they interact with nondelinquent peers (Dishion et al., 1999).

Source: Marnie E. Rice, 1997. Violent offender research and implications for the criminal justice system. *American Psychologist, 52,* 414–423.

❯ PSYCHOLOGY IN A MULTICULTURAL WORLD: INCREASING UNDERSTANDING AND REDUCING CONFLICT

FIGURE 16.21 To an increasing degree, people from different cultures are being brought into closer contact with one another, requiring greater understanding and tolerance of differences.

➤ 32. What are the major assumptions of multiculturalism?

Throughout the book we have emphasized the importance of understanding psychological phenomena from a multicultural perspective. As we have seen repeatedly, culture exerts powerful influences on humans' thoughts, motives, feelings, and behavior. No longer can psychologists assume that "laws" of behavior established within one culture apply universally (Triandis, 1994). The modern world's global economy, telecommunications, and increased immigration bring different cultures into increasingly greater contact with one another, and diverse cultural groups face the challenge of living harmoniously with one another (Figure 16.21).

In North America and many parts of Europe, minority populations struggle to retain treasured cultural traditions and at the same time try to integrate themselves into the dominant culture. The "melting pot" model of cultural assimilation seems to have been rejected by both the dominant culture and minority cultures, and the pluralistic nature of our society is being acknowledged and accepted (Locke, 1992). Whether in education, human services, medicine, work settings, or counseling, many psychologists are asserting that there can no longer be a single method of interaction and expectations based solely on the dominant culture (Marsella, 1998; Prilleltensky, 1997; D. W. Sue et al., 2000). **Multiculturalism** has evolved into "a social-intellectual movement that promotes the value of diversity as a core principle and insists that all cultural groups be treated with respect and as equals" (Fowers & Richardson, 1996, p. 609). This movement views cultural diversity as a positive force that allows different groups the freedom to follow their own paths to individual and group destiny. Additionally, it holds that interaction can enrich all cultures by exposing them to new ideas and customs and to a cultural dialogue about what is worthwhile in human living.

By providing scientifically valid information concerning important cultural factors that influence behavior, psychology can contribute to furthering multicultural understanding and tolerance. From a practical perspective, psychological research can identify the conditions that allow different ethnic groups to interact positively with one another and can inspire programs that capitalize on these factors to increase multicultural acceptance and harmony.

It is clear that we are far from achieving a global society that appreciates and tolerates cultural diversity. Racism, prejudice, and discrimination are all too common. In tragic civil wars throughout the world, different cultural groups seem intent on destroying one another in the name of "ethnic cleansing" and other euphemisms for genocide. In some ways, modern racism in North America is more difficult to detect than the more blatant forms associated with civil wars in other parts of the world, or that associated with the past history of slavery, lynchings, and cross burnings in the United States. Overt racism of that kind has been on the decrease over the past several decades (Dovidio et al., 2000). Today's prejudice and discrimination toward minority groups and people of other cultures typically is a more subtle underground phenomenon that surfaces in indirect ways when it is safe, easy to rationalize, or socially desirable. Indeed, many majority people are minimally aware of contradictions between their consciously stated values of fairness and equality and coexisting feelings of discomfort, hostility, and anxiety toward members of other racial and ethnic groups (Greenwald et al., 1998).

Approaches to Reducing Intergroup Conflict

Whether blatant or subtle, negative attitudes and behaviors toward members of other cultural or racial groups tear at the fabric of society. We offer two illustrative examples of how psychological principles can be applied in this important area.

The Contact Hypothesis: Lessons from School Integration

In 1954, the United States Supreme Court handed down one of its most momentous decisions in the case of *Brown v. Board of Education*. The Supreme Court ruled that school segregation based solely on race is a violation of the constitutional rights of racial minorities. Providing key testimony, several psychologists stated that segregation had harmful effects on the self-esteem and academic achievements of African-Americans and that it contributed to racial prejudice and hostility. Further, in accord with Gordon Allport's (1954) **contact hypothesis,** they suggested that direct contact between the races could set the stage for greater multicultural understanding and a reduction in prejudice and discrimination.

The Supreme Court's decision ushered in one of the most controversial social reforms in U.S. history. A half century later, we can ask whether school desegregation achieved its goals of reducing prejudice, increasing the self-esteem of minorities, and enhancing their school achievement. Although the results have been far from conclusive, and often have conflicted with one another, the overall answer is less positive than proponents hoped. For example, Walter Stephan (1990) reviewed more than 80 evaluation studies of desegregation programs involving African-American and Caucasian children. He concluded that increasing direct contact through desegregation does not, in and of itself, seem to reduce racial prejudice. Only 13 percent of the evaluation studies reported a decrease in prejudice among Whites, whereas 34 percent showed no change and 53 percent reported an increase in prejudice. Among African-American students, prejudice toward Whites was more likely to decrease than to increase, but some increases in prejudice were also found.

Despite the overall negative verdict, the school desegregation studies, combined with research results in other settings, helped identify the conditions under which increased contact does have its desired positive impact. For example,

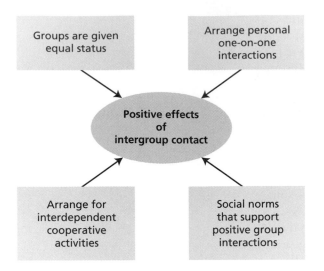

FIGURE 16.22 Under these four conditions, increasing contact between adversarial groups is most likely to reduce prejudice and promote positive attitudes and interactions.

➤ 33. What four factors influence the extent to which the effects predicted by the contact hypothesis actually occur? How are these factors incorporated into cooperative learning programs?

FIGURE 16.23 Increased contact is likely to have positive result on intergroup relations if people in authority promote the norms of positive interaction. Clearly, this did not occur in the early years of school integration.

a natural question to ask is what occurred that was different in the 13 percent of the programs that increased positive attitudes toward members of other groups. Four conditions, summarized in Figure 16.22 seem particularly important (Aronson, 1997; Pettigrew, 1991).

First, the contact situation should be arranged so that the groups in contact are of *equal status,* for unequal status serves only to perpetuate both groups' negative stereotypes of one another. Promoting equal-status contact in such diverse settings as the armed forces, housing arrangements, and athletic teams has helped reduce prejudice (Dovidio et al., 2000).

Second, successful contact requires *personal one-on-one interactions* between the groups, so that members of each group come to be judged on the basis of their individual qualities rather than in terms of stereotypes applied to all group members. In many integrated school situations, this did not occur, for students were placed in different "learning tracks" that minimized in-class contact, and they tended to associate only with members of their own racial group outside of class (Schofield & Sagar, 1979).

Third, as we saw in the classic Robbers Cave boys camp experiment described in Chapter 1, intergroup hostility breaks down most quickly when opposing groups like the Rattlers and the Eagles engage in *cooperative activities* that lead them toward goals that both groups want (Sherif et al., 1961). This produces a "we're in this together" atmosphere that helps break down psychological barriers between groups and causes "outsiders" to become "insiders," (Fiske, 2000).

Finally, intergroup contact will work only if it is supported by *social norms.* In the early years of desegregation, many White politicians, parents, teachers, and school officials militantly opposed school integration, and this factor helped counteract positive effects that might have occurred from increased contact (Figure 16.23). Where both groups are committed to improving their relations, and where relevant authorities promote and enforce this goal, the power of these norms help move people toward more positive interactions. Where there's a will, people are more likely to find a way.

In school settings, these four principles are applied in **cooperative learning programs** involving children of different ethnic groups. In the most effective programs, such as the jigsaw program described in Chapter 1, children representing different ethnic groups are placed in learning groups where each is accorded equal status and each child is given responsibility for learning and then teaching other group members one piece of the information that is needed for the group to succeed in its assignment (Aronson et al., 1978). Groups are encouraged and reinforced by the teacher for their positive interactions and mutual achievements. Such programs include all four of the group contact factors described above, and they have proven to be highly successful not only in enhancing the academic performance of children, but also in reducing prejudice and promoting appreciation of individual and ethnic group differences (Johnson, 2000). An Australian study showed that the dependence of students on one another is an especially important feature of effective cooperative learning programs (Walker & Crogan, 1998). Research that helps identify the most important "active ingredients" of social programs helps program planners to develop increasingly more effective programs.

Interactive Problem Solving: The Israeli-Palestinian Project

In an attempt to defuse conflicts around the world, a new field called *international conflict resolution* has developed over the past 30 years (Burton, 1969; Kelman, 1996). This field applies psychological principles to help groups communicate and work toward peaceful solutions to problems that divide them.

Few ethnic conflicts have caused more human tragedy and bloodshed than that involving the Israelis and Arabs. The past century's continuous cycles of violence and counterviolence between Palestinians and Jews began in the 1920s and the prospect of peace in that land has appeared virtually hopeless during the past half-century. In the early 1970s, long before the Madrid and Oslo accords of the past decade provided a glimmer of hope for peace, a group of American, Israeli, and Arab psychologists quietly began a program designed to bring influential Israelis and Palestinians together (Kelman, 1997; Rouhana & Bar-Tal, 1998). Their approach, called **interactive problem solving,** is a process that enables the parties to explore each other's perspective, develop joint ideas for mutually satisfactory resolutions to their conflict, and transfer their ideas and insights into the policy process (Kelman, 1997).

Problem-solving workshops are intensive meetings between politically influential but unofficial Israeli and Palestinian representatives, such as parliamentarians, leading figures in political parties and movements, former military leaders and politicians, journalists and editors, and Israeli and Palestinian academic scholars who specialize in Middle East affairs. The workshops take place over several days under the sponsorship of academic institutions and are led by a panel of social scientists who are experts in international conflict resolution. Group meetings typically have three to six members of each side and two to four social scientists. The meetings are entirely private and confidential, with no audience, no publicity, and no records kept. Nothing said within the workshop can be attributed to the individual who said it outside of the workshop, and all participants are to be regarded as equals. These ground rules permit a level of honest communication that is usually not possible for the participants.

Each workshop has three major phases that are designed to modify existing beliefs and to introduce new beliefs that motivate the participants to work toward a peaceful relationship that can satisfy the basic human needs of both Israelis and Palestinians. First, the participants are asked to describe to one another the conflict from their community's perspective in an analytic rather than argumentative manner, and to describe the human concerns, needs, and fears that must be addressed in any resolution. This process is designed to help each side see the conflict through the other's eyes and to realize that they have important fears and needs in common.

Once both sets of needs and concerns are on the table and have been understood and acknowledged by the other side, the participants become a single problem-solving group. They are asked to work together in developing new ways for resolving the conflict that would satisfy the fundamental human needs of both parties and allay their fears. This search for "win-win" solutions is in sharp contrast to normal perceptions that if one side wins, the other side must lose. The members are also asked to explore the political and psychological barriers that have prevented a solution in the past, and to problem-solve on how these barriers might be overcome. This mutual problem-solving approach has the added benefit of building personal relationships (and, in some cases, real friendships) between the participants that help each side see the human qualities of the other and to realize that they have a shared vision for a peaceful future. In the end, workshop participants can communicate to their respective communities ideas for building a new relationship with the other side. They also can testify from their own personal experiences that a collaborative and mutually enhancing relationship is indeed possible. We should note that the interactive problem-solving approach, like the jigsaw classroom, fulfills all four conditions that influence whether the contact hypothesis applied: equal status, personal interactions, cooperative activities, and norms that support cooperation.

Dozens of influential Israelis and Palestinians have participated in the workshops, and many of these individuals were ultimately involved in the discussions and negotiations that led to the ground-breaking Oslo accord in 1993, where both sides committed themselves to peace negotiations and acknowledged each other's right to existence and self-governance (Figure 16.24). Whether these steps

➤ 34. How have the four contact hypothesis factors been applied within the interactive problem-solving workshops conducted in the Israeli-Palestinian project?

FIGURE 16.24 The Israeli-Palestinian interactive problem solving workshops involved prominent figures on each side. They helped pave the way to agreements that may eventually bring peaceful coexistence to the region.

➤ 35. Summarize the personal and environmental factors that make some children highly resilient to stressful environments.

will ultimately lead to peace remains to be seen, but both participants and facilitators have new hope that this can eventually occur (Kelman, 1997).

As humanity enters the first decade of the new millennium, we believe that psychological science is destined to play a central role in the building of a better world. In so doing, psychology must focus not only on helping society heal the worst things in life, but also on helping people build the best things that human existence has to offer. Our final *Psychological Frontier* explores what a "positive science" has to offer.

PSYCHOLOGICAL FRONTIERS

Toward a Psychology of Human Strengths and Fulfillment

There is much that is wrong with our world, and too many people live unhappy and unfulfilling lives in environments that stifle human potential and foster pathology. A psychology that defines its goal as promoting human welfare clearly must address such issues and try to remedy them. However, an emphasis on remediation and prevention also invites an exploration of what can be when human potential is achieved. What is the good life? What makes people feel happy and fulfilled? What human strengths allow people to lead fulfilling lives and serve as buffers against the stresses of life? How can we nurture what is best within ourselves to create a life of virtue and strength? What constitutes optimal living? (Seligman & Csikszentmihalyi, 2000)

These are not new questions, although they are being approached today in a new research-oriented fashion. In earlier years, humanistic psychologists such as Abraham Maslow (1971) and Carl Rogers (1961) pioneered the study of people who were labeled as *fully functioning people* or *self-actualized individuals.* Based on their personal observations, Maslow and Rogers described such people as self-determined, spontaneous people who developed their inner potential to the fullest. Marie Jahoda (1958) captured many of these qualities in her description of *positive mental health,* which consisted of these characteristics:

- positive attitudes toward oneself—self-acceptance;
- autonomy—a sense of self-determination and inner directedness;
- growth and development, an investment in achieving one's potential;
- accurate perception of reality;

- competence in reacting to environmental demands; and
- positive interpersonal relationships.

During the 1970s and 1980s, optimal living received relatively little attention outside of the humanistic school. Behaviorism was concerned with environmental determinants of behavior, the psychodynamic perspective with psychopathology, and the cognitive perspective with analyzing human thought. But two lines of research began to bring the topics of optimal living and human strength into a new focus. One was the research on subjective well-being, or happiness, described in Chapter 10. In a sense, asking what makes people truly happy is another way of phrasing the question, "What is the good life?" (Diener, 2000). Another important stimulus to a positive psychology was the study of stress and coping, which began to identify personal characteristics, such as optimism, self-efficacy, perceived control, and coping skills, that served as protective factors against stressful events. Asking how some highly resilient people can flourish within psychologically toxic environments casts the spotlight on human strengths. Using experimental and other data-based methods that build upon the humanists' clinical observations and case studies of optimal living, psychology is now approaching terrain that humanists tried to lead it into 40 years ago.

In Chapter 10 we told you about Priscilla, a child who grew up in a terrible home environment with a psychotic mother and a father who abused her and committed suicide in her presence. Somehow, despite these experiences, Priscilla grew into a highly successful young woman. The study of people like Priscilla has much to contribute to a

—Continued

psychology that focuses on human strengths and the powerful adaptive systems that foster and protect the development of competence and well-being even under the most unfavorable conditions.

What are the factors that matter in the lives of children who cope successfully with severe life challenges? Reviewing many studies of unusually resilient children and adolescents, Ann Masten and J. Douglas Coatsworth (1998) found that these children have a consistent pattern of characteristics that contribute to a positive outcome even in the face of stressful life events. These factors are summarized in Table 16.6. They include characteristics of the child, such as an adequate level of intellectual functioning, social skills, self-efficacy, and faith (optimism and hope). They also include environmental factors, such as a relationship with at least one caring, prosocial adult (in Priscllla's case, it was a teacher who befriended, encouraged, and guided her). Obviously, a resilient child need not have all of the characteristics listed in Table 16.6, but he or she must have at least some of them. Good intellectual functioning and a good relationship with an adult seem to be the most important (Masten & Coatsworth, 1998).

The study of human strengths has an important side-benefit. It tells us what factors we should try to increase if we are interested in developing competent, resilient, and happy people. As we have seen in this chapter and throughout the book, psychology has developed an array of techniques for intervening successfully to change both personal and environmental factors in a manner that can produce successful outcomes in the lives of people. In the years to come, we may expect to see these techniques applied in new ways that release human potential.

TABLE 16.6 PERSONAL AND ENVIRONMENTAL FACTORS THAT CONTRIBUTE TO STRESS-RESILIENCE IN CHILDREN

Source	Characteristic
Individual	Good intellectual functioning
	Appealing, sociable, easygoing disposition
	Self-efficacy, self-confidence, high self-esteem
	Talents
	Faith
Family	Close relationship to caring parent figure
	Authoritative parenting: warmth, structure, high expectations
	Socioeconomic advantages
	Connections to extended supportive family networks
Extrafamilial context	Bonds to prosocial adults outside the family
	Connections to prosocial organizations
	Attending effective schools

Source: Masten & Coatsworth, 1998, p. 212.

〉 A FINAL WORD

In Chapter 1, we began our journey through the sprawling domain of modern-day psychology. That journey has taken us from the inner recesses of the human mind to the social world in which we spend our lives. We have examined the intricate workings of the brain and the biological processes that underlie our thoughts, feelings, and behaviors. We have also explored the learning mechanisms that enable us to profit from our experiences and adapt to our environment. We have seen how the environment in which we live, including our culture, exerts powerful influences over who we become and how we behave. We have achieved greater understanding of the cognitive processes that, more than anything else about us, define our humanity. We have also gained insights into the personality processes that make each of us unique. We have found repeatedly, these bio-psycho-social factors interact in complex ways to influence our behavior. As your guides through the domains of psychology, we hope that our shared journey has influenced your conception of human nature, your understanding of yourself and others, and your ability to apply psychological principles to enrich your life.

▼▼▼

CHAPTER SUMMARY

Linkages Between Theory, Research, and Intervention

- Psychological theories, research, and interventions each influence, and are influenced by, one another.

- Social interventions, properly conducted, can be conceived as experiments, with the intervention being the independent variable and the outcome the dependent variable.

- Program evaluation research measures the effects of an intervention, and an attempt is made to assess the psychological factors and processes that influence its effects. Another aspect of program evaluation is a cost-benefit analysis: the extent to which its benefits outweigh its costs.

Enhancing Children's Development

- Childhood intervention programs designed to overcome the lack of intellectual stimulation in impoverished environments date back to Head Start. The Abecedarian and High/Scope Perry Preschool programs show that early preschool intervention has long-term positive effects on the educational and social outcomes in at-risk children.

- Intervention programs designed to promote mental health have also been implemented. An example is the Penn Optimism Project, designed to reduce the likelihood that pessimistic children will develop depression as they move into adolescence and young adulthood.

Health Promotion and Illness Prevention

- Health psychology studies psychological and behavioral factors in the prevention and treatment of illness and in the maintenance and enhancement of health. It focuses on both health-enhancing and health-compromising behaviors.

- The Stages of Change model has identified six stages through which people may move during the process of successful behavioral change. Stage-matched interventions focus on the individual's current stage, with the intent of moving the person to the action, maintenance, and termination stages.

- Exercise is an important health-enhancing behavior. Many behavioral interventions have been developed to promote exercise, but many people fail to adhere to exercise programs. One factor that influences adherence is social support. People who are able to adhere for three to six months have a better chance of adhering thereafter.

- About a third of the American population is obese, as are one in six children and adolescents. Behavioral weight control programs feature self-monitoring, stimulus control procedures, and eating procedures designed to cause people to eat less, but enjoy it more. The addition of an exercise program to weight-control procedures enhances weight loss.

- Psychologists have been active in AIDS prevention programs. Behavioral changes have been accomplished in homosexual populations, and efforts are centering on high-risk heterosexual populations, such as teenagers and certain groups of women.

Combating Substance Abuse

- Substance abuse is highly associated with other disorders, often being part of a larger pattern of maladjustment. The most effective substance abuse treatment approaches are based upon psychological principles like classical conditioning, positive reinforcement, and coping skills training.

- Used alone, aversion therapies are of limited effectiveness. They tend to reduce craving within the treatment setting, but to not be maintained when the person leaves the treatment setting.

- Multimodal treatments combine a number of techniques, including aversion training, stress management and coping skills training, and positive reinforcement for change. A promising new approach is motivational interviewing, designed to engage the person's own motivation to change. Relapse prevention is designed to keep lapses from becoming relapses by building effective coping skills and countering the abstinence violation effect. It enhances the effects of many behavior change programs.

- Harm reduction approaches attempt to reduce the negative consequences that a behavior produces rather than to focus on stopping the behavior itself. Examples include needle exchange programs for drug addicts and programs designed to reduce the destructive consequences of binge drinking in college students.

Reducing Violence

- Violent acts are performed for a variety of reasons including negative reinforcement, positive reinforcement, and emotional overarousal. The causal factors provide keys for successful intervention.

- The mass media can be used to promote nonviolent solutions to problems, as in the current collaborative project involving the American Psychological Association and MTV. In some cases, cultural factors are important determinants of violent behavior, including physical abuse of women. Recent findings that serotonin inhibits aggressive behavior may provide a biological treatment for some violent individuals.

- Treatment approaches may have differential effects on different kinds of offenders. One intensive therapeutic community program reduced violent recidivism in nonpsychopaths, but increased it in psychopaths.

Psychology in a Multicultural World

- Multiculturalism as a movement promotes the value of diversity and insists that all groups be treated with respect and as equals.

- The contact hypothesis asserts that increasing contact between opposing groups will reduce hostility and promote mutual acceptance. Research has shown that increased contact results in more positive attitudes and interactions if four conditions apply: (1) equal status; (2) personal interactions between group members that break down negative stereotypes; (3) cooperative activities in the service of a common goal; and (4) support of cooperative interactions by social norms.

- An interactive problem-solving program has been used to bring warring parties like the Israelis and Palestinians together under conditions that satisfy the four conditions that promote positive effects of contact.

A Psychology of Human Strengths and Fulfillment

- Prevention approaches and the study of competent and resilient individuals have resurrected a positive psychology of human strengths that was at one time a focus of humanistic psychologists. This approach involves focusing on positive human qualities and the conditions that produce them.

▼▼

KEY TERMS AND CONCEPTS*

abstinence violation effect (686)
aerobic exercise (679)
contact hypothesis (695)
cooperative learning programs (696)
harm reduction (687)
health-compromising behaviors (677)
health-enhancing behaviors (677)

health psychology (676)
interactive problem solving (697)
interventions (671)
lapse (686)
motivational interviewing (685)
multiculturalism (694)

multimodal treatment approaches (684)
program evaluation (671)
relapse (686)
relational aggression (689)
yo-yo dieting (680)

* Each term has been boldfaced in the text on the page indicated in parentheses.

APPLYING YOUR KNOWLEDGE

1. Relying on a program evaluation, an educational review panel concludes that a program based on a new theory of reading comprehension has failed to raise children's reading comprehension scores. The committee recommends "a rethinking of how children learn to read." Which theory/research/intervention link is reflected in this statement?
   a) Theory influences interventions.
   b) Theory influences research.
   c) Research influences theory.
   d) Research influences interventions.

2. In the terminology of experimental research, the reading comprehension scores of the children in the above program may be considered.
   a) independent variables
   b) dependent variables
   c) underlying causal factors
   d) random variables

3. Educational leaders in your region propose an expensive educational enrichment program that will be administered to all children when they enter elementary school. If you were to testify before a hearing on the proposed program, what suggestion would be consistent with the results of previous programs?
   a) The program will increase educational outcomes in all children.
   b) The program will have positive outcomes only for underprivileged children.
   c) The program will only benefit children from wealthy homes.
   d) The program will probably have limited benefits because the children are too old.

4. A rash of suicides among adolescents in your community stimulates a desire for a prevention program. You are on the council considering potential programs that might be implemented. Which of the programs described in this chapter would offer the greatest potential?
   a) the Jigsaw Program
   b) the Penn Optimism Project
   c) the Abecedarian Program
   d) the High/Scope Perry Program

5. An informational program alerting unaware college students of the dire consequences that accompany binge drinking would be most relevant to which of the Stages of Change?
   a) termination
   b) preparation
   c) precontemplation
   d) contemplation

6. Clem makes a New Year's resolution to begin a regular program of daily exercise to lose weight as soon as he returns to school for the winter academic term. According to the Stages of Change model, Clem is in the _____ stage.
   a) contemplation
   b) precontemplation
   c) action
   d) preparation

7. In some European countries, the government provides drug addicts with drugs. Such programs are most likely to be based on the _____ model.
    a) harm reduction
    b) relapse prevention
    c) positive reinforcement
    d) medical

8. You are a member of a committee that is designing a program for juvenile delinquents to reduce their antisocial behavior. Which of the following programs would offer the greatest promise, based on the results in summarized in this chapter?
    a) sending them to summer camps with other delinquents where they would be treated by skilled therapists
    b) group therapy with other delinquents in an alternative school
    c) immersion in a two-year therapeutic community program for psychopaths
    d) group activities with nondelinquents

9. If you wished to lose weight permanently, which of the following methods should you most assuredly avoid?
    a) stimulus control methods, because they work only for alcohol reduction
    b) repeated yo-yo dieting until the weight stays off
    c) physical exercise, because it will make you hungrier
    d) slow eating, because you won't be satiated

10. You wish to apply the results of research on the contact hypothesis to enhance interactions among children of different ethnic groups within your local school district. Which of the following principles should you *not* implement?
    a) cooperative learning programs
    b) athletic programs in which children are randomly assigned to teams
    c) competition between segregated athletic teams
    d) "laying down the law" to parents who oppose the program

Answers

1. c) (page 671); 2. b) (page 671); 3. d) (page 673); 4. b) (page 675); 5. c) (page 678); 6. d) (page 678); 7. a) (page 687); 8. d) (page 693); 9. b) (page 680); 10. c) (page 696)

For additional quizzing and a variety of interactive resources, visit the book's Online Learning Center at www.mhhe.com/passer.

STATISTICS IN PSYCHOLOGY

At various points in the text we have briefly described statistical procedures to help you understand the information being presented. This appendix discusses statistics in more detail and focuses on the concepts underlying these procedures. Our goal is to help you understand how psychologists use statistics in their research.

For some students, the prospect of studying statistics evokes reactions of anxiety or dread. You will find, however, that if you can add, subtract, multiply, and divide, you can easily perform basic statistical operations.

❯ DESCRIPTIVE STATISTICS

Psychological research often involves a large number of measurements. Typically, it is difficult to make sense of the data merely by examining the individual scores of each participant. **Descriptive statistics** allow us to summarize and describe the characteristics of a set (also called a *distribution*) of scores.

To summarize a set of scores we might first construct a **frequency distribution,** which shows us how many participants received each score. For example, suppose that 50 college students take a 32-item psychological test that measures their level of self-esteem. The frequency distribution in Table A.1 tells us that 2 participants had scores of 30, 31, or 32; none had scores of 27, 28, or 29; 11 had scores of 15, 16, or 17, and so on. Note that the researcher chose to use *intervals* of 3 points (e.g., 30–32) rather than to show the number (frequency) of participants who obtained each of the 33 possible (0–32) scores. She could have done the latter if she had wished to break down the scores even further. The number of intervals chosen is somewhat arbitrary, but frequency distributions often contain 10 to 12 categories.

This frequency distribution tells us at a glance about certain characteristics of the data, such as whether scores tend to cluster in one region of the distribution or are scattered throughout. We can easily convert these data into a **histogram,** which is a graph of a frequency distribution. Typically, the scores (or in this case, score intervals) are plotted along the horizontal axis (i.e., *x-axis* or *abscissa*), while the frequencies are plotted on the vertical axis (i.e.,

TABLE A.1	FREQUENCY DISTRIBUTION OF SELF-ESTEEM SCORES	
Self-Esteem Scores	**Frequency**	
30–32	2	
27–29	0	
24–26	5	
21–23	6	
18–20	9	
15–17	11	
12–14	8	
9–11	3	
6–8	4	
3–5	1	
0–2	1	

y-axis or *ordinate*). This produces a column or bar above each score that shows how frequently the score occurred. Figure A.1 shows a histogram of the self-esteem scores for our sample of 50 college students.

Measures of Central Tendency

Frequency distributions and histograms give us a general picture of how scores are distributed. **Measures of central tendency** allow us to describe a distribution in terms of a single statistic which is in some way "typical" of the sample as a whole. There are three commonly used measures of central tendency: the *mode*, the *mean*, and the *median*. For example, Table A.2 shows the salaries of the 10 employees who work at Honest Al's Savings and Loan Corporation. Our task is to arrive at a single number that somehow typifies the salaries of the group as a whole.

The **mode** is defined as the most frequently occurring score in a distribution. At Honest Al's, the modal salary is $205,000, since it is the only salary received by more than one person. Although the mode is easy to identify in a distribution, it is not always the most representative score,

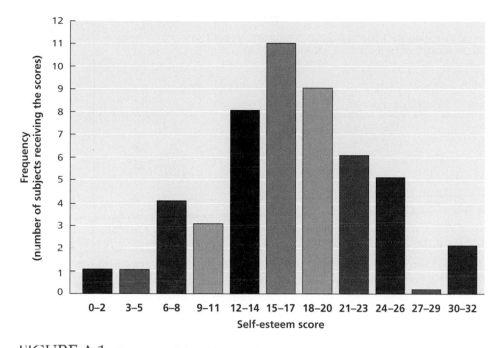

FIGURE A.1 Histogram of the self-esteem distribution shown in Table A.1.

TABLE A.2	STATISTICAL PROPERTIES AND COMPUTATION OF THE MODE, MEAN, AND MEDIAN OF THE ANNUAL SALARIES OF 10 EMPLOYEES

Employee	Annual Salary (X)
1. Honest Al	$205,000
2. Honest Al's mother	205,000
3. Johnson	20,000
4. Rodriguez	19,500
5. Jones	19,000
6. Chen	18,000
7. Brown	17,500
8. Carter	17,000
9. Mullins	16,500
10. Watson	16,000
N = 10	Σ = $553,500

Mode = The score that occurs most often—in this case, $205,000.

Mean = The arithmetic average, computed by the following formula:

$$M = \frac{\Sigma X}{N} = \frac{553,500}{10} = 55,350$$

Median = The point above and below which there is an equal number of scores. In this case, because there is an even number of scores, the median is midway between the 5th- and 6th-ranked salaries—that is, $18,500.

of scores. The mean is calculated by adding up all the scores and dividing by the number of scores. The statistical formula for computing the mean is:

$$M = \frac{\Sigma X}{N}$$

X is the symbol for an individual score, N denotes the number of scores, and M is the symbol for the mean of the individual scores. The Greek letter Σ (sigma) means "the sum." Thus to compute the mean of the salaries at Honest Al's, we simply add up the individual salaries and divide the total by 10, the number of salaries. As Table A.2 shows, the mean salary at Honest Al's is $55,350.

Would you be tempted to go to work at Honest Al's when, during a job interview, Al tells you that "our average salary is $55,350 per year"? Your negative answer to this question illustrates a shortcoming of the mean as a measure of central tendency. The mean can be strongly affected by one or more extremely high or low scores that are not representative of the group as a whole. In this case, the high salaries of Honest Al and his mother increased the mean to a figure more than twice as great as the salary of the next highest paid employee. Thus we cannot consider the mean to be representative of the salaries of his employees.

Our third measure of central tendency, the **median,** is defined as the point that divides the distribution in half when the individual scores are arranged in order from lowest to highest. In other words, half of the scores lie above the median and half below it. If there is an odd number of scores, there will be one score that is exactly in the middle. If there were 11 salaries in Table A.2, the sixth-ranked score would be the median, because 5 scores would fall above and 5 below. In a distribution having an even number of scores, the median is halfway between the 2 middle scores. In our salary distribution, the median is the point halfway between employee 5 ($19,000) and employee 6 ($18,000), or $18,500.

The median has an important property that the mean does not have: It is unaffected by extreme scores. Whether Honest Al makes $205,000 or $500,000, the median remains the same. Therefore the median is more representative of the group as a whole in instances where there are very extreme scores. In Honest Al's case, the median figure of $18,500 is more representative of the "typical" employee's salary than is the mean figure of $55,350 or the modal salary of $205,000. The median, however, can fail to capture important information. For example, suppose that employee 3 (Johnson) and employee 4 (Rodriguez) each received an $80,000 raise. In this case the median would not change, because the "middle

particularly if it falls far from the center of the distribution. Clearly, $205,000 is not the "typical" salary of the 10 employees, because 8 of them receive $20,000 or less.

The most commonly used measure of central tendency, the **mean,** represents the arithmetic average of a set

| TABLE A.3 | COMPUTATION OF THE VARIANCE AND STANDARD DEVIATION FOR TWO DISTRIBUTIONS OF SCORES WITH IDENTICAL MEANS ($M = 10$) |

	Distribution A				Distribution B		
X (score)	$X - M = x$	x^2		X (score)	$X - M = x$	x^2
12	+2	4		18	+8	64
12	+2	4		18	+8	64
11	+1	1		15	+5	25
11	+1	1		15	+5	25
10	0	0		10	0	0
10	0	0		10	0	0
9	−1	1		5	−5	25
9	−1	1		5	−5	25
8	−2	4		2	−8	64
8	−2	4		2	−8	64
$\Sigma X = 100$	$\Sigma x = 0$	$\Sigma x^2 = 20$		$\Sigma X = 100$	$\Sigma x = 0$	$\Sigma x^2 = 356$
$N = 10$				$N = 10$		
$M = 10.00$				$M = 10.00$		

x (deviation) $= X - M$

$$\text{variance} = \frac{\Sigma x^2}{N} = \frac{20}{10} = 2.00 \qquad\qquad \text{variance} = \frac{\Sigma x^2}{N} = \frac{356}{10} = 35.6$$

$$SD \text{ (standard deviation)} = \sqrt{2.00} = 1.414 \qquad\qquad SD = \sqrt{35.6} = 5.967$$

score" would still be the midpoint between employees 5 (Jones) and 6 (Chen). The mean, however, would increase to $71,350 ($713,500/10) and reflect the fact that Honest Al is being a touch more generous in paying his employees.

Measures of Variability

Measures of central tendency provide us with a single score that typifies the distribution. But to describe a distribution adequately, we need to know more. One key question concerns the amount of variability, or spread, there is among scores. Do they tend to cluster closely about the mean, or do they vary widely? **Measures of variability** provide information about the spread of scores in a distribution.

The **range,** which is the difference between the highest and the lowest score in a distribution, is the simplest but least informative measure of variability. At Honest Al's, the range is $205,000 − $16,000 = $189,000. As another example, if we have a distribution of 20 IQ scores, and the highest IQ is 160 and the lowest is 70, then the range is 160 − 70 = 90. But suppose the other 18 people all have IQs of 110. If we knew only the range of scores, we might be led to believe that the scores in this distribution vary far more than they actually do. Thus it would be more useful to know how much, on average, each IQ score varied or deviated from the mean of the distribution.

To do this we first create a *deviation score* (represented by a lowercase x) that measures the distance between each score (X) and the mean (M). To provide a simple example, suppose we have two distributions, A and B, each comprised of 10 scores. Looking at the "X (score)" column in Table A.3 for each distribution, you can see that although each distribution has a mean of 10, the scores in B are more spread out than in A. Now, for each score, we compute how much it differs from the mean (i.e., $x = X - M$). At this stage, you might think that to measure the variability of each distribution, we need only add up its deviation scores and then compute the average deviation. But we have a problem. Even though distribution B is more spread out than A, adding up the deviation scores for each distribution yields a sum of zero ($\Sigma x = 0$). In fact, the sum of deviation scores for any distribution always will add up to zero.

To avoid this, we must get rid of the plus and minus signs that end up canceling each other out. As the rightmost column under each distribution in Table A.3 shows, we achieve this goal by taking each deviation score, squaring it, and then adding up these squared deviation scores. This produces a sum of 20 for distribution A and 356 for distribution B. Now we divide by 10 (i.e., the number of scores in each distribution) to find the average squared deviation. This statistic is called the **variance;** it is the average of the squared deviation scores about the mean. You can see that the variance for distribution B (35.6) is considerably greater than the variance for distribution A (2.00), reflecting the greater spread of the scores in B.

The most popular measure of variability, the **standard deviation (SD),** is simply the square root of the variance. Because we had to square the deviation scores to

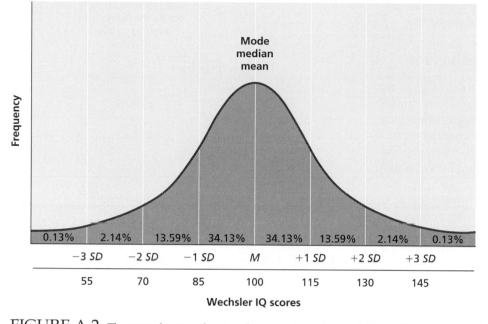

FIGURE A.2 The normal curve, showing the percentage of cases falling within each area of the normal distribution and Wechsler IQ scores corresponding to standard deviation (SD) units.

compute the variance, we now return to the original scale of measurement by taking the square root of the variance. Psychologists tend to prefer the standard deviation over the variance as a measure of variability because the SD is expressed in the same unit of measurement as the original data. You can see in Table A.3 that the standard deviation from the mean of distribution B (5.967) is more than four times greater than the average deviation from the mean of distribution A (1.414).

❭ THE NORMAL CURVE

One particularly important distribution in statistics is called the **normal curve,** a symmetrical bell-shaped curve in which 50 percent of the cases fall on each side of the mean. Additionally, in a normal curve the median and mode have the same value as the mean. Figure A.2 shows that in a normal curve, as we move away from the mean the frequency of each score steadily decreases. The normal curve is important because so many variables—weight, height, IQ, and anxiety, to name a few—are distributed in the population in this fashion. Thus a few people are extremely tall or short, a greater number people are moderately tall or short, and most are close to average in height.

The normal curve is a statistician's delight because it has several key properties. Above all, the standard deviation can be used to divide the normal curve into areas containing known percentages of the population. In a normal curve, about two thirds of the scores fall within plus or minus 1 standard deviation of the mean; about 95 percent of cases fall within plus or minus 2 standard deviations, and nearly all of the cases fall between 3 standard deviations

above and 3 standard deviations below the mean. Therefore if we know that a psychological characteristic or any other variable is normally distributed (as many are), then we can deduce more information about it. For example, IQ scores as measured by the Wechsler intelligence tests (see Chapter 8) are normally distributed with a mean of 100 and a standard deviation of 15. Knowing this, we can use our knowledge of the normal curve to answer questions like these:

1. What percentage of people have IQs between 70 and 130? (Approximately 95 percent. These scores are −2 and +2 SD from the mean. As Figure A.2 shows, this area of the curve includes 13.59 + 34.13 + 34.13 + 13.59 percent of the cases, or 95.44 percent.)

2. My IQ is 115, so where does that place me? 115 is +1 SD above the mean, so as Figure A.2 shows, about 16 percent of the population will have a higher IQ, and 84 percent will have a lower IQ. That is, the area to the right of +1 SD represents 13.59 + 2.14 + 0.13 = 15.86 percent of the cases.)

3. What is the probability that a person selected at random from the population will have an IQ of 145 or more? (About one eighth of 1 percent. This probability corresponds to the area under the curve beyond +3 SD, or 0.13 percent.)

These examples point to a major use of the normal curve: It allows us to estimate the probability that a given event will occur. Indeed, the statistical tests we describe next are methods for arriving at probability statements based on the assumption that the variables being investigated are normally distributed. Thus the normal curve not only mirrors reality in many cases, but it helps us to arrive at probability statements, which are as close as we can come to "truth" in science. We shall say more about this point shortly.

❭ STATISTICAL METHODS FOR DATA ANALYSIS

Given a set of data for any single variable, such as the scores of a sample of people on a self-esteem test or the salaries of Honest Al's employees, we use descriptive statistics to summarize the characteristics of those data. But psychologists do more than describe variables individually. They seek to explain and predict behavior by examining how variables are *related* to one another. The following statistical methods are used to analyze relations among variables and draw inferences about the meaning of those relations.

Accounting for Variance in Behavior

Behavior varies. It varies between individuals (e.g., some people are more aggressive or helpful than others) and it varies for the same individual across time and situations (we may perform a task well under some conditions, but more poorly under other circumstances). Explaining why variations in behavior occur (i.e., accounting for variance) is a central goal of psychological science.

As an example, suppose we want to examine how the number of bystanders present during an emergency influences the speed with which they assist a person in distress. In this instance the number of bystanders is the independent variable and speed of helping is the dependent variable. We conduct an experiment, randomly assign participants to different conditions (one, two, or four bystanders present), and find that overall, bystanders who are alone respond most quickly and groups of four respond most slowly. We also find that speed of response varies even within each condition; for example, among those bystanders who were alone, some simply respond more quickly than others. Maybe they were in a better mood, had more altruistic personalities, and so on.

In any experiment, the total amount of variation in people's behavior (e.g., speed of helping) may be divided into two components: the amount of *variance accounted for* by the differences in the independent variable(s) we have manipulated (e.g., being placed alone or with other bystanders), and the amount of variance that is left over and therefore must be due to other factors (e.g., participants' mood, personality). Thus

Total variance = Variance accounted for + Variance not accounted for
(due to independent   (due to random, unmeasured,
variables)   or uncontrolled factors)

Suppose that, in our experiment, a statistical analysis reveals that 20 percent of the total variance in the speed with which participants help a person in distress can be accounted for by our independent variable—the number of other bystanders who were present. Figure A.3 shows this schematically. The other 80 percent of the variance in speed of helping (the unshaded portion of the circle) is due to other factors that were not controlled in the experiment. Some of these other factors, which are random and beyond the control of the experimenter, produce what is called *error variance.* For example, some participants may have been momentarily bored or preoccupied with personal problems, and thus responded more slowly than they would have otherwise. The rest of the unexplained variance results from factors that systematically affect speed of helping but which the researcher either does not know about or were not controlled for in the experiment. Such variables may include the bystanders' personality charac-

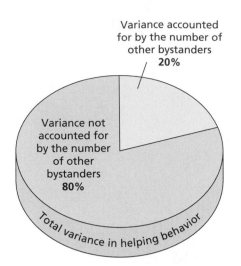

FIGURE A.3 The total amount of variation in the dependent variable (speed of responding to another person in distress) is represented within the circle. The total variance may be divided into one portion accounted for by the independent variable (number of bystanders) and another portion not accounted for by the independent variable.

teristics or mood, victim's gender, nature of the emergency, and so forth. In future research we might include additional independent variables, such as manipulating (i.e., creating) an environment that puts bystanders in a good or bad mood just prior to the emergency. By studying other independent variables we attempt to increase the amount of variance accounted for, thereby expanding the size of the green shaded area in Figure A.3. Perhaps we will find that by knowing both the number of bystanders present and the participants' mood, we can now account for 35 percent of variance in people's speed of helping.

Viewed from this perspective, understanding and/or predicting behavior involves isolating factors that account for behavioral variance. The more important a particular variable is, the more highly it relates to the behavior of interest and the more variance it helps us account for. To be sure, we can never completely eliminate the random factors that produce error variance. But as scientific research proceeds, the goal is to discover new variables that account for additional portions of the total variance in people's behavior.

Correlational Methods

The concept of *variance accounted for* applies not only to experiments, but also to correlational studies. As discussed in Chapter 2, correlational research does not involve manipulating independent variables. Rather, it involves measuring two or more variables and determining whether changes in one variable are associated with changes in the other. Suppose that we administer two psychological tests—one measuring self-esteem and the other measuring depression—to 200 adults. On each test we will find that the scores vary: Some people will have higher

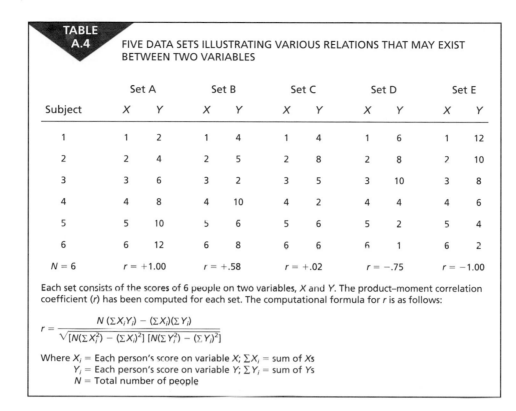

TABLE A.4	FIVE DATA SETS ILLUSTRATING VARIOUS RELATIONS THAT MAY EXIST BETWEEN TWO VARIABLES									

	Set A		Set B		Set C		Set D		Set E	
Subject	X	Y	X	Y	X	Y	X	Y	X	Y
1	1	2	1	4	1	4	1	6	1	12
2	2	4	2	5	2	8	2	8	2	10
3	3	6	3	2	3	5	3	10	3	8
4	4	8	4	10	4	2	4	4	4	6
5	5	10	5	6	5	6	5	2	5	4
6	6	12	6	8	6	6	6	1	6	2
N = 6	r = +1.00		r = +.58		r = +.02		r = −.75		r = −1.00	

Each set consists of the scores of 6 people on two variables, X and Y. The product–moment correlation coefficient (r) has been computed for each set. The computational formula for r is as follows:

$$r = \frac{N\left(\sum X_i Y_i\right) - \left(\sum X_i\right)\left(\sum Y_i\right)}{\sqrt{[N(\sum X_i^2) - (\sum X_i)^2][N(\sum Y_i^2) - (\sum Y_i)^2]}}$$

Where X_i = Each person's score on variable X; $\sum X_i$ = sum of Xs
Y_i = Each person's score on variable Y; $\sum Y_i$ = sum of Ys
N = Total number of people

self-esteem or will be more depressed than others. The question is this: Is there a relation between the variance in self-esteem scores and the variance in depression scores? Stated differently, as scores on variable X become higher or lower (i.e., as they move further away from the mean of X), do scores on Y tend to become either higher or lower (i.e., move away from the mean of Y) in a systematic manner?

The Correlation Coefficient

Relations between variables can differ in *direction* (positive or negative) and in *strength*. To illustrate, examine the relations between the five sets of X and Y scores in Table A.4. In each set we have a score on variable X and a score on variable Y for six individuals. In set A the relation is positive in direction. That is, high scores on variable X are associated with high scores on Y, and low scores on X are associated with low scores on Y. In contrast, set E reveals a negative relation. Here, high scores on X are associated with low Y scores and vice versa. In set C the pairs of X and Y scores bear no clear relation to each other: They are not correlated. As scores on X change, scores on Y do not change in any consistent manner. Thus in sets A, C, and E we see three different types of relations—positive, none, and negative.

To illustrate how relations between variables differ in strength, let us compare set A with set B. In set A there is a perfect positive relation between X and Y: As each X score increases, each Y score becomes higher by a constant amount. In set B individuals having higher X scores also tend to have higher Y scores, but the increase in Y is not con-

stant, as in set A. For example, participant 2 has a higher X score than participants 1 and 3, yet has a lower Y score. In other words, the positive relation is not as strong. Likewise, compare set E with set D. Set E displays a perfect negative relation: As each X score increases, each Y scores decreases by a constant amount. In set D, the negative relation between X and Y is not as consistent, and thus is not as strong.

The **Pearson product-moment correlation coefficient** is a statistic that provides a precise numerical index of the direction and strength of the relation between two variables. The correlation coefficient (designated r) can range in magnitude from −1.00 to +1.00. If r = +1.00, this reflects a perfect positive relation between X and Y scores, as in set A of Table A.4. A correlation coefficient of −1.00 signifies a perfect negative relation, as in set E. Correlations close to 0.00 indicate no systematic relation between the variables, as in set C.

In actual research a correlation of −1.00 or +1.00 is rare; psychological variables tend to be imperfectly correlated with one another. More typically, correlation coefficients might resemble those in sets B (r = +.58) and D (r = −.75). Remember that it is the magnitude of the correlation coefficient and not its sign (direction) that indicates the degree to which two variables are related to one another. Thus X and Y are more strongly related in set D (r = −.75) than in set B (r = +.58), even though the correlation in set D is negative.

How shall we interpret a correlation coefficient? A correlation of +.50, for example, *does not* mean that X and Y " are 50 percent related." Rather, squaring the correlation

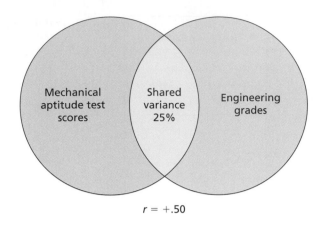

$$r = +.50$$

FIGURE A.4 Squaring the correlation coefficient provides an estimate of the amount of variance shared by two variables. In this instance, $r = .50$, indicating that 25 percent of the variance in engineering grades in this sample can be accounted for by individual differences in mechanical aptitude.

coefficient (r^2) indicates the amount of variance that the two variables share or have in common. Stated another way, r^2 tells us how much of the variance in one measure can be accounted for by differences in the other measure. For example, suppose we obtain a correlation of $+.50$ between scores on a mechanical aptitude test and grades in a college engineering course. As illustrated in Figure A.4, squaring the correlation coefficient ($+.50^2 = .25$) tells us that 25 percent of the total variance in course grades can be accounted for by differences in mechanical aptitude scores. Obviously, the more highly two variables are correlated, the more common variance they share. If the two variables in Figure A.4 correlated $-.70$, the area of overlap would include about half of each circle, since $(-.70)^2 = .49$. Finally, if two variables are perfectly correlated, the green shaded area of overlap in Figure A.4 would fill the entire circle.

Recall from Chapter 2 that a correlation between two variables does not allow us to conclude that one caused the other. We know only that they are statistically related to one another. If variables X and Y are correlated, it is possible that X causes Y, Y causes X, or that both X and Y are caused by some third variable, Z. We cannot infer causality from correlation.

Correlation and Prediction

If two variables are correlated and we know an individual's score on one variable, then this information will help us predict his or her score on the other variable. *The more highly two variables are correlated, the more accurate our predictions will be.* In fact, if two variables are perfectly correlated—if their variance overlaps completely—we can make precise predictions. For example, in set A of Table A.4, once we know a person's score on X, we can accurately predict that $Y = 2X$. (Conversely, if we know Y, we

can predict that $X = .5Y$). In statistical prediction based on correlation, we are thus taking advantage of lawful relations among variables to predict to the individual case.

There are many practical applications for predictions based on correlational analysis. Industrial-organizational psychologists, for example, often help organizations develop aptitude tests that correlate with on-the-job performance. Personnel managers can therefore use job applicants' test scores to predict which applicants are most likely to perform well, just as colleges use high school students' Scholastic Aptitude Test (SAT) scores to help predict potential college performance. The more highly a *predictor variable* (e.g., aptitude test scores) is correlated with the *criterion variable* (e.g., job performance or college grades), the more accurate the selection decisions will be.

Factor Analysis

Within a single study, researchers may measure many variables and examine the correlations among them. For example, suppose we wish to determine the mental abilities that people possess. Are there dozens of different mental abilities, or are there are only a few basic and general mental abilities that influence performance across diverse tasks? If so, what is the nature of these abilities? To answer such questions, let us assume that a psychologist administers 40 different performance tests to hundreds of participants and correlates all of the test scores with one another. She reasons that if several tests are correlated highly with one another—if performance scores on these tests "cluster" or "hang together"—then these tests are probably measuring the same underlying or basic mental ability. Further, if the tests within a cluster or group correlate highly with one another but are not correlated with tests in other clusters, then these various test clusters probably reflect different and distinct mental abilities. Thus the psychologist hopes to determine the number of test clusters and to use this information to infer the nature of the underlying abilities.

When the sets of scores for the 40 tests are correlated with one another ($N =$ the number of tests or variables), our psychologist will end up with 780 correlations [($N \times (N - 1))/2$, or $(40 \times 39)/2$] to examine. Obviously, with so many correlations, trying to visually determine which tests cluster together (while not clustering with other tests) is a hopeless task. Fortunately, a statistical technique called **factor analysis** reduces the large number of correlations among many measures to a smaller number of clusters. Today, computers can analyze the patterns of correlations and perform a factor analysis in a few seconds. The term *factor* refers to the underlying characteristic that presumably accounts for why the measures within each cluster are linked together.

Factor analysis is a complex procedure and we need not be concerned with its mathematical basis. Our interest is in how psychologists use it as a research tool, so consider a simple example. Let us assume that Table A.5 shows the

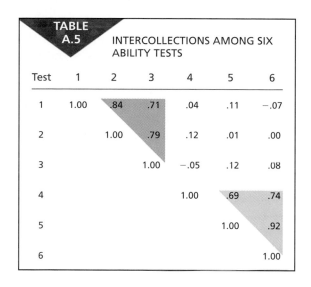

Test	1	2	3	4	5	6
1	1.00	.84	.71	.04	.11	−.07
2		1.00	.79	.12	.01	.00
3			1.00	−.05	.12	.08
4				1.00	.69	.74
5					1.00	.92
6						1.00

TABLE A.5 INTERCOLLECTIONS AMONG SIX ABILITY TESTS

correlations among only 6 of the 40 measures. Such a table is called a *correlation matrix*. The correlation coefficients of 1.00 along the diagonal of the matrix reflect the obvious fact that each variable correlates perfectly with itself. Because the bottom half of the matrix contains the same correlations as the top, we need concern ourselves only with 15 correlations [$(6 \times 5)/2$]—the upper half.

Examining Table A.5 clearly reveals two clusters of tests. Tests 1, 2, and 3 all correlate highly with one another. Likewise, Tests 4, 5, 6 correlate strongly with one another. Notice also that Tests 1, 2, and 3 have low correlations with Tests 4, 5, and 6, which indicates that the two clusters are measuring different things. But just what do these two clusters of tests measure? The factor analysis cannot answer this question directly; it can only identify the clusters for us. Now it is up to the psychologist to examine the nature of the tests in each cluster and decide what the underlying factors might be. Suppose that Test 1 measures vocabulary, Test 2 measures reading comprehension, and Test 3 requires participants to fill in sentences having missing words. Because all three tasks involve the use of words, the psychologist might decide to name the underlying factor "verbal ability" or perhaps "word fluency." What matters in Table A.5 is that we have reduced six variables and 15 correlations to two underlying factors. In our complete example, with 40 tests and 780 correlations, a typical factor analysis might identify between two to six factors. In psychology, where we often attempt to identify basic dimensions of behavior, factor analysis a valuable tool.

Inferential Statistics and Hypothesis Testing

No matter the type of research, psychologists rarely have access to the entire population of people they are interested in. Instead, they must be satisfied with studying relatively small samples of participants. Thus 80 introductory psychology students might participate in an experiment on bystander helping, and 400 adults recruited through newspaper advertisements might participate in a correlational study examining the relation between self-esteem and depression. On the basis of the results obtained from such samples, researchers seek to generalize their conclusions to the population as a whole.

In experiments, for example, we are typically interested in overall differences between the various conditions. Suppose we find that participants randomly assigned to be alone help a victim more quickly than participants assigned to groups of two or four bystanders. Before concluding that the independent variable (number of bystanders) truly influenced the dependent variable (speed of helping), we must first ask whether this difference is "real" or a merely a "chance" finding. In other words, because our data are based only on a particular sample of people in each condition, how do we know that the same results would have occurred if we had tested other samples? Perhaps for one reason or another the participants we tested were not truly representative of the populations from which they were drawn. Perhaps, despite random assignment, participants assigned to be alone happened by chance to have more highly altruistic personalities than participants in the other conditions, and this (rather than "being alone") is the reason they helped more quickly.

Methods known as **inferential statistics** tell us how confident we can be in drawing conclusions or *inferences* about a population based on findings obtained from a sample. Stated differently, inferential statistics tell us how likely it is that results obtained from a sample (e.g., differences between experimental and control groups, or a correlation between two variables) occurred by chance alone and thus do not reflect a genuine difference in the population from which the sample is drawn. Psychologists typically consider a result to be genuine—to be *statistically significant*—only if it could have occurred by chance alone less than 5 times in 100. This probability is called the **level of statistical significance.**

The logic underlying tests of statistical significance is related to our previous discussion of the normal curve and its statistical properties. Determining the level of statistical significance is in many ways similar to the IQ problem presented earlier in the appendix: If IQ is normally distributed with a mean of 100 and a standard deviation of 15, what is the likelihood of randomly selecting a person with an IQ of 145? To answer that question, all we had to do was to determine what proportion of cases are 3 standard deviations above the mean in a normal distribution. We found that proportion to be about one tenth of 1 percent. Thus we would expect to randomly select a person with an IQ that high about once in 1,000 times—pretty small odds. With this example in mind, let us consider the logic of statistical inference in greater detail.

Suppose we are interested in the effects of a stress management program on the academic performance of freshmen college students who are high in test anxiety. We hypothesize that learning to control anxiety during tests will result in better performance. We randomly assign 40 students who have received high scores on a self-report measure of test anxiety to either an experimental group (20 participants) that participates in a stress management program for test anxiety, or to a control group (20 participants) that receives no guidance or treatment. All of the students take the same required courses, and at the end of the academic year we compare the mean grade point averages of the two groups. We find that the experimental group (training program condition) obtains a mean grade point of 3.17 (A = 4.0), the control group has a mean grade point of 2.61, and the difference between the two groups therefore is 3.17 − 2.61 = 0.56 grade points. How can we decide whether this difference in the two samples reflects a difference in the respective populations (i.e., all high-test-anxious students who might participate in a stress management program and all who do not)?

If we repeated our experiment a large number of times with different samples of high-anxiety participants, we would find that the means for the two samples would vary in each experiment. The next three times we performed the study the means might be 2.94 (experimental) versus 2.77 (control), 3.34 versus 2.31, and 2.89 versus 2.83, yielding differences between the groups of 0.17, 1.04, and 0.06, respectively. By repeating the experiment numerous times, we could create a distribution of experimental versus control difference scores, and mathematical theory tells us that this distribution would be a *normal* distribution. This gives us the key. Because we have a normal distribution, we can assess the likelihood of randomly obtaining any particular size difference between our sample means, just as we could arrive at the exact likelihood of randomly selecting a person with an IQ of 145, 92, or 71. But to do this, we must know what the mean and standard deviation of our distribution of differences are. One way to determine these values would be to perform our experiment a large number of times. But, fortunately, we can estimate these values on the basis of a single experiment. Here's how it works.

If there is no real difference in grade point between the populations of trained and untrained test-anxious students, and if we repeated our experiment a great many times, then we would expect the mean of our distribution of difference scores to be around zero. The normal distribution of difference scores would cluster around this mean. The standard deviation of this normal distribution can be estimated from the standard deviations of the two samples, although the mathematics need not concern us here.

Statistical analysis involves testing the **null hypothesis,** which assumes that any observed differences between the samples are due to chance, and therefore that the difference between the two population means is zero. In our hypothetical experiment, we obtained grade point means of 3.17 for the experimental group and 2.61 for the controls, a difference of +0.56. Let us now suppose that the standard deviation of our distribution of differences between means was estimated on the basis of our samples to be .25. Thus our obtained difference is slightly more than 2 *SD* above the mean (0) of the null hypothesis distribution. From the properties of the normal curve, we know that more than 95 percent of the cases fall in the area of the curve between −2 *SD* and +2 *SD*. Thus if the null hypothesis were true, we would expect a difference in means as large as .56 (either above or below zero) less than 5 percent of the time on the basis of chance factors. This probability level meets the criterion for statistical significance described earlier. In view of this fact, we would reject the null hypothesis and conclude that there is a real difference in grade point in the two populations. Thus our experimental hypothesis that the stress management program resulted in a higher level of academic performance would be supported.

Note that we used the term *supported,* not proven, because we are making an inference based on a probability statement. There is, after all, a 5 percent chance that the null hypothesis is true and this really was a chance finding. Note also that this statistical analysis does not tell us why the stress management group performed better (e.g., was it the program's content or the mere attention that students received?). This is one reason why repeating or replicating research studies is so valuable. If another study—particularly one with more appropriate control groups—also yields statistically significant results, we can have more confidence that the difference we obtained reflects a real relation between the independent and dependent variables. But no matter how many times we repeat the experiment, we shall never escape from the world of probability into the world of absolute truth.

APPENDIX A SUMMARY

Descriptive Statistics

- Descriptive statistics summarize the characteristics of a set of data. A frequency distribution shows how many participants received each score. Histograms are graphs of frequency distributions.

- Measures of central tendency describe a distribution in terms of a single, "typical" score. The mode is the most frequently occurring score in a distribution. The mean is the arithmetic average, and the median is the point that divides the distribution in half.

- Measures of variability tell us how much variation there is among scores. The range represents the difference between the highest and lowest scores in the distribution. The variance is the average squared difference between each score and the mean of the distribution. The standard deviation is the square root of the variance.

The Normal Curve

- A normal curve is a symmetrical bell-shaped curve. Fifty percent of the cases fall on each side of the mean, and the mean, median, and mode all have the same value. The standard deviation can be used to make probability estimates by dividing the normal distribution into areas containing known percentages of a population.

Statistical Methods for Data Analysis

- A major goal of psychological research is to determine how much behavioral variance can be accounted for by relations between variables, including experimental manipulations, and how much is due to random, unmeasured, or uncontrolled factors. Random factors that are beyond the experimenter's control produce error variance.

- Two variables are correlated when changes in the scores of one variable reliably correspond with changes in the scores of the other variable. The correlation coefficient numerically represents the direction and magnitude of the relation between two variables. Correlations may be positive, negative, or zero, as well as weak or strong.

- Squaring the correlation coefficient tells us how much of the variance in one measure can be accounted for by differences in the other measure. Although correlation does not allow us to assume causality, correlations are often the basis for predictions.

- Factor analysis reduces a large number of measures to a smaller number of clusters. The measures within each cluster are highly intercorrelated and presumably reflect the same underlying psychological dimension.

- Inferential statistics allow us to draw conclusions and test hypotheses because they tell us how likely it is that differences between groups or correlations among variables are the result of chance alone. Inferential statistics are needed because most research is done with samples, and conclusions must be generalized to the population from which the sample was drawn.

- The probability that relations shown among variables do not reflect a corresponding relation in the population is called the level of statistical significance. Statistical analysis involves testing the null hypothesis, which assumes that any observed relation is due to chance, or that the difference between the two population means is zero. Inferential statistics yield probability statements, not proof.

KEY TERMS AND CONCEPTS*

descriptive statistics (A-1)	mean (A-2)	null hypothesis (A-9)
factor analysis (A-7)	measures of variability (A-3)	Pearson product-moment correlation coefficient (A-6)
frequency distribution (A-1)	measures of central tendency (A-1)	
histogram (A-1)	median (A-2)	range (A-3)
inferential statistics (A-8)	mode (A-1)	standard deviation (SD) (A-3)
level of statistical significance (A-8)	normal curve (A-4)	variance (A-3)

* Each term has been boldfaced in the text on the page indicated in parentheses.

CAREERS IN PSYCHOLOGY

Psychology is at once a discipline, a science, and a profession. First, it is a discipline, an important topic of study in colleges and universities. Psychology is also a science, a set of methods for conducting research and understanding behavior and its causes. Finally, psychology is a profession that requires an individual to apply special knowledge and skills to solve human problems.

As a career, psychology offers a panorama of vocational opportunities. The psychologists you are most likely to encounter work as teachers and perhaps researchers in universities, four-year and two-year colleges, and sometimes in high schools. As researchers, psychologists are also employed in government, business, and the military to do basic and applied science. Many other psychologists work as service providers and administrators in mental health clinics, nonprofit organizations, government agencies, hospitals, universities, and in business settings. Finally, psychologists with special expertise serve as consultants, being hired by organizations to evaluate problems and suggest solutions. For example, a consulting psychologist may work with an educational system to devise new ways of improving children's learning and mental health, or she may consult with industry to design an employee evaluation or job enrichment program. Many psychologists perform more than one of these roles, making for a varied vocational life.

Your introductory psychology course (and, hopefully, this book!), may have stimulated interest in exploring a possible career in psychology. In this Appendix we briefly describe the career options that are available in psychology and the educational background that is required to perform them. We also provide some advice for how to prepare yourself for possible advanced study in psychology.

❭ EMPLOYMENT OPPORTUNITIES IN PSYCHOLOGY

In Chapter 1 of this text we provided a brief description of the various specialty areas within psychology (Table 1.3, page 32) and described the settings in which psychologists work (Figure 1.25, page 32). These specialty areas ac-commodate people with widely varying interests. For example, if you wish to work directly with people to help them overcome psychological disorders or other problems in living, then a career in clinical or counseling psychology may be of interest to you. In either of these fields you would also have opportunities to do research on the causes and treatment of such problems. On the other hand, you may be more interested in research questions on topics such as the functioning of the brain, child development, social behavior, learning and memory, or sensation and perception. You will find specialty areas in psychology that deal with all of these topics. As you explore psychology in greater depth, you may find that one or more of its specialty areas mesh with your interest pattern. Whether you're interested in human services, education, high technology, management, aviation and space, sports, or many other fields, you are likely to find psychologists working in that field. A common denominator in the activities of all psychologists is their interest in human or animal behavior and their desire to have a challenging and personally fulfilling career.

Understandably, anyone considering a career wants to know what the employment opportunities are and what kinds of salaries are available. Where salaries are concerned, it is difficult to make any general statement because of the great variety of employment settings in which psychologists work. In addition, salaries are determined by years of experience, level of expertise and productivity, and the amount of advanced training in the field. Nonetheless, we can give you some general or "ball park" figures based upon a recent salary survey carried out by the American Psychological Association (APA, 1998). For example, a new Ph.D. (Doctor of Philosophy) who is hired as a faculty member at a major research institution may begin at a salary of around $40,000 a year for a 9- to 10-month contract (with another 20–22 percent being added for teaching or salary from a research grant or contract during the summer). A full professor with 15 to 20 years experience who is a prominent researcher might well double that salary. Applied psychologists who work in industry average about $85,000 a year. Clinical psychologists who offer direct human services average between $50,000 and

$80,000 a year, with some in private practice earning considerably more. However, managed care has cut sharply into the incomes of many private practitioners.

What is the job market like in psychology? APA's Research Office found that nearly 68 percent of 2,116 psychologists who earned their doctorate in the 1996–97 academic year secured their first choice when seeking a job. Nearly 70 percent were employed within three months of completing their degree (Chamberlin, 2000). Academia continues to accommodate many new doctorates, although competition is keen for faculty positions at top-level universities. Good opportunities also exist in nonacademic settings, such as health care settings and business and industry. Opportunities for psychologists in the public sector may also grow, particularly if federal, state, and local funding is increased for health maintenance and illness prevention and for psychological services to special populations such as the aged and the disadvantaged.

Obviously, many employment possibilities exist for which a degree in psychology is extremely useful. To make an informed vocational choice involving psychology, however, you need to evaluate the extent to which your interests and abilities match the different kinds of job opportunities as well as decide how many years you are willing to commit to your education. Although the doctoral degree is recognized as the basic credential for the profession of psychology, stimulating career opportunities in many different fields are also open to students with an education in psychology at the bachelor's and master's levels. You must also realize that planning a career is rarely a simple, logical, or orderly process. Indeed, many people change their career choices a number of times. Nonetheless, the early college years are a good time to take courses in fields that may interest you and to personally explore these vocational possibilities through volunteer work and part-time jobs. Doing so will help you to focus in on vocations that seem right for you in a more informed fashion.

Career Options with Bachelor's and Master's Degrees

A bachelor's degree in psychology is not sufficient to become a professional psychologist, but it can lay a foundation for entry-level employment in business and other settings, particularly if your work in psychology is combined with courses in economics, marketing, or business. For example, combining psychology and education courses could prepare a student to teach psychology in a high school or to work with special populations, such as those with mental disabilities. People in numerous vocations have found that a psychology major proved very useful to them in their work, particularly if their jobs involved working with people. Likewise, many undergraduate students who are preparing themselves for advanced study in medicine, law, physical therapy, rehabilitation, and other professions choose psychology as a major.

The next degree beyond the bachelor's degree is the master's degree. A master's degree typically involves two years of graduate school training. People with master's degrees in psychology can work in a variety of settings, including community mental-health centers, public and private institutions, and schools and businesses. However, career advancement in most areas is limited without the doctoral degree, and individuals with master's degrees often work under the supervision of a doctoral-level psychologist. A master's degree will usually not enable one to obtain a permanent position at four-year colleges and universities, and most states will not license master's-level individuals to provide independent psychological services. Nonetheless, such professionals can work in numerous settings, including community mental health agencies and public and private mental and custodial institutions. For example, many master's-level counselors work in programs dealing with special problems such as substance abuse, crisis intervention, spouse abuse, mental retardation, and vocational rehabilitation. With appropriate training, such individuals can also be employed in industry as personnel selection and training specialists and in school settings, where they may evaluate students with special needs and assist in the planning of appropriate educational programs for such students. Many school psychologists and counselors have master's degrees and specialized training in educational and school psychology.

Doctoral Training in Psychology

The doctoral degree in psychology, considered to be the appropriate final degree, opens up additional career opportunities. At least four years of study beyond the bachelor's degree are usually required to obtain a doctorate. In areas that provide psychological services, such as clinical and counseling psychology, another year for an internship and at least one additional year of supervised practice are required for licensing. Doctoral programs in psychology consist of a series of core courses in various areas of psychology, supervised research training, a general or comprehensive examination that advances the student to doctoral candidacy, and a doctoral dissertation that consists of original research.

In addition to the traditional university-based program, there are also so-called "professional schools" that offer the Doctor of Psychology (Psy.D.) degree rather than the traditional Ph.D. These are often referred to as "freestanding" programs because they are usually not affiliated with a university. Professional schools place primary emphasis on training students for professional practice, and their programs feature extensive practical work and little emphasis on research training. Psy.D. programs, which typically offer training in clinical, counseling, or school psychology, usually require three years of coursework and practical experience plus a supervised internship during the fourth year.

Graduate programs differ in their admission requirements and in the quality of training that they offer. In the more applied fields of psychology, *accreditation* is one important indicator of quality. In the areas of clinical, counseling, and school psychology, the American Psychological Association (APA) accredits doctoral programs that meet rigorous standards of training. A listing of accredited programs is published each year in the *American Psychologist.* The listing can also be found on the APA's website (www.apa.org). Graduation from a nonaccredited program does not prevent licensing or employment in some states, but an increasing number of states are requiring graduation from an APA-approved doctoral program for licensing in clinical psychology. Likewise, some employers decline to hire graduates of nonaccredited programs.

All fifty states and the District of Columbia require that psychologists be licensed or certified by a state board in order to offer psychological services on an independent and unsupervised basis. Licensing is based on a careful review of the psychologist's educational background and the passing of rather rigorous written and oral examinations. Before entering a doctoral program, a student who wishes to practice psychology should find out about the status of the institution offering the doctorate. As noted earlier, APA-accredited programs meet the standards of every licensing board. Your state's Examining Board for Psychology can provide information on the status of nonaccredited programs. Obviously, it behooves students to carefully investigate the quality of a graduate program before committing themselves to years of training in that program.

❯ PREPARATION FOR GRADUATE TRAINING IN PSYCHOLOGY

Graduate school is a challenging undertaking. High scholastic achievement, the ability to cope with a much heavier workload than at the undergraduate level, and a high level of self-motivation are required. However, if you have good academic ability, are truly committed to a career in psychology, and are willing to put in the effort that is required, graduate school can be a very gratifying period of your life. Most programs at major universities provide graduate students with financial aid in the form of teaching and research assistantships, traineeships, and fellowships. Such support typically pays tuition and fees as well as a modest monthly stipend ($1,000–$1,500). Thus graduate school need not involve great financial sacrifice. In contrast, most independent professional schools offer little if any financial support of this kind, and their high tuition can be a true financial hardship.

Admission to a graduate program is based on several criteria, including evidence of academic ability, scholarship as an undergraduate, previous involvement in related research or fieldwork, and promise of success in scholarly activity. These qualities are judged primarily on the basis of the applicant's record of academic achievement as an undergraduate, scores on standardized tests such as the Graduate Record Exam, and letters of recommendation from faculty members at the undergraduate institution.

Because many people are interested in graduate study in psychology, gaining acceptance to graduate school is challenging. The average program accepts only about 15% of its applicants and some prominent clinical programs accept fewer than 2% of the hundreds who apply. However, there are many high-quality doctoral programs that offer excellent training and are not as difficult to gain admission to. Some students enroll first in a master's program, then apply later to a doctoral program when they have clearly demonstrated their ability to do doctoral-level work. This course of training typically takes one or two years longer than direct entry into a program that offers the doctorate if the doctoral program is at a different university.

Although an undergraduate major in psychology is not required to be admitted to a graduate program, the bachelor's degree in psychology can provide a strong foundation for the advanced training of graduate school. Although the specifics of the undergraduate major in psychology vary from school to school, the major typically consists of courses in introductory psychology, statistics and research design, experimental psychology, personality, abnormal psychology, learning, social psychology, developmental psychology, physiological psychology, history of psychology, and tests and measurement. In addition, doctoral programs find undergraduate preparation in the natural sciences and mathematics very desirable. A high level of academic performance is required, and students accepted for graduate study in psychology typically have grade point averages that exceed 3.5 (A = 4.0).

Good academic performance is only part of the graduate school equation. Practical experience in the field is also essential. The most important aspects of this practical work are exposure to the kinds of activity that you will be engaged in during graduate school, such as research. As early as possible in your college career, you should begin developing relationships with faculty members in your psychology department who are conducting research in an area that is of interest to you. Try to get involved in their research programs, either by volunteering or by taking an independent studies course under their supervision. This will provide you with firsthand experience in research and can help you decide how much you enjoy the research enterprise. The involvement may result in research ideas of your own, and in some cases, the possibility of being an author or co-author on an article that gets published in a psychology journal or a paper that is presented at a psychology convention. Such accomplishment would be regarded as noteworthy evidence of scholarly achievement when you apply to graduate school. Moreover, being involved in one or more research programs gives the faculty member(s) the opportunity to write a truly personalized letter of recommendation for you. These letters weigh heavily in graduate school admissions decisions. Virtually all students who get accepted into top graduate programs have strong letters of recommendation from faculty members at their undergraduate institutions who have supervised their research activities. The same applies to letters received from fieldwork supervisors. If you are interested in service-oriented specialty areas such as clinical, counseling, or school psychology, you should try to get involved in fieldwork that will give you some exposure and training in those areas. Many undergraduate programs have formal relationships with community agencies where students can get fieldwork experiences. For example, undergraduates often get their first clinical experiences as volunteers at crisis clinics or telephone hotlines. Again, exposure to these experiences can help you decide whether you are truly interested in clinical work.

Other types of experience can also be helpful to you in your undergraduate preparation. For example, many psychology departments have a colloquium series at which invited speakers present their research and ideas. It is a good idea for undergraduate students to attend such colloquia. Another valuable experience is to attend a state or regional psychological association meeting. You may learn a great deal from the presentations, but even more

importantly, you will have an opportunity to meet and talk with psychologists who work in a wide variety of settings and who engage in diverse professional activities. If you talk to psychologists about their work, the chances are good that they will share the excitement that they experience in their professional lives with you. It is also possible to become acquainted with faculty from graduate programs that interest you and gain firsthand information about the "fit" that exists between your interests and their program. Such contacts could influence later admissions decisions (both yours and theirs).

For more information about careers in psychology, we direct you to the website of the American Psychological Association, which has a link devoted to students (www.apa.org/students). The APA publication *Graduate Study in Psychology and Associated Fields* provides descriptions of more than 600 programs of study as well as information about graduate education, financial assistance, and requirements for admission to various programs. This book may also be available through your university library, student counseling center, or psychology advisory office.

A career in psychology can be a wonderfully fulfilling way to live one's life. We hope that we have been able to communicate and share with you our enthusiasm for the field of psychology in the pages of this book.

CREDITS

PHOTOGRAPHS

Chapter One

Opener: © PhotoDisc/People, Lifestyles, and Vacations; **1.1:** © Jeffry W. Myers/Stock Boston; **1.2:** © Bettmann/Corbis; **1.5:** © Jim Amos/Photo Researchers; **1.6:** © Granger Collection; **1.7:** © Michael W. Tweedie/Photo Researchers; **1.9:** © Thomas Nebbia/Woodfin Camp & Associates; **1.10:** © Jake Rajs/Tony Stone Images; **1.11:** © Archives of the History of American Psychology; **1.12:** © Erich Lessing/Art Resource; **1.13:** © Yerkes Regional Primate Research Center, Emory University; **1.14:** © Anderson/ Monkmeyer; **1.16:** © Leo Baeck Institute/Archive Photos; **1.17:** © Archives of the History of American Psychology; **1.18:** © Falk/Monkmeyer; **1.19:** © Courtesy, Albert Bandura; **1.20:** © Steven E. Sutton/Duomo; **1.21(left):** *Walk in the Park,* by James J. Tissot. Musee d'Orsay, Paris/Bridgeman Art Library, London/Superstock; **1.21(right):** © Rob Tringali, Jr./SportsChrome.

Chapter Two

Opener: *Mirror Image* by Lucile Montague. The Grand Design/Superstock; **2.1a:** © Apeiron/ Corbis-Sygma; **2.1b:** © Steve Nickerson/Detroit Free Press; **2.7a:** © Bob Daemmrich/Stock Boston; **2.7b:** © Richard T. Nowitz/Photo Researchers; **2.7c:** © Jeff Greenberg/Photo Edit; **2.8:** © Bettmann/Corbis; **2.9:** © Penelope Breese/Liaison Agency; **2.15:** © Mark Rosenzweig; **2.19:** © Will & Deni McIntyre/Photo Researchers; **2.21:** © Michael Newman/Photo Edit; **2.22(left):** © Lawrence Migdale/Photo Researchers; **2.22(right):** © Will & Deni McIntyre/Photo Researchers; **2.23(left):** © Chuck Nacke/Woodfin Camp & Associates; **2.23(right):** Courtesy, Foundation for Biomedical Research, 2000.

Chapter Three

Opener: © Mehau Kulyk/SPL/Photo Researchers; **3.1:** From: Damasio H., Grabowski, T., Frank R., Galaburda A.M., Damasio A.R.: The return of Phineas Gage: Clues about the brain from the skull of a famous patient. *Science,* 264:1102–1105, 1994. Department of Neurology and Image Analysis Facility, University of Iowa.; **3.11a:** © Larry Mulvehill/Science Source/Photo Researchers; **3.11c:** © Richard T. Nowitz/Corbis; **3.11d:** © Clinique Ste. Catherine/CNRI/SPL/ Photo Researchers; **3.11e:** © Dan McCoy/ Rainbow; **3.11f:** © Mehau Kulyk/SPL/Photo Researchers; **3.12:** © Martin M. Rotker/Science Source/Photo Researchers; **3.13:** © Bill Bachmann/Stock Boston; **3.14b:** An Arthur Leipzig Photo © 1960; **3.21:** Shaywitz, et al., 1995. NMR Research/Yale Medical School; **3.23:** © Boehringer Ingelheim International GmbH, Photo by Lennart Nilsson. From The Body Victorious; **3.29(top):** © Donna Day/Stone; **3.29(bottom):** Margaret Ross/Stock Boston.

Chapter Four

Opener: © Roger Ressmeyer/Corbis; **4.1:** © Wide World Photos; **4.10:** © Matthew McVay/Stone; **4.16:** Fritz Goro, Life Magazine © Time, Inc.; **4.20:** © Culver Pictures; **4.21(both):** Robert E. Preson, courtesy of Prof J.E. Hawkins, Kresge Hearing Research Institute, U of MI; **4.23:** Courtesy, The Department of Veterans Affairs; **4.24b:** Courtesy, Richard A. Normann, Dept. of Bioengineering, University of Utah; **4.27:** © Gavin Smith/FSP/Liaison Agency; **4.29 (left):** © Johnny Crawford/Image Works; **4.29(right):** © AP/Wide World Photos; **4.31:** © Crockett Photography & Design; **4.32:** *Pinto's* by Bev Doolittle @ 1979, The Greenwich Workshop, Inc.; **4.36a:** Copyright © 11/1/1900 by the New York Times Co. Reprinted by permission; **4.37(both):** © Jeffrey Grosscup; **4.38:** © Rob Tringali, Jr./SportsChrome; **4.39:** © 1948 M.C. Escher Foundation/Baarn-Holland, All Rights Reserved.; **4.40:** School of Athens by Raphael. Scala/Art Resource, NY; **4.41:** © Holway & Lobel Globus/Stock Market; **4.43a:** © Baron Wolman/ Woodfin Camp & Associates; **4.46:** © Dawson Jones/Stock Boston; **4.48:** © J.P. Laffont/Corbis-Sygma; **4.51:** © Enrico Ferorelli; **4.52:** © Corbis Digital Stock.

Chapter Five

Opener, 5.1: © Matt Mahurin; **5.2:** Photo by Donna T. Biershwale, courtesy of UL Lafayette Institute of Cognitive Science; **5.3:** © Arthur Tilley/FPG; **5.6(both):** © Tom Ives/Corbis-Sygma; **5.10:** © Robin Thomas; **5.11a:** © Patrick L. Pfister/Medichrome; **5.16(both):** © Louis Psihoyos/Matrix; **5.17:** © The Kobal Collection; **5.25:** © The Granger Collection; **5.26:** © Claudia Andujar/Photo Researchers; **5.27:** © 1997 Newsweek, Inc. All rights reserved. Reprinted by permission; **5.29:** © Bettmann/Corbis; **5.30:** © AP/Wide World Photos; **5.31:** © Bettmann/ Corbis; **5.32a:** Courtesy, News and Publications Service, Stanford University.

Chapter Six

Opener: © Stock South/Michael W. Nelson /PictureQuest; **6.2:** © Wayne R. Bilenduke/ Stone; **6.4a:** © Bettmann/Corbis; **6.10:** Courtesy of Professor Benjamin Harris; **6.11:** © S. Rubin/ Image Works; **6.14:** Nina Leen, Life Magazine © Time, Inc.; **6.16:** © Myrleen Ferguson/Photo Edit; **6.17(all):** Robert W. Kelley, Life Magazine © Time, Inc.; **6.18:** © Gerald Davis/Woodfin Camp & Associates; **6.20:** © George Mars Cassidy/Index Stock Imagery; **6.23:** © Nubar Alexanian/Woodfin Camp & Associates; **6.24:** © Gary Payne/Liaison Agency; **6.27(both):** © Lincoln P. Brower; **6.28:** © Monte S. Buchsbaum, M.D., Mt. Sinai School of Medicine, New York, NY; **6.29(all):** © Superstock; **6.33,6.34(both):** Courtesy, Albert Bandura, Stanford University.

Chapter Seven

Opener: © Bob Krist/Corbis; **7.4:** © Pauline Cutler/Stone; **7.14:** © PhotoFest; **7.15:** © Bettmann/Corbis; **7.19(both):** Intraub, H., Gottesman, C.V., Willey, E. V., & Zuk, I.J. (1996). Boundary extension for briefly glimpsed pictures: Do common perceptual processes result in unexpected memory distortions? *Journal of Memory and Language,* 35, 118-134; **7.20(both):** © Bettmann/Corbis; **7.21:** © Shahn-Kermani/Liaison Agency; **7.23:** Courtesy, Dr. John Gabrielli.

Chapter Eight

Opener: © Tom Wurl/Stock Boston; **8.1:** © James Cachero/Corbis-Sygma; **8.5(all):** © Corbis Digital Stock; **8.7a:** © Enrico Ferorelli; **8.13a:** © AP/Wide World Photos; **8.13b:** © Douglas Levere; **8.20:** © Lew Merrim/Monkmeyer; **8.25(left, center):** © AP/Wide World Photos; **8.25(right):** © Spencer Grant/Photo Edit.

Chapter Nine

Opener: © I.D. Gordon/Image Bank; **9.1:** © AP/ Wide World Photos; **9.5b:** Courtesy, Neal E. Miller; **9.6a:** © Museo del Prado, Madrid/ Superstock; **9.6b:** © The Granger Collection; **9.6c:** © AP/Wide World Photos; **9.8:** © David Austen/Woodfin Camp & Associates; **9.11(both):** © William Thompson/Index Stock Imagery; **9.12(top):** Harlow Primate Laboratory, University of Wisconsin; **9.12(bottom):** © James Lozeau/Outside Images/PictureQuest; **9.13:** © Bettmann/Corbis; **9.18:** © Donna Day/Stone; **9.19(top):** © Richard Lord/Photo Edit; **9.19(bottom):** © Sid Bahrt/Photo Researchers; **9.22:** © Donald Dutton, PhD; **9.23:** © Andrew Brusso; **9.24:** © Irvington Publishers; **9.25(both):** © Andrew Brusso; **9.26:** © Charles Gupton/ Stock Boston.

Chapter Ten

Opener: © Vincent DeWitt/Stock Boston; **10.1(both):** © J.O. Atlanta/Liaison Agency; **10.2:** © Robert Van Der Hilgt/Stone; **10.4:** © Bob Daemmrich/Stock Boston; **10.8a:** © Michael L. Abramson/Woodfin Camp & Associates; **10.9:** © Archive Photos; **10.10:** P. Ekman and W.V. Friesen, "Pictures of Facial Affect." Consulting Psychologists Press, Palo Alto, CA. 1976; **10.14(both):** © Tony Freeman/Photo Edit; **10.19(left):** © Cindy Andrews/Liaison Agency; **10.19(right):** © Ron Sherman/Stock Boston/PictureQuest; **10.22:** © Oscar Burriel/

Latin Stock/SPL/Photo Researchers; **10.23:** © Judith Calson/The Sacramento Bee/Corbis-Sygma; **10.26:** © Felix Man/Liaison Agency.

Chapter Eleven

Opener: © Richard Hutchings/Photo Researchers; **11.1:** © The British Library; **11.3a:** © David M. Phillips/The Population Council/Photo Researchers; **11.3b:** © Biophoto Associates/ Photo Researchers; **11.3c:** © John Watney Photo Library/Photo Researchers; **11.4a:** © CNRI/SPL/Photo Researchers; **11.5a:** Streissguth, A.P., Landesman-Dwyer, S., Martin, J.C., & Smith D.W. (1980) Teratogenic effects of alcohol in humans and laboratory animals. *Science* 209 (18): 353–361.; **11.5b:** Streissguth A.P., & Little, R.E. (1994). "Unit 5: Alcohol, Pregnancy, and the Fetal Alcohol Syndrome: Second Edition" of the Project Cork Insitute Medical School Curriculum ("slide lecture series") on Biomedical Education: Alcohol Use and Its Medical Consequences, produced by Dartmouth Medical School; **11.6(all):** © Courtesy, Dr. Charles A. Nelson; **11.8a:** © Michael Siluk; **11.8b:** © Dr. Melanie Spence, University of Texas, Dallas; **11.9:** © Enrico Ferorelli; **11.13:** © Steven Raymer/National Geographic Image Collection; **11.14(both):** © Goodman/Monkmeyer; **11.16(both):** Rheta De Vries. (May 1969) Constancy of genetic identity in the years three to six. *Monographs of the Society for Research in Child Development,* Vol. 34, no. 127, Fig. 1-2, p. 8. © Society for Research in Child Development, Inc.; **11.15(all):** © Tony Freeman/Photo Edit; **11.22a:** © Nina Leen/Time Life Syndication; **11.22b:** © Myrleen Ferguson/Photo Edit; **11.23, 11.25:** Harlow Primate Laboratory, University of Wisconsin; **11.28a:** © Ian O'Leary/Stone; **11.28b:** © Rosanne Olson/Stone; **11.29:** © Bill Gillette/Stock Boston; **11.30:** © Charles Gupton/Stock Boston; **11.34:** © Figaro Magazine/Liaison Agency; **11.35a:** NASA; **11.35b:** © Gordon Trice; **11.38:** © David Burnett/Stock Boston.

Chapter Twelve

Opener: © Bettmann/Corbis; **12.1:** © John Elk/Stock Boston; **12.2a:** © Joel Gordon; **12.2b:** © R & S Michaud/Woodfin Camp & Associates; **12.7(both), 12.9:** © 1965 by Stanley Milgram. From the film OBEDIENCE, distributed by Penn State, Media Sales.; **12.10:** © AP/Wide World Photos; **12.12:** NASA; **12.15:** © Eastcott/Momatiuk/Image Works; **12.16:** © Adam Woolfitt/Corbis; **12.19:** Kobal Collection; **12.22b:** Courtesy, Dr. Natalie Porter; **12.23:** © Rosanne Olson/Allstock/PictureQuest; **12.24:** © Richard R. Hansen/Photo Researchers; **12.26:** © New York Times Pictures; **12.29a:** Photo Courtesy, National Institutes of Mental Health; **12.29b:** © Bob Daemmrich/Stock Boston/Picturequest; **12.31:** © Seth Resnick/Stock Boston.

Chapter Thirteen

Opener: © PhotoDisc/People, Lifestyles, and Vacations; **13.2:** © Mary Evans Picture Library; **13.4:** © S. Ferry/Liaison Agency; **13.5:** © Paul Chesley/Photographers Aspen/PictureQuest; **13.6:** © Gregg Mancuso/Stock Boston; **13.12a:** © Mary Evans/John Cutten Collection; **13.13(both):** © Michael Nichols/Magnum; **13.16:** © Larry Kolvoord/Image Works; **13.18a:** © Spencer Grant/Stock Boston; **13.24:** © James Shaffer/Photo Edit; **13.26:** © Laura Dwight/Corbis.

Chapter Fourteen

Opener: *Slipsliding* by Judy Castelli: www.multiple-personality.com; **14.1:** © Archive Photos/PictureQuest; **14.2:** © Kevin and Betty Collins/Visuals Unlimited; **14.3:** *Witches' Sabbath: The He-Goat.* 1798 Museo Lazaro Galdiano, Madrid, Spain. Giraudon/Art Resource, NY, 14.7(top): © Bettmann/Corbis; **14.7(bottom):** © Wide World Photos; **14.9:** © AP/Wide World Photos; **14.13:** © Donna Day/Stone; **14.16:** © Alan Oddie/Photo Edit; **14.20:** © The Everett Collection; **14.22:** © Steve Smith; **14.23:** © AP/Wide World Photos; **14.25(all):** © Derek Bayes/LIFE Magazine @Time Inc.; **14.26:** © Grunnitus/Monkmeyer; **14.28(top):** Monte S. Buchsbaum, M.D., Mt. Sinai School of Medicine, New York, NY; **14.28(bottom):** Courtesy, The Genain Quadrulplets; **14.30:** © Bettmann/Corbis; **14.32:** © Labat/Jerrican/Photo Researchers.

Chapter Fifteen

Opener: © Michael Frye/Stone; **15.1:** © Gale Zucker/Stock Boston; **15.3:** © Louie Psihoyos/Matrix; **15.5:** © Courtesy, Natalie Rogers; **15.6:** © Real People Press; **15.8:** © Courtesy, Dr. Albert Ellis; **15.9:** Courtesy, Dr. Aaron T. Beck; **15.10:** © James Wilson/Woodfin Camp & Associates; **15.13:** © David Young-Wolff/Photo Edit./PictureQuest; **15.14:** Courtesy, Hunter Hoffman; photo by Mary Levin, University of Washington; **15.15:** © Rhoda Sidney/Photo Edit; **15.21:** © Michael Newman/Photo Edit; **15.22:** © Will & Deni McIntyre/Photo Researchers; **15.25:** © David Young-Wolff/Photo Edit.

Chapter Sixteen

Opener: © David Young-Wolf/Photo Edit; **16.3:** © Christopher Brown/Stock Boston; **16.4:** © Steve Lenard/Black Star/PictureQuest; **16.7:** © David Ximeno Tejada/Stone; **16.13:** © Bruce Ayres/Stone; **16.18:** © Gregg Mancuso/Stock Boston/PictureQuest; **16.19:** © Dan McCoy/ Rainbow/PictureQuest; **16.21:** © Ron Chapple/ FPG; **16.23:** © Bettmann/Corbis; **16.24:** © Dennis Brack/Black Star/PictureQuest.

LINE ART

Chapter Two

2.2: THE FARSIDE © 1984 FARWORKS, INC. Used by permission. All rights Reserved; **2.4:** The Unresponsive Bystander, by Latane/Darley, © 1970. Reprinted by permission of Prentice-Hall, Inc., Upper Saddle River, NJ; **2.5:** © 2000 by Sidney Harris; **2.18:** © 2000 by Sidney Harris; **2.20:** © 2000 by Sidney Harris.

Chapter Four

4.15: The above/below has been reproduced from Ishihara's Tests for Colour Deficiency published by KANEHARA & CO., LTD., located at Tokyo in Japan. But tests for color deficiency cannot be conducted with this material. For accurate testing, the original plates should be used.

Chapter Five

5.7: Based on data from J.P. Guthrie, R.A. Ash, and V. Bendapudi (1995). "Additional Validity Evidence for a Measure of Morningness," *Journal of Applied Psychology,* 80, 186-190; **5.9:** From Introduction to the Problems of Shift Work," by K. Kogi. In Hours of Work by Folkard & Monk (eds.). Copyright 1985: John Wiley & Sons. Reproduced by permission of John Wiley & Sons Limited; **5.14:** H.P. Roffwarg, J.N. Muzio, and W.C. Dement (1966). Figure adapted from an updated revision of a figure in "Ontogentic development of human sleep-dream cycle," *Science,* 152, 1966, pp. 604–609. Copyright 1966 American Association for the advancement of Science; **5.15:** Data from H.W. Agnew Jr., W.B. Webb, and R.L. Williams, 1967, Comparison of stage four and 1-REM sleep deprivation. *Perceptual and Motor Skills, 24,* 851–858; **5.18:** Figure from "Eyelid Movements and Mental Activity at Sleep Onset," by Jason T. Rowley, Robert Stickgold, and J. Allan Hobson, in Consciousness and Cognition, Volume 7, 64–68, copyright © 1988 by Academic Press, reproduced by permission of the publisher; **5.24:** From T. McDonald, G.T. Fong, M.P. Zanna, & A. Martineau, 1995, "Decision Making in Altered States," Journal of Personality and Social Psychology, Vol. 68, No. 6, Figure 1, p. 979. Copyright by the American Psychological Association. Reprinted with permission.

Chapter Six

6.3: THE FARSIDE © 1984 FARWORKS, Used by permission. All rights Reserved; **6.31:** Reprinted with permission of Jester Columbia.

Chapter Seven

7.1: Adapted from J. Pinel, *Biopsychology,* 1997, Allyn & Bacon. **7.2:** From F.C. Bartlett, Remembering: A Study in Experimental and Social Psychology, 1932. Reprinted with the permission of Cambridge University Press; **7.7:** © The New Yorker Collection 1983 Ed Fisher from cartoonbank.com. All Rights Reserved; **7.9a:** Figure from "Hierarchical Retrieval Schemes in Recall of Categorized Word Lists" by G.H. Bower, M.C. Clark, M.A. Lesgold, and D. Winzenz, in Journal of Verbal Learning and Verbal Behavior, Volume 8, 323–343, copyright © 1969 by Academic Press, reproduced by permission of the publisher; **7.9b:** Figure from "Hierarchical Retrieval Schemes in Recall of

Categorized Word Lists" by G.H. Bower, M.C. Clark, M.A. Lesgold, and D. Winzenz, in Journal of Verbal Learning and Verbal Behavior, Volume 8, 323–343, copyright © 1969 by Academic Press, reproduced by permission of the publisher; **7.10:** Adapted from American Journal of Psychology. Copyright 1991 by the Board of Trustees of the University of Illinois. Used with the permission of the University of Illinois Press; **7.24:** Reprinted with permission from "Acquisition of a Memory Skill," by K. Anders Ericsson, W.G. Chase, and S. Faloon, Science, Vol. 208, June 6, 1980, Figure 1, p. 1181. Copyright © 1980 American Association for the Advancement of Science; **7.25:** Figure from Bahrick, Hall & Berger, "Accuracy and Distortion in Memory for High School Grades," Psychological Science, 7. Reprinted with permission of Blackwell Publishers.

Chapter Eight

8.5: Reprinted from Personality and Individual Differences, Vol. 25, Schutte, Malouff, et al., "Development and Validation of a Measure of Emotional Intelligence," p. 167–177. Copyright © 1998, with permission from Elsevier Science; © 2000 by Sidney Harris; © 2000 by Sidney Harris; **8.8b:** From S. Savage-Rumbaugh, et al., Journal of Experimental Psychology, General, 1986, Vol. 115 (3) Figure 1, p. 220. Copyright 1986 by the American Psychological Association. Reprinted with permission; **8.26:** From R.J. Sternberg, 1993, "Intelligence Is More Than IQ: The Practical Side of Intelligence," Journal of Cooperative Education, XXVII(2), 1993, p. 6. **8.29:** From D. Kimura, "Sex Differences in the Brain," Scientific American, 267, (3), 1992, Figure 1. Copyright © 1992 by Jared Schneidman Design; **8.30:** From C.M. Steele, "The Threat in the Air: How Stereotypes Shape Intellectual Identity and Performance," American Psychologist, 52, 1997, p. 613–629. Copyright 1997 by the American Psychological Association. Reprinted with permission.

Chapter Nine

9.10: Adapted from C.T. Halpern, et al., "Effects of Body Fat on Weight Concerns, Dating, and Sexual Activity: A Longitudinal Analysis of Black and White Adolescent Girls," Developmental Psychology, Vol. 35, No. 3, May 1999, Figure 3, p. 731. Copyright © 1999 by the American Psychological Association. Reprinted with permission; **9.15:** From Sex in America by Robert T. Michael, et al. Copyright © 1994 by CSG Enterprises, Inc., Edward O. Laumann, Robert T. Michael, and Gina Kolata. By permission of Little, Brown & Company, Inc; **9.17:** From Sex in America by Robert T. Michael, et al. Copyright © 1994 by CSG Enterprises, Inc., Edward O. Laumann, Robert T. Michael, and Gina Kolata. By permission of Little, Brown & Company, Inc; **9.27:** THE FARSIDE © 1985 FARWORKS, INC. Used by permission. All rights Reserved.

Chapter Ten

10.7: From R.J. Davidson & N.A. Fox, "Frontal Brain Asymmetry Predicts Infants' Response to Maternal Separation," Journal of Abnormal Psychology, 98, 1989, Figure 1, p. 127–131. Copyright © 1989 by the American Psychological Association. Reprinted with permission; **10.16:** From J. Speisman, et al., "Experimental Reducation of Stress Based on Ego-Defense Theory," Journal of Abnormal and Social Psychology, 68, 1964, Figure 1, p. 367–380. Copyright © 1964 by the American Psychological Association. Reprinted with permission; **10.20:** From H. Selye, The Stress of Life, 1978. Reprinted with permission of The McGraw-Hill Companies; **10.24:** From R.S. Baron, et al., "Social Support and Immune Responses Among Spouses of Cancer Patients," Journal of Personality and Social Psychology, 59, 1990, Figure 1, p. 344–352. Copyright © 1990 by the American Psychological Association. Reprinted with permission.

Chapter Eleven

11.12: Reprinted by permission of the publisher from The Postnatal Development of the Human Cerebral Cortex, Vol I–VIII by Jesse LeRoy Conel, Cambridge, Mass.: Harvard University Press, Copyright © 1939–1975 by the President and Fellows of Harvard College; **11.18:** From R. Ballargeon, "Object Permanence in 3 1/2- and 4 1/2-Month-Old Infants," Developmental Psychology, 23, p. 655–664. Copyright by the American Psychological Association. Adapted with permission; **11.19:** Figure from "The Development of Scanning Strategies and Their Relation to Visual Differentiations" by E. Vurpillot in Journal of Experimental Child Psychology, Volume 6, 632–650, copyright © 1968 by Academic Press, reproduced by permission of the publisher; **11.20:** Data from R. Kail (1988). "Developmental Functions for Speeds of Cognitive Processes," Journal of Experimental Child Psychology, 45, 339–364. **11.26:** Adapted from Maccoby & Martin, "Socialiation in the Context of the Family: Parent-Child Interaction," in Hetherington (ed.) Handbook of Child Psychology. Copyright © 1983 John Wiley & Sons. Reprinted by permission of John Wiley & Sons, Inc.; **11.27:** CATHY © 1986 Cathy Guisewite. Reprinted with permission of Universal Press Syndicate. All rights reserved; **11.36a:** From K.W. Schaie, "The Course of Adult Intellectual Development," American Psychologist, Vol. 49, No. 4, April 1994, Figure 5, p. 307. Copyright 1994 by the American Psychological Association. Adapted with permission; **11.36b:** From K.W. Schaie, "The Course of Adult Intellectual Development," American Psychologist, Vol. 49, No. 4, April 1994, Figure 6, p. 308. Copyright 1994 by the American Psychological Association. Adapted with permission; **11.37:** From R.R. McCrae and P.T. Costa, Jr., Personality in Adulthood, 1990, Guilford Press. Reprinted with permission.

Chapter Twelve

12.4: © The New Yorker Collection 1972 J.B. Handelsman from cartoonbank.com. All Rights Reserved; **12.6:** From R.S. Baron, J.A. Vandello, and B. Brunsman, "The Forgotten Variable in Conformity Research: Impact of Task Importance on Social Influence," Journal of Personality and Social Psychology, 72, 1996, Figure 1, p. 915–927. Copyright © 1996 by the American Psychological Association. Adapted with permission; **12.12a:** © The New Yorker Collection 1979 Henry Martin from cartoonbank.com. All Rights Reserved; **12.20:** From J.G. Miller, "Culture and the Development of Everyday Social Explanation," Journal of Personality and Social Psychology, 46, 1984, p. 961–978. Copyright © 1984 by the American Psychological Association. Reprinted with permission.

Chapter Thirteen

13.1: © The New Yorker Collection 1971 Dana Fradon from cartoonbank.com. All Rights Reserved; **13.9:** From S.D. Cousins, "Culture and Self-Perception in the United States and Japan," Journal of Personality and Social Psychology, 56, 1989, Figure 1, p. 124–131. Copyright © 1989 by the American Psychological Association. Reprinted with permission; **13.12:** From H.J. Eyesenck, The Biological Basis of Personality, Figure 13, 1967. Courtesy of Charles C Thomas, Publisher, Ltd., Springfield, Illinois; **13.14:** From Carver, C.S. & Scheier. M.F., Perspectives on Personality Copyright © 1988 by Allyn & Bacon. Reprinted by permission; **13.21:** From Y. Shoda, et al., "Intra-Individual Stability and Patterning of Behavior: Incorporating Psychological Situations into the Idiographic Analysis of Personality," Journal of Personality and Social Psychology, 65, 1994, figure 1, panels 2 and 3, p. 1023–1035. Copyright © 1994 by the American Psychological Association. Reprinted with permission.

Chapter Fourteen

14.10: From E.B. Foa, D.S. Riggs, & B.S. Gershuny, "Arousal, Numbing, and Intrusion: Symptom Structure of Post Traumatic Stress Disorder Following Assault," American Journal of Psychiatry, 152, 116–120. Copyright by the American Psychiatric Association. Reprinted by permission; **14.24:** Adapted from Figure 1, page 36 of F.W. Putnam (1984), "The Psychophysiologic Investigation of Multiple Personality Disorder: A Review," Psychiatric Clinics of North America, 7, pp. 31–39. Reprinted with permission of W.B. Saunders Company; **14.2:** Abstracted from DSM-IV Axis II, American 14.2: Psychiatric Association, 1994.

Chapter Fifteen

15.4: From K.I. Howard, et al., "The Dose-Effect Relationship in Psychotherapy," American Psychologist, 41, 1986, Figure 1, p. 159–164. Copyright © 1986 by the American Psychological Association. Reprinted with permission; **15.12:** From T. Ayllon & N.H. Azrin (1965). "The Measurement and Reinforcement of Behavior of Psychotics," Journal of Experimental Analyais of Behavior, 8, 357–383, figure 2. Copyright © 1965 by the Society for the Experimental Analysis of Behavior, Inc; **15.27:** From E.B. Foa, et al., "Evaluation of a Brief Cognitive-Behavioral Program for the Prevention of Chronic PTSD in Recent Assault

Victims," Journal of Consulting and Clinical Psychology, 63, 1995, Figure 1, p. 948–955. Copyright © 1995 by the American Psychological Association. Reprinted with permission.

Chapter Sixteen

16.5: Jonathan Crane, Social Programs That Work, © 1998 Russell Sage Foundation, New York, New York; **16.6:** Jonathan Crane, Social Programs That Work, © 1998 Russell Sage Foundation, New York, New York; **16.11:** Figure 3, pg. 65 from Changing for Good by James O. Prochaska and John C. Norcross and Carlo C.

Diclemente. Copyright © 1994 by James O. Prochaska, John C. Norcross and Carlo C. Diclemente. Reprinted by permission of Harper Collins Publishers, Inc; **16.12:** Adapted from N.S. Blair, et al., (1989), "Physical Factors and All-Course Mortality: A Prospective Study of Healthy Men and Women," Journal of the American Medical Association, 262, p. 2395–2401; **16.6:** From Marlat & Gordon, Relapse Prevention. Reprinted with permission of Guilford Press; **16.15:** U.S. Public Health Service, 1999; **16.17:** From G.A. Marlatt, et al., "Screening and Brief Intervention for High-Risk College Student Drinkers: Results From a 2-Year Follow-

Up Assessment," Journal of Consulting and Clinical Psychology, 66, 1998, Figure 2, p. 604–614. Copyright © 1998 by the American Psychological Association. Reprinted with permission; **16.5:** From Fawcett, et al., "Changing Community Responses to Wife Abuse: A Research & Demonstration Project in Iztacalco Mexico," American Psychologist, 54, 1999, Figure 2, p. 41–49. Copyright © 1999 by the American Psychological Association. Reprinted with permission; **16.21:** From Rice, American Psycholgist, 1997, Figure 1, p. 415. Copyright © 1997 by the American Psychological Association. Reprinted with permission.

GLOSSARY

◄ A ►

abnormal behavior behavior that is personally distressful, personally dysfunctional, and/or so culturally deviant that other people judge it to be inappropriate or maladaptive

absolute threshold the lowest intensity at which a stimulus can be detected 50 percent of the time

abstinence violation effect a response to a lapse in which a person blames him/herself and concludes that he or she is incapable of resisting high-risk situations

accommodation (cognitive development) the process by which new experiences cause existing schemas to change

accommodation (vision) the process whereby the lens changes shape in order to focus objects at varying distances onto the retina

acetylcholine (ACh) an excitatory neurotransmitter that operates at synapses with muscles and is also the transmitter in some neural networks involved in memory

achievement test a measure of an individual's degree of accomplishment in a particular subject or task based on a relatively standardized set of experiences

action potential a nerve impulse resulting from the depolarization of an axon's cell membrane

action potential threshold the intensity of stimulation (excitatory minus inhibitory) needed to produce an action potential

activation-synthesis theory the theory that dreams represent the brain's attempt to interpret random patterns of neural activation triggered by the brain stem during REM sleep

adaptive significance the manner in which a particular behavior enhances an organism's chances of survival and reproduction

adolescent egocentrism highly self-focused thinking, particularly in the earlier teenage years

adoption studies a research method in behavior genetics in which adopted people are compared on some characteristic with both their biological and adoptive parents in an attempt to determine how strong a genetic component the characteristic might have

adrenal glands endocrine glands that release stress hormones, including epinephrine and norepinephrine

aerobic exercise sustained activity that elevates the heart rate and body's need for oxygen

affect an alternate term for feelings and emotions

agoraphobia a phobia centered around open spaces and public places

alcohol myopia when intoxicated, a "shortsightedness" in thinking (a failure to consider consequences) caused by an inability to pay attention to as much information as when sober

algorithm procedures, such as mathematical formulas, that automatically generate correct solutions to problems

all-or-none law the fact that an action potential is not proportional to the intensity of stimulation; a neuron either fires with maximum intensity or it does not fire (compare with graded potential)

alpha waves a brain-wave pattern of 8 to 12 cycles per second that is characteristic of humans in a relaxed waking state

amphetamine psychosis schizophrenia-like hallucinations and delusions that occur when the brain's dopamine activity is artificially increased far beyond normal levels by continuous, heavy amphetamine use

amplitude the vertical size of the sound wave, which gives rise to perception of loudness and is measured in terms of decibels

amygdala a limbic system structure that helps organize emotional response patterns

analytic psychology Jung's expansion of Freud's notion of the unconscious; Jung believed that humans possess not only a personal unconscious based on their life experiences, but also a collective unconscious that consists of memories accumulated throughout the entire history of the human race

androgens so called "male" sex hormones

anorexia nervosa an eating disorder involving a severe and sometimes fatal restriction of food intake

anterograde amnesia memory loss for events that occur after the initial onset of amnesia

anticipatory nausea and vomiting (ANV) classically conditioned nausea and vomiting that occur when cancer patients are exposed to stimuli associated with their treatment

antigens literally, antibody generators, or foreign substances that activate the cells of the immune system

anxiety an emotional state characterized by apprehension accompanied by physiological arousal and fearful behavior

anxiety disorders a group of behavior disorders in which anxiety and associated maladaptive behaviors are the core of the disturbance

aphasia the loss of ability to understand speech (receptive aphasia) or to produce it (productive aphasia)

applied behavior analysis a process (also called "behavior modification") in which operant conditioning is combined with scientific data collection to solve individual and societal problems

applied research research involving the application of scientific knowledge to solve practical problems

approach-approach conflict a conflict in which an individual is simultaneously attracted to two incompatible positive goals

approach-avoidance conflict a conflict in which an individual is simultaneously attracted to and repelled by the same goal

aptitude test a measure of a person's ability to profit from further training or experience in an occupation or skill; usually based on a measure of skills gained over a person's lifetime rather than during a specific course of study

archetypes innate concepts and memories (e.g., God, the hero; the good mother); memories that reside in the collective unconscious (Jung)

archival measures records or documents that already exist and which contain information about some type of behavior

artificial intelligence the field within cognitive science that attempts to develop computer simulations of human mental processes

assimilation in cognitive development, the process by which new experiences are incorporated into existing schemas

association cortex the areas of the cerebral cortex that do not have sensory or motor functions but are involved in the integration of neural activity that underlies perception, language, and other higher-order mental processes

associative network the view that long-term memory is organized as a massive network of associated ideas and concepts

attachment the strong emotional bond that develops between children and their primary caregivers

attitude a positive or negative evaluative reaction toward a stimulus (e.g., toward a person, action, object, or concept)

attributions judgments about the causes of our own and other people's behavior and outcomes

authoritarian parents caregivers who exert control over their children, but do so within a cold, unresponsive, or rejecting relationship

authoritative parents caregivers who are controlling but warm; they establish and enforce clear rules within a caring, supportive atmosphere

autoimmune reactions immune disorders in which the immune system mistakenly identifies part of the body as an antigen and attacks it

automatic processing mental activities that occur automatically and require minimal or no conscious control or awareness

autonomic nervous system the branch of the peripheral nervous system that stimulates the body's involuntary muscles (e.g., heart) and internal organs

autonomic response stereotypy individual differences in patterns of physiological responses to emotion-arousing stimuli

availability heuristic a rule of thumb used to make likelihood judgments based on how easily examples of that category of events come to mind, or are "available" in memory

aversion therapy a CS, that currently evokes a positive but maladaptive response, is paired with a noxious, unpleasant UCS, in an attempt to condition a repulsion toward the CS

aversive punishment occurs when a response is weakened by the subsequent presentation of a (noxious) stimulus

avoidance-avoidance conflict a conflict in which an individual must choose between two alternatives, both of which she or he wishes to avoid

avoidance conditioning through conditioning, an organism learns to perform a response to avoid an undesirable consequence

axon an extension from one side of the neuron cell body that conducts nerve impulses to other neurons, muscles, or glands

◀ B ▶

baseline data measures of behavior that are gathered before an intervention program is implemented; these provide a standard against which to judge the outcome of a program

basic research research designed to obtain knowledge for its own sake

basilar membrane a membrane that runs the length of the cochlea and contains the organ of Corti and its sound receptor hair cells

behavior genetics the scientific study of the role of genetic inheritance in behavior

behavior modification therapeutic procedures based on operant conditioning principles, such as positive reinforcement, operant extinction, and punishment

behavioral assessment psychologists devise an explicit coding system that contains the behavioral categories of interest

behavioral coping responses behavioral attempts to cope with the demands of a situation

behavioral marital therapy a cognitive-behavioral approach to helping married couples improve their relationships by learning communication skills, negotiating behavioral contracts, and developing acceptance of unchangeable aspects of the spouse or relationship

behavioral perspective a view that emphasizes the manner in which the environment and the learning experiences it provides shape and control behavior

behavioral signatures consistent ways of responding in particular classes of situations

behaviorism a school of psychology that emphasizes the role of learning and environmental control over behavior and maintains that the proper subject matter of psychology is observable behavior; John Watson and B. F. Skinner were major figures in behaviorism

belief bias the tendency to abandon logical rules and to form a conclusion based on one's existing beliefs

beta waves a brain-wave pattern of 15 to 30 cycles per second that is characteristic of humans who are in an alert waking state

Big Five personality factors the five personality factors of Openness, Conscientious, Extraversion, Agreeableness, and Neuroticism (OCEAN) that are thought by Five Factor theorists to be the five basic and universal dimensions of personality

binocular depth cues depth cues that require the use of both eyes

binocular disparity the binocular depth cues produced by the projection of slightly different images of an object on the retinas of the two eyes

biological perspective a perspective that focuses on the role of biological factors in behavior, including biochemical and brain processes as well as genetic and evolutionary factors

biological preparedness the notion that evolutionary factors have produced an innate readiness to learn certain associations that have had survival implications in the past

bipolar cells the second layer of retinal cells with which the rods and cones synapse

bipolar disorder a mood disorder in which intermittent mania appears against a background of depression

blindsight a condition in which patients with damage to the visual cortex are able to respond adaptively to stimuli while maintaining that they cannot see them

blood-brain barrier specialized lining of cells in the brain's blood vessels that screen out foreign substances while letting nutrients pass through to neurons

bottom-up processing perceptual processes that begin with the analysis of individual elements of the stimulus and work up to the brain's integration of them into a unified perception

brain stem the portion of the brain formed by the swelling of the spinal cord as it enters the skull; its structures regulate basic survival functions of the body, such as heart rate and respiration

British empiricism a 17th-century school of philosophy championed by John Locke, according to which all the contents of the mind are gained experientially through the senses; this notion was later a cornerstone for the behaviorists' position that we are shaped through our experiences

Broca's area a region of the left frontal lobe involved in speech production

bulimia nervosa an eating disorder that involves a repeated cycle of binge eating followed by purging of the food

bystander effect the principle that the presence of multiple bystanders inhibits each person's tendency to help, largely due to social comparison or diffusion of responsibility

◄ C ►

cannaboids natural pain-killing substances in the body that resemble THC, the analgesic agent in marijuana

case study an in-depth analysis of an individual group, or event

catatonic type a schizophrenic reaction characterized by alternating stuporous states and agitated excitement during which the person can be quite dangerous

catharsis the idea that performing an act of aggression discharges aggressive energy and temporarily reduces our impulse to aggress

CCK (cholecystokinin) a peptide that appears to decrease eating and thereby helps regulate food intake

central nervous system that portion of the nervous system that includes the brain and the spinal cord

central route to persuasion occurs when people think carefully about a message and are influenced because they find the arguments compelling

cephalocaudal principle the tendency for physical development to proceed in a head-to-foot direction

cerebellum a convoluted hindbrain structure involved in motor coordination and some aspects of learning and memory

cerebral cortex the gray, convoluted outer covering of the brain that is the seat of higher-order sensory, motor, perceptual, and mental processes

chaining an operant conditioning procedure used to develop a sequence (chain) of responses by reinforcing each response with the opportunity to perform the next response

chromosomes tightly coiled strands of deoxyribonucleic acid (DNA) and protein that contain the genes

chunking combining individual items into larger units of meaning

circadian rhythms biological cycles within the body that occur on an approximately 24-hour cycle

classical conditioning a procedure in which a formerly neutral stimulus (the conditioned stimulus) comes to elicit a conditioned response by virtue of being paired with an unconditioned stimulus that naturally elicits a similar response (the unconditioned response)

cochlea a small coil-shaped structure of the inner ear that contains the receptors for sound

cognitive-affective personality system (CAPS) the five person variables that account for how a given person might respond to a particular situation are organized into this system; the dynamic interplay among these five factors, together with the characteristics of the situation, account for individual differences between people as well as differences in people's behavior across different situations

cognitive appraisal the process of making judgments about situations, personal capabilities, likely consequences, and personal meaning of consequences

cognitive-arousal model of love the view that passionate love has interacting cognitive and physiological components

cognitive behaviorism a behavioral approach that incorporates cognitive concepts, suggesting that the environment influences our behavior by affecting our thoughts and giving us information; these cognitive processes allow us to control our behavior and the environment

cognitive distortions persistent, automatic modes of illogical thinking that tend to evoke depression, anxiety and other negative emotions

cognitive map a mental representation of the spatial layout of an area

cognitive perspective a psychological perspective that views humans as rational information processors and problem solvers and focuses on the mental processes that influence behavior

cognitive-process dream theory a theory that focuses on "how" (rather than "why") we dream, and proposes that dreaming and waking thought are produced by the same mental systems in the brain

cognitive process theories approaches to intelligence that analyze the mental processes that underlie intelligent thinking

cognitive restructuring a cognitive stress-reduction approach that involves attempts to detect, dispute, and change maladaptive or irrational ideas that trigger negative emotions

collective unconscious Jung's notion of an unconscious that consists of ancestral memories that are innate

collectivism a cultural factor that emphasizes the achievement of group rather than individual goals and in which personal identity is largely defined by ties to the larger social group (see individualism)

common factors therapeutic elements that are possessed by virtually any type of therapy and which may contribute to the similar positive effects shown by many different treatment approaches

communicator credibility the degree to which an audience views a communicator as believable, largely based on the communicator's expertise and trustworthiness

comorbidity the tendency for more than one disorder, such as a mood and an anxiety disorder, to occur together in a given individual

companionate love an affectionate relationship characterized by commitment and caring about the partner's well-being; sometimes contrasted with passionate love, which is more intensely emotional

compensatory response a bodily response that opposes a drug's effects and occurs in an attempt to restore homeostasis

competency a legal decision that a defendant is mentally capable of understanding the nature of the charges, participating meaningfully in the trial, and consulting with his or her attorney

competency-focused intervention prevention programs that are designed to enhance personal resources needed to cope with situations that might otherwise cause psychological disorders

compulsion a repetitive act that the person feels compelled to carry out, often in response to an obsessive thought or image

computerized axial tomography (CT) scan a method of scanning the brain with narrow beams of x rays that are then analyzed and combined by a computer to provide pictures of brain structures from many different angles

concept mental categories containing similiar objects, people, and events

concordance the likelihood that two people share a particular characteristic

concrete operational stage in Piaget's theory, a stage of cognitive development during which children can perform basic mental operations concerning problems that involve tangible (i.e., "concrete") objects and situations

conditioned response (CR) in classical conditioning, a response to a conditioned stimulus; the CR is established by pairing a conditioned stimulus with an unconditioned stimulus that evokes a similar response

conditioned stimulus (CS) a neutral stimulus that comes to evoke a conditioned response after being paired with an unconditioned stimulus

conditioned taste aversion a learned repulsion to a food that formerly was neutral or desired, by virtue of pairing the food with an aversive UCS (e.g., nausea, stomach illness)

conditions of worth internalized standards for self-worth fostered by conditional positive regard from others

conduction deafness hearing loss caused by damage to the mechanical system that conducts sound waves to the cochlea

cones photoreceptors in the retina that function best in bright light and are differentially sensitive to red, green, or blue wavelengths; the retina's color receptors

confirmation bias the tendency to seek and favor information that reinforces our beliefs rather than to be open to disconfirming information

confounding of variables in experiments, a situation in which the independent variable is intertwined or mixed up with another, uncontrolled variable; thus, we cannot tell which variable is responsible for changes in the behavior of interest (i.e., in the dependent variable)

congruence consistency between self-perceptions and experience

consciousness our moment-to-moment awareness of ourselves and our environment; consciousness involves selective attention to ongoing thoughts, perceptions, and feelings

conservation the principle that basic properties of objects, such as their mass or quantity, stay the same (are "conserved") even though their outward appearance may change

construct validity the extent to which a test measures the psychological construct (e.g., intelligence, anxiety) that it is purported to measure

contact hypothesis Allport's hypothesis that increasing contact between hostile groups can result in positive attitudinal changes

content validity the extent to which test items adequately sample the domain that the test is supposed to measure (e.g., intelligence, mathematical reasoning)

context-dependent memory the phenomenon that it is typically easier to remember something in the same environment in which it was originally learned or experienced

continuous reinforcement schedule a reinforcement schedule in which each correct response is followed by reinforcement

control group in an experiment, the group that is not exposed to the treatment, or which receives a zero level of the independent variable

controlled (effortful) processing mental processing that requires some degree of volitional control and attentiveness

conventional moral reasoning moral judgments that are based on conformity to social expectations, laws, and duties

convergent thinking a form of creative thinking in which the problem is solved by eliminating alternative solutions to converge on the correct one

conversion disorder disorder in which serious neurological symptoms, such as paralysis, loss of sensation, or blindness suddenly occur

cooperative learning programs educational programs that place children of different ethnic groups in a setting in which they need to cooperate and teach one another if the group is to succeed

coping self-efficacy beliefs relating to our ability to deal effectively with a stressful stimulus or situation, including pain

corpus callosum a broad band of white, myelinated fibers that connect the left and right cerebral hemispheres and allow the two hemispheres to communicate with one another

correlation coefficient a statistic that indicates the direction and strength of a relation between two variables; values can range from -1.00 to $+1.00$

correlational research research that measures two or more naturally occurring variables, and examines whether they are statistically related

counterbalancing a procedure used when participants in an experiment are exposed to all the conditions; the order of conditions is varied so that no condition has an advantage relative to the others

counterconditioning the process of conditioning an incompatible response to a particular stimulus to eliminate a maladaptive response (e.g., anxiety), as occurs in systematic desensitization

critical periods limited time periods during which plasticity can occur as a result of experience or in response to injury; in development, a time period in which exposure to particular kinds of stimulation is required for normal growth to occur

cross-sectional design a research design that simultaneously compares people of different ages at a particular point in time

crystallized intelligence intellectual abilities that depend on a store of information and the acquisition of particular skills; compare to fluid intelligence

cultural competence a set of therapeutic skills, including scientific mindedness, the ability to consider both cultural and individual factors, and the capacity to introduce culture-specific elements into therapy with people from minority cultures

culture the enduring values, beliefs, behaviors, and traditions that are shared by a large group of people and passed from one generation to the next

culture-bound disorders behavior disorders whose specific forms are restricted to one particular cultural context

◄ D ►

dark adaptation the progressive increase in brightness sensitivity that occurs over time as photopigments regenerate themselves during exposure to low levels of illumination

decay theory the theory that with time and disuse the physical memory trace in the nervous system fades away

deception a procedure in which participants are misled about the purpose or nature of a study

decibel a logarithmic measure of sound intensity

decision criterion in signal detection theory, the potentially changing standard of how certain a person must be that a stimulus is present in order to report its presence

declarative memory our memory for factual knowledge, which is comprised of two subcategories: knowledge pertaining to personal experiences (episodic memory) and knowledge of general facts and language (semantic memory)

deductive reasoning reasoning from a general principle to a specific case

deep structure a linguistic term that refers to the underlying meaning of a spoken or written sentence; the meanings that make up deep structure are stored as concepts and rules in long-term memory

defense mechanisms unconscious processes by which the ego prevents the expression of anxiety-arousing impulses or allows them to appear in disguised forms

deindividuation a state of increased anonymity in which a person, often as part of a group or crowd, engages in disinhibited behavior

deinstitutionalization the attempt to move the primary locus of treatment from mental hospitals to the community

delay of gratification the ability to forego immediate rewards for delayed but more satisfying outcomes

delta waves low-frequency, high-amplitude brain waves that occur in stage 3 sleep and predominate in stage 4 sleep

delusions false beliefs, often involving themes of persecution or grandeur, that are sustained in the face of evidence that normally would be sufficient to destroy them

demand characteristics cues used by research participants to guess the purpose or hypothesis of a study, thereby causing them to alter their behavior

dendrites small branching fibers that extend from the soma of a neuron and receive messages from adjacent neurons

dependent variable in an experiment, the factor that is measured by the researcher and which presumably is influenced by the independent variable

depolarization the reversal of the resting potential of a neuron's cell membrane that produces the action potential

depressants drugs—including alcohol, barbiturates, and tranquilizers—that reduce neural activity and can decrease feelings of tension and anxiety

depressive attributional pattern the tendency of depressed people to attribute negative outcomes to their own inadequacies and positive ones to factors outside of themselves

descriptive research research in which the main goal is to carefully describe how organisms behave, particularly in natural settings

deterioration effect the tendency of some clients to deteriorate rather than improve as a result of therapy

difference threshold the smallest difference between two similar stimuli that people can detect; also termed the just noticeable difference (jnd)

discrimination (classical conditioning) the occurrence of a CR to one stimulus, but not to another stimulus

discrimination (operant conditioning) the ability to respond differentially to stimuli that signal particular consequences

discriminative stimulus an antecedent stimulus that signals the likelihood of certain consequences if a response is made

disorganized type a schizophrenic disorder marked by verbal incoherence, disordered thought processes, disorganized behavior, and inappropriate emotional responses

displacement the capacity of language to represent objects and conditions that are not physically present

display rules culturally influenced standards for the circumstances and manner in which specific emotions are expressed

dissociation theories (of hypnosis) the view that hypnosis is an altered state involving a division ("dissociation") of consciousness; one theory proposes that the hypnotized person simultaneously experiences two streams of consciousness that are cut off from one another

dissociative disorders disorders which involve a major dissociation of personal identity or memory

dissociative identity disorder (DID) a dissociative disorder in which two or more separate identities or personalities coexist within an individual

divergent thinking a creative form of thinking that involves the generating of novel ideas that diverge from the normal ways of thinking about something

divided attention the ability to perform more than one activity at the same time

dominant gene a gene that will produce a particular characteristic when it is present

door-in-the-face technique a manipulation technique in which a persuader makes a large request, expecting you to reject it, and then presents a smaller request

dopamine an excitatory neurotransmitter whose overactivity may underlie some of the disordered behaviors seen in schizophrenia

dopamine hypothesis states that the symptoms of schizophrenia are produced by overactivity of the dopamine system in areas of the brain that regulate emotional expression, motivated behavior, and cognitive functioning

double-blind procedure a procedure in which both the participant and the experimenter are kept unaware of the research condition to which the participant has been assigned

downward comparison the act of comparing oneself or one's situation with less positive alternatives

drive theory the theory that physiological disruptions to homeostasis produce states of internal tension (called drives) that motivate an organism to behave in ways that reduce this tension

dual coding theory the theory that if we encode information using both verbal and imagery codes, the chances improve that at least one of the two codes will be available later to support recall

dual-process theory the modern color vision theory that posits cones that are sensitive red, blue, and green in the cones and opponent processes at the level of ganglion cells and beyond

dysthymia a depressive mood disorder of moderate intensity that occurs over a long period of time but does not disrupt functioning as a major depression does

◄ E ►

eclectic an approach to therapy that incorporates principles and procedures from multiple therapies to provide the most suitable therapy to a client

effect size in meta-analysis, a measure of treatment effectiveness that indicates what percentage of treated clients improve more than the average untreated client

effect size statistic represents a common measure of treatment effectiveness

effectiveness Seligman's term for the outcomes achieved by therapies in real-life uncontrolled therapy settings

efficacy the extent to which therapy can be shown to achieve positive outcomes in controlled outcome studies

ego the "executive" of the personality that is partly conscious and that mediates between the impulses of the id, the prohibitions of the superego, and the dictates of reality

egocentrism difficulty in viewing the world from someone else's perspective

elaborative rehearsal focusing on the meaning of information or relating it to other things we already know

Electra complex the female version of the Oedipus complex where the girl child experiences erotic feelings toward her father, desires to possess him sexually, and views her mother as a rival

electroconvulsive therapy (ECT) a biomedical technique involving the application of electrical current to the brain that is used primarily to reduce severe depression

electroencephalograph (EEG) a device used to record the simultaneous activity of many thousands of neurons through electrodes attached to the scalp

embryo scientific term for the prenatal organism during the 2nd week through the 8th week after conception

emotion a pattern of cognitive, physiological, and behavioral responses to situations and events that have relevance to important goals or motives

emotion-focused coping coping strategies directed at minimizing or reducing emotional responses to a stressor

emotional intelligence ability to respond adaptively in the emotional realm by reading and responding appropriately to others' emotions, to be aware of one's own emotions and have the ability to control them, and to delay gratification

empathy the capacity for experiencing the same emotional response being exhibited by another person; in therapy, the ability of a therapist to view the world through the clients' eyes and to understand the client's emotions

empathy-altruism hypothesis the theory that pure altruism does exist, and that it is produced by empathy

empirical approach an approach to test construction in which items (regardless of their content) are chosen that differentiate between two groups that are known to differ on a particular personality variable

encoding getting information into the memory system by translating it into a neural code that the brain processes and stores

encoding specificity principle states that memory is enhanced when conditions present during retrieval match those that were present during encoding

endocrine system the body's system of glands that secrete hormones into the bloodstream and thereby affect many bodily functions

endorphins natural opiate-like substances that are involved in pain reduction

episodic memory our store of factual knowledge concerning personal experiences—when, where, and what happened in the *episodes* of our lives

escape conditioning a form of learning in which the organism learns to perform a behavior to escape from an aversive stimulus

estrogens so called "female" sex hormones

evolutionary/circadian sleep models the view that in the course of evolution each species developed an adaptive circadian sleep-wake pattern that increased its chances of survival in relation to its environmental demands

evolutionary personality theory a recently developed attempt to account for personality traits such as the Big Five in terms of the evolutionary history of the human species; these traits are thought to develop from processes of natural selection

evolutionary psychology a field of study that focuses on the role of evolutionary processes (especially natural selection) in the development of adaptive psychological mechanisms and social behavior in humans

expectancy × value theory a cognitive theory that goal-directed behavior is jointly influenced by (1) the person's expectancy that a particular behavior will contribute to reaching the goal and (2) how positively or negatively the person values the goal

experiment a research method in which the researcher manipulates an independent variable under controlled conditions and measures whether this produces changes in a dependent variable

experimental group in an experiment, the group that receives a treatment or is exposed to an active level of the independent variable

experimenter expectancy effects subtle and unintentional ways in which an experimenter influences participants to behave in a way that will confirm the experimenter's hypothesis

explicit memory conscious or intentional memory retrieval

exposure (therapy) a therapeutic technique designed to extinguish anxiety responses by exposing clients to anxiety-arousing stimuli or situations while preventing escape or avoidance through response prevention

expressed emotion a family interaction pattern involving criticism, hostility, and overinvolvement, that is associated with relapse when formerly hospitalized schizophrenic patients return home

expressive behaviors observable behavioral indications of subjectively experienced emotions

external validity the degree to which the results of a study can be generalized to other people, settings, and conditions

extinction (classical conditioning) a CS is presented without the UCS, causing the CR to weaken and eventually stop occurring

extinction (operant conditioning) occurs when the absence of reinforcement for a previously reinforced response causes that response to weaken and eventually stop

extrinsic motivation motivation to perform a behavior to obtain external rewards and reinforcers, such as money, status, attention, and praise

◄ F ►

facial feedback hypothesis the notion that somatic feedback from facial muscles provides feedback to the brain and influences emotional experience

factor analysis a statistical technique that permits a researcher to reduce a large number of measures to a small number of clusters or factors; it identifies the clusters of behavior or test scores that are highly correlated with one another

fantasy-prone personality the tendency of some people to spend much of their waking time living in a vivid, rich fantasy world that they control

feature detectors sensory neurons that respond to particular features of a stimulus, such as its shape, angle, or color

fetal alcohol syndrome (FAS) a severe group of abnormalities that results from prenatal exposure to alcohol

fetus the scientific term for the prenatal organism from the 9th week after conception until birth

figure-ground relations perceptual organization in which a focal stimulus is perceived as a figure against a background of other stimuli

fixation a state of arrested development due to unresolved conflicts at a particular earlier psychosexual stage

fixed action pattern an unlearned response that is automatically triggered by a simple (releaser) stimulus

fixed-interval (FI) schedule a reinforcement schedule in which the first correct response occurring after a constant time interval is reinforced

fixed-ratio schedule a reinforcement schedule in which reinforcement is given after a constant number of correct responses

flashbulb memories recollections that seem so vivid and clear that we can picture them as if they were a "snapshot" of a moment in time

fluid intelligence the ability to deal with novel problem-solving situations for which personal experience does not supply a solution; compare with crystallized intelligence

foot-in-the-door technique a manipulation technique in which the persuader gets you to comply with a small request first, and later presents a larger request

forebrain brain structures above the midbrain, including the thalamus, hypothalamus, limbic system, and the cerebral hemispheres; involved in higher-order sensory, motor, and cognitive functions

formal operational stage in Piaget's theory, a period in which individuals are able to think logically and systematically about both concrete and abstract problems, form hypotheses, and test them in a thoughtful way

fovea a small area in the center of the retina that contains only cones and where visual acuity is greatest

free association in psychoanalysis, the procedure of verbalizing all thoughts that enter consciousness without censorship

frequency in audition, the number of cycles per second in a sound wave that is responsible for the pitch of the sound; the measure of frequency is the hertz (Hz), which equals one cycle per second

frequency theory the theory of pitch perception that holds that the number of nerve impulses sent to the brain by the hair cells of the cochlea corresponds to the frequency of the sound wave; this theory is accurate at low frequencies

frontal lobe the anterior (front) portion of the cerebral hemispheres that includes Broca's speech production area, the motor cortex, and associative cortex involved in planning and problem-solving

frustration-aggression hypothesis the view that (1) frustration inevitably leads to aggression, and (2) all aggression is the result of frustration

fully functioning persons Rogers's term for self-actualized people who are free from unrealistic conditions of worth and who exhibit congruence, spontaneity, creativity, and a desire to develop still further

functional fixedness a phenomenon often found in problem-solving tasks in which the customary use of an object interferes with its use in a novel situation

functionalism an early school of American psychology that focused on the functions of consciousness and behavior in helping organisms adapt to their environment and satisfy their needs

fundamental attribution error a tendency to underestimate the impact of the situation and overestimate the role of personal factors when explaining other people's behavior

fundamental emotional patterns basic emotional response patterns that are believed to be innate

◄ G ►

ganglion cells the third layer of retinal cells with which the bipolar cells synapse and whose axons form the optic nerve

gender constancy the understanding that being male or female is a permanent part of a person

gender identity the sense of "femaleness" or "maleness" that is an integral part of our identity

gender schemas organized mental structures that contain our understanding of the attributes and behaviors that are appropriate and expected for males and females

general adaptation syndrome (GAS) Selye's description of the body's responses to a stressor, which includes successive phases of alarm, resistance, and exhaustion

generalized anxiety disorder a chronic state of diffuse, or "free-floating," anxiety that is not attached to specific situations or objects

genes the biological units of heredity, located on the chromosomes

genotype the specific genetic makeup of the individual, which may or may not be expressed in the observable phenotype

genuineness the ability of a therapist to honestly express his or her feelings to a client

Gestalt laws of perceptual organization the laws of perceptual organization advanced by the Gestalt psychologists—namely, similarity, proximity, closure, and continuity

Gestalt psychology a German school of psychology that emphasized the natural organization of perceptual elements into wholes, or patterns, as well as the role of insight in problem solving

glial cells cells of the central nervous system that provide physical support for neurons and supply neurons with needed chemicals

glove anesthesia a type of conversion symptom in which a person experiences a physiologically impossible loss of feeling below the wrist

glucose a simple sugar that is the body's (and especially the brain's) major source of immediately usable fuel

graded potential a change in the electrical potential of a neuron that is proportional to the intensity of the incoming stimulation, but not sufficient to produce an action potential

group polarization when a group of like-minded people discusses an issue, the "average" opinion of group members tends to become more extreme

groupthink the tendency of group members to suspend critical thinking because they are motivated to seek agreement

gustation the sense of taste

◄ H ►

habituation a decrease in the strength of response to a repeated stimulus

hallucinations false perceptions that have a compelling sense of reality

hallucinogens drugs—such as LSD and PCP—that distort or intensify sensory experiences and evoke hallucinations and disordered thought processes

hardiness a stress-resistant personality pattern that involves the factors of commitment, control, and challenge

harm reduction a prevention strategy that is designed not to eliminate a problem behavior, but to reduce its harmful consequences

health-compromising behaviors behaviors, such as poor dietary habits and unprotected sexual activity, that impair health and reduce longevity

health-enhancing behaviors behaviors, such as exercise and good dietary habits, that support and increase health and longevity

health psychology the study of psychological and behavioral factors in the prevention and treatment of illness and in the maintenance of health

hertz (Hz) the measure of sound wave frequency as cycles per second

heuristics a method of problem solving characterized by quick and easy search procedures similar to rules of thumb

higher-order conditioning in classical conditioning, a neutral stimulus becomes a CS after it is paired with another CS (rather than with the original UCS)

hippocampus a structure of the limbic system that plays a key role in the formation and storage of memories

homeostasis the maintenance of biological equilibrium, or balance, within the body

hormones chemical substances secreted by the glands of the endocrine system that travel in the bloodstream and affect bodily organs as well as psychological functions and development

hospitalization syndrome the adoption of a chronic sick role and the deterioration of social and vocational skills that can occur as a result of custodial psychiatric hospitalization

humanistic perspective a psychological perspective that emphasizes personal freedom, choice, and self-actualization

hyperopia a visual deficit sometimes called farsightedness in which the lens focuses the image behind the retina, reducing acuity for nearby objects

hypnosis a condition of enhanced suggestibility in which some people are able to experience imagined test suggestions as if they were real

hypnotic susceptibility scale a set of induction procedures and test questions that enable researchers to measure a person's responsiveness to hypnotic suggestions

hypochondriasis a somatoform disorder characterized by an overreaction to physical symptoms and a conviction that one has or is on the verge of a serious illness

hypothalamus a forebrain structure located below the thalamus and above the pituitary gland that controls autonomic and hormonal processes and plays a major role in many aspects of motivation and emotional behavior

hypothesis a tentative explanation or prediction about some phenomenon

hysteria a psychological disorder studied and treated by Freud in which physical symptoms appear without any apparent underlying organic cause

◄ I ►

id the primitive and unconscious part of the personality that contains the instincts

illusions incorrect perceptions based on false perceptual hypotheses that often result from constancies that do not apply to the stimuli in question

imaginal thought a form of thinking that uses images that can be from any sense modality

implicit memory occurs when memory influences our behavior without conscious awareness

imprinting in some species, a sudden, biologically primed form of attachment

incentive an environmental stimulus or condition that motivates behavior

incubation a phenomenon in which the solution to a problem suddenly appears in consciousness after a problem solver has stopped thinking about it for a while

independent variable in an experiment, the factor that is manipulated by the researcher

individualism a cultural characteristic that favors the achievement of individual over group goals and which is characteristic of many Western nations; self-identity is based primarily on one's own attributes and achievements (see collectivism)

inductive reasoning reasoning that proceeds from a set of specific facts to a general conclusion or principle

indulgent parents caregivers that have warm and caring relationships with their children, but do not provide much guidance and discipline

infantile amnesia an inability to remember personal experiences from the first few years of our lives

informational social influence following the opinions or behavior of other people because we believe they have accurate knowledge and what they are doing is "right"

informed consent the principle that, prior to agreeing to participate in research, a person should be fully informed about the procedures, risks involved, and the right to withdraw at any time without penalty

insanity a legal decision that a defendant was so severely impaired at the time a crime was committed that he or she was incapable of appreciating the wrongfulness of the act or controlling his or her behavior

insight in Gestalt psychology, the sudden perception of a useful relationship or solution to a problem; in psychoanalysis, the conscious awareness of unconscious dynamics that underlie psychological problems

insomnia a sleep disorder involving chronic difficulty in falling asleep, staying asleep, or experiencing restful sleep

instinct an inherited characteristic, common to all members of a species, that automatically produces a particular response when the organism is exposed to a particular stimulus

instinctive drift the tendency for innate behaviors to override a conditioning procedure, thus making it difficult to create or maintain a conditioned response

instrumental behaviors emotional coping behaviors that are directed at achieving the goal or performing the task that is relevant to the emotion

intelligence a concept that refers to individual differences in the ability to acquire knowledge, to think and reason effectively, and to deal adaptively with the environment

intelligence quotient (IQ) originally defined as mental age (MA) divided by chronological age (CA) multiplied by 100 (IQ = (MA/CA) × 100); an IQ of 100 indicates an individual is average for his or her age group. IQ scores are today based on norms derived from people of various ages

interaction in analyzing causal factors, the influence that the presence or strength of one factor can have on other causal factors

interactive problem solving a procedure used in the field of international conflict resolution that brings competing groups together, enables them to share their differing perspectives and work together to develop solutions that will satisfy both groups' human needs

interjudge reliability the extent to which different observers or scorers agree in their scoring of a particular test or observed behavior

internal consistency the extent to which items within a psychological test correlate with one another, indicating that they are measuring a common characteristic

internal-external locus of control Rotter's generalized expectancy that one's outcomes are under personal versus external control

internal validity the degree to which an experiment produces clear causal conclusions; internal validity is high when there is no confounding of variables

internalization the process of taking on as one's own the values and moral dictates communicated by parents and society

interneurons neurons that are neither sensory or motor neurons, but perform associative or integrative functions within the nervous system

interpersonal therapy a form of brief therapy that focuses on the client's interpersonal problems and seeks to develop new interpersonal skills

interpretation in psychoanalysis, a statement made by the analyst that is intended to promote insight in the client

interventions systematically applied programs designed to solve a practical problem by changing behavior

intrinsic motivation the motivation to perform a behavior simply because one finds it interesting or enjoyable for its own sake

introspection the method of "looking within" and verbally reporting on immediate experiences; used by the structuralists to study the contents of the mind

ion channels special protein molecules located on the membrane of a neuron that control the entry and exit of specific ions, such as sodium and potassium

◄ J ►

jigsaw program an applied research program in which knowledge gained from basic research on factors that increase and decrease intergroup hostility was translated into a cooperative learning program designed to reduce interracial hostility in racially integrated schools

job enrichment an approach to increasing employees' intrinsic motivation by making their jobs more fulfilling and providing them with opportunities for growth

just world hypothesis holds that because people want to view the world as fair, they perceive that people get what they deserve and deserve what they get

◄ K ►

kin selection the view that organisms are most likely to help others with whom they share the most genes—namely, their offspring and genetic relatives

kinesthesis the body sense that provides feedback on the position and movements of our body parts

knowledge-acquisition components allow us to learn from our experiences, store information in memory, and combine new insights with previously acquired information

◄ L ►

la belle indifference an attitude of indifference to the seriousness of one's symptom shown in some cases of conversion disorder

language a system of symbols and rules for combining them that can produce an infinite number of possible messages and meanings

lapse a one-time return to an undesirable behavior pattern, usually in a high-risk situation

latent learning learning that occurs in the absence of reinforcement, but which is not displayed until reinforcement is later introduced into the situation

lateralization the localization of a function in either the right or the left cerebral hemisphere

law of effect Thorndike's concept that a response followed by satisfying consequences will become more likely to occur, whereas a response followed by unsatisfying consequences will become less likely to occur

learned helplessness theory a theory of depression that states that if people are unable to control life events, they develop a state of helplessness that leads to depressive symptoms

learning a relatively enduring change in an organism's behavior or performance capabilities that occurs as a result of experience

lens the transparent structure behind the pupil that changes its shape to focus images on the retina

leptin a hormone secreted by fat cells that decreases general appetite

levels of analysis an approach to analyzing behavioral phenomena and their causal factors in terms of biological, psychological, and environmental factors

levels of processing the concept that the more deeply we process information, the better it will be remembered

life event scales questionnaires that measure the number (and, sometimes, the intensity) of positive and negative life events that have occurred over a specific period of time

limbic system a group of subcortical structures, including the hippocampus and amygdala, which are involved in organizing many goal-directed and emotional behaviors

linguistic relativity hypothesis the idea, suggested by Benjamin Whorf, that people's language determines the ways in which they perceive and think about their world

longitudinal design the researcher repeatedly tests the same cohort as it grows older

long-term memory our vast library of more durable stored memories

long-term potentiation an enduring increase in synaptic strength that occurs after a neural circuit is rapidly stimulated

lowballing a manipulation technique in which a persuader gets you to commit to some action and then—before you actually perform the behavior—he or she increases the "cost" of that same behavior

◄ M ►

magnetic resonance imaging (MRI) a procedure that produces a highly detailed image of living tissue based on the tissue's response to a magnetic field; can be used to study both structure and, in the case of functional MRI (FMRI), brain functions as they occur

maintenance rehearsal the simple mental repetition of information

major depression a mood disorder characterized by intense depression that interferes markedly with functioning

management by objectives (MBO) an approach to increasing employees' motivation by combining goal-setting with employee participation and feedback

matching effect in romantic relationships, the tendency for partners to have a similar level of physical attractiveness

mania a state of intense emotional and behavioral excitement in which a person feels very optimistic and energized

maturation a genetically programmed, biological process that governs our growth

means-end analysis a heuristic problem-solving device in which people first define a subgoal that they hope to achieve (and "end"), compare that subgoal with their present state of knowledge and, if there is a discrepancy between them, try to find the means to reduce the difference

medulla a brain stem structure that controls vital functions, including heartbeat and respiration

melatonin a hormone, secreted by the pineal gland, that has a relaxing effect on the body and promotes a readiness for sleep

memory the processes that allow us to record and later retrieve experiences and information

memory consolidation the creation and binding together of neural codes that allow information to be transferred from short-term memory into long-term memory

menstrual synchrony the tendency for some women who live together to become more similar to one another in the timing of their menstrual cycles over time

mental age the age determined by a "standardized interview" in which an adult examiner poses a series of questions to a child to determine the mental level at which a child is performing

mental representations cognitive representations of the world, including images, ideas, concepts, and principles, that are the foundations of thinking and problem solving

mental set the tendency to stick to problem-solving strategies or solutions that have worked in the past

mere exposure effect the tendency to evaluate a stimulus more favorably after repeated exposure to it

meta-analysis a statistical procedure for combining the results of different studies that examine the same topic

metabolism the rate of energy expenditure by the body

metacomponents higher-order processes used to plan and regulate task performance (triarchic theory)

midbrain brain structures above the hindbrain that are involved in sensory and motor functions and in attention and states of consciousness

mind-body dualism the philosophical position that the mind is a nonphysical entity that is not subject to physical laws and cannot be reduced to physical processes; body and mind are separate entities

Minnesota Multiphasic Personality Inventory (MMPI) a widely used personality test whose items were developed using the empirical approach and comparing various kinds of psychiatric patients with normals

misinformation effect the distortion of a memory by misleading postevent information

monism the philosophical position that mental events are reducible to physical events in the brain, so that "mind" and body are one and the same

monocular depth cues depth cues that require only one eye; include linear perspective, decreasing size, height in the horizontal plane, texture, clarity, light and shadow, motion parallax, and interposition

mood-congruent recall tendency to recall information or events that are congruent with our current mood

mood disorders psychological disorders whose core conditions involve maladaptive mood states, such as depression or mania

morpheme the smallest unit of meaning in a given language; English morphemes include whole words, prefixes, and suffixes; there are over 100,000 English morphemes

motherese a high-pitched intonation that seems to be used all over the world

motivation a process that influences the direction, persistence, and vigor of goal-directed behavior

motivational interviewing a treatment approach that avoids confrontation and leads the clients to their own realization of a problem and increased motivation to change

motor cortex cortical area in the back of the frontal lobes that controls voluntary movements on the opposite sides of the body

motor neurons specialized neurons that carry neural messages from the brain and spinal cord to the muscles and glands

motoric thought mental representations of motor movements, such as throwing an object

multiculturalism a social-intellectual movement that emphasizes the value of diversity and insists that all groups be treated with equality and respect

multimodal treatment approaches substance abuse interventions that combine a number of treatments, such as aversion therapy and coping skills training

myelin sheath a fatty insulating substance on the axon of some neurons that increases the speed of neural transmission

myopia a visual defect sometimes called nearsightedness in which the lens focuses distant images in front of the retina rather than on it

◄ N ►

naloxone an opiate antagonist drug that interferes with the action of endorphins by occupying the receptor sites tailored for endorphins and morphine, resulting in increased pain perception

narcolepsy a sleep disorder that involves extreme daytime sleepiness and sudden, uncontrollable sleep attacks during waking hours

natural selection the evolutionary process through which characteristics that increase the likelihood of survival are preserved in the gene pool and thereby become more common in a species over time

naturalistic observation a method in which the researcher observes behavior in a natural setting and tries to avoid influencing the participants being observed

need for achievement the desire to accomplish tasks and attain standards of excellence

need for positive regard (and positive self-regard) an innate need to be positively regarded by others and by oneself

need hierarchy Maslow's view that human needs are arranged in a progression, beginning with deficiency needs and then reaching growth needs

negative affectivity a temperamental disposition to experience negative emotional states, such as anxiety and depression

negative correlation as scores on one variable change, scores on a second variable change in the opposite direction

negative process hostile interchanges between therapist and client that may result in negative therapy outcomes

negative reinforcement a response is strengthened by the subsequent removal of a (noxious) stimulus

negative state relief model the view that empathy does not lead to pure altruism, but instead, that high empathy causes us to feel distress when we learn of others' suffering, so by helping them we reduce our own personal distress

negative symptoms schizophrenic symptoms that reflect a lack of normal reactions, such as emotions or social behaviors

neglectful parents caregivers who provide neither warmth nor rules or guidance

neoanalytic theorists former followers of Freud, such as Adler and Jung, who developed their own psychodynamic theories that generally deemphasized psychosexual factors in favor of social ones and gave increased emphasis to ego functioning

nerve deafness hearing loss caused by damage to the cochlear receptor cells or to the auditory nerve

neural network a model in which each concept stored in memory is represented by a unique pattern of distributed and simultaneously activated nodes that process information in parallel; also known as a parallel distributed processing model

neural plasticity the ability of neurons to modify their structure and function in response to experiential factors or injury

neuromodulators neurotransmitter substances that are released by neurons and circulate within the nervous system to affect the sensitivity of many neurons to their natural transmitter substances

neurons nerve cells that constitute the basic building blocks of the nervous system

neuropsychological tests psychological measures that are designed to detect sensory, cognitive, or motor deficits produced by neurological damage

neurotic anxiety in psychoanalytic theory, a state of anxiety that arises when impulses from the id threaten to break through into behavior

neuroticism a personality trait that involves the tendency to experience high levels of negative affect and to behave in self-defeating ways

neurotransmitter chemical substances that are released from the axons of one neuron, travel across the synaptic space, and bind to specially keyed receptors in another neuron, where they produce a chemical reaction that is either excitatory or inhibitory

night terrors a disorder in which a sleeper—often feeling a strong sense of dread or danger—becomes aroused to a near panic state; the sleeper may suddenly sit up, let out a blood-curdling scream, and thrash about or flee to another room, as if trying to escape

norms test scores derived from a relevant sample used to evaluate individuals' scores; behavioral "rules"

norm of reciprocity the norm that when other people treat us well, we should respond in kind

normal distribution a frequency distribution in the shape of a symmetrical or bell-shaped curve that satisfies certain mathematical conditions deduced from the theory of probability

normative social influence conformity motivated by gaining social acceptance and avoiding social rejection

◄ O ►

object permanence the recognition that an object continues to exist even when it no longer can be seen

object relations the images or mental representations that people form of themselves and other people as a result of early experiences with caregivers

observational learning learning through observing the behavior of a model

obsession an unwanted and disturbing thought or image that invades consciousness and is very difficult to control

obsessive-compulsive disorder an anxiety disorder characterized by persistent and unwanted thoughts and compulsive behaviors

occipital lobe the rearmost portion of the cerebral cortex that contains the primary visual sensory area

Oedipus complex the male child experiences erotic feelings toward his mother, desires to possess her sexually, and views his father as a rival

olfaction the sense of smell

openness a willingness of a client to invest oneself in the process of therapy that predicts favorable therapeutic outcomes

operant conditioning a type of learning in which behavior is modified by its consequences, such as by reinforcement, punishment, and extinction

operant discrimination an operant response occurs when a particular antecedent stimulus is present, but not when another antecedent stimulus is present

operant generalization an operant reponse occurs to a new antecedent stimulus that is similar to the original antecedent stimulus

operational definition defining a concept or variable in terms of the specific procedures used to produce or measure it

opiates a category of drugs consisting of opium and drugs derived from it, such as morphine, codeine, and heroin; opiates provide pain relief and cause mood changes, which may include euphoria

opponent-process theory the theory proposed by Hering that the retina contains three sets of color receptors that respond differentially to red-green, blue-yellow, and black-white; the opponent processes that result can produce a perception of any hue

optic chiasma the point at which optic nerves cross after leaving the eyes, so that half of each eye's visual field is sent to each hemisphere's visual projection area

organ of Corti structures embedded in the basilar membrane that contain the hair cell receptors for sound

overlearning continued rehearsal past the point of initial learning that significantly improves performance on memory tasks

‹ P ›

pain disorder a somatoform disorder in which the person's complaints of pain cannot be accounted for in terms of physical damage

panic disorder an anxiety disorder characterized by unpredictable panic attacks and a pervasive fear that another will occur; may also include a resulting agoraphobia

paranoid type a schizophrenic disorder marked by delusional thinking and suspiciousness

parasympathetic nervous system the branch portion of the autonomic nervous system that slows down bodily processes to conserve energy and reduce arousal

paraventricular nucleus (PVN) a cluster of neurons in the hippocampus packed with receptor sites for transmitters that stimulate or reduce appetite

parental investment theory the view, based on evolutionary theory, that the gender with a greater investment (higher costs) in producing offspring will be more selective in choosing a mate

parietal lobe the cerebral region behind the frontal lobe that contains the somatic sensory cortex and Wernicke's speech comprehension area

partial reinforcement schedule a schedule in which reinforcement follows some correct responses but not others

passionate love a form of love that involves intense emotional arousal and yearning for one's partner

perception the process of organizing stimulus input and giving it meaning

perceptual constancies the ability to recognize stimulus characteristics—size, color, and so on, under varying conditions

perceptual schemas internal representations that contain the essential features of an object of perception

perceptual set a readiness to perceive a stimulus in a particular way based on expectations, motives, emotions, or beliefs

performance components the actual mental processes used to perform a task (triarchic theory)

peripheral nervous system all of the neurons that connect the central nervous system with the sensory receptors, the muscles, and the glands

peripheral route to persuasion occurs when people do not scrutinize a message, but are influenced mostly by other factors such as a speaker's attractiveness or a message's emotional appeal

personal unconscious according to Jung, those aspects of the unconscious that arise from the individual's life experiences

personality those biologically and environmentally determined characteristics within the person that account for distinctive and relatively enduring patterns of thinking, feeling, and acting

personality disorder stable, inflexible, and maladaptive personality styles

perspective a theoretical vantage point from which to analyze behavior and its causes

phenotype the observable characteristics produced by one's genetic endowment

pheromones chemical signals found in natural body scents

phobias strong and irrational fears of particular objects or circumstances

phoneme the smallest unit of sound in a language; these are the vowel and consonant sounds that are recognized in any given language; English has 45 phonemes

photopigments protein molecules within the rods and cones whose chemical reactions when absorbing light result in nerve impulses being generated

place theory the theory of pitch perception that holds that sound frequencies are coded in terms of the portion of the basilar membrane where the fluid wave in the cochlea peaks; this theory accounts for perception of frequencies above 4,000 Hz

placebo an inactive or inert substance

placebo control group a control group that receives an intervention that is assumed to have no therapeutic value

placebo effect a change in behavior that occurs because of the expectation or belief that one is receiving a treatment

pleasure principle the drive for instant need gratification that is characteristic of the id

polygenic transmission a number of genes working together to create a particular phenotypic characteristic

polygraph a research and clinical instrument that measures a wide array of physiological responses

pons a brain stem structure having sensory and motor tracts whose functions are involved in sleep and dreaming

population in a survey, the entire set of individuals about whom we wish to draw a conclusion

positive affectivity a relatively stable disposition to experience pleasure and positive emotions

positive correlation as scores on one variable change, scores on a second variable change in the same direction

positive reinforcement a response is strengthened by the subsequent presentation of a (positive) stimulus

positive symptoms schizophrenic symptoms such as delusions, hallucinations, and disordered speech and thinking

positron emission tomography (PET) scan a procedure that provides a visual display of the absorption of a radioactive substance by neurons, indicating how actively they are involved as the brain performs a task

postconventional moral reasoning moral judgments are based on a system of internalized, well thought out moral principles

postformal thought the ability to reason logically about opposing points of view and accept contradictions and irreconcilable differences

posttraumatic stress disorder (PTSD) a pattern of distressing symptoms, such as flashbacks, nightmares, avoidance, and anxiety responses that recur after a traumatic experience

preconventional level stage at which moral judgments are based on anticipated punishments or rewards

predictive validity the ability of a test to predict future outcomes (e.g., academic performance) that are influenced by the characteristic measured by the test (e.g., intelligence)

prefrontal cortex the area of the frontal lobe just behind the eyes and forehead that is involved in the executive functions of planning, self-awareness, and responsibility

prejudice a negative attitude toward people based on their membership in a group

preoperational stage in Piaget's model, a stage of cognitive development in which children represent the world symbolically through words and mental images, but do not yet understand basic mental operations or rules

preparedness the notion that evolutionary factors have produced an innate readiness to learn certain associations that have had survival implications in the past

primacy effect (impression formation) our tendency to attach more importance to the initial information that we learn about a person

primary appraisal the initial appraisal of a situation as benign, irrelevant, or threatening; a perception of the severity of demands

primary mental abilities include spatial ability, perceptual speed, numerical ability, verbal meaning, memory, verbal fluency, and inductive reasoning; these were defined by L. L. Thurstone on the basis of his factor analysis of intelligence test items

primary reinforcer a positive reinforcer that satisfies a biological need, such as food or water

primary visual cortex the area of the occipital lobe which revives impulses generated from the retina via the thalamus and analyzes visual input using its feature detectors

priming the activation of one concept (or one unit of information) by another

proactive interference occurs when material learned in the past interferes with recall of newer material

problem-focused coping coping strategies that involve direct attempts to confront and master a stressful situation

problem-solving models (of dreaming) the view that dreams can help us find creative solutions to our problems and conflicts because they are not constrained by reality

problem-solving schemas step-by-step scripts for selecting information and solving specialized classes of problems

procedural memory (nondeclarative memory) is reflected in learned skills and actions

program evaluation research research designed to measure the outcomes of an intervention

projective tests tests, such as the Rorschach and the TAT, that present ambiguous stimuli to the subject; the responses are assumed to be based on a projection of internal characteristics of the person onto the stimuli

proposition a statement that expresses an idea in subject-predicate form

propositional thought a form of linguistically based thought that expresses a statement in subject-predicate thought

prospective memory concerns remembering to perform an activity in the future

protective factors environmental or personal resources that help people fare better in the face of stress

prototype the most typical and familiar members of a class that defines a concept

proximodistal principle the principle that physical development begins along the innermost parts of the body and continues toward the outermost parts

psychic energy generated by instinctual drives, this energy powers the mind and constantly presses for either direct or indirect release

psychodynamic behavior therapy an integration of psychoanalysis and behavior therapy

psychodynamic perspective a psychological perspective that focuses on inner personality dynamics, including the role of unconscious impulses and defenses, in understanding behavior

psychogenic amnesia an extensive but selective memory loss that occurs after a traumatic event

psychogenic fugue a dissociative phenomenon in which a person loses all sense of personal identity and may wander to another place and establish a new identity

psychological risk the degree to which research procedures may expose participants to significant mental or emotional harm

psychological test a method for measuring individual differences related to some psychological construct, based on a sample of relevant behavior obtained under standardized conditions

psychology the scientific study of behavior and its causes

psychometrics the study of the statistical properties of psychological tests; the psychometric approach to intelligence focuses on the number and nature of abilities that define intelligence

psychoneuroimmunology (PNI) the field of study that explores relations between psychological and immune functions

psychophysics the study of relations between the physical characteristics of stimuli and the sensory experiences they evoke

psychosexual stages stages of development in which psychic energy is focused on certain body parts; the major childhood stages are the oral, anal, and phallic stages; experiences during these stages are assumed to shape personality development

psychosocial stages a sequence of eight developmental stages proposed by Erikson, each of which involves a different "crisis" (i.e., conflict) over how we view ourselves in relation to other people and the world

psychosurgery surgical procedures, such as lobotomy or cingulotomy, in which brain tissue involved in a behavior disorder is removed or destroyed

puberty a period of rapid maturation in which the person becomes capable of sexual reproduction

punishment a response is weakened by an outcome that follows it

◄ R ►

random assignment a procedure in which each participant has an equal likelihood of being assigned to any one group within an experiment

random sampling a method of choosing a sample in which each member of the population has an equal opportunity to be included in the sample

randomized clinical trial a research design that involves the random assignment of clients having specific problems to an experimental (therapy) group or to a control condition so as to draw sound causal conclusions about the therapy's efficacy

rape trauma syndrome a pattern of cognitive, emotional, and behavioral responses that occurs in response to the trauma of being raped

rational-theoretical approach an approach to test construction in which test items are made up on the basis of a theorist's conception of a construct

reaction range the genetically influenced limits within which environmental factors can exert their effects on an organism

realistic conflict theory the theory that competition for limited resources fosters prejudice

reality principle the ego's tendency to take reality factors into account and to act in a rational fashion in need satisfaction

receptor sites protein molecules on neurons' dendrites or soma that are specially shaped to accommodate a specific neurotransmitter molecule

recessive gene a gene whose characteristic will be masked by a corresponding dominant gene; its characteristic will be expressed if the correspondent gene is also recessive

reciprocal determinism Bandura's model of two-way causal relations between the person, behavior, and the environment

recombinant DNA procedures gene-splicing procedures that can be used to produce new life forms, such as bacteria that can produce scarce chemical materials like human growth hormone

reflexes automatic, inborn behaviors triggered by specific stimuli

refractory period the period of time following an action potential during which the neuron cannot be stimulated to produce another nerve impulse

regression a psychoanalytic defense mechanism in which a person retreats back to an earlier stage of development in response to stress

reinforcement a response is strengthened by an outcome that follows it

relapse a complete return to a previous undesirable behavior and an abandonment of attempts to change

relapse prevention a treatment approach designed to teach coping skills, increase self-efficacy, and counter the abstinence violation effect and thus reduce the likelihood of relapse

relational aggression negative behavior that involves spreading of vicious rumors, exclusion from peer groups, and withdrawal from friendships

reliability in psychological testing, the consistency with which a measure assesses a given characteristic, or different observers agree on a given score

REM sleep a recurring sleep stage characterized by rapid eye movements, increased physiological arousal, paralysis of the voluntary muscles, and a high rate of dreaming

REM-sleep behavior disorder a sleep disorder in which the loss of muscle tone that causes normal REM-sleep paralysis is absent, thereby enabling sleepers to move about—sometimes violently—and seemingly "act out" their dreams

remote behavior sampling researchers and clinicians collect samples of behavior from respondents as they live their daily lives

replication the process of repeating a study to determine whether the original findings can be duplicated

representative sample a sample that accurately reflects the important characteristics of the population

representativeness heuristic a rule of thumb in estimating the probability that an object or event belongs to a certain category based on the extent to which it represents a prototype of that category

repression the basic defense mechanism that actively keeps anxiety-arousing material in the unconscious

resistance largely unconscious maneuvers that protect clients from dealing with anxiety-arousing material in therapy

response cost a response is weakened by the subsequent removal of a (positive) stimulus; this stimulus was not the cause of the original response (e.g., TV privileges are taken away from a misbehaving child who wants attention)

response prevention the prevention of escape or avoidance responses during exposure to an anxiety-arousing CS so that extinction can occur

restoration model the theory that sleep recharges our run-down bodies and allows us to recover from physical and mental fatigue

reticular formation a structure extending from the hindbrain into the midbrain that plays a central role in consciousness and attention, in part by alerting and activating higher brain centers (ascending portion), and by selectively blocking some inputs from admission to higher regions in the brain (descending portion)

retina the light-sensitive back surface of the eye that contains the visual receptors

retrieval the process of accessing information in long-term memory

retrieval cue any stimulus, whether internal or external, that stimulates the activation of information stored in long-term memory

retroactive interference newly acquired information interferes with the ability to recall information learned at an earlier time

retrograde amnesia memory loss for events that occurred prior to the onset of amnesia

reuptake the process whereby transmitter substances are taken back into the presynaptic neuron so that they do not continue to stimulate postsynaptic neurons

right to privacy the principle that people's right to have their behavior considered "private" depends upon the setting, the sensitivity of the behavior, and the way in which information would be reported

rods visual receptors that function under low levels of illumination and do not give rise to color sensations

◄ S ►

sample in a survey, a subset of individuals drawn from the population

savant a person who is intellectually disabled but shows some striking mental ability, such as being able to mentally compute complex mathematical problems

scatterplot a graph commonly used to examine correlational data; each pair of scores on variable X and variable Y is plotted as a single point

schema a "mental framework"—an organized pattern of thought about some aspect of the world, such as a class of people, events, situations, or objects

schizophrenia a psychotic disorder involving serious impairments of attention, thought, language, emotion, and behavior

seasonal affective disorder (SAD) a disorder in which depressive symptoms appear or worsen during certain seasons of the year (most typically, fall and winter) and then improve during the other seasons

secondary appraisal one's judgment of the adequacy of personal resources needed to cope with a stressor

secondary (conditioned) reinforcer a stimulus that acquires reinforcing qualities by being associated with a primary reinforcer

seeking social support attempts to turn to others for assistance or emotional support in times of stress

selective serotonin reuptake inhibitors (SSRIs) a class of antidepressant drugs that increase the activity of serotonin by presenting its reuptake into the presynaptic neuron

self in Rogers's theory, an organized consistent set of perceptions and beliefs about oneself

self-actualization in humanistic theories, an inborn tendency to strive toward the realization of one's full potential

self-consistency an absence of conflict among self-perceptions

self-efficacy the conviction that we can perform the behaviors necessary to produce a desired outcome

self-enhancement processes whereby one enhances positive self-regard

self-esteem how positively or negatively we feel about ourselves

self-evaluative processes the ability of humans to reinforce or punish themselves contingent upon certain behaviors that relate to internal standards

self-fulfilling prophecy occurs when people's erroneous expectations lead them to act toward others in a way that brings about the expected behaviors, thereby confirming the original impression

self-instructional training a cognitive coping approach of giving adaptive self-instructions to oneself at crucial phases of the coping process

self-monitoring a personality trait that reflects people's tendencies to regulate their social behavior in accord with situational cues as opposed to internal values, attitudes, and needs

self-perception theory the theory that we make inferences about our own attitudes by observing how we behave

self-reinforcement processes self-administered rewards and punishments that are contingent on meeting certain standards for behavior that are an important basis for self-regulation of behavior

self-regulation the ability to structure antecedent conditions and behavioral consequences in a way that increases desirable behaviors or reduces undesirable ones

self-relatedness a client's ability to be flexible to change, to listen carefully to the therapist, and to constructively use what is learned in therapy

self-serving bias the tendency to make relatively more personal attributions for success and situational attributions for failures

self-verification the tendency to try to verify or validate one's existing self-concept—that is, to satisfy congruence needs

semantics the rules for connecting the symbols to what they represent

semantic memory general factual knowledge about the world and language, including memory for words and concepts

sensation the process by which stimuli are detected, transduced into nerve impulses, and sent to the brain

sensation-seeking a motivational trait directed toward obtaining stimulation, novelty, and excitement

sensitive period an optimal age range for certain experiences, but if those experiences occur at another time, normal development will still be possible

sensorimotor stage in Piaget's theory, the stage of cognitive development in which children understand their world primarily through sensory experiences and physical (motor) interactions with objects

sensory adaptation diminishing sensitivity to an unchanging stimulus with the passage of time as sensory neurons habituate to the stimulation

sensory memory memory processes that retain incoming sensory information just long enough for it to be recognized

sensory neurons specialized neurons that carry messages from the sense organs to the spinal cord and brain

separation anxiety distress experienced by infants when they are separated from a primary caregiver, peaking around age 12 to 16 months and disappearing between 2 and 3 years of age

sequential design repeatedly testing several age cohorts as they grow older

serial position effect the finding that recall is influenced by a word's position in a series of items

serotonin a neurotransmitter that seems to underlie positive mood states; underactivity may be a factor in depression

sex-role stereotypes beliefs about the types of characteristics and behaviors that are appropriate for boys versus for girls

sexual orientation a person's emotional and erotic preference for partners of a particular sex

sexual response cycle a physiological response to sexual stimulation that involves stages of excitement, plateau, orgasm, and resolution

shadowing an experimental procedure used in attention research in which a person simultaneously receives two or more messages, is asked to focus on one of them, and then is asked to report on the other messages as well

shaping an operant conditioning procedure in which reinforcement begins with a behavior that the organism can already perform, then is made contingent upon behaviors that increasingly approximate the final desired behavior

short-term memory type of memory that holds the information that we are conscious of at any given time; also called *working memory*

signal detection theory a theory that assumes that stimulus detection is not based on a fixed absolute threshold, but rather is affected by rewards, punishments, expectations, and motivational factors

situation-focused intervention prevention efforts that focus on altering environmental conditions that are known to promote the development of psychological disorders

Skinner box an experimental chamber in which animals learn to perform operant responses, such as bar presses or pecking responses, so that the learning process can be studied

sleep apnea a disorder characterized by a repeated cycle in which the sleeper stops breathing, momentarily awakens gasping for air, and then returns to sleep

slow-wave sleep stages 3 and 4 of sleep, in which the EEG pattern shows large, slow brain waves called delta waves

social clock a set of cultural norms concerning the optimal age range for work, marriage, parenthood, and other major life experiences to occur

social cognitive theory a cognitive-behavioral approach to personality developed by Albert Bandura and Walter Mischel that emphasizes the role of social learning, cognitive processes, and self-regulation

social-cognitive theories (of hypnosis) the view that hypnotic experiences occur because people are highly motivated to assume the role of being "hypnotized"; the person develops a readiness to perceive hypnotic experiences as real and involuntary

social comparison the act of comparing one's personal attributes, abilities, and opinions with those of other people

social constructivism the position that people construct their reality and beliefs through their cognitions

social exchange theory a theory proposing that a social relationship can best be described in terms of exchanges of rewards and costs between the two partners

social facilitation an increased tendency to perform one's dominant response in the mere presence of others

social identity theory the theory that prejudice stems from a need to enhance our self-esteem

social loafing the tendency for people to expend less individual effort when working collectively in a group than when working alone

social norms shared expectations about how people should think, feel, and behave

social penetration theory a theory proposing that as a relationship deepens, exchanges (including self-disclosure) become broader and more intimate

social phobia excessive and inappropriate fear of social situations in which a person might be evaluated and possibly embarrassed

social risk the degree to which research information about individual participants could become known to others and produce negative consequences for the participants

social role a set of norms that characterizes how people in a given social position ought to behave

social skills training a technique in which a client learns more effective social behaviors by observing and imitating a skillful model

social structure theory the theory that men and women behave differently, such as expressing different mate preferences, because society directs them into different social and economic roles

socialization the process by which we acquire the beliefs, values, and behaviors of a group

socially toxic environments Garbarino's term for negative settings that involve poverty, violence, lack of intellectual stimulation, and other factors that have harmful effects on children's development

sociobiology an evolutionary theory of social behavior that emphasizes the role of adaptive behavior in maintaining one's genes in the species' gene pool

sociocultural perspective a perspective that emphasizes the role of culture and the social environment in understanding commonalties and differences in human behavior

somatoform disorder a disorder in which a person complains of bodily symptoms that cannot be accounted for in terms of actual physical damage or dysfunction

somatic nervous system the branch of the peripheral nervous system that provides input from the sensory receptors and output to the voluntary muscles of the body

somatic relaxation training a means of voluntarily reducing or preventing high levels of arousal

somatic sensory cortex cortical strips in the front portions of the parietal lobes that receive sensory input from various regions of the body

somatic theory of emotions a modern emotion theory inspired by the James-Lange theory that emphasizes the causal role of bodily responses in the experiencing of emotion

source confusion tendency to recall something or recognize it as familiar, but to forget where it was encountered

specific phobia irrational and excessive fear of specific objects or situations that pose little or no actual threat

specificity question the ultimate question of psychotherapy research: "Which types of therapy, administered by which kinds of therapists to which kinds of clients having which kinds of problems, produce which kinds of effects?"

spinal reflex a simple stimulus-response sequence that is carried out by sensory input and motor output at the level of the spinal cord without the involvement of higher brain centers

spontaneous recovery in classical conditioning, the reappearance of a previously extinguished conditioned response after a period of time has passed following extinction

spontaneous remission improvements in symptoms in the absence of any therapy

standardization in psychological testing, refers to (1) creating a standard set of procedures for administering a test or making observations, and (2) deriving norms with which an individual's performance can be compared

state-dependent memory theory that our ability to retrieve information is greater when our internal state at the time of retrieval matches our original state during learning

stereotype a generalized belief about a group or category of people

stereotype threat the anxiety created by the perceived possibility that one's behavior or performance will confirm a negative stereotype about one's group

stimulants drugs that stimulate neural activity, resulting in a state of excitement or aroused euphoria

stimulus generalization a CR occurs to stimuli other than the original CS, based on the similarity of these stimuli to the CS

stimulus hierarchy in systematic desensitization, the creation of a series of anxiety-arousing stimuli that are ranked in terms of the amount of anxiety they evoke

storage the retention of information over time

strange situation a standardized procedure used to determine the type of emotional attachment between infant and caregiver

stranger anxiety distress over contact with strangers that typically develops in the first year of infancy and dissipates in the second year

stress a pattern of cognitive appraisals, physiological responses, and behavioral tendencies that occurs in response to a perceived imbalance between situational demands and the resources available to cope with them

stress-induced analgesia a reduction in sensitivity that occurs when endorphins are released under stressful conditions

stressors situations that place demands on organisms that tax or exceed their resources

striving for superiority Adler's notion that people are driven to compensate for intrinsic feelings of inferiority and inadequacy through achievement of personal and social goals

stroboscopic movement the illusory movement produced when adjacent lights are illuminated and extinguished at specific time intervals

structuralism an early German school of psychology established by Wilhelm Wundt that attempted to study the structure of the mind by breaking it down into its basic components, thought to be sensations

subgoal analysis a problem-solving heuristic in which people attack a large problem by formulating subgoals, or intermediate steps toward a solution

subjective well-being happiness; the overall degree of satisfaction with one's life

sublimation the channeling of unacceptable impulses into socially accepted behaviors, as when aggressive drives are expressed in violent sports

subliminal psychodynamic activation a research technique in which subliminal stimuli are used in an attempt to activate unconscious conflicts and study their effects on behavior

subliminal stimuli weak stimuli below the perceptual threshold that are not consciously perceived

substance dependence a maladaptive pattern of substance use that causes a person significant distress or substantially impairs that person's life; substance dependence is diagnosed as occurring "with *physiological dependence*" if drug tolerance or withdrawal symptoms have developed

suicide the willful taking of one's own life

superego the moral arm of the personality that internalizes the standards and values of society and serves as the person's conscience

suprachiasmatic nuclei (SCN) the brain's master "biological clock," located in the hypothalamus, that regulates most circadian rhythms

surface structure a linguistic term for the words and organization of a spoken or written sentence; two sentences may have quite different surface structure, but still mean the same thing

survey research a method in which questionnaires or interviews are used to obtain information about many people

sympathetic nervous system the branch of the autonomic nervous system that has an arousal function on the body's internal organs, speeding up bodily processes and mobilizing the body

synaptic vesicles chambers within the axon that contains the neurotransmitter substance

synapse the microscopic space between neurons over which the nerve impulse is biochemically transmitted

synesthesia a condition in which stimuli are experienced not only in the normal sensory modality, but in others as well

syntax the rules for the combination of symbols within a given language

systematic desensitization an attempt to eliminate anxiety using counterconditioning, in which a new response that is compatible with anxiety is conditioned to the anxiety-arousing conditioned stimulus

◄ T ►

tardive dyskinesia an irreversible motor disorder that can occur as a side effect of certain antipsychotic drugs

target behavior when trying to modify behavior, the specific behavior that is to be changed

taste buds the receptors for taste in the tongue and in the roof and back of the mouth that are sensitive to the qualities of sweet, sour, salty, and bitter

telegraphic speech two-word sentences that consist of a noun and a verb

temperament a biologically based general style of reacting emotionally and behaviorally to the environment

temporal lobe the portion of the cortex that lies below the parietal lobes and is the major site of auditory input to the brain

teratogens environmental (nongenetic) agents that cause abnormal prenatal development

terror management theory a theory that focuses on the ways people defend against fear of death

test-retest reliability the extent to which scores on a presumably stable characteristic are consistent over time

thalamus a major sensory integration and relay center in the forebrain, sometimes referred to as the brain's sensory switchboard

THC (tetrahydrocannabinol) the major active ingredient in marijuana

theory a set of formal statements that explains how and why certain events or phenomena are related to one another

theory of cognitive dissonance the theory that people strive to maintain consistency in their beliefs and actions, and that inconsistency creates dissonance—unpleasant arousal that motivates people to restore balance by changing their cognitions

theory of mind a person's beliefs about the "mind" and ability to understand other people's mental states

theory of planned behavior the view that our intention to engage in a behavior is strongest when we have a positive attitude toward that behavior, when subjective norms (our perceptions of what other people think we should do) support our attitudes, and when we believe that the behavior is under our control

threat in Roger's theory any experience we have that is inconsistent with our self-concept, including our perceptions of our own behavior

token economy a procedure in which desirable behaviors are reinforced with tokens or points that can later be redeemed for other reinforcers

tolerance a condition in which increasingly larger doses of a drug are required to produce the same level of bodily responses; caused by the body's compensatory responses, which counter the effects of the drug

top-down processing perceptual processing in which existing knowledge, concepts, ideas, or expectations are applied in order to make sense of incoming stimulation

transduction the conversion of one form of energy into another; in sensation, the process whereby physical stimuli are translated into nerve impulses

transfer of excitation a misinterpretation of one's state of arousal that occurs when arousal actually is caused by one source, but the person attributes her or his arousal to another source

transference the psychoanalytic phenomenon in which a client responds irrationally to the analyst as if the latter were an important person from the client's past who plays an important role in the client's dynamics

trauma-dissociation theory a theory that accounts for the development of dissociative identity disorder in terms of dissociation as a defense against severe childhood abuse or trauma

triangular theory of love the view that various types of love result from different combinations of three core factors: *intimacy*, *commitment*, and *passion*

triarchic theory of intelligence Sternberg's theory of intelligence that distinguishes between analytical, practical, and creative forms of mental ability

trichromatic theory the color vision theory originally advanced by Young and Helmholtz that there are three types of color receptors in the retina—one for red, one for blue, and one for green—and that combinations of activation of these receptors can produce perception of any hue in the visible spectrum

twin studies a behavior genetics method in which identical (monozygotic) and fraternal (dizygotic) twins are compared on some characteristic; this method is particularly informative if the twins have been raised in different environments

two-factor theory of avoidance learning a theory that avoidance learning first involves the classical conditioning of fear, followed by learning operant responses that avoid an anticipated aversive stimulus and thus are reinforced by anxiety reduction

two-factor theory of emotion Schachter's theory that intensity of physiological arousal determines perceived intensity of emotion, whereas appraisal of environmental cues tells us which emotion we are experiencing

Type I schizophrenia subtype of schizophrenia characterized by a predominance of positive symptoms

Type II schizophrenia subtype of schizophrenia characterized by negative symptoms

Type A personality a behavioral pattern involving a sense of time urgency, pressured behavior, and hostility that appears to be a risk factor in coronary heart disease

Type C personality a personality pattern characterized by inhibition of negative emotions that may be a risk factor in the development of cancer

◄ U ►

unconditional positive regard a communicated attitude of total and unconditional acceptance of another person that conveys the person's intrinsic worth

unconditioned response (UCR) a response (usually reflexive or innate) that is elicited by a specific stimulus (the UCS) without prior learning

unconditioned stimulus (UCS) a stimulus that elicits a particular reflexive or innate response (the UCR) without prior learning

undifferentiated type a residual category of schizophrenia for people who show some of the symptoms of paranoid, disorganized, and catatonic types but not enough to be placed in one of those diagnostic categories

unobtrusive measurement recording behavior in a way that keeps participants unaware that they are being observed

upward comparison comparing oneself or one's current situation with more positive alternatives

◄ V ►

validity the extent to which a test actually measures what it is supposed to measure; the degree to which a diagnostic system's categories contain the core features of the behavior disorders and permit differentiation among the disorders

variable any characteristic of an organism or situation that can vary

variable-interval schedule a schedule in which reinforcement follows the first correct response that occurs after an average (but variable) time interval following the last reinforced response

variable-ratio schedule a schedule in which reinforcement is based on an average but variable number of responses

vascular theory of emotional feedback the version of the facial feedback hypothesis that attributes facial muscle effects to the warming or cooling of blood that is entering the brain

vestibular sense the sense of body orientation or equilibrium

virtual reality the use of computer-produced virtual environments that immerse an individual and produce experiences like those that would be produced by a corresponding real environment

visual acuity the ability to see fine detail

visual association cortex cortical areas in the occipital, parietal, and temporal lobes that analyze visual stimuli sent to the primary visual cortex in relation to stored knowledge and establish the "meaning" of the stimuli

vulnerability a predisposition that can have a biological basis, such as our genotype, a brain malfunction, or a hormonal factor

vulnerability factors situational or physical factors that increase susceptibility to the negative impact of stressful events

vulnerability-stress model a model that explains behavior disorders as resulting from predisposing biological or psychological vulnerability factors that are triggered by a stressor

◄ W ►

Weber's law the principle that to perceive a difference between two stimuli, the stimuli must differ by a constant percentage or ratio

Wernicke's area an area of the left temporal lobe that is involved in speech comprehension

wish fulfillment in Freudian theory, the partial or complete satisfaction of a psychological need through dreaming or waking fantasy

withdrawal the occurrence of compensatory responses after drug use is discontinued, causing the person to experience physiological reactions opposite to those that had been produced by the drug

working memory a more current name for short-term memory, reflecting the fact that it consciously processes, codes, and "works on" information

◄ Y ►

yo-yo dieting severe intermittent dieting that results in large weigh fluctuations

◄ Z ►

zone of proximal development the difference between what a child can do independently, and what the child can do with assistance from adults or more advanced peers

zygote the fertilized egg

REFERENCES

"A recovering patient" (1986). "Can we talk?" The schizophrenic patient in psychotherapy. *American Journal of Psychiatry, 143,* 68–70.

Aamodt, M. G. (1991). *Applied industrial/ organizational psychology.* Belmont, CA: Wadsworth.

Aaron, S. (1986). *Stage fright.* Chicago: University of Chicago Press.

Abel, T., & Kandel, E. (1998). Positive and negative regulatory mechanisms that mediate long-term memory storage. *Brain Research Reviews, 26,* 360–378.

Abraham, K. (1911). Notes on the psychoanalytic investigation and treatment of manic-depressive insanity and allied conditions. In K. Abraham, *Selected Papers of Karl Abraham.* New York: Basic Books, 1968.

Abramov, I., & Gordon, J. (1994). Color appearance: On seeing red—or yellow, or green, or blue. *Annual Review of Psychology, 45:* 451–485.

Adair, R. K. (1990). *The physics of baseball.* New York: Harper & Row.

Adams, G. R., & Fitch, S. A. (1982). Ego stage and identity status development: A cross-sequential analysis. *Journal of Personality and Social Psychology, 43,* 574–583.

Adelmann, P. K., & Zajonc, R. B. (1989). Facial efference and the experience of emotion. *Annual Review of Psychology, 40,* 249–280.

Ader, R. (2000). True or false: The placebo effect as seen in drug studies is definitive proof that the mind can bring about clinically relevant changes in the body. *Advances in Mind Body Medicine, 16,* 7–11.

Ader, R., & Cohen, N. (1975). Behaviorally conditioned immunosuppression. *Psychosomatic Medicine, 37,* 333–340.

Ader, R., & Cohen, N. (1990). The influence of conditioning on immune responses. In R. Ader, N. Cohen, & D. L. Felten (Eds.), *Psychoneuroimmunology II.* New York: Academic Press.

Ader, R., & Cohen, N. S. (1982). Behaviorally conditioned immunosuppression and murine systemic lupus erythematosus. *Science, 215,* 1534–1536.

Ader, R., Cohen, N., & Felten, D. (1995). Psychoneuroimmunology: Interactions between the nervous system and the immune system. *Lancet, 345,* 99–103.

Adler, A. (1927). *The practice and theory of individual psychology.* New York: Harcourt.

Adler, S. R. (1995). Refugee stress and folk belief: Hmong sudden deaths. *Social Science and Medicine, 40,* 1623–1629.

Adolphs, R., Cahill, L., Schul, R., & Babinsky, R. (1997). Impaired declarative memory for emotional material following bilateral amygdala damage in humans. *Learning and Memory, 4,* 291–300.

Aggleton, J. P. (1993). The contribution of the amygdala to normal and abnormal emotional states. *Trends in Neurosciences, 16,* 328–333.

Agnew, H. W. Jr., Webb, W. B., & Williams, R. L. (1967). Comparison of stage four and 1-REM sleep deprivation. *Perceptual and Motor Skills, 24,* 851-858.

Ahadi, S., & Diener, E. (1989). Multiple determinants and effect size. *Journal of Personality and Social Psychology, 56,* 398–406.

Ahn, S., Riccio, A., & Ginty, D. G. (2000). Spatial considerations for stimulus-dependent transcription in neurons. *Annual Review of Physiology, 62,* 803–823.

Aiken, L. R. (1999). *Psychological testing and assessment.* Needham Heights, MA: Allyn & Bacon.

Ainsworth, M. (1989). Attachments beyond infancy. *American Psychologist, 44,* 709–716.

Ainsworth, M., Blehar, M. C., Waters, E., & Wall, S. (1978). *Patterns of attachment: A psychological study of the strange situation.* Hillsdale, NJ: Erlbaum.

Ainsworth, M. D. S. (1967). *Infancy in Uganda: Infant care and the growth of love.* Baltimore: The Johns Hopkins University Press.

Ainsworth, M. S., & Bowlby, J. (1991). An etiological approach to personality development. *American Psychologist, 46,* 333–341.

Aitchison, J. (1996). *The seeds of speech: Language origin and evolution.* New York: Cambridge University Press.

Aitken, S., & Bower T. G. (1982). Intersensory substitution in the blind. *Journal of Experimental Child Psychology, 33,* 309–323.

Ajzen, I. (1991). The theory of planned behavior. *Organizational Behavior and Human Decision Processes, 50,* 179–211.

Akerstedt, T. (1988). Sleepiness and a consequence of shift work. *Sleep, 11,* 17–34.

Albee, G. W. (1996). Revolutions and counterrevolutions in prevention. *American Psychologist, 51,* 1130–1133.

Albee, G. W. (1997). Speak no evil? *American Psychologist, 52,* 1143–1144.

Aldridge, S. (1998). *The thread of life: The story of genes and genetic engineering.* New York: Cambridge University Press.

Alexander, N. (1996). Barriers to sexually transmitted diseases. *Scientific American: Science and Medicine, 3*(2), 32–41.

Alfieri, T., Ruble, D. N., & Higgins, E. T. (1996). Gender stereotypes during adolescence: Developmental changes and the transition to junior high school. *Developmental Psychology, 32,* 1129–1137.

Allen, M. (1991). Meta-analysis comparing the persuasiveness of one-sided and two-sided messages. *Western Journal of Speech Communication, 55,* 390–404.

Allen, M., D'Alessio, D., & Brezgel, K. (1995). A meta-analysis summarizing the effects of pornography: II. Aggression after exposure. *Human Communication Research, 22,* 258–283.

Alloy, L. B., Jacobson, N. S., & Acocella, J. (1999). *Abnormal psychology: Current perspectives.* Boston: McGraw-Hill.

Allport, G. W. (1935). Attitudes. In C. Murchison (Ed.), *Handbook of social psychology.* Worcester, MA: Clark University Press.

Allport, G. W. (1937). *Personality: A psychological interpretation.* New York: Holt, Rinehart & Winston.

Allport, G. W. (1954). *The nature of prejudice.* Reading, MA: Addison-Wesley.

Allport, G. W., & Odbert, H. S. (1936). Trait names: A psycho-lexical study. *Psychological Monographs, 47* (Whole No. 211).

Allport, G. W., & Postman, L. (1947). *The psychology of rumor.* New York: Holt.

Alm, H., & Nilsson, L. (1995). The effects of a mobile telephone task on driver behaviour in a car following situation. *Accident Analysis and Prevention, 27,* 707–715.

Altman, I., & Taylor, D. A. (1973). *Social penetration: The development of interpersonal relationships.* New York: Holt, Rinehart & Winston.

Altman, J., & Bayer, S. A. (1996). *Development of the cerebellar system: In relation to its evolution, structure and functions.* Boca Raton, FL: CRC Press.

Alvarado, C. S. (2000). Psi-related experiences. In E. Cardeña, S. J. Lynn, & S. Krippner, (Eds.), *Varieties of anomalous experience: Examining the scientific evidence.* Washington, DC: American Psychological Association.

Amato, P. R., & Keith, B. (1991). Parental divorce and the well-being of children: A meta-analysis. *Psychological Bulletin, 110,* 26–46.

Amato, P. R., Loomis, L. S., & Booth, A. (1995). Parental divorce, marital conflict, and offspring well-being during early adulthood. *Social Forces, 73,* 895–915.

Ameri, A. (1999). The effects of cannabinoids on the brain. *Progress in Neurobiology, 58,* 315-348.

American Cancer Society (1997). *Smoking facts and figures.* New York: Author.

American Psychiatric Association (1994). *Diagnostic and statistical manual of mental disorders (4th ed.).* Washington, DC: Author.

American Psychological Association Task Force on Psychological Intervention Guidelines (1995). *Template for developing guidelines: Interventions for mental disorders and psychological aspects of physical disorders.* Washington, DC: American Psychological Association.

Amorapanth, P., LeDoux, J. E., & Nader, K. (2000). Different lateral amygdala outputs mediate reactions and actions elicited by a fear-arousing stimulus. *Nature Neuroscience, 3,* 74–79.

Anand, B. K., & Brobeck, J. R. (1951). Hypothalamic control of food intake in rats and cats. *Yale Journal of Biology and Medicine, 24,* 123–140.

Andersen, P. A., & Guerrero, L. K. (Eds.) (1998). *Handbook of communication and emotion: Research, theory, applications, and contexts.* San Diego: Academic Press.

Anderson, C. A. (1999). Attributional style, depression, and loneliness: A cross-cultural comparison of American and Chinese students. *Personality and Social Psychology Bulletin, 25,* 482–499.

Anderson, C. A., & Anderson, K. B. (1998). Temperature and aggression: Paradox, controversy, and a (fairly) clear picture. In R. G. Geen & E. Donnerstein (Eds.), *Human aggression: Theories, research, and implications for social policy.* San Diego: Academic Press.

Anderson, C. A., & Dill, K. E. (2000). Video games and aggressive thoughts, feelings, and behavior in the laboratory and in life. *Journal of Personality and Social Psychology, 78,* 772–790.

Anderson, E. (1994, May). The code of the streets. *Atlantic Monthly,* pp. 81–94.

Anderson, E. M., & Lambert, M. J. (1995). Short-term dynamically oriented psychotherapy: A review and meta-analysis. *Clinical Psychology Review, 15,* 503–514.

Anderson, J. R. (1980). *Cognitive psychology and its implications.* San Francisco: W. H. Freeman.

Anderson, J. R. (1985). *Cognitive psychology and its implications* (2nd ed.). New York: W. H. Freeman.

Anderson, J. R. (1991). The adaptive nature of human categorization. *Psychological Review, 98,* 409–429.

Anderson, M. C., & Neely, J. H. (1996). Interference and inhibition in memory retrieval. In E. L. Bjork & R. A. Bjork (Eds), *Memory. Handbook of perception and cognition* (2nd ed). San Diego: Academic Press.

Anderson, N. D., & Craik, F. I. M. (2000). Memory in the aging brain. In E. Tulving & F. I. M. Craik (Eds.), *The Oxford handbook of memory.* New York: Oxford University Press.

Anderson, S. R., & Lightfoot, D. W. (1999). The human language faculty as an organ. *Annual Review of Physiology, 62,* 697–722.

Andreasen, N. C., Arndt, S., Swayze, V. Cizadlo, T., et al. (1994). Thalamic abnormalities in schizophrenia visualized through magnetic resonance image averaging. *Science, 266,* 294–298.

Annie E. Casey Foundation (1997, February). *City kids count.* [Online]. Available: http//www.aecf.org/aecnews/citykc.htm

Anthony, J. C., Warner, L. A., & Kessler, R. C. (1997). Comparative epidemiology of dependence on tobacco, alcohol, controlled substances, and inhalants: Basic findings from the National Comorbidity Survey. In G. A. Marlatt & G. R. VandenBos (Eds.), *Addictive behaviors: Readings on etiology, prevention and treatment.* Washington, DC: American Psychological Association.

Antonietti, A., & Colombo, B. (1997). The spontaneous occurrence of mental visualization in thinking. *Imagination, Cognition and Personality, 16,* 415–428.

Antrobus, J. (1983). REM and NREM sleep reports: Comparison of word frequencies by cognitive classes. *Psychophysiology, 20,* 562–568.

Antrobus, J. (1991). Dreaming: Cognitive processes during cortical activation and high afferent thresholds. *Psychological Review, 98,* 96–121.

Aponte, H., & Hoffman, L. (1973). The open door. A structural approach to a family with an anorectic child. *Family Process, 12,* 1–44.

Archer, J. (1996). Sex differences in social behavior: Are the social role and evolutionary explanations compatible? *American Psychologist, 51,* 909–917.

Arendt, J., Skene, D. J., Middleton, B., Lockley, S. W., & Deacon, S. (1997). Efficacy of melatonin treatment in jet lag, shift work, and blindness. *Journal of Biological Rhythms, 12,* 604–617.

Argyle, M. (1999). Causes and correlates of happiness. In D. Kahneman, E. Diener, & N. Schwarz (Eds.), *Well-being: The foundations of hedonic psychology.* New York: Russell Sage Foundation.

Armony, J. L., & LeDoux, J. E. (2000). How danger is encoded: Toward a systems, cellular, and computational understanding of cognitive-emotional interactions in fear. In M. S. Gazzaniga (Ed.), *The new cognitive neurosciences* (2nd ed.). Cambridge, MA: MIT Press.

Arnett, P. A. (1997). Autonomic responsivity in psychopaths: A critical review and theoretical proposal. *Clinical Psychology Review, 17,* 903–936.

Aron, A., & Westbay, L. (1996). Dimensions of the prototype of love. *Journal of Personality and Social Psychology, 70,* 535–551.

Aron, L. (1996). *A meeting of minds: Mutuality in psychoanalysis.* Hillsdale, NJ: Analytic Press.

Aronson, E. (1997). *The jigsaw classroom: Building cooperation in the classroom.* Reading, MA: Good Year Books.

Aronson, E., Stephan, C., Sikes, J., Blaney, N., & Snopp, M. (1978). *The jigsaw classroom.* Beverly Hills, CA: Sage Publications.

Aronson, E., Turner, J. A., & Carlsmith, J. M. (1963). Communicator credibility and communicator discrepancy as determinants of opinion change. *Journal of Abnormal and Social Psychology, 67,* 31–36.

Aronson, J., Lustina, M. J., Good, C., Keough, K., Steele, C. M., & Brown, J. (1999). When White men can't do math: Necessary and sufficient factors in stereotype threat. *Journal of Experimental Social Psychology, 35,* 29–46.

Aronson, M., & Hagberg, B. (1998). Neuropsychological disorders in children exposed to alcohol during pregnancy: A follow-up study of 24 children born to alcoholic mothers in Goeteborg, Sweden. *Alcoholism: Clinical and Experimental Research, 22,* 321–324.

Arrigo, J. M., & Pezdek, K. (1997). Lessons from the study of psychogenic amnesia. *Current Directions in Psychological Science, 6,* 148–152.

Asch, S. E. (1946). Forming impressions of personality. *Journal of Abnormal and Social Psychology, 41,* 258–290.

Asch, S. E. (1951). Effects of group pressure upon the modification and distortion of judgment. In Guetzkow, H. (Ed.), *Groups, leadership, and men.* Pittsburgh: Carnegie Press.

Asch, S. E. (1956). Studies of independence and conformity: A minority of one against a unanimous majority. *Psychological Monographs, 70,* 416.

Aserinsky, E., & Kleitman, N. (1953). Regularly occurring periods of ocular motility and concomitant phenomena during sleep. *Science, 118,* 361–375.

Aslin, R. N. (1987). Visual and auditory development in infancy. In J. Osofsky (Ed.), *Handbook of infant development.* New York: Wiley.

Assanand, S. P., John, P. J., & Lehman, D. R. (1998). Teaching theories of hunger and eating: Overcoming students' misconceptions. *Teaching of Psychology, 25,* 44–46.

Associated Press (1989, June 25) Best way to retain complex information: Sleep on it, researchers say. *Seattle Times,* p. A9.

Atkinson, D. (1977). Society and sexes in the Russian past. In D. Atkinson & G. W. Lapidus (Eds.), *Women in Russia.* Stanford, CA: Stanford University Press.

Atkinson, J. W. (Ed.) (1958). *Motives in fantasy, action, and society.* Princeton, NJ: Van Nostrand.

Atkinson, J. W. (1964). *An introduction to motivation.* Princeton, NJ: Van Nostrand.

Atkinson, J. W., & Birch, D. (1978). *An introduction to motivation.* New York: Van Nostrand.

Atkinson, R. C., & Shiffrin, R. M. (1968). Human memory: A proposed system and its control processes. In K. W. Spence & J. T. Spence (Eds.), *Advances in the psychology of learning and motivation: Research and theory* (Vol. 2). New York: Academic Press.

Auerbach, S. M. (1989). Stress management and coping research in the health care setting: An overview and methodological commentary. *Journal of Consulting and Clinical Psychology, 57,* 388–395.

Averill, J. A. (1980). A constructivist view of emotion. In R. Plutchik & H. Kellerman (Eds.), *Emotion: Theory, research and experience* (Vol. 1). New York: Academic Press.

Avery, D. H., Dahl, K., Savage, M. V., & Brengelmann, G. L. (1997). Circadian temperature and cortisol rhythms during a constant routine are phase-delayed in hypersomnic winter depression. *Biological Psychiatry, 41,* 1109–1123.

Avila-White, D., Schneider, A., & Domhoff, G. W. (1999). The most recent dreams of 12–13-year-old boys and girls: A methodological contribution to the study of dream content in teenagers. *Dreaming: Journal of the Association for the Study of Dreams, 9,* 163–171.

Avis, J., & Harris, P. L. (1991). Belief-desire reasoning among Baka children: Evidence for a universal conception of mind. *Child Development, 62,* 460–467.

Ayllon, T., & Azrin, N. H. (1965). The measurement and reinforcement of behavior of psychotics. *Journal of the Experimental Analysis of Behavior, 8,* 357–383.

Ayllon, T., & Azrin, N. H. (1968). *The token economy: A motivational system for therapy and rehabilitation.* New York: Appleton-Century-Crofts.

Ayres, J. J. B. (1998). Fear conditioning and avoidance. In W. T. O'Donohue (Ed.), *Learning and behavior therapy.* Boston: Allyn & Bacon.

Azrin, N. H., & Nunn, R. G. (1973). Habit reversal: A method of eliminating nervous habits and tics. *Behaviour Research and Therapy, 11,* 619–628.

Baars, B. J. (1997). In the theatre of consciousness: Global workspace theory, a rigorous scientific theory of consciousness. *Journal of Consciousness Studies, 4,* 292–309.

Bachman, J. G., Johnson, L. D., & O'Malley, P. M. (1987). *Monitoring the future: Questionnaire responses from the nation's high school seniors.* Ann Arbor, MI: Institute for Social Research, University of Michigan.

Backhaus, W. G., Kliegl, R., & Werner, J. S. (Eds.). (1998). *Color vision: Perspectives from different disciplines.* New York: Walter De Gruyter.

Baddeley, A. D. (1966). Short-term memory for word sequences as a function of acoustic, semantic, and formal similarity. *Quarterly Journal of Experimental Psychology, 18,* 362–365.

Baddeley, A. D. (1986). *Working memory.* Oxford, England: Oxford University Press.

Baddeley, A. D. (1990). *Human memory: Theory and practice.* Boston: Allyn & Bacon.

Baddeley, A. D. (1994). The magical number seven: Still magic after all these years? *Psychological Review, 101,* 353–356.

Baddeley, A. (1998). Recent developments in working memory. *Current Opinion in Neurobiology, 8,* 234-238.

Baddeley, A. D. (2000). Working memory: The interface between memory and cognition. In M. S. Gazzaniga (Ed.), *Cognitive neuroscience: A reader.* Malden, MA: Blackwell.

Baeyens, F., Wrzesniewski, A., de-Houwer, J., & Eelen, P. (1996). Toilet rooms, body massages, and smells: Two field studies on human evaluative odor conditioning. *Current Psychology: Developmental, Learning, Personality, & Social, 15,* 77–96.

Bagley, C., & Ramsay, R. (1997). *Suicidal behaviour in adolescents and adults: Research, taxonomy and prevention.* Ashgate, UK: Ashgate.

Bahrick, H. P. (1984). Semantic memory content in permastore: Fifty years of memory for Spanish learned in school. *Journal of Experimental Psychology: General, 113,* 1–29.

Bahrick, H. P., Bahrick, P. O., & Wittlinger, R. P. (1975). Fifty years of memory for names and faces: A cross-sectional approach. *Journal of Experimental Psychology: General, 104,* 54–75.

Bahrick, H. P., Hall, L. K., & Berger, S. A. (1996). Accuracy and distortion in memory for high school grades. *Psychological Science, 7,* 265–271.

Bailey, C. H., & Chen, M. (1992). The anatomy of long-term sensitization in *Aplysia:* Morphological insights into learning and memory. In L. R. Squire, N. M. Weinberger, G. Lynch, & J. L. McGaugh (Eds.), *Memory: Organization and locus of change.* New York: Oxford University Press.

Bailey, J. M., & Pillard, R. C. (1991). A genetic study of male sexual orientation. *Archives of General Psychiatry, 48,* 1089–1096.

Bailey, J. M., Pillard, R. C., Neale, M. C., & Agyei, Y. (1993). Heritable factors influence sexual orientation in women. *Archives of General Psychiatry, 50,* 217–223.

Baillargeon, R. (1987). Object permanence in 3 1/2- and 4 1/2-month-old infants. *Developmental Psychology, 23,* 655–664.

Baker, L. H., Cooney, N. L., & Pomerleau, O. F. (1987). Craving for alcohol: Theoretical processes and treatment procedures. In W. M. Cox (Ed.), *Treatment and prevention of alcohol problems: A resource manual.* New York: Academic Press.

Baldwin, E. (1993). The case for animal research in psychology. *Journal of Social Issues, 49,* 121–131.

Ballenger, J. C. (2000). Panic disorder and agoraphobia. In G. Fink (Ed.), *Encyclopedia of stress.* San Diego: Academic Press.

Bandura, A. (1965). Influence of models' reinforcement contingencies on the acquisition of imitated responses. *Journal of Personality and Social Psychology, 1,* 589–595.

Bandura, A. (1969). *Principles of behavior modification.* New York: Holt, Rinehart & Winston.

Bandura, A. (1973). *Aggression: A social learning analysis.* Englewood Cliffs, NJ: Prentice Hall.

Bandura, A. (1977a). Self-efficacy: Toward a unifying theory of behavioral change. *Psychological Review, 84,* 191–215.

Bandura, A. (1977b). *Social learning theory.* Englewood Cliffs, NJ: Prentice Hall.

Bandura, A. (1986). *Social foundations of thought and action: A social-cognitive theory.* Englewood Cliffs, NJ: Prentice Hall.

Bandura, A. (1988). Mechanisms of moral disengagement in terrorism. In W. Reich (Ed.), *The psychology of terrorism: Behaviors, world-views, states of mind.* New York: Cambridge University Press.

Bandura, A. (1989). Social cognitive theory. *Annals of Child Development, 6,* 3–58.

Bandura, A. (1991). Human agency: The rhetoric and the reality. *American Psychologist, 46,* 157–162.

Bandura, A. (1997). *Self-efficacy: The exercise of control.* New York: W. H. Freeman.

Bandura, A., & Cervone, D. (1983). Self-evaluative and self-efficacy mechanisms governing the motivational effects of goal systems. *Journal of Personality and Social Psychology, 45,* 1017–1028.

Bandura, A., O'Leary, A., Taylor, C. B., Gauthier, J., & Gossard, D. (1987). Perceived self-efficacy and pain control: Opioid and nonopioid mechanisms. *Journal of Personality and Social Psychology, 53,* 563–571.

Bandura, A., & Walters, R. H. (1959). *Adolescent aggression.* New York: Ronald Press.

Banks, W. P., & Krajicek, D. (1991). Perception. *Annual Review of Psychology, 42,* 305–332.

Barbalet, J. M. (1998). *Emotion, social theory and social structure: A macrosociological approach.* New York: Cambridge University Press.

Barber, J. (1977). Rapid induction analgesia. *American Journal of Clinical Hypnosis, 19,* 138–143.

Barber, J. (1998). The mysterious persistence of hypnotic analgesia. *International Journal of Clinical and Experimental Hypnosis, 46,* 28–43.

Bardo, M. T. (1998). Neuropharmacological mechanisms of drug reward: Beyond dopamine in the nucleus accumbens. *Critical Reviews in Neurobiology, 12,* 37-67.

Barefoot, J. C., Dodge, K. A., Peterson, B. L., Dahlstrom, W. G., & Williams, R. B. (1989). The Cook-Medley Hostility Scale: Item content and ability to predict survival. *Psychosomatic Medicine, 51,* 46–57.

Bargh, J. A. (1984). Automatic and conscious processing of social information. In R. S. Wyer & T. K. Srull (Eds.), *Handbook of social cognition* (Vol. 3). Hillsdale, NJ: Erlbaum.

Bargh, J. A. (1997). The automaticity of everyday life. In R. S. Wyer, Jr. (Ed.), *The automaticity of everyday life: Advances in social cognition* (Vol. 10). New York: Guilford Press.

Bargh, J. A., & Chartrand, T. L. (1999). The unbearable automaticity of being. *American Psychologist, 54,* 462–479.

Barlow, D. H. (1988). *Anxiety and its disorders: The nature and treatment of anxiety and panic.* New York: Guilford Press.

Barlow, D. H. (1991). Disorders of emotion. *Psychological Inquiry, 2,* 58–71.

Barlow, D. H. (1997). Cognitive-behavioral therapy for panic disorder: Current status. *Journal of Clinical Psychiatry, 58* (Suppl. 2), 32–36.

Barlow, D. H., & Rapee, R. M. (1991). *Mastering stress: A lifestyle approach.* Dallas: American Health.

Barnes, G. E., & Prosen, H. (1985). Parental death and depression. *Journal of Abnormal Psychology, 94,* 64–69.

Barnes, T. R. (Ed.) (1994). *Antipsychotic drugs and their side effects.* San Diego: Academic Press.

Barnett, J. E., & Porter, J. E. (1998). The suicidal patient: Clinical and risk management strategies. In L. VandeCreek & S. Knapp (Eds), *Innovations in clinical practice: A source book* (Vol. 16). Sarasota, FL: Professional Resource Press.

Baron, P., & Hanna, J. (1990). Egocentrism and depressive symptomatology in young adults. *Social Behavior and Personality, 18,* 279–285.

Baron, R. S. (1986). Distraction-conflict theory: Progress and problems. In L. Berkowitz (Ed.), *Advances in experimental social psychology* (Vol. 20). New York: Academic Press.

Baron, R. S., Cutrona, C. E., Hicklin, D., Russell, D. W., & Lubaroff, D. M. (1990). Social support and immune responses among spouses of cancer patients. *Journal of Personality and Social Psychology, 59,* 344–352.

Baron, R. S., Vandello, J. A., & Brunsman, B. (1996). The forgotten variable in conformity research: Impact of task importance on social influence. *Journal of Personality and Social Psychology, 71,* 915–927.

Barondes, S. H. (1999). *Mood genes: Hunting for origins of mania and depression.* New York: Oxford University Press.

Barrett, G. V., & Depinet, R. L. (1991). A reconsideration of testing for competence rather than for intelligence. *American Psychologist, 46,* 1012–1024.

Barrett, P. T., & Eysenck, H. J. (1992). Brain evoked potentials and intelligence: The Hendrickson paradigm. *Intelligence, 16,* 361–381.

Barsalou, L. W. (1992). *Cognitive psychology: An overview for cognitive scientists.* Hillsdale, NJ: Erlbaum.

Barsky, A. J. (1992). Amplification, somatization, and the somatoform disorders. *Psychosomatics, 33,* 28–34.

Bartlett, F. C. (1932). *Remembering: A study in experimental and social psychology.* New York: Cambridge University Press.

Bartoshuk, L. M., & Beauchamp, G. K. (1994). Chemical senses. *Annual Review of Psychology, 45,* 419–449.

Bassok, M., & Holyoak, K. J. (1989). Interdomain transfer between isomorphic topics in algebra and physics. *Journal of Experimental*

Psychology: Memory, Learning, and Cognition, 15 (1), 153–166.

Bastik, T. (1982). *Intuition: How we think and act.* New York: Wiley.

Bates, M. S., Edwards, W. T., & Anderson, K. O. (1993). Ethnocultural influences on variation in chronic pain perception. *Pain, 52,* 101–112.

Batson, C. D., Duncan, B. D., Ackerman, P., Buckley, T., & Birch, K. (1981). Is empathic emotion a source of altruistic motivation? *Journal of Personality and Social Psychology, 40,* 290–302.

Batson, C. D., Sager, K., Garst, E., & Kang, M. (1997). Is empathy-induced helping due to self-other merging? *Journal of Personality and Social Psychology, 73,* 495–509.

Batson, G. D. (1991). *The altruism question: Toward a social-psychological answer.* Hillsdale, NJ: Erlbaum.

Baudry, M., & Davis, J. L. (Eds.) (1991). *Long-term potentiation: A debate of current issues.* Cambridge, MA: MIT Press.

Bauer, K. E., & McCanne, T. R. (1980). Autonomic and central nervous system responding during hypnosis and simulation of hypnosis. *International Journal of Clinical and Experimental Hypnosis, 28,* 148–163.

Baum, A., Krantz, D. S., & Gatchel, R. J. (1997). *An introduction to health psychology* (3rd ed.). Boston: McGraw-Hill.

Baum, A., & Posluszny, D. M. (1999). Health psychology: Mapping biobehavioral contributions to health and illness. *Annual Review of Psychology, 50,* 137–164.

Baumeister, R. F. (1984). Choking under pressure: Self-consciousness and paradoxical effects of incentives on skillful performance. *Journal of Personality and Social Psychology, 46,* 610–620.

Baumeister, R. F. (1989). The optimal margin of illusion. *Journal of Social and Clinical Psychology, 8,* 176–189.

Baumeister, R. F., & Leary, M. R. (1995). The need to belong: Desire for interpersonal attachments as a fundamental human motivation. *Psychological Bulletin, 117,* 497–529.

Baumrind, D. (1964). Some thoughts on ethics of research: After reading Milgram's behavioral study of 'obedience.' *American Psychologist, 19,* 421–423.

Baumrind, D. (1967). Child care practices anteceding three patterns of preschool behavior. *Genetic Psychology Monographs, 75,* 43–88.

Baumrind, D. (1980). New directions in socialization research. *American Psychologist, 35,* 639–652.

Baumrind, D. (1983). Rejoinder to Lewis's reinterpretation of parental firm control effects: Are authoritative families really harmonious? *Psychological Bulletin, 94,* 132–142.

Baumrind, D. (1991). Parenting styles and adolescent development. In J. Brooks-Gunn, R. Lerner, & A. C. Petersen (Eds.), *The encyclopedia of adolescence.* New York: Garland.

Bauserman, R. (1996). Sexual aggression and pornography: A review of correlational research. *Basic and Applied Social Psychology, 18,* 405–427.

Baxter, L. R. (1992). Neuroimaging studies of obsessive compulsive disorder. *Psychiatric Clinics of North America, 15,* 871–884.

Beahrs, J. O. (1994). Dissociative identity disorder: Adaptive deception of self and others. *Bulletin of the American Academy of Psychiatric Law, 22,* 223–237.

Beaman, A. L., Barnes, P. J., Klentz, B., & McQuirk, B. (1978). Increasing helping rates through information dissemination: Teaching pays. *Personality and Social Psychology Bulletin, 4,* 406–411.

Beardsley, L., & Pedersen, P. (1997). Health and culture-centered intervention. In J. W. Berry, M. H. Segall, and C. Kagitçibasi (Eds.), *Handbook of Cross-Cultural Psychology: Social Behavior and Applications* (Vol 1, 2nd ed.). Boston: Allyn & Bacon.

Beauchamp, G. K., & Bartoshuk, L. (Eds.) (1997). *Tasting and smelling.* Philadelphia: Academic Press.

Bechara, A., Damasio, A. R., Damasio, H., & Anderson, S. W. (1994). Insensitivity to future consequences following damage to human prefrontal cortex. *Cognition, 50,* 7–15.

Bechara, A., Tranel, D., et al. (1995). Double dissociation of conditioning and declarative knowledge relative to the amygdala and hippocampus in humans. *Science, 29,* 1115–1118.

Beck, A. P., & Lewis, C. M. (Eds.) (2000). *The process of group psychotherapy: Systems for analyzing change.* Washington, DC: American Psychological Association.

Beck, A. T. (1976). *Cognitive therapy and the emotional disorders.* New York: International Universities Press.

Beck, A. T. (1988). Cognitive approaches to panic disorder: Theory and therapy. In S. Rachman and J. D. Maser (Eds.), *Panic: Psychological perspectives.* Hillsdale, NJ: Erlbaum.

Beck, A. T. (1991). Cognitive therapy: A 30-year retrospective. *American Psychologist, 46,* 368–375.

Beck, A. T., & Freeman, A. (1990). *Cognitive theory of personality disorders.* New York: Guilford Press.

Beck, A. T., Rush, A. J., Shaw, B. F., & Emery, G. (1979). *Cognitive therapy of depression.* New York: Guilford Press.

Becker, A. E., Grinspoon, S. K., Klibanski, A., & Herzog, D. B. (1999). Current concepts: Eating disorders. *New England Journal of Medicine, 340,* 1092–1098.

Becker, E. (1973). *The denial of death.* New York: Free Press.

Becker, J. B., Breedlove, S. M., & Crews, D. (Eds.) (1992). *Behavioral endocrinology.* Cambridge, MA: MIT Press.

Bedard, J., & Chi, M. T. (1992). Expertise. *Current Directions in Psychological Science, 4,* 135–139.

Bednekoff, P. A., & Balda, R. P. (1996). Observational spatial memory in Clark's nutcrackers and Mexican jays. *Animal Behaviour, 52,* 833–839.

Beecher, H. K. (1959). Generalization from pain of various types and diverse origins. *Science, 130,* 267–268.

Beitman, B. D. (1998). *The psychotherapist's guide to cost containment: How to survive and thrive in an age of managed care.* Newbury Park, CA: Sage Publications.

Bekesy, G. von (1957). The ear. *Scientific American, 230,* 66–78.

Bell, A. P., Weinberg, M. S., & Hammersmith, S. K. (1981). *Sexual preference: Its development in men and women.* Bloomington: Indiana University Press.

Belsky, J., & Hsieh, K. H. (1998). Patterns of marital change during the early childhood years: Parent personality, coparenting, and division-of-labor correlates. *Journal of Family Psychology, 12,* 511–528.

Bem, D. J. (1972). Self-perception theory. In L. Berkowitz (Ed.), *Advances in experimental social psychology* (Vol. 6). New York: Academic Press.

Bem, D. J. (1996). Exotic becomes erotic: A developmental theory of sexual orientation. *Psychological Review, 103,* 320–335.

Bem, D. J., & Honorton, C. (1994). Does psi exist? Replicable evidence for an anomalous process of information transfer. *Psychological Bulletin, 115,* 4–18.

Bem, S. L. (1981). Gender schema theory: A cognitive account of sex typing. *Psychological Review, 88,* 354–364.

Benjamin, L. T., Cavell, T. A. & Shallenberger, W. R. (1984). Staying with initial answers on objective tests: Is it a myth? *Teaching of Psychology, 11,* 133–141.

Bennett, H. L. (1983). Remembering drink orders: The memory skills of cocktail waitresses. *Human Learning, 2,* 157–169.

Bennett, N. G., Blanc, A. K., & Bloom, D. E. (1988). Commitment and the modern union: Assessing the link between premarital cohabitation and subsequent marital stability. *American Sociological Review, 53,* 127–138.

Benski, C., & Scientists from CRSSA. (1998). Testing new claims of dermo-optical perception. *Skeptical Inquirer, 22*(1), 21–26.

Bentley, D. R. (2000). The human genome project: An overview. *Medical Research Review, 20,* 189–196.

Benton, A. L. (1994). Neuropsychological assessment. *Annual Review of Psychology, 45,* 1–23.

Berg, K. M., & Boswell, A. E. (1998). Infants' detection of increments in low- and high-frequency noise. *Perception and Psychophysics, 60,* 1044–1051.

Bergen, R. K. (1998). *Issues in intimate violence.* Thousand Oaks, CA: Sage Publications.

Berger, M., Vollmann, J., Hohagen, F., & Konig, A. (1997). Sleep deprivation combined with consecutive sleep phase advance as a fast-acting therapy in depression: An open pilot trial in medicated and unmedicated patients. *American Journal of Psychiatry, 154,* 870–872.

Berger, R. J., & Phillips, N. H. (1995). Energy conservation and sleep. *Behavioural Brain Research, 69,* 65–73.

Berkowitz, L. (1972). Social norms, feelings, and other factors affecting helping and altruism. In L. Berkowitz (Ed.), *Advances in experimental social psychology.* New York: Academic Press.

Berkowitz, L. (1990). On the formation and regulation of anger and aggression. *American Psychologist, 45,* 494–503.

Berkowitz, L. (1998). Aggressive personalities. In D. F. Barone, M. Hersen, & V. B. Van Hasselt (Eds.), *Advanced personality.* New York: Plenum.

Berlin, R. M., & Qayyum, U. (1986). Sleepwalking: Diagnosis and treatment through the life cycle. *Psychosomatics, 27,* 755–760.

Bernstein, I. L. (1978). Learned taste aversions in children receiving chemotherapy. *Science, 200*, 1302–1303.

Berry, J., & Ataca, B. (2000). Cultural factors. In G. Fink (Ed.), *Encyclopedia of stress.* San Diego: Academic Press.

Berry, J. W., Poortinga, Y. H., Segall, M. H., & Dasen, P. (1992). *Cross-cultural psychology: Research and application.* New York: Cambridge University Press.

Berry, J. W., Segall, M. H., & Kagitçibasi (1997). *Handbook of cross-cultural psychology: Social behavior and applications.* Boston: Allyn & Bacon.

Berry, L. M. (1998). *Psychology at work* (2nd ed.). Boston: McGraw-Hill.

Berscheid, E. (1984). *The problem of emotion in close relationships.* New York: Plenum.

Best, D. L., Williams, J. E., Cloud, J. M., Davis, S. W., Robertson, L. S., Edwards, J. R., Giles, H., & Fowles, J. (1977). Development of sex-trait stereotypes among young children in the United States, England, and Ireland. *Child Development, 48*, 1375–1384.

Betancourt, H., & Blair, I. (1992). A cognition (attribution)-emotion model of violence in conflict situations. *Personality and Social Psychology Bulletin, 18*, 343–350.

Beutler, L. E., Machado, P. P., & Neufeldt, S. A. (1994). Therapist variables. In A. E. Bergin & S. L. Garfield (Eds.), *Handbook of psychotherapy and behavior change* (4th ed.). New York: Wiley.

Beyer, S. (1990). Gender differences in the accuracy of self-evaluations of performance. *Journal of Personality and Social Psychology, 59*, 960–970.

Beyerstein, B. L. (1990). Brainscams: Neuromythologies of the New Age. *International Journal of Mental Health, 19*, 27–36.

Biener, L., & Boudreau, L. (1991). Social power and influence. In R. M. Baron, W. G. Graziano, & C. Stangor (Eds.), *Social psychology.* Ft. Worth, TX: Holt, Rinehart & Winston.

Billings, A. G., & Moos, R. H. (1981). The role of coping responses and social resources in attenuating the stress of life events. *Journal of Behavioral Medicine, 4*, 139–157.

Billings, A. G., & Moos, R. H. (1984). Coping, stress, and social resources among adults with unipolar depression. *Journal of Personality and Social Psychology, 46*, 877–891.

Binder, J. L., & Strupp, H. H. (1997). "Negative process": A recurrently discovered and underestimated facet of therapeutic process and outcome in the individual psychotherapy of adults. *Clinical Psychology: Science & Practice, 4*, 121–139.

Binet, A. M., & Simon, T. (1905). Methodes nouvelles pour le diagnostic du niveau intellectuel des anormaux. *L'Anee Psychologique, 11*, 191–224.

Björkqvist, K. (1997). The inevitability of conflict, but not of violence: Theoretical considerations on conflict and aggression. In D. P. Fry & K. Björkqvist (Eds.), *Cultural variation in conflict resolution: Alternatives to violence.* Mahwah, NJ: Erlbaum.

Black, D. W. (1999). *Bad boys, bad men: Confronting antisocial personality disorder.* New York: Oxford University Press.

Black, D. W., Yates, W. R., & Andreasen, N. C. (1988). Schizophrenia, schizophreniform disorder, and delusional paranoid disorders.

In J. A. Talbott, R. E. Hales, & S. C. Yudofsky (Eds.), *Textbook of psychiatry.* Washington, DC: American Psychiatric Press.

Black, M., & Krishnakumar, A. (1998). Children in low-income, urban settings: Interventions to promote mental health and well-being. *American Psychologist, 53*, 635–646.

Blackwood, D. (2000). Genetic predispositions to stressful conditions. In G. Fink (Ed.), *Encyclopedia of stress.* San Diego: Academic Press.

Blakemore, C., & Cooper, G. F. (1970). Development of the brain depends on visual environment. *Nature, 228*, 477–478.

Blank, R. H. (1999). *Brain policy: How the new neuroscience will change our lives and our politics.* Washington, DC: Georgetown University Press.

Blascovich, J., Mendes, W. B., Hunter, S. B., & Salomon, K. (1999). Social "facilitation" as challenge and threat. *Journal of Personality and Social Psychology, 77*, 68–77.

Blascovich, J., Wyer, N. A., Swart, L. A., & Kibler, J. L. (1997). Racism and racial categorization. *Journal of Personality and Social Psychology, 72*, 1364–1372.

Blasi, A. (1980). Bridging moral cognition and moral action: A critical review of the literature. *Psychological Bulletin, 88*, 1–45.

Blass, T. (1996). Attribution of responsibility and trust in the Milgram obedience experiment. *Journal of Applied Social Psychology, 26*, 1529–1535.

Blass, T. (Ed.) (2000). *Obedience to authority: Current perspectives on the Milgram paradigm.* Mahwah, NJ: Erlbaum.

Blechman, E., & Brownell, K. D. (1998). *Behavioral medicine and women: A comprehensive handbook.* New York: Guilford Press.

Blessing, W. W. (1997). *The lower brainstem and bodily homeostasis.* New York: Oxford University Press.

Blethen, S. L., Baptista, J., Kuntze, J., Foley, T., LaFranchi, S., & Johanson, A. (1997). Adult height in growth hormone (GH)-deficient children treated with biosynthetic GH. The Genentech Growth Study Group. *Journal of Clinical Endocrinology and Metabolism, 82*, 418–420.

Bliss, T. V., & Dolphin, A.-C. (1982). What is the mechanism of long-term potentiation in the hippocampus? *Trends in Neurosciences, 5*, 289–290.

Block, L., & Keller, P. (1998). Beyond protection motivation: An integrative theory of health appeals. *Journal of Applied Social Psychology, 28*, 1584–1608.

Blodgett, H. C. (1929). The effect of the introduction of reward on the maze performance of rats. *University of California Publications in Psychology, 4*(8), 114-126.

Blodgett, R. (1986, May). Lost in the stars: Psychics strike out (again). *People Expression*, 32–35.

Bloom, F. E. (1998). *Brain, mind and behavior.* San Francisco: W. H. Freeman.

Bobo, L. (1988). Attitudes toward the black political movement: Trends, meaning, and effects of racial policy preferences. *Social Psychology Quarterly, 51*, 287–302.

Bochner, S., & Insko, C. A. (1966). Communicator discrepancy, source credibility, and opinion change. *Journal of Personality and Social Psychology, 4*, 614–621.

Boesch, C. (1991). Teaching among wild chimpanzees. *Animal Behaviour, 41*, 530–532.

Boesch, C. (1995). Innovation in wild chimpanzees (Pan troglodytes). *International Journal of Primatology, 16*, 1–16.

Bohart, A. C., & Greenberg, L. S. (Eds.) (1997). *Empathy reconsidered: New directions in psychotherapy.* Washington, DC: American Psychological Association.

Bolles, R. C. (1979). *Learning theory* (2nd ed.). New York: Holt, Rinehart & Winston.

Bolles, R. C. (1980). Some functionalistic thought about regulation. In F. M. Toates & T. R. Halliday (Eds.), *Analysis of motivational processes.* London: Academic Press.

Bolles, R. C., & Beecher, M. D. (Eds.) (1988). *Evolution and learning.* Hillsdale, NJ: Erlbaum.

Bonanno, G. A., Kaltman, S., Duberstein, P. R., & Masling, J. M. (2000). The assumed necessity of working through memories of traumatic experiences. In P. R. Duberstein & J. M. Masling (Eds.), *Psychodynamic perspectives on sickness and health.* Washington, DC: American Psychological Association.

Bond, R., & Smith, P. B. (1996). Culture and conformity: A meta-analysis of studies using Asch's (1952b, 1956) line judgment task. *Psychological Bulletin, 119*, 111-137.

Bond, C. F., Jr., & Titus, L. J. (1983). Social facilitation: A meta-analysis of 241 studies. *Psychological Bulletin, 94*, 265–292.

Bonnel, A. M., & Hafter, E. R. (1998). Divided attention between simultaneous auditory and visual signals. *Perception and Psychophysics, 60*, 179–190.

Bonvillian, J. D., & Patterson, F. G. P. (1997). Sign language acquisition and the development of meaning in a lowland gorilla. In C. Mandell & A. McCabe (Eds.), *The problem of meaning: Behavioral and cognitive perspectives.* Amsterdam, Netherlands: North-Holland/Elsevier Science.

Book, H. E. (1997). *How to practice brief psychodynamic psychotherapy: The core conflictual relationship theme method.* Washington, DC: American Psychological Association.

Booth-Kewley, S., & Friedman, H. S. (1987). Psychological predictors of heart disease: A quantitative review. *Psychological Bulletin, 101*, 343–362.

Bootzin, R. R. (1979). Effects of self-control procedures for insomnia. *American Journal of Clinical Biofeedback, 2*, 70–77.

Bootzin, R. R., Rider, S. P., Pressman, M. R., & Orr, W. C. (Eds.) (1997). *Behavioral techniques and biofeedback for insomnia. Understanding sleep: The evaluation and treatment of sleep disorders..* Washington, DC.: American Psychological Association.

Borbely, A. A., Achermann, P., Trachsel, L., & Tobler, I. (1989). Sleep initiation and initial sleep intensity: Interactions of homeostatic and circadian mechanisms. *Journal of Biological Rhythms, 4*, 149–160.

Borke, H. (1975). Piaget's mountains revisited: Changes in the egocentric landscape. *Developmental Psychology, 11*, 240–243.

Bornstein, R. F. (1989). Subliminal techniques as propaganda tools: Review and critique. *Journal of Mind and Behavior, 10*, 231–262.

Borod, J. C. (2000). *The neuropsychology of emotion.* New York: Oxford University Press.

Botman, H. I., & Crovitz, H. F. (1989–1990). Dream reports and autobiographical memory. *Imagination, Cognition and Personality, 9,* 213–224.

Bouchard, C., Tremblay, A., Despres, J. P., Nadeau, A., Lupien, P. J., & Theriault, G. (1990). The response to long-term overfeeding in identical twins. *The New England Journal of Medicine, 322,* 1477–1482.

Bouchard, T. J., Lykken, D. T., McGue, M., Segal, N. L., & Tellegen, A. (1990). Sources of human psychological differences: The Minnesota study of twins reared apart. *Science, 250,* 223–228.

Boucher, J. D., & Ekman, P. (1975). Facial areas and emotional information. *Journal of Communication, 25,* 21–29.

Boulos, Z. (1998). Bright light treatment for jet lag and shift work. In R. Lam & W. Raymond (Eds.), *Seasonal affective disorder and beyond: Light treatment for SAD and non-SAD conditions.* Washington, DC: American Psychiatric Press.

Bower, G. H. (2000). A brief history of memory research. In E. Tulving and F. I. M. Craik (Eds.), *The Oxford handbook of memory.* New York: Oxford University Press.

Bower, G. H., Clark, M. C., Lesgold, M. A., & Winzenz, D. (1969). Hierarchical retrieval schemes in recall of categorized word lists. *Journal of Verbal Learning and Verbal Behavior, 8,* 323–343.

Bowers, K. S. (1992). Imagination and dissociation in hypnotic responding. *International Journal of Clinical and Experimental Hypnosis, 40,* 253–275.

Bowlby, J. (1958). The nature of the child's tie to his mother. *International Journal of Psychoanalysis, 39,* 350–373.

Bowlby, J. (1969). *Attachment and loss: Vol. 1. Attachment.* New York: Basic Books.

Bowlby, J. (1973). *Attachment and loss: Vol. 2. Separation: Anxiety and anger.* London: Hogarth.

Bowlby, J. (2000a). *Loss: Sadness and depression.* New York: Basic Books.

Bowlby, J. (2000b). *Separation: Anxiety and anger.* New York: Basic Books.

Brandon, S., Boakes, J., Glaser, D., & Green, R. (1998). Recovered memories of childhood sexual abuse: Implications for clinical practice. *British Journal of Psychiatry, 172,* 296–307.

Bransford, J. D., & Johnson, M. K. (1972). Contextual prerequisites for understanding: Some investigations of comprehension and recall. *Journal of Verbal Learning and Verbal Behavior, 11,* 717–726.

Brantley, P., & Garrett, V. D. (1993). Psychobiological approaches to health and disease. In P. B. Sutker & H. E. Adams (Eds.), *Comprehensive handbook of psychopathology* (2nd ed.). New York: Plenum.

Bray, J. H., & Berger, S. H. (1993). Developmental Issues in Step Families Research Project: Family relationships and parent-child interactions. *Journal of Family Psychology, 7,* 76–90.

Brayfield, A. H., & Crockett, W. H. (1955). Employee attitudes and employee performance. *Psychological Bulletin, 52,* 396–424.

Breedlove, S. M. (1992). Sexual differentiation of brain and behavior. In J. B. Becker, S. M. Breedlove, & D. Crews (Eds.), *Behavioral endocrinology.* Cambridge, MA: MIT Press.

Brehm, J. W., & Self, E. A. (1989). The intensity of motivation. *Annual Review of Psychology, 40,* 109–131.

Breland, K., & Breland, M. (1961). The misbehavior of organisms. *American Psychologist, 16,* 681–684.

Breland, K., & Breland, M. (1966). *Animal behavior.* New York: Macmillan.

Bremner, J. D. (2000). Neurobiology of posttraumatic stress disorder. In G. Fink (Ed.), *Encyclopedia of stress.* San Diego: Academic Press.

Brewer, K. R., & Wann, D. L. (1998). Observational learning effectiveness as a function of model characteristics: Investigating the importance of social power. *Social Behavior and Personality, 26,* 1–10.

Brickman, P., Coates, D., & Janoff-Bulman (1978). Lottery winners and accident victims: Is happiness relative? *Journal of Personality and Social Psychology, 36,* 917–927.

Brief, A. P., Butcher, A. H., George, J. M., & Link, K. E. (1993). Integrating bottom-up and top-down theories of subjective well being: The case of health. *Journal of Personality and Social Psychology, 64,* 646–653.

Briere, J., & Lanktree, C. (1983). Sex role-related effects of sex bias in language. *Sex Roles, 9,* 625–632.

Brinton, R. D., & Berger, T. W. (2000). Hippocampal neurons. In G. Fink (Ed.), *Encyclopedia of stress.* San Diego: Academic Press.

Brislin, R. (1993). *Understanding culture's influence on behavior.* Fort Worth, TX: Harcourt Brace Jovanovich.

Broberg, D. J., & Bernstein, I. L. (1987). Candy as a scapegoat in the prevention of food aversions in children receiving chemotherapy. *Cancer, 60,* 2344–2347.

Brody, G. H., Neubaum, E., & Forehand, R. (1988). Serial marriages: A heuristic analysis of an emerging family form. *Psychological Bulletin, 103,* 211–222.

Brody, G. H., & Stoneman, Z. (1985). Peer imitation: An examination of status and competence hypotheses. *Journal of Genetic Psychology, 146,* 161–170.

Brody, J. E. (1995, September 14). Even moderate weight gain can be risky, study finds. *New York Times,* pp. A1, A11.

Bronzaft, A. L., Ahern, K. D., McGinn, R., O'Connor, J., & Savino, B. (1998). Aircraft noise: A potential health hazard. *Environment and Behavior, 30,* 101–113.

Brooks-Gunn, J., & Warren, M. P. (1985). Measuring physical status and timing in early adolescence: A developmental perspective. *Journal of Youth and Adolescence, 14,* 163–184.

Brown, A. L. (1997). Transforming schools into communities of thinking and learning about serious matters. *American Psychologist, 52,* 399–413.

Brown, A. L., Bransford, J. D., Ferrara, R. A., & Campione, J. C. (1983). Learning, remembering, and understanding. In P. Mussen (Ed.), *Handbook of child psychology: Vol. 3. Cognitive development.* New York: Wiley.

Brown, A. S. (1991). A review of the tip-of-the-tongue experience. *Psychological Bulletin, 109,* 204–223.

Brown, B. B., Clasen, D. R., & Eicher, S. A. (1986). Perceptions of peer pressure, peer conformity dispositions, and self-reported behavior among adolescents. *Developmental Psychology, 22,* 521–530.

Brown, E., Deffenbacher, K., & Sturgill, W. (1977). Memory for faces and the circumstances of encounter. *Journal of Applied Psychology, 62,* 311–318.

Brown, G. W., & Harris, T. O. (1978). *Social origins of depression.* London: Tavistock Press.

Brown, J. A. (1958). Some tests of the decay theory of immediate memory. *Quarterly Journal of Experimental Psychology, 10,* 12–21.

Brown, J. D. (1998). *The self.* Boston: McGraw-Hill.

Brown, J. M. (1998). *Self-regulation and the addictive behaviors.* In W. R. Miller & N. Heather (Eds.), *Treating addictive behaviors* (2nd ed.). New York: Plenum.

Brown, L. S. (1994). *Subversive dialogues: Theory in feminist therapy.* New York: Basic Books.

Brown, L. S. (2000). The controversy concerning recovered memory of traumatic events. In A. Y. Shalev, R. Yehuda, & A. C. McFarlane (Eds.), *International handbook of human response to trauma.* New York: Kluwer Academic/Plenum.

Brown, N. O. (1959). *Life against death.* New York: Random House.

Brown, R., & Kulik, J. (1977). Flashbulb memories. *Cognition, 5,* 73–99.

Brown, S. L., & Booth, A. (1996). Cohabitation versus marriage: A comparison of relationship quality. *Journal of Marriage and the Family, 58,* 668–678.

Brown, T. S., & Wallace, P. (1980). *Physiological psychology.* New York: Academic Press.

Brownell, K. D. (1994). *The LEARN program for weight control.* Dallas: American Health.

Brownell, K. D., & Rodin, J. (1994). The dieting maelstrom: Is it possible and advisable to lose weight? *American Psychologist, 49,* 781–791.

Bruce, T. J., & Sanderson, W. C. (1998). *Specific phobias: Clinical applications of evidence-based psychotherapy.* Northvale, NJ: Jason Aronson.

Bruch, H. (1973). *Eating disorders: Obesity, anorexia nervosa, and the person within.* New York: Basic Books.

Bruck, M., & Ceci, S. J. (1999). The suggestibility of children's memory. *Annual Review of Psychology, 50,* 419–439.

Bruck, M., Ceci, S. J., & Francoeur, E. (2000). Children's use of anatomically detailed dolls to report genital touching in a medical examination: Developmental and gender comparisons. *Journal of Experimental Psychology: Applied, 6,* 74–83.

Bruck, M., Ceci, S. J., Francoeur, E., & Barr, R. (1995). "I hardly cried when I got my shot": Influencing children's reports about a visit to their pediatrician. *Child Development, 66,* 193–208.

Bruck, M., Ceci, S. J., & Hembrooke, H. (1998). Reliability and credibility of young children's reports: From research to policy and practice. *American Psychologist, 53,* 136–151.

Bruederl, J., Diekmann, A., & Engelhardt, H. (1997). Erhoeht eine Probeehe das Scheidungsrisiko? Eine empirische Untersuchung mit dem Familiensurvey./ Does a trial marriage increase divorce risk? Empirical study of the Families Survey. *Koelner Zeitschrift fuer Soziologie und Sozialpsychologie, 49,* 205–222.

Bruunk, B., & Gibbons, F. X. (Eds.) (1997). *Health, coping, and well-being: Perspectives from social comparison theory.* Mahwah, NJ: Erlbaum.

Bryan, J., III. (1986). *Hodgepodge: A commonplace book.* New York: Ballantine.

Bryant, R. A., & Harvey, A. G. (2000). *Acute stress disorder: A handbook of theory, assessment, and treatment.* Washington, DC: American Psychological Association.

Bucci, W. (1997). *Psychoanalysis and cognitive science: A multiple code theory.* New York: Guilford Press.

Buchanan, C. M., Eccles, J. S., & Becker, J. B. (1992). Are adolescents the victims of raging hormones? Evidence for activational effects of hormones on moods and behaviors at adolescence. *Psychological Bulletin, 111,* 62–107.

Buck, L., & Axel, R. (1991). A novel multigene family may encode odorant receptors: A molecular basis for odor recognition. *Cell, 65,* 175–187.

Buck, R. & Ginsburg, B. (1991). Spontaneous communication and altruism: The communicative gene hypothesis. In M. S. Clark (Ed.), *Prosocial behavior.* Newbury Park, CA: Sage.

Buckingham, M., & Coffman, C. (1999). *Gallup's discoveries about great managers and great workplaces.* The Workplace Column. [Online]. Available: http://www.gallup.com/poll/managing/grtwrkplc.asp

Buergin, D. (1999). Psychosocial failure to thrive. In U. Eiholzer, F. Haverkamp, & Voss, L. D. (Eds.), *Growth, stature, and psychosocial well-being.* Seattle, WA: Hogrefe & Huber.

Buet, V. I., & Harris, T. (1994). The third national health and nutrition examination survey: Contributing data. *Gerontologist, 34,* 486–490.

Bugenthal, D. B. (2000). Acquisition of the algorithms of social life: A domain-based approach. *Psychological Bulletin, 126,* 187–219.

Bumpass, L. L., & Sweet, J. A. (1989). National estimates of cohabitation. *Demography, 26,* 615–625.

Bureau of the Census. (2000). *Statistical abstract of the U.S.* Washington, DC: U.S. Government Printing Office.

Burger, J. M. (1991). Changes in attributions over time: The ephemeral fundamental attribution error. *Social Cognition, 9,* 182–193.

Burger, J. M. (1999). Personality and control. In V. J. Derlega, B. A. Winstead, & W. H. Jones (Eds.), *Personality: Contemporary theory and research.* Chicago: Nelson Hall.

Burger, J. M. (2000). *Personality* (5th ed). Belmont, CA: Wadsworth.

Burger, J. M., Horita, M., Kinoshita, L., Roberts, K., & Vera, C. (1997). Effects of time on the norm of reciprocity. *Basic and Applied Social Psychology, 19,* 91-100.

Burger, J. M., & Petty, R. E. (1981). The low-ball compliance technique: Task or person commitment? *Journal of Personality and Social Psychology, 40,* 492–500.

Burgess, C. A., & Kirsch, I. (1999). Expectancy information as a moderator of the effects of hypnosis on memory. *Contemporary Hypnosis, 16,* 22–31.

Burke, K. C., Burke, J. D., Rae, D. S., & Regier, D. A. (1991). Comparing age at onset of major depression and other psychiatric disorders by birth cohorts in five U.S. community populations. *Archives of General Psychiatry, 48,* 789–795.

Burnam, M. A., Hough, R., Escobar, J. I., & Karno, N. (1987). Six months prevalence rates for specific psychiatric disorders among Mexican-American and non-Hispanic whites in Los Angeles. *Archives of General Psychiatry, 44,* 687–694.

Burns, M. O., & Seligman, M. E. P. (1989). Explanatory style across the life span: Evidence for stability over 52 years. *Journal of Personality and Social Psychology, 56,* 471–477.

Burns, M. O., & Seligman, M. E. P. (1991). Explanatory style, helplessness, and depression. In C. R. Snyder & D. R. Forsyth (Eds.), *Handbook of social and clinical psychology: The health perspective.* New York: Pergamon.

Burnstein, E. (1983). Persuasion as argument processing. In M. Brandstatter, J. H. Davis, & G. Stocker-Kreichgauer (Eds.), *Group decision processes.* London: Academic Press.

Burroughs, S. M., & Eby, L. T. (1998). Psychological sense of community at work: A measurement system and explanatory framework. *Journal of Community Psychology, 26,* 509–532.

Burton, J. W. (1969). *Conflict and communication: The use of controlled communication in international relations.* London: Macmillan.

Buske-Kirschbaum, A., Kirschbaum, C., & Hellhammer, D. H. (1994). Conditioned modulation of NK cells in humans: Alteration of cell activity and cell number by conditioning protocols. *Psychologische Beitraege, 36,* 100–111.

Buske-Kirschbaum, A., Kirschbaum, C., Stierle, H., & Lehnert, H. (1992). Conditioned increase of natural killer cell activity (NKCA) in humans. *Psychosomatic Medicine, 54,* 123-132.

Buss, D. M. (1985). Human mate selection. *American Scientist, 73,* 47–51.

Buss, D. M. (1989). Sex differences in human mate preferences: Evolutionary hypotheses tested in 37 cultures. *Behavioral and Brain Sciences, 12,* 1–49.

Buss, D. M. (1991). Evolutionary personality theory. *Annual Review of Psychology, 42,* 459–491.

Buss, D. M. (1995). Evolutionary psychology: A new paradigm for psychological science. *Psychological Inquiry, 6,* 1–30.

Buss, D. M. (1998). Sexual strategies theory: Historical origins and current status. *Journal of Sex Research, 35,* 19–31.

Buss, D. M. (1999). Human nature and individual differences: The evolution of human personality. In L. A. Pervin & O. P. John (Eds.), *Handbook of personality: Theory and research.* New York: Guilford Press.

Buss, D. M. (2000). *The dangerous passion: Why jealousy is as necessary as love and sex.* New York: Free Press.

Buss, D. M., Abbott, M., Angleitner, A., & Asherian, A. (1990). International preferences in selecting mates: A study of 37 cultures. *Journal of Cross-Cultural Psychology, 21,* 5–47.

Buysse, D. J., Frank, E., Lowe, K. K., Cherry, C. R. (1997). Electroencephalographic sleep correlates of episode and vulnerability to recurrence in depression. *Biological Psychiatry, 41,* 406–418.

Byer, C. O., Shainberg, L. W., & Galliano, G. (1999). *Dimensions of human sexuality* (5th ed.). Boston: McGraw-Hill.

Byne, W. (1997). Why we cannot conclude that sexual orientation is primarily a biological phenomenon. *Journal of Homosexuality, 34,* 73–80.

Byrne, D. (1997). An overview (and underview) of research and theory within the attraction paradigm. *Journal of Social and Personal Relationships, 14,* 417–431.

Byrne, D., Clore, G. L., & Smeaton, G. (1986). The attraction hypothesis: Do similar attitudes affect anything? *Journal of Personality and Social Psychology, 51,* 1167–1170.

Byrne, D., Ervin, C. R., & Lamberth, J. (1970). Continuity between the experimental study of attraction and real-life computer dating. *Journal of Personality and Social Psychology, 16,* 157–165.

Byrne, D., & Greendlinger, V. (1989). *Need for affiliation as a predictor of classroom friendships.* Unpublished manuscript, State University of New York at Albany.

Byrne, D., & Nelson, D. (1965). Attraction as a linear function of proportion of positive reinforcements. *Journal of Personality and Social Psychology, 1,* 659–663.

Byrne, D., & Osland, J. A. (2000). Sexual fantasy and erotica/pornography: Internal and external imagery. In L. T. Szuchman & F. Muscarella, (Eds). *Psychological perspectives on human sexuality.* New York: Wiley.

Cabeza, R., & Nyberg, L. (2000). Imaging cognition II: An empirical review of 275 PET and fMRI studies. *Journal of Cognitive Neuroscience, 12,* 1–47.

Cacioppo, J. T., & Gardner, W. L. (1999). Emotion. *Annual Review of Psychology, 50,* 101–124.

Cacioppo, J. T., Petty, R. E., Feinstein, J. A., & Jarvis, W. B. G. (1996). Dispositional differences in cognitive motivation: The life and times of individuals varying in need for cognition. *Psychological Bulletin, 119,* 197–253.

Cacioppo, J. T., Petty, R. E., & Morris, K. J. (1983). Effects of need for cognition on message evaluation, recall, and persuasion. *Journal of Personality and Social Psychology, 45,* 805–818.

Cadieu, N., & Cadieu, J. C. (1998). Is food recognition in an unfamiliar environment a long-term effect of stimulus or local enhancement? A study in the juvenile canary. *Behavioural Processes, 43,* 183–192.

Cahill, L., Babinsky, R., Markowitsch, H. J., & McGaugh, J. L. (1995). The amygdala and emotional memory. *Nature, 377,* 295–296.

Cairns, H. (1952). Disturbances of consciousness in lesions of the mid-brain and diencephalon. *Brain, 75,* 107–114.

Caldwell, A. B. (1994). *The profile of Jeffrey Dahmer* (videotape). Los Angeles: Caldwell Report, Inc.

Calhoun, J. B. (1962). Population density and social pathology. *Scientific American, 206*(2), 139-148.

Calignano, A., LaRana, G., Giuffrida, A., & Peiomelli, D. (1998). Control of pain initiation by endogenous cannabinoids. *Nature, 394,* 277–281.

Calkins, S. D., & Johnson, M. C. (1998). Toddler regulation of distress to frustrating events: Temperamental and maternal correlates. *Infant Behavior and Development, 21,* 379–395.

Camilleri, C., & Malewska-Peyre, H. (1997). Socialization and identity strategies. In J. W. Berry, P. R. Dasen, & T. S. Saraswathi (Eds.),

Handbook of cross-cultural psychology: Basic processes and human development (2nd ed, Vol. 2). Handbook of cross-cultural psychology. Boston: Allyn & Bacon.

Campbell, D. T. (1969). Reforms as experiments. *American Psychologist, 24,* 409–429.

Campbell, S. S. (1993). Seasonal effects on sleep. In M. A. Carskadon (Ed.), *Encyclopedia of sleep and dreaming.* New York: Macmillan.

Campbell, S. S., & Murphy, P. J. (1998). Extraocular circadian phototransduction in humans. *Science, 279,* 396–399.

Campfield, L. A. (1997). Metabolic and hormonal controls of food intake: Highlights of the last 25 years: 1972–1997. *Appetite, 29,* 135-152.

Campfield, L. A., Smith, F. J., Rosenbaum, M., & Hirsch, J. (1996). Human eating: Evidence for a physiological basis using a modified paradigm. *Neuroscience and Biobehavioral Reviews, 20,* 133–1137.

Campfield, L. A., Smith, F. J., & Stricker, E. M. (Eds.) (1990). Systemic factors in the control of food intake: Evidence for patterns as signals. In E. M. Stricker (Ed.), *Neurobiology of food and fluid intake.* New York: Plenum.

Canivez, G. L., & Watkins, M. W. (1998). Long-term stability of the Wechsler Intelligence Scale for Children–Third Edition. *Psychological Assessment, 10,* 285–291.

Cannon, W. B. (1929). *Bodily changes in pain, hunger, fear, and rage.* New York: Appleton-Century.

Cannon, W. B. (1932). *The wisdom of the body.* New York: W. W. Norton.

Cannon, W. B. (1942). "Voodoo" death. *American Anthropologist, 44,* 169–181.

Cannon, W. B., & Washburn, A. L. (1912). An explanation of hunger. *American Journal of Physiology, 29,* 441–454.

Capon, N., & Kuhn, D. (1979). Logical reasoning in the super-market: Adult females' use of proportional reasoning strategy in an everyday context. *Developmental Psychology, 15,* 450–452.

Caporael, L. R. (1997). The evolution of truly social cognition: The core configurations model. *Personality and Social Psychology Review, 1,* 276-298.

Cardeña, E., Lynn, S. J., & Krippner, S. (2000). Introduction: Anomalous experiences in perspective. In E. Cardeña, S. J. Lynn, & S. Krippner (Eds.), *Varieties of anomalous experience: Examining the scientific evidence.* Washington, DC: American Psychological Association.

Carew, T. J., & Kandel, E. R. (1973). Acquisition and retention of long-term habituation in *Aplysia:* Correlation of behavioral and cellular processes. *Science, 182,* 1158–1160.

Carew, T. J., Marcus, E. A., Nolen, T. G., & Rankin, C. H. (1990). The development of learning and memory in *Aplysia.* In J. L. McGaugh, N. M. Weinberger, & G. Lynch (Eds.), *Brain organization and memory: Cells, systems, and circuits.* New York: Oxford University Press.

Carey, F. (1977). The child as a word learner. In M. Halle, J. Bresnan, & G. Miller (Eds.), *Linguistic theory and psychological reality.* Cambridge, MA: MIT Press.

Carlin, A. S., Hoffman, H. G., & Weghorst, S. (1997). Virtual reality and tactile augmentation in the treatment of spider phobia: A case report. *Behaviour Research and Therapy, 35,* 153–158.

Carlson, J. G., & Hatfield, E. (1992). *Psychology of emotion.* Ft. Worth, TX: Harcourt Brace Jovanovich.

Carlson, S. M., Moses, L. J., & Hix, H. R. (1998). The role of inhibitory processes in young children's difficulties with deception and false belief. *Child Development, 69,* 672–691.

Carney, R. N., Levin, J. R., & Levin, M. E. (1994). Enhancing the psychology of memory by enhancing memory of psychology. *Teaching of Psychology, 21,* 171-174.

Carnicero, J. A. C., Perez-Lopez, J., Salinas, M. D. C. G., & Martinez-Fuentes, M. T. (2000). A longitudinal study of temperament in infancy: Stability and convergence of measures. *European Journal of Personality, 14,* 21–37.

Carpenter, R., & Robson, J. (Eds.) (1999). *Vision research: A practical guide to laboratory methods.* New York: Oxford University Press.

Carpenter, W. T., Jr., & Heinrichs, D. W. (1983). Early intervention, time-limited, targeted pharmacotherapy of schizophrenia. *Schizophrenia Bulletin, 9,* 533–542.

Carrere, S., Buehlman, K. T., Gottman, J. M., Coan, J. A., & Ruckstuhl, L. (2000). Predicting marital stability and divorce in newlywed couples. *Journal of Family Psychology, 14,* 42-58.

Carruthers, M. (1981). Field studies. Emotion and beta-blockade. In M. J. Christie & P. G. Mellett (Eds.), *Foundations of psychosomatics.* Chichester, England: Wiley.

Carson, R. C., Butcher, J. N., & Coleman, J. C. (1988). *Abnormal psychology and modern life* (8th ed.). Glenview, IL: Scott, Foresman.

Carter, S. J., & Cassaday, H. J. (1998). State dependent retrieval and chlorpheniramine. *Human Psychopharmacology: Clinical and Experimental, 13,* 513–523.

Cartledge, B. (1997). *Mind, brain and the environment.* New York: Oxford University Press.

Cartwright, R. D. (1977). *Night life: Explorations in dreaming.* Englewood Cliffs, NJ: Prentice-Hall.

Cartwright, R. D. (1991). Dreams that work: The relation of dream incorporation to adaptation to stressful events. *Dreaming: Journal of the Association for the Study of Dreams, 1,* 3–9.

Carver, C. S., & Scheier, M. F. (1988). *Perspectives on personality.* Boston: Allyn & Bacon.

Carver, C. S., & Scheier, M. F. (2000). *Perspectives on personality* (4th ed.). Boston: Allyn & Bacon.

Carver, C. S., Scheier, M. F., & Weintraub, J. K. (1989). Assessing coping strategies: A theoretically based approach. *Journal of Personality and Social Psychology, 56,* 267–283.

Caryl, P. G. (1994). Early event-related potentials correlate with inspection time and intelligence. *Intelligence, 18,* 15–46.

Case, R. (1987). The structure and process of intellectual development. *International Journal of Psychology, 22,* 571–607.

Case, R. (1996). Modeling the process of conceptual change in a continuously evolving hierarchical system. *Monographs of the Society for Research in Child Development, 61,* 283–295.

Caspi, A., Elder, G. H., & Bem, D. J. (1988). Moving away from the world: Life course patterns of shy children. *Developmental Psychology, 24,* 824–831.

Caspi, A., & Herbener, E. S. (1990). Continuity and change: Asortative marriage and the consistency of personality in adulthood. *Journal of Personality and Social Psychology, 58,* 250–258.

Caspi, A., & Roberts, B. W. (1999). Personality continuity and change across the life course. In L. A. Pervin & O. P. John (Eds.), *Handbook of personality: Theory and research.* New York: Guilford Press.

Catania, C. A. (1998). *Learning* (4th ed.). Upper Saddle River, NJ: Prentice Hall.

Catchpole, C. K., & Rowell, A. (1993). Song sharing and local dialects in a population of the European wren Troglodytes troglodytes. *Behaviour, 125,* 67–78.

Cattell, R. B. (1965). *The scientific analysis of personality.* Chicago: Aldine.

Cattell, R. B. (1971). *Abilities: Their growth, structure, and action.* Boston: Houghton Mifflin.

Cattell, R. B. (1990). Advances in Cattellian personality theory. In L. A. Pervin (Ed.), *Handbook of personality: Theory and research.* New York: Guilford Press.

Cattell, R. B. (1998). Where is intelligence? Some answers from the triadic theory. In J. J. McArdler, R. W. Woodcock, & et al. (Eds.), *Human cognitive abilities in theory and practice.* Mahwah, NJ: Erlbaum.

Ceci, S. J. (1996). *On intelligence: A bioecological treatise on intellectual development.* Cambridge, MA: Harvard University Press.

Ceci, S. J., Bruck, M., & Battin, D. B. (2000). The suggestibility of children's testimony. In D. F. Bjorklund (Ed.), *False memory creation in children and adults: Theory, research, and implications.* Mahwah, NJ: Erlbaum.

Ceci, S. J., & Huffman, M. L. C. (1997). How suggestible are preschool children? Cognitive and social factors. *Journal of the American Academy of Child and Adolescent Psychiatry 36,* 948–958.

Ceci, S. J., Loftus, E. F., Leichtman, M. D., & Bruck, M. (1994). The possible role of source misattributions in the creation of false beliefs among preschoolers. *International Journal of Clinical and Experimental Hypnosis, 42,* 304–320.

Centers for Disease Control and Prevention (1994). *Addressing emerging infectious disease threats: A prevention strategy for the United States.* Washington, DC: Author.

Centers for Disease Control and Prevention (1996). *National and international HIV seroprevalence surveys—Summary of results.* Washington, DC: Author.

Centers for Disease Control and Prevention (CDC) (1996, September 27). Youth risk behavior surveillance—United States, 1995. *Morbidity and Mortality Weekly Report, 45*(SS-4). Washington, DC: Author.

Centers for Disease Control and Prevention (CDC) (1997). *Fertility, family planning, and women's health: New data from the 1995 National Survey on Family Growth* (Series 23, No. 19). Washington DC: Author.

Cervone, D. (1992). The role of self-referent cognitions in goal-setting, motivation, and performance. In M. Rabinowitz (Ed.), *Applied Cognition.* New York: Ablex.

Cervone, D., & Shoda, Y. (1999). *The coherence of personality: Social-cognitive bases of consistency, variability, and organization.* New York: Guilford Press.

Chaiken, S. (1987). The heuristic model of persuasion. In M. P. Zanna, J. M. Olson, &

C. P. Herman (Eds.), *Social influence: The Ontario symposium* (Vol. 5). Hillsdale, NJ: Erlbaum.

Chaiken, S., & Maheswaran, D. (1994). Heuristic processing can bias systematic processing: Effects of source credibility, argument ambiguity, and task importance on attitude judgment. *Journal of Personality and Social Psychology, 66*, 460–473.

Chalmers, D. J. (1995). The puzzle of conscious experience. *Scientific American, 273*(6): 80–86.

Chambless, D. L., & Hollon, S. D. (1998). Defining empirically supported therapies. *Journal of Consulting and Clinical Psychology, 66*, 7–18.

Chang, E. C. (1996). Cultural differences in optimism, pessimism, and coping: Predictors of subsequent adjustment in American and Caucasian American college students. *Journal of Counseling Psychology, 43*, 113–123.

Chang, E. C. (1998). Dispositional optimism and primary and secondary appraisal of a stressor: Controlling for confounding influences and relations to coping and psychological and physical adjustment. *Journal of Personality and Social Psychology, 74*, 1109–1120.

Chapell, M. S., & Overton, W. F. (1998). Development of logical reasoning in the context of parental style and test anxiety. *Merrill Palmer Quarterly, 44*, 141–156.

Chappell, M., & Humphreys, M. S. (1994). An auto-associative neural network for sparse representations: Analysis and application to models of recognition and cued recall. *Psychological Review, 101*, 103–128.

Chartrand, T., Pinckert, S., & Burger, J. M. (1999). When manipulation backfires: The effects of time delay and requester on the foot-in-the-door technique. *Journal of Applied Social Psychology, 29*, 211–221.

Chartrand, T. L., & Bargh, J. A. (2000). *Consequences of automatic motivation for current mood.* Manuscript in preparation, Ohio State University.

Chase, W. G. and Simon, H. A. (1973). Perception in chess. *Cognitive Psychology, 4*, 55–81.

Chaves, J. F. (1994). Recent advances in the application of hypnosis to pain management. *American Journal of Clinical Hypnosis, 37*, 117–129.

Chen, C., Greenberger, E., Leter, J., Dong, Q., & Guo, M. S. (1998). A cross-cultural study of family and peer correlates of adolescent misconduct. *Developmental Psychology, 34*, 770–781.

Chen, H., Charlat, O., Tartaglia, L. A., Woolf, E. A., Weng, X., & Ellis, S. J. (1996). Evidence that the diabetes gene encodes the leptin receptor: Identification of a mutation in the leptin receptor gene in db/db mice. *Cell, 84*, 491–495.

Chen, H., & Lan, W. (1998). Adolescents' perceptions of their parents' academic expectations: Comparison of American, Chinese-American, and Chinese high school students. *Adolescence, 33*, 385–390.

Chen, S. C. (1937). Social modification of the activity of ants in nest-building. *Physiological Zoology, 10*, 420–436.

Cherlin, A. J., & Furstenberg, F. F. (1994). Stepfamilies in the United States: A reconsideration. *Annual Review of Sociology, 20*, 359–381.

Chi, M. T. H. (1997). Creativity: Shifting across ontological categories flexibly. In T. B. Ward & S. M. Smith (Eds.), *Creative thought: An investigation of conceptual structures and processes.* Washington, DC: American Psychological Association.

Chiappelli, F. (2000). Immune suppression. In G. Fink (Ed.), *Encyclopedia of stress.* San Diego: Academic Press.

Chiles, J. A., & Strosahl, K. D. (1995). *The suicidal patient: Principles of assessment, treatment, and case management.* Washington, DC: American Psychiatric Press.

Chiriboga, D. A. (1989). Mental health at the midpoint: Crisis, challenge, or relief? In S. Hunter & M. Sundel (Eds.), *Midlife myths: Issues, findings, and practice implications.* Newbury Park, CA: Sage Publications.

Choca, J. P., Shanley, L. A., & Van Denburg, E. (1992). *Interpretive guide to the Millon Clinical Multiaxial Inventory.* Washington, DC: American Psychological Association.

Chomsky, N. (1965). *Aspects of a theory of syntax.* Cambridge, MA: MIT Press.

Chomsky, N. (1972). *Language and mind.* New York: Harcourt.

Chomsky, N. (1987). Language in a psychological setting. *Sophia Linguistic Working Papers in Linguistics, 22.* Tokyo: Sophia University.

Christianson, S. A., & Nilsson, L. G. (1989). Hysterical amnesia: A case of aversively motivated isolation of memory. In T. Archer & L. G. Nilsson (Eds.), *Aversion, avoidance, and anxiety: Perspectives on aversively motivated behavior.* Hillsdale, NJ: Erlbaum.

Christy, C. A., & Voigt, H. (1994). Bystander responses to public episodes of child abuse. *Journal of Applied Social Psychology, 24*, 824–847.

Chwalisz, K., Diener, E., & Gallagher, D. (1988). Autonomic arousal feedback and emotional experience: Evidence from the spinal cord injured. *Journal of Personality and Social Psychology, 54*, 820–828.

Cialdini, R. B. (1988). *Influence: Science and practice* (2nd ed.). Glenview, IL: Scott, Foresman.

Cialdini, R. B., Brown, S. L., Lewis, B. P., & Luce, C. (1997). Reinterpreting the empathy-altruism relationship: When one into one equals oneness. *Journal of Personality and Social Psychology, 73*, 481–494.

Cialdini, R. B., Cacioppo, J. T., Bassett, R., & Miller, J. A. (1978). Lowball procedure for producing compliance: Commitment then cost. *Journal of Personality and Social Psychology, 36*, 463–476.

Cialdini, R. B., Schaller, M., Hoolihan, D., Arps, K., Fultz, J., & Beaman, A. L. (1987). Empathy-based helping: Is it selflessly or selfishly motivated? *Journal of Personality and Social Psychology, 52*, 749–758.

Cialdini, R. B., & Trost, M. R. (1998). Social influence: Social norms, conformity and compliance. In D. T. Gilbert, S. T. Fiske, & G. Lindzey (Eds.), *The handbook of social psychology* (4th ed., Vol. 2). Boston: McGraw-Hill.

Cialdini, R. B., Vincent, J. E., Lewis, S. K., Catalan, J., Wheeler, D., & Darby, B. L. (1975). Reciprocal concessions procedure for inducing compliance: The door-in-the-face technique. *Journal of Personality and Social Psychology, 31*, 206–215.

Cianelli, S. N., & Fouts, R. S. (1998). Chimpanzee to chimpanzee American Sign Language. *Human Evolution, 13*, 147–159.

Cicirelli, V. G. (1998). Personal meanings of death in relation to fear of death. *Death Studies, 22*, 713–733.

Cigales, M., Field, T., Lundy, B., Cuadra, A., & Hart, S. (1997). Massage enhances recovery from habituation in normal infants. *Infant Behavior and Development, 20*, 29–34.

Cirelli, S. N., Shaw, P. J., Rechtschaffen, A., & Tononi, G. (1999). No evidence of brain cell degeneration after long term sleep deprivation in rats. *Brain Research, 840*, 184–193.

Claparède, E. (1911). Recognition et moïïté. *Archives de Psychologies, 11*, 79–90.

Clark, A., & Toribio, J. (1998). *Cognitive architectures in artificial intelligence: The evolution of research.* New York: Garland.

Clark, A., & Toribio, J. (1998). *Consciousness and emotion in cognitive science: Conceptual and empirical issues.* New York: Garland.

Clark, D. A., Beck, A. T., & Alford, B. A. (1999). *Scientific foundations of cognitive theory and therapy of depression.* New York: Wiley.

Clark, D. A., Beck, A. T., & Brown, G. (1989). Cognitive mediation in general psychiatric outpatients: A test of the content-specificity hypothesis. *Journal of Personality and Social Psychology, 56*, 958–964.

Clark, D. M. (1988). A cognitive model of panic attacks. In S. Rachman & J. D. Maser (Eds.), *Panic: Psychological Perspectives.* Hillsdale, NJ: Erlbaum.

Clark, M. S., Ouellette, R., Powell, M. C., & Milberg, S. (1987). Recipient's mood, relationship type, and helping. *Journal of Personality and Social Psychology, 53*, 94–103.

Clark, R. D., & Hatfield, E. (1989). Gender differences in receptivity to sexual offers. *Journal of Psychology and Human Sexuality, 2*, 39–55.

Clarke, A. M., & Clarke, A. D. B. (2000). *Early experience and the life path.* London: Jessica Kingsley.

Clarkson-Smith, L., & Hartley, A. A. (1990). Structural equation models of relationships between exercise and cognitive abilities. *Psychology and Aging, 5*, 437–446.

Clayton, P. J. (2000). Bereavement. In G. Fink (Ed.), *Encyclopedia of stress.* San Diego: Academic Press.

Cleare, A. J., & Bond, A. J. (1997). Does central serotonergic function correlate inversely with aggression? A study using d-fenfluramine in healthy subjects. *Psychiatry Research, 69*, 89–95.

Clement, K. (1999). Leptin and the genetics of obesity. *Acta paediatrica, 88*, 51–57.

Cloninger, C. R., & Gottesman, I. I. (1989). Genetic and environmental factors in antisocial behavior disorders. In S. Mednick, T. Moffitt, & S. Strack (Eds.), *The causes of crime: New biological approaches.* New York: Cambridge University Press.

Cobb, J. M. T., & Steptoe, A. (1998). Psychosocial influences on upper respiratory infectious illness in children. *Journal of Psychosomatic Research, 45*(4), 319–330.

Coccaro, E. F., Bergeman, C. S., Kavoussi, R. J., & Seroczynski, A. D. (1997). Heritability of aggression and irritability: A twin study of the Buss-Durkee aggression scales in adult male subjects. *Biological Psychiatry, 41,* 273–284.

Coffey, C. E., Weiner, R. D., Djang, W. T., et al. (1991). Brain anatomic effects of electroconvulsive therapy: A prospective magnetic resonance imaging study. *Archives of General Psychiatry, 48,* 1013–1020.

Cohen, F. L., Ferrans, C. E., & Eshler, B. (1992). Reported accidents in narcolepsy. *Loss, Grief and Care, 5,* 71–80.

Cohen, N. J., & Squire, L. R. (1981). Retrograde amnesia and remote memory impairment. *Neuropsychologia, 19,* 337–356.

Cohen, S. (1988). Psychosocial models of the role of social support in the etiology of physical disease. *Health Psychology. 7,* 269–297.

Cohen, S., & Edwards, J. R. (1989). Personality characteristics as moderators of the relationship between stress and disorder. In R. W. J. Neufeld (Ed.), *Advances in the investigation of psychological stress.* New York: Wiley.

Cohen, S., Frank, E. D., Doyle, W. J., Skoner, D. P., Rabin, B. S., & Gwaltney, J. M., Jr. (1998). Types of stressors that increase susceptibility to the common cold in healthy adults. *Health Psychology, 17,* 214–223.

Cohen, S., & Herbert. T. B. (1996). Health psychology: Psychological factors and physical disease from the perspective of human psychoneuroimmunology. *Annual Review of Psychology, 47,* 113–142.

Cohen, S., Kessler, R. C., & Gordon, L. U. (1995). *Measuring stress.* New York: Oxford University Press.

Colby, A., Kohlberg, L., Gibbs, J., & Lieberman, M. (1983). A longitudinal study of moral judgment. *Monographs of the Society for Research in Child Development, 48* (1–2, Serial No. 200).

Coleman, D. L. (1978). Obese and diabetes: Two mutant genes causing diabetes-obesity syndromes in mice. *Diabetologia, 14,* 141–148.

Collaer, M. L., & Hines, M. (1995). Human behavioral sex differences: A role for gonadal hormones during early development? *Psychological Bulletin, 118,* 55–107.

Collins, A. M., & Loftus, E. F. (1975). A spreading activation theory of semantic processing. *Psychological Review, 82,* 407–428.

Collins, W. A., Maccoby, E. E., Steinberg, L., & Hetherington, E. M. (2000). Contemporary research on parenting: The case for nature and nurture. *American Psychologist, 55,* 218–232.

Commons, M. L., Rachlin, H., & Nevin, J. A. (Eds.) (1984). *Quantitative analyses of behavior: Vol. 5. Reinforcement value: The effect of delay and intervening events.* Cambridge, MA: Ballenger.

Comuzzie, A. G., & Allison, D. B. (1998). The search for human obesity genes. *Science, 280,* 1374–1377.

Conrad, R. (1964). Acoustic confusions in immediate memory. *British Journal of Psychology, 55,* 75–84.

Constantine, M. G., Feng, P. F., Ladany, N., Bergmann, B. M., Inman, A. G., Rechtschaffen, A., & Ponterotto, J. G. (1995). Sleep deprivation in rats with preoptic/anterior hypothalamic lesions. *Brain Research, 703,* 93–99.

Contrada, R. J., Cather, C., & O'Leary, A. (1999). Personality and health: Dispositions and processes in disease susceptibility and adaptation to illness. In L. A. Pervin & O. P. John (Eds.), *Handbook of personality: Theory and research.* New York: Guilford Press.

Cook, S. W. (1985). Experimenting on social issues: The case of school desegregation. *American Psychologist, 40,* 452–460.

Cooke, P. (1991, June 23). They cried until they couldn't see. *New York Times Magazine,* pp. 25, 43.

Coons, P. M., Milstein, V., & Marley, C. (1982). EEG studies of two multiple personalities and a control. *Archives of General Psychiatry, 39,* 823–825.

Cooper, C. R., & Denner, J. (1998). Theories linking culture and psychology: Universal and community-specific processes. *Annual Review of Psychology, 49,* 559–584.

Cooper, J. (1998). Unlearning cognitive dissonance: Toward an understanding of the development of dissonance. *Journal of Experimental Social Psychology, 34,* 562–575.

Cooper, J. Bennett, E. A., & Sukel, H. L. (1996). Complex scientific testimony: How do jurors make decisions? *Law and Human Behavior, 20,* 379–394.

Cooper, J., & Fazio, R. H. (1984). A new look at dissonance theory. In L. Berkowitz (Ed.), *Advances in experimental social psychology* (Vol. 17). New York: Academic Press.

Coopersmith, S. (1967). *The antecedents of self-esteem.* San Francisco: W. H. Freeman.

Cordova, J. V., Jacobson, N. S., & Christensen, A. (1998). Acceptance versus change interventions in behavioral couple therapy: Impact on couples' in-session communication. *Journal of Marriage and Family Counseling, 24,* 437–455.

Corina, D. P., Poizner, H., Bellugi, U., Feinberg, T., Dowd, D., & O'Grady-Batch, L. (1992). Dissociation between linguistic and nonlinguistic gestural systems: A case for compositionality. *Brain and Language, 43,* 414–447.

Cosmides, L., & Tooby, J. (1987). From evolution to behavior: Evolutionary psychology as the missing link. In J. Dupre (Ed.), *The latest on the best: Essays on evolution and optimality.* Cambridge, MA: MIT Press.

Cosmides, L., & Tooby, J. (1995). From evolution to adaptations to behavior: Toward an integrated evolutionary psychology. In R. Wong (Ed.), *Biological perspectives on motivated activities.* Norwood, NJ: Ablex

Costa, P. T., & McCrae, R. R. (1992). The five-factor model of personality and its relevance to personality disorders. *Journal of Personality Disorders, 6,* 343–359.

Cotman, C. W., Brinton, R., Galaburda, G., & McEwen, S. (1987). *The neuro-immune-endocrine connection.* Philadelphia: Lippincott-Raven.

Courneya, K. S. (1995). Understanding readiness for regular physical activity in older individuals: An application of the theory of planned behavior. *Health Psychology, 14,* 80–87.

Courneya, K. S., Friedenreich, C. M., Arthur, K., & Bobick, T. M. (1999). Understanding exercise motivation in colorectal cancer patients: A prospective study using the theory of planned behavior. *Rehabilitation Psychology, 44,* 68–84.

Cousins, S. D. (1989). Culture and self-perception in the United States and Japan. *Journal of Personality and Social Psychology, 56,* 124–131.

Cowan, C. P., & Cowan, P. A. (2000). *When partners become parents: The big life change for couples.* Mahwah, NJ: Erlbaum.

Cowan, P. A., & Cowan, C. P. (1988). Changes in marriage during the transition to parenthood: Must we blame the baby? In G. Y. Michaels, W. A. Goldberg, & A. Wendy (Eds.), *The transition to parenthood: Current theory and research. Cambridge studies in social and emotional development.* New York: Cambridge University Press.

Coyne, J. C., Burchill, S. A. L., & Stiles, W. B. (1991). An interactional perspective on depression. In C. R. Snyder & D. R. Forsyth (Eds.), *Handbook of social and clinical psychology: The health perspective.* New York: Pergamon.

Crabbe, J. C., Young, E. R., Tam, B., & Kosobud, A. (1986). Genetic differences in anticonvulsant sensitivity in mouse lines selectively bred for ethanol withdrawal severity. *Journal of Pharmacology and Experimental Therapeutics, 239,* 154–159.

Craig, T. P. (1991). Kin-selection, reciprocal altruism, and information sharing among Maine lobstermen. *Ethology and Sociobiology, 12,* 221–235.

Craik, F. I. M., & Lockhart, R. S. (1972). Levels of processing: A framework for memory research. *Journal of Verbal Learning and Verbal Behavior, 11,* 671–684.

Craik, F. I. M., & McDowd, J. M. (1998). Age differences in recall and recognition. In M. P. Lawton & T. A. Salthouse (Eds.), *Essential papers on the psychology of aging.* New York: University Press.

Craik, F. I. M., & Salthouse, T. A. (Eds.) (2000). *The handbook of aging and cognition.* Mahwah, NJ: Erlbaum.

Craik, F. I. M., & Tulving, E. (1975). Depth of processing and the retention of words in episodic memory. *Journal of Experimental Psychology: General, 104,* 268–294.

Crandall, C. S., & Martinez, R. (1996). Culture, ideology, and antifat attitudes. *Personality and Social Psychology Bulletin, 22,* 1165–1176.

Craske, M. (1999). *Anxiety disorders: Psychological approaches to theory and treatment.* Boulder, CO: Westview Press.

Crawford, C. B., & Anderson, J. L. (1989). Sociobiology: An environmentalist discipline? *American Psychologist, 44,* 1449–1459.

Crawford, M., & Chaffin, R. (1997). The meanings of difference: Cognition in social and cultural context. In P. J. Caplan, and M. Crawford (Eds.), *Gender differences in human cognition. Counterpoints: Cognition, memory, and language.* New York: Oxford University Press.

Crawford, M., Stark, A. C., & Renner, C. H. (1998). The meaning of Ms.: Social assimilation of a gender concept. *Psychology of Women Quarterly, 22,* 197–208.

Creese, I., Burd, D. R., & Snyder, S. H. (1976). Dopamine receptor binding predicts clinical and pharmacological potencies of antischizophrenic drugs. *Science, 192,* 481–483.

Crick, F., & Mitchson, G. (1983). The function of dream sleep. *Nature, 304,* 111–114.

Crick, N. R., & Bigbee, M. A. (1998). Relational and overt forms of peer victimization: A multiinformant approach. *Journal of*

Consulting and Clinical Psychology, 66, 337–347.

Criglington, A. J. (1998). Do professionals get jet lag?: A commentary on jet lag. *Aviation, Space, and Environmental Medicine, 69,* 810.

Crits-Christoph, P. (1992). The efficacy of brief dynamic psychotherapy: A meta-analysis. *American Journal of Psychiatry, 149,* 151–158.

Crits-Christoph, P., Cooper, A., & Luborsky, L. (1988). The accuracy of therapists' interpretations and the outcome of dynamic psychotherapy. *Journal of Consulting and Clinical Psychology, 56,* 490–495.

Crits-Christoph, P., & Mintz, J. (1991). Implications of therapist effects for the design and analysis of comparative studies of psychotherapies. *Journal of Consulting and Clinical Psychology, 59,* 20–26.

Crocker, P. R. E. (1989). A follow-up of cognitive-affective stress management training. *Journal of Sport and Exercise Psychology, 11,* 236–242.

Crook, J. M., & Copolov, D. L. (2000). Schizophrenia. In G. Fink (Ed.), *Encyclopedia of stress.* San Diego: Academic Press.

Cross, S., & Markus, H. (1991). Possible selves across the life span. *Human Development, 34,* 230–255.

Cross, S. E., & Markus, H. R. (1999). The cultural constitution of personality. In L. A. Pervin & O. P. John (Eds.), *Handbook of personality: Theory and research.* New York: Guilford Press.

Crovitz, H. F. (1971). The capacity of memory loci in artificial memory. *Psychonomic Science, 24,* 187–188.

Crowe, L. C., & George, W. H. (1989). Alcohol and human sexuality: Review and integration. *Psychological Bulletin, 105,* 374–386.

Croyle, R. T., & Cooper, J. (1983). Dissonance arousal: Physiological evidence. *Journal of Personality and Social Psychology, 45,* 782–791.

Csikszentmihalyi, M. (1990). *Flow: The psychology of optimal experience.* New York: Harper & Row.

Csikszentmihalyi, M., & Larson, R. (1984). *Being adolescent: Conflict and growth in the teenage years.* New York: Basic Books.

Culbertson, F. M. (1997). Depression and gender: An international review. *American Psychologist, 52,* 25–31.

Cummins, H. J. (1999, March 2). Kids learn to kill like soldiers do, author says. *Seattle Post-Intelligencer,* p. E4.

Curran, T., & Schacter, D. L. (2000). Amnesia II: Cognitive neuropsychological issues. In M. J. Martha & T. E. Feinberg (Eds.), *Patient-based approaches to cognitive neuroscience. Issues in clinical and cognitive neuropsychology.* Cambridge, MA: MIT Press.

Curtiss, S. (1977). *Genie: A psychological study of a modern day "wild child."* New York: Academic Press.

Cytowic, R. E. (1989). *Synesthesia: A union of the senses.* New York: Springer-Verlag.

Czeisler, C. A., Moore, E., Martin, C., & Coleman, R. M. (1982). Rotating shift work schedules that disrupt sleep are improved by applying circadian principles. *Science, 217,* 460–463.

Dantzer, R. (2000). Psychoneuroimmunology. In G. Fink (Ed.), *Encyclopedia of stress.* San Diego: Academic Press.

Dark, K., Peeke, H. V., Ellman, G., & Salfi, M. (1987). Behaviorally conditioned histamine release: Prior stress and conditionability and

extinction of the response. *Annals of the New York Academy of Sciences, 496,* 578–582.

Darley, J. M. (1995). Constructive and destructive obedience: A taxonomy of principal-agent relationships. *Journal of Social Issues, 51,* 125–154.

Darley, J. M., & Gross, P. H. (1983). A hypothesis-confirming bias in labeling effects. *Journal of Personality and Social Psychology, 44,* 20–33.

Darley, J. M., & Latane, B. (1968). Bystander intervention in emergencies: Diffusion of responsibility. *Journal of Personality and Social Psychology, 8,* 377–383.

Darwin, C. J., Turvey, M. T., & Crowder, R. G. (1972). An auditory analogue of the Sperling partial report procedures. *Cognitive Psychology, 3,* 255–267.

Darwin, C. R. (1872/1965). *The expression of emotions in man and animals.* Chicago: University of Chicago Press.

Dasen, P. R. (1975). Concrete operational development in Canadian Eskimos. *International Journal of Psychology, 10,* 165–180.

Davey, G. C. L. (1995). Preparedness and phobias: Specific evolved associations or a generalized expectancy bias? *Behavioral and Brain Sciences, 18,* 289–325.

Davidson, R. J. (1988). Cerebral asymmetry, affective style, and psychopathology. In M. Kinsbourne (Ed.), *Cerebral hemisphere function in depression.* Washington, DC: American Psychiatric Press.

Davidson, R. J. (1998). *Neuropsychological perspectives on affective and anxiety disorders.* Chicago: Psychology Press.

Davidson, R. J., & Fox, N. A. (1988). Cerebral asymmetry and emotion: Developmental and individual differences. In D. L. Molfese & S. J. Segalowitz (Eds.), *Brain lateralization in children: Developmental implications.* New York, Guilford Press.

Davidson, R. J., & Fox, N. A. (1989). Frontal brain asymmetry predicts infants' response to maternal separation. *Journal of Abnormal Psychology, 98,* 127–131.

Davidson, R. J., Marshall, J. R., Tomarken, A. J., & Henriques, J. B. (2000). While a phobic waits: Regional brain electrical and autonomic activity in social phobics during anticipation of public speaking. *Biological Psychiatry 47,* 85–95.

Davidson, W. B., & Cotter, P. R. (1997). Psychological sense of community and newspaper readership. *Psychological Reports, 80,* 659-665.

Davis, C. G., Nolen, H. S., & Larson, J. (1998). Making sense of loss and benefiting from the experience: Two construals of meaning. *Journal of Personality and Social Psychology, 75,* 561–574.

Davis, C. M., & Bauserman, R. (1993). Exposure to sexually explicit materials: An attitude change perspective. *Annual Review of Sex Research, 4,* 121–209.

Davis, M. (1992). The role of the amygdala in fear and anxiety. *Annual Review of Neuroscience, 15,* 311–327.

Davis, M. H., Luce, C., & Kraus, S. J. (1994). The heritability of characteristics associated with dispositional empathy. *Journal of Personality, 62,* 369–391.

Dawes, R. M. (1994). *House of cards: Psychology and psychotherapy built on myth.* New York: Free Press.

Dawidowicz, L. S. (1975). *The war against the Jews, 1933–1945.* New York: Holt, Rinehart & Winston.

Dawson, W. A. (1993). Aboriginal dreaming. In M. A. Carskadon (Ed.), *Encyclopedia of sleep and dreaming.* New York: Macmillan.

Day, R., et al. (1987). Stressful life events preceding the acute onset of schizophrenia. *Culture, Medicine, and Psychiatry, 11,* 123–205.

De Silva, P., & Rachman, J. (1998). *Obsessive-compulsive disorders.* New York: Oxford University Press.

de Waal, F. (1982). *Chimpanzee politics: Power and sex among apes.* Baltimore: John Hopkins University Press.

DeCasper, A. J., & Fifer, W. P. (1980). Of human bonding: Newborns prefer their mothers' voices. *Science, 208*(4448), 1174-1176.

DeCasper, A. J., & Spence, M. J. (1986). Prenatal maternal speech influences newborns' perceptions of speech sounds. *Infant Behavior and Development, 9,* 133–150.

deCharms, R. C., & Zador, A. (2000). Neural representation and the cortical code. *Annual Review of Neuroscience, 23,* 613–647.

DeCharms, R., & Moeller, G. H. (1962). Values expressed in American children's readers: 1800 to 1950. *Journal of Abnormal and Social Psychology, 64,* 135–142.

Deci, E. L. (1971). Effects of externally mediated rewards on intrinsic motivation. *Journal of Personality and Social Psychology, 18,* 105–115.

Deci, E. L., Koestner, R., & Ryan, R. M. (1999). A meta-analytic review of experiments examining the effects of extrinsic rewards on intrinsic motivation. *Psychological Bulletin, 125,* 627–668.

Deckel, A. W., & Fuqua, L. (1998). Effects of serotonergic drugs on lateralized aggression and aggressive displays in *Anolis carolinensis. Behavioural Brain Research, 95,* 227–232.

Decety, J., Grezes, J., Costes, N., Perani, D., Jeannerod, M., Procyk, E., Grassi, F., & Fazio, F. (1997). Brain activity during observation of actions: Influence of action content and subject's strategy. *Brain, 120,* 1763–1777.

deGeus, E. J. C. (2000). Aerobics in stress reduction. In G. Fink (Ed.), *Encyclopedia of stress.* San Diego: Academic Press.

Dekker, E., & Groen, J. (1956). Reproducible psychogenic attacks of asthma. *Journal of Psychosomatic Research, 1,* 56–67.

DeLongis, A. (2000). Coping skills. In G. Fink (Ed.), *Encyclopedia of stress.* San Diego: Academic Press.

Dement, W. C. (1974). *Some must watch while some must sleep.* San Francisco: W. H. Freeman.

DeMoranville, B. M., Jackson, I., Ader, R., Madden, K. S., Felten, D. L., & Bellinger, D. L. (2000). Endocrine and immune systems. In B. S. Fogel, R. B. Schiffer, & S. M. Rao (Eds.), *Synopsis of neuropsychiatry.* Philadelphia: Lippincott-Raven.

Dennis, W. (1973). *Children of the creche.* New York: Appleton-Century-Crofts.

Department of Health and Human Services (1998). *National Household Survey On Drug Abuse: Population Estimates 1997.* Rockville, MD: Author.

Department of Health and Human Services (1999). *Child maltreatment 1997: Reports from the states to the National Child Abuse and*

Neglect Data System. Washington, DC: U.S. Government Printing Office.

Depue, R. A. (1992). *Neurobehavioral systems, personality, and psychopathology.* New York: Springer-Verlag.

Derogatis, L. R. (1986). *Clinical psychopharmacology.* Menlo Park, CA: Addison-Wesley.

DeRubeis, R. J., & Crits-Christoph, P. (1998). Empirically supported individual and group psychological treatments for adult mental disorders. *Journal of Consulting and Clinical Psychology, 66,* 37–52.

Desmond, S. M., Price, J. H., Hallinan, C., & Smith, D. (1989). Black and white adolescents' perceptions of their ideal weight. *Journal of School Health, 59,* 353-358.

Dessens, A. B., Cohen, K. P. T., Mellenbergh, G. J., van der Poll, N., Koppe, J. G., & Boer, K. (1999). Prenatal exposure to anticonvulsants and psychosexual development. *Archives of Sexual Behavior, 28,* 31–44.

Deutsch, M., & Gerard, H. B. (1955). A study of normative and informational social influence upon individual judgment. *Journal of Abnormal and Social Psychology, 51,* 629–636.

DeValois, R. L., & DeValois, K. K. (1988). *Spatial vision.* New York: Oxford University Press.

Devane, W. A., Hanus, L., Breuer, A., Pertwee, R. G., Stevenson, L. A., & Griffin, G., (1992). Isolation and structure of a brain constituent that binds to the cannabinoid receptor. *Science, 18,* 1946–1949.

DeVries, R. (1969). Constancy of genetic identity in the years three to six. *Monographs of the Society for Research in Child Development, 34* (Serial No. 127).

DeVries, H., Mudde, A. N., Dijkstra, A., & Willemsen, M. C. (1998). Differential beliefs, perceived social influences, and self-efficacy expectations among smokers in various motivational phases. *Preventive Medicine, 27,* 681–689.

DeVries, R., Hildebrandt, C., & Zan, B. (2000). Constructivist early education for moral development. *Early Education and Development, 11,* 9–35.

Dewsbury, D. A. (1997). In celebration of the centennial of Ivan P. Pavlov's (1897/1902). The Work of the Digestive Glands. *American Psychologist, 52,* 933–935.

Diaz, J. (1997). *How drugs influence behavior: A neuro-behavioral approach.* Upper Saddle River, NJ: Prentice Hall.

Dickinson, A. (1997). Bolles's psychological syllogism. In M. E. Bouton, M. S. Fanselow, & S. Michael (Eds.), *Learning, motivation, and cognition: The functional behaviorism of Robert C. Bolles.* Washington, DC: American Psychological Association.

DiClemente, C. C., & Prochaska, J. C. (1998). Toward a comprehensive, transtheoretical model of change: Stages of change and addictive behaviors. In W. R. Miller & N. Heather (Eds.), *Treating addictive behaviors* (2nd ed.). New York: Plenum.

Diener, E. (2000). Subjective well-being: The science of happiness and a proposal for a national index. *American Psychologist, 55,* 34–43.

Diener, E., & Fujita, F. (1997). Social comparisons and subjective well-being. In B. Bruunk & F. X. Gibbons (Eds.), *Health, coping, and well-being: Perspectives from social comparison theory.* Mahwah, NJ: Erlbaum.

Diener, E., Suh, E., Lucas, R. E., & Smith, H. L. (1999). Subjective well-being: Three decades of progress. *Psychological Bulletin, 125,* 276–302.

Dienstbier, R. A. (1989). Arousal and physiological toughness: Implications for mental and physical health. *Psychological Review, 96,* 84–100.

Dietz, T. L. (1998). An examination of violence and gender role portrayals in video games: Implications for gender socialization and aggressive behavior. *Sex Roles, 38,* 425–442.

Digman, J. M. (1990). Personality structure: Emergence of the five-factor model. *Annual Review of Psychology, 41,* 417–440.

DiLalla, D. L., Carey, G., Gottesman, I. I., & Bouchard, T. J. (1996). Heritability of MMPI personality indicators of psychopathology in twins reared apart. *Journal of Abnormal Psychology, 105,* 491–499.

Dimberg, U. (1997). Psychophysiological reactions to facial expressions. In U. C. Segerstrale, et al. (Eds.), *Nonverbal communication: Where nature meets culture.* Mahwah, NJ: Erlbaum.

Dimberg, U., & Thunberg, M. (1998). Rapid facial reactions to emotional facial expressions. *Scandinavian Journal of Psychology, 39,* 39–46.

Dimberg, U., Thunberg, M., & Elmehed, K. (2000). Unconscious facial reactions to emotional facial expressions. *Psychological Science, 11,* 86–89.

Dion, K. K., Berscheid, E., & Walster, E. (1972). What is beautiful is good. *Journal of Personality and Social Psychology, 24,* 285–290.

Dishion, T. J., McCord, J., & Poulin, F. (1999). When interventions harm: Peer groups and problem behavior. *American-Psychologist, 54,* 755–764.

Dishion, T. J., & Patterson, G. R. (1999). Model building in developmental psychopathology: A pragmatic approach to understanding and intervention. *Journal of Clinical Child Psychology, 28,* 502–512.

Dishman, R. K. (1982). Compliance/adherence in health related exercise. *Health Psychology, 1,* 237–267.

Dittmann, R. W., Kappes, M. H., & Kappes, M. E. (1993). Cognitive functioning in female patients with 21-hydroxylase deficiency. *European Child and Adolescent Psychiatry, 2,* 34–43.

Dixon, M., & Laurence, J. R. (1992). Two hundred years of hypnosis research: Questions resolved. Questions unanswered. In E.Fromm & M. R. Nash (Eds.), *Contemporary hypnosis research.* New York: Guilford.

Dixon, N. F. (1981). *Preconscious processing.* New York: Wiley.

Dobson, V., & Teller, D. Y. (1978). Visual acuity in human infants: A review and comparison of behavioral and electrophysiological studies. *Vision Research, 18,* 1469–1483.

Dodge, K. A. (1986). A social information processing model of social competence. *Minnesota Symposium on Child Psychology, 18,* 77–125.

Doell, R. G. (1995). Sexuality in the brain. *Journal of Homosexuality, 28,* 345–354.

Doka, K. J. (1995). Coping with life-threatening illness: A task model. *Omega: Journal of Death and Dying, 32,* 111–122.

Dolezal, H. F. (1977). Long-term adaptation to up-down reversing the field of view: Complex changes afforded by optical invariants. *Dissertation Abstracts International, 37*(12-B, Pt 1): 6364–6365.

Dollard, J., Doob, L., Miller, N., Mowrer, O. H., & Sears, R. R. (1939). *Frustration and aggression.* New Haven, CT: Yale University Press.

Domhoff, G. W. (1999). Drawing theoretical implications from descriptive empirical findings on dream content. *Dreaming: Journal of the Association for the Study of Dreams, 9,* 201–210.

Domino, G. (2000). *Psychological testing.* Upper Saddle River, NJ: Prentice Hall.

Domjan, M., Greene, P., & North, N. C. (1989). Contextual conditioning and the control of copulatory behavior by species-specific sign stimuli in male Japanese quail. *Journal of Experimental Psychology: Animal Behavior Processes, 15,* 147–153.

Domjan, M., O'Vary, D., & Green, P. (1988). Conditioning of appetitive and consummatory sexual behavior in male Japanese quail. *Journal of the Experimental Analysis of Behavior, 50,* 505–519.

Donaldson, D. (1998). *Psychiatric disorders with a biochemical basis.* New York: Parthenon.

Donnerstein, E., & Berkowitz, L. (1981). Victim reactions in aggressive erotic films as a factor in violence against women. *Journal of Personality and Social Psychology, 41,* 710–724.

Donnerstein, E., & Donnerstein, M. (1976). Research on the control of interracial aggression. In R. G. Geen & E. C. O'Neal (Eds.), *Perspectives on aggression.* New York: Academic Press.

Donnerstein, E., & Malamuth, N. (1997). Pornography: Its consequences on the observer. In L. B. Schlesinger & E. Revitch (Eds.), *Sexual dynamics of anti-social behavior* (2nd ed.). Springfield, IL: Charles C Thomas.

Doppelt, J. E., & Wallace, W. L. (1955). Standardization of the Wechsler Adult Intelligence Scale for older persons. *Journal of Abnormal and Social Psychology, 51,* 312–330.

Dornbusch, S. M., Ritter, P. L., Liederman, P. H., Roberts, D. F., & Fraleigh, M. J. (1987). The relation of parenting style to adolescent school performance. *Child Development, 58,* 1244–1257.

Dossenbach, M., & Dossenbach, H. D. (1998). *All about animal vision.* Chicago: Blackbirch Press.

Douglas, N. J. (1998). The psychosocial aspects of narcolepsy. *Neurology, 50,* S27–S30.

Dovidio, J. F. (1984). Helping behavior and altruism: An empirical and conceptual overview. In L. Berkowitz (Ed.), *Advances in experimental social psychology* (Vol. 17). New York: Academic Press.

Dovidio, J. F., & Gaertner, S. L. (1997). On the nature of contemporary prejudice: The causes, consequences, and challenges of aversive racism. In J. L. Eberhardt & S. T. Fiske (Eds.), *Racism: The problem and the response.* Thousand Oaks, CA: Sage Publications.

Dovidio, J. F., Kawakami, K., & Gaertner, S. L. (2000). Reducing contemporary prejudice: Combatting bias at the individual and intergroup levels. In S. Oskamp (Ed.), *Reducing prejudice and discrimination.* Mahwah, NJ: Erlbaum.

Dovidio, J. F., Kawakami, K., Johnson, C., Johnson, B., & Howard, A. (1997). On the nature of prejudice: Automatic and controlled processes. *Journal of Experimental Social Psychology, 33,* 510–540.

Dovidio, J. F., Piliavin, J. A., Gaertner, S. L., Schroeder, D. A., & Clark, R. D. III. (1991). The arousal cost-reward model and the process of intervention: A review of the evidence. In M. S. Clark (Ed.), *Prosocial behavior. Review of personality and social psychology* (Vol. 12). Newbury Park, CA: Sage Publications.

Downey, G., & Feldman, S. L. (1996). Implications of rejection sensitivity for intimate relationships. *Journal of Personality and Social Psychology, 70,* 1327–1343.

Downey, G., Freitas, A. L., Michaelis, B., & Khouri, H. (1998). The self-fulfilling prophecy in close relationships: Rejection sensitivity and rejection by romantic partners. *Journal of Personality and Social Psychology, 75,* 545–560.

Drake, M. E., Pakalnis, A., & Denio, L. C. (1988). Differential diagnosis of epilepsy and multiple personality: Clinical and EEG findings in 15 cases. *Neuropsychiatry, Neuropsychology, and Behavioral Neurology, 1,* 131–140.

Draycott, S., & Dabbs, A. (1998). Cognitive dissonance 2: A theoretical grounding of motivational interviewing. *British Journal of Clinical Psychology, 37,* 355–364.

Driskell, J. E., Willis, R. P., & Copper, C. (1992). Effect of overlearning on retention. *Journal of Applied Psychology, 77,* 615–622.

Drukin, K. (1998). Implicit content and implicit processes in mass media use. In K. Kirsner et al. (Eds.), *Implicit and explicit mental processes.* Mahwah, NJ: Erlbaum.

Dukas, R. (1998). Evolutionary ecology of learning. In R. Dukas et al. (Eds.), *Cognitive ecology: The evolutionary ecology of information processing and decision making.* Chicago: University of Chicago Press.

Duncan, B. L. (1976). Differential social perception and attribution of intergroup violence: Testing the lower limits of stereotyping of blacks. *Journal of Personality and Social Psychology, 34,* 590–598.

Duncan, D. F., Donnelly, J. W., Nicholson, T., & Hees, A. J. (1992). Cultural diversity, superstitions, and pseudoscientific beliefs among allied health students. *College Student Journal, 26,* 525–530.

Duncan, I. J. H., Widowski, T. M., Malleau, A. E., Lindberg, A. C., & Petherick, J. C. (1998). External factors and causation of dustbathing in domestic hens. *Behavioural Processes, 43,* 219–228.

Duncan, R. (1997). *SPECT imaging of the brain.* New York: Kluwer Academic.

Dunn, J., & Plomin, R. (1990). *Separate lives: Why siblings are so different.* New York: Basic Books.

Dutton, D. G., & Aron, A. P. (1974). Some evidence for heightened sexual attraction under conditions of high anxiety. *Journal of Personality and Social Psychology, 30,* 510–517.

Duvander, A. Z. E. (1999). The transition from cohabitation to marriage: A longitudinal study of the propensity to marry in Sweden in the early 1990s. *Journal of Family Issues, 20,* 698–717.

Duvernoy, H. M. (1997). *The human hippocampus: Functional anatomy, vascularization and serial sections with MRI.* New York: Springer-Verlag.

Dyken, M. E., Lin-Dyken, D. C., Seaba, P., & Yamada, T. (1995). Violent sleep-related behavior leading to subdural hemorrhage. *Archives of Neurology, 52,* 318–321.

Eacott, M. J., & Crawley, R. A. (1998). The offset of childhood amnesia: Memory for events that occurred before age 3. *Journal of Experimental Psychology: General, 127,* 22–33.

Eagly, A. H., & Carli, L. L. (1981). Sex of researcher and sex-typed communications as determinants of sex differences in influenceability: A meta-analysis of social influence studies. *Psychological Bulletin, 90,* 1–20.

Eagly, A. H., & Crowley, M. (1986). Gender and helping behavior: A meta-analytic review of the social psychological literature. *Psychological Bulletin, 100,* 283–308.

Eagly, A. H., & Wood, W. (1999). The origins of sex differences in human behavior: Evolved dispositions versus social roles. *American Psychologist, 54,* 408–423.

Eastman, C. I., Hoese, E. K., Youngstedt, S. D., & Liu, L. (1995). Phase-shifting human circadian rhythms with exercise during the night shift. *Physiology and Behavior, 58,* 1287–1291.

Ebbinghaus, H. (1964). *Über das Gedächtnis: Untersuchungen Zur Experimentellen Psychologie (Memory: A contribution to experimental psychology).* (H. A. Ruger & C. E. Bussenius, Trans.). New York: Dover. (Original work published 1885)

Ebmeier, K. (2000). Cerebral metabolism, brain imaging. In G. Fink (Ed.), *Encyclopedia of stress.* San Diego: Academic Press.

Eccles, J. (1991). Gender-role socialization. In R. M. Baron, W. G. Graziano, & C. Stangor (Eds.), *Social psychology.* Ft. Worth, TX: Holt, Rinehart & Winston.

Echt, K. V., Morrell, R. W., & Park, D. C. (1998). Effects of age and training formats on basic computer skill acquisition in older adults. *Educational Gerontology, 24,* 3–25.

Eckensberger, L. H., & Zimba, R. F. (1997). The development of moral judgment. In J. W. Berry, P. R. Dasen, & T. S. Saraswathi (Eds.), *Handbook of cross-cultural psychology* (2nd ed., Vol. 2). Boston: Allyn & Bacon.

Eckhardt, C. I., & Kassinove, H. (1998). Articulated cognitive distortions and cognitive deficiencies in maritally violent men. *Journal of Cognitive Psychotherapy, 12,* 231–250.

Edwards, A. E. (1962). A demonstration of the long-term retention of a conditioned galvanic skin response. *Psychosomatic Medicine, 24,* 459–463.

Edwards, D. C. (1998). *Motivation and emotion: Evolutionary, physiological, cognitive and social influences.* Thousand Oaks, CA: Sage Publications.

Edwards, K. (1998). The face of time: Temporal cues in facial expressions of emotion. *Psychological Science, 9,* 270–276.

Efran, J. F., & Greene, M. A. (2000). The limits of change: Heredity, environment, and family influence. In W. C. Nichols & M. A. Pace-Nichols (Eds.), *Handbook of family development and intervention.* New York: Wiley.

Eibl-Eibesfeldt, I. (1973). The expressive behavior of the deaf-and-blind children. In M. von Cranach & I. Vine (Eds.), *Social communication and movement.* New York: Academic Press.

Eich, J. E., Weingartner, H., Stillman, R. C., & Gillin, J. C. (1975). State-dependent accessibility of retrieval cues in the retention of a categorized list. *Journal of Verbal Learning and Verbal Behavior, 14,* 408–417.

Eichenbaum, H. (1997). How does the brain organize memories. *Science, 277,* 330–332.

Einstein, G. O., McDaniel, M. A., Smith, R., & Shaw, P. (1998). Habitual prospective memory and aging: Remembering instructions and forgetting actions. *Psychological Science, 9,* 284–288.

Eiseley, L. (1946). *The immense journey.* New York: Random House.

Eisenberg, N. (2000). Emotion, regulation, and moral development. *Annual Review of Psychology, 51,* 665–697.

Eisenberg, N., & Mussen, P. H. (1989). *The roots of prosocial behavior in children.* Cambridge, England: Cambridge University Press.

Eisenberg, N., Shepard, S. A., Fabes, R. A., Murphy, B. C., & Guthrie, I. K. (1998). Shyness and children's emotionality, regulation, and coping: Contemporaneous, longitudinal, and across-context relations. *Child Development, 69,* 767–790.

Eisenstadt, S. A., & Simon, H. A. (1997). Logic and thought. *Minds & Machines, 7,* 365–385.

Ekman, P. (1973). *Darwin and facial expression: A century of research in review.* New York: Academic Press.

Ekman, P. (1999a). Basic emotions. In T. Dalgleish & M. J. Power (Eds.), *Handbook of cognition and emotion.* Chichester, England: Wiley.

Ekman, P. (1999b). Facial expressions. In T. Dalgleish & M. J. Power (Eds.), *Handbook of cognition and emotion.* Chichester, England: Wiley.

Ekman, P., & Davidson, R. (1994). *The nature of emotion: Fundamental questions.* New York: Oxford University Press.

Ekman, P., Davidson, R. J., & Friesen, W. V. (1990). The Duchenne smile: Emotional expression and brain physiology II. *Journal of Personality and Social Psychology, 58,* 342–353.

Ekman, P., & Friesen, W. V. (1987). *Facial action coding system.* Palo Alto, CA: Consulting Psychologists Press.

Ekman, P., et al. (1976). Universal and cultural difference in the judgments of social expressions of emotions. *Journal of Personality and Social Psychology, 53,* 712–717.

Ekman, P., Friesen, W. V., & O'Sullivan, M. (1988). Smiles when lying. *Journal of Personality and Social Psychology, 54,* 414–420.

Ekman, P., Levenson, R. W., & Friesen, W. V. (1983). Autonomic nervous system activity distinguishes among emotions. *Science, 221,* 1208–1210.

Elbert, T., Pantev, C., Wienbruch, C., Rockstroh, B., & Taub, E. (1995). Increased cortical representation of the fingers of the left hand in string players. *Science, 270,* 305–307.

Elkind, D. (1967). Egocentrism in adolescence. *Child Development, 38,* 1025–1034.

Elliot, A. J., & Church, M. A. (1997). A hierarchical model of approach and avoidance achievement motivation. *Journal of Personality and Social Psychology, 72,* 218–232.

Elliot, A. J., & Devine, P. G. (1994). On the motivational nature of cognitive dissonance: Dissonance as psychological discomfort. *Journal of Personality and Social Psychology, 67,* 382–394.

Elliot, A. J., & McGregor, H. A. (1999). Test anxiety and the hierarchical model of approach and avoidance achievement motivation. *Journal of Personality and Social Psychology, 76*, 628–644.

Elliot, A. J., McGregor, H. A., & Gable, S. (1999). Achievement goals, study strategies, and exam performance: A mediational analysis. *Journal of Educational Psychology, 91*, 549-563.

Ellis, A. (1962). *Reason and emotion in psychotherapy.* New York: Lyle Stuart.

Ellis, L., & Ames, M. A. (1987). Neurohormonal functioning and sexual orientation: A theory of homosexuality-heterosexuality. *Psychology Bulletin, 101*, 233–258.

Ellis, N. R., & Hope, R. (1968). Memory processes and the serial position curve. *Journal of Experimental Psychology, 77*, 613–619.

Emerson, R. M. (1966). Mount Everest: A case study of communication feedback and sustained group goalstriving. *Sociometry, 29*, 213–227.

Emery, R. E. (1982). Interparental conflict and the children of discord and divorce. *Psychological Bulletin, 92*, 310–330.

Emery, R. E., & Laumann-Billings, L. (1998). An overview of the nature, causes, and consequences of abusive family relationships: Toward differentiating maltreatment and violence. *American Psychologist, 53*, 121–135.

Emlen, S. T. (1975, August). The stellar-orientation system of a migratory bird. *Scientific American*, 102–111.

Emler, N. (1998). Sociomoral understanding. In A. Campbell & S. Muncer (Eds.), *The social child.* Hove, England: Psychology Press/Erlbaum.

Enquist, M., & Leimar, O. (1990). The evolution of fatal fighting. *Animal Behaviour, 39*, 1–9.

Epps, J., & Kendall, P. C. (1995). Hostile attributional bias in adults. *Cognitive Therapy and Research, 19*, 159–178.

Epstein, J. A., & Harackiewicz, J. M. (1992). Winning is not enough: The effects of competition and achievement orientation on intrinsic interest. *Personality and Social Psychology Bulletin, 18*, 128–138.

Epstein, R., Kirshnit, C. E., Lanza, R. P., & Rubin, L. C. (1984). "Insight" in the pigeon: Antecedents and determinants of an intelligent performance. *Nature, 308*, 61–62.

Epstein, S. (1983). Aggregation and beyond: Some basic issues on the production of behavior. *Journal of Personality, 51*, 360–392.

Epstein, S. (1994). Integration of the cognitive and the psychodynamic unconscious. *American Psychologist, 49*, 709–724.

Epstein, S. (1998). *Constructive thinking: The key to emotional intelligence.* Westport, CT: Praeger.

Epstein, S. (1999). The interpretation of dreams from the perspective of cognitive experiential self-theory. In J. A. Singer & P. Salovey (Eds.), *At play in the fields of consciousness: Essays in honor of Jerome L. Singer.* Mahwah, NJ: Erlbaum.

Erdberg, P. (1990). Rorschach assessment. In G. Goldstern & M. Hersen (Eds.), *Handbook of psychological assessment.* New York: Pergamon.

Erdberg, P. (2000). Rorschach assessment. In G. Goldstein & M. Hersen (Eds.), *Handbook of psychological assessment* (3rd ed.). New York: Elsevier.

Erdelyi, M. H. (1985). *Psychoanalysis: Freud's cognitive psychology.* New York: W. H. Freeman.

Erdelyi, M. H. (1988). Repression, reconstruction and defense: History and integration of the psychoanalytic and experimental frameworks. In J. Singer (Ed.), *Repression: Defense mechanism and cognitive style.* Chicago: University of Chicago Press.

Erdelyi, M. H. (1995). *Psychoanalysis: Freud's cognitive psychology.* New York: W. H. Freeman.

Ericsson, K. A., & Chase, W. G. (1982). Exceptional memory. *American Scientist, 70*, 607–615.

Ericsson, K. A., Chase, W. G., & Faloon, S. (1980). Acquisition of a memory skill. *Science, 208*, 1181–1182.

Ericsson, K. A., & Polson, P. G. (1988). An experimental analysis of the mechanisms of a memory skill. *Journal of Experimental Psychology: Learning, Memory, and Cognition, 14*, 305–316.

Erikson, E. H. (1950, 1963). *Childhood and society.* New York: W. W. Norton.

Erikson, E. H. (1968). *Identity, youth and crisis.* New York: W. W. Norton.

Erikson, E. H. (1980). *Identity and the life cycle.* New York: W. W. Norton. (Original work published 1959)

Erikson, E. H., Erikson, J. M., & Kivnick, H. Q. (1986). *Vital involvement in old age.* New York: W. W. Norton.

Eriksson, P. S., Perfilieva, E., Bjork-Erikkson, T., Alborn, A. M., Nordborg, C., Peterson, D. A., & Gage, F. H. (1998). Neurogenesis in the adult human hippocampus. *Nature Medicine, 4*(11), 1313–1317.

Eron, L. D. (1987). The development of aggressive behavior from the perspective of a developing behaviorism. *American Psychologist, 42*, 435–442.

Eron, L. D. (2000). A psychological perspective. In V. B. Van Hasselt & M. Hersen (Eds.), *Aggression and violence: An introductory text.* Boston: Allyn & Bacon.

Escorihuela, R. M., Fernandez, T. A., Tobena, A., & Vivas, N. M. (1995). Early environmental stimulation produces long-lasting changes on !b-adrenoceptor transduction system. *Neurobiology of Learning and Memory, 64*, 49–57.

Esparza, J., Fox, C., Harper, I. T., Bennett, P. H., Schulz, L. O., Valencia, M. E., & Ravussin, E. (2000). Daily energy expenditure in Mexican and USA Pima indians: Low physical activity as a possible cause of obesity. *International Journal of Obesity and Related Metabolic Disorders, 24*, 55–59.

Essau, C. A., & Petermann, F. (1999). *Depressive disorders in children and adolescents: Epidemiology, risk factors, and treatment.* Northvale, NJ: Jason Aronson.

Essau, C. A., & Trommsdorff, G. Coping with university-related problems: A cross-cultural comparison. *Journal of Cross-Cultural Psychology, 27*, 315–328.

Esser, J. K. (1998). Alive and well after 25 years: A review of groupthink research. *Organizational Behavior and Human Decision Processes, 73*, 116–141.

Esser, J. K., & Lindoerfer, J. S. (1989). Groupthink and the space shuttle Challenger accident: Toward a quantitative case analysis. *Journal of Behavioral Decision Making, 2*, 167–177.

Estes, T. H., & Vaughn, J. L. (1985). *Reading and learning in the content classroom: Diagrams and instructional strategies* (3rd ed.). Boston: Allyn & Bacon.

Estes, W. K. (1991). Cognitive architectures from the standpoint of an experimental psychologist. *Annual Review of Psychology, 42*, 1–28.

Everitt, B. J., Parkinson, J. A., Olmstead, M. C., Arroyo, M., Robledo, P., Robbins, T. W. (1999). Associative processes in addiction and reward. The role of amygdala-ventral striatal subsystems. *Annals of the New York Academy of Sciences, 877*, 412–438.

Evers, K. E., Harlow, H. L., Redding, C. A., & LaForge, R. G. (1998). Longitudinal changes in stages of change for condom use in women. *American Journal of Health Promotion, 13*, 19–25.

Exner, J. E. (1991). *The Rorschach—A comprehensive system: Assessment of personality and psychopathology* (Vol. 2). New York: Wiley.

Eysenck, H. J. (1952). The effects of psychotherapy: An evaluation. *Journal of Consulting Psychology, 16*, 319–324.

Eysenck, H. J. (1964). *Crime and personality.* Boston: Houghton Mifflin.

Eysenck, H. J. (1967). *The biological basis of personality.* Springfield, IL: Charles C Thomas.

Eysenck, H. J. (1990). Biological dimensions of personality. In L. A. Pervin (Ed.), *Handbook of personality: Theory and research.* New York: Guilford Press.

Eysenck, H. J. (1994). Cancer, personality, and stress: Prediction and prevention. *Advances in Behaviour Research and Therapy, 16*, 167–215.

Eysenck, H. J., & Grossarth-Marticek, R. (1991). Creative novation behavior therapy as a prophylactic treatment for cancer and coronary heart disease: Part II—Effects of treatment. *Behavior Research and Therapy, 29*, 17–31.

Eysenck, M. W. (1989). Personality, stress arousal, and cognitive processes in stress transactions. In R. W. J. Newfeld (Ed.), *Advances in the investigation of psychological stress.* New York: Wiley.

Eysenck, M. W., & Eysenck, M. C. (1980). Effects of processing depth, distinctiveness, and word frequency on retention. *British Journal of Psychology, 71*, 263–274.

Fagley, N. S. (1987). Positional response bias in multiple-choice tests of learning: Its relation to testwiseness and guessing strategy. *Journal of Educational Psychology, 79*, 95–97.

Fagot, B. I., Leinbach, M. D., & O'Boyle, C. (1992). Gender labeling, gender stereotyping, and parenting behaviors. *Developmental Psychology, 28*, 225–230.

Fallon, A. E., & Rozin, P. (1985). Sex differences in perceptions of desirable body shape. *Journal of Abnormal Psychology, 94*, 102–105.

Fanselow, M. S. (1991). Analgesia as a response to aversive Pavlovian conditional stimuli: Cognitive and emotional mediators. In M. R. Denny (Ed.), *Fear, avoidance, and phobias: A fundamental analysis.* Hillsdale, NJ: Erlbaum.

Fanselow, M. S. (2000). Amygdala. In G. Fink (Ed.), *Encyclopedia of stress.* San Diego: Academic Press.

Fantz, R. L. (1961, May). The origin of form perception. *Scientific American*, 66–72.

Farthing, G. W., Venturino, M., Brown, S. W., & Lazar, J. D. (1997). Internal and external distraction in the control of cold-pressor pain as a function of hypnotizability. *International Journal of Clinical and Experimental Hypnosis, 45,* 433–446.

Fawcett, G. M., Heise, L. L., Isita-Espejel, L., & Pick, S. (1999). Changing community responses to wife abuse: A research and demonstration project in Iztacalco, Mexico. *American Psychologist, 54,* 41–49.

Fazio, R. H., Jackson, J. R., Dunton, B. C., & Williams, C. J. (1995). Variability in automatic activation as an unobstrusive measure of racial attitudes: A bona fide pipeline? *Journal of Personality and Social Psychology, 69,* 1013–1027.

Fazio, R. H., Zanna, M. P., & Cooper, J. (1977). Dissonance and self-perception: An integrative view of each theory's proper domain of application. *Journal of Experimental Social Psychology, 13,* 464–479.

Federal Bureau of Investigation (1999). *FBI supplementary homicide reports.* Washington, DC: Author.

Feeny, N. C., & Foa, E. B. (2000). Sexual assault. In G. Fink (Ed.), *Encyclopedia of stress.* San Diego: Academic Press.

Fein, S., & Spencer, S. J. (1997). Prejudice as self-image maintenance: Affirming the self through derogating others. *Journal of Personality and Social Psychology, 73,* 31–44.

Feingold, A. (1988). Matching for attractiveness in romantic partners and same-sex friends: A meta-analysis and theoretical critique. *Psychological Bulletin, 104,* 226–235.

Feingold, A. (1992). Good-looking people are not what we think. *Psychological Bulletin, 11,* 304–341.

Feingold, A. (1994). Gender differences in personality: A meta-analysis. *Psychological Bulletin, 116,* 429–456.

Feingold, A., & Mazzella, R. (1998). Gender differences in body image are increasing. *Psychological Science, 9,* 190–195.

Feist, J., & Brannon, L. (2000). *Health psychology.* Boston: Allyn & Bacon.

Felder, C. C., & Glass, M. (1998). Cannabinoid receptors and their endogenous agonists. *Annual Review of Pharmacology and Toxicology, 38,* 179–200.

Felmlee, D. H. (1998). "Be careful what you wish for . . ." : A quantitative and qualitative investigation of "fatal attractions." *Personal Relationships, 5,* 235–253.

Felton, D. L., & Maida, M. E. (2000). Neuroimmunomodulation. In G. Fink (Ed.), *Encyclopedia of stress.* San Diego: Academic Press.

Feng, A. S., & Ratnam, R. (2000). Neural basis of hearing in real-world situations. *Annual Review of Psychology, 51,* 699–726.

Fenton, W. S., & McGlaskan, T. H. (1991a). Natural history of schizophrenia subtypes: I. Longitudinal study of paranoid, hebephonic, and undifferentiated schizophrenia. *Archives of General Psychiatry, 48,* 969–977.

Fenton, W. S., & McGlaskan, T. H. (1991b). Natural history of schizophrenia subtypes: II. Positive and negative symptoms and long-term course. *Archives of General Psychiatry, 48,* 978–986.

Ferguson, E. D. (1999). *Motivation: A biosocial and cognitive integration of motivation and emotion.* New York: Oxford University Press.

Fergusson, D. M., & Lynskey, M. T. (1997). Physical punishment/maltreatment during childhood and adjustment in young adulthood. *Child Abuse and Neglect, 21,* 617–630.

Fernald, A., Taeschner, T., Dunn, J., Papousek, M., De Boysson-Bardies, B., & Fukui, I. (1989). A cross-cultural study of prosodic modification in mothers' and fathers' speech to preverbal infants. *Journal of Child Language, 16,* 477–501.

Ferster, C. B., & Skinner, B. F. (1957). *Schedules of reinforcement.* Englewood Cliffs, NJ: Prentice-Hall.

Fessler, R. G. (1989). Physiology, anatomy and pharmacology of pain perception. In P. M. Camic & F. D. Brown, (Eds.), *Assessing chronic pain: A multidisciplinary approach.* New York: Springer-Verlag.

Festinger, L. (1954). A theory of social comparison processes. *Human Relations, 2,* 117–140.

Festinger, L. (1957). *A theory of cognitive dissonance.* Stanford, CA: Stanford University Press.

Festinger, L., & Carlsmith, J. M. (1959). Cognitive consequences of forced compliance. *Journal of Abnormal and Social Psychology, 58,* 203–210.

Festinger, L., Pepitone, A., & Newcomb, T. (1952). Some consequences of deindividuation in a group. *Journal of Abnormal and Social Psychology, 47,* 382–389.

Festinger, L., Schachter, S., & Back, K. (1950). *Social pressures in informal groups: A study of a housing community.* New York: Harper.

Fetterman, D. M. (1988). *Excellence and equality: A qualitatively different perspective on gifted and talented education.* Albany, NY: State University of New York Press.

Feunekes, G. I. J., De Graaf, C., & Van Staveren, W. A. (1995). Social facilitation of food intake is mediated by meal duration. *Physiology and Behavior, 58,* 551–558.

Fichera, L. V., & Andreassi, J. L. (1998). Stress and personality as factors in women's cardiovascular reactivity. *International Journal of Psychophysiology, 28,* 143–155.

Fichter, M. M., & Noegel, R. (1990). Concordance for bulimia nervosa in twins. *International Journal of Eating Disorders, 9,* 255–263.

Fiedler, K. (2000). Toward an integrative account of affect and cognition phenomena using the BIAS computer algorithm. In J. P. Forgas (Ed.), *Feeling and thinking: The role of affect in social cognition.* New York: Cambridge University Press.

Field, T. (1995). Massage therapy for infants and children. *Journal of Developmental and Behavioral Pediatrics, 16,* 105–111.

Field, T. (2000). Infant massage therapy. In C. H. Zeanah, Jr. (Ed.), *Handbook of infant mental health* (2nd ed.). New York: Guilford Press.

Field, T., Grizzle, N., Scafidi, F., Abrams, S., Richardson, S., Kuhn, C., & Schanberg, S. (1996). Massage therapy for infants of depressed mothers. *Infant Behavior and Development, 19,* 107-112.

Field, T., Woodson, R., Cohen, D., Garcia, R., & Greenberg, R. (1983). Discrimination and imitation of facial expressions by term and pre-term neonates. *Infant Behavior and Development, 6,* 485–490.

Field, T. M., Schanberg, S. M., Scafidi, F., Bauer, C. R., Vega-Lahr, N., Garcia, R., Nystrom, J., & Kuhn, C. M. (1986). Tactile/kinesthetic stimulation effects on preterm neonates. *Pediatrics, 77,* 654–658.

Filogamo, G. (1998). *Brain plasticity: Development and aging: Advances in neurobiology: plasticity and regeneration.* New York: Plenum.

Finell, J. S. (1997). *Mind-body problems: Psychotherapy with psychosomatic disorders.* Northvale, NJ: Jason Aronson.

Fischer, K. W., Shaver, P. R., & Carnochan, P. (1990). How emotions develop and how they organize development. *Cognition and Emotion, 4,* 81–127.

Fishbein, M. (1980). A theory of reasoned action: Some applications and implications. In H. E. Howe & M. M. Page (Eds.), *Nebraska Symposium on Motivation* (Vol. 27, pp. 65–116). Lincoln: University of Nebraska Press.

Fishbein, M., & Ajzen, I. (1974). Attitudes toward objects as predictors of single and multiple behavioral criteria. *Psychological Review, 81,* 59–74.

Fisher, C., Kahn E., Edwards, A., Davis, D. M., & Fine, J. (1974). A psychophysiological study of nightmares and night terrors: III. Mental content and recall of stage 4 night terrors. *Journal of Nervous and Mental Disease, 158,* 174–188.

Fisher, S., & Greenberg, R. P. (1996). *Freud scientifically reappraised: Testing the theories and therapy.* New York: Wiley.

Fiske, S. T. (1998). Stereotyping, prejudice, and discrimination. In D. T. Gilbert, S. T. Fiske, & G. Lindzey (Eds.), *The handbook of social psychology* (4th ed., Vol. 2). Boston: McGraw-Hill.

Fiske, S. T. (2000). Interdependence reduces stereotyping and prejudice. In S. Oskamp (Ed.), *Reducing prejudice and discrimination.* Mahwah, NJ: Erlbaum.

Fiske, S. T., & Taylor, S. E. (1991). *Social cognition* (2nd ed.). New York: McGraw-Hill.

Fivush, R. (1994). Young children's event recall: Are memories constructed through discourse? *Consciousness and Cognition: An International Journal, 3,* 356–373.

Flavell, J. H. (1970). Developmental studies of mediated behavior. In H. W. Reese and L. P. Lipsett (Eds.), *Advances in child development and behavior* (Vol. 5). New York: Academic Press.

Flavell, J. H. (1985). *Cognitive development* (2nd ed.). Englewood Cliffs, NJ: Prentice Hall.

Flavell, J. H., Green, F. L., & Flavell, E. R. (1990). Developmental changes in young children's knowledge about the mind. *Cognitive Development, 5,* 1–27.

Flegal, K. M., Carroll, M. D., Kuczmarski, R. J., & Johnson, C. L. (1998). Overweight and obesity in the United States: Prevalence and trends, 1960–1994. *International Journal of Obesity Related Metabolic Disorders, 22,* 39–47.

Fleming, I., Baum, A., & Weiss, L. (1987). Social density and perceived control as mediators of crowding stress in high-density residential neighborhoods. *Journal of Personality and Social Psychology, 52,* 899–906.

Flett, G. L., Vredenbrug, K., & Krames, L. (1997). The continuity of depression in clinical and nonclinical samples. *Psychological Bulletin, 121,* 395–416.

Flinn, M. V. (1997). Culture and the evolution of social learning. *Evolution and Human Behavior, 18,* 23–67.

Floyd, F. J., & Wasner, G. H. (1994). Social exchange, equity, and commitment:

Structural equation modeling of dating relationships. *Journal of Family Psychology, 8,* 55–73.

Flynn, J. P. (1975). Experimental analysis of aggression and its neural basis. In J. P. Flynn (Ed.), *Advances in behavioral biology, the neurophysiology of aggression.* New York: Academic Press.

Flynn, J. R. (1987). Massive IQ gains in 14 nations. What IQ tests really measure. *Psychological Bulletin, 101*(2), 171–191.

Flynn, J. R. (1998). IQ gains over time: Toward finding the causes. In U. Neisser et al. (Eds.). *The rising curve: Long-term gains in IQ and related measures.* Washington, DC: American Psychological Association.

Foa, E. B., Hearst-Ikeda, D., & Perry, K. J. (1995). Evaluation of a brief cognitive-behavioral program for the prevention of chronic PTSD in recent assault victims. *Journal of Consulting and Clinical Psychology, 63,* 948–955.

Foa, E. B., & Meadows, E. A. (1997). Psychosocial treatments for posttraumatic stress disorder: A critical review. *Annual Review of Psychology, 48,* 449–480.

Foa, E. B., Riggs, D. S., & Gershuny, B. S. (1995). Arousal, numbing, and intrusion: Symptom structure of post traumatic stress disorder following assault. *American Journal of Psychology, 152,* 116–120.

Foa, E. B., Steketee, G., & Grayson, J. B. (1985). Imaginal and in vivo exposure: A comparison with obsessive-compulsive checkers. *Behavior Therapy, 16,* 292–302.

Folkman, S., & Lazarus, R. S. (1988) Coping as a mediator of emotion. *Journal of Personality and Social Psychology, 54,* 466–475.

Ford, T. M., Liwag, M., Michelle, G., Foley, L. A. (1998). Perceptions of rape based on sex and sexual orientation of victim. *Journal of Social Behavior and Personality, 13,* 253–262.

Fordyce, W. E. (1988). Pain and suffering: A reappraisal. *American Psychologist, 43,* 276–283.

Forgas, J. P. (Ed.) (2000). *Feeling and thinking: The role of affect in social cognition.* New York: Cambridge University Press.

Foster, C. A., Witcher, B. S., Campbell, W. K., & Green, J. D. (1998). Arousal and attraction: Evidence for automatic and controlled processes. *Journal of Personality and Social Psychology, 74,* 86–101.

Foulkes, D. (1962). Dream reports from different states of sleep. *Journal of Abnormal and Social Psychology, 65,* 14-25.

Foulkes, D. (1982). REM-dream perspectives on the development of affect and cognition. *Psychiatric Journal of the University of Ottawa, 7,* 48–55.

Foulkes, D. (1996). Dream research: 1953–1993. *Sleep, 19,* 609–624.

Foulkes, D. (1999). *Children's dreaming and the development of consciousness.* Cambridge, MA: Harvard University Press.

Foulks, F. F., Bland, I. J., & Shervington, D. (1995). Psychotherapy across cultures. *Review of Psychiatry, 14,* 511.

Foushee, H. C. (1984). Dyads and triads at 35,000 feet: Factors affecting group process and aircrew performance. *American Psychologist, 39,* 885–893.

Fouts, D. H. (1994). The use of remote video recordings to study the use of American Sign Language by chimpanzees when no humans

are present. In R. A. Gardner, B. T. Gardner, A. B. Chiarelli, & F. X. Plooij (Eds.), *The ethological roots of culture.* Dordrecht, Netherlands: Kluwer.

Fouts, R. S. (1972). Use of guidance in teaching sign language to a chimpanzee (Pan troglodytes). *Journal of Comparative and Physiological Psychology, 80,* 515–522.

Fouts, R. S., Fouts, D. H., & Van Cantfort, T. E. (1989). The infant Loulis learns signs from other cross-fostered chimpanzees. In R. A. Gardner, B. T. Gardner, & T. E. Van Cantfort (Eds.), *Teaching sign language to chimpanzees.* Albany, NY: State University of New York Press.

Fowers, B. J., & Richardson, F. C. (1996). Why is multiculturalism good? *American Psychologist, 51,* 609–621.

Fowles, D. C. (1992). Schizophrenia: Diathesis-stress revisited. *Annual Review of Psychology, 43,* 303–336.

Fox, D. K., Hopkins, B. L., & Anger, W. K. (1987). The long-term effects of a token economy on safety performance in open-pit mining. *Journal of Applied Behavior Analysis, 20,* 215–224.

Fox, N. A., & Davidson, R. J. (1991). Hemispheric specialization and attachment behaviors: Developmental processes and individual differences in separation process. In J. L. Gewirtz & W. M. Kurtines (Eds.). *Interactions with attachment.* Hillsdale, NJ: Erlbaum.

Frank, N. C., Spirito, A., Stark, L., Owens-Stively, J. (1997). The use of scheduled awakenings to eliminate childhood sleepwalking. *Journal of Pediatric Psychology, 22,* 345–353.

Frankenhaeuser, M., Lundberg, U., & Chesney, M. (1991). *Women, work, and health: Stress and opportunities.* New York: Plenum.

Franklin, J. (1987). *Molecules of the mind: The brave new science of molecular psychology.* New York: Atheneum.

Franzek, E., & Beckmann, H. (1999). *Psychoses of the schizophrenic spectrum in twins: A discussion on the nature-nurture debate in the etiology of "endogenous" psychoses.* New York: Springer-Verlag.

Franzer, K. (Ed.) (1980). *Science confronts the paranormal.* Buffalo, NY: Prometheus Books.

Fredrickson, B. L. (1998). What good are positive emotions? *Review of General Psychology, 2,* 300–319.

Fredrickson, B. L., & Roberts, T. A. (1997). Objectification theory: Toward understanding women's lived experiences and mental health risks. *Psychology of Women Quarterly, 21,* 173–206.

Fredrickson, B. L., Roberts, T. A., Noll, S. M., Quinn, D. M., & Twenge, J. M. (1998). That swimsuit becomes you: Sex differences in self-objectification, restrained eating, and math performance. *Journal of Personality and Social Psychology, 75,* 269–284.

Freedman, J. L., & Fraser, S. C. (1966). Compliance without pressure: The foot-in-the-door technique. *Journal of Personality and Social Psychology, 4,* 195–202.

Freeman, H. (1994). Schizophrenia and city residence. *British Journal of Psychiatry, 164* (Suppl. 23), 39–50.

Freud, S. (1923). *The ego and the id.* New York: W. W. Norton.

Freud, S. (1935). *A general introduction to psychoanalysis.* New York: Washington Square Press.

Freud, S. (1953). *A general introduction to psychoanalysis.* New York: Perma-books.

Freud, S. (1950). Project for a scientific psychology. In J. Strachey (Ed. and Trans.), *The standard edition of the complete works of Sigmund Freud* (Vol. 5). London: Hogarth Press. (Original work published 1893)

Freud, S. (1953). The interpretation of dreams. In J. Strachey (Ed.), *The standard edition of the complete psychological works of Sigmund Freud* (Vols. 4 & 5). London: Hogarth. (Original work published 1900)

Freud, S. (1957). Mourning and melancholia. In J. Strachey (Ed.), *The standard edition of the complete psychological works of Sigmund Freud* (Vol. 14). London: Hogarth. (Original work published 1917)

Freud, S. (1964). *New introductory lectures in psychoanalysis.* New York: Norton. (Original work published 1933)

Friedberg, J. (1975). Let's stop blasting the brain. *Psychology Today, 35,* 18–26.

Friedman, H. (Ed.) (1991). *Hostility, coping, and health.* Washington, DC: American Psychological Association.

Friedman, H. & DiMatteo, M. R. (1989). *Health psychology.* New York: Prentice Hall.

Friedman, H. S., & Booth-Kewley, S. (1987). The "disease-prone personality": A meta-analytic view of the construct. *American Psychologist, 42,* 539–555.

Friedman, H. S., Tucker, J. S., Schwartz, J. E., Tomlinson-Keasy, C., Wingard, L., & Criqui, M. H. (1995). Psychosocial and behavioral predictors of longevity: The aging and death of the Termites. *American Psychologist, 50,* 69–78.

Friedman, W. J., Robinson, A. B., & Friedman, B. L. (1987). Sex differences in moral judgments? A test of Gilligan's theory. *Psychology of Women Quarterly, 11,* 37–46.

Frisby, J. P. (1980). *Seeing: Illusion, brain, and mind.* Oxford, England: Oxford University Press.

Fristoe, N. M., Salthouse, T. A., & Woodard, J. L. (1997). Examination of age-related deficits on the Wisconsin Card Sorting Test. *Neuropsychology, 11,* 428–436.

Fritsch, J. (1999, May 25). 95% Regain Lost Weight. Or Do They? *The New York Times,* F7.

Frodi, A. M., et al. (1978). Fathers' and mothers' responses to the faces and cries of normal and premature infants. *Developmental Psychology, 14,* 490–498.

Fromm, E. (1956). *The art of loving.* New York, Harper.

Fry, J. M. (1998). Treatment modalities for narcolepsy. *Neurology, 50* (2, Suppl. 1), S43–S48.

Fuligni, A. J. (1998). Authority, autonomy, and parent-adolescent conflict and cohesion: A study of adolescents from Mexican, Chinese, Filipino, and European backgrounds. *Developmental Psychology, 34,* 782–792.

Funk, S. C. (1992). Hardiness: A review of theory and research. *Health Psychology 11,* 335–345.

Gabbard, G. O. (1990). *Psychodynamic psychiatry in clinical practice.* Washington, DC: American Psychiatric Press.

Gabrieli, J. D. E. (1998). Cognitive neuroscience of human memory. *Annual Review of Psychology, 49,* 87–115.

Gabrieli, J. D. E., Desmond, J. E., Demb, J. B., & Wagner, A. D. (1996). Functional magnetic resonance imaging of semantic memory processes in the frontal lobes. *Psychological Science, 7,* 278–283.

Gacsaly, S. A., & Borges, C. A. (1979). The male physique and behavioral expectancies. *Journal of Psychology, 101,* 97–102.

Gaertner, S. L., Dovidio, J. F., Banker, B. S., Houletter, M., Johnson, K. M., & McGlynn, E. A. (2000). Reducing intergroup conflict: From superordinate goals to decategorization, recategorization, and mutual differentiation. *Group Dynamics, 4,* 98–114.

Gainotti, G. (1972). Emotional behavior and hemispheric side of lesion. *Cortex, 8,* 41–55.

Galati, D., & Lavelli, M. (1997). Neonate and infant emotion expression perceived by adults. *Journal of Nonverbal Behavior, 21,* 57–83.

Galavotti, C., Saltzman, L. E., Sauter, S. L., & Sumartojo, E. (1997). Behavioral science activities at the Centers for Disease Control and Prevention: A selected overview of exemplary programs. *American Psychologist, 52,* 154–166.

Galef, B. G., Jr. (1985). Social learning in wild Norway rats. In T. D. Johnson & A. T. Pietrewicz (Eds.), *Issues in the ecological study of learning.* Hillsdale, N.J.: Erlbaum.

Gallup, G. G., Jr. (1970). Chimpanzees: Self-recognition. *Science, 167*(3914), 86-87.

Gallup, G. G., Jr. (1979). Self-awareness in primates. *American Scientist, 67,* 417–421.

Gallup, G. G., Jr., & Suarez, S. D. (1986). Self-awareness and the emergence of mind in humans and other primates. In J. Suls & A. G. Greenwald (Eds.), *Psychological perspectives on the self* (Vol. 3). Hillsdale, NJ: Erlbaum.

Gallup, G. H., Jr., & Newport, F. (1991, Winter). Belief in paranormal phenomena among adult Americans. *Skeptical Inquirer,* pp. 137–146.

Gallup Organization (1988). *American's youth 1977–1988.* Princeton, NJ: Author.

Galton, F. (1869). *Hereditary genius: An inquiry into its laws and consequences.* New York: Appleton.

Galton, F. (1883). *Inquiries into human faculty and its development.* London: Dent.

Gamwell, L., & Tomes, N. (1995). *Madness in America: Cultural and medical perceptions of mental illness before 1914.* Ithaca, NY: Cornell University Press.

Gander, P. H., Nguyen, D., Rosekind, M. R., & Connell, L. J. (1993). Age, circadian rhythms, and sleep loss in flight crews. *Aviation, Space, and Environmental Medicine, 64,* 189–195.

Garbarino, J. (1995). *Raising children in a socially toxic environment.* San Francisco: Jossey-Bass.

Garber, H. L. (1988). *The Milwaukee Project: Preventing mental retardation in children at risk.* Washington, DC: American Association on Mental Retardation.

Garcia, J., & Koelling, R. A. (1966). The relation of cue to consequence in avoidance learning. *Psychonomic Science, 4,* 123–124.

Garcia, J., Lasiter, P. S., Bermudez, R. F., & Deems, D. A. (1985). A general theory of aversion learning. *Annals of the New York Academy of Sciences, 443,* 8–21.

Gardiner, J. M., Gawlick, B., & Richardson, K. A. (1994). Maintenance rehearsal affects knowing, not remembering; elaborative rehearsal affects remembering, not knowing. *Psychonomic Bulletin and Review, 1,* 107–110.

Gardner, B. T., & Gardner, R. A. (1975). Evidence for sentence constituents in the early utterances of child and chimpanzee. *Journal of Experimental Psychology: General, 104,* 244–267.

Gardner, B. T., & Gardner, R. A. (1998). Development of phrases in the early utterances of children and cross-fostered chimpanzees. *Human Evolution, 13,* 161–188.

Gardner, H. (1983). *Frames of mind: The theory of multiple intelligences.* New York: Basic Books.

Gardner, R. A., & Gardner, B. T. (1969). Teaching language to a chimpanzee. *Science, 165,* 664–672.

Garfinkel, P. E. (1992). Evidence in support of attitudes to shape and weight as a diagnostic criterion of bulimia nervosa. *International Journal of Eating Disorders, 11,* 321–325.

Garfinkel, P. E., & Garner, D. M. (1982). *Anorexia nervosa: A multidimensional perspective.* New York: Brunner-Mazel.

Garland, D. J., & Barry, J. R. (1991). Cognitive advantage in sport: The nature of perceptual structures. *American Journal of Psychology, 104,* 211–228.

Garmezy, N. (1983). *Stress, coping and development in children.* New York: McGraw-Hill.

Garnefski, N., & Arends, E. (1998). Sexual abuse and adolescent maladjustment: Differences between male and female victims. *Journal of Adolescence, 21,* 99–107.

Garner, D. M., Garfinkel, P. E., Schwartz, D., & Thompson, M. (1980). Cultural expectations of thinness in women. *Psychological Reports, 47,* 483–491.

Gatchel, R. J., & Weisberg, J. N. (2000). *Personality characteristics of patients with pain.* Washington, DC: American Psychological Association.

Gathercole, S. E. (1998). The development of memory. *Journal of Child Psychology and Psychiatry and Allied Disciplines, 39,* 3–27.

Gauci, M., Husband, A. J., Saxarra, H., & King, M. G. (1994). Pavlovian conditioning of nasal tryptase release in human subjects with allergic rhinitis. *Physiology and Behavior, 55,* 823–825.

Gaylord-Ross, R. (1990). *Issues and research in special education.* New York: Teachers College Press.

Gazzaniga, M. S. (1985). *The social brain.* New York: Basic Books.

Gazzaniga, M. S., Fendrich, R., & Wessinger, C. M. (1994). Blindsight reconsidered. *Current Directions in Psychological Science, 3,* 93–95.

Gazzaniga, M. S., & Smylie, C. S. (1983). Facial recognition and brain asymmetries: Clues to underlying mechanisms. *Annals of Neurology, 13,* 536–540.

Gazzaniga, M. S., Steen, D., & Volpe, B. T. (1979). *Functional neuroscience.* New York: Harper & Row.

Ge, X., Conger, R. D., & Elder, G. H., Jr. (1996). Coming of age too early: Pubertal influences on girls' vulnerability to psychological distress. *Child Development, 67,* 3386–3400.

Geary, D. (1995). Reflections of evolution and culture in children's cognition: Implications for mathematical instruction and development. *American Psychologist, 50,* 24–37.

Geiger, M. A. (1991). Changing multiple choice answers: A validation and extension. *College Student Journal, 25,* 181–186.

Geiselman, R. E., Fisher, R. P., MacKinnon, D. P., & Holland, H. L. (1985). Eyewitness memory enhancement in the police interview: Cognitive retrieval mnemonics versus hypnosis. *Journal of Applied Psychology, 70,* 401–412.

George, C., & Main, M. (1979). Social interactions of young abused children: Approach, avoidance, and aggression. *Child development, 50,* 306–318.

George, L. (1980). *Role transitions in later life.* Monterey, CA: Brooks/Cole.

George, W. H., Lehman, G. L., Cue, K. L., & Martinez, L. J. (1997). Postdrinking sexual inferences: Evidence for linear rather than curvilinear dosage effects. *Journal of Applied Social Psychology, 27,* 629–648.

George, W. H., Stoner, S. A., Norris, J., Lopez, P. A., & Lehman, G. L. (2000). Alcohol expectancies and sexuality: A self-fulfilling prophecy analysis of dyadic perceptions and behavior. *Journal of Studies on Alcohol, 61,* 168–176.

Geracioti, T. D., Loosen, P. T., Ebert, M. H., & Schmidt, D. (1995). Fasting and postprandial cerebrospinal fluid glucose concentrations in healthy women and in an obese binge eater. *International Journal of Eating Disorders, 18,* 365–369.

Gerben, R., deCraen, A. J. M., DeBoer, A., & Kessels, A. G. H. (1998). Is placebo analgesia mediated by endogenous opioids? A systematic review. *Pain, 76,* 273–275.

Gergen, K. (2000). *An invitation to social constructivism.* Thousand Oaks, CA: Sage Publications.

Gerhart, B. (1990). Voluntary turnover and alternative job opportunities. *Journal of Applied Psychology, 75,* 467-476.

Gershon, E. S., Berrettini, W. H., & Golden, L. E. (1989). Mood disorders: Genetic aspects. In H. I. Kaplan & B. J. Sadock (Eds.), *Comprehensive textbook of psychiatry/V.* Baltimore: Williams & Wilkins.

Gewirtz, J. C., & Davis, M. (1998). Application of Pavlovian higher-order conditioning to the analysis of the neural substrates of fear conditioning. *Neuropharmacology, 37,* 453–459.

Gibbs, J., Young, R. C., & Smith, G. P. (1973). Cholecystokinin decreases food intake in rats. *Journal of Comparative and Physiological Psychology, 84,* 488–495.

Gibson, E. J., & Walk, R. D. (1960). The "visual cliff." *Scientific American, 202,* 64–71.

Gibson, J. J. (1979). *The ecological approach to visual perception.* Boston: Houghton Mifflin.

Gilbert, D. T., & Malone, P. S. (1995). The correspondence bias. *Psychological Bulletin, 117,* 21–38.

Gillespie, M. (1999, April 30). *Americans have very mixed opinions about blame for Littleton shootings.* Gallup News Service. Princeton, NJ: Gallup Organization.

Gillett, E. (1997). Revising Freud's structural theory. *Psychoanalysis and Contemporary Thought, 20,* 471–499.

Gillette, M. U. (1986). The suprachiasmatic nuclei: Circadian phase-shifts induced at the time of hypothalamic slice preparation are preserved in vitro. *Brain Research, 379,* 176–181.

Gillham, J. E., Reivich, K. J., Jaycox, L. H., & Seligman, M. E. P. (1995). Prevention of depressive symptoms in school-children: Two year follow-up. *Psychological Science, 6,* 343–351.

Gilligan, C. (1982). *In a different voice: Psychological theory and women's development.* Cambridge, MA: Harvard University Press.

Glantz, K., Durlach, N. I., Barnett, R. C., & Aviles, W. A. (1996). Virtual reality (VR) for psychotherapy: From the physical to the social environment. *Psychotherapy, 33,* 464–473.

Glanzer, M., & Cunitz, A. R. (1966). Two storage mechanisms in free recall. *Journal of Verbal Learning and Verbal Behavior, 5,* 351–360.

Glaser, R., & Bassok, M. (1989). Learning theory and the study of instruction. *Annual Review of Psychology, 40,* 631–666.

Glaser, R., & Kiecolt-Glaser, J. (Eds.) (1995). *Handbook of human stress and immunity.* New York: Academic Press.

Gleaves, D. H. (1996). The sociocognitive model of dissociative identity disorder: A reexamination of the evidence. *Psychological Bulletin, 120,* 42–59.

Glenberg, A. M., Sanocki, T., Epstein, W., & Morris, C. (1987). Enhancing calibration of comprehension. *Journal of Experimental Psychology: General, 116,* 119–136.

Glenn, N. D. (1998). The course of marital success and failure in five American 10-year marriage cohorts. *Journal of Marriage and the Family, 60*(3), 569–576.

Glick, P., & Fiske, S. T. (1999). Gender, power dynamics, and social interaction. In M. M. Ferree, J. Lorber, & B. B. Hess (Eds.), *Revisioning gender. The gender lens.* (Vol. 5). Thousand Oaks, CA: Sage Publications.

Gobet, F., & Simon, H. A. (1998). Expert chess memory: Revisiting the chunking hypothesis. *Memory, 6,* 225–255.

Godden, D. R., & Baddeley, A. D. (1975). Context-dependent memory in two natural environments: On land and under water. *British Journal of Psychology, 66,* 325–332.

Goffman, E. (1961). *Asylums: Essays on the social situation of mental patients and other inmates.* New York: Doubleday.

Gold, E. R. (1997). *Body parts: Property rights and ownership of human biological materials.* Washington, DC: Georgetown University Press.

Gold, S. R., & Reilly, J. P. (1985–1986). Daydreaming, current concerns and personality. *Imagination, Cognition and Personality, 5,* 117–125.

Goldberg, J. L., & Barres, B. A. (2000). The relationship between neuronal survival and regeneration. *Annual Review of Neuroscience, 23,* 579–612.

Goldberg, L. R. (1981). Unconfounding situational attributions from uncertain, neutral, and ambiguous ones: A psychometric analysis of descriptions of oneself and various types of others. *Journal of Personality and Social Psychology, 41,* 517–552.

Goldman, D., Kohn, P. M., & Hunt, R. W. (1983). Sensation seeking, augmenting-reducing, and absolute auditory threshold: A strength of the nervous system perspective. *Journal of Personality and Social Psychology, 45,* 405–411.

Goldstein, B. (1999). *Sensation and perception.* Pacific Grove, CA: Brooks/Cole.

Goldstein, G. (2000). Comprehensive neuropsychological assessment batteries. In G. Goldstein & M. Hersen (Eds.), *Handbook of psychological assessment* (3rd ed.). New York: Elsevier.

Goldstein, J. H., Cajko, L., Oosterbroek, M., Michielsen, M., Houten, O., & Salverda, F. (1997). Video games and the elderly. *Social Behavior and Personality, 25,* 345–352.

Goleman, D. (1995, December 5). Making room on the couch for culture. *New York Times,* pp. C1, C3.

Gonzales, R. A., Jaworski, J. N. (1997). Alcohol and glutamate. *Alcohol Health and Research World, 21,* 120–127.

Goodall, J. (1986). *The chimpanzees of Gombe: Patterns of behavior.* Cambridge, MA: Harvard University Press.

Goodman, G. S., Quas, J. A., Batterman-Faunce, J. M., Riddlesberger, M. M., & Kuhn, J. (1994). Predictors of accurate and inaccurate memories of traumatic events experienced in childhood. *Consciousness and Cognition: An International Journal, 3,* 269–294.

Goodman, W. (1982, August 9). Of mice, monkeys and men. *Newsweek,* p. 61.

Goody, E. N. (1997). Social intelligence and language: Another rubicon? In A. Whiten, et al. (Eds.), *Machiavellian intelligence II: Extensions and evaluations.* Cambridge, England: Cambridge University Press.

Gordon, R. A. (1997). The moderation of distinctiveness-based illusory correlation: The impact of circadian variations and personal need for structure. *Journal of Social Psychology, 137,* 514–526.

Gothard, S. I., & Ivker, N. A. C. (2000). The evolving law of alleged delayed memories of childhood sexual abuse. *Child Maltreatment Journal of the American Professional Society on the Abuse of Children, 5,* 176–189.

Gottesman, I. I. (1991). *Schizophrenia genesis: The origins of madness.* New York: W. H. Freeman.

Gottfried, A. E., Fleming, J. S., & Gottfried, A. W. (1998). Role of cognitively stimulating home environment in children's academic intrinsic motivation: A longitudinal study. *Child Development, 69,* 1440–1460.

Gottfried, T. (2000). *Should drugs be legalized?* Brookfield: Twenty First Century.

Gottman, J. M. (1994). *What predicts divorce? The relationship between marital processes and marital outcomes.* Hillsdale, NJ: Erlbaum.

Gottman, J. M., & Levinson, R. (1992). Marital processes predictive of later dissolution: Behavior, psychology and health. *Journal of Personality and Social Psychology, 63,* 221–233.

Gottman, J. M., Coan, J., Carrere, S., & Swanson, C. (1998). Predicting marital happiness and stability from newlywed interactions. *Journal of Marriage and the Family, 60,* 5–22.

Gottman, J., Swanson, C., & Murray, J. (1999). The mathematics of marital conflict: Dynamic mathematical nonlinear modeling of newlywed marital interaction. *Journal of Family Psychology, 13,* 3-19.

Gould, E., Reeves, A. J., Graziano, M. S. A., & Gross, C. G. (1999). Neurogenesis in the neocortex of adult primates. *Science* (October 15), 548–552.

Gouze, K. R., & Nadelman, L. (1980). Constancy of gender identity for self and others in children between the ages of three and seven. *Child Development, 51,* 275–278.

Gow, K. M. (1999). Recovered memories of abuse: Real, fabricated, or both? *Australian Journal of Clinical and Experimental Hypnosis, 27,* 81–97.

Graber, J. A., Brooks-Gunn, J., & Warren, M. (1995). The antecedents of menarcheal age: Heredity, family environment and stressful life events. *Child Development, 66,* 346–359.

Graf, P., & Schacter, D. L. (1985). Implicit and explicit memory for new associations in normal and amnesic subjects. *Journal of Experimental Psychology: Learning, Memory, and Cognition, 11,* 501–518.

Graham, S., Hudley, C., & Williams, E. (1992). Attributional and emotional determinants of aggression among African-American and Latino young adolescents. *Developmental Psychology, 28,* 731–740.

Grant, H. M., Bredahl, L. C., Clay, J., Ferrie, J., Groves, J. E., McDorman, T. A., & Dark, V. J. (1998). Context-dependent memory for meaningful material: Information for students. *Applied Cognitive Psychology, 12,* 617–623.

Green, J. T., & Woodruff-Pak, D. S. (2000). Eyeblink classical conditioning: Hippocampal formation is for neutral stimulus associations as cerebellum is for association-response. *Psychological Bulletin, 126,* 138-158.

Green, M. F. (1997). *Schizophrenia from a neurocognitive perspective: Probing the impenetrable darkness.* Boston: Allyn & Bacon.

Greenberg, J., Solomon, S., & Pyszynski, T. (1997). Terror management theory of self-esteem and cultural worldviews: Empirical assessments and conceptual refinements. In M. P. Zanna (Ed.), *Advances in experimental social psychology* (Vol. 29). San Diego: Academic Press.

Greenberg, L. S., & Rice, L. N. (1997). Humanistic approaches to psychotherapy. In P. L. Wachtel & S. B. Messer (Eds.), *Theories of psychotherapy: Origins and evolution.* Washington, DC: American Psychological Association.

Greene, R. L. (1992). *Human memory: Paradigms and paradoxes.* Hillsdale, NJ: Erlbaum.

Greene, R. W., & Ollendick, T. H. (2000). Behavioral assessment of children. In G. Goldstein & M. Hersen (Eds.), *Handbook of psychological assessment* (3rd ed.). New York: Elsevier.

Greenfield, P. M. (1997). Culture as process: Empirical methods for cultural psychology. In J. W. Berry, Y. H. Poortinga, & J. Pandey (Eds.), *Cross-cultural psychology: Theory and method* (2nd ed., Vol. 1). Boston: Allyn & Bacon.

Greenleaf, E. (1973). "Senoi" dream groups. *Psychotherapy:Theory, Research and Practice, 10,* 218–222.

Greeno, C. G., & Wing, R. R. (1994). Stress-induced eating. *Psychological Bulletin, 115,* 444-464.

Greenwald, A. G. (1992). New look 3: Unconscious cognition reclaimed. *American Psychologist, 47,* 766–779.

Greenwald, A. G., McGhee, D. E., & Schwartz, J. (1998). Measuring individual differences in implicit cognition: The implicit association test. *Journal of Personality and Social Psychology, 74,* 1464–1480.

Greenwald, A. G., Spangenberg, E. R., Pratkanis, A. R., & Eskenazi, J. (1991). Double-blind tests of subliminal self-help tapes. *Psychological Science, 2,* 119–122.

Greer, H. S., Morris, T., & Pettingale, K. W. (1979). Psychological response to breast cancer: Effect on outcome. *Lancet, 2,* 785–787.

Gregory, R. J. (1998). *Foundations of intellectual assessment: The WAIS-III and other tests in clinical practice.* Boston: Allyn & Bacon.

Gregory, R. L. (1966). *Eye and brain.* New York: McGraw-Hill.

Griffiths, M. (1997). Video games and aggression. *Psychologist, 10,* 397–401.

Grimes, K., & Walker, E. F. (1994). Childhood emotional expressions, educational attainment, and age at onset of illness in schizophrenia. *Journal of Abnormal Psychology, 103,* 784–790.

Grissom, R. J. (1996). The magical number 7 plus or minus 2: Meta-meta-analysis of the probability of superior outcome in comparisons involving therapy, placebo, and control. *Journal of Consulting and Clinical Psychology, 64,* 973–982.

Gross, J. J. (1999). Emotion and emotion regulation. In L. A. Pervin & O. P. John (Eds.), *Handbook of personality: Theory and research* (2nd ed.). New York: Guilford Press.

Grossman, D. (1995). *On killing: The psychological cost of learning to kill in war and society.* Boston: Little, Brown.

Grossman, R. P., & Till, B. D. (1998). The persistence of classically conditioned brand attitudes. *Journal of Advertising, 27,* 23–31.

Groth-Marnat, G. (1999). *Handbook of psychological assessment.* New York: Wiley.

Gruber, A. J., Pope, H. G., & Oliva, P. (1997). Very long-term users of marijuana in the United States: A pilot study. *Substance Use and Misuse, 32,* 249–264.

Guilford, J. P. (1959). Three faces of intellect. *American Psychologist, 14,* 469–479.

Guilford, J. P. (1967). *The nature of human intelligence.* New York: McGraw-Hill.

Guilleminault, C. (1987). Obstructive sleep apnea syndrome: A review. *Psychiatric Clinics of North America, 10,* 607–621.

Guinness book of records (2000). Stamford, CT: Guinness Media.

Gulevich, G., Dement, W., & Johnson, L. (1966). Psychiatric and EEG observations on a case of prolonged (264 hours) wakefulness. *Archives of General Psychiatry, 15,* 29–35.

Gump, L. S., Baker, R. C., & Roll, S. (2000). Cultural and gender differences in moral judgment: A study of Mexican Americans and Anglo-Americans. *Hispanic Journal of Behavioral Sciences, 22,* 78–93.

Gur, R. E., Cowell, P., Turetsky, B. I., Gallacher, F., Cannon, T., Bilker, W., & Gur, R. B. (1998). A follow-up magnetic resonance imaging study of schizophrenia: Relationship of neuroanatomical changes to clinical and neurobehavioral measures. *Archives of General Psychiatry, 55,* 145–152.

Gustafson, S. B., & Magnusson, D. (1991). *Female life careers: A pattern approach.* Hillsdale, NJ: Erlbaum.

Gustavson, C. R., Garcia, J., Hankins, W. G., & Rusiniak, K. W. (1974). Coyote predation control by aversive conditioning. *Science, 184,* 581–583.

Gustavson, C. R., & Gustavson, J. C. (1985). Predation control using conditioned food aversion methodology: Theory, practice, and implications. *Annals of the New York Academy of Sciences, 443,* 348–356.

Guthrie, J. P., Ash, R. A., & Bendapudi, V. (1995). Additional validity evidence for a measure of morningness: *Journal of Applied Psychology, 80,* 186-190.

Guze, S. B. (1993). Genetics of Briquet's syndrome and somatization disorder: A review of family, adoption, and twin studies. *Annals of Clinical Psychiatry, 5,* 225–230.

Haaga, D. A. F., Dyck, M. J., & Ernst, D. (1991). Empirical status of cognitive theory of depression. *Psychological Bulletin, 110,* 215–236.

Haas, H., Fink, H., & Hartfelder, G. (1959). Das placeboproblem (translation). *Psychopharmacology Service Center Bulletin, 2,* 1–65. (U.S. Public Health Service.)

Hackman, J. R., & Lawler, E. E. (1971). Employee reactions to job characteristics. *Journal of Applied Psychology, 55,* 259–286.

Hafen, B. Q., & Hoeger, W. W. K. (1998). *Wellness: Guidelines for a healthy lifestyle.* Englewood, CO: Morton.

Haier, R. J., Siegel, B. V., Crinella, F. M., & Buchsbaum, M. S. (1993). Biological and psychometric intelligence: Testing an animal model in humans with positron emission tomography. In D. K. Detterman (Ed.), *Individual differences and cognition. Current topics in human intelligence* (Vol. 3). Norwood, NJ: Ablex.

Hailey, B. J., & White, J. G. (1983). Systematic desensitization for anticipatory nausea associated with chemotherapy. *Psychosomatics, 24,* 287–291.

Hailman, J. P. (1967). The ontogeny of an instinct. *Behaviour Supplements, 15,* 1–159.

Halaas, J. L., Gajiwala, K. S., Maffei, M., & Cohen, S. L., Chait, B. T., & Rabinowitz, D. (1995). Weight-reducing effects of the plasma protein encoded by the obese gene. *Science, 269,* 543–546.

Hall, C. S. (1984). "A ubiquitous sex difference in dreams" revisited. *Journal of Personality and Social Psychology, 46,* 1109–1117.

Hall, C. S., & Van de Castle, R. (1966). *The content analysis of dreams.* New York: Appleton-Century-Crofts.

Hall, D. R., & Zhao, J. Z. (1995). Cohabitation and divorce in Canada: Testing the selectivity hypothesis. *Journal of Marriage and the Family, 57,* 421–427.

Hall, G. S. (1904). *Adolescence* (Vols. 1 & 2). New York: Appleton-Century-Crofts.

Halpern, C. T., Udry, J. R., Campbell, B., & Suchindran, C. (1999). Effects of body fat on weight concerns, dating, and sexual activity: A longitudinal analysis of Black and White adolescent girls. *Developmental Psychology, 35,* 721–736.

Halpern, D. F. (2000). *Sex differences in cognitive abilities* (3rd ed.). Mahwah, NJ: Erlbaum.

Hamer, D. H., & Copeland, P. (1998). *Living with our genes: Why they matter more than you think.* New York: Doubleday.

Hamilton, R. J. (1985). A framework for the evaluation of the effectiveness of adjunct questions and objectives. *Review of Educational Research, 55,* 47–85.

Hamilton, W. D. (1964). The genetical theory of social behaviour, I, II. *Journal of Theoretical Biology, 12,* 12–45.

Hammen, C. (1991). *Depression runs in families: The social context of risk and resilience in children of depressed mothers.* New York: Springer-Verlag.

Hampson, E., & Kimura, D. (1992). Sex differences and hormonal influences on cognitive function in humans. In J. B. Becker, S. M. Breedlove, & D. Crews (Eds.), *Behavioral endocrinology.* Cambridge, MA: MIT Press.

Haney, C., & Zimbardo, P. (1998). The past and future of U.S. prison policy: Twenty-five years after the Stanford Prison Experiment. *American Psychologist, 53,* 709–727.

Hankin, B. L., Abramson, L. Y., et al. (1998). Development of depression from preadolescence to young adulthood: Emerging gender differences in a 10-year longitudinal study. *Journal of Abnormal Psychology, 107,* 128–140.

Hansen, C. H., & Hansen, R. D. (1988). Finding the face in the crowd: An anger superiority effect. *Journal of Personality and Social Psychology, 54,* 917–924.

Happé, F. G. E., Winner, E., & Brownell, H. (1998). The getting of wisdom: Theory of mind in old age. *Developmental Psychology, 34,* 358–362.

Hardy, C., & Latané, B. (1986). Social loafing on a cheering task. *Social Science, 71,* 165–172.

Hardy, M. A., & Quadagno, J. (1995). Satisfaction with early retirement: Making choices in the auto industry. *Journals of Gerontology: Psychological Sciences and Social Sciences, 50B,* S217–S228.

Hare, R. D. (1978). Psychopathy and electrodermal responses to nonsignal stimulation. *Biological Psychology, 6,* 237–246.

Harley, K., & Reese, E. (1999). Origins of autobiographical memory. *Developmental Psychology, 35,* 1338–1348.

Harlow, H. F. (1958). The nature of love. *The American Psychologist, 13,* 673–685.

Harlow, H. F., & Suomi, S. J. (1970). The nature of love-simplified. *American Psychologist, 25,* 161–168.

Harlow, J., & Roll, S. (1992). Frequency of day residue in dreams of young adults. *Perceptual and Motor Skills, 74,* 832–834.

Harlow, J. M. (1868). Recovery from the passage of an iron bar through the head. *Massachusetts Medical Society, 2,* 327.

Harman, R. L. (Ed.) (1990). *Gestalt therapy: Discussions with the masters.* Springfield, IL: Charles C Thomas.

Harmon-Jones, E., Brehm, J. W., Greenberg, J., Simon, L., & Nelson, D. E. (1996). Evidence that the production of aversive consequences is not necessary to create cognitive dissonance. *Journal of Personality and Social Psychology, 70,* 5–16.

Harre, R., & Parrot, W. G. (1996). *Emotion: Social, cultural and physical dimensions.* Thousand Oaks, CA: Sage Publications.

Harrington, D. M., Block, J. H., & Black, J. (1987). Testing aspects of Carl Rogers's theory of creative environments: Child-rearing antecedents of creative potential in young adolescents. *Journal of Personality and Social Psychology, 52,* 851–856.

Harris, R. J. (1977). Comprehension of pragmatic implications in advertising. *Journal of Applied Psychology, 62*, 603–608.

Harris, S. L. (1981). A letter from the editor on loss and trust. *The Clinical Psychologist, 34*(3), 3.

Harrison, J. E., & Baron, S. C. (1997). Synaesthesia: A review of psychological theories. In S. C. Baron, J. E. Harrison et al. (Eds.), *Synaesthesia: Classic and contemporary readings*. Oxford, England: Blackwell.

Hart, C. H., Nelson, D. A., Robinson, C. C., Olsen, S. F., & McNeilly, C. M. K. (1998). Overt and relational aggression in Russian nursery-school-age children: Parenting style and marital linkages. *Developmental Psychology, 34*, 687–697.

Hartigan, J. A., & Wigdor, A. K. (Eds.). (1989). *Fairness in employment testing*. Washington, DC: National Academy Press.

Hartshorne, H., & May, A. (1928). *Studies in the nature of character, Vol. 1: Studies in deceit*. New York: Macmillan.

Harvey, J. H., & Omarzu, J. (1997). Minding the close relationship. *Personality and Social Psychology Review, 1*, 224–240.

Hasher, L., & Zacks, R. T. (1979). Automatic and effortful processes in memory. *Journal of Experimental Psychology: General, 108*, 356–388.

Hasher, L., & Zacks, R. T. (1984). Automatic processing of fundamental information: The case of frequency of occurrence. *American Psychologist, 39*, 1372–1388.

Hastorf, A., & Cantril, H. (1954). They saw a game: A case study. *Journal of Abnormal and Social Psychology, 49*, 129–134.

Hatfield, E. (1988). Passionate and companionate love. In R. J. Sternberg & M. L. Barnes (Eds.), *The psychology of love*. New Haven, CT: Yale University Press.

Hatfield, E., & Rapson, R. L. (1987). Passionate love/sexual desire: Can the same paradigm explain both? Archives of Sexual Behavior, 16, 259-278.

Hathaway, S. R., & McKinley, J. C. (1983). *The Minnesota Multiphasic Personality Inventory manual*. New York: Psychological Corporation.

Haugtvedt, C. P., Petty, R. E., & Cacioppo, J. T. (1992). Need for cognition and advertising: Understanding the role of personality variables in consumer behavior. *Journal of Consumer Psychology, 1*, 239–260.

Hauri, P. (1982). *The sleep disorders* (2nd ed.). Kalamazoo, MI: Upjohn Corp.

Hauri, P. J. (1997). Can we mix behavioral therapy with hypnotics when treating insomniacs? *Sleep, 20*, 1111-1118.

Hawkins, K. A., & Trobst, K. K. (2000). Frontal lobe dysfunction and aggression: Conceptual issues and research findings. *Aggression and Violent Behavior, 5*, 147–157.

Haynes, S. G., Feinleib, M., and Kannel, W. B. (1980).The relationship of psycho-social factors in coronary heart disease in the Framingham study: Study III: Eight-year incidence of coronary heart disease. *American Journal of Epidemiology, 111*, 37–58.

Haynes, S. N. (1990). Behavioral assessment of adults. In G. Goldstein & M. Hersen (Eds.), *Handbook of psychological assessment*. Elmsford, NY: Pergamon.

Haynes, S. N. (2000). Behavioral assessment of adults. In G. Goldstein & M. Hersen (Eds.), *Handbook of psychological assessment* (3rd ed.). New York: Elsevier.

Haynes, S. N., Price, M. G., & Simons, J. P. (1975). Stimulus control treatment of insomnia. *Journal of Behavior Therapy and Experimental Psychiatry, 6*, 279–282.

Hayslip, B., & Panek, P. E. (1989). *Adult development and aging*. New York: Harper & Row.

Hazen, N. L., & Durrett, M. E. (1982). Relationship of security of attachment to exploration and cognitive mapping abilities in 2-year-olds. *Developmental Psychology, 18*, 751–759.

He, X. X., Nebert, D. W., Vasiliou, V., Zhu, H., & Shertzer, H. G. (1997). Genetic differences in alcohol drinking preference between inbred strains of mice. *Pharmacogenetics, 7*, 223–233.

Hearold, S. (1986). A synthesis of 1043 effects of television on social behavior. In G. Comstock (Ed.), *Public communications and behavior* (Vol. 1). New York: Academic Press.

Heath, A. C., Bucholz, K. K., Madden, P. A. F., Dinwiddie, S. H., Slutske, W. S., & Bierut, L. J. (1997). Genetic and environmental contributions to alcohol dependence risk in a national twin sample: Consistency of findings in women and men. *Psychological Medicine, 27*, 1381–1396.

Heath, A. C., Kendler, K. S., Eaves, L. J., & Martin, N. G. (1990). Evidence for genetic influences on sleep disturbance and sleep pattern in twins. *Sleep, 13*, 318–335.

Heath, R. G. (1972). Pleasure and brain activity in man. *Journal of Nervous and Mental Disease, 154*, 3–18.

Heatherton, T. F., Herman, C. P., & Polivy, J. (1991). Effects of physical threat and ego threat on eating behavior. *Journal of Personality and Social Psychology, 60*, 138–143.

Hebb, D. O. (1949). *The organization of behavior*. New York: Wiley.

Heckers, S., & Konradi, C. (2000). Anatomic and molecular principles of psychopharmacology: A primer for psychiatrists. *Child and Adolescent Psychiatric Clinics of North America, 9*, 1–22.

Heckhausen, H. (1991). *Motivation and action* (2nd ed.). New York: Springer-Verlag.

Heider, F. (1958). *The psychology of interpersonal relations*. New York: Wiley.

Heiman, J. R. (1977). A psychophysiological exploration of sexual arousal patterns in females and males. *Psychophysiology, 14*, 266–274.

Heller, M. A., & Schiff, W. (Eds.) (1991). *The psychology of touch*. Hillsdale, NJ: Erlbaum.

Hellerstein, D., Yankowitch, P., Rosenthal, J., et al. (1993). A randomized double-blind study of fluoxetine versus placebo in the treatment of dysthymia. *American Journal of Psychiatry, 150*, 1169–1175.

Hellriegel, D., Slocum, J. W., Jr., & Woodman, R. W. (1989). *Organizational behavior* (5th ed.). St. Paul, MN: West.

Helmreich, R. L. (1997, May). Managing human error in aviation. *Scientific American*, 62–67.

Helmreich, R. L., Merritt, A. C., & Wilhelm, J. A. (1999). The evolution of crew resource management training in commercial aviation. *International Journal of Aviation Psychology, 9*, 19–32.

Hendrick, C. (Ed.) (1989). *Close relationships*. Newbury Park, CA: Sage Publications.

Hendy, H. M., & Raudenbush, B. (2000). Effectiveness of teacher modeling to encourage food acceptance in preschool children. *Appetite, 34*, 61–76.

Herdt, G., & Lindenbaum, S. (Eds.) (1992). *Social analysis in the time of AIDS*. Newbury Park, CA: Sage Publications.

Herek, G. M. (2000). The psychology of sexual prejudice. *Current Directions in Psychological Science, 9*, 19–22.

Herman, D. B., Susser, E. S., Jandorf, L., Lavelle, J., & Bromet, E. J. (1998). Homelessness among individuals with psychotic disorders hospitalized for the first time: Findings from the Suffolk County Mental Health Project. *American Journal of Psychiatry, 155*, 109–113.

Herrington, R., & Lader, M. H. (1996). *Biological treatments in psychiatry* (2nd ed.). New York: Oxford University Press.

Herskovits, M. J. (1948). *Man and his works*. New York: Knopf.

Herz, R. S., & Cupchik, C. G. (1995). The emotional distinctiveness of odor-evoked memories. *Chemical Senses, 20*, 517–528.

Hess, E. H. (1959). Imprinting. *Science, 130*, 133–141.

Hess, W. R. (1965). Sleep as phenomenon of the integral organism. In: K. Akert, C. Bally, & J. P. Schade (Eds), *Sleep mechanisms*. New York: Elsevier.

Hetherington, A. W., & Ranson, S. W. (1942). The spontaneous activity and food intake of rats with hypothalamic lesions. *American Journal of Physiology, 136*, 609–617.

Hetherington, E. M. (1989). Coping with family transitions: Winners, losers, and survivors. *Child Development, 60*, 1–14.

Hetherington, E. M. (1998). Relevant issues in developmental science: Introduction to the special issue. *American Psychologist, 53*, 93–94.

Hetherington, E. M., Bridges, M., & Insabella, G. M. (1998). What matters? What does not? Five perspectives on the association between marital transitions and children's adjustment. *American Psychologist, 53*, 167–184.

Hetherington, E. M., Parke, R. D., & Locke, V. O. (1999). *Child psychology: A contemporary viewpoint* (5th ed.). Boston: McGraw-Hill.

Heylighen, F. (1992). A cognitive-systemic reconstruction of Maslow's theory of self-actualization. *Behavioral Science, 37*, 39–58.

Higgins, A. (1991). The Just Community approach to moral education: Evolution of the idea and recent findings. In W. M. Kurtines & J. L. Gewirtz (Eds.), *Handbook of moral behavior and development*, (Vol. 3). Hillsdale, NJ: Erlbaum.

Higgins, E. T. (1996). The "self digest": Self-knowledge serving self-regulatory functions. *Journal of Personality and Social Psychology, 71*, 1062–1083.

Hilgard, E. R. (1977). *Divided consciousness: Multiple controls in human thought and action*. New York: Wiley.

Hilgard, E. R. (1991). A neodissociation interpretation of hypnosis. In S. J. Lynn & J. W. Rhue (Eds.), *Theories of hypnosis: Current models and perspectives*. New York: Guilford Press.

Hill, C. A. (1987). Affiliation motivation: People who need people but in different ways. *Journal of Personality and Social Psychology, 52*, 1008–1018.

Hill, J. O., & Peters, J. C. (1998). Environmental contributions to the obesity epidemic. *Science, 280,* 1371–1374.

Hill, M. M., Dodson, B. B., Hill, E. W., & Fox, J. (1995). An infant sonicguide intervention program for a child with a visual disability. *Journal of Visual Impairment and Blindness, 89,* 329–336.

Hill, S. Y., Locke, J., Zezza, N., Kaplan, B., Neiswanger, K., & Steinhauer, S. R. (1998). Genetic association between reduced P300 amplitude and the DRD2 dopamine receptor A1 allele in children at high risk for alcoholism. *Biological Psychiatry, 43,* 40–51.

Hillman, D. C., Siffre, M., Milano, G., & Halberg, F. (1994). Free-running psycho-physiologic circadians and three-month pattern in a woman isolated in a cave. *New Trends in Experimental and Clinical Psychiatry, 10,* 127–133.

Hirshkowitz, M. (2000). Nightmares. In G. Fink (Ed.), *Encyclopedia of stress.* San Diego: Academic Press.

Hirshman, E., & Jackson, E. (1997). Distinctive perceptual processing and memory. *Journal of Memory and Language, 36,* 2–12.

Hirst, R. A., Lambert D. G., & Notcutt, W. G. (1998). Pharmacology and potential therapeutic uses of cannabis. *British Journal of Anaesthesia, 81,* 77–84.

Hixon, M. D. (1998). Ape language research: A review and behavioral perspective. *Analysis of Verbal Behavior, 15,* 17–39.

Hobson, A. (1988). Psychoanalytic dream theory: A critique based upon modern neurophysiology. In P. Clark & C. Wright (Eds.), *Mind, psychoanalysis and science.* Oxford, England: Basil Blackwell.

Hobson, J. A. (1996). *Chemistry of conscious states: How the brain changes its mind.* Boston: Little, Brown.

Hobson, J. A., & McCarley, R. W. (1977). The brain as a dream state generator: An activation-synthesis hypothesis of the dream process. *American Journal of Psychiatry, 134,* 1335–1348.

Hobson, J. A., Stickgold, R., Pace, S., & Edward, F. (1998). The neuropsychology of REM sleep dreaming. *Neuroreport: An International Journal for the Rapid Communication of Research in Neuroscience, 9,* R1–R14.

Hodges, J., & Tizard, B. (1989). Social and family relationships of ex-institutional adolescents. *Journal of Child Psychology and Psychiatry, 30,* 77–97.

Hoeksema, V. O., Claudia, Y. D., Gaillard, A. W. K., & Buunk, B. P. (1998). Social loafing under fatigue. *Journal of Personality and Social Psychology, 75,* 1179–1190.

Hoffart, A., & Martinson, E. W. (1991). Mental health locus of control in agoraphobia and depression: A longitudinal study of inpatients. *Psychological Reports, 68,* 1011–1018.

Hofmann, A. (1980). *LSD, my problem child.* New York: McGraw-Hill.

Hogue, M. E., Beaugrand, J. P., & Lauguee, P. C. (1996). Coherent use of information by hens observing their former dominant defeating or being defeated by a stranger. *Behavioural Processes, 38,* 241–252.

Holahan, C. J., & Moos, R. H. (1986). Personality, coping, and family resources in stress resistance: A longitudinal analysis. *Journal of Personality and Social Psychology 51,* 389–395.

Holahan, C. J., & Moos, R. H. (1990). Life stressors, resistance factors, and improved psychological functioning: An extension of the stress resistance paradigm. *Journal of Personality and Social Psychology, 58,* 909–917.

Holahan, C. J., Moos, R. H., Holahan, C. K., & Cronkite, R. C. (2000). Long-term posttreatment functioning among patients with unipolar depression: An integrative model. *Journal of Consulting and Clinical Psychology, 68,* 226–232.

Holland, J. L. (1985). *Making vocational choices: A theory of vocational personalities and work environments* (2nd ed.). Englewood Cliffs, NJ: Prentice Hall.

Hollis, K. L. (1997). Contemporary research on Pavlovian conditioning: A "new" functional analysis. *American Psychologist, 52,* 956–965.

Hollon, S. D. (1996). The efficacy and effectiveness of psychotherapy relative to medications. *American Psychologist, 51,* 1025–1030.

Hollon, S. D., & Beck, A. T. (1994). Cognitive and cognitive-behavioral therapies. In A. E. Bergin & S. L. Garfield (Eds.), *Handbook of psychotherapy and behavior change.* New York: Wiley.

Hollon, S. D., Shelton, R. C., & Loosen, P. T. (1991). Cognitive therapy and pharmacotherapy for depression. *Journal of Consulting and Clinical Psychology, 59,* 88–99.

Holloway, M. (1991). Rx for addiction. *Scientific American, 264,* 95–103.

Holmes, D. S. (1990). The evidence for repression: An examination of sixty years of research. In J. L. Singer (Ed.), *Repression and dissociation.* Chicago: University of Chicago Press.

Holmes, M. R., & St.-Lawrence, J. S. (1983). Treatment of rape-induced trauma: Proposed behavioral conceptualization and review of the literature. *Clinical Psychology Review; 3,* 417–433.

Holmes, T. H., & Rahe, R. H. (1987). The Social Readjustment Rating Scale. *Journal of Psychosomatic Research, 11,* 213–218.

Honeycutt, J. M. (1995). Predicting relational trajectory beliefs as a consequence of typicality and necessity ratings of relationship behaviors. *Communication Research Reports, 12,* 3–14.

Honts, C. R. (1991). The emperor's new clothes: Application of polygraph tests in the American workplace. *Forensic Reports, 4,* 91–116.

Honts, C. R., Devitt, M. K., Winbush, M., & Kircher, J. C. (1996). Mental and physical countermeasures reduce the accuracy of the concealed knowledge test. *Psychophysiology, 33,* 84–92.

Honts, C. R., & Perry, M. V. (1992). Polygraph admissibility: Changes and challenges. *Law and Human Behavior, 16,* 357–379.

Hooper, J., & Teresi, M. (1986). *The three-pound universe.* New York: Macmillan.

Hopkins, W. D., & Leavens, D. A. (1998). Hand use and gestural communication in chimpanzees (Pan troglodytes). *Journal of Comparative Psychology, 112,* 95–99.

Horn, J. L., & Cattell, R. C. (1966). Refinement and test of the theory of fluid and crystallized general intelligences. *Journal of Educational Psychology, 57,* 253–270.

Horne, J. A. (1977). Factors relating to energy conservation during sleep in mammals. *Physiological Psychology, 5,* 403–408.

Horne, J. A. (1992). Sleep and its disorders in children. *Journal of Child Psychology and Psychiatry and Allied Disciplines, 33,* 473–487.

Horne, S. (1999). Domestic violence in Russia. *American Psychologist, 54,* 55–61.

Houpt, T. A., Boulos, Z., Moore, E., & Martin, C. (1996). MidnightSun: Software for determining light exposure and phase-shifting schedules during global travel. *Physiology and Behavior, 59,* 561–568.

House, J. S., Landis, K. R., & Umberson, D. (1988). Social relationships and health. *Science, 241,* 540–545.

Houston, J. P. (1992). *Fundamentals of learning and memory.* Ft. Worth: Harcourt Brace Jovanovich.

Hovland, C. I., Janis, I., and Kelley, H. H. (1953). *Communication and persuasion.* New Haven, CT: Yale University Press.

Hovland, C. I., & Sears, R. (1940). Minor studies of aggression: Correlation of lynchings with economic indices. *Journal of Psychology, 9,* 301–310.

Howard, I. P., & Rogers, B. J. (1995). *Binocular vision and stereopsis.* New York: Oxford University Press.

Howard, K. I., Kopta, S. M., Krause, M. S., & Orlinsky, D. E. (1986). The dose-effect relationship in psychotherapy. *American Psychologist, 41,* 159–164.

Howard, K. I., Lueger, R. J., Maling, M. S., & Martinovich, Z. (1993). A phase model of psychotherapy outcome: Causal mediation of change. *Journal of Consulting and Clinical Psychology, 61,* 678–685.

Howard, M. O., Walker, R. D., Walker, P. S., Cottler, L. B., & Compton, W. M. (1999). Inhalant use among urban American Indian youth. *Addiction, 94,* 83-95.

Howe, Mark L., & Courage, M. L. (1993). On resolving the enigma of infantile amnesia. *Psychological Bulletin, 113,* 305–326.

Hryshko-Mullen, A. S., Broeckl, L. S., Haddock, C. K., & Peterson, A. L. (2000). Behavioral treatment of insomnia: The Wilford Hall Insomnia Program. *Military Medicine, 165,* 200–207.

Hubbard, K., O'Neill, A. M., & Cheakalos, C. (1999, April 12). Out of control. *People,* 52–72.

Hublin, C., Kaprio, J., Partinen, M., Heikkila, K., Koskenvuo, M. (1997). Prevalence and genetics of sleepwalking: A population-based twin study. *Neurology, 48,* 177–181.

Huddy, L., & Birtanen, S. (1995). Subgroup differentiation and subgroup bias among Latinos as a function of familiarity and positive distinctiveness. *Journal of Personality and Social Psychology, 68,* 97–108.

Huesmann, L. R. (1997). Observational learning of violent behavior: Social and biosocial processes. In A. Raine, P. A. Brennan, D. P. Farrington, & S. A. Mednick (Eds.), *Biosocial bases of violence.* New York: Plenum.

Huff, R. M., Kline, M. V. (Eds.) (1999). *Promoting health in multicultural populations: A handbook for practitioners.* Thousand Oaks, CA: Sage Publications.

Hughes, C., Lorden, S. W., Scott, S. V., Hwang, B., Derer, K. R., & Rodi, M. S., (1998). *Journal of Applied Behavior Analysis, 31,* 431-446.

Hui, C. H., Yee, C., & Eastman, K. L. (1995). The relationship between individualism-collectivism and job satisfaction. *Applied Psychology: An International Review, 44,* 276–282.

Hull, C. L. (1933). *Hypnosis and suggestibility: An experimental approach.* New York: Appleton-Century.

Hull, C. L. (1943). *Principles of behavior, an introduction to behavior theory.* New York: Appleton-Century.

Hull, C. L. (1951). *Essentials of behavior.* New Haven, CT: Yale University Press.

Humphriss, N. (1989, November 20). Letters. *Time,* p. 12.

Hunt, E. (1993). A proposal for computer modeling of animal linguistic comprehension. In H. L. Roitblat, L. M. Herman, et al. (Eds.), *Language and communication: Comparative perspectives. Comparative cognition and neuroscience.* Hillsdale, NJ: Erlbaum.

Hunt, E. (1997). The status of the concept of intelligence. *Japanese Psychological Research, 39,* 1–11.

Hunt, E., & Agnoli, F. (1991). The Whorfian hypothesis: A cognitive psychology perspective. *Psychological Review, 98,* 377–389.

Hunt, E., Streissguth, A. P., Kerr, B., & Olson, H. C. (1995). Mothers' alcohol consumption during pregnancy: Effects on spatial-visual reasoning in 14-year-old children. *Psychological Science, 6,* 339–342.

Hunt, R. R., & Ellis, H. C. (1999). *Fundamentals of cognitive psychology* (6th ed.). New York: McGraw-Hill.

Hunter, F. T., & Youniss, J. (1982). Changes in functions of three relations during adolescence. *Developmental Psychology, 18,* 806–811.

Hunter, J. E., & Hunter, R. F. (1984). Validity and utility of alternative predictors of job performance. *Psychological Bulletin, 96,* 72–98.

Hunter, J. E., & Schmidt, F. L. (1982). Fitting people to jobs: The impact of personnel selection on national productivity. In M. D. Dunnette & E. A. Fleishman (Eds.), *Human performance and productivity: Vol. 1. Human capability assessment.* Hillsdale, NJ: Erlbaum.

Hurst, L. C., & Mulhall, D. J. (1988). Another calendar Savant. *British Journal of Psychiatry, 152,* 274–277.

Huston, T. L. (1973). Ambiguity of acceptance, social desirability, and dating choice. *Journal of Experimental Social Psychology, 9,* 32–42.

Huttenlocher, P. R. (1979). Synaptic density in human frontal cortex: Developmental changes and effects of aging. *Brain Research, 163,* 195–205.

Huxley, A. (1950). *Science, liberty, and peace.* London: Chato and Winders.

Hyde, J. S., & DeLamater, J. (2000). *Understanding human sexuality* (7th ed.). Boston: McGraw-Hill.

Hyde, J. S., & Oliver, M. B. (2000). Gender differences in sexuality: Results from meta-analysis. In C. B. Travis & J. W. White (Eds.), *Sexuality, society, and feminism.* Washington, DC: American Psychological Association.

Hyman, R. (1994). Anomaly or artifact? Comments on Bem and Honorton. *Psychological Bulletin, 115,* 19–24.

Iaffaldano, M. T., & Muchinsky, P. M. (1985). Job satisfaction and job performance: A meta-analysis. *Psychological Bulletin, 97,* 251–273.

Ichimaru, Y., & Miyamoto, M. (1998). Cardiovascular diseases. *Nippon-Rinsho, 56,* 461–468.

Iidaka, T., Anderson, N. D., Kapur, S., Cabeza, R., & Craik, F. I. M. (2000). The effect of divided attention on encoding and retrieval in episodic memory revealed by positron emission tomography. *Journal of Cognitive Neuroscience, 12,* 267–280.

Ikemi, Y., & Nakagawa, A. (1962). A psychosomatic study of contagious dermatitis. *Kyushu Journal of Medical Science, 13,* 335–350.

Ingelhart, R., & Rabier, J. R. (1986). Aspirations adapt to situations—but why are the Belgians so much happier than the French? A cross-cultural study of the quality of life. In F. M. Andrews (Ed.), *Research on the quality of life.* Ann Arbor, MI: Institute for Social Research, University of Michigan.

Ingham, A. G., Levinger, G., Graves, J., & Peckham, V. (1974). The Ringelmann effect: Studies of group size and group performance. *Journal of Experimental Social Psychology, 10,* 371–384.

Ingold, C. H. (1989). Locus of control and use of public information. *Psychological Reports, 64,* 603–607.

Inhelder, B., & Piaget, J. (1958). *The growth of logical thinking from childhood to adolescence.* New York: Basic Books.

Intraub, H., Gottesman, C. V., & Bills, A. J. (1998). Effects of perceiving and imagining scenes on memory for pictures. *Journal of Experimental Psychology: Learning, Memory, and Cognition, 24,* 186–201.

Intraub, H., Gottesman, C. V., Willey, E. V., & Zuk, I. J. (1996). Boundary extension for briefly glimpsed photographs: Do common perceptual processes result in unexpected memory distortions? *Journal of Memory and Language, 35,* 118–134.

Ip, M. S. M., Tsang, W. T., Lam, W. K., & Lam, B. (1998). Obstructive sleep apnea syndrome: An experience in Chinese adults in Hong Kong. *Chinese Medical Journal, 111,* 257–260.

Irwin, A. R., & Gross, A. M. (1995). Cognitive tempo, violent video games, and aggressive behavior in young boys. *Journal of Family Violence, 10,* 337–350.

Irwin, J. R., & McCarthy, D. (1998). Psychophysics: Methods and analyses of signal detection. In K. A. Lattal & M. Perone (Eds.), *Handbook of research methods in human operant behavior: Applied clinical psychology.* New York: Plenum.

Irwin, M., Daniels, M., & Weiner, H. (1987). Immune and neuroendocrine changes during bereavement. *Psychiatric Clinics of North America, 10,* 449–465.

Irwin, W., Davidson, R. J., Lowe, M. J., Mock, B. J., Sorenson, J. A. & Turski, P. A. (1996). Human amygdala activation detected with echo-planar functional magnetic resonance imaging. *Neuroreport: An International Journal for the Rapid Communication of Research in Neuroscience, 7,* 1765–1769.

Isaacs, K. S. (1998). *Uses of emotion: Nature's vital gift.* New York: Praeger.

Ishihara, K., Miyake, S., Miyasita, A., & Miyata, Y. (1992). Morningness-eveningness preference and sleep habits in Japanese office workers of different ages. *Chronobiologia, 19,* 9–16.

Ito, T., Suzuki, T., Wellman, S. E., & Ho, I. K. (1996). Pharmacology of barbiturate tolerance/dependence: GABA-sub(A) receptors and molecular aspects. *Life Sciences, 59,* 169–195.

Itard, J. M. G. (1962). *The wild boy of Aveyron* (G. Humphrey & M. Humphrey, Trans.). New York: Appleton-Century-Crofts. (Original work published 1894)

Izard, C. E. (1989). The structure and functions of emotions: Implications for cognition, motivation, and personality. In I. S. Cohen (Ed.), *The G. Stanley Hall lecture series* (Vol. 9). Washington, DC: American Psychological Association.

Izard, C. E., & Malatesta, C. Z. (1987). Perspectives on emotional development: I. Differential emotions theory of early emotional development. In J. D. Osofsky (Ed.), *Handbook of infant development* (2nd ed.). New York: Wiley Interscience.

Jablensky, A., Sartorius, N., Enberg, C., Anker, M., Korten, A., et al. (1992). Schizophrenia: Manifestation, incidence, and course in different cultures: A World Health Organization ten country study. *Psychological Medicine Monograph Supplement 20.* Cambridge, England: Cambridge University Press.

Jack, S. J., & Ronan, K. R. (1998). Sensation seeking among high- and low-risk sports participants. *Personality and Individual Differences, 25,* 1063–1083.

Jackendoff, R. (1996). The architecture of the linguistic-spatial interface. In P. Bloom, M. A. Peterson, L. Nadel, & M. F. Garrett, (Eds.), *Language and space. Language, speech, and communication.* Cambridge, MA: MIT Press.

Jacobs, W. J., Thomas, K. G. F., Laurance, H. E., & Hadel, L. (1998). Place learning in virtual space: Topographical relations as one dimension of stimulus control. *Learning and Motivation, 29,* 288–308.

Jacobson, N. S., & Christensen, A. (1996). *Integrative couple therapy: Promoting acceptance and change.* New York: W. W. Norton.

Jacobson, N. S., Christensen, A., Prince, S. E., Cordova, J., & Eldridge, K. (2000). Integrative couple behavior therapy: An acceptance-based, promising new treatment for couple discord. *Journal of Consulting and Clinical Psychology, 68,* 351–355.

Jacobson, N. S., & Gottman, J. M. (1998). *When men batter women: New insights into ending abusive relationships.* New York: Simon & Schuster.

Jacobson, N. S., Gottman, J. M., Gortner, E., Berns, S., & Shortt, J. W. (1996). Psychological factors in the longitudinal course of battering: When do the couples split up? When does the abuse decrease? *Violence & Victims, 11,* 371–392.

Jaggar, S. I., Hasnie, F. S., Sellaturay, S., Rice, A. S. (1998). The anti-hyperalgesic actions of the cannabinoid anandamide and the putative CB2 receptor agonist palmitoylethanolamide in visceral and somatic inflammatory pain. *Pain, 76,* 189–199.

Jahoda, G. (1983). European "lag" in the development of an economic concept: A study in Zimbabwe. *British Journal of Developmental Psychology, 1,* 113–120.

Jahoda, M. (1958). *Current concepts of positive mental health.* New York: Basic Books.

James, W. (1879). Are we automata? *Mind, 4,* 1–22.

James, W. (1902). *The varieties of religious experience: A study in human nature.* New York: Longmans, Green.

James, W. (1950). *Principles of psychology* (Vol. 2). New York: Dover Publications. (Original work published 1890)

Jamison, K. (1995, February). Manic-depressive illness and creativity. *Scientific American,* pp. 63–67.

Jamison, K. R. (1995). *An unquiet mind.* New York: Vantage Books.

Janis, I. L. (1983). *Groupthink: Psychological studies of policy decisions and fiascos* (2nd ed.). Boston: Houghton Mifflin.

Janis, I. L., & Mann, L. (1977). Emergency decision making: A theoretical analysis of responses to disaster warnings. *Journal of Human Stress,* 3(2), 35-48.

Janoski, T., Musick, M., & Wilson, J. (1998). Being volunteered? The impact of social participation and pro-social attitudes on volunteering. *Sociological Forum, 13,* 495–519.

Janssens, Jan M. A. M., & Dekovic, M. (1997). Child rearing, prosocial moral reasoning, and prosocial behaviour. *International Journal of Behavioral Development, 20,* 509–527.

Janssens, R. (1998). Structuring complex concepts. In C. E. Dowling & F. S. Roberts (Eds.), *Recent progress in mathematical psychology: Psychophysics, knowledge, representation, cognition, and measurement.* Mahwah, NJ: Erlbaum.

Janus, S. S., & Janus, C. L. (1993). *The Janus report on sexual behavior.* New York: Wiley.

Jasper, H. H. (1995). A historical perspective: The rise and fall of prefrontal lobotomy. In H. H. Jasper & S. Riggio (Eds.), *Epilepsy and the functional anatomy of the frontal lobe. Advances in neurology* (Vol. 66). New York: Raven Press.

Jeffery, R. W., Epstein, L. H., Wilson, G. T., Drewnowski, A., Stunkard, A. J., & Wing, R. R. (2000). Long-term maintenance of weight loss: Current status. *Health Psychology, 19,* 5–16.

Jeffery, R. W., & Wing, R. R. (1995). Long-term effects of interventions for weight loss using food provisions and money incentives. *Journal of Consulting and Clinical Psychology, 63,* 793–796.

Jemmott, J. B., Jemmott, L. S., & Fong, G. T. (1998). Abstinence and safer sex HIV risk-reduction interventions for African American adolescents. *Journal of the American Medical Association, 279,* 1529–1536.

Jenike, M. A. (1998). *Obsessive-compulsive disorders.* St. Louis: Mosby.

Jennings, B. M. (1990). Stress, locus of control, social support, and psychological symptoms among head nurses. *Research in Nursing and Health, 13,* 393–401.

Jensen, A. R. (1980). *Bias in mental testing.* New York: Free Press.

Jensen, A. R. (1998). The g factor and the design of education. In R. J. Sternberg & W. M. Williams (Eds.), *Intelligence, instruction, and assessment: Theory into practice.* Mahwah, NJ: Erlbaum.

Jensen, J. P., Bergin, A. E., & Greaves, D. W. (1990). The meaning of eclecticism: New survey and analysis of components. *Professional Psychology: Research and Practice, 21,* 124–130.

Jentsch, J. D., Wise, A., Katz, Z., & Roth, R. H. (1998). Alpha-noradrenergic receptor modulation of the phencyclidine- and delta9-tetrahydrocannabinol-induced increases in dopamine utilization in rat prefrontal cortex. *Synapse, 28,* 21–26.

Jepson, C., & Chaiken, S. (1990). Chronic issue-specific fear inhibits systematic processing of persuasive communications. *Journal of Social Behaviors and Personality, 5,* 61–84.

Jequier, E., & Tappy, L. (1999). Regulation of body weight in humans. *Physiological Reviews, 79,* 451–480.

Jernigan, T. L., Zisook, S., Heaton, R. K., Moranville, J. T., Hesselink, J. R., & Braff, D. L. (1991). Magnetic resonance imaging abnormalities in lenticular nuclei and cerebral cortex in schizophrenia. *Archives of General Psychiatry, 48,* 881–890.

Jeste, D., & Heaton, S. (1994). How does late-onset compare with early-onset schizophrenia? *Harvard Mental Health Letter, 49,* 132–139.

John, O. P., & Srivastava, S. (1999). The Big Five trait taxonomy: History, measurement, and theoretical perspectives. In L. A. Pervin & O. P. John (Eds.), *Handbook of personality: Theory and research.* New York: Guilford Press.

Johnson, A. M., Wadsworth, J., Wellings, K., & Bradshaw, S. (1992). Sexual lifestyles and HIV risk. *Nature, 360,* 410–412.

Johnson, B. T. (1991). Insights about attitudes: Meta-analytic perspectives. *Personality and Social Psychology Bulletin, 17,* 289–299.

Johnson, D. W. (2000). Cooperative learning processes reduce prejudice. In S. Oskamp (Ed.), *Reducing prejudice and discrimination.* Mahwah, NJ: Erlbaum.

Johnson, J. S., & Newport, E. L. (1991). Critical period effects on universal properties of language: The status of subjacency in the acquisition of a second language. *Cognition, 39,* 215–258.

Johnson, L. P. N. (1997). An end to the controversy? A reply to Rips. *Minds & Machines, 7,* 425–432.

Johnson, T. J., & Cropsey, K. L. (2000). Sensation seeking and drinking game participation in heavy-drinking college students. *Addictive Behaviors 25,* 109–116.

Johnston, L. D., O'Malley, P. M., & Bachman, J. G. (1999). *National survey results on drug use from the Monitoring the Future Study, 1975–1998* (Vol. 2). U.S. Department of Health and Human Services. Washington, DC: U.S. Government Printing Office.

Johnston, M. S., Kelley, C. S., Harris, F. F., & Wolf, M. M. (1966). An application of reinforcement principles to development of motor skills of a young child. *Child Development, 37,* 379–387.

Johnstone, E. C., Humphreys, M. S., Lang, F. H., et al. (Eds.) (1999). *Schizophrenia: Concepts and clinical management.* New York: Cambridge University Press.

Joiner, T. E., Alfano, M. S., & Metalsky, G. I. (1992). When depression breeds contempt: Reassurance seeking, self-esteem, and rejection of depressed college students by their roommates. *Journal of Abnormal Psychology, 101,* 165–173.

Joiner, T. E., & Coyne, J. C. (Eds.) (1999). *The interactional nature of depression: Advances in interpersonal approaches.* Washington, DC: American Psychological Association.

Jones, E., Cumming, J. D., & Horowitz, M. J. (1988). Another look at the nonspecific hypothesis of therapeutic effectiveness. *Journal of Consulting and Clinical Psychology, 56,* 48–55.

Jones, E. E., & Harris, V. A. (1967). The attribution of attitudes. *Journal of Experimental Social Psychology, 3,* 2–24.

Jones, E. G. (2000). Cortical and subcortical contributions to activity-dependent plasticity in primate somatosensory cortex. *Annual Review of Neuroscience, 23,* 1–37.

Jones, E. G., Steriade, M., & McCormick, D. A. (1997). *Thalamus.* New York: Elsevier Science.

Jones, G. V. (1990). Misremembering a common object: When left is not right. *Memory and Cognition, 18,* 174–182.

Jones, M. C. (1924). A laboratory study of fear: The case of Peter. *Pedagogical Seminary, 31,* 308–315.

Judge, T. A., Bono, J. E., & Locke, E. A. (2000). Personality and job satisfaction: The mediating role of job characteristics. *Journal of Applied Psychology, 85,* 237–249.

Julien, R. M. (1991). *A primer of drug action* (6th ed.). New York: W. H. Freeman.

Jung, J. (1995). Ethnic group and gender differences in the relationship between personality and coping. *Anxiety, Stress & Coping: An International Journal 8,* 113–126.

Kaemingk, K., & Paquette, A. (1999). Effects of prenatal alcohol exposure on neuropsychological functioning. *Developmental Neuropsychology, 15,* 111–140.

Kagan, J. (1972) Do infants think? *Scientific American, 226,* 74–82.

Kagan, J. (1989). Temperamental contributions to social behavior. *American Psychologist, 44,* 668–674.

Kagan, J., Kearsley, R. B., & Zelazo, P. (1978). *Infancy: Its place in human development.* Cambridge, MA: Harvard University Press.

Kagan, J., Reznick, S., & Snidman, N. (1988). Biological bases of childhood shyness. *Science, 240,* 167–171.

Kagan, J., & Snidman, N. (1991). Infant predictors of inhibited and uninhibited profiles. *Psychological Science, 2,* 40–44.

Kagitçibasi, C. (1997). Individualism and collectivism. In J. W. Berry, M. H. Segall, & C. Kagitçibasi (Eds.), *Handbook of cross-cultural psychology* (Vol. 3). Handbook of cross-cultural psychology. Boston: Allyn & Bacon

Kagitçibasi, C., & Poortinga, Y. H. (2000). Cross-cultural psychology: Issues and overarching themes. *Journal of Cross Cultural Psychology, 31,* 129–147.

Kahn, S., Zimmerman, G., Csikszentmihalyi, M., & Getzels, J. W. (1985). Relations between identity in young adulthood and intimacy at midlife. *Journal of Personality and Social Psychology, 49,* 1316–1322.

Kahneman, D., & Tversky, A. (1979). Prospect theory: An analysis of decisions under risk. *Econometrica, 47,* 263–291.

Kahneman, D., & Tversky, A. (1982). On the study of statistical intuitions. *Cognition, 11,* 123–141.

Kail, R. (1991). Developmental change in speed of processing during childhood and adolescence. *Psychological Bulletin, 109,* 490–501.

Kales, J. D., & Kales, A. (1975). Nocturnal psychophysiological correlates of somatic conditions and sleep disorders. *International Journal of Psychiatry in Medicine, 6,* 43–62.

Kalick, S. M., & Hamilton, T. E., III. (1988). Closer look at a matching simulation: Reply to Aron. *Journal of Personality and Social Psychology, 54*, 447–451.

Kalin, N. H., Larson, C., Shelton, S. E., & Davidson, R. R. (1998). Asymmetric frontal brain activity, cortisol, and behavior associated with fearful temperament in rhesus monkeys. *Behavioral Neuroscience, 112*, 286–292.

Kalish, R. A., & Reynolds, D. K. (1977). The role of age in death attitudes. *Death Education, 1*, 205–230.

Kallen, D. J. (1971). Nutrition and society. *Journal of the American Medical Association, 215*, 94–100.

Kandel, E. R., & Hawkins, R. D. (1992). The biological basis of learning and individuality. *Scientific American, 267*(3), 78-87.

Kane, J. M. (Ed.) (1992). *Tardive dyskinesia: A task force report of the American Psychiatric Association.* Washington, DC: American Psychiatric Press.

Kaner, A. (1995). Physical attractiveness and women's lives: Findings from a longitudinal study. *Dissertation Abstracts International: Section B: The Sciences and Engineering, 56*, 2942.

Kanfer, F. H. (1996). Motivation and emotion in behavior therapy. In K. S. Dobson & K. D. Craig (Eds.), *Advances in cognitive-behavioral therapy* (Vol. 2). Thousand Oaks, CA: Sage Publications.

Kanfer, F. H., & Goldstein, A. P. (Eds.). (1991). *Helping people change: A textbook of methods* (4th ed.). New York: Pergamon.

Kanwisher, N. (1998). The modular structure of human visual recognition: Evidence from functional imaging. In M. Sabourin, C. Fergus et al. (Eds.), *Advances in psychological science, Vol. 2: Biological and cognitive aspects.* Hove, England: Psychology Press/Erlbaum (UK), Taylor & Francis.

Kaplan, H., & Dove, H. (1987). Infant development among the Ache of eastern Paraguay. *Development Psychology, 23*, 190–198.

Kaplan, H. S., & Owett, T. (1993). The female androgen deficiency syndrome. *Journal of Sex and Marital Therapy, 19*, 3–24.

Kaprio, J., Koskenvu, M., & Rita, H. (1987). Mortality after bereavement: A prospective study of 95,647 widowed persons. *American Journal of Public Health, 77*, 283–287.

Karau, S. J., & Hart, J. W. (1998). Group cohesiveness and social loafing: Effects of a social interaction manipulation on individual motivation within groups. *Group Dynamics, 2*, 185–191.

Karau, S. J., & Williams, K. D. (1993). Social loafing: A meta-analytic review and theoretical integration. *Journal of Personality and Social Psychology, 65*, 681–706.

Karper, L. P., & Krystal, J. H. (1997). Pharmacotherapy of violent behavior. In D. M. Stroff, J. Breiling, & J. D. Maser (Eds.), *Handbook of antisocial behavior.* New York: Wiley.

Kashima, Y., Yamaguchi, S., Kim, U., Choi, S., Gelfand, M., & Yuki, M. (1995). Culture, gender, and self: A perspective from individualism-collectivism research. *Journal of Personality and Social Psychology, 69*, 925–937.

Kastenbaum, R. (2000). Death anxiety. In G. Fink (Ed.), *Encyclopedia of stress.* San Diego: Academic Press.

Katz, J., & Melzack, R. (1990). Pain "memories" in phantom limbs: Review and clinical observations. *Pain, 43*, 319–336.

Katz, L. J., & Slomka, G. T. (2000). Achievement testing. In G. Goldstein & M. Hersen (Eds.), *Handbook of psychological assessment* (3rd ed.). New York: Elsevier.

Kay, L. (1982). *Spatial perception through an acoustic sensor.* Christchurch, New Zealand: University of Canterbury Press.

Kayser, J., Tenke, C., Nordby, H., Hammerborg, D., et. al. (1997). Event-related potential (ERP) asymmetries to emotional stimuli in a visual half-field paradigm. *Psychophysiology, 34*(4), 414–426.

Kazdin, A. E. (1975). The impact of applied behavior analysis on diverse areas of research. *Journal of Applied Behavior Analysis, 8*, 213–229.

Kazdin, A. E. (Ed.) (1998). *Methodological issues and strategies in clinical research* (2nd ed.). Washington, DC: American Psychological Association.

Keating, N., & Jeffrey, B. (1983). Work careers of ever married and never married retired women. *Gerontologist, 23*, 416–421.

Keefe, F. J., Lefebvre, J. C., Maixner, W., Salley, A. N., & Caldwell, D. S. (1997). Self-efficacy for arthritis pain: Relationship to perception of thermal laboratory pain stimuli. *Arthritis Care & Research, 10*, 177–184.

Keller, H. (1955). *The story of my life.* New York: Doubleday.

Kelley, H. H. (1973). The process of causal attribution. *American Psychologist, 28*, 107–128.

Kellner, R. (1992). *Psychosomatic syndromes and somatic symptoms.* Washington, DC: American Psychiatric Press.

Kelly, G. F. (2001). *Sexuality today: The human perspective* (7th ed.). Boston: McGraw-Hill.

Kelly, J. A., St. Lawrence, J. S., & Brasfield, T. L. (1991). Predictors of vulnerability to AIDS risk behavior relapse. *Journal of Consulting and Clinical Psychology, 59*, 163–166.

Kelly, J. A., St. Lawrence, J. S., Hood. H. V., & Brasfield, T. L. (1989). Behavioral intervention to reduce AIDS risk activities. *Journal of Consulting and Clinical Psychology, 57*, 60–67.

Kelly, T. A., & Strupp, H. H. (1992). Patient and therapist values in psychotherapy: Perceived changes, assimilation, similarity, and outcome. *Journal of Consulting and Clinical Psychology, 60*, 34–40.

Kelman, H. C. (1996). Negotiation as interactive problem solving. *International Negotiation, 1*, 99–123.

Kelman, H. C. (1997). Group processes in the resolution of international conflicts: Experiences from the Israeli-Palestinian case. *American Psychologist, 52*, 212–220.

Kendall, D. (1998). *Social problems in a diverse society.* Boston: Allyn & Bacon.

Kenrick, D. T., & Funder, D. C. (1988). Profiting from controversy: Lessons from the person-situation debate. *American Psychologist, 43*, 23–34.

Kenrick, D. T., & Funder, D. C. (1991). The person-situation debate: Do personality traits really exist? In N. J. Derlega, B. A. Winstead, & W. H. Jones, (Eds.), *Personality: Contemporary theory and research.* Chicago: Nelson-Hall.

Kernberg, O. (1976). *Object relations theory and clinical psychoanalysis.* New York: Jason Aronsen.

Kernberg, O. E. (1984). *Severe personality disorders.* New Haven, CT: Yale University Press.

Kernberg, O. F. (1984). *Severe personality disorders: Psychotherapeutic strategies.* New Haven, CT: Yale University Press.

Kernberg, O. F. (1999). *Personality disorders in children and adolescents.* Poulsbo, WA: H-R Press.

Kerr, M., Lambert, W. W., & Bem, D. J. (1996). Life course sequelae of childhood shyness in Sweden: Comparison with the United States. *Developmental Psychology, 32*, 1100–1105.

Kessler, R. C., McGonagle, K. A., Zhao, S., & Nelson, C. (1994). Lifetime and 12-month prevalence of DSM-III-R psychiatric disorder in the United States: Results from the National Comorbidity Survey. *Archives of General Psychiatry, 51*, 8–19.

Kety, S., Rosenthal, D., Wender, P. H., Schulsinger, F., & Jacobson, B. (1978). The biological and adoptive families of adopted individuals who become schizophrenic: Prevalence of mental illness and other characteristics. In L. C. Wynne, R. L. Cromwell, & S. Matthysse (Eds.), *The nature of schizophrenia: New approaches to research and treatment.* New York: Wiley.

Kety, S. S. (1988). Schizophrenic illness in the families of schizophrenic adoptees: Findings from the Danish national sample. *Schizophrenia Bulletin, 1988; 14*, 217–222.

Keyes, D. (1982). *The minds of Billy Milligan.* New York: Bantam.

Khan, A. U., & Olson, D. L. (1977). Deconditioning of exercise-induced asthma. *Psychosomatic Medicine, 39*, 382–392.

Khoury, R. M. (1985). Norm formation, social conformity, and the confederating function of humor. *Social Behavior and Personality, 13*, 159–165.

Kiecolt-Glaser, J. K., Glaser, R., Cacioppo, J. T., & Malarkey, W. B. (1998). Marital stress: Immunologic, neuroendocrine, and autonomic correlates. *Annals of the New York Academy of Sciences, 840*, 656–663.

Kiesler, C. A. (1992). U.S. mental health policy: Doomed to fail. *American Psychologist, 47*, 1077–1082.

Kihlstrom, J. F. (1982). Hypnosis and the dissociation of memory, with special reference to posthypnotic amnesia. *Research Communications in Psychology, Psychiatry and Behavior, 7*, 181–197.

Kihlstrom, J. F. (1985). Posthypnotic amnesia and the dissociation of memory. *Psychology of Learning and Motivation, 19*, 131–178.

Kihlstrom, J. F. (1998). Dissociations and dissociation theory in hypnosis: Comment on Kirsch and Lynn. *Psychological Bulletin, 123*, 186–191.

Kihlstrom, J. F. (1999). The psychological unconscious. In L. A. Pervin & O. P. John (Eds.), *Handbook of personality: Theory and research.* New York: Guilford Press.

Killen, M., Ardila-Rey, R., Barakkatz, M., & Wang, P. L. (2000). Preschool teacher's perceptions about conflict resolution, autonomy, and the group in four countries: United States, Colombia, El Salvador, and Taiwan. *Early Education and Development, 11*, 73–92.

Kim, J., Lim, J. S., & Bhargava, M. (1998). The role of affect in attitude formation: A classical conditioning approach. *Journal of the Academy of Marketing Science, 26,* 143-152.

Kimble, D. P. (1992). *Biological psychology* (2nd ed.). Ft. Worth, TX: Harcourt Brace Jovanovich.

Kimura, D. (1992). Sex differences in the brain. *Scientific American, 267*(3), 119–195.

Kimura, D., & Hampson, E. (1994). Cognitive pattern in men and women is influenced by fluctuations in sex hormones. *Current Directions in Psychological Science, 3*(2), 57–61.

Kimura, K., Tachibana, N., Aso, T., Kimura, J., & Shibasaki, H. (1997). Subclinical REM sleep behavior disorder in a patient with corticobasal degeneration. *Sleep, 20,* 891–894.

King, C. R. (1997). Nonpharmacologic management of chemotherapy-induced nausea and vomiting. *Oncology Nursing Forum, Aug. 24* (7 Suppl.), 41–48.

Kinsey, A. C., Pomeroy, W. B., & Martin, C. E. (1948). *Sexual behavior in the human male.* Philadelphia: Saunders.

Kinsey, A. C., Pomeroy, W. B., Martin, C. E., & Gebhard, P. H. (1953). *Sexual behavior in the human female.* Philadelphia: Saunders.

Kirchner, W. H., & Grasser, A. (1998). The significance of odor cues and dance language information for the food search behavior of honeybees (Hymenoptera Apidae). *Journal of Insect Behavior, 11,* 169–178.

KIRO News (1998, January 17). *KIRO evening news.* Seattle, WA.

Kirsch, I. (1999). Clinical hypnosis as a nondeceptive placebo. In I. Kirsch, A. Capafons, B. E. Cardeña, & S. (Eds,)., *Clinical hypnosis and self-regulation: Cognitive behavioral perspectives.* Washington, DC: American Psychological Association.

Kirsch, I., & Lynn, S. J. (1998a). Dissociation theories of hypnosis. *Psychological Bulletin, 123,* 100–115.

Kirsch, I., & Lynn, S. J. (1998b). Social cognitive alternatives to dissociation theories of hypnotic involuntariness. *Review of General Psychology, 2,* 66–80.

Kirsch, I., & Lynn, S. J. (1999). Automaticity in clinical psychology. *American Psychologist, 54,* 504–515.

Kirschbaum, A. K., Krischbaum, C., Stierle, H., & Lehnert, H. (1992). Conditioned increase of natural killer cell activity (NKCA) in humans. *Psychosomatic Medicine, 54,* 123–132.

Kirsh, S. J. (1998). Seeing the world through Mortal Kombat–colored glasses: Violent video games and the development of a short-term hostile attribution bias. *Childhood: A Global Journal of Child Research, 5,* 177–184.

Klahr, D., & Simon, H. A. (1999). Studies of scientific discovery: Complementary approaches and convergent findings. *Psychological Bulletin, 125,* 524–543.

Klein, M. (1975). *The writings of Melanie Klein.* London: Hogarth Press.

Klein, S. B., & Mowrer, R. R. (1989). *Contemporary learning theories. Vol I: Pavlovian conditioning and the status of tradition.* Hillsdale, NJ: Erlbaum.

Kleinknecht, R. A., Dinnel, D. L., Kleinknecht, E. E. & Hiruma, N. et al. (1997). Cultural factors in social anxiety: A comparison of social phobia symptoms and Taijin Kyofusho. *Journal of Anxiety Disorders, 2,* 157–177.

Kleinmuntz, B. (1980). *Essentials of abnormal psychology* (2nd ed.). New York: Harper & Row.

Kleinmuntz, B., & Szucko, J. (1984). Lie detection in ancient and modern times: A call for contemporary scientific study. *American Psychologist, 39,* 766–776.

Kleitman, N. (1963). *Sleep and wakefulness* (2nd ed.). Chicago: University of Chicago Press.

Klimesch, W. (1979). Reminiscence and visual memory: Implications for the respective kind of the forgetting process. *Psychologische Beitraege, 21,* 40-48.

Klinger, E. (1993). What will they think of next? Understanding daydreaming. In G. G. Brannigan & M. R. Merrens, (Eds.), *The undaunted psychologist: Adventures in research.* Philadelphia: Temple University Press.

Kluckhohn, C., & Murray, H. A. (1953). Personality formation: The determinants. In C. Kluckhohn, H. A. Murray, & D. M. Schneider (Eds.), *Personality in nature, society, and culture.* New York: Alfred A. Knopf.

Kluft, R. P. (1999). True lies, false truths, and naturalistic raw data: Applying clinical research findings to the false memory debate. In L. M. Williams & V. L. Banyard, (Eds), *Trauma and Memory.* Thousand Oaks, CA: Sage Publications.

Knauth, P. (1996). Designing better shift systems. *Applied Ergonomics, 27,* 39–44.

Kobasa, S. C., Maddi, S. R., Puccetti, M. C., & Zola, M. A. (1985). Effectiveness of hardiness, exercise and social support as resources against illness. *Journal of Psychosomatic Research, 29,* 525–533.

Koenig, H. G., Pargament, K. L., & Nielsen, J. (1998). Religious coping and health status in medically ill hospitalized older adults. *Journal of Nervous and Mental Disease, 186,* 513–521.

Koestner, R., & McClelland, D. C. (1990). Perspectives on competence motivation. In L. A. Pervin (Ed.), *Handbook of personality theory and research.* New York: Guilford Press.

Kohlberg, L. (1963). The development of children's orientations toward a moral order: I. Sequence in the development of moral thought. *Human Development, 6,* 11–33.

Kohlberg, L. (1984). *The psychology of moral development: Essays on moral development* (Vol. 2). New York: Harper & Row.

Köhler, W. (1925). *The mentality of apes.* New York: Harcourt. (Trans. from the 2nd rev. ed. by Ella Winter)

Kohut, H. (1971). *Analysis of the self.* New York: International Universities Press.

Kohut, H. (1977). *The restoration of self.* New York: International Universities Press.

Kolb, B. (1989). Brain development, plasticity, and behavior. *American Psychologist, 44,* 1203–1212.

Kolb, B., & Whishaw, I. Q. (1989). Plasticity in the neocortex: Mechanisms underlying recovery from early brain damage. *Progress in Neurobiology, 32,* 235–276.

Kolb, B., & Whishaw, I. Q. (1998). Brain plasticity and behavior. *Annual Review of Psychology, 49,* 43–64.

Kollar, E. J., & Fisher, C. (1980). Tooth induction in chick epithelium: Expression of quiescent genes for enamel synthesis. *Science, 207,* 993–995.

Koluchova, J. (1972). Severe deprivation in twins: A case study. *Journal of Child Psychology and Psychiatry, 13,* 107–114.

Koluchova, J. (1991). Severely deprived twins after 22 years of observation. *Studiea Psychologica, 33,* 23–28.

Konkle, A. T. M., Kubela, S. L., & Bielajew, C. (2000). The effects of cholecystokinin on stimulation-induced feeding and self-stimulation. *Behavioural Brain Research, 107,* 145–152.

Kopelman, M. D., Stanhope, N., & Kingsley, D. (1999). Retrograde amnesia in patients with diencephalic, temporal lobe or frontal lesions. *Neuropsychologia, 37,* 939–958.

Koriat, A., Goldsmith, M., & Pansky, A. (2000). Toward a psychology of memory accuracy. *Annual Review of Psychology, 51,* 481–537.

Korpi, E. R. (1994). Role of GABA-sub(A) receptors in the actions of alcohol and in alcoholism: Recent advances. *Alcohol and Alcoholism, 29,* 115–129.

Kosambi, D. D. (1967). Living prehistory in India. *Scientific American, 216,* 105.

Koss, M. P., & Ingram, M. (2000). Male partner violence. In G. Fink (Ed.), *Encyclopedia of stress.* San Diego: Academic Press.

Koss, M. P., Gidycz, C. A., & Wisniewski, N. (1987). The scope of rape: Incidence and prevalence of sexual aggression and victimization in a national sample of higher education students. *Journal of Consulting and Clinical Psychology, 55,* 162–170.

Kottak, C. P. (2000). *Cultural anthropology* (8th ed.). Boston: McGraw-Hill.

Kraft, C. L. (1978). A psychophysical contribution to air safety: Simulator studies of visual illusions in night visual approaches. In H. L. Pick, Jr., H. W. Leibowitz, J. E. Singer, A. Steinschneider, & H. W. Stevenson (Eds.), *Psychology: From research to practice.* New York: Plenum.

Kramer, D. A. (1983). Post-formal operations? A need for further conceptualization. *Human Development, 26,* 91–105.

Krasnegor, N. A., Lyon, G. R., & Goldman, R. P. S. (1997). *Development of the prefrontal cortex: Evolution, neurobiology, and behavior.* Baltimore: Paul H. Brookes.

Kraus, S. J. (1995). Attitudes and the prediction of behavior: A meta-analysis of the empirical literature. *Personality and Social Psychology Bulletin, 21,* 58–75.

Krause, M. A., & Fouts, R. S. (1997). Chimpanzee (Pan troglodytes) pointing: Hand shapes, accuracy, and the role of eye gaze. *Journal of Comparative Psychology, 111,* 330–336.

Krausz, M. (1982). Policies of organizational choice at different vocational life stages. *Vocational Guidance Quarterly, 31,* 60–68.

Krebs, D. L., & Denton, K. (1997). Social illusions and self-deception: The evolution of biases in person perception. In J. A. Simpson & D. T. Kenrick (Eds.), *Evolutionary social psychology.* Mahwah, NJ: Lawrence Erlbaum.

Krech, D. (1978). Quoted in M. C. Diamond, The aging brain: Some enlightening and optimistic results. *American Scientist, 66,* 66–71.

Krevans, J., & Gibbs, J. C. (1996). Parents' use of inductive discipline: Relations to children's empathy and prosocial behavior. *Child Development, 67,* 3263–3277.

Kribbs, N. B. (1993). Siesta. In M. A. Carskadon (Ed.), *Encyclopedia of sleep and dreaming*. New York: Macmillan.

Kroeber, A. L. (1948). *Anthropology*. New York: Harcourt Brace Jovanovich.

Kron, J. H. (1998). The reality of deception. *American Psychologist, 53*, 805.

Krosnick, J. A., Betz, A. L., Jussim, L. J., & Lynn, A. R. (1992). Subliminal conditioning of attitudes. *Personality and Social Psychology Bulletin, 18*, 152–162.

Krueger, R. F., & Caspi, A. (1993). Personality, arousal, and pleasure: A test of competing models of interpersonal attraction. *Personality and Individual Differences, 14*, 105–111.

Kruglanski, A. W., & Webster, D. M. (1996). Motivated closing of the mind: "Seizing" and "freezing." *Psychological Review, 103*, 263–283.

Kubler-Ross, E. (1969). *On death and dying*. New York: Macmillan.

Kuhn, C. M., & Schanberg, S. M. (1998). Responses to maternal separation: Mechanisms and mediators. *International Journal of Developmental Neuroscience, 16*, 261–270.

Kulik, J. A., & Mahler, H. I. M. (1989). Stress and affiliation in a hospital setting: Preoperative roommate preferences. *Personality and Social Psychology Bulletin, 15*, 183–193.

Kulik, J. A., Mahler, H. I. M., & Moore, P. J. (1996). Social comparison and affiliation under threat: Effects of recovery from major surgery. *Journal of Personality and Social Psychology, 66*, 301–309.

Kumar, P., & Dhyani, J. (1996). Marital adjustment: A study of some related factors. *Indian Journal of Clinical Psychology, 23*, 112–116.

Kunzendorf, R. G., Hartmann, E., Cohen, R., & Cutler, J. (1997). Bizarreness of the dreams and daydreams reported by individuals with thin and thick boundaries. *Dreaming: Journal of the Association for the Study of Dreams, 7*, 265–271.

Kurdek, L. A. (1991). Marital stability and changes in marital quality in newlywed couples: A test of the contextual model. *Journal of Social and Personal Relationships, 8*, 27–48.

Kurdek, L. A. (1998). The nature and predictors of the trajectory of change in marital quality over the first 4 years of marriage for first-married husbands and wives. *Journal of Family Psychology, 12*, 494–510.

Kurdek, L. A. (1999). The nature and predictors of the trajectory of change in marital quality for husbands and wives over the first 10 years of marriage. *Developmental Psychology, 35*, 1283–1296.

Kurzweil, E. (1989). *The Freudians: A comparative perspective*. New Haven, CT: Yale University Press.

Kutter, P. (Ed.) (1995). *Psychoanalysis international: A guide to psychoanalysis throughout the world*. New York: Analytic Press.

LaBar, K. S., & Phelps, E. A. (1998). Arousal-mediated memory consolidation: Role of the medial temporal lobe in humans. *Psychological Science, 9*, 490–493.

Lacks, P., Bertelson, A. D., Gans, L., & Kunkel, J. (1983). The effectiveness of three behavioral treatments for different degrees of sleep onset insomnia. *Behavior Therapy, 14*, 593–605.

Lafferty, P., Beutler, L. E., & Crago, M. (1989). Differences between more and less effective psychotherapists: A study of select therapist variables. *Journal of Consulting and Clinical Psychology, 57*, 76–80.

Lagerspetz, K. Y., Tirri, R., & Lagerspetz, K. M. (1968). Neurochemical and endocrinological studies of mice selectively bred for aggressiveness. *Scandinavian Journal of Psychology, 9*, 157–160.

Laing, R. D. (1967). *The politics of experience*. New York: Pantheon Books.

Lakein, A. (1973). *How to get control of your time and your life*. New York: Peter H. Wyden.

Lakin, M. (1998). Carl Rogers and the culture of psychotherapy. In G. A. Kimble & M. Wertheimer (Eds.), *Portraits of pioneers in psychology* (Vol. 3). Washington, DC: American Psychological Association.

Lamal, P. A. (Ed.) (1991). *Behavioral analysis of societies and cultural practices*. Bristol, PA: Hemisphere.

Lambert, M. J., Shapiro, D. A., & Bergin, A. E. (1986). The effectiveness of psychotherapy. In S. L. Garfield & A. E. Bergin (Eds.), *Handbook of psychotherapy and behavior change* (3rd ed.). New York: Wiley.

Lambert, W. E., Genesee, F., Holobow, N., & Chartrand, L. (1993). Bilingual education for majority English-speaking children. *European Journal of Psychology of Education, 8*, 3–22.

Lamble, D., Kauranen, T., Laakso, M., & Summala, H. (1999). Cognitive load and detection thresholds in car following situations: Safety implications for using mobile (cellular) telephones while driving. *Accident Analysis and Prevention, 31*, 617–623.

Lamborn, S. D., Mounts, N. S., Steinberg, L., & Dornbusch, S. M. (1991). Patterns of competence and adjustment among adolescents from authoritative, authoritarian, indulgent, and neglectful families. *Child Development, 62*, 1049–1065.

Lamke, L. K. (1982). The impact of sex-role orientation on self-esteem in early adolescence. *Child Development, 53*, 1530–1535.

Landesman, S., & Ramey, C. T. (1989). Developmental psychology and mental retardation: Integrating scientific principles with treatment practices. *American Psychologist, 44*, 409–415.

Lane, R. D., Reiman, E. M., Ahern, G. L., & Schwartz, G. E. (1997). Neuroanatomical correlates of happiness, sadness, and disgust. *American Journal of Psychiatry, 154*, 926–933.

Langer, E. (1989). *Mindlessness*. Reading, MA: Addison-Wesley.

Langs, R. J. (1996). *The evolution of the emotion-processing mind: With an introduction to mental Darwinism*. New York: International Universal Press.

LaPiere, R. T. (1934). Attitudes and actions. *Social Forces, 13*, 230–237.

Larimer, M. E., Baer, J. S., Quigley, L. A., Blume, A. W., & Hawkins, E. H. (1998). Harm reduction for alcohol problems: Expanding access to and acceptability of prevention and treatment services. In G. A. Marlatt (Ed.), *Harm reduction: Pragmatic strategies for managing high-risk behaviors*. New York: Guilford Press.

Larroque, B., & Kaminski, M. (1998). Prenatal alcohol exposure and development at preschool age: Main results of a French

study. *Alcoholism: Clinical and Experimental Research, 22*, 295–303.

Larsen, R. J., & Zarate, M. A. (1991). Extending reducer/augmenter theory into the emotion domain: The role of affect in regulating stimulation level. *Personality and Individual Differences, 12*, 713–723.

Larson, S. J., & Siegel, S. (1998). Learning and tolerance to the ataxic effect of ethanol. *Pharmacology, Biochemistry and Behavior, 61*, 131–142.

Lashley, K. S. (1930). The mechanism of vision: 1. A method for rapid analysis of pattern-vision in the rat. *Journal of Genetic Psychology, 37*, 453–460.

Lashley, K. S. (1950). In search of the engram. In *Symposium of the Society for Experimental Biology* (Vol. 4). New York: Cambridge University Press.

Laska, M., & Metzker, K. (1998). Food avoidance learning in squirrel monkeys and common marmosets. *Learning and Memory, 5*, 193–203.

Latané, B. (1981). The psychology of social impact. *American Psychologist, 36*, 343–356.

Latané, B., & Darley, J. M. (1968). Group inhibition of bystander intervention in emergencies. *Journal of Personality and Social Psychology, 10*, 215–221.

Latané, B., & Darley, J. M. (1970). *The unresponsive bystander: Why doesn't he help?* New York: Appleton-Century-Crofts.

Latané, B., Liu, J. H., Nowak, A., Bonevento, M., & Zheng, L. (1995). Distance matters: Physical space and social impact. *Personality and Social Psychology Bulletin, 21*, 795–805.

Latané, B., & Nida, S. (1981). Ten years of research on group size and helping. *Psychological Bulletin, 89*, 308–324.

Latané, B., & Rodin, J. (1969). A lady in distress: Inhibiting effects of friends and strangers on bystander intervention. *Journal of Experimental Social Psychology, 5*, 189–202.

Lau, R. R., & Russell, D. (1980). Attribution in the sports pages. *Journal of Personality and Social Psychology, 39*, 29–38.

Laughlin, H. P. (1967). *The neuroses*. Washington, DC: Butterworth.

Laumann, E. O., Gagnon, J. H., Michael, R. T., & Michaels, S. (1994). *The social organization of sexuality: Sexual practices in the United States*. Chicago: University of Chicago Press.

Lawler, K. A., Kline, K. A., Harriman, H. L., & Kelly, K. M. (1999). Stress and illness. In V. J. Derlega, B. A. Winstead, et al. (Eds.), *Personality: Contemporary theory and research* (2nd ed.). Chicago: Nelson-Hall.

Lazarus, A. A. (1995). Multimodal therapy. In R. J. Corsini & D. Wedding (Eds.), *Current psychotherapies* (5th ed.). Itaska, IL: Peacock.

Lazarus, R. S. (1991). Progress on a cognitive-motivational-relational theory of emotion. *American Psychologist, 46*, 819–834.

Lazarus, R. S. (1998). *Fifty years of the research and theory of R. S. Lazarus: An analysis of historical and perennial issues*. Mahwah, NJ: Erlbaum.

Lazarus, R. S., & Folkman, S. (1984). *Stress, appraisal, and coping*. New York: Springer.

Leaper, C., Anderson, K. J., & Sanders, P. (1998). Moderators of gender effects on parents' talk to their children: A meta-analysis. *Developmental Psychology, 34*, 3–27.

LeBon, G. (1895). *Psychologies des foules*. Paris: Oleon.

LeDoux, J. E. (1989). Cognitive-emotional interactions in the brain. *Cognition and Emotion, 3,* 267–289.

LeDoux, J. E. (1992). Systems and synapses of emotional memory. In L. R. Squire, N. M. Weinberger, G. Lynch, & J. L. McGaugh (Eds.), *Memory: Organization and locus of change.* New York: Oxford University Press.

LeDoux, J. E. (1996, 1998). *The emotional brain.* New York: Simon & Schuster.

LeDoux, J. E. (2000). Emotion circuits in the brain. *Annual Review of Neuroscience, 23,* 155–184.

LeDoux, J. E., Wilson, D. H., & Gazzaniga, M. S. (1977). A divided mind: Observations on the conscious properties of the separated hemispheres. *Annals of Neurology, 2,* 417–421.

Lee, J. A. (1973). *Colors of love.* Toronto: New Press.

Lee, J. D. (1998). Which kids can "become" scientists? Effects of gender, self-concepts, and perceptions of scientists. *Social Psychology Quarterly, 61,* 199–219.

Lee, R. M. (2000). *Unobtrusive methods in social research.* Buckingham, UK: Open University Press.

Lehmann-Haupt, C. (1988, August 4). Books of the times: How an actor found success, and himself. *New York Times,* p. 2.

Leibowitz, S. F. (1992). Hypothalamic neurochemical systems mediate drug effects on food intake. *International Journal of Obesity and Related Metabolic Disorders, 15,* 701A–702A.

Leibowitz, S. F., Xuereb, M., & Kim, T. (1992). Blockade of natural and neuropeptide Y-induced carbohydrate feeding by a receptor antagonist PYX-2. *Neuroreport, 3,* 1023–1026.

Leichliter, J. S., Meilman, P. W., Presley, C. A., & Cashin, J. R. (1998). Alcohol use and related consequences among students with varying levels of involvement in college athletics. *Journal of American College Health, 46,* 257–262.

Leichtman, M. D., & Ceci, S. J. (1995). The effects of stereotypes and suggestions on preschoolers' reports. *Developmental Psychology, 31,* 568–578.

Leigh, B. C., & Stall, R. (1993). Substance use and risky sexual behavior for exposure to HIV: Issues in methodology, interpretation, and prevention. *American Psychologist, 48,* 1035–1045.

Leigland, S. (2000). On cognitivism and behaviorism. *American Psychologist, 55,* 273–274.

Leitenberg, H., & Henning, K. (1995). Sexual fantasy. *Psychological Bulletin, 117,* 469–496.

LeMoal, H. (1999). *Dopamine and the brain: From neurons to networks.* New York: Academic Press.

Lenneberg, E. H. (1967). *Biological foundations of language.* New York: Wiley.

Leondes, C. T. (1997). *Medical imaging systems techniques and applications: Brain and skeletal systems.* New York: Gordon and Breach.

Lepage, M., Habib, R., & Tulving, E. (1998). Hippocampal PET activations of memory encoding and retrieval: The HIPER model. *Hippocampus, 8,* 313–322.

Lepper, M. R. (1998). A whole much less than the sum of its parts. *American Psychologist, 53,* 675–676.

Lepper, M. R., Greene, D., & Nisbett, R. E. (1973). Undermining children's intrinsic interest with extrinsic reward: A test of the "overjustification" hypothesis. *Journal of Personality and Social Psychology, 28,* 129-137.

Lerner, M. J. (1980). *The belief in a just world: A fundamental delusion.* New York: Plenum.

Lerner, R. M. (1987). A life-span perspective for early adolescence. In R. M. Lerner & T. T. Foch (Eds.), *Biological-psychosocial interactions in early adolescence.* Hillsdale, NJ: Erlbaum.

Lerner, R. M. (1995). *America's youth in crisis: Challenges and options for programs and policies.* Thousand Oaks, CA: Sage Publications.

Leventhal, H. (2000). Emotions: Structures and adaptive functions. In G. Fink (Ed.), *Encyclopedia of stress.* San Diego: Academic Press.

Levine, D. S. (2000). *Introduction to neural and cognitive modeling* (2nd ed.). Mahwah, NJ: Lawrence Erlbaum.

Levine, R., Sato, S., Hashimoto, T., & Verma, J. (1995). Love and marriage in eleven cultures. *Journal of Cross-Cultural Psychology, 26,* 554–571.

Levinson, D. J. (1986). A conception of adult development. *American Psychologist, 41,* 3–13.

Levinson, D. J. (1990). A theory of life structure development in adulthood. In C. N. Alexander & E. J. Langer. (Eds.), Higher stages of human development: Perspectives on adult growth. New York: Oxford University Press.

Levinson, D. J., Darow, C. N., Klein, E. B., Levinson, M. H., & McKee, B. (1978). *The seasons of a man's life.* New York: Knopf.

Levinthal, C. F. (1996). *Drugs, behavior, and modern society.* Boston: Allyn & Bacon.

Levis, D. J. (1989). The case for a return to a two-factor theory of avoidance: The failure of non-fear interpretations. In S. B. Klein, B. Stephen, & R. R. Mowrer (Eds.), *Contemporary learning theories: Pavlovian conditioning and the status of traditional learning theory.* Hillsdale, NJ: Erlbaum.

Levy, S., Marrow, L., Bagley, C., & Lippman, M. (1989). Survival hazards analysis in first recurrent breast cancer patients: Seven-year follow-up. *Psychosomatic Medicine, 50,* 520–528.

Lewin, K. (1935). *A dynamic theory of personality.* New York: McGraw-Hill.

Lewinsohn, P. M., Gotlib, I. H., Lewinsohn, M., Seeley, J. R., & Allen, N. B. (1998). Gender differences in anxiety disorders and anxiety symptoms in adolescents. *Journal of Abnormal Psychology, 107,* 109–117.

Lewinsohn, P. M., Hoberman, H., Teri, L., & Hantzinger, M. (1985). An integrative theory of depression. In S. Reiss & R. Bootzin (Eds.), *Theoretical issues in behavior therapy.* New York: Academic Press.

Lewinsohn, P. M., Hops, H., Roberts, R. E., Seeley, J. R., et al. (1993). Adolescent psychopathology: I. Prevalence and incidence of depression and other DSM-III–R disorders in high school students. *Journal of Abnormal Psychology, 102,* 133–144.

Lewis, B. P., & Linder, D. E. (1997). Thinking about choking? Attentional processes and paradoxical performance. *Personality and Social Psychology Bulletin, 23,* 937–944.

Lewis, C., O'Sullivan, C., & Barraclough, J. (Eds.) (1995). *The psychoimmunology of human cancer.* New York: Oxford University Press.

Lewis, M. (1999). On the development of personality. In L. A. Pervin & O. P. John (Eds.), *Handbook of personality: Theory and research.* New York: Guilford Press.

Lewy, A. J., Bauer, V. K., Cutler, N. L., Sack, R. L., Ahmed, S., Thomas, K. H., Blood, M. L., & Jackson, J. M. L. (1998). Morning vs evening light treatment of patients with winter depression. *Archives of General Psychiatry, 55,* 890–896.

Lewy, A. J., Sack, R. L., & Cutler, N. L. (1998). Melatonin in circadian phase sleep and mood disorders. In M. Shafii, S. Mohammad, & L. Sharon (Eds.), *Melatonin in psychiatric and neoplastic disorders. Progress in Psychiatry, 55,* Washington, DC: American Psychiatric Press.

Leyens, J. P., Camino, L., Parke, R. D., & Berkowitz, L. (1975). Effects of movie violence on aggression in a field setting as a function of group dominance and cohesion. *Journal of Personality and Social Psychology, 32,* 346–360.

Lezak, M. (1995). *Neuropsychological assessment* (3rd ed.). New York: Oxford Press.

Li, T. K. (2000). Pharmacogenetics of responses to alcohol and genes that influence alcohol drinking. *Journal of Studies on Alcohol, 61,* 5–12.

Lickey, M. E., & Gordon, B. (1991). *Medicine and mental illness: The use of drugs in psychiatry.* New York: W. H. Freeman.

Lieberman, J. A. (1998). *Psychiatric drugs.* Philadelphia: Saunders.

Lieberman, P. (1984). *The biology and evolution of language.* Cambridge: Harvard University Press.

Lilienfeld, S. O., Kirsch, I., Sarbin, T. R., Lynn, S. J., Chaves, J. F., Ganaway, G. K., & Powell, R. A. (1999). Dissociative identity disorder and the sociocognitive model: Recalling the lessons of the past. *Psychological Bulletin, 125,* 507–523.

Linn, R. L. (Ed.) (1989). *Intelligence: Measurement, theory, and public policy.* Urbana, IL: University of Illinois Press.

Linville, P. W., & Jones, E. E. (1980). Polarized appraisals of out-group members. *Journal of Personality and Social Psychology, 38,* 689–703.

Linz, D., & Donnerstein, E. (1989). The effects of countertransformation on the acceptance of rape myths. In D. Zillmann & J. Bryant (Eds.), *Pornography: Research advances and policy considerations.* Hillsdale, NJ: Erlbaum.

Lipsey, M. W., & Cordray, C. S. (2000). Evaluation methods for social intervention. *Annual Review of Psychology, 51,* 345–376.

Lipsitt, L. P. (1990). Learning processes in the human newborn: Sensitization, habituation, and classical conditioning. *Annals of the New York Academy of Sciences, 608,* 113–127.

Little, B. (1999). Personality and motivation: Personal action and the conative evolution. In L. A. Pervin & O. P. John (Eds.), *Handbook of personality: Theory and research.* New York: Guilford Press.

Litz, B. T., Orsillo, S. M., Kaloupek, D., & Weathers, F. (2000). Emotional processing in posttraumatic stress disorder. *Journal of Abnormal Psychology, 109,* 26–39.

Liu, J. H., & Latane, B. (1998). Extremitization of attitudes: Does thought- and discussion-induced polarization cumulate? *Basic and Applied Social Psychology, 20,* 103–110.

Livingstone, M., & Hubel, D. (1994). Segregation of form, color, movement, and depth: Anatomy, physiology, and perception. In H. Gutfreund, & G. Toulouse (Eds.), *Biology and computation: A physicist's choice. Advanced series in neuroscience.* Singapore: World Scientific.

Locke, D. C. (1992). *Multicultural understanding: A comprehensive model.* Newbury Park, CA: Sage Publications.

Locke, E. A. (1996). Motivation through conscious goal setting. *Applied and Preventive Psychology, 5,* 117–124.

Locke, E. A., & Latham, G. P. (1990). *A theory of goal setting and task performance.* Englewood Cliffs, NJ: Prentice Hall.

Locke, E. A., & Latham, G. P. (1994). Goal setting theory. In H. F. O'Neil Jr., & M. Drillings (Eds.), *Motivation: Theory and research.* Hillsdale, NJ: Erlbaum.

Lockwood, P., & Kunda, Z. (1997). Superstars and me: Predicting the impact of role models on the self. *Journal of Personality and Social Psychology, 73,* 91–103.

Loehlin, J. C. (1992). *Genes and environment in personality development.* Newbury Park, CA: Sage Publications.

Loehlin, J. C., Willerman, L., & Horn, J. M. (1988). Genetics and human behavior. *Annual Review of Psychology, 39,* 101–134.

Loewenstein, R. J. (1991). Psychogenic amnesia and psychogenic fuge: A comprehensive review. In A. Tasman & S. M. Goldfinger (Eds.), *American Psychiatric Press review of psychiatry* (Vol. 10). Washington, DC: American Psychiatric Association.

Loftus, E. F. (1979) *Eyewitness testimony.* Cambridge, MA: Harvard University Press.

Loftus, E. F. (2000). Remembering what never happened. In E. Tulving (Ed.), *Memory, consciousness, and the brain: The Tallinn Conference.* Philadelphia: Psychology Press/Taylor & Francis.

Loftus, E. F., & Burns, T. E. (1982). Mental shock can produce retrograde amnesia. *Memory and Cognition, 10,* 318–323.

Loftus, E. F., & Loftus, G. R. (1980). On the permanence of stored information in the human brain. *American Psychologist, 35,* 409–420.

Loftus, E. F., & Palmer, J. C. (1974). Reconstruction of automobile destruction: An example of the interaction between language and memory. *Journal of Verbal Learning and Verbal Behavior, 13,* 585–589.

Loftus, E. F., & Pickrell, J. E. (1995). The formation of false memories. *Psychiatric Annals, 25,* 720–725.

Logue, A. W. (1991). *The psychology of eating and drinking* (2nd ed.). New York: W. H. Freeman.

Lopez, S. R., & Guarnaccia, P. J. (2000). Cultural psychopathology: Uncovering the social world of mental illness. *Annual Review of Psychology, 51,* 571–598.

Lopez-Mendoza, D., Aguilar, B. H., & Swanson, H. H. (1998). Combined effects of gepirone and (+)WAY 100135 on territorial aggression in mice. *Pharmacology, Biochemistry and Behavior, 61,* 1–8.

Lorenz, K. (1937). The companion in the bird's world. *Auk, 54,* 245–273.

Lorenz, K. (1966). *On aggression.* New York: Harcourt Brace Jovanovich.

Lovaas, O. I. (1977). *The autistic child.* New York: Irvington.

Lubinski, D. (2000). Scientific and social significance of assessing individual differences: "Sinking shafts at a few critical points." *Annual Review of Psychology, 51,* 405–444.

Luborsky, L. (1987). Research can now affect clinical practice: A happy turnaround. *Clinical Psychologist 40,* 56–60.

Luborsky, L., & Crits-Christoph, O. (1998). *Understanding transference: The core conflictual relationship theme method* (2nd ed.). Washington, DC: American Psychological Association.

Luchins, A. (1957a). Primacy-recency in impression formation. In C. Hovland, W. Mandell, E. Campbell, T. Brock, A. Luchins, & A.Cohen (Eds.), *The order of presentation in persuasion.* New Haven, CT: Yale University Press.

Luchins, A. (1957b). Experimental attempts to minimize the impact of first impressions. In C. Hovland, W. Mandell, E. Campbell, T. Brock, A. Luchins, & A. Cohen (Eds.), *The order of presentation in persuasion.* New Haven, CT: Yale University Press.

Luchins, A. J. (1942). Mechanization in problem solving: The effect of Einstellung. *Psychological Monographs, 54,* 6 (Whole No. 248).

Lucker, W., Rosenfield, D., Sikes, J., & Aronson, E. (1977). Performance in the interdependent classroom: A field study. *American Educational Research Journal, 13,* 115–123.

Lundh, L. G. (1998). Cognitive-behavioural analysis and treatment of insomnia. *Scandinavian Journal of Behaviour Therapy, 27,* 10–29.

Lupien, S. J., & Briere, S. (2000). Memory and stress. In G. Fink (Ed.), *Encyclopedia of stress.* San Diego: Academic Press.

Luria, A. R. (1968). *The mind of a mnemonist: A little book about a vast memory.* New York: Basic Books.

Luthans, F., Paul, R., & Baker, D. (1981). An experimental analysis of the impact of contingent reinforcement on salespersons' performance behavior. *Journal of Applied Psychology, 66,* 314–323.

Lydic, R., & Biebuyck, J. F. (Eds.). *Clinical physiology of sleep.* New York: Oxford.

Lykken, D. T. (1984). Polygraph interrogation. *Nature, 307,* 681–684.

Lykken, D. T. (1998). *A tremor in the blood: Uses and abuses of the lie detector.* New York: Plenum.

Lykken, D. T., McGue, M., Tellegen, A., & Bouchard, T. J. (1992). Emergenesis: Genetic traits that may not run in families. *American Psychologist, 47,* 1565–1577.

Lykken, D., & Tellegen, A. (1996). Happiness is a stochastic phenomenon. *Psychological Science, 7,* 186–189.

Lynn, E. J. (1971). Amphetamine abuse: A "speed" trap. *Psychiatric Quarterly, 45,* 92–101.

Lynn, M. (1989). Race differences in sexual behavior: A critique of Rushton and Bogaert's evolutionary hypothesis. *Journal of Research in Personality, 23,* 1–6.

Lynn, R. (1998a). Has the black-white intelligence difference in the United States been narrowing over time? *Personality and Individual Differences, 25,* 999–1002.

Lynn, R. (1998b). The decline of genotypic intelligence. In U. Neisser, et al. (Eds.), *The rising curve: Long-term gains in IQ and related measures.* Washington, DC: American Psychological Association.

Lytton, H., & Romney, D. M. (1991). Parents' differential socialization of boys and girls: A meta-analysis. *Psychological Bulletin, 109,* 267–296.

Lyvers, M. F., & Maltzman, I. (1991). The balanced placebo design: Effects of alcohol and beverage instructions cannot be independently assessed. *International Journal of the Addictions, 26,* 963–972.

Maass, A., & Clark, R. D. III. (1984). Hidden impact of minorities: Fifteen years of minority influence research. *Psychological Bulletin, 95,* 428–450.

MacAndrew, C., & Edgerton, R. B. (1969). *Drunken comportment: A social explanation.* Chicago: Aldine.

Maccoby, E. E. (1988). Gender as a social category. *Developmental Psychology, 24,* 755–765.

Maccoby, E. E., & Jacklin, C. N. (1974). *The psychology of sex differences.* Stanford, CA: Stanford University Press.

Maccoby, E. E., & Maccoby, N. (1954). The interview: A tool of social science. In G. Lindzey (Ed.), *Handbook of social psychology.* Cambridge, MA: Addison-Wesley.

Maccoby, E. E., & Martin, J. A. (1983). Socialization in the context of the family: Parent-child interaction. In E. M. Hetherington (Ed.), *Handbook of child psychology: Socialization, personality, and social development.* New York: Wiley.

MacCoun, R. J. (1998). Toward a psychology of harm reduction. *American Psychologist, 53,* 1199–1208.

MacDonald, T. K., Fong, G. T., Zanna, M. P., & Martineau, A. M. (2000). Alcohol myopia and condom use: Can alcohol intoxication be associated with more prudent behavior? *Journal of Personality and Social Psychology, 78,* 605–619.

MacDonald, T. K., Zanna, M. P., & Fong, G. T. (1995). Decision making in altered states: Effects of alcohol on attitudes toward drinking and driving. *Journal of Personality and Social Psychology, 68,* 973–985.

MacFarlane, J. A. (1975). Olfaction in the development of social preferences in the human neonate. In M. A. Hofer (Ed.), *Parent-infant interaction.* Amersterdam: Elsevier.

MacLeod, C. (1998). Implicit perception: Perceptual processing without awareness. In K. Kirsner, et al. (Eds.), *Implicit and explicit mental processes.* Mahwah, NJ: Erlbaum.

Maddux, J. E. (1999). Personal efficacy. In V. J. Derlega, B. A. Winstead, & W. H. Jones (Eds.), *Personality: Contemporary theory and research.* Chicago: Nelson-Hall.

Madraza, I., Drucker-Colin, R., Diaz, V., Martinez-Mata, J., Torres, C., & Becerril, J. J. (1987). Open microsurgical autograph of adrenal medulla to the right candate nucleus in two patients with intractable Parkinson's disease. *New England Journal of Medicine, 316,* 831–834.

Maes, H. H. M., Neale, M. C., & Eaves, L. J. (1997). Genetic and environmental factors in relative body weight and human adiposity. *Behavior Genetics, 27,* 325–351.

Magels, J. A. (1997). Strategic processing and memory for temporal order in patients with frontal lobe lesions. *Neuropsychology, 11,* 207–221.

Magnuson, S. (1986). "A serious deficiency": The Rogers Commission faults NASA's "flawed" decision-making process. *Time* (Intl. Ed.), pp. 40–42.

Mahler, M. (1968). *On human symbiosis and the vicissitudes of individuation: Infantile psychosis.* New York: Basic Books.

Mahoney, M. J. (1980). *Abnormal psychology: Perspectives on human variance.* New York: Harper & Row.

Mahoney, W. J., & Ayres, J. J. (1976). One-trial simultaneous and backward fear conditioning as reflected in conditioned suppression of licking in rats. *Animal Learning and Behavior, 4,* 357–362.

Mai, J. K., Assheuer, J. K., & George, W. (1997). *Atlas of the human brain.* San Diego: Academic Press.

Maier, S. F., & Watkins, L. R. (1998). Cytokines for psychologists: Implications of bidirectional immune-to-brain communication for understanding behavior, mood, and cognition. *Psychological Review, 105,* 83–107.

Maier, S. F., & Watkins, L. R. (1999). Bidirectional communication between the brain and the immune system: Implications for behaviour. *Animal Behaviour, 57*(4), 741–751.

Maier, S. F., Watkins, L. R., & Fleshner, M. (1994). Psychoneuroimmunology: The interface between brain, behavior, and immunity. *American Psychologist, 49,* 1004–1017.

Maio, G. R., & Olson, J. M. (Eds.) (2000). *Why we evaluate: Functions of attitudes.* Mahwah, NJ: Erlbaum.

Major, B., Carrington, P. I., & Carnevale, P. J. D. (1984). Physical attractiveness and self-esteem: Attributions for praise from an other-sex evaluator. *Personality and Social Psychology Bulletin, 10,* 43–50.

Major, B., Spencer, S., Schmader, T., Wolfe, C., & Crocker, J. (1998). Coping with negative stereotypes about intellectual performance: The role of psychological disengagement. *Personality and Social Psychology Bulletin, 24,* 34–50.

Mäkelä, K. (1997). Drinking, the majority fallacy, cognitive dissonance and social pressure. *Addiction, 92,* 729–736.

Malamuth, N. M. (1998). The confluence model as an organizing framework for research on sexually aggressive men: Risk moderators, imagined aggression, and pornography consumption. In R. G. Geen & E. Donnerstein (Eds.), *Human aggression: Theories, research, and implications for social policy.* San Diego: Academic Press.

Malcangi, G. (1997). *Evelyn's hearing.* [Online]. Available: http://www.evelyn.co.uk/hearing.htm

Malott, R. W. (1994). From the tabula rasa to murder, massacre, and genocide. *The ADA International Newsletter, 17*(4), 10.

Mandler, G. (1984). *Mind and body: Psychology of emotion and stress.* New York: W. W. Norton.

Mangels, J. A. (1997). Strategic processing and memory for temporal order in patients with frontal lobe lesions. *Neuropsychology, 11,* 207-221.

Mann, L. (1981). The baiting crowd in episodes of threatened suicide. *Journal of Personality and Social Psychology, 41,* 703–709.

Manning, B. (1967). "Pre-imaginal conditioning" in Drosophila." *Nature, 216,* 338–340.

Manson, S. M. (1994). Culture and depression: Discovering variations in the experience of illness. In W. J. Lonner & R. S. Malpass (Eds.), *Psychology and culture.* Boston: Allyn & Bacon.

Mäntylä, T. (1986). Optimizing cue effectiveness: Recall of 500 and 600 incidentally learned words. *Journal of Experimental Psychology: Learning, Memory, and Cognition, 12,* 66–71.

Mäntylä, T. N., & Nilsson, L. G. (1997). Remembering to remember in adulthood: A population-based study on aging and prospective memory. *Aging, Neuropsychology, and Cognition, 4,* 81–92.

Mäntylä, T., & Nilsson, L. G. (1988). Cue distinctiveness and forgetting: Effectiveness of self-generated retrieval cues in delayed recall. *Journal of Experimental Psychology: Learning, Memory, and Cognition, 14,* 502–509.

Mantzoros, C., Flier, J. S., Lesem, M. D., Brewerton, T. D., & Jimerson, D. C. (1997). Cerebrospinal fluid leptin in anorexia nervosa: Correlation with nutritional status and potential role in resistance to weight gain. *The Journal of Clinical Endocrinology and Metabolism, 82,* 1845–1851.

Manuck, S. F., Flory, J. D., McCaffery, J. M., Matthews, K. A., Mann, J. J., & Muldoon, M. F. (1998). Aggression, impulsivity, and central nervous system serotonergic responsivity in a nonpatient sample. *Neuropsychopharmacology, 19,* 287–299.

Marcia, J. E. (1966). Development and validation of ego identity status. *Journal of Personality and Social Psychology, 3,* 551–558.

Marcia, J. E. (1994). The empirical study of ego identity. In H. A. Bosma, T. L. G. Graafsma, H. D. Grotevant, & D. J. de Levita (Eds.), *Identity and development: An interdisciplinary approach.* Thousand Oaks, CA: Sage Publications.

Marek, G. (1982). Toscanini's memory. In U. Neisser (Ed.), *Memory observed.* San Francisco: W. H. Freeman.

Margolin, G., & Gordis, E. B. (2000). The effects of family and community violence on children. *Annual Review of Psychology, 51,* 445–480.

Margolin, G., & Wampold, B. E. (1981). Sequential analysis of conflict and accord in distressed and nondistressed marital partners. *Journal of Consulting and Clinical Psychology, 49,* 554–567.

Markovitz, H., & Nantel, G. (1989). The belief-bias effect in the production and evaluation of logical conclusions. *Memory and Cognition, 17,* 11–17.

Marks, D., Murray, M., Evans, B., & Willig, C. (2000). *Health psychology: Theory, research, and practice.* Thousand Oaks, CA: Sage Publications.

Marks, I. M. (1991). Self-administered behavioural treatment. *Behavioural Psychotherapy, 19,* 42–46.

Marks, I. M. (1977). Phobias and obsessions: Clinical phenomena in search of laboratory models. In J. Maser & M. E. P. Seligman (Eds.), *Psychopathology: Experimental models.* San Francisco: W. H. Freeman.

Markus, H., & Nurius, P. (1986). Possible selves. *American Psychologist. 41,* 954–969.

Markus, H., & Oyserman, D. (1989). Gender and thought: The role of the self-concept. In M. Crawford & M. Gentry (Eds.), *Gender and thought: Psychological perspectives.* New York: Springer-Verlag.

Markus, H. R., & Kitayama, S. (1991). Culture and the self: Implications for cognition, emotion, and motivation. *Psychological Review, 98,* 224–253.

Marlatt, G. A. (1987). Alcohol, the magic elixir: Stress, expectancy, and the transformation of emotional states. In E. Gottheil, K. A. Druley, S. Pashko, & S. P. Weinstein (Eds.), *Stress and addiction.* New York: Brunner/Mazel.

Marlatt, G. A. (1996). Taxonomy of high-risk situations for alcohol relapse: Evolution and development of a cognitive-behavioral model. *Addiction, 91* (Suppl.), S37–S49.

Marlatt, G. A. (Ed.) (1998). *Harm reduction: Pragmatic strategies for managing high-risk behaviors.* New York: Guilford Press.

Marlatt, G. A., Baer, J. S. et al. (1998). Screening and brief intervention for high-risk college student drinkers: Results from a 2-year follow-up assessment. *Journal of Consulting and Clinical Psychology, 66,* 604–615.

Marlatt, G. A., Demming, B., & Reid, J. B. (1973). Loss of control drinking in alcoholics: An experimental analogue. *Journal of Abnormal Psychology, 81,* 233–241.

Marlatt, G. A., & Gordon, J. R. (1985). *Relapse prevention: Maintenance strategies in the treatment of addiction.* New York: Guilford Press.

Marlatt, G. A., & Kaplan, B. E. (1972). Self-initiated attempts to change behavior: A study of New Year's resolutions. *Psychological Reports, 30,* 123–131.

Marlatt, G. A., & VandenBos, G. R. (Eds.) (1997). *Addictive behaviors: Readings on etiology, prevention and treatment.* Washington, DC: American Psychological Association.

Marler, P. (1970). A comparative approach to vocal learning: Song development in white-crowned sparrows. *Journal of Comparative and Physiological Psychology, 71,* 1–25.

Marschark, M., & Mayer, T. S. (1998). Interactions of language and memory in deaf children and adults. *Scandinavian Journal of Psychology, 39,* 145–148.

Marsella, A. J. (1994, August). *Cross-cultural psychopathology: Foundations, issues, and directions.* Address presented at Annual Meeting of American Psychological Association, Los Angeles.

Marsella, A. J. (1998). Toward a "global-community psychology": Meeting the needs of a changing world. *American Psychologist, 53,* 1282–1291.

Marsh, H. W. (1990). A multidimensional, hierarchical model of self-concept: Theoretical and empirical justification. *Educational Psychology Review, 2,* 77–172.

Marsh, R. L., Hicks, J. L., & Landau, J. D. (1998). An investigation of everyday prospective memory. *Memory and Cognition, 26,* 633–643.

Marshall, G. N. (1991). A multidimensional analysis of internal health locus of control beliefs: Separating the wheat from the chaff? *Journal of Personality and Social Psychology, 61,* 483–491.

Marshall, L. H., & Magoun, H. W. (1997). *Discoveries in the human brain: Neuroscience prehistory, brain structure, and function.* New York: Humana Press.

Martin, G., & Pear, J. (1998). *Behavior modification: What it is and how to do it.* Paramus, NJ: Prentice Hall.

Martin, J. E., & Dubbert, P. M. (1985). Adherence in exercise. In R. I. Terjung (Ed.), *Exercise and sport sciences review* (Vol. 13). New York: Macmillan.

Martin, K. C., Bartsch, D., Bailey, C. H., & Kandel, E. R. (2000). Molecular mechanisms underlying learning-related long-lasting synaptic plasticity. In M. S. Gazzaniga (Ed.), *The new cognitive neurosciences* (2nd ed.). Cambridge, MA: MIT Press.

Martin, S. J., Grimwood, P. D., & Morris, G. M. (2000). Synaptic plasticity and memory: An evaluation of the hypothesis. *Annual Review of Neuroscience, 23,* 649–711.

Martinez, J. L., Jr., Barea-Rodriguez, E. J., & Derrick, B. E. (1998). Long-term potentiation, long-term depression, and learning. In J. L. Martinez, Jr., & R. P. Kesner (Eds.), *Neurobiology of learning and memory.* San Diego: Academic Press.

Maslow, A. H. (1954). *Motivation and personality.* New York: Harper.

Maslow, A. H. (1971). *The further reaches of human nature.* New York: Viking Press.

Masten, A. S., & Coatsworth, J. D. (1998). The development of competence in favorable and unfavorable environments: Lessons from research on successful children. *American Psychologist, 53,* 205–220.

Masters, W., & Johnson, V. (1966). *Human sexual response.* London: Churchill.

Masters, W. H., Johnson, V. E., & Kolodny, R. C. (1988). *Human Sexuality* (3rd ed.). Boston: Little, Brown.

Matson, J. L., & Gardner, W. I. (1991). Behavioral learning theory and current applications to severe behavior problems in persons with mental retardation. *Clinical Psychology Review, 11,* 175–183.

Matsumoto, D. (1994). *People: Psychology from a cultural perspective.* Pacific Grove, CA: Brooks/Cole.

Matsumoto, D., & Hull, P. (1994). Cognitive development and intelligence. In D. Matsumoto (Ed.), *People: Psychology from a cultural perspective,* Pacific Grove, CA: Brooks/Cole.

Matt, G. E., & Navarro, A. M. (1997). What meta-analyses have and have not taught us about psychotherapy effects. A review and future directions. *Clinical Psychology Review, 17,* 1–32.

Mattaini, M. A., Twyman, J. S., Chin, W., & Lee, K. N. (1996). Youth violence. In M. A. Mattaini & B. A. Thyer (Eds.), *Finding solutions to social problems: Behavioral strategies for change.* Washington, DC: American Psychological Association.

Matthews, K. (2000). Depression models. In G. Fink (Ed.), *Encyclopedia of stress.* San Diego: Academic Press.

Mauro, R., Sato, K., & Tucker, J. (1992). The role of appraisal in human emotions: A cross-cultural study. *Journal of Personality and Social Psychology, 62,* 301–317.

May, R. (1961). The emergence of existential psychology. In R. May (Ed.), *Existential psychology.* New York: Random House.

Mayer, J. D., & Salovey, P. (1997). What is emotional intelligence? In P. Salovey & D. J. Sluyter (Eds.), *Emotional development and emotional intelligence: Educational implications.* New York: Basic Books.

Mayes, L. C., Grillon, C., Granger, R., & Schottenfeld, R. (1998). Regulation of arousal and attention in preschool children exposed to cocaine prenatally. *Annals of the New York Academy of Sciences. 846,* 126–143.

Mayne, T. J., Norcross, J. C., & Sayette, M. A. (1994). Admission requirements, acceptance rates, and financial assistance in clinical psychology programs. *American Psychologist, 49,* 806–811.

McAdams, D. P., & deSt., Aubin (Eds.) (1998). *Generativity and adult development: How and why we care for the next generation.* Washington, DC: American Psychological Association.

McAdams, D. T. (1992). The five-factor model in personality: A critical appraisal. *Journal of Personality and Social Psychology, 60,* 329–361.

McAuley, E. (1992). The role of efficacy cognitions in the prediction of exercise behavior in middle-aged adults. *Journal of Behavioral Medicine, 15,* 65–88.

McCall, R. B. (1977). Childhood IQs as predictors of adult educational and occupational status. *Science, 1977,* 482–483.

McCall, W. V., & Edinger, J. D. (1992). Subjective total insomnia: An example of sleep state misperception. *Sleep, 15,* 71–73.

McCarley, R. W. (1998). Dreams: Disguise of forbidden wishes or transparent reflections of a distinct brain state? In R. M. Bilder & F. F. LeFever (Eds.), *Neuroscience of the mind on the centennial of Freud's Project for a Scientific Psychology: Annals of the New York Academy of Sciences* (Vol. 843). New York: New York Academy of Sciences.

McCarty, R., & Pacek, K. (2000). Alarm phase and general adaptation syndrome. In G. Fink (Ed.), *Encyclopedia of stress.* San Diego: Academic Press.

McClelland, D. C. (1989). *Human motivation.* New York: Cambridge University Press.

McClelland, D. C., Atkinson, J. W., Clark, R. A., & Lowell, E. L. (1953). *The achievement motive.* New York, Appleton-Century-Crofts.

McClelland, J. L., & Rumelhart, D. E. (1985). Distributed memory and the representation of general and specific information. *Journal of Experimental Psychology: General, 114,* 159–188.

McClintock, M. K. (1971). Menstrual synchrony and suppression. *Nature, 229,* 244–245.

McConnell, J. V. (1962). Memory transfer through cannibalism in planarians. *Journal of Neuropsychiatry, 3* (Suppl. 1), 542–548.

McCoy, D. F., Roszman, T. L., Miller, J. S., Kelly, K. S., & Titus, M. J. (1986). Some parameters of conditioned immunosuppression. Species difference and CS-US delay. *Physiology and Behavior, 36,* 731–736.

McCracken, L. M. (1998). Learning to live with pain: Acceptance of pain predicts adjustment in persons with chronic pain. *Pain, 74,* 21–27.

McCrae, R. R., & Costa, P. T. (1990). *Personality in adulthood.* New York: Guilford Press.

McCrae, R. R., & Costa, P. T. (1999). The five-factor model of personality. In L. A. Pervin & O. P. John (Eds.), *Handbook of personality: Theory and research.* New York: Guilford Press.

McCullough, M. E., Worthington, E. L., Jr., & Rachal, Kenneth C. (1997). Interpersonal forgiving in close relationships. *Journal of Personality and Social Psychology, 73,* 321–336.

McCusker, C. G., & Brown, K. (1990). Alcohol-predictive cues enhance tolerance to and precipitate "craving" for alcohol in social drinkers. *Journal of Studies on Alcohol, 51,* 494–499.

McDaniel, M. A., & Einstein, G. O. (1993). The importance of cue familiarity and cue distinctiveness in prospective memory. *Memory, 1,* 23–41.

McDaniel, M. A., Glisky, E. L., Guynn, M. J., & Routhieaux, B. C. (1999). Prospective memory: A neuropsychological study. *Neuropsychology, 13,* 103-110.

McDermott, P. A., & Weiss, R. V. (1995). A normative typology of healthy, subclinical, and clinical behavior styles among American children and adolescents. *Psychological Assessment, 7,* 162–170.

McFarland, P. T., & Christensen, A. (2000). Marital conflict. In G. Fink (Ed.), *Encyclopedia of stress.* San Diego: Academic Press.

McGinty, D. (1993). Energy conservation. In M. A. Carskadon (Ed.), *Encyclopedia of sleep and dreaming.* New York: Macmillan.

McGinty, D. J., & Sterman, M. B. (1968). Sleep suppression after basal forebrain lesions in the cat. *Science, 160,* 1253–1255.

McGlaskan, T. H., & Fenton, W. S. (1992). The positive-negative distinction in schizophrenia: Review of natural history validators. *Archives of General Psychiatry, 49,* 63–72.

McGregor, D. (1960). *The human side of enterprise.* New York: McGraw-Hill.

McIntosh, D. N., Silver, R. C., & Wortman, C. B. (1993). Religion's role in adjustment to a negative life event: Coping with the loss of a child. *Journal of Personality and Social Psychology, 65,* 812–821.

McIntosh, D. N., Zajonc, R. B., Vig, P. S., & Emerick, S. W. (1997). Facial movement, breathing, temperature, and affect: Implications of the vascular theory of emotional efference. *Cognition and Emotion, 11*(2), 171–195.

McKey, R. H., Condelli, L., Ganson, H., Barrett, B. J., McConkey, C., & Platz, M. C. (1985). *The impact of Head Start on children, families, and communities.* Department of Health and Human Services Publication OHDS 90-31193. Washington, DC: U.S. Government Printing Office.

McMillan, T. M., Robertson, I. H., & Wilson, B. A. (1999). Neurogenesis after brain injury: Implications for neurorehabilitation. *Neuropsychological Rehabilitation, 9,* 129–133.

McNatt, D. B. (2000). Ancient Pygmalion joins contemporary management: A meta-analysis of the result. *Journal of Applied Psychology, 85,* 314–322.

McNeil, E. B. (1967). *The quiet furies: Man and disorder.* Englewood Cliffs, NJ: Prentice Hall.

Meacham, J. A., & Singer, J. (1977). Incentive effects in prospective memory. *Journal of Psychology, 97,* 191–197.

Mead, M. (1935). *Sex and temperament in three primitive societies.* New York: Morrow.

Meaney, M. J., Mitchell, J. B., Aitken, D. H., & Bhatnagar, S. (Eds.) (1991). The effects of neonatal handling on the development of the adrenocortical response to stress: Implications for neuropathology and cognitive deficits in later life. *Psychoneuroendocrinology, 16,* 85–103.

Meddis, R., Pearson, A. J., & Langford, G. (1973). An extreme case of healthy insomnia.

Electroencephalography and Clinical Neurophysiology, 35, 213–214.

Medin, D. L., & Coley, J. D. (1998). Concepts and categorization. In H. Julian et al. (Eds.), *Perception and cognition at century's end. Handbook of perception and cognition* (2nd ed.). San Diego: Academic Press.

Medin, D. L., Lynch, E. B., & Solomon, K. O. (2000). Are there kinds of concepts? *Annual Review of Psychology, 51,* 121–147.

Meehl, P. E. (1995). "Is psychoanalysis one science, two sciences, or no science at all? A discourse among friendly antagonists": Comment. *Journal of the American Psychoanalytic Association, 43,* 1015–1023.

Meeus, W. H. J., & Raaijmakers, Q. A. W. (1986). Administrative obedience: Carrying out orders to use psychological-administrative violence. *European Journal of Social Psychology, 16,* 311–324.

Meeus, W. H. J., & Raaijmakers, Q. A. W. (1995). Obedience in modern society: The Utrecht studies. *Journal of Social Issues, 51,* 155–175.

Megargee, E. I. (1966). Undercontrolled and overcontrolled personality types in extreme anti-social aggression. *Psychological Monographs, 80* (Whole No. 611).

Mehnert, T., Krauss, H. H., Nadler, R., & Boyd, M. (1990). Correlates of life satisfaction in those with disabling conditions. *Rehabilitation Psychology, 35,* 3–17.

Meichenbaum, D. (1985). *Stress inoculation training.* New York: Pergamon.

Meier, R. P. (1991). Language acquisition by deaf children. *American Scientist, 79,* 61–70.

Meilman, P. W. (1979). Cross-sectional age changes in ego identity status during adolescence. *Developmental Psychology, 15,* 230–231.

Meltzoff, A. N. (1988). Infant imitation and memory: Nine-month-olds in immediate and deferred tests. *Child Development, 59,* 217–225.

Meltzoff, A. N., & Moore, M. K. (1977). Imitation of facial and manual gestures by human neonates. *Science, 198,* 75–78.

Meltzoff, A. N., & Moore, M. K. (1999). A new foundation for cognitive development in infancy: The birth of the representational infant. In E. K. Scholnick, K. Nelson, S. A. Gelman, & P. H. Miller (Eds.), *Conceptual development: Piaget's legacy.* Mahwah, NJ: Erlbaum.

Melzack, R. (1998). Pain and stress. Clues toward understanding chronic pain. In M. Sabourin et al. (Eds.), *Advances in psychological science.* Hove, England: Psychology Press/Erlbaum.

Mendelson, W. B. (2000). Sleep-inducing effects of adenosine microinjections into the medial preoptic area are blocked by flumazenil. *Brain Research, 852,* 479–481.

Menon, U., & Schweder, R. A. (1994). Cultural psychology and the power of shame in Orissa, India. In S. Kitayama & H. Markus (Eds.), *Emotion and culture.* Washington, DC: American Psychological Association.

Menzies, R. G., & Clarke, J. C. (1995). The etiology of acrophobia and its relationship to severity and individual response patterns. *Behaviour Research and Therapy, 33,* 795–803.

Meredith, N. (1986). Testing the talking cure. *Science, 232,* 31–37.

Merikle, P. M., & Daneman, M. (1998). Psychological investigations of unconscious perception. *Journal of Consciousness Studies, 5,* 5–18.

Mersch, P. P. A., Middendorp, H. M., Bouhuys, A. L., Beersma, D. G. M., & van den Hoofdakker, R. H. (1999). Seasonal affective disorder and latitude: A review of the literature. *Journal of Affective Disorders, 53,* 35-48.

Mershon, B., & Gorsuch, R. L. (1988). Number of factors in the personality sphere: Does increase in factors increase predictability of real-life criteria. *Journal of Personality and Social Psychology, 55,* 675–680.

Messenger, J. C. (1971). Sex and repression in an Irish folk community. In D. S. Marshall & R. C. Suggs (Eds.), *Human sexual behavior.* Englewood Cliffs, NJ: Prentice Hall.

Metcalfe, J., & Mischel, W. (1999). A hot/cool-system analysis of delay of gratification: Dynamics of willpower. *Psychological Review, 106,* 3–19.

Methot, L. L., & Heuitema, B. E. (1998). Effects of signal probability on individual differences in vigilance. *Human Factors, 40,* 78–90.

Meyer, C. B., & Taylor, S. E. (1986). Adjustment to rape. *Journal of Personality and Social Psychology, 50,* 1226–1234.

Meyer, R. G., & Osborne, Y. H. (1987). *Case studies in abnormal behavior* (2nd ed.). Boston: Allyn & Bacon.

Meyer, T. A., Svirsky, M. A., Kirk, K. I., & Miyamoto, R. T. (1998). Improvements in speech perception by children with profound prelingual hearing loss: Effects of device, communication mode, and chronological age. *Journal of Speech, Language, & Hearing Research, 41,* 846–858.

Michael, R. T., Gagnon, J. H., Laumman, E. O., & Kolata, G. (1994). *Sex in America: A definitive survey.* Boston: Little, Brown.

Michaels, J. W., Blommel, J. M., Brocato, R. M., Linkous, R. A., & Rowe, J. S. (1982). Social facilitation and inhibition in a natural setting. *Replications in Social Psychology, 2,* 21–24.

Middlebrooks, J. C., & Green, D. M. (1991). Sound localization by human listeners. *Annual Review of Psychology, 42,* 135–159.

Mignot, E. (1998). Genetic and familial aspects of narcolepsy. *Neurology, 50,* S16–S22.

Miles, C., & Hardman, E. (1998). State dependent memory produced by aerobic exercise. *Ergonomics, 41,* 20–28.

Miles, H. L., Mitchell, R. W., & Harper, S. E. (1996). Simon says: The development of imitation in an enculturated orangutan. In A. E. Russon, K. A. Bard, & A. Kim (Eds.), *Reaching into thought: The minds of the great apes.* Cambridge, England: Cambridge University Press.

Milgram, S. (1974). *Obedience to authority: An experimental view.* New York: Harper & Row.

Millar, M. G., & Millar, K. U. (1996). The effects of direct and indirect experience on affective and cognitive responses and the attitude-behavior relation. *Journal of Experimental Social Psychology, 32,* 561–579.

Miller, A. G. (1986). *The obedience experiments: A case study of controversy in social science.* New York: Praeger.

Miller, C. T., & Downey, K. T. (1999). A meta-analysis of heavyweight and self-esteem.

Personality and Social Psychology Review, 3, 68–84.

Miller, G. A. (1956). The magical number seven, plus or minus two: Some limits on our capacity for processing information. *Psychological Review, 63,* 81–97.

Miller, J. D., Morin, L. P., Schwartz, W. J., & Moore, R. Y. (1996). New insights into the mammalian circadian clock. State of the art review. *Sleep, 19,* 641–667.

Miller, J. G. (1984). Culture and the development of everyday social explanation. *Journal of Personality and Social Psychology, 46,* 961–978.

Miller, J. G., Bersoff, D. M., & Harwood, R. L. (1990). Perceptions of social responsibility in India and in the United States: Moral imperatives or personal decisions? *Journal of Personality and Social Psychology, 58,* 33–47.

Miller, K. F., & Stigler, J. F. (1987). Counting in Chinese: Cultural variation in a basic cognitive skill. *Cognitive Development. 2,* 279–305.

Miller, K. J., Gleaves, D. H., Hirsch, T. G., Green, B. A., Snow, A. C., & Corbett, C. C. (2000). Comparisons of body image dimensions by race/ethnicity and gender in a university population. *International Journal of Eating Disorders, 27,* 310–316.

Miller, L., & Budd, J. (1999). The development of occupational sex-role stereotypes, occupational preferences and academic subject preferences in children at ages 8, 12, and 16. *Educational Psychology, 19,* 17–35.

Miller, L. C. (1990). Intimacy and liking: Mutual influence and the role of unique relationships. *Journal of Personality and Social Psychology, 59,* 50–60.

Miller, L. K. (1999). The Savant Syndrome: Intellectual impairment and exceptional skill. *Psychological Bulletin, 125,* 31–46.

Miller, N. E. (1944). Experimental studies of conflict. In J. McV Hunt (Ed.), *Personality and the behavior disorders* (Vol. 1). New York: Ronald Press.

Miller, S. D., Blackburn, T., Scholes, G., White, G. L., & Mamales, N. (1991). Optical differences in multiple personality disorder: A second look. *Journal of Nervous and Mental Disease, 179,* 132–135.

Miller, T. Q. (2000). Type A behavior. In G. Fink (Ed.), *Encyclopedia of stress.* San Diego: Academic Press.

Miller, W. R. (1996). Motivational interviewing: Research, practice, and puzzles. *Addictive Behaviors, 21,* 835–842.

Miller, W. R., & Brown, S. A. (1997). Why psychologists should treat alcohol and drug problems. *American Psychologist, 52,* 1269–1279.

Miller, W. R., & Rollnick, S. (1991). *Motivational interviewing: Preparing people to change addictive behavior.* New York: Guilford Press.

Millman, J., Bishop, C. H., & Ebel, R. (1965). An analysis of testwiseness. *Educational and Psychological Measurement, 25,* 707–726.

Millon, T., Simonsen, E., Birket-Smith, M., & Davis, R. D. (Eds). *Psychopathy: Antisocial, criminal and violent behavior.* New York: Guilford Press.

Milner, B. (1965). Memory disturbances after bilateral hippocampal lesions. In P. Milner & S. Glickman (Eds.), *Cognitive processes and the brain.* Princeton, NJ: D. Van Nostrand.

Milner, B. R. (1970). Memory and medial temporal regions of the brain. In K. H. Pribram & D. R. Broadbent (Eds.), *Biology of memory.* Orlando, FL: Academic Press.

Milner, B., Corkin, S., & Teuber, H. L. (1968). Further analysis of the hippocampal syndrome: 14-year follow-up study of H. M. *Neuropsychologia, 6,* 215-234.

Milrod, B., Busch, F., Cooper, A., & Shapiro, T. (1997). *Manual of panic-focused psychodynamic psychotherapy.* Washington, DC: American Psychiatric Press.

Miltenberger, R. G., Fuqua, R. W., & Woods, D. W. (1998). Applying behavior analysis to clinical problems: Review and analysis of habit reversal. *Journal of Applied Behavior Analysis, 31,* 447-469.

Milton, J., & Wiseman, R. (1999). Does psi exist? Lack of replication of an anomalous process of information transfer. *Psychological Bulletin, 125,* 387-391.

Mineka, S., & Cook, M. (1993). Mechanisms involved in the observational conditioning of fear. *Journal of Experimental Psychology: General, 122,* 23-38.

Mineka, S., Davidson, M., Cook, M., & Kier, R. (1984). Observational conditioning of snake fear in rhesus monkeys. *Journal of Abnormal Psychology, 93,* 355-372.

Mineka, S., Watson, D., & Clark, L. A. (1998). Comorbidity of anxiety and unipolar mood disorder. *Annual Review of Psychology, 49,* 377-412.

Mineka, S., & Zinbarg, R. (1998). Experimental approaches to the anxiety and mood disorders. In J. G. Adair, D. Belanger, & K. L. Dion (Eds.), *Advances in psychological science, Vol. 1: Social, personal, and cultural aspects.* Hove, England: Psychology Press/Erlbaum.

Minuchin, S. (1974). *Families and family therapy.* Cambridge, MA: Harvard University Press.

Mischel, W. (1984). Convergences and challenges in the search for consistency. *American Psychologist, 39,* 351-364.

Mischel, W. (1999). Personality coherence and dispositions in a cognitive-affective processing system (CAPS) approach. In D. Cervone and Y. Shoda (Eds.), *The coherence of personality: Social-cognitive bases of consistency, variability, and organization.* New York: Guilford Press.

Mischel, W., Ebbesen, E. B., & Raskoff, Z. A. (1972). Cognitive and attentional mechanisms in delay of gratification. *Journal of Personality and Social Psychology, 21,* 204-218.

Mischel, W., Shoda, Y., & Rodriguez, M. L. (1989). Delay of gratification in children. *Science, 244*(4907), 933-938.

Misumi, J. (1985). *The behavioral science of leadership: An interdisciplinary Japanese research program.* Ann Arbor, MI: University of Michigan Press.

Mitler, M. M., Carskadon, M. A., Czeisler, C. A., Dement, W. C., Dinges, D. F. & Graeber, R. C. (1988). Catastrophes, sleep, and public policy: Consensus report. *Sleep, 11*(1), 100-109.

Money, J. (1987). Sin, sickness or status. *American Psychologist, 42,* 384-399.

Monk, T. H., Folkard, S., Wedderburn, A. I. (1996). Maintaining safety and high performance on shiftwork. *Applied Ergonomics, 27,* 17-23.

Monroe, S. M., & Peterman, A. M. (1988). Life stress and psychopathology. In L. H. Cohen (Ed.), *Life events and psychological functioning: Theoretical and methodological issues.* Newbury Park, CA: Sage Publications.

Monti, P. M., & Smith, N. F. (1976). Residual fear of the conditioned stimulus as a function of response prevention after avoidance or classical defensive conditioning in the rat. *Journal of Experimental Psychology: General, 105,* 148-162.

Moody, M. S. (1997). Changes in scores on the Mental Rotations Test during the menstrual cycle. *Perceptual and Motor Skills, 84,* 955-961.

Moon, C., & Fifer, W. P. (1990). Syllables as signals for 2-day-old infants. *Infant Behavior and Development, 13,* 377-390.

Moore, L. P., Moore, J. W., & Hauck, W. E. (1982). Conditioning children's attitudes toward alcohol, smoking, and drugs. *Journal of Experimental Education, 50,* 154-158.

Moorhead, G., Ference, R., & Neck, C. P. (1991). Group decision fiascoes continue: Space shuttle Challenger and a revised groupthink framework. *Human Relations, 44,* 539-550.

Moreland, J. L., Dansereau, D. F., & Chmielewski, T. L. (1997). Recall of descriptive information: The roles of presentation format, annotation strategy, and individual differences. *Contemporary Educational Psychology, 22,* 521-533.

Morey, L. C. (1988). Personality disorders in DSM-III and DSM-III-R: Convergence, coverage, and internal consistency. *American Journal of Psychiatry, 145,* 573-577.

Morgenstern, J., Labouvie, E., McCrady, B. S., Kahler, C. W., & Frey, R. M. (1997). Affiliation with Alcoholics Anonymous after treatment: A study of therapeutic effects and mechanisms of action. *Journal of Consulting and Clinical Psychology, 65,* 768-777.

Mori, D., Chaiken, S., & Pliner, P. (1987). "Eating lightly" and the self-presentation of femininity. *Journal of Personality and Social Psychology, 53,* 693-702.

Morrell, M. J., Dixen, J. M., Carter, C. S. & Davidson, J. M. (1984). The influence of age and cycling status on sexual arousability in women. *American Journal of Obstetrics and Gynecology, 148,* 66-71.

Morrell, R. W., Park, D. C., & Poon, L. W. (1989). Quality of instructions on prescription drug labels: Effects on memory and comprehension in young and old adults. *Gerontologist, 29,* 345-354.

Morris, D., Collett, P., Marsh, P., & O'Shaughnessy, M. (1979). *Gestures.* New York: Stein & Day.

Morris, J. S., Oehman, A., & Dolan, R. J. (1998). Conscious and unconscious emotional learning in the human amygdala. *Nature, 393*(6684), 467-470.

Morrison, D. C. (1988). Marine mammals join the navy. *Science, 242,* 1503-1504.

Morrison, D. R., & Coiro, M. J. (1999). Parental conflict and marital disruption: Do children benefit when high-conflict marriages are dissolved? *Journal of Marriage and the Family, 61,* 626-637.

Morrow, G. W., Roscoe, J. A., Kirshner, J. J., Hynes, H. E., & Rosenbluth, R. J. (1998). *Support Care Cancer, 6,* 244-247.

Morton, J., & Johnson, M. H. (1991). Conspec and Conlern: A two-process theory of infant face recognition. *Psychological Review, 98,* 164-181.

Moscovici, S. (1985). Social influence and conformity. In G. Lindzey & E. Aronson (Eds.), *Handbook of social psychology* (3rd ed.). New York: Random House.

Moscovici, S., & Zavalloni, M. (1969). The group as a polarizer of attitudes. *Journal of Personality and Social Psychology, 12,* 124-135.

Moss, C. S. (1972). *Recovery with aphasia.* Urbana: University of Illinois Press.

Moss, D. (Ed.) (1998). *Humanistic psychology: A historical and biographical sourcebook.* Westport, CT: Greenwood.

Motta, R. W., & Joseph, J. M. (2000). Group intelligence tests. In G. Goldstein & M. Hersen (Eds.), *Handbook of psychological assessment* (3rd ed.). New York: Elsevier.

Mowrer, O. H. (1947). On the dual nature of learning: A reinterpretation of "conditioning" and "problem solving." *Harvard Educational Review, 17,* 102-150.

Mowrer, R. R., Krug, D. E., & Klein, S. B. (1988). Backward second-order conditioning in flavor aversion learning. *Psychological Record, 38,* 259-269.

Muchinsky, P. M. (1997). *Psychology applied to work* (5th ed.). Pacific Grove, CA: Brooks/Cole.

Muchinsky, P. M. (2000). *Psychology applied to work* (6th ed.). Pacific Grove, CA: Brooks/Cole.

Mullen, B., Anthony, T., Salas, E., & Driskell, J. E. (1994). Group cohesiveness and quality of decision making: An integration of tests of the groupthink hypothesis. *Small Group Research, 25,* 189-204.

Mumme, D. L., Fernald, A., & Herrera, C. (1996). Infants' responses to facial and vocal emotional signals in a social referencing paradigm. *Child Development, 67,* 3229-3237.

Munoz, R. F., Mrazek, P. J., & Haggerty, R. J. (1996). Institute of Medicine Report on Prevention of Mental Disorders. Summary and commentary. *American Psychologist, 51,* 1116-1122.

Murdoch, H. (1984). Maternal rubella: The implications. *AEP Association of Educational Psychologists Journal, 6,* 3-6.

Murray, J. B. (1995). Evidence for acupuncture's analgesic effectiveness and proposals for the physiological mechanisms involved. *Journal of Psychology, 129,* 443-461.

Myers, D. G. (2000). The funds, friends, and faith of happy people. *American Psychologist, 55,* 56-67.

Myers, D. G., & Diener, E. (1995). Who is happy? *Psychological Science, 6,* 10-19.

Na, E. Y., & Loftus, E. F. (1998). Attitudes toward law and prisoners, conservative authoritarianism, attribution, and internal-external locus of control: Korean and American law students and undergraduates. *Journal of Cross Cultural Psychology, 29,* 595-615.

Nadelson, C. C., & Reinburg, C. E. (Eds.) (1999). *Schizophrenia: Losing touch with reality.* Broomall, England: Chelsea House.

Nadler, A., & Ben-Slushan, D. (1989). Forty years later: Long-term consequences of massive traumatization as manifested by holocaust survivors from the city and the Kibbutz. *Journal of Consulting and Clinical Psychology, 57*, 287–293.

Nakayama, K., & Tyler, C. W. (1981). Psychophysical isolation of movement sensitivity by removal of familiar position cues. *Vision Research, 21*, 427–433.

Natale, V., & Lorenzetti, R. (1997). Influences of morningness-eveningness and time of day on narrative comprehension. *Personality and Individual Differences, 23*, 685–690.

Nathan, P. E. (1985). Aversion therapy in the treatment of alcoholism: Success and failure. *Annals of the New York Academy of Sciences, 443*, 357–364.

Nathan, P. E. (1997). Substance use disorders in the DSM-IV. In G. A. Marlatt & G. R. VandenBos (Eds.), *Addictive behaviors: Readings on etiology, prevention and treatment.* Washington, DC: American Psychological Association.

National Center for Health Statistics (1995). *Healthy people 2000.* Washington, DC: Author.

National Center for Health Statistics (1996). *Health, United States, 1995.* Hyattsville, MD: U.S. Public Health Service.

National Highway Traffic Safety Administration (2000). *Traffic Safety Facts 1998: Alcohol* (DOT HS 808 950). [Online]. PDF file available: http://www.nhtsa.dot.gov/people/ncsa/factsheet.html.

National Sleep Foundation (2000). *2000 omnibus sleep in America poll* [Online]. Available: http://www.sleepfoundation.org/publications/2000poll.html#9

National Task Force on the Prevention and Treatment of Obesity (1994). Weight cycling. *Journal of the American Medical Association, 272*, 1196-1202.

National Television Violence Study (Vol. 3) (1998). Thousand Oaks, CA: Sage Publications. Author.

National Transportation Safety Board (NTSB) (1979, June). *Aircraft accident report* (NTSB-AAR-79-7). Washington. DC: NTSB Bureau of Accident Investigations.

National Weight Control Registry. (2000). [On-line]. Available: http://www.uchsc.edu/nutrition/nwcr.htm

Natsoulas, T. (1999). An ecological and phenomenological perspective on consciousness and perception: Contact with the world at the very heart of the being of consciousness. *Review of General Psychology, 3*, 224–245.

Naveh, B. M., & Jonides, J. (1984). Cognitive load and maintenance rehearsal. *Journal of Verbal Learning and Verbal Behavior, 23*, 494–507.

Nayak, A., Zastrow, D. J., Lickteig, R., Zahniser, N. R., & Browning, M. D. (1998). Maintenance of late-phase LTP is accompanied by PKA-dependent increase in AMPA receptor synthesis. *Nature, 394*, 680–683.

Nederhof, A. J. (1985). Methods of coping with social desirability bias: A review. *European Journal of Social Psychology, 15*, 263–280.

Neiderhiser, J. M., Reiss, D., Hetherington, E. M., & Plomin, R. (1999). Relationships between parenting and adolescent adjustment over time: Genetic and environmental contributions. *Developmental Psychology, 35*, 680, 692.

Neimeyer, R. A., & Raskin, J. D. (Eds.) (2000). *Constructions of disorder: Meaning-making frameworks for psychotherapy.* Washington, DC: American Psychological Association.

Neisser, U., Bouchard, T. J., Jr., Boykin, A. W., Brody, N., Ceci, S. J., Halpern, D. F., Loehlin, J. C., Perloff, R., Sternberg, R. J., & Urbina, S. (1998). Intelligence: Knowns and unknowns. In M. E. Hertzig, E. A. Farber et al. (Eds.), *Annual progress in child psychiatry and child development: 1997.* Bristol, PA: Brunner/Mazel.

Neisser, U., & Harsch, N. (1993). Phantom flashbulbs: False recollections of hearing the news about Challenger. In E. Winograd & U. Neisser (Eds.), *Affect and accuracy in recall: Studies of "flashbulb" memories.* New York: Cambridge University Press.

Nelson, C. A., Monk, C. S., Lin, J., Carver, L. J., Thomas, K. M., & Truwit, C. L. (2000). Functional neuroanatomy of spatial working memory in children. *Developmental Psychology, 36*, 109–116.

Nelson, F. V., Zimmerman, L., Barnason, S., Nieveen, J., & Schmaderer, M. (1998). The relationship and influence of anxiety on postoperative pain in the coronary artery bypass graft patient. *Journal of Pain and Symptom Management, 15*, 102–109.

Nemiah, J. C. (1978). Psychoneurotic disorders. In A. M. Nicholi (Ed.), *Harvard guide to modern psychiatry.* Cambridge, MA: Harvard University Press.

Nesbitt, E. B. (1973). An escalator phobia overcome in one session of flooding in vivo. *Journal of Behavior Therapy and Experimental Psychiatry, 4*, 405–406.

Neugarten, B. L. (1979). Time, age, and the life cycle. *American Journal of Psychiatry, 136*, 887–894.

Neugarten, B. L., & Hall, E. (1980, April). Acting one's age: New roles for old. *Psychology Today*, pp. 66–80.

Neumäker, K. J. (2000). Mortality rates and causes of death. *European Eating Disorders Review, 8*, 181–187.

New York Times (1999, January 30). Driver on Long Island saves a woman trapped in her burning car. *New York Times*, p. B2.

Newcomb, M. D., & Harlow, L. L. (1986). Life events and substance use among adolescents: Mediating effects of perceived loss of control and meaninglessness in life. *Journal of Personality and Social Psychology, 51*, 564–577.

Newcomb, M. D., & McGee, L. (1991). Influence of sensation seeking on general deviance and specific problem behaviors from adolescence to young adulthood. *Journal of Personality and Social Psychology, 61*, 614–628.

Newcombe, N., & Fox, N. A. (1994). Infantile amnesia: Through a glass darkly. *Child Development, 65*, 31–40.

Newell, A., & Simon, H. A. (1972). *Human problem solving.* Englewood Cliffs, NJ: Prentice Hall.

Newlin, D. B., & Thomson, J. B. (1997). Alcohol challenge with sons of alcoholics: A critical review and analysis. In G. A. Marlatt & G. R. VandenBos (Eds.), *Addictive behaviors: Readings on etiology, prevention and treatment.* Washington, DC: American Psychological Association.

Newman, D. L., Caspi, A., Moffitt, T. E., & Silva, P. A. (1997). Antecedents of adult interpersonal functioning: Effects of individual differences in age 3 temperament. *Developmental Psychology, 33*, 206–217.

Newport, F. (1999, March 1). *Some change over time in American attitudes towards homosexuality, but negativity remains.* Gallup News Service. Princeton, NJ: Gallup Organization.

Newport, F. (1999, March 29). *Americans today much more accepting of a woman, Black, Catholic, or Jew as president.* Gallup News Service. Princeton, NJ: Gallup Organization.

Newport, F. (1999, May 10). *Media portrayals of violence seen by many as causes of real-life violence.* Gallup News Service. Princeton, NJ. Gallup Organization.

Nezami, E., & Butcher, J. N. (2000). Objective personality assessment. In G. Goldstein & M. Hersen (Eds.), *Handbook of psychological assessment* (3rd ed.). New York: Elsevier.

Nezlek, J. B., Hampton, C. P., & Shean, G. (2000). Clinical depression and day-to-day social interaction in a community sample. *Journal of Abnormal Psychology, 109*, 11–19.

Nezu, A. M., Nezu, C. M., & D'Zurilla (2000). Problem-solving skills training. In G. Fink (Ed.), *Encyclopedia of stress.* San Diego: Academic Press.

NICHD Early Child Care Research Network (1997). The effects of infant child care on infant-mother attachment security: Results of the NICHD study of early child care. *Child Development, 68*, 860–879.

NICHD Early Child Care Research Network (1999). Child care and mother-child interaction in the first three years of life. *Developmental Psychology, 35*, 1399–1413.

Nichter, M. & Vuckovic, N. (1994). Fat talk: Body image among adolescent girls. In N. Sault (Ed.), *Many mirrors: Body image and social relations.* New Brunswick, NJ: Rutgers University Press.

Nickerson, R. S., & Adams, M. J. (1979). Long term memory for a common object. *Cognitive Psychology, 11*, 287–307.

Nicks, S. D., Korn, J. H., & Mainieri, T. (1997). The rise and fall of deception in social psychology and personality research, 1921 to 1994. *Ethics and Behavior, 7*, 69–77.

Nigg, J. T., Lohr, N. E., Westen, D., & Gold, L. J. (1992). Malevolent object representation in borderline personality disorder and major depression. *Journal of Abnormal Psychology, 101*, 61–67.

Niles, S. (1998). Achievement goals and means: A cultural comparison. *Journal of Cross Cultural Psychology, 29*, 656–667.

Nisbett, R. E. (1998). Race, genetics, and IQ. In C. Jencks & M. Phillips et al. (Eds.), *The Black-White test score gap.* Washington DC: Brookings Institution.

Nishith, P., Mechanic, M. B., & Resick, P. A. (2000). Prior interpersonal trauma: The contribution to current PTSD symptoms in female rape victims. *Journal of Abnormal Psychology, 109*, 20–25.

Noble, E. P. (1998). The D_2 dopamine receptor gene: A review of association studies in alcoholism and phenotypes. *Alcohol, 16*, 33–45.

Noble, R. E. (1997). The incidence of parental obesity in overweight individuals. *International Journal of Eating Disorders, 22*, 265–271.

Nolen-Hoeksema, S. (1990). *Sex differences in depression.* Stanford, CA: Stanford University Press.

Nolen-Hoeksema, S., & Morrow, J. (1991). A prospective study of depression and post-traumatic stress symptoms following a natural disaster: The 1989 Loma Prieta earthquake. *Journal of Personality and Social Psychology, 61,* 115–121.

Noll, S. M., & Fredrickson, B. L. (1998). A mediational model linking self-objectification, body shame, and disordered eating. *Psychology of Women Quarterly, 22,* 623–636.

Nolte, J. (1998). *The human brain: An introduction to its functional anatomy.* St. Louis: Mosby.

Norcross, J. C. (1991). Prescriptive matching in psychotherapy: An introduction. *Psychotherapy, 28,* 439–443.

Norcross, J. C., Karg-Bray, R. S., & Prochaska, J. O. (1995). *Clinical psychologists in the 1990s.* Unpublished manuscript, University of Scranton.

Norcross, J. C., Ratzin, A. C., & Payne, D. (1989). Ringing in the New Year: The change processes and reported outcomes of resolutions. *Addictive Behaviors, 14,* 205–212.

Normann, R. A. (1995). Visual neuroprosthetics—functional vision for the blind. *IEEE Engineering in Medicine and Biology, 14,* 77–83.

Normann, R. A., Maynard, E. M., Guillory, K. S., & Warren, D. J. (1996). Cortical implants for the blind. *IEEE Spectrum, 33,* 54–59.

Norris, J. (1994). Alcohol and female sexuality: A look at expectancies and risks. *Alcohol Health and Research World, 18,* 197–201.

North, M. M., North, S. M., & Coble, J. R. (1997). Virtual reality therapy for fear of flying. *American Journal of Psychiatry, 154,* 130.

Norton, G. R., Harrison, B., Haunch, J., & Rhodes, L. (1985). Characteristics of people with infrequent panic attacks. *Abnormal Psychiatry, 94,* 216–221.

Nossal, C. J. V., & Hall, F. (1995). Choices following antigen entry: Antibody formation or immunologic tolerance? *Annual Review of Immunology, 13,* 171–204.

Novaco, R. (1975). *Anger control.* Lexington, MA: Lexington Books.

Noveck, J. (1997, August 4). Oldest person to ever live dies in France at 122. *Seattle Times.* p. A2.

Noyes, R., & Hoehn, S. R. (1999). *The anxiety disorders.* New York: Cambridge University Press.

Nyberg, L., Persson, J., Habib, R., Tulving, E., McIntosh, A. R., Cabeza, R., & Houle, S. (2000). Large scale neurocognitive networks underlying episodic memory. *Journal of Cognitive Neuroscience, 12,* 163-173.

Nye, R. D. (1992). *Three psychologies: Perspectives from Freud, Skinner, and Rogers* (4th ed.). Pacific Grove, CA: Brooks/Cole.

Oatley, K., & Jenkins, J. M. (1992). Human emotions: Function and dysfunction. *Annual Review of Psychology, 43,* 55–85.

O'Brien, C. P. (1997). Recent developments in the pharmacotherapy of substance abuse. In G. A. Marlatt & G. R. VandenBos (Eds.), *Addictive behaviors: Readings on etiology, prevention and treatment.* Washington, DC: American Psychological Association.

O'Connor, T. G., Deater, D. K., Fulker, D., Rutter, M., & Plomin, R. (1998). Genotype-environment correlations in late childhood and early adolescence: Antisocial behavioral problems and coercive parenting. *Developmental Psychology, 34,* 970–981.

O'Connor, T. G., Thorpe, K., Dunn, J., & Golding, J. (1999). Parental divorce and adjustment in adulthood: Findings from a community sample. *Journal of Child Psychology and Psychiatry and Allied Disciplines, 40,* 777–789.

O'Donnell, C. R. (1995). Firearm deaths among children and youth. *American Psychologist, 50,* 771–776.

O'Donohue, W., & Elliot, A. (1992). The current status of posttraumatic stress disorder as a diagnostic category: Problems and proposals. *Journal of Traumatic Stress, 5,* 421–439.

Ohayon, M. M., Guilleminault, C., & Priest, R. G. (1999). Night terrors, sleepwalking, and confusional arousals in the general population: Their frequency and relationship to other sleep and mental disorders. *Journal of Clinical Psychiatry, 60,* 268–276.

Ohbuchi, K., & Kambara, T. (1985). Attacker's intent and awareness of outcome, impression management, and retaliation. *Journal of Experimental Social Psychology, 21,* 321–330.

Öhman, A. (1993). Fear and anxiety as emotional phenomena: Clinical phenomenology, evolutionary perspectives, and information-processing mechanisms. In M. Lewis & J. M. Haviland (Eds.), *Handbook of emotions.* New York: Guilford Press.

Öhman, A. (2000). Anxiety. In G. Fink (Ed.), *Encyclopedia of stress.* San Diego: Academic Press.

Öhman, A., Fredrikson, M., & Hugdahl, K. (1978). Towards an experimental model for simple phobic reactions. *Behavioural Analysis and Modification, 2,* 97–114.

Öhman, A., & Soares, J. J. F. (1998). Emotional conditioning to masked stimuli: Expectancies for aversive outcomes following nonrecognized fear-relevant stimuli. *Journal of Experimental Psychology: General, 127,* 69–82.

Okawa, M., Nanami, T., Wada, S., Shimizu, T., & et al. (Eds.) (1987). Four congenitally blind children with circadian sleep-wake rhythm disorder. *Sleep, 10,* 101–110.

O'Keefe, D. J., & Figge, M. (1997). A guilt-based explanation of the door-in-the-face influence strategy. *Human Communication Research, 24,* 64–81.

Oldenburg, D. (1990, April 3). Hidden messages. *Washington Post,* p. C5.

Oldridge, N. B. (1984). Adherence to adult exercise fitness programs. In J. D. Matarzzo, Sh.M. Weiss, J. A. Herd, N. E. Miller, & St.M. Weiss (Eds.), *Behavioral health: A handbook of health enhancement and disease prevention.* New York: Wiley.

Olds, J. (1956). Pleasure centers in the brain. *Scientific American, 193,* 105–116.

Olds, J. (1958). Self-stimulation of the brain. *Science, 127,* 315–324.

O'Leary, K. D., & Wilson, G. T. (1987). *Behavior therapy: Application and outcome.* Englewood Cliffs, NJ: Prentice Hall.

Olness, K., & Ader, R. (1992). Conditioning as an adjunct in the pharmacotherapy of lupus erythematosus. *Journal of Developmental and Behavioral Pediatrics, 13,* 124–125.

Olson, E. J., Boeve, B. F., & Silber, M. H. (2000). Rapid eye movement sleep behaviour disorder: Demographic, clinical and laboratory findings in 93 cases. *Brain, 123,* 331–339.

Olson, J. M., & Zanna, M. P. (1991). Attitude change and attitude-behavior consistency. In R. M. Baron, W. G. Graziano, & C. Stangor (Eds.), *Social psychology.* Ft. Worth, TX: Holt, Rinehart & Winston.

Orbuch, T. L., House, J. S., Mero, R. P., & Webster, P. S. (1996). Marital quality over the life course. *Social Psychology Quarterly, 59,* 162–171.

Oren, D. A., & Terman, M. (1998). Tweaking the human circadian clock with light. *Science, 279,* 333–334.

Ormel, J., & Wohlforth, T. (1991). How neuroticism, long-term difficulties, and life situation change influence psychological distress. *Journal of Personality and Social Psychology, 60,* 744–755.

Orne, M. T. (1959). The nature of hypnosis: Artifact and essence. *Journal of Abnormal and Social Psychology, 58,* 277–299.

Orne, M. T. (1962). On the social psychology of the psychological experiment: With particular reference to demand characteristics and their implications. *American Psychologist, 17,* 776–783.

Orne, M. T., & Evans, F. J. (1965). Social control in the psychological experiment: Antisocial behavior and hypnosis. *Journal of Personality and Social Psychology, 1,* 189–200.

Ornstein, R. (1997). *Right mind.* Ft. Worth, TX: Harcourt Brace.

Orr, A. L. (1998). *Issues in aging and vision: A curriculum.* Washington, DC: American Foundation for the Blind Press.

Ortmann, A., & Hertwig, R. (1997). Is deception acceptable? *American Psychologist, 52,* 746–747.

Osborn, A. F. (1963). *Applied imagination: Principles and procedures for creative problem-solving* (3rd ed.). New York: Scribners.

Ost, L. (1987). Age of onset in different phobias. *Journal of Abnormal Psychology, 96,* 223–229.

Ouchi W. G. (1981). *Theory Z: How American business can meet the Japanese challenge.* Reading, MA: Addison-Wesley.

Ouellette, J. A., & Wood, W. (1998). Habit and intention in everyday life: The multiple processes by which past behavior predicts future behavior. *Psychological Bulletin, 124,* 54–74.

Ouimette, P. C., Finney, J. W., & Moos, R. H. (1997). Twelve-step and cognitive-behavioral treatment for substance abuse: A comparison of treatment effectiveness. *Journal of Consulting and Clinical Psychology, 65,* 230–240.

Ozer, D. J. (1989). Construct validity in personality assessment. In D. M. Buss & N. Cantor (Eds.), *Personality psychology: Recent trends and emerging directions.* New York: Springer-Verlag.

Ozer, E. M., & Bandura, A. (1990). Mechanisms governing empowerment effects: A self-efficacy analysis. *Journal of Personality and Social Psychology, 58,* 472–486.

Paffenbarger, R. S., Jr., Hyde, R. T., Wing, A. L., & Hsieh, C. C. (1986). Physical activity, all-cause mortality, and longevity of college alumni. *New England Journal of Medicine, 314,* 605–613.

Paivio, A. (1969). Mental imagery is associative learning and memory. *Psychological Review, 76,* 241–263.

Paivio, A. (1986). *Mental representations: A dual coding approach.* New York: Oxford University Press.

Paivio, A. (1995). Imagery and memory. In M. S. Gazzaniga (Ed.). *The cognitive neurosciences.* Cambridge, MA: MIT Press.

Pajer, K. (2000a). Antisocial disorders. In G. Fink (Ed.), *Encyclopedia of stress.* San Diego: Academic Press.

Pajer, K. (2000b). Hysteria. In G. Fink (Ed.), *Encyclopedia of stress.* San Diego: Academic Press.

Palfai, T., & Jankiewicz, H. (1991). *Drugs and human behavior.* Dubuque, IA: Wm. C. Brown.

Palmer, C. T. (1991). Kin-selection, reciprocal altruism, and information sharing among Maine lobstermen. *Ethology and Sociobiology, 12,* 221-235.

Palmere, M., Benton, S. L., Glover, J. A., & Ronning, R. (1983). Elaboration and recall of main ideas in prose. *Journal of Education Psychology, 75,* 898-907.

Panksepp, J. (1998). *Affective neuroscience: The foundations of human and animal emotions.* Oxford, England: Oxford University Press.

Papanicolaou, A. C. (1989). *Emotion: A reconsideration of the somatic theory.* New York: Gordon and Breach.

Papolos, D. F., & Lachman, H. M. (1994). *Genetic studies in affective disorders: Overview of basic methods, current directions, and critical research issues.* New York: Wiley.

Parchman, S. W., Ellis, J. A., Christinaz, D., & Vogel, M. (2000). An evaluation of three computer-based instructional strategies in basic electricity and electronics training. *Military Psychology, 12,* 73-87.

Park, D. C., Smith, A. D., & Cavanaugh, J. C. (1990). Metamemories of memory researchers. *Memory and Cognition, 18,* 321-327.

Parker, A. (2000). A review of the ganzfeld work at Gothenburg University. *Journal of the Society for Psychical Research, 64,* 1-15.

Parker, C. R., Bolling, M. Y., & Kohlenberg, R. J. (1998). Operant theory of personality. In D. F. Barone, M. Hersen, & V. B. Van Hasselt (Eds.), *Advanced personality.* New York: Plenum.

Parkes, J. D., Clift, S. J., Dahlitz, M. J., & Chen, S. Y. (Eds.) (1995). The narcoleptic syndrome. *Journal of Neurology, Neurosurgery and Psychiatry, 59,* 221-224.

Parkin, A. J. (2000). Memory impairment. In G. Fink (Ed.), *Encyclopedia of stress.* San Diego: Academic Press.

Parkinson, A. J., Parkinson, W. S., Tyler, R. S., Lowder, M. W., & Gantz, B. J. (1998). Speech perception performance in experienced cochlear-implant patients receiving the SPEAK processing strategy in the Nucleus Spectra-22 cochlear implant. *Journal of Speech, Language, and Hearing Research, 41,* 1073-1087.

Parrott, A. C. (1999). Does cigarette smoking cause stress? *American Psychologist, 54,* 817-820.

Partinen, M., Kaprio, J., Koskenvuo, M., Putkonen, P., & Langinvainio, H. (1983). Genetic and environmental determination of human sleep. *Sleep, 6,* 179-185.

Partonen, T. (1994). Effects of morning light treatment on subjective sleepiness and mood in winter depression. *Journal of Affective Disorders, 30,* 47-56.

Pascalis, O., DeSchoenen, S., Morton, J., & Deruelle, C. (1995). Mother's face recognition by neonates: A replication and an extension. *Infant Behavior and Development, 18,* 79-85.

Patrick, C. J., Cuthbert, B. N., & Lang, P. J. (1994). Emotion in the criminal psychopath: Fear image processing. *Journal of Abnormal Psychology, 103,* 523-534.

Patterson, G. R. (1982). *Coercive family processes.* Eugene, OR: Castalia Press.

Patterson, G. R., Littman, R. A., & Bricker, W. (1967). Assertive behavior in children: A step toward a theory of aggression. *Monographs of the Society for Research in Child Development, 32* (Whole No. 5).

Pauk, W., & Fiore, J. P. (2000). *Succeed in college!* Boston: Houghton Mifflin.

Paul, G. L., & Lentz, R. J. (1977). *Psychosocial treatment of chronic mental patients: Milieu versus social learning programs.* Cambridge, MA: Harvard University Press.

Pavlov, I. P. (1902). *The work of the digestive glands* (W. H. Thompson, Trans.). London: Griffin. (Original work published 1897)

Pavlov, I. P. (1906). The scientific investigation of the psychical faculties or processes in the higher animals. *Science, 24,* 613-619.

Pavlov, I. P. (1928). *Lectures on conditioned reflexes: Twenty-five years of objective study of the higher nervous activity (behaviour) of animals* (W. H. Gantt, Trans.). New York: International Publishers. (Original work published 1923)

Pearlin, L. I., & Schooler, C. (1978). The structure of coping. *Journal of Health and Social Behavior, 19,* 2-21.

Pearson, R. (1998). *Physical anthropology.* New York: Scott-Townsend.

Pecchinenda, A., & Zoccolotti, P. (1993). Facial expressions as modulators of emotional experiences. *Rassegna di Psicologia, 10(3),* 55-75.

Pedalino, E., & Gamboa, V. U. (1974). Behavior modification and absenteeism: Intervention in one industrial setting. *Journal of Applied Psychology, 59,* 694-698.

Pedersen-Pietersen, L. (1997, January 12). You're sober at last: Now prove it to the boss. *New York Times,* p. F10.

Pederson, N. L., Plomin, R., McClearn, G. E., & Griberg, L. (1988). Neuroticism, extraversion, and related traits in adult twins reared apart and reared together. *Journal of Personality and Social Psychology, 55,* 950-957.

Pedrotti, F. L., & Pedrottie, L. S. (1997). *Optics and vision.* Englewood Cliffs, NJ: Prentice Hall.

Pellino, T. A., & Ward, S. E. (1998). Perceived control mediates the relationship between pain severity and patient satisfaction. *Journal of Pain and Symptom Management, 15,* 110-116.

Penfield, W., & Perot P. (1963). The brain's record of auditory and visual experience. *Brain, 86,* 595-696.

Pennebaker, J. W. (1995). *Emotion, disclosure and health.* Washington, DC: American Psychological Association.

Pennebaker, J. W. (1997). *Opening up: The healing power of expressing emotions.* New York: Guilford Press.

Peplau, L. A., Garnets, L. D., Spalding, L. R., Conley, T. D., & Veniegas, R. C. (1998). A critique of Bem's "Exotic Becomes Erotic" theory of sexual orientation. *Psychological Review, 105,* 387-394.

Pepler, D. J., & Craig, W. M. (1995). A peek behind the fence: Naturalistic observations of aggressive children with remote audiovisual recording. *Developmental Psychology, 31,* 548-553.

Perani, D., Paulesu, E., Galles, N. S., Dupoux, E., & Dehaene, S. (1998). The bilingual brain: Proficiency and age of acquisition of the second language. *Brain, 121,* 1841-1852.

Perdue, C. W., Dovidio, J. F., Gurtman, M. B., & Tyler, R. B. (1990). Us and them: Social categorization and the process of intergroup bias. *Journal of Personality and Social Psychology, 59,* 475-486.

Perls, F. S. (1972). Gestalt therapy. In A. Bry (Ed.), *Inside psychotherapy.* New York: Basic Books.

Perna, F. M., Schneiderman, N., & LaPerriere, A. (1997). Psychological stress, exercise, and immunity. *International Journal of Sports Medicine, 18* (Suppl.), S78-S83.

Perse, E. M. (1996). Sensation seeking and the use of television for arousal. *Communication Reports, 9,* 37-48.

Pert, C. B. (1986). The wisdom of the receptors: Neuropeptides, the emotions, and bodymind. *Advances, 3,* 8-16.

Pert, C. B. (1997). *Molecules of emotion: Why you feel the way you feel.* New York: Simon & Schuster.

Peters, R., & McGee, R. (1982). Cigarette smoking and state-dependent memory. *Psychopharmacology, 76,* 232-235.

Peterson, A. C. (1987). The nature of biological-psychosocial interactions: The sample case of early adolescence. In R. M. Lerner & T. T. Foch (Eds.), *Biological-psychosocial interactions in early adolescence.* Hillsdale, NJ: Erlbaum.

Peterson, C., & Park, C. (1998). Learned helplessness and explanatory style. In D. F. Barone, M. Hersen, & V. B. Van Hasselt (Eds.), *Advanced personality.* New York: Plenum.

Peterson, C., & Seligman, M. E. P. (1987). Explanatory style and illness. *Journal of Personality, 55,* 237-265.

Peterson, C., Seligman, M. E. P., Yurko, K. H., Martin, L. R. & Friedman, H. S. (1998). Catastrophizing and untimely death. *Psychological Science, 9,* 127-130.

Peterson, L. R., & Peterson, M. J. (1959). Short term retention of individual verbal items. *Journal of Experimental Psychology, 58,* 193-198.

Petitto, J. M., Gariepy, J. L., Gendreau, P. L., Rodriguiz, R., Lewis, M. H., & Lysle, D. T. (1999). Differences in NK cell function in mice bred for high and low aggression: Genetic linkage between complex behavioral and immunological traits? *Brain, Behavior and Immunity, 13,* 175-186.

Petrinovich, L. F. (1999). *Darwinian dominion: Animal welfare and human interests.* Cambridge, MA.: MIT Press.

Pettigrew, T. F. (1969). Racially separate or together? *Journal of Social Issues, 25,* 43-69.

Pettigrew, T. F. (1979). The ultimate attribution error: Extending Allport's cognitive analysis of prejudice. *Personality and Social Psychology Bulletin, 55,* 461-476.

Pettigrew, T. F. (1991). Normative theory in intergroup relations: Explaining bad harmony and conflict. *Psychology and Developing Societies, 3,* 3-16.

Pettigrew, T. F., & Meertens, R. W. (1995). Subtle and blatant prejudice in western Europe. *European Journal of Social Psychology, 25,* 57-76.

Petty, R. E., & Cacioppo, J. T. (1986). *Communication and persuasion: Central and peripheral routes to attitude change.* New York: Springer-Verlag.

Petty, R. E., & Wegener, D. T. (1998). Attitude change: Multiple roles for persuasion variables. In D. T. Gilbert, S. T. Fiske, & G. Lindzey (Eds.), *The handbook of social psychology* (4th ed., Vol. 1). Boston: McGraw-Hill.

Pfeffer, K., Cole, B., & Dada, M. K. (1998). Attributions for youth crime among British and Nigerian primary school children. *Journal of Social Psychology, 138,* 251–253.

Phares, E. J. (1992). *Clinical psychology: Concepts, methods, and profession.* Pacific Grove, CA: Brooks/Cole.

Phillips, M., Brooks, G. J., Duncan, G. J., Klebanov, P., & Crane, J. (1998). Family background, parenting practices, and the Black-White test score gap. In C. Jencks & M. Phillips (Eds.), *The Black-White test score gap.* Washington, DC: Brookings Institution.

Piaget, J. (1926). *The language and thought of the child.* New York: Meridian Books.

Piaget, J. (1932). *The moral judgement of the child.* New York: Harcourt Brace.

Piaget, J. (1970). Piaget's theory. In P. H. Mussen (Ed.), *Carmichael's manual of child psychology* (Vol.1). New York: Wiley.

Piaget, J. (1977). *The development of thought: Equilibration of cognitive structure.* New York: Viking.

Piaget, J., & Inhelder, B. (1956). *The child's conception of space.* London: Routledge & Kegan Paul.

Piccione, C., Hilgard, E. R., & Zimbardo, P. G. (1989). On the degree of measured hypnotizability over a 25-year period. *Journal of Personality and Social Psychology, 56,* 289–295.

Pickering, A. D., & Gray, J. A. (1999). The neuroscience of personality. In L. A. Pervin & O. P. John (Eds.), *Handbook of personality: Theory and research.* New York: Guilford Press.

Pierce, G. R., Sarason, B. R., & Sarason, I. G. (1996). *Cognitive interference: Theories, methods, and findings.* Mahwah, NJ: Erlbaum.

Pierce, W. D., & Epling, W. F. (1999). *Behavior analysis and learning* (2nd ed.). Englewood Cliffs, NJ: Prentice-Hall.

Pies, R. W. (1998). *Handbook of essential psychopharmacology.* Washington, DC: American Psychiatric Press.

Pilbeam, D. (1984). The descent of hominoids and hominids. *Scientific American, 250,* 84–87.

Pilcher, J. J., & Huffcutt, A. J. (1996). Effects of sleep deprivation on performance: A meta-analysis. *Sleep, 19,* 318–326.

Pilcher, J. J., & Walters, A. S. (1997). How sleep deprivation affects psychological variables related to college students' cognitive performance. *Journal of American College Health, 46,* 121–126.

Pilgrim, C., Luo, Q., Urberg, K. A., & Fang, X. (1999). Influence of peers, parents, and individual characteristics on adolescent drug use in two cultures. *Merrill-Palmer Quarterly, 45,* 85-107.

Pilla, M., Perachon, S., Sautel, F., Garrido, F., Mann, A., Wermuth, C. G., Schwartz, J. C., Everitt, B. J., & Sokoloff, P. (1999). Selective inhibition of cocaine-seeking behaviour by a partial dopamine D_3 receptor agonist. *Nature, 400,* 371–375.

Pina, P. (1995, December 5). No rest for many weary Americans. *USA Today,* p. D5.

Pinel, J. P. J. (1997). *Biopsychology.* Boston: Allyn & Bacon.

Pinker, S. (2000). *Words and rules: The ingredients of language.* New York: Basic Books.

Pisklakova, M. (1992, Spring). Another perspective on domestic violence. *You and We: The Women's Dialogue,* 22.

Pitman, R. K., Shalev, A. Y., & Orr, S. P. (2000). Posttraumatic stress disorder: Emotion, conditioning, and memory. In M. S. Gazzaniga (Ed.), *The new cognitive neurosciences* (2nd ed.). Cambridge, MA: MIT Press.

Pitz, G. F., & Sachs, N. J. (1984). Judgment and decision: Theory and application. *Annual Review of Psychology, 35,* 139–163.

Plaud, J. J., & Plaud, D. M. (1998). Clinical behavior therapy and the experimental analysis of behavior. *Journal of Clinical Psychology, 54,* 905–921.

Pliner, P., Hart, H., Kohl, J., & Saari, D. (1974). Compliance without pressure: Some further data on the foot-in-the-door technique. *Journal of Experimental Social Psychology, 10,* 17–22.

Plomin, R. (1997). *Behavioral genetics.* New York: St. Martins Press.

Plomin, R., & Caspi, A. (1999). Behavior genetics and personality. In L. A. Pervin & O. P. John (Eds.), *Handbook of personality: Theory and research* (2nd ed.). New York: Guilford Press.

Plomin, R., De Fries, J. C., & McClearn, G. E. (1990). *Behavior genetics: A primer* (2nd ed.). New York: W. H. Freeman.

Plomin, R., Emde, R. N., Braungart, J. M., & Campos, J. (1993). Genetic change and continuity from fourteen to twenty months: The MacArthur Longitudinal Twin Study. *Child Development, 64,* 1354–1376.

Plomin, R., & Rende, R. (1991). Human behavioral genetics. *Annual Review of Psychology, 42,* 161–190.

Plous, S. (1996a). Attitudes toward the use of animals in psychological research and education: Results from a national survey of psychologists. *American Psychologist, 51,* 1167–1180.

Plous, S. (1996b). Attitudes toward the use of animals in psychological research and education: Results from a national survey of psychology majors. *Psychological Science, 7,* 352–358.

Plumert, J. M., & Nichols, W. P. (1996). Parental scaffolding of young children's spatial communication. *Developmental Psychology, 32,* 523–532.

Plutchik, R. (1994). *Psychology of emotion.* Reading, MA: Addison-Wesley.

Polivy, J., & Herman, C. P. (1992). Undieting: A program to help people stop dieting. *International Journal of Eating Disorders, 11,* 261–268.

Pollak, C. P. (1991). The effects of noise on sleep. In T. Fay (Ed.), *Noise and health.* New York: New York Academy of Medicine.

Pollner, M. (1989). Divine relations, social relations, and well-being. *Journal of Health and Social Behavior, 30,* 92–104.

Polster, E., & Polster, M. (1973). *Gestalt therapy integrated: Contours of theory and practice.* New York: Brunner/Mazel.

Pool, G. J., Wood, W., & Leck, K. (1998). The self-esteem motive in social influence: Agreement with valued majorities and disagreement with derogated minorities. *Journal of Personality and Social Psychology, 75,* 967–975.

Pool, R. (1994). *The dynamic brain.* Washington, DC: National Academy Press.

Porkka, H. T., Strecker, R. E., Thakkar, M., & Bjorkun, A. A. (1997). Adenosine: A mediator of the sleep-inducing effects of prolonged wakefulness. *Science, 276,* 1265–1267.

Porter, N. P., & Geis, F. L. (1981). Women and nonverbal leadership cues: When seeing is not believing. In C. Mayo & N. M. Henley (Eds.), *Gender and nonverbal behavior.* New York: Springer-Verlag.

Porter, R. H., & Winberg, J. (1999). Unique salience of maternal breast odors for newborn infants. *Neuroscience and Biobehavioral Reviews, 23,* 439–449.

Postle, B. R., & Corkin, S. (1998). Impaired word-stem completion priming but intact perceptual identification priming with novel words: Evidence from the amnesic patient H. M. *Neuropsychologia, 36,* 421-440.

Postman, L., & Phillips, L. W. (1965). Short-term temporal changes in free recall. *Quarterly Journal of Experimental Psychology, 17,* 132–138.

Postman, L., & Underwood, B. J. (1973). Critical issues in interference theory. *Memory and Cognition, 1,* 19–40.

Postmes, T., & Spears, R. (1998). Deindividuation and antinormative behavior: A meta-analysis. *Psychological Bulletin, 123,* 238–259.

Powell, M. C., & Fazio, R. M. (1984). Attitude accessibility as a function of repeated attitudinal expression. *Personality and Social Psychology Bulletin, 10,* 139–148.

Powell, R. W., & Curley, M. (1976). Instinctive drift in nondomesticated rodents. *Bulletin of the Psychonomic Society, 8,* 175–178.

Powley, T. L., & Kessey, R. E. (1970). Relationship of body weight to the lateral hypothalamic feeding syndrome. *Journal of Comparative and Physiological Psychology, 70,* 25–36.

Pratkanis, A. R., Eskenazi, J., & Greenwald, A. G. (1994). What you expect is what you believe (but not necessarily what you get): A test of the effectiveness of subliminal self-help audiotapes. *Basic and Applied Social Psychology, 15,* 251–276.

Pressley, M., Snyder, B. L., Levin, J. R., Murray, H. G., & Ghatala, E. S. (1987). Perceived readiness for examination performance (PREP) produced by initial reading of text and text containing adjunct questions. *Reading Research Quarterly, 22,* 219 236.

Pressman, J. D. (1998). *Last resort: Psychosurgery and the limits of medicine.* New York: Cambridge University Press.

Preti, G., Cutler, W. B., Garcia, G. R., Huggins, G. R., & Lawley, J. J. (1986). Human axillary secretions influences women's menstrual cycles: The role of donor extract from females. *Hormones and Behavior, 20,* 473–480.

Price, R. A., Charles, M. A., Pettitt, D. J., & Knowler, W. C. (1993). Obesity in Pima Indians: Large increases among post–World War II birth cohorts. *American Journal of Physical Anthropology, 92,* 473–479.

Prilleltensky, I. (1997). Values, assumptions, and practices: Assessing the moral implications of psychological discourse and action. *American Psychologist, 52,* 517–535.

Pritchard, R. D., Hollenback, J., & DeLeo, P. J. (1980). The effects of continuous and partial schedules of reinforcement on effort, performance, and satisfaction. *Organizational Behavior and Human Decision Processes, 25,* 336–353.

Pritchard, R. M. (1961, June). Stabilized images on the retina. *Scientific American,* pp. 72–78.

Probst, L. R., Ostrom, R., Watkins, P., Dean, T., & Mashburn, D. (1992). Comparative efficacy of religious and non-religious cognitive-behavioral therapy for the treatment of clinical depression in religious individuals. *Journal of Consulting and Clinical Psychology, 60,* 94–103.

Prochaska, J. O., Johnson, S., & Lee, P. (1998). The transtheoretical model of behavior change. In S. A. Shumaker & E. B. Schron (Eds.), *The handbook of health behavior change* (2nd ed.). New York: Springer.

Prochaska, J. O., Norcross, J. C., & DiClemente, C. C. (1994). *Changing for good.* New York: Avon Books.

Project MATCH Research Group (1997). Matching alcoholism treatments to client heterogeneity: Project MATCH posttreatment drinking outcomes. *Journal of Studies on Alcohol, 58,* 7–29.

Prout, P. I., & Dobson, K. S. (1998). Recovered memories of childhood sexual abuse: Searching for the middle ground in clinical practice. *Canadian Psychology, 39,* 257-265.

Ptacek, J. T., Smith, R. E., & Zanas, J. (1992). Gender, appraisal, and coping: A longitudinal analysis. *Journal of Personality, 60,* 747–770.

Pugh, G. E. (1977). *The biological origin of human values.* New York: Basic Books.

Punamaeki, R. L., & Joustie, M. (1998). The role of culture, violence, and personal factors affecting dream content. *Journal of Cross-Cultural Psychology, 29,* 320–342.

Putnam, F. W. (1984). The psychophysiologic investigation of multiple personality disorder: A review. *Psychiatric Clinics of North America, 7,* 31–39.

Putnam, F. W. (1989). *Diagnosis and treatment of multiple personality disorder.* New York: Guilford Press.

Putnam, F. W. (1991). Recent research on multiple personality disorder. *Psychiatric Clinics of North America, 14*(3), 489–502.

Putnam, F. W. (1993). Diagnosis and clinical phenomenology of multiple personality disorder: A North American perspective. *Dissociation: Progress in the Dissociative Disorders, 6*(2–3), 80–86.

Putnam, F. W. (1998). *Dissociation in children and adolescents: A developmental perspective.* New York: Guilford Press.

Pyszczynski, T., & Greenberg, J. (1987). Toward an integration of cognitive and motivational perspectives on social inference: A biased hypothesis-testing model. In L. Berkowitz (Ed.), *Advances in experimental social psychology* (Vol. 20). Orlando, FL: Academic Press.

Pyszczynski, T., Hamilton, J. C., Greenberg, J., & Becker, S. E. (1991). Self-awareness and psychological dysfunction. In C. R. Snyder & D. O. Forsyth (Eds.), *Handbook of social and clinical psychology: The health perspective.* New York: Pergamon.

Quera-Salva, M. A., Guillenminault, C., Claustrat, B. & Defrance, A., et al. (1997). Rapid shift in peak melatonin secretion associated with

improved performance in short shift work schedule. *Sleep, 20,* 1145–1150.

Quinsey, V. L., Maguire, A., & Varney, G. W. (1983). Assertion and overcontrolled hostility among mentally disordered murderers. *Journal of Consulting and Clinical Psychology, 51,* 550–566.

Quintero, N. (1980, February). Coming of age the Apache way. *National Geographic, 157* (2), 262–271.

Rachlin, H. (1995). *Introduction to modern behaviorism.* New York: W. H. Freeman.

Rachman, S. (1998). *Anxiety.* Mahwah, NJ: Erlbaum.

Rachman, S. (2000). Joseph Wolpe: Obituary. *American Psychologist, 55,* 431–432.

Rachman, S., Hodgson, R. J. (1968). Experimentally-induced "sexual fetishism": Replication and development. *Psychological Record, 18,* 25–27.

Rachman, S. J., & Hodgson, R. J. (1980). *Obsessions and compulsions.* Englewood Cliffs, NJ: Prentice Hall.

Rahe, R. (2000). Acute reactions to combat. In G. Fink (Ed.), *Encyclopedia of stress.* San Diego: Academic Press.

Raichle, M. E. (1994). Images of the mind: Studies with modern imaging techniques. *Annual Review of Psychology, 45,* 333–356.

Rail, T. W. (1980). Central nervous system stimulants: The xanthines. In A. G. Gilman, L. Goodman, & A. Gilman (Eds.), *The pharmacological basis of therapeutics.* New York: Macmillan.

Raine, A., Buchsbaum, M., & LaCasse, L. (1997). Brain abnormalities in murderers indicated by positron tomography. *Biological Psychiatry, 42,* 495–508.

Raine, A., Lencz, T., Bihrle, S., LaCasse, L., & Colletti, P. (2000). Reduced prefrontal gray matter volume and reduced autonomic activity in antisocial personality disorder. *Archives of General Psychiatry, 57,* 119–127.

Raine, A., Meloy, J. R., Bihrle, S., Stoddard, J., LaCasse, L., & Buchsbaum, M. S. (1998). Reduced prefrontal and increased subcortical brain functioning assessed using positron emission tomography in predatory and affective murderers. *Behavioral Sciences and the Law, 16,* 319–332.

Raine, A., Venables, P. H., & Williams, M. (1996). Better autonomic conditioning and faster electrodermal half-recovery time at age 15 years as possible protective factors against crime at age 29 years. *Developmental Psychology, 32,* 624–630.

Rakfeldt, J., Rybash, J. M., & Roodin, P. A. (1996). Affirmative coping: A marker of success in adult therapeutic intervention. In M. L. Commons, J. Demick, & C. Goldberg (Eds.), *Clinical approaches to adult development.* Norwood, NJ: Ablex.

Rakic, P. (1995). Corticogenesis in human and nonhuman primates. In M. S. Gazzaniga (Ed.), *The cognitive neurosciences.* Cambridge, MA: MIT Press.

Ramey, C. T., Campbell, F. A., & Blair, C. (1998). Enhancing the life course for high-risk children: Results from the Abecedarian Project. In J. Crane (Ed.), *Social programs that work.* New York: Russell Sage Foundation.

Ramey, C. T., & Ramey, S. L. (1998a). Early intervention and early experience. *American Psychologist, 53,* 109–120.

Ramey, C. T., & Ramey, S. L. (1998b). In defense of special education. *American Psychologist, 53,* 1159–1160.

Ramirez, J. C., & Uribe, G. (1993). Mujer y violencia: Un hecho cotidiano [Women and violence: A daily occurrence]. *Salud Publica de Mexico, 35,* 148–160.

Raphling, D. L. (1998). Aggression: Its relation to desire and self-interest. *Journal of the American Psychoanalytic Association, 46,* 797–811.

Rasmussen, A. M., & Charney, D. S. (2000). Posttraumatic therapy. In G. Fink (Ed.), *Encyclopedia of stress.* San Diego: Academic Press.

Raven, B. H. (1998). Groupthink, Bay of Pigs, and Watergate reconsidered. *Organizational Behavior and Human Decision Processes, 73,* 352–361.

Ravussin, E., & Gautier, J. F. (1999). Metabolic predictors of weight gain. *International Journal of Obesity and Related Metabolic Disorders, 23* (Suppl 1), 37–41.

Ravussin, E., Valencia, M. E., Esparza, J., Bennett, P. H., & Schulz, L. O. (1994). Effects of a traditional lifestyle on obesity in Pima Indians. *Diabetes Care, 17,* 1067–1074.

Ray, O. S. (1983). *Drugs, society, and human behavior* (3rd ed.). St. Louis: Mosby.

Ray, O. S., & Ksir, C. (1987). *Drugs, society and human behavior* (4th ed.). St. Louis: Mosby.

Ray, W. J. (2000). Methods: Toward a science of behavior and experience (6th ed.). Belmont, CA: Wadsworth.

Read, M. S. (1982). Malnutrition and behavior. *Applied Research in Mental Retardation, 3,* 279–291.

Ready, D. J., Bothwell, R. K., & Brigham, J. C. (1997). The effects of hypnosis, context reinstatement, and anxiety on eyewitness memory. *International Journal of Clinical and Experimental Hypnosis, 45,* 55–68.

Rechtschaffen, A., Bergmann, B. M., Gilliland, M. A., & Bauer, K. (1999). Effects of method, duration, and sleep stage on rebounds from sleep deprivation in the rat. *Sleep, 22,* 11–31.

Redelmeier, D. A., & Tibshirani, R. J. (1997). Association between cellular telephone calls and motor vehicle collisions. *New England Journal of Medicine, 336,* 453–458.

Reeve, J. (1992). *Understanding motivation and emotion.* Ft. Worth, TX: Harcourt Brace Jovanovich.

Regan, D. T., & Fazio, R. (1977). On the consistency between attitudes and behavior: Look to the method of attitude formation. *Journal of Experimental Social Psychology, 13,* 28–45.

Regan, D. T., Williams, M., & Sparling, S. (1972). Voluntary expiation of guilt: A field experiment. *Journal of Personality and Social Psychology, 24,* 42-45.

Reichl, A. J. (1997). Ingroup favouritism and outgroup favouritism in low status minimal groups: Differential responses to status-related and status-unrelated measures. *European Journal of Social Psychology, 27,* 617–633.

Reid, A. K., & Staddon, J. E. F. (1998). A dynamic route finder for the cognitive map. *Psychological Review, 105,* 585–601.

Reisberg, D. (1997). *Cognition: Exploring the science of the mind.* New York: W. W. Norton.

Reiss, A. J., Jr., & Roth, J. A. (Eds.) (1993). *Understanding and preventing violence: Vol III.*

Social influences. Washington, DC: National Academy Press.

Reiss, M., & Straughan, R. (1998). *Improving nature?: The science and ethics of genetic engineering.* New York: Cambridge University Press.

Reitzes, D. C., Mutran, E. J., & Fernandez, M. E. (1998). The decision to retire: A career perspective. *Social Science Quarterly, 79,* 607–619.

Remland, M. S., Jones, T. S., & Brinkman, H. (1995). Interpersonal distance, body orientation, and touch: Effects of culture, gender, and age. *Journal of Social Psychology, 135,* 281–297.

Rendell, P. G., & Thomson, D. M. (1993). The effect of ageing on remembering to remember: An investigation of simulated medication regimens. *Australian Journal on Ageing, 12,* 11–18.

Rendell, P. G., & Thomson, D. M. (1999). Aging and prospective memory: Differences between naturalistic and laboratory tasks. *Journals of Gerontology: Series B: Psychological Sciences and Social Sciences, 54B(4),* 256–269.

Renzulli, J. S. (1986). The three-ring conception of intelligence: A developmental model for creative productivity. In R. J. Sternberg & J. E. Davidson (Eds.), *Conceptions of giftedness.* Cambridge, England: Cambridge University Press.

Reppucci, N. D., Woolard, J. L., & Fried, C. S. (1999). Social, community, and preventive interventions. *Annual Review of Psychology, 50,* 387–418.

Reschly, D. J., & Robinson-Zanurtu, C. (2000). Evaluation of aptitudes. In G. Goldstein & M. Hersen (Eds.), *Handbook of psychological assessment* (3rd ed.). New York: Elsevier.

Rescorla, R. A. (1968). Probability of shock in the presence and absence of CS in fear. *Journal of Comparative and Physiological Psychology, 66,* 1–5.

Rescorla, R. A. (1988). Pavlovian conditioning: It's not what you think it is. *American Psychologist, 43,* 151–160.

Rescorla, R. A., & Solomon, R. L. (1967). Two-process learning theory: Relationships between pavlovian conditioning and instrumental learning. *Psychological Review, 74,* 151–182.

Rescorla, R. A., & Wagner, A. R. (1972). A theory of Pavlovian conditioning: Variations in the effectiveness of reinforcement and nonreinforcement. In A. H. Black & W. F. Prokasky (Eds.), *Classical conditioning: II. Current research and theory.* New York: Appleton-Century-Crofts.

Rey, J. M., & Walter, G. (1997). Half a century of ECT use in young people. *American Journal of Psychiatry, 154,* 595–602.

Reznick, J. S., Gibbons, J., Johnson, M. O., & McDonough, P. (1992). Behavioral inhibition in a normative sample. In J. S. Reznick (Ed.), *Perspectives in behavioral inhibition.* Chicago: University of Chicago Press.

Rice, M. E. (1997). Violent offender research and implications for the criminal justice system. *American Psychologist, 52,* 414–423.

Rice, M. E., Harris, G. T., & Cormier, C. A. (1992). An evaluation of a maximum security therapeutic community for psychopaths and other mentally disordered offenders. *Law and Human Behavior, 16,* 399–412.

Richard, S., Davies, D. C., & Faure, J. M. (2000). The role of fear in one-trial passive avoidance learning in Japanese quail chicks genetically selected for long or short duration of the tonic immobility reaction. *Behavioural Processes, 48,* 165–170.

Richards, H. C., Bear, G. G., Stewart, A. L., & Norman, A. D. (1992). Moral reasoning and classroom conduct: Evidence of a curvilinear relationship. *Merrill Palmer Quarterly, 38,* 176–190.

Richardson, D. R. (1991). Interpersonal attraction and love. In R. M. Baron, W. G. Graziano, & C. Stangor (Eds.), *Social psychology.* Ft. Worth, TX: Holt, Rinehart & Winston.

Riefer, D. M., Keveri, M. K., & Kramer, D. L. F. (1995). Name that tune: Eliciting the tip-of-the-tongue experience using auditory stimuli. *Psychological Reports, 77,* 1379-1390.

Riegel, K. (1973). Dialectic operations: The final period of cognitive development. *Human Development, 16,* 346–370.

Riesen, A. R. (1965). Effects of early deprivation of photic stimulation. In S. Oster & R. Cooke (Eds.), *The biosocial basis of mental retardation.* Baltimore, MD: The Johns Hopkins University Press.

Rilling, M. (1996). The mystery of the vanished citations: James McConnell's forgotten 1960s quest for planarian learning, a biochemical engram, and celebrity. *American Psychologist, 51,* 589–598.

Rips, L. J. (1994). *The psychology of proof: Deductive reasoning in human thinking.* Cambridge, MA: MIT Press.

Rips, L. J. (1997). Goals for a theory of deduction: Reply to Johnson-Laird. *Minds & Machines, 7,* 409–424.

Ritblatt, S. N. (2000). Children's level of participation in a false-belief task, age, and theory of mind. *Journal of Genetic Psychology, 161,* 53–64.

Rivera-Tovar, L. A., & Jones, R. T. (1990). Effect of elaboration on the acquisition and maintenance of cardiopulmonary resuscitation. *Journal of Pediatric Psychology, 15,* 123–130.

Robbe, H. (1998). Marijuana's impairing effects on driving are moderate when taken alone but severe when combined with alcohol. *Human Psychopharmacology Clinical and Experimental, 13* (Suppl. 2), S70–S78.

Robers, P. J., & Blundell, J. E. (1984). Meal patterns and food selections during the development of obesity in rats fed a cafeteria diet. *Neuroscience and Biobehavioral Reviews, 8,* 441–453.

Robins, L. N., & Regier, D. A. (Eds.) (1991). *Psychiatric disorders in America: The Epidemiological Catchment Area Study.* New York: Free Press.

Robins, L. N. (1966). *Deviant children grow up.* Baltimore: Williams & Wilkins.

Robins, R. W., Gosling, S. D, & Craik, K. H. (1999). An empirical analysis of trends in psychology. *American Psychologist, 54,* 117–128.

Robins, R. W., Norem, J. K., & Cheek, J. M. (1999). Naturalizing the self. In L. A. Pervin & O. P. John (Eds.), *Handbook of personality: Theory and research.* New York: Guilford Press.

Robinson, D. (1997). *Neurobiology.* New York: Springer-Verlag.

Roche, A. F. (1979). Secular trends in human growth, maturation, and development. *Monographs of the Society for Research and Child Development, 44* (3–4, Serial No. 179).

Rodgers, J. E. (1982). The malleable memory of eyewitnesses. *Science Digest, 3,* 32–35.

Rodgers, R., & Hunter, J. E. (1991). Impact of management by objectives on organizational productivity. *Journal of Applied Psychology, 76,* 322–336.

Rodin, J., Bartoshuk, L., Peterson, C., & Schank, D. (1990). Bulimia and taste: Possible interactions. *Journal of Abnormal Psychology, 99,* 32–39.

Rodin, J., & Salovey, P. (1989). Health psychology. *Annual Review of Psychology, 40,* 533–579.

Roediger, H. L. (1980). The effectiveness of four mnemonics in ordering recall. *Journal of Experimental Psychology: Human Learning and Memory, 6,* 558–567.

Rogers, C. R. (1951). *Client-centered therapy.* Boston: Houghton Mifflin.

Rogers, C. R. (1959). A theory of therapy, personality and interpersonal relationships, as developed in the client-centered framework. In S. Koch (Ed.), *Psychology: A study of a science* (Vol. 3). New York: McGraw-Hill.

Rogers, C. R. (1961). *On becoming a person: A therapist's view of psychotherapy.* Boston: Houghton Mifflin.

Rogers, C. R. (Ed.) (1967). *The therapeutic relationship and its impact: A study of psychotherapy with schizophrenics.* Madison, WI: University of Wisconsin Press.

Rogers, C. R. (1980). *A way of being.* Boston: Houghton Mifflin.

Rogers, C. R., & Dymond, R. F. (1954). *Psychotherapy and personality change: Coordinated studies in the client-centered approach.* Chicago: University of Chicago Press.

Rogers, P. J., & Blundell, J. E. (1984). Meal patterns and food selections during the development of obesity in rats fed a cafeteria diet. *Neuroscience and Biobehavioral Reviews, 8,* 441-453.

Rogers, R. W. (1983). Cognitive and psychological processes in fear appeals and attitude change: A revised theory of protection motivation. In J. Cacioppo & R. Petty (Eds.), *Social psychophysiology: A sourcebook.* New York: Guilford Press.

Rohrer, J. H., Baron, S. H., Hoffman, E. L., & Swander, D. V. (1954). The stability of autokinetic judgments. *Journal of Abnormal and Social Psychology, 49,* 595–597.

Rohsenow, D. J., & Marlatt, G. A. (1981). The balanced placebo design: Methodological considerations. *Addictive Behaviors, 6,* 107–122.

Rohsenow, D. J., & Smith, R. E. (1985). Stress management training as a prevention program for heavy social drinkers: Cognitions, affect, drinking, and individual differences. *Addictive Behaviors, 10,* 45–54.

Roitblat, H. L., & von Ferson, L. (1992). Comparative cognition: Representations and processes in learning and memory. *Annual Review of Psychology, 43,* 671–710.

Roland, P. E. (1997). *Brain activation.* New York: Wiley.

Rollin, S. A., Anderson, C. W., Buncher, Robert M., & Frydenberg, E. (Eds.) (1999). Coping in children and adolescents: A prevention model for helping kids avoid or reduce at-risk behaviour. *Learning to cope: Developing as a person in complex societies.* New York: Oxford University Press.

Rollins, B. C., & Feldman, H. (1970). Marital satisfaction over the family life cycle. *Journal of Marriage and the Family, 32,* 20–28.

Rollman, G. (1998). Culture and pain. In S. S. Kazarian, et al. (Eds.) *Cultural clinical psychology: Theory, research, and practice.* New York: Oxford University Press.

Rolls, E. T. (2000). Memory systems in the brain. *Annual Review of Psychology, 5,* 599-630.

Rolls, B. J., Rolls, E. T., Rowe, E. A., & Sweeney, K. (1981). Sensory specific satiety in man. *Physiology and Behavior, 27,* 137–142.

Ron, M. A., & David, A. S. (1997). *Disorders of brain and mind.* Cambridge, England: Cambridge University Press.

Rosch, E. (1973). On the internal structure of perceptual and semantic categories. In T. E. Moore (Ed.), *Cognitive development and the acquisition of language.* New York: Academic Press.

Rosch, E. (1977). Human categorization. In N. Warren (Ed.), *Advances in cross-cultural psychology* (Vol. 1). London: Academic Press.

Rose, R. J. (1995). Genes and human behavior. *Annual Review of Psychology, 46,* 625–654.

Rose, S. (1973). *The conscious brain.* New York: Knopf.

Rosen, C. S. (2000). Integrating stage and continuum models to explain processing of exercise messages and exercise initiation among sedentary college students. *Health Psychology, 19,* 172–180.

Rosen, J. C., & Leitenberg, H. (1982). Bulimia nervosa: Treatment with exposure and response prevention. *Behavior Therapy, 13,* 117–124.

Rosenbaum, A., Abend, S. S., Gearan, P. J., & Fletcher, K. E. (1997). Serotonergic functioning in partner-abusive men. In A. Raine, P. A. Brennan, D. P. Farrington, & S. A. Mednick (Eds.), *Biosocial bases of violence.* New York: Plenum.

Rosenbaum, M. E. (1986). The repulsion hypothesis: On the nondevelopment of relationships. *Journal of Personality and Social Psychology, 51,* 1156–1166.

Rosenberg, M. (1985). Self-concept and psychological well-being in adolescence. In R. L. Leahy (Ed.), *The development of the self.* Orlando, FL: Academic Press.

Rosenfarb, I. S., Goldstein, M. J., Mintz, J., Nuechterlein, K. H. (1995). Expressed emotion and subclinical psychopathology observable within the transactions between schizophrenic patients and their family members. *Journal of Abnormal Psychology, 104,* 259–267.

Rosenhan, D. L (1973). On being sane in insane places. *Science, 179,* 250–258.

Rosenhan, D. L., & Seligman, M. E. P. (1989). *Abnormal psychology* (2nd ed.). New York: W. W. Norton.

Rosenman, R. H., Brand, R. J., Jenkins, C. D., et al. (1975). Coronary heart disease in the Western Collaborative Group Study. *Journal of the American Medical Association, 233,* 872–877.

Rosenthal, N. E., & Wehr, T. A. (1987). Seasonal affective disorders. *Psychiatric Annals, 17,* 670–674.

Rosenthal, R. (1985). From unconscious experimenter bias to teacher expectancy effects. In J. B. Dusek, V. C. Hall, & W. J.

Meyer (Eds.), *Teacher expectancies.* Hillsdale, NJ: Erlbaum.

Rosenthal, R. (1991). Teacher expectancy effects: A brief update 25 years after the Pygmalion experiment. *Journal of Research in Education, 1,* 3-12.

Rosenthal, R. (1994). Interpersonal expectancy effects: A 30-year perspective. *Current Directions in Psychological Science, 3,* 176–179.

Rosenthal, R., Archer, D., DiMatteo, M. R., Koivumaki, J. H., & Rogers, P. L. (1974). Body talk and tone of voice: The language without words. *Psychology Today, 8,* 64–71.

Rosenthal, R., & Jacobson, L. (1968). *Pygmalion in the classroom: Teacher expectations and pupils' intellectual development.* New York: Holt, Rinehart & Winston.

Rosenzweig, M. R. (1984). Experience, memory, and the brain. *American Psychologist, 39,* 365–376.

Rosenzweig, M. R., & Bennett, E. L. (1996). Psychobiology of plasticity: Effects of training and experience on brain and behavior. *Behavioural Brain Research, 78,* 57–65.

Rosenzweig, S. (1992). Freud and experimental psychology: The emergence of idiodynamics. In S. Koch & D. E. Leary (Eds.), *A century of psychology as science.* Washington, DC: American Psychological Association.

Ross, L. (1977). The intuitive psychologist and his shortcomings: Distortions in the attribution process. In L. Berkowitz (Ed.), *Advances in experimental social psychology* (Vol. 10). New York: Academic Press.

Ross, L., & Nisbett, R. E. (1991). *The person and the situation: Perspectives of social psychology.* New York: McGraw-Hill.

Ross, R. J., Ball, W. A., Sullivan, K. A., & Caroff, S. N. (1989). Sleep disturbance as the hallmark of posttraumatic stress disorder. *American Journal of Psychiatry, 146,* 697–707.

Rothbaum, B. O., Hodges, L. F., Kooper, I. R., et al. (1995). Effectiveness of computer-generated (virtual reality) graded exposure in the treatment of acrophobia. *American Journal of Psychiatry, 52,* 626–628.

Rotton, J., & Cohn, E. G. (2000). Violence is a curvilinear function of temperature in Dallas: A replication. *Journal of Personality and Social Psychology, 78,* 1074–1081.

Rouhana, N. N., & Bar-Tal, D. (1998). Psychological dynamics of intractable ethnonational conflicts: The Israeli-Palestinian case. *American Psychologist, 53,* 761–770.

Rousche, P. J., & Normann, R. A. (1998). Chronic recording capability of the Utah intracortical electrode array in cat sensory cortex. *Journal of Neuroscience Methods, 82,* 1–15.

Rowatt, W. C., Cunningham, M. R., & Druen, P. B. (1999). Lying to get a date: The effect of facial physical attractiveness on the willingness to deceive prospective dating partners. *Journal of Social and Personal Relationships, 16,* 209–223.

Rowe, D. C. (1999). Heredity. In V. J. Derlega, B. A. Winstead, & W. H. Jones (Eds.), *Personality: Contemporary theory and research.* Chicago: Nelson-Hall.

Rowley, J. T., Stickgold, R., & Hobson, J. A. (1998). Eyelid movements and mental activity at sleep onset. *Consciousness and Cognition: An International Journal, 7,* 67–84.

Rozin, P., Dow, S., Moscovitch, M., & Rajaram, S. (1998). What causes humans to begin and end a meal? A role for memory for what has been eaten, as evidenced by a study of multiple meal eating in amnesic patients. *Psychological Science, 9,* 392–396.

Rubin, D. C., & Kozin, M. (1984). Vivid memories. *Cognition, 16,* 81–95.

Rubin, R. T. (2000). Depression and manic-depressive illness. In G. Fink (Ed.), *Encyclopedia of stress.* San Diego: Academic Press.

Rubonis, A. V., & Bickman, L. (1991). Psychological impairment in the wake of disaster: The disaster-psychopathology relationship. *Psychological Bulletin, 109,* 384–399.

Ruffman, R., Perner, J., Naito, M., Parkin, L., & Clements, W. A. (1998). Older (but not younger) siblings facilitate false belief understanding. *Developmental Psychology, 34,* 161–174.

Rugg, M. (1995). La difference vive. *Nature, 373* (16 February), 561.

Runge, C. B. (2000). *Clinical MRI.* St. Louis: Harcourt Health Sciences.

Runquist, W. N. (1975). Interference among memory traces. *Memory and Cognition, 3,* 143–159.

Rush, A. J., Crismon, M. L. et al. (1998). Consensus guidelines in the treatment of major depressive disorder. *Journal of Clinical Psychiatry, 59* (Suppl. 20), 73–84.

Rushton, J. P. (1989). Genetic similarity, human altruism, and group selection. *Behavioral and Brain Sciences, 12,* 503–559.

Russell, J., & Fernandez-Dols, J. M. (1994). Is there universal recognition of emotion from facial expression? A review of cross-cultural studies. *Psychological Bulletin, 115,* 102–141.

Russell, J. A. (1994). Is there universal recognition of emotion from facial expressions? A review of the cross-cultural studies. *Psychological Bulletin, 115,* 102–141.

Russell, J. C. (1989). Anxiety disorders in Japan: A review of the Japanese literature on Shinkeishitsu and Taijin Kyofushu. *Culture, Medicine, and Psychiatry, 13,* 391–403.

Russell, M., Dark, K. A., Cummins, R. W., Ellman, G., Callaway, E., & Peeke, H. V. (1984). Learned histamine release. *Science, 225,* 733–734.

Russell, P. A., Deregowski, J. B., & Kinnear, P. R. (1997). Perception and aesthetics. In J. W. Berry & P. R. (Eds.), *Handbook of cross-cultural psychology, Vol. 2: Basic processes and human development* (2nd ed.). Boston: Allyn & Bacon.

Russian Association of Crisis Centers for Women (1995). *Report for the non-governmental forum of the United Nations' fourth world congress on the status of women: Violence against women in Russia.* Moscow: Author.

Ruttenber, A. J., Lawler, H. J., Yin, M., & Wetli, C. V. (1997). Fatal excited delirium following cocaine use: Epidemiologic findings provide new evidence for mechanisms of cocaine toxicity. *Journal of Forensic Sciences, 42,* 25–31.

Rutter, D. R. (2000). Attendance and reattendance for breast cancer screening: A prospective 3-year test of the Theory of Planned Behaviour. *British Journal of Health Psychology, 5,* 1-13.

Rutter, M. L. (1997). Nature-nurture integration: The example of antisocial behavior. *American Psychologist, 52,* 390–398.

Ryan, L., & Eich, E. (2000). Mood dependence and implicit memory. In E. Tulving (Ed.), *Memory, consciousness, and the brain: The Tallinn Conference.* Philadelphia: Psychology Press/Taylor & Francis.

Rys, G. S., & Bear, G. G. (1997). Relational aggression and peer relations: Gender and developmental issues. *Merrill Palmer Quarterly, 43,* 87–106.

Saad, L. (1999, April 23). *Public views Littleton tragedy as sign of deeper problems in country.* Gallup News Service. Princeton, NJ: Gallup Organization.

Saari, L. M., Johnson, T. R., McLaughlin, S. D., & Zimmerle, D. M. (1988). A survey of management training and education practices in U.S. companies. *Personnel Psychology, 41,* 731–743.

Sack, R. L., Hughes, R. J., Edgar, D. M., & Lewy, A. J. (1997). Sleep-promoting effects of melatonin: At what dose, in whom, under what conditions, and by what mechanisms? *Sleep, 20,* 908–915.

Sack, R. L., & Lewy, A. J. (1997). Melatonin as a chronobiotic: Treatment of circadian desynchrony in night workers and the blind. *Journal of Biological Rhythms, 12,* 595–603.

Sack, R. L., Lewy, A. J., & Hughes, R. J. (1998). Use of melatonin for sleep and circadian rhythm disorders. *Annals of Medicine, 30,* 115–121.

Sacks, O. (1985, 1986). *The man who mistook his wife for a hat and other clinical tales.* New York: Summit Books and Simon & Schuster.

Sadoski, M., Kealy, W. A., Goetz, E. T., & Paivio, A. (1997). Concreteness and imagery effects in the written composition of definitions. *Journal of Educational Psychology, 89,* 518–526.

Sagi, A., & Hoffman, M. L. (1976). Empathic distress in the newborn. *Developmental Psychology, 12,* 175–176.

Salovey, P., Mayer, J. D., Goldman, S. L., Turvey, C., & Palfai, T. P. (1995). Emotional attention, clarity, and repair: Exploring emotional intelligence using the Trait Meta-Mood Scale. In J. W. Pennebaker, et. al. (Eds.), *Emotion, disclosure and health.* Washington, DC: American Psychological Association.

Salovey, P., Mayer, J. D., & Rosenhan, D. L. (1991). Mood and helping: Mood as a motivator of helping and helping as a regulator of mood. In M. S. Clark (Ed.), *Prosocial behavior* (Vol. 12). Newbury Park, CA: Sage Publications.

Salovey, P., Rothman, A. J., Detweiler, J. B., & Steward, W. T. (2000). Emotional states and physical health. *American Psychologist, 55,* 110–121.

Salovey, P., Sluyter, D., & Goleman, D. (1997). *Emotional development and emotional intelligence.* New York: Basic Books.

Salthouse, T. A. (1994). The nature of the influence of speed on adult age differences in cognition. *Developmental Psychology, 30,* 240–259.

Saltz, B., et al. (1991). Prospective study of tardive dyskinesia incidence in the elderly. *Journal of the American Medical Association, 266,* 2402–2406.

Sampaio, E. (1989). Is there a critical age for using the Sonicguide with blind infants? *Journal of Visual Impairment & Blindness, 82,* 105–108.

Sampson, R. J. (1997). The embeddedness of adolescent and child development: A community level perspective on urban violence. In J. McCord (Ed.), *Violence and childhood in the inner-city.* New York: Cambridge University Press.

Sandler, J. (1986). Aversion methods. In F. H. Kanfer & A. P. Goldstein (Eds.), *Helping people change: A textbook of methods* (3rd ed.). New York: Pergamon.

Sanes, J. N., Dimitrov, B., & Hallett, M. (1990). Motor learning in patients with cerebellar dysfunction. *Brain, 113,* 103-120.

Saphier, D. (1992). Electrophysiological studies of the effects of interleukin-1 and interferon on the EEG and pituitary-adrenocortical activity. In J. J. Rothwell & R. D. Dantzer (Eds.), *Interleukin-1 in the brain.* Oxford, England: Pergamon.

Sapse, A. T. (1997). Cortisol, high cortisol diseases, and anticortisol therapy. *Psychoneuroendocrinology, 22,* 3–8.

Sarason, I. G., & Sarason, B. R. (1990). Test anxiety. In H. Leitenberg (Ed.), *Handbook of social and evaluation anxiety.* New York: Plenum.

Sarason, I. G., Sarason, B. R., Pierce, G. R., Shearin, E. N., & Sayers, M. H. (1991). A social learning approach to increasing blood donations. *Journal of Applied Social Psychology, 21,* 896–918.

Sarbin, T. R., & Coe, W. C. (1972). *Hypnosis: A social psychological analysis of influence communication.* New York: Holt, Rinehart and Winston.

Satcher, D. (1999). *Mental health: A report of the Surgeon General.* Washington, DC.: U.S. Department of Health and Human Services.

Satir, V. (1967). *Conjoint family therapy.* Palo Alto, CA: Sciences and Behavior Books.

Sauer, M. V. (1998). *Principles of oocyte and embryo donation.* New York: Springer-Verlag.

Savage, P. J., & Bennett, P. H. (1992). Obesity and diabetes in American Indians and their interrelationships among the Pima Indians of Arizona. In E. W. Haller & L. P. Aitken (Eds.), *Mashkiki: Old medicine nourishing the new. American Indians and Alaska Natives in biomedical research careers.* Lanham, MD: University Press of America.

Savage-Rumbaugh, E. S., Murphy, J., et al. (1993). Language comprehension in ape and child. *Monographs of the Society for Research in Child Development, 58* (no. 233), 1–254.

Savage-Rumbaugh, E. S., Pate, J. L., Lawson, J., Smith, S. T., & Rosenbaum, S. (1983). Can a chimpanzee make a statement? *Journal of Experimental Psychology: General. 112,* 457–492.

Scarr, S. (1992). Developmental theories for the 1990s: Development and individual differences. *Child Development, 63,* 1–19.

Scarr, S. (1998a). American child care today. *American Psychologist, 53,* 95–108.

Scarr, S. (1998b). How do families affect intelligence? Social environmental and behavior genetic predictions. In J. J. McArdle & R. W. Woodcock et al. (Eds.). *Human cognitive abilities in theory and practice.* Mahwah, NJ: Erlbaum.

Schachter, S. (1959). *The psychology of affiliation: Experimental studies of the sources of gregariousness.* Stanford, CA: Stanford University Press.

Schachter, S. (1966). The interaction of cognitive and physiological determinants of emotional state. In C. D. Spielberger (Ed.), *Anxiety and behavior.* New York: Academic Press.

Schachter, S. (1968). Obesity and eating. *Science, 16,* 751–756.

Schachter, S. (1982). Recidivism and self-cure of smoking and obesity. *American Psychologist, 37,* 436–444.

Schachter, S., & Latane, B. (1964). Crime, cognition, and the autonomic nervous system. In D. Levine (Ed.), *Nebraska Symposium on Maturation.* Lincoln: University of Nebraska Press.

Schachter, S., & Wheeler, L. (1962). Epinephrine, chlorpromazine, and amusement. *Journal of Abnormal and Social Psychology, 65,* 121–128.

Schacter, D. L. (1992). Understanding implicit memory: A cognitive neuroscience approach. *American Psychologist, 47,* 559–569.

Schacter, D. L., & Curran, T. (2000). Memory without remembering and remembering without memory: Implicit and false memories. In M. S. Gazzaniga (Ed.), *The new cognitive neurosciences* (2nd ed.). Cambridge, MA: MIT Press.

Schacter, D. L., Norman, K. A., & Koutstaal, W. (1998). The cognitive neuroscience of constructive memory. *Annual Review of Psychology, 49,* 289–318.

Schaeff, C. M., Boness, D. J., & Bowen, W. D. (1999). Female distribution, genetic relatedness, and fostering behaviour in harbour seals, Phoca vitulina. *Animal Behaviour, 57,* 427–431.

Schaie, K. W. (1994). The course of adult intellectual development. *American Psychologist, 49,* 304–313.

Schaie, K. W. (1998). The Seattle Longitudinal Studies of adult intelligence. In M. Lawton & T. A. Salthouse (Eds.), *Essential papers on the psychology of aging.* New York: University Press.

Scheff, T. J. (1966). *Being mentally ill: A sociological theory.* Chicago: Aldine.

Scheflin, A. W., Spiegel, H., & Spiegel, D. (1999). Forensic uses of hypnosis. In A. K. Hess & I. B. Weiner (Eds.), *The handbook of forensic psychology* (2nd ed.). New York: John Wiley & Sons.

Scheier, M. F. (2000). Optimism. In G. Fink (Ed.), *Encyclopedia of stress,* San Diego: Academic Press.

Scheier, M. F., & Carver, C. S. (1985). Optimism, coping, and health: Assessment and implications of generalized outcome expectancies. *Health Psychology, 4,* 219–247.

Schenck, C. H., Milner, D. M., Hurwitz, T. D., & Bundlie, S. R. (1989). A polysomnographic and clinical report on sleep-related injury in 100 adult patients. *American Journal of Psychiatry, 146,* 1166–1173.

Scher, S. J. (1999). Are adaptations necessarily genetic? *American Psychologist, 54,* 436–437.

Scherer, K. (1984). On the nature and function of emotion: A component process approach. In K. Scherer & P. Ekman (Eds.), *Approaches to emotion.* Hillsdale, NJ: Erlbaum.

Scherer, K. R. (1988). *Facets of emotion: Recent research.* Hillsdale, NJ: Erlbaum.

Scherer, Klaus R. (1999). Appraisal theory. In T. Dalgleish & M. J. Power (Eds.), *Handbook of cognition and emotion.* Chichester, England: Wiley.

Schlegel, A., & Barry, H. (1991). *Adolescence: An anthropological inquiry.* New York: Free Press.

Schlenker, B. R., & Weigold, M. F. (1992). Interpersonal processes involving impression regulation and management. *Annual Review of Psychology, 43,* 133–168.

Schlink, B. (1997). *The reader.* New York: Random House.

Schmajuk, N. A., & Holland, P. C. (Eds.) (1998). *Occasion setting: Associative learning and cognition in animals.* Washington, DC: American Psychological Association.

Schmajuk, N. A., Lamoureux, J. A., & Holland, P. C. (1998). Occasion setting: A neural network approach. *Psychological Review, 105,* 3-32.

Schmidt, P. J., & Rubinow, D. R. (1997). Neuroregulatory role of gonadal steroids in humans. *Psychopharmacology Bulletin, 33*(2), 219–220.

Schmolck, H., Buffalo, E. A., & Squire, L. R. (2000). Memory distortions develop over time: Recollections of the O.J. Simpson trial verdict after 15 and 32 months. *Psychological Science, 11,* 39–45.

Schneer, J. A., & Reitman, F. (1995). The impact of gender as managerial careers unfold. *Journal of Vocational Behavior, 47,* 290–315.

Schneer, J. A., & Reitman, F. (1997). The interrupted managerial career path: A longitudinal study of MBAs. *Journal of Vocational Behavior, 51,* 411–434.

Schnurr, P. P., Spiro III, A., Aldwin, C. M., & Stukel, T. A. (1998). Physical symptom trajectories following trauma exposure: Longitudinal findings from the Normative Aging Study. *Journal of Nervous and Mental Disease, 186,* 522–528.

Schoen, L. M. (1996). Monopoly: Board games and mnemonics. *Teaching of Psychology, 23,* 30–32.

Schofeld, J. W., & Wagar, H. A. (1979). Unplanned social learning in an interracial school. In R. Rist (Ed.), *Inside desegregated schools: Taking stock of a great American experiment.* New York: Academic Press.

Schooler, J. W., & Eich, E. (2000). Memory for emotional events. In E. Tulving and F. I. M. Craik (Eds.), *The Oxford handbook of memory.* New York: Oxford University Press.

Schore, A. N. (1996). The experience-dependent maturation of a regulatory system in the orbital prefrontal cortex and the origin of developmental psychopathology. *Development and Psychopathology, 8,* 59–87.

Schriever, S. H. (1990). Comparison of beliefs and practices of ethnic Viet and Lao Hmong concerning illness, healing, death and mourning: Implications for hospice care with refugees in Canada. *Journal of Palliative Care, 6,* 42–49.

Schulz, R., & Aderman, D. (1980). Clinical research and the stages of dying. In R. A. Kalish (Ed.), *Death, dying, and transcending.* Farmingdale, New York: Baywood.

Schutte, N. S., Malouff, J. M., Hall, L. E., Haggerty, D. J., Cooper, J. T., Golden, C. J., & Dornheim, L. (1998). Development and validation of a measure of emotional intelligence. *Personality and Individual Differences, 25,* 167–177.

Schwartz, B. L. (1998). Illusory tip-of-the-tongue states. *Memory, 6,* 623–642.

Schwartz, B. L., Travis, D. M., Castro, A. M., & Smith, S. M. (2000). The phenomenology of real and illusory tip-of-the-tongue states. *Memory and Cognition, 28,* 18–27.

Schwartz, R. (1984). Body weight regulation. *University of Washington Medicine, 10,* 16–20.

Schwarzer, R. (1998). Stress and coping from a social-cognitive perspective. *Annals of the New York Academy of Sciences, 851,* 531–537.

Schweder, R. A., & Sullivan, L. (1990). The semiotic subject of cultural psychology. In L. A. Pervin (Ed.), *Handbook of personality: Theory and research.* New York: Guilford Press.

Schweinhart, L. J., & Weikart, D. P. (1998). Hign/Scope Perry Preschool Program effects at age twenty-seven. In J. Crane (Ed.), *Social programs that work.* New York: Russell Sage Foundation.

Scialfa, C. T., & Joffe, K. M. (1997). Age differences in feature and conjunction search: Implications for theories of visual search and generalized slowing. *Aging, Neuropsychology, and Cognition, 4,* 227–246.

Scott, C. S., Arthur, D. P., Panizo, M. I., & Owen, R. (1989). Menarche: The Black American experience. *Journal of Adolescent Health Care, 10,* 363, 368.

Scott, T. R. (1992). Taste, feeding, and pleasure. In A. N. Epstein, et al. (Eds.), *Progress in psychobiology and physiological psychology.* San Diego: Academic Press.

Scott, T. R., & Giza, B. K. (1993). Gustatory control of ingestion. In D. A. Booth, et al. (Eds.), *Neurophysiology of ingestion. Pergamon studies in neuroscience.* Oxford, England: Pergamon.

Scoville, W. B., & Milner, B. (1957). Loss of recent memory after bilateral hippocampal lesions. *Journal of Neurology, Neurosurgery, and Psychiatry, 20,* 11–21.

Seale, C. (1998). *Constructing death: The sociology of dying and bereavement.* New York: Cambridge University Press.

Sears, R. R. (1977). Sources of life satisfaction of the Terman gifted men. *American Psychologist, 32,* 119–128.

Sears, R. R., Maccoby, E. E., & Levin, H. (1957). *Patterns of child rearing.* Evanston, IL: Row, Peterson.

Seattle Times (1997, December 11). Paralyzed woman is good Samaritan. *Seattle Times,* p. B3.

Segerstrom, S. C., Taylor, S. E., Kemeny, M. E., & Fahey, J. L. (1998). Optimism is associated with mood, coping and immune change in response to stress. *Journal of Personality and Social Psychology, 74,* 1646–1655.

Seligman, M. E. P. (1970). On the generality of the laws of learning. *Psychological Review, 77,* 406–418.

Seligman, M. E. P. (1971). Phobias and preparedness. *Behavior Therapy, 2,* 307–320.

Seligman, M. E. P. (1975). *Helplessness: On depression, development, and death.* New York: W. H. Freeman.

Seligman, M. E. P. (1989). Research in clinical psychology: Why is there so much depression today? In I. S. Cohen (Ed.), *The G. Stanley Hall lecture series* (Vol. 9). Washington, DC: American Psychological Association.

Seligman, M. E. P. (1991). *Learned optimism.* New York: Knopf.

Seligman, M. E. P. (1995). The effectiveness of psychotherapy: The Consumer Reports study. *American Psychologist, 50,* 965–974.

Seligman, M. E. P., & Csikszentmihalyi, M. (2000). Positive psychology: An introduction. *American Psychologist, 55,* 5–14.

Seligman, M. E. P., & Isaacowitz, D. M. (2000). Learned helplessness. In G. Fink (Ed.), *Encyclopedia of stress.* San Diego: Academic Press.

Selye, H. (1976). *The stress of life.* New York: McGraw-Hill.

Sen, D., Jefferson, J. W., & Greist, J. H. (1999). *Depression and antidepressants: A guide.* Madison, WI: Madison Institute of Medicine.

Senden, M. von (1960). *Space and sight: The perception of space and shape in the congenitally blind before and after operation.* New York: Free Press. (P. Heath, Trans.)

Sergios, P. A., & Cody, J. (1985–1986). Importance of physical attractiveness and social assertiveness skills in male homosexual dating behavior and partner selection. *Journal of Homosexuality, 12,* 71–84.

Seto, M. C., & Barbaree, H. E. (1995). The role of alcohol in sexual aggression. *Clinical Psychology Review, 15,* 545–566.

Shaffer, D. R. (1989). *Developmental psychology: Childhood and adolescence* (2nd ed.). Pacific Grove, CA: Brooks/Cole.

Shair, H. N., Barr, G. A., & Hofer, M. A. (Eds.). (1991). *Developmental psychobiology.* New York: Oxford University Press.

Shallice, T., & Burgess, P. (1991). Higher-order cognitive impairments and frontal-lobe lesions in man. In H. S. Levin, H. M. Eisenberg, & A. L. Benton (Eds.), *Frontal lobe function and dysfunction.* New York: Oxford University Press.

Shanab, M. E., & Yahya, L. A. (1977). A behavioral study of obedience in children. *Journal of Personality and Social Psychology, 35,* 530–536.

Shanahan, T. L., Kronauer, R. E., Duffy, J. F., Williams, G. H., & Czeisler, C. A. (1999). Melatonin rhythm observed throughout a three-cycle bright-light stimulus designed to reset the human circadian pacemaker. *Journal of Biological Rhythms, 14,* 237–253.

Shapiro, A. F., Gottman, J. M., & Carrere, S. (2000). The baby and the marriage: Identifying factors that buffer against decline in marital satisfaction after the first baby arrives. *Journal of Family Psychology, 14,* 59–70.

Shapiro, C. M., Bortz, R., Mitchell, D., Bartel, P., & Jooste, P. (1981). Slow-wave sleep: A recovery period after exercise. *Science, 214,* 1253–1254.

Shapiro, K. J. (1997). The separate world of animal research. *American Psychologist, 52,* 1250.

Sharkey, K. M. (1993). Short sleepers in history and legend. In M. A. Carskadon (Ed.), *Encyclopedia of sleep and dreaming.* New York: Macmillan.

Sharma, J., Angelucci, A., & Sur, M. (2000). Induction of visual orientation modules in auditory cortex. *Nature, 404,* 841–847.

Sharp, S. (1995). How much does bullying hurt? The effects of bullying on the personal wellbeing and educational progress of secondary aged students. *Educational and Child Psychology, 12,* 81–88.

Shaver, P. R., & Clark, C. L. (1996). Forms of adult romantic attachment and their cognitive and emotional underpinnings. In G. G. Noam, K. W. Fischer et al. (Eds.), *Development and vulnerability in close relationships. The Jean Piaget symposium series.* Mahwah, NJ: Erlbaum.

Shavit, Y. (1990). Stress-induced immune modulation in animals: Opiates and endogenous opioid peptides. In R. Ader, N. Cohen, & D. L. Felten (Eds.), *Psychoneuroimmunology II*. New York: Academic Press.

Shaw, W. S., & Dimsdale, J. E. (2000). Type A personality, Type B personality. In G. Fink (Ed.), *Encyclopedia of stress*. San Diego: Academic Press.

Shaywitz, B. A., Shaywitz, S. E., & Pugh, K. R., et al. (1995). Sex differences in the functional organization of the brain for language. *Nature, 373* (16 February), 607–609.

Sheehan, P. W., Green, V., & Truesdale, P. (1992). Influence of rapport on hypnotically induced pseudomemory. *Journal of Abnormal Psychology, 101*, 690–700.

Shek, D. T. L. (1998). A longitudinal study of the relations between parent-adolescent conflict and adolescent psychological well-being. *Journal of Genetic Psychology, 159*, 53–67.

Shepherd, G. (1997). *The synaptic organizer of the brain*. New York: Oxford University Press.

Sherif, M. (1935). A study of some social factors in perception. *Archives of Psychology* (No. 187).

Sherif, M., Harvey, O., White, B., Hood, W., & Sherif, C. (1961). *Intergroup conflict and cooperation: The Robbers Cave experiment*. Norman, OK: University of Oklahoma Press.

Sherwood, L. (1991). *Fundamentals of physiology: A human perspective*. St. Paul, MN: West.

Shevrin, H., Bond, J. A., Brakel, L. A. W., Hertel, R. K., & Williams, W. J. (1996). *Conscious and unconscious processes: Psychodynamic, cognitive, and neurophysiological convergences*. New York: Guilford Press.

Shevrin, H., Bond, J. A., Brakel, L. A. W., Hertel, R. K., & Williams, W. J. (1998). The Freud-Rapaport theory of consciousness. In R. F. Bronstein, J. M. Masling et al. (Eds.), *Empirical perspectives on the psychoanalytic unconscious. Empirical studies of psychoanalytic theories*. Washington, DC: American Psychological Association.

Shiner, R. L. (1998). How shall we speak of children's personalities in middle childhood? A preliminary taxonomy. *Psychological Bulletin, 124*, 308–332.

Shneidman, E. S. (1998). *The suicidal mind*. New York: Oxford University Press.

Shoda, Y. (1999). Behavioral expressions of a personality system: Generation and perception of behavioral signatures. In D. Cervone & Y. Shoda (Eds.), *The coherence of personality: Social-cognitive bases of consistency, variability, and organization*. New York: Guilford Press.

Shoda, Y., & Mischel, W. (2000). Reconciling contextualism with the core assumptions of personality psychology. *European Journal of Personality, 14*, 462–484.

Shoda, Y., Mischel, W., & Wright, J. C. (1994). Intra-individual stability and patterning of behavior: Incorporating psychological situations into the idiographic analysis of personality. *Journal of Personality and Social Psychology, 65*, 1023–1035.

Shorter, E. (1998). *A history of psychiatry: From the era of the asylum to the age of Prozac*. New York: Wiley.

Shultz, K. S., Morton, K. R., & Weckerle, J. R. (1998). The influence of push and pull factors on voluntary and involuntary early retirees' retirement decision and adjustment. *Journal of Vocational Behavior, 53*, 45–57.

Shumaker, S. A., & Hill, D. R. (1991). Gender differences in social support and physical health. *Health Psychology, 10*, 102–111.

Siegal, M. P., & Cadida, C. (1998). Preschoolers' understanding of lies and innocent and negligent mistakes. *Developmental Psychology, 34*, 332–341.

Siegel, A., Roeling, T. A. P., Gregg, T. R., & Kruk, M. R. (1999). Neuropharmacology of brain-stimulation-evoked aggression. *Neuroscience and Biobehavioral Reviews, 23*, 359–389.

Siegel, S. (1984). Pavlovian conditioning and heroin overdose: Reports from overdose victims. *Bulletin of the Psychonomic Society, 22*, 428–430.

Siegel, S., & Allan, L. G. (1996). The widespread influence of the Rescorla-Wagner model. *Psychonomic Bulletin and Review, 3*, 314–321.

Siegler, R. S. (1981). Developmental sequences within and between concepts. *Monographs of the Society for Research in Child Development, 46*, 84.

Siegler, R. S. (1986). *Children's thinking*. Englewood Cliffs, NJ: Prentice Hall.

Siegler, R. S. (1996). *Emerging minds: The process of change in children's thinking*. New York: Oxford University Press.

Siever, L. J., Buchsbaum, M. S., New, A. S., Spiegel, C. J., Wei, T., & Hazlett, E. A., (1999). d,l-Fenfluramine response in impulsive personality disorder assessed with [-sup-1-sup-8F]flurodeoxyglucose positron emission tomography. *Neuropsychopharmacology, 20*, 413–423.

Sigall, H., & Page, R. (1971). Current stereotypes: A little fading, a little faking. *Journal of Personality and Social Psychology, 18*, 247–255.

Sigelman, C. K., & Shaffer, D. R. (1991). *Life-span human development*. Pacific Grove, CA: Brooks/Cole.

Sigman, M. (1995). Nutrition and child development: More food for thought. *Current Directions in Psychological Science, 4*, 52–55.

Silva, A. J., Paylor, R., Wehner, J. M., & Tonegawa, S. (1992). Impaired spatial learning in !a-calcium-calmodulin kinase II mutant mice. *Science, 257*, 206–211.

Simion, F., Valenza, E., Umilta, C., & Barba, B. D. (1998). Preferential orienting to faces in newborns: A temporal-nasal asymmetry. *Journal of Experimental Psychology: Human Perception and Performance, 24*, 1399–1405.

Simkin, L. R., & Gross, A. M. (1994). Assessment of coping with high risk situations for exercise relapse among healthy women. *Health Psychology, 13*, 274–277.

Simmons, J. V. (1981). *Project sea hunt: A report on prototype development and tests*. Naval Ocean Systems Center, San Diego: Technical Report 746.

Simon, H. A. (1990). Invariants of human behavior. *Annual Review of Psychology, 41*, 1–20.

Simon, L., Greenberg, J., & Brehm, J. (1995). Trivialization: The forgotten mode of dissonance reduction. *Journal of Personality and Social Psychology, 68*, 247–260.

Simons, R. L., & Chao, W. (1996). Conduct problems. In R. L. Simon (Ed.), *Understanding differences between divorced and intact families: Stress, interaction, and child outcome*. Thousand Oaks, CA: Sage Publications.

Simonton, D. K. (1999). Creativity and genius. In L. A. Pervin & O. P. John (Eds.), *Handbook of personality: Theory and research* (2nd ed.). New York: Guilford Press.

Sinclair, S. V., & Mistlberger, R. E. (1997). Scheduled activity reorganizes circadian phase of Syrian hamsters under full and skeleton photoperiods. *Behavioural Brain Research, 87*, 127–137.

Singer, J. A., Singer, J. L., & Zittel, C. (2000). Personality variations in autobiographical memories, self-representations, and daydreaming. In R. G. Kunzendorf & B. Wallace (Eds.), *Individual differences in conscious experience. Advances in consciousness research* (Vol. 20). Amsterdam: John Benjamins.

Singer, J. L. (1988). Sampling ongoing consciousness and emotional experience: Implications for health. In M. J. Horowitz (Ed.), *Psychodynamics and cognition*. Chicago: University of Chicago Press.

Singer, J. L. (1990). *Repression and dissociation*. Chicago: University of Chicago Press.

Singer, J. L. (1999). Repression, dissociation and our human stream of consciousness: Memory as a constructive, creative process. In S. Taub (Ed.), *Recovered memories of child sexual abuse: Psychological, social, and legal perspectives on a contemporary mental health controversy*. Springfield, IL: Charles C Thomas.

Singh, R., Gupta, M., & Dalal, A. K. (1979). Cultural difference in attribution of performance: An integration-theoretical analysis. *Journal of Personality and Social Psychology, 37*, 1342-1351.

Sistler, A. B., & Moore, G. M. (1996). Cultural diversity in coping with marital stress. *Journal of Clinical Geropsychology, 2*, 77–82.

Skinner, B. F. (1938). *The behavior of organisms; an experimental analysis*. New York: Appleton-Century.

Skinner, B. F. (1948). *Walden two*. New York: Macmillan.

Skinner, B. F. (1953). *Science and human behavior*. New York: Macmillan.

Skinner, B. F. (1957). *Verbal behavior*. New York: Prentice Hall.

Skinner, B. F. (1968). *The technology of teaching*. New York: Appleton-Century-Crofts.

Skinner, B. F. (1971). *Beyond freedom and dignity*. New York: Knopf.

Skinner, B. F. (1977). *Upon further reflection*. Englewood Cliffs, NJ: Prentice Hall.

Skinner, B. F. (1983). *A matter of consequences*. New York: Knopf.

Skinner, B. F. (1986). The evolution of verbal behavior. *Journal of the Experimental Analysis of Behavior, 45*, 115–122.

Skinner, B. F. (1989a). Teaching machines. *Science, 243*, 1535.

Skinner, B. F. (1989b). The origins of cognitive thought. *American Psychologist, 44*, 13–18.

Skinner, B. F. (1990). Can psychology be a science of mind? *American Psychologist, 45*, 1206–1210.

Sklar, L. S., & Anisman, H. (1981). Stress and cancer. *Psychological Bulletin, 89*, 369–406.

Skorikov, V., & Vondracek, F. W. (1998). Vocational identity development: Its relationship to other identity domains and to overall identity development. *Journal of Career Assessment, 6*, 13–35.

Slavin, R. E. (1900). *Cooperative learning: Theory, research and practice*. Englewood Cliffs, NJ: Prentice Hall.

Slavney, P. R. (1990). *Perspectives on hysteria.* Baltimore: The Johns Hopkins University Press.

Slobin, D. I. (1996). From "thought and language" to "thinking for speaking." In J. J. Gumperz, et al. (Eds.), *Rethinking linguistic relativity. Studies in the social and cultural foundations of language.* Cambridge, England: Cambridge University Press.

Sloman, S. A., Hayman, C. G., Ohta, N., & Law, J. (1988). Forgetting in primed fragment completion. *Journal of Experimental Psychology: Learning, Memory, and Cognition, 14,* 223–239.

Smeets, M. A. M. (1999).Body size categorization in anorexia nervosa using a morphing instrument. *International Journal of Eating Disorders, 25,* 451-455.

Smetana, J. (1988). Adolescents' and parents' conceptions of parental authority. *Child Development, 59,* 321–335.

Smetana, J., & Gaines, C. (1999). Adolescent-parent conflict in middle-class African American families. *Child Development, 70,* 1447–1463.

Smiley, A. (1986). Marijuana: On-road and driving simulator studies. *Alcohol, Drugs and Driving, 2,* 121–134.

Smith, C. A., & Ellsworth, P. C. (1985). Patterns of cognitive approach in emotion. *Journal of Personality and Social Psychology, 48,* 813–838.

Smith, C. A., & Lazarus, R. S. (1990). Emotion and adaptation. In L. A. Pervin (Ed.), *Handbook of personality: Theory and research.* New York: Guilford Press.

Smith, E. R., & Zarate, M. A. (1992). Exemplar-based model of social judgment. *Psychological Review, 99,* 3–21.

Smith, J. W., & Frawley, P. J. (1993). Treatment outcome of 600 chemically dependent patients treated in a multimodal inpatient program including aversion therapy and pentothal interviews. *Journal of Substance Abuse Treatment, 10,* 359–369.

Smith, L. D., & Woodward, W. R. (Eds.) (1996). *B. F. Skinner and behaviorism in American culture.* Bethlehem, PA: Lehigh University Press.

Smith, M. E. (1926). An investigation of the development of the sentence and the extent of vocabulary in young children. *University of Iowa Studies in Child Welfare, 3* (No. 5).

Smith, M. L., & Glass, G. V. (1977). Meta-analyses of psychotherapy outcome studies. *American Psychologist, 32,* 752–760.

Smith, R. E. (1989). Effects of coping skills training on generalized self-efficacy and locus of control. *Journal of Personality and Social Psychology, 56,* 228–233.

Smith, R. E. (1993). *Enhancing human performance: A psychological skills approach.* Minneapolis: West.

Smith, R. E. (1996). Performance anxiety, cognitive interference, and concentration enhancement strategies in sports. In I. G. Sarason, G. R. Pierce, & B. R. Sarason (Eds.), *Cognitive interference: Theories, methods, and findings.* Mahwah, NJ: Erlbaum.

Smith, R. E., Johnson, J. H., & Sarason, I. G. (1978). Life change, the sensation seeking motive, and psychological distress. *Journal of Consulting and Clinical Psychology, 46,* 348–349.

Smith, R. E., Leffingwell, T. R., & Ptacek, J. T. (1999). Can people remember how they coped? Factors associated with discordance between same-day and retrospective reports.

Journal of Personality and Social Psychology, 76, 1050–1061.

Smith, R. E., & Nye, S. L. (1989). A comparison of induced affect and covert rehearsal in the acquisition of stress management coping skills. *Journal of Counseling Psychology, 36,* 17–23.

Smith, R. E., & Rohsenow, D. J. (1987). Cognitive-affective stress management training: A treatment and resource manual. *Social and Behavioral Science Documents, 17*(2), Document No. 2829.

Smith, R. E., & Smoll, F. L. (1990). Sport performance anxiety. In H. Leitenberg (Ed.), *Handbook of social and evaluation anxiety.* New York: Plenum.

Smith, R. E., & Smoll, F. L. (1997). Coaching the coaches: Youth sports as a scientific and applied behavioral setting. *Current Directions in Psychological Science, 6,* 16–21.

Smith, R. E., Smoll, F. L., & Ptacek, J. T. (1989). Conjunctive moderator variables in vulnerability and resiliency research: Life stress, social support and coping skills, and adolescent sport injuries. *Journal of Personality and Social Psychology, 58,* 360–370.

Smith, R. E., Smoll, F. L., & Schutz, R. W. (1990). Measurement and correlates of sport-specific cognitive and somatic trait anxiety: The Sport Anxiety Scale. *Anxiety Research, 2,* 263–280.

Smith, S. L., & Donnerstein, E. (1998). Harmful effects of exposure to media violence: Learning of aggression, emotional desensitization, and fear. In R. G. Geen, G. Russell, & E. Donnerstein (Eds.), *Human aggression: Theories, research, and implications for social policy.* San Diego: Academic Press.

Smith, S. M., McIntosh, W. D., & Bazzini, D. G. (1999). Are the beautiful good in Hollywood? An investigation of the beauty-and-goodness stereotype on film. *Basic and Applied Social Psychology, 21,* 69–80.

Smith, S. M., & Rothkopf, E. Z. (1984). Contextual enrichment and distribution of practice in the classroom. *Cognition and Instruction, 1,* 341-358.

Snow, M. E., Jacklin, C. N., & Maccoby, E. E. (1983). Sex-of-child-differences in father-child interaction at one year of age. *Child Development, 54,* 227–232.

Snyder, F. (1970). The phenomenology of dreaming. In L. Madow & L. Snow (Eds.), *The psychodynamic implications of the physiological studies on dreams.* Springfield, IL: Charles C Thomas.

Snyder, H. N., & Sickmund, M. (1995). *Juvenile offenders and victims: A national report.* Washington, DC: Office of Juvenile Justice and Delinquency Prevention.

Snyder, M. (1987). *Public appearances/private realities: The psychology of self-monitoring.* New York: W. H. Freeman.

Snyder, M., Berscheid, E., & Glick, P. (1985). Focusing on the exterior and the interior: Two investigations of the initiation of personal relationships. *Journal of Personality and Social Psychology, 48,* 1427–1439.

Snyder, M., & Gangestad, S. (1986). On the nature of self-monitoring: Matters of assessment, matters of validity. *Journal of Personality and Social Psychology, 51,* 125–139.

Snyder, M., & Swann, W. B., Jr. (1976). When actions reflect attitudes: The politics of

impression management. *Journal of Personality and Social Psychology, 34,* 1034–1042.

Snyder, S. H. (1977). Opiate receptors and internal opiates. *Scientific American, 236,* 44–56.

Sober, E., & Wilson, D. S. (1998). *Unto others: The evolution and psychology of unselfish behavior.* Cambridge, MA: Harvard University Press.

Soler, M. J., & Ruiz, J. C. (1996). The spontaneous use of memory aids at different educational levels. *Applied Cognitive Psychology, 10,* 41-51.

Solomon, G. F., Segerstrom, S. C., Grohr, P., Kemeny, M., & Fahey, J. (1997). Shaking up immunity: Psychological and immunologic changes after a natural disaster. *Psychosomatic Medicine, 59,* 114–127.

Solomon, R. L., & Wynne, L. C. (1953). Traumatic avoidance learning: Acquisition in normal dogs. *Journal of Abnormal and Social Psychology, 48,* 291–302.

Solomon, Z., & Ginzburg, K. (1998). War trauma and the aged: An Israeli perspective. In J. Lomaranz (Ed.), *Handbook of aging and mental health: An integrative approach.* New York: Plenum.

Solso, R. L. (1999). *Mind and brain sciences in the 21st century.* Cambridge, MA: MIT Press.

Somse, P., Chapko, M. K., Wata, J. B., & et al. (1998). Evaluation of an AIDS training program for traditional healers in the Central African Republic. *AIDS Education and Prevention, 10,* 558–564.

Sorensen, T., & Snow, B. (1991). How children tell: The process of disclosure in child sexual abuse. *Child Welfare, 70,* 3–15.

Spanos, N. P. (1986). Hypnotic behavior: A social-psychological interpretation of amnesia, analgesia, and "trance logic." *Behavioral and Brain Sciences, 9,* 449–467.

Spanos, N. P. (1991). A sociocognitive approach to hypnosis. In S. J. Lynn & J. W. Rhue (Eds.), *Theories of hypnosis: Current models and perspectives.* New York: Guilford Press.

Spanos, N. P. (1994). Multiple identity enactments and multiple personality disorder: A sociocognitive perspective. *Psychological Bulletin, 116,* 143–165.

Spanos, N. P. (1996). *Multiple identities and false memories: A sociocognitive perspective.* Washington, DC: American Psychological Association.

Spanos, N. P., & Chaves, J. F. (Eds.) (1988). *Hypnosis: The cognitive-behavioral perspective.* Buffalo, NY: Prometheus Books.

Spanos, N. P., DuBreuil, S. C., & Gabora, N. J. (1991). Four-month follow-up of skill-training-induced enhancements in hypnotizability. *Contemporary Hypnosis, 8,* 25-32.

Spanos, N. P., & Katsanis, J. (1989). Effects of institutional set on attributions of nonvolition during hypnotic and nonhypnotic analgesia. *Journal of Personality and Social Psychology, 56,* 182–188.

Spearman, C. (1923). *The nature of "intelligence" and the principles of cognition.* London: Macmillan.

Spector, P. E. (1997). The role of frustration in antisocial behavior at work. In R. A. Giacalone & J. Greenberg (Eds.), *Antisocial behavior in organizations.* Thousand Oaks, CA: Sage Publications.

Speisman, J., Lazarus, R. S., Mordkoff, A., & Davidson, L. (1964). Experimental reduction of stress based on ego-defense theory.

Journal of Abnormal and Social Psychology, 68, 367–380.

Spencer, S. J., Steele, C. M., & Quinn, D. M. (1999). Stereotype threat and women's math performance. *Journal of Experimental Social Psychology, 35,* 4–28.

Sperling, G. (1960). The information available in brief visual presentations. *Psychological Monographs 74* (Whole No. 11).

Sperling, G. (1984). A unified theory of attention and signal detection. In R. Parasuraman & D. R. Davies (Eds.), *Varieties of attention.* New York: Academic Press.

Sperry, R. W. (1970). Perception in the absence of neocortical commissures. In Association for Research in Nervous and Mental Disease, *Perception and its disorders.* New York: Williams & Wilkins.

Spiegel, D. (2000). Cancer. In G. Fink (Ed.), *Encyclopedia of stress.* San Diego: Academic Press.

Spiegel, D., Bloom, J. R., Kraemer, H. C., & Gottleib, E. (1989, October 14). Effect of psychosocial treatment on survival of patients with metastatic breast cancer. *The Lancet,* 888–891.

Spiegler, M. D., & Guevremont, D. C. (1998). *Contemporary behavior therapy* (3rd ed.). Pacific Grove, CA: Brooks/Cole.

Spielberger, C. D., & DeNike, L. D. (1966). Descriptive behaviorism versus cognitive theory in verbal operant conditioning. *Psychological Review, 73,* 306–326.

Sprafkin, J. N., Liebert, R. M., & Poulos, R. W. (1975). Effects of a prosocial televised example on children's helping. *Journal of Experimental Child Psychology, 20,* 119–126.

Sprecher, S., Barbee, A., & Schwartz, P. (1995). "Was it good for you, too?" Gender differences in first sexual intercourse experiences. *Journal of Sex Research, 32,* 13–15.

Sprecher, S., & Regan, P. C. (1998). Passionate and companionate love in courting and young married couples. *Sociological Inquiry, 68,* 163–185.

Springer, S. (1997). *Left brain, right brain.* San Francisco: W. H. Freeman.

Squier, L. H., & Domhoff, G. W. (1998). The presentation of dreaming and dreams in introductory psychology textbooks: A critical examination with suggestions for textbook authors and course instructors. *Dreaming: Journal of the Association for the Study of Dreams, 8,* 149–168.

Squire, L. R. (1987). *Memory and brain.* Oxford: Oxford University Press.

Squire, L. R. (1992). Memory and the hippocampus: A synthesis from findings with rats, monkeys, and humans. *Psychological Review, 99,* 195–231.

Squire, L. R., & Zola-Morgan, S. (1991). The medial temporal lobe memory system. *Science, 253,* 1380–1386.

Staats, H., van Leeuwen, E., & Wit, A. (2000). A longitudinal study of informational interventions to save energy in an office building. *Journal of Applied Behavior Analysis, 33,* 101–104.

Stahl, S. M. (1998). *Essential psychopharmacology: Neuroscientific basis and clinical applications.* New York: Cambridge University Press.

Stalder, D. R., & Baron, R. S. (1998). Attributional complexity as a moderator of

dissonance-produced attitude change. *Journal of Personality and Social Psychology, 75,* 449–455.

Stanford Center for Narcolepsy (2000). *Basic mechanisms involved in the disease.* [Online]. Available: http://www.med.stanford.edu/school/Psychiatry/narcolepsy/research1.html

Stanley, B. G., Kyrkouli, S. E., Lampert, S., & Leibowitz, S. F. (1986). Neuropeptide Y chronically injected into the hypothalamus: A powerful neurochemical inducer of hyperphagia and obesity. *Peptides, 7,* 1189–1192.

Stark, E. (1989, May). Teen sex: Not for love. *Psychology Today,* 10–11.

Staub, E. (1996). Cultural-society roots of violence: The examples of genocidal violence and of contemporary youth violence in the United States. *American Psychologist, 51,* 117–132.

Steele, C. M. (1988). The psychology of self-affirmation: Sustaining the integrity of the self. In L. Berkowitz (Ed.), *Advances in experimental social psychology* (Vol. 21). New York: Academic Press.

Steele, C. M. (1997). A threat in the air: How stereotypes shape intellectual identity and performance. *American Psychologist, 52,* 613–629.

Steele, C. M., & Aronson, J. (1995). Stereotype threat and the intellectual test performance of African Americans. *Journal of Personality and Social Psychology, 69,* 797–811.

Steele, C. M., & Josephs, R. A. (1990). Alcohol myopia: Its prized and dangerous effects. *American Psychologist, 45,* 921–933.

Steers, R. M., & Porter, L. W. (1991) (Eds.). *Motivation and work behavior* (5th ed.). New York: McGraw-Hill.

Stein, D. J. (1997) (Ed.). *Cognitive science and the unconscious.* Washington, DC: American Psychiatric Press.

Stein, M., Miller, A. H., & Trestman, R. L. (1990). Depression and the immune system. In R. Ader, N. Cohen, & D. L. Felten (Eds), *Psychoneuroimmunology II.* New York: Academic Press.

Steinberg, L., Lamborn, S. D., Darling, N., & Mount, N. S. (1994). Over-time changes in adjustment and competence among adolescents from authoritative, authoritarian, indulgent, and neglectful families. *Child Development, 65,* 754–770.

Steinberg, R. J. (1988). *The triarchic mind.* New York: Viking Press.

Stella, N., Schweitzer, P., & Piomelli, D. (1997). A second endogenous cannabinoid that modulates long-term potentiation. *Nature, 388* (6644), 773–778.

Stellar, E. (1954). The physiology of motivation. *Psychological Review, 61,* 5–22.

Stephan, W. G. (1990). School desegregation: Short-term and long-term effects. In H. Knopke (Ed.), *Opening Doors: An appraisal of race relations in America.* Tuscaloosa: University of Alabama Press.

Stephan, W. G. (1991). Intergroup relations and prejudice. In R. M. Baron, W. G. Graziano, & C. Stangor (Eds.), *Social psychology.* Ft. Worth, TX: Holt, Rinehart & Winston.

Stephenson, J. (1998). Ethics group drafts guidelines for control of genetic material and information [news]. *Journal of the American Medical Association, 279*(3), 184.

Steptoe, A. (2000). Control and stress. In G. Fink (Ed.), *Encyclopedia of stress.* San Diego: Academic Press.

Sternberg, R. J. (1988). Triangulating love. In R. J. Sternberg & M. L. Barnes (Eds.), *The psychology of love.* New Haven, CT: Yale University Press.

Sternberg, R. J. (1997). Construct validation of a triangular love scale. *European Journal of Social Psychology, 27,* 313–335.

Sternberg, R. J. (1998a). Principles of teaching for successful intelligence. *Educational Psychologist, 33,* 65–72.

Sternberg, R. J. (1998b). Applying the triarchic theory of human intelligence in the classroom. In R. J. Sternberg & W. M. Williams (Eds.), *Intelligence, instruction, and assessment: Theory into practice.* Mahwah, NJ: Erlbaum.

Sternberg, R. J., Torff, B., & Grigorenko, E. L. (1998). Teaching triarchically improves school achievement. *Journal of Educational Psychology, 90,* 374–384.

Stetson, B. A., Rahn, J. M., Dubbert, P. M., Wilner, B. I., & Mercury, M. G. (1997). Prospective evaluation of the effects of stress on exercise adherence in community-residing women. *Health Psychology, 16,* 515–520.

Stickgold, R., Pace, S. E., & Hobson, J. A. (1994). A new paradigm for dream research: Mentation reports following spontaneous arousal from REM and NREM sleep recorded in a home setting. *Consciousness and Cognition: An International Journal, 3,* 16–29.

Stockhorst, U., Klosterhalfen, S., & Steingrueber, H. J. (1998). Conditioned nausea and further side-effects in cancer chemotherapy: A review. *Journal of Psychophysiology, 12,* 14–33.

Stokols, D. (1995). The paradox of environmental psychology. *American Psychologist, 50,* 821–837.

Stone, A. A., Shiffman, S. S., & DeVries, M. (2000). Rethinking our self-report assessment methodologies: An argument for collecting ecologically valid, momentary measurements. In D. Kahneman, E. Diener, & N. Schwarz (Eds.), *Understanding quality of life: Scientific perspectives on enjoyment and suffering.* New York: Russel Sage Foundation.

Storms, M. D. (1973). Videotape and the attribution process: Reversing actors' and observers' points of view. *Journal of Personality and Social Psychology, 27,* 165–175.

Stormshak, E. A., Bierman, K. L., McMahon, R. J., Lengua, L. J. Conduct Problems Prevention Research Group. (2000). Parenting practices and child disruptive behavior problems in early elementary school. *Journal of Clinical Child Psychology, 29,* 17–29.

Strack, F., Martin, L. L., & Stepper, S. (1988). Inhibiting and facilitating conditions of facial expressions: A non-obtrusive test of the facial feedback hypothesis. *Journal of Personality and Social Psychology, 54,* 768–777.

Strawbridge, W. J., Shema, S. J., Cohen, R. D., Roberts, R. E., & Kaplan, G. A. (1998). Religion buffers effects of some stressors on depression but exacerbates others. *Journal of Gerontology, 53,* 118–126.

Streissguth, A. P., Bookstein, F. L., Barr, H. M., Press, S., & Sampson, P. D. (1998). A Fetal Alcohol Behavior Scale. *Alcoholism: Clinical and Experimental Research, 22,* 325–333.

Streissguth, A. P., Clarren, S. K., & Jones, K. L. (1985). Natural history of the fetal alcohol syndrome: A 10-year follow-up of eleven patients. *The Lancet, 2* (8446), 85–91.

Streissguth, A. P., Landesman, D. S., Martin, J. C., & Smith, D. W. (1982). Clinical effects of fetal alcohol syndrome. *Digest of Alcoholism Theory and Application, 1,* 5–10.

Strentz, H. (1984, December 25). The road to imbecility. *Cleveland Plain Dealer,* p. B23.

Strentz, T., & Auerbach, S. M. (1988). Adjustment to the stress of simulated captivity: Effects of emotion-focused versus problem-focused preparation on hostages differing in locus of control. *Journal of Personality and Social Psychology, 55,* 652–660.

Stricker, E. M., & Verbalis, J. G. (1987). Biological bases of hunger and satiety. *Annals of Behavioral Medicine, 9,* 3–8.

Stricker, G. (1992). The relation of research to clinical practice. *American Psychologist, 47,* 543–549.

Strober, M., & Humphrey, L. L. (1987). Familial contributions to the etiology and course of anorexia nervosa and bulimia. *Journal of Consulting and Clinical Psychology, 55,* 654–659.

Stouffer, S. A., Lumsdaine, A. A., Lumsdaine, M. H., Williams, R. M., Jr. (1949b). *The American soldier: Combat and its aftermath.* Princeton, NJ: Princeton University Press.

Stouffer, S. A., Suchman, E. A., De Vinney, L. C., Star, S. A., & Williams, R. M., Jr. (1949a). *The American soldier: Adjustments during army life.* Princeton, NJ: Princeton University Press.

Strough, J., Berg, C. A., & Sandone, C. (1996). Goals for solving everyday problems across the life span: Age and gender differences in the salience of interpersonal concerns. *Developmental Psychology, 32,* 1106–1115.

Strupp, H. H. (1989). Psychotherapy: Can the practitioner learn from the researcher? *American Psychologist, 44,* 717–724.

Stryer, L. (1987). The molecules of visual excitation. *Scientific American, 257*(1), 42–50.

Stukas, A. A., Snyder, M., & Clary, E. G. (1999). The effects of "mandatory volunteerism" on intentions to volunteer. *Psychological Science, 10,* 59–64.

Stunkard, A. J., Harris, J. R., Pedersen, N. L., & McClearn, G. E. (1990). The body-mass index of twins who have been reared apart. *New England Journal of Medicine, 322,* 1483–1487.

Stuss, D., & Broughton, R. (1978). Extreme short sleep: Personality profiles and a case study of sleep requirement. *Waking and Sleeping, 2,* 101–105.

Sue, D. W., & Sue, D. (1990). *Counseling the culturally different: Theory and practice.* New York: Wiley.

Sue, S. (1977). Community mental health services to minority groups: Some optimism, some pessimism. *American Psychologist, 32,* 616–624.

Sue, S. (1998). In search of cultural competence in psychotherapy and counseling. *American Psychologist, 53,* 440–448.

Sue, S., Fujino, D., Hu, L. N., Takeuchi, D., & Zane, N. (1991). Community mental health services for ethnic minority groups: A test of the cultural responsiveness hypothesis. *Journal of Consulting and Clinical Psychology, 59,* 533–540.

Sue, S., & Zane, N. (1987). The role of culture and cultural techniques in psychotherapy. *American Psychologist, 42,* 37–45.

Suggs, R. (1962). *The hidden worlds of Polynesia.* New York: Harcourt.

Suh, E., Diener, E., & Fujita, F. (1996). Events and subjective well-being: Only recent events matter. *Journal of Personality and Social Psychology, 70,* 1091–1102.

Suh, E., Diener, E., Oishi, S., & Triandis, H. (1998). The shifting basis of life satisfaction judgments across cultures: Emotions versus norms. *Journal of Personality and Social Psychology, 74,* 482–493.

Suinn, R. M., Osborne, D., & Winfree, P. (1962). The self-concept and accuracy of recall of inconsistent self-related information. *Journal of Clinical Psychology, 18,* 473–474.

Sullivan, M. A., & O'Leary, S. G. (1990). Maintenance following reward and cost token programs. *Behavior Therapy, 21,* 139–149.

Suls, J., Green, P., & Hillis, S. (1998). Emotional reactivity to everyday problems, affective inertia, and neuroticism. *Personality and Social Psychology Bulletin, 24,* 127–136.

Suomi, S. J., & Harlow, H. F. (1972). Social rehabilitation of isolate-reared monkeys. *Developmental Psychology, 6,* 487–496.

Super, C. M. (1976). Environmental effects on motor development: A case of African infant precocity. *Developmental Medicine and Child Neurology, 18,* 561–567.

Super, D. E. (1981). A developmental theory: Implementing a self-concept. In D. H. Montross & C. J. Shinkman (Eds.), *Career development in the 1980s: Theory and practice.* Springfield, IL: Charles C Thomas.

Super, C. M., Harkness, S. (1997). The cultural structuring of child development. In J. W. Berry, P. R. Dasen, & T. S. Saraswathi (Eds.), *Handbook of cross-cultural psychology* (2nd ed., Vol. 2). Boston: Allyn & Bacon.

Super, D. E. (1957). *The psychology of careers.* New York: Harper & Row.

Sussman, N. M., & Rosenfeld, H. M. (1982). Influence of culture, language, and sex on conversational distance. *Journal of Personality and Social Psychology, 42,* 66–74.

Sutton, S. K., & Davidson, R. J. (1997). Prefrontal brain asymmetry: A biological substrate of the behavioral approach and inhibition systems. *Psychological Science, 8,* 204–210.

Swain, J. C., & McLaughlin, T. F. (1998). The effects of bonus contingencies in a classwide token program on math accuracy with middle-school students with behavioral disorders. *Behavioral Interventions, 13,* 11–19.

Swan, G. E., Dame, A., & Carmelli, D. (1991). Involuntary retirement, Type A behavior, and current functioning in elderly men: 27-year followup of the Western Collaborative Group Study. *Psychology and Aging, 6,* 384–391.

Swann, W. B. (1966). *Self-traps: The elusive quest for higher self-esteem.* New York: W. H. Freeman.

Swann, W. B., Jr., Stein-Seroussi, A., & Giesler, R. B. (1992). Why people self-verify. *Journal of Personality and Social Psychology, 62,* 392–401.

Swets, J. A. (1992). The science of choosing the right decision threshold in high-stakes diagnostics. *American Psychologist, 47,* 522–532.

Swets, J. A. (1998). Enhancing diagnostic decisions. In R. R. Hoffman & M. F. Sherrick (Eds.), *Viewing psychology as a whole: The integrative science of William N. Dember.* Washington, DC: American Psychological Association.

Szasz, T. (1974). *The myth of mental illness* (revised edition). New York: Harper & Row.

Szasz, T. (1987). *Insanity: The idea and its consequences.* New York: Wiley.

Szkrybalo, J., & Ruble, D. N. (1999). "God made me a girl": Sex-category constancy judgments and explanations revisited. *Developmental Psychology, 35,* 392–402.

Szymusiak, R., & McGinty, D. (1986). Sleep-related neuronal discharge in the basal forebrain of cats. *Brain Research, 370,* 82–92.

't Hooft, G. (2000). Physics and the paranormal: A theoretical physicist's view. *Skeptical Inquirer, 24* (2), 27–33.

Tajfel, H., Billig, M. G., Bundy, R. P., & Flament, C. (1971). Social categorization and intergroup behavior. *European Journal of Social Psychology, 1,* 149–178.

Tajfel, H., & Turner, J. C. (1986). The social identity theory of intergroup behavior. In S. Worchel & W. G. Austin (Eds.), *The psychology of intergroup relations* (2nd ed.). Chicago, IL: Nelson-Hall.

Takahashi, Y. (1990). Is multiple personality disorder really rare in Japan? *Dissociation: Progress in the Dissociative Disorders, 3,* 57–59.

Tan, E. S. (1980). Transcultural aspects of anxiety. In G. Burrows and G. Davies (Eds.), *Handbook of studies on anxiety.* Amsterdam, The Netherlands: Elsevier.

Tanaka-Matsumi, J. (1979). Taijin Kyofushu: Diagnostic and cultural issues in Japanese psychiatry. *Culture, Medicine, and Psychiatry, 3,* 231–245.

Tanaka-Matsumi, J., & Draguns, J. (1997). Culture and psychopathology. In J. W. Berry, M. H. Segall, & C. Kagitçibasi (Eds.), *Handbook of cross-cultural psychology* (Vol. 3). Boston: Allyn & Bacon.

Tanda, G., Pontieri, F. E., & Di-Chiara, G. (1997). Cannabinoid and heroin activation of mesolimbic dopamine transmission by a common mu1 opioid receptor mechanism. *Science, 276,* 2048–2050.

Tanner, J. M. (1978). *Fetus into man: Physical growth from conception to maturity.* Cambridge, MA: Harvard University Press.

Taylor, F. W. (1911). *The principles of scientific management.* New York: Harper.

Taylor, H. G. (1998). Analysis of the medical use of marijuana and its societal implications. *Journal of the American Pharmaceutical Association, 38,* 126.

Taylor, S. E. (1999). *Health psychology* (2nd ed.). Boston: McGraw-Hill.

Taylor, S. E., & Brown, J. D. (1988). Illusion and well-being: A social psychological perspective on mental health. *Psychological Bulletin, 103,* 193–210.

Taylor, S. E., & Brown, J. D. (1994). "Illusion" of mental health does not explain positive illusions. *American-Psychologist, 49,* 972–973.

Taylor, S. E., Kemeny, M. E., Reed, G. M., Bower, J. E., & Gruenwald, T. L. (2000). Psychological resources, positive illusions, and health. *American Psychologist, 55,* 99–109.

Taylor, R. D., & Wang, M. C. (Eds.) (2000). *Resilience across contexts: Family, work, culture, and community.* Mahwah, NJ: Erlbaum.

Teasdale, J. D., & Fogarty, F. J. (1979). Differential affects of induced mood on retrieval of pleasant and unpleasant events from episodic memory. *Journal of Abnormal Psychology, 88,* 248–257.

Teghtsoonian, R. (1971). On the exponents in Stevens' law and the constant in Ekman's law. *Psychological Review, 78,* 71–80.

Teicher, M. H., Glod, C. A., Magnus, E., & Harper, D. (1997). Circadian rest-activity disturbances in seasonal affective disorder. *Archives of General Psychiatry, 54,* 124–130.

Teicher, M., Glod, C. A., Magnus, E., & Harper, D. (1997). Circadian rest-activity disturbances in seasonal affective disorder. *Archives of General Psychiatry, 54,* 124–130.

Teitelbaum, S., & Geiselman, R. E. (1997). Observer mood and cross-racial cognition of faces. *Journal of Cross-Cultural Psychology, 28,* 93–106.

Tellegen, A., Lykken, D. T., Bouchard, T. J., Wilcox, K. J., Segal, N. L., & Rich, S. (1988). Personality similarity in twins reared apart and together. *Journal of Personality and Social Psychology, 54,* 1031–1039.

Templeton, J. J. (1998). Learning from others' mistakes: A paradox revisited. *Animal Behaviour, 55,* 79–85.

Templeton, L. M., & Wilcox, S. A. (2000). A tale of two representations: The misinformation effect and children's developing theory of mind. *Child Development, 71,* 402–416.

Terrace, H. M., Petitto, L. A., Sanders, R. J & Bever, T. G. (1979). Can an ape create a sentence? *Science, 206,* 891–902.

Terrace, H. S. (1979). *Nim.* New York: Knopf.

Tesser, A. (1988). Toward a self-evaluation maintenance model of social behavior. In L. Berkowitz (Ed.), *Advances in experimental social psychology* (Vol. 21). Orlando, FL: Academic Press.

Tesser, A., & Shaffer, D. (1990). Attitudes and attitude change. *Annual Review of Psychology, 41,* 479–523.

Teyber, E. (1992). *Interpersonal process in psychotherapy: A guide for clinical training.* Pacific Grove, CA: Brooks/Cole.

Thase, M. E., Greenhouse, J. B., Frank, E. et al. (1997). Treatment of major depression with psychotherapy or psychotherapy-pharmacotherapy combinations. *Archives of General Psychiatry, 54,* 1009–1015.

Thatch, W. T., Goodkin, H. P., & Keating, J. G. (1992). The cerebellum and the adaptive coordination of movement. *Annual Review of Neuroscience, 15,* 161–182.

Thatcher, R. W., Hallett, M., Zeffiro, T., John, E. R., & Huerta, M. (Eds.) (1994). *Functional neuroimaging: Technical foundations.* New York: Academic Press.

Thibaut, J. W., & Kelley, H. H. (1959). *The social psychology of groups.* New York: Wiley.

Thoits, P. (1983). Dimensions of life events that influence psychological distress: An evaluation and synthesis of the literature. In H. B. Kaplan (Ed.), *Psychological stress: Trends in theory and research.* New York: Academic Press.

Thomas, A., & Chess, S. (1977). *Temperament and development.* New York: Brunner/Mazel.

Thomas, A., & Chess, S. (1986). The New York Longitudinal Study: From infancy to early adult life. In R. Plomin & J. Dunn (Eds.), *The study of temperament: Changes, continuities, and challenges.* New York: Brunner/Mazel.

Thomas, L. (1974). *The lives of a cell.* New York: Viking Press.

Thomas, R. M. (2000). *Human development theories: Windows on culture.* Thousand Oaks, CA: Sage Publications.

Thomas, S. A., & Palmiter, R. D. (1997). Disruption of the dopamine beta-hydroxylase gene in mice suggests roles for norepinephrine in motor function, learning, and memory. *Behavioral Neuroscience, 111,* 579–589.

Thomas, W. P., & Collier, V. P. (1997). *School effectiveness for language minority students.* Washington, DC: National Clearinghouse for Bilingual Education.

Thompson, C. P., Cowan, T., Frieman, J., Mahadevan, R. S., et al. (1991). Rajan: A study of a memorist. *Journal of Memory and Language, 30,* 702-724.

Thompson, J. G. (1988). *The psychobiology of emotions.* New York: Plenum.

Thompson, R. F. (1985). *The brain: An introduction to neuroscience.* New York: W. H. Freeman.

Thompson, R. F. (1997). *The brain: Introduction to neuroscience* (3rd ed.). San Francisco: W. H. Freeman.

Thompson, R. F., & Robinson, D. N. (1979). Physiological psychology. In E. Hearsh (Ed.), *The first century of experimental psychology.* Hillsdale, NJ: Erlbaum.

Thompson, R. F., & Steinmetz, J. E. (1992). The essential memory trace circuit for a basic form of associative learning. In I. Gormezano & E. A. Wasserman (Eds.), *Learning and memory: The behavioral and biological substrates.* Hillsdale, NJ: Erlbaum.

Thorndike, E. L. (1898). *Animal intelligence, an experimental study of the associative processes in animals.* New York: Macmillan.

Thorndike, E. L. (1911). *Animal intelligence; experimental studies.* New York: Macmillan.

Thorndike, R. L., Hagen, E. P., & Sattler, J. M. (1986). *What is intelligence?: Contemporary viewpoints on its nature and definition.* Chicago: Riverside Press.

Tienari, P., Wynne, L. C., Moring, J., & Lahti, I. et al. (Eds.) (1994). The Finnish adoptive family study of schizophrenia: Implications for family research. *British Journal of Psychiatry, 164,* 20–26.

Tilker, H. A. (1970). Socially responsible behavior as a function of observer responsibility and victim feedback. *Journal of Personality and Social Psychology, 14,* 95–100.

Timiras, P. S. (1972). *Developmental psychology and aging.* New York: Macmillan.

Tinbergen, N. (1951). *The study of instinct.* Oxford, England: Clarendon Press.

Tizard, B., & Hodges, J. (1978). The effect of early institutional rearing on the development of eight-year-old children. *Journal of Child Psychology and Psychiatry, 19,* 99–118.

Tobin, J. J., & Friedman, J. (1983). Spirits, shamans, and nightmare death: Survivor stress in a Hmong refugee. *American Journal of Orthopsychiatry, 53,* 439–448.

Toch, H. (1992). *Violent men: An inquiry into the psychology of violence* (rev. ed.). Washington, DC: American Psychological Association.

Tollefson, G. D. (1993). Major depression. In D. L. Dunner (Ed.), *Current psychiatric therapy.* Philadelphia: Saunders.

Tolman, E. C. (1948). Cognitive maps in rats and men. *Psychological Review, 55,* 189–208.

Tolman, E. C., & Honzik, C. H. (1930). Introduction and removal of reward and maze performance in rats. *University of California Publications in Psychology, 4,* 257–275.

Tolson, J. M., & Urberg, K. A. (1993). Similarity between adolescent best friends. *Journal of Adolescent Research, 8,* 274–288.

Tomaka, J., Blascovich, J., Kibler, J., & Ernst, J. M. (1997). Cognitive and physiological antecedents of threat and challenge appraisal. *Journal of Personality and Social Psychology, 73,* 63–72.

Tomarken, A. J., Davidson, R. J., Wheeler, R. E., & Doss, R. C. (1992). Individual differences in anterior brain symmetry and fundamental dimensions of emotion. *Journal of Personality and Social Psychology, 62,* 676–687.

Tomarken, A. J., & Keener, A. D. (1998). Frontal brain asymmetry and depression: A self-regulatory perspective. Special Issue: Neuropsychological perspectives on affective and anxiety disorders. *Cognition and Emotion, 12(3),* 387–420.

Tomkins, S. S. (1991). *Affect, imagery, consciousness. Vol. 3: Anger and fear.* New York: Springer.

Tonigan, J. S., Toscova, R., & Miller, W. R. (1996). Meta-analysis of the literature on Alcoholics Anonymous: Sample and study characteristics moderate findings. *Journal of Studies on Alcohol, 57,* 65–72.

Tooby, J., & Cosmides, L. (1992). The psychological foundations of culture. In J. H. Barkow, L. Cosmides, & J. Tooby (Eds.), *The adapted mind.* New York: Oxford University Press.

Torrey, E. F. (1997). *Out of the shadows: Confronting America's mental illness crisis.* New York: Wiley.

Toth, L. A., & Williams, R. W. (1999). A quantitative genetic analysis of slow-wave sleep and rapid-eye movement sleep in CXB recombinant inbred mice. *Behavior Genetics, 29,* 329–337.

Toufexis, A. (1989, June 5). The times of your life. *Time, 66-67.*

Trakas, K., Lawrence, K., & Shear, N. H. (1999). Utilization of health care resources by obese Canadians. *Canadian Medical Association Journal, 160,* 1457–1462.

Traue, H. C., & Deighton, R. M. (2000). Emotional inhibition. In G. Fink (Ed.), *Encyclopedia of stress.* San Diego: Academic Press.

Tremblay, R. E., Schaal, B., Boulerice, B., Arseneault, L., Soussignan, R., & Perusse, D. (1997). Male physical aggression, social dominance, and testosterone levels at puberty: A developmental perspective. In A. Raine, P. A. Brennan, D. P. Farrington, & S. A. Mednick (Eds.), *Biosocial bases of violence.* New York: Plenum.

Triandis, H. C. (1989). Cross-cultural studies of individualism and collectivism. In J. J. Berman (Ed.), *Nebraska Symposium on Motivation* (Vol. 37). Lincoln: University of Nebraska Press.

Triandis, H. C. (1994). *Culture and social behavior.* Boston: McGraw-Hill.

Triplett, N. (1898). The dynamogenic factors in pace-making and competition. *American Journal of Psychology, 9,* 507–533.

Trivers, R. (1971). The evolution of reciprocal altruism. *Quarterly Review of Biology, 46,* 35–57.

Trivers, R. L. (1972). Parental investment and sexual selection. In B. Campbell (Ed.), *Sexual selection and the descent of man.* Chicago: Aldine-Atherton.

Troiano, R. P., & Flegal, K. M. (1999). Overweight prevalence among youth in the United States: Why so many different numbers? *International Journal of Obesity and Related Metabolic Disorders, 23,* S22–27.

Troll, L. E. (1985). *Early and middle adulthood* (2nd ed.). Monterey, CA: Brooks/Cole.

Trommald, M., Hulleberg, G., & Andersen, P. (1996). Long-term potentiation is associated with new excitatory spine synapses on rat dentate granule cells. *Learning and Memory, 3,* 218–228.

Trull, T. J., & Geary, D. C. (1997). Comparison of the Big Five Factor structure across samples of Chinese and American adults. *Journal of Personality Assessment, 69,* 324–341.

Trull, T. J., & McCrae, R. R. (1994). A five-factor perspective on personality disorder research. In P. T. Costa, Jr., & T. A. Widiger (Eds.), *Personality disorders and the five-factor model of personality.* Washington, DC: American Psychological Association.

Trulson, M. E., & Jacobs, B. L. (1979). Dissociations between the effects of LSD on behavior and raphe unit activity in freely moving cats. *Science, 204* (4405), 515-518.

Tsai, J. L., & Levenson, R. W. (1997). Cultural influences of emotional responding: Chinese-American and European-American dating couples during interpersonal conflict. *Journal of Cross-Cultural Psychology, 28,* 600–625.

Tseng, W. S., Asai, M., Liu, J., Pismai, W. et al. (1990). Multi-cultural study of minor psychiatric disorders in Asia: Symptom manifestations. *International Journal of Social Psychiatry, 36,* 252–264.

Tucker, P., & Aron, A. (1993). Passionate love and marital satisfaction at key transition points in the family life cycle. *Journal of Social and Clinical Psychology, 12,* 135–147.

Tuckfelt, S., Fink, J., & Warren, M. P. (1997). *The psychotherapists' guide to managed care in the 21st century: Surviving big brother.* Northvale, NJ: Jason Aronson.

Tulving, E. (2000) (Ed.). *Memory, consciousness, and the brain: The Tallinn Conference.* Philadelphia: Psychology Press/Taylor & Francis.

Tulving, E., Markowitsch, H. J., Kapur, S., Habib, R., et al. (1994). Novelty encoding networks in the human brain: Positron emission tomography data. *Neuroreport: An International Journal for the Rapid Communication of Research in Neuroscience, 5,* 2525-2528.

Tulving, E., & Psotka, J. (1971). Retroactive inhibition in free recall: Inaccessibility of information available in the memory store. *Journal of Experimental Psychology, 87,* 1–8.

Tulving, E., & Schacter, D. L. (1990). Timing and human memory systems. *Science, 247,* 301–306.

Tulving, E., & Thomson, D. M. (1973). Encoding specificity and retrieval processes in episodic memory. *Psychological Review, 80,* 359-380.

Turnbull, C. M. (1961). Some observations regarding the experiences and behavior of the Ba Mbuti pygmies. *American Journal of Psychology, 74,* 304–308.

Turner, J. A., Deyo, R. A., et al. (1994). The importance of placebo effects in pain treatment and research. *Journal of the American Medical Association, 271,* 1609–1614.

Tusing, K. J., & Dillard, J. P. (2000). The psychological reality of the door-in-the-face: It's helping, not bargaining. *Journal of Language and Social Psychology, 19,* 5–25.

Tversky, A., & Kahneman, D. (1980). Causal schemas in judgments under uncertainty. In M. Fishbein (Ed.), *Progress in social psychology.* Hillsdale, NJ: Erlbaum.

Tversky, A., & Kahneman, D. (1981). The framing of decisions and the psychology of choice. *Science, 211,* 453–458.

Tversky, A. & Kahneman, D. (1982). Judgements of and by representativeness. In D. Kahneman, P. Slovic, & A. Tversky (Eds.), *Judgement under uncertainty: Heuristics and biases.* Cambridge, MA: Cambridge University Press.

Tversky, B., & Tuchin, M. (1989). A reconciliation of the evidence on eyewitness testimony: Comments on McCloskey and Zaragoza. *Journal of Experimental Psychology: General, 118,* 86–91.

Tyc, V. L., Mulhern, R. K., & Bieberich, A. A. (1997). Anticipatory nausea and vomiting in pediatric cancer patients: An analysis of conditioning and coping variables. *Journal of Developmental and Behavioral Pediatrics, 18,* 27–33.

Tye, M. (1991). *The imagery debate.* Cambridge, MA: MIT Press.

Tzeng, O. J., Hung, W., Cohen, F. J., & Wang, P. (1979). Visual lateralization effect in reading Chinese characters. *Nature, 282,* 499–501.

Tzeng, J. M., & Mare, R. D. (1995). Labor market and socioeconomic effects on marital stability. *Social Science Research, 24,* 329–351.

U.S. Bureau of the Census (1996). *Statistical abstracts of the United States, 1995* (115th ed.). Washington, DC: U.S. Government Printing Office.

U.S. Department of Justice (1999). *National crime victimization survey.* Washington, DC: Author.

U.S. Department of Labor (1998). Supplement to the May 1997 Current Population Survey (CPS). *Bureau of Labor Statistics* [Online]. Available: ftp://146.142.4.23/pub/news.release/flex.txt

U.S. Public Health Service (1979). *Healthy people: The Surgeon General's report on health promotion and disease prevention.* Washington, DC: U.S. Government Printing Office.

Underwood, B. J. (1970). A breakdown of the total-time law in free-recall learning. *Journal of Verbal Learning and Verbal Behavior, 9,* 573–580.

Usher, J. A., & Neisser, U. (1993). Childhood amnesia and the beginnings of memory for four early life events. *Journal of Experimental Psychology: General, 122,* 155–165.

Vaillant, G. E. (1977). *Adaptation to life.* Boston: Little, Brown.

Valent, P. (2000a). Stress effects of the Holocaust. In G. Fink (Ed.), *Encyclopedia of stress.* San Diego: Academic Press.

Valent, P. (2000b). Survivor guilt. In G. Fink (Ed.), *Encyclopedia of stress.* San Diego: Academic Press.

Valsiner, J. (2000). *Culture and human development.* Thousand Oaks, CA: Sage Publications.

Valsiner, J., & Lawrence, J. A. (1997). Human development in culture across the life span. In J. W. Berry, P. R. Dasen, & T. S. Saraswathi (Eds.), *Handbook of cross-cultural psychology* (Vol. 2). Boston: Allyn & Bacon.

Van Cauter, E. (2000). Sleep loss, jet lag, and shift work. In G. Fink (Ed.), *Encyclopedia of stress.* San Diego: Academic Press.

Van De Castle, R. L., & Kinder, P. (1968). Dream content during pregnancy. *Psychophysiology, 4,* 375.

Vandell, D. L., & Ramanan, J. (1991). Children of the National Longitudinal Survey of Youth: Choices in after-school care and child development. *Developmental Psychology, 27,* 637–643.

van der Heijden, A. H. C. (1991). *Selective attention in vision.* New York: Routledge.

van der Vegt, G., Emans, B., & Van de Vliert, E. (1998). Motivating effects of task and outcome interdependence in work teams. *Group and Organization Management, 23,* 124–143.

Vander Zanden, J. W. (1997). Human development (6th ed.). Boston: McGraw-Hill.

van Ijzendoorn, M. (1995). Adult attachment representations, parental responsiveness, and infant attachment: A meta-analysis of the Adult Attachment Interview. *Psychological Bulletin, 117,* 387–403.

Van Wel, F. (1994). A culture gap between the generations? Social influences on youth cultural style. *International Journal of Adolescence and Youth, 4,* 211–228.

Van Zomeren, A. H., & Brouwer, W. H. (1994). *Clinical neuropsychology of attention.* New York: Oxford University Press.

Vargha-Khadem, F., Gadian, D. G., Watkins, K. E., Connelly, A., Van Paesschen, W., & Mishkin, M. (1997). Differential effects of early hippocampal pathology on episodic and semantic memory. *Science, 277,* 376–380.

Varney, N. R., & Roberts, R. J. (1999). *The evaluation and treatment of mild traumatic brain injury.* Mahwah, NJ: Erlbaum.

Vartanian, L. R. (1997). Separation-individuation, social support, and adolescent egocentrism: An exploratory study. *Journal of Early Adolescence, 17,* 245–270.

Vaughn, C., & Leff, J. (1976). The measurement of expressed emotion in the families of psychiatric patients. *British Journal of Social and Clinical Psychology, 15,* 157–165.

Verbrugge, L. M. (1979). Marital status and health. *Journal of Marriage and the Family, 41,* 267–285.

Vgonitzas, A. N., Bixler, E. O., & Kales, A. K. (2000). Sleep, sleep disorders, and stress. In G. Fink (Ed.), *Encyclopedia of stress.* San Diego: Academic Press.

Vickery, A. R., & Kirsch, I. (1991). The effects of brief expectancy manipulations on hypnotic responsiveness. *Contemporary Hypnosis, 8,* 167–171.

Viemerö, V. (1996). Factors in childhood that predict later criminal behavior. *Aggressive Behavior, 22,* 87-97.

Violanti, J. M., & Marshall, J. R. (1996). Cellular phones and traffic accidents: An epidemiological approach. *Accident Analysis and Prevention, 28,* 265–270.

Vogel, G. W. (1978). An alternative view of the neurobiology of dreaming. *American Journal of Psychiatry, 135,* 1531–1535.

von Frisch, K. (1974). Decoding the language of the bee. *Science, 185,* 663–668.

Vonk, R. (1997). Attitudes toward animal research. *American Psychologist, 52,* 1248–1249.

Von Melchner, L., Pallas, S. L., & Sur, M. (2000). Visual behaviour mediated by retinal projections directed to the auditory pathway. *Nature, 404,* 871–876.

Vrij, A., van der Steen, J., & Koppelaar, L. (1994). Aggression of police officers as a function of temperature: An experiment with the Fire Arms Training System. *Journal of Community and Applied Social Psychology. 1994, 4,* 365–370.

Vurpillot, E. (1968). The development of scanning strategies and their relation to visual differentiations. *Journal of Experimental Child Psychology, 6,* 632–650.

Vygotsky, L. S. (1935/1978). *Mind in society: The development of higher psychological processes.* In Cambridge, MA: Harvard University Press.

Wachs, T. D. (2000). *Necessary but not sufficient: The respective roles of single and multiple influences of individual development.* Washington, DC: American Psychological Association.

Wachtel, P. L. (1997). *Psychoanalysis, behavior therapy, and the relational world.* Washington, DC: American Psychological Association.

Wadden, T. A., Vogt, R. A., Andersen, R. E., et al. (1997). Exercise in the treatment of obesity: Effects of four interventions on body composition, resting energy expenditure, appetite, and mood. *Journal of Consulting and Clinical Psychology, 654,* 269–277.

Wade, C., & Cirese, S. (1992). *Human sexuality* (2nd ed.). Chicago: Harcourt Brace Jovanovich.

Wade, N. J., & Swanston, M. (1991). *Visual perception: An introduction.* New York: Routledge.

Wade, P., & Bernstein, B. (1991). Culture sensitivity training and counselor's race: Effects on Black female client's perceptions and attrition. *Journal of Counseling Psychology, 38,* 9–15.

Wagman, M. (1997). *Cognitive science and the symbolic operations of human and artificial intelligence: Theory and research into the intellective processes.* Westport, CT: Greenwood.

Wagman, M. (1998). *Cognitive science and the mind-body problem: From philosophy to psychology to artificial intelligence to imaging of the brain.* Westport, CT: Greenwood.

Wagner, E. H., La Croix, A. Z., Buckner, D. M., & Larson, E. B. (1992). Effects of physical activity on health status in older adults: I: Observational studies. *Annual Review of Public Health, 13,* 368–392.

Wagstaff, G. F. (1999). Hypnosis and forensic psychology. In I. Kirsch & A. Capafons (Eds.), *Clinical hypnosis and self-regulation: Cognitive-behavioral perspectives.* Washington, DC: American Psychological Association.

Wahlberg, K. E., Wynne, L. C., Oja, H., Keskitalo, P., et al. (1997). Gene-environment interaction in vulnerability to schizophrenia: Findings from the Finnish Family Study of Schizophrenia. *American Journal of Psychiatry, 154,* 355–362.

Wakefield, M., Reid, Y., Roberts, L., Mullins, R., & Gillies, P. (1998). Smoking and smoking cessation among men whose partners are pregnant: A qualitative study. *Social Science and Medicine, 47,* 657–664.

Walen, S. (1980). Cognitive factors in sexual behavior. *Journal of Sex and Marital Therapy, 6,* 87–101.

Walen, S. R., & Roth, D. (1987). A cognitive approach. In J. H. Geer & W. T. O'Donohue (Eds.), *Theories of human sexuality.* New York: Plenum.

Walk, R. D. (1981). *Perceptual development.* Monterey, CA: Brooks/Cole.

Walker, L. E. (1999). Psychology and domestic violence around the world. *American Psychologist, 54,* 21–29.

Walker, L. J. (1987, April). *Moral orientations: A comparison of two models.* Paper presented at biennial meetings of Society for Research in Child Development, Baltimore.

Walker, T. G., & Main, E. C. (1973). Choice-shifts in political decision making: Federal judges and civil liberties cases. *Journal of Applied Social Psychology, 2,* 39–48.

Wallbott, H., & Scherer, K. (1988). How universal and specific is emotional experience? Evidence from 27 countries and five continents. In K. Scherer (Ed.), *Facets of emotion: Recent research.* Hillsdale, NJ: Erlbaum.

Waller, G., & Hartley, P. (1994). Perceived parental style and eating psychopathology. *European Eating Disorders Review, 2,* 76–92.

Wallerstein, J. S. (1989). *Second chances.* New York: Tickner & Fields.

Wallerstein, J. S. (1984). Children of divorce: Preliminary report of a ten-year follow-up of young children. *American Journal of Orthopsychiatry, 54,* 444–458.

Wallerstein, J. S., & Kelly, J. B. (1980). *Surviving the break-up: How children actually cope with divorce.* New York: Basic Books.

Walling, D. P., Baker, J. M., & Dott, S. G. (1998). Scope of hypnosis education in academia: Results of a national survey. *International Journal of Clinical and Experimental Hypnosis, 46,* 150–156.

Wallston, K. A. (1993). Hocus-pocus, the focus isn't strictly on locus: Rotter's social learning theory modified for health. *Cognitive Therapy and Research, 16,* 183–199.

Walsh, B. T., & Devlin, M. J. (1998). Eating disorders: Progress and problems. *Science, 280,* 1387–1390.

Walster, E., Aronson, V., Abrahams, D., & Rottman, L. (1966). The importance of physical attractiveness in dating behavior. *Journal of Personality and Social Psychology, 4,* 508–516.

Wang, T., Brownstein, R., & Katzev, R. (1989). Promoting charitable behaviour with compliance techniques. *Applied Psychology: An International Review, 38,* 165–183.

Ward, S. L., & Overton, W. F. (1990). Semantic familiarity, relevance, and the development of deductive reasoning. *Developmental Psychology, 26,* 488–493.

Warga, C. (1987). Pain's gatekeeper. *Psychology Today, 21,* 50–59.

Warren, M. P. (1992). Eating, body weight, and menstrual function. In K. D. Brownell, J. Rodin, & J. H. Wilmore (Eds.), *Eating, body weight, and performance in athletes: Disorders of modern society.* Philadelphia: Lea & Febiger.

Washington Post (1994, October 30). *Gunman trains rifle fire on White House. Washington Post,* p. A1.

Wason, P. C., & Johnson-Laird, P. N. (1972). *Psychology of reasoning.* London: Batsford.

Wasserman, E. A, & Berglan, L. R. (1998). Backward blocking and recovery from overshadowing in human causal judgement: The role of within-compound associations. *Quarterly Journal of Experimental Psychology: Comparative and Physiological Psychology, 51B,* 121–138.

Watkins, L. R., & Maier, S. F. (2000). The pain of being sick: Implications of immune-to-brain communication for understanding pain. *Annual Review of Psychology, 51,* 29–58.

Watkins, L. R., Wiertelak, E. P., McGorry, M., Martinez, J., Schwartz, B., Sisk, D., & Maier, S. F. (1998). Neurocircuitry of conditioned inhibition of analgesia: Effects of amygdala, dorsal raphe, ventral medullary, and spinal cord lesions on antianalgesia in the rat. *Behavioral Neuroscience, 112.*

Watson, C. G., Barnett, M., Nikunen, L., Schultz, C., Randolph, E. T., & Mendez, C. M. (1997). Lifetime prevalences of nine common psychiatric/personality disorders in female domestic abuse survivors. *Journal of Nervous and Mental Disease, 185,* 645–647.

Watson, D., & Clark, L. A. (1992). Affects separable and inseparable: On the hierarchical arrangement of the negative affects. *Journal of Personality and Social Psychology, 62,* 489–505.

Watson, D. L. & Tharp., R. G. (1989). *Self-directed behavior: Self modification for personal adjustment* (4th ed.). Pacific Grove, CA: Brooks/Cole.

Watson, D. L., & Tharp, R. G. (1997). *Self-directed behavior: Self-modification for personal adjustment* (6th ed.) Belmont, CA: Brooks/Cole.

Watson, J. B. (1924). *Behaviorism.* New York: People's Institute.

Watson, J. B., & Rayner, R. (1920). Conditioned emotional reactions. *Journal of Experimental Psychology, 3,* 1–14.

Watson, J. C., & Greenberg, L. S. (1998). Humanistic and experiential theories of personality. In D. F. Barone, M. Hersen, & V. B. Van Hasselt (Eds.), *Advanced personality.* New York: Plenum.

Watten, R. G., Vassend, D., Myhrer, T., & Syversen, J. L. (1997). Personality factors and somatic symptoms. *European Journal of Personality, 11,* 57–68.

Weaver, C. A. (1993). Do you need a "flash" to form a flashbulb memory? *Journal of Experimental Psychology: General, 122,* 39–46.

Webb, E. J., Campbell, D. T., Schwartz, R. D., & Sechrest, L. (1966). *Unobtrusive measures: Nonreactive research in the social sciences.* Chicago: Rand McNally.

Webb, W. B. (1974). Sleep as an adaptive response. *Perceptual and Motor Skills, 38,* 1023–1027.

Webb, W. B. (1992). *Sleep: The gentle tyrant* (2nd ed.). Bolton, MA: Anker.

Webb, W. B. (1994). Prediction of sleep onset. In R. D. Ogilvie & J. R. Harsh. (Eds.), *Sleep onset: Normal and abnormal processes.* Washington, DC: American Psychological Association.

Webb, W. B., & Campbell, S. S. (1983). Relationships in sleep characteristics of identical and fraternal twins. *Archives of General Psychiatry, 40,* 1093–1095.

Webster, D. M., Richter, L., & Kruglanski, A. W. (1996). On leaping to conclusions when feeling tired: Mental fatigue effects on impressional primacy. *Journal of Experimental Social Psychology, 32,* 181–195.

Wechsler, D. (1991). *WISC III: Wechsler Intelligence Scale for Children—Third Edition* (1991). San Antonio, TX: The Psychological Corporation.

Weg, R. B. (1983). Changing physiology of aging: Normal and pathological. In D. S. Woodruff & J. E. Birren (Eds.), *Aging: Scientific perspectives and social issues* (2nd ed.). Monterey, CA: Brooks/Cole.

Weil, A. (1986). *The natural mind: An investigation of drugs and the higher consciousness.* Boston: Houghton Mifflin.

Weinberg, R. S., & Genuchi, M. (1980). Relationship between competitive trait anxiety, state anxiety, and golf performance: A field study. *Journal of Sport Psychology, 2*, 148–154.

Weinberger, D. A. (1990). The construct validity of the repressive coping style. In J. L. Singer (Ed.), *Repression and dissociation*. Chicago: University of Chicago Press.

Weiner, B. (1985). An attributional theory of achievement motivation and emotion. *Psychological Review, 92*, 548–573.

Weiner, B. (1992). *Human motivation: Metaphors, theories, and research*. Newbury Park, CA: Sage Publications.

Weiner, B. (1996). Searching for order in social motivation. *Psychological Inquiry, 7*, 199–216.

Weiner, R. D., & Coffey, C. E. (1988). Indications for the use of electroconvulsive therapy. In A. J. Francis & R. E. Hales (Eds.), *Review of Psychiatry* (Vol. 7), Washington, DC: American Psychiatric Press.

Weingardt, K. R., & Marlatt, G. A. (1998). Harm reduction and public policy. In G. A. Marlatt (Ed.), *Harm reduction: Pragmatic strategies for managing high-risk behaviors*. New York: Guilford Press.

Weingarten, H. P. (1983). Conditioned cues elicit feeding in sated rats: A role for learning in meal initiation. *Science, 220*, 431–433.

Weinstein, C. S. (1991). The classroom as a social context for learning. *Annual Review of Psychology, 42*, 493–525.

Weinstock, M. (1997). Does prenatal stress impair coping and regulation of hypothalamic-pituitary-adrenal axis? *Neuroscience and Biobehavioral Reviews, 21*, 1–10.

Weisenberg, M. (1998). Cognitive aspects of pain and pain control. *International Journal of Clinical and Experimental Hypnosis, 46*, 44–61.

Weiskrantz, L. (1986). *Blindsight: A case study and implications*. Oxford, England: Oxford University Press.

Weiskrantz, L. (1998). Consciousness and commentaries, *International Journal of Psychology, 33*, 227–223.

Weiss, J. M., Glazer, H. I., & Pohoresky, L. A. (1976). Coping behavior and neurochemical change in rats: An alternative explanation for the original "learned helplessness" experiments. In G. Serban & A. King (Eds.), *Animal models in human psychobiology*. New York: Plenum.

Weissberg, R. P., & Bell, D. N. (1997). A meta-analytic review of primary prevention in programs for children and adolescents: Contributions and caveats. *American Journal of Community Psychology, 25*, 207–214.

Weissman, M. M., Bland, R. C., Canino, G. J., et al. (1994). The cross-national epidemiology of obsessive-compulsive disorder: The Cross National Collaborative Group. *Journal of Clinical Psychiatry, 55*, 5–10.

Weissman, M. M., Geshon, E. S., Kidd, K. K., Prusoff, B. A., Leckman, J. F., Dibble, E., Hamovit, J., Thompson, W. D., Pauls, D. L., & Guroff, J. J. (1984). Psychiatric disorders in the relatives of probands with affective disorders. *Archives of General Psychiatry, 41*, 13–21.

Weissman, M. M., & Markowitz, J. C. (1994). Interpersonal psychotherapy: Current status. *Archives of General Psychiatry, 51*, 599–606.

Weller, A., & Weller, L. (1997). Menstrual synchrony under optimal conditions: Bedouin families. *Journal of Comparative Psychology, 111*, 143–151.

Weller, A., & Weller, L. (1998). Prolonged and very intensive contact may not be conducive to menstrual synchrony. *Psychoneuroendocrinology, 23*, 19–32.

Weller, L., Weller, A., Koresh, H. K., & Shoshan, B. R. (1999). Menstrual synchrony in a sample of working women. *Psychoneuroendocrinology, 24*, 449–459.

Wender, P. H., Kety, S. S., Rosenthal, D., Schulsinger, F., Ortmann, J., & Lunde, I. (1986). Psychiatric disorders in the biological and adoptive families of adopted individuals with affective disorders. *Archives of General Psychiatry, 43*, 923–929.

Wenning, G. K., Odin, P., Morrish, P., et al. (1997). Short- and long-term survival and function of intrastriatal dopaminergic grafts in Parkinson's disease. *Annals of Neurology, 42*, 95–107.

Wenzlaff, R. M., & Wegner, D. M. (2000). Thought suppression. *Annual Review of Psychology, 51*, 59–91.

Wenzlaff, R. M., Wegner, D. M., & Roper, D. W. (1988). Depression and mental control: The resurgence of unwanted negative thoughts. *Journal of Personality and Social Psychology, 55*, 882–892.

Werker, J. F., & Tees, R. C. (1992). The organization and reorganization of human speech perception. *Annual Review of Neuroscience, 15*, 86–101.

Werner, E. E., & Smith, R. S. (1982). *Vulnerable but invincible: A longitudinal study of resilient children*. New York: McGraw-Hill.

Westen, D. (1998). The scientific legacy of Sigmund Freud: Toward a psychodynamically informed psychological science. *Psychological Bulletin, 24*, 333–371.

Westen, D., & Gabbard, G. (1999). Psychoanalytic approaches to personality. In L. A. Pervin & O. P. John (Eds.), *Handbook of personality: Theory and research*. New York: Guilford Press.

Wethington, E. (2000). Life events scale. In G. Fink (Ed.), *Encyclopedia of stress*. San Diego: Academic Press.

Wetter, D. W., Fiore, M. C., et al. (1998). The Agency for Health Care Policy and Research Smoking cessation clinical practice guideline: Findings and implications for psychologists. *American Psychologist, 53*, 657–669.

Wever, R. A. (1979). *The circadian system of man: Results of experiments under temporal isolation*. New York: Springer-Verlag.

Wever, R. A. (1989). Light effects on human circadian rhythms: A review of recent Andechs experiments. *Journal of Biological Rhythms, 4*, 161–185.

Wexley, K. N., & Yukl, G. A. (1977). *Organizational behavior and personnel psychology*. Homewood, IL: Irwin.

Wheeden, A., Scafidi, F. A., Field, T., & Ironson, G. (1993). Massage effects on cocaine-exposed preterm neonates. *Journal of Developmental and Behavioral Pediatrics, 14*, 318–322.

Wheeler, L., & Miyake, K. (1992). Social comparison in everyday life. *Journal of Personality and Social Psychology, 62*, 760–773.

Whitam, F. L., & Mathy, R. M. (1991). Childhood cross-gender behavior of homosexual females in Brazil, Peru, the Philippines, and the United States. *Archives of Sexual Behavior, 20*, 151–170.

Whitbourne, S. K. (1985). *The aging body: Physiological changes and psychological consequences*. New York: Springer-Verlag.

White, G. L. (1980). Physical attractiveness and courtship progress. *Journal of Personality and Social Psychology, 39*, 660–668.

White, M. (1987). *The Japanese educational challenge: A commitment to children*. New York: Free Press.

White, N. M., & Milner, P. M. (1992). The psychobiology of reinforcers. *Annual Review of Psychology, 43*, 443–472.

White, R. K. (1968). *Nobody wanted war*. Garden City, NY: Doubleday.

Whiten, A., Goodall, J., McGrew, W. C., Nishida, T., Reynolds, V., Sugiyama, Y., & Tutin, C. E. G. (1999). Cultures in chimpanzees. *Nature, 399*, 682–685.

Whitney, G., McClearn, G. E., & DeFries, J. C. (1970). Heritability of alcohol preference in laboratory mice and rats. *The Journal of Heredity, 61*, 165–169.

Whorf, B. L. (1956). Science and linguistics. In J. B. Carroll (Ed.), *Language, thought and reality: Selected writings of Benjamin Lee Whorf*. Cambridge, MA: MIT Press.

Wicker, A. W. (1969). Attitudes versus actions: The relationship between verbal and overt behavioral responses to attitude objects. *Journal of Social Issues, 25*, 41–78.

Widiger, T. A. (1995). Detection of self-defeating and sadistic personality disorders. In W. J. Livesley (Ed.), *The DSM-IV personality disorders*. New York: Guilford Press.

Widiger, T. A., & Sankis, L. M. (2000). Adult psychopathology: Issues and controversies. *Annual Review of Psychology, 51*, 377–405.

Widom, C. S. (1983). A methodology for studying noninstitutionalized psychopaths. In R. D. Hare & D. A. Schaling (Eds.), *Psychopathic behavior: Approaches to research*. Chichester, England: Wiley.

Wiedenfeld, S. A., O'Leary, A., Bandura, A., Brown, S., Levine, S., & Raska, K. (1990). Impact of perceived self-efficacy in coping with stressors on components of the immune system. *Journal of Personality and Social Psychology, 59*, 1082–1094.

Wiederman, M. W., & Dubois, S. L. (1998). Evolution and sex differences in preferences for short-term mates: Results from a policy capturing study. *Evolution and Human Behavior, 19*, 153–170.

Wiens, A. N., & Menustik, C. E. (1983). Treatment outcome and patient characteristics in an aversion therapy program for alcoholism. *American Psychologist, 38*, 1089–1096.

Wilcox, S., & Storandt, M. (1996). Relations among age, exercise, and psychological variables in a community sample of women. *Health Psychology, 15*, 110–113.

Wilder, D. A. (1986). Social categorization: Implications for creation and reduction of intergroup bias. In L. Berkowitz (Ed.), *Advances in experimental social psychology* (Vol. 19). New York: Academic Press.

Wilk, L. A., & Redmon, W. K. (1998). The effects of feedback and goal setting on the productivity and satisfaction of university admissions staff. *Journal of Organizational Behavior Management, 18*, 45–68.

Wilkins, A. J., & Baddeley, A. D. (1978). Remembering to recall in everyday life: An approach to absentmindedness. In M. M.

Grueneberg, P. E. Morris, & R. N. Sykes (Eds.), *Practical aspects of memory*. London: Academic Press.

Willenberg, H. S., Bornstein, S. R., & Crousos, G. P. (2000). Stress-induced disease: Overview. In G. Fink (Ed.), *Encyclopedia of stress*. San Diego: Academic Press.

Williams, L. M. (1994). Recall of childhood trauma: A prospective study of women's memories of child sexual abuse. *Journal of Consulting and Clinical Psychology, 62*, 1167–1176.

Williams, S. L., Kinney, P. J., & Falbo, J. (1989). Generalization of therapeutic changes in agoraphobia: The role of perceived self-efficacy. *Journal of Consulting and Clinical Psychology, 57*, 436–442.

Williams, T. J., Pepitone, M. E., Christensen, S. E., Cooke, B. M., Huberman, A. D., & Breedlove, N. J. (2000). Finger length patterns and human sexual orientation. *Nature, 404*, 455–456.

Williams, W. M. (1998). Are we raising smarter children today? School- and home-related influences on IQ. In U. Neisser, et al. (Eds.), *The rising curve: Long-term gains in IQ and related measures*. Washington, DC: American Psychological Association.

Willingham, W. W., Rock, D. A., & Pollack, J. (1990). Predictability of college grades: Three tests and three national samples. In W. W. Willingham & C. Lewis (Eds.), *Predicting college grades: An analysis of institutional trends over two decades*. Princeton, NJ: Educational Testing Service.

Wilson, E. O. (1980). *Sociobiology*. Cambridge, MA: Harvard University Press.

Wilson, G. T., & Lawson, D. M. (1976). Expectancies, alcohol, and sexual arousal in male social drinkers. *Journal of Abnormal Psychology, 85*, 587–594.

Wilson, S. C., & Barber, T. X. (1982). The fantasy-prone personality: Implications for understanding imagery, hypnosis, and parapsychological phenomena. *PSI-Research, 1*, 94–116.

Wilson, S. C., & Barber, T. X. (1983). The fantasy-prone personality: Implications for understanding imagery, hypnosis, and parapsychological phenomena. In A. A. Sheikh (Ed.), *Imagery: Current theory, research and applications*. New York: Wiley.

Windholz, G. (1997). Ivan P. Pavlov: An overview of his life and psychological work. *American Psychologist, 52*, 941–946.

Winner, E. (2000). The origins and ends of giftedness. *American Psychologist, 55*, 159–169.

Winograd, E., Goldstein, F. C., Monarch, E. S., Peluso, J. P., & Goldman, W. P. (1999). The mere exposure effect in patients with Alzheimer's disease. *Neuropsychology, 13*, 41–46.

Winson, J. (1990). The meaning of dreams. *Scientific American, 260*(11), 86–96.

Wise, R. A., & Rompre, P. P. (1989). Brain dopamine and reward. *Annual Review of Psychology, 40*, 191–226.

Wiseman, C. V., Gray, J. J., Mosimann, J. E., & Ahrens, A. H. (1992). Cultural expectations of thinness in women: An update. *International Journal of Eating Disorders, 11*, 85–89.

Wiseman, R., Smith, M., & Kornbrot, D. (1996). Exploring possible sender to experimenter acoustic leakage in the PRL autoganzfeld experiments. *Journal of Parapsychology, 60*, 97–128.

Wittchen, H. U., Zhao, S., Kessler, R. C., & Eaton, W. W. (1994). DSM-III-R generalized anxiety disorder in the National Comorbidity Survey. *Archives of General Psychiatry, 51*, 355–364.

Witter, R. A., Okun, M. A., Stock, W. A., & Haring, M. J. (1984). Education and subjective well-being: A meta-analysis. *Educational Evaluation and Policy Analysis, 6*, 165–173.

Wixted, J. T. (1991). Conditions and consequences of maintenance rehearsal. *Journal of Experimental Psychology: Learning, Memory, and Cognition, 17*, 963–973.

Wolberg, L. R. (1967). *The technique of psychotherapy* (2nd ed.). New York: Grune & Stratton.

Wolken, J. J. (1995). *Light detectors, photoreceptors, and imaging systems in nature*. New York: Oxford University Press.

Wolpe, J. (1958). *Psychotherapy by reciprocal inhibition*. Stanford, CA: Stanford University Press.

Wolpe, J., & Plau, J. J. (1997). Pavlov's contributions to behavior therapy: The obvious and the not so obvious. *American Psychologist, 52*, 966–972.

Wonderly, D. M. (1996). *The selfish gene pool: An evolutionarily stable system*. Lanham, MD: University Press of America.

Wong, D. F., et al. (1986). Positron emission tomography reveals elevated D_2 dopamine receptors in drug-naive schizophrenics. *Science, 234*, 1558–1563.

Wong, M. M., & Csikszentmahalyi, M. (1991). Affiliation motivation and daily experience: Some issues on gender differences. *Journal of Personality and Social Psychology, 60*, 154–164.

Wood, J. M., Bootzin, R. R., Rosenhan, D., Nolen-Hoeksema, S. (1992). Effects of the 1989 San Francisco earthquake on frequency and content of nightmares. *Journal of Abnormal Psychology, 101*, 219–224.

Wood, J. M., Nezworski, M. T., & Stejskal, W. J. (1996). The comprehensive system for the Rorschach: A critical examination. *Psychological Science, 7*, 3–10.

Wood, N. (1997). Genes and parkinsonism. *Journal of Neurology, Neurosurgery and Psychiatry, 62*, 305–309.

Wood, W. (2000). Attitude change: Persuasion and social influence. *Annual Review of Psychology, 51*, 539–570.

Wood, W., & Eagly, A. H. (2000). A call to recognize the breadth of evolutionary perspectives: Sociocultural theories and evolutionary psychology. *Psychological Inquiry, 11*, 52–55.

Wood, W., Lundgren, S., Ouellete, J. A., Busceme, S., & Blackstone, T. (1994). Minority influence: A meta-analytic review of social influence processes. *Psychological Bulletin, 115*, 323–345.

Wood, W., Pool, G. J., Leck, K., & Purvis, D. (1996). Self-definition, defensive processing, and influence: The normative impact of majority and minority groups. *Journal of Personality and Social Psychology, 71*, 1181–1193.

Wood, W., Rhodes, N., & Whelan, M. (1989). Sex differences in positive well-being: A consideration of emotional style and marital status. *Psychological Bulletin, 106*, 249–264.

Woodruff-Pak, D. S. (1993). Eyeblink classical conditioning in H. M.: Delay and trace

paradigms. *Behavioral Neuroscience, 107*, 911–925.

Woods, S. C., Schwartz, M. W., Baskin, D. S., & Seeley, R. J. (2000). Food intake and the regulation of body weight. *Annual Review of Psychology, 51*, 255–277.

Woods, S. C., Seely, R. J., Porte, D., Jr., & Schwartz, M. W. (1998). Signals that regulate food intake and energy homeostasis. *Science, 280*, 1378–1383.

Woodside, D. B., Field, L. L., Garfinkel, P. E., & Heinmaa, M. (1998). Specificity of eating disorders diagnoses in families of probands with anorexia nervosa and bulimia nervosa. *Comprehensive Psychiatry, 39*, 261–264.

Woody, E., & Sadler, P. (1998). On reintegrating dissociated theories: Comment on Kirsch and Lynn. *Psychological Bulletin, 123*, 192–197.

Word, C. O., Zanna, M. P., & Cooper, J. (1974). The nonverbal mediation of self-fulfilling prophecies in interracial interaction. *Journal of Experimental Social Psychology, 10*, 109–120.

Worell, J., & Remer, P. (1992). *Feminist perspectives in therapy: An empowerment model for women*. New York: Wiley.

Wright, B. A. (1991). Labeling: The need for greater person-environment individuation. In C. R. Snyder & D. R. Forsyth (Eds.), *Handbook of social and clinical psychology: The health perspective*. New York: Pergamon.

Wright, J. H., & Thase, M. E. (1997) (Eds.). *Cognitive therapy*. Washington, DC: American Psychiatric Press.

Wyer, R. S., Bodenhausen, G. V., & Gorman, T. F. (1985). Cognitive mediators of reactions to rape. *Journal of Personality and Social Psychology, 48*, 324–338.

Wylie, R. C. (1979). *The self-concept* (Vol. 2). Lincoln: University of Nebraska Press.

Wylie, R. C. (1989). *Measures of self-concept*. Lincoln: University of Nebraska Press.

Yablonsky, L. (1962). *The violent gang*. New York: Macmillan.

Yalom, I. D. (1980). *Existential psychotherapy*. New York: Basic Books.

Yerkes, R. M., & Dodson, J. D. (1908). The relation of strength of stimulus to rapidity of habit-formation. *Journal of Comparative and Physiological Psychology, 18*, 459–482.

Yin, T. C. T., & Kuwada, S. (1984). Neuronal mechanisms of binaural interaction. In G. M. Edelman, W. M. Cowan, & W. E. Gall (Eds.), *Dynamic aspects of neocortical function*. New York: Wiley.

Young, L. R., & Joffe, R. T. (1997). *Bipolar disorder: Biological models and their clinical application*. New York: Marcel Dekker.

Youngstedt, S. D., O'Connor, P. J., & Dishman, R. K. (1997). The effects of acute exercise on sleep: A quantitative synthesis. *Sleep, 20*, 203–214.

Zabriskie, J. (1999, February). APA teams with MTV to prevent violence. *APA Monitor*, 24.

Zahn-Waxler, C., Radke-Yarrow, M., & King, R. A. (1979). Child rearing and children's prosocial initiations towards victims of distress. *Child Development, 50*, 319–330.

Zahn-Waxler, C., Radke-Yarrow, M., Wagner, E., & Chapman, M. (1992). Development of concern for others. *Developmental Psychology, 28*, 126–136.

Zajonc, R. B. (1965). Social facilitation. *Science, 149*, 269–274.

Zajonc, R. B. (1968). Attitudinal effects of mere exposure. *Journal of Personality and Social Psychology, 9* (2, Part 2), 1–27.

Zajonc, R. B. (1980). Compresence. In P. Paulus (Ed.), *The psychology of group influence.* Hillsdale, NJ: Erlbaum.

Zajonc, R. B. (1984). On the primacy of affect. *American Psychologist, 39*, 117–123.

Zajonc, R. B. (1985). Emotion and facial efference: A theory reclaimed. *Science, 228*, 15–21.

Zajonc, R. B., Murphy, S. T., & Inglehart, M. (1989). Feeling and facial efference: Implications of a vascular theory of emotion. *Psychological Review, 96*, 395–416.

Zakzanis, K. K. (1998). Neuropsychological correlates of positive vs. negative schizophrenic symptomatology. *Schizophrenia Research, 29*, 227–233.

Zangari, W., & Machado, F. R. (1996). Survey: Incidence and social relevance of Brazilian university students' psychic experiences. *European Journal of Parapsychology, 12*, 75–87.

Zanna, M. P., & Cooper, J. (1974). Dissonance and the pill: An attribution approach to studying the arousal properties of dissonance. *Journal of Personality and Social Psychology, 29*, 703–709.

Zaragoza, M. S., & Mitchell, K. J. (1996). Repeated exposure to suggestion and the creation of false memories. *Psychological Science, 7*, 294–300.

Zatzick, D. F., & Dimsdale, J. E. (1990). Cultural variations in response to painful stimuli. *Psychosomatic Medicine, 52*, 544–557.

Zebrowitz, L. A., Voinescu, L., & Collins, M. A. (1996). "Wide-eyed" and "crooked-faced": Determinants of perceived and real honesty across the life span. *Personality and Social Psychology Bulletin, 22*, 1258–1269.

Zhang, A. Y., & Snowden, L. R. (1999). Ethnic characteristics of mental disorders in five U.S. communities. *Cultural Diversity and Ethnic Minority Psychology, 5*, 134–146.

Zhang, Y., Proenca, R., Maffei, M., & Barone, M. et al. (1994). Positional cloning of the mouse obese gene and its human homologue. *Nature, 372*, 425–432.

Zhdanova, I. V., & Wurtman, R. J. (1997). Efficacy of melatonin as a sleep-promoting agent. *Journal of Biological Rhythms, 12*, 644–650.

Zhuikov, A. Y., Couvillon, P. A., & Bitterman, M. E. (1994). Quantitative two-process analysis of avoidance conditioning in goldfish. *Journal of Experimental Psychology: Animal Behavior Processes, 20*, 32–43.

Zillmann, D. (1979). *Hostility and aggression.* New York: Halsted Press.

Zillmann, D. (1984). *Connections between sex and aggression.* Hillsdale, NJ: Erlbaum.

Zillmann, D. (1994). Erotica and family values. In D. Zillmann, J. Bryant, & A. C. Huston (Eds.), *Media, children, and the family: Social scientific, psychodynamic, and clinical perspectives.* Hillsdale, NJ: Erlbaum.

Zimbardo, P. G., Haney, C., Banks, W. C., & Jaffe, D. (1973, April 8). The mind is a formidable jailer: A Pirandellian prison. *New York Times Magazine*, pp. 38–60.

Zimmerman, M. (1995). Diagnosing personality disorders: A review of issues and research methods. *Archives of General Psychiatry, 51*, 225–245.

Zinbarg, R. E., Barlow, D. H., Brown, T. A., & Hertz, R. M. (1992). Cognitive-behavioral approaches to the nature and treatment of anxiety disorders. *Annual Review of Psychology, 43*, 235–268.

Zucker, T. P., Flesche, C. W., Germing, U., Schroeter, S., Willers, R., Wolf, H. H., & Heyll, A. (1998). Patient-controlled versus staff-controlled analgesia with pethidine after allogeneic bone marrow transplantation. *Pain, 75*, 305–312.

Zuckerman, M. (1979). *Sensation seeking: Beyond the optimum level of arousal.* Hillsdale, NJ: Erlbaum.

Zuckerman, M. (1991). *Psychobiology of personality.* New York: Cambridge University Press.

Zuckerman, M. (1996). The psychobiological model for impulsive unsocialized sensation seeking: A comparative approach. *Neuropsychobiology, 34*, 125–129.

Zuckerman, M., Hall, J. A., DeFrank, R. S., & Rosenthal, R. (1976). Encoding and decoding of spontaneous and posed facial expressions. *Journal of Personality and Social Psychology, 34*, 966–977.

Zuckerman, M., & Link, K. (1968). Construct validity for the Sensation-Seeking Scale. *Journal of Consulting and Clinical Psychology, 32*, 420–426.

NAME INDEX

‹ A ›

Aamodt, M. G., 405
Aaron, S., 442
Abbott, M., 394, 395, 397
Abel, T., 307
Abend, S. S., 531
Abraham, K., 604
Abrahams, D., 393
Abramov, I., 143, 144
Abramson, 605
Ackerman, P., 527
Adair, R. K., 164
Adams, M. J., 281, 295, 296
Adelmann, P. K., 429
Ader, R., 118, 119, 239
Aderman, D., 494
Adler, A., 369, 550
Adler, S. R., 51
Aggleton, J. P., 530
Agnew, H. W., 196
Agnoli, F., 322
Aguilar, B. H., 692
Agyei, Y., 391
Ahern, G. L., 105
Ahern, K. D., 193
Ahrens, A. H., 375
Aiello, 147
Aiken, L. R., 343
Ainsworth, M., 474, 475, 479
Aitchison, J., 319
Aitken, D. H., 61, 258
Aitken, S., 152
Ajzen, I., 512, 513
Akerstedt, T., 188
Albee, G. W., 661
Alborn, A. M., 112
Aldridge, S., 122
Aldwin, 444
Aldwin, C. M., 437
Alexander, N., 384
Alfano, M. S., 438
Alfieri, T., 480
Alford, B. A., 601, 604, 636
Allan, L. G., 261
Allen, L., 110
Allen, M., 389, 515
Allen, N. B., 598
Allison, D. B., 378
Allport, G. W., 512, 524, 526, 555, 695
Alm, H., 185
Altman, I., 397
Altman, J., 96
Amato, P. R., 478
Ameri, 213
Ames, M. A., 391
Amorapanth, P., 306
Anand, B. K., 373
Andersen, P., 308
Andersen, R. E., 681
Anderson, C. A., 520, 532, 536
Anderson, E., 690
Anderson, J. L., 255
Anderson, J. R., 300, 324, 337
Anderson, K. B., 532
Anderson, K. J., 480
Anderson, K. O., 171
Anderson, M. C., 296
Anderson, N. D., 298
Anderson, S. R., 319
Anderson, S. W., 105, 420
Andreasen, N. C., 99, 616
Andreassi, J. L., 564
Andrews, 417
Anger, W. K., 253
Angleitner, A., 394, 395, 397
Anisman, H., 439
Anker, M., 618
Anthony, J. C., 208, 211, 212, 213, 214
Anthony, T., 511

Antonietti, A., 204
Antrobus, J., 192, 200, 202, 203
Aponte, H., 643
Archer, D., 425
Archer, J., 25
Ardila-Rey, R., 471
Arends, E., 607
Arendt, J., 190
Argyle, M., 417
Arndt, S., 99, 136, 616
Arnett, P. A., 620
Aron, A. P., 398, 399
Aron, L., 551
Aronson, E., 6, 7, 516, 696
Aronson, J., 356, 526
Aronson, M., 457
Aronson, V., 393
Arps, K., 528
Arrigo, J. M., 304
Arroyo, M., 208
Arseneault, L., 531
Arthur, D. P., 481
Arthur, K., 513
Asai, M., 606
Asch, S. E., 503
Aserinsky, E., 192
Asherian, A., 394, 395, 397
Aso, T., 198
Assanand, S. P., 371
Atchison, 611
Atkinson, J. W., 367, 401, 402, 580
Atkinson, R. C., 276, 277
Auerbach, S. M., 444, 445
Averill, J. A., 444
Avery, D. H., 188
Avila-White, D., 201
Aviles, W. A., 645
Avis, J., 468
Axel, R., 155
Ayllon, T., 611, 642
Ayres, J. J., 233, 237
Azrin, N. H., 255, 641, 642

‹ B ›

Baars, B. J., 183
Bachman, J. G., 485
Back, K., 393
Backhaus, W. G., 142, 143
Baddeley, A. D., 277, 278, 281, 292, 298
Baer, J. S., 684, 688, 689
Baert, 95
Baeyens, F., 237
Bagley, C., 442, 564, 608
Bahrick, H. P., 279, 294, 295, 310, 487
Bahrick, P. O., 487
Bailey, C. H., 307
Bailey, J. M., 391
Baillargeon, R., 465, 466
Baker, D., 405
Baker, J. M., 216
Baker, L. H., 686
Baker, R. C., 471
Balda, R. P., 263
Baldwin, E., 72
Ballenger, J. C., 595

Bandura, A., 22, 34, 36, 172, 231, 245, 262, 263, 264, 441, 480, 532, 565, 567, 568, 569, 573, 621, 638, 643, 691
Banker, B. S., 526
Banks, W. C., 500, 509
Banks, W. P., 133
Banon, 118
Baptista, J., 122
Barakkatz, M., 471
Barba, B. D., 458
Barbaree, H. E., 63, 66
Barbee, A., 383
Barber, J., 218
Barber, T. X., 204
Bard, L. L., 428
Bardo, M. T., 212
Barea-Rodriguez, E. J., 308
Barefoot, J. C., 564
Bargh, J. A., 20, 158, 184, 185, 370, 416, 419, 420, 547, 549
Barlow, D. H., 446, 447, 598, 599, 639, 640
Barnes, G. E., 604
Barnes, T. R., 657
Barnett, J. E., 608
Barnett, M., 597
Barnett, R. C., 645
Baron, P., 483
Baron, R. S., 440, 504, 514
Baron, S. C., 132, 133
Baron, S. H., 502
Barondes, S. H., 603, 604
Barone, M., 373
Barr, G. A., 104
Barr, H. M., 457
Barr, R., 49
Barraclough, J., 119
Barrett, D. J., 670
Barrett, G. V., 352
Barrett, P. T., 349
Barry, H., 481
Barry, J. R., 286
Barsky, A. J., 609
Bar-Tal, D., 17, 697
Bartel, P., 195
Bartlett, F. C., 284, 298, 299
Bartoshuk, L. M., 154, 155, 381, 680
Bartsch, D., 307
Baskin, D. S., 368, 371, 373, 374
Bassett, R., 517
Bassok, M., 34, 329
Bastik, T., 337
Batson, C. D., 527, 528
Batterman-Faunce, J. M., 302
Battin, D. B., 302, 303
Baudry, M., 307
Bauer, C. R., 62, 111, 156
Bauer, K. E., 196, 220
Baum, A., 434, 438, 531, 679, 680, 686
Baumeister, R. F., 185, 391, 553
Baumrind, D., 478, 506, 672
Bauserman, R., 387, 388
Baxter, L. R., 659
Bayer, S. A., 96
Bazzini, D. G., 394
Beahrs, J. O., 612
Beaman, A. L., 528, 530

Bear, G. G., 471
Beardsley, L., 215
Beauchamp, G. K., 154, 155
Beaugrand, J. P., 263
Becerril, J. J., 114
Bech, 172
Bechara, A., 105, 420
Beck, A. P., 643
Beck, A. T., 16, 29, 416, 588, 601, 604, 607, 636, 638
Becker, A. E., 380, 381, 600
Becker, E., 23, 24
Becker, J. B., 115, 355, 481
Becker, S. E., 292
Beckmann, H., 615
Bedard, J., 332
Bednekoff, P. A., 263
Beecher, H. K., 171, 172
Beecher, M. D., 229
Beitman, B. D., 663
Bekesy, G. von, 149
Bell, A. P., 390
Bell, D. N., 674
Bellinger, D. L., 239
Bellugi, U., 109
Belsky, J., 491
Bem, D. J., 391, 473, 514
Bem, S. L., 554
Benaji, 136
Benjamin, L. T., 35
Bennett, E. A., 515
Bennett, E. L., 61, 461
Bennett, H. L., 294
Bennett, N. G., 491
Bennett, P. H., 378, 379
Benski, C., 69
Ben-Slushan, D., 437
Benton, S. L., 282, 293
Berg, C. A., 490
Berg, K. M., 248
Bergeman, C. S., 550
Bergen, R. K., 621
Berger, M., 29
Berger, R. J., 196
Berger, S. A., 294, 310
Berger, S. H., 478
Bergin, A. E., 645, 652
Bergmann, B. M., 195, 196
Berkowitz, L., 388, 527, 531, 533, 534, 571
Berlin, R. M., 199
Bermudez, R. F., 255
Bern, D. J., 69
Bernstein, B., 648
Bernstein, I. L., 256
Berrettini, W. H., 603
Berry, J. W., 465
Berry, L. M., 404, 492, 493
Berscheid, E., 394, 399, 522
Bersoff, D. M., 527
Best, D. L., 480
Betancourt, H., 532
Betz, N., 136
Beutler, L. E., 628, 635, 652
Beyer, S., 555
Bhatnagar, S., 61, 258
Bickman, L., 437
Bieberich, A. A., 238
Biebuyck, J. F., 197
Bielajew, C., 372
Biener, L., 503
Bierman, K. L., 245, 532
Bierut, L. J., 214

Bigbee, M. A., 689
Bihrle, S., 531, 533, 620
Bilker, W., 615
Billings, A. G., 445
Bills, A. J., 300
Binder, J. L., 628, 652
Birch, D., 402
Birch, K., 527
Birket-Smith, M., 618
Birtanen, S., 524
Bishop, C. H., 35
Bitterman, M. E., 251
Bjork-Erikkson, T., 112
Björkqvist, K., 531, 533
Black, D. W., 616, 619
Black, J., 553
Black, M., 672
Blackburn, T., 611
Blackstone, T., 504
Blackwood, D., 598
Blair, C., 672, 673
Blair, I., 532
Blakemore, C., 175
Blanc, A. K., 491
Bland, I. J., 647
Bland, R. C., 596
Blaney, N., 6, 7, 696
Blank, R. H., 114
Blascovich, J., 436, 501, 525
Blasi, A., 471
Blass, T., 506, 507
Blechman, E., 171
Blehar, M. C., 475
Blessing, W. W., 96
Blethen, S. L., 122
Bliss, T. V., 308
Block, J. H., 553
Blodgett, R., 69, 262
Blommel, J. M., 501
Bloom, D. E., 491
Bloom, F. E., 81
Bloom, J. R., 119
Blosser, 112
Blume, A. W., 684
Blundell, J. E., 377
Boakes, R., 304
Bobick, T. M., 513
Bobo, L., 525
Bochner, S., 516
Bodenhausen, G. V., 529
Boer, K., 391
Boesch, C., 52, 55
Boeve, B. F., 198
Bogart, 682
Bohart, A. C., 635, 652
Bolles, R. C., 229, 260, 371
Bolling, M. Y., 565
Bonanno, G. A., 297
Bond, A. J., 692
Bond, C. F., Jr., 501
Bond, J. A., 548, 549
Bond, R., 504
Boness, D. J., 527
Bonevento, M., 292
Bonnel, A. M., 158
Bonvillian, J. D., 325
Bookstein, F. L., 457
Booth, A., 478, 491
Booth-Kewley, S., 564
Bootzin, R. R., 197
Borbely, A. A., 196
Borges, C. A., 522
Borke, H., 465
Bornstein, S. R., 439
Borod, J. C., 100, 116, 418, 433, 436
Bortz, R., 195
Boswell, A. E., 248
Bothwell, R. K., 219
Botman, H. I., 201
Bouchard, C., 125, 378
Bouchard, T. J., 13, 125, 339, 350, 530, 560, 598
Boucher, J. D., 425

SUBJECT INDEX